PROFESSIONAL RESPONSIBILITY STANDARDS, RULES & STATUTES

2002–2003 Edition

Selected and Edited

By

John S. Dzienkowski
Professor of Law & John S. Redditt Professor in State and Local Government, University of Texas

WEST GROUP

A THOMSON COMPANY

Material # 40054901

TEXT IS PRINTED ON 10% POST CONSUMER RECYCLED PAPER

PREFACE

In recent years, the ABA, the states, and other entities have been active in the promulgation of standards, rules, and statutes that regulate lawyers' conduct. These sources of the law of professional responsibility have significantly affected the manner in which lawyers analyze problems in this area. Similarly, the existence of different formal sources of professional responsibility have altered the way in which lawyers and law students are taught about ethical problems. This pamphlet of Professional Responsibility Standards, Rules, and Statutes is designed to provide teachers and students with easy access to the important sources of professional responsibility.

Beginning with the 1995 edition of Professional Responsibility Standards Rules and Statutes, this book is now published in a full version and an abridged version. The full version will continue to include various sources of professional responsibility including standards for specialized areas of practice and standards for the organized regulation of the profession. The abridged edition will present the ABA versions of the codes governing lawyers and judges as well as several selected rules of procedure and evidence and selected rules from California and New York. The purpose of the two editions is to allow professors to choose which version best fits the class that they plan to teach. This preface will however cover materials in both versions.

The full version of Professional Responsibility Standards Rules and Statutes is organized into seven different parts: (1) Codes Regulating Lawyers' Conduct; (2) Code of Judicial Conduct; (3) Rules of Evidence and Procedure that Affect the Legal Profession; (4) Statutes that Affect the Legal Profession; (5) Standards for Specialized Areas of Practice; and (6) Standards for the Organized Regulation of Lawyers. The abridged edition includes the first three parts which focus on the ABA's pronouncements as well as the federal rules of evidence and procedure that influence the legal profession.

In February 2000, the ABA House of Delegates amended the Model Rules to reflect the revisions proposed by the Ethics 2000 Commission. The 2002 version of the Model Rules is reproduced in the marked up version to reflect changes from the prior draft. This supplement will continue to reproduce the 2001 version of the Model Rules in the annotated format because this document is more representative of the rules currently in effect in the majority of states. The annotated version of the Model Rules contained in this pamphlet allows students to compare the current version with the prior version, which appears in a footnote on the same page with the current version. The annotated Model Rules should also facilitate the study of cases and ethics opinions that are based upon prior versions of the Model Rules. Where appropriate, the annotations also

PREFACE

contain the text of a prior draft of the Model Rules to illustrate a shift in the final ABA position. In light of the fact that the states have made significant modifications to the ABA's version of the Model Rules, it has become desirable to include a section on selected significant state modifications to the Model Rules. This section allows teachers and students to examine how various states have chosen to modify specific provisions of the Model Rules. Both the full and abridged editions now contain the California and New York state materials.

Both the full and abridged versions include the ABA Model Code of Professional Conduct and the 1908 Canons, as well as the 1990 Code of Judicial Conduct. The prior standards are included to facilitate study of the evolution of professional standards as well as cases and jurisdictions that rely on the prior rules.

The full edition contains the text of the sections in the Restatement of Law Governing Lawyers and selected Reporters Comments. This project will occupy a significant role in shaping the law of professional responsibility.

I welcome comments and suggestions on the materials contained in this edition. My E mail address is jsd@mail.law.utexas.edu.

The materials are current through April 2002, and this supplement will be updated periodically to reflect new and amended statutes and rules.

JOHN S. DZIENKOWSKI

Austin, Texas
May 2002

TABLE OF CONTENTS

PART ONE: CODES REGULATING LAWYERS' CONDUCT

PART TWO: CODES OF JUDICIAL CONDUCT

PART THREE: RULES OF EVIDENCE AND PROCEDURE THAT AFFECT THE LEGAL PROFESSION

TABLE OF CONTENTS

PART FOUR: RESTATEMENT (THIRD) OF LAW GOVERNING LAWYERS

PART FIVE: STATUTES THAT AFFECT THE LEGAL PROFESSION

PART SIX: STANDARDS FOR SPECIALIZED AREAS OF PRACTICE

PART SEVEN: STANDARDS FOR THE ORGANIZED REGULATION OF LAWYERS

PROFESSIONAL RESPONSIBILITY STANDARDS, RULES & STATUTES

2002–2003 EDITION

PART ONE

CODES AND STANDARDS REGULATING LAWYERS' CONDUCT

Table of Contents

Introduction

One of the traditional characteristics of a profession is the attempt to achieve self regulation. Throughout history, professions have enacted codes of conduct to assert control over their members. Various groups within the legal profession have similarly sought to exercise a degree of self regulation by enacting codes of conduct. This part includes several codes and standards which have attempted to regulate the conduct of all lawyers in their practice of law.

The first three codes contained in this section were promulgated by the American Bar Association (ABA), a national voluntary organization of lawyers. The ABA has assumed the primary responsibility for promulgating national ethical standards for the legal profession. In 1908, the ABA enacted 32 Canons of Professional Ethics. In 1969, it replaced the Canons with the Model Code of Professional Responsibility. In 1983, the Model Code was replaced with the Model Rules of Professional Conduct.

3

REGULATING LAWYERS' CONDUCT

In 1997, the ABA established an Ethics 2000 Committee to revise the Model Rules in light of developments in law and practice. The ABA House of Delegates adopted a series of revisions in 2002 to reflect the Ethics 2000 project. Because no state has adopted the 2002 version of the Model Rules, this supplement will reproduce both the 2002 and 2001 versions of the Model Rules. The 2001 version is also needed to understand the cases decided under this prior standard.

Although the ABA's codes of conduct have been influential in shaping the law of professional responsibility, they only have force as a body of rules with its voluntary members. However, the various states and the federal courts have looked to the ABA versions as a basis for regulating lawyers within the jurisdiction. Thus, the ABA's codes have been used as the basis for state and federal codes. With the Model Code, many states adopted the ABA version without many significant changes. However, with the ABA's promulgation of the Model Rules, the states have been less deferential. Many states have made significant modifications to the ABA version. Thus, this part includes a section on significant state modifications to the Model Rules.

A final series of documents in this part reflect a recent trend on the part of the ABA and the states to focus on lawyer professionalism as a basis for regulating lawyers' conduct. The origin of this movement was a study on professionalism commissioned by the ABA. The results of the study identified several reasons for the decline in lawyer professionalism and offered several suggestions to address this problem. The ABA Creed of Professionalism and the ABA Pledge of Professionalism illustrate attempts to implement the suggestions of the Commission on Professionalism. The Texas Creed on Professionalism provides a similar example of a state effort to address this problem. The ABA's Aspirational Goals on Lawyer Advertising provide a more concrete example of urging standards of professionalism in the communication of advertising to the general public.

2002 VERSION OF THE AMERICAN BAR ASSOCIATION MODEL RULES OF PROFESSIONAL CONDUCT

Redlined by the ABA to reflect amendment from the 2001 Version of the ABA Model Rules

Adopted February 2002.

[In 1997, the ABA formed the Ethics 2000 Commission on the Evaluation of the Rules of Professional Conduct. The role of the E2K Commission was to update the Model Rules in light of developments in the law and the legal profession. The project was considered timely in light of the nearing of the completion of the Restatement (Third) of Law Governing Lawyers. The E2K Commission held hearings and circulated proposed drafts for comments from the profession. In November 2000, the Commission prepared a report, which was presented to the ABA House of Delegates. The ABA considered the Report at the August 2001 meeting and the February 2002 meeting, and a majority of amendments proposed by the E2K Commission were adopted by the ABA House of Delegates. As of February 2002, the Model Rules have been amended to reflect the E2K Commission recommendations. However, the name of the document continues to be referred to as the Model Rules of Professional Conduct (2002). It is not called the Ethics 2000 version or any other new title. The document reproduced below is redlined by the ABA for comparison with the 2001 version of the Model Rules. Note that no state currently has adopted the 2002 version of the Model Rules and very few authorities have had a chance to examine or analyze the changed language. Thus, the 2001 version of the Model Rules will be reproduced after this document so that professors and students can examine the case law and other authorities in light of the rules in effect at the time of the decisions. The 2002 Model Rules draft has been annotated to note where the House of Delegates rejected the recommendation of the E2K Commission Report. These issues indicate areas over which there is significant disagreement in the organized bar. Ed.]

CONTENTS

2002 ABA MODEL RULES

CLIENT–LAWYER RELATIONSHIP

COUNSELOR

ADVOCATE

TRANSACTIONS WITH PERSONS OTHER THAN CLIENTS

LAW FIRMS AND ASSOCIATIONS

PREAMBLE: A LAWYER'S RESPONSIBILITIES

[1] A lawyer, as a member of the legal profession, is a representative of clients, an officer of the legal system and a public citizen having special responsibility for the quality of justice.

[2] As a representative of clients, a lawyer performs various functions. As advisor, a lawyer provides a client with an informed understanding of the client's legal rights and obligations and explains their practical implications. As advocate, a lawyer zealously asserts the client's position under the rules of the adversary system. As negotiator, a lawyer seeks a result advantageous to the client but consistent with requirements of honest dealings with others. As intermediary between clients, a lawyer seeks to reconcile their divergent interests as an advisor and, to a limited extent, as a spokesperson for each client. A As an evaluator, a lawyer acts as evaluator by examining a client's legal affairs and reporting about them to the client or to others.

[3] In addition to these representational functions, a lawyer may serve as a third-party neutral, a nonrepresentational role helping the

7

parties to resolve a dispute or other matter. Some of these Rules apply directly to lawyers who are or have served as third-party neutrals. See, e.g., Rules 1.12 and 2.4. In addition, there are Rules that apply to lawyers who are not active in the practice of law or to practicing lawyers even when they are acting in a nonprofessional capacity. For example, a lawyer who commits fraud in the conduct of a business is subject to discipline for engaging in conduct involving dishonesty, fraud, deceit or misrepresentation. See Rule 8.4.

[3] [4] In all professional functions a lawyer should be competent, prompt and diligent. A lawyer should maintain communication with a client concerning the representation. A lawyer should keep in confidence information relating to representation of a client except so far as disclosure is required or permitted by the Rules of Professional Conduct or other law.

[4] [5] A lawyer's conduct should conform to the requirements of the law, both in professional service to clients and in the lawyer's business and personal affairs. A lawyer should use the law's procedures only for legitimate purposes and not to harass or intimidate others. A lawyer should demonstrate respect for the legal system and for those who serve it, including judges, other lawyers and public officials. While it is a lawyer's duty, when necessary, to challenge the rectitude of official action, it is also a lawyer's duty to uphold legal process.

[5] [6] As a public citizen, a lawyer should seek improvement of the law, access to the legal system, the administration of justice and the quality of service rendered by the legal profession. As a member of a learned profession, a lawyer should cultivate knowledge of the law beyond its use for clients, employ that knowledge in reform of the law and work to strengthen legal education. In addition, a lawyer should further the public's understanding of and confidence in the rule of law and the justice system because legal institutions in a constitutional democracy depend on popular participation and support to maintain their authority. A lawyer should be mindful of deficiencies in the administration of justice and of the fact that the poor, and sometimes persons who are not poor, cannot afford adequate legal assistance, and. Therefore, all lawyers should therefore devote professional time and resources and use civic influence in their behalf to ensure equal access to our system of justice for all those who because of economic or social barriers cannot afford or secure adequate legal counsel. A lawyer should aid the legal profession in pursuing these objectives and should help the bar regulate itself in the public interest.

[6] [7] Many of a lawyer's professional responsibilities are prescribed in the Rules of Professional Conduct, as well as substantive and procedural law. However, a lawyer is also guided by personal conscience and the approbation of professional peers. A lawyer should strive to attain the highest level of skill, to improve the law and the legal profession and to exemplify the legal profession's ideals of public service.

~~[7]~~ [8] A lawyer's responsibilities as a representative of clients, an officer of the legal system and a public citizen are usually harmonious. Thus, when an opposing party is well represented, a lawyer can be a zealous advocate on behalf of a client and at the same time assume that justice is being done. So also, a lawyer can be sure that preserving client confidences ordinarily serves the public interest because people are more likely to seek legal advice, and thereby heed their legal obligations, when they know their communications will be private.

~~[8]~~ [9] In the nature of law practice, however, conflicting responsibilities are encountered. Virtually all difficult ethical problems arise from conflict between a lawyer's responsibilities to clients, to the legal system and to the lawyer's own interest in remaining an ~~upright~~ ethical person while earning a satisfactory living. The Rules of Professional Conduct often prescribe terms for resolving such conflicts. Within the framework of these Rules, however, many difficult issues of professional discretion can arise. Such issues must be resolved through the exercise of sensitive professional and moral judgment guided by the basic principles underlying the Rules. These principles include the lawyer's obligation zealously to protect and pursue a client's legitimate interests, within the bounds of the law, while maintaining a professional, courteous and civil attitude toward all persons involved in the legal system.

~~[9]~~ [10] The legal profession is largely self-governing. Although other professions also have been granted powers of self-government, the legal profession is unique in this respect because of the close relationship between the profession and the processes of government and law enforcement. This connection is manifested in the fact that ultimate authority over the legal profession is vested largely in the courts.

~~[10]~~ [11] To the extent that lawyers meet the obligations of their professional calling, the occasion for government regulation is obviated. Self-regulation also helps maintain the legal profession's independence from government domination. An independent legal profession is an important force in preserving government under law, for abuse of legal authority is more readily challenged by a profession whose members are not dependent on government for the right to practice.

~~[11]~~ [12] The legal profession's relative autonomy carries with it special responsibilities of self-government. The profession has a responsibility to assure that its regulations are conceived in the public interest and not in furtherance of parochial or self-interested concerns of the bar. Every lawyer is responsible for observance of the Rules of Professional Conduct. A lawyer should also aid in securing their observance by other lawyers. Neglect of these responsibilities compromises the independence of the profession and the public interest which it serves.

~~[12]~~ [13] Lawyers play a vital role in the preservation of society. The fulfillment of this role requires an understanding by lawyers of their relationship to our legal system. The Rules of Professional Conduct, when properly applied, serve to define that relationship.

SCOPE

[~~13~~] [14] The Rules of Professional Conduct are rules of reason. They should be interpreted with reference to the purposes of legal representation and of the law itself. Some of the Rules are imperatives, cast in the terms "shall" or "shall not." These define proper conduct for purposes of professional discipline. Others, generally cast in the term "may," are permissive and define areas under the Rules in which the lawyer has ~~professional~~ discretion to exercise professional judgment. No disciplinary action should be taken when the lawyer chooses not to act or acts within the bounds of such discretion. Other Rules define the nature of relationships between the lawyer and others. The Rules are thus partly obligatory and disciplinary and partly constitutive and descriptive in that they define a lawyer's professional role. Many of the Comments use the term "should." Comments do not add obligations to the Rules but provide guidance for practicing in compliance with the Rules.

[~~14~~] [15] The Rules presuppose a larger legal context shaping the lawyer's role. That context includes court rules and statutes relating to matters of licensure, laws defining specific obligations of lawyers and substantive and procedural law in general. The Comments are sometimes used to alert lawyers to their responsibilities under such other law.

[16] Compliance with the Rules, as with all law in an open society, depends primarily upon understanding and voluntary compliance, secondarily upon reinforcement by peer and public opinion and finally, when necessary, upon enforcement through disciplinary proceedings. The Rules do not, however, exhaust the moral and ethical considerations that should inform a lawyer, for no worthwhile human activity can be completely defined by legal rules. The Rules simply provide a framework for the ethical practice of law.

[~~15~~] [17] Furthermore, for purposes of determining the lawyer's authority and responsibility, principles of substantive law external to these Rules determine whether a client-lawyer relationship exists. Most of the duties flowing from the client-lawyer relationship attach only after the client has requested the lawyer to render legal services and the lawyer has agreed to do so. But there are some duties, such as that of confidentiality under Rule 1.6, that ~~may~~ attach when the lawyer agrees to consider whether a client-lawyer relationship shall be established. See Rule 1.18. Whether a client-lawyer relationship exists for any specific purpose can depend on the circumstances and may be a question of fact.

[~~16~~] [18] Under various legal provisions, including constitutional, statutory and common law, the responsibilities of government lawyers may include authority concerning legal matters that ordinarily reposes in the client in private client-lawyer relationships. For example, a lawyer for a government agency may have authority on behalf of the government to decide upon settlement or whether to appeal from an adverse judgment. Such authority in various respects is generally vested in the attorney general and the state's attorney in state government, and their federal counterparts, and the same may be true of other government law officers. Also, lawyers under the supervision of these officers may be authorized to represent several government agencies in intragovernmental legal controversies in circumstances where a private lawyer could not represent multiple private clients. ~~They also may have authority to represent the "public interest" in circumstances where a private lawyer would not be authorized to do so.~~ These Rules do not abrogate any such authority.

~~[17]~~ [19] Failure to comply with an obligation or prohibition imposed by a Rule is a basis for invoking the disciplinary process. The Rules presuppose that disciplinary assessment of a lawyer's conduct will be made on the basis of the facts and circumstances as they existed at the time of the conduct in question and in recognition of the fact that a lawyer often has to act upon uncertain or incomplete evidence of the situation. Moreover, the Rules presuppose that whether or not discipline should be imposed for a violation, and the severity of a sanction, depend on all the circumstances, such as the willfulness and seriousness of the violation, extenuating factors and whether there have been previous violations.

~~[18]~~ [20] Violation of a Rule should not itself give rise to a cause of action against a lawyer nor should it create any presumption in such a case that a legal duty has been breached. In addition, violation of a Rule does not necessarily warrant any other nondisciplinary remedy, such as disqualification of a lawyer in pending litigation. The Rules are designed to provide guidance to lawyers and to provide a structure for regulating conduct through disciplinary agencies. They are not designed to be a basis for civil liability. Furthermore, the purpose of the Rules can be subverted when they are invoked by opposing parties as procedural weapons. The fact that a Rule is a just basis for a lawyer's self-assessment, or for sanctioning a lawyer under the administration of a disciplinary authority, does not imply that an antagonist in a collateral proceeding or transaction has standing to seek enforcement of the Rule. ~~Accordingly, nothing in the Rules should be deemed to augment any substantive legal duty of lawyers or the extra-disciplinary consequences of violating such a duty.~~ Nevertheless, since the Rules do establish standards of conduct by lawyers, a lawyer's violation of a Rule may be evidence of breach of the applicable standard of conduct.

~~[19] Moreover, these Rules are not intended to govern or affect judicial application of either the attorney-client or work product privilege. Those privileges were developed to promote compliance with law and fairness in litigation. In reliance on the attorney-client privilege, clients are entitled to expect that communications within the scope of the privilege will be protected against compelled disclosure. The attorney-client privilege is that of the client and not of the lawyer. The fact that in exceptional situations the lawyer under the rules has a limited discretion to disclose a client confidence does not vitiate the proposition that, as a general matter, the client has a reasonable expectation that~~

~~information relating to the client will not be voluntarily disclosed and that disclosure of such information may be judicially compelled only in accordance with recognized exceptions to the attorney-client and work product privileges.~~

~~[20] The lawyer's exercise of discretion not to disclose information under Rule 1.6 should not be subject to reexamination. Permitting such reexamination would be incompatible with the general policy of promoting compliance with law through assurances that communications will be protected against disclosure.~~

[21] The Comment accompanying each Rule explains and illustrates the meaning and purpose of the Rule. The Preamble and this note on Scope provide general orientation. The Comments are intended as guides to interpretation, but the text of each Rule is authoritative. ~~Research notes were prepared to compare counterparts in the ABA Model Code of Professional Responsibility (adopted 1969, as amended) and to provide selected references to other authorities. The notes have not been adopted, do not constitute part of the Model Rules, and are not intended to affect the application or interpretation of the Rules and Comments.~~

CLIENT–LAWYER RELATIONSHIP

Rule 1.0 Terminology

(a) "Belief" or "believes" denotes that the person involved actually supposed the fact in question to be true. A person's belief may be inferred from circumstances.

~~"Consult" or "consultation" denotes communication of information reasonably sufficient to permit the client to appreciate the significance of the matter in question.~~

(b) "Confirmed in writing," when used in reference to the informed consent of a person, denotes informed consent that is given in writing by the person or a writing that a lawyer promptly transmits to the person confirming an oral informed consent. See paragraph (e) for the definition of "informed consent." If it is not feasible to obtain or transmit the writing at the time the person gives informed consent, then the lawyer must obtain or transmit it within a reasonable time thereafter.

(c) "Firm" or "law firm" denotes a lawyer or lawyers in a ~~private firm,~~ law partnership, professional corporation, sole proprietorship or other association authorized to practice law; or lawyers employed in a legal services organization or the legal department of a corporation or other organization ~~and lawyers employed in a legal services organization. See Comment, Rule 1.10.~~

(d) "Fraud" or "fraudulent" denotes conduct ~~having~~ that is fraudulent under the substantive or procedural law of the applicable jurisdiction and has a purpose to deceive ~~and not merely negligent misrepresentation or failure to apprise another of relevant information.~~

(e) "Informed consent" denotes the agreement by a person to a proposed course of conduct after the lawyer has communicated adequate information and explanation about the material risks of and reasonably available alternatives to the proposed course of conduct.

(f) "Knowingly," "known," or "knows" denotes actual knowledge of the fact in question. A person's knowledge may be inferred from circumstances.

(g) "Partner" denotes a member of a partnership ~~and~~, a shareholder in a law firm organized as a professional corporation, or a member of an association authorized to practice law.

(h) "Reasonable" or "reasonably" when used in relation to conduct by a lawyer denotes the conduct of a reasonably prudent and competent lawyer.

(i) "Reasonable belief" or "reasonably believes" when used in reference to a lawyer denotes that the lawyer believes the matter in question and that the circumstances are such that the belief is reasonable.

(j) "Reasonably should know" when used in reference to a lawyer denotes that a lawyer of reasonable prudence and competence would ascertain the matter in question.

(k) "Screened" denotes the isolation of a lawyer from any participation in a matter through the timely imposition of procedures within a firm that are reasonably adequate under the circumstances to protect information that the isolated lawyer is obligated to protect under these Rules or other law.

(*l*) "Substantial" when used in reference to degree or extent denotes a material matter of clear and weighty importance.

(m) "Tribunal" denotes a court, an arbitrator in a binding arbitration proceeding or a legislative body, administrative agency or other body acting in an adjudicative capacity. A legislative body, administrative agency or other body acts in an adjudicative capacity when a neutral official, after the presentation of evidence or legal argument by a party or parties, will render a binding legal judgment directly affecting a party's interests in a particular matter.

(n) "Writing" or "written" denotes a tangible or electronic record of a communication or representation, including handwriting, typewriting, printing, photostating, photography, audio or videorecording and e-mail. A "signed" writing includes an electronic sound, symbol or process attached to or logically associated with a writing and executed or adopted by a person with the intent to sign the writing.

COMMENT

Confirmed in Writing

[1] If it is not feasible to obtain or transmit a written confirmation at the time the client gives informed consent, then the lawyer must obtain or transmit it within a reasonable time thereafter. If a lawyer has obtained a client's informed consent, the lawyer may act in reliance on

that consent so long as it is confirmed in writing within a reasonable time thereafter.

Firm

[2]   Whether two or more lawyers constitute a firm within paragraph (c) can depend on the specific facts. For example, two practitioners who share office space and occasionally consult or assist each other ordinarily would not be regarded as constituting a firm. However, if they present themselves to the public in a way that suggests that they are a firm or conduct themselves as a firm, they should be regarded as a firm for purposes of the Rules. The terms of any formal agreement between associated lawyers are relevant in determining whether they are a firm, as is the fact that they have mutual access to information concerning the clients they serve. Furthermore, it is relevant in doubtful cases to consider the underlying purpose of the Rule that is involved. A group of lawyers could be regarded as a firm for purposes of the Rule that the same lawyer should not represent opposing parties in litigation, while it might not be so regarded for purposes of the Rule that information acquired by one lawyer is attributed to another.

[3]   With respect to the law department of an organization, including the government, there is ordinarily no question that the members of the department constitute a firm within the meaning of the Rules of Professional Conduct. There can be uncertainty, however, as to the identity of the client. For example, it may not be clear whether the law department of a corporation represents a subsidiary or an affiliated corporation, as well as the corporation by which the members of the department are directly employed. A similar question can arise concerning an unincorporated association and its local affiliates.

[4]   Similar questions can also arise with respect to lawyers in legal aid and legal services organizations. Depending upon the structure of the organization, the entire organization or different components of it may constitute a firm or firms for purposes of these Rules.

Fraud

[5]   When used in these Rules, the terms "fraud" or "fraudulent" refer to conduct that is characterized as such under the substantive or procedural law of the applicable jurisdiction and has a purpose to deceive. This does not include merely negligent misrepresentation or negligent failure to apprise another of relevant information. For purposes of these Rules, it is not necessary that anyone has suffered damages or relied on the misrepresentation or failure to inform.

Informed Consent

[6]   Many of the Rules of Professional Conduct require the lawyer to obtain the informed consent of a client or other person (e.g., a former client or, under certain circumstances, a prospective client) before ac-

cepting or continuing representation or pursuing a course of conduct. See, e.g, Rules 1.2(c), 1.6(a) and 1.7(b). The communication necessary to obtain such consent will vary according to the Rule involved and the circumstances giving rise to the need to obtain informed consent. The lawyer must make reasonable efforts to ensure that the client or other person possesses information reasonably adequate to make an informed decision. Ordinarily, this will require communication that includes a disclosure of the facts and circumstances giving rise to the situation, any explanation reasonably necessary to inform the client or other person of the material advantages and disadvantages of the proposed course of conduct and a discussion of the client's or other person's options and alternatives. In some circumstances it may be appropriate for a lawyer to advise a client or other person to seek the advice of other counsel. A lawyer need not inform a client or other person of facts or implications already known to the client or other person; nevertheless, a lawyer who does not personally inform the client or other person assumes the risk that the client or other person is inadequately informed and the consent is invalid. In determining whether the information and explanation provided are reasonably adequate, relevant factors include whether the client or other person is experienced in legal matters generally and in making decisions of the type involved, and whether the client or other person is independently represented by other counsel in giving the consent. Normally, such persons need less information and explanation than others, and generally a client or other person who is independently represented by other counsel in giving the consent should be assumed to have given informed consent.

[7] Obtaining informed consent will usually require an affirmative response by the client or other person. In general, a lawyer may not assume consent from a client's or other person's silence. Consent may be inferred, however, from the conduct of a client or other person who has reasonably adequate information about the matter. A number of Rules require that a person's consent be confirmed in writing. See Rules 1.7(b) and 1.9(a). For a definition of "writing" and "confirmed in writing," see paragraphs (n) and (b). Other Rules require that a client's consent be obtained in a writing signed by the client. See, e.g., Rules 1.8(a) and (g). For a definition of "signed," see paragraph (n).

Screened

[8] This definition applies to situations where screening of a personally disqualified lawyer is permitted to remove imputation of a conflict of interest under Rules 1.11, 1.12 or 1.18.

[9] The purpose of screening is to assure the affected parties that confidential information known by the personally disqualified lawyer remains protected. The personally disqualified lawyer should acknowledge the obligation not to communicate with any of the other lawyers in the firm with respect to the matter. Similarly, other lawyers in the firm who are working on the matter should be informed that the screening is

15

in place and that they may not communicate with the personally disqualified lawyer with respect to the matter. Additional screening measures that are appropriate for the particular matter will depend on the circumstances. To implement, reinforce and remind all affected lawyers of the presence of the screening, it may be appropriate for the firm to undertake such procedures as a written undertaking by the screened lawyer to avoid any communication with other firm personnel and any contact with any firm files or other materials relating to the matter, written notice and instructions to all other firm personnel forbidding any communication with the screened lawyer relating to the matter, denial of access by the screened lawyer to firm files or other materials relating to the matter and periodic reminders of the screen to the screened lawyer and all other firm personnel.

[10] In order to be effective, screening measures must be implemented as soon as practical after a lawyer or law firm knows or reasonably should know that there is a need for screening.

Rule 1.1: Competence

A lawyer shall provide competent representation to a client. Competent representation requires the legal knowledge, skill, thoroughness and preparation reasonably necessary for the representation.

COMMENT

Legal Knowledge and Skill

[1] In determining whether a lawyer employs the requisite knowledge and skill in a particular matter, relevant factors include the relative complexity and specialized nature of the matter, the lawyer's general experience, the lawyer's training and experience in the field in question, the preparation and study the lawyer is able to give the matter and whether it is feasible to refer the matter to, or associate or consult with, a lawyer of established competence in the field in question. In many instances, the required proficiency is that of a general practitioner. Expertise in a particular field of law may be required in some circumstances.

[2] A lawyer need not necessarily have special training or prior experience to handle legal problems of a type with which the lawyer is unfamiliar. A newly admitted lawyer can be as competent as a practitioner with long experience. Some important legal skills, such as the analysis of precedent, the evaluation of evidence and legal drafting, are required in all legal problems. Perhaps the most fundamental legal skill consists of determining what kind of legal problems a situation may involve, a skill that necessarily transcends any particular specialized knowledge. A lawyer can provide adequate representation in a wholly novel field through necessary study. Competent representation can also be provided

through the association of a lawyer of established competence in the field in question.

[3] In an emergency a lawyer may give advice or assistance in a matter in which the lawyer does not have the skill ordinarily required where referral to or consultation or association with another lawyer would be impractical. Even in an emergency, however, assistance should be limited to that reasonably necessary in the circumstances, for ill-considered action under emergency conditions can jeopardize the client's interest.

[4] A lawyer may accept representation where the requisite level of competence can be achieved by reasonable preparation. This applies as well to a lawyer who is appointed as counsel for an unrepresented person. See also Rule 6.2.

Thoroughness and Preparation

[5] Competent handling of a particular matter includes inquiry into and analysis of the factual and legal elements of the problem, and use of methods and procedures meeting the standards of competent practitioners. It also includes adequate preparation. The required attention and preparation are determined in part by what is at stake; major litigation and complex transactions ordinarily require more ~~elaborate~~ extensive treatment than matters of lesser complexity and consequence. An agreement between the lawyer and the client regarding the scope of the representation may limit the matters for which the lawyer is responsible. See Rule 1.2(c).

Maintaining Competence

[6] To maintain the requisite knowledge and skill, a lawyer should keep abreast of changes in the law and its practice, engage in continuing study and education and comply with all continuing legal education requirements to which the lawyer is subject. ~~If a system of peer review has been established, the lawyer should consider making use of it in appropriate circumstance.~~

Rule 1.2 Scope of Representation <u>and Allocation of Authority Between Client and Lawyer</u>

(a) A <u>Subject to paragraphs (c) and (d),</u> a lawyer shall abide by a client's decisions concerning the objectives of representation, ~~subject to paragraphs (c), (d) and (e),~~ and, <u>as required by Rule 1.4,</u> shall consult with the client as to the means by which they are to be pursued. A lawyer may take such action on behalf of the client as is impliedly authorized to carry out the representation. A lawyer shall abide by a client's decision whether to ~~accept an offer of settlement of~~ settle a matter. In a criminal case, the lawyer shall abide by the client's decision, after consul-

tation with the lawyer, as to a plea to be entered, whether to waive jury trial and whether the client will testify.

(b) A lawyer's representation of a client, including representation by appointment, does not constitute an endorsement of the client's political, economic, social or moral views or activities.

(c) A lawyer may limit the ~~objectives~~ scope of the representation if the limitation is reasonable under the circumstances and the client ~~consents after consultation~~ gives informed consent.

(d) A lawyer shall not counsel a client to engage, or assist a client, in conduct that the lawyer knows is criminal or fraudulent, but a lawyer may discuss the legal consequences of any proposed course of conduct with a client and may counsel or assist a client to make a good faith effort to determine the validity, scope, meaning or application of the law.

~~(e) When a lawyer knows that a client expects assistance not permitted by the rules of professional conduct or other law, the lawyer shall consult with the client regarding the relevant limitations on the lawyer's conduct.~~

COMMENT

~~Scope of Representation~~ Allocation of Authority between Client and Lawyer

[1]   ~~Both lawyer and client have authority and responsibility in the objectives and means of representation.~~ The Paragraph (a) confers upon the client ~~has~~ the ultimate authority to determine the purposes to be served by legal representation, within the limits imposed by law and the lawyer's professional obligations. ~~Within those limits, a client also has a right to consult with the lawyer about the means to be used in pursuing those objectives. At the same time, a lawyer is not required to pursue objectives or employ means simply because a client may wish that the lawyer do so. A clear distinction between objectives and means sometimes cannot be drawn, and in many cases the client-lawyer relationship partakes of a joint undertaking. In questions of means the lawyer should assume responsibility for technical and legal tactical issues, but should defer to the client regarding such questions as the expense to be incurred and concern for third persons who might be adversely affected. Law defining the lawyer's scope of authority in litigation varies among jurisdictions.~~ The decisions specified in paragraph (a), such as whether to settle a civil matter, must also be made by the client. See Rule 1.4(a)(1) for the lawyer's duty to communicate with the client about such decisions. With respect to the means by which the client's objectives are to be pursued, the lawyer shall consult with the client as required by Rule 1.4(a)(2) and may take such action as is impliedly authorized to carry out the representation.

[2]   On occasion, however, a lawyer and a client may disagree about the means to be used to accomplish the client's objectives. Clients normally defer to the special knowledge and skill of their lawyer with respect to the means to be used to accomplish their objectives, particularly with respect to technical, legal and tactical matters. Conversely, lawyers usually defer to the client regarding such questions as the expense to be incurred and concern for third persons who might be adversely affected. Because of the varied nature of the matters about which a lawyer and client might disagree and because the actions in question may implicate the interests of a tribunal or other persons, this Rule does not prescribe how such disagreements are to be resolved. Other law, however, may be applicable and should be consulted by the lawyer. The lawyer should also consult with the client and seek a mutually acceptable resolution of the disagreement. If such efforts are unavailing and the lawyer has a fundamental disagreement with the client, the lawyer may withdraw from the representation. See Rule 1.16(b)(4). Conversely, the client may resolve the disagreement by discharging the lawyer. See Rule 1.16(a)(3).

[3]   At the outset of a representation, the client may authorize the lawyer to take specific action on the client's behalf without further consultation. Absent a material change in circumstances and subject to Rule 1.4, a lawyer may rely on such an advance authorization. The client may, however, revoke such authority at any time.

[2] [4] In a case in which the client appears to be suffering ~~mental disability~~ diminished capacity, the lawyer's duty to abide by the client's decisions is to be guided by reference to Rule 1.14.

Independence from Client's Views or Activities

[3] [5] Legal representation should not be denied to people who are unable to afford legal services, or whose cause is controversial or the subject of popular disapproval. By the same token, representing a client does not constitute approval of the client's views or activities.

~~Services Limited in Objectives or Means~~ Agreements Limiting Scope of Representation

[4] [6] The ~~objectives or~~ scope of services to be provided by a lawyer may be limited by agreement with the client or by the terms under which the lawyer's services are made available to the client. ~~For example, a retainer may be for a specifically defined purpose. Representation provided through a legal aid agency may be subject to limitations on the types of cases the agency handles.~~ When a lawyer has been retained by an insurer to represent an insured, for example, the representation may be limited to matters related to the insurance coverage. ~~The~~ A limited representation may be appropriate because the client has limited objectives for the representation. In addition, the terms upon which representation is undertaken may exclude specific ~~objectives or~~

means that might otherwise be used to accomplish the client's objectives. Such limitations may exclude ~~objectives or means~~ actions that the client thinks are too costly or that the lawyer regards as repugnant or imprudent.

[7] Although this Rule affords the lawyer and client substantial latitude to limit the representation, the limitation must be reasonable under the circumstances. If, for example, a client's objective is limited to securing general information about the law the client needs in order to handle a common and typically uncomplicated legal problem, the lawyer and client may agree that the lawyer's services will be limited to a brief telephone consultation. Such a limitation, however, would not be reasonable if the time allotted was not sufficient to yield advice upon which the client could rely. Although an agreement for a limited representation does not exempt a lawyer from the duty to provide competent representation, the limitation is a factor to be considered when determining the legal knowledge, skill, thoroughness and preparation reasonably necessary for the representation. See Rule 1.1.

~~[5]~~ [8] ~~An agreement~~ All agreements concerning ~~the scope of~~ a lawyer's representation of a client must accord with the Rules of Professional Conduct and other law. ~~Thus, the client may not be asked to agree to representation so limited in scope as to violate Rule 1.1, or to surrender the right to terminate the lawyer's services or the right to settle litigation that the lawyer might wish to continue.~~ See, e.g., Rules 1.1, 1.8 and 5.6.

Criminal, Fraudulent and Prohibited Transactions

~~[6]~~ [9] ~~A~~ Paragraph (d) prohibits a lawyer from knowingly counseling or assisting a client to commit a crime or fraud. This prohibition, however, does not preclude the lawyer ~~is required to give~~ from giving an honest opinion about the actual consequences that appear likely to result from a client's conduct. ~~The~~ Nor does the fact that a client uses advice in a course of action that is criminal or fraudulent ~~does not,~~ of itself~~,~~ make a lawyer a party to the course of action. ~~However, a lawyer may not knowingly assist a client in criminal or fraudulent conduct.~~ There is a critical distinction between presenting an analysis of legal aspects of questionable conduct and recommending the means by which a crime or fraud might be committed with impunity.

~~[7]~~ [10] When the client's course of action has already begun and is continuing, the lawyer's responsibility is especially delicate. ~~The lawyer is not permitted to reveal the client's wrongdoing, except where permitted by Rule 1.6. However, the~~ The lawyer is required to avoid ~~furthering the purpose~~ assisting the client, for example, by drafting or delivering documents that the lawyer knows are fraudulent or by suggesting how ~~it~~ the wrongdoing might be concealed. A lawyer may not continue assisting a client in conduct that the lawyer originally ~~supposes is~~ supposed was legally proper but then discovers is criminal or fraudulent. ~~Withdrawal~~ The lawyer must, therefore, withdraw from the representation~~, there-~~

fore, ~~may be required~~ of the client in the matter. See Rule 1.16(a). In some cases, withdrawal alone might be insufficient. It may be necessary for the lawyer to give notice of the fact of withdrawal and to disaffirm any opinion, document, affirmation or the like. See Rule 4.1.

~~[8]~~ [11] Where the client is a fiduciary, the lawyer may be charged with special obligations in dealings with a beneficiary.

~~[9]~~ [12] Paragraph (d) applies whether or not the defrauded party is a party to the transaction. Hence, a lawyer ~~should~~ must not participate in a ~~sham~~ transaction; ~~for example, a transaction~~ to effectuate criminal or fraudulent ~~escape~~ avoidance of tax liability. Paragraph (d) does not preclude undertaking a criminal defense incident to a general retainer for legal services to a lawful enterprise. The last clause of paragraph (d) recognizes that determining the validity or interpretation of a statute or regulation may require a course of action involving disobedience of the statute or regulation or of the interpretation placed upon it by governmental authorities.

[13]   If a lawyer comes to know or reasonably should know that a client expects assistance not permitted by the Rules of Professional Conduct or other law or if the lawyer intends to act contrary to the client's instructions, the lawyer must consult with the client regarding the limitations on the lawyer's conduct. See Rule 1.4(a)(5).

Rule 1.3   Diligence

A lawyer shall act with reasonable diligence and promptness in representing a client.

COMMENT

[1]   A lawyer should pursue a matter on behalf of a client despite opposition, obstruction or personal inconvenience to the lawyer, and ~~may~~ take whatever lawful and ethical measures are required to vindicate a client's cause or endeavor. A lawyer ~~should~~ must also act with commitment and dedication to the interests of the client and with zeal in advocacy upon the client's behalf. ~~However, a~~ A lawyer is not bound, however, to press for every advantage that might be realized for a client. ~~A~~ For example, a lawyer ~~has~~ may have authority to exercise professional discretion in determining the means by which a matter should be pursued. See Rule 1.2. ~~A lawyer's work load should be controlled so that each matter can be handled adequately.~~ The lawyer's duty to act with reasonable diligence does not require the use of offensive tactics or preclude the treating of all persons involved in the legal process with courtesy and respect.

[2]   A lawyer's work load must be controlled so that each matter can be handled competently.

~~[2]~~ [3] Perhaps no professional shortcoming is more widely resented than procrastination. A client's interests often can be adversely affected by the passage of time or the change of conditions; in extreme instances, as when a lawyer overlooks a statute of limitations, the client's legal position may be destroyed. Even when the client's interests are not affected in substance, however, unreasonable delay can cause a client needless anxiety and undermine confidence in the lawyer's trustworthiness. A lawyer's duty to act with reasonable promptness, however, does not preclude the lawyer from agreeing to a reasonable request for a postponement that will not prejudice the lawyer's client.

[3] [4] Unless the relationship is terminated as provided in Rule 1.16, a lawyer should carry through to conclusion all matters undertaken for a client. If a lawyer's employment is limited to a specific matter, the relationship terminates when the matter has been resolved. If a lawyer has served a client over a substantial period in a variety of matters, the client sometimes may assume that the lawyer will continue to serve on a continuing basis unless the lawyer gives notice of withdrawal. Doubt about whether a client-lawyer relationship still exists should be clarified by the lawyer, preferably in writing, so that the client will not mistakenly suppose the lawyer is looking after the client's affairs when the lawyer has ceased to do so. For example, if a lawyer has handled a judicial or administrative proceeding that produced a result adverse to the client but has not been specifically instructed concerning pursuit of an and the lawyer and the client have not agreed that the lawyer will handle the matter on appeal, the lawyer should advise must consult with the client of about the possibility of appeal before relinquishing responsibility for the matter. See Rule 1.4(a)(2). Whether the lawyer is obligated to prosecute the appeal for the client depends on the scope of the representation the lawyer has agreed to provide to the client. See Rule 1.2.

[5] To prevent neglect of client matters in the event of a sole practitioner's death or disability, the duty of diligence may require that each sole practitioner prepare a plan, in conformity with applicable rules, that designates another competent lawyer to review client files, notify each client of the lawyer's death or disability, and determine whether there is a need for immediate protective action. Cf. Rule 28 of the American Bar Association Model Rules for Lawyer Disciplinary Enforcement (providing for court appointment of a lawyer to inventory files and take other protective action in absence of a plan providing for another lawyer to protect the interests of the clients of a deceased or disabled lawyer).

Rule 1.4 Communication

(a) A lawyer shall keep a client reasonably informed about the status of a matter and promptly comply with reasonable requests for information.:

    (1) promptly inform the client of any decision or circumstance with respect to which the client's informed consent, as defined in Rule 1.0(e), is required by these Rules;

(2) reasonably consult with the client about the means by which the client's objectives are to be accomplished;

(3) keep the client reasonably informed about the status of the matter;

(4) promptly comply with reasonable requests for information; and

(5) consult with the client about any relevant limitation on the lawyer's conduct when the lawyer knows that the client expects assistance not permitted by the Rules of Professional Conduct or other law.

(b) A lawyer shall explain a matter to the extent reasonably necessary to permit the client to make informed decisions regarding the representation.

COMMENT

[1] Reasonable communication between the lawyer and the client is necessary for the client effectively to participate in the representation.

Communicating with Client

[2] If these Rules require that a particular decision about the representation be made by the client, paragraph (a)(1) requires that the lawyer promptly consult with and secure the client's consent prior to taking action unless prior discussions with the client have resolved what action the client wants the lawyer to take. For example, a lawyer who receives from opposing counsel an offer of settlement in a civil controversy or a proffered plea bargain in a criminal case must promptly inform the client of its substance unless the client has previously indicated that the proposal will be acceptable or unacceptable or has authorized the lawyer to accept or to reject the offer. See Rule 1.2(a).

[3] Paragraph (a)(2) requires the lawyer to reasonably consult with the client about the means to be used to accomplish the client's objectives. In some situations—depending on both the importance of the action under consideration and the feasibility of consulting with the client—this duty will require consultation prior to taking action. In other circumstances, such as during a trial when an immediate decision must be made, the exigency of the situation may require the lawyer to act without prior consultation. In such cases the lawyer must nonetheless act reasonably to inform the client of actions the lawyer has taken on the client's behalf. Additionally, paragraph (a)(3) requires that the lawyer keep the client reasonably informed about the status of the matter, such as significant developments affecting the timing or the substance of the representation.

[4] A lawyer's regular communication with clients will minimize the occasions on which a client will need to request information concerning the representation. When a client makes a reasonable request for

information, however, paragraph (a)(4) requires prompt compliance with the request, or if a prompt response is not feasible, that the lawyer, or a member of the lawyer's staff, acknowledge receipt of the request and advise the client when a response may be expected. Client telephone calls should be promptly returned or acknowledged.

Explaining Matters

[1] [5] The client should have sufficient information to participate intelligently in decisions concerning the objectives of the representation and the means by which they are to be pursued, to the extent the client is willing and able to do so. For example, a lawyer negotiating on behalf of a client should provide the client with facts relevant to the matter, inform the client of communications from another party and take other reasonable steps that permit the client to make a decision regarding a serious offer from another party. A lawyer who receives from opposing counsel an offer of settlement in a civil controversy or a proffered plea bargain in a criminal case should promptly inform the client of its substance unless prior discussions with the client have left it clear that the proposal will be unacceptable. See Rule 1.2(a). Even when a client delegates authority to the lawyer, the client should be kept advised of the status of the matter. [2] Adequacy of communication depends in part on the kind of advice or assistance that is involved. For example, in negotiations where when there is time to explain a proposal made in a negotiation, the lawyer should review all important provisions with the client before proceeding to an agreement. In litigation a lawyer should explain the general strategy and prospects of success and ordinarily should consult the client on tactics that might are likely to result in significant expense or to injure or coerce others. On the other hand, a lawyer ordinarily cannot will not be expected to describe trial or negotiation strategy in detail. The guiding principle is that the lawyer should fulfill reasonable client expectations for information consistent with the duty to act in the client's best interests, and the client's overall requirements as to the character of representation. In certain circumstances, such as when a lawyer asks a client to consent to a representation affected by a conflict of interest, the client must give informed consent, as defined in Rule 1.0(e).

[3] [6] Ordinarily, the information to be provided is that appropriate for a client who is a comprehending and responsible adult. However, fully informing the client according to this standard may be impracticable, for example, where the client is a child or suffers from mental disability diminished capacity. See Rule 1.14. When the client is an organization or group, it is often impossible or inappropriate to inform every one of its members about its legal affairs; ordinarily, the lawyer should address communications to the appropriate officials of the organization. See Rule 1.13. Where many routine matters are involved, a system of limited or occasional reporting may be arranged with the

client. ~~Practical exigency may also require a lawyer to act for a client without prior consultation.~~

Withholding Information

~~[4]~~ [7] In some circumstances, a lawyer may be justified in delaying transmission of information when the client would be likely to react imprudently to an immediate communication. Thus, a lawyer might withhold a psychiatric diagnosis of a client when the examining psychiatrist indicates that disclosure would harm the client. A lawyer may not withhold information to serve the lawyer's own interest or convenience or the interests or convenience of another person. Rules or court orders governing litigation may provide that information supplied to a lawyer may not be disclosed to the client. Rule 3.4(c) directs compliance with such rules or orders.

RULE 1.5 Fees*

(a) A ~~lawyer's fee~~ **lawyer** shall ~~be reasonable~~ **not make an agreement for, charge, or collect an unreasonable fee or an unreasonable amount for expenses. The factors to be considered in determining the reasonableness of a fee include the following:**

(1) the time and labor required, the novelty and difficulty of the questions involved, and the skill requisite to perform the legal service properly;

(2) the likelihood, if apparent to the client, that the acceptance of the particular employment will preclude other employment by the lawyer;

(3) the fee customarily charged in the locality for similar legal services;

(4) the amount involved and the results obtained;

(5) the time limitations imposed by the client or by the circumstances;

(6) the nature and length of the professional relationship with the client;

(7) the experience, reputation, and ability of the lawyer or lawyers performing the services; and

(8) whether the fee is fixed or contingent.

(b) ~~When the lawyer has not regularly represented the client,~~ **The** scope of the representation **and** the basis or rate of the fee **and expenses for which the client will be responsible**

---

* The Ethics 2000 Commission's Report recommended amending Rule 1.5 to include a requirement that all fee agreements or changes in the fee be in writing. The provision included an exception "when the lawyer will charge a regularly represented client on the same basis or rate" or "in any matter in which it is reasonably foreseeable that total cost to a client, including attorney fees, will be [$500] or less." The House of Delegates rejected this proposed change.

shall be communicated to the client, preferably in writing, before or within a reasonable time after commencing the representation, except when the lawyer will charge a regularly represented client on the same basis or rate. Any changes in the basis or rate of the fee or expenses shall also be communicated to the client.

(c) A fee may be contingent on the outcome of the matter for which the service is rendered, except in a matter in which a contingent fee is prohibited by paragraph (d) or other law. A contingent fee agreement shall be in a writing signed by the client and shall state the method by which the fee is to be determined, including the percentage or percentages that shall accrue to the lawyer in the event of settlement, trial or appeal; litigation and other expenses to be deducted from the recovery; and whether such expenses are to be deducted before or after the contingent fee is calculated. The agreement must clearly notify the client of any expenses for which the client will be liable whether or not the client is the prevailing party. Upon conclusion of a contingent fee matter, the lawyer shall provide the client with a written statement stating the outcome of the matter and, if there is a recovery, showing the remittance to the client and the method of its determination.

(d) A lawyer shall not enter into an arrangement for, charge, or collect:

(1) any fee in a domestic relations matter, the payment or amount of which is contingent upon the securing of a divorce or upon the amount of alimony or support, or property settlement in lieu thereof; or

(2) a contingent fee for representing a defendant in a criminal case.

(e) A division of a fee between lawyers who are not in the same firm may be made only if:

(1) the division is in proportion to the services performed by each lawyer or, ~~by written agreement with the client,~~ each lawyer assumes joint responsibility for the representation;

(2) the client ~~is advised of and does not object to the participation of all the lawyers involved~~ agrees to the arrangement, including the share each lawyer will receive, and the agreement is confirmed in writing; and

(3) the total fee is reasonable.

COMMENT

Reasonableness of Fee and Expenses

[1] Paragraph (a) requires that lawyers charge fees that are reasonable under the circumstances. The factors specified in (1) through (8)

are not exclusive. Nor will each factor be relevant in each instance. Paragraph (a) also requires that expenses for which the client will be charged must be reasonable. A lawyer may seek reimbursement for the cost of services performed in-house, such as copying, or for other expenses incurred in-house, such as telephone charges, either by charging a reasonable amount to which the client has agreed in advance or by charging an amount that reasonably reflects the cost incurred by the lawyer.

Basis or Rate of Fee

[1] [2] When the lawyer has regularly represented a client, they ordinarily will have evolved an understanding concerning the basis or rate of the fee and the expenses for which the client will be responsible. In a new client-lawyer relationship, however, an understanding as to the fee fees and expenses should must be promptly established. It is not necessary to recite all the factors that underlie the basis of the fee, but only those that are directly involved in its computation. It is sufficient, for example, to state that the basic rate is an hourly charge or a fixed amount or an estimated amount, or to identify the factors that may be taken into account in finally fixing the fee. When developments occur during the representation that render an earlier estimate substantially inaccurate, a revised estimate should be provided to the client. Generally, it is desirable to furnish the client with at least a simple memorandum or copy of the lawyer's customary fee arrangements that states the general nature of the legal services to be provided, the basis, rate or total amount of the fee and whether and to what extent the client will be responsible for any costs, expenses or disbursements in the course of the representation. A written statement concerning the fee terms of the engagement reduces the possibility of misunderstanding. Furnishing the client with a simple memorandum or a copy of the lawyer's customary fee schedule is sufficient if the basis or rate of the fee is set forth.

[3] Contingent fees, like any other fees, are subject to the reasonableness standard of paragraph (a) of this Rule. In determining whether a particular contingent fee is reasonable, or whether it is reasonable to charge any form of contingent fee, a lawyer must consider the factors that are relevant under the circumstances. Applicable law may impose limitations on contingent fees, such as a ceiling on the percentage allowable, or may require a lawyer to offer clients an alternative basis for the fee. Applicable law also may apply to situations other than a contingent fee, for example, government regulations regarding fees in certain tax matters.

Terms of Payment

[2] [4] A lawyer may require advance payment of a fee, but is obliged to return any unearned portion. See Rule 1.16(d). A lawyer may accept property in payment for services, such as an ownership interest in

an enterprise, providing this does not involve acquisition of a proprietary interest in the cause of action or subject matter of the litigation contrary to Rule 1.8(j)(i). However, a fee paid in property instead of money may be subject to ~~special scrutiny because it involves questions concerning both the value of the services and the lawyer's special knowledge of the value of the property~~ the requirements of Rule 1.8(a) because such fees often have the essential qualities of a business transaction with the client.

~~[3]~~ [5] An agreement may not be made whose terms might induce the lawyer improperly to curtail services for the client or perform them in a way contrary to the client's interest. For example, a lawyer should not enter into an agreement whereby services are to be provided only up to a stated amount when it is foreseeable that more extensive services probably will be required, unless the situation is adequately explained to the client. Otherwise, the client might have to bargain for further assistance in the midst of a proceeding or transaction. However, it is proper to define the extent of services in light of the client's ability to pay. A lawyer should not exploit a fee arrangement based primarily on hourly charges by using wasteful procedures. ~~When there is doubt whether a contingent fee is consistent with the client's best interest, the lawyer should offer the client alternative bases for the fee and explain their implications. Applicable law may impose limitations on contingent fees, such as a ceiling on the percentage.~~

Prohibited Contingent Fees

[6]   Paragraph (d) prohibits a lawyer from charging a contingent fee in a domestic relations matter when payment is contingent upon the securing of a divorce or upon the amount of alimony or support or property settlement to be obtained. This provision does not preclude a contract for a contingent fee for legal representation in connection with the recovery of post-judgment balances due under support, alimony or other financial orders because such contracts do not implicate the same policy concerns.

Division of Fee

~~[4]~~ [7] A division of fee is a single billing to a client covering the fee of two or more lawyers who are not in the same firm. A division of fee facilitates association of more than one lawyer in a matter in which neither alone could serve the client as well, and most often is used when the fee is contingent and the division is between a referring lawyer and a trial specialist. Paragraph (e) permits the lawyers to divide a fee ~~on~~ either on the basis of the proportion of services they render or ~~by agreement between the participating lawyers~~ if ~~all assume~~ each lawyer assumes responsibility for the representation as a whole. ~~and~~ In addition, the client ~~is advised and does not object. It does not require disclosure to the client of~~ must agree to the arrangement, including the share that each lawyer is to receive, and the agreement must be confirmed in writing. Contingent fee agreements must be in a writing signed by the client and must otherwise comply with paragraph (c) of this Rule. Joint responsibility for the representation entails ~~the obligations stated in Rule 5.1 for purposes of the matter involved~~ financial and ethical responsibility for the representation as if the lawyers were associated in a partnership. A lawyer should only refer a matter to a lawyer whom the referring lawyer reasonably believes is competent to handle the matter. See Rule 1.1.

[8] Paragraph (e) does not prohibit or regulate division of fees to be received in the future for work done when lawyers were previously associated in a law firm.

Disputes over Fees

~~[5]~~ [9] If a procedure has been established for resolution of fee disputes, such as an arbitration or mediation procedure established by the bar, the lawyer must comply with the procedure when it is mandatory, and, even when it is voluntary, the lawyer should conscientiously consider submitting to it. Law may prescribe a procedure for determining a lawyer's fee, for example, in representation of an executor or administrator, a class or a person entitled to a reasonable fee as part of the measure of damages. The lawyer entitled to such a fee and a lawyer representing another party concerned with the fee should comply with the prescribed procedure.

RULE 1.6   Confidentiality of Information*

(a) A lawyer shall not reveal information relating to the representation of a client unless the client ~~consents after consultation, except for disclosures that are~~ gives informed consent, the disclosure is impliedly authorized in order to carry out the representation, ~~and except as stated in~~ or the disclosure is permitted by paragraph (b).

(b) A lawyer may reveal ~~such~~ information relating to the representation of a client to the extent the lawyer reasonably believes necessary:

* The Ethics 2000 Commission's Report recommended amending Rule 1.6 to include the following exceptions to subsection (b) of the confidentiality rule:

(2) to prevent the client from committing a crime or fraud that is reasonably certain to result in substantial injury to the financial interests or property of another and in furtherance of which the client has used or is using the lawyer's services;

(3) to prevent, mitigate or rectify substantial injury to the financial interests or property of another that is reasonably certain to result or has resulted from the client's commission of a crime or fraud in furtherance of which the client has used the lawyer's services;

The ABA House of Delegates rejected (b)(2) and the Ethics 2000 Commission withdrew (b)(3) from consideration.

(1) to prevent ~~the client from committing a criminal act that the lawyer believes is likely to result in imminent~~ <u>reasonably certain</u> death or substantial bodily harm; ~~or~~

(2) to secure legal advice about the lawyer's compliance with these Rules;

~~(2)~~ <u>(3)</u> to establish a claim or defense on behalf of the lawyer in a controversy between the lawyer and the client, to establish a defense to a criminal charge or civil claim against the lawyer based upon conduct in which the client was involved, or to respond to allegations in any proceeding concerning the lawyer's representation of the client; <u>or</u>

(4) to comply with other law or a court order.

COMMENT

~~[1]   The lawyer is part of a judicial system charged with upholding the law. One of the lawyer's functions is to advise clients so that they avoid any violation of the law in the proper exercise of their rights.~~

~~[2]   The observance of the ethical obligation of a lawyer to hold inviolate confidential information of the client not only facilitates the full development of facts essential to proper representation of the client but also encourages people to seek early legal assistance.~~

~~[3]   Almost without exception, clients come to lawyers in order to determine what their rights are and what is, in the maze of laws and regulations, deemed to be legal and correct. The common law recognizes that the client's confidences must be protected from disclosure. Based upon experience, lawyers know that almost all clients follow the advice given, and the law is upheld.~~

<u>[1]   This Rule governs the disclosure by a lawyer of information relating to the representation of a client during the lawyer's representation of the client. See Rule 1.18 for the lawyer's duties with respect to information provided to the lawyer by a prospective client, Rule 1.9(c)(2) for the lawyer's duty not to reveal information relating to the lawyer's prior representation of a former client and Rules 1.8(b) and 1.9(c)(1) for the lawyer's duties with respect to the use of such information to the disadvantage of clients and former clients.</u>

~~[4]~~ <u>[2]</u> A fundamental principle in the client-lawyer relationship is that<u>, in the absence of the client's informed consent,</u> the lawyer ~~maintain confidentiality of~~ <u>must not reveal</u> information relating to the representation. <u>See Rule 1.0(e) for the definition of informed consent. This</u> contributes to the trust that is the hallmark of the client-lawyer relationship. The client is thereby encouraged to <u>seek legal assistance and to</u> communicate fully and frankly with the lawyer even as to embarrassing or legally damaging subject matter. <u>The lawyer needs this information to represent the client effectively and, if necessary, to advise the client to refrain from wrongful conduct. Almost without exception, clients come to lawyers in order to determine their rights and what is, in the complex of</u>

laws and regulations, deemed to be legal and correct. Based upon experience, lawyers know that almost all clients follow the advice given, and the law is upheld.

[5] [3] The principle of client-lawyer confidentiality is given effect in two by related bodies of law,: the attorney-client privilege, (which includes the work product doctrine) in the law of evidence and the rule of confidentiality established in professional ethics. The attorney-client privilege applies and work-product doctrine apply in judicial and other proceedings in which a lawyer may be called as a witness or otherwise required to produce evidence concerning a client. The rule of client-lawyer confidentiality applies in situations other than those where evidence is sought from the lawyer through compulsion of law. The confidentiality rule, for example, applies not merely only to matters communicated in confidence by the client but also to all information relating to the representation, whatever its source. A lawyer may not disclose such information except as authorized or required by the Rules of Professional Conduct or other law. See also Scope.

[6] The requirement of maintaining confidentiality of information relating to representation applies to government lawyers who may disagree with the policy goals that their representation is designed to advance.

[4] Paragraph (a) prohibits a lawyer from revealing information relating to the representation of a client. This prohibition also applies to disclosures by a lawyer that do not in themselves reveal protected information but could reasonably lead to the discovery of such information by a third person. A lawyer's use of a hypothetical to discuss issues relating to the representation is permissible so long as there is no reasonable likelihood that the listener will be able to ascertain the identity of the client or the situation involved.

Authorized Disclosure

[7] [5] A Except to the extent that the client's instructions or special circumstances limit that authority, a lawyer is impliedly authorized to make disclosures about a client when appropriate in carrying out the representation, except to the extent that the client's instructions or special circumstances limit that authority. In litigation some situations, for example, a lawyer may disclose information by admitting be impliedly authorized to admit a fact that cannot properly be disputed or, in negotiation by making to make a disclosure that facilitates a satisfactory conclusion to a matter. [8] Lawyers in a firm may, in the course of the firm's practice, disclose to each other information relating to a client of the firm, unless the client has instructed that particular information be confined to specified lawyers.

Disclosure Adverse to Client

[9] [6] The Although the public interest is usually best served by a strict rule requiring lawyers to preserve the confidentiality of informa-

tion relating to the representation of their clients, the confidentiality rule is subject to limited exceptions. ~~In becoming privy to information about a client, a lawyer may foresee that the client intends serious harm to another person. However, to the extent a lawyer is required or permitted to disclose a client's purposes, the client will be inhibited from revealing facts which would enable the lawyer to counsel against a wrongful course of action. The public is better protected if full and open communication by the client is encouraged than if it is inhibited.~~ Paragraph (b)(1) recognizes the overriding value of life and physical integrity and permits disclosure reasonably necessary to prevent reasonably certain death or substantial bodily harm. Such harm is reasonably certain to occur if it will be suffered imminently or if there is a present and substantial threat that a person will suffer such harm at a later date if the lawyer fails to take action necessary to eliminate the threat. Thus, a lawyer who knows that a client has accidentally discharged toxic waste into a town's water supply may reveal this information to the authorities if there is a present and substantial risk that a person who drinks the water will contract a life-threatening or debilitating disease and the lawyer's disclosure is necessary to eliminate the threat or reduce the number of victims.

~~[10]   Several situations must be distinguished.~~

~~[11]   First, the lawyer may not counsel or assist a client in conduct that is criminal or fraudulent. See Rule 1.2(d). Similarly, a lawyer has a duty under Rule 3.3(a)(4) not to use false evidence. This duty is essentially a special instance of the duty prescribed in Rule 1.2(d) to avoid assisting a client in criminal or fraudulent conduct.~~

~~[12]   Second, the lawyer may have been innocently involved in past conduct by the client that was criminal or fraudulent. In such a situation the lawyer has not violated Rule 1.2(d), because to "counsel or assist" criminal or fraudulent conduct requires knowing that the conduct is of that character.~~

~~[13]   Third, the lawyer may learn that a client intends prospective conduct that is criminal and likely to result in imminent death or substantial bodily harm. As stated in paragraph (b)(1), the lawyer has professional discretion to reveal information in order to prevent such consequences. The lawyer may make a disclosure in order to prevent homicide or serious bodily injury which the lawyer reasonably believes is intended by a client. It is very difficult for a lawyer to "know" when such a heinous purpose will actually be carried out, for the client may have a change of mind.~~

~~[14]   The lawyer's exercise of discretion requires consideration of such factors as the nature of the lawyer's relationship with the client and with those who might be injured by the client, the lawyer's own involvement in the transaction and factors that may extenuate the conduct in question. Where practical, the lawyer should seek to persuade the client to take suitable action. In any case, a disclosure adverse to the client's interest should be no greater than the lawyer reasonably believes~~

~~necessary to the purpose. A lawyer's decision not to take preventive action permitted by paragraph (b)(1) does not violate this Rule.~~

[7] A lawyer's confidentiality obligations do not preclude a lawyer from securing confidential legal advice about the lawyer's personal responsibility to comply with these Rules. In most situations, disclosing information to secure such advice will be impliedly authorized for the lawyer to carry out the representation. Even when the disclosure is not impliedly authorized, paragraph (b)(2) permits such disclosure because of the importance of a lawyer's compliance with the Rules of Professional Conduct.

~~Dispute Concerning a Lawyer's Conduct~~

~~[18]~~ [8] Where a legal claim or disciplinary charge alleges complicity of the lawyer in a client's conduct or other misconduct of the lawyer involving representation of the client, the lawyer may respond to the extent the lawyer reasonably believes necessary to establish a defense. The same is true with respect to a claim involving the conduct or representation of a former client. Such a charge can arise in a civil, criminal, disciplinary or other proceeding and can be based on a wrong allegedly committed by the lawyer against the client or on a wrong alleged by a third person, for example, a person claiming to have been defrauded by the lawyer and client acting together. The lawyer's right to respond arises when an assertion of such complicity has been made. Paragraph (b)~~(2)~~(3) does not require the lawyer to await the commencement of an action or proceeding that charges such complicity, so that the defense may be established by responding directly to a third party who has made such an assertion. The right to defend also applies, of course, ~~applies~~ where a proceeding has been commenced. ~~Where practicable and not prejudicial to the lawyer's ability to establish the defense, the lawyer should advise the client of the third party's assertion and request that the client respond appropriately. In any event, disclosure should be no greater than the lawyer reasonably believes is necessary to vindicate innocence, the disclosure should be made in a manner which limits access to the information to the tribunal or other persons having a need to know it, and appropriate protective orders or other arrangements should be sought by the lawyer to the fullest extent practicable.~~

~~[19]~~ [9] ~~If the lawyer is charged with wrongdoing in which the client's conduct is implicated, the rule of confidentiality should not prevent the lawyer from defending against the charge. Such a charge can arise in a civil, criminal or professional disciplinary proceeding, and can be based on a wrong allegedly committed by the lawyer against the client, or on a wrong alleged by a third person; for example, a person claiming to have been defrauded by the lawyer and client acting together.~~ A lawyer entitled to a fee is permitted by paragraph (b)~~(2)~~(3) to prove the services rendered in an action to collect it. This aspect of the rule expresses the principle that the beneficiary of a fiduciary relationship may not exploit it to the detriment of the fiduciary. ~~As stated above, the~~

~~lawyer must make every effort practicable to avoid unnecessary disclo-~~
~~sure of information relating to a representation, to limit disclosure to~~
~~those having the need to know it, and to obtain protective orders or~~
~~make other arrangements minimizing the risk of disclosure.~~

[10]   Other law may require that a lawyer disclose information about a client. Whether such a law supersedes Rule 1.6 is a question of law beyond the scope of these Rules. When disclosure of information relating to the representation appears to be required by other law, the lawyer must discuss the matter with the client to the extent required by Rule 1.4. If, however, the other law supersedes this Rule and requires disclosure, paragraph (b)(4) permits the lawyer to make such disclosures as are necessary to comply with the law.

[11]   A lawyer may be ordered to reveal information relating to the representation of a client by a court or by another tribunal or governmental entity claiming authority pursuant to other law to compel the disclosure. Absent informed consent of the client to do otherwise, the lawyer should assert on behalf of the client all nonfrivolous claims that the order is not authorized by other law or that the information sought is protected against disclosure by the attorney-client privilege or other applicable law. In the event of an adverse ruling, the lawyer must consult with the client about the possibility of appeal to the extent required by Rule 1.4. Unless review is sought, however, paragraph (b)(4) permits the lawyer to comply with the court's order.

[12]   Paragraph (b) permits disclosure only to the extent the lawyer reasonably believes the disclosure is necessary to accomplish one of the purposes specified. Where practicable, the lawyer should first seek to persuade the client to take suitable action to obviate the need for disclosure. In any case, a disclosure adverse to the client's interest should be no greater than the lawyer reasonably believes necessary to accomplish the purpose. If the disclosure will be made in connection with a judicial proceeding, the disclosure should be made in a manner that limits access to the information to the tribunal or other persons having a need to know it and appropriate protective orders or other arrangements should be sought by the lawyer to the fullest extent practicable.

[13]   Paragraph (b) permits but does not require the disclosure of information relating to a client's representation to accomplish the purposes specified in paragraphs (b)(1) through (b)(4). In exercising the discretion conferred by this Rule, the lawyer may consider such factors as the nature of the lawyer's relationship with the client and with those who might be injured by the client, the lawyer's own involvement in the transaction and factors that may extenuate the conduct in question. A lawyer's decision not to disclose as permitted by paragraph (b) does not violate this Rule. Disclosure may be required, however, by other Rules. Some Rules require disclosure only if such disclosure would be permitted by paragraph (b). See Rules 1.2(d), 4.1(b), 8.1 and 8.3. Rule 3.3, on the other hand, requires disclosure in some circumstances regardless of whether such disclosure is permitted by this Rule. See Rule 3.3(c).

Withdrawal

[15] [14] If the lawyer's services will be used by the client in materially furthering a course of criminal or fraudulent conduct, the lawyer must withdraw, as stated in Rule 1.16(a)(1). [16] After withdrawal the lawyer is required to refrain from making disclosure of the client's confidences, except as otherwise permitted in Rule 1.6. Neither this Rule nor Rule 1.8(b) nor Rule 1.16(d) prevents the lawyer from giving notice of the fact of withdrawal, and the lawyer may also withdraw or disaffirm any opinion, document, affirmation, or the like. [17] Where the client is an organization, the lawyer may be in doubt whether contemplated conduct will actually be carried out by the organization. Where necessary to guide conduct in connection with this Rule, the lawyer may make inquiry within the organization as indicated in Rule 1.13(b).

~~Disclosures Otherwise Required or Authorized~~

~~[20] The attorney-client privilege is differently defined in various jurisdictions. If a lawyer is called as a witness to give testimony concerning a client, absent waiver by the client, paragraph (a) requires the lawyer to invoke the privilege when it is applicable. The lawyer must comply with the final orders of a court or other tribunal of competent jurisdiction requiring the lawyer to give information about the client.~~

~~[21] The Rules of Professional Conduct in various circumstances permit or require a lawyer to disclose information relating to the representation. See Rules 2.2, 2.3, 3.3 and 4.1. In addition to these provisions, a lawyer may be obligated or permitted by other provisions of law to give information about a client. Whether another provision of law supercedes Rule 1.6 is a matter of interpretation beyond the scope of these Rules, but a presumption should exist against such a supersession.~~

Acting Competently to Preserve Confidentiality

[15] A lawyer must act competently to safeguard information relating to the representation of a client against inadvertent or unauthorized disclosure by the lawyer or other persons who are participating in the representation of the client or who are subject to the lawyer's supervision. See Rules 1.1, 5.1 and 5.3.

[16] When transmitting a communication that includes information relating to the representation of a client, the lawyer must take reasonable precautions to prevent the information from coming into the hands of unintended recipients. This duty, however, does not require that the lawyer use special security measures if the method of communication affords a reasonable expectation of privacy. Special circumstances, however, may warrant special precautions. Factors to be considered in determining the reasonableness of the lawyer's expectation of confidentiality include the sensitivity of the information and the extent to which the privacy of the communication is protected by law or by a confidentiality agreement. A client may require the lawyer to implement special

security measures not required by this Rule or may give informed consent to the use of a means of communication that would otherwise be prohibited by this Rule.

Former Client

[22] [17] The duty of confidentiality continues after the client-lawyer relationship has terminated. See Rule 1.9(c)(2). See Rule 1.9(c)(1) for the prohibition against using such information to the disadvantage of the former client.

Rule 1.7   Conflict of Interest: ~~General Rule~~ Current Clients

~~(a) A lawyer shall not represent a client if the representation of that client will be directly adverse to another client, unless:~~

~~(1) the lawyer reasonably believes the representation will not adversely affect the relationship with the other client; and~~

~~(2) each client consents after consultation.~~

~~(b) A lawyer shall not represent a client if the representation of that client may be materially limited by the lawyer's responsibilities to another client or to a third person, or by the lawyer's own interests, unless:~~

~~(1) the lawyer reasonably believes the representation will not be adversely affected; and~~

~~(2) the client consents after consultation. When representation of multiple clients in a single matter is undertaken, the consultation shall include explanation of the implications of the common representation and the advantages and risks involved.~~

(a) Except as provided in paragraph (b), a lawyer shall not represent a client if the representation involves a concurrent conflict of interest. A concurrent conflict of interest exists if:

(1) the representation of one client will be directly adverse to another client; or

(2) there is a significant risk that the representation of one or more clients will be materially limited by the lawyer's responsibilities to another client, a former client or a third person or by a personal interest of the lawyer.

(b) Notwithstanding the existence of a concurrent conflict of interest under paragraph (a), a lawyer may represent a client if:

(1) the lawyer reasonably believes that the lawyer will be able to provide competent and diligent representation to each affected client;

(2) the representation is not prohibited by law;

(3) the representation does not involve the assertion of a claim by one client against another client represented by the lawyer in the same litigation or other proceeding before a tribunal; and

(4) each affected client gives informed consent, confirmed in writing.

COMMENT

~~Loyalty to a Client~~ General Principles

[1] Loyalty ~~is an~~ and independent judgment are essential ~~element~~ elements in the lawyer's relationship to a client. Concurrent conflicts of interest can arise from the lawyer's responsibilities to another client, a former client or a third person or from the lawyer's own interests. For specific Rules regarding certain concurrent conflicts of interest, see Rule 1.8. For former client conflicts of interest, see Rule 1.9. For conflicts of interest involving prospective clients, see Rule 1.18. For definitions of "informed consent" and "confirmed in writing," see Rule 1.0(e) and (b).

[2] Resolution of a conflict of interest problem under this Rule requires the lawyer to: 1) clearly identify the client or clients; 2) determine whether a conflict of interest exists; 3) decide whether the representation may be undertaken despite the existence of a conflict, i.e., whether the conflict is consentable; and 4) if so, consult with the clients affected under paragraph (a) and obtain their informed consent, confirmed in writing. The clients affected under paragraph (a) include both of the clients referred to in paragraph (a)(1) and the one or more clients whose representation might be materially limited under paragraph (a)(2).

[3] ~~An impermissible~~ A conflict of interest may exist before representation is undertaken, in which event the representation ~~should~~ must be declined, unless the lawyer obtains the informed consent of each client under the conditions of paragraph (b). ~~The~~ To determine whether a conflict of interest exists, a lawyer should adopt reasonable procedures, appropriate for the size and type of firm and practice, to determine in both litigation and non-litigation matters the ~~parties~~ persons and issues involved ~~and to determine whether there are actual or potential conflicts of interest~~. See also Comment to Rule 5.1. Ignorance caused by a failure to institute such procedures will not excuse a lawyer's violation of this Rule. As to whether a client-lawyer relationship exists or, having once been established, is continuing, see Comment to Rule 1.3 and Scope.

~~[2]~~ [4] If ~~such~~ a conflict arises after representation has been undertaken, the lawyer ~~should~~ ordinarily must withdraw from the representation, unless the lawyer has obtained the informed consent of the client under the conditions of paragraph (b). See Rule 1.16. Where more than one client is involved ~~and the lawyer withdraws because a conflict arises after representation~~, whether the lawyer may continue to represent any of the clients is determined <u>both</u> by <u>the lawyer's ability to</u> comply with duties owed to the former <u>client and by the lawyer's ability</u> <u>to represent adequately the remaining client or clients, given the law-</u> <u>yer's duties to the former client.</u> See Rule 1.9. See also ~~Rule 2.2(c)~~ Comments [5] and [29]. ~~As to whether a client-lawyer relationship exists~~ ~~or, having once been established, is continuing, see Comment to Rule 1.3~~ ~~and Scope.~~

[5] Unforeseeable developments, such as changes in corporate and other organizational affiliations or the addition or realignment of parties in litigation, might create conflicts in the midst of a representation, as when a company sued by the lawyer on behalf of one client is bought by another client represented by the lawyer in an unrelated matter. De-pending on the circumstances, the lawyer may have the option to withdraw from one of the representations in order to avoid the conflict. The lawyer must seek court approval where necessary and take steps to minimize harm to the clients. See Rule 1.16. The lawyer must continue to protect the confidences of the client from whose representation the lawyer has withdrawn. See Rule 1.9(c).

Identifying Conflicts of Interest: Directly Adverse

~~[3]~~ [6] ~~As a general proposition, loyalty~~ <u>Loyalty</u> to a <u>current</u> client prohibits undertaking representation directly adverse to that client without that client's <u>informed</u> consent. ~~Paragraph (a) expresses that~~ ~~general rule.~~ Thus, <u>absent consent,</u> a lawyer ~~ordinarily~~ may not act as an advocate <u>in one matter</u> against a person the lawyer represents in some other matter, even ~~if it is~~ <u>when the matters are</u> wholly unrelated. <u>The</u> <u>client as to whom the representation is directly adverse is likely to feel</u> <u>betrayed, and the resulting damage to the client-lawyer relationship is</u> <u>likely to impair the lawyer's ability to represent the client effectively. In</u> addition, the client on whose behalf the adverse representation is under-taken reasonably may fear that the lawyer will pursue that client's case less effectively out of deference to the other client, i.e., that the represen-tation may be materially limited by the lawyer's interest in retaining the current client. <u>Similarly, a directly adverse conflict may arise when a</u> <u>lawyer is required to cross-examine a client who appears as a witness in</u> <u>a lawsuit involving another client, as when the testimony will be damag-</u> <u>ing to the client who is represented in the lawsuit.</u> On the other hand, simultaneous representation in unrelated matters of clients whose inter-ests are only ~~generally~~ <u>economically</u> adverse, such as <u>representation of</u> competing economic enterprises <u>in unrelated litigation,</u> does not <u>ordi-</u> <u>narily constitute a conflict of interest and thus may not</u> require consent of the respective clients. ~~Paragraph (a) applies only when the representa-~~ ~~tion of one client would be directly adverse to the other.~~

[7] Directly adverse conflicts can also arise in transactional mat-ters. For example, if a lawyer is asked to represent the seller of a business in negotiations with a buyer represented by the lawyer, not in the same transaction but in another, unrelated matter, the lawyer could

not undertake the representation without the informed consent of each client.

Identifying Conflicts of Interest: Material Limitation

[4] [8] ~~Loyalty to a client is also impaired when~~ Even where there is no direct adverseness, a conflict of interest exists if there is a significant risk that a ~~lawyer cannot~~ lawyer's ability to consider, recommend or carry out an appropriate course of action for the client ~~because~~ will be materially limited as a result of the lawyer's other responsibilities or interests. For example, a lawyer asked to represent several individuals seeking to form a joint venture is likely to be materially limited in the lawyer's ability to recommend or advocate all possible positions that each might take because of the lawyer's duty of loyalty to the others. The conflict in effect forecloses alternatives that would otherwise be available to the client. ~~Paragraph (b) addresses such situations. A possible conflict~~ The mere possibility of subsequent harm does not itself ~~preclude the representation~~ require disclosure and consent. The critical questions are the likelihood that a ~~conflict~~ difference in interests will eventuate and, if it does, whether it will materially interfere with the lawyer's independent professional judgment in considering alternatives or foreclose courses of action that reasonably should be pursued on behalf of the client. ~~Consideration should be given to whether the client wishes to accommodate the other interest involved.~~

Lawyer's ~~Interests~~ Responsibilities to Former Clients and Other Third Persons

[9] In addition to conflicts with other current clients, a lawyer's duties of loyalty and independence may be materially limited by responsibilities to former clients under Rule 1.9 or by the lawyer's responsibilities to other persons, such as fiduciary duties arising from a lawyer's service as a trustee, executor or corporate director.

Personal Interest Conflicts

[6] [10] The lawyer's own interests should not be permitted to have an adverse effect on representation of a client. For example, ~~a lawyer's need for income should not lead the lawyer to undertake matters that cannot be handled competently and at a reasonable fee. See Rules 1.1 and 1.5. If~~ if the probity of a lawyer's own conduct in a transaction is in serious question, it may be difficult or impossible for the lawyer to give a client detached advice. ~~A~~ Similarly, when a lawyer has discussions concerning possible employment with an opponent of the lawyer's client, or with a law firm representing the opponent, such discussions could materially limit the lawyer's representation of the client. In addition, a lawyer may not allow related business interests to affect representation, for example, by referring clients to an enterprise in which the lawyer has an undisclosed financial interest. See Rule 1.8 for specific Rules pertaining to a number of personal interest conflicts,

including business transactions with clients. See also Rule 1.10 (personal interest conflicts under Rule 1.7 ordinarily are not imputed to other lawyers in a law firm).

[11]   When lawyers representing different clients in the same matter or in substantially related matters are closely related by blood or marriage, there may be a significant risk that client confidences will be revealed and that the lawyer's family relationship will interfere with both loyalty and independent professional judgment. As a result, each client is entitled to know of the existence and implications of the relationship between the lawyers before the lawyer agrees to undertake the representation. Thus, a lawyer related to another lawyer, e.g., as parent, child, sibling or spouse, ordinarily may not represent a client in a matter where that lawyer is representing another party, unless each client gives informed consent. The disqualification arising from a close family relationship is personal and ordinarily is not imputed to members of firms with whom the lawyers are associated. See Rule 1.10.

[12]   A lawyer is prohibited from engaging in sexual relationships with a client unless the sexual relationship predates the formation of the client-lawyer relationship. See Rule 1.8(j).

Interest of Person Paying for a Lawyer's Service

~~[10]~~ [13] A lawyer may be paid from a source other than the client, including a co-client, if the client is informed of that fact and consents and the arrangement does not compromise the lawyer's duty of loyalty or independent judgment to the client. See Rule 1.8(f). ~~For example, when an insurer and its insured have conflicting interests in a matter arising from a liability insurance agreement, and the insurer is required to provide special counsel for the insured, the arrangement should assure the special counsel's professional independence. So also, when a corporation and its directors or employees are involved in a controversy in which they have conflicting interests, the corporation may provide funds for separate legal representation of the directors or employees, if the clients consent after consultation and the arrangement ensures the lawyer's professional independence.~~ If acceptance of the payment from any other source presents a significant risk that the lawyer's representation of the client will be materially limited by the lawyer's own interest in accommodating the person paying the lawyer's fee or by the lawyer's responsibilities to a payer who is also a co-client, then the lawyer must comply with the requirements of paragraph (b) before accepting the representation, including determining whether the conflict is consentable and, if so, that the client has adequate information about the material risks of the representation.

~~Consultation and Consent~~ Prohibited Representations

~~[5]~~ [14] ~~A client~~ Ordinarily, clients may consent to representation notwithstanding a conflict. However, as indicated in paragraph ~~(a)(1)~~

~~with respect to representation directly adverse to a client, and paragraph~~
~~(b)(1) with respect to material limitations on representation of a client,~~
~~when a disinterested lawyer would conclude that the client should not~~
~~agree to the representation under the circumstances,~~ some conflicts are
nonconsentable, meaning that the lawyer involved cannot properly ask
for such agreement or provide representation on the basis of the client's
consent. When the lawyer is representing more than one client ~~is~~
~~involved~~, the question of ~~conflict~~ consentability must be resolved as to
each client. ~~Moreover, there may be circumstances where it is impossible~~
~~to make the disclosure necessary to obtain consent. For example, when~~
~~the lawyer represents different clients in related matters and one of the~~
~~clients refuses to consent to the disclosure necessary to permit the other~~
~~client to make an informed decision, the lawyer cannot properly ask the~~
~~latter to consent.~~

[15]   Consentability is typically determined by considering whether
the interests of the clients will be adequately protected if the clients are
permitted to give their informed consent to representation burdened by
a conflict of interest. Thus, under paragraph (b)(1), representation is
prohibited if in the circumstances the lawyer cannot reasonably conclude
that the lawyer will be able to provide competent and diligent representation. See Rule 1.1 (competence) and Rule 1.3 (diligence).

[16]   Paragraph (b)(2) describes conflicts that are nonconsentable
because the representation is prohibited by applicable law. For example,
in some states substantive law provides that the same lawyer may not
represent more than one defendant in a capital case, even with the
consent of the clients, and under federal criminal statutes certain
representations by a former government lawyer are prohibited, despite
the informed consent of the former client. In addition, decisional law in
some states limits the ability of a governmental client, such as a
municipality, to consent to a conflict of interest.

[17]   Paragraph (b)(3) describes conflicts that are nonconsentable
because of the institutional interest in vigorous development of each
client's position when the clients are aligned directly against each other
in the same litigation or other proceeding before a tribunal. Whether
clients are aligned directly against each other within the meaning of this
paragraph requires examination of the context of the proceeding. Although this paragraph does not preclude a lawyer's multiple representation of adverse parties to a mediation (because mediation is not a
proceeding before a "tribunal" under Rule 1.0(m)), such representation
may be precluded by paragraph (b)(1).

Informed Consent

[18]   Informed consent requires that each affected client be aware
of the relevant circumstances and of the material and reasonably foreseeable ways that the conflict could have adverse effects on the interests
of that client. See Rule 1.0(e) (informed consent). The information
required depends on the nature of the conflict and the nature of the

risks involved. When representation of multiple clients in a single matter is undertaken, the information must include the implications of the common representation, including possible effects on loyalty, confidentiality and the attorney-client privilege and the advantages and risks involved. See Comments [30] and [31] (effect of common representation on confidentiality).

[19] Under some circumstances it may be impossible to make the disclosure necessary to obtain consent. For example, when the lawyer represents different clients in related matters and one of the clients refuses to consent to the disclosure necessary to permit the other client to make an informed decision, the lawyer cannot properly ask the latter to consent. In some cases the alternative to common representation can be that each party may have to obtain separate representation with the possibility of incurring additional costs. These costs, along with the benefits of securing separate representation, are factors that may be considered by the affected client in determining whether common representation is in the client's interests.

Consent Confirmed in Writing

[20] Paragraph (b) requires the lawyer to obtain the informed consent of the client, confirmed in writing. Such a writing may consist of a document executed by the client or one that the lawyer promptly records and transmits to the client following an oral consent. See Rule 1.0(b). See also Rule 1.0(n) (writing includes electronic transmission). If it is not feasible to obtain or transmit the writing at the time the client gives informed consent, then the lawyer must obtain or transmit it within a reasonable time thereafter. See Rule 1.0(b). The requirement of a writing does not supplant the need in most cases for the lawyer to talk with the client, to explain the risks and advantages, if any, of representation burdened with a conflict of interest, as well as reasonably available alternatives, and to afford the client a reasonable opportunity to consider the risks and alternatives and to raise questions and concerns. Rather, the writing is required in order to impress upon clients the seriousness of the decision the client is being asked to make and to avoid disputes or ambiguities that might later occur in the absence of a writing.

Revoking Consent

[21] A client who has given consent to a conflict may revoke the consent and, like any other client, may terminate the lawyer's representation at any time. Whether revoking consent to the client's own representation precludes the lawyer from continuing to represent other clients depends on the circumstances, including the nature of the conflict, whether the client revoked consent because of a material change in circumstances, the reasonable expectations of the other client and whether material detriment to the other clients or the lawyer would result.

Consent to Future Conflict

[22]   Whether a lawyer may properly request a client to waive conflicts that might arise in the future is subject to the test of paragraph (b). The effectiveness of such waivers is generally determined by the extent to which the client reasonably understands the material risks that the waiver entails. The more comprehensive the explanation of the types of future representations that might arise and the actual and reasonably foreseeable adverse consequences of those representations, the greater the likelihood that the client will have the requisite understanding. Thus, if the client agrees to consent to a particular type of conflict with which the client is already familiar, then the consent ordinarily will be effective with regard to that type of conflict. If the consent is general and open-ended, then the consent ordinarily will be ineffective, because it is not reasonably likely that the client will have understood the material risks involved. On the other hand, if the client is an experienced user of the legal services involved and is reasonably informed regarding the risk that a conflict may arise, such consent is more likely to be effective, particularly if, e.g., the client is independently represented by other counsel in giving consent and the consent is limited to future conflicts unrelated to the subject of the representation. In any case, advance consent cannot be effective if the circumstances that materialize in the future are such as would make the conflict nonconsentable under paragraph (b).

Conflicts in Litigation

[7] [23] Paragraph (a) (b)(3) prohibits representation of opposing parties in the same litigation, regardless of the clients' consent. Simultaneous On the other hand, simultaneous representation of parties whose interests in litigation may conflict, such as coplaintiffs or codefendants, is governed by paragraph (b) (a)(2). An impermissible A conflict may exist by reason of substantial discrepancy in the parties' testimony, incompatibility in positions in relation to an opposing party or the fact that there are substantially different possibilities of settlement of the claims or liabilities in question. Such conflicts can arise in criminal cases as well as civil. The potential for conflict of interest in representing multiple defendants in a criminal case is so grave that ordinarily a lawyer should decline to represent more than one codefendant. On the other hand, common representation of persons having similar interests in civil litigation is proper if the risk of adverse effect is minimal and the requirements of paragraph (b) are met. Compare Rule 2.2 involving intermediation between clients.

[8] Ordinarily, a lawyer may not act as advocate against a client the lawyer represents in some other matter, even if the other matter is wholly unrelated. However, there are circumstances in which a lawyer may act as advocate against a client. For example, a lawyer representing an enterprise with diverse operations may accept employment as an

43

advocate against the enterprise in an unrelated matter if doing so will not adversely affect the lawyer's relationship with the enterprise or conduct of the suit and if both clients consent upon consultation. By the same token, government lawyers in some circumstances may represent government employees in proceedings in which a government agency is the opposing party. The propriety of concurrent representation can depend on the nature of the litigation. For example, a suit charging fraud entails conflict to a degree not involved in a suit for a declaratory judgment concerning statutory interpretation.

[9] A lawyer may represent parties having antagonistic positions on a legal question that has arisen in different cases, unless representation of either client would be adversely affected. Thus, it is ordinarily not improper to assert such positions in cases pending in different trial courts, but it may be improper to do so in cases pending at the same time in an appellate court.

[24]   Ordinarily a lawyer may take inconsistent legal positions in different tribunals at different times on behalf of different clients. The mere fact that advocating a legal position on behalf of one client might create precedent adverse to the interests of a client represented by the lawyer in an unrelated matter does not create a conflict of interest. A conflict of interest exists, however, if there is a significant risk that a lawyer's action on behalf of one client will materially limit the lawyer's effectiveness in representing another client in a different case; for example, when a decision favoring one client will create a precedent likely to seriously weaken the position taken on behalf of the other client. Factors relevant in determining whether the clients need to be advised of the risk include: where the cases are pending, whether the issue is substantive or procedural, the temporal relationship between the matters, the significance of the issue to the immediate and long-term interests of the clients involved and the clients' reasonable expectations in retaining the lawyer. If there is significant risk of material limitation, then absent informed consent of the affected clients, the lawyer must refuse one of the representations or withdraw from one or both matters.

[25]   When a lawyer represents or seeks to represent a class of plaintiffs or defendants in a class-action lawsuit, unnamed members of the class are ordinarily not considered to be clients of the lawyer for purposes of applying paragraph (a)(1) of this Rule. Thus, the lawyer does not typically need to get the consent of such a person before representing a client suing the person in an unrelated matter. Similarly, a lawyer seeking to represent an opponent in a class action does not typically need the consent of an unnamed member of the class whom the lawyer represents in an unrelated matter.

Other Conflict Situations Nonlitigation Conflicts

[11] [26] Conflicts of interest under paragraphs (a)(1) and (a)(2) arise in contexts other than litigation sometimes may be difficult to assess. For a discussion of directly adverse conflicts in transactional

matters, see Comment [7]. Relevant factors in determining whether there is significant potential for ~~adverse effect~~ material limitation include the duration and intimacy of the lawyer's relationship with the client or clients involved, the functions being performed by the lawyer, the likelihood that ~~actual conflict~~ disagreements will arise and the likely prejudice to the client from the conflict ~~if it does arise~~. The question is often one of proximity and degree. See Comment [8].

~~[13]~~ [27] ~~Conflict~~ For example, conflict questions may ~~also~~ arise in estate planning and estate administration. A lawyer may be called upon to prepare wills for several family members, such as husband and wife, and, depending upon the circumstances, a conflict of interest may ~~arise~~ be present. In estate administration the identity of the client may be unclear under the law of a particular jurisdiction. Under one view, the client is the fiduciary; under another view the client is the estate or trust, including its beneficiaries. ~~The~~ In order to comply with conflict of interest rules, the lawyer should make clear the lawyer's relationship to the parties involved.

~~[12]~~ [28] Whether a conflict is consentable depends on the circumstances. For example, a lawyer may not represent multiple parties to a negotiation whose interests are fundamentally antagonistic to each other, but common representation is permissible where the clients are generally aligned in interest even though there is some difference in interest among them. Thus, a lawyer may seek to establish or adjust a relationship between clients on an amicable and mutually advantageous basis; for example, in helping to organize a business in which two or more clients are entrepreneurs, working out the financial reorganization of an enterprise in which two or more clients have an interest or arranging a property distribution in settlement of an estate. The lawyer seeks to resolve potentially adverse interests by developing the parties' mutual interests. Otherwise, each party might have to obtain separate representation, with the possibility of incurring additional cost, complication or even litigation. Given these and other relevant factors, the clients may prefer that the lawyer act for all of them.

Special Considerations in Common Representation

[29] In considering whether to represent multiple clients in the same matter, a lawyer should be mindful that if the common representation fails because the potentially adverse interests cannot be reconciled, the result can be additional cost, embarrassment and recrimination. Ordinarily, the lawyer will be forced to withdraw from representing all of the clients if the common representation fails. In some situations, the risk of failure is so great that multiple representation is plainly impossible. For example, a lawyer cannot undertake common representation of clients where contentious litigation or negotiations between them are imminent or contemplated. Moreover, because the lawyer is required to be impartial between commonly represented clients, representation of multiple clients is improper when it is unlikely that impartiality can be

maintained. Generally, if the relationship between the parties has already assumed antagonism, the possibility that the clients' interests can be adequately served by common representation is not very good. Other relevant factors are whether the lawyer subsequently will represent both parties on a continuing basis and whether the situation involves creating or terminating a relationship between the parties.

[30] A particularly important factor in determining the appropriateness of common representation is the effect on client-lawyer confidentiality and the attorney-client privilege. With regard to the attorney-client privilege, the prevailing rule is that, as between commonly represented clients, the privilege does not attach. Hence, it must be assumed that if litigation eventuates between the clients, the privilege will not protect any such communications, and the clients should be so advised.

[31] As to the duty of confidentiality, continued common representation will almost certainly be inadequate if one client asks the lawyer not to disclose to the other client information relevant to the common representation. This is so because the lawyer has an equal duty of loyalty to each client, and each client has the right to be informed of anything bearing on the representation that might affect that client's interests and the right to expect that the lawyer will use that information to that client's benefit. See Rule 1.4. The lawyer should, at the outset of the common representation and as part of the process of obtaining each client's informed consent, advise each client that information will be shared and that the lawyer will have to withdraw if one client decides that some matter material to the representation should be kept from the other. In limited circumstances, it may be appropriate for the lawyer to proceed with the representation when the clients have agreed, after being properly informed, that the lawyer will keep certain information confidential. For example, the lawyer may reasonably conclude that failure to disclose one client's trade secrets to another client will not adversely affect representation involving a joint venture between the clients and agree to keep that information confidential with the informed consent of both clients.

[32] When seeking to establish or adjust a relationship between clients, the lawyer should make clear that the lawyer's role is not that of partisanship normally expected in other circumstances and, thus, that the clients may be required to assume greater responsibility for decisions than when each client is separately represented. Any limitations on the scope of the representation made necessary as a result of the common representation should be fully explained to the clients at the outset of the representation. See Rule 1.2(c).

[33] Subject to the above limitations, each client in the common representation has the right to loyal and diligent representation and the protection of Rule 1.9 concerning the obligations to a former client. The client also has the right to discharge the lawyer as stated in Rule 1.16.

Organizational Clients

[34]   A lawyer who represents a corporation or other organization does not, by virtue of that representation, necessarily represent any constituent or affiliated organization, such as a parent or subsidiary. See Rule 1.13(a). Thus, the lawyer for an organization is not barred from accepting representation adverse to an affiliate in an unrelated matter, unless the circumstances are such that the affiliate should also be considered a client of the lawyer, there is an understanding between the lawyer and the organizational client that the lawyer will avoid representation adverse to the client's affiliates, or the lawyer's obligations to either the organizational client or the new client are likely to limit materially the lawyer's representation of the other client.

[~~14~~] [35] A lawyer for a corporation or other organization who is also a member of its board of directors should determine whether the responsibilities of the two roles may conflict. The lawyer may be called on to advise the corporation in matters involving actions of the directors. Consideration should be given to the frequency with which such situations may arise, the potential intensity of the conflict, the effect of the lawyer's resignation from the board and the possibility of the corporation's obtaining legal advice from another lawyer in such situations. If there is material risk that the dual role will compromise the lawyer's independence of professional judgment, the lawyer should not serve as a director or should cease to act as the corporation's lawyer when conflicts of interest arise. The lawyer should advise the other members of the board that in some circumstances matters discussed at board meetings while the lawyer is present in the capacity of director might not be protected by the attorney-client privilege and that conflict of interest considerations might require the lawyer's recusal as a director or might require the lawyer and the lawyer's firm to decline representation of the corporation in a matter.

~~Conflict Charged by an Opposing Party~~

~~[15]   Resolving questions of conflict of interest is primarily the responsibility of the lawyer undertaking the representation. In litigation, a court may raise the question when there is reason to infer that the lawyer has neglected the responsibility. In a criminal case, inquiry by the court is generally required when a lawyer represents multiple defendants. Where the conflict is such as clearly to call in question the fair or efficient administration of justice, opposing counsel may properly raise the question. Such an objection should be viewed with caution, however, for it can be misused as a technique of harassment. See Scope.~~

Rule 1.8   Conflict of Interest: ~~Prohibited Transactions~~ Current Clients: Specific Rules

(a) A lawyer shall not enter into a business transaction with a client or knowingly acquire an ownership, possessory, security or other pecuniary interest adverse to a client unless:

47

(1) the transaction and terms on which the lawyer acquires the interest are fair and reasonable to the client and are fully disclosed and transmitted in writing ~~to the client~~ in a manner ~~which~~ <u>that</u> can be reasonably understood by the client;

(2) the client is <u>advised in writing of the desirability of seeking and is</u> given a reasonable opportunity to seek the advice of independent <u>legal</u> counsel ~~in~~ <u>on</u> the transaction; and

(3) the client ~~consents~~ <u>gives informed consent, in a</u> writing ~~thereto~~ <u>signed by the client, to the essential terms of the transaction and the lawyer's role in the transaction, including whether the lawyer is representing the client in the transaction.</u>

(b) A lawyer shall not use information relating to representation of a client to the disadvantage of the client unless the client ~~consents after consultation~~ <u>gives informed consent,</u> except as permitted or required by ~~Rule 1.6 or Rule 3.3~~ <u>these Rules.</u>

(c) A lawyer shall not <u>solicit any substantial gift from a client, including a testamentary gift, or</u> prepare <u>on behalf of a client</u> an instrument giving the lawyer or a person related to the lawyer ~~as parent, child, sibling, or spouse~~ <u>any substantial gift</u> ~~from a client, including a testamentary~~ <u>unless the lawyer or other recipient of the</u> gift~~, except where the client~~ <u>is related to</u> the ~~donee~~ <u>client. For purposes of this paragraph, related persons include a spouse, child, grandchild, parent, grandparent or other relative or individual with whom the lawyer or the client maintains a close, familial relationship.</u>

(d) Prior to the conclusion of representation of a client, a lawyer shall not make or negotiate an agreement giving the lawyer literary or media rights to a portrayal or account based in substantial part on information relating to the representation.

(e) A lawyer shall not provide financial assistance to a client in connection with pending or contemplated litigation, except that:

(1) a lawyer may advance court costs and expenses of litigation, the repayment of which may be contingent on the outcome of the matter; and

(2) a lawyer representing an indigent client may pay court costs and expenses of litigation on behalf of the client.

(f) A lawyer shall not accept compensation for representing a client from one other than the client unless:

(1) the client ~~consents after consultation~~ <u>gives informed consent</u>;

(2) there is no interference with the lawyer's independence of professional judgment or with the client-lawyer relationship; and

(3) information relating to representation of a client is protected as required by Rule 1.6.

(g) A lawyer who represents two or more clients shall not participate in making an aggregate settlement of the claims of or against the clients, or in a criminal case an aggregated agreement as to guilty or nolo contendere pleas, unless each client ~~consents after consultation, including~~ <u>gives informed consent, in a writing signed by the client. The lawyer's disclosure</u> ~~of~~ <u>shall include</u> the existence and nature of all the claims or pleas involved and of the participation of each person in the settlement.

(h) A lawyer shall not<u>:</u>

<u>(1)</u> make an agreement prospectively limiting the lawyer's liability to a client for malpractice unless ~~permitted by law and~~ the client is independently represented in making the agreement<u>,</u>; or

<u>(2)</u> settle a claim <u>or potential claim</u> for such liability with an unrepresented client or former client ~~without first advising~~ <u>unless</u> that person <u>is advised</u> in writing ~~that~~ <u>of the desirability of seeking and is given a reasonable opportunity to seek the advice of</u> independent ~~representation is appropriate~~ <u>legal counsel</u> in connection therewith.

~~(i) A lawyer related to another lawyer as parent, child, sibling or spouse shall not represent a client in a representation directly adverse to a person whom the lawyer knows is represented by the other lawyer except upon consent by the client after consultation regarding the relationship.~~

~~(j)~~ <u>(i)</u> A lawyer shall not acquire a proprietary interest in the cause of action or subject matter of litigation the lawyer is conducting for a client, except that the lawyer may:

(1) acquire a lien ~~granted~~ <u>authorized</u> by law to secure the lawyer's fee or expenses; and

(2) contract with a client for a reasonable contingent fee in a civil case.

<u>(j) A lawyer shall not have sexual relations with a client unless a consensual sexual relationship existed between them when the client-lawyer relationship commenced.</u>

(k) While lawyers are associated in a firm, a prohibition in the foregoing paragraphs (a) through (i) that applies to any one of them shall apply to all of them.

COMMENT

Business Transactions Between Client and Lawyer

[1] ~~As a general principle, all transactions between client and lawyer should be fair and reasonable to the client. In such transactions a review by independent counsel on behalf of the client is often advisable. Furthermore, a lawyer may not exploit information relating to the representation to the client's disadvantage. For example, a lawyer who has learned that the client is investing in specific real estate may not, without the client's consent, seek to acquire nearby property where doing so would adversely affect the client's plan for investment. Paragraph (a)~~ A lawyer's legal skill and training, together with the relationship of trust and confidence between lawyer and client, create the possibility of overreaching when the lawyer participates in a business, property or financial transaction with a client, for example, a loan or sales transaction or a lawyer investment on behalf of a client. The requirements of paragraph (a) must be met even when the transaction is not closely related to the subject matter of the representation, as when a lawyer drafting a will for a client learns that the client needs money for unrelated expenses and offers to make a loan to the client. The Rule applies to lawyers engaged in the sale of goods or services related to the practice of law, for example, the sale of title insurance or investment services to existing clients of the lawyer's legal practice. See Rule 5.7. It also applies to lawyers purchasing property from estates they represent. It does not apply to ordinary fee arrangements between client and lawyer, which are governed by Rule 1.5, although its requirements must be met when the lawyer accepts an interest in the client's business or other nonmonetary property as payment of all or part of a fee. In addition, the Rule does not~~, however,~~ apply to standard commercial transactions between the lawyer and the client for products or services that the client generally markets to others, for example, banking or brokerage services, medical services, products manufactured or distributed by the client, and utilities' services. In such transactions, the lawyer has no advantage in dealing with the client, and the restrictions in paragraph (a) are unnecessary and impracticable.

[2] Paragraph (a)(1) requires that the transaction itself be fair to the client and that its essential terms be communicated to the client, in writing, in a manner that can be reasonably understood. Paragraph (a)(2) requires that the client also be advised, in writing, of the desirability of seeking the advice of independent legal counsel. It also requires that the client be given a reasonable opportunity to obtain such advice. Paragraph (a)(3) requires that the lawyer obtain the client's informed consent, in a writing signed by the client, both to the essential terms of

the transaction and to the lawyer's role. When necessary, the lawyer should discuss both the material risks of the proposed transaction, including any risk presented by the lawyer's involvement, and the existence of reasonably available alternatives and should explain why the advice of independent legal counsel is desirable. See Rule 1.0(e) (definition of informed consent).

[3] The risk to a client is greatest when the client expects the lawyer to represent the client in the transaction itself or when the lawyer's financial interest otherwise poses a significant risk that the lawyer's representation of the client will be materially limited by the lawyer's financial interest in the transaction. Here the lawyer's role requires that the lawyer must comply, not only with the requirements of paragraph (a), but also with the requirements of Rule 1.7. Under that Rule, the lawyer must disclose the risks associated with the lawyer's dual role as both legal adviser and participant in the transaction, such as the risk that the lawyer will structure the transaction or give legal advice in a way that favors the lawyer's interests at the expense of the client. Moreover, the lawyer must obtain the client's informed consent. In some cases, the lawyer's interest may be such that Rule 1.7 will preclude the lawyer from seeking the client's consent to the transaction.

[4] If the client is independently represented in the transaction, paragraph (a)(2) of this Rule is inapplicable, and the paragraph (a)(1) requirement for full disclosure is satisfied either by a written disclosure by the lawyer involved in the transaction or by the client's independent counsel. The fact that the client was independently represented in the transaction is relevant in determining whether the agreement was fair and reasonable to the client as paragraph (a)(1) further requires.

Use of Information Related to Representation

[5] Use of information relating to the representation to the disadvantage of the client violates the lawyer's duty of loyalty. Paragraph (b) applies when the information is used to benefit either the lawyer or a third person, such as another client or business associate of the lawyer. For example, if a lawyer learns that a client intends to purchase and develop several parcels of land, the lawyer may not use that information to purchase one of the parcels in competition with the client or to recommend that another client make such a purchase. The Rule does not prohibit uses that do not disadvantage the client. For example, a lawyer who learns a government agency's interpretation of trade legislation during the representation of one client may properly use that information to benefit other clients. Paragraph (b) prohibits disadvantageous use of client information unless the client gives informed consent, except as permitted or required by these Rules. See Rules 1.2(d), 1.6, 1.9(c), 3.3, 4.1(b), 8.1 and 8.3.

Gifts to Lawyers

[2] [6] A lawyer may accept a gift from a client, if the transaction meets general standards of fairness. For example, a simple gift such as a present given at a holiday or as a token of appreciation is permitted. If a client offers the lawyer a more substantial gift, paragraph (c) does not prohibit the lawyer from accepting it, although such a gift may be voidable by the client under the doctrine of undue influence, which treats client gifts as presumptively fraudulent. In any event, due to concerns about overreaching and imposition on clients, a lawyer may not suggest that a substantial gift be made to the lawyer or for the lawyer's benefit, except where the lawyer is related to the client as set forth in paragraph (c).

[7] If effectuation of a substantial gift requires preparing a legal instrument such as a will or conveyance, however, the client should have the detached advice that another lawyer can provide. Paragraph (c) recognizes an The sole exception to this Rule is where the client is a relative of the donee or the gift is not substantial.

[8] This Rule does not prohibit a lawyer from seeking to have the lawyer or a partner or associate of the lawyer named as executor of the client's estate or to another potentially lucrative fiduciary position. Nevertheless, such appointments will be subject to the general conflict of interest provision in Rule 1.7 when there is a significant risk that the lawyer's interest in obtaining the appointment will materially limit the lawyer's independent professional judgment in advising the client concerning the choice of an executor or other fiduciary. In obtaining the client's informed consent to the conflict, the lawyer should advise the client concerning the nature and extent of the lawyer's financial interest in the appointment, as well as the availability of alternative candidates for the position.

Literary Rights

[3] [9] An agreement by which a lawyer acquires literary or media rights concerning the conduct of the representation creates a conflict between the interests of the client and the personal interests of the lawyer. Measures suitable in the representation of the client may detract from the publication value of an account of the representation. Paragraph (d) does not prohibit a lawyer representing a client in a transaction concerning literary property from agreeing that the lawyer's fee shall consist of a share in ownership in the property, if the arrangement conforms to Rule 1.5 and paragraph (j) paragraphs (a) and (i).

Financial Assistance

[10] Lawyers may not subsidize lawsuits or administrative proceedings brought on behalf of their clients, including making or guaranteeing loans to their clients for living expenses, because to do so would encourage clients to pursue lawsuits that might not otherwise be

brought and because such assistance gives lawyers too great a financial stake in the litigation. These dangers do not warrant a prohibition on a lawyer lending a client court costs and litigation expenses, including the expenses of medical examination and the costs of obtaining and presenting evidence, because these advances are virtually indistinguishable from contingent fees and help ensure access to the courts. Similarly, an exception allowing lawyers representing indigent clients to pay court costs and litigation expenses regardless of whether these funds will be repaid is warranted.

Person Paying for a Lawyer's Services

~~[4] Paragraph (f) requires disclosure of the fact that the lawyer's services are being paid for by a third party. Such an arrangement must also conform to the requirements of Rule 1.6 concerning confidentiality and Rule 1.7 concerning conflict of interest. Where the client is a class, consent may be obtained on behalf of the class by court-supervised procedure.~~

[11] Lawyers are frequently asked to represent a client under circumstances in which a third person will compensate the lawyer, in whole or in part. The third person might be a relative or friend, an indemnitor (such as a liability insurance company) or a co-client (such as a corporation sued along with one or more of its employees). Because third-party payers frequently have interests that differ from those of the client, including interests in minimizing the amount spent on the representation and in learning how the representation is progressing, lawyers are prohibited from accepting or continuing such representations unless the lawyer determines that there will be no interference with the lawyer's independent professional judgment and there is informed consent from the client. See also Rule 5.4(c) (prohibiting interference with a lawyer's professional judgment by one who recommends, employs or pays the lawyer to render legal services for another).

[12] Sometimes, it will be sufficient for the lawyer to obtain the client's informed consent regarding the fact of the payment and the identity of the third-party payer. If, however, the fee arrangement creates a conflict of interest for the lawyer, then the lawyer must comply with Rule. 1.7. The lawyer must also conform to the requirements of Rule 1.6 concerning confidentiality. Under Rule 1.7(a), a conflict of interest exists if there is significant risk that the lawyer's representation of the client will be materially limited by the lawyer's own interest in the fee arrangement or by the lawyer's responsibilities to the third-party payer (for example, when the third-party payer is a co-client). Under Rule 1.7(b), the lawyer may accept or continue the representation with the informed consent of each affected client, unless the conflict is nonconsentable under that paragraph. Under Rule 1.7(b), the informed consent must be confirmed in writing.

Aggregate Settlements

[13]   Differences in willingness to make or accept an offer of settlement are among the risks of common representation of multiple clients by a single lawyer. Under Rule 1.7, this is one of the risks that should be discussed before undertaking the representation, as part of the process of obtaining the clients' informed consent. In addition, Rule 1.2(a) protects each client's right to have the final say in deciding whether to accept or reject an offer of settlement and in deciding whether to enter a guilty or nolo contendere plea in a criminal case. The rule stated in this paragraph is a corollary of both these Rules and provides that, before any settlement offer or plea bargain is made or accepted on behalf of multiple clients, the lawyer must inform each of them about all the material terms of the settlement, including what the other clients will receive or pay if the settlement or plea offer is accepted. See also Rule 1.0(e) (definition of informed consent). Lawyers representing a class of plaintiffs or defendants, or those proceeding derivatively, may not have a full client-lawyer relationship with each member of the class; nevertheless, such lawyers must comply with applicable rules regulating notification of class members and other procedural requirements designed to ensure adequate protection of the entire class.

Limiting Liability and Settling Malpractice Claims

[5]   Paragraph (h) is not intended to apply to customary qualifications and limitations in legal opinions and memoranda.

[14]   Agreements prospectively limiting a lawyer's liability for malpractice are prohibited unless the client is independently represented in making the agreement because they are likely to undermine competent and diligent representation. Also, many clients are unable to evaluate the desirability of making such an agreement before a dispute has arisen, particularly if they are then represented by the lawyer seeking the agreement. This paragraph does not, however, prohibit a lawyer from entering into an agreement with the client to arbitrate legal malpractice claims, provided such agreements are enforceable and the client is fully informed of the scope and effect of the agreement. Nor does this paragraph limit the ability of lawyers to practice in the form of a limited-liability entity, where permitted by law, provided that each lawyer remains personally liable to the client for his or her own conduct and the firm complies with any conditions required by law, such as provisions requiring client notification or maintenance of adequate liability insurance. Nor does it prohibit an agreement in accordance with Rule 1.2 that defines the scope of the representation, although a definition of scope that makes the obligations of representation illusory will amount to an attempt to limit liability.

[15]   Agreements settling a claim or a potential claim for malpractice are not prohibited by this Rule. Nevertheless, in view of the danger that a lawyer will take unfair advantage of an unrepresented client or

former client, the lawyer must first advise such a person in writing of the appropriateness of independent representation in connection with such a settlement. In addition, the lawyer must give the client or former client a reasonable opportunity to find and consult independent counsel.

~~Family Relationships Between Lawyers~~

~~[6] Paragraph (i) applies to related lawyers who are in different firms. Related lawyers in the same firm are governed by Rules 1.7, 1.9, and 1.10. The disqualification stated in paragraph (i) is personal and is not imputed to members of firms with whom the lawyers are associated.~~

~~Acquisition of~~ Acquiring Proprietary Interest in Litigation

~~[7]~~ [16] Paragraph ~~(j)~~ (i) states the traditional general rule that lawyers are prohibited from acquiring a proprietary interest in litigation. ~~This~~ Like paragraph (e), the general rule~~, which~~ has its basis in common law champerty and maintenance~~,~~ and is designed to avoid giving the lawyer too great an interest in the representation. In addition, when the lawyer acquires an ownership interest in the subject of the representation, it will be more difficult for a client to discharge the lawyer if the client so desires. The Rule is subject to specific exceptions developed in decisional law and continued in these Rules~~, such as the exception for reasonable contingent fees set forth in Rule 1.5 and the exception for certain advances of the costs of litigation set forth in paragraph (e).~~ The exception for certain advances of the costs of litigation is set forth in paragraph (e). In addition, paragraph (i) sets forth exceptions for liens authorized by law to secure the lawyer's fees or expenses and contracts for reasonable contingent fees. The law of each jurisdiction determines which liens are authorized by law. These may include liens granted by statute, liens originating in common law and liens acquired by contract with the client. When a lawyer acquires by contract a security interest in property other than that recovered through the lawyer's efforts in the litigation, such an acquisition is a business or financial transaction with a client and is governed by the requirements of paragraph (a). Contracts for contingent fees in civil cases are governed by Rule 1.5.

Client-Lawyer Sexual Relationships

[17] The relationship between lawyer and client is a fiduciary one in which the lawyer occupies the highest position of trust and confidence. The relationship is almost always unequal; thus, a sexual relationship between lawyer and client can involve unfair exploitation of the lawyer's fiduciary role, in violation of the lawyer's basic ethical obligation not to use the trust of the client to the client's disadvantage. In addition, such a relationship presents a significant danger that, because of the lawyer's emotional involvement, the lawyer will be unable to represent the client without impairment of the exercise of independent professional judgment. Moreover, a blurred line between the professional

and personal relationships may make it difficult to predict to what extent client confidences will be protected by the attorney-client evidentiary privilege, since client confidences are protected by privilege only when they are imparted in the context of the client-lawyer relationship. Because of the significant danger of harm to client interests and because the client's own emotional involvement renders it unlikely that the client could give adequate informed consent, this Rule prohibits the lawyer from having sexual relations with a client regardless of whether the relationship is consensual and regardless of the absence of prejudice to the client.

[18]   Sexual relationships that predate the client-lawyer relationship are not prohibited. Issues relating to the exploitation of the fiduciary relationship and client dependency are diminished when the sexual relationship existed prior to the commencement of the client-lawyer relationship. However, before proceeding with the representation in these circumstances, the lawyer should consider whether the lawyer's ability to represent the client will be materially limited by the relationship. See Rule 1.7(a)(2).

[19]   When the client is an organization, paragraph (j) of this Rule prohibits a lawyer for the organization (whether inside counsel or outside counsel) from having a sexual relationship with a constituent of the organization who supervises, directs or regularly consults with that lawyer concerning the organization's legal matters.

Imputation of Prohibitions

[20]   Under paragraph (k), a prohibition on conduct by an individual lawyer in paragraphs (a) through (i) also applies to all lawyers associated in a firm with the personally prohibited lawyer. For example, one lawyer in a firm may not enter into a business transaction with a client of another member of the firm without complying with paragraph (a), even if the first lawyer is not personally involved in the representation of the client. The prohibition set forth in paragraph (j) is personal and is not applied to associated lawyers.

Rule 1.9   ~~Conflict of Interest:~~ Duties to Former ~~Client~~ Clients

(a) A lawyer who has formerly represented a client in a matter shall not thereafter represent another person in the same or a substantially related matter in which that person's interests are materially adverse to the interests of the former client unless the former client ~~consents after consultation~~ gives informed consent, confirmed in writing.

(b) A lawyer shall not knowingly represent a person in the same or a substantially related matter in which a firm with which the lawyer formerly was associated had previously represented a client

(1) whose interests are materially adverse to that person; and

(2) about whom the lawyer had acquired information protected by Rules 1.6 and 1.9(c) that is material to the matter;

unless the former client ~~consents after consultation~~ gives informed consent, confirmed in writing.

(c) A lawyer who has formerly represented a client in a matter or whose present or former firm has formerly represented a client in a matter shall not thereafter:

(1) use information relating to the representation to the disadvantage of the former client except as ~~Rule 1.6 or Rule 3.3~~ these Rules would permit or require with respect to a client, or when the information has become generally known; or

(2) reveal information relating to the representation except as ~~Rule 1.6 or Rule 3.3~~ these Rules would permit or require with respect to a client.

COMMENT

[1] After termination of a client-lawyer relationship, a lawyer has certain continuing duties with respect to confidentiality and conflicts of interest and thus may not represent another client except in conformity with this Rule. ~~The principles in Rule 1.7 determine whether the interests of the present and former client are adverse. Thus~~ Under this Rule, for example, a lawyer could not properly seek to rescind on behalf of a new client a contract drafted on behalf of the former client. So also a lawyer who has prosecuted an accused person could not properly represent the accused in a subsequent civil action against the government concerning the same transaction. Nor could a lawyer who has represented multiple clients in a matter represent one of the clients against the others in the same or a substantially related matter after a dispute arose among the clients in that matter, unless all affected clients give informed consent. See Comment [9]. Current and former government lawyers must comply with this Rule to the extent required by Rule 1.11.

[2] The scope of a "matter" for purposes of this Rule ~~may depend~~ depends on the facts of a particular situation or transaction. The lawyer's involvement in a matter can also be a question of degree. When a lawyer has been directly involved in a specific transaction, subsequent representation of other clients with materially adverse interests in that transaction clearly is prohibited. On the other hand, a lawyer who recurrently handled a type of problem for a former client is not precluded from later representing another client in a ~~wholly~~ factually distinct problem of that type even though the subsequent representation involves a position adverse to the prior client. Similar considerations can apply to

the reassignment of military lawyers between defense and prosecution functions within the same military jurisdictions. The underlying question is whether the lawyer was so involved in the matter that the subsequent representation can be justly regarded as a changing of sides in the matter in question.

[3] Matters are "substantially related" for purposes of this Rule if they involve the same transaction or legal dispute or if there otherwise is a substantial risk that confidential factual information as would normally have been obtained in the prior representation would materially advance the client's position in the subsequent matter. For example, a lawyer who has represented a businessperson and learned extensive private financial information about that person may not then represent that person's spouse in seeking a divorce. Similarly, a lawyer who has previously represented a client in securing environmental permits to build a shopping center would be precluded from representing neighbors seeking to oppose rezoning of the property on the basis of environmental considerations; however, the lawyer would not be precluded, on the grounds of substantial relationship, from defending a tenant of the completed shopping center in resisting eviction for nonpayment of rent. Information that has been disclosed to the public or to other parties adverse to the former client ordinarily will not be disqualifying. Information acquired in a prior representation may have been rendered obsolete by the passage of time, a circumstance that may be relevant in determining whether two representations are substantially related. In the case of an organizational client, general knowledge of the client's policies and practices ordinarily will not preclude a subsequent representation; on the other hand, knowledge of specific facts gained in a prior representation that are relevant to the matter in question ordinarily will preclude such a representation. A former client is not required to reveal the confidential information learned by the lawyer in order to establish a substantial risk that the lawyer has confidential information to use in the subsequent matter. A conclusion about the possession of such information may be based on the nature of the services the lawyer provided the former client and information that would in ordinary practice be learned by a lawyer providing such services.

Lawyers Moving Between Firms

[3̶] [4] When lawyers have been associated within a firm but then end their association, the question of whether a lawyer should undertake representation is more complicated. There are several competing considerations. First, the client previously represented by the former firm must be reasonably assured that the principle of loyalty to the client is not compromised. Second, the rule should not be so broadly cast as to preclude other persons from having reasonable choice of legal counsel. Third, the rule should not unreasonably hamper lawyers from forming new associations and taking on new clients after having left a previous association. In this connection, it should be recognized that today many lawyers practice in firms, that many lawyers to some degree limit their practice to one field or another, and that many move from one association to another several times in their careers. If the concept of imputation were applied with unqualified rigor, the result would be radical curtailment of the opportunity of lawyers to move from one practice setting to another and of the opportunity of clients to change counsel.

[4] ~~Reconciliation of these competing principles in the past has been attempted under two rubrics. One approach has been to seek per se rules of disqualification. For example, it has been held that a partner in a law firm is conclusively presumed to have access to all confidences concerning all clients of the firm. Under this analysis, if a lawyer has been a partner in one law firm and then becomes a partner in another law firm, there may be a presumption that all confidences known by the partner in the first firm are known to all partners in the second firm. This presumption might properly be applied in some circumstances, especially where the client has been extensively represented, but may be unrealistic where the client was represented only for limited purposes. Furthermore, such a rigid rule exaggerates the difference between a partner and an associate in modern law firms.~~

[5] ~~The other rubric formerly used for dealing with disqualification is the appearance of impropriety proscribed in Canon 9 of the ABA Model Code of Professional Responsibility. This rubric has a two-fold problem. First, the appearance of impropriety can be taken to include any new client-lawyer relationship that might make a former client feel anxious. If that meaning were adopted, disqualification would become little more than a question of subjective judgment by the former client. Second, since "impropriety" is undefined, the term "appearance of impropriety" is question-begging. It therefore has to be recognized that the problem of disqualification cannot be properly resolved either by simple analogy to a lawyer practicing alone or by the very general concept of appearance of impropriety.~~

~~Confidentiality~~

[~~8~~] [5] Paragraph (b) operates to disqualify the lawyer only when the lawyer involved has actual knowledge of information protected by Rules 1.6 and 1.9~~(b)~~(c). Thus, if a lawyer while with one firm acquired no knowledge or information relating to a particular client of the firm, and that lawyer later joined another firm, neither the lawyer individually nor the second firm is disqualified from representing another client in the same or a related matter even though the interests of the two clients conflict. See Rule 1.10(b) for the restrictions on a firm once a lawyer has terminated association with the firm.

[6] ~~Preserving confidentiality is a question of access to information. Access to information, in turn, is essentially a question of fact in~~ Application of paragraph (b) depends on a situation's particular ~~circumstances~~ facts, aided by inferences, deductions or working presumptions that reasonably may be made about the way in which lawyers work

59

together. A lawyer may have general access to files of all clients of a law firm and may regularly participate in discussions of their affairs; it should be inferred that such a lawyer in fact is privy to all information about all the firm's clients. In contrast, another lawyer may have access to the files of only a limited number of clients and participate in discussions of the affairs of no other clients; in the absence of information to the contrary, it should be inferred that such a lawyer in fact is privy to information about the clients actually served but not those of other clients. In such an inquiry, the burden of proof should rest upon the firm whose disqualification is sought.

[7] Application of paragraph (b) depends on a situation's particular facts. In such an inquiry, the burden of proof should rest upon the firm whose disqualification is sought.

[9] [7] Independent of the question of disqualification of a firm, a lawyer changing professional association has a continuing duty to preserve confidentiality of information about a client formerly represented. See Rules 1.6 and 1.9(c).

Adverse Positions

[10] The second aspect of loyalty to a client is the lawyer's obligation to decline subsequent representations involving positions adverse to a former client arising in substantially related matters. This obligation requires abstention from adverse representation by the individual lawyer involved, but does not properly entail abstention of other lawyers through imputed disqualification. Hence, this aspect of the problem is governed by Rule 1.9(a). Thus, if a lawyer left one firm for another, the new affiliation would not preclude the firms involved from continuing to represent clients with adverse interests in the same or related matters, so long as the conditions of paragraphs (b) and (c) concerning confidentiality have been met.

[11] [8] Information Paragraph (c) provides that information acquired by the lawyer in the course of representing a client may not subsequently be used or revealed by the lawyer to the disadvantage of the client. However, the fact that a lawyer has once served a client does not preclude the lawyer from using generally known information about that client when later representing another client.

[12] [9] Disqualification from subsequent representation is The provisions of this Rule are for the protection of former clients and can be waived by them. A waiver is effective only if there is disclosure of the circumstances, including the lawyer's intended role in behalf of the new client if the client gives informed consent, which consent must be confirmed in writing under paragraphs (a) and (b). See Rule 1.0(e). [13] With regard to an opposing party's raising a question of conflict of interest the effectiveness of an advance waiver, see Comment [22] to Rule 1.7. With regard to disqualification of a firm with which a lawyer is or was formerly associated, see Rule 1.10.

RULE 1.10 ~~Imputed Disqualification~~ Imputation of Conflicts of Interest: General Rule*

(a) While lawyers are associated in a firm, none of them shall knowingly represent a client when any one of them practicing alone would be prohibited from doing so by Rules 1.7, ~~1.8(c),~~ or 1.9 ~~or 2.2,~~ unless the prohibition is based on a personal interest of the prohibited lawyer and does not present a significant risk of materially limiting the representation of the client by the remaining lawyers in the firm.

(b) When a lawyer has terminated an association with a firm, the firm is not prohibited from thereafter representing a person with interests materially adverse to those of a client represented by the formerly associated lawyer and not currently represented by the firm, unless:

(1) the matter is the same or substantially related to that in which the formerly associated lawyer represented the client; and

(2) any lawyer remaining in the firm has information protected by Rules 1.6 and 1.9(c) that is material to the matter.

(c) A disqualification prescribed by this rule may be waived by the affected client under the conditions stated in Rule 1.7.

(d) The disqualification of lawyers associated in a firm with former or current government lawyers is governed by Rule 1.11.

COMMENT

Definition of "Firm"

[1] For purposes of the Rules of Professional Conduct, the term "firm" ~~includes~~ denotes lawyers in a ~~private firm, and~~ law partnership, professional corporation, sole proprietorship or other association authorized to practice law; or lawyers employed in a legal services organization or the legal department of a corporation or other organization, ~~or in a legal services organization.~~ See Rule 1.0(c). Whether two or more lawyers constitute a firm within this definition can depend on the specific facts. ~~For example, two practitioners who share office space and occasionally~~

---

* The Ethics 2000 Commission Report included a proposed subsection (c) on screening:

(c) When a lawyer becomes associated with a firm, no lawyer associated in the firm shall knowingly represent a person in a matter in which that lawyer is disqualified under Rule 1.9 unless:

(1) the personally disqualified lawyer is timely screened from any participation in the matter and is apportioned no part of the fee therefrom; and

(2) written notice is promptly given to any affected former client to enable it to ascertain compliance with the provisions of this Rule.

The ABA House of Delegates rejected this attempt to include screening of migratory lawyers.

~~consult or assist each other ordinarily would not be regarded as constituting a firm. However, if they present themselves to the public in a way suggesting that they are a firm or conduct themselves as a firm, they should be regarded as a firm for purposes of the Rules. The terms of any formal agreement between associated lawyers are relevant in determining whether they are a firm, as is the fact that they have mutual access to information concerning the clients they serve. Furthermore, it is relevant in doubtful cases to consider the underlying purpose of the Rule that is involved. A group of lawyers could be regarded as a firm for purposes of the rule that the same lawyer should not represent opposing parties in litigation, while it might not be so regarded for purposes of the rule that information acquired by one lawyer is attributed to another. See Rule 1.0, Comments [2]–[4].~~

~~[2]   With respect to the law department of an organization, there is ordinarily no question that the members of the department constitute a firm within the meaning of the Rules of Professional Conduct. However, there can be uncertainty as to the identity of the client. For example, it may not be clear whether the law department of a corporation represents a subsidiary or an affiliated corporation, as well as the corporation by which the members of the department are directly employed. A similar question can arise concerning an unincorporated association and its local affiliates.~~

~~[3]   Similar questions can also arise with respect to lawyers in legal aid. Lawyers employed in the same unit of a legal service organization constitute a firm, but not necessarily those employed in separate units. As in the case of independent practitioners, whether the lawyers should be treated as associated with each other can depend on the particular rule that is involved, and on the specific facts of the situation.~~

~~[5]   Different provisions are thus made for movement of a lawyer from one private firm to another and for movement of a lawyer between a private firm and the government. The government is entitled to protection of its client confidences and, therefore, to the protections provided in Rules 1.6, 1.9 and 1.11. However, if the more extensive disqualification in Rule 1.10 were applied to former government lawyers, the potential effect on the government would be unduly burdensome. The government deals with all private citizens and organizations and, thus, has a much wider circle of adverse legal interests than does any private law firm. In these circumstances, the government's recruitment of lawyers would be seriously impaired if Rule 1.10 were applied to the government. On balance, therefore, the government is better served in the long run by the protections stated in Rule 1.11.~~

Principles of Imputed Disqualification

~~[6]~~ [2] The rule of imputed disqualification stated in paragraph (a) gives effect to the principle of loyalty to the client as it applies to lawyers who practice in a law firm. Such situations can be considered from the premise that a firm of lawyers is essentially one lawyer for purposes of the rules governing loyalty to the client, or from the premise that each lawyer is vicariously bound by the obligation of loyalty owed by each lawyer with whom the lawyer is associated. Paragraph (a) operates only among the lawyers currently associated in a firm. When a lawyer moves from one firm to another, the situation is governed by Rules 1.9(b) and 1.10(b).

[3]   The rule in paragraph (a) does not prohibit representation where neither questions of client loyalty nor protection of confidential information are presented. Where one lawyer in a firm could not effectively represent a given client because of strong political beliefs, for example, but that lawyer will do no work on the case and the personal beliefs of the lawyer will not materially limit the representation by others in the firm, the firm should not be disqualified. On the other hand, if an opposing party in a case were owned by a lawyer in the law firm, and others in the firm would be materially limited in pursuing the matter because of loyalty to that lawyer, the personal disqualification of the lawyer would be imputed to all others in the firm.

[4]   The rule in paragraph (a) also does not prohibit representation by others in the law firm where the person prohibited from involvement in a matter is a nonlawyer, such as a paralegal or legal secretary. Nor does paragraph (a) prohibit representation if the lawyer is prohibited from acting because of events before the person became a lawyer, for example, work that the person did while a law student. Such persons, however, ordinarily must be screened from any personal participation in the matter to avoid communication to others in the firm of confidential information that both the nonlawyers and the firm have a legal duty to protect. See Rules 1.0(k) and 5.3.

[7] [5] Rule 1.10(b) operates to permit a law firm, under certain circumstances, to represent a person with interests directly adverse to those of a client represented by a lawyer who formerly was associated with the firm. The Rule applies regardless of when the formerly associated lawyer represented the client. However, the law firm may not represent a person with interests adverse to those of a present client of the firm, which would violate Rule 1.7. Moreover, the firm may not represent the person where the matter is the same or substantially related to that in which the formerly associated lawyer represented the client and any other lawyer currently in the firm has material information protected by Rules 1.6 and 1.9(c).

[6]   Rule 1.10(c) removes imputation with the informed consent of the affected client or former client under the conditions stated in Rule 1.7. The conditions stated in Rule 1.7 require the lawyer to determine that the representation is not prohibited by Rule 1.7(b) and that each affected client or former client has given informed consent to the representation, confirmed in writing. In some cases, the risk may be so severe that the conflict may not be cured by client consent. For a discussion of the effectiveness of client waivers of conflicts that might

arise in the future, see Rule 1.7, Comment [22]. For a definition of informed consent, see Rule 1.0(e).

[4] [7] Where a lawyer has joined a private firm after having represented the government, the situation imputation is governed by Rule 1.11(a) and (b) and (c);, not this Rule. Under Rule 1.11(d), where a lawyer represents the government after having served private clients, the situation is governed by Rule 1.11(c)(1). The individual lawyer involved is bound by the Rules generally, including Rules 1.6, 1.7 and 1.9 in private practice, nongovernmental employment or in another government agency, former-client conflicts are not imputed to government lawyers associated with the individually disqualified lawyer.

[8] Where a lawyer is prohibited from engaging in certain transactions under Rule 1.8, paragraph (k) of that Rule, and not this Rule, determines whether that prohibition also applies to other lawyers associated in a firm with the personally prohibited lawyer.

Rule 1.11 ~~Successive~~ Special Conflicts of Interest for Former and Current Government Officers and ~~Private Employment~~ Employees

(a) Except as law may otherwise expressly permit, a lawyer who has formerly served as a public officer or employee of the government:

(1) is subject to Rule 1.9(c); and

(2) shall not otherwise represent a ~~private~~ client in connection with a matter in which the lawyer participated personally and substantially as a public officer or employee, unless the appropriate government agency ~~consents after consultation~~ gives its informed consent, confirmed in writing, to the representation.

(b) ~~No~~ When a lawyer is disqualified from representation under paragraph (a), no lawyer in a firm with which that lawyer is associated may knowingly undertake or continue representation in such a matter unless:

(1) the disqualified lawyer is timely screened from any participation in the matter and is apportioned no part of the fee therefrom; and

(2) written notice is promptly given to the appropriate government agency to enable it to ascertain compliance with the provisions of this rule.

~~(b)~~ (c) Except as law may otherwise expressly permit, a lawyer having information that the lawyer knows is confidential government information about a person acquired when the lawyer was a public officer or employee, may not represent a private client whose interests are adverse to that person in a matter in which the information could be used to the material disadvantage of that person. As used in this Rule, the term "confidential government information" means information that has been obtained under governmental authority and which, at the time this Rule is applied, the government is prohibited by law from disclosing to the public or has a legal privilege not to disclose and which is not otherwise available to the public. A firm with which that lawyer is associated may undertake or continue representation in the matter only if the disqualified lawyer is timely screened from any participation in the matter and is apportioned no part of the fee therefrom.

~~(c)~~ (d) Except as law may otherwise expressly permit, a lawyer currently serving as a public officer or employee:

(1) is subject to Rules 1.7 and 1.9; and

(2) shall not:

~~(1)~~ (i) participate in a matter in which the lawyer participated personally and substantially while in private practice or nongovernmental employment, unless ~~under applicable law no one is, or by lawful delegation may be, authorized to act in the lawyer's stead in the matter~~ the appropriate government agency gives its informed consent, confirmed in writing; or

~~(2)~~ (ii) negotiate for private employment with any person who is involved as a party or as lawyer for a party in a matter in which the lawyer is participating personally and substantially, except that a lawyer serving as a law clerk to a judge, other adjudicative officer or arbitrator may negotiate for private employment as permitted by Rule 1.12(b) and subject to the conditions stated in Rule 1.12(b).

~~(d)~~ (e) As used in this Rule, the term "matter" includes:

(1) any judicial or other proceeding, application, request for a ruling or other determination, contract, claim, controversy, investigation, charge, accusation, arrest or other particular matter involving a specific party or parties, and

(2) any other matter covered by the conflict of interest rules of the appropriate government agency.

~~(e) As used in this Rule, the term "confidential government information" means information which has been obtained under governmental authority and which, at the time this rule is applied, the government is prohibited by law from disclosing to the public or has a legal privilege not to disclose, and which is not otherwise available to the public.~~

COMMENT

[1] This Rule prevents a lawyer from exploiting public office for the advantage of a private client. It is a counterpart of Rule 1.10(b), which applies to lawyers moving from one firm to another.

[2] [1] A lawyer representing a government agency, whether employed or specially retained by the government, who has served or is currently serving as a public officer or employee is personally subject to the Rules of Professional Conduct, including the prohibition against representing adverse interests concurrent conflicts of interest stated in Rule 1.7 and the protections afforded former clients in Rule 1.9. In addition, such a lawyer is may be subject to Rule 1.11 and to statutes and government regulations regarding conflict of interest. Such statutes and regulations may circumscribe the extent to which the government agency may give consent under this Rule. See Rule 1.0(e) for the definition of informed consent.

[2] Paragraphs (a)(1), (a)(2) and (d)(1) restate the obligations of an individual lawyer who has served or is currently serving as an officer or employee of the government toward a former government or private client. Rule 1.10 is not applicable to the conflicts of interest addressed by this Rule. Rather, paragraph (b) sets forth a special imputation rule for former government lawyers that provides for screening and notice. Because of the special problems raised by imputation within a government agency, paragraph (d) does not impute the conflicts of a lawyer currently serving as an officer or employee of the government to other associated government officers or employees, although ordinarily it will be prudent to screen such lawyers.

[3] Paragraphs (a)(2) and (d)(2) apply regardless of whether a lawyer is adverse to a former client and are thus designed not only to protect the former client, but also to prevent a lawyer from exploiting public office for the advantage of another client. For example, a lawyer who has pursued a claim on behalf of the government may not pursue the same claim on behalf of a later private client after the lawyer has left government service, except when authorized to do so by the government agency under paragraph (a). Similarly, a lawyer who has pursued a claim on behalf of a private client may not pursue the claim on behalf of the government, except when authorized to do so by paragraph (d). As with paragraphs (a)(1) and (d)(1), Rule 1.10 is not applicable to the conflicts of interest addressed by these paragraphs.

[3] [4] Where This Rule represents a balancing of interests. On the one hand, where the successive clients are a public government agency and a private another client, public or private, the risk exists that power or discretion vested in that agency public authority might be used for the special benefit of a private the other client. A lawyer should not be in a position where benefit to a private the other client might affect performance of the lawyer's professional functions on behalf of the government public authority. Also, unfair advantage could accrue to the private other client by reason of access to confidential government information about the client's adversary obtainable only through the lawyer's government

66

service. ~~However~~ On the other hand, the rules governing lawyers presently or formerly employed by a government agency should not be so restrictive as to inhibit transfer of employment to and from the government. The government has a legitimate need to attract qualified lawyers as well as to maintain high ethical standards. Thus a former government lawyer is disqualified only from particular matters in which the lawyer participated personally and substantially. The provisions for screening and waiver in paragraph (b) are necessary to prevent the disqualification rule from imposing too severe a deterrent against entering public service. The limitation of disqualification in paragraphs (a)(2) and (d)(2) to matters involving a specific party or parties, rather than extending disqualification to all substantive issues on which the lawyer worked, serves a similar function.

~~[4]~~ [5] When ~~the client is an agency of~~ a lawyer has been employed by one government agency and then moves to a second government agency, it may be appropriate to treat that second agency ~~should be treated~~ as ~~a private~~ another client for purposes of this Rule ~~if the lawyer thereafter represents an agency of another government~~, as when a lawyer ~~represents~~ is employed by a city and subsequently is employed by a federal agency. However, because the conflict of interest is governed by paragraph (d), the latter agency is not required to screen the lawyer as paragraph (b) requires a law firm to do. The question of whether two government agencies should be regarded as the same or different clients for conflict of interest purposes is beyond the scope of these Rules. See Rule 1.13 Comment [6].

~~[5]~~ [6] Paragraphs ~~(a)(1) and~~ (b) and (c) contemplate a screening arrangement. See Rule 1.0(k) (requirements for screening procedures). These paragraphs do not prohibit a lawyer from receiving a salary or partnership share established by prior independent agreement. ~~They prohibit,~~ but that lawyer may not receive compensation directly relating the lawyer's compensation to the fee in the matter in which the lawyer is disqualified.

[7] Notice, including a description of the screened lawyer's prior representation and of the screening procedures employed, generally should be given as soon as practicable after the need for screening becomes apparent.

~~[6]   Paragraph (a)(2) does not require that a lawyer give notice to the government agency at a time when premature disclosure would injure the client; a requirement for premature disclosure might preclude engagement of the lawyer. Such notice is, however, required to be given as soon as practicable in order that the government agency will have a reasonable opportunity to ascertain that the lawyer is complying with Rule 1.11 and to take appropriate action if it believes the lawyer is not complying.~~

~~[7]~~ [8] Paragraph ~~(b)~~ (c) operates only when the lawyer in question has knowledge of the information, which means actual knowledge; it does not operate with respect to information that merely could be imputed to the lawyer.

[8] [9] Paragraphs (a) and (c) (d) do not prohibit a lawyer from jointly representing a private party and a government agency when doing so is permitted by Rule 1.7 and is not otherwise prohibited by law.

[9] Paragraph (c) does not disqualify other lawyers in the agency with which the lawyer in question has become associated.

[10] For purposes of paragraph (e) of this Rule, a "matter" may continue in another form. In determining whether two particular matters are the same, the lawyer should consider the extent to which the matters involve the same basic facts, the same or related parties, and the time elapsed.

Rule 1.12 Former Judge Or, Arbitrator, Mediator or Other Third–Party Neutral

(a) Except as stated in paragraph (d), a lawyer shall not represent anyone in connection with a matter in which the lawyer participated personally and substantially as a judge or other adjudicative officer, arbitrator or law clerk to such a person or as an arbitrator, mediator or other third-party neutral, unless all parties to the proceeding give informed consent after consultation, confirmed in writing.

(b) A lawyer shall not negotiate for employment with any person who is involved as a party or as lawyer for a party in a matter in which the lawyer is participating personally and substantially as a judge or other adjudicative officer or as an arbitrator, mediator or other third-party neutral. A lawyer serving as a law clerk to a judge, or other adjudicative officer or arbitrator may negotiate for employment with a party or lawyer involved in a matter in which the clerk is participating personally and substantially, but only after the lawyer has notified the judge, or other adjudicative officer or arbitrator.

(c) If a lawyer is disqualified by paragraph (a), no lawyer in a firm with which that lawyer is associated may knowingly undertake or continue representation in the matter unless:

(1) the disqualified lawyer is timely screened from any participation in the matter and is apportioned no part of the fee therefrom; and

(2) written notice is promptly given to the parties and any appropriate tribunal to enable it them to ascertain compliance with the provisions of this rule.

(d) An arbitrator selected as a partisan of a party in a multimember arbitration panel is not prohibited from subsequently representing that party.

COMMENT

[1] This Rule generally parallels Rule 1.11. The term "personally and substantially" signifies that a judge who was a member of a

multimember court, and thereafter left judicial office to practice law, is not prohibited from representing a client in a matter pending in the court, but in which the former judge did not participate. So also the fact that a former judge exercised administrative responsibility in a court does not prevent the former judge from acting as a lawyer in a matter where the judge had previously exercised remote or incidental administrative responsibility that did not affect the merits. Compare the Comment to Rule 1.11. The term "adjudicative officer" includes such officials as judges pro tempore, referees, special masters, hearing officers and other parajudicial officers, and also lawyers who serve as part-time judges. Compliance Canons A(2), B(2) and C of the Model Code of Judicial Conduct provide that a part-time judge, judge pro tempore or retired judge recalled to active service, may not "act as a lawyer in any proceeding in which he served as a judge or in any other proceeding related thereto." Although phrased differently from this Rule, those Rules correspond in meaning.

[2]   Like former judges, lawyers who have served as arbitrators, mediators or other third-party neutrals may be asked to represent a client in a matter in which the lawyer participated personally and substantially. This Rule forbids such representation unless all of the parties to the proceedings give their informed consent, confirmed in writing. See Rule 1.0(e) and (b). Other law or codes of ethics governing third-party neutrals may impose more stringent standards of personal or imputed disqualification. See Rule 2.4.

[3]   Although lawyers who serve as third-party neutrals do not have information concerning the parties that is protected under Rule 1.6, they typically owe the parties an obligation of confidentiality under law or codes of ethics governing third-party neutrals. Thus, paragraph (c) provides that conflicts of the personally disqualified lawyer will be imputed to other lawyers in a law firm unless the conditions of this paragraph are met.

[4]   Requirements for screening procedures are stated in Rule 1.0(k). Paragraph (c)(1) does not prohibit the screened lawyer from receiving a salary or partnership share established by prior independent agreement, but that lawyer may not receive compensation directly related to the matter in which the lawyer is disqualified.

[5]   Notice, including a description of the screened lawyer's prior representation and of the screening procedures employed, generally should be given as soon as practicable after the need for screening becomes apparent.

Rule 1.13   Organization as Client

(a) A lawyer employed or retained by an organization represents the organization acting through its duly authorized constituents.

(b) If a lawyer for an organization knows that an officer, employee or other person associated with the organization is engaged in action, intends to act or refuses to act in a matter related to the representation that is a violation of a legal obligation to the organization, or a violation of law which reasonably might be imputed to the organization, and is likely to result in substantial injury to the organization, the lawyer shall proceed as is reasonably necessary in the best interest of the organization. In determining how to proceed, the lawyer shall give due consideration to the seriousness of the violation and its consequences, the scope and nature of the lawyer's representation, the responsibility in the organization and the apparent motivation of the person involved, the policies of the organization concerning such matters and any other relevant considerations. Any measures taken shall be designed to minimize disruption of the organization and the risk of revealing information relating to the representation to persons outside the organization. Such measures may include among others:

(1) asking for reconsideration of the matter;

(2) advising that a separate legal opinion on the matter be sought for presentation to appropriate authority in the organization; and

(3) referring the matter to higher authority in the organization, including, if warranted by the seriousness of the matter, referral to the highest authority that can act in on behalf of the organization as determined by applicable law.

(c) If, despite the lawyer's efforts in accordance with paragraph (b), the highest authority that can act on behalf of the organization insists upon action, or a refusal to act, that is clearly a violation of law and is likely to result in substantial injury to the organization, the lawyer may resign in accordance with Rule 1.16.

(d) In dealing with an organization's directors, officers, employees, members, shareholders or other constituents, a lawyer shall explain the identity of the client when it is apparent the lawyer knows or reasonably should know that the organization's interests are adverse to those of the constituents with whom the lawyer is dealing.

(e) A lawyer representing an organization may also represent any of its directors, officers, employees, members, shareholders or other constituents, subject to the provisions of Rule 1.7. If the organization's consent to the dual representation is required by Rule 1.7, the consent shall be given by an appropriate official of the organization other than the individual who is to be represented, or by the shareholders.

COMMENT

The Entity as the Client

[1]   An organizational client is a legal entity, but it cannot act except through its officers, directors, employees, shareholders and other constituents. Officers, directors, employees and shareholders are the constituents of the corporate organizational client. The duties defined in this Comment apply equally to unincorporated associations. "Other constituents" as used in this Comment means the positions equivalent to officers, directors, employees and shareholders held by persons acting for organizational clients that are not corporations.

[2]   When one of the constituents of an organizational client communicates with the organization's lawyer in that person's organizational capacity, the communication is protected by Rule 1.6. Thus, by way of example, if an organizational client requests its lawyer to investigate allegations of wrongdoing, interviews made in the course of that investigation between the lawyer and the client's employees or other constituents are covered by Rule 1.6. This does not mean, however, that constituents of an organizational client are the clients of the lawyer. The lawyer may not disclose to such constituents information relating to the representation except for disclosures explicitly or impliedly authorized by the organizational client in order to carry out the representation or as otherwise permitted by Rule 1.6.

[3]   When constituents of the organization make decisions for it, the decisions ordinarily must be accepted by the lawyer even if their utility or prudence is doubtful. Decisions concerning policy and operations, including ones entailing serious risk, are not as such in the lawyer's province. However, different considerations arise when the lawyer knows that the organization may be substantially injured by action of a constituent that is in violation of law. In such a circumstance, it may be reasonably necessary for the lawyer to ask the constituent to reconsider the matter. If that fails, or if the matter is of sufficient seriousness and importance to the organization, it may be reasonably necessary for the lawyer to take steps to have the matter reviewed by a higher authority in the organization. Clear justification should exist for seeking review over the head of the constituent normally responsible for it. The stated policy of the organization may define circumstances and prescribe channels for such review, and a lawyer should encourage the formulation of such a policy. Even in the absence of organization policy, however, the lawyer may have an obligation to refer a matter to higher authority, depending on the seriousness of the matter and whether the constituent in question has apparent motives to act at variance with the organization's interest. Review by the chief executive officer or by the board of directors may be required when the matter is of importance commensurate with their authority. At some point it may be useful or essential to obtain an independent legal opinion.

[4] ~~In an extreme case, it may be reasonably necessary for the lawyer to refer the matter to the~~ The organization's highest authority~~.~~ ~~Ordinarily, that is~~ to whom a matter may be referred ordinarily will be the board of directors or similar governing body. However, applicable law may prescribe that under certain conditions the highest authority reposes elsewhere, for example, in the independent directors of a corporation.

Relation to Other Rules

[5] The authority and responsibility provided in ~~paragraph (b)~~ this Rule are concurrent with the authority and responsibility provided in other Rules. In particular, this Rule does not limit or expand the lawyer's responsibility under Rule 1.6, 1.8, 1.16, 3.3 or 4.1. If the lawyer's services are being used by an organization to further a crime or fraud by the organization, Rule 1.2(d) can be applicable.

Government Agency

[6] The duty defined in this Rule applies to governmental organizations. ~~However, when the client is a governmental organization, a different balance may be appropriate between maintaining confidentiality and assuring that the wrongful official act is prevented or rectified, for public business is involved. In addition, duties of lawyers employed by the government or lawyers in military service may be defined by statutes and regulation. Therefore, defining~~ Defining precisely the identity of the client and prescribing the resulting obligations of such lawyers may be more difficult in the government context and is a matter beyond the scope of these Rules. See Scope [18]. Although in some circumstances the client may be a specific agency, it ~~is generally~~ may also be a branch of government, such as the executive branch, or the government as a whole. For example, if the action or failure to act involves the head of a bureau, either the department of which the bureau is a part or the relevant branch of government ~~as a whole~~ may be the client for ~~purpose~~ purposes of this Rule. Moreover, in a matter involving the conduct of government officials, a government lawyer may have authority under applicable law to question such conduct more extensively than that of a lawyer for a private organization in similar circumstances. Thus, when the client is a governmental organization, a different balance may be appropriate between maintaining confidentiality and assuring that the wrongful act is prevented or rectified, for public business is involved. In addition, duties of lawyers employed by the government or lawyers in military service may be defined by statutes and regulation. This Rule does not limit that authority. See ~~note on~~ Scope.

Clarifying the Lawyer's Role

[7] There are times when the organization's interest may be or become adverse to those of one or more of its constituents. In such circumstances the lawyer should advise any constituent, whose interest

the lawyer finds adverse to that of the organization of the conflict or potential conflict of interest, that the lawyer cannot represent such constituent, and that such person may wish to obtain independent representation. Care must be taken to assure that the individual understands that, when there is such adversity of interest, the lawyer for the organization cannot provide legal representation for that constituent individual, and that discussions between the lawyer for the organization and the individual may not be privileged.

[8]   Whether such a warning should be given by the lawyer for the organization to any constituent individual may turn on the facts of each case.

Dual Representation

[9]   Paragraph (e) recognizes that a lawyer for an organization may also represent a principal officer or major shareholder.

Derivative Actions

[10]   Under generally prevailing law, the shareholders or members of a corporation may bring suit to compel the directors to perform their legal obligations in the supervision of the organization. Members of unincorporated associations have essentially the same right. Such an action may be brought nominally by the organization, but usually is, in fact, a legal controversy over management of the organization.

[11]   The question can arise whether counsel for the organization may defend such an action. The proposition that the organization is the lawyer's client does not alone resolve the issue. Most derivative actions are a normal incident of an organization's affairs, to be defended by the organization's lawyer like any other suit. However, if the claim involves serious charges of wrongdoing by those in control of the organization, a conflict may arise between the lawyer's duty to the organization and the lawyer's relationship with the board. In those circumstances, Rule 1.7 governs who should represent the directors and the organization.

Rule 1.14   Client ~~Under a Disability~~ With Diminished Capacity

(a) When a client's ~~ability~~ capacity to make adequately considered decisions in connection with ~~the~~ a representation is ~~impaired~~ diminished, whether because of minority, mental ~~disability~~ impairment or for some other reason, the lawyer shall, as far as reasonably possible, maintain a normal client-lawyer relationship with the client.

(b) ~~A lawyer may seek the appointment of a guardian or take other protective action with respect to a client only when~~ When the lawyer reasonably believes that the client has diminished capacity, is at risk of substantial physical, financial or other harm unless action is taken and cannot adequately act in the client's own interest, the lawyer may take reasonably neces-

73

sary protective action, including consulting with individuals or entities that have the ability to take action to protect the client and, in appropriate cases, seeking the appointment of a guardian ad litem, conservator or guardian.

(c) Information relating to the representation of a client with diminished capacity is protected by Rule 1.6. When taking protective action pursuant to paragraph (b), the lawyer is impliedly authorized under Rule 1.6(a) to reveal information about the client, but only to the extent reasonably necessary to protect the client's interests.

COMMENT

[1]   The normal client-lawyer relationship is based on the assumption that the client, when properly advised and assisted, is capable of making decisions about important matters. When the client is a minor or suffers from a diminished mental capacity disorder or disability, however, maintaining the ordinary client-lawyer relationship may not be possible in all respects. In particular, an a severely incapacitated person may have no power to make legally binding decisions. Nevertheless, a client lacking legal competence with diminished capacity often has the ability to understand, deliberate upon, and reach conclusions about matters affecting the client's own well-being. Furthermore, to an increasing extent the law recognizes intermediate degrees of competence. For example, children as young as five or six years of age, and certainly those of ten or twelve, are regarded as having opinions that are entitled to weight in legal proceedings concerning their custody. So also, it is recognized that some persons of advanced age can be quite capable of handling routine financial matters while needing special legal protection concerning major transactions.

[2]   The fact that a client suffers a disability does not diminish the lawyer's obligation to treat the client with attention and respect. If the person has no guardian or legal representative, the lawyer often must act as de facto guardian. Even if the person does have has a legal representative, the lawyer should as far as possible accord the represented person the status of client, particularly in maintaining communication.

[3]   The client may wish to have family members or other persons participate in discussions with the lawyer. When necessary to assist in the representation, the presence of such persons generally does not affect the applicability of the attorney-client evidentiary privilege. Nevertheless, the lawyer must keep the client's interests foremost and, except for protective action authorized under paragraph (b), must to look to the client, and not family members, to make decisions on the client's behalf.

[3] [4] If a legal representative has already been appointed for the client, the lawyer should ordinarily look to the representative for decisions on behalf of the client. If a legal representative has not been appointed, the lawyer should see to such an appointment where it would

~~serve the client's best interests. Thus, if a disabled client has substantial~~ ~~property that should be sold for the client's benefit, effective completion~~ ~~of the transaction ordinarily requires appointment of a legal representa-~~ ~~tive. In many circumstances, however, appointment of a legal represen-~~ ~~tative may be expensive or traumatic for the client. Evaluation of these~~ ~~considerations is a matter of professional judgment on the lawyer's part.~~ In matters involving a minor, whether the lawyer should look to the parents as natural guardians may depend on the type of proceeding or matter in which the lawyer is representing the minor. [4] If the lawyer represents the guardian as distinct from the ward, and is aware that the guardian is acting adversely to the ward's interest, the lawyer may have an obligation to prevent or rectify the guardian's misconduct. See Rule 1.2(d).

Taking Protective Action

[5] If a lawyer reasonably believes that a client is at risk of substantial physical, financial or other harm unless action is taken, and that a normal client-lawyer relationship cannot be maintained as provided in paragraph (a) because the client lacks sufficient capacity to communicate or to make adequately considered decisions in connection with the representation, then paragraph (b) permits the lawyer to take protective measures deemed necessary. Such measures could include: consulting with family members, using a reconsideration period to permit clarification or improvement of circumstances, using voluntary surrogate decisionmaking tools such as durable powers of attorney or consulting with support groups, professional services, adult-protective agencies or other individuals or entities that have the ability to protect the client. In taking any protective action, the lawyer should be guided by such factors as the wishes and values of the client to the extent known, the client's best interests and the goals of intruding into the client's decisionmaking autonomy to the least extent feasible, maximizing client capacities and respecting the client's family and social connections.

[6] In determining the extent of the client's diminished capacity, the lawyer should consider and balance such factors as: the client's ability to articulate reasoning leading to a decision, variability of state of mind and ability to appreciate consequences of a decision; the substantive fairness of a decision; and the consistency of a decision with the known long-term commitments and values of the client. In appropriate circumstances, the lawyer may seek guidance from an appropriate diagnostician.

[7] If a legal representative has not been appointed, the lawyer should consider whether appointment of a guardian ad litem, conservator or guardian is necessary to protect the client's interests. Thus, if a client with diminished capacity has substantial property that should be sold for the client's benefit, effective completion of the transaction may require appointment of a legal representative. In addition, rules of

procedure in litigation sometimes provide that minors or persons with diminished capacity must be represented by a guardian or next friend if they do not have a general guardian. In many circumstances, however, appointment of a legal representative may be more expensive or traumatic for the client than circumstances in fact require. Evaluation of such circumstances is a matter entrusted to the professional judgment of the lawyer. In considering alternatives, however, the lawyer should be aware of any law that requires the lawyer to advocate the least restrictive action on behalf of the client.

Disclosure of the Client's Condition

[5] [8] ~~Rules of procedure in litigation generally provide that minors or persons suffering mental disability shall be represented by a guardian or next friend if they do not have a general guardian. However, disclosure~~ Disclosure of the client's ~~disability can~~ diminished capacity could adversely affect the client's interests. For example, raising the question of ~~disability~~ diminished capacity could, in some circumstances, lead to proceedings for involuntary commitment. Information relating to the representation is protected by Rule 1.6. Therefore, unless authorized to do so, the lawyer may not disclose such information. When taking protective action pursuant to paragraph (b), the lawyer is impliedly authorized to make the necessary disclosures, even when the client directs the lawyer to the contrary. Nevertheless, given the risks of disclosure, paragraph (c) limits what the lawyer may disclose in consulting with other individuals or entities or seeking the appointment of a legal representative. At the very least, the lawyer should determine whether it is likely that the person or entity consulted with will act adversely to the client's interests before discussing matters related to the client. The lawyer's position in such cases is an unavoidably difficult one. ~~The lawyer may seek guidance from an appropriate diagnostician.~~

Emergency Legal Assistance

[6] [9] In an emergency where the health, safety or a financial interest of a person ~~under a disability~~ with seriously diminished capacity is threatened with imminent and irreparable harm, a lawyer may take legal action on behalf of such a person even though the person is unable to establish a client-lawyer relationship or to make or express considered judgments about the matter, when the ~~disabled~~ person or another acting in good faith on that person's behalf has consulted with the lawyer. Even in such an emergency, however, the lawyer should not act unless the lawyer reasonably believes that the person has no other lawyer, agent or other representative available. The lawyer should take legal action on behalf of the ~~disabled~~ person only to the extent reasonably necessary to maintain the status quo or otherwise avoid imminent and irreparable harm. A lawyer who undertakes to represent a person in such an exigent

situation has the same duties under these Rules as the lawyer would with respect to a client.

[7] [10] A lawyer who acts on behalf of a ~~disabled~~ person with seriously diminished capacity in an emergency should keep the confidences of the ~~disabled~~ person as if dealing with a client, disclosing them only to the extent necessary to accomplish the intended protective action. The lawyer should disclose to any tribunal involved and to any other counsel involved the nature of his or her relationship with the ~~disabled~~ person. The lawyer should take steps to regularize the relationship or implement other protective solutions as soon as possible. Normally, a lawyer would not seek compensation for such emergency actions taken ~~on behalf of a disabled person~~.

Rule 1.15 Safekeeping Property

(a) A lawyer shall hold property of clients or third persons that is in a lawyer's possession in connection with a representation separate from the lawyer's own property. Funds shall be kept in a separate account maintained in the state where the lawyer's office is situated, or elsewhere with the consent of the client or third person. Other property shall be identified as such and appropriately safeguarded. Complete records of such account funds and other property shall be kept by the lawyer and shall be preserved for a period of [five years] after termination of the representation.

(b) A lawyer may deposit the lawyer's own funds in a client trust account for the sole purpose of paying bank service charges on that account, but only in an amount necessary for that purpose.

(c) A lawyer shall deposit into a client trust account legal fees and expenses that have been paid in advance, to be withdrawn by the lawyer only as fees are earned or expenses incurred.

~~(b)~~ (d) Upon receiving funds or other property in which a client or third person has an interest, a lawyer shall promptly notify the client or third person. Except as stated in this rule or otherwise permitted by law or by agreement with the client, a lawyer shall promptly deliver to the client or third person any funds or other property that the client or third person is entitled to receive and, upon request by the client or third person, shall promptly render a full accounting regarding such property.

~~(c)~~ (e) When in the course of representation a lawyer is in possession of property in which ~~both~~ two or more persons (one of whom may be the lawyer ~~and another person~~) claim interests, the property shall be kept separate by the lawyer until ~~there is an accounting and severance of their interests. If a dispute arises concerning their respective interests, the portion in dis-~~

~~pute shall be kept separate by the lawyer until~~ the dispute is resolved. The lawyer shall promptly distribute all portions of the property as to which the interests are not in dispute.

COMMENT

[1]   A lawyer should hold property of others with the care required of a professional fiduciary. Securities should be kept in a safe deposit box, except when some other form of safekeeping is warranted by special circumstances. All property that is the property of clients or third persons ~~should~~, including prospective clients, must be kept separate from the lawyer's business and personal property and, if monies, in one or more trust accounts. Separate trust accounts may be warranted when administering estate monies or acting in similar fiduciary capacities. A lawyer should maintain on a current basis books and records in accordance with generally accepted accounting practice and comply with any recordkeeping rules established by law or court order. See, e.g., ABA Model Financial Recordkeeping Rule.

[2]   While normally it is impermissible to commingle the lawyer's own funds with client funds, paragraph (b) provides that it is permissible when necessary to pay bank service charges on that account. Accurate records must be kept regarding which part of the funds are the lawyer's.

~~[2]~~ [3] Lawyers often receive funds from ~~third parties from~~ which the lawyer's fee will be paid. ~~If there is risk that the client may divert the funds without paying the fee, the~~ The lawyer is not required to remit ~~the portion from which the fee is to be paid~~ to the client funds that the lawyer reasonably believes represent fees owed. However, a lawyer may not hold funds to coerce a client into accepting the lawyer's contention. The disputed portion of the funds ~~should~~ must be kept in a trust account and the lawyer should suggest means for prompt resolution of the dispute, such as arbitration. The undisputed portion of the funds shall be promptly distributed.

~~[3]~~ [4] ~~Third~~ Paragraph (e) also recognizes that third parties, ~~such as a client's creditors,~~ may have ~~just~~ lawful claims against specific funds or other property in a lawyer's custody, such as a client's creditor who has a lien on funds recovered in a personal injury action. A lawyer may have a duty under applicable law to protect such third-party claims against wrongful interference by the client~~, and accordingly may~~. In such cases, when the third-party claim is not frivolous under applicable law, the lawyer must refuse to surrender the property to the client until the claims are resolved. ~~However, a~~ A lawyer should not unilaterally assume to arbitrate a dispute between the client and the third party, but, when there are substantial grounds for dispute as to the person entitled to the funds, the lawyer may file an action to have a court resolve the dispute.

~~[4]~~ [5] The obligations of a lawyer under this Rule are independent of those arising from activity other than rendering legal services. For example, a lawyer who serves only as an escrow agent is governed by the applicable law relating to fiduciaries even though the lawyer does not render legal services in the transaction and is not governed by this Rule.

[5] [6] A "clients' security lawyers' fund" for client protection provides a means through the collective efforts of the bar to reimburse persons who have lost money or property as a result of dishonest conduct of a lawyer. Where such a fund has been established, a lawyer must participate where it is mandatory, and, even when it is voluntary, the lawyer should participate.

Rule 1.16   Declining or Terminating Representation

(a) Except as stated in paragraph (c), a lawyer shall not represent a client or, where representation has commenced, shall withdraw from the representation of a client if:

(1) the representation will result in violation of the rules of professional conduct or other law;

(2) the lawyer's physical or mental condition materially impairs the lawyer's ability to represent the client; or

(3) the lawyer is discharged.

(b) Except as stated in paragraph (c), a lawyer may withdraw from representing a client if:

(1) withdrawal can be accomplished without material adverse effect on the interests of the client, or if:;

(1) (2) the client persists in a course of action involving the lawyer's services that the lawyer reasonably believes is criminal or fraudulent;

(2) (3) the client has used the lawyer's services to perpetrate a crime or fraud;

(3) (4) a the client insists upon pursuing an objective taking action that the lawyer considers repugnant or imprudent with which the lawyer has a fundamental disagreement;

(4) (5) the client fails substantially to fulfill an obligation to the lawyer regarding the lawyer's services and has been given reasonable warning that the lawyer will withdraw unless the obligation is fulfilled;

(5) (6) the representation will result in an unreasonable financial burden on the lawyer or has been rendered unreasonably difficult by the client; or

(6) (7) other good cause for withdrawal exists.

(c) A lawyer must comply with applicable law requiring notice to or permission of a tribunal when terminating a representation. When ordered to do so by a tribunal, a lawyer shall continue representation notwithstanding good cause for terminating the representation.

(d) Upon termination of representation, a lawyer shall take steps to the extent reasonably practicable to protect a client's interests, such as giving reasonable notice to the client, allowing time for employment of other counsel, surrendering papers and property to which the client is entitled and refunding any advance payment of fee or expense that has not been earned or incurred. The lawyer may retain papers relating to the client to the extent permitted by other law.

COMMENT

[1]   A lawyer should not accept representation in a matter unless it can be performed competently, promptly, without improper conflict of interest and to completion. Ordinarily, a representation in a matter is completed when the agreed-upon assistance has been concluded. See Rules 1.2(c) and 6.5. See also Rule 1.3, Comment [4].

Mandatory Withdrawal

[2]   A lawyer ordinarily must decline or withdraw from representation if the client demands that the lawyer engage in conduct that is illegal or violates the Rules of Professional Conduct or other law. The lawyer is not obliged to decline or withdraw simply because the client suggests such a course of conduct; a client may make such a suggestion in the hope that a lawyer will not be constrained by a professional obligation.

[3]   When a lawyer has been appointed to represent a client, withdrawal ordinarily requires approval of the appointing authority. See also Rule 6.2. Similarly, court approval or notice to the court is often required by applicable law before a lawyer withdraws from pending litigation. Difficulty may be encountered if withdrawal is based on the client's demand that the lawyer engage in unprofessional conduct. The court may ~~wish~~ request an explanation for the withdrawal, while the lawyer may be bound to keep confidential the facts that would constitute such an explanation. The lawyer's statement that professional considerations require termination of the representation ordinarily should be accepted as sufficient. Lawyers should be mindful of their obligations to both clients and the court under Rules 1.6 and 3.3.

Discharge

[4]   A client has a right to discharge a lawyer at any time, with or without cause, subject to liability for payment for the lawyer's services. Where future dispute about the withdrawal may be anticipated, it may be advisable to prepare a written statement reciting the circumstances.

[5]   Whether a client can discharge appointed counsel may depend on applicable law. A client seeking to do so should be given a full

explanation of the consequences. These consequences may include a decision by the appointing authority that appointment of successor counsel is unjustified, thus requiring self-representation by the client.

[6] If the client ~~is mentally incompetent~~ has severely diminished capacity, the client may lack the legal capacity to discharge the lawyer, and in any event the discharge may be seriously adverse to the client's interests. The lawyer should make special effort to help the client consider the consequences and~~, in an extreme case,~~ may ~~initiate proceedings for a conservatorship or similar protection of the client. See~~ take reasonably necessary protective action as provided in Rule 1.14.

Optional Withdrawal

[7] A lawyer may withdraw from representation in some circumstances. The lawyer has the option to withdraw if it can be accomplished without material adverse effect on the client's interests. Withdrawal is also justified if the client persists in a course of action that the lawyer reasonably believes is criminal or fraudulent, for a lawyer is not required to be associated with such conduct even if the lawyer does not further it. Withdrawal is also permitted if the lawyer's services were misused in the past even if that would materially prejudice the client. The lawyer may also withdraw where the client insists on ~~a~~ taking action that the lawyer considers repugnant or ~~imprudent objective~~ with which the lawyer has a fundamental disagreement.

[8] A lawyer may withdraw if the client refuses to abide by the terms of an agreement relating to the representation, such as an agreement concerning fees or court costs or an agreement limiting the objectives of the representation.

Assisting the Client upon Withdrawal

[9] Even if the lawyer has been unfairly discharged by the client, a lawyer must take all reasonable steps to mitigate the consequences to the client. The lawyer may retain papers as security for a fee only to the extent permitted by law. ~~Whether or not a lawyer for an organization may under certain unusual circumstances have a legal obligation to the organization after withdrawing or being discharged by the organization's highest authority is beyond the scope of these Rules.~~ See Rule 1.15.

RULE 1.17   Sale of Law Practice*

A lawyer or a law firm may sell or purchase a law practice, or an area of practice, including good will, if the following conditions are satisfied:

(a) The seller ceases to engage in the private practice of law, or in the area of practice that has been sold, [in the geographic

---

* The ABA House of Delegates amended the Ethics 2000 Commission Report to allow a lawyer to cease part of a practice that has been sold without leaving the practice of law entirely. See Model Rule 1.17(a).

area] [in the jurisdiction] (a jurisdiction may elect either version) in which the practice has been conducted;

   (b) The entire practice, or the entire area of practice, is sold ~~as an entirety~~ to ~~another lawyer~~ one or more lawyers or law ~~firm~~ firms;

   (c) ~~Actual~~ The seller gives written notice ~~is given~~ to each of the seller's clients regarding:

      (1) the proposed sale;

      ~~(2) the terms of any proposed change in the fee arrangement authorized by paragraph (d);~~

      ~~(3)~~ (2) the client's right to retain other counsel or to take possession of the file; and

      ~~(4)~~ (3) the fact that the client's consent to the ~~sale~~ transfer of the client's files will be presumed if the client does not take any action or does not otherwise object within ninety (90) days of receipt of the notice.

   If a client cannot be given notice, the representation of that client may be transferred to the purchaser only upon entry of an order so authorizing by a court having jurisdiction. The seller may disclose to the court in camera information relating to the representation only to the extent necessary to obtain an order authorizing the transfer of a file.

   (d) The fees charged clients shall not be increased by reason of the sale. ~~The purchaser may, however, refuse to undertake the representation unless the client consents to pay the purchaser fees at a rate not exceeding the fees charged by the purchaser for rendering substantially similar services prior to the initiation of the purchase negotiations.~~

COMMENT

   [1] The practice of law is a profession, not merely a business. Clients are not commodities that can be purchased and sold at will. Pursuant to this Rule, when a lawyer or an entire firm ceases to practice, or ceases to practice in an area of law, and ~~another lawyer~~ other lawyers or ~~firm takes~~ firms take over the representation, the selling lawyer or firm may obtain compensation for the reasonable value of the practice as may withdrawing partners of law firms. See Rules 5.4 and 5.6.

Termination of Practice by the Seller

   [2] The requirement that all of the private practice, or all of an area of practice, be sold is satisfied if the seller in good faith makes the entire practice, or the area of practice, available for sale to the ~~purchaser~~ purchasers. The fact that a number of the seller's clients decide not to be represented by the ~~purchaser~~ purchasers but take their matters else-

where, therefore, does not result in a violation. ~~Neither does a return~~ Return to private practice as a result of an unanticipated change in circumstances does not necessarily result in a violation. For example, a lawyer who has sold the practice to accept an appointment to judicial office does not violate the requirement that the sale be attendant to cessation of practice if the lawyer later resumes private practice upon being defeated in a contested or a retention election for the office or resigns from a judiciary position.

[3] The requirement that the seller cease to engage in the private practice of law does not prohibit employment as a lawyer on the staff of a public agency or a legal services entity that provides legal services to the poor, or as in-house counsel to a business.

[4] The Rule permits a sale of an entire practice attendant upon retirement from the private practice of law within the jurisdiction. Its provisions, therefore, accommodate the lawyer who sells the practice upon the occasion of moving to another state. Some states are so large that a move from one locale therein to another is tantamount to leaving the jurisdiction in which the lawyer has engaged in the practice of law. To also accommodate lawyers so situated, states may permit the sale of the practice when the lawyer leaves the geographic area rather than the jurisdiction. The alternative desired should be indicated by selecting one of the two provided for in Rule 1.17(a).

[5] This Rule also permits a lawyer or law firm to sell an area of practice. If an area of practice is sold and the lawyer remains in the active practice of law, the lawyer must cease accepting any matters in the area of practice that has been sold, either as counsel or co-counsel or by assuming joint responsibility for a matter in connection with the division of a fee with another lawyer as would otherwise be permitted by Rule 1.5(e). For example, a lawyer with a substantial number of estate planning matters and a substantial number of probate administration cases may sell the estate planning portion of the practice but remain in the practice of law by concentrating on probate administration; however, that practitioner may not thereafter accept any estate planning matters. Although a lawyer who leaves a jurisdiction or geographical area typically would sell the entire practice, this Rule permits the lawyer to limit the sale to one or more areas of the practice, thereby preserving the lawyer's right to continue practice in the areas of the practice that were not sold.

~~Single Purchaser~~ Sale of Entire Practice or Entire Area of Practice

~~[5]~~ [6] The Rule requires ~~a single purchaser~~ that the seller's entire practice, or an entire area of practice, be sold. The prohibition against ~~piecemeal~~ sale of ~~a~~ less than an entire practice area protects those clients whose matters are less lucrative and who might find it difficult to secure other counsel if a sale could be limited to substantial fee-generating matters. The ~~purchaser is~~ purchasers are required to undertake all client matters in the practice or practice area, subject to client consent. ~~If~~ This

83

requirement is satisfied, however, ~~the~~ even if a purchaser is unable to undertake ~~all~~ a particular client ~~matters~~ matter because of a conflict of interest ~~in a specific matter respecting which the purchaser is not permitted by Rule 1.7 or another rule to represent the client, the requirement that there be a single purchaser is nevertheless satisfied~~.

Client Confidences, Consent and Notice

~~[6]~~ [7] Negotiations between seller and prospective purchaser prior to disclosure of information relating to a specific representation of an identifiable client no more violate the confidentiality provisions of Model Rule 1.6 than do preliminary discussions concerning the possible association of another lawyer or mergers between firms, with respect to which client consent is not required. Providing the purchaser access to client-specific information relating to the representation and to the file, however, requires client consent. The Rule provides that before such information can be disclosed by the seller to the purchaser the client must be given actual written notice of the contemplated sale, including the identity of the purchaser ~~and any proposed change in the terms of future representation~~, and must be told that the decision to consent or make other arrangements must be made within 90 days. If nothing is heard from the client within that time, consent to the sale is presumed.

~~[7]~~ [8] A lawyer or law firm ceasing to practice cannot be required to remain in practice because some clients cannot be given actual notice of the proposed purchase. Since these clients cannot themselves consent to the purchase or direct any other disposition of their files, the Rule requires an order from a court having jurisdiction authorizing their transfer or other disposition. The Court can be expected to determine whether reasonable efforts to locate the client have been exhausted, and whether the absent client's legitimate interests will be served by authorizing the transfer of the file so that the purchaser may continue the representation. Preservation of client confidences requires that the petition for a court order be considered in camera. (A procedure by which such an order can be obtained needs to be established in jurisdictions in which it presently does not exist.)

~~[8]~~ [9] All the elements of client autonomy, including the client's absolute right to discharge a lawyer and transfer the representation to another, survive the sale of the practice or area of practice.

Fee Arrangements Between Client and Purchaser

~~[9]~~ [10] The sale may not be financed by increases in fees charged the clients of the practice. Existing agreements between the seller and the client as to fees and the scope of the work must be honored by the purchaser~~, unless the client consents after consultation. The purchaser may, however, advise the client that the purchaser will not undertake the representation unless the client consents to pay the higher fees the purchaser usually charges. To prevent client financing of the sale, the~~

~~higher fee the purchaser may charge must not exceed the fees charged by the purchaser for substantially similar service rendered prior to the initiation of the purchase negotiations.~~

~~[10] The purchaser may not intentionally fragment the practice which is the subject of the sale by charging significantly different fees in substantially similar matters. Doing so would make it possible for the purchaser to avoid the obligation to take over the entire practice by charging arbitrarily higher fees for less lucrative matters, thereby increasing the likelihood that those clients would not consent to the new representation.~~

Other Applicable Ethical Standards

[11] Lawyers participating in the sale of a law practice <u>or a practice area</u> are subject to the ethical standards applicable to involving another lawyer in the representation of a client. These include, for example, the seller's obligation to exercise competence in identifying a purchaser qualified to assume the practice and the purchaser's obligation to undertake the representation competently (see Rule 1.1); the obligation to avoid disqualifying conflicts, and to secure ~~client~~ <u>the client's informed</u> consent ~~after consultation~~ for those conflicts that can be agreed to (see Rule 1.7 <u>regarding conflicts and Rule 1.0(e) for the definition of informed consent</u>); and the obligation to protect information relating to the representation (see Rules 1.6 and 1.9).

[12] If approval of the substitution of the purchasing lawyer for the selling lawyer is required by the rules of any tribunal in which a matter is pending, such approval must be obtained before the matter can be included in the sale (see Rule 1.16).

Applicability of the Rule

[13] This Rule applies to the sale of a law practice by representatives of a deceased, disabled or disappeared lawyer. Thus, the seller may be represented by a non-lawyer representative not subject to these Rules. Since, however, no lawyer may participate in a sale of a law practice which does not conform to the requirements of this Rule, the representatives of the seller as well as the purchasing lawyer can be expected to see to it that they are met.

[14] Admission to or retirement from a law partnership or professional association, retirement plans and similar arrangements, and a sale of tangible assets of a law practice, do not constitute a sale or purchase governed by this Rule.

[15] This Rule does not apply to the transfers of legal representation between lawyers when such transfers are unrelated to the sale of a practice <u>or an area of practice</u>.

<u>Rule 1.18   Duties to Prospective Client</u>

(a) A person who discusses with a lawyer the possibility of forming a client-lawyer relationship with respect to a matter is a prospective client.

(b) Even when no client-lawyer relationship ensues, a law-yer who has had discussions with a prospective client shall not use or reveal information learned in the consultation, except as Rule 1.9 would permit with respect to information of a former client.

(c) A lawyer subject to paragraph (b) shall not represent a client with interests materially adverse to those of a prospective client in the same or a substantially related matter if the lawyer received information from the prospective client that could be significantly harmful to that person in the matter, except as provided in paragraph (d). If a lawyer is disqualified from repre-sentation under this paragraph, no lawyer in a firm with which that lawyer is associated may knowingly undertake or continue representation in such a matter, except as provided in para-graph (d).

(d) When the lawyer has received disqualifying information as defined in paragraph (c), representation is permissible if:

(1) both the affected client and the prospective client have given informed consent, confirmed in writing, or:

(2) the lawyer who received the information took rea-sonable measures to avoid exposure to more disqualifying information than was reasonably necessary to determine whether to represent the prospective client; and

(i) the disqualified lawyer is timely screened from any participation in the matter and is apportioned no part of the fee therefrom; and

(ii) written notice is promptly given to the prospec-tive client.

COMMENT

[1] Prospective clients, like clients, may disclose information to a lawyer, place documents or other property in the lawyer's custody, or rely on the lawyer's advice. A lawyer's discussions with a prospective client usually are limited in time and depth and leave both the prospec-tive client and the lawyer free (and sometimes required) to proceed no further. Hence, prospective clients should receive some but not all of the protection afforded clients.

[2] Not all persons who communicate information to a lawyer are entitled to protection under this Rule. A person who communicates information unilaterally to a lawyer, without any reasonable expectation that the lawyer is willing to discuss the possibility of forming a client-lawyer relationship, is not a "prospective client" within the meaning of paragraph (a).

[3] It is often necessary for a prospective client to reveal informa-tion to the lawyer during an initial consultation prior to the decision about formation of a client-lawyer relationship. The lawyer often must

learn such information to determine whether there is a conflict of interest with an existing client and whether the matter is one that the lawyer is willing to undertake. Paragraph (b) prohibits the lawyer from using or revealing that information, except as permitted by Rule 1.9, even if the client or lawyer decides not to proceed with the representation. The duty exists regardless of how brief the initial conference may be.

[4] In order to avoid acquiring disqualifying information from a prospective client, a lawyer considering whether or not to undertake a new matter should limit the initial interview to only such information as reasonably appears necessary for that purpose. Where the information indicates that a conflict of interest or other reason for non-representation exists, the lawyer should so inform the prospective client or decline the representation. If the prospective client wishes to retain the lawyer, and if consent is possible under Rule 1.7, then consent from all affected present or former clients must be obtained before accepting the representation.

[5] A lawyer may condition conversations with a prospective client on the person's informed consent that no information disclosed during the consultation will prohibit the lawyer from representing a different client in the matter. See Rule 1.0(e) for the definition of informed consent. If the agreement expressly so provides, the prospective client may also consent to the lawyer's subsequent use of information received from the prospective client.

[6] Even in the absence of an agreement, under paragraph (c), the lawyer is not prohibited from representing a client with interests adverse to those of the prospective client in the same or a substantially related matter unless the lawyer has received from the prospective client information that could be significantly harmful if used in the matter.

[7] Under paragraph (c), the prohibition in this Rule is imputed to other lawyers as provided in Rule 1.10, but, under paragraph (d)(1), imputation may be avoided if the lawyer obtains the informed consent, confirmed in writing, of both the prospective and affected clients. In the alternative, imputation may be avoided if the conditions of paragraph (d)(2) are met and all disqualified lawyers are timely screened and written notice is promptly given to the prospective client. See Rule 1.0(k) (requirements for screening procedures). Paragraph (d)(2)(i) does not prohibit the screened lawyer from receiving a salary or partnership share established by prior independent agreement, but that lawyer may not receive compensation directly related to the matter in which the lawyer is disqualified.

[8] Notice, including a general description of the subject matter about which the lawyer was consulted, and of the screening procedures employed, generally should be given as soon as practicable after the need for screening becomes apparent.

[9] For the duty of competence of a lawyer who gives assistance on the merits of a matter to a prospective client, see Rule 1.1. For a lawyer's

duties when a prospective client entrusts valuables or papers to the lawyer's care, see Rule 1.15.

COUNSELOR

Rule 2.1 Advisor

In representing a client, a lawyer shall exercise independent professional judgment and render candid advice. In rendering advice, a lawyer may refer not only to law but to other considerations such as moral, economic, social and political factors, that may be relevant to the client's situation.

COMMENT

Scope of Advice

[1] A client is entitled to straightforward advice expressing the lawyer's honest assessment. Legal advice often involves unpleasant facts and alternatives that a client may be disinclined to confront. In presenting advice, a lawyer endeavors to sustain the client's morale and may put advice in as acceptable a form as honesty permits. However, a lawyer should not be deterred from giving candid advice by the prospect that the advice will be unpalatable to the client.

[2] Advice couched in narrow legal terms may be of little value to a client, especially where practical considerations, such as cost or effects on other people, are predominant. Purely technical legal advice, therefore, can sometimes be inadequate. It is proper for a lawyer to refer to relevant moral and ethical considerations in giving advice. Although a lawyer is not a moral advisor as such, moral and ethical considerations impinge upon most legal questions and may decisively influence how the law will be applied.

[3] A client may expressly or impliedly ask the lawyer for purely technical advice. When such a request is made by a client experienced in legal matters, the lawyer may accept it at face value. When such a request is made by a client inexperienced in legal matters, however, the lawyer's responsibility as advisor may include indicating that more may be involved than strictly legal considerations.

[4] Matters that go beyond strictly legal questions may also be in the domain of another profession. Family matters can involve problems within the professional competence of psychiatry, clinical psychology or social work; business matters can involve problems within the competence of the accounting profession or of financial specialists. Where consultation with a professional in another field is itself something a competent lawyer would recommend, the lawyer should make such a recommendation. At the same time, a lawyer's advice at its best often consists of recommending a course of action in the face of conflicting recommendations of experts.

Offering Advice

[5] In general, a lawyer is not expected to give advice until asked by the client. However, when a lawyer knows that a client proposes a course of action that is likely to result in substantial adverse legal consequences to the client, the lawyer's duty to the client under Rule 1.4 may require that the lawyer ~~act~~ offer advice if the client's course of action is related to the representation. Similarly, when a matter is likely to involve litigation, it may be necessary under Rule 1.4 to inform the client of forms of dispute resolution that might constitute reasonable alternatives to litigation. A lawyer ordinarily has no duty to initiate investigation of a client's affairs or to give advice that the client has indicated is unwanted, but a lawyer may initiate advice to a client when doing so appears to be in the client's interest.

~~Rule 2.2   Intermediary~~

~~(a) A lawyer may act as intermediary between clients if:~~

~~(1) the lawyer consults with each client concerning the implications of the common representation, including the advantages and risks involved, and the effect on the attorney-client privileges, and obtains each client's consent to the common representation;~~

~~(2) the lawyer reasonably believes that the matter can be resolved on terms compatible with the clients' best interests, that each client will be able to make adequately informed decisions in the matter and that there is little risk of material prejudice to the interests of any of the clients if the contemplated resolution is unsuccessful; and~~

~~(3) the lawyer reasonably believes that the common representation can be undertaken impartially and without improper effect on other responsibilities the lawyer has to any of the clients.~~

~~(b) While acting as intermediary, the lawyer shall consult with each client concerning the decisions to be made and the considerations relevant in making them, so that each client can make adequately informed decisions.~~

~~(c) A lawyer shall withdraw as intermediary if any of the clients so requests, or if any of the conditions stated in paragraph (a) is no longer satisfied. Upon withdrawal, the lawyer shall not continue to represent any of the clients in the matter that was the subject of the intermediation.~~

~~COMMENT~~

~~[1]   A lawyer acts as intermediary under this Rule when the lawyer represents two or more parties with potentially conflicting interests. A key factor in defining the relationship is whether the parties share~~

responsibility for the lawyer's fee, but the common representation may be inferred from other circumstances. Because confusion can arise as to the lawyer's role where each party is not separately represented, it is important that the lawyer make clear the relationship.

[2] The Rule does not apply to a lawyer acting as arbitrator or mediator between or among parties who are not clients of the lawyer, even where the lawyer has been appointed with the concurrence of the parties. In performing such a role the lawyer may be subject to applicable codes of ethics, such as the Code of Ethics for Arbitration in Commercial Disputes prepared by a joint Committee of the American Bar Association and the American Arbitration Association.

[3] A lawyer acts as intermediary in seeking to establish or adjust a relationship between clients on an amicable and mutually advantageous basis; for example, in helping to organize a business in which two or more clients are entrepreneurs, working out the financial reorganization of an enterprise in which two or more clients have an interest, arranging a property distribution in settlement of an estate or mediating a dispute between clients. The lawyer seeks to resolve potentially conflicting interests by developing the parties' mutual interests. The alternative can be that each party may have to obtain separate representation, with the possibility in some situations of incurring additional cost, complication or even litigation. Given these and other relevant factors, all the clients may prefer that the lawyer act as intermediary.

[4] In considering whether to act as intermediary between clients, a lawyer should be mindful that if the intermediation fails the result can be additional cost, embarrassment and recrimination. In some situations the risk of failure is so great that intermediation is plainly impossible. For example, a lawyer cannot undertake common representation of clients between whom contentious litigation is imminent or who contemplate contentious negotiations. More generally, if the relationship between the parties has already assumed definite antagonism, the possibility that the clients' interests can be adjusted by intermediation ordinarily is not very good.

[5] The appropriateness of intermediation can depend on its form. Forms of intermediation range from informal arbitration, where each client's case is presented by the respective client and the lawyer decides the outcome, to mediation, to common representation where the clients' interests are substantially though not entirely compatible. One form may be appropriate in circumstances where another would not. Other relevant factors are whether the lawyer subsequently will represent both parties on a continuing basis and whether the situation involves creating a relationship between the parties or terminating one.

Confidentiality and Privilege

[6] A particularly important factor in determining the appropriateness of intermediation is the effect on client-lawyer confidentiality and the attorney-client privilege. In a common representation, the lawyer is

still required both to keep each client adequately informed and to maintain confidentiality of information relating to the representation. See Rules 1.4 and 1.6. Complying with both requirements while acting as intermediary requires a delicate balance. If the balance cannot be maintained, the common representation is improper. With regard to the attorney-client privilege, the prevailing rule is that as between commonly represented clients the privilege does not attach. Hence, it must be assumed that if litigation eventuates between the clients, the privilege will not protect any such communications, and the clients should be so advised.

[7] Since the lawyer is required to be impartial between commonly represented clients, intermediation is improper when that impartiality cannot be maintained. For example, a lawyer who has represented one of the clients for a long period and in a variety of matters might have difficulty being impartial between that client and one to whom the lawyer has only recently been introduced.

Consultation

[8] In acting as intermediary between clients, the lawyer is required to consult with the clients on the implications of doing so, and proceed only upon consent based on such a consultation. The consultation should make clear that the lawyer's role is not that of partisanship normally expected in other circumstances.

[9] Paragraph (b) is an application of the principle expressed in Rule 1.4. Where the lawyer is intermediary, the clients ordinarily must assume greater responsibility for decisions than when each client is independently represented.

Withdrawal

[10] Common representation does not diminish the rights of each client in the client-lawyer relationship. Each has the right to loyal and diligent representation, the right to discharge the lawyer as stated in Rule 1.16, and the protection of Rule 1.9 concerning obligations to a former client.

Rule 2.3   Evaluation for Use by Third Persons

(a) A lawyer may ~~undertake~~ provide an evaluation of a matter affecting a client for the use of someone other than the client if: ~~(1)~~ the lawyer reasonably believes that making the evaluation is compatible with other aspects of the lawyer's relationship with the client; ~~and~~.

~~(2)~~ (b) When the lawyer knows or reasonably should know that the evaluation is likely to affect the client's interests materially and adversely, the lawyer shall not provide the evaluation unless the client ~~consents after consultation~~ gives informed consent.

~~(b)~~ (c) **Except as disclosure is ~~required~~ authorized in connection with a report of an evaluation, information relating to the evaluation is otherwise protected by Rule 1.6.**

COMMENT

Definition

[1] An evaluation may be performed at the client's direction ~~but~~ or when impliedly authorized in order to carry out the representation. See Rule 1.2. Such an evaluation may be for the primary purpose of establishing information for the benefit of third parties; for example, an opinion concerning the title of property rendered at the behest of a vendor for the information of a prospective purchaser, or at the behest of a borrower for the information of a prospective lender. In some situations, the evaluation may be required by a government agency; for example, an opinion concerning the legality of the securities registered for sale under the securities laws. In other instances, the evaluation may be required by a third person, such as a purchaser of a business.

~~[2] Lawyers for the government may be called upon to give a formal opinion on the legality of contemplated government agency action. In making such an evaluation, the government lawyer acts at the behest of the government as the client but for the purpose of establishing the limits of the agency's authorized activity. Such an opinion is to be distinguished from confidential legal advice given agency officials. The critical question is whether the opinion is to be made public.~~

~~[3]~~ [2] A legal evaluation should be distinguished from an investigation of a person with whom the lawyer does not have a client-lawyer relationship. For example, a lawyer retained by a purchaser to analyze a vendor's title to property does not have a client-lawyer relationship with the vendor. So also, an investigation into a person's affairs by a government lawyer, or by special counsel by a government lawyer, or by special counsel employed by the government, is not an evaluation as that term is used in this Rule. The question is whether the lawyer is retained by the person whose affairs are being examined. When the lawyer is retained by that person, the general rules concerning loyalty to client and preservation of confidences apply, which is not the case if the lawyer is retained by someone else. For this reason, it is essential to identify the person by whom the lawyer is retained. This should be made clear not only to the person under examination, but also to others to whom the results are to be made available.

~~Duty~~ Duties Owed to Third Person and Client

~~[4]~~ [3] When the evaluation is intended for the information or use of a third person, a legal duty to that person may or may not arise. That legal question is beyond the scope of this Rule. However, since such an evaluation involves a departure from the normal client-lawyer relationship, careful analysis of the situation is required. The lawyer must be satisfied as a matter of professional judgment that making the evaluation is compatible with other functions undertaken in behalf of the client. For example, if the lawyer is acting as advocate in defending the client against charges of fraud, it would normally be incompatible with that responsibility for the lawyer to perform an evaluation for others concerning the same or a related transaction. Assuming no such impediment is apparent, however, the lawyer should advise the client of the implications of the evaluation, particularly the lawyer's responsibilities to third persons and the duty to disseminate the findings.

Access to and Disclosure of Information

[5] [4] The quality of an evaluation depends on the freedom and extent of the investigation upon which it is based. Ordinarily a lawyer should have whatever latitude of investigation seems necessary as a matter of professional judgment. Under some circumstances, however, the terms of the evaluation may be limited. For example, certain issues or sources may be categorically excluded, or the scope of search may be limited by time constraints or the noncooperation of persons having relevant information. Any such limitations that are material to the evaluation should be described in the report. If after a lawyer has commenced an evaluation, the client refuses to comply with the terms upon which it was understood the evaluation was to have been made, the lawyer's obligations are determined by law, having reference to the terms of the client's agreement and the surrounding circumstances. In no circumstances is the lawyer permitted to knowingly make a false statement of material fact or law in providing an evaluation under this Rule. See Rule 4.1.

Obtaining Client's Informed Consent

[5] Information relating to an evaluation is protected by Rule 1.6. In many situations, providing an evaluation to a third party poses no significant risk to the client; thus, the lawyer may be impliedly authorized to disclose information to carry out the representation. See Rule 1.6(a). Where, however, it is reasonably likely that providing the evaluation will affect the client's interests materially and adversely, the lawyer must first obtain the client's consent after the client has been adequately informed concerning the important possible effects on the client's interests. See Rules 1.6(a) and 1.0(e).

Financial Auditors' Requests for Information

[6] When a question concerning the legal situation of a client arises at the instance of the client's financial auditor and the question is referred to the lawyer, the lawyer's response may be made in accordance with procedures recognized in the legal profession. Such a procedure is set forth in the American Bar Association Statement of Policy Regarding

Lawyers' Responses to Auditors' Requests for Information, adopted in 1975.

Rule 2.4   Lawyer Serving as Third–Party Neutral

(a) A lawyer serves as a third-party neutral when the lawyer assists two or more persons who are not clients of the lawyer to reach a resolution of a dispute or other matter that has arisen between them. Service as a third-party neutral may include service as an arbitrator, a mediator or in such other capacity as will enable the lawyer to assist the parties to resolve the matter.

(b) A lawyer serving as a third-party neutral shall inform unrepresented parties that the lawyer is not representing them. When the lawyer knows or reasonably should know that a party does not understand the lawyer's role in the matter, the lawyer shall explain the difference between the lawyer's role as a third-party neutral and a lawyer's role as one who represents a client.

COMMENT

[1]   Alternative dispute resolution has become a substantial part of the civil justice system. Aside from representing clients in dispute-resolution processes, lawyers often serve as third-party neutrals. A third-party neutral is a person, such as a mediator, arbitrator, conciliator or evaluator, who assists the parties, represented or unrepresented, in the resolution of a dispute or in the arrangement of a transaction. Whether a third-party neutral serves primarily as a facilitator, evaluator or decisionmaker depends on the particular process that is either selected by the parties or mandated by a court.

[2]   The role of a third-party neutral is not unique to lawyers, although, in some court-connected contexts, only lawyers are allowed to serve in this role or to handle certain types of cases. In performing this role, the lawyer may be subject to court rules or other law that apply either to third-party neutrals generally or to lawyers serving as third-party neutrals. Lawyer-neutrals may also be subject to various codes of ethics, such as the Code of Ethics for Arbitration in Commercial Disputes prepared by a joint committee of the American Bar Association and the American Arbitration Association or the Model Standards of Conduct for Mediators jointly prepared by the American Bar Association, the American Arbitration Association and the Society of Professionals in Dispute Resolution.

[3]   Unlike nonlawyers who serve as third-party neutrals, lawyers serving in this role may experience unique problems as a result of differences between the role of a third-party neutral and a lawyer's service as a client representative. The potential for confusion is significant when the parties are unrepresented in the process. Thus, paragraph (b) requires a lawyer-neutral to inform unrepresented parties that the lawyer is not representing them. For some parties, particularly parties

who frequently use dispute-resolution processes, this information will be sufficient. For others, particularly those who are using the process for the first time, more information will be required. Where appropriate, the lawyer should inform unrepresented parties of the important differences between the lawyer's role as third-party neutral and a lawyer's role as a client representative, including the inapplicability of the attorney-client evidentiary privilege. The extent of disclosure required under this paragraph will depend on the particular parties involved and the subject matter of the proceeding, as well as the particular features of the dispute-resolution process selected.

[4]   A lawyer who serves as a third-party neutral subsequently may be asked to serve as a lawyer representing a client in the same matter. The conflicts of interest that arise for both the individual lawyer and the lawyer's law firm are addressed in Rule 1.12.

[5]   Lawyers who represent clients in alternative dispute-resolution processes are governed by the Rules of Professional Conduct. When the dispute-resolution process takes place before a tribunal, as in binding arbitration (see Rule 1.0(m)), the lawyer's duty of candor is governed by Rule 3.3. Otherwise, the lawyer's duty of candor toward both the third-party neutral and other parties is governed by Rule 4.1.

ADVOCATE

Rule 3.1   Meritorious Claims and Contentions

A lawyer shall not bring or defend a proceeding, or assert or controvert an issue therein, unless there is a basis in law and fact for doing so that is not frivolous, which includes a good faith argument for an extension, modification or reversal of existing law. A lawyer for the defendant in a criminal proceeding, or the respondent in a proceeding that could result in incarceration, may nevertheless so defend the proceeding as to require that every element of the case be established.

COMMENT

[1]   The advocate has a duty to use legal procedure for the fullest benefit of the client's cause, but also a duty not to abuse legal procedure. The law, both procedural and substantive, establishes the limits within which an advocate may proceed. However, the law is not always clear and never is static. Accordingly, in determining the proper scope of advocacy, account must be taken of the law's ambiguities and potential for change.

[2]   The filing of an action or defense or similar action taken for a client is not frivolous merely because the facts have not first been fully substantiated or because the lawyer expects to develop vital evidence only by discovery. What is required of lawyers, however, is that they inform themselves about the facts of their clients' cases and the applicable law and determine that they can make good faith arguments in

support of their clients' positions. Such action is not frivolous even though the lawyer believes that the client's position ultimately will not prevail. The action is frivolous, however, if the ~~client desires to have the action taken primarily for the purpose of harassing or maliciously injuring a person, or, if the~~ lawyer is unable either to make a good faith argument on the merits of the action taken or to support the action taken by a good faith argument for an extension, modification or reversal of existing law.

[3]   The lawyer's obligations under this Rule are subordinate to federal or state constitutional law that entitles a defendant in a criminal matter to the assistance of counsel in presenting a claim or contention that otherwise would be prohibited by this Rule.

Rule 3.2   Expediting Litigation

A lawyer shall make reasonable efforts to expedite litigation consistent with the interests of the client.

COMMENT

[1]   Dilatory practices bring the administration of justice into disrepute. ~~Delay should not be indulged merely for the convenience of the advocates, or~~ Although there will be occasions when a lawyer may properly seek a postponement for personal reasons, it is not proper for a lawyer to routinely fail to expedite litigation solely for the convenience of the advocates. Nor will a failure to expedite be reasonable if done for the purpose of frustrating an opposing party's attempt to obtain rightful redress or repose. It is not a justification that similar conduct is often tolerated by the bench and bar. The question is whether a competent lawyer acting in good faith would regard the course of action as having some substantial purpose other than delay. Realizing financial or other benefit from otherwise improper delay in litigation is not a legitimate interest of the client.

Rule 3.3   Candor Toward the Tribunal

(a) A lawyer shall not knowingly:

(1) make a false statement of ~~material~~ fact or law to a tribunal or fail to correct a false statement of material fact or law previously made to the tribunal by the lawyer;

~~(2) fail to disclose a material fact to a tribunal when disclosure is necessary to avoid assisting a criminal or fraudulent act by the client;~~

~~(3)~~ (2) fail to disclose to the tribunal legal authority in the controlling jurisdiction known to the lawyer to be directly adverse to the position of the client and not disclosed by opposing counsel; or

~~(4)~~ (3) **offer evidence that the lawyer knows to be false. If a lawyer, the lawyer's client, or a witness called by the lawyer, has offered material evidence and the lawyer comes to know of its falsity, the lawyer shall take reasonable remedial measures, including, if necessary, disclosure to the tribunal. A lawyer may refuse to offer evidence, other than the testimony of a defendant in a criminal matter, that the lawyer reasonably believes is false.**

(b) A lawyer who represents a client in an adjudicative proceeding and who knows that a person intends to engage, is engaging or has engaged in criminal or fraudulent conduct related to the proceeding shall take reasonable remedial measures, including, if necessary, disclosure to the tribunal.

~~(b)~~ **(c) The duties stated in** ~~paragraph~~ **paragraphs (a) and (b) continue to the conclusion of the proceeding, and apply even if compliance requires disclosure of information otherwise protected by Rule 1.6.**

~~(c) A lawyer may refuse to offer evidence that the lawyer reasonably believes is false.~~

(d) In an ex parte proceeding, a lawyer shall inform the tribunal of all material facts known to the lawyer that will enable the tribunal to make an informed decision, whether or not the facts are adverse.

COMMENT

[1]   This Rule governs the conduct of a lawyer who is representing a client in the proceedings of a tribunal. See Rule 1.0(m) for the definition of "tribunal." It also applies when the lawyer is representing a client in an ancillary proceeding conducted pursuant to the tribunal's adjudicative authority, such as a deposition. Thus, for example, paragraph (a)(3) requires a lawyer to take reasonable remedial measures if the lawyer comes to know that a client who is testifying in a deposition has offered evidence that is false.

~~[1]~~ [2] ~~The advocate's task is~~ This Rule sets forth the special duties of lawyers as officers of the court to avoid conduct that undermines the integrity of the adjudicative process. A lawyer acting as an advocate in an adjudicative proceeding has an obligation to present the client's case with persuasive force. Performance of that duty while maintaining confidences of the client, however, is qualified by the advocate's duty of candor to the tribunal. ~~However~~ Consequently, ~~an advocate does~~ although a lawyer in an adversary proceeding is not required to present an impartial exposition of the law or to vouch for the evidence submitted in a cause~~;~~, the lawyer must not allow the tribunal ~~is responsible for assessing its probative value~~ to be misled by false statements of law or fact or evidence that the lawyer knows to be false.

Representations by a Lawyer

~~[2]~~ [3] An advocate is responsible for pleadings and other documents prepared for litigation, but is usually not required to have personal knowledge of matters asserted therein, for litigation documents ordinarily present assertions by the client, or by someone on the client's behalf, and not assertions by the lawyer. Compare Rule 3.1. However, an assertion purporting to be on the lawyer's own knowledge, as in an affidavit by the lawyer or in a statement in open court, may properly be made only when the lawyer knows the assertion is true or believes it to be true on the basis of a reasonably diligent inquiry. There are circumstances where failure to make a disclosure is the equivalent of an affirmative misrepresentation. The obligation prescribed in Rule 1.2(d) not to counsel a client to commit or assist the client in committing a fraud applies in litigation. Regarding compliance with Rule 1.2(d), see the Comment to that Rule. See also the Comment to Rule 8.4(b).

~~Misleading~~ Legal Argument

~~[3]~~ [4] Legal argument based on a knowingly false representation of law constitutes dishonesty toward the tribunal. A lawyer is not required to make a disinterested exposition of the law, but must recognize the existence of pertinent legal authorities. Furthermore, as stated in paragraph (a)~~(3)~~(2), an advocate has a duty to disclose directly adverse authority in the controlling jurisdiction that has not been disclosed by the opposing party. The underlying concept is that legal argument is a discussion seeking to determine the legal premises properly applicable to the case.

~~False~~ Offering Evidence

~~[4]   When evidence that a lawyer knows to be false is provided by a person who is not the client, the lawyer must refuse to offer it regardless of the client's wishes.~~

~~[5]   When false evidence is offered by the client, however, a conflict may arise between the lawyer's duty to keep the client's revelations confidential and the duty of candor to the court. Upon ascertaining that material evidence is false, the lawyer should seek to persuade the client that the evidence should not be offered or, if it has been offered, that its false character should immediately be disclosed. If the persuasion is ineffective, the lawyer must take reasonable remedial measures.~~

[5]   Paragraph (a)(3) requires that the lawyer refuse to offer evidence that the lawyer knows to be false, regardless of the client's wishes. This duty is premised on the lawyer's obligation as an officer of the court to prevent the trier of fact from being misled by false evidence. A lawyer does not violate this Rule if the lawyer offers the evidence for the purpose of establishing its falsity.

[6]   If a lawyer knows that the client intends to testify falsely or wants the lawyer to introduce false evidence, the lawyer should seek to

98

persuade the client that the evidence should not be offered. If the persuasion is ineffective and the lawyer continues to represent the client, the lawyer must refuse to offer the false evidence. If only a portion of a witness's testimony will be false, the lawyer may call the witness to testify but may not elicit or otherwise permit the witness to present the testimony that the lawyer knows is false.

[7] The duties stated in paragraphs (a) and (b) apply to all lawyers, including defense counsel in criminal cases. In some jurisdictions, however, courts have required counsel to present the accused as a witness or to give a narrative statement if the accused so desires, even if counsel knows that the testimony or statement will be false. The obligation of the advocate under the Rules of Professional Conduct is subordinate to such requirements. See also Comment [9].

[8] The prohibition against offering false evidence only applies if the lawyer knows that the evidence is false. A lawyer's reasonable belief that evidence is false does not preclude its presentation to the trier of fact. A lawyer's knowledge that evidence is false, however, can be inferred from the circumstances. See Rule 1.0(f). Thus, although a lawyer should resolve doubts about the veracity of testimony or other evidence in favor of the client, the lawyer cannot ignore an obvious falsehood.

Refusing to Offer Proof Believed to Be False

[14] [9] ~~Generally speaking,~~ Although paragraph (a)(3) only prohibits a lawyer ~~has authority~~ from offering evidence the lawyer knows to be false, it permits the lawyer to refuse to offer testimony or other proof that the lawyer reasonably believes is ~~untrustworthy~~ false. Offering such proof may reflect adversely on the lawyer's ability to discriminate in the quality of evidence and thus impair the lawyer's effectiveness as an advocate. ~~In criminal cases, however, a lawyer may, in some jurisdictions, be denied this authority by constitutional requirements governing the right to counsel.~~ Because of the special protections historically provided criminal defendants, however, this Rule does not permit a lawyer to refuse to offer the testimony of such a client where the lawyer reasonably believes but does not know that the testimony will be false. Unless the lawyer knows the testimony will be false, the lawyer must honor the client's decision to testify. See also Comment [7].

Perjury by a Criminal Defendant

~~[7] Whether an advocate for a criminally accused has the same duty of disclosure has been intensely debated. While it is agreed that the lawyer should seek to persuade the client to refrain from perjurious testimony, there has been dispute concerning the lawyer's duty when that persuasion fails. If the confrontation with the client occurs before trial, the lawyer ordinarily can withdraw. Withdrawal before trial may not be possible, however, either because trial is imminent, or because the~~

~~confrontation with the client does not take place until the trial itself, or because no other counsel is available.~~

~~[8]   The most difficult situation, therefore, arises in a criminal case where the accused insists on testifying when the lawyer knows that the testimony is perjurious. The lawyer's effort to rectify the situation can increase the likelihood of the client's being convicted as well as opening the possibility of a prosecution for perjury. On the other hand, if the lawyer does not exercise control over the proof, the lawyer participates, although in a merely passive way, in deception of the court.~~

~~[9]   Three resolutions of this dilemma have been proposed. One is to permit the accused to testify by a narrative without guidance through the lawyer's questioning. This compromises both contending principles; it exempts the lawyer from the duty to disclose false evidence but subjects the client to an implicit disclosure of information imparted to counsel. Another suggested resolution, of relatively recent origin, is that the advocate be entirely excused from the duty to reveal perjury if the perjury is that of the client. This is a coherent solution but makes the advocate a knowing instrument of perjury.~~

~~[10]   The other resolution of the dilemma is that the lawyer must reveal the client's perjury if necessary to rectify the situation. A criminal accused has a right to the assistance of an advocate, a right to testify and a right of confidential communication with counsel. However, an accused should not have a right to assistance of counsel in committing perjury. Furthermore, an advocate has an obligation, not only in professional ethics but under the law as well, to avoid implication in the commission of perjury or other falsification of evidence. See Rule 1.2(d).~~

Remedial Measures

[~~11~~] [10] ~~If perjured testimony or false~~ Having offered material evidence ~~has been offered~~ in the belief that it was true, a lawyer may subsequently come to know that the evidence is false. Or, a lawyer may be surprised when the lawyer's client, or another witness called by the lawyer, offers testimony the lawyer knows to be false, either during the lawyer's direct examination or in response to cross-examination by the opposing lawyer. In such situations or if the lawyer knows of the falsity of testimony elicited from the client during a deposition, the lawyer must take reasonable remedial measures. In such situations, the advocate's proper course ~~ordinarily~~ is to remonstrate with the client confidentially, advise the client of the lawyer's duty of candor to the tribunal and seek the client's cooperation with respect to the withdrawal or correction of the false statements or evidence. If that fails, the advocate ~~should seek to withdraw if that will remedy the situation~~ must take further remedial action. If withdrawal from the representation is not permitted or will not ~~remedy the situation or is impossible~~ undo the effect of the false evidence, the advocate ~~should~~ must make such disclosure to the ~~court~~ tribunal as is reasonably necessary to remedy the situation, even if doing so requires the lawyer to reveal information that otherwise would be protected by Rule 1.6. It is for the ~~court~~ <u>tribunal</u> then to determine what should be done—making a statement about the matter to the trier of fact, ordering a mistrial or perhaps nothing. ~~If the false testimony was that of the client, the client may controvert the lawyer's version of their communication when the lawyer discloses the situation to the court. If there is an issue whether the client has committed perjury, the lawyer cannot represent the client in resolution of the issue, and a mistrial may be unavoidable. An unscrupulous client might in this way attempt to produce a series of mistrials and thus escape prosecution. However, a second such encounter could be construed as a deliberate abuse of the right to counsel and as such a waiver of the right to further representation.~~

~~[6]~~ <u>[11]</u> ~~Except in the defense of a criminal accused, the rule generally recognized is that, if necessary to rectify the situation, an advocate must disclose the existence of the client's deception to the court or to the other party. Such a~~ <u>The</u> disclosure <u>of a client's false testimony</u> can result in grave consequences to the client, including not only a sense of betrayal but also loss of the case and perhaps a prosecution for perjury. But the alternative is that the lawyer cooperate in deceiving the court, thereby subverting the truth-finding process which the adversary system is designed to implement. See Rule 1.2(d). Furthermore, unless it is clearly understood that the lawyer will act upon the duty to disclose the existence of false evidence, the client can simply reject the lawyer's advice to reveal the false evidence and insist that the lawyer keep silent. Thus the client could in effect coerce the lawyer into being a party to fraud on the court.

Preserving Integrity of Adjudicative Process

[12]   Lawyers have a special obligation to protect a tribunal against criminal or fraudulent conduct that undermines the integrity of the adjudicative process, such as bribing, intimidating or otherwise unlawfully communicating with a witness, juror, court official or other participant in the proceeding, unlawfully destroying or concealing documents or other evidence or failing to disclose information to the tribunal when required by law to do so. Thus, paragraph (b) requires a lawyer to take reasonable remedial measures, including disclosure if necessary, whenever the lawyer knows that a person, including the lawyer's client, intends to engage, is engaging or has engaged in criminal or fraudulent conduct related to the proceeding.

~~Constitutional Requirements~~

[12]   The general rule that an advocate must reveal the existence of perjury with respect to a material fact, even that of a client—applies to defense counsel in criminal cases, as well as in other instances. However, the definition of the lawyer's ethical duty in such a situation may be qualified by constitutional provisions for due process and the right to

101

counsel in criminal cases. In some jurisdictions these provisions have been construed to require that counsel present an accused as a witness if the accused wishes to testify, even if counsel knows the testimony will be false. The obligation of the advocate under these Rules is subordinate to such a constitutional requirement.

Duration of Obligation

[13]   A practical time limit on the obligation to rectify ~~the presentation of~~ false evidence or false statements of law and fact has to be established. The conclusion of the proceeding is a reasonably definite point for the termination of the obligation. A proceeding has concluded within the meaning of this Rule when a final judgment in the proceeding has been affirmed on appeal or the time for review has passed.

Ex Parte Proceedings

~~[15]~~ [14] Ordinarily, an advocate has the limited responsibility of presenting one side of the matters that a tribunal should consider in reaching a decision; the conflicting position is expected to be presented by the opposing party. However, in any ex parte proceeding, such as an application for a temporary restraining order, there is no balance of presentation by opposing advocates. The object of an ex parte proceeding is nevertheless to yield a substantially just result. The judge has an affirmative responsibility to accord the absent party just consideration. The lawyer for the represented party has the correlative duty to make disclosures of material facts known to the lawyer and that the lawyer reasonably believes are necessary to an informed decision.

Withdrawal

[15]   Normally, a lawyer's compliance with the duty of candor imposed by this Rule does not require that the lawyer withdraw from the representation of a client whose interests will be or have been adversely affected by the lawyer's disclosure. The lawyer may, however, be required by Rule 1.16(a) to seek permission of the tribunal to withdraw if the lawyer's compliance with this Rule's duty of candor results in such an extreme deterioration of the client-lawyer relationship that the lawyer can no longer competently represent the client. Also see Rule 1.16(b) for the circumstances in which a lawyer will be permitted to seek a tribunal's permission to withdraw. In connection with a request for permission to withdraw that is premised on a client's misconduct, a lawyer may reveal information relating to the representation only to the extent reasonably necessary to comply with this Rule or as otherwise permitted by Rule 1.6.

Rule 3.4   Fairness to Opposing Party and Counsel

A lawyer shall not:

    (a) unlawfully obstruct another party's access to evidence or unlawfully alter, destroy or conceal a document or other material having potential evidentiary value. A lawyer shall not counsel or assist another person to do any such act;

    (b) falsify evidence, counsel or assist a witness to testify falsely, or offer an inducement to a witness that is prohibited by law;

    (c) knowingly disobey an obligation under the rules of a tribunal, except for an open refusal based on an assertion that no valid obligation exists;

    (d) in pretrial procedure, make a frivolous discovery request or fail to make reasonably diligent effort to comply with a legally proper discovery request by an opposing party;

    (e) in trial, allude to any matter that the lawyer does not reasonably believe is relevant or that will not be supported by admissible evidence, assert personal knowledge of facts in issue except when testifying as a witness, or state a personal opinion as to the justness of a cause, the credibility of a witness, the culpability of a civil litigant or the guilt or innocence of an accused; or

    (f) request a person other than a client to refrain from voluntarily giving relevant information to another party unless:

        (1) the person is a relative or an employee or other agent of a client; and

        (2) the lawyer reasonably believes that the person's interests will not be adversely affected by refraining from giving such information.

COMMENT

[1] The procedure of the adversary system contemplates that the evidence in a case is to be marshalled competitively by the contending parties. Fair competition in the adversary system is secured by prohibitions against destruction or concealment of evidence, improperly influencing witnesses, obstructive tactics in discovery procedure, and the like.

[2] Documents and other items of evidence are often essential to establish a claim or defense. Subject to evidentiary privileges, the right of an opposing party, including the government, to obtain evidence through discovery or subpoena is an important procedural right. The exercise of that right can be frustrated if relevant material is altered, concealed or destroyed. Applicable law in many jurisdictions makes it an offense to destroy material for purpose of impairing its availability in a pending proceeding or one whose commencement can be foreseen. Falsifying evidence is also generally a criminal offense. Paragraph (a) applies to evidentiary material generally, including computerized information. Applicable law may permit a lawyer to take temporary possession of physical evidence of client crimes for the purpose of conducting a limited

examination that will not alter or destroy material characteristics of the evidence. In such a case, applicable law may require the lawyer to turn the evidence over to the police or other prosecuting authority, depending on the circumstances.

[3] With regard to paragraph (b), it is not improper to pay a witness's expenses or to compensate an expert witness on terms permitted by law. The common law rule in most jurisdictions is that it is improper to pay an occurrence witness any fee for testifying and that it is improper to pay an expert witness a contingent fee.

[4] Paragraph (f) permits a lawyer to advise employees of a client to refrain from giving information to another party, for the employees may identify their interests with those of the client. See also Rule 4.2.

Rule 3.5 Impartiality and Decorum of the Tribunal

A lawyer shall not:

(a) seek to influence a judge, juror, prospective juror or other official by means prohibited by law;

(b) communicate ex parte with such a person ~~except as permitted~~ **during the proceeding unless authorized to do so by law or court order;**

(c) communicate with a juror or prospective juror after discharge of the jury if:

> **(1) the communication is prohibited by law or court order;**

> **(2) the juror has made known to the lawyer a desire not to communicate; or**

> **(3) the communication involves misrepresentation, coercion, duress or harassment; or**

~~(c)~~ **(d) engage in conduct intended to disrupt a tribunal.**

COMMENT

[1] Many forms of improper influence upon a tribunal are proscribed by criminal law. Others are specified in the ABA Model Code of Judicial Conduct, with which an advocate should be familiar. A lawyer is required to avoid contributing to a violation of such provisions.

[2] During a proceeding a lawyer may not communicate ex parte with persons serving in an official capacity in the proceeding, such as judges, masters or jurors, unless authorized to do so by law or court order.

[3] A lawyer may on occasion want to communicate with a juror or prospective juror after the jury has been discharged. The lawyer may do so unless the communication is prohibited by law or a court order but must respect the desire of the juror not to talk with the lawyer. The lawyer may not engage in improper conduct during the communication.

~~[2]~~ [4] The advocate's function is to present evidence and argument so that the cause may be decided according to law. Refraining from abusive or obstreperous conduct is a corollary of the advocate's right to speak on behalf of litigants. A lawyer may stand firm against abuse by a judge but should avoid reciprocation; the judge's default is no justification for similar dereliction by an advocate. An advocate can present the cause, protect the record for subsequent review and preserve professional integrity by patient firmness no less effectively than by belligerence or theatrics.

[5]   The duty to refrain from disruptive conduct applies to any proceeding of a tribunal, including a deposition. See Rule 1.0(m).

Rule 3.6   Trial Publicity

(a) A lawyer who is participating or has participated in the investigation or litigation of a matter shall not make an extrajudicial statement that ~~a reasonable person would expect to~~ the lawyer knows or reasonably should know will be disseminated by means of public communication ~~if the lawyer knows or reasonably should know that it~~ and will have a substantial likelihood of materially prejudicing an adjudicative proceeding in the matter.

(b) Notwithstanding paragraph (a), a lawyer may state:

(1) the claim, offense or defense involved and, except when prohibited by law, the identity of the persons involved;

(2) information contained in a public record;

(3) that an investigation of a matter is in progress;

(4) the scheduling or result of any step in litigation;

(5) a request for assistance in obtaining evidence and information necessary thereto;

(6) a warning of danger concerning the behavior of a person involved, when there is reason to believe that there exists the likelihood of substantial harm to an individual or to the public interest; and

(7) in a criminal case, in addition to subparagraphs (1) through (6):

(i) the identity, residence, occupation and family status of the accused;

(ii) if the accused has not been apprehended, information necessary to aid in apprehension of that person;

(iii) the fact, time and place of arrest; and

(iv) the identity of investigating and arresting officers or agencies and the length of the investigation.

(c) Notwithstanding paragraph (a), a lawyer may make a statement that a reasonable lawyer would believe is required to protect a client from the substantial undue prejudicial effect of recent publicity not initiated by the lawyer or the lawyer's client. A statement made pursuant to this paragraph shall be limited to such information as is necessary to mitigate the recent adverse publicity.

(d) No lawyer associated in a firm or government agency with a lawyer subject to paragraph (a) shall make a statement prohibited by paragraph (a).

COMMENT

[1]   It is difficult to strike a balance between protecting the right to a fair trial and safeguarding the right of free expression. Preserving the right to a fair trial necessarily entails some curtailment of the information that may be disseminated about a party prior to trial, particularly where trial by jury is involved. If there were no such limits, the result would be the practical nullification of the protective effect of the rules of forensic decorum and the exclusionary rules of evidence. On the other hand, there are vital social interests served by the free dissemination of information about events having legal consequences and about legal proceedings themselves. The public has a right to know about threats to its safety and measures aimed at assuring its security. It also has a legitimate interest in the conduct of judicial proceedings, particularly in matters of general public concern. Furthermore, the subject matter of legal proceedings is often of direct significance in debate and deliberation over questions of public policy.

[2]   Special rules of confidentiality may validly govern proceedings in juvenile, domestic relations and mental disability proceedings, and perhaps other types of litigation. Rule 3.4(c) requires compliance with such rules.

[3]   The Rule sets forth a basic general prohibition against a lawyer's making statements that the lawyer knows or should know will have a substantial likelihood of materially prejudicing an adjudicative proceeding. Recognizing that the public value of informed commentary is great and the likelihood of prejudice to a proceeding by the commentary of a lawyer who is not involved in the proceeding is small, the rule applies only to lawyers who are, or who have been involved in the investigation or litigation of a case, and their associates.

[4]   Paragraph (b) identifies specific matters about which a lawyer's statements would not ordinarily be considered to present a substantial likelihood of material prejudice, and should not in any event be considered prohibited by the general prohibition of paragraph (a). Paragraph (b) is not intended to be an exhaustive listing of the subjects upon which a lawyer may make a statement, but statements on other matters may be subject to paragraph (a).

[5] There are, on the other hand, certain subjects that are more likely than not to have a material prejudicial effect on a proceeding, particularly when they refer to a civil matter triable to a jury, a criminal matter, or any other proceeding that could result in incarceration. These subjects relate to:

(1) the character, credibility, reputation or criminal record of a party, suspect in a criminal investigation or witness, or the identity of a witness, or the expected testimony of a party or witness;

(2) in a criminal case or proceeding that could result in incarceration, the possibility of a plea of guilty to the offense or the existence or contents of any confession, admission, or statement given by a defendant or suspect or that person's refusal or failure to make a statement;

(3) the performance or results of any examination or test or the refusal or failure of a person to submit to an examination or test, or the identity or nature of physical evidence expected to be presented;

(4) any opinion as to the guilt or innocence of a defendant or suspect in a criminal case or proceeding that could result in incarceration;

(5) information that the lawyer knows or reasonably should know is likely to be inadmissible as evidence in a trial and that would, if disclosed, create a substantial risk of prejudicing an impartial trial; or

(6) the fact that a defendant has been charged with a crime, unless there is included therein a statement explaining that the charge is merely an accusation and that the defendant is presumed innocent until and unless proven guilty.

[6] Another relevant factor in determining prejudice is the nature of the proceeding involved. Criminal jury trials will be most sensitive to extrajudicial speech. Civil trials may be less sensitive. Non-jury hearings and arbitration proceedings may be even less affected. The Rule will still place limitations on prejudicial comments in these cases, but the likelihood of prejudice may be different depending on the type of proceeding.

[7] Finally, extrajudicial statements that might otherwise raise a question under this Rule may be permissible when they are made in response to statements made publicly by another party, another party's lawyer, or third persons, where a reasonable lawyer would believe a public response is required in order to avoid prejudice to the lawyer's client. When prejudicial statements have been publicly made by others, responsive statements may have the salutary effect of lessening any resulting adverse impact on the adjudicative proceeding. Such responsive statements should be limited to contain only such information as is necessary to mitigate undue prejudice created by the statements made by others.

[8]   See Rule 3.8(f) for additional duties of prosecutors in connection with extrajudicial statements about criminal proceedings.

Rule 3.7   Lawyer as Witness

(a) A lawyer shall not act as advocate at a trial in which the lawyer is likely to be a necessary witness ~~except where~~ unless:

   (1) the testimony relates to an uncontested issue;

   (2) the testimony relates to the nature and value of legal services rendered in the case; or

   (3) disqualification of the lawyer would work substantial hardship on the client.

(b) A lawyer may act as advocate in a trial in which another lawyer in the lawyer's firm is likely to be called as a witness unless precluded from doing so by Rule 1.7 or Rule 1.9.

COMMENT

[1] · Combining the roles of advocate and witness can prejudice the tribunal and the opposing party and can also involve a conflict of interest between the lawyer and client.

Advocate-Witness Rule

[2]   The tribunal has proper objection when the trier of fact may be confused or misled by a lawyer serving as both advocate and witness. The opposing party has proper objection where the combination of roles may prejudice that party's rights in the litigation. A witness is required to testify on the basis of personal knowledge, while an advocate is expected to explain and comment on evidence given by others. It may not be clear whether a statement by an advocate-witness should be taken as proof or as an analysis of the proof.

[3]   To protect the tribunal, paragraph (a) prohibits a lawyer from simultaneously serving as advocate and necessary witness except in those circumstances specified in paragraphs (a)(1) through (a)(3). Paragraph (a)(1) recognizes that if the testimony will be uncontested, the ambiguities in the dual role are purely theoretical. Paragraph (a)(2) recognizes that where the testimony concerns the extent and value of legal services rendered in the action in which the testimony is offered, permitting the lawyers to testify avoids the need for a second trial with new counsel to resolve that issue. Moreover, in such a situation the judge has firsthand knowledge of the matter in issue; hence, there is less dependence on the adversary process to test the credibility of the testimony.

[4]   Apart from these two exceptions, paragraph (a)(3) recognizes that a balancing is required between the interests of the client and those of the tribunal and the opposing party. Whether the tribunal is likely to be misled or the opposing party is likely to suffer prejudice depends on

the nature of the case, the importance and probable tenor of the lawyer's testimony, and the probability that the lawyer's testimony will conflict with that of other witnesses. Even if there is risk of such prejudice, in determining whether the lawyer should be disqualified, due regard must be given to the effect of disqualification on the lawyer's client. It is relevant that one or both parties could reasonably foresee that the lawyer would probably be a witness. The ~~principle of imputed disqualification~~ conflict of interest principles stated in ~~Rule~~ Rules 1.7, 1.9 and 1.10 ~~has~~ have no application to this aspect of the problem.

[5] Because the tribunal is not likely to be misled when a lawyer acts as advocate in a trial in which another lawyer in the lawyer's firm will testify as a necessary witness, paragraph (b) permits the lawyer to do so except in situations involving a conflict of interest.

Conflict of Interest

~~[5]~~ [6] ~~Whether the combination of roles involves an improper~~ In determining if it is permissible to act as advocate in a trial in which the lawyer will be a necessary witness, the lawyer must also consider that the dual role may give rise to a conflict of interest ~~with respect to the client is determined by Rule~~ that will require compliance with Rules 1.7 or 1.9. For example, if there is likely to be substantial conflict between the testimony of the client and that of the lawyer ~~or a member of the lawyer's firm~~, the representation ~~is improper~~ involves a conflict of interest that requires compliance with Rule 1.7. This would be true even though the lawyer might not be prohibited by paragraph (a) from simultaneously serving as advocate and witness because the lawyer's disqualification would work a substantial hardship on the client. Similarly, a lawyer who might be permitted to simultaneously serve as an advocate and a witness by paragraph (a)(3) might be precluded from doing so by Rule 1.9. The problem can arise whether the lawyer is called as a witness on behalf of the client or is called by the opposing party. Determining whether or not such a conflict exists is primarily the responsibility of the lawyer involved. If there is a conflict of interest, the lawyer must secure the client's informed consent, confirmed in writing. In some cases, the lawyer will be precluded from seeking the client's consent. See ~~Comment to~~ Rule 1.7. ~~If a lawyer who is a member of a firm may not act as both advocate and witness by reason of conflict of interest, Rule 1.10 disqualifies the firm also.~~ See Rule 1.0(b) for the definition of "confirmed in writing" and Rule 1.0(e) for the definition of "informed consent."

[7] Paragraph (b) provides that a lawyer is not disqualified from serving as an advocate because a lawyer with whom the lawyer is associated in a firm is precluded from doing so by paragraph (a). If, however, the testifying lawyer would also be disqualified by Rule 1.7 or Rule 1.9 from representing the client in the matter, other lawyers in the firm will be precluded from representing the client by Rule 1.10 unless the client gives informed consent under the conditions stated in Rule 1.7.

Rule 3.8   Special Responsibilities of a Prosecutor

The prosecutor in a criminal case shall:

(a) refrain from prosecuting a charge that the prosecutor knows is not supported by probable cause;

(b) make reasonable efforts to assure that the accused has been advised of the right to, and the procedure for obtaining, counsel and has been given reasonable opportunity to obtain counsel;

(c) not seek to obtain from an unrepresented accused a waiver of important pretrial rights, such as the right to a preliminary hearing;

(d) make timely disclosure to the defense of all evidence or information known to the prosecutor that tends to negate the guilt of the accused or mitigates the offense, and, in connection with sentencing, disclose to the defense and to the tribunal all unprivileged mitigating information known to the prosecutor, except when the prosecutor is relieved of this responsibility by a protective order of the tribunal;

~~(e)~~ [See paragraph (f).]

~~(f)~~ (e) not subpoena a lawyer in a grand jury or other criminal proceeding to present evidence about a past or present client unless the prosecutor reasonably believes:

(1) the information sought is not protected from disclosure by any applicable privilege;

(2) the evidence sought is essential to the successful completion of an ongoing investigation or prosecution; and

(3) there is no other feasible alternative to obtain the information.~~.~~;

~~(g)~~ (f) except for statements that are necessary to inform the public of the nature and extent of the prosecutor's action and that serve a legitimate law enforcement purpose, refrain from making extrajudicial comments that have a substantial likelihood of heightening public condemnation of the accused and ~~(e)~~ exercise reasonable care to prevent investigators, law enforcement personnel, employees or other persons assisting or associated with the prosecutor in a criminal case from making an extrajudicial statement that the prosecutor would be prohibited from making under Rule 3.6 or this Rule.

COMMENT

[1]   A prosecutor has the responsibility of a minister of justice and not simply that of an advocate. This responsibility carries with it specific obligations to see that the defendant is accorded procedural justice and that guilt is decided upon the basis of sufficient evidence. Precisely how far the prosecutor is required to go in this direction is a matter of debate

and varies in different jurisdictions. Many jurisdictions have adopted the ABA Standards of Criminal Justice Relating to the Prosecution Function, which in turn are the product of prolonged and careful deliberation by lawyers experienced in both criminal prosecution and defense. ~~See also Rule 3.3(d), governing ex parte proceedings, among which grand jury proceedings are included.~~ Applicable law may require other measures by the prosecutor and knowing disregard of those obligations or a systematic abuse of prosecutorial discretion could constitute a violation of Rule 8.4.

[2]   In some jurisdictions, a defendant may waive a preliminary hearing and thereby lose a valuable opportunity to challenge probable cause. Accordingly, prosecutors should not seek to obtain waivers of preliminary hearings or other important pretrial rights from unrepresented accused persons. Paragraph (c) does not apply, however, to an accused appearing pro se with the approval of the tribunal. Nor does it forbid the lawful questioning of ~~a~~ an uncharged suspect who has knowingly waived the rights to counsel and silence.

[3]   The exception in paragraph (d) recognizes that a prosecutor may seek an appropriate protective order from the tribunal if disclosure of information to the defense could result in substantial harm to an individual or to the public interest.

[4]   Paragraph ~~(f)~~ (e) is intended to limit the issuance of lawyer subpoenas in grand jury and other criminal proceedings to those situations in which there is a genuine need to intrude into the client-lawyer relationship.

[5]   Paragraph ~~(g)~~ (f) supplements Rule 3.6, which prohibits extrajudicial statements that have a substantial likelihood of prejudicing an adjudicatory proceeding. In the context of a criminal prosecution, a prosecutor's extrajudicial statement can create the additional problem of increasing public condemnation of the accused. Although the announcement of an indictment, for example, will necessarily have severe consequences for the accused, a prosecutor can, and should, avoid comments which have no legitimate law enforcement purpose and have a substantial likelihood of increasing public opprobrium of the accused. Nothing in this Comment is intended to restrict the statements which a prosecutor may make which comply with Rule 3.6(b) or 3.6(c).

[6]   Like other lawyers, prosecutors are subject to Rules 5.1 and 5.3, which relate to responsibilities regarding lawyers and nonlawyers who work for or are associated with the lawyer's office. Paragraph (f) reminds the prosecutor of the importance of these obligations in connection with the unique dangers of improper extrajudicial statements in a criminal case. In addition, paragraph (f) requires a prosecutor to exercise reasonable care to prevent persons assisting or associated with the prosecutor from making improper extrajudicial statements, even when such persons are not under the direct supervision of the prosecutor. Ordinarily, the reasonable care standard will be satisfied if the prosecutor issues the

appropriate cautions to law-enforcement personnel and other relevant individuals.

Rule 3.9   Advocate in Nonadjudicative Proceedings

A lawyer representing a client before a legislative <u>body</u> or administrative ~~tribunal~~ <u>agency</u> in a nonadjudicative proceeding shall disclose that the appearance is in a representative capacity and shall conform to the provisions of Rules 3.3(a) through (c), 3.4(a) through (c), and 3.5.

COMMENT

[1]   In representation before bodies such as legislatures, municipal councils, and executive and administrative agencies acting in a rule-making or policy-making capacity, lawyers present facts, formulate issues and advance argument in the matters under consideration. The decision-making body, like a court, should be able to rely on the integrity of the submissions made to it. A lawyer appearing before such a body ~~should~~ <u>must</u> deal with ~~the tribunal~~ <u>it</u> honestly and in conformity with applicable rules of procedure. <u>See Rules 3.3(a) through (c), 3.4(a) through (c) and 3.5.</u>

[2]   Lawyers have no exclusive right to appear before nonadjudicative bodies, as they do before a court. The requirements of this Rule therefore may subject lawyers to regulations inapplicable to advocates who are not lawyers. However, legislatures and administrative agencies have a right to expect lawyers to deal with them as they deal with courts.

[3]   This Rule <u>only applies when a lawyer represents a client in connection with an official hearing or meeting of a governmental agency or a legislative body to which the lawyer or the lawyer's client is presenting evidence or argument.</u> It does not apply to representation of a client in a negotiation or other bilateral transaction with a governmental agency~~; representation~~ <u>or in connection with an application for a license or other privilege or the client's compliance with generally applicable reporting requirements, such as the filing of income-tax returns. Nor does it apply to the representation of a client in connection with an investigation or examination of the client's affairs conducted by govern-ment investigators or examiners. Representation</u> in such ~~a transaction~~ <u>matters</u> is governed by Rules 4.1 through 4.4.

TRANSACTIONS WITH PERSONS OTHER THAN CLIENTS

Rule 4.1   Truthfulness in Statements to Others

In the course of representing a client a lawyer shall not knowingly:

(a) make a false statement of material fact or law to a third person; or

(b) fail to disclose a material fact when disclosure is necessary to avoid assisting a criminal or fraudulent act by a client, unless disclosure is prohibited by Rule 1.6.

COMMENT

Misrepresentation

[1]　A lawyer is required to be truthful when dealing with others on a client's behalf, but generally has no affirmative duty to inform an opposing party of relevant facts. A misrepresentation can occur if the lawyer incorporates or affirms a statement of another person that the lawyer knows is false. Misrepresentations can also occur by ~~failure to act~~ partially true but misleading statements or omissions that are the equivalent of affirmative false statements. For dishonest conduct that does not amount to a false statement or for misrepresentations by a lawyer other than in the course of representing a client, see Rule 8.4.

Statements of Fact

[2]　This Rule refers to statements of fact. Whether a particular statement should be regarded as one of fact can depend on the circumstances. Under generally accepted conventions in negotiation, certain types of statements ordinarily are not taken as statements of material fact. Estimates of price or value placed on the subject of a transaction and a party's intentions as to an acceptable settlement of a claim are ordinarily in this category, and so is the existence of an undisclosed principal except where nondisclosure of the principal would constitute fraud. Lawyers should be mindful of their obligations under applicable law to avoid criminal and tortious misrepresentation.

Crime or Fraud by Client

[3]　Under Rule 1.2(d), a lawyer is prohibited from counseling or assisting a client in conduct that the lawyer knows is criminal or fraudulent. Paragraph (b) ~~recognizes that~~ states a specific application of the principle set forth in Rule 1.2(d) and addresses the situation where a client's crime or fraud takes the form of a lie or misrepresentation. Ordinarily, a lawyer can avoid assisting a client's crime or fraud by withdrawing from the representation. Sometimes it may be necessary for the lawyer to give notice of the fact of withdrawal and to disaffirm an opinion, document, affirmation or the like. In extreme cases, substantive law may require a lawyer to disclose ~~certain~~ information relating to the representation to avoid being deemed to have assisted the client's crime or fraud. ~~The requirement of~~ If the lawyer can avoid assisting a client's crime or fraud only by disclosing this information, then under paragraph (b) the lawyer is required to do so, unless the disclosure ~~created by this paragraph is, however, subject to the obligations created~~ is prohibited by Rule 1.6.

Rule 4.2 Communication With Person Represented by Counsel

In representing a client, a lawyer shall not communicate about the subject of the representation with a person the lawyer knows to be represented by another lawyer in the matter, unless the lawyer has the consent of the other lawyer or is authorized to do so by law ~~to do so~~ **or a court order.**

COMMENT

[1] This Rule contributes to the proper functioning of the legal system by protecting a person who has chosen to be represented by a lawyer in a matter against possible overreaching by other lawyers who are participating in the matter, interference by those lawyers with the client-lawyer relationship and the uncounselled disclosure of information relating to the representation.

~~[3]~~ [2] This Rule ~~also~~ applies to communications with any person, ~~whether or not a party to a formal adjudicative proceeding, contract or negotiation,~~ who is represented by counsel concerning the matter to which the communication relates.

[3] The Rule applies even though the represented person initiates or consents to the communication. A lawyer must immediately terminate communication with a person if, after commencing communication, the lawyer learns that the person is one with whom communication is not permitted by this Rule.

~~[1]~~ [4] This Rule does not prohibit communication with a represented person, or an employee or agent of such a person, concerning matters outside the representation. For example, the existence of a controversy between a government agency and a private party, or between two organizations, does not prohibit a lawyer for either from communicating with nonlawyer representatives of the other regarding a separate matter. ~~Also, parties~~ Nor does this Rule preclude communication with a represented person who is seeking advice from a lawyer who is not otherwise representing a client in the matter. A lawyer may not make a communication prohibited by this Rule through the acts of another. See Rule 8.4(a). Parties to a matter may communicate directly with each other, and a lawyer is not prohibited from advising a client concerning a communication that the client is legally entitled to make. Also, a lawyer having independent justification or legal authorization for communicating with a represented person is permitted to do so. ~~Communications authorized by law include, for example, the right of a party to a controversy with a government agency to speak with government officials about the matter.~~

[5] Communications authorized by law may include communications by a lawyer on behalf of a client who is exercising a constitutional or other legal right to communicate with the government. ~~[2]~~ Communications authorized by law may also include ~~constitutionally permissible~~ investigative activities of lawyers representing governmental entities,

114

directly or through investigative agents, prior to the commencement of criminal or civil enforcement proceedings, ~~when there is applicable judicial precedent that either has found the activity permissible under this Rule or has found this Rule inapplicable. However, the Rule imposes ethical restrictions that go beyond those imposed by constitutional provisions.~~ When communicating with the accused in a criminal matter, a government lawyer must comply with this Rule in addition to honoring the constitutional rights of the accused. The fact that a communication does not violate a state or federal constitutional right is insufficient to establish that the communication is permissible under this Rule.

[6] A lawyer who is uncertain whether a communication with a represented person is permissible may seek a court order. A lawyer may also seek a court order in exceptional circumstances to authorize a communication that would otherwise be prohibited by this Rule, for example, where communication with a person represented by counsel is necessary to avoid reasonably certain injury.

~~[4]~~ [7] In the case of ~~an~~ a represented organization, this Rule prohibits communications ~~by a lawyer for another person or entity concerning the matter in representation~~ with ~~persons having a managerial responsibility on behalf~~ a constituent of the organization, ~~and with any other person~~ who supervises, directs or regularly consults with the organization's lawyer concerning the matter or has authority to obligate the organization with respect to the matter or whose act or omission in connection with ~~that~~ the matter may be imputed to the organization for purposes of civil or criminal liability ~~or whose statement may constitute an admission on the part of the organization~~. Consent of the organization's lawyer is not required for communication with a former constituent. If ~~an agent or employee~~ a constituent of the organization is represented in the matter by his or her own counsel, the consent by that counsel to a communication will be sufficient for purposes of this Rule. Compare Rule 3.4(f). In communicating with a current or former constituent of an organization, a lawyer must not use methods of obtaining evidence that violate the legal rights of the organization. See Rule 4.4.

~~[5]~~ [8] The prohibition on communications with a represented person only applies, ~~however,~~ in circumstances where the lawyer knows that the person is in fact represented in the matter to be discussed. This means that the lawyer has actual knowledge of the fact of the representation; but such actual knowledge may be inferred from the circumstances. See ~~Terminology~~ Rule 1.0(f). ~~Such an inference may arise in circumstances where there is substantial reason to believe that the person with whom communication is sought is represented in the matter to be discussed.~~ Thus, the lawyer cannot evade the requirement of obtaining the consent of counsel by closing eyes to the obvious.

~~[6]~~ [9] In the event the person with whom the lawyer communicates is not known to be represented by counsel in the matter, the lawyer's communications are subject to Rule 4.3.

Rule 4.3 Dealing With Unrepresented Person

In dealing on behalf of a client with a person who is not represented by counsel, a lawyer shall not state or imply that the lawyer is disinterested. When the lawyer knows or reasonably should know that the unrepresented person misunderstands the lawyer's role in the matter, the lawyer shall make reasonable efforts to correct the misunderstanding. **The lawyer shall not give legal advice to an unrepresented person, other than the advice to secure counsel, if the lawyer knows or reasonably should know that the interests of such a person are or have a reasonable possibility of being in conflict with the interests of the client.**

COMMENT

[1] An unrepresented person, particularly one not experienced in dealing with legal matters, might assume that a lawyer is disinterested in loyalties or is a disinterested authority on the law even when the lawyer represents a client. ~~During the course of a lawyer's representation of a client, the lawyer should not give advice to an unrepresented person other than the advice to obtain counsel.~~ In order to avoid a misunderstanding, a lawyer will typically need to identify the lawyer's client and, where necessary, explain that the client has interests opposed to those of the unrepresented person. For misunderstandings that sometimes arise when a lawyer for an organization deals with an unrepresented constituent, see Rule 1.13(d).

[2] The Rule distinguishes between situations involving unrepresented persons whose interests may be adverse to those of the lawyer's client and those in which the person's interests are not in conflict with the client's. In the former situation, the possibility that the lawyer will compromise the unrepresented person's interests is so great that the Rule prohibits the giving of any advice, apart from the advice to obtain counsel. Whether a lawyer is giving impermissible advice may depend on the experience and sophistication of the unrepresented person, as well as the setting in which the behavior and comments occur. This Rule does not prohibit a lawyer from negotiating the terms of a transaction or settling a dispute with an unrepresented person. So long as the lawyer has explained that the lawyer represents an adverse party and is not representing the person, the lawyer may inform the person of the terms on which the lawyer's client will enter into an agreement or settle a matter, prepare documents that require the person's signature and explain the lawyer's own view of the meaning of the document or the lawyer's view of the underlying legal obligations.

Rule 4.4 Respect For Rights of Third Persons

(a) In representing a client, a lawyer shall not use means that have no substantial purpose other than to embarrass, delay, or burden a third person, or use methods of obtaining evidence that violate the legal rights of such a person.

(b) A lawyer who receives a document relating to the representation of the lawyer's client and knows or reasonably should know that the document was inadvertently sent shall promptly notify the sender.

COMMENT

[1] Responsibility to a client requires a lawyer to subordinate the interests of others to those of the client, but that responsibility does not imply that a lawyer may disregard the rights of third persons. It is impractical to catalogue all such rights, but they include legal restrictions on methods of obtaining evidence from third persons and unwarranted intrusions into privileged relationships, such as the client-lawyer relationship.

[2] Paragraph (b) recognizes that lawyers sometimes receive documents that were mistakenly sent or produced by opposing parties or their lawyers. If a lawyer knows or reasonably should know that a such a document was sent inadvertently, then this Rule requires the lawyer to promptly notify the sender in order to permit that person to take protective measures. Whether the lawyer is required to take additional steps, such as returning the original document, is a matter of law beyond the scope of these Rules, as is the question of whether the privileged status of a document has been waived. Similarly, this Rule does not address the legal duties of a lawyer who receives a document that the lawyer knows or reasonably should know may have been wrongfully obtained by the sending person. For purposes of this Rule, "document" includes e-mail or other electronic modes of transmission subject to being read or put into readable form.

[3] Some lawyers may choose to return a document unread, for example, when the lawyer learns before receiving the document that it was inadvertently sent to the wrong address. Where a lawyer is not required by applicable law to do so, the decision to voluntarily return such a document is a matter of professional judgment ordinarily reserved to the lawyer. See Rules 1.2 and 1.4.

LAW FIRMS AND ASSOCIATIONS

Rule 5.1 Responsibilities of a ~~Partner or~~ Partners, Managers, and Supervisory ~~Lawyer~~ Lawyers

(a) A partner in a law firm, and a lawyer who individually or together with other lawyers possesses comparable managerial authority in a law firm, shall make reasonable efforts to ensure that the firm has in effect measures giving reasonable assurance that all lawyers in the firm conform to the Rules of Professional Conduct.

(b) A lawyer having direct supervisory authority over another lawyer shall make reasonable efforts to ensure that the other lawyer conforms to the Rules of Professional Conduct.

(c) A lawyer shall be responsible for another lawyer's violation of the Rules of Professional Conduct if:

(1) the lawyer orders or, with knowledge of the specific conduct, ratifies the conduct involved; or

(2) the lawyer is a partner or has comparable managerial authority in the law firm in which the other lawyer practices, or has direct supervisory authority over the other lawyer, and knows of the conduct at a time when its consequences can be avoided or mitigated but fails to take reasonable remedial action.

COMMENT

[1]   ~~Paragraphs~~ Paragraph (a) ~~and (b) refer~~ applies to lawyers who have ~~supervisory~~ managerial authority over the professional work of a firm ~~or legal department of a government agency~~. See Rule 1.0(c). This includes members of a partnership ~~and~~, the shareholders in a law firm organized as a professional corporation, and members of other associations authorized to practice law; lawyers having ~~supervisory~~ comparable managerial authority in ~~the~~ a legal services organization or a law department of an enterprise or government agency; and lawyers who have intermediate managerial responsibilities in a firm. Paragraph (b) applies to lawyers who have supervisory authority over the work of other lawyers in a firm.

[2]   Paragraph (a) requires lawyers with managerial authority within a firm to make reasonable efforts to establish internal policies and procedures designed to provide reasonable assurance that all lawyers in the firm will conform to the Rules of Professional Conduct. Such policies and procedures include those designed to detect and resolve conflicts of interest, identify dates by which actions must be taken in pending matters, account for client funds and property and ensure that inexperienced lawyers are properly supervised.

~~[2]~~ [3] ~~The~~ Other measures that may be required to fulfill the responsibility prescribed in ~~paragraphs~~ paragraph (a) ~~and (b)~~ can depend on the firm's structure and the nature of its practice. In a small firm of experienced lawyers, informal supervision and ~~occasional admonition~~ periodic review of compliance with the required systems ordinarily ~~might be sufficient~~ will suffice. In a large firm, or in practice situations in which ~~intensely~~ difficult ethical problems frequently arise, more elaborate ~~procedures~~ measures may be necessary. Some firms, for example, have a procedure whereby junior lawyers can make confidential referral of ethical problems directly to a designated senior partner or special committee. See Rule 5.2. Firms, whether large or small, may also rely on continuing legal education in professional ethics. In any event, the

118

ethical atmosphere of a firm can influence the conduct of all its members and ~~a lawyer having authority over the work of another~~ the partners may not assume that ~~the subordinate lawyer~~ all lawyers associated with the firm will inevitably conform to the Rules.

~~[3]~~ [4] Paragraph (c)~~(1)~~ expresses a general principle of personal responsibility for acts of another. See also Rule 8.4(a).

~~[4]~~ [5] Paragraph (c)(2) defines the duty of a partner or other lawyer having comparable managerial authority in a law firm, as well as a lawyer who has direct supervisory authority over performance of specific legal work by another lawyer. Whether a lawyer has supervisory authority in particular circumstances is a question of fact. Partners ~~of a private firm~~ and lawyers with comparable authority have at least indirect responsibility for all work being done by the firm, while a partner or manager in charge of a particular matter ordinarily also has ~~direct authority over~~ supervisory responsibility for the work of other firm lawyers engaged in the matter. Appropriate remedial action by a partner or managing lawyer would depend on the immediacy of ~~the partner's~~ that lawyer's involvement and the seriousness of the misconduct. ~~The~~ A supervisor is required to intervene to prevent avoidable consequences of misconduct if the supervisor knows that the misconduct occurred. Thus, if a supervising lawyer knows that a subordinate misrepresented a matter to an opposing party in negotiation, the supervisor as well as the subordinate has a duty to correct the resulting misapprehension.

~~[5]~~ [6] Professional misconduct by a lawyer under supervision could reveal a violation of paragraph (b) on the part of the supervisory lawyer even though it does not entail a violation of paragraph (c) because there was no direction, ratification or knowledge of the violation.

~~[6]~~ [7] Apart from this Rule and Rule 8.4(a), a lawyer does not have disciplinary liability for the conduct of a partner, associate or subordinate. Whether a lawyer may be liable civilly or criminally for another lawyer's conduct is a question of law beyond the scope of these Rules.

[8] The duties imposed by this Rule on managing and supervising lawyers do not alter the personal duty of each lawyer in a firm to abide by the Rules of Professional Conduct. See Rule 5.2(a).

Rule 5.2   Responsibilities of a Subordinate Lawyer

(a) A lawyer is bound by the Rules of Professional Conduct notwithstanding that the lawyer acted at the direction of another person.

(b) A subordinate lawyer does not violate the Rules of Professional Conduct if that lawyer acts in accordance with a supervisory lawyer's reasonable resolution of an arguable question of professional duty.

COMMENT

[1]   Although a lawyer is not relieved of responsibility for a violation by the fact that the lawyer acted at the direction of a supervisor, that fact may be relevant in determining whether a lawyer had the knowledge required to render conduct a violation of the Rules. For example, if a subordinate filed a frivolous pleading at the direction of a supervisor, the subordinate would not be guilty of a professional violation unless the subordinate knew of the document's frivolous character.

[2]   When lawyers in a supervisor-subordinate relationship encounter a matter involving professional judgment as to ethical duty, the supervisor may assume responsibility for making the judgment. Otherwise a consistent course of action or position could not be taken. If the question can reasonably be answered only one way, the duty of both lawyers is clear and they are equally responsible for fulfilling it. However, if the question is reasonably arguable, someone has to decide upon the course of action. That authority ordinarily reposes in the supervisor, and a subordinate may be guided accordingly. For example, if a question arises whether the interests of two clients conflict under Rule 1.7, the supervisor's reasonable resolution of the question should protect the subordinate professionally if the resolution is subsequently challenged.

Rule 5.3   Responsibilities Regarding Nonlawyer Assistants

With respect to a nonlawyer employed or retained by or associated with a lawyer:

(a) a partner, and a lawyer who individually or together with other lawyers possesses comparable managerial authority in a law firm shall make reasonable efforts to ensure that the firm has in effect measures giving reasonable assurance that the person's conduct is compatible with the professional obligations of the lawyer;

(b) a lawyer having direct supervisory authority over the nonlawyer shall make reasonable efforts to ensure that the person's conduct is compatible with the professional obligations of the lawyer; and

(c) a lawyer shall be responsible for conduct of such a person that would be a violation of the Rules of Professional Conduct if engaged in by a lawyer if:

> **(1) the lawyer orders or, with the knowledge of the specific conduct, ratifies the conduct involved; or**

> **(2) the lawyer is a partner or has comparable managerial authority in the law firm in which the person is employed, or has direct supervisory authority over the person, and knows of the conduct at a time when its consequences can be avoided or mitigated but fails to take reasonable remedial action.**

COMMENT

[1] Lawyers generally employ assistants in their practice, including secretaries, investigators, law student interns, and paraprofessionals. Such assistants, whether employees or independent contractors, act for the lawyer in rendition of the lawyer's professional services. A lawyer ~~should~~ must give such assistants appropriate instruction and supervision concerning the ethical aspects of their employment, particularly regarding the obligation not to disclose information relating to representation of the client, and should be responsible for their work product. The measures employed in supervising nonlawyers should take account of the fact that they do not have legal training and are not subject to professional discipline.

[2] Paragraph (a) requires lawyers with managerial authority within a law firm to make reasonable efforts to establish internal policies and procedures designed to provide reasonable assurance that nonlawyers in the firm will act in a way compatible with the Rules of Professional Conduct. See Comment [1] to Rule 5.1. Paragraph (b) applies to lawyers who have supervisory authority over the work of a nonlawyer. Paragraph (c) specifies the circumstances in which a lawyer is responsible for conduct of a nonlawyer that would be a violation of the Rules of Professional Conduct if engaged in by a lawyer.

Rule 5.4 Professional Independence of a Lawyer

(a) A lawyer or law firm shall not share legal fees with a nonlawyer, except that:

(1) an agreement by a lawyer with the lawyer's firm, partner, or associate may provide for the payment of money, over a reasonable period of time after the lawyer's death, to the lawyer's estate or to one or more specified persons;

(2) a lawyer who purchases the practice of a deceased, disabled, or disappeared lawyer may, pursuant to the provisions of Rule 1.17, pay to the estate or other representative of that lawyer the agreed-upon purchase price; ~~and~~

(3) a lawyer or law firm may include nonlawyer employees in a compensation or retirement plan, even though the plan is based in whole or in part on a profit-sharing arrangement; and

(4) a lawyer may share court-awarded legal fees with a nonprofit organization that employed, retained or recommended employment of the lawyer in the matter.

(b) A lawyer shall not form a partnership with a nonlawyer if any of the activities of the partnership consist of the practice of law.

(c) A lawyer shall not permit a person who recommends, employs, or pays the lawyer to render legal services for another to direct or regulate the lawyer's professional judgment in rendering such legal services.

(d) A lawyer shall not practice with or in the form of a professional corporation or association authorized to practice law for a profit, if:

(1) a nonlawyer owns any interest therein, except that a fiduciary representative of the estate of a lawyer may hold the stock or interest of the lawyer for a reasonable time during administration;

(2) a nonlawyer is a corporate director or officer thereof or occupies the position of similar responsibility in any form of association other than a corporation ; or

(3) a nonlawyer has the right to direct or control the professional judgment of a lawyer.

COMMENT

[1] The provisions of this Rule express traditional limitations on sharing fees. These limitations are to protect the lawyer's professional independence of judgment. Where someone other than the client pays the lawyer's fee or salary, or recommends employment of the lawyer, that arrangement does not modify the lawyer's obligation to the client. As stated in paragraph (c), such arrangements should not interfere with the lawyer's professional judgment.

[2] This Rule also expresses traditional limitations on permitting a third party to direct or regulate the lawyer's professional judgment in rendering legal services to another. See also Rule 1.8(f) (lawyer may accept compensation from a third party as long as there is no interference with the lawyer's independent professional judgment and the client gives informed consent).

RULE 5.5 UNAUTHORIZED PRACTICE OF LAW*

A lawyer shall not:

(a) practice law in a jurisdiction where doing so violates the regulation of the legal profession in that jurisdiction; or

(b) assist a person who is not a member of the bar in the performance of activity that constitutes the unauthorized practice of law.

COMMENT

[1] The definition of the practice of law is established by law and varies from one jurisdiction to another. Whatever the definition, limiting the practice of law to members of the bar protects the public against

* This rule along with Model Rule 8.5 will be reconsidered along with the final report of the Multijurisdictional Practice of Law Commission (MJP) possibly as early as August 2002.

rendition of legal services by unqualified persons. Paragraph (b) does not prohibit a lawyer from employing the services of paraprofessionals and delegating functions to them, so long as the lawyer supervises the delegated work and retains responsibility for their work. See Rule 5.3. Likewise, it does not prohibit lawyers from providing professional advice and instruction to nonlawyers whose employment requires knowledge of law; for example, claims adjusters, employees of financial or commercial institutions, social workers, accountants and persons employed in government agencies. In addition, a lawyer may counsel nonlawyers who wish to proceed pro se.

Rule 5.6   Restrictions on Right to Practice

A lawyer shall not participate in offering or making:

(a) a partnership ~~or,~~ **shareholders, operating, employment, or other similar type of agreement that restricts the right of a lawyer to practice after termination of the relationship, except an agreement concerning benefits upon retirement; or**

(b) an agreement in which a restriction on the lawyer's right to practice is part of the settlement of a client controversy ~~between private parties.~~

COMMENT

[1]   An agreement restricting the right of ~~partners or associates~~ lawyers to practice after leaving a firm not only limits their professional autonomy but also limits the freedom of clients to choose a lawyer. Paragraph (a) prohibits such agreements except for restrictions incident to provisions concerning retirement benefits for service with the firm.

[2]   Paragraph (b) prohibits a lawyer from agreeing not to represent other persons in connection with settling a claim on behalf of a client.

[3]   This Rule does not apply to prohibit restrictions that may be included in the terms of the sale of a law practice pursuant to Rule 1.17.

Rule 5.7   Responsibilities Regarding Law–Related Services

(a) A lawyer shall be subject to the Rules of Professional Conduct with respect to the provision of law-related services, as defined in paragraph (b), if the law-related services are provided:

(1) by the lawyer in circumstances that are not distinct from the lawyer's provision of legal services to clients; or

(2) in other circumstances by ~~a separate~~ **an entity controlled by the lawyer individually or with others if the lawyer fails to take reasonable measures to assure that a person obtaining the law-related services knows that the services** ~~of the separate entity~~ **are not legal services and that the protections of the client-lawyer relationship do not exist.**

(b) The term "law-related services" denotes services that might reasonably be performed in conjunction with and in substance are related to the provision of legal services, and that are not prohibited as unauthorized practice of law when provided by a nonlawyer.

COMMENT

[1] When a lawyer performs law-related services or controls an organization that does so, there exists the potential for ethical problems. Principal among these is the possibility that the person for whom the law-related services are performed fails to understand that the services may not carry with them the protections normally afforded as part of the client-lawyer relationship. The recipient of the law-related services may expect, for example, that the protection of client confidences, prohibitions against representation of persons with conflicting interests, and obligations of a lawyer to maintain professional independence apply to the provision of law-related services when that may not be the case.

[2] Rule 5.7 applies to the provision of law-related services by a lawyer even when the lawyer does not provide any legal services to the person for whom the law-related services are performed and whether the law-related services are performed through a law firm or a separate entity. The Rule identifies the circumstances in which all of the Rules of Professional Conduct apply to the provision of law-related services. Even when those circumstances do not exist, however, the conduct of a lawyer involved in the provision of law-related services is subject to those Rules that apply generally to lawyer conduct, regardless of whether the conduct involves the provision of legal services. See, e.g., Rule 8.4.

[3] When law-related services are provided by a lawyer under circumstances that are not distinct from the lawyer's provision of legal services to clients, the lawyer in providing the law-related services must adhere to the requirements of the Rules of Professional Conduct as provided in Rule 5.7 paragraph (a)(1). Even when the law-related and legal services are provided in circumstances that are distinct from each other, for example through separate entities or different support staff within the law firm, the Rules of Professional Conduct apply to the lawyer as provided in paragraph (a)(2) unless the lawyer takes reasonable measures to assure that the recipient of the law-related services knows that the services are not legal services and that the protections of the client-lawyer relationship do not apply.

[4] Law-related services also may be provided through an entity that is distinct from that through which the lawyer provides legal services. If the lawyer individually or with others has control of such an entity's operations, the Rule requires the lawyer to take reasonable measures to assure that each person using the services of the entity knows that the services provided by the entity are not legal services and that the Rules of Professional Conduct that relate to the client-lawyer relationship do not apply. A lawyer's control of an entity extends to the

ability to direct its operation. Whether a lawyer has such control will depend upon the circumstances of the particular case.

[5] When a client-lawyer relationship exists with a person who is referred by a lawyer to a separate law-related service entity controlled by the lawyer, individually or with others, the lawyer must comply with Rule 1.8(a).

[6] In taking the reasonable measures referred to in paragraph (a)(2) to assure that a person using law-related services understands the practical effect or significance of the inapplicability of the Rules of Professional Conduct, the lawyer should communicate to the person receiving the law-related services, in a manner sufficient to assure that the person understands the significance of the fact, that the relationship of the person to the business entity will not be a client-lawyer relationship. The communication should be made before entering into an agreement for provision of or providing law-related services, and preferably should be in writing.

[7] The burden is upon the lawyer to show that the lawyer has taken reasonable measures under the circumstances to communicate the desired understanding. For instance, a sophisticated user of law-related services, such as a publicly held corporation, may require a lesser explanation than someone unaccustomed to making distinctions between legal services and law-related services, such as an individual seeking tax advice from a lawyer-accountant or investigative services in connection with a lawsuit.

[8] Regardless of the sophistication of potential recipients of law-related services, a lawyer should take special care to keep separate the provision of law-related and legal services in order to minimize the risk that the recipient will assume that the law-related services are legal services. The risk of such confusion is especially acute when the lawyer renders both types of services with respect to the same matter. Under some circumstances the legal and law-related services may be so closely entwined that they cannot be distinguished from each other, and the requirement of disclosure and consultation imposed by paragraph (a)(2) of the Rule cannot be met. In such a case a lawyer will be responsible for assuring that both the lawyer's conduct and, to the extent required by Rule 5.3, that of nonlawyer employees in the distinct entity that the lawyer controls complies in all respects with the Rules of Professional Conduct.

[9] A broad range of economic and other interests of clients may be served by lawyers' engaging in the delivery of law-related services. Examples of law-related services include providing title insurance, financial planning, accounting, trust services, real estate counseling, legislative lobbying, economic analysis, social work, psychological counseling, tax preparation, and patent, medical or environmental consulting.

[10] When a lawyer is obliged to accord the recipients of such services the protections of those Rules that apply to the client-lawyer relationship, the lawyer must take special care to heed the proscriptions

of the Rules addressing conflict of interest (Rules 1.7 through 1.11, especially Rules 1.7~~(b)~~(a)(2) and 1.8(a), (b) and (f)), and to scrupulously adhere to the requirements of Rule 1.6 relating to disclosure of confidential information. The promotion of the law-related services must also in all respects comply with Rules 7.1 through 7.3, dealing with advertising and solicitation. In that regard, lawyers should take special care to identify the obligations that may be imposed as a result of a jurisdiction's decisional law.

[11]   When the full protections of all of the Rules of Professional Conduct do not apply to the provision of law-related services, principles of law external to the Rules, for example, the law of principal and agent, govern the legal duties owed to those receiving the services. Those other legal principles may establish a different degree of protection for the recipient with respect to confidentiality of information, conflicts of interest and permissible business relationships with clients. See also Rule 8.4 (Misconduct).

PUBLIC SERVICE

RULE 6.1   Voluntary Pro Bono Publico Service*

Every lawyer has a professional responsibility to provide legal services to those unable to pay. A lawyer should aspire to render at least (50) hours of pro bono publico legal services per year. In fulfilling this responsibility, the lawyer should:

(a) provide a substantial majority of the (50) hours of legal services without fee or expectation of fee to:

(1) persons of limited means or

(2) charitable, religious, civic, community, governmental and educational organizations in matters that are designed primarily to address the needs of persons of limited means; and

(b) provide any additional services through:

(1) delivery of legal services at no fee or substantially reduced fee to individuals, groups or organizations seeking to secure or protect civil rights, civil liberties or public rights, or charitable, religious, civic, community, governmental and educational organizations in matters in furtherance of their organizational purposes, where the payment of standard legal fees would significantly deplete the organization's economic resources or would be otherwise inappropriate;

---

* The ABA House of Delegates amended comment 11 from the original Ethics 2000 Commission Report to add the concept that lawyers should encourage pro bono as well as enabling it.

(2) delivery of legal services at a substantially reduced fee to persons of limited means; or

(3) participation in activities for improving the law, the legal system or the legal profession.

In addition, a lawyer should voluntarily contribute financial support to organizations that provide legal services to persons of limited means.

COMMENT

[1]   Every lawyer, regardless of professional prominence or professional work load, has a responsibility to provide legal services to those unable to pay, and personal involvement in the problems of the disadvantaged can be one of the most rewarding experiences in the life of a lawyer. The American Bar Association urges all lawyers to provide a minimum of 50 hours of pro bono services annually. States, however, may decide to choose a higher or lower number of hours of annual service (which may be expressed as a percentage of a lawyer's professional time) depending upon local needs and local conditions. It is recognized that in some years a lawyer may render greater or fewer hours than the annual standard specified, but during the course of his or her legal career, each lawyer should render on average per year, the number of hours set forth in this Rule. Services can be performed in civil matters or in criminal or quasi-criminal matters for which there is no government obligation to provide funds for legal representation, such as post-conviction death penalty appeal cases.

[2]   Paragraphs (a)(1) and (2) recognize the critical need for legal services that exists among persons of limited means by providing that a substantial majority of the legal services rendered annually to the disadvantaged be furnished without fee or expectation of fee. Legal services under these paragraphs consist of a full range of activities, including individual and class representation, the provision of legal advice, legislative lobbying, administrative rule making and the provision of free training or mentoring to those who represent persons of limited means. The variety of these activities should facilitate participation by government lawyers, even when restrictions exist on their engaging in the outside practice of law.

[3]   Persons eligible for legal services under paragraphs (a)(1) and (2) are those who qualify for participation in programs funded by the Legal Services Corporation and those whose incomes and financial resources are slightly above the guidelines utilized by such programs but nevertheless, cannot afford counsel. Legal services can be rendered to individuals or to organizations such as homeless shelters, battered women's centers and food pantries that serve those of limited means. The term "governmental organizations" includes, but is not limited to, public protection programs and sections of governmental or public sector agencies.

[4]   Because service must be provided without fee or expectation of fee, the intent of the lawyer to render free legal services is essential for the work performed to fall within the meaning of paragraphs (a)(1) and (2). Accordingly, services rendered cannot be considered pro bono if an anticipated fee is uncollected, but the award of statutory attorneys' fees in a case originally accepted as pro bono would not disqualify such services from inclusion under this section. Lawyers who do receive fees in such cases are encouraged to contribute an appropriate portion of such fees to organizations or projects that benefit persons of limited means.

[5]   While it is possible for a lawyer to fulfill the annual responsibility to perform pro bono services exclusively through activities described in paragraphs (a)(1) and (2), to the extent that any hours of service remained unfulfilled, the remaining commitment can be met in a variety of ways as set forth in paragraph (b). Constitutional, statutory or regulatory restrictions may prohibit or impede government and public sector lawyers and judges from performing the pro bono services outlined in paragraphs (a)(1) and (2). Accordingly, where those restrictions apply, government and public sector lawyers and judges may fulfill their pro bono responsibility by performing services outlined in paragraph (b).

[6]   Paragraph (b)(1) includes the provision of certain types of legal services to those whose incomes and financial resources place them above limited means. It also permits the pro bono lawyer to accept a substantially reduced fee for services. Examples of the types of issues that may be addressed under this paragraph include First Amendment claims, Title VII claims and environmental protection claims. Additionally, a wide range of organizations may be represented, including social service, medical research, cultural and religious groups.

[7]   Paragraph (b)(2) covers instances in which lawyers agree to and receive a modest fee for furnishing legal services to persons of limited means. Participation in judicare programs and acceptance of court appointments in which the fee is substantially below a lawyer's usual rate are encouraged under this section.

[8]   Paragraph (b)(3) recognizes the value of lawyers engaging in activities that improve the law, the legal system or the legal profession. Serving on bar association committees, serving on boards of pro bono or legal services programs, taking part in Law Day activities, acting as a continuing legal education instructor, a mediator or an arbitrator and engaging in legislative lobbying to improve the law, the legal system or the profession are a few examples of the many activities that fall within this paragraph.

[9]   Because the provision of pro bono services is a professional responsibility, it is the individual ethical commitment of each lawyer. Nevertheless, there may be times when it is not feasible for a lawyer to engage in pro bono services. At such times a lawyer may discharge the pro bono responsibility by providing financial support to organizations providing free legal services to persons of limited means. Such financial

support should be reasonably equivalent to the value of the hours of service that would have otherwise been provided. In addition, at times it may be more feasible to satisfy the pro bono responsibility collectively, as by a firm's aggregate pro bono activities.

[10] Because the efforts of individual lawyers are not enough to meet the need for free legal services that exists among persons of limited means, the government and the profession have instituted additional programs to provide those services. Every lawyer should financially support such programs, in addition to either providing direct pro bono services or making financial contributions when pro bono service is not feasible.

[11] Law firms should act reasonably to enable and encourage all lawyers in the firm to provide the pro bono legal services called for by this Rule.

[11] [12] The responsibility set forth in this Rule is not intended to be enforced through disciplinary process.

Rule 6.2 Accepting Appointments

A lawyer shall not seek to avoid appointment by a tribunal to represent a person except for good cause, such as:

(a) representing the client is likely to result in violation of the Rules of Professional Conduct or other law;

(b) representing the client is likely to result in an unreasonable financial burden on the lawyer; or

(c) the client or the cause is so repugnant to the lawyer as to be likely to impair the client-lawyer relationship or the lawyer's ability to represent the client.

COMMENT

[1] A lawyer ordinarily is not obliged to accept a client whose character or cause the lawyer regards as repugnant. The lawyer's freedom to select clients is, however, qualified. All lawyers have a responsibility to assist in providing pro bono publico service. See Rule 6.1. An individual lawyer fulfills this responsibility by accepting a fair share of unpopular matters or indigent or unpopular clients. A lawyer may also be subject to appointment by a court to serve unpopular clients or persons unable to afford legal services.

Appointed Counsel

[2] For good cause a lawyer may seek to decline an appointment to represent a person who cannot afford to retain counsel or whose cause is unpopular. Good cause exists if the lawyer could not handle the matter competently, see Rule 1.1, or if undertaking the representation would result in an improper conflict of interest, for example, when the client or the cause is so repugnant to the lawyer as to be likely to impair the client-lawyer relationship or the lawyer's ability to represent the client.

A lawyer may also seek to decline an appointment if acceptance would be unreasonably burdensome, for example, when it would impose a financial sacrifice so great as to be unjust.

[3]   An appointed lawyer has the same obligations to the client as retained counsel, including the obligations of loyalty and confidentiality, and is subject to the same limitations on the client-lawyer relationship, such as the obligation to refrain from assisting the client in violation of the Rules.

Rule 6.3   Membership in Legal Services Organization

A lawyer may serve as a director, officer or member of a legal services organization, apart from the law firm in which the lawyer practices, notwithstanding that the organization serves persons having interests adverse to a client of the lawyer. The lawyer shall not knowingly participate in a decision or action of the organization:

(a) if participating in the decision or action would be incompatible with the lawyer's obligations to a client under Rule 1.7; or

(b) where the decision or action could have a material adverse effect on the representation of a client of the organization whose interests are adverse to a client of the lawyer.

COMMENT

[1]   Lawyers should be encouraged to support and participate in legal service organizations. A lawyer who is an officer or a member of such an organization does not thereby have a client-lawyer relationship with persons served by the organization. However, there is potential conflict between the interests of such persons and the interests of the lawyer's clients. If the possibility of such conflict disqualified a lawyer from serving on the board of a legal services organization, the profession's involvement in such organizations would be severely curtailed.

[2]   It may be necessary in appropriate cases to reassure a client of the organization that the representation will not be affected by conflicting loyalties of a member of the board. Established, written policies in this respect can enhance the credibility of such assurances.

Rule 6.4   Law Reform Activities Affecting Client Interests

A lawyer may serve as a director, officer or member of an organization involved in reform of the law or its administration notwithstanding that the reform may affect the interests of a client of the lawyer. When the lawyer knows that the interests of a client may be materially benefitted by a decision in which the lawyer participates, the lawyer shall disclose that fact but need not identify the client.

COMMENT

[1]   Lawyers involved in organizations seeking law reform generally do not have a client-lawyer relationship with the organization. Otherwise, it might follow that a lawyer could not be involved in a bar association law reform program that might indirectly affect a client. See also Rule 1.2(b). For example, a lawyer specializing in antitrust litigation might be regarded as disqualified from participating in drafting revisions of rules governing that subject. In determining the nature and scope of participation in such activities, a lawyer should be mindful of obligations to clients under other Rules, particularly Rule 1.7. A lawyer is professionally obligated to protect the integrity of the program by making an appropriate disclosure within the organization when the lawyer knows a private client might be materially benefitted.

Rule 6.5   Nonprofit and Court–Annexed Limited Legal Services Programs

(a) A lawyer who, under the auspices of a program sponsored by a nonprofit organization or court, provides short-term limited legal services to a client without expectation by either the lawyer or the client that the lawyer will provide continuing representation in the matter:

(1) is subject to Rules 1.7 and 1.9(a) only if the lawyer knows that the representation of the client involves a conflict of interest; and

(2) is subject to Rule 1.10 only if the lawyer knows that another lawyer associated with the lawyer in a law firm is disqualified by Rule 1.7 or 1.9(a) with respect to the matter.

(b) Except as provided in paragraph (a)(2), Rule 1.10 is inapplicable to a representation governed by this Rule.

COMMENT

[1]   Legal services organizations, courts and various nonprofit organizations have established programs through which lawyers provide short-term limited legal services—such as advice or the completion of legal forms—that will assist persons to address their legal problems without further representation by a lawyer. In these programs, such as legal-advice hotlines, advice-only clinics or pro se counseling programs, a client-lawyer relationship is established, but there is no expectation that the lawyer's representation of the client will continue beyond the limited consultation. Such programs are normally operated under circumstances in which it is not feasible for a lawyer to systematically screen for conflicts of interest as is generally required before undertaking a representation. See, e.g., Rules 1.7, 1.9 and 1.10.

[2]   A lawyer who provides short-term limited legal services pursuant to this Rule must secure the client's informed consent to the limited

scope of the representation. See Rule 1.2(c). If a short-term limited representation would not be reasonable under the circumstances, the lawyer may offer advice to the client but must also advise the client of the need for further assistance of counsel. Except as provided in this Rule, the Rules of Professional Conduct, including Rules 1.6 and 1.9(c), are applicable to the limited representation.

[3] Because a lawyer who is representing a client in the circumstances addressed by this Rule ordinarily is not able to check systematically for conflicts of interest, paragraph (a) requires compliance with Rules 1.7 or 1.9(a) only if the lawyer knows that the representation presents a conflict of interest for the lawyer, and with Rule 1.10 only if the lawyer knows that another lawyer in the lawyer's firm is disqualified by Rules 1.7 or 1.9(a) in the matter.

[4] Because the limited nature of the services significantly reduces the risk of conflicts of interest with other matters being handled by the lawyer's firm, paragraph (b) provides that Rule 1.10 is inapplicable to a representation governed by this Rule except as provided by paragraph (a)(2). Paragraph (a)(2) requires the participating lawyer to comply with Rule 1.10 when the lawyer knows that the lawyer's firm is disqualified by Rules 1.7 or 1.9(a). By virtue of paragraph (b), however, a lawyer's participation in a short-term limited legal services program will not preclude the lawyer's firm from undertaking or continuing the representation of a client with interests adverse to a client being represented under the program's auspices. Nor will the personal disqualification of a lawyer participating in the program be imputed to other lawyers participating in the program.

[5] If, after commencing a short-term limited representation in accordance with this Rule, a lawyer undertakes to represent the client in the matter on an ongoing basis, Rules 1.7, 1.9(a) and 1.10 become applicable.

INFORMATION ABOUT LEGAL SERVICES

Rule 7.1   Communications Concerning a Lawyer's Services

A lawyer shall not make a false or misleading communication about the lawyer or the lawyer's services. A communication is false or misleading if it: (a) contains a material misrepresentation of fact or law, or omits a fact necessary to make the statement considered as a whole not materially misleading;

(b) is likely to create an unjustified expectation about results the lawyer can achieve, or states or implies that the lawyer can achieve results by means that violate the Rules of Professional Conduct or other law; or

(c) compares the lawyer's services with other lawyers' services, unless the comparison can be factually substantiated.

COMMENT

[1] This Rule governs all communications about a lawyer's services, including advertising permitted by Rule 7.2. Whatever means are used to make known a lawyer's services, statements about them ~~should~~ <u>must</u> be truthful. ~~The prohibition in paragraph (b) of statements that may create "unjustified expectations" would ordinarily preclude advertisements about results obtained on behalf of a client, such as the amount of a damage award or the lawyer's record in obtaining favorable verdicts, and advertisements containing client endorsements. Such information may create the unjustified expectation that similar results can be obtained for others without reference to the specific factual and legal circumstances.~~

[2] Truthful statements that are misleading are also prohibited by this Rule. A truthful statement is misleading if it omits a fact necessary to make the lawyer's communication considered as a whole not materially misleading. A truthful statement is also misleading if there is a substantial likelihood that it will lead a reasonable person to formulate a specific conclusion about the lawyer or the lawyer's services for which there is no reasonable factual foundation.

[3] An advertisement that truthfully reports a lawyer's achievements on behalf of clients or former clients may be misleading if presented so as to lead a reasonable person to form an unjustified expectation that the same results could be obtained for other clients in similar matters without reference to the specific factual and legal circumstances of each client's case. Similarly, an unsubstantiated comparison of the lawyer's services or fees with the services or fees of other lawyers may be misleading if presented with such specificity as would lead a reasonable person to conclude that the comparison can be substantiated. The inclusion of an appropriate disclaimer or qualifying language may preclude a finding that a statement is likely to create unjustified expectations or otherwise mislead a prospective client.

[4] See also Rule 8.4(e) for the prohibition against stating or implying an ability to influence improperly a government agency or official or to achieve results by means that violate the Rules of Professional Conduct or other law.

Rule 7.2 Advertising

(a) **Subject to the requirements of Rules 7.1 and 7.3, a lawyer may advertise services through ~~public media, such as a telephone directory, legal directory, newspaper or other periodical, outdoor advertising, radio or television, or through~~ written ~~or,~~ recorded <u>or electronic</u> communication, including public media.**

~~(b) A copy or recording of an advertisement or communication shall be kept for two years after its last dissemination along with a record of when and where it was used.~~

133

~~(c)~~ (b) **A lawyer shall not give anything of value to a person for recommending the lawyer's services except that a lawyer may**

> **(1) pay the reasonable costs of advertisements or communications permitted by this Rule;**

> **(2) pay the usual charges of a ~~not-for-profit lawyer referral service or~~ legal service ~~organization~~ plan or a not-for-profit or qualified lawyer referral service. A qualified lawyer referral service is a lawyer referral service that has been approved by an appropriate regulatory authority; and**

> **(3) pay for a law practice in accordance with Rule 1.17.**

~~(d)~~ (c) **Any communication made pursuant to this rule shall include the name and office address of at least one lawyer or law firm responsible for its content.**

COMMENT

[1]   To assist the public in obtaining legal services, lawyers should be allowed to make known their services not only through reputation but also through organized information campaigns in the form of advertising. Advertising involves an active quest for clients, contrary to the tradition that a lawyer should not seek clientele. However, the public's need to know about legal services can be fulfilled in part through advertising. This need is particularly acute in the case of persons of moderate means who have not made extensive use of legal services. The interest in expanding public information about legal services ought to prevail over considerations of tradition. Nevertheless, advertising by lawyers entails the risk of practices that are misleading or overreaching.

[2]   This Rule permits public dissemination of information concerning a lawyer's name or firm name, address and telephone number; the kinds of services the lawyer will undertake; the basis on which the lawyer's fees are determined, including prices for specific services and payment and credit arrangements; a lawyer's foreign language ability; names of references and, with their consent, names of clients regularly represented; and other information that might invite the attention of those seeking legal assistance.

[3]   Questions of effectiveness and taste in advertising are matters of speculation and subjective judgment. Some jurisdictions have had extensive prohibitions against television advertising, against advertising going beyond specified facts about a lawyer, or against "undignified" advertising. Television is now one of the most powerful media for getting information to the public, particularly persons of low and moderate income; prohibiting television advertising, therefore, would impede the flow of information about legal services to many sectors of the public. Limiting the information that may be advertised has a similar effect and assumes that the bar can accurately forecast the kind of information that the public would regard as relevant. Similarly, electronic media,

such as the Internet, can be an important source of information about legal services, and lawful communication by electronic mail is permitted by this Rule. But see Rule 7.3(a) for the prohibition against the solicitation of a prospective client through a real-time electronic exchange that is not initiated by the prospective client.

[4] Neither this Rule nor Rule 7.3 prohibits communications authorized by law, such as notice to members of a class in class action litigation.

~~Record of Advertising~~

~~[5] Paragraph (b) requires that a record of the content and use of advertising be kept in order to facilitate enforcement of this Rule. It does not require that advertising be subject to review prior to dissemination. Such a requirement would be burdensome and expensive relative to its possible benefits, and may be of doubtful constitutionality.~~

Paying Others to Recommend a Lawyer

~~[6]~~ [5] ~~A lawyer is allowed to pay for advertising permitted by this Rule and for the purchase of a law practice in accordance with the provisions of Rule 1.17, but otherwise is~~ Lawyers are not permitted to pay ~~another person~~ others for channeling professional work. ~~This restriction does not prevent an organization or person other than the lawyer from advertising or recommending the lawyer's services. Thus, a legal aid agency or prepaid legal services plan may pay to advertise legal services provided under its auspices. Likewise, a lawyer may participate in not-for-profit lawyer referral programs and pay the usual fees charged by such programs. Paragraph (c) does not prohibit paying regular compensation to an assistant, such as a secretary, to prepare communications permitted by this Rule.~~ Paragraph (b)(1), however, allows a lawyer to pay for advertising and communications permitted by this Rule, including the costs of print directory listings, on-line directory listings, newspaper ads, television and radio airtime, domain-name registrations, sponsorship fees, banner ads, and group advertising. A lawyer may compensate employees, agents and vendors who are engaged to provide marketing or client-development services, such as publicists, public-relations personnel, business-development staff and website designers. See Rule 5.3 for the duties of lawyers and law firms with respect to the conduct of nonlawyers who prepare marketing materials for them.

[6] A lawyer may pay the usual charges of a legal service plan or a not-for-profit or qualified lawyer referral service. A legal service plan is a prepaid or group legal service plan or a similar delivery system that assists prospective clients to secure legal representation. A lawyer referral service, on the other hand, is any organization that holds itself out to the public as a lawyer referral service. Such referral services are understood by laypersons to be consumer-oriented organizations that provide unbiased referrals to lawyers with appropriate experience in the subject

matter of the representation and afford other client protections, such as complaint procedures or malpractice insurance requirements. Consequently, this Rule only permits a lawyer to pay the usual charges of a not-for-profit or qualified lawyer referral service. A qualified lawyer referral service is one that is approved by an appropriate regulatory authority as affording adequate protections for prospective clients. See, e.g., the American Bar Association's Model Supreme Court Rules Governing Lawyer Referral Services and Model Lawyer Referral and Information Service Quality Assurance Act (requiring that organizations that are identified as lawyer referral services (i) permit the participation of all lawyers who are licensed and eligible to practice in the jurisdiction and who meet reasonable objective eligibility requirements as may be established by the referral service for the protection of prospective clients; (ii) require each participating lawyer to carry reasonably adequate malpractice insurance; (iii) act reasonably to assess client satisfaction and address client complaints; and (iv) do not refer prospective clients to lawyers who own, operate or are employed by the referral service.)

[7] A lawyer who accepts assignments or referrals from a legal service plan or referrals from a lawyer referral service must act reasonably to assure that the activities of the plan or service are compatible with the lawyer's professional obligations. See Rule 5.3. Legal service plans and lawyer referral services may communicate with prospective clients, but such communication must be in conformity with these Rules. Thus, advertising must not be false or misleading, as would be the case if the communications of a group advertising program or a group legal services plan would mislead prospective clients to think that it was a lawyer referral service sponsored by a state agency or bar association. Nor could the lawyer allow in-person, telephonic, or real-time contacts that would violate Rule 7.3.

Rule 7.3 Direct Contact With Prospective Clients

(a) A lawyer shall not by in-person ~~or,~~ live telephone **or real-time electronic** contact solicit professional employment from a prospective client ~~with whom the lawyer has no family or prior professional relationship~~ when a significant motive for the lawyer's doing so is the lawyer's pecuniary gain, **unless the person contacted:**

(1) **is a lawyer; or**

(2) **has a family, close personal, or prior professional relationship with the lawyer.**

(b) A lawyer shall not solicit professional employment from a prospective client by written ~~or,~~ recorded **or electronic** communication or by in-person ~~or,~~ telephone **or real-time electronic** contact even when not otherwise prohibited by paragraph (a), if:

(1) the prospective client has made known to the lawyer a desire not to be solicited by the lawyer; or

(2) the solicitation involves coercion, duress or harassment.

(c) Every written ~~or~~, recorded <u>or electronic</u> communication from a lawyer soliciting professional employment from a prospective client known to be in need of legal services in a particular matter, ~~and with whom the lawyer has no family or prior professional relationship,~~ shall include the words "Advertising Material" on the outside envelope, <u>if any,</u> and at the beginning and ending of any recorded <u>or electronic</u> communication, <u>unless the recipient of the communication is a person specified in paragraphs (a)(1) or (a)(2).</u>

(d) Notwithstanding the prohibitions in paragraph (a), a lawyer may participate with a prepaid or group legal service plan operated by an organization not owned or directed by the lawyer that uses in-person or telephone contact to solicit memberships or subscriptions for the plan from persons who are not known to need legal services in a particular matter covered by the plan.

COMMENT

[1] There is a potential for abuse inherent in direct in-person ~~or~~, live telephone <u>or real-time electronic</u> contact by a lawyer with a prospective client known to need legal services. These forms of contact between a lawyer and a prospective client subject the layperson to the private importuning of the trained advocate in a direct interpersonal encounter. The prospective client, who may already feel overwhelmed by the circumstances giving rise to the need for legal services, may find it difficult fully to evaluate all available alternatives with reasoned judgment and appropriate self-interest in the face of the lawyer's presence and insistence upon being retained immediately. The situation is fraught with the possibility of undue influence, intimidation, and over-reaching.

[2] This potential for abuse inherent in direct in-person ~~or~~, live telephone <u>or real-time electronic</u> solicitation of prospective clients justifies its prohibition, particularly since lawyer advertising and written and recorded communication permitted under Rule 7.2 offer alternative means of conveying necessary information to those who may be in need of legal services. Advertising and written and recorded communications which may be mailed or autodialed make it possible for a prospective client to be informed about the need for legal services, and about the qualifications of available lawyers and law firms, without subjecting the prospective client to direct in-person ~~or~~, telephone <u>or real-time electronic</u> persuasion that may overwhelm the client's judgment.

[3] The use of general advertising and written ~~and~~, recorded <u>or electronic</u> communications to transmit information from lawyer to prospective client, rather than direct in-person ~~or~~, live telephone <u>or real-time electronic</u> contact, will help to assure that the information flows

cleanly as well as freely. The contents of advertisements and communications permitted under Rule 7.2 ~~are~~ can be permanently recorded so that they cannot be disputed and may be shared with others who know the lawyer. This potential for informal review is itself likely to help guard against statements and claims that might constitute false and misleading communications, in violation of Rule 7.1. The contents of direct in-person ~~or~~, live telephone or real-time electronic conversations between a lawyer ~~to~~ and a prospective client can be disputed and ~~are~~ may not be subject to third-party scrutiny. Consequently, they are much more likely to approach (and occasionally cross) the dividing line between accurate representations and those that are false and misleading.

[4] There is far less likelihood that a lawyer would engage in abusive practices against an individual who is a former client, or with whom the lawyer has a ~~prior~~ close personal or ~~professional~~ family relationship, or ~~where~~ in situations in which the lawyer is motivated by considerations other than the lawyer's pecuniary gain. Nor is there a serious potential for abuse when the person contacted is a lawyer. Consequently, the general prohibition in Rule 7.3(a) and the requirements of Rule 7.3(c) are not applicable in those situations. Also, paragraph (a) is not intended to prohibit a lawyer from participating in constitutionally protected activities of public or charitable legal-service organizations or bona fide political, social, civic, fraternal, employee or trade organizations whose purposes include providing or recommending legal services to its members or beneficiaries.

[5] But even permitted forms of solicitation can be abused. Thus, any solicitation which contains information which is false or misleading within the meaning of Rule 7.1, which involves coercion, duress or harassment within the meaning of Rule 7.3(b)(2), or which involves contact with a prospective client who has made known to the lawyer a desire not to be solicited by the lawyer within the meaning of Rule 7.3(b)(1) is prohibited. Moreover, if after sending a letter or other communication to a client as permitted by Rule 7.2 the lawyer receives no response, any further effort to communicate with the prospective client may violate the provisions of Rule 7.3(b).

[6] This Rule is not intended to prohibit a lawyer from contacting representatives of organizations or groups that may be interested in establishing a group or prepaid legal plan for their members, insureds, beneficiaries or other third parties for the purpose of informing such entities of the availability of and details concerning the plan or arrangement which the lawyer or lawyer's firm is willing to offer. This form of communication is not directed to a prospective client. Rather, it is usually addressed to an individual acting in a fiduciary capacity seeking a supplier of legal services for others who may, if they choose, become prospective clients of the lawyer. Under these circumstances, the activity which the lawyer undertakes in communicating with such representatives and the type of information transmitted to the individual are

functionally similar to and serve the same purpose as advertising permitted under Rule 7.2.

[7] The requirement in Rule 7.3(c) that certain communications be marked "Advertising Material" does not apply to communications sent in response to requests of potential clients or their spokespersons or sponsors. General announcements by lawyers, including changes in personnel or office location, do not constitute communications soliciting professional employment from a client known to be in need of legal services within the meaning of this Rule.

[8] Paragraph (d) of this Rule ~~would permit~~ permits a lawyer to participate with an organization which uses personal contact to solicit members for its group or prepaid legal service plan, provided that the personal contact is not undertaken by any lawyer who would be a provider of legal services through the plan. The organization ~~referred to in paragraph (d)~~ must not be owned by or directed (whether as manager or otherwise) by any lawyer or law firm that participates in the plan. For example, paragraph (d) would not permit a lawyer to create an organization controlled directly or indirectly by the lawyer and use the organization for the in-person or telephone solicitation of legal employment of the lawyer through memberships in the plan or otherwise. The communication permitted by these organizations also must not be directed to a person known to need legal services in a particular matter, but is to be designed to inform potential plan members generally of another means of affordable legal services. Lawyers who participate in a legal service plan must reasonably assure that the plan sponsors are in compliance with Rules 7.1, 7.2 and 7.3(b). See 8.4(a).

Rule 7.4 Communication of Fields of Practice <u>and Specialization</u>

(a) **A lawyer may communicate the fact that the lawyer does or does not practice in particular fields of law.** ~~A lawyer shall not state or imply that the lawyer has been recognized or certified as a specialist in a particular field of law except as follows:~~

~~(a)~~ **(b)** ~~a~~ **A lawyer admitted to engage in patent practice before the United States Patent and Trademark Office may use the designation "Patent Attorney" or a substantially similar designation**~~;~~**.**

~~(b)~~ **(c)** ~~a~~ **A lawyer engaged in Admiralty practice may use the designation "Admiralty," "Proctor in Admiralty" or a substantially similar designation**~~; and~~**.**

~~(c) [for jurisdictions where there is a regulatory authority granting certification or approving organizations that grant certification] a lawyer may communicate the fact that the lawyer has been certified as a specialist in a field of law by a named organization or authority but only if:~~

139

~~(1) such certification is granted by the appropriate regulatory authority or by an organization which has been approved by the appropriate regulatory authority to grant such certification; or~~

~~(2) such certification is granted by an organization that has not yet been approved by, or has been denied the approval available from, the appropriate regulatory authority, and the absence or denial of approval is clearly stated in the communication, and in any advertising subject to Rule 7.2, such statement appears in the same sentence that communicates the certification.~~

~~(c) [for jurisdictions where there is no procedure either for certification of specialties or for approval of organizations granting certification] a lawyer may communicate the fact that the lawyer has been certified as a specialist in a field of law by a named organization, provided that the communication clearly states that there is no procedure in this jurisdiction for approving certifying organizations. If, however, the named organization has been accredited by the American Bar Association to certify lawyers as specialists in a particular field of law, the communication need not contain such a statement.~~

(d) A lawyer shall not state or imply that a lawyer is certified as a specialist in a particular field of law, unless:

(1) the lawyer has been certified as a specialist by an organization that has been approved by an appropriate state authority or that has been accredited by the American Bar Association; and

(2) the name of the certifying organization is clearly identified in the communication.

COMMENT

[1] ~~This~~ Paragraph (a) of this Rule permits a lawyer to indicate areas of practice in communications about the lawyer's services. If a lawyer practices only in certain fields, or will not accept matters except in a specified field or fields, the lawyer is permitted to so indicate. A lawyer is generally permitted to state that the lawyer is a "specialist," practices a "specialty," or "specializes in" particular fields, but such communications are subject to the "false and misleading" standard applied in Rule 7.1 to communications concerning a lawyer's services.

[2] ~~However, a lawyer may not communicate that the lawyer has been recognized or certified as a specialist in a particular field of law, except as provided by this Rule. Recognition of specialization in patent matters is a matter of~~ Paragraph (b) recognizes the long-established policy of the Patent and Trademark Office, ~~as reflected in paragraph (a)~~ for the designation of lawyers practicing before the Office. Paragraph ~~(b)~~ (c) recognizes that designation of ~~admiralty~~ Admiralty practice has a

long historical tradition associated with maritime commerce and the federal courts.

[3] Paragraph ~~(c) provides for certification~~ (d) permits a lawyer to state that the lawyer is certified as a specialist in a field of law ~~when a state authorizes an appropriate regulatory authority to grant such certification or when the state grants other organizations the right to grant certification~~ if such certification is granted by an organization approved by an appropriate state authority or accredited by the American Bar Association or another organization, such as a state bar association, that has been approved by the state authority to accredit organizations that certify lawyers as specialists. Certification ~~procedures imply~~ signifies that an objective entity has recognized ~~a lawyer's higher~~ an advanced degree of ~~specialized ability~~ knowledge and experience in the specialty area greater than is suggested by general licensure to practice law. ~~Those objective entities~~ Certifying organizations may be expected to apply standards of ~~competence,~~ experience ~~and,~~ knowledge and proficiency to insure that a lawyer's recognition as a specialist is meaningful and reliable. In order to insure that consumers can obtain access to useful information about an organization granting certification, the name of the certifying organization ~~or agency~~ must be included in any communication regarding the certification.

[4] ~~Lawyers may also be certified as specialists by organizations that either have not yet been approved to grant such certification or have been disapproved. In such instances, the consumer may be misled as to the significance of the lawyer's status as a certified specialist. The Rule therefore requires that a lawyer who chooses to communicate recognition by such an organization also clearly state the absence or denial of the organization's authority to grant such certification. Since lawyer advertising through public media and written or recorded communications invites the greatest danger of misleading consumers, the absence or denial of the organization's authority to grant certification must be clearly stated in such advertising in the same sentence that communicates the certification.~~

[5] ~~In jurisdictions where no appropriate regulatory authority has a procedure for approving organizations granting certification, the Rule requires that a lawyer clearly state such lack of procedure. If, however, the named organization has been accredited by the American Bar Association to certify lawyers as specialists in a particular field of law, the communication need not contain such a statement.~~

Rule 7.5   Firm Names and Letterheads

(a) A lawyer shall not use a firm name, letterhead or other professional designation that violates Rule 7.1. A trade name may be used by a lawyer in private practice if it does not imply a connection with a government agency or with a public or chari-

table legal services organization and is not otherwise in violation of Rule 7.1.

(b) A law firm with offices in more than one jurisdiction may use the same name or other professional designation in each jurisdiction, but identification of the lawyers in an office of the firm shall indicate the jurisdictional limitations on those not licensed to practice in the jurisdiction where the office is located.

(c) The name of a lawyer holding a public office shall not be used in the name of a law firm, or in communications on its behalf, during any substantial period in which the lawyer is not actively and regularly practicing with the firm.

(d) Lawyers may state or imply that they practice in a partnership or other organization only when that is the fact.

COMMENT

[1]   A firm may be designated by the names of all or some of its members, by the names of deceased members where there has been a continuing succession in the firm's identity or by a trade name such as the "ABC Legal Clinic." A lawyer or law firm may also be designated by a distinctive website address or comparable professional designation. Although the United States Supreme Court has held that legislation may prohibit the use of trade names in professional practice, use of such names in law practice is acceptable so long as it is not misleading. If a private firm uses a trade name that includes a geographical name such as "Springfield Legal Clinic," an express disclaimer that it is a public legal aid agency may be required to avoid a misleading implication. It may be observed that any firm name including the name of a deceased partner is, strictly speaking, a trade name. The use of such names to designate law firms has proven a useful means of identification. However, it is misleading to use the name of a lawyer not associated with the firm or a predecessor of the firm.

[2]   With regard to paragraph (d), lawyers sharing office facilities, but who are not in fact ~~partners~~ associated with each other in a law firm, may not denominate themselves as, for example, "Smith and Jones," for that title suggests ~~partnership in the practice of~~ that they are practicing law together in a firm.

Rule 7.6   Political Contributions to Obtain Government Legal Engagements or Appointments by Judges

A lawyer or law firm shall not accept a government legal engagement or an appointment by a judge if the lawyer or law firm makes a political contribution or solicits political contributions for the purpose of obtaining or being considered for that type of legal engagement or appointment.

COMMENT

[1] Lawyers have a right to participate fully in the political process, which includes making and soliciting political contributions to candidates for judicial and other public office. Nevertheless, when lawyers make or solicit political contributions in order to obtain an engagement for legal work awarded by a government agency, or to obtain appointment by a judge, the public may legitimately question whether the lawyers engaged to perform the work are selected on the basis of competence and merit. In such a circumstance, the integrity of the profession is undermined.

[2] The term "political contribution" denotes any gift, subscription, loan, advance or deposit of anything of value made directly or indirectly to a candidate, incumbent, political party or campaign committee to influence or provide financial support for election to or retention in judicial or other government office. Political contributions in initiative and referendum elections are not included. For purposes of this Rule, the term "political contribution" does not include uncompensated services.

[3] Subject to the exceptions below, (i) the term "government legal engagement" denotes any engagement to provide legal services that a public official has the direct or indirect power to award; and (ii) the term "appointment by a judge" denotes an appointment to a position such as referee, commissioner, special master, receiver, guardian or other similar position that is made by a judge. Those terms do not, however, include (a) substantially uncompensated services; (b) engagements or appointments made on the basis of experience, expertise, professional qualifications and cost following a request for proposal or other process that is free from influence based upon political contributions; and (c) engagements or appointments made on a rotational basis from a list compiled without regard to political contributions.

[4] The term "lawyer or law firm" includes a political action committee or other entity owned or controlled by a lawyer or law firm.

[5] Political contributions are for the purpose of obtaining or being considered for a government legal engagement or appointment by a judge if, but for the desire to be considered for the legal engagement or appointment, the lawyer or law firm would not have made or solicited the contributions. The purpose may be determined by an examination of the circumstances in which the contributions occur. For example, one or more contributions that in the aggregate are substantial in relation to other contributions by lawyers or law firms, made for the benefit of an official in a position to influence award of a government legal engagement, and followed by an award of the legal engagement to the contributing or soliciting lawyer or the lawyer's firm would support an inference that the purpose of the contributions was to obtain the engagement, absent other factors that weigh against existence of the proscribed purpose. Those factors may include among others that the contribution or solicitation was made to further a political, social, or

economic interest or because of an existing personal, family, or professional relationship with a candidate.

[6] If a lawyer makes or solicits a political contribution under circumstances that constitute bribery or another crime, Rule 8.4(b) is implicated.

MAINTAINING THE INTEGRITY OF THE PROFESSION

Rule 8.1 Bar Admission and Disciplinary Matters

An applicant for admission to the bar, or a lawyer in connection with a bar admission application or in connection with a disciplinary matter, shall not:

(a) knowingly make a false statement of material fact; or

(b) fail to disclose a fact necessary to correct a misapprehension known by the person to have arisen in the matter, or knowingly fail to respond to a lawful demand for information from an admissions or disciplinary authority, except that this rule does not require disclosure of information otherwise protected by Rule 1.6.

COMMENT

[1] The duty imposed by this Rule extends to persons seeking admission to the bar as well as to lawyers. Hence, if a person makes a material false statement in connection with an application for admission, it may be the basis for subsequent disciplinary action if the person is admitted, and in any event may be relevant in a subsequent admission application. The duty imposed by this Rule applies to a lawyer's own admission or discipline as well as that of others. Thus, it is a separate professional offense for a lawyer to knowingly make a misrepresentation or omission in connection with a disciplinary investigation of the lawyer's own conduct. ~~This~~ Paragraph (b) of this Rule also requires correction of any prior misstatement in the matter that the applicant or lawyer may have made and affirmative clarification of any misunderstanding on the part of the admissions or disciplinary authority of which the person involved becomes aware.

[2] This Rule is subject to the provisions of the fifth amendment of the United States Constitution and corresponding provisions of state constitutions. A person relying on such a provision in response to a question, however, should do so openly and not use the right of nondisclosure as a justification for failure to comply with this Rule.

[3] A lawyer representing an applicant for admission to the bar, or representing a lawyer who is the subject of a disciplinary inquiry or proceeding, is governed by the rules applicable to the client-lawyer relationship, including Rule 1.6 and, in some cases, Rule 3.3.

144

Rule 8.2   Judicial and Legal Officials

(a) **A lawyer shall not make a statement that the lawyer knows to be false or with reckless disregard as to its truth or falsity concerning the qualifications or integrity of a judge, adjudicatory officer or public legal officer, or of a candidate for election or appointment to judicial or legal office.**

(b) **A lawyer who is a candidate for judicial office shall comply with the applicable provisions of the Code of Judicial Conduct.**

COMMENT

[1]   Assessments by lawyers are relied on in evaluating the professional or personal fitness of persons being considered for election or appointment to judicial office and to public legal offices, such as attorney general, prosecuting attorney and public defender. Expressing honest and candid opinions on such matters contributes to improving the administration of justice. Conversely, false statements by a lawyer can unfairly undermine public confidence in the administration of justice.

[2]   When a lawyer seeks judicial office, the lawyer should be bound by applicable limitations on political activity.

[3]   To maintain the fair and independent administration of justice, lawyers are encouraged to continue traditional efforts to defend judges and courts unjustly criticized.

Rule 8.3   Reporting Professional Misconduct

(a) **A lawyer ~~having knowledge~~ who knows that another lawyer has committed a violation of the Rules of Professional Conduct that raises a substantial question as to that lawyer's honesty, trustworthiness or fitness as a lawyer in other respects, shall inform the appropriate professional authority.**

(b) **A lawyer ~~having knowledge~~ who knows that a judge has committed a violation of applicable rules of judicial conduct that raises a substantial question as to the judge's fitness for office shall inform the appropriate authority.**

(c) **This Rule does not require disclosure of information otherwise protected by Rule 1.6 or information gained by a lawyer or judge while ~~serving as a member of~~ participating in an approved lawyers assistance program ~~to the extent that such information would be confidential if it were communicated subject to the attorney-client privilege.~~**

COMMENT

[1]   Self-regulation of the legal profession requires that members of the profession initiate disciplinary investigation when they know of a violation of the Rules of Professional Conduct. Lawyers have a similar obligation with respect to judicial misconduct. An apparently isolated

violation may indicate a pattern of misconduct that only a disciplinary investigation can uncover. Reporting a violation is especially important where the victim is unlikely to discover the offense.

[2]   A report about misconduct is not required where it would involve violation of Rule 1.6. However, a lawyer should encourage a client to consent to disclosure where prosecution would not substantially prejudice the client's interests.

[3]   If a lawyer were obliged to report every violation of the Rules, the failure to report any violation would itself be a professional offense. Such a requirement existed in many jurisdictions but proved to be unenforceable. This Rule limits the reporting obligation to those offenses that a self-regulating profession must vigorously endeavor to prevent. A measure of judgment is, therefore, required in complying with the provisions of this Rule. The term "substantial" refers to the seriousness of the possible offense and not the quantum of evidence of which the lawyer is aware. A report should be made to the bar disciplinary agency unless some other agency, such as a peer review agency, is more appropriate in the circumstances. Similar considerations apply to the reporting of judicial misconduct.

[4]   The duty to report professional misconduct does not apply to a lawyer retained to represent a lawyer whose professional conduct is in question. Such a situation is governed by the Rules applicable to the client-lawyer relationship.

[5]   Information about a lawyer's or judge's misconduct or fitness may be received by a lawyer in the course of that lawyer's participation in an approved lawyers or judges assistance program. In that circumstance, providing for ~~the confidentiality of such information~~ an exception to the reporting requirements of paragraphs (a) and (b) of this Rule encourages lawyers and judges to seek treatment through such a program. Conversely, without such ~~confidentiality~~ an exception, lawyers and judges may hesitate to seek assistance from these programs, which may then result in additional harm to their professional careers and additional injury to the welfare of clients and the public. ~~The Rule therefore exempts the lawyer from the reporting requirements of paragraphs (a) and (b) with respect to information that would be privileged if the relationship between the impaired lawyer or judge and the recipient of the information were that of a client and a lawyer. On the other hand, a lawyer who receives such information would nevertheless be required to comply with the Rule 8.3 reporting provisions to report misconduct if the impaired lawyer or judge indicates an intent to engage in illegal activity, for example, the conversion of client funds to his or her use.~~ These Rules do not otherwise address the confidentiality of information received by a lawyer or judge participating in an approved lawyers assistance program; such an obligation, however, may be imposed by the rules of the program or other law.

Rule 8.4 Misconduct

It is professional misconduct for a lawyer to:

(a) violate or attempt to violate the **Rules of Professional Conduct, knowingly assist or induce another to do so, or do so through the acts of another;**

(b) commit a criminal act that reflects adversely on the lawyer's honesty, trustworthiness or fitness as a lawyer in other respects;

(c) engage in conduct involving dishonesty, fraud, deceit or misrepresentation;

(d) engage in conduct that is prejudicial to the administration of justice;

(e) state or imply an ability to influence improperly a government agency or official **or to achieve results by means that violate the Rules of Professional Conduct or other law; or**

(f) knowingly assist a judge or judicial officer in conduct that is a violation of applicable rules of judicial conduct or other law.

COMMENT

[1] Lawyers are subject to discipline when they violate or attempt to violate the Rules of Professional Conduct, knowingly assist or induce another to do so or do so through the acts of another, as when they request or instruct an agent to do so on the lawyer's behalf. Paragraph (a), however, does not prohibit a lawyer from advising a client concerning action the client is legally entitled to take.

[1] [2] Many kinds of illegal conduct reflect adversely on fitness to practice law, such as offenses involving fraud and the offense of willful failure to file an income tax return. However, some kinds of offenses carry no such implication. Traditionally, the distinction was drawn in terms of offenses involving "moral turpitude." That concept can be construed to include offenses concerning some matters of personal morality, such as adultery and comparable offenses, that have no specific connection to fitness for the practice of law. Although a lawyer is personally answerable to the entire criminal law, a lawyer should be professionally answerable only for offenses that indicate lack of those characteristics relevant to law practice. Offenses involving violence, dishonesty, breach of trust, or serious interference with the administration of justice are in that category. A pattern of repeated offenses, even ones of minor significance when considered separately, can indicate indifference to legal obligation.

[2] [3] A lawyer who, in the course of representing a client, knowingly manifests by words or conduct, bias or prejudice based upon race, sex, religion, national origin, disability, age, sexual orientation or socioeconomic status, violates paragraph (d) when such actions are prejudicial to the administration of justice. Legitimate advocacy respect-

ing the foregoing factors does not violate paragraph (d). A trial judge's finding that peremptory challenges were exercised on a discriminatory basis does not alone establish a violation of this rule.

{3} [4] A lawyer may refuse to comply with an obligation imposed by law upon a good faith belief that no valid obligation exists. The provisions of Rule 1.2(d) concerning a good faith challenge to the validity, scope, meaning or application of the law apply to challenges of legal regulation of the practice of law.

{4} [5] Lawyers holding public office assume legal responsibilities going beyond those of other citizens. A lawyer's abuse of public office can suggest an inability to fulfill the professional role of lawyers. The same is true of abuse of positions of private trust such as trustee, executor, administrator, guardian, agent and officer, director or manager of a corporation or other organization.

RULE 8.5 Disciplinary Authority; Choice of Law*

(a) Disciplinary Authority. A lawyer admitted to practice in this jurisdiction is subject to the disciplinary authority of this jurisdiction, regardless of where the lawyer's conduct occurs. A lawyer may be subject to the disciplinary authority of both this jurisdiction and another jurisdiction where the lawyer is admitted for the same conduct.

(b) Choice of Law. In any exercise of the disciplinary authority of this jurisdiction, the rules of professional conduct to be applied shall be as follows:

(1) for conduct in connection with a proceeding in a court before which a lawyer has been admitted to practice (either generally or for purposes of that proceeding), the rules to be applied shall be the rules of the jurisdiction in which the court sits, unless the rules of the court provide otherwise; and

(2) for any other conduct,

(i) if the lawyer is licensed to practice only in this jurisdiction, the rules to be applied shall be the rules of this jurisdiction, and

(ii) if the lawyer is licensed to practice in this and another jurisdiction, the rules to be applied shall be the rules of the admitting jurisdiction in which the lawyer principally practices; provided, however, that if particular conduct clearly has its predominant effect in another jurisdiction in which the lawyer is licensed to practice,

---

* This rule along with Model Rule 5.5 will be reconsidered along with the final report of the Multijurisdictional Practice of Law Commission (MJP) possibly as early as August 2002.

the rules of that jurisdiction shall be applied to that conduct.

COMMENT

Disciplinary Authority

[1] Paragraph (a) restates longstanding law.

Choice of Law

[2] A lawyer may be potentially subject to more than one set of rules of professional conduct which impose different obligations. The lawyer may be licensed to practice in more than one jurisdiction with differing rules, or may be admitted to practice before a particular court with rules that differ from those of the jurisdiction or jurisdictions in which the lawyer is licensed to practice. In the past, decisions have not developed clear or consistent guidance as to which rules apply in such circumstances.

[3] Paragraph (b) seeks to resolve such potential conflicts. Its premise is that minimizing conflicts between rules, as well as uncertainty about which rules are applicable, is in the best interest of both clients and the profession (as well as the bodies having authority to regulate the profession). Accordingly, it takes the approach of (i) providing that any particular conduct of a lawyer shall be subject to only one set of rules of professional conduct, and (ii) making the determination of which set of rules applies to particular conduct as straightforward as possible, consistent with recognition of appropriate regulatory interests of relevant jurisdictions.

[4] Paragraph (b) provides that as to a lawyer's conduct relating to a proceeding in a court before which the lawyer is admitted to practice (either generally or pro hac vice), the lawyer shall be subject only to the rules of professional conduct of that court. As to all other conduct, paragraph (b) provides that a lawyer licensed to practice only in this jurisdiction shall be subject to the rules of professional conduct of this jurisdiction, and that a lawyer licensed in multiple jurisdictions shall be subject only to the rules of the jurisdiction where he or she (as an individual, not his or her firm) principally practices, but with one exception: if particular conduct clearly has its predominant effect in another admitting jurisdiction, then only the rules of that jurisdiction shall apply. The intention is for the latter exception to be a narrow one. It would be appropriately applied, for example, to a situation in which a lawyer admitted in, and principally practicing in, State A, but also admitted in State B, handled an acquisition by a company whose headquarters and operations were in State B of another, similar such company. The exception would not appropriately be applied, on the other hand, if the lawyer handled an acquisition by a company whose headquarters and operations were in State A of a company whose headquar-

ters and main operations were in State A, but which also had some operations in State B.

[5]   If two admitting jurisdictions were to proceed against a lawyer for the same conduct, they should, applying this rule, identify the same governing ethics rules. They should take all appropriate steps to see that they do apply the same rule to the same conduct, and in all events should avoid proceeding against a lawyer on the basis of two inconsistent rules.

[6]   The choice of law provision is not intended to apply to transnational practice. Choice of law in this context should be the subject of agreements between jurisdictions or of appropriate international law.

2001 VERSION OF THE AMERICAN BAR ASSOCIATION MODEL RULES OF PROFESSIONAL CONDUCT

Annotated to Reflect Amendments and Prior Text of the Model Rules in Footnotes.

Adopted August 1983, as Amended to February 2001.

NOTE: The 2001 version has been completely replaced by the 2002 version as of February 2002.

[Less than a decade after the Model Code of Professional Responsibility was promulgated in 1969, the ABA established a commission to create another code of ethics for the legal profession. Between 1977 to 1983 the Kutak Commission, named after its chairman Robert Kutak, proceeded to write several drafts of a new code of conduct for lawyers. In 1983, the ABA enacted the Model Rules of Professional Conduct based upon the work of the Kutak Commission. The Model Rules were a response to criticisms about the Model Code's focus on litigation and its three tier structure of canons, ethical considerations, and disciplinary rules. The Model Rules follow a UCC or restatement-like approach by placing the rule of professional responsibility in text and including elaborative material in the comments. Since its adoption in 1983, the ABA has amended the Model Rules several times, and thus this version of the Model Rules is annotated to indicate in footnotes the manner in which the ABA has amended the Model Rules since the original adoption in 1983. Although the current ABA version is important, the original version of the Model Rules is more likely to form the basis for the state adoptions of the Model Rules. When studying a case or an ethics opinion in the various states, one should examine whether the decision is based upon the current version of the Model Rules or a prior version. In several instances, the annotations include the text of a prior Kutak draft of the Model Rules to indicate a shift in the ABA position. Additionally, the comments to the Model Rules are numbered sequentially under each Model Rule provision to facilitate citation of a particular comment. Ed.]

CONTENTS

2001 ABA MODEL RULES

CLIENT–LAWYER RELATIONSHIP

COUNSELOR

ADVOCATE

TRANSACTIONS WITH PERSONS OTHER THAN CLIENTS

LAW FIRMS AND ASSOCIATIONS

PROFESSIONAL CONDUCT

PREAMBLE, SCOPE, AND TERMINOLOGY

Preamble: A Lawyer's Responsibilities

[1] A lawyer is a representative of clients, an officer of the legal system and a public citizen having special responsibility for the quality of justice.

[2] As a representative of clients, a lawyer performs various functions. As advisor, a lawyer provides a client with an informed understanding of the client's legal rights and obligations and explains their practical implications. As advocate, a lawyer zealously asserts the client's position under the rules of the adversary system. As negotiator, a lawyer seeks a result advantageous to the client but consistent with requirements of honest dealing with others. As intermediary between clients, a lawyer seeks to reconcile their divergent interests as an advisor and, to a limited extent, as a spokesperson for each client. A lawyer acts as evaluator by examining a client's legal affairs and reporting about them to the client or to others.

[3] In all professional functions a lawyer should be competent, prompt and diligent. A lawyer should maintain communication with a client concerning the representation. A lawyer should keep in confidence information relating to representation of a client except so far as disclosure is required or permitted by the Rules of Professional Conduct or other law.

[4] A lawyer's conduct should conform to the requirements of the law, both in professional service to clients and in the lawyer's business and personal affairs. A lawyer should use the law's procedures only for legitimate purposes and not to harass or intimidate others. A lawyer should demonstrate respect for the legal system and for those who serve it, including judges, other lawyers and public officials. While it is a lawyer's duty, when necessary, to challenge the rectitude of official action, it is also a lawyer's duty to uphold legal process.

[5] As a public citizen, a lawyer should seek improvement of the law, the administration of justice and the quality of service rendered by the legal profession. As a member of a learned profession, a lawyer should cultivate knowledge of the law beyond its use for clients, employ that knowledge in reform of the law and work to strengthen legal education. A lawyer should be mindful of deficiencies in the administration of justice and of the fact that the poor, and sometimes persons who are not poor, cannot afford adequate legal assistance, and should therefore devote professional time and civic influence in their behalf. A lawyer should aid the legal profession in pursuing these objectives and should help the bar regulate itself in the public interest.

[6] Many of a lawyer's professional responsibilities are prescribed in the Rules of Professional Conduct, as well as substantive and procedural law. However, a lawyer is also guided by personal conscience and the approbation of professional peers. A lawyer should strive to attain the highest level of skill, to improve the law and the legal profession and to exemplify the legal profession's ideals of public service.

[7] A lawyer's responsibilities as a representative of clients, an officer of the legal system and a public citizen are usually harmonious. Thus, when an opposing party is well represented, a lawyer can be a zealous advocate on behalf of a client and at the same time assume that justice is being done. So also, a lawyer can be sure that preserving client confidences ordinarily serves the public interest because people are more likely to seek legal advice, and thereby heed their legal obligations, when they know their communications will be private.

[8] In the nature of law practice, however, conflicting responsibilities are encountered. Virtually all difficult ethical problems arise from conflict between a lawyer's responsibilities to clients, to the legal system and to the lawyer's own interest in remaining an upright person while earning a satisfactory living. The Rules of Professional Conduct prescribe terms for resolving such conflicts. Within the framework of these Rules many difficult issues of professional discretion can arise. Such

issues must be resolved through the exercise of sensitive professional and moral judgment guided by the basic principles underlying the Rules.

[9] The legal profession is largely self-governing. Although other professions also have been granted powers of self-government, the legal profession is unique in this respect because of the close relationship between the profession and the processes of government and law enforcement. This connection is manifested in the fact that ultimate authority over the legal profession is vested largely in the courts.

[10] To the extent that lawyers meet the obligations of their professional calling, the occasion for government regulation is obviated. Self-regulation also helps maintain the legal profession's independence from government domination. An independent legal profession is an important force in preserving government under law, for abuse of legal authority is more readily challenged by a profession whose members are not dependent on government for the right to practice.

[11] The legal profession's relative autonomy carries with it special responsibilities of self-government. The profession has a responsibility to assure that its regulations are conceived in the public interest and not in furtherance of parochial or self-interested concerns of the bar. Every lawyer is responsible for observance of the Rules of Professional Conduct. A lawyer should also aid in securing their observance by other lawyers. Neglect of these responsibilities compromises the independence of the profession and the public interest which it serves.

[12] Lawyers play a vital role in the preservation of society. The fulfillment of this role requires an understanding by lawyers of their relationship to our legal system. The Rules of Professional Conduct, when properly applied, serve to define that relationship.

Scope

[1] The Rules of Professional Conduct are rules of reason. They should be interpreted with reference to the purposes of legal representation and of the law itself. Some of the Rules are imperatives, cast in the terms "shall" or "shall not." These define proper conduct for purposes of professional discipline. Others, generally cast in the term "may," are permissive and define areas under the Rules in which the lawyer has professional discretion. No disciplinary action should be taken when the lawyer chooses not to act or acts within the bounds of such discretion. Other Rules define the nature of relationships between the lawyer and others. The Rules are thus partly obligatory and disciplinary and partly constitutive and descriptive in that they define a lawyer's professional role. Many of the Comments use the term "should." Comments do not add obligations to the Rules but provide guidance for practicing in compliance with the Rules.

[2] The Rules presuppose a larger legal context shaping the lawyer's role. That context includes court rules and statutes relating to matters of licensure, laws defining specific obligations of lawyers and substantive and procedural law in general. Compliance with the Rules,

as with all law in an open society, depends primarily upon understanding and voluntary compliance, secondarily upon reinforcement by peer and public opinion and finally, when necessary, upon enforcement through disciplinary proceedings. The Rules do not, however, exhaust the moral and ethical considerations that should inform a lawyer, for no worthwhile human activity can be completely defined by legal rules. The Rules simply provide a framework for the ethical practice of law.

[3] Furthermore, for purposes of determining the lawyer's authority and responsibility, principles of substantive law external to these Rules determine whether a client-lawyer relationship exists. Most of the duties flowing from the client-lawyer relationship attach only after the client has requested the lawyer to render legal services and the lawyer has agreed to do so. But there are some duties, such as that of confidentiality under Rule 1.6, that may attach when the lawyer agrees to consider whether a client-lawyer relationship shall be established. Whether a client-lawyer relationship exists for any specific purpose can depend on the circumstances and may be a question of fact.

[4] Under various legal provisions, including constitutional, statutory and common law, the responsibilities of government lawyers may include authority concerning legal matters that ordinarily reposes in the client in private client-lawyer relationships. For example, a lawyer for a government agency may have authority on behalf of the government to decide upon settlement or whether to appeal from an adverse judgment. Such authority in various respects is generally vested in the attorney general and the state's attorney in state government, and their federal counterparts, and the same may be true of other government law officers. Also, lawyers under the supervision of these officers may be authorized to represent several government agencies in intragovernmental legal controversies in circumstances where a private lawyer could not represent multiple private clients. They also may have authority to represent the "public interest" in circumstances where a private lawyer would not be authorized to do so. These Rules do not abrogate any such authority.

[5] Failure to comply with an obligation or prohibition imposed by a Rule is a basis for invoking the disciplinary process. The Rules presuppose that disciplinary assessment of a lawyer's conduct will be made on the basis of the facts and circumstances as they existed at the time of the conduct in question and in recognition of the fact that a lawyer often has to act upon uncertain or incomplete evidence of the situation. Moreover, the Rules presuppose that whether or not discipline should be imposed for a violation, and the severity of a sanction, depend on all the circumstances, such as the willfulness and seriousness of the violation, extenuating factors and whether there have been previous violations.

[6] Violation of a Rule should not give rise to a cause of action nor should it create any presumption that a legal duty has been breached. The Rules are designed to provide guidance to lawyers and to provide a

structure for regulating conduct through disciplinary agencies. They are not designed to be a basis for civil liability. Furthermore, the purpose of the Rules can be subverted when they are invoked by opposing parties as procedural weapons. The fact that a Rule is a just basis for a lawyer's self-assessment, or for sanctioning a lawyer under the administration of a disciplinary authority, does not imply that an antagonist in a collateral proceeding or transaction has standing to seek enforcement of the Rule. Accordingly, nothing in the Rules should be deemed to augment any substantive legal duty of lawyers or the extra-disciplinary consequences of violating such a duty.

[7] Moreover, these Rules are not intended to govern or affect judicial application of either the attorney-client or work product privilege. Those privileges were developed to promote compliance with law and fairness in litigation. In reliance on the attorney-client privilege, clients are entitled to expect that communications within the scope of the privilege will be protected against compelled disclosure. The attorney-client privilege is that of the client and not of the lawyer. The fact that in exceptional situations the lawyer under the Rules has a limited discretion to disclose a client confidence does not vitiate the proposition that, as a general matter, the client has a reasonable expectation that information relating to the client will not be voluntarily disclosed and that disclosure of such information may be judicially compelled only in accordance with recognized exceptions to the attorney-client and work product privileges.

[8] The lawyer's exercise of discretion not to disclose information under Rule 1.6 should not be subject to reexamination. Permitting such reexamination would be incompatible with the general policy of promoting compliance with law through assurances that communications will be protected against disclosure.

[9] The Comment accompanying each Rule explains and illustrates the meaning and purpose of the Rule. The Preamble and this note on Scope provide general orientation. The Comments are intended as guides to interpretation, but the text of each Rule is authoritative. Research notes were prepared to compare counterparts in the ABA Model Code of Professional Responsibility (adopted 1969, as amended) and to provide selected references to other authorities. The notes have not been adopted, do not constitute part of the Model Rules, and are not intended to affect the application or interpretation of the Rules and Comments.

Terminology

[1] "Belief" or "Believes" denotes that the person involved actually supposed the fact in question to be true. A person's belief may be inferred from circumstances.

[2] "Consult" or "Consultation" denotes communication of information reasonably sufficient to permit the client to appreciate the significance of the matter in question.

[3] "Firm" or "Law firm" denotes a lawyer or lawyers in a private firm, lawyers employed in the legal department of a corporation or other organization and lawyers employed in a legal services organization. See Comment, Rule 1.10.

[4] "Fraud" or "Fraudulent" denotes conduct having a purpose to deceive and not merely negligent misrepresentation or failure to apprise another of relevant information.

[5] "Knowingly," "Known," or "Knows" denotes actual knowledge of the fact in question. A person's knowledge may be inferred from circumstances.

[6] "Partner" denotes a member of a partnership and a shareholder in a law firm organized as a professional corporation.

[7] "Reasonable" or "Reasonably" when used in relation to conduct by a lawyer denotes the conduct of a reasonably prudent and competent lawyer.

[8] "Reasonable belief" or "Reasonably believes" when used in reference to a lawyer denotes that the lawyer believes the matter in question and that the circumstances are such that the belief is reasonable.

[9] "Reasonably should know" when used in reference to a lawyer denotes that a lawyer of reasonable prudence and competence would ascertain the matter in question.

[10] "Substantial" when used in reference to degree or extent denotes a material matter of clear and weighty importance.

MODEL RULES OF PROFESSIONAL CONDUCT

CLIENT–LAWYER RELATIONSHIP

RULE 1.1   Competence

A Lawyer shall provide competent representation to a client. Competent representation requires the legal knowledge, skill, thoroughness and preparation reasonably necessary for the representation.

COMMENT:

Legal Knowledge and Skill

[1] In determining whether a lawyer employs the requisite knowledge and skill in a particular matter, relevant factors include the relative complexity and specialized nature of the matter, the lawyer's general experience, the lawyer's training and experience in the field in question, the preparation and study the lawyer is able to give the matter and whether it is feasible to refer the matter to, or associate or consult with, a lawyer of established competence in the field in question. In many instances, the required proficiency is that of a general practitioner.

Expertise in a particular field of law may be required in some circumstances.

[2] A lawyer need not necessarily have special training or prior experience to handle legal problems of a type with which the lawyer is unfamiliar. A newly admitted lawyer can be as competent as a practitioner with long experience. Some important legal skills, such as the analysis of precedent, the evaluation of evidence and legal drafting, are required in all legal problems. Perhaps the most fundamental legal skill consists of determining what kind of legal problems a situation may involve, a skill that necessarily transcends any particular specialized knowledge. A lawyer can provide adequate representation in a wholly novel field through necessary study. Competent representation can also be provided through the association of a lawyer of established competence in the field in question.

[3] In an emergency a lawyer may give advice or assistance in a matter in which the lawyer does not have the skill ordinarily required where referral to or consultation or association with another lawyer would be impractical. Even in an emergency, however, assistance should be limited to that reasonably necessary in the circumstances, for ill considered action under emergency conditions can jeopardize the client's interest.

[4] A lawyer may accept representation where the requisite level of competence can be achieved by reasonable preparation. This applies as well to a lawyer who is appointed as counsel for an unrepresented person. See also Rule 6.2.

Thoroughness and Preparation

[5] Competent handling of a particular matter includes inquiry into and analysis of the factual and legal elements of the problem, and use of methods and procedures meeting the standards of competent practitioners. It also includes adequate preparation. The required attention and preparation are determined in part by what is at stake; major litigation and complex transactions ordinarily require more elaborate treatment than matters of lesser consequence.

Maintaining Competence

[6] To maintain the requisite knowledge and skill, a lawyer should engage in continuing study and education. If a system of peer review has been established, the lawyer should consider making use of it in appropriate circumstances.

MODEL CODE COMPARISON:

DR 6–101(A)(1) provided that a lawyer shall not handle a matter "which he knows or should know that he is not competent to handle, without associating himself with a lawyer who is competent to handle it"; DR 6–101(A)(2) requires "preparation adequate in the circumstances." Rule 1.1 more fully particularizes the elements of competence. Whereas DR 6–101(A)(3) prohibited the "[N]eglect of a legal matter," Rule 1.1 does not contain such a prohibition. Instead, Rule 1.1 affirmatively requires the lawyer to be competent.

RULE 1.2 Scope of Representation

(a) A lawyer shall abide by a client's decisions concerning the objectives of representation, subject to paragraphs (c), (d) and (e), and shall consult with the client as to the means by which they are to be pursued. A lawyer shall abide by a client's decision whether to accept an offer of settlement of a matter. In a criminal case, the lawyer shall abide by the client's decision, after consultation with the lawyer, as to a plea to be entered, whether to waive jury trial and whether the client will testify.

(b) A lawyer's representation of a client, including representation by appointment, does not constitute an endorsement of the client's political, economic, social or moral views or activities.

(c) A lawyer may limit the objectives of the representation if the client consents after consultation.

(d) A lawyer shall not counsel a client to engage, or assist a client, in conduct that the lawyer knows is criminal or fraudulent, but a lawyer may discuss the legal consequences of any proposed course of conduct with a client and may counsel or assist a client to make a good faith effort to determine the validity, scope, meaning or application of the law.

(e) When a lawyer knows that a client expects assistance not permitted by the rules of professional conduct or other law, the lawyer shall consult with the client regarding the relevant limitations on the lawyer's conduct.

COMMENT:

Scope of Representation

[1] Both lawyer and client have authority and responsibility in the objectives and means of representation. The client has ultimate authority to determine the purposes to be served by legal representation, within the limits imposed by law and the lawyer's professional obligations. Within those limits, a client also has a right to consult with the lawyer about the means to be used in pursuing those objectives. At the same time, a lawyer is not required to pursue objectives or employ means simply because a client may wish that the lawyer do so. A clear distinction between objectives and means sometimes cannot be drawn, and in many cases the client-lawyer relationship partakes of a joint undertaking. In questions of means, the lawyer should assume responsibility for technical and legal tactical issues, but should defer to the client regarding such questions as the expense to be incurred and concern for

third persons who might be adversely affected. Law defining the lawyer's scope of authority in litigation varies among jurisdictions.

[2] In a case in which the client appears to be suffering mental disability, the lawyer's duty to abide by the client's decisions is to be guided by reference to Rule 1.14.

Independence from Client's Views or Activities

[3] Legal representation should not be denied to people who are unable to afford legal services, or whose cause is controversial or the subject of popular disapproval. By the same token, representing a client does not constitute approval of the client's views or activities.

Services Limited in Objectives or Means

[4] The objectives or scope of services provided by a lawyer may be limited by agreement with the client or by the terms under which the lawyer's services are made available to the client. For example, a retainer may be for a specifically defined purpose. Representation provided through a legal aid agency may be subject to limitations on the types of cases the agency handles. When a lawyer has been retained by an insurer to represent an insured, the representation may be limited to matters related to the insurance coverage. The terms upon which representation is undertaken may exclude specific objectives or means. Such limitations may exclude objectives or means that the lawyer regards as repugnant or imprudent.

[5] An agreement concerning the scope of representation must accord with the Rules of Professional Conduct and other law. Thus, the client may not be asked to agree to representation so limited in scope as to violate Rule 1.1, or to surrender the right to terminate the lawyer's services or the right to settle litigation that the lawyer might wish to continue.

Criminal, Fraudulent and Prohibited Transactions

[6] A lawyer is required to give an honest opinion about the actual consequences that appear likely to result from a client's conduct. The fact that a client uses advice in a course of action that is criminal or fraudulent does not, of itself, make a lawyer a party to the course of action. However, a lawyer may not knowingly assist a client in criminal or fraudulent conduct. There is a critical distinction between presenting an analysis of legal aspects of questionable conduct and recommending the means by which a crime or fraud might be committed with impunity.

[7] When the client's course of action has already begun and is continuing, the lawyer's responsibility is especially delicate. The lawyer is not permitted to reveal the client's wrongdoing, except where permitted by Rule 1.6. However, the lawyer is required to avoid furthering the purpose, for example, by suggesting how it might be concealed. A lawyer may not continue assisting a client in conduct that the lawyer

originally supposes is legally proper but then discovers is criminal or fraudulent. Withdrawal from the representation, therefore, may be required.

[8] Where the client is a fiduciary, the lawyer may be charged with special obligations in dealings with a beneficiary.

[9] Paragraph (d) applies whether or not the defrauded party is a party to the transaction. Hence, a lawyer should not participate in a sham transaction; for example, a transaction to effectuate criminal or fraudulent escape of tax liability. Paragraph (d) does not preclude undertaking a criminal defense incident to a general retainer for legal services to a lawful enterprise. The last clause of paragraph (d) recognizes that determining the validity or interpretation of a statute or regulation may require a course of action involving disobedience of the statute or regulation or of the interpretation placed upon it by governmental authorities.

MODEL CODE COMPARISON:

Paragraph (a) has no counterpart in the Disciplinary Rules of the Model Code. EC 7–7 stated: "In certain areas of legal representation not affecting the merits of the cause or substantially prejudicing the rights of a client, a lawyer is entitled to make decisions on his own. But otherwise the authority to make decisions is exclusively that of the client...." EC 7–8 stated that "[I]n the final analysis, however, the ... decision whether to forego legally available objectives or methods because of nonlegal factors is ultimately for the client.... In the event that the client in a nonadjudicatory matter insists upon a course of conduct that is contrary to the judgment and advice of the lawyer but not prohibited by Disciplinary Rules, the lawyer may withdraw from the employment." DR 7–101(A)(1) provided that a lawyer "shall not intentionally ... fail to seek the lawful objectives of his client through reasonably available means permitted by law.... A lawyer does not violate this Disciplinary Rule, however, by ... avoiding offensive tactics...."

Paragraph (b) has no counterpart in the Model Code.

With regard to paragraph (c), DR 7–101(B)(1) provided that a lawyer may, "where permissible, exercise his professional judgment to waive or fail to assert a right or position of his client."

With regard to paragraph (d), DR 7–102(A)(7) provided that a lawyer shall not "counsel or assist his client in conduct that the lawyer knows to be illegal or fraudulent." DR 7–102(A)(6) provided that a lawyer shall not "participate in the creation or preservation of evidence when he knows or it is obvious that the evidence is false." DR 7–106 provided that a lawyer shall not "advise his client to disregard a standing rule of a tribunal or a ruling of a tribunal ... but he may take appropriate steps in good faith to test the validity of such rule or ruling." EC 7–5 stated that a lawyer "should never encourage or aid his client to commit criminal acts or counsel his client on how to violate the law and avoid punishment therefor."

With regard to Rule 1.2(e), DR 2–110(C)(1)(c) provided that a lawyer may withdraw from representation if a client "insists" that the lawyer engage in "conduct that is illegal or that is prohibited under the Disciplinary Rules." DR 9–101(C) provided that "a lawyer shall not state or imply that he is able to influence improperly ... any tribunal, legislative body or public official."

RULE 1.3 Diligence

A lawyer shall act with reasonable diligence and promptness in representing a client.

COMMENT:

[1] A lawyer should pursue a matter on behalf of a client despite opposition, obstruction or personal inconvenience to the lawyer, and may take whatever lawful and ethical measures are required to vindicate a client's cause or endeavor. A lawyer should act with commitment and dedication to the interests of the client and with zeal in advocacy upon the client's behalf. However, a lawyer is not bound to press for every advantage that might be realized for a client. A lawyer has professional discretion in determining the means by which a matter should be pursued. See Rule 1.2. A lawyer's workload should be controlled so that each matter can be handled adequately.

[2] Perhaps no professional shortcoming is more widely resented than procrastination. A client's interests often can be adversely affected by the passage of time or the change of conditions; in extreme instances, as when a lawyer overlooks a statute of limitations, the client's legal position may be destroyed. Even when the client's interests are not affected in substance, however, unreasonable delay can cause a client needless anxiety and undermine confidence in the lawyer's trustworthiness.

[3] Unless the relationship is terminated as provided in Rule 1.16, a lawyer should carry through to conclusion all matters undertaken for a client. If a lawyer's employment is limited to a specific matter, the relationship terminates when the matter has been resolved. If a lawyer has served a client over a substantial period in a variety of matters, the client sometimes may assume that the lawyer will continue to serve on a continuing basis unless the lawyer gives notice of withdrawal. Doubt about whether a client-lawyer relationship still exists should be clarified by the lawyer, preferably in writing, so that the client will not mistakenly suppose the lawyer is looking after the client's affairs when the lawyer has ceased to do so. For example, if a lawyer has handled a judicial or administrative proceeding that produced a result adverse to the client but has not been specifically instructed concerning pursuit of an appeal,

the lawyer should advise the client of the possibility of appeal before relinquishing responsibility for the matter.

MODEL CODE COMPARISON:

DR 6–101(A)(3) required that a lawyer not "[n]eglect a legal matter entrusted to him." EC 6–4 stated that a lawyer should "give appropriate attention to his legal work." Canon 7 stated that "a lawyer should represent a client zealously within the bounds of the law." DR 7–101(A)(1) provided that a lawyer "shall not intentionally . . . fail to seek the lawful objectives of his client through reasonably available means permitted by law and the Disciplinary Rules. . . ." DR 7–101(A)(3) provided that a lawyer "shall not intentionally . . . [p]rejudice or damage his client during the course of the relationship. . . ."

RULE 1.4   Communication

(a) A lawyer shall keep a client reasonably informed about the status of a matter and promptly comply with reasonable requests for information.

(b) A lawyer shall explain a matter to the extent reasonably necessary to permit the client to make informed decisions regarding the representation.

COMMENT:

[1] The client should have sufficient information to participate intelligently in decisions concerning the objectives of the representation and the means by which they are to be pursued, to the extent the client is willing and able to do so. For example, a lawyer negotiating on behalf of a client should provide the client with facts relevant to the matter, inform the client of communications from another party and take other reasonable steps that permit the client to make a decision regarding a serious offer from another party. A lawyer who receives from opposing counsel an offer of settlement in a civil controversy or a proffered plea bargain in a criminal case should promptly inform the client of its substance unless prior discussions with the client have left it clear that the proposal will be unacceptable. See Rule 1.2(a). Even when a client delegates authority to the lawyer, the client should be kept advised of the status of the matter.

[2] Adequacy of communication depends in part on the kind of advice or assistance involved. For example, in negotiations where there is time to explain a proposal the lawyer should review all important provisions with the client before proceeding to an agreement. In litigation a lawyer should explain the general strategy and prospects of success and ordinarily should consult the client on tactics that might injure or coerce others. On the other hand, a lawyer ordinarily cannot be expected to describe trial or negotiation strategy in detail. The guiding principle is that the lawyer should fulfill reasonable client

expectations for information consistent with the duty to act in the client's best interests, and the client's overall requirements as to the character of representation.

[3] Ordinarily, the information to be provided is that appropriate for a client who is a comprehending and responsible adult. However, fully informing the client according to this standard may be impracticable, for example, where the client is a child or suffers from mental disability. See Rule 1.14. When the client is an organization or group, it is often impossible or inappropriate to inform every one of its members about its legal affairs; ordinarily, the lawyer should address communications to the appropriate officials of the organization. See Rule 1.13. Where many routine matters are involved, a system of limited or occasional reporting may be arranged with the client. Practical exigency may also require a lawyer to act for a client without prior consultation.

Withholding Information

[4] In some circumstances, a lawyer may be justified in delaying transmission of information when the client would be likely to react imprudently to an immediate communication. Thus, a lawyer might withhold a psychiatric diagnosis of a client when the examining psychiatrist indicates that disclosure would harm the client. A lawyer may not withhold information to serve the lawyer's own interest or convenience. Rules or court orders governing litigation may provide that information supplied to a lawyer may not be disclosed to the client. Rule 3.4(c) directs compliance with such rules or orders.

MODEL CODE COMPARISON:

Rule 1.4 has no direct counterpart in the Disciplinary Rules of the Model Code. DR 6–101(A)(3) provided that a lawyer shall not "[n]eglect a legal matter entrusted to him." DR 9–102(B)(1) provided that a lawyer shall "[p]romptly notify a client of the receipt of his funds, securities, or other properties." EC 7–8 stated that a lawyer "should exert his best efforts to insure that decisions of his client are made only after the client has been informed of relevant considerations." EC 9–2 stated that "a lawyer should fully and promptly inform his client of material developments in the matters being handled for the client."

RULE 1.5 Fees

(a) **A lawyer's fee shall be reasonable. The factors to be considered in determining the reasonableness of a fee include the following:**

(1) **the time and labor required, the novelty and difficulty of the questions involved, and the skill requisite to perform the legal service properly;**

(2) the likelihood, if apparent to the client, that the acceptance of the particular employment will preclude other employment by the lawyer;

(3) the fee customarily charged in the locality for similar legal services;

(4) the amount involved and the results obtained;

(5) the time limitations imposed by the client or by the circumstances;

(6) the nature and length of the professional relationship with the client;

(7) the experience, reputation, and ability of the lawyer or lawyers performing the services; and

(8) whether the fee is fixed or contingent.

(b) When the lawyer has not regularly represented the client, the basis or rate of the fee shall be communicated to the client, preferably in writing, before or within a reasonable time after commencing the representation.

(c) A fee may be contingent on the outcome of the matter for which the service is rendered, except in a matter in which a contingent fee is prohibited by paragraph (d) or other law. A contingent fee agreement shall be in writing and shall state the method by which the fee is to be determined, including the percentage or percentages that shall accrue to the lawyer in the event of settlement, trial or appeal, litigation and other expenses to be deducted from the recovery, and whether such expenses are to be deducted before or after the contingent fee is calculated. Upon conclusion of a contingent fee matter, the lawyer shall provide the client with a written statement stating the outcome of the matter and, if there is a recovery, showing the remittance to the client and the method of its determination.

(d) A lawyer shall not enter into an arrangement for, charge, or collect:

(1) any fee in a domestic relations matter, the payment or amount of which is contingent upon the securing of a divorce or upon the amount of alimony or support, or property settlement in lieu thereof; or

(2) a contingent fee for representing a defendant in a criminal case.

(e) A division of fee between lawyers who are not in the same firm may be made only if:

(1) the division is in proportion to the services performed by each lawyer or, by written agreement with the

client, each lawyer assumes joint responsibility for the representation;

(2) the client is advised of and does not object to the participation of all the lawyers involved; and

(3) the total fee is reasonable.

COMMENT:

Basis or Rate of Fee

[1] When the lawyer has regularly represented a client, they ordinarily will have evolved an understanding concerning the basis or rate of the fee. In a new client-lawyer relationship, however, an understanding as to the fee should be promptly established. It is not necessary to recite all the factors that underlie the basis of the fee, but only those that are directly involved in its computation. It is sufficient, for example, to state that the basic rate is an hourly charge or a fixed amount or an estimated amount, or to identify the factors that may be taken into account in finally fixing the fee. When developments occur during the representation that render an earlier estimate substantially inaccurate, a revised estimate should be provided to the client. A written statement concerning the fee reduces the possibility of misunderstanding. Furnishing the client with a simple memorandum or a copy of the lawyer's customary fee schedule is sufficient if the basis or rate of the fee is set forth.

Terms of Payment

[2] A lawyer may require advance payment of a fee, but is obliged to return any unearned portion. See Rule 1.16(d). A lawyer may accept property in payment for services, such as an ownership interest in an enterprise, providing this does not involve acquisition of a proprietary interest in the cause of action or subject matter of the litigation contrary to Rule 1.8(j).* However, a fee paid in property instead of money may be subject to special scrutiny because it involves questions concerning both the value of the services and the lawyer's special knowledge of the value of the property.

[3] An agreement may not be made whose terms might induce the lawyer improperly to curtail services for the client or perform them in a way contrary to the client's interest. For example, a lawyer should not enter into an agreement whereby services are to be provided only up to a stated amount when it is foreseeable that more extensive services probably will be required, unless the situation is adequately explained to the client. Otherwise, the client might have to bargain for further assistance in the midst of a proceeding or transaction. However, it is

---

* In 1987, the ABA added the following clause to the 1983 version of the Model Rules: "providing this does not involve acquisition of a proprietary interest in the cause of action or subject matter of the litigation contrary to Rule 1.8(j)."

proper to define the extent of services in light of the client's ability to pay. A lawyer should not exploit a fee arrangement based primarily on hourly charges by using wasteful procedures. When there is doubt whether a contingent fee is consistent with the client's best interest, the lawyer should offer the client alternative bases for the fee and explain their implications. Applicable law may impose limitations on contingent fees, such as a ceiling on the percentage.

Division of Fee

[4] A division of fee is a single billing to a client covering the fee of two or more lawyers who are not in the same firm. A division of fee facilitates association of more than one lawyer in a matter in which neither alone could serve the client as well, and most often is used when the fee is contingent and the division is between a referring lawyer and a trial specialist. Paragraph (e) permits the lawyers to divide a fee on either the basis of the proportion of services they render or by agreement between the participating lawyers if all assume responsibility for the representation as a whole and the client is advised and does not object. It does not require disclosure to the client of the share that each lawyer is to receive. Joint responsibility for the representation entails the obligations stated in Rule 5.1 for purposes of the matter involved.

Disputes Over Fees

[5] If a procedure has been established for resolution of fee disputes, such as an arbitration or mediation procedure established by the bar, the lawyer should conscientiously consider submitting to it. Law may prescribe a procedure for determining a lawyer's fee, for example, in representation of an executor or administrator, a class or a person entitled to a reasonable fee as part of the measure of damages. The lawyer entitled to such a fee and a lawyer representing another party concerned with the fee should comply with the prescribed procedure.

MODEL CODE COMPARISON:

DR 2–106(A) provided that a lawyer "shall not enter into an agreement for, charge, or collect an illegal or clearly excessive fee." DR 2–106(B) provided that a fee is "clearly excessive when, after a review of the facts, a lawyer of ordinary prudence would be left with a definite and firm conviction that the fee is in excess of a reasonable fee." The factors of a reasonable fee in Rule 1.5(a) are substantially identical to those listed in DR 2–106(B). EC 2–17 states that a lawyer "should not charge more than a reasonable fee...."

There was no counterpart to Rule 1.5(b) in the Disciplinary Rules of the Model Code. EC 2–19 stated that it is "usually beneficial to reduce to writing the understanding of the parties regarding the fee, particularly when it is contingent."

There was no counterpart to paragraph (c) in the Disciplinary Rules of the Model Code. EC 2–20 provided that "[c]ontingent fee arrangements in civil cases have long been commonly accepted in the United States," but that "a lawyer generally should decline to accept employment on a contingent fee basis by one who is able to pay a reasonable fixed fee. . . . "

With regard to paragraph (d), DR 2–106(C) prohibited "a contingent fee in a criminal case." EC 2–20 provided that "contingent fee arrangements in domestic relation cases are rarely justified."

With regard to paragraph (e), DR 2–107(A) permitted division of fees only if: "(1) The client consents to employment of the other lawyer after a full disclosure that a division of fees will be made. (2) The division is in proportion to the services performed and responsibility assumed by each. (3) The total fee does not exceed clearly reasonable compensation. . . . " Paragraph (e) permits division without regard to the services rendered by each lawyer if they assume joint responsibility for the representation.

RULE 1.6 Confidentiality of Information*

(a) A lawyer shall not reveal information relating to representation of a client unless the client consents after consultation, except for disclosures that are impliedly authorized in order to carry out the representation, and except as stated in paragraph (b).

(b) A lawyer may reveal such information to the extent the lawyer reasonably believes necessary:

(1) to prevent the client from committing a criminal act that the lawyer believes is likely to result in imminent death or substantial bodily harm; or

* In 1991, The ABA House of Delegates rejected the ethics committee recommendation that it modify Model Rule 1.6. The rejected language would have inserted the following exception to the general rule of confidentiality under Model Rule 1.6(b): "to rectify the consequences of a client's criminal or fraudulent act in the furtherance of which the lawyer's services had been used." This language is identical to an exception listed in the Kutak Commission's 1982 Final Revised Draft of Model Rule 1.6. The proposed Kutak Rule 1.6(b) would have contained the following exceptions:

(1) to prevent the client from committing a criminal or fraudulent act that the lawyer reasonably believes is likely to result in death or substantial bodily harm, or in substantial injury to the financial interests or property of another;

(2) to rectify the consequences of a client's criminal or fraudulent act in the furtherance of which the lawyer's financial services had been used;

(3) to establish a claim or defense on behalf of the lawyer in a controversy between the lawyer and the client, or to establish a defense to a criminal charge, civil claim or disciplinary complaint against the lawyer based upon conduct in which the client was involved; or

(4) to comply with other law.

Proposed Model Rule 1.6(b) (Revised Final Draft) (June 20, 1982).

(2) to establish a claim or defense on behalf of the lawyer in a controversy between the lawyer and the client, to establish a defense to a criminal charge or civil claim against the lawyer based upon conduct in which the client was involved, or to respond to allegations in any proceeding concerning the lawyer's representation of the client.

COMMENT:

[1] The lawyer is part of a judicial system charged with upholding the law. One of the lawyer's functions is to advise clients so that they avoid any violation of the law in the proper exercise of their rights.

[2] The observance of the ethical obligation of a lawyer to hold inviolate confidential information of the client not only facilitates the full development of facts essential to proper representation of the client but also encourages people to seek early legal assistance.

[3] Almost without exception, clients come to lawyers in order to determine what their rights are and what is, in the maze of laws and regulations, deemed to be legal and correct. The common law recognizes that the client's confidences must be protected from disclosure. Based upon experience, lawyers know that almost all clients follow the advice given, and the law is upheld.

[4] A fundamental principle in the client-lawyer relationship is that the lawyer maintain confidentiality of information relating to the representation. The client is thereby encouraged to communicate fully and frankly with the lawyer even as to embarrassing or legally damaging subject matter.

[5] The principle of confidentiality is given effect in two related bodies of law, the attorney-client privilege (which includes the work product doctrine) in the law of evidence and the rule of confidentiality established in professional ethics. The attorney-client privilege applies in judicial and other proceedings in which a lawyer may be called as a witness or otherwise required to produce evidence concerning a client. The rule of client-lawyer confidentiality applies in situations other than those where evidence is sought from the lawyer through compulsion of law. The confidentiality rule applies not merely to matters communicated in confidence by the client but also to all information relating to the representation, whatever its source. A lawyer may not disclose such information except as authorized or required by the Rules of Professional Conduct or other law. See also Scope.

[6] The requirement of maintaining confidentiality of information relating to representation applies to government lawyers who may disagree with the policy goals that their representation is designed to advance.

Authorized Disclosure

[7] A lawyer is impliedly authorized to make disclosures about a client when appropriate in carrying out the representation, except to the

extent that the client's instructions or special circumstances limit that authority. In litigation, for example, a lawyer may disclose information by admitting a fact that cannot properly be disputed, or in negotiation by making a disclosure that facilitates a satisfactory conclusion.

[8] Lawyers in a firm may, in the course of the firm's practice, disclose to each other information relating to a client of the firm, unless the client has instructed that particular information be confined to specified lawyers.

Disclosure Adverse to Client

[9] The confidentiality rule is subject to limited exceptions. In becoming privy to information about a client, a lawyer may foresee that the client intends serious harm to another person. However, to the extent a lawyer is required or permitted to disclose a client's purposes, the client will be inhibited from revealing facts which would enable the lawyer to counsel against a wrongful course of action. The public is better protected if full and open communication by the client is encouraged than if it is inhibited.

Several situations must be distinguished.

[10] First, the lawyer may not counsel or assist a client in conduct that is criminal or fraudulent. See Rule 1.2(d). Similarly, a lawyer has a duty under Rule 3.3(a)(4) not to use false evidence. This duty is essentially a special instance of the duty prescribed in Rule 1.2(d) to avoid assisting a client in criminal or fraudulent conduct.

[11] Second, the lawyer may have been innocently involved in past conduct by the client that was criminal or fraudulent. In such a situation the lawyer has not violated Rule 1.2(d), because to "counsel or assist" criminal or fraudulent conduct requires knowing that the conduct is of that character.

[12] Third, the lawyer may learn that a client intends prospective conduct that is criminal and likely to result in imminent death or substantial bodily harm. As stated in paragraph (b)(1), the lawyer has professional discretion to reveal information in order to prevent such consequences. The lawyer may make a disclosure in order to prevent homicide or serious bodily injury which the lawyer reasonable believes is intended by a client. It is very difficult for a lawyer to "know" when such a heinous purpose will actually be carried out, for the client may have a change of mind.

[13] The lawyer's exercise of discretion requires consideration of such factors as the nature of the lawyer's relationship with the client and with those who might be injured by the client, the lawyer's own involvement in the transaction and factors that may extenuate the conduct in question. Where practical, the lawyer should seek to persuade the client to take suitable action. In any case, a disclosure adverse to the client's interest should be no greater than the lawyer reasonably believes necessary to the purpose. A lawyer's decision not to

take preventive action permitted by paragraph (b)(1) does not violate this Rule.

Withdrawal

[14]   If the lawyer's services will be used by the client in materially furthering a course of criminal or fraudulent conduct, the lawyer must withdraw, as stated in Rule 1.16(a)(1).

[15]   After withdrawal the lawyer is required to refrain from making disclosure of the clients' confidences, except as otherwise provided in Rule 1.6.   Neither this Rule nor Rule 1.8(b) nor Rule 1.16(d) prevents the lawyer from giving notice of the fact of withdrawal, and the lawyer may also withdraw or disaffirm any opinion, document, affirmation, or the like.

[16]   Where the client is an organization, the lawyer may be in doubt whether contemplated conduct will actually be carried out by the organization.   Where necessary to guide conduct in connection with this Rule, the lawyer may make inquiry within the organization as indicated in Rule 1.13(b).

Dispute Concerning Lawyer's Conduct

[17]   Where a legal claim or disciplinary charge alleges complicity of the lawyer in a client's conduct or other misconduct of the lawyer involving representation of the client, the lawyer may respond to the extent the lawyer reasonably believes necessary to establish a defense. The same is true with respect to a claim involving the conduct or representation of a former client.   The lawyer's right to respond arises when an assertion of such complicity has been made.   Paragraph (b)(2) does not require the lawyer to await the commencement of an action or proceeding that charges such complicity, so that the defense may be established by responding directly to a third party who has made such an assertion.   The right to defend, of course, applies where a proceeding has been commenced.   Where practicable and not prejudicial to the lawyer's ability to establish the defense, the lawyer should advise the client of the third party's assertion and request that the client respond appropriately. In any event, disclosure should be no greater than the lawyer reasonably believes is necessary to vindicate innocence, the disclosure should be made in a manner which limits access to the information to the tribunal or other persons having a need to know it, and appropriate protective orders or other arrangements should be sought by the lawyer to the fullest extent practicable.

[18]   If the lawyer is charged with wrongdoing in which the client's conduct is implicated, the rule of confidentiality should not prevent the lawyer from defending against the charge.   Such a charge can arise in a civil, criminal or professional disciplinary proceeding, and can be based on a wrong allegedly committed by the lawyer against the client, or on a wrong alleged by a third person; for example, a person claiming to have

been defrauded by the lawyer and client acting together. A lawyer entitled to a fee is permitted by paragraph (b)(2) to prove the services rendered in an action to collect it. This aspect of the rule expresses the principle that the beneficiary of a fiduciary relationship may not exploit it to the detriment of the fiduciary. As stated above, the lawyer must make every effort practicable to avoid unnecessary disclosure of information relating to a representation, to limit disclosure to those having the need to know it, and to obtain protective orders or make other arrangements minimizing the risk of disclosure.

Disclosures Otherwise Required or Authorized

[19] The attorney-client privilege is differently defined in various jurisdictions. If a lawyer is called as a witness to give testimony concerning a client, absent waiver by the client, Rule 1.6(a) requires the lawyer to invoke the privilege when it is applicable. The lawyer must comply with the final orders of a court or other tribunal of competent jurisdiction requiring the lawyer to give information about the client.

[20] The Rules of Professional Conduct in various circumstances permit or require a lawyer to disclose information relating to the representation. See Rules 2.2, 2.3, 3.3 and 4.1. In addition to these provisions, a lawyer may be obligated or permitted by other provisions of law to give information about a client. Whether another provision of law supersedes Rule 1.6 is a matter of interpretation beyond the scope of these Rules, but a presumption should exist against such a supersession.

Former Client

[21] The duty of confidentiality continues after the client-lawyer relationship has terminated.

MODEL CODE COMPARISON:

Rule 1.6 eliminates the two-pronged duty under the Model Code in favor of a single standard protecting all information about a client "relating to the representation." Under DR 4–101, the requirement applied only to information protected by the attorney-client privilege and to information "gained in" the professional relationship that "the client has requested be held inviolate or the disclosure of which would be embarrassing or would be likely to be detrimental to the client." EC 4–4 added that the duty differed from the evidentiary privilege in that it existed "without regard to the nature or source of information or the fact that others share the knowledge." Rule 1.6 imposes confidentiality on information relating to the representation even if it is acquired before or after the relationship existed. It does not require the client to indicate information that is to be confidential, or permit the lawyer to speculate whether particular information might be embarrassing or detrimental.

Paragraph (a) permits a lawyer to disclose information where impliedly authorized to do so in order to carry out the representation. Under DR 4–101(B) and (C), a lawyer was not permitted to reveal "confidences" unless the client first consented after disclosure.

Paragraph (b) redefines the exceptions to the requirement of confidentiality. Regarding paragraph (b)(1), DR 4–101(C)(3) provided that a lawyer "may reveal ... [t]he intention of his client to commit a crime and the information necessary to prevent the crime." This option existed regardless of the seriousness of the proposed crime.

With regard to paragraph (b)(2), DR 4–101(C)(4) provided that a lawyer may reveal "[c]onfidences or secrets necessary to establish or collect his fee or to defend himself or his employers or associates against an accusation of wrongful conduct." Paragraph (b)(2) enlarges the exception to include disclosure of information relating to claims by the lawyer other than for the lawyer's fee; for example, recovery of property from the client.

RULE 1.7   Conflict of Interest: General Rule

(a) A lawyer shall not represent a client if the representation of that client will be directly adverse to another client, unless:

(1) the lawyer reasonably believes the representation will not adversely affect the relationship with the other client; and

(2) each client consents after consultation.

(b) A lawyer shall not represent a client if the representation of that client may be materially limited by the lawyer's responsibilities to another client or to a third person, or by the lawyer's own interests, unless:

(1) the lawyer reasonably believes the representation will not be adversely affected; and

(2) the client consents after consultation. When representation of multiple clients in a single matter is undertaken, the consultation shall include explanation of the implications of the common representation and the advantages and risks involved.

COMMENT:

Loyalty to a Client

[1]   Loyalty is an essential element in the lawyer's relationship to a client. An impermissible conflict of interest may exist before representation is undertaken, in which event the representation should be declined. The lawyer should adopt reasonable procedures, appropriate for the size and type of firm and practice, to determine in both litigation and non-

litigation matters the parties and issues involved and to determine whether there are actual or potential conflicts of interest.*

[2]   If such a conflict arises after representation has been undertaken, the lawyer should withdraw from the representation. See Rule 1.16. Where more than one client is involved and the lawyer withdraws because a conflict arises after representation, whether the lawyer may continue to represent any of the clients is determined by Rule 1.9. See also Rule 2.2(c). As to whether a client-lawyer relationship exists or, having once been established, is continuing, see Comment to Rule 1.3 and Scope.

[3]   As a general proposition, loyalty to a client prohibits undertaking representation directly adverse to that client without that client's consent. Paragraph (a) expresses that general rule. Thus, a lawyer ordinarily may not act as advocate against a person the lawyer represents in some other matter, even if it is wholly unrelated. On the other hand, simultaneous representation in unrelated matters of clients whose interests are only generally adverse, such as competing economic enterprises, does not require consent of the respective clients. Paragraph (a) applies only when the representation of one client would be directly adverse to the other.

[4]   Loyalty to a client is also impaired when a lawyer cannot consider, recommend or carry out an appropriate course of action for the client because of the lawyer's other responsibilities or interests. The conflict in effect forecloses alternatives that would otherwise be available to the client. Paragraph (b) addresses such situations. A possible conflict does not itself preclude the representation. The critical questions are the likelihood that a conflict will eventuate and, if it does, whether it will materially interfere with the lawyer's independent professional judgment in considering alternatives or foreclose courses of action that reasonably should be pursued on behalf of the client. Consideration should be given to whether the client wishes to accommodate the other interest involved.

Consultation and Consent

[5]   A client may consent to representation notwithstanding a conflict. However, as indicated in paragraph (a)(1) with respect to representation directly adverse to a client, and paragraph (b)(1) with respect to material limitations on representation of a client, when a disinterested lawyer would conclude that the client should not agree to the representation under the circumstances, the lawyer involved cannot properly ask for such agreement or provide representation on the basis of the client's consent. When more than once client is involved, the question of conflict must be resolved as to each client. Moreover, there

---

* The ABA added this sentence in the comments to the Model Rules in 1987. The remainder of paragraph 1 in the original version of this comment now appears in the current paragraph 2.

may be circumstances where it is impossible to make the disclosure necessary to obtain consent. For example, when the lawyer represents different clients in related matters and one of the clients refuses to consent to the disclosure necessary to permit the other client to make an informed decision, the lawyer cannot properly ask the latter to consent.

Lawyer's Interests

[6] The lawyer's own interests should not be permitted to have adverse effect on representation of a client. For example, a lawyer's need for income should not lead the lawyer to undertake matters that cannot be handled competently and at a reasonable fee. See Rules 1.1 and 1.5. If the probity of a lawyer's own conduct in a transaction is in serious question, it may be difficult or impossible for the lawyer to give a client detached advice. A lawyer may not allow related business interests to affect representation, for example, by referring clients to an enterprise in which the lawyer has an undisclosed interest.

Conflicts in Litigation

[7] Paragraph (a) prohibits representation of opposing parties in litigation. Simultaneous representation of parties whose interests in litigation may conflict, such as co-plaintiffs or co-defendants, is governed by paragraph (b). An impermissible conflict may exist by reason of substantial discrepancy in the parties' testimony, incompatibility in positions in relation to an opposing party or the fact that there are substantially different possibilities of settlement of the claims or liabilities in question. Such conflicts can arise in criminal cases as well as civil. The potential for conflict of interest in representing multiple defendants in a criminal case is so grave that ordinarily a lawyer should decline to represent more than one codefendant. On the other hand, common representation of persons having similar interests is proper if the risk of adverse effect is minimal and the requirements of paragraph (b) are met. Compare Rule 2.2 involving intermediation between clients.

[8] Ordinarily, a lawyer may not act as advocate against a client the lawyer represents in some other matter, even if the other matter is wholly unrelated. However, there are circumstances in which a lawyer may act as advocate against a client. For example, a lawyer representing an enterprise with diverse operations may accept employment as an advocate against the enterprise in an unrelated matter if doing so will not adversely affect the lawyer's relationship with the enterprise or conduct of the suit and if both clients consent upon consultation. By the same token, government lawyers in some circumstances may represent government employees in proceedings in which a government agency is the opposing party. The propriety of concurrent representation can depend on the nature of the litigation. For example, a suit charging fraud entails conflict to a degree not involved in a suit for a declaratory judgment concerning statutory interpretation.

[9] A lawyer may represent parties having antagonistic positions on a legal question that has arisen in different cases, unless representation of either client would be adversely affected. Thus, it is ordinarily not improper to assert such positions in cases pending in different trial courts, but it may be improper to do so in cases pending at the same time in an appellate court.

Interest of Person Paying for a Lawyer's Service

[10] A lawyer may be paid from a source other than the client, if the client is informed of that fact and consents and the arrangement does not compromise the lawyer's duty of loyalty to the client. See Rule 1.8(f). For example, when an insurer and its insured have conflicting interests in a matter arising from a liability insurance agreement, and the insurer is required to provide special counsel for the insured, the arrangement should assure the special counsel's professional independence. So also, when a corporation and its directors or employees are involved in a controversy in which they have conflicting interests, the corporation may provide funds for separate legal representation of the directors or employees, if the clients consent after consultation and the arrangement ensures the lawyer's professional independence.

Other Conflict Situations

[11] Conflicts of interest in contexts other than litigation sometimes may be difficult to assess. Relevant factors in determining whether there is potential for adverse effect include the duration and intimacy of the lawyer's relationship with the client or clients involved, the functions being performed by the lawyer, the likelihood that actual conflict will arise and the likely prejudice to the client from the conflict if it does arise. The question is often one of proximity and degree.

[12] For example, a lawyer may not represent multiple parties to a negotiation whose interests are fundamentally antagonistic to each other, but common representation is permissible where the clients are generally aligned in interest even though there is some difference of interest among them.

[13] Conflict questions may also arise in estate planning and estate administration. A lawyer may be called upon to prepare wills for several family members, such as husband and wife, and, depending upon the circumstances, a conflict of interest may arise. In estate administration the identity of the client may be unclear under the law of a particular jurisdiction. Under one view, the client is the fiduciary; under another view the client is the estate or trust, including its beneficiaries. The lawyer should make clear the relationship to the parties involved.

[14] A lawyer for a corporation or other organization who is also a member of its board of directors should determine whether the responsibilities of the two roles may conflict. The lawyer may be called on to advise the corporation in matters involving actions of the directors.

Consideration should be given to the frequency with which such situations may arise, the potential intensity of the conflict, the effect of the lawyer's resignation from the board and the possibility of the corporation's obtaining legal advice from another lawyer in such situations. If there is material risk that the dual role will compromise the lawyer's independence of professional judgment, the lawyer should not serve as a director.

Conflict Charged by an Opposing Party

[15] Resolving questions of conflict of interest is primarily the responsibility of the lawyer undertaking the representation. In litigation, a court may raise the question when there is reason to infer that the lawyer has neglected the responsibility. In a criminal case, inquiry by the court is generally required when a lawyer represents multiple defendants. Where the conflict is such as clearly to call in question the fair or efficient administration of justice, opposing counsel may properly raise the question. Such an objection should be viewed with caution, however, for it can be misused as a technique of harassment. See Scope.

MODEL CODE COMPARISON:

DR 5–101(A) provided that "[e]xcept with the consent of his client after full disclosure, a lawyer shall not accept employment if the exercise of his professional judgment on behalf of the client will be or reasonably may be affected by his own financial, business, property, or personal interests." DR 5–105(A) provided that a lawyer "shall decline proffered employment if the exercise of his independent professional judgment in behalf of a client will be or is likely to be adversely affected by the acceptance of the proffered employment, or if it would be likely to involve him in representing differing interests, except to the extent permitted under DR 5–105(C)." DR 5–105(C) provided that "a lawyer may represent multiple clients if it is obvious that he can adequately represent the interest of each and if each consents to the representation after full disclosure of the possible effect of such representation on the exercise of his independent professional judgment on behalf of each." DR 5–107(B) provided that a lawyer "shall not permit a person who recommends, employs, or pays him to render legal services for another to direct or regulate his professional judgment in rendering such services."

Rule 1.7 clarifies DR 5–105(A) by requiring that, when the lawyer's other interests are involved, not only must the client consent after consultation but also that, independent of such consent, the representation reasonably appears not to be adversely affected by the lawyer's other interests. This requirement appears to be the intended meaning of the provision in DR 5–105(C) that "it is obvious that he can adequately represent" the client, and was implicit in EC 5–2, which stated that a lawyer "should not accept proffered employment if his personal interests or desires will, or there is a reasonable probability that they will, affect adversely the advice to be given or services to be rendered the prospective client."

RULE 1.8 Conflict of Interest: Prohibited Transactions

(a) A lawyer shall not enter into a business transaction with a client or knowingly acquire an ownership, possessory, security or other pecuniary interest adverse to a client unless:

(1) the transaction and terms on which the lawyer acquires the interest are fair and reasonable to the client and are fully disclosed and transmitted in writing to the client in a manner which can be reasonably understood by the client;

(2) the client is given a reasonable opportunity to seek the advice of independent counsel in the transaction; and

(3) the client consents in writing thereto.

(b) A lawyer shall not use information relating to representation of a client to the disadvantage of the client unless the client consents after consultation, except as permitted or required by Rule 1.6 or Rule 3.3.

(c) A lawyer shall not prepare an instrument giving the lawyer or a person related to the lawyer as parent, child, sibling, or spouse any substantial gift from a client, including a testamentary gift, except where the client is related to the donee.

(d) Prior to the conclusion of representation of a client, a lawyer shall not make or negotiate an agreement giving the lawyer literary or media rights to a portrayal or account based in substantial part on information relating to the representation.

(e) A lawyer shall not provide financial assistance to a client in connection with pending or contemplated litigation, except that:

(1) a lawyer may advance court costs and expenses of litigation, the repayment of which may be contingent on the outcome of the matter; and

(2) a lawyer representing an indigent client may pay court costs and expenses of litigation on behalf of the client.

(f) A lawyer shall not accept compensation for representing a client from one other than the client unless:

(1) the client consents after consultation;

(2) there is no interference with the lawyer's independence of professional judgment or with the client–lawyer relationship; and

(3) Information relating to representation of a client is protected as required by rule 1.6.

(g) A lawyer who represents two or more clients shall not participate in making an aggregate settlement of the claims of or against the clients, or in a criminal case an aggregated agreement as to guilty or nolo contendere pleas, unless each client consents after consultation, including disclosure of the existence and nature of all the claims or pleas involved and of the participation of each person in the settlement.

(h) A lawyer shall not make an agreement prospectively limiting the lawyer's liability to a client for malpractice unless permitted by law and the client is independently represented in making the agreement, or settle a claim for such liability with an unrepresented client or former client without first advising that person in writing that independent representation is appropriate in connection therewith.

(i) A lawyer related to another lawyer as parent, child, sibling or spouse shall not represent a client in a representation directly adverse to a person who the lawyer knows is represented by the other lawyer except upon consent by the client after consultation regarding the relationship.

(j) A lawyer shall not acquire a proprietary interest in the cause of action or subject matter of litigation the lawyer is conducting for a client, except that the lawyer may:

> (1) acquire a lien granted by law to secure the lawyer's fee or expenses; and

> (2) contract with a client for a reasonable contingent fee in a civil case.

COMMENT:

Transactions Between Client and Lawyer

[1] As a general principle, all transactions between client and lawyer should be fair and reasonable to the client. In such transactions a review by independent counsel on behalf of the client is often advisable. Furthermore, a lawyer may not exploit information relating to the representation to the client's disadvantage. For example, a lawyer who has learned that the client is investing in specific real estate may not, without the client's consent, seek to acquire nearby property where doing so would adversely affect the client's plan for investment. Paragraph (a) does not, however, apply to standard commercial transactions between the lawyer and the client for products or services that the client generally markets to others, for example, banking or brokerage services, medical services, products manufactured or distributed by the client, and utilities services. In such transactions, the lawyer has no advantage in dealing with the client, and the restrictions in paragraph (a) are unnecessary and impracticable.

[2] A lawyer may accept a gift from a client, if the transaction meets general standards of fairness. For example, a simple gift such as

a present given at a holiday or as a token of appreciation is permitted. If effectuation of a substantial gift requires preparing a legal instrument such as a will or conveyance, however, the client should have the detached advice that another lawyer can provide. Paragraph (c) recognizes an exception where the client is a relative of the donee or the gift is not substantial.

Literary Rights

[3] An agreement by which a lawyer acquires literary or media rights concerning the conduct of the representation creates a conflict between the interests of the client and the personal interests of the lawyer. Measures suitable in the representation of the client may detract from the publication value of an account of the representation. Paragraph (d) does not prohibit a lawyer representing a client in a transaction concerning literary property from agreeing that the lawyer's fee shall consist of a share in ownership in the property, if the arrangement conforms to Rule 1.5 and paragraph (j).

Person Paying for Lawyer's Services

[4] Rule 1.8(f) requires disclosure of the fact that the lawyer's services are being paid for by a third party. Such an arrangement must also conform to the requirements of Rule 1.6 concerning confidentiality and Rule 1.7 concerning conflict of interest. Where the client is a class, consent may be obtained on behalf of the class by court-supervised procedure.

Family Relationships Between Lawyers

[5] Rule 1.8(i) applies to related lawyers who are in different firms. Related lawyers in the same firm are governed by Rules 1.7, 1.9, and 1.10. The disqualification stated in Rule 1.8(i) is personal and is not imputed to members of firms with whom the lawyers are associated.

Acquisition of Interest in Litigation

[6] Paragraph (j) states the traditional general rule that lawyers are prohibited from acquiring a proprietary interest in litigation. This general rule, which has its basis in common law champerty and maintenance, is subject to specific exceptions developed in decisional law and continued in these Rules, such as the exception for reasonable contingent fees set forth in Rule 1.5 and the exception for certain advances of the costs of litigation set forth in paragraph (e).

[7] This Rule is not intended to apply to customary qualification and limitations in legal opinions and memoranda.

MODEL CODE COMPARISON:

With regard to paragraph (a), DR 5–104(A) provided that a lawyer "shall not enter into a business transaction with a client if they have differing interests therein and if the client expects the lawyer to exercise his professional judgment therein for the protection of the client, unless the client has consented after full disclosure." EC 5–3 stated that a lawyer "should not seek to persuade his client to permit him to invest in an undertaking of his client nor make improper use of his professional relationship to influence his client to invest in an enterprise in which the lawyer is interested."

With regard to paragraph (b), DR 4–101(B)(3) provided that a lawyer should not use "a confidence or secret of his client for the advantage of himself, or of a third person, unless the client consents after full disclosure."

There was no counterpart to paragraph (c) in the Disciplinary Rules of the Model Code. EC 5–5 stated that a lawyer "should not suggest to his client that a gift be made to himself or for his benefit. If a lawyer accepts a gift from his client, he is peculiarly susceptible to the charge that he unduly influenced or overreached the client. If a client voluntarily offers to make a gift to his lawyer, the lawyer may accept the gift, but before doing so, he should urge that the client secure disinterested advice from an independent, competent person who is cognizant of all the circumstances. Other than in exceptional circumstances, a lawyer should insist that an instrument in which his client desires to name him beneficially be prepared by another lawyer selected by the client."

Paragraph (d) is substantially similar to DR 5–104(B), but refers to "literary or media" rights, a more generally inclusive term than "publication" rights.

Paragraph (e)(1) is similar to DR 5–103(B), but eliminates the requirement that "the client remains ultimately liable for such expenses."

Paragraph (e)(2) has no counterpart in the Model Code.

Paragraph (f) is substantially identical to DR 5–107(A)(1).

Paragraph (g) is substantially identical to DR 5–106.

The first clause of paragraph (h) is similar to DR 6–102(A). There was no counterpart in the Model Code to the second clause of paragraph (h).

Paragraph (i) has no counterpart in the Model Code.

Paragraph (j) is substantially identical to DR 5–103(A).

RULE 1.9 Conflict of Interest: Former Client *

(a) A lawyer who has formerly represented a client in a matter shall not thereafter represent another person in the

---

* In 1989, the ABA amended Model Rule 1.9 by moving some of the text in original Model Rule 1.10(b) into current Model Rule 1.9(b). The original Model Rule 1.9(b) was moved to Model Rule 1.9(c). The impetus behind this change was to clarify an overlap between Model Rule 1.9 and 1.10 and to address the question of duties to former clients when a lawyer changes firms and did not represent the former client but may have acquired confidential information about a former client of the old firm. The same or a substantially related matter in which that person's interests are materially adverse to the interests of the former client unless the former client consents after consultation.

(b) A lawyer shall not knowingly represent a person in the same or a substantially related matter in which a firm with which the lawyer formerly was associated had previously represented a client,

(1) whose interests are materially adverse to that person; and

(2) about whom the lawyer had acquired information protected by Rules 1.6 and 1.9(c) that is material to the matter;

unless the former client consents after consultation.

(c) A lawyer who has formerly represented a client in a matter or whose present or former firm has formerly represented a client in a matter shall not thereafter:

(1) use information relating to the representation to the disadvantage of the former client except as Rule 1.6 or Rule 3.3 would permit or require with respect to a client, or when the information has become generally known; or

(2) reveal information relating to the representation except as Rule 1.6 or Rule 3.3 would permit or require with respect to a client.

COMMENT:

[1]   After termination of a client-lawyer relationship, a lawyer may not represent another client except in conformity with this Rule. The principles in Rule 1.7 determine whether the interests of the present and former client are adverse. Thus, a lawyer could not properly seek to rescind on behalf of a new client a contract drafted on behalf of the former client. So also a lawyer who has prosecuted an accused person could not properly represent the accused in a subsequent civil action against the government concerning the same transaction.

[2]   The scope of a "matter" for purposes of this Rule may depend on the facts of a particular situation or transaction. The lawyer's

following represents Model Rule 1.9 as adopted in 1983:

RULE 1.9   Conflict of Interest: Former Client

A Lawyer who has formerly represented a client in a matter shall not thereafter:

(a) Represent another person in the same or a substantially related matter in which that person's interests are materially adverse to the interests of the former client unless the former client consents after consultation; or

(b) Use information relating to the representation to the disadvantage of the former client except as Rule 1.6 would permit with respect to a client or when the information has become generally known.

involvement in a matter can also be a question of degree. When a lawyer has been directly involved in a specific transaction, subsequent representation of other clients with materially adverse interests clearly is prohibited. On the other hand, a lawyer who recurrently handled a type of problem for a former client is not precluded from later representing another client in a wholly distinct problem of that type even though the subsequent representation involves a position adverse to the prior client. Similar considerations can apply to the reassignment of military lawyers between defense and prosecution functions within the same military jurisdiction. The underlying question is whether the lawyer was so involved in the matter that the subsequent representation can be justly regarded as a changing of sides in the matter in question.

*Lawyers Moving Between Firms**

[3]   When lawyers have been associated within a firm but then end their association, the question of whether a lawyer should undertake representation is more complicated. There are several competing considerations. First, the client previously represented by the former firm must be reasonably assured that the principle of loyalty to the client is not compromised. Second, the rule should not be so broadly cast as to preclude other persons from having reasonable choice of legal counsel. Third, the rule should not unreasonably hamper lawyers from forming new associations and taking on new clients after having left a previous association. In this connection, it should be recognized that today many lawyers practice in firms, that many lawyers to some degree limit their practice to one field or another, and that many move from one association to another several times in their careers. If the concept of imputation were applied with unqualified rigor, the result would be radical curtailment of the opportunity of lawyers to move from one practice setting to another and of the opportunity of clients to change counsel.

[4]   Reconciliation of these competing principles in the past has been attempted under two rubrics. One approach has been to seek per se rules of disqualification. For example, it has been held that a partner in a law firm is conclusively presumed to have access to all confidences concerning all clients of the firm. Under this analysis, if a lawyer has been a partner in one law firm and then becomes a partner in another law firm, there may be a presumption that all confidences known by the partner in the first firm are known to all partners in the second firm. This presumption might properly be applied in some circumstances, especially where the client has been extensively represented, but may be unrealistic where the client was represented only for limited purposes. Furthermore, such a rigid rule exaggerates the difference between a partner and an associate in modern law firms.

* The comments under this topic originally appeared under Model Rule 1.10. With the modification of Model Rule 1.9, the ABA moved these comments under Model Rule 1.9 without significant change.

[5] The other rubric formerly used for dealing with disqualification is the appearance of impropriety proscribed in Canon 9 of the ABA Model Code of Professional Responsibility. This rubric has a two fold problem. First, the appearance of impropriety can be taken to include any new client-lawyer relationship that might make a former client feel anxious. If that meaning were adopted, disqualification would become little more than a question of subjective judgment by the former client. Second, since "impropriety" is undefined, the term "appearance of impropriety" is question-begging. It therefore has to be recognized that the problem of disqualification cannot be properly resolved either by simple analogy to a lawyer practicing alone or by the very general concept of appearance of impropriety.

Confidentiality*

[6] Preserving confidentiality is a question of access to information. Access to information, in turn, is essentially a question of fact in particular circumstances, aided by inferences, deductions or working presumptions that reasonably may be made about the way in which lawyers work together. A lawyer may have general access to files of all clients of a law firm and may regularly participate in discussions of their affairs; it should be inferred that such a lawyer in fact is privy to all information about all the firm's clients. In contrast, another lawyer may have access to the files of only a limited number of clients and participate in discussions of the affairs of no other clients; in the absence of information to the contrary, it should be inferred that such a lawyer in fact is privy to information about the clients actually served but not those of other clients.

[7] Application of paragraph (b) depends on a situation's particular facts. In such an inquiry, the burden of proof should rest upon the firm whose disqualification is sought.

[8] Paragraph (b) operates to disqualify the lawyer only when the lawyer involved has actual knowledge of information protected by Rules 1.6 and 1.9(b). Thus, if a lawyer while with one firm acquired no knowledge or information relating to a particular client of the firm, and that lawyer later joined another firm, neither the lawyer individually nor the second firm is disqualified from representing another client in the same or a related matter even though the interests of the two clients conflict. See Rule 1.10(b) for the restrictions on a firm once a lawyer has terminated association with the firm.

[9] Independent of the question of disqualification of a firm, a lawyer changing professional association has a continuing duty to preserve confidentiality of information about a client formerly represented. See Rules 1.6 and 1.9.

---

* The comments under this topic originally appeared under Model Rule 1.10. With the modification of Model Rule 1.9, the ABA moved these comments under Model Rule 1.9 without significant change.

*Adverse Positions**

[10] The second aspect of loyalty to a client is the lawyer's obligation to decline subsequent representations involving positions adverse to a former client arising in substantially related matters. This obligation requires abstention from adverse representation by the individual lawyer involved, but does not properly entail abstention of other lawyers through imputed disqualification. Hence, this aspect of the problem is governed by Rule 1.9(a). Thus, if a lawyer left one firm for another, the new affiliation would not preclude the firms involved from continuing to represent clients with adverse interests in the same or related matters, so long as the conditions of paragraphs (b) and (c) concerning confidentiality have been met.

[11] Information acquired by the lawyer in the course of representing a client may not subsequently be used or revealed by the lawyer to the disadvantage of the client. However, the fact that a lawyer has once served a client does not preclude the lawyer from using generally known information about that client when later representing another client.

[12] Disqualification from subsequent representation is for the protection of former clients and can be waived by them. A waiver is effective only if there is disclosure of the circumstances, including the lawyer's intended role in behalf of the new client.

[13] With regard to an opposing party's raising a question of conflict of interest, see Comment to Rule 1.7. With regard to disqualification of a firm with which a lawyer is or was formerly associated, see Rule 1.10.

MODEL CODE COMPARISON: **

There was no counterpart to this Rule in the Disciplinary Rules of the Model Code. Representation adverse to a former client was sometimes dealt with under the rubric of Canon 9 of the Model Code, which provided: "A lawyer should avoid even the appearance of impropriety." Also applicable were EC 4–6 which stated that the "obligation of a lawyer to preserve the confidences and secrets of his client continues after the termination of his employment" and Canon 5 which stated that "[a] lawyer should exercise independent professional judgment on behalf of a client."

The provision in paragraph (a) for waiver by the former client is similar to DR 5–105(C).

The exception in the last clause of paragraph (c)(1) permits a lawyer to use information relating to a former client that is in the "public

---

** When ABA modified Model Rule 1.9 in 1989, it did not change the text of the Model Code Comparison. Thus, the current Model Code Comparison only refers to the Model Rule 1.9 as originally enacted. To understand the amended Model Rule 1.9, one must read the following text quoted from the Code Comparison to Model Rule 1.10: "DR 5–105(D) provided that '[i]f a lawyer is required to decline or to withdraw from employment under a Disciplinary Rule, no partner, or associate, or any other lawyer affiliated with him or his firm, may accept or continue such employment.' "

domain," a use that was also not prohibited by the Model Code, which protected only "confidences and secrets." Since the scope of paragraph (a) is much broader than "confidences and secrets," it is necessary to define when a lawyer may make use of information about a client after the client-lawyer relationship has terminated.

RULE 1.10 Imputed Disqualification: General Rule***

(a) While lawyers are associated in a firm, none of them shall knowingly represent a client when any one of them practicing alone would be prohibited from doing so by Rules 1.7, 1.8(c), 1.9 or 2.2.

(b) When a lawyer has terminated an association with a firm, the firm is not prohibited from thereafter representing a person with interests materially adverse to those of a client represented by the formerly associated lawyer and not currently represented by the firm, unless:

(1) the matter is the same or substantially related to that in which the formerly associated lawyer represented the client; and

*** In 1989, the ABA amended Model Rule 1.10 to remove original Rule 1.10(b) and move it to Model Rule 1.9(b). The ABA thus renumbered original Model Rule 1.10(c) and 1.10(d) as new Model Rule 1.10(b) and 1.10(c). The impetus behind this change was to clarify an overlap between Model Rule 1.9 and 1.10 and to address the question of duties to former clients when a lawyer changes firms and did not represent the former client but may have acquired confidential information about a former client of the old firm. Also, the ABA added the words "and, not currently represented by the firm" to current Model Rule 1.10(b). This was added to clarify the problem that when a lawyer leaves a firm, Model Rule 1.7's general prohibition of a directly adverse conflict still applies to the situation. The original version of Model Rule 1.10 is reproduced below:

RULE 1.10 Imputed Disqualification: General Rule

(a) While lawyers are associated in a firm, none of them shall knowingly represent a client when any one of them practicing alone would be prohibited from doing so by Rules 1.7, 1.8(c), 1.9 or 2.2.

(b) When a lawyer becomes associated with a firm, the firm may not knowingly represent a person in the same or a substantially related matter in which that lawyer, or a firm with which the lawyer was associated, had previously represented a client whose interests are materially adverse to that person and about whom the lawyer had acquired information protected by Rules 1.6 and 1.9(b) that is material to the matter.

(c) When a lawyer has terminated an association with a firm, the firm is not prohibited from thereafter representing a person with interests materially adverse to those of a client represented by the formerly associated lawyer unless:

(1) the matter is the same or substantially related to that in which the formerly associated lawyer represented the client; and

(2) any lawyer remaining in the firm has information protected by Rules 1.6 and 1.9(b) that is material to the matter.

(d) A disqualification prescribed by this rule may be waived by the affected client under the conditions stated in Rule 1.7.

(2) any lawyer remaining in the firm has information protected by Rules 1.6 and 1.9(c) that is material to the matter.

(c) A disqualification prescribed by this rule may be waived by the affected client under the conditions stated in Rule 1.7.

COMMENT: *

Definition of "Firm"

[1] For purposes of the Rules of Professional Conduct, the term "firm" includes lawyers in a private firm, and lawyers in the legal

---

* When the ABA amended Model Rule 1.10 in 1989, it moved several paragraphs of comments from Model Rule 1.10 to Model Rule 1.9. The paragraphs which appeared in the original version of the Model Rules are reproduced below:

Lawyers Moving Between Firms

When lawyers have been associated in a firm but then end their association, however, the problem is more complicated. The fiction that the law firm is the same as a single lawyer is no longer wholly realistic. There are several competing considerations. First, the client previously represented must be reasonably assured that the principle of loyalty to the client is not compromised. Second, the rule of disqualification should not be so broadly cast as to preclude other persons from having reasonable choice of legal counsel. Third, the rule of disqualification should not unreasonably hamper lawyers from forming new associations and taking on new clients after having left a previous association. In this connection, it should be recognized that today many lawyers practice in firms, that many to some degree limit their practice to one field or another, and that many move from one association to another several times in their careers. If the concept of imputed disqualification were defined with unqualified rigor, the result would be radical curtailment of the opportunity of lawyers to move from one practice setting to another and of the opportunity of clients to change counsel.

Reconciliation of these competing principles in the past has been attempted under two rubrics. One approach has been to seek per se rules of disqualifica-

tion. For example, it has been held that a partner in a law firm is conclusively presumed to have access to all confidences concerning all clients of the firm. Under this analysis, if a lawyer has been a partner in one law firm and then becomes a partner in another law firm, there is a presumption that all confidences known by a partner in the first firm are known to all partners in the second firm. This presumption might properly be applied in some circumstances, especially where the client has been extensively represented, but may be unrealistic where the client was represented only for limited purposes. Furthermore, such a rigid rule exaggerates the difference between a partner and an associate in modern law firms.

The other rubric formerly used for dealing with vicarious disqualification is the appearance of impropriety proscribed in Canon 9 of the ABA Model Code of Professional Responsibility. This rubric has a twofold problem. First, the appearance of impropriety can be taken to include any new client-lawyer relationship that might make a former client feel anxious. If that meaning were adopted, disqualification would become little more than a question of subjective judgment by the former client. Second, since "impropriety" is undefined, the term "appearance of impropriety" is question-begging. It therefore has to be recognized that the problem of imputed disqualification cannot be properly resolved either by simple analogy to a lawyer practicing alone or by the very general concept of appearance of impropriety.

A rule based on a functional analysis is more appropriate for determining the department of a corporation or other organization, or in a legal services organization. Whether two or more lawyers constitute a firm within this definition can depend on the specific facts. For example, two practitioners who share office space and occasionally consult or assist each other ordinarily would not be regarded as constituting a firm. However, if they present themselves to the public in a way suggesting that they are a firm or conduct themselves as a firm, they should be regarded as a firm for the purposes of the Rules. The terms of any formal agreement between associated lawyers are relevant in determining whether they are a firm, as is the fact that they have mutual access to information concerning the clients they serve. Furthermore, it is relevant in doubtful cases to consider the underlying purpose of the Rule that is involved. A group of lawyers could be regarded as a firm for purposes of the rule that the same lawyer should not represent opposing

question of vicarious disqualification. Two functions are involved: preserving confidentiality and avoiding positions adverse to a client.

Confidentiality

Preserving confidentiality is a question of access to information. Access to information, in turn, is essentially a question of fact in particular circumstances, aided by inferences, deductions or working presumptions that reasonably may be made about the way in which lawyers work together. A lawyer may have general access to files of all clients of a law firm and may regularly participate in discussions of their affairs; it should be inferred that such a lawyer in fact is privy to all information about all the firm's clients. In contrast, another lawyer may have access to the files of only a limited number of clients and participate in discussion of the affairs of no other clients; in the absence of information to the contrary, it should be inferred that such a lawyer in fact is privy to information about the clients actually served but not those of other clients.

Application of paragraphs (b) and (c) depends on a situation's particular facts. In any such inquiry, the burden of proof should rest upon the firm whose disqualification is sought.

Paragraphs (b) and (c) operate to disqualify the firm only when the lawyer involved has actual knowledge of information protected by Rules 1.6 and 1.9(b). Thus, if a lawyer while with one firm acquired no knowledge of information relating to a particular client of the firm, and that lawyer later joined another firm, neither the lawyer individually nor the second firm is disqualified from representing another client in the same or a related matter even though the interests of the two clients conflict.

Independent of the question of disqualification of a firm, a lawyer changing professional association has a continuing duty to preserve confidentiality of information about a client formerly represented. See Rules 1.6 and 1.9.

Adverse Positions

The second aspect of loyalty to client is the lawyer's obligation to decline subsequent representations involving positions adverse to a former client arising in substantially related matters. This obligation requires abstention from adverse representation by the individual lawyer involved, but does not properly entail abstention of other lawyers through imputed disqualification. Hence, this aspect of the problem is governed by Rule 1.9(a). Thus, if a lawyer left one firm for another, the new affiliation would not preclude the firms involved from continuing to represent clients with adverse interests in the same or related matters, so long as the conditions of Rule 1.10(b) and (c) concerning confidentiality have been met.

parties in litigation, while it might not be so regarded for purposes of the rule that information acquired by one lawyer is attributed to the other.

[2]   With respect to the law department of an organization, there is ordinarily no question that the members of the department constitute a firm within the meaning of the Rules of Professional Conduct. However, there can be uncertainty as to the identity of the client. For example, it may not be clear whether the law department of a corporation represents a subsidiary or an affiliated corporation, as well as the corporation by which the members of the department are directly employed. A similar question can arise concerning an unincorporated association and its local affiliates.

[3]   Similar questions can also arise with respect to lawyers in legal aid. Lawyers employed in the same unit of a legal service organization constitute a firm, but not necessarily those employed in separate units. As in the case of independent practitioners, whether the lawyers should be treated as associated with each other can depend on the particular rule that is involved, and on the specific facts of the situation.

[4]   Where a lawyer has joined a private firm after having represented the government, the situation is governed by Rule 1.11(a) and (b); where a lawyer represents the government after having served private clients, the situation is governed by Rule 1.11(c)(1). The individual lawyer involved is bound by the Rules generally, including Rules 1.6, 1.7 and 1.9.

[5]   Different provisions are thus made for movement of a lawyer from one private firm to another and for movement of a lawyer between a private firm and the government. The government is entitled to protection of its client confidences and, therefore, to the protections provided in Rules 1.6, 1.9 and 1.11. However, if the more extensive disqualification in Rule 1.10 were applied to former government lawyers, the potential effect on the government would be unduly burdensome. The government deals with all private citizens and organizations and, thus, has a much wider circle of adverse legal interests than does any private law firm. In these circumstances, the government's recruitment of lawyers would be seriously impaired if Rule 1.10 were applied to the government. On balance, therefore, the government is better served in the long run by the protections stated in Rule 1.11.

Principles of Imputed Disqualification

[6]   The rule of imputed disqualification stated in paragraph (a) gives effect to the principle of loyalty to the client as it applies to lawyers who practice in a law firm. Such situations can be considered from the premise that a firm of lawyers is essentially one lawyer for purposes of the rules governing loyalty to the client, or from the premise that each lawyer is vicariously bound by the obligation of loyalty owed by each lawyer with whom the lawyer is associated. Paragraph (a) operates only among the lawyers currently associated in a firm. When a lawyer moves

from one firm to another, the situation is governed by Rules 1.9(b) and 1.10(b).

[7] * Rule 1.10(b) operates to permit a law firm, under certain circumstances, to represent a person with interests directly adverse to those of a client represented by a lawyer who formerly was associated with the firm. The Rule applies regardless of when the formerly associated lawyer represented the client. However, the law firm may not represent a person with interests adverse to those of a present client of the firm, which would violate Rule 1.7. Moreover, the firm may not represent the person where the matter is the same or substantially related to that in which the formerly associated lawyer represented the client and any other lawyer currently in the firm has material information protected by Rules 1.6 and 1.9(c).

MODEL CODE COMPARISON:

DR 5–105(D) provided that "[i]f a lawyer is required to decline or to withdraw from employment under a Disciplinary Rule, no partner, or associate, or any other lawyer affiliated with him or his firm, may accept or continue such employment."

RULE 1.11 Successive Government and Private Employment

(a) **Except as law may otherwise expressly permit, a lawyer shall not represent a private client in connection with a matter in which the lawyer participated personally and substantially as a public officer or employee, unless the appropriate government agency consents after consultation. No lawyer in a firm with which that lawyer is associated may knowingly undertake or continue representation in such a matter unless:**

(1) **the disqualified lawyer is screened from any participation in the matter and is apportioned no part of the fee therefrom; and**

(2) **written notice is promptly given to the appropriate government agency to enable it to ascertain compliance with the provisions of this rule.**

(b) **Except as law may otherwise expressly permit, a lawyer having information that the lawyer knows is confidential government information about a person acquired when the lawyer was a public officer or employee, may not represent a private client whose interests are adverse to that person in a matter in which the information could be used to the material disadvantage of that person. A firm with which that lawyer is associated may undertake or continue representation in the matter only if**

---

* The ABA added this entire paragraph to the comments to Model Rule 1.10 in 1989. Thus, this language does not appear in the original version of the Model Rules.

the disqualified lawyer is screened from any participation in the matter and is apportioned no part of the fee therefrom.

(c) Except as law may otherwise expressly permit, a lawyer serving as a public officer or employee shall not:

(1) participate in a matter in which the lawyer participated personally and substantially while in private practice or nongovernmental employment, unless under applicable law no one is, or by lawful delegation may be, authorized to act in the lawyer's stead in the matter; or

(2) negotiate for private employment with any person who is involved as a party or as attorney for a party in a matter in which the lawyer is participating personally and substantially, except that a lawyer serving as a law clerk to a judge, other adjudicative officer or arbitrator may negotiate for private employment as permitted by Rule 1.12(b) and subject to the conditions stated in Rule 1.12(b).

(d) As used in this rule, the term "matter" includes:

(1) any judicial or other proceeding, application, request for a ruling or other determination, contract, claim, controversy, investigation, charge, accusation, arrest or other particular matter involving a specific party or parties; and

(2) any other matter covered by the conflict of interest rules of the appropriate government agency.

(e) As used in this rule, the term "confidential government information" means information which has been obtained under governmental authority and which, at the time this rule is applied, the government is prohibited by law from disclosing to the public or has a legal privilege not to disclose, and which is not otherwise available to the public.

COMMENT:

[1] This Rule prevents a lawyer from exploiting public office for the advantage of a private client. It is a counterpart of Rule 1.10(b), which applies to lawyers moving from one firm to another.

[2] A lawyer representing a government agency, whether employed or specially retained by the government, is subject to the Rules of Professional Conduct, including the prohibition against representing adverse interests stated in Rule 1.7 and the protections afforded former clients in Rule 1.9. In addition, such a lawyer is subject to Rule 1.11 and to statutes and government regulations regarding conflict of interest. Such statutes and regulations may circumscribe the extent to which the government agency may give consent under this Rule.

[3] Where the successive clients are a public agency and a private client, the risk exists that power or discretion vested in public authority might be used for the special benefit of a private client. A lawyer should

not be in a position where benefit to a private client might affect performance of the lawyer's professional functions on behalf of public authority. Also, unfair advantage could accrue to the private client by reason of access to confidential government information about the client's adversary obtainable only through the lawyer's government service. However, the rules governing lawyers presently or formerly employed by a government agency should not be so restrictive as to inhibit transfer of employment to and from the government. The government has a legitimate need to attract qualified lawyers as well as to maintain high ethical standards. The provisions for screening and waiver are necessary to prevent the disqualification rule from imposing too severe a deterrent against entering public service.

[4] When the client is an agency of one government, that agency should be treated as a private client for purposes of this Rule if the lawyer thereafter represents an agency of another government, as when a lawyer represents a city and subsequently is employed by a federal agency.

[5] Paragraphs (a)(1) and (b) do not prohibit a lawyer from receiving a salary or partnership share established by prior independent agreement. They prohibit directly relating the attorney's compensation to the fee in the matter in which the lawyer is disqualified.

[6] Paragraph (a)(2) does not require that a lawyer give notice to the government agency at a time when premature disclosure would injure the client; a requirement for premature disclosure might preclude engagement of the lawyer. Such notice is, however, required to be given as soon as practicable in order that the government agency will have a reasonable opportunity to ascertain that the lawyer is complying with Rule 1.11 and to take appropriate action if it believes the lawyer is not complying.

[7] Paragraph (b) operates only when the lawyer in question has knowledge of the information, which means actual knowledge; it does not operate with respect to information that merely could be imputed to the lawyer.

[8] Paragraphs (a) and (c) do not prohibit a lawyer from jointly representing a private party and a government agency when doing so is permitted by Rule 1.7 and is not otherwise prohibited by law.

[9] Paragraph (c) does not disqualify other lawyers in the agency with which the lawyer in question has become associated.

MODEL CODE COMPARISON:

Paragraph (a) is similar to DR 9–101(B), except that the latter used the terms "in which he had substantial responsibility while he was a public employee."

Paragraphs (b), (c), (d) and (e) have no counterparts in the Model Code.

RULE 1.12   Former Judge or Arbitrator

(a) Except as stated in paragraph (d), a lawyer shall not represent anyone in connection with a matter in which the lawyer participated personally and substantially as a judge or other adjudicative officer, arbitrator or law clerk to such a person, unless all parties to the proceeding consent after consultation.

(b) A lawyer shall not negotiate for employment with any person who is involved as a party or as attorney for a party in a matter in which the lawyer is participating personally and substantially as a judge or other adjudicative officer, or arbitrator. A lawyer serving as a law clerk to a judge, other adjudicative officer or arbitrator may negotiate for employment with a party or attorney involved in a matter in which the clerk is participating personally and substantially, but only after the lawyer has notified the judge, other adjudicative officer or arbitrator.

(c) If a lawyer is disqualified by paragraph (a), no lawyer in a firm with which that lawyer is associated may knowingly undertake or continue representation in the matter unless:

(1) the disqualified lawyer is screened from any participation in the matter and is apportioned no part of the fee therefrom; and

(2) written notice is promptly given to the appropriate tribunal to enable it to ascertain compliance with the provisions of this rule.

(d) An arbitrator selected as a partisan of a party in a multi-member arbitration panel is not prohibited from subsequently representing that party.

COMMENT:

This Rule generally parallels Rule 1.11. The term "personally and substantially" signifies that a judge who was a member of a multi-member court, and thereafter left judicial office to practice law, is not prohibited from representing a client in a matter pending in the court, but in which the former judge did not participate. So also the fact that a former judge exercised administrative responsibility in a court does not prevent the former judge from acting as a lawyer in a matter where the judge had previously exercised remote or incidental administrative responsibility that did not affect the merits. Compare the Comment to Rule 1.11. The term "adjudicative officer" includes such officials as judges pro tempore, referees, special masters, hearing officers and other parajudicial officers, and also lawyers who serve as part-time judges. Compliance Canons A(2), B(2) and C of the Model Code of Judicial Conduct provide that a part-time judge, judge pro tempore or retired judge recalled to active service, may not "act as a lawyer in any proceeding in which he served as a judge or in any other proceeding related thereto." Although phrased differently from this Rule, those Rules correspond in meaning.

MODEL CODE COMPARISON:

Paragraph (a) is substantially similar to DR 9–101(A), which provided that a lawyer "shall not accept private employment in a matter upon the merits of which he has acted in a judicial capacity." Paragraph (a) differs, however, in that it is broader in scope and states more specifically the persons to whom it applies. There was no counterpart in the Model Code to paragraphs (b), (c) or (d).

With regard to arbitrators, EC 5–20 stated that "a lawyer [who] has undertaken to act as an impartial arbitrator or mediator, ... should not thereafter represent in the dispute any of the parties involved." DR 9–101(A) did not permit a waiver of the disqualification applied to former judges by consent of the parties. However, DR 5–105(C) was similar in effect and could be construed to permit waiver.

RULE 1.13   Organization as Client *

(a) A lawyer employed or retained by an organization represents the organization acting through its duly authorized constituents.

(b) If a lawyer for an organization knows that an officer, employee or other person associated with the organization is engaged in action, intends to act or refuses to act in a matter related to the representation that is a violation of a legal obligation to the organization, or a violation of law which reasonably might be imputed to the organization, and is likely to

---

* The Kutak Commission's Revised Final Draft contained substantially different language on the lawyer's duty to rectify third party acts which are likely to result in substantial injury to the corporation. Proposed Rule 1.13(a) and (c) are reproduced below. Proposed provision (b) of 1.13 was substantially similar to the final version.

Rule 1.13   Organization as Client

(a) A lawyer employed or retained to represent an organization represents the organization as distinct from its directors, officers, employees, members, shareholders or other constituents.

. . .

(c) When the organization's highest authority insists upon action, or refuses to take action, that is clearly a violation of a legal obligation to the organization, or a violation of law which reasonably might be imputed to the organization,

and is likely to result in substantial injury to the organization, the lawyer may take further remedial action that the lawyer reasonably believes to be in the best interest of the organization. Such action may include revealing information otherwise protected by Rule 1.6 only if the lawyer reasonably believes that:

(1) the highest authority in the organization has acted to further the personal or financial interests of members of that authority which are in conflict with the interests of the organization; and

(2) revealing the information is necessary in the best interest of the organization.

Proposed Model Rule 1.13(a), (c) (Revised Final Draft) (June 20, 1982).

195

result in substantial injury to the organization, the lawyer shall proceed as is reasonably necessary in the best interest of the organization. In determining how to proceed, the lawyer shall give due consideration to the seriousness of the violation and its consequences, the scope and nature of the lawyer's representation, the responsibility in the organization and the apparent motivation of the person involved, the policies of the organization concerning such matters and any other relevant considerations. Any measures taken shall be designed to minimize disruption of the organization and the risk of revealing information relating to the representation to persons outside the organization. Such measures may include among others:

(1) asking reconsideration of the matter;

(2) advising that a separate legal opinion on the matter be sought for presentation to appropriate authority in the organization; and

(3) referring the matter to higher authority in the organization, including, if warranted by the seriousness of the matter, referral to the highest authority that can act in behalf of the organization as determined by applicable law.

(c) If, despite the lawyer's efforts in accordance with paragraph (b), the highest authority that can act on behalf of the organization insists upon action, or a refusal to act, that is clearly a violation of law and is likely to result in substantial injury to the organization, the lawyer may resign in accordance with rule 1.16.

(d) In dealing with an organization's directors, officers, employees, members, shareholders or other constituents, a lawyer shall explain the identity of the client when it is apparent that the organization's interests are adverse to those of the constituents with whom the lawyer is dealing.

(e) A lawyer representing an organization may also represent any of its directors, officers, employees, members, shareholders or other constituents, subject to the provisions of rule 1.7. If the organization's consent to the dual representation is required by rule 1.7, the consent shall be given by an appropriate official of the organization other than the individual who is to be represented, or by the shareholders.

COMMENT:

The Entity as the Client

[1] An organizational client is a legal entity, but it cannot act except through its officers, directors, employees, shareholders and other constituents.

[2] Officers, directors, employees and shareholders are the constituents of the corporate organizational client. The duties defined in this Comment apply equally to unincorporated associations. "Other constituents" as used in this Comment means the positions equivalent to officers, directors, employees and shareholders held by persons acting for organizational clients that are not corporations.

[3] When one of the constituents of an organizational client communicates with the organization's lawyer in that person's organizational capacity, the communication is protected by Rule 1.6. Thus, by way of example, if an organizational client requests its lawyer to investigate allegations of wrongdoing, interviews made in the course of that investigation between the lawyer and the client's employees or other constituents are covered by Rule 1.6. This does not mean, however, that constituents of an organizational client are the clients of the lawyer. The lawyer may not disclose to such constituents information relating to the representation except for disclosures explicitly or impliedly authorized by the organizational client in order to carry out the representation or as otherwise permitted by Rule 1.6.

[4] When constituents of the organization make decisions for it, the decisions ordinarily must be accepted by the lawyer even if their utility or prudence is doubtful. Decisions concerning policy and operations, including ones entailing serious risk, are not as such in the lawyer's province. However, different considerations arise when the lawyer knows that the organization may be substantially injured by action of [a] constituent that is in violation of law. In such a circumstance, it may be reasonably necessary for the lawyer to ask the constituent to reconsider the matter. If that fails, or if the matter is of sufficient seriousness and importance to the organization, it may be reasonably necessary for the lawyer to take steps to have the matter reviewed by a higher authority in the organization. Clear justification should exist for seeking review over the head of the constituent normally responsible for it. The stated policy of the organization may define circumstances and prescribe channels for such review, and a lawyer should encourage the formulation of such a policy. Even in the absence of organization policy, however, the lawyer may have an obligation to refer a matter to higher authority, depending on the seriousness of the matter and whether the constituent in question has apparent motives to act at variance with the organization's interest. Review by the chief executive officer or by the board of directors may be required when the matter is of importance commensurate with their authority. At some point it may be useful or essential to obtain an independent legal opinion.

[5] In an extreme case, it may be reasonably necessary for the lawyer to refer the matter to the organization's highest authority. Ordinarily, that is the board of directors or similar governing body. However, applicable law may prescribe that under certain conditions

highest authority reposes elsewhere; for example, in the independent directors of a corporation.

Relation to Other Rules

[6] The authority and responsibility provided in paragraph (b) are concurrent with the authority and responsibility provided in other Rules. In particular, this Rule does not limit or expand the lawyer's responsibility under Rules 1.6, 1.8, and 1.16, 3.3 or 4.1. If the lawyer's services are being used by an organization to further a crime or fraud by the organization, Rule 1.2(d) can be applicable.

Government Agency

[7] The duty defined in this Rule applies to governmental organizations. However, when the client is a governmental organization, a different balance may be appropriate between maintaining confidentiality and assuring that the wrongful official act is prevented or rectified, for public business is involved. In addition, duties of lawyers employed by the government or lawyers in military service may be defined by statutes and regulation. Therefore, defining precisely the identity of the client and prescribing the resulting obligations of such lawyers may be more difficult in the government context. Although in some circumstances the client may be a specific agency, it is generally the government as a whole. For example, if the action or failure to act involves the head of a bureau, either the department of which the bureau is a part or the government as a whole may be the client for purpose of this Rule. Moreover, in a matter involving the conduct of government officials, a government lawyer may have authority to question such conduct more extensively than that of a lawyer for a private organization in similar circumstances. This Rule does not limit that authority. See note on Scope.

Clarifying the Lawyer's Role

[8] There are times when the organization's interest may be or become adverse to those of one or more of its constituents. In such circumstances the lawyer should advise any constituent, whose interest the lawyer finds adverse to that of the organization of the conflict or potential conflict of interest, that the lawyer cannot represent such constituent, and that such person may wish to obtain independent representation. Care must be taken to assure that the individual understands that, when there is such adversity of interest, the lawyer for the organization cannot provide legal representation for that constituent individual, and that discussions between the lawyer for the organization and the individual may not be privileged.

[9] Whether such a warning should be given by the lawyer for the organization to any constituent individual may turn on the facts of each case.

Dual Representation

[10] Paragraph (e) recognizes that a lawyer for an organization may also represent a principal officer or major shareholder.

Derivative Actions

[11] Under generally prevailing law, the shareholders or members of a corporation may bring suit to compel the directors to perform their legal obligations in the supervision of the organization. Members of unincorporated associations have essentially the same right. Such an action may be brought nominally by the organization, but usually is, in fact, a legal controversy over management of the organization.

[12] The question can arise whether counsel for the organization may defend such an action. The proposition that the organization is the lawyer's client does not alone resolve the issue. Most derivative actions are a normal incident of an organization's affairs, to be defended by the organization's lawyer like any other suit. However, if the claim involves serious charges of wrongdoing by those in control of the organization, a conflict may arise between the lawyer's duty to the organization and the lawyer's relationship with the board. In those circumstances, Rule 1.7 governs who should represent the directors and the organization.

MODEL CODE COMPARISON:

There was no counterpart to this Rule in the Disciplinary Rules of the Model Code. EC 5–18 stated that a "lawyer employed or retained by a corporation or similar entity owes his allegiance to the entity and not to a stockholder, director, officer, employee, representative, or other person connected with the entity. In advising the entity, a lawyer should keep paramount its interests and his professional judgment should not be influenced by the personal desires of any person or organization. Occasionally, a lawyer for an entity is requested by a stockholder, director, officer, employee, representative, or other person connected with the entity to represent him in an individual capacity; in such case the lawyer may serve the individual only if the lawyer is convinced that differing interests are not present." EC 5–24 stated that although a lawyer "may be employed by a business corporation with non-lawyers serving as directors or officers, and they necessarily have the right to make decisions of business policy, a lawyer must decline to accept direction of his professional judgment from any layman." DR 5–107(B) provided that a lawyer "shall not permit a person who ... employs ... him to render legal services for another to direct or regulate his professional judgment in rendering such legal services."

RULE 1.14 Client Under a Disability

(a) When a client's ability to make adequately considered decisions in connection with the representation is impaired, whether because of minority, mental disability or for some other

reason, the lawyer shall, as far as reasonably possible, maintain a normal client–lawyer relationship with the client.

(b) A lawyer may seek the appointment of a guardian or take other protective action with respect to a client, only when the lawyer reasonably believes that the client cannot adequately act in the client's own interest.

COMMENT:

[1]   The normal client-lawyer relationship is based on the assumption that the client, when properly advised and assisted, is capable of making decisions about important matters.   When the client is a minor or suffers from a mental disorder or disability, however, maintaining the ordinary client-lawyer relationship may not be possible in all respects. In particular, an incapacitated person may have no power to make legally binding decisions.   Nevertheless, a client lacking legal competence often has the ability to understand, deliberate upon, and reach conclusions about matters affecting the client's own well-being.   Furthermore, to an increasing extent the law recognizes intermediate degrees of competence.   For example, children as young as five or six years of age, and certainly those of ten or twelve, are regarded as having opinions that are entitled to weight in legal proceedings concerning their custody.   So also, it is recognized that some persons of advanced age can be quite capable of handling routine financial matters while needing special legal protection concerning major transactions.

[2]   The fact that a client suffers a disability does not diminish the lawyer's obligation to treat the client with attention and respect.   If the person has no guardian or legal representative, the lawyer often must act as de facto guardian.   Even if the person does have a legal representative, the lawyer should as far as possible accord the represented person the status of client, particularly in maintaining communication.

[3]   If a legal representative has already been appointed for the client, the lawyer should ordinarily look to the representative for decisions on behalf of the client.   If a legal representative has not been appointed, the lawyer should see to such an appointment where it would serve the client's best interests.   Thus, if a disabled client has substantial property that should be sold for the client's benefit, effective completion of the transaction ordinarily requires appointment of a legal representative.   In many circumstances, however, appointment of a legal representative may be expensive or traumatic for the client.   Evaluation of these considerations is a matter of professional judgment on the lawyer's part.

[4]   If the lawyer represents the guardian as distinct from the ward, and is aware that the guardian is acting adversely to the ward's interest, the lawyer may have an obligation to prevent or rectify the guardian's misconduct.   See Rule 1.2(d).

Disclosure of the Client's Condition

[5] Rules of procedure in litigation generally provide that minors or persons suffering mental disability shall be represented by a guardian or next friend if they do not have a general guardian. However, disclosure of the client's disability can adversely affect the client's interests. For example, raising the question of disability could, in some circumstances, lead to proceedings for involuntary commitment. The lawyer's position in such cases is an unavoidably difficult one. The lawyer may seek guidance from an appropriate diagnostician.

Emergency Legal Assistance *

[6] In an emergency where the health, safety or a financial interest of a person under a disability is threatened with imminent and irreparable harm, a lawyer may take legal action on behalf of such a person even though the person is unable to establish a client-lawyer relationship or to make or express considered judgments about the matter, when the disabled person or another acting in good faith on that person's behalf has consulted the lawyer. Even in such an emergency, however, the lawyer should not act unless the lawyer reasonably believes that the person has no other lawyer, agent or other representative available. The lawyer should take legal action on behalf of the disabled person only to the extent reasonably necessary to maintain the status quo or otherwise avoid imminent and irreparable harm. A lawyer who undertakes to represent a person in such an exigent situation has the same duties under these Rules as the lawyer would with respect to a client.

[7] A lawyer who acts on behalf of a disabled person in an emergency should keep the confidences of the disabled person as if dealing with a client, disclosing them only to the extent necessary to accomplish the intended protective action. The lawyer should disclose to any tribunal involved and to any other counsel involved the nature of his or her relationship with the disabled person. The lawyer should take steps to regularize the relationship or implement other protective solutions as soon as possible. Normally, a lawyer would not seek compensation for such emergency actions taken on behalf of a disabled person.

MODEL CODE COMPARISON:

There was no counterpart to this Rule in the Disciplinary Rules of the Model Code. EC 7–11 stated that the "responsibilities of a lawyer may vary according to the intelligence, experience, mental condition or age of a client. . . . Examples include the representation of an illiterate or an incompetent." EC 7–12 stated that "[a]ny mental or physical condition of a client that renders him incapable of making a considered judgment on his own behalf casts additional responsibilities upon his

---

* In 1997, the ABA House of Delegates added comments 6 and 7 to Model Rule 1.14 in order to clarify a lawyer's role when a disabled person is in need of emergency legal services.

lawyer. Where an incompetent is acting through a guardian or other legal representative, a lawyer must look to such representative for those decisions which are normally the prerogative of the client to make. If a client under disability has no legal representative, his lawyer may be compelled in court proceedings to make decisions on behalf of the client. If the client is capable of understanding the matter in question or of contributing to the advancement of his interests, regardless of whether he is legally disqualified from performing certain acts, the lawyer should obtain from him all possible aid. If the disability of a client and the lack of a legal representative compel the lawyer to make decisions for his client, the lawyer should consider all circumstances then prevailing and act with care to safeguard and advance the interests of his client. But obviously a lawyer cannot perform any act or make any decision which the law requires his client to perform or make, either acting for himself if competent, or by a duly constituted representative if legally incompetent.''

RULE 1.15 Safekeeping Property

(a) A lawyer shall hold property of clients or third persons that is in a lawyer's possession in connection with a representation separate from the lawyer's own property. Funds shall be kept in a separate account maintained in the state where the lawyer's office is situated, or elsewhere with the consent of the client or third person. Other property shall be identified as such and appropriately safeguarded. Complete records of such account funds and other property shall be kept by the lawyer and shall be preserved for a period of [five years] after termination of the representation.

(b) Upon receiving funds or other property in which a client or third person has an interest, a lawyer shall promptly notify the client or third person. Except as stated in this rule or otherwise permitted by law or by agreement with the client, a lawyer shall promptly deliver to the client or third person any funds or other property that the client or third person is entitled to receive and, upon request by the client or third person, shall promptly render a full accounting regarding such property.

(c) When in the course of representation a lawyer is in possession of property in which both the lawyer and another person claim interests, the property shall be kept separate by the lawyer until there is an accounting and severance of their interest. If a dispute arises concerning their respective interests, the portion in dispute shall be kept separate by the lawyer until the dispute is resolved.

COMMENT:

[1] A lawyer should hold property of others with the care required of a professional fiduciary. Securities should be kept in a safe deposit

box, except when some other form of safekeeping is warranted by special circumstances. All property which is the property of clients or third persons should be kept separate from the lawyer's business and personal property and, if monies, in one or more trust accounts. Separate trust accounts may be warranted when administering estate monies or acting in similar fiduciary capacities.

[2] Lawyers often receive funds from third parties from which the lawyer's fee will be paid. If there is risk that the client may divert the funds without paying the fee, the lawyer is not required to remit the portion from which the fee is to be paid. However, a lawyer may not hold funds to coerce a client into accepting the lawyer's contention. The disputed portion of the funds should be kept in trust and the lawyer should suggest means for prompt resolution of the dispute, such as arbitration. The undisputed portion of the funds shall be promptly distributed.

[3] Third parties, such as a client's creditors, may have just claims against funds or other property in a lawyer's custody. A lawyer may have a duty under applicable law to protect such third-party claims against wrongful interference by the client, and accordingly may refuse to surrender the property to the client. However, a lawyer should not unilaterally assume to arbitrate a dispute between the client and the third party.

[4] The obligations of a lawyer under this Rule are independent of those arising from activity other than rendering legal services. For example, a lawyer who serves as an escrow agent is governed by the applicable law relating to fiduciaries even though the lawyer does not render legal services in the transaction.

[5] A "client's security fund" provides a means through the collective efforts of the bar to reimburse persons who have lost money or property as a result of dishonest conduct of a lawyer. Where such a fund has been established, a lawyer should participate.

MODEL CODE COMPARISON:

With regard to paragraph (a), DR 9–102(A) provided that "funds of clients" are to be kept in an identifiable bank account in the state in which the lawyer's office is situated. DR 9–102(B)(2) provided that a lawyer shall "identify and label securities and properties of a client ... and place them in ... safekeeping...." DR 9–102(B)(3) required that a lawyer "[m]aintain complete records of all funds, securities, and other properties of a client...." Paragraph (a) extends these requirements to property of a third person that is in the lawyer's possession in connection with the representation.

Paragraph (b) is substantially similar to DR 9–102(B)(1), (3) and (4).

Paragraph (c) is similar to DR 9–102(A)(2), except that the requirement regarding disputes applies to property concerning which an interest is claimed by a third person as well as by a client.

RULE 1.16   Declining or Terminating Representation

(a) Except as stated in paragraph (c), a lawyer shall not represent a client or, where representation has commenced, shall withdraw from the representation of a client if:

(1) the representation will result in violation of the rules of professional conduct or other law;

(2) the lawyer's physical or mental condition materially impairs the lawyer's ability to represent the client; or

(3) the lawyer is discharged.

(b) Except as stated in paragraph (c), a lawyer may withdraw from representing a client if withdrawal can be accomplished without material adverse effect on the interests of the client, or if:

(1) the client persists in a course of action involving the lawyer's services that the lawyer reasonably believes is criminal or fraudulent;

(2) the client has used the lawyer's services to perpetrate a crime or fraud;

(3) a client insists upon pursuing an objective that the lawyer considers repugnant or imprudent;

(4) the client fails substantially to fulfill an obligation to the lawyer regarding the lawyer's services and has been given reasonable warning that the lawyer will withdraw unless the obligation is fulfilled;

(5) the representation will result in an unreasonable financial burden on the lawyer or has been rendered unreasonably difficult by the client; or

(6) other good cause for withdrawal exists.

(c) When ordered to do so by a tribunal, a lawyer shall continue representation notwithstanding good cause for terminating the representation.

(d) Upon termination of representation, a lawyer shall take steps to the extent reasonably practicable to protect a client's interests, such as giving reasonable notice to the client, allowing time for employment of other counsel, surrendering papers and property to which the client is entitled and refunding any advance payment of fee that has not been earned. The lawyer may retain papers relating to the client to the extent permitted by other law.

COMMENT:

[1] A lawyer should not accept representation in a matter unless it can be performed competently, promptly, without improper conflict of interest and to completion.

Mandatory Withdrawal

[2]   A lawyer ordinarily must decline or withdraw from representation if the client demands that the lawyer engage in conduct that is illegal or violates the Rules of Professional Conduct or other law.   The lawyer is not obliged to decline or withdraw simply because the client suggests such a course of conduct; a client may make such a suggestion in the hope that a lawyer will not be constrained by a professional obligation.

[3]   When a lawyer has been appointed to represent a client, withdrawal ordinarily requires approval of the appointing authority.   See also Rule 6.2.   Difficulty may be encountered if withdrawal is based on the client's demand that the lawyer engage in unprofessional conduct. The court may wish an explanation for the withdrawal, while the lawyer may be bound to keep confidential the facts that would constitute such an explanation.   The lawyer's statement that professional considerations require termination of the representation ordinarily should be accepted as sufficient.

Discharge

[4]   A client has a right to discharge a lawyer at any time, with or without cause, subject to liability for payment for the lawyer's services. Where future dispute about the withdrawal may be anticipated, it may be advisable to prepare a written statement reciting the circumstances.

[5]   Whether a client can discharge appointed counsel may depend on applicable law.   A client seeking to do so should be given a full explanation of the consequences.   These consequences may include a decision by the appointing authority that appointment of successor counsel is unjustified, thus requiring the client to represent himself.

[6]   If the client is mentally incompetent, the client may lack the legal capacity to discharge the lawyer, and in any event the discharge may be seriously adverse to the client's interests.   The lawyer should make special effort to help the client consider the consequences and, in an extreme case, may initiate proceedings for a conservatorship or similar protection of the client.   See Rule 1.14.

Optional Withdrawal

[7]   A lawyer may withdraw from representation in some circumstances.   The lawyer has the option to withdraw if it can be accomplished without material adverse effect on the client's interests.   Withdrawal is also justified if the client persists in a course of action that the lawyer reasonably believes is criminal or fraudulent, for a lawyer is not required to be associated with such conduct even if the lawyer does not further it.   Withdrawal is also permitted if the lawyer's services were misused in the past even if that would materially prejudice the client. The lawyer also may withdraw where the client insists on a repugnant or imprudent objective.

[8] A lawyer may withdraw if the client refuses to abide by the terms of an agreement relating to the representation, such as an agreement concerning fees or court costs or an agreement limiting the objectives of the representation.

Assisting the Client Upon Withdrawal

[9] Even if the lawyer has been unfairly discharged by the client, a lawyer must take all reasonable steps to mitigate the consequences to the client. The lawyer may retain papers as security for a fee only to the extent permitted by law.

[10] Whether or not a lawyer for an organization may under certain unusual circumstances have a legal obligation to the organization after withdrawing or being discharged by the organization's highest authority is beyond the scope of these Rules.

MODEL CODE COMPARISON:

With regard to paragraph (a), DR 2–109(A) provided that a lawyer "shall not accept employment ... if he knows or it is obvious that [the prospective client] wishes to ... [b]ring a legal action ... or otherwise have steps taken for him, merely for the purpose of harassing or maliciously injuring any person...." Nor may a lawyer accept employment if the lawyer is aware that the prospective client wishes to "[p]resent a claim or defense ... that is not warranted under existing law, unless it can be supported by good faith argument for an extension, modification, or reversal of existing law." DR 2–110(B) provided that a lawyer "shall withdraw from employment ... if:

"(1) He knows or it is obvious that his client is bringing the legal action ... or is otherwise having steps taken for him, merely for the purpose of harassing or maliciously injuring any person.

"(2) He knows or it is obvious that his continued employment will result in violation of a Disciplinary Rule.

"(3) His mental or physical condition renders it unreasonably difficult for him to carry out the employment effectively.

"(4) He is discharged by his client."

With regard to paragraph (b), DR 2–110(C) permitted withdrawal regardless of the effect on the client if:

"(1) His client: (a) Insists upon presenting a claim or defense that is not warranted under existing law and cannot be supported by good faith argument for an extension, modification, or reversal of existing law; (b) Personally seeks to pursue an illegal course of conduct; (c) Insists that the lawyer pursue a course of conduct that is illegal or that is prohibited under the Disciplinary Rules; (d) By other conduct renders it unreasonably difficult for the lawyer to carry out his employment effectively; (e) Insists, in a matter not pending before a tribunal, that the lawyer engage in conduct that is contrary to the judgment and advice of the lawyer but not prohibited under the Disciplinary Rules; (f)

Deliberately disregards an agreement or obligation to the lawyer as to expenses and fees.

"(2) His continued employment is likely to result in a violation of a Disciplinary Rule.

"(3) His inability to work with co-counsel indicates that the best interest of the client likely will be served by withdrawal.

"(4) His mental or physical condition renders it difficult for him to carry out the employment effectively.

"(5) His client knowingly and freely assents to termination of his employment.

"(6) He believes in good faith, in a proceeding pending before a tribunal, that the tribunal will find the existence of other good cause for withdrawal."

With regard to paragraph (c), DR 2–110(A)(1) provided: "If permission for withdrawal from employment is required by the rules of a tribunal, the lawyer shall not withdraw ... without its permission."

RULE 1.17   Sale of Law Practice*

A lawyer or a law firm may sell or purchase a law practice, including good will, if the following conditions are satisfied:

(a) The seller ceases to engage in the private practice of law [in the geographic area] [in the jurisdiction] (a jurisdiction may elect either version) in which the practice has been conducted;

(b) The practice is sold as an entirety to another lawyer or law firm;

(c) Actual written notice is given to each of the seller's clients regarding:

(1) the proposed sale;

(2) the terms of any proposed change in the fee arrangement authorized by paragraph (d);

(3) the client's right to retain other counsel or to take possession of the file; and

(4) the fact that the client's consent to the sale will be presumed if the client does not take any action or does not otherwise object within ninety (90) days of receipt of the notice.

If a client cannot be given notice, the representation of that client may be transferred to the purchaser only upon entry of an order so authorizing by a court having jurisdiction. The seller may disclose to the court *in camera* information relating to the representation only to the extent necessary to obtain an order authorizing the transfer of a file.

---

* Model Rule 1.17 did not appear in the original version of the Model Rules. This provision and its comments were added by the ABA in 1990.

(d) The fees charged clients shall not be increased by reason of the sale. The purchaser may, however, refuse to undertake the representation unless the client consents to pay the purchaser fees at a rate not exceeding the fees charged by the purchaser for rendering substantially similar services prior to the initiation of the purchase negotiations.

COMMENT:

[1]   The practice of law is a profession, not merely a business. Clients are not commodities that can be purchased and sold at will. Pursuant to this Rule, when a lawyer or an entire firm ceases to practice and another lawyer or firm takes over the representation, the selling lawyer or firm may obtain compensation for the reasonable value of the practice as may withdrawing partners of law firms. See Rules 5.4 and 5.6.

Termination of Practice by the Seller

[2]   The requirement that all of the private practice be sold is satisfied if the seller in good faith makes the entire practice available for sale to the purchaser. The fact that a number of the seller's clients decide not to be represented by the purchaser but take their matters elsewhere, therefore, does not result in a violation. Neither does a return to private practice as a result of an unanticipated change in circumstances result in a violation. For example, a lawyer who has sold the practice to accept an appointment to judicial office does not violate the requirement that the sale be attendant to cessation of practice if the lawyer later resumes private practice upon being defeated in a contested or a retention election for the office.

[3]   The requirement that the seller cease to engage in the private practice of law does not prohibit employment as a lawyer on the staff of a public agency or a legal services entity which provides legal services to the poor, or as in-house counsel to a business.

[4]   The Rule permits a sale attendant upon retirement from the private practice of law within the jurisdiction. Its provisions, therefore, accommodate the lawyer who sells the practice upon the occasion of moving to another state. Some states are so large that a move from one locale therein to another is tantamount to leaving the jurisdiction in which the lawyer has engaged in the practice of law. To also accommodate lawyers so situated, states may permit the sale of the practice when the lawyer leaves the geographic area rather than the jurisdiction. The alternative desired should be indicated by selecting one of the two provided for in Rule 1.17(a).

Single Purchaser

[5]   The Rule requires a single purchaser. The prohibition against piecemeal sale of a practice protects those clients whose matters are less

lucrative and who might find it difficult to secure other counsel if a sale could be limited to substantial fee-generating matters. The purchaser is required to undertake all client matters in the practice, subject to client consent. If, however, the purchaser is unable to undertake all client matters because of a conflict of interest in a specific matter respecting which the purchaser is not permitted by Rule 1.7 or another rule to represent the client, the requirement that there be a single purchaser is nevertheless satisfied.

Client Confidences, Consent and Notice

[6] Negotiations between seller and prospective purchaser prior to disclosure of information relating to a specific representation of an identifiable client no more violate the confidentiality provisions of Model Rule 1.6 than do preliminary discussions concerning the possible association of another lawyer or mergers between firms, with respect to which client consent is not required. Providing the purchaser access to client-specific information relating to the representation and to the file, however, requires client consent. The Rule provides that before such information can be disclosed by the seller to the purchaser the client must be given actual written notice of the contemplated sale, including the identity of the purchaser and any proposed change in the terms of future representation, and must be told that the decision to consent or make other arrangements must be made within 90 days. If nothing is heard from the client within that time, consent to the sale is presumed.

[7] A lawyer or law firm ceasing to practice cannot be required to remain in practice because some clients cannot be given actual notice of the proposed purchase. Since these clients cannot themselves consent to the purchase or direct any other disposition of their files, the Rule requires an order from a court having jurisdiction authorizing their transfer or other disposition. The Court can be expected to determine whether reasonable efforts to locate the client have been exhausted, and whether the absent client's legitimate interests will be served by authorizing the transfer of the file so that the purchaser may continue the representation. Preservation of client confidences requires that the petition for a court order be considered *in camera*. (A procedure by which such an order can be obtained needs to be established in jurisdictions in which it presently does not exist.)

[8] All the elements of client autonomy, including the client's absolute right to discharge a lawyer and transfer the representation to another, survive the sale of the practice.

Fee Arrangements Between Client and Purchaser

[9] The sale may not be financed by increases in fees charged the clients of the practice. Existing agreements between the seller and the client as to fees and the scope of the work must be honored by the purchaser, unless the client consents after consultation. The purchaser

may, however, advise the client that the purchaser will not undertake the representation unless the client consents to pay the higher fees the purchaser usually charges. To prevent client financing of the sale, the higher fee the purchaser may charge must not exceed the fees charged by the purchaser for substantially similar service rendered prior to the initiation of the purchase negotiations.

[10] The purchaser may not intentionally fragment the practice which is the subject of the sale by charging significantly different fees in substantially similar matters. Doing so would make it possible for the purchaser to avoid the obligation to take over the entire practice by charging arbitrarily higher fees for less lucrative matters, thereby increasing the likelihood that those clients would not consent to the new representation.

Other Applicable Ethical Standards

[11] Lawyers participating in the sale of a law practice are subject to the ethical standards applicable to involving another lawyer in the representation of a client. These include, for example, the seller's obligation to exercise competence in identifying a purchaser qualified to assume the practice and the purchaser's obligation to undertake the representation competently (see Rule 1.1); the obligation to avoid disqualifying conflicts, and to secure client consent after consultation for those conflicts which can be agreed to (see Rule 1.7); and the obligation to protect information relating to the representation (see Rules 1.6 and 1.9).

[12] If approval of the substitution of the purchasing attorney for the selling attorney is required by the rules of any tribunal in which a matter is pending, such approval must be obtained before the matter can be included in the sale (see Rule 1.16).

Applicability of the Rule

[13] This Rule applies to the sale of a law practice by representatives of a deceased, disabled or disappeared lawyer. Thus, the seller may be represented by a non-lawyer representative not subject to these Rules. Since, however, no lawyer may participate in a sale of a law practice which does not conform to the requirements of this Rule, the representatives of the seller as well as the purchasing lawyer can be expected to see to it that they are met.

[14] Admission to or retirement from a law partnership or professional association, retirement plans and similar arrangements, and a sale of tangible assets of a law practice, do not constitute a sale or purchase governed by this Rule.

[15] This Rule does not apply to the transfers of legal representation between lawyers when such transfers are unrelated to the sale of a practice.

MODEL CODE COMPARISON:

There was no counterpart to this Rule in the Model Code.

COUNSELOR

RULE 2.1 Advisor

In representing a client, a lawyer shall exercise independent professional judgment and render candid advice. In rendering advice, a lawyer may refer not only to law but to other considerations such as moral, economic, social and political factors, that may be relevant to the client's situation.

COMMENT:

Scope of Advice

[1] A client is entitled to straightforward advice expressing the lawyer's honest assessment. Legal advice often involves unpleasant facts and alternatives that a client may be disinclined to confront. In presenting advice, a lawyer endeavors to sustain the client's morale and may put advice in as acceptable a form as honesty permits. However, a lawyer should not be deterred from giving candid advice by the prospect that the advice will be unpalatable to the client.

[2] Advice couched in narrowly legal terms may be of little value to a client, especially where practical considerations, such as cost or effects on other people, are predominant. Purely technical legal advice, therefore, can sometimes be inadequate. It is proper for a lawyer to refer to relevant moral and ethical considerations in giving advice. Although a lawyer is not a moral advisor as such, moral and ethical considerations impinge upon most legal questions and may decisively influence how the law will be applied.

[3] A client may expressly or impliedly ask the lawyer for purely technical advice. When such a request is made by a client experienced in legal matters, the lawyer may accept it at face value. When such a request is made by a client inexperienced in legal matters, however, the lawyer's responsibility as advisor may include indicating that more may be involved than strictly legal considerations.

[4] Matters that go beyond strictly legal questions may also be in the domain of another profession. Family matters can involve problems within the professional competence of psychiatry, clinical psychology or social work; business matters can involve problems within the competence of the accounting profession or of financial specialists. Where consultation with a professional in another field is itself something a competent lawyer would recommend, the lawyer should make such a recommendation. At the same time, a lawyer's advice at its best often consists of recommending a course of action in the face of conflicting recommendations of experts.

211

Offering Advice

[5] In general, a lawyer is not expected to give advice until asked by the client. However, when a lawyer knows that a client proposes a course of action that is likely to result in substantial adverse legal consequences to the client, duty to the client under Rule 1.4 may require that the lawyer act if the client's course of action is related to the representation. A lawyer ordinarily has no duty to initiate investigation of a client's affairs or to give advice that the client has indicated is unwanted, but a lawyer may initiate advice to a client when doing so appears to be in the client's interest.

MODEL CODE COMPARISON:

There was no direct counterpart to this Rule in the Disciplinary Rules of the Model Code. DR 5–107(B) provided that a lawyer "shall not permit a person who recommends, employs, or pays him to render legal services for another to direct or regulate his professional judgment in rendering such legal services." EC 7–8 stated that "[a]dvice of a lawyer to his client need not be confined to purely legal considerations.... In assisting his client to reach a proper decision, it is often desirable for a lawyer to point out those factors which may lead to a decision that is morally just as well as legally permissible.... In the final analysis, however, ... the decision whether to forego legally available objectives or methods because of nonlegal factors is ultimately for the client...."

RULE 2.2   Intermediary

(a) A lawyer may act as intermediary between clients if:

(1) the lawyer consults with each client concerning the implications of the common representation, including the advantages and risks involved, and the effect on the attorney–client privileges, and obtains each client's consent to the common representation;

(2) the lawyer reasonably believes that the matter can be resolved on terms compatible with the clients' best interests, that each client will be able to make adequately informed decisions in the matter and that there is little risk of material prejudice to the interest of any of the clients if the contemplated resolution is unsuccessful; and

(3) the lawyer reasonably believes that the common representation can be undertaken impartially and without improper effect on other responsibilities the lawyer has to any of the clients.

(b) While acting as intermediary, the lawyer shall consult with each client concerning the decisions to be made and the considerations relevant in making them, so that each client can make adequately informed decisions.

(c) A lawyer shall withdraw as intermediary if any of the clients so request, or if any of the conditions stated in paragraph (a) is no longer satisfied. Upon withdrawal, the lawyer shall not continue to represent any of the clients in the matter that was the subject of the intermediation.

COMMENT:

[1] A lawyer acts as intermediary under this Rule when the lawyer represents two or more parties with potentially conflicting interests. A key factor in defining the relationship is whether the parties share responsibility for the lawyer's fee, but the common representation may be inferred from other circumstances. Because confusion can arise as to the lawyer's role where each party is not separately represented, it is important that the lawyer make clear the relationship.

[2] The Rule does not apply to a lawyer acting as arbitrator or mediator between or among parties who are not clients of the lawyer, even where the lawyer has been appointed with the concurrence of the parties. In performing such a role the lawyer may be subject to applicable codes of ethics, such as the Code of Ethics for Arbitration in Commercial Disputes prepared by a joint Committee of the American Bar Association and the American Arbitration Association.

[3] A lawyer acts as intermediary in seeking to establish or adjust a relationship between clients on an amicable and mutually advantageous basis; for example, in helping to organize a business in which two or more clients are entrepreneurs, working out the financial reorganization of an enterprise in which two or more clients have an interest, arranging a property distribution in settlement of an estate or mediating a dispute between clients. The lawyer seeks to resolve potentially conflicting interests by developing the parties' mutual interests. The alternative can be that each party may have to obtain separate representation, with the possibility in some situations of incurring additional cost, complication or even litigation. Given these and other relevant factors, all the clients may prefer that the lawyer act as intermediary.

[4] In considering whether to act as intermediary between clients, a lawyer should be mindful that if the intermediation fails the result can be additional cost, embarrassment and recrimination. In some situations the risk of failure is so great that intermediation is plainly impossible. For example, a lawyer cannot undertake common representation of clients between whom contentious litigation is imminent or who contemplate contentious negotiations. More generally, if the relationship between the parties has already assumed definite antagonism, the possibility that the clients' interests can be adjusted by intermediation ordinarily is not very good.

[5] The appropriateness of intermediation can depend on its form. Forms of intermediation range from informal arbitration, where each client's case is presented by the respective client and the lawyer decides the outcome, to mediation, to common representation where the clients'

interests are substantially though not entirely compatible. One form may be appropriate in circumstances where another would not. Other relevant factors are whether the lawyer subsequently will represent both parties on a continuing basis and whether the situation involves creating a relationship between the parties or terminating one.

Confidentiality and Privilege

[6] A particularly important factor in determining the appropriateness of intermediation is the effect on client-lawyer confidentiality and the attorney-client privilege. In a common representation, the lawyer is still required both to keep each client adequately informed and to maintain confidentiality of information relating to the representation. See Rules 1.4 and 1.6. Complying with both requirements while acting as intermediary requires a delicate balance. If the balance cannot be maintained, the common representation is improper. With regard to the attorney-client privilege, the prevailing rule is that as between commonly represented clients the privilege does not attach. Hence, it must be assumed that if litigation eventuates between the clients, the privilege will not protect any such communications, and the clients should be so advised.

[7] Since the lawyer is required to be impartial between commonly represented clients, intermediation is improper when that impartiality cannot be maintained. For example, a lawyer who has represented one of the clients for a long period and in a variety of matters might have difficulty being impartial between that client and one to whom the lawyer has only recently been introduced.

Consultation

[8] In acting as intermediary between clients, the lawyer is required to consult with the clients on the implications of doing so, and proceed only upon consent based on such a consultation. The consultation should make clear that the lawyer's role is not that of partisanship normally expected in other circumstances.

[9] Paragraph (b) is an application of the principle expressed in Rule 1.4. Where the lawyer is intermediary, the clients ordinarily must assume greater responsibility for decisions than when each client is independently represented.

Withdrawal

[10] Common representation does not diminish the rights of each client in the client-lawyer relationship. Each has the right to loyal and diligent representation, the right to discharge the lawyer as stated in Rule 1.16, and the protection of Rule 1.9 concerning obligations to a former client.

MODEL CODE COMPARISON:

There was no direct counterpart to this Rule in the Disciplinary Rules of the Model Code. EC 5–20 stated that a "lawyer is often asked to serve as an impartial arbitrator or mediator in matters which involve present or former clients. He may serve in either capacity if he first discloses such present or former relationships." DR 5–105(B) provided that a lawyer "shall not continue multiple employment if the exercise of his independent judgment in behalf of a client will be or is likely to be adversely affected by his representation of another client, or if it would be likely to involve him in representation of differing interests, except to the extent permitted under DR 5–105(C)." DR 5–105(C) provided that "a lawyer may represent multiple clients if it is obvious that he can adequately represent the interests of each and if each consents to the representation after full disclosure of the possible effect of such representation on the exercise of his independent professional judgment on behalf of each."

RULE 2.3 Evaluation for Use by Third Persons

(a) A lawyer may undertake an evaluation of a matter affecting a client for the use of someone other than the client if:

(1) the lawyer reasonably believes that making the evaluation is compatible with other aspects of the lawyer's relationship with the client; and

(2) the client consents after consultation.

(b) Except as disclosure is required in connection with a report of an evaluation, information relating to the evaluation is otherwise protected by rule 1.6.

COMMENT:

Definition

[1] An evaluation may be performed at the client's direction but for the primary purpose of establishing information for the benefit of third parties; for example, an opinion concerning the title of property rendered at the behest of a vendor for the information of a prospective purchaser, or at the behest of a borrower for the information of a prospective lender. In some situations, the evaluation may be required by a government agency; for example, an opinion concerning the legality of the securities registered for sale under the securities laws. In other instances, the evaluation may be required by a third person, such as a purchaser of a business.

[2] Lawyers for the government may be called upon to give a formal opinion on the legality of contemplated government agency action. In making such an evaluation, the government lawyer acts at the behest of the government as the client but for the purpose of establishing the limits of the agency's authorized activity. Such an opinion is to

be distinguished from confidential legal advice given agency officials. The critical question is whether the opinion is to be made public.

[3] A legal evaluation should be distinguished from an investigation of a person with whom the lawyer does not have a client-lawyer relationship. For example, a lawyer retained by a purchaser to analyze a vendor's title to property does not have a client-lawyer relationship with the vendor. So also, an investigation into a person's affairs by a government lawyer, or by special counsel employed by the government, is not an evaluation as that term is used in this Rule. The question is whether the lawyer is retained by the person whose affairs are being examined. When the lawyer is retained by that person, the general rules concerning loyalty to client and preservation of confidences apply, which is not the case if the lawyer is retained by someone else. For this reason, it is essential to identify the person by whom the lawyer is retained. This should be made clear not only to the person under examination, but also to others to whom the results are to be made available.

Duty to Third Person

[4] When the evaluation is intended for the information or use of a third person, a legal duty to that person may or may not arise. That legal question is beyond the scope of this Rule. However, since such an evaluation involves a departure from the normal client-lawyer relationship, careful analysis of the situation is required. The lawyer must be satisfied as a matter of professional judgment that making the evaluation is compatible with other functions undertaken in behalf of the client. For example, if the lawyer is acting as advocate in defending the client against charges of fraud, it would normally be incompatible with that responsibility for the lawyer to perform an evaluation for others concerning the same or a related transaction. Assuming no such impediment is apparent, however, the lawyer should advise the client of the implications of the evaluation, particularly the lawyer's responsibilities to third persons and the duty to disseminate the findings.

Access to and Disclosure of Information

[5] The quality of an evaluation depends on the freedom and extent of the investigation upon which it is based. Ordinarily a lawyer should have whatever latitude of investigation seems necessary as a matter of professional judgment. Under some circumstances, however, the terms of the evaluation may be limited. For example, certain issues or sources may be categorically excluded, or the scope of search may be limited by time constraints or the noncooperation of persons having relevant information. Any such limitations which are material to the evaluation should be described in the report. If after a lawyer has commenced an evaluation, the client refuses to comply with the terms upon which it was understood the evaluation was to have been made, the

lawyer's obligations are determined by law, having reference to the terms of the client's agreement and the surrounding circumstances.

Financial Auditors' Requests for Information

[6] When a question concerning the legal situation of a client arises at the instance of the client's financial auditor and the question is referred to the lawyer, the lawyer's response may be made in accordance with procedures recognized in the legal profession. Such a procedure is set forth in the American Bar Association Statement of Policy Regarding Lawyers' Responses to Auditors' Requests for Information, adopted in 1975.

MODEL CODE COMPARISON:

There was no counterpart to this Rule in the Model Code.

ADVOCATE

RULE 3.1 Meritorious Claims and Contentions

A lawyer shall not bring or defend a proceeding, or assert or controvert an issue therein, unless there is a basis for doing so that is not frivolous, which includes a good faith argument for an extension, modification or reversal of existing law. A lawyer for the defendant in a criminal proceeding, or the respondent in a proceeding that could result in incarceration, may nevertheless so defend the proceeding as to require that every element of the case be established.

COMMENT:

[1] The advocate has a duty to use legal procedure for the fullest benefit of the client's cause, but also a duty not to abuse legal procedure. The law, both procedural and substantive, establishes the limits within which an advocate may proceed. However, the law is not always clear and never is static. Accordingly, in determining the proper scope of advocacy, account must be taken of the law's ambiguities and potential for change.

[2] The filing of an action or defense or similar action taken for a client is not frivolous merely because the facts have not first been fully substantiated or because the lawyer expects to develop vital evidence only by discovery. Such action is not frivolous even though the lawyer believes that the client's position ultimately will not prevail. The action is frivolous, however, if the client desires to have the action taken primarily for the purpose of harassing or maliciously injuring a person or if the lawyer is unable either to make a good faith argument on the merits of the action taken or to support the action taken by a good faith argument for an extension, modification or reversal of existing law.

MODEL CODE COMPARISON:

DR 7–102(A)(1) provided that a lawyer may not "[f]ile a suit, assert a position, conduct a defense, delay a trial, or take other action on behalf of his client when he knows or when it is obvious that such action would serve merely to harass or maliciously injure another." Rule 3.1 is to the same general effect as DR 7–102(A)(1), with three qualifications. First, the test of improper conduct is changed from "merely to harass or maliciously injure another" to the requirement that there be a basis for the litigation measure involved that is "not frivolous." This includes the concept stated in DR 7–102(A)(2) that a lawyer may advance a claim or defense unwarranted by existing law if "it can be supported by good faith argument for an extension, modification, or reversal of existing law." Second, the test in Rule 3.1 is an objective test, whereas DR 7–102(A)(1) applied only if the lawyer "knows or when it is obvious" that the litigation is frivolous. Third, Rule 3.1 has an exception that in a criminal case, or a case in which incarceration of the client may result (for example, certain juvenile proceedings), the lawyer may put the prosecution to its proof even if there is no nonfrivolous basis for defense.

RULE 3.2   Expediting Litigation

A lawyer shall make reasonable efforts to expedite litigation consistent with the interests of the client.

COMMENT:

Dilatory practices bring the administration of justice into disrepute. Delay should not be indulged merely for the convenience of the advocates, or for the purpose of frustrating an opposing party's attempt to obtain rightful redress or repose. It is not a justification that similar conduct is often tolerated by the bench and bar. The question is whether a competent lawyer acting in good faith would regard the course of action as having some substantial purpose other than delay. Realizing financial or other benefit from otherwise improper delay in litigation it not a legitimate interest of the client.

MODEL CODE COMPARISON:

DR 7–101(A)(1) stated that a lawyer does not violate the duty to represent a client zealously "by being punctual in fulfilling all professional commitments." DR 7–102(A)(1) provided that a lawyer "shall not ... file a suit, assert a position, conduct a defense [or] delay a trial ... when he knows or when it is obvious that such action would serve merely to harass or maliciously injure another."

RULE 3.3   Candor Toward the Tribunal

(a) A lawyer shall not knowingly:

(1) make a false statement of material fact or law to a tribunal;

(2) fail to disclose a material fact to a tribunal when disclosure is necessary to avoid assisting a criminal or fraudulent act by the client;

(3) fail to disclose to the tribunal legal authority in the controlling jurisdiction known to the lawyer to be directly adverse to the position of the client and not disclosed by opposing counsel; or

(4) offer evidence that the lawyer knows to be false. If a lawyer has offered material evidence and comes to know of its falsity, the lawyer shall take reasonable remedial measures.

(b) The duties stated in paragraph (a) continue to the conclusion of the proceeding, and apply even if compliance requires disclosure of information otherwise protected by rule 1.6.

(c) A lawyer may refuse to offer evidence that the lawyer reasonably believes is false.

(d) In an ex parte proceeding, a lawyer shall inform the tribunal of all material facts known to the lawyer which will enable the tribunal to make an informed decision, whether or not the facts are adverse.

COMMENT:

[1] The advocate's task is to present the client's case with persuasive force. Performance of that duty while maintaining confidences of the client is qualified by the advocate's duty of candor to the tribunal. However, an advocate does not vouch for the evidence submitted in a cause; the tribunal is responsible for assessing its probative value.

Representations by a Lawyer

[2] An advocate is responsible for pleadings and other documents prepared for litigation, but is usually not required to have personal knowledge of matters asserted therein, for litigation documents ordinarily present assertions by the client, or by someone on the client's behalf, and not assertions by the lawyer. Compare Rule 3.1. However, an assertion purporting to be on the lawyer's own knowledge, as in an affidavit by the lawyer or in a statement in open court, may properly be made only when the lawyer knows the assertion is true or believes it to be true on the basis of a reasonably diligent inquiry. There are circumstances where failure to make a disclosure is the equivalent of an affirmative misrepresentation. The obligation prescribed in Rule 1.2(d) not to counsel a client to commit or assist the client in committing a fraud applies in litigation. Regarding compliance with Rule 1.2(d), see the Comment to that Rule. See also the Comment to Rule 8.4(b).

219

Misleading Legal Argument

[3] Legal argument based on a knowingly false representation of law constitutes dishonesty toward the tribunal. A lawyer is not required to make a disinterested exposition of the law, but must recognize the existence of pertinent legal authorities. Furthermore, as stated in paragraph (a)(3), an advocate has a duty to disclose directly adverse authority in the controlling jurisdiction which has not been disclosed by the opposing party. The underlying concept is that legal argument is a discussion seeking to determine the legal premises properly applicable to the case.

False Evidence

[4] When evidence that a lawyer knows to be false is provided by a person who is not the client, the lawyer must refuse to offer it regardless of the client's wishes.

[5] When false evidence is offered by the client, however, a conflict may arise between the lawyer's duty to keep the client's revelations confidential and the duty of candor to the court. Upon ascertaining that material evidence is false, the lawyer should seek to persuade the client that the evidence should not be offered or, if it has been offered, that its false character should immediately be disclosed. If the persuasion is ineffective, the lawyer must take reasonable remedial measures.

[6] Except in the defense of a criminal accused, the rule generally recognized is that, if necessary to rectify the situation, an advocate must disclose the existence of the client's deception to the court or to the other party. Such a disclosure can result in grave consequences to the client, including not only a sense of betrayal but also loss of the case and perhaps a prosecution for perjury. But the alternative is that the lawyer cooperate in deceiving the court, thereby subverting the truth-finding process which the adversary system is designed to implement. See Rule 1.2(d). Furthermore, unless it is clearly understood that the lawyer will act upon the duty to disclose the existence of false evidence, the client can simply reject the lawyer's advice to reveal the false evidence and insist that the lawyer keep silent. Thus the client could in effect coerce the lawyer into being a party to fraud on the court.

Perjury by a Criminal Defendant

[7] Whether an advocate for a criminally accused has the same duty of disclosure has been intensely debated. While it is agreed that the lawyer should seek to persuade the client to refrain from perjurious testimony, there has been dispute concerning the lawyer's duty when that persuasion fails. If the confrontation with the client occurs before trial, the lawyer ordinarily can withdraw. Withdrawal before trial may not be possible, however, either because trial is imminent, or because the confrontation with the client does not take place until the trial itself, or because no other counsel is available.

[8]   The most difficult situation, therefore, arises in a criminal case where the accused insists on testifying when the lawyer knows that the testimony is perjurious. The lawyer's effort to rectify the situation can increase the likelihood of the client's being convicted as well as opening the possibility of a prosecution for perjury. On the other hand, if the lawyer does not exercise control over the proof, the lawyer participates, although in a merely passive way, in deception of the court.

[9]   Three resolutions of this dilemma have been proposed. One is to permit the accused to testify by a narrative without guidance through the lawyer's questioning. This compromises both contending principles; it exempts the lawyer from the duty to disclose false evidence but subjects the client to an implicit disclosure of information imparted to counsel. Another suggested resolution, of relatively recent origin, is that the advocate be entirely excused from the duty to reveal perjury if the perjury is that of the client. This is a coherent solution but makes the advocate a knowing instrument of perjury.

[10]   The other resolution of the dilemma is that the lawyer must reveal the client's perjury if necessary to rectify the situation. A criminal accused has a right to the assistance of an advocate, a right to testify and a right of confidential communication with counsel. However, an accused should not have a right to assistance of counsel in committing perjury. Furthermore, an advocate has an obligation, not only in professional ethics but under the law as well, to avoid implication in the commission of perjury or other falsification of evidence. See Rule 1.2(d).

Remedial Measures

[11]   If perjured testimony or false evidence has been offered, the advocate's proper course ordinarily is to remonstrate with the client confidentially. If that fails, the advocate should seek to withdraw if that will remedy the situation. If withdrawal will not remedy the situation or is impossible, the advocate should make disclosure to the court. It is for the court then to determine what should be done—making a statement about the matter to the trier of fact, ordering a mistrial or perhaps nothing. If the false testimony was that of the client, the client may controvert the lawyer's version of their communication when the lawyer discloses the situation to the court. If there is an issue whether the client has committed perjury, the lawyer cannot represent the client in resolution of the issue and a mistrial may be unavoidable. An unscrupulous client might in this way attempt to produce a series of mistrials and thus escape prosecution. However, a second such encounter could be construed as a deliberate abuse of the right to counsel and as such a waiver of the right to further representation.

Constitutional Requirements

[12]   The general rule—that an advocate must disclose the existence of perjury with respect to a material fact, even that of a client—

applies to defense counsel in criminal cases, as well as in other instances. However, the definition of the lawyer's ethical duty in such a situation may be qualified by constitutional provisions for due process and the right to counsel in criminal cases. In some jurisdictions these provisions have been construed to require that counsel present an accused as a witness if the accused wishes to testify, even if counsel knows the testimony will be false. The obligation of the advocate under these Rules is subordinate to such a constitutional requirement.

Duration of Obligation

[13] A practical time limit on the obligation to rectify the presentation of false evidence has to be established. The conclusion of the proceeding is a reasonably definite point for the termination of the obligation.

Refusing to Offer Proof Believed to be False

[14] Generally speaking, a lawyer has authority to refuse to offer testimony or other proof that the lawyer believes is untrustworthy. Offering such proof may reflect adversely on the lawyer's ability to discriminate in the quality of evidence and thus impair the lawyer's effectiveness as an advocate. In criminal cases, however, a lawyer may, in some jurisdictions, be denied this authority by constitutional requirements governing the right to counsel.

Ex Parte Proceedings

[15] Ordinarily, an advocate has the limited responsibility of presenting one side of the matters that a tribunal should consider in reaching a decision; the conflicting position is expected to be presented by the opposing party. However, in an ex parte proceeding, such as an application for a temporary restraining order, there is no balance of presentation by opposing advocates. The object of an ex parte proceeding is nevertheless to yield a substantially just result. The judge has an affirmative responsibility to accord the absent party just consideration. The lawyer for the represented party has the correlative duty to make disclosures of material facts known to the lawyer and that the lawyer reasonably believes are necessary to an informed decision.

MODEL CODE COMPARISON:

Paragraph (a)(1) is substantially identical to DR 7–102(A)(5), which provided that a lawyer shall not "knowingly make a false statement of law or fact."

Paragraph (a)(2) is implicit in DR 7–102(A)(3), which provided that "a lawyer shall not ... knowingly fail to disclose that which he is required by law to reveal."

Paragraph (a)(3) is substantially identical to DR 7–106(B)(1).

With regard to paragraph (a)(4), the first sentence of this subparagraph is similar to DR 7–102(A)(4), which provided that a lawyer shall not "knowingly use" perjured testimony or false evidence. The second sentence of paragraph (a)(4) resolves an ambiguity in the Model Code concerning the action required of a lawyer who discovers that the lawyer has offered perjured testimony or false evidence. DR 7–102(A)(4), quoted above, did not expressly deal with this situation, but the prohibition against "use" of false evidence can be construed to preclude carrying through with a case based on such evidence when that fact has become known during the trial. DR 7–102(B)(1), also noted in connection with Rule 1.6, provided that a lawyer "who receives information clearly establishing that ... [h]is client has ... perpetrated a fraud upon ... a tribunal shall [if the client does not rectify the situation] ... reveal the fraud to the ... tribunal. ..." Since use of perjured testimony or false evidence is usually regarded as "fraud" upon the court, DR 7–102(B)(1) apparently required disclosure by the lawyer in such circumstances. However, some states have amended DR 7–102(B)(1) in conformity with an ABA-recommended amendment to provide that the duty of disclosure does not apply when the "information is protected as a privileged communication." This qualification may be empty, for the rule of attorney-client privilege has been construed to exclude communications that further a crime, including the crime of perjury. On this interpretation of DR 7–102(B)(1), the lawyer has a duty to disclose the perjury.

Paragraph (c) confers discretion on the lawyer to refuse to offer evidence that the lawyer "reasonably believes" is false. This gives the lawyer more latitude than DR 7–102(A)(4), which prohibited the lawyer from offering evidence the lawyer "knows" is false.

There was no counterpart in the Model Code to paragraph (d).

RULE 3.4 Fairness to Opposing Party and Counsel

A lawyer shall not:

(a) unlawfully obstruct another party's access to evidence or unlawfully alter, destroy or conceal a document or other material having potential evidentiary value. A lawyer shall not counsel or assist another person to do any such act;

(b) falsify evidence, counsel or assist a witness to testify falsely, or offer an inducement to a witness that is prohibited by law;

(c) knowingly disobey an obligation under the rules of a tribunal except for an open refusal based on an assertion that no valid obligation exists;

(d) in pretrial procedure, make a frivolous discovery request or fail to make reasonably diligent effort to comply with a legally proper discovery request by an opposing party;

(e) in trial, allude to any matter that the lawyer does not reasonably believe is relevant or that will not be supported by

admissible evidence, assert personal knowledge of facts in issue except when testifying as a witness, or state a personal opinion as to the justness of a cause, the credibility of a witness, the culpability of a civil litigant or the guilt or innocence of an accused; or

(f) request a person other than a client to refrain from voluntarily giving relevant information to another party unless:

(1) the person is a relative or an employee or other agent of a client; and

(2) the lawyer reasonably believes that the person's interests will not be adversely affected by refraining from giving such information.

COMMENT:

[1] The procedure of the adversary system contemplates that the evidence in a case is to be marshalled competitively by the contending parties. Fair competition in the adversary system is secured by prohibitions against destruction or concealment of evidence, improperly influencing witnesses, obstructive tactics in discovery procedure, and the like.

[2] Documents and other items of evidence are often essential to establish a claim or defense. Subject to evidentiary privileges, the right of an opposing party, including the government, to obtain evidence through discovery or subpoena is an important procedural right. The exercise of that right can be frustrated if relevant material is altered, concealed or destroyed. Applicable law in many jurisdictions makes it an offense to destroy material for purpose of impairing its availability in a pending proceeding or one whose commencement can be foreseen. Falsifying evidence is also generally a criminal offense. Paragraph (a) applies to evidentiary material generally, including computerized information.

[3] With regard to paragraph (b), it is not improper to pay a witness's expenses or to compensate an expert witness on terms permitted by law. The common law rule in most jurisdictions is that it is improper to pay an occurrence witness any fee for testifying and that it is improper to pay an expert witness a contingent fee.

[4] Paragraph (f) permits a lawyer to advise employees of a client to refrain from giving information to another party, for the employees may identify their interests with those of the client. See also Rule 4.2.

MODEL CODE COMPARISON:

With regard to paragraph (a), DR 7–109(A) provided that a lawyer "shall not suppress any evidence that he or his client has a legal obligation to reveal." DR 7–109(B) provided that a lawyer "shall not advise or cause a person to secrete himself . . . for the purpose of making him unavailable as a witness. . . ." DR 7–106(C)(7) provided that a lawyer shall not "[i]ntentionally or habitually violate any established rule of procedure or of evidence."

With regard to paragraph (b), DR 7–102(A)(6) provided that a lawyer shall not participate "in the creation or preservation of evidence when he knows or it is obvious that the evidence is false." DR 7–109(C) provided that a lawyer "shall not pay, offer to pay, or acquiesce in the payment of compensation to a witness contingent upon the content of his testimony or the outcome of the case. But a lawyer may advance, guarantee or acquiesce in the payment of: (1) Expenses reasonably incurred by a witness in attending or testifying; (2) Reasonable compensation to a witness for his loss of time in attending or testifying; [or] (3) A reasonable fee for the professional services of an expert witness." EC 7–28 stated that witnesses "should always testify truthfully and should be free from any financial inducements that might tempt them to do otherwise."

Paragraph (c) is substantially similar to DR 7–106(A), which provided that "A lawyer shall not disregard ... a standing rule of a tribunal or a ruling of a tribunal made in the course of a proceeding, but he may take appropriate steps in good faith to test the validity of such rule or ruling."

Paragraph (d) has no counterpart in the Model Code.

Paragraph (e) substantially incorporates DR 7–106(C)(1), (2), (3) and (4). DR 7–106(C)(2) proscribed asking a question "intended to degrade a witness or other person," a matter dealt with in Rule 4.4. DR 7–106(C)(5), providing that a lawyer shall not "fail to comply with known local customs of courtesy or practice," was too vague to be a rule of conduct enforceable as law.

With regard to paragraph (f), DR 7–104(A)(2) provided that a lawyer shall not "give advice to a person who is not represented ... other than the advice to secure counsel, if the interests of such person are or have a reasonable possibility of being in conflict with the interests of his client."

RULE 3.5 Impartiality and Decorum of the Tribunal

A lawyer shall not:

(a) seek to influence a judge, juror, prospective juror or other official by means prohibited by law;

(b) communicate ex parte with such a person except as permitted by law; or

(c) engage in conduct intended to disrupt a tribunal.

COMMENT:

[1] Many forms of improper influence upon a tribunal are proscribed by criminal law. Others are specified in the ABA Model Code of Judicial Conduct, with which an advocate should be familiar. A lawyer is required to avoid contributing to a violation of such provisions.

225

[2] The advocate's function is to present evidence and argument so that the cause may be decided according to law. Refraining from abusive or obstreperous conduct is a corollary of the advocate's right to speak on behalf of litigants. A lawyer may stand firm against abuse by a judge but should avoid reciprocation; the judge's default is no justification for similar dereliction by an advocate. An advocate can present the cause, protect the record for subsequent review and preserve professional integrity by patient firmness no less effectively than by belligerence or theatrics.

MODEL CODE COMPARISON:

With regard to paragraphs (a) and (b), DR 7–108(A) provided that "[b]efore the trial of a case a lawyer ... shall not communicate with ... anyone he knows to be a member of the venire...." DR 7–108(B) provided that during the trial of a case a lawyer "shall not communicate with ... any member of the jury." DR 7–110(B) provided that a lawyer shall not "communicate ... as to the merits of the cause with a judge or an official before whom the proceeding is pending, except ... upon adequate notice to opposing counsel," or as "otherwise authorized by law."

With regard to paragraph (c), DR 7–106(C)(6) provided that a lawyer shall not engage in "undignified or discourteous conduct which is degrading to a tribunal."

RULE 3.6 Trial Publicity*

(a) A lawyer who is participating or has participated in the investigation or litigation of a matter shall not make an extraju-

* In August 1994, the ABA House of Delegates amended Model Rule 3.6 to reflect the Supreme Court's decision in Gentile v. Nevada State Bar, 501 U.S. 1030 (1991). The original version of Model Rule 3.6 read as follows:

(a) A lawyer shall not make an extrajudicial statement that a reasonable person would expect to be disseminated by means of public communication if the lawyer knows or reasonably should know that it will have a substantial likelihood of materially prejudicing an adjudicative proceeding.

(b) A statement referred to in paragraph (a) ordinarily is likely to have such an effect when it refers to a civil matter triable to a jury, a criminal matter, or any other proceeding that could result in incarceration, and the statement relates to:

(1) the character, credibility, reputation or criminal record of a party, suspect in a criminal investigation or witness, or the identity of a witness, or the expected testimony of a party or witness;

(2) in a criminal case or proceeding that could result in incarceration, the possibility of a plea of guilty to the offense or the existence or contents of any confession, admission, or statement given by a defendant or suspect or that person's refusal or failure to make a statement;

(3) the performance or results of any examination or test or the refusal or failure of a person to submit to an examination or test, or the identity or nature of physical evidence expected to be presented;

dicial statement that a reasonable person would expect to be disseminated by means of public communication if the lawyer knows or reasonably should know that it will have a substantial likelihood of materially prejudicing an adjudicative proceeding in the matter.

(b) Notwithstanding paragraph (a), a lawyer may state:

(1) the claim, offense or defense involved and, except when prohibited by law, the identity of the persons involved;

(2) information contained in a public record;

(3) that an investigation of a matter is in progress;

(4) the scheduling or result of any step in litigation;

(5) a request for assistance in obtaining evidence and information necessary thereto;

(6) a warning of danger concerning the behavior of a person involved, when there is reason to believe that there exists the likelihood of substantial harm to an individual or to the public interest; and

(4) any opinion as to the guilt or innocence of a defendant or suspect in a criminal case or proceeding that could result in incarceration;

(5) information the lawyer knows or reasonably should know is likely to be inadmissible as evidence in a trial and would if disclosed create a substantial risk of prejudicing an impartial trial; or

(6) the fact that a defendant has been charged with a crime, unless there is included therein a statement explaining that the charge is merely an accusation and that the defendant is presumed innocent until and unless proven guilty.

(c) Notwithstanding paragraph (a) and (b)(1–5), a lawyer involved in the investigation or litigation of a matter may state without elaboration:

(1) the general nature of the claim or defense;

(2) the information contained in a public record;

(3) that an investigation of the matter is in progress, including the general scope of the investigation, the offense or claim or defense in-

volved and, except when prohibited by law, the identity of the persons involved;

(4) the scheduling or result of any step in litigation;

(5) a request for assistance in obtaining evidence and information necessary thereto;

(6) a warning of danger concerning the behavior of a person involved, when there is reason to believe that there exists the likelihood of substantial harm to an individual or to the public interest; and

(7) in a criminal case:

(i) the identity, residence, occupation and family status of the accused;

(ii) if the accused has not been apprehended, information necessary to aid in apprehension of that person;

(iii) the fact, time and place of arrest; and

(iv) the identity of investigating and arresting officers or agencies and the length of the investigation.

(7) in a criminal case, in addition to subparagraphs (1) through (6):

(i) the identity, residence, occupation and family status of the accused;

(ii) if the accused has not been apprehended, information necessary to aid in apprehension of that person;

(iii) the fact, time and place of arrest; and

(iv) the identity of investigating and arresting officers or agencies and the length of the investigation.

(c) Notwithstanding paragraph (a), a lawyer may make a statement that a reasonable lawyer would believe is required to protect a client from the substantial undue prejudicial effect of recent publicity not initiated by the lawyer or the lawyer's client. A statement made pursuant to this paragraph shall be limited to such information as is necessary to mitigate the recent adverse publicity.

(d) No lawyer associated in a firm or government agency with a lawyer subject to paragraph (a) shall make a statement prohibited by paragraph (a).

COMMENT:*

[1] It is difficult to strike a balance between protecting the right to a fair trial and safeguarding the right of free expression. Preserving the right to a fair trial necessarily entails some curtailment of the information that may be disseminated about a party prior to trial, particularly where trial by jury is involved. If there were no such limits, the result would be the practical nullification of the protective effect of the rules of forensic decorum and the exclusionary rules of evidence. On the other hand, there are vital social interests served by the free dissemination of information about events having legal consequences and about legal proceedings themselves. The public has a right to know about threats to its safety and measures aimed at assuring its security. It also has a legitimate interest in the conduct of judicial proceedings, particularly in matters of general public concern. Furthermore, the subject matter of legal proceedings is often of direct significance in debate and deliberation over questions of public policy.

[2] Special rules of confidentiality may validly govern proceedings in juvenile, domestic relations and mental disability proceedings, and

---

* The ABA's amendment of Model Rule 3.6 in August 1994 deleted the original comment 2 and renumbered comment 3 as comment 2 and added comments 3, 4, 5, 6 and 7. The deleted comment 2 read as follows:

[2] No body of rules can simultaneously satisfy all interests of fair trial and all those of free expression. The formula in this Rule is based upon the ABA Model Code of Professional Responsibility and the ABA Standards Relating to Fair Trial and Free Press, as amended in 1978.

perhaps other types of litigation. Rule 3.4(c) requires compliance with such Rules.

[3] The Rule sets forth a basic general prohibition against a lawyer's making statements that the lawyer knows or should know will have a substantial likelihood of materially prejudicing an adjudicative proceeding. Recognizing that the public value of informed commentary is great and the likelihood of prejudice to a proceeding by the commentary of a lawyer who is not involved in the proceeding is small, the rule applies only to lawyers who are, or who have been involved in the investigation or litigation of a case, and their associates.

[4] Paragraph (b) identifies specific matters about which a lawyer's statements would not ordinarily be considered to present a substantial likelihood of material prejudice, and should not in any event be considered prohibited by the general prohibition of paragraph (a). Paragraph (b) is not intended to be an exhaustive listing of the subjects upon which a lawyer may make a statement, but statements on other matters may be subject to paragraph (a).

[5] There are, on the other hand, certain subjects which are more likely than not to have a material prejudicial effect on a proceeding, particularly when they refer to a civil matter triable to a jury, a criminal matter, or any other proceeding that could result in incarceration. These subjects relate to:

(1) the character, credibility, reputation or criminal record of a party, suspect in a criminal investigation or witness, or the identity of a witness, or the expected testimony of a party or witness;

(2) in a criminal case or proceeding that could result in incarceration, the possibility of a plea of guilty to the offense or the existence or contents of any confession, admission, or statement given by a defendant or suspect or that person's refusal or failure to make a statement;

(3) the performance or results of any examination or test or the refusal or failure of a person to submit to an examination or test, or the identity or nature of physical evidence expected to be presented;

(4) any opinion as to the guilt or innocence of a defendant or suspect in a criminal case or proceeding that could result in incarceration;

(5) information that the lawyer knows or reasonably should know is likely to be inadmissible as evidence in a trial and that would, if disclosed, create a substantial risk of prejudicing an impartial trial; or

(6) the fact that a defendant has been charged with a crime, unless there is included therein a statement explaining that the charge is merely an accusation and that the defendant is presumed innocent until and unless proven guilty.

[6] Another relevant factor in determining prejudice is the nature of the proceeding involved. Criminal jury trials will be most sensitive to extrajudicial speech. Civil trials may be less sensitive. Non-jury hearings and arbitration proceedings may be even less affected. The Rule will still place limitations on prejudicial comments in these cases, but the likelihood of prejudice may be different depending on the type of proceeding.

[7] Finally, extrajudicial statements that might otherwise raise a question under this Rule may be permissible when they are made in response to statements made publicly by another party, another party's lawyer, or third persons, where a reasonable lawyer would believe a public response is required in order to avoid prejudice to the lawyer's client. When prejudicial statements have been publicly made by others, responsive statements may have the salutary effect of lessening any resulting adverse impact on the adjudicative proceeding. Such responsive statements should be limited to contain only such information as is necessary to mitigate undue prejudice created by the statements made by others.

MODEL CODE COMPARISON:

Rule 3.6 is similar to DR 7–107, except as follows: First, Rule 3.6 adopts the general criteria of "substantial likelihood of materially prejudicing an adjudicative proceeding" to describe impermissible conduct. Second, Rule 3.6 makes clear that only attorneys who are, or have been involved in a proceeding, or their associates, are subject to the Rule. Third, Rule 3.6 omits the particulars in DR 7–107(b), transforming them instead into an illustrative compilation as part of the Rule's commentary that is intended to give fair notice of the kinds of statements that are generally thought to be more likely than other kinds of statements to pose unacceptable dangers to the fair administration of justice. Whether any statement will have a substantial likelihood of materially prejudicing an adjudicatory proceeding will depend upon the facts of each case. The particulars of DR 7–107(c) are retained in Rule 3.6(b), except DR 7–107(C)(7), which provided that a lawyer may reveal "[a]t the time of seizure, a description of the physical evidence seized, other than a confession, admission or statement." Such revelations may be substantially prejudicial and are frequently the subject of pretrial suppression motions whose success would be undermined by disclosure of the suppressed evidence to the press. Finally, Rule 3.6 authorizes a lawyer to protect a client by making a limited reply to adverse publicity substantially prejudicial to the client.

RULE 3.7 Lawyer as Witness

(a) A lawyer shall not act as advocate at a trial in which the lawyer is likely to be a necessary witness except where:

    (1) the testimony relates to an uncontested issue;

(2) the testimony relates to the nature and value of legal services rendered in the case; or

(3) disqualification of the lawyer would work substantial hardship on the client.

(b) A lawyer may act as advocate in a trial in which another lawyer in the lawyer's firm is likely to be called as a witness unless precluded from doing so by rule 1.7 or rule 1.9.

COMMENT:

[1] Combining the roles of advocate and witness can prejudice the opposing party and can involve a conflict of interest between the lawyer and client.

[2] The opposing party has proper objection where the combination of roles may prejudice that party's rights in the litigation. A witness is required to testify on the basis of personal knowledge, while an advocate is expected to explain and comment on evidence given by others. It may not be clear whether a statement by an advocate-witness should be taken as proof or as an analysis of the proof.

[3] Paragraph (a)(1) recognizes that if the testimony will be uncontested, the ambiguities in the dual role are purely theoretical. Paragraph (a)(2) recognizes that where the testimony concerns the extent and value of legal services rendered in the action in which the testimony is offered, permitting the lawyers to testify avoids the need for a second trial with new counsel to resolve that issue. Moreover, in such a situation the judge has first hand knowledge of the matter in issue; hence, there is less dependence on the adversary process to test the credibility of the testimony.

[4] Apart from these two exceptions, paragraph (a)(3) recognizes that a balancing is required between the interests of the client and those of the opposing party. Whether the opposing party is likely to suffer prejudice depends on the nature of the case, the importance and probable tenor of the lawyer's testimony, and the probability that the lawyer's testimony will conflict with that of other witnesses. Even if there is risk of such prejudice, in determining whether the lawyer should be disqualified due regard must be given to the effect of disqualification on the lawyer's client. It is relevant that one or both parties could reasonably foresee that the lawyer would probably be a witness. The principle of imputed disqualification stated in Rule 1.10 has no application to this aspect of the problem.

[5] Whether the combination of roles involves an improper conflict of interest with respect to the client is determined by Rule 1.7 or 1.9. For example, if there is likely to be substantial conflict between the testimony of the client and that of the lawyer or a member of the lawyer's firm, the representation is improper. The problem can arise whether the lawyer is called as a witness on behalf of the client or is called by the opposing party. Determining whether or not such a

conflict exists is primarily the responsibility of the lawyer involved. See Comment to Rule 1.7. If a lawyer who is a member of a firm may not act as both advocate and witness by reason of conflict of interest, Rule 1.10 disqualifies the firm also.

MODEL CODE COMPARISON:

DR 5-102(A) prohibited a lawyer, or the lawyer's firm, from serving as advocate if the lawyer "learns or it is obvious that he or a lawyer in his firm ought to be called as a witness on behalf of his client." DR 5-102(B) provided that a lawyer, and the lawyer's firm, may continue representation if the "lawyer learns or it is obvious that he or a lawyer in his firm may be called as a witness other than on behalf of his client ... until it is apparent that his testimony is or may be prejudicial to his client." DR 5-101(B) permitted a lawyer to testify while representing a client: "(1) If the testimony will relate solely to an uncontested matter; (2) If the testimony will relate solely to a matter of formality and there is no reason to believe that substantial evidence will be offered in opposition to the testimony; (3) If the testimony will relate solely to the nature and value of legal services rendered in the case by the lawyer or his firm to the client; (4) As to any matter if refusal would work a substantial hardship on the client because of the distinctive value of the lawyer or his firm as counsel in the particular case."

The exception stated in paragraph (a)(1) consolidates provisions of DR 5-101(B)(1) and (2). Testimony relating to a formality, referred to in DR 5-101(B)(2), in effect defines the phrase "uncontested issue," and is redundant.

RULE 3.8 Special Responsibilities of a Prosecutor*

The prosecutor in a criminal case shall:

(a) refrain from prosecuting a charge that the prosecutor knows is not supported by probable cause;

(b) make reasonable efforts to assure that the accused has been advised of the right to, and the procedure for obtaining,

---

* In 1990, the ABA House of Delegates added subparagraph (f) to Model Rule 3.8 to address the profession's concerns over the increased use of subpoenas by prosecutors towards attorneys for information about their clients. The original amendment included a statement limiting the situations in which a prosecutor may subpoena a lawyer in a grand jury or criminal proceeding to cases in which "the prosecutor obtains prior judicial approval after an opportunity for an adversarial hearing." This statement was removed by the House of Delegates in August 1995, because several judicial decisions had invalidated this ABA requirement. Thus, under the current rule, a prosecutor must continue to meet the remaining standards in subparagraph (f) to obtain a subpoena against a criminal defense lawyer; however, the prosecutor does not need to obtain prior court approval.

In August 1994, the ABA added the text in subparagraph (g) to the original Model Rule 3.8. This amendment reflects the changes that the ABA made to Model Rule 3.6 as it applies to prosecutors.

counsel and has been given reasonable opportunity to obtain counsel;

(c) not seek to obtain from an unrepresented accused a waiver of important pretrial rights, such as the right to a preliminary hearing;

(d) make timely disclosure to the defense of all evidence or information known to the prosecutor that tends to negate the guilt of the accused or mitigates the offense, and, in connection with sentencing, disclose to the defense and to the tribunal all unprivileged mitigating information known to the prosecutor, except when the prosecutor is relieved of this responsibility by a protective order of the tribunal; and

(e) exercise reasonable care to prevent investigators, law enforcement personnel, employees or other persons assisting or associated with the prosecutor in a criminal case from making an extrajudicial statement that the prosecutor would be prohibited from making under rule 3.6.

(f) not subpoena a lawyer in a grand jury or other criminal proceeding to present evidence about a past or present client unless:

(i) the prosecutor reasonably believes:

(1) the information sought is not protected from disclosure by any applicable privilege;

(2) the evidence sought is essential to the successful completion of an ongoing investigation or prosecution;

(3) there is no other feasible alternative to obtain the information.

(g) except for statements that are necessary to inform the public of the nature and extent of the prosecutor's action and that serve a legitimate law enforcement purpose, refrain from making extrajudicial comments that have a substantial likelihood of heightening public condemnation of the accused.

COMMENT:

[1] A prosecutor has the responsibility of a minister of justice and not simply that of an advocate. This responsibility carries with it specific obligations to see that the defendant is accorded procedural justice and that guilt is decided upon the basis of sufficient evidence. Precisely how far the prosecutor is required to go in this direction is a matter of debate and varies in different jurisdictions. Many jurisdictions have adopted the ABA Standards of Criminal Justice Relating to Prosecution Function, which in turn are the product of prolonged and careful deliberation by lawyers experienced in both criminal prosecution and defense. See also Rule 3.3(d), governing ex parte proceedings, among which grand jury proceedings are included. Applicable law may require

other measures by the prosecutor and knowing disregard of those obligations or a systematic abuse of prosecutorial discretion could constitute a violation of Rule 8.4.

[2] Paragraph (c) does not apply to an accused appearing pro se with the approval of the tribunal. Nor does it forbid the lawful questioning of a suspect who has knowingly waived the rights to counsel and silence.

[3] The exception in paragraph (d) recognizes that a prosecutor may seek an appropriate protective order from the tribunal if disclosure of information to the defense could result in substantial harm to an individual or to the public interest.

[4]* Paragraph (f) is intended to limit the issuance of lawyer subpoenas in grand jury and other criminal proceedings to those situations in which there is a genuine need to intrude into the client-lawyer relationship.

[5] ** Paragraph (g) supplements Rule 3.6, which prohibits extrajudicial statements that have a substantial likelihood of prejudicing an adjudicatory proceeding. In the context of a criminal prosecution, a prosecutor's extrajudicial statement can create the additional problem of increasing public condemnation of the accused. Although the announcement of an indictment, for example, will necessarily have severe consequences for the accused, a prosecutor can, and should, avoid comments which have no legitimate law enforcement purpose and have a substantial likelihood of increasing public opprobrium of the accused. Nothing in this Comment is intended to restrict the statements which a prosecutor may make which comply with Rule 3.6(b) or 3.6(c).

MODEL CODE COMPARISON:

DR 7–103(A) provided that a "public prosecutor ... shall not institute ... criminal charges when he knows or it is obvious that the charges are not supported by probable cause." DR 7–103(B) provided that "[a] public prosecutor ... shall make timely disclosure ... of the existence of evidence, known to the prosecutor ... that tends to negate the guilt of the accused, mitigate the degree of the offense, or reduce the punishment."

RULE 3.9 Advocate in Nonadjudicative Proceedings

A lawyer representing a client before a legislative or administrative tribunal in a nonadjudicative proceeding shall disclose

---

* The ABA added paragraph [4] in 1990 when it amended Model Rule 3.8 by adding subparagraph (f). The 1995 amendment to subparagraph (f) deleted the following sentence: "The prosecutor is required to obtain court approval for the issuance of the subpoena after an opportunity for an adversarial hearing is afforded in order to assure an independent determination that the applicable standards are met."

** The ABA added paragraph [5] in 1994 when it amended Model Rule 3.8 by adding subparagraph (g).

that the appearance is in a representative capacity and shall conform to the provisions of rules 3.3(a) through (c), 3.4(a) through (c), and 3.5.

COMMENT:

[1] In representation before bodies such as legislatures, municipal councils, and executive and administrative agencies acting in a rule-making or policy-making capacity, lawyers present facts, formulate issues and advance argument in the matters under consideration. The decision-making body, like a court, should be able to rely on the integrity of the submissions made to it. A lawyer appearing before such a body should deal with the tribunal honestly and in conformity with applicable rules of procedure.

[2] Lawyers have no exclusive right to appear before nonadjudicative bodies, as they do before a court. The requirements of this Rule therefore may subject lawyers to regulations inapplicable to advocates who are not lawyers. However, legislatures and administrative agencies have a right to expect lawyers to deal with them as they deal with courts.

[3] This Rule does not apply to representation of a client in a negotiation or other bilateral transaction with a governmental agency; representation in such a transaction is governed by Rules 4.1 through 4.4.

MODEL CODE COMPARISON:

EC 7–15 stated that a lawyer "appearing before an administrative agency, regardless of the nature of the proceeding it is conducting, has the continuing duty to advance the cause of his client within the bounds of the law." EC 7–16 stated that "[w]hen a lawyer appears in connection with proposed legislation, he . . . should comply with applicable laws and legislative rules." EC 8–5 stated that "[f]raudulent, deceptive, or otherwise illegal conduct by a participant in a proceeding before a . . . legislative body . . . should never be participated in . . . by lawyers." DR 7–106(B)(1) provided that "[i]n presenting a matter to a tribunal, a lawyer shall disclose . . . [u]nless privileged or irrelevant, the identity of the clients he represents and of the persons who employed him."

TRANSACTIONS WITH PERSONS OTHER THAN CLIENTS

RULE 4.1   Truthfulness in Statements to Others *

In the course of representing a client a lawyer shall not knowingly:

(a) make a false statement of material fact or law to a third person; or

---

* The Kutak Commission's Revised Final Draft contained substantially different language on the interaction of Rules 1.6 and 4.1: "The duties stated in this Rule apply even if compliance requires disclosure of information otherwise protected by Rule 1.6." Proposed Model Rule 4.1(b) (Revised Final Draft) (June 20, 1982).

(b) fail to disclose a material fact to a third person when disclosure is necessary to avoid assisting a criminal or fraudulent act by a client, unless disclosure is prohibited by rule 1.6.

COMMENT:

Misrepresentation

[1]   A lawyer is required to be truthful when dealing with others on a client's behalf, but generally has no affirmative duty to inform an opposing party of relevant facts. A misrepresentation can occur if the lawyer incorporates or affirms a statement of another person that the lawyer knows is false. Misrepresentations can also occur by failure to act.

Statements of Fact

[2]   This Rule refers to statements of fact. Whether a particular statement should be regarded as one of fact can depend on the circumstances. Under generally accepted conventions in negotiation, certain types of statements ordinarily are not taken as statements of material fact. Estimates of price or value placed on the subject of a transaction and a party's intentions as to an acceptable settlement of a claim are in this category, and so is the existence of an undisclosed principal except where nondisclosure of the principal would constitute fraud.

Fraud by Client

[3]   Paragraph (b) recognizes that substantive law may require a lawyer to disclose certain information to avoid being deemed to have assisted the client's crime or fraud. The requirement of disclosure created by this paragraph is, however, subject to the obligations created by Rule 1.6.

MODEL CODE COMPARISON:

Paragraph (a) is substantially similar to DR 7–102(A)(5), which stated that "[i]n his representation of a client, a lawyer shall not ... [k]nowingly make a false statement of law or fact."

With regard to paragraph (b), DR 7–102(A)(3) provided that a lawyer shall not "[c]onceal or knowingly fail to disclose that which he is required by law to reveal."

RULE 4.2 Communication With Person Represented by Counsel*

In representing a client, a lawyer shall not communicate about the subject of the representation with a person the lawyer

---

* In August 1995, the ABA House of Delegates amended Model Rule 4.2 to substitute the word "person" for the word "party" so as to clarify that the rule applies to

knows to be represented by another lawyer in the matter, unless the lawyer has the consent of the other lawyer or is authorized by law to do so.

COMMENT:†

[1]   This Rule does not prohibit communication with a represented person, or an employee or agent of such a person, concerning matters outside the representation. For example, the existence of a controversy between a government agency and a private party, or between two organizations, does not prohibit a lawyer for either from communicating with nonlawyer representatives of the other regarding a separate matter. Also, parties to a matter may communicate directly with each other and a lawyer having independent justification for communicating with the other party is permitted to do so. Communications authorized by law include, for example, the right of a party to a controversy with a government agency to speak with government officials about the matter.

[2]   Communications authorized by law also include constitutionally permissible investigative activities of lawyers representing governmental entities, directly or through investigative agents, prior to the commencement of criminal or civil enforcement proceedings, when there is applicable judicial precedent that either has found the activity permissible under this Rule or has found this Rule inapplicable. However, the Rule imposes ethical restrictions that go beyond those imposed by constitutional provisions.

[3]   This rule applies to communications with any person, whether or not a party to a formal adjudicative proceeding, contract or negotiation, who is represented by counsel concerning the matter to which the communication relates.

[4]   In the case of an organization, this Rule prohibits communications by a lawyer for another person or entity concerning the matter in representation with persons having a managerial responsibility on behalf of the organization, and with any other person whose act or omission in connection with that matter may be imputed to the organization for purposes of civil or criminal liability or whose statement may constitute an admission on the part of the organization. If an agent or employee of

situations where a lawyer seeks to contact a represented individual in pre-litigation or pre-custodial settings as well or when a lawyer seeks to contact a non-party such as an informant or undercover agent who is represented by counsel.

† The ABA's amendment of Rule 4.2 in August 1995 included a substantial revision of the comments: (1) to clarify that knowledge of the fact that a person is represented by counsel may be inferred from the circumstances; (2) to elaborate on the situations in which the communication with rep-resented persons is authorized by law; (3) to make clear that the rule applies to persons represented by counsel in all matters (for example, contract or negotiation matters) and not just to parties in formal proceedings; and (4) to cross reference discussions of situations where the person is not represented by counsel to Model Rule 4.3 Comments 2, 5, and 6 are added in this amendment. Comments 1, 3, and 4 are based upon prior comments and rewritten to reflect the clarifications discussed above.

the organization is represented in the matter by his or her own counsel, the consent by that counsel to a communication will be sufficient for purposes of this Rule. Compare Rule 3.4(f).

[5] The prohibition on communications with a represented person only applies, however, in circumstances where the lawyer knows that the person is in fact represented in the matter to be discussed. This means that the lawyer has actual knowledge of the fact of the representation; but such actual knowledge may be inferred from the circumstances. See Terminology. Such an inference may arise in circumstances where there is substantial reason to believe that the person with whom communication is sought is represented in the matter to be discussed. Thus, a lawyer cannot evade the requirement of obtaining the consent of counsel by closing eyes to the obvious.

[6] In the event the person with whom the lawyer communicates is not known to be represented by counsel in the matter, the lawyer's communications are subject to Rule 4.3.

MODEL CODE COMPARISON:

This Rule is substantially identical to DR 7–104(A)(1).

RULE 4.3   Dealing With Unrepresented Person

In dealing on behalf of a client with a person who is not represented by counsel, a lawyer shall not state or imply that the lawyer is disinterested. When the lawyer knows or reasonably should know that the unrepresented person misunderstands the lawyer's role in the matter, the lawyer shall make reasonable efforts to correct the misunderstanding.

COMMENT:

An unrepresented person, particularly one not experienced in dealing with legal matters, might assume that a lawyer is disinterested in loyalties or is a disinterested authority on the law even when the lawyer represents a client. During the course of a lawyer's representation of a client, the lawyer should not give advice to an unrepresented person other than the advice to obtain counsel.

MODEL CODE COMPARISON:

There was no direct counterpart to this Rule in the Model Code. DR 7–104(A)(2) provided that a lawyer shall not "[g]ive advice to a person who is not represented by a lawyer, other than the advice to secure counsel...."

RULE 4.4   Respect for Rights of Third Persons

In representing a client, a lawyer shall not use means that have no substantial purpose other than to embarrass, delay, or

burden a third person, or use methods of obtaining evidence that violate the legal rights of such a person.

COMMENT:

Responsibility to a client requires a lawyer to subordinate the interests of others to those of the client, but that responsibility does not imply that a lawyer may disregard the rights of third persons. It is impractical to catalogue all such rights, but they include legal restrictions on methods of obtaining evidence from third persons.

MODEL CODE COMPARISON:

DR 7–106(C)(2) provided that a lawyer shall not "[a]sk any question that he has no reasonable basis to believe is relevant to the case and that is intended to degrade a witness or other person." DR 7–102(A)(1) provided that a lawyer shall not "take ... action on behalf of his client when he knows or when it is obvious that such action would serve merely to harass or maliciously injure another." DR 7–108(D) provided that "[a]fter discharge of the jury ... the lawyer shall not ask questions or make comments to a member of that jury that are calculated merely to harass or embarrass the juror...." DR 7–108(E) provided that a lawyer "shall not conduct ... a vexatious or harassing investigation of either a venireman or a juror."

LAW FIRMS AND ASSOCIATIONS

RULE 5.1 Responsibilities of a Partner or Supervisory Lawyer

(a) A partner in a law firm shall make reasonable efforts to ensure that the firm has in effect measures giving reasonable assurance that all lawyers in the firm conform to the rules of professional conduct.

(b) A lawyer having direct supervisory authority over another lawyer shall make reasonable efforts to ensure that the other lawyer conforms to the rules of professional conduct.

(c) A lawyer shall be responsible for another lawyer's violation of the rules of professional conduct if:

(1) the lawyer orders or, with knowledge of the specific conduct, ratifies the conduct involved; or

(2) the lawyer is a partner in the law firm in which the other lawyer practices, or has direct supervisory authority over the other lawyer, and knows of the conduct at a time when its consequences can be avoided or mitigated but fails to take reasonable remedial action.

COMMENT:

[1] Paragraphs (a) and (b) refer to lawyers who have supervisory authority over the professional work of a firm or legal department of a

government agency. This includes members of a partnership and the shareholders in a law firm organized as a professional corporation; lawyers having supervisory authority in the law department of an enterprise or government agency; and lawyers who have intermediate managerial responsibilities in a firm.

[2]   The measures required to fulfill the responsibility prescribed in paragraphs (a) and (b) can depend on the firm's structure and the nature of its practice. In a small firm, informal supervision and occasional admonition ordinarily might be sufficient. In a large firm, or in practice situations in which intensely difficult ethical problems frequently arise, more elaborate procedures may be necessary. Some firms, for example, have a procedure whereby junior lawyers can make confidential referral of ethical problems directly to a designated senior partner or special committee. See Rule 5.2. Firms, whether large or small, may also rely on continuing legal education in professional ethics. In any event, the ethical atmosphere of a firm can influence the conduct of all its members and a lawyer having authority over the work of another may not assume that the subordinate lawyer will inevitably conform to the Rules.

[3]   Paragraph (c)(1) expresses a general principle of responsibility for acts of another. See also Rule 8.4(a).

[4]   Paragraph (c)(2) defines the duty of a lawyer having direct supervisory authority over performance of specific legal work by another lawyer. Whether a lawyer has such supervisory authority in particular circumstances is a question of fact. Partners of a private firm have at least indirect responsibility for all work being done by the firm, while a partner in charge of a particular matter ordinarily has direct authority over other firm lawyers engaged in the matter. Appropriate remedial action by a partner would depend on the immediacy of the partner's involvement and the seriousness of the misconduct. The supervisor is required to intervene to prevent avoidable consequences of misconduct if the supervisor knows that the misconduct occurred. Thus, if a supervising lawyer knows that a subordinate misrepresented a matter to an opposing party in negotiation, the supervisor as well as the subordinate has a duty to correct the resulting misapprehension.

[5]   Professional misconduct by a lawyer under supervision could reveal a violation of paragraph (b) on the part of the supervisory lawyer even though it does not entail a violation of paragraph (c) because there was no direction, ratification or knowledge or the violation.

[6]   Apart from this Rule and Rule 8.4(a), a lawyer does not have disciplinary liability for the conduct of a partner, associate or subordinate. Whether a lawyer may be liable civilly or criminally for another lawyer's conduct is a question of law beyond the scope of these Rules.

MODEL CODE COMPARISON:

There was no direct counterpart to this Rule in the Model Code. DR 1–103(A) provided that a lawyer "possessing unprivileged knowledge of a violation of DR 1–102 shall report such knowledge to … authority empowered to investigate or act upon such violation."

RULE 5.2 Responsibilities of a Subordinate Lawyer

(a) A lawyer is bound by the rules of professional conduct notwithstanding that the lawyer acted at the direction of another person.

(b) A subordinate lawyer does not violate the rules of professional conduct if that lawyer acts in accordance with a supervisory lawyer's reasonable resolution of an arguable question of professional duty.

COMMENT:

[1] Although a lawyer is not relieved of responsibility for a violation by the fact that the lawyer acted at the direction of a supervisor, that fact may be relevant in determining whether a lawyer had the knowledge required to render conduct a violation of the Rules. For example, if a subordinate filed a frivolous pleading at the direction of a supervisor, the subordinate would not be guilty of a professional violation unless the subordinate knew of the document's frivolous character.

[2] When lawyers in a supervisor-subordinate relationship encounter a matter involving professional judgment as to ethical duty, the supervisor may assume responsibility for making the judgment. Otherwise a consistent course of action or position could not be taken. If the question can reasonably be answered only one way, the duty of both lawyers is clear and they are equally responsible for fulfilling it. However, if the question is reasonably arguable, someone has to decide upon the course of action. That authority ordinarily reposes in the supervisor, and a subordinate may be guided accordingly. For example, if a question arises whether the interests of two clients conflict under Rule 1.7, the supervisor's reasonable resolution of the question should protect the subordinate professionally if the resolution is subsequently challenged.

MODEL CODE COMPARISON:

There was no counterpart to this Rule in the Model Code.

RULE 5.3 Responsibilities Regarding Nonlawyer Assistants

With respect to a nonlawyer employed or retained by or associated with a lawyer:

(a) a partner in a law firm shall make reasonable efforts to ensure that the firm has in effect measures giving reasonable assurance that the person's conduct is compatible with the professional obligations of the lawyer;

(b) a lawyer having direct supervisory authority over the nonlawyer shall make reasonable efforts to ensure that the

person's conduct is compatible with the professional obligations of the lawyer; and

(c) a lawyer shall be responsible for conduct of such a person that would be a violation of the rules of professional conduct if engaged in by a lawyer if:

(1) the lawyer orders or, with the knowledge of the specific conduct, ratifies the conduct involved; or

(2) the lawyer is a partner in the law firm in which the person is employed, or has direct supervisory authority over the person, and knows of the conduct at a time when its consequences can be avoided or mitigated but fails to take reasonable remedial action.

COMMENT:

Lawyers generally employ assistants in their practice, including secretaries, investigators, law student interns, and paraprofessionals. Such assistants, whether employees or independent contractors, act for the lawyer in rendition of the lawyer's professional services. A lawyer should give such assistants appropriate instruction and supervision concerning the ethical aspects of their employment, particularly regarding the obligation not to disclose information relating to representation of the client, and should be responsible for their work product. The measures employed in supervising nonlawyers should take account of the fact that they do not have legal training and are not subject to professional discipline.

MODEL CODE COMPARISON:

There was no direct counterpart to this Rule in the Model Code. DR 4–101(D) provided that a lawyer "shall exercise reasonable care to prevent his employees, associates, and others whose services are utilized by him from disclosing or using confidences or secrets of a client...." DR 7–107(J) provided that "[a] lawyer shall exercise reasonable care to prevent his employees and associates from making an extrajudicial statement that he would be prohibited from making under DR 7–107."

RULE 5.4   Professional Independence of a Lawyer*

(a) A lawyer or law firm shall not share legal fees with a nonlawyer, except that:

* In 1990, the ABA amended the text of Model Rule 5.4(a)(2) to recognize the addition of Model Rule 1.17 on the sale of a law practice. The original Model Rule 5.4(a)(2) read as follows:

RULE 5.4 Professional Independence of a Lawyer

(a) A lawyer or law firm shall not share legal fees with a nonlawyer, except that:

* * *

(1) an agreement by a lawyer with the lawyer's firm, partner, or associate may provide for the payment of money, over a reasonable period of time after the lawyer's death, to the lawyer's estate or to one or more specified persons;

(2) a lawyer who purchases the practice of a deceased, disabled, or disappeared lawyer may, pursuant to the provisions of Rule 1.17, pay to the estate or other representative of that lawyer the agreed-upon purchase price; and

(3) a lawyer or law firm may include nonlawyer employees in a compensation or retirement plan, even though the plan is based in whole or in part on a profit-sharing arrangement.

(b) A lawyer shall not form a partnership with a nonlawyer if any of the activities of the partnership consist of the practice of law.

(c) A lawyer shall not permit a person who recommends, employs, or pays the lawyer to render legal services for another to direct or regulate the lawyer's professional judgment in rendering such legal services.

(d) A lawyer shall not practice with or in the form of a professional corporation or association authorized to practice law for a profit, if:

(1) a nonlawyer owns any interest therein, except that a fiduciary representative of the estate of a lawyer may hold the stock or interest of the lawyer for a reasonable time during administration;

(2) a nonlawyer is a corporate director or officer thereof; or

(3) a nonlawyer has the right to direct or control the professional judgment of a lawyer.

COMMENT:

The provisions of this Rule express traditional limitations on sharing fees. These limitations are to protect the lawyer's professional independence of judgment. Where someone other than the client pays the lawyer's fee or salary, or recommends employment of the lawyer, that arrangement does not modify the lawyer's obligation to the client. As stated in paragraph (c), such arrangements should not interfere with the lawyer's professional judgment.

(2) a lawyer who undertakes to complete unfinished legal business of a deceased lawyer may pay to the estate of the deceased lawyer that proportion of the total compensation which fairly represents the services rendered by the deceased lawyer; and

* * *

MODEL CODE COMPARISON:

Paragraph (a) is substantially identical to DR 3–102(A).

Paragraph (b) is substantially identical to DR 3–103(A).

Paragraph (c) is substantially identical to DR 5–107(B).

Paragraph (d) is substantially identical to DR 5–107(C).

RULE 5.5 Unauthorized Practice of Law

A lawyer shall not:

(a) practice law in a jurisdiction where doing so violates the regulation of the legal profession in that jurisdiction; or

(b) assist a person who is not a member of the bar in the performance of activity that constitutes the unauthorized practice of law.

COMMENT:

The definition of the practice of law is established by law and varies from one jurisdiction to another. Whatever the definition, limiting the practice of law to members of the bar protects the public against rendition of legal services by unqualified persons. Paragraph (b) does not prohibit a lawyer from employing the services of paraprofessionals and delegating functions to them, so long as the lawyer supervises the delegated work and retains responsibility for their work. See Rule 5.3. Likewise, it does not prohibit lawyers from providing professional advice and instruction to nonlawyers whose employment requires knowledge of law; for example, claims adjusters, employees of financial or commercial institutions, social workers, accountants and persons employed in government agencies. In addition, a lawyer may counsel nonlawyers who wish to proceed pro se.

MODEL CODE COMPARISON:

With regard to paragraph (a), DR 3–101(B) of the Model Code provided that "[a] lawyer shall not practice law in a jurisdiction where to do so would be in violation of regulations of the profession in that jurisdiction."

With regard to paragraph (b), DR 3–101(A) of the Model Code provided that "[a] lawyer shall not aid a non-lawyer in the unauthorized practice of law."

RULE 5.6 Restrictions on Right to Practice

A lawyer shall not participate in offering or making:

(a) a partnership or employment agreement that restricts the rights of a lawyer to practice after termination of the relationship, except an agreement concerning benefits upon retirement; or

(b) an agreement in which a restriction on the lawyer's right to practice is part of the settlement of a controversy between private parties.

COMMENT:

[1]   An agreement restricting the right of partners or associates to practice after leaving a firm not only limits their professional autonomy but also limits the freedom of clients to choose a lawyer. Paragraph (a) prohibits such agreements except for restrictions incident to provisions concerning retirement benefits for service with the firm.

[2]   Paragraph (b) prohibits a lawyer from agreeing not to represent other persons in connection with settling a claim on behalf of a client.

[3] *   This Rule does not apply to prohibit restrictions that may be included in the terms of the sale of a law practice pursuant to Rule 1.17.

MODEL CODE COMPARISON:

This Rule is substantially similar to DR 2–108.

RULE 5.7   Responsibilities Regarding Law–Related Services[†]

(a) A lawyer shall be subject to the Rules of Professional Conduct with respect to the provision of law-related services, as defined in paragraph (b), if the law-related services are provided:

(1) by the lawyer in circumstances that are not distinct from the lawyer's provision of legal services to clients; or

(2) by a separate entity controlled by the lawyer individually or with others if the lawyer fails to take reasonable measures to assure that a person obtaining the law-related services knows that the services of the separate entity are not legal services and that the protections of the client-lawyer relationship do not exist.

(b) The term "law-related services" denotes services that might reasonably be performed in conjunction with and in substance are related to the provision of legal services, and that are not prohibited as unauthorized practice of law when provided by a nonlawyer.

COMMENT:

[1]   When a lawyer performs law-related services or controls an organization that does so, there exists the potential for ethical problems.

* This paragraph was added by the ABA in 1990 to resolve the potential overlap between this provision and the restrictions placed in Model Rule 1.17 regarding the sale of a law practice.

† See footnote a, page 245 infra, for text and comment to former Rule 5.7, Provision of Ancillary Services (Repealed).

Principal among these is the possibility that the person for whom the law-related services are performed fails to understand that the services may not carry with them the protections normally afforded as part of the client-lawyer relationship. The recipient of the law-related services may expect, for example, that the protection of client confidences, prohibitions against representation of persons with conflicting interests, and obligations of a lawyer to maintain professional independence apply to the provision of law-related services when that may not be the case. Rule 5.7 applies to the provision of law-related services by a lawyer even when the lawyer does not provide any legal services to the person for whom the law-related services are performed. The Rule identifies the circumstances in which all of the Rules of Professional Conduct apply to the provision of law-related services. Even when those circumstances do not exist, however, the conduct of a lawyer involved in the provision of law-related services is subject to those Rules that apply generally to lawyer conduct, regardless of whether the conduct involves the provision of legal services. See, e.g., Rule 8.4.

[2] When law-related services are provided by a lawyer under circumstances that are not distinct from the lawyer's provision of legal services to clients, the lawyer in providing the law-related services must adhere to the requirements of the Rules of Professional Conduct as provided in Rule 5.7(a)(1).

[3] Law-related services also may be provided through an entity that is distinct from that through which the lawyer provides legal services. If the lawyer individually or with others has control of such an entity's operations, the Rule requires the lawyer to take reasonable measures to assure that each person using the services of the entity knows that the services provided by the entity are not legal services and that the Rules of Professional Conduct that relate to the client-lawyer relationship do not apply. A lawyer's control of an entity extends to the ability to direct its operation. Whether a lawyer has such control will depend upon the circumstances of the particular case.

[4] When a client-lawyer relationship exists with a person who is referred by a lawyer to a separate law-related service entity controlled by the lawyer, individually or with others, the lawyer must comply with Rule 1.8(a).

[5] In taking the reasonable measures referred to in paragraph (a)(2) to assure that a person using law-related services understands the practical effect or significance of the inapplicability of the Rules of Professional Conduct, the lawyer should communicate to the person receiving the law-related services, in a manner sufficient to assure that the person understands the significance of the fact, that the relationship of the person to the business entity will not be a client-lawyer relationship. The communication should be made before entering into an agreement for provision of or providing law-related services, and preferably should be in writing.

[6] The burden is upon the lawyer to show that the lawyer has taken reasonable measures under the circumstances to communicate the desired understanding. For instance, a sophisticated user of law-related services, such as a publicly held corporation, may require a lesser explanation than someone unaccustomed to making distinctions between legal services and law-related services, such as an individual seeking tax advice from a lawyer-accountant or investigative services in connection with a lawsuit.

[7] Regardless of the sophistication of potential recipients of law-related services, a lawyer should take special care to keep separate the provision of law-related and legal services in order to minimize the risk that the recipient will assume that the law-related services are legal services. The risk of such confusion is especially acute when the lawyer renders both types of services with respect to the same matter. Under some circumstances the legal and law-related services may be so closely entwined that they cannot be distinguished from each other, and the requirement of disclosure and consultation imposed by paragraph (a)(2) of the Rule cannot be met. In such a case a lawyer will be responsible for assuring that both the lawyer's conduct and, to the extent required by Rule 5.3, that of nonlawyer employees in the distinct entity which the lawyer controls complies in all respects with the Rules of Professional Conduct.

[8] A broad range of economic and other interests of clients may be served by lawyers' engaging in the delivery of law-related services. Examples of law-related services include providing title insurance, financial planning, accounting, trust services, real estate counseling, legislative lobbying, economic analysis social work, psychological counseling, tax return preparation, and patient, medical or environmental consulting. When a lawyer is obliged to accord the recipients of such services the protections of those Rules that apply to the client-lawyer relationship, the lawyer must take special care to heed the proscriptions of the Rules addressing conflict of interest (Rules 1.7 through 1.11, especially Rules 1.7(b) and 1.8(a), (b) and (f)), and to scrupulously adhere to the requirements of Rule 1.6 relating to disclosure of confidential information. The promotion of the law-related services must also in all respects comply with Rules 7.1 through 7.3, dealing with advertising and solicitation. In that regard, lawyers should take special care to identify the obligations that may be imposed as a result of a jurisdiction's decisional law.

[9] When the full protections of all of the Rules of Professional Conduct do not apply to the provision of law-related services, principles of law external to the Rules, for example, the law of principal and agent, govern the legal duties owed to those receiving the services. Those other legal principles may establish a different degree of protection for the recipient with respect to confidentiality of information, conflicts of interest and permissible business relationships with clients. See also Rule 8.4 (Misconduct).

a. Model Rule 5.7 did not appear in the original version of the Model Rules. In 1991, the ABA added the provision reproduced in this footnote and its comments in response to the debate created by the adoption of the District of Columbia rule that allows lawyers and non-lawyers to practice together in the same law firm. D.C. Rule 5.4 is contained on pages 200–203. Model Rule 5.7 was passed by a vote of 197 to 186 in the House of Delegates.

In the August 1992 ABA meeting, the House of Delegates voted 190 to 183 to repeal the provision reproduced in this footnote. In February 1994, the ABA passed a new rule dealing with ancillary services. The short-lived Model Rule 5.7 text and comment are reprinted below:

(a) A lawyer shall not practice law in a law firm which owns a controlling interest in, or operates, an entity which provides non-legal services which are ancillary to the practice of law, or otherwise provides such ancillary non-legal services, except as provided in paragraph (b).

(b) A lawyer may practice law in a law firm which provides non-legal services which are ancillary to the practice of law if:

(1) The ancillary services are provided solely to clients of the law firm and are incidental to, in connection with and concurrent to, the provision of legal services by the law firm to such clients;

(2) Such ancillary services are provided solely by employees of the law firm itself and not by a subsidiary or other affiliate of the law firm;

(3) The law firm makes appropriate disclosure in writing to its clients; and

(4) The law firm does not hold itself out as engaging in any non-legal activities except in conjunction with the provision of legal services, as provided in this rule.

(c) One or more lawyers who engage in the practice of law in a law firm shall neither own a controlling interest in, nor operate, an entity which provides non-legal services which are ancillary to the practice of law, nor otherwise provide such ancillary non-legal services, except that their firms may provide such services as provided in paragraph (b).

(d) Two or more lawyers who engage in the practice of law in separate law firms shall neither own a controlling interest in, nor operate, an entity which provides non-legal services which are ancillary to the practice of law, nor otherwise provide such ancillary non-legal services.

COMMENT:

General

[1] For many years, lawyers have provided to their clients non-legal services which are ancillary to the practice of law. Such services included title insurance, trust services and patent consulting. In most instances, these ancillary nonlegal services were provided to law firm clients in connection with, and concurrent to, the provision of legal services by the lawyer or law firm. The provision of such services afforded benefits to clients, including making available a greater range of services from one source and maintaining technical expertise in various fields within a law firm. However, the provision of both legal and ancillary nonlegal services raises ethical concerns, including conflicts of interest, confusion on the part of clients and possible loss (or inapplicability) of the attorney-client privilege, which may not have been addressed adequately by the other Model Rules of Professional Conduct.

[2] Eventually, law firms began to form affiliates, largely staffed by nonlawyers, to provide ancillary nonlegal services to both clients and customers who were not clients for legal services. In addition to exacerbating the ethical problems of conflicts of interest, confusion and threats to confidentiality, the large-scale movement of law firms into ancillary nonlegal businesses raised serious professionalism concerns, including compromising lawyers' independent judg-

ment, the loss of the bar's right to self-regulation and the provision of legal services by entities controlled by nonlawyers.

[3] Rule 5.7 addresses both the ethical and professionalism concerns implicated by the provision of ancillary nonlegal services by lawyers and law firms. It preserves the ability of lawyers to provide additional services to their clients and maintain within the law firm a broad range of technical expertise. However, Rule 5.7 restricts the ability of law firms to provide ancillary nonlegal services through affiliates to nonclient customers and clients alike, the rendition of which raises serious ethical and professionalism concerns.

Limitations on the Provision of Nonlegal Services Which Are Ancillary to the Practice of Law

[4] Paragraph (a) attempts to forestall the ethical and professional concerns which are raised when law firms own or operate nonlegal businesses which are ancillary to the practice of law or otherwise provide such services. The provision of such ancillary services by law firms has the potential of compromising a lawyer's independent professional judgment and otherwise causing harm to law firm clients (*e.g.*, creating conflicts of interest, jeopardizing clients' expectations of confidentiality and causing confusion on the part of clients). Additionally, serious threats to lawyers' professionalism are also posed when law firms own or operate ancillary businesses which provide services to persons who are not concurrently seeking legal services from the law firm.

[5] Paragraph (a) prohibits lawyers from practicing in a law firm which owns a controlling interest in, or operates, an entity which provides nonlegal services which are ancillary to the practice of law, or which provides such ancillary services from within the law firm, unless such services are incidental to the law firm's provision of legal services as set forth in Paragraph (b).

[6] The term "nonlegal services which are ancillary to the practice of law" refers to those services which satisfy all or most of the following indicia: (1) are provided to clients of a law firm (or customers of a business owned or controlled by a law firm); (2) clearly do not constitute the practice of law; (3) are readily available from those not licensed to practice law; (4) are functionally connected to the provision of legal services, i.e., services which are often sought or needed in connection with (and in addition to) legal services; (5) involve intellectual ability or learning; and (6) have the potential for creating serious ethical problems in the lawyer-client relationship, such as compromising the independent professional judgment of lawyers; creating conflicts of interest; threatening the clients' (or customers') expectations of confidentiality and/or causing confusion on the part of clients or customers.

[7] Among those activities which are not included in the term "nonlegal services which are ancillary to the practice of law" because they do not pose serious ethical problems in the lawyer-client relationship are:

(1) law firms or lawyers owning, for example, restaurants, shops or taxi services (since these services are not functionally connected to the practice of law);

(2) law firms providing copying services or other clerical services incidental to the practice of law;

(3) law firms owning and managing the buildings in which their offices are located or other property (since owning and managing property—even through a subsidiary or affiliate—is not functionally connected to the provision of legal services to clients);

(4) a law firm providing services or products intended for use by other lawyers, such as publications, software programs, or legal malpractice insurance (since such services or products are not functionally connected to the provision of legal services to clients);

(5) lawyers serving as fiduciaries of trusts or corporate directors or lawyers serving in quasi-judicial positions such as mediators or arbitrators.

[8] When services provided by a law firm are performed by nonlawyers, there should be an initial presumption that the

services do not constitute the practice of law and may be a "nonlegal service which is ancillary to the practice of law." In addition, a presumption that a service is "ancillary to the practice of law" should exist if the service is normally provided by nonlawyers in discrete professions or occupations, e.g., doctors, architects, engineers, real estate brokers, investment bankers or financial consultants.

[9] Note that Paragraph (a) does not prohibit a lawyer from practicing in a law firm which acquires a passive financial interest in an entity which provides nonlegal ancillary services (i.e., purchasing shares of an investment banking firm or a consulting company), provided that the interest is not a controlling one. This rule does not define the concept of control, which is generally a fact-based inquiry dependent on the particular facts and circumstances. However, the existence of an ownership interest by lawyers in other entities (especially clients) may implicate conflict of interest concerns (see Model Rules of Professional Conduct 1.7 and 1.8) and may require disclosure by the lawyers pursuant to these rules.

Connection Between the Provision of Legal and Ancillary Nonlegal Services

[10] Paragraph (b) preserves the ability of law firms to provide nonlegal services which are ancillary to the practice of law, but under conditions designed to ensure that such services are closely related to the firms' provision of legal services and not independent of, and unrelated to, such legal services.

[11] Subsection (1) of Paragraph (b) requires that ancillary nonlegal services be provided solely to law firm clients (as opposed to persons who are not currently seeking legal services from a law firm) and be incidental to, in connection with, and concurrent to, the provision of legal services by the law firm. The requirement that ancillary services be "incidental to" and "in connection with" the firm's provision of legal services seeks to ensure that any nonlegal services be secondary to, strictly related to, and under the supervision of those responsible for, the provision of legal services.

[12] Paragraph (b) permits law firms to employ the services of other professionals if their services are connected to the firm's provision of legal services. For example, an architect on staff at a law firm would be permitted to help clients and lawyers understand the technical issues in a construction contract negotiation, a building accident litigation or the like. However, the requirement in Paragraph (b) that such services be "incidental to" and "in connection with" the provision of legal services would proscribe a law firm from employing architects to design buildings for law firm clients or for nonclient customers who do not use the law firm's legal services. Similarly, an investment banker on staff at a law firm would be permitted to assist lawyers in the negotiation of a transaction or the litigation of valuation issues or the like, as well as to consult with law firm clients when the firm is providing legal services to them, but a law firm would be prohibited from employing investment bankers to seek out acquisitions, sell securities (or otherwise secure financing) or perform other investment banking services unrelated to a pending legal representation. Likewise, a corporation pursuing an acquisition might need the assistance of nonlawyer lobbyists before a state legislature considering anti-takeover legislation. Such lobbying designed to forestall (or attain) a change in the law, if provided by nonlawyers within a law firm, could reasonably be construed to be incidental to the firm's provision of legal services.

[13] Paragraph (b) also requires that the provision of nonlegal services be concurrent with the provision of legal services. In essence, law firm clients (like nonlegal services customers generally) may not obtain ancillary nonlegal services from the law firm (e.g., investment banking services or medical tests), and the firm may not provide them, at a time when the client is not obtaining legal services from the law firm on a related matter.

Provision of Ancillary Nonlegal Services by Employees of Law Firms

[14] Subsection (2) of Paragraph (b), in an effort to vitiate risks of compromise to lawyers' professional judgment, con-

flicts of interest, client confusion and potential loss of confidentiality, provides that any ancillary services provided by a law firm must be performed within the law firm by employees of the law firm itself (who work together with, and are supervised by, the firm's lawyers), and not through a subsidiary or affiliate of the law firm. This requirement closely unites the provision of legal and nonlegal services under the supervision of lawyers and thereby affords lawyers the opportunity to ensure that their nonlawyer employees are acting responsibly and in accordance with the rules of legal ethics. Such a requirement minimizes the risks of nonlegal employees either providing advice with which the firm's lawyers will disagree and/or engaging in improper behavior for which the firm's lawyers would be responsible. In addition, structuring the provision of nonlegal services in such a way forestalls confusion on the part of clients as to whether the nonlegal services are provided subject to the limitations of the Model Rules (and will prevent lawyers from seeking to provide services outside of the protections afforded to clients by the Model Rules). Finally, if lawyers are present (or otherwise involved) in the provision of nonlegal services ancillary to the practice of law, there is a greater likelihood that client confidences will be protected and a client will be able to maintain evidentiary privileges with respect to communications made by the client to the providers of nonlegal ancillary services. Paragraph (b)(2) is not designed to limit the ability of lawyers to retain outside (*i.e.*, nonaffiliated) consultants such as experts, private investigators or accountants to help them provide legal services to clients.

Disclosure Requirements Relating to the Provision of Ancillary Nonlegal Services

[15] Subsection (3) of Paragraph (b) requires that before providing ancillary services to a client, a law firm must comply with appropriate disclosure requirements (as mandated in Model Rule of Professional Conduct 1.8, relevant case law and other authorities) and fully disclose in writing the firm's interest in the providers of nonlegal services em-

ployed by the firm and the potential conflicts of interest inherent in the provision of such services. The law firm should also consider, in appropriate circumstances, recommending that the client seek the advice of independent counsel (or independent providers of nonlegal services) before obtaining nonlegal services from the firm.

Representations Concerning Ancillary and Nonlegal Services

[16] Subsection (4) of Paragraph (b) ensures that when law firms deal with clients (whether prospective or actual) or the public, they do not represent themselves as providing any ancillary nonlegal services independent of the firm's provision of legal services. This proscription attempts to obviate the risks of confusion on the part of clients and the public, actual or apparent overreaching by attorneys and improper solicitation. It ensures that clients and the public are aware that they are dealing with a law firm and can therefore assume that representatives of the firm are bound by the rules of legal ethics; prospective or actual clients do not feel compelled to use the firm's ancillary services; and law firms do not engage in improper solicitation by seeking business for the firm's nonlegal services with an expectation that these nonlegal services will serve as a "feeder" for the firm's legal services. Paragraph (b)(4) also seeks to preserve the unique and independent status of the legal profession in the public's perception by preventing law firms from representing themselves to clients and the public as multidisciplinary conglomerates or otherwise emphasizing their nonlegal activities.

[17] Paragraph (b)(4) is not intended to preclude law firms from making the existence of their nonlegal business known to clients who have retained the firm for legal services, and who, in the attorney's opinion, might have a need for the firm's ancillary services in addition to legal services (subject to appropriate disclosure requirements). In addition, Paragraph (b)(4) is not intended to prevent individual lawyers from indicating that they are qualified or licensed in other

professions, e.g., accounting, where relevant jurisdictions so permit.

Provision of Ancillary Nonlegal Services By One or More Lawyers in a Law Firm

[18] Paragraph (c) prevents one or more lawyers in a single law firm from owning or operating an entity which provides nonlegal services which are ancillary to the practice of law. Paragraph (c) attempts to prevent lawyers or law firms from circumventing the restrictions on law firm ownership and operation of ancillary businesses by vesting ownership not in the entire law firm, but in one or more of the attorneys in a law firm. The ethical and professional concerns inherent in the ownership of ancillary businesses are not vitiated when ownership or operation is vested in several partners in a law firm (as opposed to an entire law firm). However, a law firm itself may provide such ancillary nonlegal services in accordance with Paragraph (b).

Provision of Ancillary Nonlegal Services by Lawyers from Different Law Firms

[19] Paragraph (d) addresses the concerns which may result when lawyers in separate law firms own or operate an entity which provides nonlegal services which are ancillary to the practice of law. The ethical and professional concerns inherent in the ownership and operation of such ancillary businesses by law firms (or one or more lawyers in a firm) are also present (or may be exacerbated) when lawyers in different firms own or operate such businesses.

MODEL CODE COMPARISON

There was no counterpart to this Rule in the Model Code.

PUBLIC SERVICE

RULE 6.1   Voluntary Pro Bono Publico Service *

A lawyer should aspire to render at least (50) hours of pro bono publico legal services per year. In fulfilling this responsibility, the lawyer should:

* In February 1993, the ABA House of Delegates replaced the original version of Model Rule 6.1 with an aspirational plea for 50 hours a year from each lawyer. The amended language also seeks to direct lawyers to provide pro bono services to the economically disadvantaged rather than to charitable and nonprofit organizations. The new rule was adopted by a vote of 228 to 215. The following represents the original text of Model Rule 6.1 and its comments:

RULE 6.1   Pro Bono Publico Service

A lawyer should render public interest legal service. A lawyer may discharge this responsibility by providing professional services at no fee or a reduced fee to persons of limited means or to public service or charitable groups or organizations, by service in activities for improving the law, the legal system or the legal profession, and by financial support for organizations that provide legal services to persons of limited means.

COMMENT:

[1] The ABA House of Delegates has formally acknowledged "the basic responsibility of each lawyer engaged in the practice of law to provide public interest legal services" without fee, or at a substantially reduced fee, in one or more of the following areas: poverty law, civil rights law, public rights law, charitable organization representation and the administration of justice. This Rule expresses that policy but is not intended to be enforced through disciplinary process.

[2] The rights and responsibilities of individuals and organizations in the United States are increasingly defined in legal terms. As a consequence, legal assis-

(a) provide a substantial majority of the (50) hours of legal services without fee or expectation of fee to:

(1) persons of limited means or

(2) charitable, religious, civic, community, governmental and educational organizations in matters which are designed primarily to address the needs of persons of limited means; and

(b) provide any additional services through:

(1) delivery of legal services at no fee or substantially reduced fee to individuals, groups or organizations seeking to secure or protect civil rights, civil liberties or public rights, or charitable, religious, civic, community, governmental and educational organizations in matters in furtherance of their organizational purposes, where the payment of standard legal fees would significantly deplete the organization's economic resources or would be otherwise inappropriate;

(2) delivery of legal services at a substantially reduced fee to persons of limited means; or

(3) participation in activities for improving the law, the legal system or the legal profession.

In addition, a lawyer should voluntarily contribute financial support to organizations that provide legal services to persons of limited means.

COMMENT:

[1] Every lawyer, regardless of professional prominence or professional work load, has a responsibility to provide legal services to those unable to pay, and personal involvement in the problems of the disadvantaged can be one of the most rewarding experiences in the life of a

tance in coping with the web of statutes, rules and regulations is imperative for persons of modest and limited means, as well as for the relatively well-to-do.

[3] The basic responsibility for providing legal services for those unable to pay ultimately rests upon the individual lawyer, and personal involvement in the problems of the disadvantaged can be one of the most rewarding experiences in the life of a lawyer. Every lawyer, regardless of professional prominence or professional workload, should find time to participate in or otherwise support the provision of legal services to the disadvantaged. The provision of free legal services to

those unable to pay reasonable fees continues to be an obligation of each lawyer as well as the profession generally, but the efforts of individual lawyers are often not enough to meet the need. Thus, it has been necessary for the profession and government to institute additional programs to provide legal services. Accordingly, legal aid offices, lawyer referral services and other related programs have been developed, and others will be developed by the profession and government. Every lawyer should support all proper efforts to meet this need for legal services.

lawyer. The American Bar Association urges all lawyers to provide a minimum of 50 hours of pro bono services annually. States, however, may decide to choose a higher or lower number of hours of annual service (which may be expressed as a percentage of a lawyer's professional time) depending upon local needs and local conditions. It is recognized that in some years a lawyer may render greater or fewer hours than the annual standard specified, but during the course of his or her legal career, each lawyer should render on average per year, the number of hours set forth in this Rule. Services can be performed in civil matters or in criminal or quasi-criminal matters for which there is no government obligation to provide funds for legal representation, such as post-conviction death penalty appeal cases.

[2] Paragraphs (a)(1) and (2) recognize the critical need for legal services that exists among persons of limited means by providing that a substantial majority of the legal services rendered annually to the disadvantaged be furnished without fee or expectation of fee. Legal services under these paragraphs consist of a full range of activities, including individual and class representation, the provision of legal advice, legislative lobbying, administrative rule making and the provision of free training or mentoring to those who represent persons of limited means. The variety of these activities should facilitate participation by government attorneys, even when restrictions exist on their engaging in the outside practice of law.

[3] Persons eligible for legal services under paragraphs (a)(1) and (2) are those who qualify for participation in programs funded by the Legal Services Corporation and those whose incomes and financial resources are slightly above the guidelines utilized by such programs but nevertheless, cannot afford counsel. Legal services can be rendered to individuals or to organizations such as homeless shelters, battered women's centers and food pantries that serve those of limited means. The term ''governmental organizations'' includes, but is not limited to, public protection programs and sections of governmental or public sector agencies.

[4] Because service must be provided without fee or expectation of fee, the intent of the lawyer to render free legal services is essential for the work performed to fall within the meaning of paragraphs (a)(1) and (2). Accordingly, services rendered cannot be considered pro bono if an anticipated fee is uncollected, but the award of statutory attorneys' fees in a case originally accepted as pro bono would not disqualify such services from inclusion under this section. Lawyers who do receive fees in such cases are encouraged to contribute an appropriate portion of such fees to organizations or projects that benefit persons of limited means.

[5] While it is possible for a lawyer to fulfill the annual responsibility to perform pro bono services exclusively through activities described in paragraphs (a)(1) and (2), to the extent that any hours of service remained unfulfilled, the remaining commitment can be met in a variety

of ways as set forth in paragraph (b). Constitutional, statutory or regulatory restrictions may prohibit or impede government and public sector lawyers and judges from performing the pro bono services outlined in paragraphs (a)(1) and (2). Accordingly, where those restrictions apply, government and public sector lawyers and judges may fulfill their pro bono responsibility by performing services outlined in paragraph (b).

[6] Paragraph (b)(1) includes the provision of certain types of legal services to those whose incomes and financial resources place them above limited means. It also permits the pro bono attorney to accept a substantially reduced fee for services. Example of the types of issues that may be addressed under this paragraph include First Amendment claims, Title VII claims and environmental protection claims. Additionally, a wide range of organizations may be represented, including social service, medical research, cultural and religious groups.

[7] Paragraph (b)(2) covers instances in which attorneys agree to and receive a modest fee for furnishing legal services to persons of limited means. Participation in judicare programs and acceptance of court appointments in which the fee is substantially below a lawyer's usual rate are encouraged under this section.

[8] Paragraph (b)(3) recognizes the value of lawyers engaging in activities that improve the law, the legal system or the legal profession. Serving on bar association committees, serving on boards of pro bono or legal services programs, taking part in Law Day activities, acting as a continuing legal education instructor, a mediator or an arbitrator and engaging in legislative lobbying to improve the law, the legal system or the profession are a few examples of the many activities that fall within this paragraph.

[9] Because the provision of pro bono services is a professional responsibility, it is the individual ethical commitment of each lawyer. Nevertheless, there may be times when it is not feasible for a lawyer to engage in pro bono services. At such times a lawyer may discharge the pro bono responsibility by providing financial support to organizations providing free legal services to persons of limited means. Such financial support should be reasonably equivalent to the value of the hours of service that would have otherwise been provided. In addition, at times it may be more feasible to satisfy the pro bono responsibility collectively, as by a firm's aggregate pro bono activities.

[10] Because the efforts of individual lawyers are not enough to meet the need for free legal services that exists among persons of limited means, the government and the profession have instituted additional programs to provide those services. Every lawyer should financially support such programs, in addition to either providing direct pro bono services or making financial contributions when pro bono service is not feasible.

[11] The responsibility set forth in this Rule is not intended to be enforced through disciplinary process.

MODEL CODE COMPARISON:

There was no counterpart of this Rule in the Disciplinary Rules of the Model Code. EC 2–25 stated that the "basic responsibility for providing legal services for those unable to pay ultimately rests upon the individual lawyer.... Every lawyer, regardless of professional prominence or professional work load, should find time to participate in serving the disadvantaged." EC 8–9 stated that "[t]he advancement of our legal system is of vital importance in maintaining the rule of law ... [and] lawyers should encourage, and should aid in making, needed changes and improvements." EC 8–3 stated that "[t]hose persons unable to pay for legal services should be provided needed services."

RULE 6.2   Accepting Appointments

A lawyer shall not seek to avoid appointment by a tribunal to represent a person except for good cause, such as:

(a) representing the client is likely to result in violation of the rules of professional conduct or other law;

(b) representing the client is likely to result in an unreasonable financial burden on the lawyer; or

(c) the client or the cause is so repugnant to the lawyer as to be likely to impair the client-lawyer relationship or the lawyer's ability to represent the client.

COMMENT:

[1] A lawyer ordinarily is not obliged to accept a client whose character or cause the lawyer regards as repugnant. The lawyer's freedom to select clients is, however, qualified. All lawyers have a responsibility to assist in providing pro bono publico service. See Rule 6.1. An individual lawyer fulfills this responsibility by accepting a fair share of unpopular matters or indigent or unpopular clients. A lawyer may also be subject to appointment by a court to serve unpopular clients or persons unable to afford legal services.

Appointed Counsel

[2] For good cause a lawyer may seek to decline an appointment to represent a person who cannot afford to retain counsel or whose cause is unpopular. Good cause exists if the lawyer could not handle the matter competently, see Rule 1.1, or if undertaking the representation would result in an improper conflict of interest, for example, when the client or the cause is so repugnant to the lawyer as to be likely to impair the client-lawyer relationship or the lawyer's ability to represent the client. A lawyer may also seek to decline an appointment if acceptance would be unreasonably burdensome, for example, when it would impose a financial sacrifice so great as to be unjust.

[3] An appointed lawyer has the same obligations to the client as retained counsel, including the obligations of loyalty and confidentiality,

and is subject to the same limitations on the client-lawyer relationship, such as the obligation to refrain from assisting the client in violation of the Rules.

MODEL CODE COMPARISON:

There was no counterpart to this Rule in the Disciplinary Rules of the Model Code. EC 2–29 stated that when a lawyer is "appointed by a court or requested by a bar association to undertake representation of a person unable to obtain counsel, whether for financial or other reasons, he should not seek to be excused from undertaking the representation except for compelling reasons. Compelling reasons do not include such factors as the repugnance of the subject matter of the proceeding, the identity or position of a person involved in the case, the belief of the lawyer that the defendant in a criminal proceeding is guilty, or the belief of the lawyer regarding the merits of the civil case." EC 2–30 stated that "a lawyer should decline employment if the intensity of his personal feelings, as distinguished from a community attitude, may impair his effective representation of a prospective client."

RULE 6.3 Membership in Legal Services Organization

A lawyer may serve as a director, officer or member of a legal services organization, apart from the law firm in which the lawyer practices, notwithstanding that the organization serves persons having interests adverse to a client of the lawyer. The lawyer shall not knowingly participate in a decision or action of the organization:

(a) if participating in the decision or action would be incompatible with the lawyer's obligations to a client under rule 1.7; or

(b) where the decision or action could have a material adverse effect on the representation of a client of the organization whose interests are adverse to a client of the lawyer.

COMMENT:

[1] Lawyers should be encouraged to support and participate in legal service organizations. A lawyer who is an officer or a member of such an organization does not thereby have a client-lawyer relationship with persons served by the organization. However, there is potential conflict between the interests of such persons and the interests of the lawyer's clients. If the possibility of such conflict disqualified a lawyer from serving on the board of a legal services organization, the profession's involvement in such organizations would be severely curtailed.

[2] It may be necessary in appropriate cases to reassure a client of the organization that the representation will not be affected by conflicting loyalties of a member of the board. Established, written policies in this respect can enhance the credibility of such assurances.

MODEL CODE COMPARISON:

There was no counterpart to this Rule in the Model Code.

RULE 6.4   Law Reform Activities Affecting Client Interests

A lawyer may serve as a director, officer or member of an organization involved in reform of the law or its administration notwithstanding that the reform may affect the interests of a client of the lawyer. When the lawyer knows that the interests of a client may be materially benefitted by a decision in which the lawyer participates, the lawyer shall disclose that fact but need not identify the client.

COMMENT:

Lawyers involved in organizations seeking law reform generally do not have a client-lawyer relationship with the organization. Otherwise, it might follow that a lawyer could not be involved in a bar association law reform program that might indirectly affect a client. See also Rule 1.2(b). For example, a lawyer specializing in antitrust litigation might be regarded as disqualified from participating in drafting revisions of rules governing that subject. In determining the nature and scope of participation in such activities, a lawyer should be mindful of obligations to clients under other Rules, particularly Rule 1.7. A lawyer is professionally obligated to protect the integrity of the program by making an appropriate disclosure within the organization when the lawyer knows a private client might be materially benefitted.

MODEL CODE COMPARISON:

There was no counterpart to this Rule in the Model Code.

INFORMATION ABOUT LEGAL SERVICES

RULE 7.1   Communications Concerning a Lawyer's Services

A lawyer shall not make a false or misleading communication about the lawyer or the lawyer's services. A communication is false or misleading if it:

(a) contains a material misrepresentation of fact or law, or omits a fact necessary to make the statement considered as a whole not materially misleading;

(b) is likely to create an unjustified expectation about results the lawyer can achieve, or states or implies that the lawyer can achieve results by means that violate the rules of professional conduct or other law; or

(c) compares the lawyer's services with other lawyers' services, unless the comparison can be factually substantiated.

COMMENT:

This Rule governs all communications about a lawyer's services, including advertising permitted by Rule 7.2. Whatever means are used to make known a lawyer's services, statements about them should be truthful. The prohibition in paragraph (b) of statements that may create "unjustified expectations" would ordinarily preclude advertisements about results obtained on behalf of a client, such as the amount of a damage award or the lawyer's record in obtaining favorable verdicts, and advertisements containing client endorsements. Such information may create the unjustified expectation that similar results can be obtained for others without reference to the specific factual and legal circumstances.

MODEL CODE COMPARISON:

DR 2–101 provided that "[a] lawyer shall not ... use ... any form of public communication containing a false, fraudulent, misleading, deceptive, self-laudatory or unfair statement or claim." DR 2–101(B) provided that a lawyer "may publish or broadcast ... the following information ... in the geographic area or areas in which the lawyer resides or maintains offices or in which a significant part of the lawyer's clientele resides, provided that the information ... complies with DR 2–101(A), and is presented in a dignified manner...." DR 2–101(B) then specified twenty-five categories of information that may be disseminated. DR 2–101(C) provided that "[a]ny person desiring to expand the information authorized for disclosure in DR 2–101(B), or to provide for its dissemination through other forums may apply to [the agency having jurisdiction under state law].... The relief granted in response to any such application shall be promulgated as an amendment to DR 2–101(B), universally applicable to all lawyers."

RULE 7.2 Advertising*

(a) Subject to the requirements of rule 7.1 and 7.3, a lawyer may advertise services through public media, such as a tele-

* The ABA amended Model Rule 7.2 in 1989 to conform to the holding in Shapero v. Kentucky Bar Ass'n, 486 U.S. 466 (1988) and in 1990 to reflect the addition of Model Rule 1.17 on the sale of a law practice. The original version of Model Rule 7.2 read as follows:

RULE 7.2 Advertising

(a) Subject to the requirements of Rules 7.1, a lawyer may advertise services through public media, such as a telephone directory, legal directory, newspaper or other periodical, outdoor, radio or television, or through written communication not involving solicitation as defined in Rule 7.3.

(b) A copy or recording of an advertisement or written communication shall be kept for two years after its last dissemination along with a record of when and where it was used.

(c) A lawyer shall not give anything of value to a person for recommending the lawyer's services, except that a lawyer may pay the

phone directory, legal directory, newspaper or other periodical, outdoor advertising, radio or television, or through written or recorded communication.

(b) A copy or recording of an advertisement or written communication shall be kept for two years after its last dissemination along with a record of when and where it was used.

(c) A lawyer shall not give anything of value to a person for recommending the lawyer's services, except that a lawyer may

(1) pay the reasonable costs of advertisements or communications permitted by this Rule;

(2) pay the usual charges of a not-for-profit lawyer referral service or legal service organization; and

(3) pay for a law practice in accordance with Rule 1.17.

(d) Any communication made pursuant to this rule shall include the name of at least one lawyer responsible for its content.

COMMENT:

[1]   To assist the public in obtaining legal services, lawyers should be allowed to make known their services not only through reputation but also through organized information campaigns in the form of advertising.   Advertising involves an active quest for clients, contrary to the tradition that a lawyer should not seek clientele.   However, the public's need to know about legal services can be fulfilled in part through advertising.   This need is particularly acute in the case of persons of moderate means who have not made extensive use of legal services.   The interest in expanding public information about legal services ought to prevail over considerations of tradition.   Nevertheless, advertising by lawyers entails the risk of practices that are misleading or overreaching.

[2]   This Rule permits public dissemination of information concerning a lawyer's name or firm name, address and telephone number;   the kinds of services the lawyer will undertake;   the basis on which the lawyer's fees are determined, including prices for specific services and payment and credit arrangements;   a lawyer's foreign language ability;   names of references and, with their consent, names of clients regularly represented;   and other information that might invite the attention of those seeking legal assistance.

[3]   Questions of effectiveness and taste in advertising are matters of speculation and subjective judgment.   Some jurisdictions have had extensive prohibitions against television advertising, against advertising

reasonable cost of advertising or written communication permitted by this rule and may pay the usual charges of a not-for-profit lawyer referral service or other legal service organization.

(d) Any communication made pursuant to this rule shall include the name of at least one lawyer responsible for its content.

going beyond specified facts about a lawyer, or against "undignified" advertising. Television is now one of the most powerful media for getting information to the public, particularly persons of low and moderate income; prohibiting television advertising, therefore, would impede the flow of information about legal services to many sectors of the public. Limiting the information that may be advertised has a similar effect and assumes that the bar can accurately forecast the kind of information that the public would regard as relevant.

[4] Neither this Rule nor Rule 7.3 prohibits communications authorized by law, such as notice to members of a class in class action litigation.

Record of Advertising

[5] Paragraph (b) requires that a record of the content and use of advertising be kept in order to facilitate enforcement of this Rule. It does not require that advertising be subject to review prior to dissemination. Such a requirement would be burdensome and expensive relative to its possible benefits, and may be of doubtful constitutionality.

Paying Others to Recommend a Lawyer*

[6] A lawyer is allowed to pay for advertising permitted by this Rule and for the purchase of a law practice in accordance with the provisions of Rule 1.17, but otherwise is not permitted to pay another person for channeling professional work. This restriction does not prevent an organization or person other than the lawyer from advertising or recommending the lawyer's services. Thus, a legal aid agency or prepaid legal services plan may pay to advertise legal services provided under its auspices. Likewise, a lawyer may participate in not-for-profit lawyer referral programs and pay the usual fees charged by such programs. Paragraph (c) does not prohibit paying regular compensation to an assistant, such as a secretary, to prepare communications permitted by this Rule.

MODEL CODE COMPARISON:

With regard to paragraph (a), DR 2–101(B) provided that a lawyer "may publish or broadcast, subject to DR 2–103, ... in print media ... or television or radio...."

With regard to paragraph (b), DR 2–101(D) provided that if the advertisement is "communicated to the public over television or radio, ... a recording of the actual transmission shall be retained by the lawyer."

With regard to paragraph (c), DR 2–103(B) provided that a lawyer "shall not compensate or give anything of value to a person or organiza-

---

* In 1990, the ABA added the clause "and for the purchase of a law practice in accordance with the provisions of Rule 1.17" to reflect to addition of this provision to the Model Rules.

tion to recommend or secure his employment ... except that he may pay the usual and reasonable fees or dues charged by any of the organizations listed in DR 2–103(D)." (DR 2–103(D) referred to legal aid and other legal services organizations.) DR 2–101(I) provided that a lawyer "shall not compensate or give anything of value to representatives of the press, radio, television, or other communication medium in anticipation of or in return for professional publicity in a news item."

There was no counterpart to paragraph (d) in the Model Code.

RULE 7.3 Direct Contact With Prospective Clients*

(a) A lawyer shall not by in-person or live telephone contact solicit professional employment from a prospective client with whom the lawyer has no family or prior professional relationship when a significant motive for the lawyer's doing so is the lawyer's pecuniary gain.

(b) A lawyer shall not solicit professional employment from a prospective client by written or recorded communication or by in-person or telephone contact even when not otherwise prohibited by paragraph (a), if:

(1) the prospective client has made known to the lawyer a desire not to be solicited by the lawyer; or

(2) the solicitation involves coercion, duress or harassment.

(c) Every written or recorded communication from a lawyer soliciting professional employment from a prospective client known to be in need of legal services in a particular matter, and with whom the lawyer has no family or prior professional relationship, shall include the words "Advertising Material" on the outside envelope and at the beginning and ending of any recorded communication.

---

* The ABA amended the original version of Model Rule 7.3 in 1989 because in 1988 the Supreme Court had declared a blanket restriction on targeted mailings unconstitutional under the First Amendment. See Shapero v. Kentucky Bar Ass'n, 486 U.S. 466 (1988). The Kentucky rule which was the subject of the Supreme Court decision was identical to the original Model Rule 7.3. This provision read as follows:

RULE 7.3 Direct Contact With Prospective Clients

A lawyer may not solicit professional employment from a prospective client with whom the lawyer has no family or prior professional rela-

tionship, by mail, in-person or otherwise, when a significant motive for the lawyer's doing so is the lawyer's pecuniary gain. The term "solicit" includes contact in person, by telephone or telegraph, by letter or other writing or by other communication directed to a specific recipient, but does not include letters addressed or advertising circulars distributed generally to persons not known to need legal services of the kind provided by the lawyer in a particular matter, but who are so situated that they might in general find such services useful.

(d) Notwithstanding the prohibitions in paragraph (a), a lawyer may participate with a prepaid or group legal service plan operated by an organization not owned or directed by the lawyer which uses in-person or telephone contact to solicit memberships or subscriptions for the plan from persons who are not known to need legal services in a particular matter covered by the plan.

COMMENT: *

[1]   There is a potential for abuse inherent in direct in-person or live telephone contact by a lawyer with a prospective client known to

* The ABA amended the comments to Model Rule 7.3 in 1989 to reflect changes made in the text of the Rule brought about by the *Shapero* decision. The text of the original comment reads as follows:

COMMENT:

There is a potential for abuse inherent in direct solicitation by a lawyer of prospective clients known to need legal services. It subjects the lay person to the private importuning of a trained advocate, in a direct interpersonal encounter. A prospective client often feels overwhelmed by the situation giving rise to the need for legal services, and may have an impaired capacity for reason, judgment and protective self-interest. Furthermore, the lawyer seeking the retainer is faced with a conflict stemming from the lawyer's own interest, which may color the advice and representation offered the vulnerable prospect.

The situation is therefore fraught with the possibility of undue influence, intimidation, and over-reaching. This potential for abuse inherent in direct solicitation of prospective clients justifies its prohibition, particularly since lawyer advertising permitted under Rule 7.2 offers an alternative means of communicating necessary information to those who may be in need of legal services.

Advertising makes it possible for a prospective client to be informed about the need for legal services, and about the qualifications of available lawyers and law firms, without subjecting the prospective client to direct personal persuasion that may overwhelm the client's judgment.

The use of general advertising to transmit information from lawyer to prospective client, rather than direct private contact, will help to assure that the information flows cleanly as well as freely. Advertising is out in public view, thus subject to scrutiny by those who know the lawyer. This informal review is itself likely to help guard against statements and claims that might constitute false or misleading communications, in violation of Rule 7.1. Direct, private communications from a lawyer to a prospective client are not subject to such third-scrutiny and consequently are much more likely to approach (and occasionally cross) the dividing line between accurate representations and those that are false and misleading.

These dangers attend direct solicitation whether in-person or by mail. Direct mail solicitation cannot be effectively regulated by means less drastic than outright prohibition. One proposed safeguard is to require that the designation "Advertising" be stamped on any envelope containing a solicitation letter. This would do nothing to assure the accuracy and reliability of the contents. Another suggestion is that solicitation letters be filed with a state regulatory agency. This would be ineffective as a practical matter. State lawyer discipline agencies struggle for resources to investigate specific complaints, much less for those necessary to screen lawyers' mail solicitation material. Even if they could examine such materials, agency staff members are unlikely to know anything about the lawyer or about the prospective client's underlying problem. Without such knowlneed legal services. These forms of contact between a lawyer and a prospective client subject the layperson to the private importuning of the trained advocate in a direct interpersonal encounter. The prospective client, who may already feel overwhelmed by the circumstances giving rise to the need for legal services, may find it difficult fully to evaluate all available alternatives with reasoned judgment and appropriate self-interest in the face of the lawyer's presence and insistence upon being retained immediately. The situation is fraught with the possibility of undue influence, intimidation, and over-reaching.

[2] This potential for abuse inherent in direct in-person or live telephone solicitation of prospective clients justifies its prohibition, particularly since lawyer advertising and written and recorded communication permitted under Rule 7.2 offer alternative means of conveying necessary information to those who may be in need of legal services. Advertising and written and recorded communications which may be mailed or autodialed make it possible for a prospective client to be informed about the need for legal services, and about the qualifications of available lawyers and law firms, without subjecting the prospective client to direct in-person or telephone persuasion that may overwhelm the client's judgment.

[3] The use of general advertising and written and recorded communications to transmit information from lawyer to prospective client, rather than direct in-person or live telephone contact, will help to assure that the information flows cleanly as well as freely. The contents of advertisements and communications permitted under Rule 7.2 are per-

edge they cannot determine whether the lawyer's representations are misleading. In any event, such review would be after the fact, potentially too late to avert the undesirable consequences of disseminating false and misleading material.

General mailings not speaking to a specific matter do not pose the same danger of abuse as targeted mailings, and therefore are not prohibited by this Rule. The representations made in such mailings are necessarily general rather than tailored, less importuning than informative. They are addressed to recipients unlikely to be specially vulnerable at the time, hence who are likely to be more skeptical about unsubstantiated claims. General mailings not addressed to recipients involved in a specific legal matter or incident, therefore, more closely resemble permissible advertising rather than prohibited solicitation.

Similarly, this Rule would not prohibit a lawyer from contacting representatives of organizations or groups that may be interested in establishing a group or prepaid legal plan for its members, insureds, beneficiaries or other third parties for the purpose of informing such entities of the availability of and details concerning the plan or arrangement which he or his firm is willing to offer. This form of communication is not directed to a specific prospective client known to need legal services related to a particular matter. Rather, it is usually addressed to an individual acting in a fiduciary capacity seeking a supplier of legal services for others who may, if they choose, become prospective clients of the lawyer. Under these circumstances, the activity which the lawyer undertakes in communicating with such representatives and the type of information transmitted to the individual are functionally similar to and serve the same purpose as advertising permitted under Rule 7.2.

manently recorded so that they cannot be disputed and may be shared with others who know the lawyer. This potential for informal review is itself likely to help guard against statements and claims that might constitute false and misleading communications, in violation of Rule 7.1. The contents of direct in-person or live telephone conversations between a lawyer to a prospective client can be disputed and are not subject to third-party scrutiny. Consequently, they are much more likely to approach (and occasionally cross) the dividing line between accurate representations and those that are false and misleading.

[4] There is far less likelihood that a lawyer would engage in abusive practices against an individual with whom the lawyer has a prior personal or professional relationship or where the lawyer is motivated by considerations other than the lawyer's pecuniary gain. Consequently, the general prohibition in Rule 7.3(a) and the requirements of Rule 7.3(c) are not applicable in those situations.

[5] But even permitted forms of solicitation can be abused. Thus, any solicitation which contains information which is false or misleading within the meaning of Rule 7.1, which involves coercion, duress or harassment within the meaning of Rule 7.3(b)(2), or which involves contact with a prospective client who has made known to the lawyer a desire not to be solicited by the lawyer within the meaning of Rule 7.3(b)(1) is prohibited. Moreover, if after sending a letter or other communication to a client as permitted by Rule 7.2 the lawyer receives no response, any further effort to communicate with the prospective client may violate the provisions of Rule 7.3(b).

[6] This Rule is not intended to prohibit a lawyer from contacting representatives of organizations or groups that may be interested in establishing a group or prepaid legal plan for their members, insureds, beneficiaries or other third parties for the purpose of informing such entities of the availability of and details concerning the plan or arrangement which the lawyer or lawyer's firm is willing to offer. This form of communication is not directed to a prospective client. Rather, it is usually addressed to an individual acting in a fiduciary capacity seeking a supplier of legal services for others who may, if they choose, become prospective clients of the lawyer. Under these circumstances, the activity which the lawyer undertakes in communicating with such representatives and the type of information transmitted to the individual are functionally similar to and serve the same purpose as advertising permitted under Rule 7.2.

[7] The requirement in Rule 7.3(c) that certain communications be marked "Advertising Material" does not apply to communications sent in response to requests of potential clients or their spokespersons or sponsors. General announcements by lawyers, including changes in personnel or office location, do not constitute communications soliciting professional employment from a client known to be in need of legal services within the meaning of this Rule.

[8]   Paragraph (d) of this Rule would permit an attorney to participate with an organization which uses personal contact to solicit members for its group or prepaid legal service plan, provided that the personal contact is not undertaken by any lawyer who would be a provider of legal services through the plan.   The organization referred to in paragraph (d) must not be owned by or directed (whether as manager or otherwise) by any lawyer or law firm that participates in the plan.   For example, paragraph (d) would not permit a lawyer to create an organization controlled directly or indirectly by the lawyer and use the organization for the in-person or telephone solicitation of legal employment of the lawyer through memberships in the plan or otherwise.   The communication permitted by these organizations also must not be directed to a person known to need legal services in a particular matter, but is to be designed to inform potential plan members generally of another means of affordable legal services.   Lawyers who participate in a legal service plan must reasonably assure that the plan sponsors are in compliance with Rules 7.1, 7.2 and 7.3(a).   See 8.4(a).

MODEL CODE COMPARISON:

DR 2–104(A) provided with certain exceptions that "[a] lawyer who has given in-person unsolicited advice to a layperson that he should obtain counsel or take legal action shall not accept employment resulting from that advice...."   The exceptions include DR 2–104(A)(1), which provided that a lawyer "may accept employment by a close friend, relative, former client (if the advice is germane to the former employment), or one whom the lawyer reasonably believes to be a client."   DR 2–104(A)(2) through DR 2–104(A)(5) provided other exceptions relating, respectively, to employment resulting from public educational programs, recommendation by a legal assistance organization, public speaking or writing and representing members of a class in class action litigation.

RULE 7.4   Communication of Fields of Practice *

A lawyer may communicate the fact that the lawyer does or does not practice in particular fields of law. A lawyer shall not

* In August 1992, the ABA House of Delegates modified Model Rule 7.4(c) as a reaction to the Supreme Court's decision in Peel v. Attorney Registration and Disciplinary Commission, 496 U.S. 91 (1990).   The 1983 version of 7.4(c) read as follows: "(c) (provisions on designation of specialization of the particular state)."   The original intent of the rule was to limit the right of lawyers to state or imply that they are specialists except when a state has an organized plan of specialization or in the two well defined area of law (admiralty and patent) in which a long tradition of specialization exists.   In Peel, the Supreme Court held that a state could not prohibit a lawyer from stating that he or she is a civil trial specialist certified by the National Board of Trial Advocacy.   The revised rule encourages the states to create organizations to certify organizations that seek to qualify lawyers as specialists and requires lawyers who wish to advertise specialties by organizations that have either been denied or not approved to disclose such information in the advertisement.   In its February 1993 meeting, the ABA adopted "Standards for

state or imply that the lawyer is a specialist in a particular field of law except as follows:

(a) a lawyer admitted to engage in patent practice before the United States Patent and Trademark Office may use the designation "Patent Attorney" or a substantially similar designation;

(b) a lawyer engaged in admiralty practice may use the designation "Admiralty," "Proctor in Admiralty" or a substantially similar designation; and

(c) [for jurisdictions where there is a regulatory authority granting certification or approving organizations that grant certification] a lawyer may communicate the fact that the lawyer has been certified as a specialist in a field of law by a named organization or authority, but only if:

(1) such certification is granted by the appropriate regulatory authority or by an organization which has been approved by the appropriate regulatory authority to grant such certification; or

(2) such certification is granted by an organization that has not yet been approved by, or has been denied the approval available from, the appropriate regulatory authority, and the absence or denial of approval is clearly stated in the communication, and in any advertisement subject to Rule 7.2, such statement appears in the same sentence that communicates the certification.

(c) [for jurisdictions where there is no procedure either for certification of specialties or for approval of organizations granting certification] a lawyer may communicate the fact that the lawyer has been certified as a specialist in a field of law by a named organization, provided that the communication clearly states that there is no procedure in this jurisdiction for approving certifying organizations. If, however, the named organization has been accredited by the American Bar Association to certify lawyers as specialists in a particular field of law, the communication need not contain such a statement.

Accreditation of Specialty Certification Programs for Lawyers." These standards seek to ensure that certification programs ensure that the lawyer has a special proficiency in the specialty and devotes a substantial amount of time to this type of work. They also require that certifying organizations be made up primarily of lawyer members.

In August 1994, the ABA House of Delegates added the last line to alternative paragraph (c): "If, however, the named organization has been accredited by the American Bar Association to certify lawyers as specialists in a particular field of law, the communication need not contain such a statement."

This line reflects the new role of the ABA committee on specialization to accredit organizations.

COMMENT: *

[1] This Rule permits a lawyer to indicate areas of practice in communications about the lawyer's services. If a lawyer practices only in certain fields, or will not accept matters in a specified field or fields, the lawyer is permitted to so indicate. A lawyer is generally permitted to state that the lawyer is a "specialist," practices a "specialty," or "specializes in" particular fields, but such communications are subject to the "false and misleading" standard applied in Rule 7.1 to communications concerning a lawyer's services.

[2] However, a lawyer may not communicate that the lawyer has been recognized or certified as a specialist in a particular field of law, except as provided by this Rule. Recognition of specialization in patent matters is a matter of long-established policy of the Patent and Trademark Office, as reflected in paragraph (a). Paragraph (b) recognizes that designation of admiralty practice has a long historical tradition associated with maritime commerce and the federal courts.

[3] Paragraph (c) provides for certification as a specialist in a field of law when a state authorizes an appropriate regulatory authority to grant such certification or when the state grants other organizations the right to grant certification. Certification procedures imply that an objective entity has recognized a lawyer's higher degree of specialized ability than is suggested by general licensure to practice law. Those

---

* In 1989, the ABA amended the comment to Model Rule 7.3 to reflect concerns that the language in the original comment may violate the Supreme Court's legal advertising decisions. The original language read as follows:

COMMENT:

This Rule permits a lawyer to indicate areas of practice in communications about the lawyer's services; for example, in a telephone directory or other advertising. If a lawyer practices only in certain fields, or will not accept matters except in such fields, the lawyer is permitted so to indicate. However, stating that the lawyer is a "specialist" or that the lawyer's practice "is limited to" or "concentrated in" particular fields is not permitted. These terms have acquired a secondary meaning implying formal recognition as a specialist. Hence, use of these terms may be misleading unless the lawyer is certified or recognized in accordance with procedures in the state where the lawyer is licensed to practice.

The 1989 amendment adopted the following language:

COMMENT:

[1] This Rule permits a lawyer to indicate areas of practice in communications about the lawyer's services; for example, in a telephone directory or other advertising. If a lawyer practices only in certain fields, or will not accept matters except in such fields, the lawyer is permitted so to indicate. However, a lawyer is not permitted to state that the lawyer is a "specialist," practices a "specialty," or "specializes in" particular fields. These terms have acquired a secondary meaning implying formal recognition as a specialist and therefore, use of these terms is misleading. [An exception would apply in those states which provide procedures for certification or recognition of specialization and the lawyer has complied with such procedures.]

[2] Recognition of specialization in patent matters is a matter of long-established policy of the Patent and Trademark Office. Designation of admiralty practice has a long historical tradition associated with maritime commerce and the federal courts.

objective entities may be expected to apply standards of competence, experience and knowledge to insure that a lawyer's recognition as a specialist is meaningful and reliable. In order to insure that consumers can obtain access to useful information about an organization granting certification, the name of the certifying organization or agency must be included in any communication regarding the certification.

[4] Lawyers may also be certified as specialists by organizations that either have not yet been approved to grant such certification or have been disapproved. In such instances, the consumer may be misled as to the significance of the lawyer's status as a certified specialist. The Rule therefore requires that a lawyer who chooses to communicate recognition by such an organization also clearly state the absence or denial of the organization's authority to grant such certification. Since lawyer advertising through public media and written or recorded communications invites the greatest danger of misleading consumers, the absence or denial of the organization's authority to grant certification must be clearly stated in such advertising in the same sentence that communicates the certification.

[5]* In jurisdictions where no appropriate regulatory authority has a procedure for approving organizations granting certification, the Rule requires that a lawyer clearly state such lack of procedure.

If, however, the named organization has been accredited by the American Bar Association to certify lawyers as specialists in a particular field of law, the communication need not contain such a statement.

MODEL CODE COMPARISON:

DR 2–105(A) provided that a lawyer "shall not hold himself out publicly as a specialist, as practicing in certain areas of law or as limiting his practice . . . except as follows:

"(1) A lawyer admitted to practice before the United States Patent and Trademark Office may use the designation 'Patents,' 'Patent Attorney,' 'Patent Lawyer,' or 'Registered Patent Attorney' or any combination of those terms, on his letterhead and office sign.

"(2) A lawyer who publicly discloses fields of law in which the lawyer . . . practices or states that his practice is limited to one or more fields of law shall do so by using designations and definitions authorized and approved by [the agency having jurisdiction of the subject under state law].

"(3) A lawyer who is certified as a specialist in a particular field of law or law practice by [the authority having jurisdiction under state law over the subject of specialization by lawyers] may hold himself out as such, but only in accordance with the rules prescribed by that authority."

* The ABA added the last line in this paragraph when it amended alternative paragraph (c).

EC 2–14 stated that "In the absence of state controls to insure the existence of special competence, a lawyer should not be permitted to hold himself out as a specialist, ... other than in the fields of admiralty, trademark, and patent law where a holding out as a specialist historically has been permitted."

RULE 7.5 Firm Names and Letterheads

(a) A lawyer shall not use a firm name, letterhead or other professional designation that violates rule 7.1. A trade name may be used by a lawyer in private practice if it does not imply a connection with a government agency or with a public or charitable legal services organization and is not otherwise in violation of rule 7.1.

(b) A law firm with offices in more than one jurisdiction may use the same name in each jurisdiction, but identification of the lawyers in an office of the firm shall indicate the jurisdictional limitations on those not licensed to practice in the jurisdiction where the office is located.

(c) The name of a lawyer holding a public office shall not be used in the name of a law firm, or in communications on its behalf, during any substantial period in which the lawyer is not actively and regularly practicing with the firm.

(d) Lawyers may state or imply that they practice in a partnership or other organization only when that is the fact.

COMMENT:

[1] A firm may be designated by the names of all or some of its members, by the names of deceased members where there has been a continuing succession in the firm's identity or by a trade name such as the "ABC Legal Clinic." Although the United States Supreme Court has held that legislation may prohibit the use of trade names in professional practice, use of such names in law practice is acceptable so long as it is not misleading. If a private firm uses a trade name that includes a geographical name such as "Springfield Legal Clinic," an express disclaimer that it is a public legal aid agency may be required to avoid a misleading implication. It may be observed that any firm name including the name of a deceased partner is, strictly speaking, a trade name. The use of such names to designate law firms has proven a useful means of identification. However, it is misleading to use the name of a lawyer not associated with the firm or a predecessor of the firm.

[2] With regard to paragraph (d), lawyers sharing office facilities, but who are not in fact partners, may not denominate themselves as, for example, "Smith and Jones," for that title suggests partnership in the practice of law.

MODEL CODE COMPARISON:

With regard to paragraph (a), DR 2–102(A) provided that "[a] lawyer ... shall not use ... professional announcement cards ... letterheads, or similar professional notices or devices, except ... if they are in dignified form...." DR 2–102(B) provided that "[a] lawyer in private practice shall not practice under a trade name, a name that is misleading as to the identity of the lawyer or lawyers practicing under such name, or a firm name containing names other than those of one or more of the lawyers in the firm, except that ... a firm may use as ... its name the name or names of one or more deceased or retired members of the firm or of a predecessor firm in a continuing line of succession."

With regard to paragraph (b), DR 2–102(D) provided that a partnership "shall not be formed or continued between or among lawyers licensed in different jurisdictions unless all enumerations of the members and associates of the firm on its letterhead and in other permissible listings make clear the jurisdictional limitations on those members and associates of the firm not licensed to practice in all listed jurisdictions; however, the same firm name may be used in each jurisdiction."

With regard to paragraph (c), DR 2–102(B) provided that "[a] lawyer who assumes a judicial, legislative, or public executive or administrative post or office shall not permit his name to remain in the name of a law firm ... during any significant period in which he is not actively and regularly practicing law as a member of the firm...."

Paragraph (d) is substantially identical to DR 2–102(C).

RULE 7.6 Political Contributions to Obtain Government Legal Engagements or Appointments by Judges*

A lawyer or law firm shall not accept a government legal engagement or an appointment by a judge if the lawyer or law firm makes a political contribution or solicits political contributions for the purpose of obtaining or being considered for that type of legal engagement or appointment.

COMMENT:

[1] Lawyers have a right to participate fully in the political process, which includes making and soliciting political contributions to candidates for judicial and other public office. Nevertheless, when lawyers make or solicit political contributions in order to obtain an engagement for legal work awarded by a government agency, or to obtain appointment by a judge, the public may legitimately question whether the lawyers engaged to perform the work are selected on the basis of

---

* In February 2000, the ABA enacted the new Model Rule 7.6 to address ethical problems with the "pay to play" practice in effect in some jurisdictions.

competence and merit. In such a circumstance, the integrity of the profession is undermined.

[2] The term "political contribution" denotes any gift, subscription, loan, advance or deposit of anything of value made directly or indirectly to a candidate, incumbent, political party or campaign committee to influence or provide financial support for election to or retention in judicial or other government office. Political contributions in initiative and referendum elections are not included. For purposes of this Rule, the term "political contribution" does not include uncompensated services.

[3] Subject to the exceptions below, (i) the term "government legal engagement" denotes any engagement to provide legal services that a public official has the direct or indirect power to award; and (ii) the term "appointment by a judge" denotes an appointment to a position such as referee, commissioner, special master, receiver, guardian or other similar position that is made by a judge. Those terms do not, however, include (a) substantially uncompensated services; (b) engagements or appointments made on the basis of experience, expertise, professional qualifications and cost following a request for proposal or other process that is free from influence based upon political contributions; and (c) engagements or appointments made on a rotational basis from a list compiled without regard to political contributions.

[4] The term "lawyer or law firm" includes a political action committee or other entity owned or controlled by a lawyer or law firm.

[5] Political contributions are for the purpose of obtaining or being considered for a government legal engagement or appointment by a judge if, but for the desire to be considered for the legal engagement or appointment, the lawyer or law firm would not have made or solicited the contributions. The purpose may be determined by an examination of the circumstances in which the contributions occur. For example, one or more contributions that in the aggregate are substantial in relation to other contributions by lawyers or law firms, made for the benefit of an official in a position to influence award of a government legal engagement, and followed by an award of the legal engagement to the contributing or soliciting lawyer or the lawyer's firm would support an inference that the purpose of the contributions was to obtain the engagement, absent other factors that weigh against existence of the proscribed purpose. Those factors may include among others that the contribution or solicitation was made to further a political, social, or economic interest or because of an existing personal, family, or professional relationship with a candidate.

[6] If a lawyer makes or solicits a political contribution under circumstances that constitute bribery or another crime, Rule 8.4(b) is implicated.

MAINTAINING THE INTEGRITY OF THE PROFESSION

RULE 8.1 Bar Admission and Disciplinary Matters

An applicant for admission to the bar, or a lawyer in connection with a bar admission application or in connection with a disciplinary matter, shall not:

(a) knowingly make a false statement of material fact; or

(b) fail to disclose a fact necessary to correct a misapprehension known by the person to have arisen in the matter, or knowingly fail to respond to a lawful demand for information from an admission or disciplinary authority, except that this rule does not require disclosure of information otherwise protected by rule 1.6.

COMMENT:

[1] The duty imposed by this Rule extends to persons seeking admission to the bar as well as to lawyers. Hence, if a person makes a material false statement in connection with an application for admission, it may be the basis for subsequent disciplinary action if the person is admitted, and in any event may be relevant in a subsequent admission application. The duty imposed by this Rule applies to a lawyer's own admission or discipline as well as that of others. Thus, it is a separate professional offense for a lawyer to knowingly make a misrepresentation or omission in connection with a disciplinary investigation of the lawyer's own conduct. This Rule also requires affirmative clarification of any misunderstanding on the part of the admissions or disciplinary authority of which the person involved becomes aware.

[2] This Rule is subject to the provisions of the Fifth Amendment of the United States Constitution and corresponding provisions of state constitutions. A person relying on such a provision in response to a question, however, should do so openly and not use the right of nondisclosure as a justification for failure to comply with this Rule.

[3] A lawyer representing an applicant for admission to the bar, or representing a lawyer who is the subject of a disciplinary inquiry or proceeding, is governed by the rules applicable to the client-lawyer relationship.

MODEL CODE COMPARISON:

DR 1–101(A) provided that a lawyer is "subject to discipline if he has made a materially false statement in, or if he has deliberately failed to disclose a material fact requested in connection with, his application for admission to the bar." DR 1–101(B) provided that a lawyer "shall not further the application for admission to the bar of another person known by him to be unqualified in respect to character, education, or other relevant attribute." With respect to paragraph (b), DR 1–

102(A)(5) provided that a lawyer shall not engage in "conduct that is prejudicial to the administration of justice."

RULE 8.2   Judicial and Legal Officials

(a) A lawyer shall not make a statement that the lawyer knows to be false or with reckless disregard as to its truth or falsity concerning the qualifications or integrity of a judge, adjudicatory officer or public legal officer, or of a candidate for election or appointment to judicial or legal office.

(b) A lawyer who is a candidate for judicial office shall comply with the applicable provisions of the code of judicial conduct.

COMMENT:

[1]   Assessments by lawyers are relied on in evaluating the professional or personal fitness of persons being considered for election or appointment to judicial office and to public legal offices, such as attorney general, prosecuting attorney and public defender. Expressing honest and candid opinions on such matters contributes to improving the administration of justice. Conversely, false statements by a lawyer can unfairly undermine public confidence in the administration of justice.

[2]   When a lawyer seeks judicial office, the lawyer should be bound by applicable limitations on political activity.

[3]   To maintain the fair and independent administration of justice, lawyers are encouraged to continue traditional efforts to defend judges and courts unjustly criticized.

MODEL CODE COMPARISON:

With regard to paragraph (a), DR 8–102(A) provided that a lawyer "shall not knowingly make false statements of fact concerning the qualifications of a candidate for election or appointment to a judicial office." DR 8–102(B) provided that a lawyer "shall not knowingly make false accusations against a judge or other adjudicatory officer."
Paragraph (b) is substantially identical to DR 8–103.

RULE 8.3   Reporting Professional Misconduct*

(a) A lawyer having knowledge that another lawyer has committed a violation of the rules of professional conduct that raises a substantial question as to that lawyer's honesty, trustworthiness or fitness as a lawyer in other respects, shall inform the appropriate professional authority.

---

* In 1991, the ABA amended Model Rule 8.3(c) to include the reference to the protection of certain information obtained in lawyer assistance programs. The original version of 8.3(c) read as follows: "This rule does not require disclosure of information otherwise protected by Rule 1.6."

(b) A lawyer having knowledge that a judge has committed a violation of applicable rules of judicial conduct that raises a substantial question as to the judge's fitness for office shall inform the appropriate authority.

(c) This rule does not require disclosure of information otherwise protected by Rule 1.6 or information gained by a lawyer or judge while serving as a member of an approved lawyers assistance program to the extent that such information would be confidential if it were communicated subject to the attorney-client privilege.

COMMENT:

[1] Self-regulation of the legal profession requires that members of the profession initiate disciplinary investigation when they know of a violation of the Rules of Professional Conduct. Lawyers have a similar obligation with respect to judicial misconduct. An apparently isolated violation may indicate a pattern of misconduct that only a disciplinary investigation can uncover. Reporting a violation is especially important where the victim is unlikely to discover the offense.

[2] A report about misconduct is not required where it would involve violation of Rule 1.6. However, a lawyer should encourage a client to consent to disclosure where prosecution would not substantially prejudice the client's interests.

[3] If a lawyer were obliged to report every violation of the Rules, the failure to report any violation would itself be a professional offense. Such a requirement existed in many jurisdictions but proved to be unenforceable. This Rule limits the reporting obligation to those offenses that a self-regulating profession must vigorously endeavor to prevent. A measure of judgment is, therefore, required in complying with the provisions of this Rule. The term "substantial" refers to the seriousness of the possible offense and not the quantum of evidence of which the lawyer is aware. A report should be made to the bar disciplinary agency unless some other agency, such as a peer review agency, is more appropriate in the circumstances. Similar considerations apply to the reporting of judicial misconduct.

[4] The duty to report professional misconduct does not apply to a lawyer retained to represent a lawyer whose professional conduct is in question. Such a situation is governed by the rules applicable to the client-lawyer relationship.

[5] Information about a lawyer's or judge's misconduct or fitness may be received by a lawyer in the course of that lawyer's participation in an approved lawyers' or judges' assistance program. In that circumstance, providing for the confidentiality of such information encourages lawyers and judges to seek treatment through such program. Conversely, without such confidentiality, lawyers and judges may hesitate to seek assistance from these programs, which may then result in additional harm to their professional careers and additional injury to the welfare of

275

clients and the public. The Rule therefore exempts the lawyer from the reporting requirements of paragraphs (a) and (b) with respect to information that would be privileged if the relationship between the impaired lawyer or judge and the recipient of the information were that of a client and a lawyer. On the other hand, a lawyer who receives such information would nevertheless be required to comply with the Rule 8.3 reporting provisions to report misconduct if the impaired lawyer or judge indicates an intent to engage in illegal activity, for example, the conversion of client funds to his or her use.

MODEL CODE COMPARISON:

DR 1–103(A) provided that "[a] lawyer possessing unprivileged knowledge of a violation of [a Disciplinary Rule] shall report such knowledge to ... authority empowered to investigate or act upon such violation."

RULE 8.4 Misconduct

It is professional misconduct for a lawyer to:

(a) violate or attempt to violate the rules of professional conduct, knowingly assist or induce another to do so, or do so through the acts of another;

(b) commit a criminal act that reflects adversely on the lawyer's honesty, trustworthiness or fitness as a lawyer in other respects;

(c) engage in conduct involving dishonesty, fraud, deceit or misrepresentation;

(d) engage in conduct that is prejudicial to the administration of justice;

(e) state or imply an ability to influence improperly a government agency or official; or

(f) knowingly assist a judge or judicial officer in conduct that is a violation of applicable rules of judicial conduct or other law.

COMMENT:

[1] Many kinds of illegal conduct reflect adversely on fitness to practice law, such as offenses involving fraud and the offense of willful failure to file an income tax return. However, some kinds of offense carry no such implication. Traditionally, the distinction was drawn in terms of offenses involving "moral turpitude." That concept can be construed to include offenses concerning some matters of personal morality, such as adultery and comparable offenses, that have no specific connection to fitness for the practice of law. Although a lawyer is personally answerable to the entire criminal law, a lawyer should be professionally answerable only for offenses that indicate lack of those characteristics relevant to law practice. Offenses involving violence,

276

dishonesty or breach of trust, or serious interference with the administration of justice are in that category. A pattern of repeated offenses, even ones of minor significance when considered separately, can indicate indifference to legal obligation.

[2] * A lawyer who, in the course of representing a client, knowingly manifests by words or conduct, bias or prejudice based upon race, sex, religion, national origin, disability, age, sexual orientation or socioeconomic status, violates paragraph (d) when such actions are prejudicial to the administration of justice. Legitimate advocacy respecting the foregoing factors does not violate paragraph (d). A trial judge's finding that peremptory challenges were exercised on a discriminatory basis does not alone establish a violation of this rule.

[3] A lawyer may refuse to comply with an obligation imposed by law upon a good faith belief that no valid obligation exists. The provisions of Rule 1.2(d) concerning a good faith challenge to the validity, scope, meaning or application of the law apply to challenges of legal regulation of the practice of law.

[4] Lawyers holding public office assume legal responsibilities going beyond those of other citizens. A lawyer's abuse of public office can suggest an inability to fulfill the professional role of attorney. The same is true of abuse of positions of private trust such as trustee, executor, administrator, guardian, agent and officer, director or manager of a corporation or other organization.

MODEL CODE COMPARISON:

With regard to paragraphs (a) through (d) DR 1–102(A) provided that a lawyer shall not:

"(1) Violate a Disciplinary Rule.

"(2) Circumvent a Disciplinary Rule through actions of another.

"(3) Engage in illegal conduct involving moral turpitude.

"(4) Engage in conduct involving dishonesty, fraud, deceit, or misrepresentation.

"(5) Engage in conduct that is prejudicial to the administration of justice.

"(6) Engage in any other conduct that adversely reflects on his fitness to practice law."

Paragraph (e) is substantially similar to DR 9–101(C).

There was no direct counterpart to paragraph (f) in the Disciplinary Rules of the Model Code. EC 7–34 stated in part that "[a] lawyer . . . is never justified in making a gift or a loan to a [judicial officer] except as permitted by . . . the Code of Judicial Conduct." EC 9–1 stated that a

---

* The ABA House of Delegates added this comment to Model Rule 8.4 in 1998 after pressure from many groups to amend the text of the rule to prohibit attorney conduct or words based upon bias or prejudice unrelated to the merits of the representation.

lawyer "should promote public confidence in our [legal] system and in the legal profession."

RULE 8.5 Disciplinary Authority; Choice of Law*

(a) **Disciplinary Authority.** A lawyer admitted to practice in this jurisdiction is subject to the disciplinary authority of this jurisdiction, regardless of where the lawyer's conduct occurs. A lawyer may be subject to the disciplinary authority of both this jurisdiction and another jurisdiction where the lawyer is admitted for the same conduct.

(b) **Choice of Law.** In any exercise of the disciplinary authority of this jurisdiction, the rules of professional conduct to be applied shall be as follows:

(1) for conduct in connection with a proceeding in a court before which a lawyer has been admitted to practice (either generally or for purposes of that proceeding), the rules to be applied shall be the rules of the jurisdiction in which the court sits, unless the rules of the court provide otherwise; and

(2) for any other conduct,

(i) if the lawyer is licensed to practice only in this jurisdiction, the rules to be applied shall be the rules of this jurisdiction, and

(ii) if the lawyer is licensed to practice in this and another jurisdiction, the rules to be applied shall be the rules of the admitting jurisdiction in which the lawyer

---

* In August 1993, the ABA amended Model Rule 8.5 to more clearly address the problem of choice of professional responsibility rules when more than one jurisdiction's rules may potentially apply to the lawyer's conduct. The original Model Rule 8.5 text and comments are reprinted below:

RULE 8.5 Jurisdiction

A lawyer admitted to practice in this jurisdiction is subject to the disciplinary authority of this jurisdiction although engaged in practice elsewhere.

COMMENT:

[1] In modern practice lawyers frequently act outside the territorial limits of the jurisdiction in which they are licensed to practice, either in another state or outside the United States. In doing so, they remain subject to the governing authority of the jurisdiction in which they are licensed to practice. If their activity in another jurisdiction is substantial and continuous, it may constitute practice of law in that jurisdiction. See Rule 5.5.

[2] If the rules of professional conduct in the two jurisdictions differ, principles of conflict of laws may apply. Similar problems can arise when a lawyer is licensed to practice in more than one jurisdiction.

[3] Where the lawyer is licensed to practice law in two jurisdictions which impose conflicting obligations, applicable rules of choice of law may govern the situation. A related problem arises with respect to practice before a federal tribunal, where the general authority of the states to regulate the practice of law must be reconciled with such authority as federal tribunals may have to regulate practice before them.

principally practices; provided, however, that if particular conduct clearly has its predominant effect in another jurisdiction in which the lawyer is licensed to practice, the rules of that jurisdiction shall be applied to that conduct.

COMMENT:

Disciplinary Authority

[1] Paragraph (a) restates longstanding law.

Choice of Law

[2] A lawyer may be potentially subject to more than one set of rules of professional conduct which impose different obligations. The lawyer may be licensed to practice in more than one jurisdiction with differing rules, or may be admitted to practice before a particular court with rules that differ from those of the jurisdiction or jurisdictions in which the lawyer is licensed to practice. In the past, decisions have not developed clear or consistent guidance as to which rules apply in such circumstances.

[3] Paragraph (b) seeks to resolve such potential conflicts. Its premise is that minimizing conflicts between rules, as well as uncertainty about which rules are applicable, is in the best interest of both clients and the profession (as well as the bodies having authority to regulate the profession). Accordingly, it takes the approach of (i) providing that any particular conduct of an attorney shall be subject to only one set of rules of professional conduct, and (ii) making the determination of which set of rules applies to particular conduct as straightforward as possible, consistent with recognition of appropriate regulatory interests of relevant jurisdictions.

[4] Paragraph (b) provides that as to a lawyer's conduct relating to a proceeding in a court before which the lawyer is admitted to practice (either generally or pro hac vice), the lawyer shall be subject only to the rules of professional conduct of that court. As to all other conduct, paragraph (b) provides that a lawyer licensed to practice only in this jurisdiction shall be subject to the rules of professional conduct of this jurisdiction, and that a lawyer licensed in multiple jurisdictions shall be subject only to the rules of the jurisdiction where he or she (as an individual, not his or her firm) principally practices, but with one exception: if particular conduct clearly has its predominant effect in another admitting jurisdiction, then only the rules of that jurisdiction shall apply. The intention is for the latter exception to be a narrow one. It would be appropriately applied, for example, to a situation in which a lawyer admitted in, and principally practicing in, State A, but also admitted in State B, handled an acquisition by a company whose headquarters and operations were in State B of another, similar such company. The exception would not appropriately be applied, on the other hand, if the lawyer handled an acquisition by a company whose

headquarters and operations were in State A of a company whose headquarters and main operations were in State A, but which also had some operations in State B.

[5] If two admitting jurisdictions were to proceed against a lawyer for the same conduct, they should, applying this rule, identify the same governing ethics rules. They should take all appropriate steps to see that they do apply the same rule to the same conduct, and in all events should avoid proceeding against a lawyer on the basis of two inconsistent rules.

[6]   The choice of law provision is not intended to apply to transnational practice. Choice of law in this context should be the subject of agreements between jurisdictions or of appropriate international law.

MODEL CODE COMPARISON:

There was no counterpart to this Rule in the Model Code.

TABLES A AND B: RELATED SECTIONS IN THE ABA MODEL CODE OF PROFESSIONAL RESPONSIBILITY

TABLE A *

ABA Model Rules	ABA Model Code	ABA Model Rules	ABA Model Code
Competence		*Conflict of Interest*	
Rule 1.1	EC 1–1, EC 1–2, EC 6–1, EC 6–2, EC 6–3, EC 6–4, EC 6–5, DR 6–101(A)	Rule 1.7(a)	EC 5–1, EC 5–14, EC 5–15, EC 5–17, EC 5–21, EC 5–22, DR 5–101(A), DR 5–105(A) & (B), DR 5–107(B)
Scope of Representation		Rule 1.7(b) & (b)(1)	EC 2–21, EC 5–1, EC 5–2, EC 5–3, EC 5–9, EC 5–11, EC 5–13, EC 5–14, EC 5–15, EC 5–16, EC 5–17, EC 5–19, EC 5–21, EC 5–22, EC 5–23, DR 5–101(A) & (B), DR 5–102, DR 5–104(A), DR 5–105(A), (B) & (C), DR 5–107(A)
Rule 1.2(a)	EC 5–12, EC 7–7, EC 7–8, DR 7–101(A)(1)		
Rule 1.2(b)	EC 7–17		
Rule 1.2(c)	EC 7–8, EC 7–9, DR 7–101(B)(1)		
Rule 1.2(d)	EC 7–1, EC 7–2, EC 7–5, EC 7–22, DR 7–102(A)(6), (7) & (8), DR 7–106		
Rule 1.2(e)	DR 2–110(C)(1)(c), DR 9–101(C)	Rule 1.7(b)(2)	EC 5–16, EC 5–17, DR 7–106(B)(2)
Diligence		*Prohibited Transactions*	
Rule 1.3	EC 2–31, EC 6–4, EC 7–1, EC 7–38, DR 6–101(A)(3), DR 7–101(A)(1) & (3)	Rule 1.8(a)	EC 5–3, EC 5–5, DR 5–104(A)
		Rule 1.8(b)	EC 4–5, DR 4–101(B)
Communication		Rule 1.8(c)	EC 5–1, EC 5–2, EC 5–5, EC 5–6
Rule 1.4(a)	EC 7–8, EC 9–2, DR 6–101(A)(3), DR 9–102(B)(1)	Rule 1.8(d)	EC 5–1, EC 5–3, EC 5–4, DR 5–104(B)
Rule 1.4(b)	EC 7–8	Rule 1.8(e)	EC 5–1, EC 5–3, EC 5–7, EC 5–8, DR 5–103(B)
Fees			
Rule 1.5(a)	EC 2–16, EC 2–17, EC 2–18, DR 2–106(A) & (B)	Rule 1.8(f)	EC 2–21, EC 5–1, DR 5–107(A) & (B)
Rule 1.5(b)	EC 2–19	Rule 1.8(g)	EC 5–1, DR 5–106(A)
Rule 1.5(c)	EC 2–20, EC 5–7		
Rule 1.5(d)	EC 2–20, DR 2–106(C)	Rule 1.8(h)	EC 6–6, DR 6–102(A)
Rule 1.5(e)	EC 2–22, DR 2–107(A)	Rule 1.8(i)	None
		Rule 1.8(j)	EC 5–1, EC 5–7, DR 5–101(A), DR 5–103(A)
Confidentiality of Information			
Rule 1.6(a)	EC 4–1, EC 4–2, EC 4–3, EC 4–4, DR 4–101(A), (B) & (C)	*Former Client*	
		Rule 1.9(a)	DR 5–105(C)
Rule 1.6(b)(1)	EC 4–2, DR 4–101(C)(3), DR 7–102(B)	Rule 1.9(b)	EC 4–5, EC 4–6
		Imputed Disqualification	
Rule 1.6(b)(2)	DR 4–101(C)(4)	Rule 1.10(a)	EC 4–5, DR 5–105(D)

* Table A provides cross-references to related provisions, but only in the sense that the provisions consider substantially similar subject matter or reflect similar concerns. A cross-reference does not indicate that a provision of the ABA Model Code of Professional Responsibility has been incorporated by the provision of a Model Rule. The Canons of the Code are not cross-referenced.

ABA MODEL RULES

ABA Model Rules	ABA Model Code	ABA Model Rules	ABA Model Code
Imputed Disqualification		*Declining or Terminating Representation*	
Rule 1.10(b)	EC 4–5, DR 5–105(D)	Rule 1.16(b)(5)	EC 2–32, DR 2–110(C)(1)(d) & (e)
Rule 1.10(c)	DR 5–105(A)	Rule 1.16(b)(6)	EC 2–32, DR 2–110(C)(6)
Rule 1.10(d)	EC 5–16	Rule 1.16(c)	EC 2–32, DR 2–110(A)(1)
Successive Government and Private Employment		Rule 1.16(d)	EC 2–32, DR 2–110(A)(2) & (3)
Rule 1.11(a)	EC 9–3, DR 9–101(B)	*Advisor*	
Rule 1.11(b)	None	Rule 2.1	EC 5–11, EC 7–3, EC 7–8, DR 5–107(B)
Rule 1.11(c)	EC 8–8		
Rule 1.11(d)	None	*Intermediary*	
Rule 1.11(e)	None	Rule 2.2(a)(1)	EC 4–2, EC 5–14, EC 5–15, EC 5–16, EC 5–20, DR 5–105(A) & (C)
Former Judge or Arbitrator			
Rule 1.12(a) & (b)	EC 5–20, EC 9–3, DR 9–101(A) & (B)	Rule 2.2(a)(2) & (3)	EC 5–14, EC 5–15, DR 5–105(A) & (C)
Rule 1.12(c)	DR 5–105(D)	Rule 2.2(b)	EC 5–16
Rule 1.12(d)	None	Rule 2.2(c)	EC 5–15, EC 5–19, DR 5–105(B) & (C)
Organization as Client			
Rule 1.13(a)	EC 5–18, EC 5–24	*Evaluation for Use by Third Persons*	
Rule 1.13(b)	EC 5–18, EC 5–24, DR 5–107(B)	Rule 2.3	None
		Meritorious Claims and Contentions	
Rule 1.13(c)	EC 5–18, EC 5–24, DR 5–105(D), DR 5–107(B)	Rule 3.1	EC 7–1, EC 7–4, EC 7–5, EC 7–14, EC 7–25, DR 1–102(A)(5), DR 2–109(A)(B)(1), DR 7–102(A)(1) & (2)
Rule 1.13(d)	EC 5–16		
Rule 1.13(e)	EC 4–4, EC 5–16, DR 5–105(B) & (C)		
Disabled Client		*Expediting Litigation*	
Rule 1.14(a)	EC 7–11, EC 7–12	Rule 3.2	EC 7–20, DR 1–102(A)(5), DR 7–101(A)(1) & (2)
Rule 1.14(b)	EC 7–12		
Safekeeping Property		*Candor Toward the Tribunal*	
Rule 1.15	EC 5–7, EC 9–5, EC 9–7, DR 5–103(A)(1), DR 9–102	Rule 3.3(a)(1)	EC 7–4, EC 7–32, EC 8–5, DR 1–102(A)(4) & (5), DR 7–102(A)(4) & (5)
Declining or Terminating Representation		Rule 3.3(a)(2)	EC 8–5, DR 1–102(A)(4) & (5), DR 7–102(A)(3), DR 7–102(B)(1), DR 7–109(A)
Rule 1.16(a)(1)	EC 2–30, EC 2–31, EC 2–32, DR 2–103(E), DR 2–104(A), DR 2–109(A), DR 2–110(B)(1) & (2)		
		Rule 3.3(a)(3)	EC 7–23, DR 1–102(A)(5), DR 7–106(B)(1)
Rule 1.16(a)(2)	EC 1–6, EC 2–30, EC 2–31, EC 2–32, DR 2–110(B)(3), DR 2–110(C)(4)	Rule 3.3(a)(4)	EC 7–5, EC 7–26, EC 8–5, DR 1–102(A)(4) & (5), DR 7–102(A)(7), DR 7–102(B)(1)
Rule 1.16(a)(3)	EC 2–31, EC 2–32, DR 2–110(B)(4)		
Rule 1.16(b)(1)	EC 2–31, EC 2–32, DR 2–110(C)(1)(b) & (c), DR 2–110(C)(2)	Rule 3.3(b)	EC 8–5, DR 7–102(B)
		Rule 3.3(c)	EC 7–24, EC 7–25
Rule 1.16(b)(2)	EC 2–31, EC 2–32, DR 2–110(C)(2)	Rule 3.3(d)	EC 7–24, EC 7–27
		Fairness to Opposing Party and Counsel	
Rule 1.16(b)(3)	EC 2–30, EC 2–31, EC 2–32, DR 2–110(C)(1)(d)	Rule 3.4(a)	EC 7–6, EC 7–27, DR 1–102(A)(4) & (5), DR 7–106(C)(7), DR 7–109(A) & (B)
Rule 1.16(b)(4)	EC 2–31, EC 2–32, DR 2–110(C)(1)(f)(i)(j)		

TABLES

ABA Model Rules	ABA Model Code	ABA Model Rules	ABA Model Code
Fairness to Opposing Party and Counsel		*Truthfulness to Others*	
Rule 3.4(b)	EC 7–6, EC 7–28, DR 1–102(A)(4), (5) & (6), DR 7–102(A)(6), DR 7–109(C)	Rule 4.1	EC 7–5, DR 7–102(A)(3), (4), (5) & (7), DR 7–102(B)
		Communication With Represented Persons	
Rule 3.4(c)	EC 7–22, EC 7–25, EC 7–38, DR 1–102(A)(5), DR 7–106(A), DR 7–106(C)(5) & (7)	Rule 4.2	EC 2–30, EC 7–18, DR 7–104(A)(1)
		Dealing With Unrepresented Persons	
		Rule 4.3	EC 2–3, EC 7–18, DR 7–104(A)(2)
Rule 3.4(d)	DR 1–102(A)(5), DR 7–106(A), DR 7–106(C)(7)	*Respect for Rights of Third Persons*	
		Rule 4.4	EC 7–10, EC 7–14, EC 7–21, EC 7–25, EC 7–29, EC 7–30, EC 7–37, DR 2–110(B)(1), DR 7–101(A)(1), DR 7–102(A)(1), DR 7–106(C)(2), DR 7–107(D), (E) & (F), DR 7–108(D), (E) & (F)
Rule 3.4(e)	EC 7–24, EC 7–25, DR 1–102(A)(5), DR 7–106(C)(1), (2), (3) & (4)		
Rule 3.4(f)	EC 7–27, DR 1–102(A)(5), DR 7–104(A)(2), DR 7–109(B)		
Impartiality and Decorum		*Responsibilities of a Partner or Supervisory Lawyer*	
Rule 3.5(a)	EC 7–20, EC 7–29, EC 7–31, EC 7–32, EC 7–34, DR 7–106, DR 7–108, DR 7–109, DR 7–110, DR 8–101(A)	Rule 5.1(a) & (b)	EC 4–5, DR 4–101(D), DR 7–107(J)
		Rule 5.1(c)	DR 1–102(A)(2), DR 1–103(A), DR 7–108(E)
Rule 3.5(b)	EC 7–35, DR 7–108, DR 7–110(A) & (B)	*Responsibilities of a Subordinate Lawyer*	
		Rule 5.2	None
Rule 3.5(c)	EC 7–20, EC 7–25, EC 7–36, EC 7–37, DR 7–101(A)(1), DR 7–106(C)(6)	*Responsibilities Regarding Nonlawyer Assistants*	
		Rule 5.3(a)	EC 3–6, EC 4–2, EC 4–5, EC 7–28, DR 4–101(D), DR 7–107(J)
Trial Publicity		Rule 5.3(b)	DR 1–102(A)(2), DR 7–107(J), DR 7–108(B), DR 7–108(E)
Rule 3.6	EC 7–25, EC 7–33, DR 7–107		
Lawyer as Witness		Rule 5.3(c)	None
		Professional Independence of Lawyer	
Rule 3.7(a)	EC 5–9, EC 5–10, DR 5–101(B)(1) & (2), DR 5–102	Rule 5.4(a)	EC 2–33, EC 3–8, EC 5–24, DR 2–103(D)(4)(d), (e) & (f), DR 3–102(A), DR 5–107(C)(3)
Rule 3.7(b)	EC 5–9, DR 5–101(B), DR 5–102		
Special Responsibilities of a Prosecutor		Rule 5.4(b)	EC 2–33, EC 3–8, DR 3–103(A)
Rule 3.8(a)	EC 7–11, EC 7–13, EC 7–14, DR 7–103(A)	Rule 5.4(c)	EC 2–33, EC 5–23, DR 2–103(C), DR 5–107(B)
Rule 3.8(b)	EC 7–11, EC 7–13	Rule 5.4(d)	EC 2–33, EC 3–8, DR 5–107(C)
Rule 3.8(c)	EC 7–11, EC 7–13, EC 7–18	*Unauthorized Practice of Law*	
Rule 3.8(d)	EC 7–11, EC 7–13, DR 7–103(B)	Rule 5.5	DR 3–101(A) & (B)
		Restrictions on Right to Practice	
Rule 3.8(e)	None	Rule 5.6	DR 2–108
Advocate in Nonadjudicative Proceedings		*Pro Bono Publico Service*	
Rule 3.9	EC 7–11, EC 7–15, EC 7–16, EC 8–4, EC 8–5, DR 7–106(B)(2), DR 9–101(C)	Rule 6.1	EC 1–2, EC 1–4, EC 2–1, EC 2–2, EC 2–16, EC 2–24, EC 2–25, EC 6–2, EC 8–1,

ABA Model Rules	ABA Model Code	ABA Model Rules	ABA Model Code
Pro Bono Publico Service	EC 8–2, EC 8–3, EC 8–7, EC 8–9	*Communication of Fields of Practice*	
		Rule 7.4	EC 2–1, EC 2–7, EC 2–8, EC 2–14, DR 2–101(B)(2), DR 2–102(A)(3), DR 2–102(E), DR 2–105(A)
Accepting Appointments			
Rule 6.2(a)	EC 2–1, EC 2–25, EC 2–27, EC 2–28, EC 2–29, EC 8–3	Rule 7.4(a)	DR 2–105(A)(1)
		Rule 7.4(b)	EC 2–14
Rule 6.2(b)	EC 2–16, EC 2–25, EC 2–29, EC 2–30	Rule 7.4(c)	DR 2–105(A)(2) & (3)
Rule 6.2(c)	EC 2–25, EC 2–27, EC 2–29, EC 2–30	*Firm Names and Letterheads*	
		Rule 7.5(a)	EC 2–11, EC 2–13, DR 2–102(A)(4), DR 2–102(B), (D) & (E), DR 2–105
Membership in Legal Services Organization			
Rule 6.3	EC 2–33, DR 5–101(A)	Rule 7.5(b)	EC 2–11, DR 2–102(D)
Law Reform Activities Affecting Client Interests		Rule 7.5(c)	EC 2–11, EC 2–12, DR 2–102(B)
Rule 6.4	EC 2–33, DR 5–101(A), DR 8–101	Rule 7.5(d)	EC 2–11, EC 2–13, DR 2–102(C)
Communication Concerning Lawyer's Services		*Bar Admission and Disciplinary Matters*	
Rule 7.1(a)	EC 2–8, EC 2–9, EC 2–10, DR 2–101(A), (B), (C), (E), (F) & (G), DR 2–102(E)	Rule 8.1(a)	EC 1–1, EC 1–2, EC 1–3, DR 1–101(A) & (B)
		Rule 8.1(b)	DR 1–102(A)(5), DR 1–103(B)
Rule 7.1(b)	EC 2–5, EC 2–8, EC 2–9, EC 9–4, DR 2–101(A), (B), (C), (E), (F) & (G), DR 9–101(C)	*Judges and Legal Officials*	
		Rule 8.2(a)	EC 8–6, DR 8–102
		Rule 8.2(b)	DR 8–103
Rule 7.1(c)	EC 2–8, EC 2–9, EC 2–10, DR 2–101(A), (B), (C), (E), (F) & (G)	*Reporting Professional Misconduct*	
		Rule 8.3	EC 1–3, DR 1–103(A)
Advertising		*Misconduct*	
Rule 7.2(a)	EC 2–1, EC 2–2, EC 2–6, EC 2–7, EC 2–8, EC 2–15, DR 2–101(B) & (H), DR 2–102(A) & (B), DR 2–103(B), DR 2–104(A)(4) & (5)	Rule 8.4(a)	EC 1–5, EC 1–6, EC 9–6, DR 1–102(A)(1) & (2), DR 2–103(E), DR 7–102(A) & (B)
		Rule 8.4(b)	EC 1–5, DR 1–102(A)(3) & (6), DR 7–102(A)(8), DR 8–101(A)(3)
		Rule 8.4(c)	EC 1–5, EC 9–4, DR 1–102(A)(4), DR 8–101(A)(3)
Rule 7.2(b)	DR 2–101(D)	Rule 8.4(d)	EC 3–9, EC 8–3, DR 1–102(A)(5), DR 3–101(B)
Rule 7.2(c)	EC 2–8, EC 2–15, DR 2–101(I), DR 2–103(B), (C) & (D)		
		Rule 8.4(e)	EC 1–5, EC 9–2, EC 9–4, EC 9–6, DR 9–101(C)
Rule 7.2(d)	None		
Direct Contact With Prospective Clients		Rule 8.4(f)	EC 1–5, EC 7–34, EC 9–1, DR 1–102(A)(3), (4), (5) & (6), DR 7–110(A), DR 8–101(A)(2)
Rule 7.3	EC 2–3, EC 2–4, EC 5–6, DR 2–103(A), DR 2–103(C)(1), DR 2–103(D)(4)(b) & (c), DR 2–104(A)(1), (2), (3) & (5)	*Jurisdiction*	
		Rule 8.5	None

TABLE B*

TABLES

ABA Model Code	ABA Model Rules	ABA Model Code	ABA Model Rules

Canon 1: Integrity of Profession

ABA Model Code	ABA Model Rules
EC 1–1	Rules 1.1, 8.1(a)
EC 1–2	Rules 1.1, 6.1, 8.1(a)
EC 1–3	Rules 8.1(a), 8.3
EC 1–4	Rule 6.1
EC 1–5	Rule 8.4(a), (b), (c), (e) & (f)
EC 1–6	Rules 1.16(a)(2), 8.4(a)
DR 1–101	Rule 8.1(a)
DR 1–102(A)(1)	Rule 8.4(a)
DR 1–102(A)(2)	Rules 5.1(c), 5.3(b), 8.4(a)
DR 1–102(A)(3)	Rule 8.4(b) & (f)
DR 1–102(A)(4)	Rules 3.3(a)(1), (2) & (4), 3.4(a) & (b), 8.4(c) & (f)
DR 1–102(A)(5)	Rules 3.1, 3.2, 3.3(a)(1), (2) & (4), 3.4, 8.4(d) & (f)
DR 1–102(A)(6)	Rules 3.4(b), 8.4(b) & (f)
DR 1–103(A)	Rules 5.1(c), 8.3
DR 1–103(B)	Rule 8.1(b)

Canon 2: Making Counsel Available

ABA Model Code	ABA Model Rules
EC 2–1	Rules 6.1, 6.2(a), 7.2(a), 7.4
EC 2–2	Rules 6.1, 7.2(a)
EC 2–3	Rules 4.3, 7.3
EC 2–4	Rule 7.3
EC 2–5	Rule 7.1(b)
EC 2–6	Rule 7.2(a)
EC 2–7	Rules 7.2(a), 7.4
EC 2–8	Rules 7.1, 7.2(a) & (c), 7.4
EC 2–9	Rule 7.1
EC 2–10	Rule 7.1(a) & (c)
EC 2–11	Rule 7.5
EC 2–12	Rule 7.5(c)
EC 2–13	Rule 7.5(a) & (d)
EC 2–14	Rule 7.4
EC 2–15	Rule 7.2(a) & (c)
EC 2–16	Rules 1.5(a), 6.1, 6.2(b)
EC 2–17	Rule 1.5(a)
EC 2–18	Rule 1.5(a)
EC 2–19	Rule 1.5(b)
EC 2–20	Rule 1.5(c) & (d)
EC 2–21	Rules 1.7(b), 1.8(f)
EC 2–22	Rule 1.5(e)
EC 2–23	None
EC 2–24	Rule 6.1
EC 2–25	Rules 6.1, 6.2
EC 2–26	None
EC 2–27	Rule 6.2(a) & (c)

Canon 2: Making Counsel Available

ABA Model Code	ABA Model Rules
EC 2–28	Rule 6.2(a)
EC 2–29	Rule 6.2
EC 2–30	Rules 1.16(a)(1) & (2), 1.16(b)(3), 4.2, 6.2(b) & (c)
EC 2–31	Rules 1.3, 1.16(a) & (b)
EC 2–32	Rule 1.16(a), (b), (c) & (d)
EC 2–33	Rules 5.4, 6.3, 6.4
DR 2–101(A)	Rule 7.1
DR 2–101(B)	Rules 7.1, 7.2(a)
DR 2–101(C)	Rule 7.1
DR 2–101(D)	Rule 7.2(b)
DR 2–101(E)	Rule 7.1
DR 2–101(F)	Rule 7.1
DR 2–101(G)	Rule 7.1
DR 2–101(H)	Rule 7.2
DR 2–101(I)	Rule 7.2(c)
DR 2–102(A)	Rules 7.2(a), 7.4
DR 2–102(B)	Rules 7.2(a), 7.5(a) & (c)
DR 2–102(C)	Rule 7.5(d)
DR 2–102(D)	Rule 7.5(a) & (b)
DR 2–102(E)	Rules 7.1(a), 7.4, 7.5(a)
DR 2–103(A)	Rule 7.3
DR 2–103(B)	Rule 7.2(a) & (c)
DR 2–103(C)	Rules 5.4(a), 7.2(c), 7.3
DR 2–103(D)	Rules 1.16(a)(1), 5.4(a), 7.2(c), 7.3
DR 2–103(E)	Rules 1.16(a), 7.2(a), 7.3
DR 2–104	Rules 1.16(a), 7.3
DR 2–105	Rule 7.4
DR 2–106(A)	Rule 1.5(a)
DR 2–106(B)	Rule 1.5(a)
DR 2–106(C)	Rule 1.5(d)
DR 2–107(A)	Rule 1.5(e)
DR 2–107(B)	Rule 5.4(a)(1)
DR 2–108(A)	Rule 5.6
DR 2–108(B)	Rule 5.6
DR 2–109(A)	Rules 1.16(a)(1), 3.1
DR 2–110(A)	Rule 1.16(c) & (d)
DR 2–110(B)	Rules 1.16(a), 3.1, 4.4
DR 2–110(C)	Rules 1.2(e), 1.16(a) & (b)

Canon 3: Unauthorized Practice

ABA Model Code	ABA Model Rules
EC 3–1	None
EC 3–2	None
EC 3–3	Rule 8.4(e)
EC 3–4	None
EC 3–5	None
EC 3–6	Rule 5.3(a)
EC 3–7	None

* Table B provides cross-references to related provisions, but only in the sense that the provisions consider substantially similar subject matter or reflect similar concerns. A cross-reference does not indicate that a provision of the ABA Model Code of Professional Responsibility has been incorporated by the provision of a Model Rule. The Canons of the Code are not cross-referenced.

285

ABA Model Code	ABA Model Rules	ABA Model Code	ABA Model Rules
Canon 3: Unauthorized Practice		*Canon 5: Independent Judgment*	
EC 3–8	Rule 5.49(a), (b) & (d)	DR 5–102(B)	Rules 1.7(b), 3.7
EC 3–9	Rule 8.4(d)	DR 5–103(A)	Rules 1.8(j), 1.15
DR 3–101(A)	Rule 5.5	DR 5–103(B)	Rule 1.8(e)
DR 3–101(B)	Rules 5.5, 8.4(d)	DR 5–104(A)	Rules 1.7(b), 1.8(a)
DR 3–102	Rule 5.4(a)	DR 5–104(B)	Rule 1.8(d)
DR 3–103	Rule 5.4(b)	DR 5–105(A)	Rules 1.7, 1.10(c), 2.2(a)
Canon 4: Confidences and Secrets		DR 5–105(B)	Rules 1.7, 1.13(e), 2.2(c)
EC 4–1	Rule 1.6(a)		
EC 4–2	Rules 1.6(a) & (b)(1), 2.2(a)(1), 5.3(a)	DR 5–105(C)	Rules 1.7(b), 1.13(e), 1.9(a), 2.2
EC 4–3	Rule 1.6(a)	DR 5–105(D)	Rules 1.10(a), 1.12(c), 1.13(c)
EC 4–4	Rules 1.6(a), 1.13(e)		
EC 4–5	Rules 1.8(b), 1.9(b), 1.10(a) & (b), 5.1(a) & (c), 5.3(a)	DR 5–106	Rule 1.8(g)
		DR 5–107(A)	Rules 1.7(b), 1.8(f)
EC 4–6	Rule 1.9(b)	DR 5–107(B)	Rules 1.7(a), 1.8(f), 1.13(b) & (c), 2.1, 5.4(c)
DR 4–101(A)	Rule 1.6(a)		
DR 4–101(B)	Rules 1.6(a), 1.8(b), 1.9(b)		
		DR 5–107(C)	Rule 5.4(a) & (d)
DR 4–101(C)	Rules 1.6(a) & (b)	*Canon 6: Competence*	
DR 4–101(D)	Rules 5.1(a) & (b), 5.3(a) & (b)	EC 6–1	Rule 1.1
Canon 5: Independent Judgment		EC 6–2	Rules 1.1, 5.1(a) & (b), 6.1
EC 5–1	Rules 1.7(a) & (b), 1.8(c), (d), (e), (f), (g) & (j)	EC 6–3	Rule 1.1
		EC 6–4	Rules 1.1, 1.3
		EC 6–5	Rule 1.1
EC 5–2	Rules 1.7(b), 1.8(c)	EC 6–6	Rule 1.8(h)
EC 5–3	Rules 1.7(b), 1.8(a), (d) & (e)	DR 6–101	Rules 1.1, 1.3, 1.4(a)
		DR 6–102	Rule 1.8(h)
EC 5–4	Rule 1.8(d)	*Canon 7: Zeal Within the Law*	
EC 5–5	Rule 1.8(a) & (c)	EC 7–1	Rules 1.2(d), 1.3, 3.1
EC 5–6	Rules 1.8(c), 7.3	EC 7–2	Rule 1.2(d)
EC 5–7	Rules 1.5(c), 1.8(e) & (j), 1.15	EC 7–3	Rule 2.1
		EC 7–4	Rules 3.1, 3.3(a)(1)
EC 5–8	Rule 1.8(e)	EC 7–5	Rules 1.2(d), 3.1, 3.3(a)(4), 4.1
EC 5–9	Rules 1.7(b), 3.7		
EC 5–10	Rule 3.7(a)	EC 7–6	Rule 3.4(a) & (b)
EC 5–11	Rules 1.7(b), 2.1	EC 7–7	Rule 1.2(a)
EC 5–12	Rule 1.2(a)	EC 7–8	Rules 1.2(a) & (c), 1.4, 2.1
EC 5–13	Rule 1.7(b)		
EC 5–14	Rules 1.7(a), 2.2(a)		
EC 5–15	Rules 1.7, 2.2(a) & (c)	EC 7–9	Rule 1.2(c)
		EC 7–10	Rule 4.4
EC 5–16	Rules 1.7(b), 1.10(d), 1.13(d) & (e), 2.2(a)(1) & (b)	EC 7–11	Rules 1.14(a), 3.8(a), (b), (c) & (d), 3.9
		EC 7–12	Rule 1.14
EC 5–17	Rule 1.7	EC 7–13	Rule 3.8
EC 5–18	Rule 1.13(a), (b) & (c)	EC 7–14	Rules 3.1, 3.8(a), 4.4
		EC 7–15	Rule 3.9
EC 5–19	Rules 1.7(b), 2.2(c)	EC 7–16	Rule 3.9
EC 5–20	Rules 1.12(a) & (b), 2.2(a)(1)	EC 7–17	Rule 1.2(b)
		EC 7–18	Rules 3.8(c), 4.2, 4.3
EC 5–21	Rule 1.7	EC 7–19	None
EC 5–22	Rule 1.7	EC 7–20	Rules 3.2, 3.5(a) & (c)
EC 5–23	Rules 1.7(b), 5.4(c)		
EC 5–24	Rules 1.13(a), (b) & (c), 5.4(a)	EC 7–21	Rule 4.4
DR 5–101(A)	Rules 1.7, 1.8(j), 6.3, 6.4	EC 7–22	Rules 1.2(d), 3.4(c)
		EC 7–23	Rule 3.3(a)(3)
DR 5–101(B)	Rules 1.7(b), 3.7		
DR 5–102(A)	Rules 1.7(b), 3.7		

TABLES

ABA Model Code	ABA Model Rules	ABA Model Code	ABA Model Rules
Canon 7: Zeal Within the Law		*Canon 7: Zeal Within the Law*	
EC 7–24	Rules 3.3(c) & (d), 3.4(e)	DR 7–107(J)	Rules 5.1(a) & (b), 5.3(a) & (b)
EC 7–25	Rules 3.1, 3.3(c), 3.4(c) & (e), 3.5(c), 3.6, 4.4	DR 7–108(A)	Rule 3.5(a) & (b)
		DR 7–108(B)	Rules 3.5(a), (b), (c), (d) & (f), 5.3(b)
EC 7–26	Rule 3.3(a)(4)	DR 7–108(C)	Rule 3.5(a) & (b)
EC 7–27	Rules 3.3(d), 3.4(a) & (f)	DR 7–108(D)	Rule 4.4
		DR 7–108(E)	Rules 4.4, 5.1(c), 5.3(b)
EC 7–28	Rules 3.4(b), 5.3(a)	DR 7–108(F)	Rule 4.4
EC 7–29	Rules 3.5(a), 4.4	DR 7–108(G)	None
EC 7–30	Rule 4.4	DR 7–109(A)	Rules 3.3(a)(2), 3.4(a)
EC 7–31	Rule 3.5(a)		
EC 7–32	Rules 3.3(a)(1), 3.5(a)	DR 7–109(B)	Rule 3.4(a) & (f)
		DR 7–109(C)	Rule 3.4(b)
EC 7–33	Rule 3.6	DR 7–110(A)	Rules 3.5(a), 8.4(f)
EC 7–34	Rules 3.5(a), 8.4(f)	DR 7–110(B)	Rule 3.5(a) & (b)
EC 7–35	Rule 3.5(b)	*Canon 8: Improving Legal System*	
EC 7–36	Rule 3.5(c)	EC 8–1	Rule 6.1
EC 7–37	Rules 3.5(c), 4.4	EC 8–2	Rule 6.1
EC 7–38	Rules 1.3, 3.4(c)	EC 8–3	Rules 6.1, 6.2(a), 8.4(d)
EC 7–39	None		
DR 7–101(A)	Rules 1.2(a), 1.3, 3.2, 3.5(c), 4.4	EC 8–4	Rule 3.9
		EC 8–5	Rules 3.3(a)(1), (2) & (4), 3.3(b), 3.9
DR 7–101(B)	Rules 1.2, 1.16(b)		
DR 7–102(A)(1)	Rules 3.1, 4.4	EC 8–6	Rule 8.2(a)
DR 7–102(A)(2)	Rule 3.1	EC 8–7	Rule 6.1
DR 7–102(A)(3)	Rules 3.3(a)(2), 4.1	EC 8–8	Rule 1.11(c)
DR 7–102(A)(4)	Rules 3.3(a) & (c), 4.1	EC 8–9	Rule 6.1
		DR 8–101	Rules 3.5, 8.4(b), (c) & (f)
DR 7–102(A)(5)	Rules 3.3(a)(1), 4.1		
DR 7–102(A)(6)	Rules 1.2(d), 3.4(b)	DR 8–102	Rule 8.2(a)
DR 7–102(A)(7)	Rules 1.2(d), 3.3(a)(4), 4.1	DR 8–103	Rule 8.2(b)
		Canon 9: Appearance of Impropriety	
DR 7–102(A)(8)	Rules 1.2(d), 8.4(a) & (b)	EC 9–1	Rule 8.4(f)
		EC 9–2	Rules 1.4(a), 8.4(e)
DR 7–102(B)	Rules 1.6(b)(1), 3.3(b), 4.1	EC 9–3	Rules 1.11(a), 1.12(a) & (b)
DR 7–103(A)	Rule 3.8(a)	EC 9–4	Rules 7.1(b), 8.4(c) & (e)
DR 7–103(B)	Rule 3.8(d)		
DR 7–104	Rules 3.4(f), 4.2, 4.3	EC 9–5	Rule 1.15
DR 7–105	None	EC 9–6	Preamble, Rule 8.4(e)
DR 7–106(A)	Rules 1.2(d), 3.4(c) & (d), 3.5(a)		
		EC 9–7	Rule 1.15
DR 7–106(B)	Rules 1.7(b)(2), 3.3(a)(3), 3.9	DR 9–101(A)	Rule 1.12(a) & (b)
		DR 9–101(B)	Rules 1.11(a), 1.12(a) & (b)
DR 7–106(C)	Rules 3.4(a), (c), (d) & (e), 3.5(c), 4.4	DR 9–101(C)	Rules 1.2(e), 3.9, 7.1(b), 8.4(e)
DR 7–107(A)–(I)	Rule 3.6		
DR 7–107(D)–(F)	Rule 4.4	DR 9–102	Rules 1.4(a), 1.15

INDEX TO ABA MODEL RULES

D

INDEX

INDEX

N

Negotiation,
    conflicting interest, representation of,
        Rule 1.7 (Comment)
    statements made during, Rule 4.1 (Comment)
Negotiator,
    lawyer as, Preamble
Nonlawyers,
    division of fees with, Rule 5.4(a)
    partnership with, Rule 5.4(b)

O

Objectives of the representation,
    client's right to determine, Rule 1.2(a)
    lawyer's right to limit, Rule 1.2(c)
Opposing party,
    communications with represented party,
        Rule 4.2
    duty of fairness to, Rule 3.4
Organization, representation of,
    board of directors, lawyer for serving on,
        Rule 1.7 (Comment)
    communication with, Rule 1.4 (Comment)
    conflicting interests among officers and
        employees, Rule 1.7 (Comment)
    conflict of interest, Rule 1.7 (Comment)
    constituents, representing, Rule 1.13(e)
    identity of client, Rule 1.13(a); Rule
        1.13(d)
    misconduct, client engaged in, Rule
        1.13(b)

P

Partner,
    defined, Terminology
Patent practice,
    advertising, Rule 7.4(a)
Perjury,
    criminal defendant, Rule 3.3 (Comment)
    disclosure of, Rule 3.3(b)
Personal affairs of lawyer,
    duty to conduct in compliance with law,
        Preamble
Plea bargain,
    client's right to accept or reject, Rule
        1.2(a)
Pleadings,
    verification of, Rule 3.3 (Comment)
Precedent,
    failure to disclose to court, Rule 3.3(a)(3)
Prepaid legal services,
    advertising for, Rule 7.2 (Comment)
Pro bono publico service, Rule 6.1

Procedural law,
    lawyer's professional responsibilities
        proscribed by, Preamble
Professional corporation,
    defined, Terminology
    formation of, Rule 5.4(d)
Prompt,
    lawyer's duty to be, Preamble
Property of client,
    safekeeping, Rule 1.15
Prosecutor,
    representing former defendant, Rule 1.9
        (Comment)
    special responsibilities of, Rule 3.8
Public citizen,
    lawyer's duty as, Preamble
Public interest,
    government lawyer's authority to represent, Scope
Public interest legal services, *See Pro bono publico* service.
Public office, lawyer holding,
    negotiating private employment while,
        Rule 1.11(c)(2)
Public officials,
    lawyer's duty to show respect for,
        Preamble

R

Recordkeeping,
    property of client, Rule 1.15(a)
Referral,
    when lawyer not competent to handle
        matter, Rule 1.1
Regulation of the legal profession,
    self-governance, Preamble
Relatives of lawyer,
    representing interests adverse to, Rule
        1.8(h)
Representation of client,
    decisionmaking authority of lawyer and
        client, Rule 1.2(a)
    objectives, lawyer's right to limit, Rule
        1.2(c)
    termination of, Rule 1.2 (Comment)
Restrictions on right to practice,
    partnership or employment agreement
        imposes, Rule 5.6(a)
    settlement imposes, Rule 5.6(b)

S

Sanction,
    severity of, Scope
Scope of representation, Rule 1.2
Settlement,
    aggregate settlement on behalf of
        clients, Rule 1.8(g)

293

SELECTED SIGNIFICANT STATE MODIFICATIONS TO THE ABA MODEL RULES

The ABA Model Rules are designed to serve as a model for the states to consider and adopt. The enactment of the Model Rules caused most of the states to at least reconsider their local codes of ethics. As of the date of this publication, thirty-nine states have replaced codes based upon the Model Code and have enacted codes based upon the structure and content of the Model Rules. Every one of these states has in some way amended the Model Rules provisions. Three states (New York, Oregon, and Virginia) have amended their version of the Model Code to reflect certain Model Rules' provisions. One state, California, did not base its code on the Model Code originally and refused to base a 1989 revision on the Model Rules.

In light of the many state modifications to the Model Rules, it is useful to examine selected significant state amendments. Some of these amendments illustrate substantive disagreements with the position adopted by the ABA in the Model Rules. Other modifications reflect local practices that the states have chosen to memorialize in the local code. Still other changes illustrate the desire to be more elaborative with respect to the language in the text. The selected state variations presented in this section fall within each of these categories.

The selected significant state modifications to the ABA Model Rules are presented under the order of the rules and within this framework by alphabetical order of the states. In the advertising section, however, the Arizona and Texas rules are grouped under each state. This section is intended to be illustrative and not exhaustive of the many state modifications. The comments to the state rule are included only if they are relevant to the difference that is illustrated.

TABLE OF CONTENTS

Illinois Rule 1.8.
Indiana Rule 1.8(k).
Minnesota Rule 1.8(e)(3).
Texas Rule 1.09 (Modification of Model Rule 1.9).
Utah Rule 1.9(a).
District of Columbia Rule 1.11.
New Hampshire Rule 1.11A.
Montana Rule 1.17.

Counsellor

Oregon Rule DR 5–106 (Modification to Model Rule 2.2).

Advocate

Wyoming Rule 3.1.
Kansas Rule 3.5.

Transactions With Persons Other Than Clients

Louisiana Rule 4.2.
New Mexico Rule 16–402 (Modification of Model Rule 4.2).
Texas Rule 4.02 (Modification of Model Rule 4.2).
Minnesota Rule 4.3.
Texas Rule 4.04 (Modification of Model Rule 4.4).

Law Firms and Associations

Texas Rule 5.01 (Modification of Model Rule 5.1).
Texas Rule 5.02 (Modification of Model Rule 5.2).
District of Columbia Rule 5.4.
Pennsylvania Rule 5.7.

Public Service

South Dakota Rule 6.1.

Information About Legal Services

Arizona Rule 7.1.
Arizona Rule 7.2.
Arizona Rule 7.3.
Texas Rule 7.01.
Texas Rule 7.02.
Texas Rule 7.03.
Texas Rule 7.04.
Texas Rule 7.05.
Texas Rule 7.06.
Texas Rule 7.07.

Maintaining the Integrity of the Profession

Kansas Rule 8.3.
Florida Rule 4–8.4(d).
Louisiana Rule 8.4.
Minnesota Rule 8.4.
New Jersey Rule 8.4(g).

District of Columbia Rule 9.1.
Appendix: States That Have Adopted a Version of the Model Rules.

CLIENT–LAWYER RELATIONSHIP

Texas Rule 1.01 *(Modification of Model Rules 1.1 and 1.3)*

[Texas has combined Model Rule 1.1 (competence) and 1.3 (diligence) into one rule.]

RULE 1.01   Competent and Diligent Representation

(a) A lawyer shall not accept or continue employment in a legal matter which the lawyer knows or should know is beyond the lawyer's competence, unless:

(1) another lawyer who is competent to handle the matter is, with the prior informed consent of the client, associated in the matter; or

(2) the advice or assistance of the lawyer is reasonably required in an emergency and the lawyer limits the advice and assistance to that which is reasonably necessary in the circumstances.

(b) In representing a client, a lawyer shall not:

(1) neglect a legal matter entrusted to the lawyer; or

(2) frequently fail to carry out completely the obligations that the lawyer owes to a client or clients.

(c) As used in this Rule, "neglect" signifies inattentiveness involving a conscious disregard for the responsibilities owed to a client or clients.

COMMENT:

Accepting Employment

[1]   A lawyer generally should not accept or continue employment in any area of the law in which the lawyer is not and will not be prepared to render competent legal services. "Competence" is defined in Terminology as possession of the legal knowledge, skill, and training reasonably necessary for the representation. Competent representation contemplates appropriate application by the lawyer of that legal knowledge, skill and training, reasonable thoroughness in the study and analysis of the law and facts, and reasonable attentiveness to the responsibilities owed to the client.

[2]   In determining whether a matter is beyond a lawyer's competence, relevant factors include the relative complexity and specialized nature of the matter, the lawyer's general experience in the field in

question, the preparation and study the lawyer will be able to give the matter, and whether it is feasible either to refer the matter to or associate a lawyer of established competence in the field in question. The required attention and preparation are determined in part by what is at stake; major litigation and complex transactions ordinarily require more elaborate treatment than matters of lesser consequences.

[3] A lawyer may not need to have special training or prior experience to accept employment to handle legal problems of a type with which the lawyer is unfamiliar. Although expertise in a particular field of law may be useful in some circumstances, the appropriate proficiency in many instances is that of a general practitioner. A newly admitted lawyer can be as competent in some matters as a practitioner with long experience. Some important legal skills, such as the analysis of precedent, the evaluation of evidence and legal drafting, are required in all legal problems. Perhaps the most fundamental legal skill consists of determining what kind of legal problems a situation may involve, a skill that necessarily transcends any particular specialized knowledge.

[4] A lawyer possessing the normal skill and training reasonably necessary for the representation of a client in an area of law is not subject to discipline for accepting employment in a matter in which, in order to represent the client properly, the lawyer must become more competent in regard to relevant legal knowledge by additional study and investigation. If the additional study and preparation will result in unusual delay or expense to the client, the lawyer should not accept employment except with the informed consent of the client.

[5] A lawyer offered employment or employed in a matter beyond the lawyer's competence generally must decline or withdraw from the employment or, with the prior informed consent of the client, associate a lawyer who is competent in the matter. Paragraph (a)(2) permits a lawyer, however, to give advice or assistance in an emergency in a matter even though the lawyer does not have the skill ordinarily required if referral to or consultation with another lawyer would be impractical and if the assistance is limited to that which is reasonably necessary in the circumstances.

Competent and Diligent Representation

[6] Having accepted employment, a lawyer should act with competence, commitment and dedication to the interest of the client and with zeal in advocacy upon the client's behalf. A lawyer should feel a moral or professional obligation to pursue a matter on behalf of a client with reasonable diligence and promptness despite opposition, obstruction or personal inconvenience to the lawyer. A lawyer's workload should be controlled so that each matter can be handled with diligence and competence. As provided in paragraph (a), an incompetent lawyer is subject to discipline.

Neglect

[7] Perhaps no professional shortcoming is more widely resented than procrastination. A client's interests often can be adversely affected by the passage of time or the change of conditions; in extreme instances, as when a lawyer overlooks a statute of limitations, the client's legal position may be destroyed. Under paragraph (b), a lawyer is subject to professional discipline for neglecting a particular legal matter as well as for frequent failures to carry out fully the obligations owed to one or more clients. A lawyer who acts in good faith is not subject to discipline, under those provisions for an isolated inadvertent or unskilled act or omission, tactical error, or error of judgment. Because delay can cause a client needless anxiety and undermine confidence in the lawyer's trust-worthiness, there is a duty to communicate reasonably with clients; see Rule 1.03.

Maintaining Competence

[8] Because of the vital role of lawyers in the legal process, each lawyer should strive to become and remain proficient and competent in the practice of law. To maintain the requisite knowledge and skill of a competent practitioner, a lawyer should engage in continuing study and education. If a system of peer review has been established, the lawyer should consider making use of it in appropriate circumstances. Isolated instances of faulty conduct or decision should be identified for purposes of additional study or instruction.

Michigan Rule 1.2

[Michigan has amended Model Rule 1.2(a) to read as follows:]

RULE 1.2   Scope of Representation

(a) A lawyer shall seek the lawful objectives of a client through reasonably available means permitted by law and these rules. A lawyer does not violate this rule by acceding to reasonable requests of opposing counsel that do not prejudice the rights of the client, by being punctual in fulfilling all professional commitments, by avoiding offensive tactics. A lawyer shall abide by a client's decision whether to accept an offer of settlement or mediation evaluation of a matter. In a criminal case, the lawyer shall abide by the client's decision, after consultation with the lawyer, as to a plea to be entered, whether to waive jury trial, and whether the client will testify. In representing a client, a lawyer may, where permissible, exercise professional judgment to waive or fail to assert a right or position of the client.

* * *

299

Florida Rule 4–1.5 (Modification of Model Rule 1.5)

[Florida has amended Model Rule 1.5 to read as follows:]

RULE 4–1.5   Fees for Legal Services

(a) Illegal, Prohibited, or Clearly Excessive Fees. An attorney shall not enter into an agreement for, charge, or collect an illegal, prohibited, or clearly excessive fee or a fee generated by employment that was obtained through advertising or solicitation not in compliance with the Rules Regulating The Florida Bar. A fee is clearly excessive when:

(1) after a review of the facts, a lawyer of ordinary prudence would be left with a definite and firm conviction that the fee exceeds a reasonable fee for services provided to such a degree as to constitute clear overreaching or an unconscionable demand by the attorney; or

(2) the fee is sought or secured by the attorney by means of intentional misrepresentation or fraud upon the client, a nonclient party, or any court, as to either entitlement to, or amount of, the fee.

(b) Factors to Be Considered in Determining Reasonable Fee. Factors to be considered as guides in determining a reasonable fee include:

(1) the time and labor required, the novelty, complexity, and difficulty of the questions involved, and the skill requisite to perform the legal service properly;

(2) the likelihood that the acceptance of the particular employment will preclude other employment by the lawyer;

(3) the fee, or rate of fee, customarily charged in the locality for legal services of a comparable or similar nature;

(4) the significance of, or amount involved in, the subject matter of the representation, the responsibility involved in the representation, and the results obtained;

(5) the time limitations imposed by the client or by the circumstances and, as between attorney and client, any additional or special time demands or requests of the attorney by the client;

(6) the nature and length of the professional relationship with the client;

(7) the experience, reputation, diligence, and ability of the lawyer or lawyers performing the service and the skill, expertise, or efficiency of effort reflected in the actual providing of such services; and

(8) whether the fee is fixed or contingent, and, if fixed as to amount or rate, then whether the client's ability to pay rested to any significant degree on the outcome of the representation.

(c) Consideration of All Factors. In determining a reasonable fee, the time devoted to the representation and customary rate of fee need not be the sole or controlling factors. All factors set forth in this rule should be considered, and may be applied, in justification of a fee higher or lower than that which would result from application of only the time and rate factors.

(d) Enforceability of Fee Contracts. Contracts or agreements for attorney's fees between attorney and client will ordinarily be enforceable according to the terms of such contracts or agreements, unless found to be illegal, obtained through advertising or solicitation not in compliance with the Rules Regulating The Florida Bar, prohibited by this rule, or clearly excessive as defined by this rule.

(e) Duty to Communicate Basis or Rate of Fee to Client. When the lawyer has not regularly represented the client, the basis or rate of the fee shall be communicated to the client, preferably in writing, before or within a reasonable time after commencing the representation.

(f) Contingent Fees. As to contingent fees:

(1) A fee may be contingent on the outcome of the matter for which the service is rendered, except in a matter in which a contingent fee is prohibited by paragraph (f)(3) or by law. A contingent fee agreement shall be in writing and shall state the method by which the fee is to be determined, including the percentage or percentages that shall accrue to the lawyer in the event of settlement, trial, or appeal, litigation and other expenses to be deducted from the recovery, and whether such expenses are to be deducted before or after the contingent fee is calculated. Upon conclusion of a contingent fee matter, the lawyer shall provide the client with a written statement stating the outcome of the matter and, if there is a recovery, showing the remittance to the client and the method of its determination.

(2) Every lawyer who accepts a retainer or enters into an agreement, express or implied, for compensation for services rendered or to be rendered in any action, claim, or proceeding whereby the lawyer's compensation is to be dependent or contingent in whole or in part upon the successful prosecution or settlement thereof shall do so only where such fee arrangement is reduced to a written contract, signed by the client, and by a lawyer for the lawyer or for the law firm representing the client. No lawyer or firm may participate in the fee without the consent of the client in writing. Each participating lawyer or law firm shall sign the contract with the client and shall agree to assume joint legal responsibility to the client for the performance of the services in question as if each were partners of the other lawyer or law firm involved. The client shall be furnished with a copy of the signed contract and any subsequent notices or consents. All provisions of this rule shall apply to such fee contracts.

(3) A lawyer shall not enter into an arrangement for, charge, or collect:

> (A) any fee in a domestic relations matter, the payment or amount of which is contingent upon the securing of a divorce or upon the amount of alimony or support, or property settlement in lieu thereof; or

301

(B) a contingent fee for representing a defendant in a criminal case.

(4) A lawyer who enters into an arrangement for, charges, or collects any fee in an action or claim for personal injury or for property damages or for death or loss of services resulting from personal injuries based upon tortious conduct of another, including products liability claims, whereby the compensation is to be dependent or contingent in whole or in part upon the successful prosecution or settlement thereof shall do so only under the following requirements:

(A) The contract shall contain the following provisions:

(i) "The undersigned client has, before signing this contract, received and read the statement of client's rights and understands each of the rights set forth therein. The undersigned client has signed the statement and received a signed copy to refer to while being represented by the undersigned attorney(s)."

(ii) "This contract may be cancelled by written notification to the attorney at any time within 3 business days of the date the contract was signed, as shown below, and if cancelled the client shall not be obligated to pay any fees to the attorney for the work performed during that time. If the attorney has advanced funds to others in representation of the client, the attorney is entitled to be reimbursed for such amounts as the attorney has reasonably advanced on behalf of the client."

(B) The contract for representation of a client in a matter set forth in subdivision (f)(4) may provide for a contingent fee arrangement as agreed upon by the client and the lawyer, except as limited by the following provisions:

(i) Without prior court approval as specified below, any contingent fee that exceeds the following standards shall be presumed, unless rebutted, to be clearly excessive:

a. Before the filing of an answer or the demand for appointment of arbitrators or, if no answer is filed or no demand for appointment of arbitrators is made, the expiration of the time period provided for such action:

1. 33–1/3% of any recovery up to $1 million; plus

2. 30% of any portion of the recovery between $1 million and $2 million; plus

3. 20% of any portion of the recovery exceeding $2 million.

b. After the filing of an answer or the demand for appointment of arbitrators or, if no answer is filed or no demand for appointment of arbitrators is made, the expiration of the time period provided for such action, through the entry of judgment.

1. 40% of any recovery up to $1 million; plus

2. 30% of any portion of the recovery between $1 million and $2 million; plus

3. 20% of any portion of the recovery exceeding $2 million.

c. If all defendants admit liability at the time of filing their answers and request a trial only on damages:

1. 33⅓% of any recovery up to $1 million; plus

2. 20% of any portion of the recovery between $1 million and $2 million; plus

3. 15% of any portion of the recovery for any amount exceeding $2 million.

d. An additional 5% of any recovery after notice of appeal is filed or post-judgment relief or action is required for recovery on the judgment.

(ii) If any client is unable to obtain an attorney of the client's choice because of the limitations set forth in (f)(4)(B)(i), the client may petition the court in which the matter would be filed, if litigation is necessary, or if such court will not accept jurisdiction for the fee division, the circuit court wherein the cause of action arose, for approval of any fee contract between the client and an attorney of the client's choosing. Such authorization shall be given if the court determines the client has a complete understanding of the client's rights and the terms of the proposed contract. The application for authorization of such a contract can be filed as a separate proceeding before suit or simultaneously with the filing of a complaint. Proceedings thereon may occur before service on the defendant and this aspect of the file may be sealed. Authorization of such a contract shall not bar subsequent inquiry as to whether the fee actually claimed or charged is clearly excessive under subdivisions (a) and (b).

(iii) In cases where the client is to receive a recovery that will be paid to the client on a future structured or periodic basis, the contingent fee percentage shall only be calculated on the cost of the structured verdict or settlement or, if the cost is unknown, on the present money value of the structured verdict or settlement, whichever is less. If the damages and the fee are to be paid out over the long term future schedule, then this limitation does not apply. No attorney may separately negotiate with the defendant for that attorney's fee in a structured verdict or settlement where such separate negotiations would place the attorney in a position of conflict.

(C) Before a lawyer enters into a contingent fee contract for representation of a client in a matter set forth in this rule, the lawyer shall provide the client with a copy of the statement of client's rights and shall afford the client a full and complete opportunity to understand each of the rights as set forth therein. A copy of the statement, signed by both the client and the lawyer, shall be given to the client to retain and the lawyer shall keep a copy in the client's file. The statement shall be retained by the lawyer with the written fee contract and closing statement under the same conditions and requirements as subdivision (f)(5).

(D) As to lawyers not in the same firm, a division of any fee within subdivision (f)(4) shall be on the following basis:

(i) To the lawyer assuming primary responsibility for the legal services on behalf of the client, a minimum of 75% of the total fee.

(ii) To the lawyer assuming secondary responsibility for the legal services on behalf of the client, a maximum of 25% of the total fee. Any fee in excess of 25% shall be presumed to be clearly excessive.

(iii) The 25% limitation shall not apply to those cases in which 2 or more lawyers or firms accept substantially equal active participation in the providing of legal services. In such circumstances counsel shall apply for circuit court authorization of the fee division in excess of 25%, based upon a sworn petition signed by all counsel that shall disclose in detail those services to be performed. The application for authorization of such a contract may be filed as a separate proceeding before suit or simultaneously with the filing of a complaint. Proceedings thereon may occur before service of process on any party and this aspect of the file may be sealed. Authorization of such contract shall not bar subsequent inquiry as to whether the fee actually claimed or charged is clearly excessive. An application under this subdivision shall contain a certificate showing service on the client and The Florida Bar. Counsel may proceed with representation of the client pending court approval.

(iv) The percentages required by this subdivision shall be applicable after deduction of any fee payable to separate counsel retained especially for appellate purposes.

(5) In the event there is a recovery, upon the conclusion of the representation, the lawyer shall prepare a closing statement reflecting an itemization of all costs and expenses, together with the amount of fee received by each participating lawyer or law firm. A copy of the closing statement shall be executed by all participating lawyers, as well as the client, and each shall receive a copy. Each participating lawyer shall retain a copy of the written fee contract and closing statement for 6

years after execution of the closing statement. Any contingent fee contract and closing statement shall be available for inspection at reasonable times by the client, by any other person upon judicial order, or by the appropriate disciplinary agency.

(g) Division of Fees Between Lawyers in Different Firms. Subject to the provisions of subdivision (f)(4)(D), a division of fee between lawyers who are not in the same firm may be made only if the total fee is reasonable and:

(1) the division is in proportion to the services performed by each lawyer; or

(2) by written agreement with the client:

(A) each lawyer assumes joint legal responsibility for the representation and agrees to be available for consultation with the client; and

(B) the agreement fully discloses that a division of fees will be made and the basis upon which the division of fees will be made.

(h) Credit Plans. Charges made by any lawyer or law firm under an approved credit plan shall be only for services actually rendered or cash actually paid on behalf of the client. No higher fee shall be charged and no additional charge shall be imposed by reason of a lawyer's or law firm's participation in an approved credit plan.

STATEMENT OF CLIENT'S RIGHTS
FOR CONTINGENCY FEES

Before you, the prospective client, arrange a contingent fee agreement with a lawyer, you should understand this statement of your rights as a client. This statement is not a part of the actual contract between you and your lawyer, but, as a prospective client, you should be aware of these rights:

1. There is no legal requirement that a lawyer charge a client a set fee or a percentage of money recovered in a case. You, the client, have the right to talk with your lawyer about the proposed fee and to bargain about the rate or percentage as in any other contract. If you do not reach an agreement with one lawyer you may talk with other lawyers.

2. Any contingent fee contract must be in writing and you have 3 business days to reconsider the contract. You may cancel the contract without any reason if you notify your lawyer in writing within 3 business days of signing the contract. If you withdraw from the contract within the first 3 business days, you do not owe the lawyer a fee although you may be responsible for the lawyer's actual costs during that time. If your lawyer begins to represent you, your lawyer may not withdraw from the case without giving you notice, delivering necessary papers to you, and allowing you time to employ another lawyer. Often, your lawyer must obtain court approval before withdrawing from a case. If you discharge your lawyer without good cause after the 3–day period, you may have to pay a fee for work the lawyer has done.

3.   Before hiring a lawyer, you, the client, have the right to know about the lawyer's education, training, and experience. If you ask, the lawyer should tell you specifically about the lawyer's actual experience dealing with cases similar to yours. If you ask, the lawyer should provide information about special training or knowledge and give you this information in writing if you request it.

4.   Before signing a contingent fee contract with you, a lawyer must advise you whether the lawyer intends to handle your case alone or whether other lawyers will be helping with the case. If your lawyer intends to refer the case to other lawyers, the lawyer should tell you what kind of fee sharing arrangement will be made with the other lawyers. If lawyers from different law firms will represent you, at least 1 lawyer from each law firm must sign the contingent fee contract.

5.   If your lawyer intends to refer your case to another lawyer or counsel with other lawyers, your lawyer should tell you about that at the beginning. If your lawyer takes the case and later decides to refer it to another lawyer or to associate with other lawyers, you should sign a new contract that includes the new lawyers. You, the client, also have the right to consult with each lawyer working on your case and each lawyer is legally responsible to represent your interests and is legally responsible for the acts of the other lawyers involved in the case.

6.   You, the client, have the right to know in advance how you will need to pay the expenses and the legal fees at the end of the case. If you pay a deposit in advance for costs, you may ask reasonable questions about how the money will be or has been spent and how much of it remains unspent. Your lawyer should give a reasonable estimate about future necessary costs. If your lawyer agrees to lend or advance you money to prepare or research the case, you have the right to know periodically how much money your lawyer has spent on your behalf. You also have the right to decide, after consulting with your lawyer, how much money is to be spent to prepare a case. If you pay the expenses, you have the right to decide how much to spend. Your lawyer should also inform you whether the fee will be based on the gross amount recovered or on the amount recovered minus the costs.

7.   You, the client, have the right to be told by your lawyer about possible adverse consequences if you lose the case. Those adverse consequences might include money that you might have to pay to your lawyer for costs and liability you might have for attorney's fees to the other side.

8.   You, the client, have the right to receive and approve a closing statement at the end of the case before you pay any money. The statement must list all of the financial details of the entire case, including the amount recovered, all expenses, and a precise statement of your lawyer's fee. Until you approve the closing statement you need not pay any money to anyone, including your lawyer. You also have the right to have every lawyer or law firm working on your case sign this closing statement.

9. You, the client, have the right to ask your lawyer at reasonable intervals how the case is progressing and to have these questions answered to the best of your lawyer's ability.

10. You, the client, have the right to make the final decision regarding settlement of a case. Your lawyer must notify you of all offers of settlement before and after the trial. Offers during the trial must be immediately communicated and you should consult with your lawyer regarding whether to accept a settlement. However, you must make the final decision to accept or reject a settlement.

11. If at any time you, the client, believe that your lawyer has charged an excessive or illegal fee, you have the right to report the matter to The Florida Bar, the agency that oversees the practice and behavior of all lawyers in Florida. For information on how to reach The Florida Bar, call 850–561–5600, or contact the local bar association. Any disagreement between you and your lawyer about a fee can be taken to court and you may wish to hire another lawyer to help you resolve this disagreement. Usually fee disputes must be handled in a separate lawsuit unless your fee contract provides for arbitration. You can request, but may not require, that a provision for arbitration (under chapter 682, Florida Statutes, or under the fee arbitration rule of the Rules Regulating The Florida Bar) be included in your fee contract.

_____   _____
Client Signature   Attorney Signature

_____   _____
Date   Date

COMMENT:

Basis or rate of fee

When the lawyer has regularly represented a client, they ordinarily will have evolved an understanding concerning the basis or rate of the fee. In a new client-lawyer relationship, however, an understanding as to the fee should be promptly established. It is not necessary to recite all the factors that underlie the basis of the fee but only those that are directly involved in its computation. It is sufficient, for example, to state the basic rate is an hourly charge or a fixed amount or an estimated amount, or to identify the factors that may be taken into account in finally fixing the fee. When developments occur during the representation that render an earlier estimate substantially inaccurate, a revised estimate should be provided to the client. A written statement concerning the fee reduces the possibility of misunderstanding. Furnishing the client with a simple memorandum or a copy of the lawyer's customary fee schedule is sufficient if the basis or rate of the fee is set forth.

Rule 4–1.8(e) should be consulted regarding a lawyer's providing financial assistance to a client in connection with litigation.

Terms of payment

A lawyer may require advance payment of a fee but is obliged to return any unearned portion. See rule 4–1.16(d). A lawyer is not, however, required to return retainers that, pursuant to an agreement with a client, are not refundable. A lawyer may accept property in payment for services, such as an ownership interest in an enterprise, providing this does not involve acquisition of a proprietary interest in the cause of action or subject matter of the litigation contrary to rule 4–1.8(i). However, a fee paid in property instead of money may be subject to special scrutiny because it involves questions concerning both the value of the services and the lawyer's special knowledge of the value of the property.

An agreement may not be made whose terms might induce the lawyer improperly to curtail services for the client or perform them in a way contrary to the client's interest. For example, a lawyer should not enter into an agreement whereby services are to be provided only up to a stated amount when it is foreseeable that more extensive services probably will be required, unless the situation is adequately explained to the client. Otherwise, the client might have to bargain for further assistance in the midst of a proceeding or transaction. However, it is proper to define the extent of services in light of the client's ability to pay. A lawyer should not exploit a fee arrangement based primarily on hourly charges by using wasteful procedures. When there is doubt whether a contingent fee is consistent with the client's best interest, the lawyer should offer the client alternative bases for the fee and explain their implications. Applicable law may impose limitations on contingent fees, such as a ceiling on the percentage.

Rule 4–1.5(f)(3) does not apply to lawyers seeking to obtain or enforce judgments for arrearages.

Contingent fee regulation

Rule 4–1.5(f)(4) should not be construed to apply to actions or claims seeking property or other damages arising in the commercial litigation context.

Rule 4–1.5(f)(4)(B) is intended to apply only to contingent aspects of fee agreements. In the situation where a lawyer and client enter a contract for part noncontingent and part contingent attorney's fees, rule 4–1.5(f)(4)(B) should not be construed to apply to and prohibit or limit the noncontingent portion of the fee agreement. An attorney could properly charge and retain the noncontingent portion of the fee even if the matter was not successfully prosecuted or if the noncontingent portion of the fee exceeded the schedule set forth in rule 4–1.5(f)(4)(B). Rule 4–1.5(f)(4)(B) should, however, be construed to apply to any additional contingent portion of such a contract when considered together with earned noncontingent fees. Thus, under such a contract a lawyer may demand or collect only such additional contingent fees as would not cause the total fees to exceed the schedule set forth in rule 4–1.5(f)(4)(B).

The limitations in rule 4–1.5(f)(4)(B)(i)c are only to be applied in the case where all the defendants admit liability at the time they file their initial answer and the trial is only on the issue of the amount or extent of the loss or the extent of injury suffered by the client. If the trial involves not only the issue of damages but also such questions as proximate cause, affirmative defenses, seat belt defense, or other similar matters, the limitations are not to be applied because of the contingent nature of the case being left for resolution by the trier of fact.

Rule 4–1.5(f)(4)(B)(ii) provides the limitations set forth in subdivision (f)(4)(B)(i) may be waived by the client upon approval by the appropriate judge. This waiver provision may not be used to authorize a lawyer to charge a client a fee that would exceed rule 4–1.5(a) or (b). It is contemplated that this waiver provision will not be necessary except where the client wants to retain a particular lawyer to represent the client or the case involves complex, difficult, or novel questions of law or fact that would justify a contingent fee greater than the schedule but not a contingent fee that would exceed rule 4–1.5(b).

Upon a petition by a client, the trial court reviewing the waiver request must grant that request if the trial court finds the client: (a) understands the right to have the limitations in rule 4–1.5(f)(4)(B) applied in the specific matter; and (b) understands and approves the terms of the proposed contract. The consideration by the trial court of the waiver petition is not to be used as an opportunity for the court to inquire into the merits or details of the particular action or claim that is the subject of the contract.

The proceedings before the trial court and the trial court's decision on a waiver request are to be confidential and not subject to discovery by any of the parties to the action or by any other individual or entity except The Florida Bar. However, terms of the contract approved by the trial court may be subject to discovery if the contract (without court approval) was subject to discovery under applicable case law or rules of evidence.

Rule 4–1.5(f)(4)(B)(iii) prohibits a lawyer from charging the contingent fee percentage on the total, future value of a recovery being paid on a structured or periodic basis. This prohibition does not apply if the lawyer's fee is being paid over the same length of time as the schedule of payments to the client.

Contingent fees are prohibited in criminal and certain domestic relations matters. In domestic relations cases, fees that include a bonus provision or additional fee to be determined at a later time and based on results obtained have been held to be impermissible contingency fees and therefore subject to restitution and disciplinary sanction as elsewhere stated in these Rules Regulating The Florida Bar.

Division of fee

A division of fee is a single billing to a client covering the fee of 2 or more lawyers who are not in the same firm. A division of fee facilitates association of more than 1 lawyer in a matter in which neither alone could serve the client as well, and most often is used when the fee is contingent and the division is between a referring lawyer and a trial specialist. Subject to the provisions of subdivision (f)(4)(D), subdivision (g) permits the lawyers to divide a fee on either the basis of the proportion of services they render or by agreement between the participating lawyers if all assume responsibility for the representation as a whole and the client is advised and does not object. It does require disclosure to the client of the share that each lawyer is to receive. Joint responsibility for the representation entails the obligations stated in rule 4–5.1 for purposes of the matter involved.

Disputes over fees

Since the fee arbitration rule (Chapter 14) has been established by the bar to provide a procedure for resolution of fee disputes, the lawyer should conscientiously consider submitting to it. Where law prescribes a procedure for determining a lawyer's fee, for example, in representation of an executor or administrator, a class, or a person entitled to a reasonable fee as part of the measure of damages, the lawyer entitled to such a fee and a lawyer representing another party concerned with the fee should comply with the prescribed procedure.

Referral fees and practices

A secondary lawyer shall not be entitled to a fee greater than the limitation set forth in rule 4–1.5(f)(4)(D)(ii) merely because the lawyer agrees to do some or all of the following: (a) consults with the client; (b) answers interrogatories; (c) attends depositions; (d) reviews pleadings; (e) attends the trial; or (f) assumes joint legal responsibility to the client. However, the provisions do not contemplate that a secondary lawyer who does more than the above is necessarily entitled to a larger percentage of the fee than that allowed by the limitation.

The provisions of rule 4–1.5(f)(4)(D)(iii) only apply where the participating lawyers have for purposes of the specific case established a co-counsel relationship. The need for court approval of a referral fee arrangement under rule 4–1.5(f)(4)(D)(iii) should only occur in a small percentage of cases arising under rule 4–1.5(f)(4).

In determining if a co-counsel relationship exists, the court should look to see if the lawyers have established a special partnership agreement for the purpose of the specific case or matter. If such an agreement does exist, it must provide for a sharing of services or responsibility and the fee division is based upon a division of the services to be rendered or the responsibility assumed. It is contemplated that a co-counsel situation would exist where a division of responsibility is based

310

upon, but not limited to, the following: (a) based upon geographic considerations, the lawyers agree to divide the legal work, responsibility, and representation in a convenient fashion. Such a situation would occur when different aspects of a case must be handled in different locations; (b) where the lawyers agree to divide the legal work and representation based upon their particular expertise in the substantive areas of law involved in the litigation; or (c) where the lawyers agree to divide the legal work and representation along established lines of division, such as liability and damages, causation and damages, or other similar factors.

The trial court's responsibility when reviewing an application for authorization of a fee division under rule 4–1.5(f)(4)(D)(iii) is to determine if a co-counsel relationship exists in that particular case. If the court determines a co-counsel relationship exists and authorizes the fee division requested, the court does not have any responsibility to review or approve the specific amount of the fee division agreed upon by the lawyers and the client.

Rule 4–1.5(f)(4)(D)(iv) applies to the situation where appellate counsel is retained during the trial of the case to assist with the appeal of the case. The percentages set forth in subdivision (f)(4)(D) are to be applicable after appellate counsel's fee is established. However, the effect should not be to impose an unreasonable fee on the client.

Illinois Rule 1.5

[Illinois has added subsections (g) through (j) to Model Rule 1.5]

RULE 1.5   Fees

* * *

(g) A division of fees shall be made in proportion to the services performed and responsibility assumed by each lawyer, except where the primary service performed by one lawyer is the referral of the client to another lawyer and

> **(1) the receiving lawyer discloses that the referring lawyer has received or will receive economic benefit from the referral and the extent and basis of such economic benefit, and**

> **(2) the referring lawyer agrees to assume the same legal responsibility for the performance of the services in question as would a partner of the receiving lawyer.**

(h) The total fee of the lawyers shall be reasonable.

(i) For purposes of Rule 1.5 "economic benefit" shall include:

> **(1) the amount of participation in the fee received with regard to the particular matter;**

(2) any other form of remuneration passing to the referring lawyer from the receiving lawyer, whether or not with regard to the particular matter; and

(3) an established practice of referrals to and from or from and to the receiving lawyer and the referring lawyer.

(j) Notwithstanding Rule 1.5(f), a payment may be made to a lawyer formerly in the firm, pursuant to a separation or retirement agreement.

Kansas Rule 1.5

[Kansas has substituted the following provisions for Model Rule 1.5(c) through (e):]

RULE 1.5

(c) A lawyer's fee shall be reasonable but a court determination that a fee is not reasonable shall not be presumptive evidence of a violation that requires discipline of the attorney.

(d) A fee may be contingent on the outcome of the matter for which the service is rendered, except in a matter in which a contingent fee is prohibited by paragraph (f) or other law. A contingent fee agreement shall be in writing and shall state the method by which the fee is to be determined, including the percentage or percentages that shall accrue to the lawyer in the event of settlement, trial or appeal, and the litigation and other expenses to be deducted from the recovery. All such expenses shall be deducted before the contingent fee is calculated. Upon conclusion of a contingent fee matter, the lawyer shall provide the client with a written statement stating the outcome of the matter and, if there is a recovery, showing the client's share and amount and the method of its determination. The statement shall advise the client of the right to have the fee reviewed as provided in subsection (e).

(e) Upon application by the client, all fee contracts shall be subject to review and approval by the appropriate court having jurisdiction of the matter and the court shall have the authority to determine whether the contract is reasonable. If the court finds the contract is not reasonable, it shall set and allow a reasonable fee.

Texas Rule 1.04 *(Modification of Model Rule 1.5)*

[Texas has modified several subsections of Model Rule 1.5 (fees) to read as follows:]

RULE 1.04   Fees

(a) A lawyer shall not enter into an arrangement for, charge, or collect an illegal fee or unconscionable fee. A fee is

unconscionable if a competent lawyer could not form a reasonable belief that the fee is reasonable.

* * *

(f) A division or agreement for division of a fee between lawyers who are not in the same firm shall not be made unless:
> **(1) the division is:**
>> **(i) in proportion to the professional services performed by each lawyer;**
>>
>> **(ii) made with a forwarding lawyer; or**
>>
>> **(iii) made, by written agreement with the client, with a lawyer who assumes joint responsibility for the representation;**
>
> **(2) the client is advised of, and does not object to, the participation of all the lawyers involved; and**
>
> **(3) the aggregate fee does not violate paragraph (a).**

* * *

COMMENT:

1. A lawyer in good conscience should not charge or collect more than a reasonable fee, although he may charge less or no fee at all. The determination of the reasonableness of a fee, or of the range of reasonableness, can be a difficult question, and a standard of "reasonableness" is too vague and uncertain to be an appropriate standard in a disciplinary action. For this reason, paragraph (a) adopts, for disciplinary purposes only, a clearer standard: the lawyer is subject to discipline for an illegal fee or an unconscionable fee. Paragraph (a) defines an unconscionable fee in terms of the reasonableness of the fee but in a way to eliminate factual disputes as to the fee's reasonableness. The Rule's "unconscionable" standard, however, does not preclude use of the "reasonableness" standard of paragraph (b) in other settings.

Basis or Rate of Fee

2. When the lawyer has regularly represented a client, they ordinarily will have evolved an understanding concerning the basis or rate of the fee. If, however, the basis or rate of fee being charged to a regularly represented client differs from the understanding that has evolved, the lawyer should so advise the client. In a new client-lawyer relationship, an understanding as to the fee should be promptly established. It is not necessary to recite all the factors that underlie the basis of the fee, but only those that are directly involved in its computation. It is sufficient, for example, to state that the basic rate is an hourly charge or a fixed amount or an estimated amount, in order to identify the factors that may be taken into account in finally fixing the fee. When developments occur during the representation that render an earlier estimate substan-

tially inaccurate, a revised estimate should be provided to the client. A written statement concerning the fee reduces the possibility of misunderstanding, and when the lawyer has not regularly represented the client it is preferable for the basis or rate of the fee to be communicated to the client in writing. Furnishing the client with a simple memorandum or a copy of the lawyer's customary fee schedule is sufficient if the basis or rate of the fee is set forth. In the case of a contingent fee, a written agreement is mandatory.

* * *

Unconscionable Fees

7. Two principal circumstances combine to make it difficult to determine whether a particular fee is unconscionable within the disciplinary test provided by paragraph (a) of this Rule. The first is the subjectivity of a number of the factors relied on to determine the reasonableness of fees under paragraph (b). Because those factors do not permit more than an approximation of a range of fees that might be found reasonable in any given case, there is a corresponding degree of uncertainty in determining whether a given fee is unconscionable. Secondly, fee arrangements normally are made at the outset of representation, a time when many uncertainties and contingencies exist, while claims of unconscionability are made in hindsight when the contingencies have been resolved. The "unconscionability" standard adopts that difference in perspective and requires that a lawyer be given the benefit of any such uncertainties for disciplinary purposes only. Except in very unusual situations, therefore, the circumstances at the time a fee arrangement is made should control in determining a question of unconscionability.

8. Two factors in otherwise borderline cases might indicate a fee may be unconscionable. The first is overreaching by a lawyer, particularly of a client who was unusually susceptible to such overreaching. The second is a failure of the lawyer to give at the outset a clear and accurate explanation of how a fee was to be calculated. For example, a fee arrangement negotiated at arm's length with an experienced business client would rarely be subject to question. On the other hand, a fee arrangement with an uneducated or unsophisticated individual having no prior experience in such matters should be more carefully scrutinized for overreaching. While the fact that a client was at a marked disadvantage in bargaining with a lawyer over fees will not make a fee unconscionable, application of the disciplinary test may require some consideration of the personal circumstances of the individuals involved.

* * *

Division of Fees

10. A division of fees is a sharing of a single billing to a client between two or more lawyers who are not in the same firm. A division

of fees facilitates association of more than one lawyer in a matter in which neither alone could serve the client as well, and most often is used when the fee is contingent and the division is between a referring lawyer and a trial specialist. Because the association of additional counsel normally will result in a further disclosure of client confidences and have a financial impact on a client, advance disclosure of the existence of that proposed association and client consent generally are required. Where those consequences will not arise, however, disclosure is not mandated by this Rule. For example, if a lawyer hires a second lawyer for consultation and advice on a specialized aspect of a matter and that consultation will not necessitate the disclosure of confidential information and the hiring lawyer both absorbs the entire cost of the second lawyer's fees and assumes all responsibility for the advice ultimately given the client, a division of fees within the meaning of this Rule is not involved. See also Comment 3 to Rule 5.04.

11. Paragraph (f) permits lawyers to divide a fee on one of three bases. The first is in proportion to the professional services performed by each. The second continues the Texas practice of permitting a division of fees with a forwarding attorney. The third permits fees to be divided with a lawyer who, by written agreement with the client, assumes joint responsibility for the representation. The second and the third methods permit the fees to be divided in any mutually agreeable proportion. If the third method is used, a lawyer may satisfy his or her obligations of "joint responsibility" for the representation either by being an attorney of record in the matter or by discharging the responsibilities imposed on a "supervised lawyer" under these rules. See Rule 5.02. Paragraph (f) does not require disclosure to the client of the share that each lawyer is to receive.

Fee Disputes and Determinations

12. If a procedure has been established for resolution of fee disputes, such as an arbitration or mediation procedure established by a bar association, the lawyer should conscientiously consider submitting to it. Law may prescribe a procedure for determining a lawyer's fee, for example, in representation of an executor or administrator, or when a class or a person is entitled to recover a reasonable attorney's fee as part of the measure of damages. All involved lawyers should comply with any prescribed procedures.

Michigan Rule 1.6

[Michigan has modified Model Rule 1.6 to read as follows:]

RULE 1.6 Confidentiality of Information

(a) "Confidence" refers to information protected by the client-lawyer privilege under applicable law, and "secret" refers to other information gained in the professional relationship that

the client has requested be held inviolate or the disclosure of which would be embarrassing or would be likely to be detrimental to the client.

(b) Except when permitted under paragraph (c), a lawyer shall not knowingly:

(1) reveal a confidence or secret of a client;

(2) use a confidence or secret of a client to the disadvantage of the client; or

(3) use a confidence or secret of a client for the advantage of the lawyer or of a third person, unless the client consents after full disclosure.

(c) A lawyer may reveal:

(1) confidences or secrets with the consent of the client or clients affected, but only after full disclosure to them;

(2) confidences or secrets when permitted or required by these rules, or when required by law or by court order;

(3) confidences and secrets to the extent reasonably necessary to rectify the consequences of a client's illegal or fraudulent act in the furtherance of which the lawyer's services have been used;

(4) the intention of a client to commit a crime and the information necessary to prevent the crime; and

(5) confidences or secrets necessary to establish or collect a fee, or to defend the lawyer or the lawyer's employees or associates against an accusation of wrongful conduct.

(d) A lawyer shall exercise reasonable care to prevent employees, associates, and others whose services are utilized by the lawyer from disclosing or using confidences or secrets of a client, except that a lawyer may reveal the information allowed by paragraph (c) through an employee.

COMMENT:

The lawyer is part of a judicial system charged with upholding the law. One of the lawyer's functions is to advise clients so that they avoid any violation of the law in the proper exercise of their rights.

The observance of the ethical obligation of a lawyer to hold inviolate confidential information of the client not only facilitates the full development of facts essential to proper representation of the client, but also encourages people to seek early legal assistance.

Almost without exception, clients come to lawyers in order to determine what their rights are and what is, in the maze of laws and regulations, deemed to be legal and correct. The common law recognizes that the client's confidences must be protected from disclosure. Upon the basis of experience, lawyers know that almost all clients follow the advice given and that the law is upheld.

A fundamental principle in the client-lawyer relationship is that the lawyer maintain confidentiality of information relating to the representation. The client is thereby encouraged to communicate fully and frankly with the lawyer even as to embarrassing or legally damaging subject matter.

The principle of confidentiality is given effect in two related bodies of law, the client-lawyer privilege (which includes the work-product doctrine) in the law of evidence and the rule of confidentiality established in professional ethics. The client-lawyer privilege applies in judicial and other proceedings in which a lawyer may be called as a witness or otherwise required to produce evidence concerning a client. The rule of client-lawyer confidentiality applies in situations other than those where evidence is sought from the lawyer through compulsion of law. The confidentiality rule applies to confidences and secrets as defined in the rule. A lawyer may not disclose such information except as authorized or required by the Rules of Professional Conduct or other law. See also Scope, ante.

The requirement of maintaining confidentiality of information relating to representation applies to government lawyers who may disagree with the policy goals that their representation is designed to advance.

Authorized Disclosure. A lawyer is impliedly authorized to make disclosures about a client when appropriate in carrying out the representation, except to the extent that the client's instructions or special circumstances limit that authority. In litigation, for example, a lawyer may disclose information by admitting a fact that cannot properly be disputed, or, in negotiation, by making a disclosure that facilitates a satisfactory conclusion.

Lawyers in a firm may, in the course of the firm's practice, disclose to each other information relating to a client of the firm, unless the client has instructed that particular information be confined to specified lawyers, or unless the disclosure would breach a screen erected within the firm in accordance with Rules 1.10(b), 1.11(a), or 1.12(c).

Disclosure Adverse to Client. The confidentiality rule is subject to limited exceptions. In becoming privy to information about a client, a lawyer may foresee that the client intends to commit a crime. To the extent a lawyer is prohibited from making disclosure, the interests of the potential victim are sacrificed in favor of preserving the client's confidences even though the client's purpose is wrongful. To the extent a lawyer is required or permitted to disclose a client's purposes, the client may be inhibited from revealing facts which would enable the lawyer to counsel against a wrongful course of action. A rule governing disclosure of threatened harm thus involves balancing the interests of one group of potential victims against those of another. On the assumption that lawyers generally fulfill their duty to advise against the commission of deliberately wrongful acts, the public is better protected if full and open communication by the client is encouraged than if it is inhibited.

Generally speaking, information relating to the representation must be kept confidential as stated in paragraph (b). However, when the client is or will be engaged in criminal conduct, or the integrity of the lawyer's own conduct is involved, the principle of confidentiality may appropriately yield, depending on the lawyer's knowledge about and relationship to the conduct in question, and the seriousness of that conduct. Several situations must be distinguished.

First, the lawyer may not counsel or assist a client in conduct that is illegal or fraudulent. See Rule 1.2(c). Similarly, a lawyer has a duty under Rule 3.3(a)(4) not to use false evidence. This duty is essentially a special instance of the duty prescribed in Rule 1.2(c) to avoid assisting a client in illegal or fraudulent conduct. The same is true of compliance with Rule 4.1 concerning truthfulness of a lawyer's own representations.

Second, the lawyer may have been innocently involved in past conduct by the client that was criminal or fraudulent. In such a situation the lawyer has not violated Rule 1.2(c), because to "counsel or assist" criminal or fraudulent conduct requires knowing that the conduct is of that character. Even if the involvement was innocent, however, the fact remains that the lawyer's professional services were made the instrument of the client's crime or fraud. The lawyer, therefore, has a legitimate interest in being able to rectify the consequences of such conduct, and has the professional right, although not a professional duty, to rectify the situation. Exercising that right may require revealing information relating to the representation. Paragraph (c)(3) gives the lawyer professional discretion to reveal such information to the extent necessary to accomplish rectification. However, the constitutional rights of defendants in criminal cases may limit the extent to which counsel for a defendant may correct a misrepresentation that is based on information provided by the client. See comment to Rule 3.3.

Third, the lawyer may learn that a client intends prospective conduct that is criminal. Inaction by the lawyer is not a violation of Rule 1.2(c), except in the limited circumstances where failure to act constitutes assisting the client. See comment to Rule 1.2(c). However, the lawyer's knowledge of the client's purpose may enable the lawyer to prevent commission of the prospective crime. If the prospective crime is likely to result in substantial injury, the lawyer may feel a moral obligation to take preventive action. When the threatened injury is grave, such as homicide or serious bodily injury, a lawyer may have an obligation under tort or criminal law to take reasonable preventive measures. Whether the lawyer's concern is based on moral or legal considerations, the interest in preventing the harm may be more compelling than the interest in preserving confidentiality of information relating to the client. As stated in paragraph (c)(4), the lawyer has professional discretion to reveal information in order to prevent a client's criminal act.

It is arguable that the lawyer should have a professional obligation to make a disclosure in order to prevent homicide or serious bodily injury which the lawyer knows is intended by the client. However, it is very difficult for a lawyer to "know" when such a heinous purpose will actually be carried out, for the client may have a change of mind. To require disclosure when the client intends such an act, at the risk of professional discipline if the assessment of the client's purpose turns out to be wrong, would be to impose a penal risk that might interfere with the lawyer's resolution of an inherently difficult moral dilemma.

The lawyer's exercise of discretion requires consideration of such factors as magnitude, proximity, and likelihood of the contemplated wrong; the nature of the lawyer's relationship with the client and with those who might be injured by the client; the lawyer's own involvement in the transaction; and factors that may extenuate the conduct in question. Where practical, the lawyer should seek to persuade the client to take suitable action. In any case, a disclosure adverse to the client's interest should be no greater than the lawyer reasonably believes necessary to the purpose. A lawyer's decision not to make a disclosure permitted by paragraph (c) does not violate this rule.

Where the client is an organization, the lawyer may be in doubt whether contemplated conduct will actually be carried out by the organization. Where necessary to guide conduct in connection with this rule, the lawyer should make an inquiry within the organization as indicated in Rule 1.13(b).

Paragraph (c)(3) does not apply where a lawyer is employed after a crime or fraud has been committed to represent the client in matters ensuing therefrom.

Withdrawal. If the lawyer's services will be used by the client in materially furthering a course of criminal or fraudulent conduct, the lawyer must withdraw, as stated in Rule 1.16(a)(1).

After withdrawal the lawyer is required to refrain from making disclosure of the client's confidences, except as otherwise provided in Rule 1.6. Neither this rule nor Rule 1.8(b) nor Rule 1.16(d) prevents the lawyer from giving notice of the fact of withdrawal, and the lawyer may also withdraw or disaffirm any opinion, document, affirmation, or the like.

Dispute Concerning Lawyer's Conduct. Where a legal claim or disciplinary charge alleges complicity of the lawyer in a client's conduct or other misconduct of the lawyer involving representation of the client, the lawyer may respond to the extent the lawyer reasonably believes necessary to establish a defense. The same is true with respect to a claim involving the conduct or representation of a former client. The lawyer's right to respond arises when an assertion of complicity or other misconduct has been made. Paragraph (c)(5) does not require the lawyer to await the commencement of an action or proceeding that charges complicity or other misconduct, so that the defense may be established by responding directly to a third party who has made such an assertion. The right to defend, of course, applies where a proceeding has been commenced. Where practicable and not prejudicial to the lawyer's ability to establish the defense, the lawyer should advise the client of the third party's assertion and request that the client respond appropriately. In any event, disclosure should be no greater than the lawyer reasonably believes is necessary to vindicate innocence, the disclosure should be made in a manner which limits access to the information to the tribunal or other persons having a need to know it, and appropriate protective orders or other arrangements should be sought by the lawyer to the fullest extent practicable.

If the lawyer is charged with wrongdoing in which the client's conduct is implicated, the rule of confidentiality should not prevent the lawyer from defending against the charge. Such a charge can arise in a civil, criminal, or professional disciplinary proceeding, and can be based on a wrong allegedly committed by the lawyer against the client, or on a wrong alleged by a third person, for example, a person claiming to have been defrauded by the lawyer and client acting together.

A lawyer entitled to a fee is permitted by paragraph (c)(5) to prove the services rendered in an action to collect it. This aspect of the rule expresses the principle that the beneficiary of a fiduciary relationship may not exploit it to the detriment of the fiduciary. As stated above, the lawyer must make every effort practicable to avoid unnecessary disclosure of information relating to a representation, to limit disclosure to those having the need to know it, and to obtain protective orders or make other arrangements minimizing the risk of disclosure.

Disclosures Otherwise Required or Authorized. The scope of the client-lawyer privilege is a question of law. If a lawyer is called as a witness to give testimony concerning a client, absent waiver by the client, paragraph (b)(1) requires the lawyer to invoke the privilege when it is applicable. The lawyer must comply with the final orders of a court or other tribunal of competent jurisdiction requiring the lawyer to give information about the client.

The Rules of Professional Conduct in various circumstances permit or require a lawyer to disclose information relating to the representation. See Rules 2.2, 2.3, 3.3 and 4.1. In addition to these provisions, a lawyer may be obligated or permitted by other provisions of law to give information about a client. Whether another provision of law supersedes Rule 1.6 is a matter of interpretation beyond the scope of these rules, but a presumption should exist against such a supersession.

Former Client. The duty of confidentiality continues after the client-lawyer relationship has terminated. See Rule 1.9.

Minnesota Rule 1.6

[Minnesota has modified Model Rule 1.6 to read as follows:]

RULE 1.6 Confidentiality of Information

(a) Except when permitted under paragraph (b), a lawyer shall not knowingly:

(1) **reveal a confidence or secret of a client;**

(2) **use a confidence or secret of a client to the disadvantage of the client;**

(3) **use a confidence or secret of a client for the advantage of the lawyer or a third person, unless the client consents after consultation.**

(b) **A lawyer may reveal:**

(1) **confidences or secrets with the consent of the client or clients affected, but only after consultation with them;**

(2) **confidences or secrets when permitted under the Rules of Professional Conduct or required by law or court order;**

(3) **the intention of a client to commit a crime and the information necessary to prevent a crime;**

(4) **confidences and secrets necessary to rectify the consequences of a client's criminal or fraudulent act in the furtherance of which the lawyer's services were used;**

(5) **confidences or secrets necessary to establish or collect a fee or to defend the lawyer or employees or associates against an accusation of wrongful conduct.**

(6) **secrets necessary to inform the Office of Lawyers Professional Responsibility of knowledge of another lawyer's violation of the Rules of Professional Conduct that raises a substantial question as to that lawyer's honesty, trustworthiness or fitness as a lawyer in other respects. See Rule 8.3.**

(c) **A lawyer shall exercise reasonable care to prevent employees, associates and others whose services the lawyer utilizes from disclosing or using confidences or secrets of a client, except that a lawyer may reveal the information allowed by paragraph (b) through an employee.**

(d) **"Confidence" refers to information protected by the attorney-client privilege under applicable law, and "secret" refers to other information gained in the professional relationship that the client has requested be held inviolate or the disclosure of which would be embarrassing or would be likely to be detrimental to the client.**

COMMENT—1991

General

Both the fiduciary relationship existing between lawyer and client and the proper functioning of the legal system require the lawyer to preserve confidences and secrets of one who has employed or sought to employ the lawyer. A client must feel free to discuss whatever the client wishes with the lawyer and a lawyer must be equally free to obtain information beyond what the client volunteers. A lawyer should be fully informed of all the facts of the matter the lawyer is handling in order for the client to obtain the full advantage of our legal system. It is for the lawyer in the exercise of independent professional judgment to separate the relevant and important from the irrelevant and unimportant.

Observance of the lawyer's ethical obligation to hold inviolate the client's confidences and secrets not only facilitates the full development of facts essential to proper representation of the client but also encourages people to seek early legal assistance.

Authorized Disclosure

The obligation to protect confidences and secrets obviously does not preclude a lawyer from revealing information when the client consents after consultation, when necessary to perform professional employment, when permitted by the Rules of Professional Conduct or when required by law.

The confidentiality required under this rule should not allow a client to utilize the lawyer's services in committing a criminal or fraudulent act. A lawyer is permitted to reveal the intention of a client to commit a crime and the information necessary to prevent the crime. In addition, where the lawyer finds out, after the fact, that the lawyer's services were used by the client to commit a criminal or fraudulent act, the lawyer has discretion to reveal information necessary to rectify the consequences of the client's crime or fraud. A lawyer is not permitted, however, to disclose a client's criminal or fraudulent act committed prior to the client's retention of the lawyer's services.

Unless the client otherwise directs, a lawyer may disclose the client's affairs to partners or associates.

It is a matter of common knowledge that the normal operation of a law office exposes confidential professional information to non-lawyer employees of the office, particularly secretaries and those having access to the files; and this obligates a lawyer to exercise care in selecting and training employees so that the sanctity of all confidences and secrets of clients may be preserved.

If the obligation extends to two or more clients as to the same information, a lawyer should obtain the permission of all before revealing the information.

A lawyer must always be sensitive to the client's rights and wishes and act scrupulously in making decisions which may involve disclosure of information obtained in the professional relationship. Thus, in the absence of the client's consent after consultation, a lawyer should not associate another lawyer in handling a matter; nor, in the absence of consent, seek counsel from another lawyer if there is a reasonable possibility that the client's identity or confidences or secrets would be revealed to that lawyer. Both social amenities and professional duty should cause a lawyer to shun indiscreet conversations concerning clients.

Unless the client otherwise directs, it is not improper for a lawyer to give limited information from the lawyer's files to an outside agency necessary for statistical, bookkeeping, accounting, data processing, banking, printing, or other legitimate purposes, provided the lawyer exercises due care in selecting the agency and warns the agency that the information must be kept confidential.

Protecting Confidences

The attorney-client privilege is more limited than the lawyer's ethical obligation to guard the client's confidences and secrets. The ethical obligation, unlike the evidentiary privilege, exists without regard to the nature or source of information or the fact that others share the knowledge.

A lawyer should endeavor to act in a manner which preserves the evidentiary privilege; for example, the lawyer should avoid professional discussions in the presence of persons to whom the privilege does not extend. A lawyer owes an obligation to advise the client of the attorney-client privilege and timely to assert the privilege unless it is waived by the client.

Using Confidences or Secrets

A lawyer should not use information acquired in the course of the representation of a client to the client's disadvantage and a lawyer should not use, except with the client's consent after full disclosure, such information for the lawyer's own purposes.

Likewise, a lawyer should be diligent in efforts to prevent misuse of such information by employees and associates.

A lawyer should exercise care to prevent disclosure of confidences and secrets of one client to another and should accept no employment that might require such disclosure.

Former Client

The lawyer's obligation to preserve the client's confidences and secrets continues after termination of the employment. Thus, a lawyer should not attempt to sell a law practice as a going business because, among other reasons, to do so would involve disclosure of confidences and secrets.

A lawyer should also provide for the protection of the client's confidences and secrets following the termination of the practice of the lawyer, whether termination is due to death, disability or retirement. For example, a lawyer might provide for the client's personal papers to be returned to the client and for the lawyer's papers to be delivered to another lawyer or to be destroyed. In determining the method of

323

disposition, the client's instructions and wishes should be a dominant consideration.

Reporting Obligation

In the course of representation a lawyer may acquire knowledge of another lawyer's violations of the Rules of Professional Conduct. In that instance, a lawyer's obligation to protect client confidences and secrets under Rule 1.6 may appear to conflict with that lawyer's obligations under Rule 8.3 to report professional misconduct by another lawyer. Where "confidences" are involved, the importance of the fiduciary relationship between lawyer and client and the proper functioning of the legal system require that the client retain the veto power over the lawyer's ability to divulge knowledge of another lawyer's violations of the Rules of Professional Conduct.

Until the Rules of Professional Conduct superseded the Code of Professional Responsibility in 1985, Minnesota lawyers were required to report professional misconduct only if their knowledge of the misconduct was "unprivileged." Until 1985, if a lawyer's knowledge of misconduct was a "secret," reporting was required; if the knowledge acquired involved a "confidence," reporting was not allowed, unless some other exception to the confidentiality rule applied. Since September 1, 1985, reporting of misconduct has been forbidden without client consent, if either a confidence or secret is involved.

Under subsection 1.6(b)(6), a lawyer now has the discretion to reveal "secrets," but not client confidences, when necessary to report the lawyer's knowledge of another lawyer's misconduct. This subsection incorporates the language of Rule 8.3 as to the type of reportable misconduct, requiring that the misconduct "raise a substantial question" about the lawyer's honesty, trustworthiness or fitness as a lawyer in other respects.

This discretion to report a lawyer's misconduct balances the policy of confidentiality with the legal profession's obligation to enforce high ethical standards. If the client consents to the lawyer reporting another lawyer's misconduct, no conflict exists between these two policies. Therefore, the lawyer with knowledge of another lawyer's misconduct should seek the client's permission to report the misconduct to the disciplinary authority.

When the client opposes such disclosure, the lawyer then must determine whether knowledge of the misconduct stemmed from a client confidence. If so, the confidentiality rule prevails: disclosure is prohibited. If the knowledge stemmed from a secret, however, the lawyer faces the discretionary decision whether to report the misconduct. Factors pertinent to the discretionary decision include the nature of the lawyer's misconduct, the likelihood that such misconduct will recur if not reported, the possible emotional harm to the client if required to testify in a disciplinary proceeding and/or the likelihood of recovery of embezzled funds.

Other factors that may merit consideration would be the ability to recover funds, such as through frozen assets or a client security fund, in which case, the client's preference might be given less weight.

Texas Rule 1.05 *(Modification of Model Rule 1.6)*

[Texas has modified Model Rule 1.6 (Confidentiality) to read as follows:]

RULE 1.05   Confidentiality of Information

(a) "Confidential information" includes both "privileged information" and "unprivileged client information." "Privileged information" refers to the information of a client protected by the lawyer-client privilege of Rule 503 of the Texas Rules of Evidence or of Rule 503 of the Texas Rules of Criminal Evidence or by the principles of attorney-client privilege governed by Rule 501 of the Federal Rules of Evidence for United States Courts and Magistrates. "Unprivileged client information" means all information relating to a client or furnished by the client, other than privileged information, acquired by the lawyer during the course of or by reason of the representation of the client.

(b) Except as permitted by paragraphs (c) and (d), or as required by paragraphs (e) and (f), a lawyer shall not knowingly:

(1) Reveal confidential information of a client or a former client to:

(i) a person that the client has instructed is not to receive the information; or

(ii) anyone else, other than the client, the client's representatives, or the members, associates, or employees of the lawyer's law firm.

(2) Use confidential information of a client to the disadvantage of the client unless the client consents after consultation.

(3) Use confidential information of a former client to the disadvantage of the former client after the representation is concluded unless the former client consents after consultation or the confidential information has become generally known.

(4) Use privileged information of a client for the advantage of the lawyer or of a third person, unless the client consents after consultation.

(c) A lawyer may reveal confidential information:

(1) When the lawyer has been expressly authorized to do so in order to carry out the representation.

(2) When the client consents after consultation.

(3) To the client, the client's representatives, or the members, associates, and employees of the lawyer's firm, except when otherwise instructed by the client.

(4) When the lawyer has reason to believe it is necessary to do so in order to comply with a court order, a Texas Disciplinary Rule of Professional Conduct, or other law.

(5) To the extent reasonably necessary to enforce a claim or establish a defense on behalf of the lawyer in a controversy between the lawyer and the client.

(6) To establish a defense to a criminal charge, civil claim or disciplinary complaint against the lawyer or the lawyer's associates based upon conduct involving the client or the representation of the client.

(7) When the lawyer has reason to believe it is necessary to do so in order to prevent the client from committing a criminal or fraudulent act.

(8) To the extent revelation reasonably appears necessary to rectify the consequences of a client's criminal or fraudulent act in the commission of which the lawyer's services had been used.

(d) A lawyer also may reveal unprivileged client information:

(1) When impliedly authorized to do so in order to carry out the representation.

(2) When the lawyer has reason to believe it is necessary to do so in order to:

(i) carry out the representation effectively;

(ii) defend the lawyer or the lawyer's employees or associates against a claim of wrongful conduct;

(iii) respond to allegations in any proceeding concerning the lawyer's representation of the client; or

(iv) prove the services rendered to a client, or the reasonable value thereof, or both, in an action against another person or organization responsible for the payment of the fee for services rendered to the client.

(e) When a lawyer has confidential information clearly establishing that a client is likely to commit a criminal or fraudulent act that is likely to result in death or substantial bodily harm to a person, the lawyer shall reveal confidential information to the extent revelation reasonably appears necessary to prevent the client from committing the criminal or fraudulent act.

(f) A lawyer shall reveal confidential information when required to do so by Rule 3.03(a)(2), 3.03(b), or by Rule 4.01(b).

COMMENT:

Confidentiality Generally

1. Both the fiduciary relationship existing between lawyer and client and the proper functioning of the legal system require the preservation by the lawyer of confidential information of one who has employed or sought to employ the lawyer. Free discussion should prevail between lawyer and client in order for the lawyer to be fully informed and for the client to obtain the full benefit of the legal system. The ethical obligation of the lawyer to protect the confidential information of the client not only facilitates the proper representation of the client but also encourages potential clients to seek early legal assistance.

2. Subject to the mandatory disclosure requirements of paragraphs (e) and (f) the lawyer generally should be required to maintain confidentiality of information acquired by the lawyer during the course of or by reason of the representation of the client. This principle involves an ethical obligation not to use the information to the detriment of the client or for the benefit of the lawyer or a third person. In regard to an evaluation of a matter affecting a client for use by a third person, see Rule 2.02.

3. The principle of confidentiality is given effect not only in the Texas Rules of Professional Conduct but also in the law of evidence regarding the attorney-client privilege and in the law of agency. The attorney-client privilege, developed through many decades, provides the client a right to prevent certain confidential communications from being revealed by compulsion of law. Several sound exceptions to confidentiality have been developed in the evidence law of privilege. Exceptions exist in evidence law where the services of the lawyer were sought or used by a client in planning or committing a crime or fraud as well as where issues have arisen as to breach of duty by the lawyer or by the client to the other.

4. Rule 1.05 reinforces the principles of evidence law relating to the attorney-client privilege. Rule 1.05 also furnishes considerable protection to other information falling outside the scope of the privilege. Rule 1.05 extends ethical protection generally to unprivileged information relating to the client or furnished by the client during the course of or by reason of the representation of the client. In this respect Rule 1.05 accords with general fiduciary principles of agency.

5. The requirement of confidentiality applies to government lawyers who may disagree with the policy goals that their representation is designed to advance.

Disclosure for Benefit of Client

6. A lawyer may be expressly authorized to make disclosures to carry out the representation and generally is recognized as having

implied-in-fact authority to make disclosures about a client when appropriate in carrying out the representation to the extent that the client's instructions do not limit that authority. In litigation, for example, a lawyer may disclose information by admitting a fact that cannot properly be disputed, or in negotiation by making a disclosure that facilitates a satisfactory conclusion. The effect of Rule 1.05 is to require the lawyer to invoke, for the client, the attorney-client privilege when applicable; but if the court improperly denies the privilege, under paragraph (c)(4) the lawyer may testify as ordered by the court or may test the ruling as permitted by Rule 3.04(d).

7. In the course of a firm's practice, lawyers may disclose to each other and to appropriate employees information relating to a client, unless the client has instructed that particular information be confined to specified lawyers. Subparagraphs (b)(1) and (c)(3) continue these practices concerning disclosure of confidential information within the firm.

Use of Information

8. Following sound principles of agency law, subparagraphs (b)(2) and (4) subject a lawyer to discipline for using information relating to the representation in a manner disadvantageous to the client or beneficial to the lawyer or a third person, absent the informed consent of the client. The duty not to misuse client information continues after the client-lawyer relationship has terminated. Therefore, the lawyer is forbidden by subparagraph (b)(3) to use, in absence of the client's informed consent, confidential information of the former client to the client's disadvantage, unless the information is generally known.

Discretionary Disclosure Adverse to Client

9. In becoming privy to information about a client, a lawyer may foresee that the client intends serious and perhaps irreparable harm. To the extent a lawyer is prohibited from making disclosure, the interests of the potential victim are sacrificed in favor of preserving the client's information—usually unprivileged information—even though the client's purpose is wrongful. On the other hand, a client who knows or believes that a lawyer is required or permitted to disclose a client's wrongful purposes may be inhibited from revealing facts which would enable the lawyer to counsel effectively against wrongful action. Rule 1.05 thus involves balancing the interests of one group of potential victims against those of another. The criteria provided by the Rule are discussed below.

10. Rule 503(d)(1), Texas Rules of Civil Evidence (Tex.R.Civ.Evid.), and Rule 503(d)(1), Texas Rules of Criminal Evidence (Tex.R.Crim. Evid.), indicate the underlying public policy of furnishing no protection to client information where the client seeks or uses the services of the lawyer to aid in the commission of a crime or fraud. That public policy governs the dictates of Rule 1.05. Where the client is planning or

engaging in criminal or fraudulent conduct or where the culpability of the lawyer's conduct is involved, full protection of client information is not justified.

11. Several other situations must be distinguished. First, the lawyer may not counsel or assist a client in conduct that is criminal or fraudulent. See Rule 1.02(c). As noted in the Comment to that Rule, there can be situations where the lawyer may have to reveal information relating to the representation in order to avoid assisting a client's criminal or fraudulent conduct, and sub-paragraph (c)(4) permits doing so. A lawyer's duty under Rule 3.03(a) not to use false or fabricated evidence is a special instance of the duty prescribed in Rule 1.02(c) to avoid assisting a client in criminal or fraudulent conduct, and sub-paragraph (c)(4) permits revealing information necessary to comply with Rule 3.03(a) or (b). The same is true of compliance with Rule 4.01. See also paragraph (f).

12. Second, the lawyer may have been innocently involved in past conduct by the client that was criminal or fraudulent. In such a situation the lawyer has not violated Rule 1.02(c), because to "counsel or assist" criminal or fraudulent conduct requires knowing that the conduct is of that character. Since the lawyer's services were made an instrument of the client's crime or fraud, the lawyer has a legitimate interest both in rectifying the consequences of such conduct and in avoiding charges that the lawyer's participation was culpable. Sub-paragraph (c)(6) and (8) give the lawyer professional discretion to reveal both unprivileged and privileged information in order to serve those interests. See paragraph (g). In view of Tex.R.Civ.Evid. Rule 503(d)(1), and Tex.R.Crim.Evid. 503(d)(1), however, rarely will such information be privileged.

13. Third, the lawyer may learn that a client intends prospective conduct that is criminal or fraudulent. The lawyer's knowledge of the client's purpose may enable the lawyer to prevent commission of the prospective crime or fraud. When the threatened injury is grave, the lawyer's interest in preventing the harm may be more compelling than the interest in preserving confidentiality of information. As stated in subparagraph (c)(7), the lawyer has professional discretion, based on reasonable appearances, to reveal both privileged and unprivileged information in order to prevent the client's commission of any criminal or fraudulent act. In some situations of this sort, disclosure is mandatory. See paragraph (e) and Comments 18–20.

14. The lawyer's exercise of discretion under paragraphs (c) and (d) involves consideration of such factors as the magnitude, proximity, and likelihood of the contemplated wrong, the nature of the lawyer's relationship with the client and with those who might be injured by the client, the lawyer's own involvement in the transaction, and factors that may extenuate the client's conduct in question. In any case, a disclosure adverse to the client's interest should be no greater than the lawyer believes necessary to the purpose. Although preventive action is permit-

ted by paragraphs (c) and (d), failure to take preventive action does not violate those paragraphs. But see paragraphs (e) and (f). *Because these rules do not define standards of civil liability of lawyers for professional conduct, paragraphs (c) and (d) do not create a duty on the lawyer to make any disclosure and no civil liability is intended to arise from the failure to make such disclosure.*

15. A lawyer entitled to a fee necessarily must be permitted to prove the services rendered in an action to collect it, and this necessity is recognized by sub-paragraphs (c)(5) and (d)(2)(iv). This aspect of the rule, in regard to privileged information, expresses the principle that the beneficiary of a fiduciary relationship may not exploit the relationship to the detriment of the fiduciary. Any disclosure by the lawyer, however, should be as protective of the client's interests as possible.

16. If the client is an organization, a lawyer also should refer to Rule 1.12 in order to determine the appropriate conduct in connection with this Rule.

Client Under a Disability

17. In some situations, Rule 1.02(g) requires a lawyer representing a client under a disability to seek the appointment of a legal representative for the client or to seek other orders for the protection of the client. The client may or may not, in a particular matter, effectively consent to the lawyer's revealing to the court confidential information and facts reasonably necessary to secure the desired appointment or order. Nevertheless, the lawyer is authorized by paragraph (c)(4) to reveal such information in order to comply with Rule 1.02(g). See also paragraph 5, Comment to Rule 1.03.

Mandatory Disclosure Adverse to Client

18. Rule 1.05(e) and (f) place upon a lawyer professional obligations in certain situations to make disclosure in order to prevent certain serious crimes by a client or to prevent involvement by the lawyer in a client's crimes or frauds. Except when death or serious bodily harm is likely to result, a lawyer's obligation is to dissuade the client from committing the crime or fraud or to persuade the client to take corrective action; see Rule 1.02(d) and (e).

19. Because it is very difficult for a lawyer to know when a client's criminal or fraudulent purpose actually will be carried out, the lawyer is required by paragraph (e) to act only if the lawyer has information "clearly establishing" the likelihood of such acts and consequences. If the information shows clearly that the client's contemplated crime or fraud is likely to result in death or serious injury, the lawyer must seek to avoid those lamentable results by revealing information necessary to prevent the criminal or fraudulent act. When the threatened crime or fraud is likely to have the less serious result of substantial injury to the financial interests or property of another, the lawyer is not required to

reveal preventive information but may do so in conformity to paragraph (c)(7). See also paragraph (f); Rule 1.02(d) and (e); and Rule 3.03(b) and (c).

20. Although a violation of paragraph (e) will subject a lawyer to disciplinary action, the lawyer's decisions whether or how to act should not constitute grounds for discipline unless the lawyer's conduct in the light of those decisions was unreasonable under all existing circumstances as they reasonably appeared to the lawyer. This construction necessarily follows from the fact that paragraph (e) bases the lawyer's affirmative duty to act on how the situation "reasonably appears" to the lawyer, while that imposed by paragraph (f) arises only when a lawyer "knows" that the lawyer's services have been misused by the client. See also Rule 3.03(b).

Withdrawal

21. If the lawyer's services will be used by the client in materially furthering a course of criminal or fraudulent conduct, the lawyer must withdraw, as stated in Rule 1.15(a)(1). After withdrawal, a lawyer's conduct continues to be governed by Rule 1.05. However, the lawyer's duties of disclosure under paragraph (e) of the Rule, insofar as such duties are mandatory, do not survive the end of the relationship even though disclosure remains permissible under paragraphs (6), (7), and (8) if the further requirements of such paragraph are met. Neither this Rule nor Rule 1.15 prevents the lawyer from giving notice of the fact of withdrawal, and no rule forbids the lawyer to withdraw or disaffirm any opinion, document, affirmation, or the like.

Other Rules

22. Various other Texas Rules of Professional Conduct permit or require a lawyer to disclose information relating to the representation. See Rules 1.07, 1.12, 2.02, 3.03 and 4.01. In addition to these provisions, a lawyer may be obligated by other provisions of statutes or other law to give information about a client. Whether another provision of law supersedes Rule 1.05 is a matter of interpretation beyond the scope of these Rules, but sub-paragraph (c)(4) protects the lawyer from discipline who acts on reasonable belief as to the effect of such laws.

Texas Rule 1.06 *(Modification of Model Rule 1.7)*

[Texas has modified Model Rule 1.7 (Conflict of Interest) as follows:]

RULE 1.06   Conflict of Interest: General Rule

(a) A lawyer shall not represent opposing parties to the same litigation.

(b) In other situations and except to the extent permitted by paragraph (c), a lawyer shall not represent a person if the representation of that person:

331

(1) involves a substantially related matter in which that person's interests are materially and directly adverse to the interests of another client of the lawyer or the lawyer's firm; or

(2) reasonably appears to be or become adversely limited by the lawyer's or law firm's responsibilities to another client or to a third person or by the lawyer's or law firm's own interests.

(c) A lawyer may represent a client in the circumstances described in (b) if:

(1) the lawyer reasonably believes the representation of each client will not be materially affected; and

(2) each affected or potentially affected client consents to such representation after full disclosure of the existence, nature, implications, and possible adverse consequences of the common representation and the advantages involved, if any.

(d) A lawyer who has represented multiple parties in a matter shall not thereafter represent any of such parties in a dispute among the parties arising out of the matter, unless prior consent is obtained from all such parties to the dispute.

(e) If a lawyer has accepted representation in violation of this Rule, or if multiple representation properly accepted becomes improper under this Rule, the lawyer shall promptly withdraw from one or more representations to the extent necessary for any remaining representation not to be in violation of these Rules.

(f) If a lawyer would be prohibited by this Rule from engaging in particular conduct, no other lawyer while a member or associated with that lawyer's firm may engage in that conduct.

COMMENT:

Loyalty to a Client

1. Loyalty is an essential element in the lawyer's relationship to a client. An impermissible conflict of interest may exist before representation is undertaken, in which event the representation should be declined. If such a conflict arises after representation has been undertaken, the lawyer must take effective action to eliminate the conflict, including withdrawal if necessary to rectify the situation. See also Rule 1.16. When more than one client is involved and the lawyer withdraws because a conflict arises after representation, whether the lawyer may continue to represent any of the clients is determined by this Rule and Rules 1.05 and 1.09. See also Rule 1.07(c). Under this Rule, any conflict that prevents a particular lawyer from undertaking or continuing a representation of a client also prevents any other lawyer who is or

becomes a member of or an associate with that lawyer's firm from doing so. See paragraph (f).

2. A fundamental principle recognized by paragraph (a) is that a lawyer may not represent opposing parties in litigation. The term "opposing parties" as used in this Rule contemplates a situation where a judgment favorable to one of the parties will directly impact unfavorably upon the other party. Moreover, as a general proposition loyalty to a client prohibits undertaking representation directly adverse to the representation of that client in a substantially related matter unless that client's fully informed consent is obtained and unless the lawyer reasonably believes that the lawyer's representation will be reasonably protective of that client's interests. Paragraphs (b) and (c) express that general concept.

Conflicts in Litigation

3. Paragraph (a) prohibits representation of opposing parties in litigation. Simultaneous representation of parties whose interests in litigation are not actually directly adverse but where the potential for conflict exists, such as co-plaintiffs or co-defendants, is governed by paragraph (b). An impermissible conflict may exist or develop by reason of substantial discrepancy in the parties' testimony, incompatibility in positions in relation to an opposing party or the fact that there are substantially different possibilities of settlement of the claims or liabilities in question. Such conflicts can arise in criminal cases as well as civil. The potential for conflict of interest in representing multiple defendants in a criminal case is so grave that ordinarily a lawyer should decline to represent more than one co-defendant. On the other hand, common representation of persons having similar interests is proper if the risk of adverse effect is minimal and the requirements of paragraph (b) are met. Compare Rule 1.07 involving intermediation between clients.

Conflict with Lawyer's Own Interests

4. Loyalty to a client is impaired not only by the representation of opposing parties in situations within paragraphs (a) and (b)(1) but also in any situation when a lawyer may not be able to consider, recommend or carry out an appropriate course of action for one client because of the lawyer's own interests or responsibilities to others. The conflict in effect forecloses alternatives that would otherwise be available to the client. Paragraph (b)(2) addresses such situations. A potential possible conflict does not itself necessarily preclude the representation. The critical questions are the likelihood that a conflict exists or will eventuate and, if it does, whether it will materially and adversely affect the lawyer's independent professional judgment in considering alternatives or foreclose courses of action that reasonably should be pursued on behalf of the client. It is for the client to decide whether the client

wishes to accommodate the other interest involved. However, the client's consent to the representation by the lawyer of another whose interests are directly adverse is insufficient unless the lawyer also believes that there will be no materially adverse effect upon the interests of either client. See paragraph (c).

5. The lawyer's own interests should not be permitted to have adverse effect on representation of a client, even where paragraph (b)(2) is not violated. For example, a lawyer's need for income should not lead the lawyer to undertake matters that cannot be handled competently and at a reasonable fee. See Rules 1.01 and 1.04. If the probity of a lawyer's own conduct in a transaction is in question, it may be difficult for the lawyer to give a client detached advice. A lawyer should not allow related business interests to affect representation, for example, by referring clients to an enterprise in which the lawyer has an undisclosed interest.

Meaning of Directly Adverse

6. Within the meaning of Rule 1.06(b), the representation of one client is "directly adverse" to the representation of another client if the lawyer's independent judgment on behalf of a client or the lawyer's ability or willingness to consider, recommend or carry out a course of action will be or is reasonably likely to be adversely affected by the lawyer's representation of, or responsibilities to, the other client. The dual representation also is directly adverse if the lawyer reasonably appears to be called upon to espouse adverse positions in the same matter or a related matter. On the other hand, simultaneous representation in unrelated matters of clients whose interests are only generally adverse, such as competing economic enterprises, does not constitute the representation of directly adverse interests. Even when neither paragraph (a) nor (b) is applicable, a lawyer should realize that a business rivalry or personal differences between two clients or potential clients may be so important to one or both that one or the other would consider it contrary to its interests to have the same lawyer as its rival even in unrelated matters; and in those situations a wise lawyer would forego the dual representation.

Full Disclosure and Informed Consent

7. A client under some circumstances may consent to representation notwithstanding a conflict or potential conflict. However, as indicated in paragraph (c)(1), when a disinterested lawyer would conclude that the client should not agree to the representation under the circumstances, the lawyer involved should not ask for such agreement or provide representation on the basis of the client's consent. When more than one client is involved, the question of conflict must be resolved as to each client. Moreover, there may be circumstances where it is impossible to make the full disclosure necessary to obtain informed consent.

For example, when the lawyer represents different clients in related matters and one of the clients refuses to consent to the disclosure necessary to permit the other client to make an informed decision, the lawyer cannot properly ask the latter to consent.

8. Disclosure and consent are not formalities. Disclosure sufficient for sophisticated clients may not be sufficient to permit less sophisticated clients to provide fully informed consent. While it is not required that the disclosure and consent be in writing, it would be prudent for the lawyer to provide potential dual clients with at least a written summary of the considerations disclosed.

9. In certain situations, such as in the preparation of loan papers or the preparation of a partnership agreement, a lawyer might have properly undertaken multiple representation and be confronted subsequently by a dispute among those clients in regard to that matter. Paragraph (d) forbids the representation of any of those parties in regard to that dispute unless informed consent is obtained from all of the parties to the dispute who had been represented by the lawyer in that matter.

10. A lawyer may represent parties having antagonistic positions on a legal question that has arisen in different cases, unless representation of either client would be adversely affected. Thus, it is ordinarily not improper to assert such positions in cases pending in different trial courts, but it may be improper to do so in cases pending at the same time in an appellate court.

11. Ordinarily, it is not advisable for a lawyer to act as advocate against a client the lawyer represents in some other matter, even if the other matter is wholly unrelated and even if paragraphs (a), (b), and (d) are not applicable. However, there are circumstances in which a lawyer may act as advocate against a client, for a lawyer is free to do so unless this Rule or another rule of the Texas Rules of Professional Conduct would be violated. For example, a lawyer representing an enterprise with diverse operations may accept employment as an advocate against the enterprise in a matter unrelated to any matter being handled for the enterprise if the representation of one client is not directly adverse to the representation of the other client. The propriety of concurrent representation can depend on the nature of the litigation. For example, a suit charging fraud entails conflict to a degree not involved in a suit for declaratory judgment concerning statutory interpretation.

Interest of Person Paying for a Lawyer's Service

12. A lawyer may be paid from a source other than the client, if the client is informed of that fact and consents and the arrangement does not compromise the lawyer's duty of loyalty to the client. See Rule 1.08(e). For example, when an insurer and its insured have conflicting interests in a matter arising from a liability insurance agreement, and the insurer is required to provide special counsel for the insured, the arrangement should assure the special counsel's professional indepen-

dence. So also, when a corporation and its directors or employees are involved in a controversy in which they have conflicting interests, the corporation may provide funds for separate legal representation of the directors or employees, if the clients consent after consultation and the arrangement ensures the lawyer's professional independence.

Non-litigation Conflict Situations

13. Conflicts of interest in contexts other than litigation sometimes may be difficult to assess. Relevant factors in determining whether there is potential for adverse effect include the duration and intimacy of the lawyer's relationship with the client or clients involved, the functions being performed by the lawyer, the likelihood that actual conflict will arise and the likely prejudice to the client from the conflict if it does arise. The question is often one of proximity and degree.

14. For example, a lawyer may not represent multiple parties to a negotiation whose interests are fundamentally antagonistic to each other, but common representation may be permissible where the clients are generally aligned in interest even though there is some difference of interest among them.

15. Conflict questions may also arise in estate planning and estate administration. A lawyer may be called upon to prepare wills for several family members, such as husband and wife, and, depending upon the circumstances, a conflict of interest may arise. In estate administration it may be unclear whether the client is the fiduciary or is the estate or trust, including its beneficiaries. The lawyer should make clear the relationship to the parties involved.

16. A lawyer for a corporation or other organization who is also a member of its board of directors should determine whether the responsibilities of the two roles may conflict. The lawyer may be called on to advise the corporation in matters involving actions of the directors. Consideration should be given to the frequency with which such situations may arise, the potential intensity of the conflict, the effect of the lawyer's resignation from the board and the possibility of the corporation's obtaining legal advice from another lawyer in such situations. If there is material risk that the dual role will compromise the lawyer's independence of professional judgment, the lawyer should not serve as a director.

Conflict Charged by an Opposing Party

17. Raising questions of conflict of interest is primarily the responsibility of the lawyer undertaking the representation. In litigation, a court may raise the question when there is reason to infer that the lawyer has neglected the responsibility. In a criminal case, inquiry by the court is generally required when a lawyer represents multiple defendants. Where the conflict is such as clearly to call in question the fair or efficient administration of justice, opposing counsel may properly

raise the question. Such an objection should be viewed with great caution, however, for it can be misused as a technique of harassment. See Preamble: Scope.

18. Except when the absolute prohibition of this rule applies or in litigation when a court passes upon issues of conflicting interests in determining a question of disqualification of counsel, resolving questions of conflict of interests may require decisions by all affected clients as well as by the lawyer.

District of Columbia Rule 1.8

[The District of Columbia has added subsection (i) to Model Rule 1.8]

RULE 1.8   Conflict of Interest: Prohibited Transactions

* * *

(i) A lawyer may acquire and enforce a lien granted by law to secure the lawyer's fees or expenses, but a lawyer shall not impose a lien upon any part of a client's files, except upon the lawyer's own work product, and then only to the extent that the work product has not been paid for. This work product exception shall not apply when the client has become unable to pay, or when withholding the lawyer's work product would present a significant risk to the client of irreparable harm.

Lawyer's Liens

[8] The substantive law of the District of Columbia has long permitted lawyers to assert and enforce liens against the property of clients. See, e.g., Redevelopment Land Agency v. Dowdey, 618 A.2d 153, 159–60 (D.C.1992), and cases cited therein. Whether a lawyer has a lien on money or property belonging to a client is generally a matter of substantive law as to which the ethics rules take no position. Exceptions to what the common law might otherwise permit are made with respect to contingent fees and retaining liens. See, respectively, Rule 1.5(c) and Rule 1.8(i).

[9] Rule 1.16(d) requires a lawyer to surrender papers and property to which the client is entitled when representation of the client terminates. Paragraph (i) of this Rule states a narrow exception to Rule 1.16(d): a lawyer may retain anything the law permits—including property—except for files. As to files, a lawyer may retain only the lawyer's own work product, and then only if the client has not paid for the work. However, if the client has paid for the work product, the client is entitled to receive it, even if the client has not previously seen or received a copy of the work product. Furthermore, the lawyer may not retain the work product for which the client has not paid, if the client has become unable to pay or if withholding the work product might irreparably harm the client's interest.

[10]   Under Rule 1.16(d), for example, a lawyer would be required to return all papers received from a client, such as birth certificates, wills, tax returns, or "green cards." Rule 1.8(i) does not permit retention of such papers to secure payment of any fee due. Only the lawyer's own work product—results of factual investigations, legal research and analysis, and similar materials generated by the lawyer's own effort— could be retained. (The term "work product" as used in paragraph (i) is limited to materials falling within the "work product doctrine," but includes any material generated by the lawyer that would be protected under that doctrine whether or not created in connection with pending or anticipated litigation.) And a lawyer could not withhold all of the work product merely because a portion of the lawyer's fees had not been paid.

[11]   There are situations in which withholding the work product would not be permissible because of irreparable harm to the client. The possibility of involuntary incarceration or criminal conviction constitutes one category of irreparable harm. The realistic possibility that a client might irretrievably lose a significant right or become subject to a significant liability because of the withholding of the work product constitutes another category of irreparable harm. On the other hand, the mere fact that the client might have to pay another lawyer to replicate the work product does not, standing alone, constitute irreparable harm. These examples are merely indicative of the meaning of the term "irreparable harm," and are not exhaustive.

Illinois Rule 1.8

[Illinois has added the following provision to Model Rule 1.8]

RULE 1.8   Conflict of Interest: Prohibited Transactions

   * * *

(h) A lawyer shall not enter into an agreement with a client or former client limiting or purporting to limit the right of the client or former client to file or pursue any complaint before the Attorney Registration and Disciplinary Commission.

Indiana Rule 1.8(k)

[Indiana has added the following provision to Model Rule 1.8.]

RULE 1.8   Conflict of Interest: Prohibited Transactions

   * * *

(k) A part-time prosecutor or deputy prosecutor authorized by statute to otherwise engage in the practice of law shall refrain from representing a private client in any matter wherein exists an issue upon which said prosecutor has statutory prosecutorial authority or responsibilities. This restriction is not

intended to prohibit representation in tort cases in which investigation and any prosecution of infractions has terminated, nor to prohibit representation in family law matters involving no issue subject to prosecutorial authority or responsibilities. Upon a prior, express written limitation of responsibility to exclude prosecutorial authority in matters related to family law, a part-time deputy prosecutor may fully represent private clients in cases involving family law.

Minnesota Rule 1.8(e)(3) & (k)

[Minnesota has added the following provision to Model Rule 1.8:]

RULE 1.8   Conflict of Interest: Prohibited Transactions

* * *

(e) A lawyer shall not provide financial assistance to a client in connection with pending or contemplated litigation, except that:

* * *

(3) a lawyer may guarantee a loan reasonably needed to enable the client to withstand delay in litigation that would otherwise put substantial pressure on the client to settle a case because of financial hardship rather than on the merits, provided the client remains ultimately liable for repayment of the loan without regard to the outcome of the litigation and, further provided, that no promise of such financial assistance was made to the client by the lawyer, or by another in the lawyer's behalf, prior to the employment of that lawyer by that client.

* * *

(k) A lawyer shall not have sexual relations with a current client unless a consensual sexual relationship existed between them when the lawyer-client relationship commenced. For purposes of this paragraph:

(1) "Sexual relations" means sexual intercourse or any other intentional touching of the intimate parts of a person or causing the person to touch the intimate parts of the lawyer.

(2) If the client is an organization, any individual who oversees the representation and gives instructions to the lawyer on behalf of the organization shall be deemed to be the client. In-house attorneys while representing governmental or corporate entities are governed by Rule 1.7(b) rather than by this rule with respect to sexual relations with other employees of the entity they represent.

(3) This paragraph does not prohibit a lawyer from engaging in sexual relations with a client of the lawyer's firm provided that the lawyer has no involvement in the performance of the legal work for the client.

(4) If a party other than the client alleges violation of this paragraph, and the complaint is not summarily dismissed, the Director, in determining whether to investigate the allegation and whether to charge any violation based on the allegations, shall consider the client's statement regarding whether the client would be unduly burdened by the investigation or charge.

Texas Rule 1.09 (Modification of Model Rule 1.9)

[Texas has modified Rule 1.9 (Former Client Conflicts) as follows:]

RULE 1.09   Conflict of Interest: Former Client

(a) Without prior consent, a lawyer who personally has formerly represented a client in a matter shall not thereafter represent another person in a matter adverse to the former client:

(1) in which such other person questions the validity of the lawyer's services or work product for the former client; or

(2) if the representation in reasonable probability will involve a violation of Rule 1.05.

(3) if it is the same or a substantially related matter;

(b) Except to the extent authorized by Rule 1.10, when lawyers are or have become members of or associated with a firm, none of them shall knowingly represent a client if any one of them practicing alone would be prohibited from doing so by paragraph (a).

(c) When the association of a lawyer with a firm has terminated, the lawyers who were then associated with that lawyer shall not knowingly represent a client if the lawyer whose association with that firm has terminated would be prohibited from doing so by paragraph (a)(1) or if the representation in reasonable probability will involve a violation of Rule 1.05.

COMMENT:

1. Rule 1.09 addresses the circumstances in which a lawyer in private practice, and other lawyers who were, are or become members of or associated with a firm in which that lawyer practiced or practices, may represent a client against a former client of that lawyer or the lawyer's former firm. Whether a lawyer, or that lawyer's present or former firm, is prohibited from representing a client in a matter by

reason of the lawyer's successive government and private employment is governed by Rule 1.10 rather than by this Rule.

2. Paragraph (a) concerns the situation where a lawyer once personally represented a client and now wishes to represent a second client against that former client. Whether such a personal attorney-client relationship existed involves questions of both fact and law that are beyond the scope of these Rules. See Preamble: Scope. Among the relevant factors, however, would be how the former representation actually was conducted within the firm; the nature and scope of the former client's contacts with the firm (including any restrictions the client may have placed on the dissemination of confidential information within the firm); and the size of the firm.

3. Although paragraph (a) does not absolutely prohibit a lawyer from representing a client against a former client, it does provide that the latter representation is improper if any of three circumstances exists, except with prior consent. The first prohibition is against representation adverse to a former client if it is the same or a substantially related matter. The second circumstance is that the lawyer may not represent a client who questions the validity of the lawyer's services or work product for the former client. Thus, for example, a lawyer who drew a will leaving a substantial portion of the testator's property to a designated beneficiary would violate paragraph (a) by representing the testator's heirs at law in an action seeking to overturn the will.

4. Paragraph (a)'s third limitation on undertaking a representation against a former client is that it may not be done if there is a "reasonable probability" that the representation would cause the lawyer to violate the obligations owed the former client under Rule 1.05. Thus, for example, if there were a reasonable probability that the subsequent representation would involve either an unauthorized disclosure of confidential information under Rule 1.05(b)(1) or an improper use of such information to the disadvantage of the former client under Rule 1.05(b)(3), that representation would be improper under paragraph (a). Whether such a reasonable probability exists in any given case will be a question of fact.

5. Paragraph (b) extends paragraph (a)'s limitations on an individual lawyer's freedom to undertake a representation against that lawyer's former client to all other lawyers who are or become members of or associated with the firm in which that lawyer is practicing. Thus, for example, if a client severs the attorney-client relationship with a lawyer who remains in a firm, the entitlement of that individual lawyer to undertake a representation against that former client is governed by paragraph (a); and all other lawyers who are or become members of or associated with that lawyer's firm are treated in the same manner by paragraph (b). Similarly, if a lawyer severs his or her association with a firm and that firm retains as a client a person whom the lawyer personally represented while with the firm, that lawyer's ability thereafter to undertake a representation against that client is governed by

paragraph (a); and all other lawyers who are or become members of or associates with that lawyer's new firm are treated in the same manner by paragraph (b).

6. Paragraph (c) addresses the situation of former partners or associates of a lawyer who once had represented a client when the relationship between the former partners or associates and the lawyer has been terminated. In that situation, the former partners or associates are prohibited from questioning the validity of such lawyer's work product and from undertaking representation which in reasonable probability will involve a violation of Rule 1.05. Such a violation could occur, for example, when the former partners or associates retained materials in their files from the earlier representation of the client that, if disclosed or used in connection with the subsequent representation, would violate Rule 1.05(b)(1) or (b)(3).

7. Thus, the effect of paragraphs (b) and (c) is to extend any inability of a particular lawyer under paragraph (a) to undertake a representation against a former client to all other lawyers who are or become members of or associated with any firm in which that lawyer is practicing. Should those other lawyers cease to be members of the same firm as the lawyer affected by paragraph (a) without themselves coming within its restrictions, they thereafter may undertake the representation against the lawyer's former client unless prevented from doing so by some other of these Rules.

8. Although not required to do so by Rule 1.05 or this Rule, some courts, as a procedural decision, disqualify a lawyer for representing a present client against a former client when the subject matter of the present representation is so closely related to the subject matter of the prior representation that confidences obtained from the former client might be useful in the representation of the present client. See Comment 17 to Rule 1.06. This so-called "substantial relationship" test is defended by asserting that to require a showing that confidences of the first client were in fact used for the benefit of the subsequent client as a condition to procedural disqualification would cause disclosure of the confidences that the court seeks to protect. A lawyer is not subject to discipline under Rule 1.05(b)(1), (3), or (4), however, unless the protected information is actually used. Likewise, a lawyer is not subject to discipline under this Rule unless the new representation by the lawyer in reasonable probability would result in a violation of those provisions.

9. Whether the "substantial relationship" test will continue to be employed as a standard for procedural disqualification is a matter beyond the scope of these Rules. See Preamble: Scope. The possibility that such a disqualification might be sought by the former client or granted by a court, however, is a matter that could be of substantial importance to the present client in deciding whether or not to retain or continue to employ a particular lawyer or law firm as its counsel. Consequently, a lawyer should disclose those possibilities, as well as their potential consequences for the representation, to the present client

as soon as the lawyer becomes aware of them; and the client then should be allowed to decide whether or not to obtain new counsel. See Rules 1.03(b) and 1.06(b).

10. This Rule is primarily for the protection of clients and its protections can be waived by them. A waiver is effective only if there is consent after disclosure of the relevant circumstances, including the lawyer's past or intended role on behalf of each client, as appropriate. See Comments 7 and 8 to Rule 1.06.

Utah Rule 1.9(a)

[Utah has modified Model Rule 1.9(a) as follows:]

RULE 1.9 Conflict of Interest: Former Client

A lawyer who has formerly represented a client in a matter shall not thereafter:

(a) Represent another person in the same or a substantially factually related matter in which that person's interests are materially adverse to the interests of the former client unless the former client consents after consultation; or

(b) Use information relating to the representation to the disadvantage of the former client except as Rule 1.6 would permit with respect to a client or when the information has become generally known.

COMMENT:

After termination of a client-lawyer relationship, a lawyer may not represent another client except in conformity with this Rule. The principles in Rule 1.7 determine whether the interests of the present and former client are adverse. Thus, a lawyer could not properly seek to rescind on behalf of a new client a contract drafted on behalf of the former client. So also a lawyer who has prosecuted an accused person could not properly represent the accused in a subsequent civil action against the government concerning the same transaction.

The scope of a "matter" for purposes of Rule 1.9(a) may depend on the facts of a particular situation or transaction. The lawyer's involvement in a matter can also be a question of degree. When a lawyer has been directly involved in a specific transaction, subsequent representation of other clients with materially adverse interests clearly is prohibited. On the other hand, a lawyer who recurrently handled a type of problem for a former client is not precluded from later representing another client in a wholly distinct problem of that type even though the subsequent representation involves a position adverse to the prior client. Similar considerations can apply to the reassignment of military lawyers between defense and prosecution functions within the same military jurisdiction. The underlying question is whether the lawyer was so involved in the matter that the subsequent representation can be justly regarded as a changing of sides in the matter in question.

Information acquired by the lawyer in the course of representing a client may not subsequently be used by the lawyer to the disadvantage of the client. However, the fact that a lawyer has once served a client does not preclude the lawyer from using generally known information about the client when later representing another client.

Disqualification from subsequent representation is for the protection of clients and can be waived by them. A waiver is effective only if there is disclosure of the circumstances, including the lawyer's intended role in behalf of the new client.

With regard to an opposing party's raising a question of conflict of interest, see Comment to Rule 1.7. With regard to disqualification of a firm with which a lawyer is associated, see Rule 1.10.

District of Columbia Rule 1.11

[The District of Columbia has added the following provisions to Model Rule 1.11]

RULE 1.11 Successive Government and Private Employment

* * *

(d) Except as provided in paragraph (e), when any of counsel, lawyer, partner, or associate of a lawyer personally disqualified under paragraph (a) accepts employment in connection with a matter giving rise to the personal disqualification, the following notifications shall be required:

(1) The personally disqualified lawyer shall submit to the public department or agency by which the lawyer was formerly employed and serve on each other party to any pertinent proceeding a signed document attesting that during the period of disqualification the personally disqualified lawyer will not participate in any manner in the matter or the representation, will not discuss the matter or the representation with any partner, associate, or of counsel lawyer, and will not share in any fees for the matter or the representation.

(2) At least one affiliated lawyer shall submit to the same department or agency and serve on the same parties a signed document attesting that all affiliated lawyers are aware of the requirement that the personally disqualified lawyer be screened from participating in or discussing the matter or the representation and describing the procedures being taken to screen the personally disqualified lawyer.

(e) If a client requests in writing that the fact and subject matter of a representation subject to paragraph (d) not be

disclosed by submitting the signed statements referred to in paragraph (d), such statements shall be prepared concurrently with undertaking the representation and filed with bar counsel under seal. If at any time thereafter the fact and subject matter of the representation are disclosed to the public or become a part of the public record, the signed statements previously pre-pared shall be promptly submitted as required by paragraph (d).

(f) Signed documents filed pursuant to paragraph (d) shall be available to the public, except to the extent that a lawyer submitting a signed document demonstrates to the satisfaction of the public department or agency upon which such documents are served that public disclosure is inconsistent with Rule 1.6 or provisions of law.

(g) This Rule applies to any matter involving a specific party or parties.

(h) A lawyer who participates in a program of temporary service to the office of corporation counsel of the kind described in Rule 1.10(e) shall be treated as having served as a public officer or employee for purposes of paragraph (a), and the provisions of paragraphs (b)–(e) shall apply to the lawyer and to lawyers affiliated with the lawyer.

New Hampshire Rule 1.11A

[New Hampshire has added the following provision to address the conduct of lawyer officials:]

RULE 1.11A Conduct of Lawyer–Officials

(a) **Definitions.** As used in this rule:

(1) lawyer-official means a lawyer actively engaged in the practice of law, who is a member of the governmental body;

(2) government body means any state or local govern-mental agency, board, body, council or commission; and

(3) interest means a direct, personal and pecuniary in-terest, individually or on a client's behalf, in a matter which is under consideration by the governmental body of which the lawyer-official is a member.

(b) No lawyer-official shall:

(1) participate in any hearing, debate, discussion or vote, or in any manner otherwise attempt to influence the outcome of a matter in which he or she has an interest;

(2) utilize information obtained in such capacity for his or her own personal benefit or that of his or her clients or the clients of the firm with which the lawyer-official is associated;

(3) appear on behalf of a client before any governmental body of which the lawyer-official is a member or whose members have been appointed by the governmental body of which the lawyer-official is a member;

(4) accept anything of value from any person or organization when the lawyer-official knows or reasonably should know that the offer is for the purpose of influencing the lawyer-official's actions or decisions;

(5) use his or her official position to influence or to attempt to influence any governmental body to act in favor of the lawyer-official or the lawyer-official's clients or clients of the firm with which the lawyer-official is associated.

(c) Other lawyers in the firm with which the lawyer-official is associated may not appear on behalf of clients before the governmental body of which the lawyer-official is a member, or any governmental body whose members have been appointed by the body of which the lawyer-official is a member, unless the lawyer-official publicly disqualifies himself or herself and refrains from participation in the matter in accordance with paragraph (b)(1) of this Rule, and otherwise conducts himself or herself with respect to the matter in accordance with paragraph (b) of this Rule.

Montana Rule 1.17

[Montana has added Rule 1.17 which has no counterpart in the Model Rules]

RULE 1.17   Government Employment

An attorney employed by a department of the State of Montana or municipality on a part-time or fee basis shall not accept other employment during the course of which it would be possible to use or otherwise rely on information obtained by reason of government employment that is injurious, confidential or privileged and not otherwise discoverable.

COUNSELLOR

Oregon Rule DR 5–106 (Modification to Model Rule 2.2)

[Oregon has modified Model Rule 2.2 to read as follows:]

DR 5–106.   Mediation

(A) A lawyer serving as a mediator:

(1) shall not act as a lawyer for any party against another party in the matter in mediation or in any related proceeding, and

(2) must clearly inform the parties of and obtain the parties' consent to the lawyer's role as mediator.

(B) A lawyer serving as a mediator:

(1) may prepare documents that memorialize and implement the agreement reached in mediation,

(2) shall recommend that each party seek independent legal advice before executing the documents, and

(3) with the consent of all parties, may record or may file the documents in court.

(C) Notwithstanding DR 5–105(G), when a lawyer is serving or has served as a mediator in a matter, a member of the lawyer's firm may accept or continue the representation of a party in the matter in mediation or in a related matter if all parties to the mediation consent after full disclosure.

(D) The requirements of (A)(2) and (B)(2) shall not apply to mediation programs established by operation of law or court order.

[Amended December 17, 1991; November 5, 1998; February 20, 2001.]

ADVOCATE

Wyoming Rule 3.1

[Wyoming has modified Model Rule 3.1 to read as follows:]

RULE 3.1   Meritorious Claims and Contentions

A lawyer shall not bring or defend a proceeding, or assert or controvert an issue therein, unless there is a basis for doing so that is not frivolous, which includes a good faith argument for an extension, modification or reversal of existing law. A lawyer for the defendant in a criminal proceeding, or the respondent in a proceeding that could result in incarceration, may nevertheless so defend the proceeding as to require that every element of the case be established. The signature of an attorney constitutes a certificate by him that he has read the pleading, motion, or other court document; that to the best of his knowledge, information, and belief, formed after reasonable inquiry, it is well grounded in fact and is warranted by existing law or a good faith argument for the extension, modification, or reversal of existing law; and that it is not interposed for any improper purpose such as to harass or to cause unnecessary delay or needless increase in the cost of litigation.

COMMENT:

[1]   The advocate has a duty to use legal procedure for the fullest benefit of the client's cause, but also a duty not to abuse legal procedure. The law, both procedural and substantive, establishes the limits within

which an advocate may proceed. However, the law is not always clear and never is static. Accordingly, in determining the proper scope of advocacy, account must be taken of the law's ambiguities and potential for change.

[2] The filing of an action, defense or other document in court is not frivolous merely because the facts have not first been fully substantiated or because the lawyer expects to develop vital evidence by discovery. Such action is not frivolous even though the lawyer believes that the client's position ultimately will not prevail. The action is frivolous, however, if the client or attorney desires to have the action taken primarily for the purpose of harassing, delaying or causing unnecessary expense or if the lawyer is unable either to make a good faith argument on the merits of the action taken or to support the action taken by a good faith argument for an extension, modification or reversal of existing law. The last sentence of Rule 3.1 is based on Rule 11 of the Federal Rules of Civil Procedure. It imposes an affirmative duty on an advocate to make reasonable inquiry, both as to the facts and law, before filing a pleading or other court document. A violation subjects the lawyer to discipline.

Kansas Rule 3.5

[Kansas has modified Model Rule 3.5 to read as follows:]

RULE 3.5 Impartiality and Decorum of the Tribunal

A lawyer shall not:

(a) give or lend anything of value to a judge, official, or employee of a tribunal except as permitted by Section C(4) of Canon 5 of the Code of Judicial Conduct as it may, from time to time be adopted in Kansas, nor may a lawyer attempt to improperly influence a judge, official or employee of a tribunal, but a lawyer may make a contribution to the campaign fund of a candidate for judicial office in conformity with Section B(2) under Canon 7 of the Code of Judicial Conduct;

(b) communicate or cause another to communicate with a member of a jury or the venire from which the jury will be selected about the matters under consideration other than in the course of official proceedings until after the discharge of the jury from further consideration of the case;

(c) communicate or cause another to communicate as to the merits of a cause with a judge or official before whom an adversary proceeding is pending except:

(1) in the course of official proceedings in the cause;

(2) in writing, if the lawyer promptly delivers a copy of the writing to opposing counsel or to the adverse party if unrepresented;

(3) **orally upon adequate notice to opposing counsel or the adverse party if unrepresented;**

(4) **as otherwise authorized by law or court rule;**

(d) **engage in undignified or discourteous conduct degrading to a tribunal.**

KANSAS COMMENT:

Rule 3.5 in the proposed Model Rules as adopted by the ABA has been substantially modified to include more specific guidelines and prohibitions such as were included in the Model Code. The reason for this is that the Kansas committee felt that existing disciplinary rules, 7.106(C)(6), 7.108, 7.109, 7.110 were more specific and preferable in many respects to the proposed model rule. Model Rule 3.5 prohibits a lawyer from seeking to influence a judge, juror, prospective juror or other official by means prohibited by law. The Kansas committee felt that this is too narrow a prohibition and would permit some things that should not be permitted. The committee has reimposed the absolute prohibition of DR 7–110(A) upon a lawyer giving or lending anything of value to a judge or official; except as permitted by the Canons of Judicial Ethics. In other words, a lawyer may ethically give what a judge may ethically receive. It was felt that such a *per se* rule is preferable to one that would require proof that the gift or loan was prompted by an attempt to influence the official.

Similarly, it was felt by the Kansas committee that the more specific provisions found in DR 7–108 regarding communication with jurors was preferable in that they give more guidance to the lawyer as to what communications are permitted and what communications are not permitted and further would give more guidance to the disciplinary authority as to when a violation had been committed.

Section (c) of the Model Rule prohibited conduct intended to disrupt a tribunal and, therefore, impliedly would authorize undignified or discourteous conduct degrading to a tribunal, prohibited under DR 7–106(C)(6), unless the intent to disrupt is established. The Kansas committee is of the opinion that standards of lawyer conduct in the courtroom should not be lowered as the model rule would appear to do.

TRANSACTIONS WITH PERSONS OTHER THAN CLIENTS

Louisiana Rule 4.2

[Louisiana has modified Model Rule 4.2 to read as follows:]

RULE 4.2 Communication With Person Represented by Counsel

In representing a client, a lawyer shall not communicate about the subject of the representation with a party the lawyer knows to be represented by another lawyer in the matter, unless

349

the lawyer has the consent of the other lawyer or is authorized by law to do so. A lawyer shall not effect the prohibited communication through a third person, including the lawyer's client.

New Mexico Rule 16–402 (Modification of Model Rule 4.2)

[New Mexico has modified Model Rule 4.2 to read as follows:]

RULE 16–402. Communication With Person Represented by Counsel

In representing a client, a lawyer shall not communicate about the subject of the representation with a party the lawyer knows to be represented by another lawyer in the matter, unless the lawyer has the consent of the other lawyer or is authorized by law to do so. Except for persons having a managerial responsibility on behalf of the organization, an attorney is not prohibited from communicating directly with employees of a corporation, partnership or other entity about the subject matter of the representation even though the corporation, partnership or entity itself is represented by counsel.

Texas Rule 4.02 (Modification of Model Rule 4.2)

[Texas has modified Model Rule 4.2 as follows:]

RULE 4.02. Communication With One Represented by Counsel

(a) In representing a client, a lawyer shall not communicate or cause or encourage another to communicate about the subject of the representation with a person, organization or entity of government the lawyer knows to be represented by another lawyer regarding that subject, unless the lawyer has the consent of the other lawyer or is authorized by law to do so.

(b) In representing a client a lawyer shall not communicate or cause another to communicate about the subject of representation with a person or organization a lawyer knows to be employed or retained for the purpose of conferring with or advising another lawyer about the subject of the representation, unless the lawyer has the consent of the other lawyer or is authorized by law to do so.

(c) For the purpose of this rule, "organization or entity of government" includes: (1) those persons presently having a managerial responsibility with an organization or entity of government that relates to the subject of the representation, or (2) those persons presently employed by such organization or entity and whose act or omission in connection with the subject of representation may make the organization or entity of government vicariously liable for such act or omission.

(d) When a person, organization, or entity of government that is represented by a lawyer in a matter seeks advice regarding that matter from another lawyer, the second lawyer is not prohibited by paragraph (a) from giving such advice without notifying or seeking consent of the first lawyer.

COMMENT:

1. Paragraph (a) of this Rule is directed at efforts to circumvent the lawyer-client relationship existing between other persons, organizations or entities of government and their respective counsel. It prohibits communications that in form are between a lawyer's client and another person, organization or entity of government represented by counsel where, because of the lawyer's involvement in devising and controlling their content, such communications in substance are between the lawyer and the represented person, organization or entity of government.

2. Paragraph (a) does not, however, prohibit communication between a lawyer's client and persons, organizations, or entities of government represented by counsel, as long as the lawyer does not cause or encourage the communication without the consent of the lawyer for the other party. Consent may be implied as well as expressed, as, for example, where the communication occurs in the form of a private placement memorandum or similar document that obviously is intended for multiple recipients and that normally is furnished directly to persons, even if known to be represented by counsel. Similarly, that paragraph does not impose a duty on a lawyer to affirmatively discourage communication between the lawyer's client and other represented persons, organizations or entities of government. Furthermore, it does not prohibit client communications concerning matters outside the subject of the representation with any such person, organization, or entity of government. Finally, it does not prohibit a lawyer from furnishing a "second opinion" in a matter to one requesting such opinion, nor from discussing employment in the matter if requested to do so. But see Rule 7.02.

3. Paragraph (b) of this Rule provides that unless authorized by law, experts employed or retained by a lawyer for a particular matter should not be contacted by opposing counsel regarding that matter without the consent of the lawyer who retained them. However, certain governmental agents or employees such as police may be contacted due to their obligations to the public at large.

4. In the case of an organization or entity of government, this Rule prohibits communications by a lawyer for one party concerning the subject of the representation with persons having a managerial responsibility on behalf of the organization that relates to the subject of the representation and with those persons presently employed by such organization or entity whose act or omission may make the organization or entity vicariously liable for the matter at issue, without the consent of the lawyer for the organization or entity of government involved. This Rule is based on the presumption that such persons are so closely

identified with the interests of the organization or entity of government that its lawyers will represent them as well. If, however, such an agent or employee is represented in the matter by his or her own counsel that presumption is inapplicable. In such cases, the consent by that counsel to communicate will be sufficient for purposes of this Rule. Compare Rule 3.04(f). Moreover, this Rule does not prohibit a lawyer from contacting a former employee of a represented organization or entity of a government, nor from contacting a person presently employed by such an organization or entity whose conduct is not a matter at issue but who might possess knowledge concerning the matter at issue.

Minnesota Rule 4.3

[Minnesota has modified Model Rule 4.3 to read as follows:]

RULE 4.3   Dealing With Unrepresented Person

(a) In dealing on behalf of a client with a person who is not represented by counsel, a lawyer shall clearly disclose whether the client's interests are adverse to the interests of such person and shall not state or imply that the lawyer is disinterested.

(b) When the lawyer knows or reasonably should know that the unrepresented person misunderstands the lawyer's role in the matter, the lawyer shall make reasonable efforts to correct the misunderstanding.

(c) During the course of representation of a client a lawyer shall not give advice to a person who is not represented by a lawyer, other than the advice to secure counsel, on those issues as to which the interests of each person are or have a reasonable possibility of being in conflict with the interests of the client.

COMMENT—1985:

An unrepresented person, particularly one not experienced in dealing with legal matters, might assume that a lawyer is disinterested in loyalties or is a disinterested authority on the law even when the lawyer represents a client.

Texas Rule 4.04 (Modification of Model Rule 4.4)

[Texas has modified Model Rule 4.4 as follows:]

RULE 4.04   Respect for Rights of Third Persons
    * * *

(b) A lawyer shall not present, participate in presenting, or threaten to present:

(1) criminal or disciplinary charges solely to gain an advantage in a civil matter; or

(2) civil, criminal or disciplinary charges against a complainant, a witness, or a potential witness in a bar disciplinary proceeding solely to prevent participation by the complainant, witness or potential witness therein.

LAW FIRMS AND ASSOCIATIONS

Texas Rule 5.01 *(Modification of Model Rule 5.1)*

[Texas has modified Model Rule 5.1 as follows:]

RULE 5.01 Responsibilities of a Partner or Supervisory Lawyer

A lawyer shall be subject to discipline because of another lawyer's violation of these rules of professional conduct if:

(a) The lawyer is a partner or supervising lawyer and orders, encourages, or knowingly permits the conduct involved; or

(b) The lawyer is a partner in the law firm in which the other lawyer practices, is the general counsel of a government agency's legal department in which the other lawyer is employed, or has direct supervisory authority over the other lawyer, and with knowledge of the other lawyer's violation of these rules knowingly fails to take reasonable remedial action to avoid or mitigate the consequences of the other lawyer's violation.

COMMENT:

1. Rule 5.01 conforms to the general principle that a lawyer is not vicariously subjected to discipline for the misconduct of another person, under Rule 8.04, a lawyer is subject to discipline if the lawyer knowingly assists or induces another to violate these rules. Rule 5.01(a) additionally provides that a partner or supervising lawyer is subject to discipline for ordering or encouraging another lawyer's violation of these rules. Moreover, a partner or supervising lawyer is in a position of authority over the work of other lawyers and the partner or supervising lawyer may be disciplined for permitting another lawyer to violate these rules.

2. Rule 5.01(b) likewise is concerned with the lawyer who is in a position of authority over another lawyer and who knows that the other lawyer has committed a violation of a rule of professional conduct. A partner in a law firm, the general counsel of a government agency's legal department, or a lawyer having direct supervisory authority over specific legal work by another lawyer, occupies the position of authority contemplated by Rule 5.01(b).

3. Whether a lawyer has "direct supervisory authority over the other lawyer" in particular circumstances is a question of fact. In some instances, a senior associate may be a supervising attorney.

4. The duty imposed upon the partner or other authoritative lawyer by Rule 5.01(b) is to take reasonable remedial action to avoid or mitigate the consequences of the other lawyer's known violation. Ap-

propriate remedial action by a partner or other supervisory lawyer would depend on may factors, such as the immediacy of the partner's or supervisory lawyer's knowledge and involvement, the nature of the action that can reasonably be expected to avoid or mitigate injurious consequences, and the seriousness of the anticipated consequences. In some circumstances, it may be sufficient for a junior partner to refer the ethical problem directly to a designated senior partner or a management committee. A lawyer supervising a specific legal matter may be required to intervene more directly. For example if a supervising lawyer knows that a supervised lawyer misrepresented a matter to an opposing party in negotiation, the supervisor as well as the other lawyer may be required by Rule 5.01(b) to correct the resulting misapprehension.

5. Thus, neither Rule 5.01(a) nor Rule 5.01(b) visits vicarious disciplinary liability upon the lawyer in a position of authority. Rather, the lawyer in such authoritative position is exposed to discipline only for his or her own knowing actions or failures to act. Whether a lawyer may be liable civilly or criminally for another lawyer's conduct is a question of law beyond the scope of these rules.

6. Wholly aside from the dictates of these rules for discipline, a lawyer in a position of authority in a firm or government agency or over another lawyer should feel a moral compunction to make reasonable efforts to ensure that the office, firm, or agency has in effect appropriate procedural measures giving reasonable assurance that all lawyers in the office conform to these rules. This moral obligation, although not required by these rules, should fall also upon lawyers who have intermediate managerial responsibilities in the law department of an organization or government agency.

7. The measures that should be undertaken to give such reasonable assurance may depend on the structure of the firm or organization and upon the nature of the legal work performed. In a small firm, informal supervision and an occasional admonition ordinarily will suffice. In a large firm, or in practice situations where intensely difficult ethical problems frequently arise, more elaborate procedures may be called for in order to give such assurance. Obviously, the ethical atmosphere of a firm influences the conduct of all of its lawyers. Lawyers may rely also on continuing legal education in professional ethics to guard against unintentional misconduct by members of their firm or organization.

Texas Rule 5.02 *(Modification of Model Rule 5.2)*

[Texas has modified Model Rule 5.2 as follows:]

RULE 5.02 Responsibilities of a Supervised Lawyer

A lawyer is bound by these rules notwithstanding that the lawyer acted under the supervision of another person, except that a supervised lawyer does not violate these rules if that

lawyer acts in accordance with a supervisory lawyer's reasonable resolution of an arguable question of professional conduct.

COMMENT:

1. Rule 5.02 embodies the fundamental concept that every lawyer is a trained, mature, licensed professional who has sworn to uphold ethical standards and who is responsible for the lawyer's own conduct. Accordingly, a lawyer is not relieved from compliance with these rules because the lawyer acted under the supervision of an employer or other person. In some situations, the fact that a lawyer acted at the direction or order of another person may be relevant in determining whether the lawyer had the knowledge required to render the conduct a violation of these rules. The fact of supervision may also, of course, be a circumstance to be considered by a grievance committee or court in mitigation of the penalty to be imposed for violation of a rule.

2. In many law firms and organizations, the relatively inexperienced lawyer works as an assistant to a more experienced lawyer or is directed, supervised or given guidance by an experienced lawyer in the firm. In the normal course of practice the senior lawyer has the responsibility for making the decisions involving professional judgment as to procedures to be taken, the status of the law, and the propriety of actions to be taken by the lawyers. Otherwise a consistent course of action could not be taken on behalf of clients. The junior lawyer reasonably can be expected to acquiesce in the decisions made by the senior lawyer unless the decision is clearly wrong.

3. Rule 5.02 take a realistic attitude toward those prevailing modes of practice by lawyers not engaged in solo practice. Accordingly, Rule 5.02 provides the supervised lawyer with a special defense in a disciplinary proceeding in which the lawyer is charged with having violated a rule of professional conduct. The supervised lawyer is entitled to this defense only if it appears that an arguable question of professional conduct was resolved by a supervising lawyer and that a resolution made by the supervising lawyer was a reasonable resolution. The resolution is a reasonable one, even if it is ultimately found to be officially unacceptable, provided it would have appeared reasonable to a disinterested, competent lawyer based on the information reasonably available to the supervising lawyer at the time the resolution was made. "Supervisory lawyer" as used in Rule 5.02 should be construed in conformity with prevailing modes of practice in firms and other groups and, therefore, should include a senior lawyer who undertakes to resolve the question of professional propriety as well as a lawyer who more directly supervises the supervised lawyer.

4. By providing such a defense to the supervised lawyer, Rule 5.02 recognizes that the inexperienced lawyer working under the direction or supervision of an employer or senior attorney is not in a favorable position to disagree with reasonable decisions made by the experienced lawyer. Often, the only choices available to the supervised lawyer would

be to accept the decision made by the senior lawyer or to resign or otherwise lose the employment. This provision of Rule 5.02 also recognizes that it is not necessarily improper for the inexperienced lawyer to rely, reasonably and in good faith, upon decisions made in unclear matters by senior lawyers in the organization.

5. The defense provided by this Rule is available without regard to whether the conduct in question was originally proposed by the supervised lawyer or another person. Nevertheless, the supervised lawyer is not permitted to accept an unreasonable decision as to the propriety of professional conduct. The Rule obviously provides no defense to the supervised lawyer who participates in clearly wrongful conduct. Reliance can be placed only upon a reasonable resolution made by the supervisory lawyer.

6. The protection afforded by Rule 5.02 to a supervised lawyer relates only to professional disciplinary proceedings. Whether a similar defense may exist in actions in tort or for breach of contract is a question beyond the scope of the Texas Rules of Professional Conduct.

District of Columbia Rule 5.4

RULE 5.4 Professional Independence of a Lawyer

(a) A lawyer or law firm shall not share legal fees with a nonlawyer, except that:

(1) an agreement by a lawyer with the lawyer's firm, partner, or associate may provide for the payment of money, over a reasonable period of time after the lawyer's death, to the lawyer's estate or to one or more specified persons;

(2) a lawyer who undertakes to complete unfinished legal business of a deceased lawyer may pay to the estate of the deceased lawyer that proportion of the total compensation which fairly represents the services rendered by the deceased lawyer;

(3) a lawyer or law firm may include nonlawyer employees in a compensation or retirement plan, even though the plan is based in whole or in part on a profit-sharing arrangement; and

(4) sharing of fees is permitted in a partnership or other form of organization which meets the requirements of paragraph (b).

(b) A lawyer may practice law in a partnership or other form of organization in which a financial interest is held or managerial authority is exercised by an individual nonlawyer who performs professional services which assist the organization in providing legal services to clients, but only if:

(1) the partnership or organization has as its sole purpose providing legal services to clients;

(2) all persons having such managerial authority or holding a financial interest undertake to abide by these rules of professional conduct;

(3) the lawyers who have a financial interest or managerial authority in the partnership or organization undertake to be responsible for the nonlawyer participants to the same extent as if nonlawyer participants were lawyers under rule 5.1;

(4) the foregoing conditions are set forth in writing.

(c) A lawyer shall not permit a person who recommends, employs, or pays the lawyer to render legal services for another to direct or regulate the lawyer's professional judgment in rendering such legal services.

COMMENT:

[1]   The provisions of this Rule express traditional limitations on sharing fees with nonlawyers. (On sharing fees among lawyers not in the same firm, see Rule 1.5(e).)   These limitations are to protect the lawyer's professional independence of judgment.   Where someone other than the client pays the lawyer's fee or salary, or recommends employment of the lawyer, that arrangement does not modify the lawyer's obligation to the client.   As stated in paragraph (c), such arrangements should not interfere with the lawyer's professional judgment.

[2]   Traditionally, the canons of legal ethics and disciplinary rules prohibited lawyers from practicing law in a partnership that includes nonlawyers or in any other organization where a nonlawyer is a shareholder, director, or officer.   Notwithstanding these strictures, the profession implicitly recognized exceptions for lawyers who work for corporate law departments, insurance companies, and legal service organizations.

[3]   As the demand increased for a broad range of professional services from a single source, lawyers employed professionals from other disciplines to work for them.   So long as the nonlawyers remained employees of the lawyers, these relationships did not violate the disciplinary rules.   However, when lawyers and nonlawyers considered forming partnerships and professional corporations to provide a combination of legal and other services to the public, they faced serious obstacles under the former rules.

[4]   This Rule rejects an absolute prohibition against lawyers and nonlawyers joining together to provide collaborative services, but continues to impose traditional ethical requirements with respect to the organization thus created.   Thus, a lawyer may practice law in an organization where nonlawyers hold a financial interest or exercise managerial authority, but only if the conditions set forth in subpara-

357

graphs (b)(1), (b)(2), and (b)(3) are satisfied, and, pursuant to subparagraph (b)(4), satisfaction of these conditions is set forth in a written instrument. The requirement of a writing helps ensure that these important conditions are not overlooked in establishing the organizational structure of entities in which nonlawyers enjoy an ownership or managerial role equivalent to that of a partner in a traditional law firm.

[5] Nonlawyer participants under Rule 5.4 ought not be confused with nonlawyer assistants under Rule 5.3. Nonlawyer participants are persons having managerial authority or financial interests in organizations which provide legal services. Within such organizations, lawyers with financial interests or managerial authority are held responsible for ethical misconduct by nonlawyer participants about which the lawyers know or reasonably should know. This is the same standard of liability contemplated by Rule 5.1, regarding the responsibilities of lawyers with direct supervisory authority over other lawyers.

[6] Nonlawyer assistants under Rule 5.3 do not have managerial authority or financial interests in the organization. Lawyers having direct supervisory authority over nonlawyer assistants are held responsible only for ethical misconduct by assistants about which the lawyers actually know.

[7] As the introductory portion of Subparagraph (b) makes clear, the purpose of liberalizing the rules regarding the possession of a financial interest or the exercise of management authority by a nonlawyer is to permit nonlawyer professionals to work with lawyers in the delivery of legal services without being relegated to the role of an employee. For example, the Rule permits economists to work in a firm with antitrust or public utility practitioners, psychologists or psychiatric social workers to work with family law practitioners to assist in counseling clients, nonlawyer lobbyists to work with lawyers who perform legislative services, certified public accountants to work in conjunction with tax lawyers or others who use accountants' services in performing legal services, and professional managers to serve as office managers, executive directors, or in similar positions. In all of these situations, the professionals may be given financial interests or managerial responsibility, so long as all of the requirements of subparagraph (c) are met.

[8] Subparagraph (b) does not permit an individual or entity to acquire all or any part of the ownership of a law partnership or other form of law practice organization for investment or other purposes. It thus does not permit a corporation, an investment banking firm, an investor, or any other person or entity to entitle itself to all or any portion of the income or profits of a law firm or other similar organization. Since such an investor would not be an individual performing professional services within the law firm or other organization, the requirements of subparagraph (b) would not be met.

[9] The term "individual" in subparagraph (b) is not intended to preclude the participation in a law firm or other organization by an individual professional corporation in the same manner as lawyers who

have incorporated as a professional corporation currently participate in partnerships which include professional corporations.

[10]   Some sharing of fees is likely to occur in the kinds of organizations permitted by paragraph (b). Subparagraph (a)(4) makes it clear that such fee-sharing is not prohibited.

* * *

Pennsylvania Rule 5.7

[Pennsylvania has enacted its own Rule 5.7 to govern lawyer involvement in nonlegal services.]

Rule 5.7.   Responsibilities Regarding Nonlegal Services

(a) **A lawyer who provides nonlegal services to a recipient that are not distinct from legal services provided to that recipient is subject to the Rules of Professional Conduct with respect to the provision of both legal and nonlegal services.**

(b) **A lawyer who provides nonlegal services to a recipient that are distinct from any legal services provided to the recipient is subject to the Rules of Professional Conduct with respect to the nonlegal services if the lawyer knows or reasonably should know that the recipient might believe that the recipient is receiving the protection of a client-lawyer relationship.**

(c) **A lawyer who is an owner, controlling party, employee, agent, or is otherwise affiliated with an entity providing nonlegal services to a recipient is subject to the Rules of Professional Conduct with respect to the nonlegal services if the lawyer knows or reasonably should know that the recipient might believe that the recipient is receiving the protection of a client-lawyer relationship.**

(d) **Paragraph (b) or (c) does not apply if the lawyer makes reasonable efforts to avoid any misunderstanding by the recipient receiving nonlegal services. Those efforts must include advising the recipient that the services are not legal services and that the protection of a client-lawyer relationship does not exist with respect to the provision of nonlegal services to the recipient.**

COMMENT

For many years, lawyers have provided to their clients nonlegal services that are ancillary to the practice of law. Nonlegal services are those that are not prohibited as unauthorized practice of law when provided by a nonlawyer. Examples of nonlegal services include providing title insurance, financial planning, accounting, trust services, real estate counseling, legislative lobbying, economic analysis, social work, psychological counseling, tax return preparation, and patent, medical or

359

environmental consulting. A broad range of economic and other interests of clients may be served by lawyers participating in the delivery of these services. In recent years, however, there has been significant debate about the role the Rules of Professional Conduct should play in regulating the degree and manner in which a lawyer participates in the delivery of nonlegal services. The ABA, for example, adopted, repealed and then adopted a different version of Rule 5.7. In the course of this debate, several ABA sections offered competing versions of Rule 5.7.

One approach to the issue of nonlegal services is to try to substantively limit the type of nonlegal services a lawyer may provide to a recipient or the manner in which the services are provided. A competing approach does not try to substantively limit the lawyer's provision of nonlegal services, but instead attempts to clarify the conduct to which the Rules of Professional Conduct apply and to avoid misunderstanding on the part of the recipient of the nonlegal services. This Rule adopts the latter approach.

The Potential for Misunderstanding

Whenever a lawyer directly provides nonlegal services, there exists the potential for ethical problems. Principal among these is the possibility that the person for whom the nonlegal services are performed may fail to understand that the services may not carry with them the protection normally afforded by the client-lawyer relationship. The recipient of the nonlegal services may expect, for example, that the protection of client confidences, prohibitions against representation of persons with conflicting interests, and obligations of a lawyer to maintain professional independence apply to the provision of nonlegal services when that may not be the case. The risk of such confusion is especially acute when the lawyer renders both types of services with respect to the same matter.

Providing Nonlegal Services That Are Not Distinct From Legal Services

Under some circumstances, the legal and nonlegal services may be so closely entwined that they cannot be distinguished from each other. In this situation, confusion by the recipient as to when the protection of the client-lawyer relationship applies are likely to be unavoidable. Therefore, Rule 5.7(a) requires that the lawyer providing the nonlegal services adhere to all of the requirements of the Rules of Professional Conduct.

In such a case, a lawyer will be responsible for assuring that both the lawyer's conduct and, to the extent required by Rule 5.3, that of nonlawyer employees comply in all respects with the Rules of Professional Conduct. When a lawyer is obliged to accord the recipients of such nonlegal services the protection of those Rules that apply to the client-lawyer relationship, the lawyer must take special care to heed the proscriptions of the Rules addressing conflict of interest (Rules 1.7

through 1.11, especially Rules 1.7(b) and 1.8(a), (b) and (f)), and to scrupulously adhere to the requirements of Rule 1.6 relating to disclosure of confidential information. The promotion of the nonlegal services must also in all respects comply with Rules 7.1 through 7.3, dealing with advertising and solicitation.

Rule 5.7(a) applies to the provision of nonlegal services by a lawyer even when the lawyer does not personally provide any legal services to the person for whom the nonlegal services are performed if the person is also receiving legal services from another lawyer that are not distinct from the nonlegal services.

Avoiding Misunderstanding When A Lawyer Directly Provides Nonlegal Services That Are Distinct From Legal Services

Even when the lawyer believes that his or her provision of nonlegal services is distinct from any legal services provided to the recipient, there is still a risk that the recipient of the nonlegal services will misunderstand the implications of receiving nonlegal services from a lawyer; the recipient might believe that the recipient is receiving the protection of a client-lawyer relationship. Where there is such a risk of misunderstanding, Rule 5.7(b) requires that the lawyer providing the nonlegal services adhere to all the Rules of Professional Conduct, unless exempted by Rule 5.7(d).

Avoiding Misunderstanding When a Lawyer is Indirectly Involved in the Provision of Nonlegal Services

Nonlegal services also may be provided through an entity with which a lawyer is somehow affiliated, for example, as owner, employee, controlling party or agent. In this situation, there is still a risk that the recipient of the nonlegal services might believe that the recipient is receiving the protection of a client-lawyer relationship. Where there is such a risk of misunderstanding, Rule 5.7(c) requires that the lawyer involved with the entity providing nonlegal services adhere to all the Rules of Professional Conduct, unless exempted by Rule 5.7(d).

Avoiding the Application of Paragraphs (b) and (c)

Paragraphs (b) and (c) specify that the Rules of Professional Conduct apply to a lawyer who directly provides or is otherwise involved in the provision of nonlegal services if there is a risk that the recipient might believe that the recipient is receiving the protection of a client-lawyer relationship. Neither the Rules of Professional Conduct nor paragraphs (b) or (c) will apply, however, if pursuant to paragraph (d), the lawyer takes reasonable efforts to avoid any misunderstanding by the recipient. In this respect, Rule 5.7 is analogous to Rule 4.3(c).

In taking the reasonable measures referred to in paragraph (d), the lawyer must communicate to the person receiving the nonlegal services that the relationship will not be a client-lawyer relationship. The communication should be made before entering into an agreement for the provision of nonlegal services, in a manner sufficient to assure that the person understands the significance of the communication, and preferably should be in writing.

The burden is upon the lawyer to show that the lawyer has taken reasonable measures under the circumstances to communicate the desired understanding. For instance, a sophisticated user of nonlegal services, such as a publicly-held corporation, may require a lesser explanation than someone unaccustomed to making distinctions between legal services and nonlegal services, such as an individual seeking tax advice from a lawyer-accountant or investigative services in connection with a lawsuit.

The Relationship Between Rule 5.7 and Other Rules of Professional Conduct

Even before Rule 5.7 was adopted, a lawyer involved in the provision of nonlegal services was subject to those Rules of Professional Conduct that apply generally. For example, Rule 8.4(c) makes a lawyer responsible for fraud committed with respect to the provision of nonlegal services. Such a lawyer must also comply with Rule 1.8(a). Nothing in this rule is intended to suspend the effect of any otherwise applicable Rule of Professional Conduct such as Rule 1.7(b), Rule 1.8(a) and Rule 8.4(c).

In addition to the Rules of Professional Conduct, principles of law external to the Rules, for example, the law of principal and agent, may govern the legal duties owed by a lawyer to those receiving the nonlegal services.

PUBLIC SERVICE

South Dakota Rule 6.1

[South Dakota has modified Model Rule 6.1 to read as follows:]

RULE 6.1   Pro Bono Publico Service

A lawyer should render public interest legal service.

A lawyer may discharge this responsibility by:

(a) providing professional services at no fee or a reduced fee to persons of limited means or to public service or charitable groups or organizations; or

(b) by service without compensation in public interest activities that improve the law, the legal system or the legal profession; or

(c) by financial support for organizations that provide legal services to persons of limited means.

COMMENT:

Each lawyer engaged in the practice of law has a responsibility to provide public interest legal services without fee, or at a substantially reduced fee, in one or more of the following areas: poverty law, civil rights law, public rights law, charitable organization representation and the administration of justice. This Rule expresses that policy but is not intended to be enforced through disciplinary process.

The rights and responsibilities of individuals and organizations in the United States are increasingly defined in legal terms. As a consequence, legal assistance in coping with the web of statutes, rules and regulations is imperative for all persons.

The basic responsibility for providing legal services for those unable to pay ultimately rests upon the individual lawyer, and personal involvement in the problems of the disadvantaged can be one of the most rewarding experiences in the life of a lawyer. Every lawyer, regardless of professional prominence or professional workload, should find time to participate in or otherwise support the provision of legal services to the disadvantaged. The provision of free legal services to those unable to pay reasonable fees continues to be an obligation of each lawyer as well as the profession generally, but the efforts of individual lawyers are often not enough to meet the need. Thus, it has been necessary for the profession and government to institute additional programs to provide legal services. Accordingly, legal aid offices, lawyer referral services and other related programs have been developed, and others will be developed by the profession and government. Every lawyer should support all proper efforts to meet this need for legal services.

The Rule has been restructured to make it clear that the "pro bono publico" obligation can also be discharged by uncompensated service in public interest activities and by financial support for legal service organizations.

INFORMATION ABOUT LEGAL SERVICES

Arizona Rule 7.1

[Arizona has modified Model Rule 7.1 to read as follows:]

ER 7.1 Communications and Advertising Concerning a Lawyer's Services

(a) A lawyer shall not make a false or misleading communication about the lawyer or the lawyer's services. A communication is false or misleading if it:

(1) contains a material misrepresentation of fact or law or omits a fact necessary to make the statement considered as a whole not materially misleading;

(2) is likely to create an unjustified expectation about results the lawyer can achieve or states or implies that the

lawyer can achieve results by means that violate the rules of professional conduct or other law;

(3) compares the lawyer's services with any other lawyers' services, unless the comparison can be factually substantiated;

(4) is a factual statement which cannot be factually substantiated.

(b) All communications and advertising concerning a lawyer's services shall be predominantly informational. As used in this rule, "predominantly informational" shall mean that, in both quantity and quality, the communication of factual information rationally related to the need for and selection of an attorney predominates.

(c) Subject to all the requirements set forth in these rules, a lawyer may advertise services through public media, such as a telephone directory, legal directory, newspaper or other periodical, billboards and other signs, radio, television and recorded messages the public may access by dialing a telephone number, or through written communication. These rules shall not apply to any advertisement broadcast or disseminated in another jurisdiction in which the advertising lawyer is admitted if such advertisement complies with the rules governing lawyer advertising in that jurisdiction and is not intended for broadcast or dissemination within the State of Arizona.

(d) The following information in advertisements and written communications, if truthful, shall be presumed not to violate the provisions of ER 7.1:

(1) the name of the lawyer or law firm, a listing of lawyers associated with the firm, office addresses and telephone numbers, office and telephone service hours, and a designation such as "attorney" or "law firm";

(2) date of admission to the State Bar of Arizona and any other bar associations and a listing of federal courts and jurisdictions other than Arizona where the lawyer is licensed to practice;

(3) technical and professional licenses granted by the state or other recognized licensing authorities;

(4) language ability in addition to English;

(5) fields of law in which the lawyer is certified subject to the requirements of ER 7.4;

(6) prepaid or group legal service plans or programs in which the lawyer participates;

(7) acceptance of credit cards;

(8) information concerning fees and costs, or the availability of such information on request, subject to the requirements of these rules;

(9) a listing of a lawyer or law firm as a sponsor of charitable, civic or community program or event or public service announcement. Such listing shall not exceed the traditional description of sponsors of or contributors to the charitable, civic or community program or event or public service announcement, and such listing must comply with the provisions of these rules;

(10) schools attended, with dates of graduation, degrees and other scholastic distinctions;

(11) public or quasi-public offices;

(12) military service;

(13) legal authorships;

(14) legal teaching positions;

(15) memberships, offices and committee assignments in bar associations;

(16) memberships and offices in legal fraternities and legal societies;

(17) memberships in scientific, technical and professional associations and societies;

(18) names and addresses of bank references;

(19) with their written consent, names of clients regularly represented;

(20) office and telephone answering service hours;

(21) availability upon request of written schedule of fees and/or an estimate of the fee to be charged for specific services.

(e) Every advertisement (including advertisement by written solicitation) that contains information about the lawyer's fees shall be subject to the following requirements:

(1) Advertisements and written communications indicating that the charging of a fee is contingent on outcome or that the fee will be a percentage of the recovery shall disclose (A) that the client will be liable for expenses regardless of outcome and (B) whether the percentage fee will be computed before expenses are deducted from the recovery.

(2) Range of fees or hourly rates for services may be communicated provided that the client is informed in writing at the commencement of any attorney-client relationship that the total fee within the range which will be charged or

the total hours to be devoted will vary depending upon that particular matter to be handled for each client and the client is entitled without obligation to an estimate of the fee within the range likely to be charged.

(3) Fixed fees for specific routine legal services, the description of which would not be misunderstood or be deceptive, may be communicated provided that the client is informed in writing at the commencement of any attorney-client relationship that the quoted fee will be available only to clients whose matters fall within the services described and that the client is entitled without obligation to a specific estimate of the fee likely to be charged.

(4) A lawyer who advertises a specific fee, range of fees or hourly rate for a particular service shall honor the advertised fee, or range of fees, for at least ninety (90) days unless the advertisement specifies a shorter period; provided, for advertisements in the yellow pages of telephone directories or other media not published more frequently than annually, the advertised fee or range of fees shall be honored for no less than one year following publication.

(f) A lawyer shall not advertise services or communicate in writing under a name that violates the provisions of these rules.

(g) All advertisements and written communications provided for under these rules shall disclose the cities, towns or counties in which the lawyer or lawyers who will actually perform the services advertised maintain an office or principally practice law.

(h) No lawyer shall, directly or indirectly, pay all or a part of the cost of an advertisement by a lawyer not in the same firm unless the advertisement discloses the name and address of the non-advertising lawyer, the relationship between the advertising lawyer and the non-advertising lawyer, and whether the advertising lawyer may refer any case received through the advertisement to the non-advertising lawyer.

(i) Nothing in this rule prohibits a lawyer or law firm from permitting the inclusion in reputable law lists and law directories intended primarily for the use of the legal profession of such information as has traditionally been included in these publications, subject to the requirements of these rules.

(j) A lawyer shall not give anything of value to a person for recommending the lawyer's services, except that a lawyer may pay the reasonable cost of advertising or written or recorded communications permitted by these rules and may pay the usual charges of a lawyer referral service or other legal service organization.

(k) This rule does not apply to identification of a lawyer as a lawyer as well as by name:

(1) in political advertisements when the professional status is germane to the political campaign or to a political issue;

(2) in public notices when the name and profession of a lawyer are required or authorized by law or are reasonably pertinent for a purpose other than the attraction of potential clients;

(3) in routine reports and announcements of a bona fide business, civic, professional, or political organization in which the lawyer serves as a director or officer;

(4) in and on legal documents prepared by the lawyer;

(5) in and on legal textbooks, treatises, and other legal publications, and in dignified advertisements thereof;

(6) in communications by a qualified legal assistance organization, along with the biographical information permitted in these rules, directed to a member or beneficiary of such organization;

(7) in a brief announcement in any of the public media that identifies a lawyer or law firm as a contributor to a specified charity or as a sponsor of a specified charitable, community or public interest program, activity or event;

(8) in a newsletter mailed only to existing clients or other lawyers;

(9) in professional announcement cards stating new or changed associations, new offices, and similar changes relating to a lawyer or law firm, and which are mailed only to other lawyers, relatives, close personal friends and existing clients.

(l) A lawyer shall not, on behalf of himself, his partner or associate, or any other lawyer affiliated with him or his firm, use or participate in the use of any form of public communication which:

(1) is intended or is likely to result in a legal action or a legal position being asserted merely to harass or maliciously injure another;

(2) contains a prediction of future success; or

(3) contains an opinion, representation or implication regarding the quality of legal services which is not susceptible of reasonable verification by the public.

(m) A lawyer shall not accept employment when he knows or should know that the person who seeks his services does so as a result of conduct prohibited under this rule.

(n) All advertisements and written communications pursuant to these rules shall include the name of at least one lawyer or the lawyer referral service responsible for its content.

(o) A copy or recording of an advertisement or written or recorded communication shall be kept for three years after its last dissemination along with a record of when and where it was used.

(p) No communication, advertisement or other professional designation shall state or imply a relationship between any member in private practice and a government agency or instrumentality, or a public or non-public legal services organization; or that a member has a relationship to any other member or a law firm as a partner or associate, or officer or shareholder unless such relationship in fact exists or that a member or a law firm is "of counsel" to another member or law firm unless the former has a relationship with the latter which is close, personal, continuous and regular.

(q) Advertisements on the electronic media, such as television and radio, may contain the same information as permitted in advertisements in the print media, subject to the following requirements:

(1) Impersonations, dramatizations and recreations shall comply with all the requirements set forth in these rules, and shall be designed to further the informational purposes of legal advertisement.

(2) If a law firm advertises on television and a person appears on screen purporting to be a lawyer, such person shall in fact be a lawyer employed full-time at the advertising law firm. If a law firm advertises a particular legal service on television, and a lawyer appears on screen as the person purporting to render the service, the lawyer appearing on screen shall be the lawyer who will actually perform the service advertised unless the advertisement discloses that the service may be performed by other lawyers in the firm.

(r) A lawyer or his partner or associate or any other lawyer affiliated with him or his firm may be recommended, employed or paid by, or may cooperate with, one of the following offices or organizations that promote the use of his services or those of his partner or associate or any other lawyer affiliated with him or his firm if there is no interference with the exercise of independent professional judgment in behalf of his client:

(1) a legal aid office or public defender office which is operated or sponsored by a duly accredited law school, by a bona fide non-profit community organization, or by a governmental agency; or which is operated, sponsored, or approved by a bar association;

(2) a military legal assistance office;

(3) a lawyer referral service operated, sponsored, or approved by a bar association. A lawyer shall not accept referrals from a lawyer referral service unless the service:

(A) engages in no communication with the public and in no direct contact with prospective clients in a manner that would violate the rules of professional conduct if the communication or contact were made by the lawyer;

(B) receives no fee or charge that constitutes a division or sharing of fees;

(C) refers clients only to lawyers lawfully permitted to practice law in Arizona when the services to be rendered constitute the practice of law in Arizona;

(D) furnishes the state bar on a quarterly basis with the names of all lawyers participating in the service; and

(E) neither represents nor implies to the public that this service is operated, endorsed, sponsored or approved by the state bar, unless the service is operated, endorsed, sponsored or expressly approved by the state bar.

(4) any bona fide organization that recommends, furnishes or pays for legal services to its members or beneficiaries, provided the following conditions are satisfied:

(A) such organization, including any affiliate, is so organized and operated that no profit is derived by it from the rendition of legal services by lawyers, and that, if the organization is organized for profit, the legal services are not rendered by lawyers employed, directed, supervised or selected by it, except in connection with matters where such organization bears ultimate liability of its members or beneficiary;

(B) neither the lawyer, nor his partner or associate, nor any other lawyer affiliated with him or his firm, nor any non-lawyer, shall have initiated or promoted such organization for the primary purpose of providing financial or other benefit to such lawyer, partner, associate or affiliated lawyer;

(C) such organization is not operated for the purpose of procuring legal work or financial benefit for any lawyer as a private practitioner outside of the legal services program of the organization;

(D) the member or beneficiary to whom the legal services are furnished, and not such organization, is recognized as the client of the lawyer in the matter;

(E) any member or beneficiary who is entitled to have legal services furnished or paid for by the organization may, if such member or beneficiary so desires, select counsel other than that furnished, selected or approved by the organization for the particular matter involved; and the legal service plan of such organization provides appropriate relief for any member or beneficiary who asserts a claim that representation by counsel furnished, selected or approved would be unethical, improper or inadequate under the circumstances of the matter involved and the plan provides an appropriate procedure for seeking such relief;

(F) the lawyer does not know or have cause to know that such organization is in violation of applicable laws, rules of court and other legal requirements that govern its legal service operations; and

(G) such organization has filed with the appropriate disciplinary authority at least annually a report with respect to its legal service plan, if any, showing its terms, schedule of benefits, subscription charges, agreements with counsel, and financial results of its legal service activities, or if it has failed to do so, the lawyer does not know or have cause to know of such failure.

(5) A public interest law firm, which is defined as: A nonprofit firm which provides, without cost or at a substantially reduced fee, legal services which would not be provided by a governmental agency or by any other means, and has been recognized and approved as such by the Board of Governors of the State Bar of Arizona, and which falls exclusively into one or more of the following areas:

(A) Poverty Law: Legal services in civil and criminal matters of importance to a client who does not have the financial resources to compensate counsel.

(B) Individual Civil Rights Laws: Legal representation of an important right of an individual which society has a special interest in protecting, but which the client would not otherwise seek to vindicate.

(C) Public Rights Law: Legal representation of an important right belonging to the public at large, where those asserting the right would not otherwise seek its vindication.

(D) Charitable Organization Representation: Legal service to charitable, religious, civic and educational institutions in matters in furtherance of their organizational purpose where the payment of customary legal fees would significantly deplete the organization's economic resources.

Arizona Rule 7.2

[Arizona has modified Model Rule 7.2 to read as follows:]

ER 7.2 Legal Service Information

(a) Each lawyer or law firm that advertises (including by written solicitation) his, her or its availability to provide legal services shall have a factual statement detailing the background, training and experience of each lawyer or law firm available for delivery upon request to any potential client in a form to be prescribed by the state bar and approved by the court.

(b) If the lawyer or law firm claims expertise beyond that possessed by competent and experienced lawyers in general practice in the representation of clients in particular matters or publicly designated or limits the lawyer's or law firm's practice to particular types of cases or clients, the written information shall comply with ER 7.4.

(c) Whenever a potential client requests information regarding a lawyer or law firm for the purpose of making a decision regarding employment of the lawyer or law firm:

(1) the lawyer or law firm shall promptly furnish (by mail if requested) the written information described in paragraphs (a) and (b).

(2) the lawyer or law firm may furnish such additional factual information regarding the lawyer or law firm deemed valuable to assist the client.

(d) A copy of all information furnished to clients by reason of this rule shall be retained by the lawyer or law firm for a period of three (3) years after last regular use of the information.

(e) Upon reasonable request by the state bar, a lawyer shall promptly provide proof that any statement or claim made in any advertisement or written communication, as well as the information furnished to a prospective client as authorized by these rules, is in compliance with paragraphs (a) and (b) above.

Amended July 27, 1989, effective Aug. 1, 1989; July 16, 1992, effective Dec. 1, 1992.

STATE BAR OF ARIZONA
LAW FIRM INFORMATION STATEMENT
(eff. Dec. 1, 1994)

1. Firm name _____
2. Firm address(es) _____
3. Telephone number(s) _____
4. Number of Lawyers in firm _____
5. Areas of law firm practice _____
6. Courts to which members of the law firm are admitted to practice
    _____

7. Areas in which lawyers are certified by the Arizona Board of Legal Specialization or Equivalent Certification, and number of lawyers certified by each organization in each area of specialization _____

8. Year in which firm originally was established _____
9. List attorneys in firm having experience in each advertised area of practice. (For a description of the experience, see each attorney's Lawyer Information Statement.) _____

STATE BAR OF ARIZONA
LAWYER INFORMATION STATEMENT

1. Lawyer's name _____
2. Office address(es) _____
3. Telephone number(s) _____
4. Date of admission to State Bar of Arizona _____
5. Courts to which lawyer is admitted and dates of admission to each
    _____

6. Technical and professional licenses granted by state or other licensing authorities _____
7. Areas of law in which lawyer practices _____
8. Areas of law in which lawyer is certified by the Arizona Board of Legal Specialization or equivalent certification _____
9. For each advertised area of law in which the lawyer practices, please give the following information:
    —Number of years of experience in the area of law _____
    —Percentage of practice devoted to the area of law, and for how long _____
    —Approximate total number of cases or matters in the area which have been handled by the lawyer _____
    —Pertinent publications, if any _____
    —Special training in the area _____
    —Pertinent awards and recognition _____
    If the advertised area of law is litigation or personal injury law, please specify the following information for cases in which you have served either as sole or lead counsel or associate counsel:
    Arizona Superior Court or U.S. District Court

Number of civil jury trials completed
  sole or lead counsel _____
  associate counsel _____
Number of civil bench trials completed
  sole or lead counsel _____
  associate counsel _____
Number of criminal jury trials completed
  sole or lead counsel _____
  associate counsel _____
Number of criminal bench trials completed
  sole or lead counsel _____
  associate counsel _____

Municipal or Justice Courts

Number of civil jury trials completed
  sole or lead counsel _____
  associate counsel _____
Number of civil bench trials completed
  sole or lead counsel _____
  associate counsel _____
Number of criminal jury trials completed
  sole or lead counsel _____
  associate counsel _____
Number of criminal bench trials completed
  sole or lead counsel _____
  associate counsel _____

Contested Arbitration Proceedings

Number of completed arbitration hearings
  sole or lead counsel _____
  associate counsel _____

Other Evidentiary Hearings

Number of other evidentiary hearings that have exceeded three
  hours of in-court appearance (e.g., judicial administrative
  hearings, temporary restraining orders, preliminary injunctions, provisional remedy hearings, criminal motions to suppress, temporary orders in marital dissolutions, etc.).
  sole or lead counsel _____
  associate counsel _____

10. Membership in professional organizations _____
11. School(s) attended, dates of graduation, degrees received, honors or
    distinctions _____
12. Public or quasi-public offices held _____
13. Military service _____
14. Legal authorships _____
15. Legal teaching positions _____
16. Memberships, offices and committee assignments in bar associa-
    tions _____
17. Language ability in addition to English _____

Arizona Rule 7.3

[Arizona has modified Model Rule 7.3 to read as follows:]

ER 7.3   Direct Contact With Prospective Clients

(a) A lawyer may not solicit professional employment from a prospective client with whom the lawyer has no family or prior professional relationship in person or by telephone, when a motive for the lawyer's doing so is the lawyer's pecuniary gain.

(b) Subject to all of the requirements of these rules concerning communications and advertising and the specific additional requirements of this section, a lawyer may initiate written communication, not involving personal or telephone contact, with persons known to need legal services of the kind provided by the lawyer in a particular matter, for the purpose of obtaining professional employment. Such written communication shall be clearly marked on the envelope and on the first page of the communication contained in the envelope, as follows:

ADVERTISING MATERIAL:

THIS IS A COMMERCIAL SOLICITATION

Said notification shall be printed in red ink, in all capital letters, in type size at least double the largest type size used in the body of the communication. No other statement shall be placed on the envelope which makes reference to the contents of the solicitation. If the solicitation advertises representation on a contingent or "no recovery, no fee" basis, it shall also state that the client may be liable for costs and expenses.

(c) At the time of dissemination of such written communication, a copy shall be forwarded to the Clerk of the Arizona Supreme Court and the State Bar of Arizona at its Phoenix office. If a written communication identical in content is sent to two or more prospective clients, the lawyer may comply with this requirement by forwarding a single copy together with a list of the names and addresses of persons to whom the written communication was sent.

(d) A lawyer shall not send, or knowingly permit to be sent, on behalf of himself, his firm, his partner, an associate, or any other lawyer affiliated with him or his firm a written communication to a prospective client for the purpose of obtaining professional employment if:

(1) it has been made known to the lawyer that the person does not want to receive such communications from the lawyer;

(2) the communication involves coercion, duress, fraud, overreaching, harassment, intimidation, or undue influence;

(3) the communication contains a false, fraudulent, misleading, deceptive or unfair statement or claim or is otherwise improper under these rules;

(4) the lawyer knows or reasonably should know that the physical, emotional, or mental state of the person makes it unlikely that the person would exercise reasonable judgment in employing a lawyer.

(e) Written communications mailed to prospective clients shall be sent only by regular U.S. mail, not by registered mail or other forms of restricted delivery.

(f) No reference shall be made in the communication to the communication having received any kind of approval from the state bar.

(g) If a contract for representation is mailed with the written communication, the contract shall be marked "sample" in red ink and shall contain the words "do not sign" on the client signature line.

(h) Written communications shall be on letter-sized paper rather than legal-sized paper and shall not be made to resemble legal pleadings or other legal documents. This provision does not preclude the mailing of brochures and pamphlets.

(i) If a lawyer other than the lawyer whose name or signature appears on the communication will actually handle the case or matter or if the case or matter will be referred to another lawyer or law firm, any written communication concerning a specific matter shall include a statement so advising the client.

(j) Any written communication prompted by a specific occurrence involving or affecting the intended recipient of the communication or a family member shall disclose how the lawyer obtained the information prompting the communication. If the information prompting the communication is a public document obtained from a commercial service or subscription, the disclosure shall identify the fact and role of the commercial service or subscription.

(k) A written communication seeking employment by a specific prospective client in a specific matter shall not reveal on the envelope, or on the outside of a self-mailing brochure or pamphlet, the nature of the client's legal problem.

(*l*) All statements required by this rule shall be displayed conspicuously in type size at least equal to the largest type used in the communication.

(m) The lawyer initiating the communication shall bear the burden of proof regarding the truthfulness of all facts contained in the communication, and shall, upon request of the State Bar or the recipient of the communication, disclose:

(1) how the identity and specific legal need of the potential recipient were discovered; and

(2) how the identity and knowledge of the specific need of the potential recipient were verified by the soliciting lawyer.

Texas Disciplinary Rules 7.01–7.07

[In 1995, Texas substantially revised its advertising rules as follows:]

RULE 7.01   Firm Names and Letterhead

(a) A lawyer in private practice shall not practice under a trade name, a name that is misleading as to the identity of the lawyer or lawyers practicing under such name, or a firm name containing names other than those of one or more of the lawyers in the firm, except that the names of a professional corporation, professional association, limited liability partnership, or professional limited liability company may contain "P.C.," "P.A.," "L.L.P.," "P.L.L.C.," or similar symbols indicating the nature of the organization, and if otherwise lawful a firm may use as, or continue to include in, its name the name or names of one or more deceased or retired members of the firm or of a predecessor firm in a continuing line of succession. Nothing herein shall prohibit a married woman from practicing under her maiden name.

(b) A firm with offices in more than one jurisdiction may use the same name in each jurisdiction, but identification of the lawyers in an office of the firm shall indicate the jurisdictional limitations on those not licensed to practice in the jurisdiction where the office is located.

(c) The name of a lawyer occupying a judicial, legislative, or public executive or administrative position shall not be used in the name of a firm, or in communications on its behalf, during any substantial period in which the lawyer is not actively and regularly practicing with the firm.

(d) A lawyer shall not hold himself or herself out as being a partner, shareholder, or associate with one or more other lawyers unless they are in fact partners, shareholders, or associates.

(e) A lawyer shall not advertise in the public media or seek professional employment by written communication under a trade or fictitious name, except that a lawyer who practices under a trade name as authorized by paragraph (a) of this Rule may use that name in such advertisement or such written communication but only if that name is the firm name that appears on the lawyer's letterhead, business cards, office sign, fee contracts, and with the lawyer's signature on pleadings and other legal documents.

(f) A lawyer shall not use a firm name, letterhead, or other professional designation that violates Rule 7.02(a).

(Former Rule 7.04 adopted eff. Jan. 1, 1990; redesignated and amended to be eff. April 1, 1995; on March 31, 1995, the Texas Supreme Court extended the effective date 120 days after the date of judgment of the U.S. District Court in Texans Against Censorship, Inc. v. State Bar of Texas, 888 F.Supp. 1328 (E.D.Tex. 1995).)

COMMENT

1. A lawyer or law firm may not practice law using a name that is misleading as to the identity of the lawyers practicing under such name, but the continued use of the name of a deceased or retired member of the firm or of a predecessor firm is not considered to be misleading. Trade names are generally considered inherently misleading. Other types of firm names can be misleading as well, such as a firm name that creates the appearance that lawyers are partners or employees of a single law firm when in fact they are merely associated for the purpose of sharing expenses. In such cases, the lawyers involved may not denominate themselves in any manner suggesting such an ongoing professional relationship as, for example, "Smith and Jones" or "Smith and Jones Associates" or "Smith and Associates." Such titles create the false impression that the lawyers named have assumed a joint professional responsibility for clients' legal affairs. See paragraph (d).

2. The practice of law firms having offices in more than one state is commonplace. Although it is not necessary that the name of an interstate firm include Texas lawyers, a letterhead including the name of any lawyer not licensed in Texas must indicate the lawyer is not licensed in Texas.

3. Paragraph (c) is designed to prevent the exploitation of a lawyer's public position for the benefit of the lawyer's firm. Likewise, because it may be misleading under paragraph (a), a lawyer who occupies a judicial, legislative, or public executive or administrative position should not indicate that fact on a letterhead which identifies that person as an attorney in the private practice of law. However, a firm name may include the name of a public official who is actively and regularly practicing law with the firm. But see Rule 7.02(a)(4).

4. With certain limited exceptions, paragraph (a) forbids a lawyer from using a trade name or fictitious name. Paragraph (e) sets out this same prohibition with respect to advertising in public media or written communications seeking professional employment and contains additional restrictions on the use of trade names or fictitious names in those contexts. In a largely overlapping measure, paragraph (f) forbids the use of any such name or designation if it would amount to a "false or misleading communication" under Rule 7.02(a).

(Comment amended by State Bar Board of Directors Jan. 20, 1995.)

RULE 7.02 Communications Concerning a Lawyer's Services

(a) A lawyer shall not make a false or misleading communication about the qualifications or the services of any lawyer or firm. A communication is false or misleading if it:

(1) contains a material misrepresentation of fact or law, or omits a fact necessary to make the statement considered as a whole not materially misleading;

(2) is likely to create an unjustified expectation about results the lawyer can achieve, or states or implies that the lawyer can achieve results by means that violate these rules or other law;

(3) compares the lawyer's services with other lawyers' services, unless the comparison can be substantiated by reference to verifiable, objective data;

(4) states or implies that the lawyer is able to influence improperly or upon irrelevant grounds any tribunal, legislative body, or public official; or

(5) designates one or more specific areas of practice in an advertisement in the public media or in a written solicitation unless the advertising lawyer is competent to handle legal matters in each such area of practice.

(b) Rule 7.02(a)(5) does not require that a lawyer be certified by the Texas Board of Legal Specialization at the time of advertising in a specific area of practice, but such certification shall conclusively establish that such lawyer satisfies the requirements of Rule 7.02(a)(5) with respect to the area(s) of practice in which such lawyer is certified.

(c) A lawyer shall not advertise in the public media that the lawyer is a specialist, except as permitted under Rule 7.04.

(d) Any statement or disclaimer required by these rules shall be made in each language used in the advertisement or writing with respect to which such required statement or disclaimer relates; provided however, the mere statement that a particular language is spoken or understood shall not alone result in the need for a statement or disclaimer in that language.

(Former Rule 7.01 adopted eff. Jan. 1, 1990; redesignated and amended to be eff. April 1, 1995; on March 31, 1995, the Texas Supreme Court extended the effective date 120 days after the date of judgment of the U.S. District Court in Texans Against Censorship, Inc. v. State Bar of Texas, 888 F.Supp. 1328 (E.D.Tex. 1995).)

COMMENT

1. The Rules within Part VII are intended to regulate communications made for the purpose of obtaining professional employment. They are not intended to affect other forms of speech by lawyers, such as political advertisements or political commentary, except insofar as a

lawyer's effort to obtain employment is linked to a matter of current public debate.

2. Whatever means are used to make known a lawyer's services, statements about them should be truthful and nondeceptive. Sub-paragraph (a)(1) recognizes that statements can be misleading both by what they contain and what they leave out. Statements that are false or misleading for either reason are prohibited. The prohibitions in sub-paragraph (a)(2) of statements that may create an "unjustified expecta-tion" and in sub-paragraph (a)(3) of comparisons of lawyers' services unless those comparisons "can be substantiated by reference to verifia-ble objective data" are each designated to prevent lawyers from mislead-ing members of the public as they seek legal services. Those provisions would ordinarily preclude advertisements in the public media and writ-ten solicitation communications that discuss the results obtained on behalf of a client, such as the amount of a damage award, the lawyer's record in obtaining favorable settlements or verdicts, as well as those that contain client endorsements. Unless accompanied by appropriate, prominent qualifications and disclaimers, that information can readily mislead prospective clients into believing that similar results can be obtained for them without reference to their specific factual and legal circumstances. Similarly, statements comparing a lawyer's services with those of another where the comparisons are not susceptible of precise measurement or verification, such as "we are the toughest lawyers in town", "we will get money for you when other lawyers can't", or "we are the best law firm in Texas if you want a large recovery" can deceive or mislead prospective clients. On the other hand, a simple statement of a lawyer's own qualifications devoid of comparisons to other lawyers does not pose the same risk of being misleading and does not fall within this Rule. See Rule 7.04. A lawyer making a referral to another lawyer may, of course, express a good faith subjective opinion regarding that lawyer.

3. This Rule does not prohibit communication of information con-cerning a lawyer's name or firm name, address and telephone numbers; the basis on which the lawyer's fees are determined, including prices for specific services and payment and credit arrangements; names of refer-ences and, with their consent, names of clients regularly represented; and other truthful information that might invite the attention of those seeking legal assistance. When a communication permitted by Rule 7.02 is made in the public media, the lawyer should consult Rule 7.04 for further guidance and restrictions. When a communication permitted by Rule 7.02 is made by a lawyer through a written solicitation, the lawyer should consult Rule 7.05 for further guidance and restrictions.

Communication of Fields of Practice

4. Paragraphs (a)(5), (b) and (c) of Rule 7.02 regulate communica-tions concerning a lawyer's fields of practice and should be construed together with Rule 7.04 or 7.05, as applicable. If a lawyer in a public

media advertisement or in a written solicitation designates one or more specific areas of practice, that designation is at least an implicit representation that the lawyer is qualified in the areas designated. Accordingly, Rule 7.02(a)(5) prohibits the designation of a field of practice unless the communicating lawyer is in fact competent in the area.

5.   Typically, one would expect competency to be measured by special education, training, or experience in the particular area of law designated. Because certification by the Texas Board of Legal Specialization involves special education, training, and experience, certification by the Texas Board of Legal Specialization conclusively establishes that a lawyer meets the requirements of Rule 7.02(a)(5) in any area in which the Board has certified the lawyer. However, competency may be established by means other than certification by the Texas Board of Legal Specialization. See Rule 7.04(b).

6.   Lawyers who wish to advertise in the public media that they specialize should refer to Rule 7.04(a), (b) and (c). Lawyers who wish to assert a specialty in a written solicitation should refer to Rule 7.05(a)(4) and (b)(1).

Communication in a Second Language

7.   The ability of lawyers to communicate in a second language can facilitate the delivery and receipt of legal services. Accordingly, it is in the best interest of the public that potential clients be made aware of a lawyer's language ability. A lawyer may state an ability to communicate in a second language without any further elaboration. However, if a lawyer chooses to communicate with potential clients in a second language, all statements or disclaimers required by the Texas Disciplinary Rules of Professional Conduct must also be made in that language. See paragraph (d). Communicating some information in one language while communicating the rest in another is potentially misleading if the recipient understands only one of the languages.

(Comment amended by State Bar Board of Directors Jan. 20, 1995.)

RULE 7.03   Prohibited Solicitations and Payments

(a) A lawyer shall not by in-person or telephone contact seek professional employment concerning a matter arising out of a particular occurrence or event, or series of occurrences or events, from a prospective client or nonclient who has not sought the lawyer's advice regarding employment or with whom the lawyer has no family or past or present attorney-client relationship when a significant motive for the lawyer's doing so is the lawyer's pecuniary gain. Notwithstanding the provisions of this paragraph, a lawyer for a qualified nonprofit organization may communicate with the organization's members for the purpose of educating the members to understand the law, to recognize legal problems, to make intelligent selection of counsel, or to use legal services. In those situations where in-person or telephone contact is permitted by this paragraph, a lawyer shall not have such a contact with a prospective client if:

(1) the communication involves coercion, duress, fraud, overreaching, intimidation, undue influence, or harassment;

(2) the communication contains information prohibited by Rule 7.02(a); or

(3) the communication contains a false, fraudulent, misleading, deceptive, or unfair statement or claim.

(b) A lawyer shall not pay, give, or offer to pay or give anything of value to a person not licensed to practice law for soliciting prospective clients for, or referring clients or prospective clients to, any lawyer or firm, except that a lawyer may pay reasonable fees for advertising and public relations services rendered in accordance with this Rule and may pay the usual charges of a lawyer referral service that meets the requirements of Article 320d, Revised Statutes.

(c) A lawyer, in order to solicit professional employment, shall not pay, give, advance, or offer to pay, give, or advance anything of value, other than actual litigation expenses and other financial assistance as permitted by Rule 1.08(d), to a prospective client or any other person; provided however, this provision does not prohibit the payment of legitimate referral fees as permitted by paragraph (b) of this Rule.

(d) A lawyer shall not enter into an agreement for, charge for, or collect a fee for professional employment obtained in violation of Rule 7.03(a), (b), or (c).

(e) A lawyer shall not participate with or accept referrals from a lawyer referral service unless the lawyer knows or reasonably believes that the lawyer referral service meets the requirements of Article 320d, Revised Statutes.

(Former Rule 7.02 adopted eff. Jan. 1, 1990; redesignated and amended to be eff. April 1, 1995; on March 31, 1995, the Texas Supreme Court extended the effective date 120 days after the date of judgment of the U.S. District Court in Texans Against Censorship, Inc. v. State Bar of Texas, 888 F.Supp. 1328 (E.D.Tex. 1995).)

COMMENT

1. In many situations, in-person or telephone solicitations by lawyers involve well-known opportunities for abuse of prospective clients. Nonetheless, paragraph (a) unconditionally prohibits those activities only when profit for the lawyer is a significant motive and the solicitation concerns matters arising out of a particular occurrence, event, or series of occurrences or events. The reason for this limited outright ban is that there are circumstances where the dangers of such contacts can be reduced. As long as the conditions of subparagraphs (a)(1) through (a)(3) are not violated by a given contact, a lawyer may engage in telephone or in-person solicitations when the solicitation is unrelated to

a specific occurrence, event, or series of occurrences or events. Similarly, subject to the same restrictions, in-person or telephone solicitations are permitted where the prospective client either has a family or past or present attorney-client relationship with the lawyer or where the potential client had previously contacted the lawyer about possible employment in the matter.

2. In addition, Rule 7.03(a) does not prohibit a lawyer for a qualified non-profit organization from in-person or telephone solicitation of prospective clients for purposes related to that organization. Historically and by law, nonprofit legal aid agencies, unions, and other qualified nonprofit organizations and their lawyers have been permitted to solicit clients in-person or by telephone, and Rule 7.03(a) is not in derogation of their constitutional rights to do so. Attorneys for such nonprofit organizations, however, remain subject to this Rule's general prohibitions against undue influence, intimidation, overreaching, and the like.

Paying for Solicitation

3. Rule 7.03(b) does not prohibit a lawyer from paying standard commercial fees for advertising or public relations services rendered in accordance with these Rules. In addition, a lawyer may pay the fees required by a lawyer referral service that meets the requirements of Article 320(d), Revised Statutes. However, paying, giving, or offering to pay or give anything of value to persons not licensed to practice law who solicit prospective clients for lawyers has always been considered to be against the best interest of both the public and the legal profession. Such actions circumvent these Rules by having a nonlawyer do what a lawyer is ethically proscribed from doing. Accordingly, the practice is forbidden by Rule 7.03(b). As to payments or gifts of value to licensed lawyers for soliciting prospective clients, see Rule 1.04(f).

4. Rule 7.03(c) prohibits a lawyer from paying or giving value directly to a prospective client or any other person as consideration for employment by that client except as permitted by Rule 1.08(d).

5. Paragraph (d) prohibits a lawyer from agreeing to or charging for professional employment obtained in violation of Rule 7.03. Paragraph (e) further requires a lawyer to decline business generated by a lawyer referral service unless the lawyer knows or reasonably believes that service is operated in conformity with statutory requirements.

6. References to "a lawyer" in this and other Rules include lawyers who practice in law firms. A lawyer associated with a firm cannot circumvent these Rules by soliciting or advertising in the name of that firm in a way that violates these Rules. See Rule 7.04(e).

(Comment amended by State Bar Board of Directors Jan. 20, 1995.)

RULE 7.04   Advertisements in the Public Media

(a) A lawyer shall not advertise in the public media that the lawyer is a specialist, except as permitted under Rule 7.04(b) or as follows:

(1) A lawyer admitted to practice before the United States Patent Office may use the designation "Patents," "Patent Attorney," or "Patent Lawyer," or any combination of those terms. A lawyer engaged in the trademark practice may use the designation "Trademark," "Trademark Attorney," or "Trademark Lawyer," or any combination of those terms. A lawyer engaged in patent and trademark practice may hold himself or herself out as specializing in "Intellectual Property Law," "Patent, Trademark, Copyright Law and Unfair Competition," or any of those terms.

(2) A lawyer may permit his or her name to be listed in lawyer referral service offices that meet the requirements of Article 320d, Revised Statutes, according to the areas of law in which the lawyer will accept referrals.

(3) A lawyer available to practice in a particular area of law or legal service may distribute to other lawyers and publish in legal directories and legal newspapers a listing or an announcement of such availability. The listing shall not contain a false or misleading representation of special competence or experience, but may contain the kind of information that traditionally has been included in such publications.

(b) A lawyer who advertises in the public media:

(1) shall publish or broadcast the name of at least one lawyer who is responsible for the content of such advertisement.

(2) shall not include a statement that the lawyer has been certified or designated by an organization as possessing special competence or a statement that the lawyer is a member of an organization the name of which implies that its members possess special competence, except that:

(i) a lawyer who has been awarded a Certificate of Special Competence by the Texas Board of Legal Specialization in the area so advertised, may state with respect to each such area, "Board Certified, [area of specialization]—Texas Board of Legal Specialization;" and

(ii) a lawyer who is a member of an organization the name of which implies that its members possess special competence, or who has been certified or designated by an organization as possessing special competence, may include a factually accurate statement of such membership or may include a factually accurate statement, "Certified [area of specialization] [name of certifying organization]," but such statements may be made only if

383

that organization has been accredited by the Texas Board of Legal Specialization as a bona fide organization that admits to membership or grants certification only on the basis of objective, exacting, publicly available standards (including high standards of individual character, conduct, and reputation) that are reasonably relevant to the special training or special competence that is implied and that are in excess of the level of training and competence generally required for admission to the Bar.

(3) shall state with respect to each area advertised in which the lawyer has not been awarded a Certificate of Special Competence by the Texas Board of Legal Specialization, "Not Certified by the Texas Board of Legal Specialization," however, if an area of law so advertised has not been designated as an area in which a lawyer may be awarded a Certificate of Special Competence by the Texas Board of Legal Specialization, the lawyer may also state, "No designation has been made by the Texas Board of Legal Specialization for a Certificate of Special Competence in this area."

(c) Separate and apart from any other statements, the statements referred to in paragraph (b) shall be displayed conspicuously with no abbreviations, changes, or additions in the quoted language set forth in paragraph (b) so as to be easily seen or understood by an ordinary consumer.

(d) Subject to the requirements of Rule 7.02 and of paragraphs (a), (b), and (c) of this Rule, a lawyer may, either directly or through a public relations or advertising representative, advertise services in the public media, such as (but not limited to) a telephone directory, legal directory, newspaper or other periodical, outdoor display, radio, or television.

(e) All advertisements in the public media for a lawyer or firm must be reviewed and approved in writing by the lawyer or a lawyer in the firm.

(f) A copy or recording of each advertisement in the public media and relevant approval referred to in paragraph (e), and a record of when and where the advertisement was used, shall be kept by the lawyer or firm for four years after its last dissemination.

(g) In advertisements utilizing video or comparable visual images, any person who portrays a lawyer whose services or whose firm's services are being advertised, or who narrates an advertisement as if he or she were such a lawyer, shall be one or more of the lawyers whose services are being advertised. In advertisements utilizing audio recordings, any person who narrates an advertisement as if he or she were a lawyer whose services or whose firm's services are being advertised, shall be one or more of the lawyers whose services are being advertised.

(h) If an advertisement in the public media by a lawyer or firm discloses the willingness or potential willingness of the lawyer or firm to render services on a contingent fee basis, the advertisement must state whether the client will be obligated to pay all or any portion of the court costs and, if a client may be liable for other expenses, this fact must be disclosed. If specific percentage fees or fee ranges of contingent fee work are disclosed in such advertisement, it must also disclose whether the percentage is computed before or after expenses are deducted from the recovery.

(i) A lawyer who advertises in the public media a specific fee or range of fees for a particular service shall conform to the advertised fee or range of fees for the period during which the advertisement is reasonably expected to be in circulation or otherwise expected to be effective in attracting clients, unless the advertisement specifies a shorter period; but in no instance is the lawyer bound to conform to the advertised fee or range of fees for a period of more than one year after the date of publication.

* (j) A lawyer or firm who advertises in the public media must disclose the geographic location, by city or town, of the lawyer's or firm's principal office. A lawyer or firm shall not advertise the existence of any office other than the principal office unless:

(1) that other office is staffed by a lawyer at least three days a week; or

(2) the advertisement discloses the days and times during which a lawyer will be present at that office.

* **Publisher's Note**: In Texans Against Censorship, Inc. v. State Bar of Texas, 888 F.Supp. 1328 (E.D.Tex. 1995), the U.S. District Court for the Eastern District of Texas held Rule 7.04(j) unconstitutional as applied to one of the plaintiffs. Affirmed, Texans v. State Bar of Texas, 100 F.3d 953 (5th Cir. 1996).

(k) A lawyer may not, directly or indirectly, pay all or a part of the cost of an advertisement in the public media for a lawyer not in the same firm unless such advertisement discloses the name and address of the financing lawyer, the relationship between the advertising lawyer and the financing lawyer, and whether the advertising lawyer is likely to refer cases received through the advertisement to the financing lawyer.

(*l*) If an advertising lawyer knows or should know at the time of an advertisement in the public media that a case or matter will likely be referred to another lawyer or firm, a statement of such fact shall be conspicuously included in such advertisement.

(m) **No motto, slogan, or jingle that is false or misleading may be used in any advertisement in the public media.**

(n) **A lawyer shall not include in any advertisement in the public media the lawyer's association with a lawyer referral service unless the lawyer knows or reasonably believes that the lawyer referral service meets the requirements of Article 320d, Revised Statutes.**

(o) **A lawyer may not advertise in the public media as part of an advertising cooperative or venture of two or more lawyers not in the same firm unless each such advertisement:**

(1) **states that the advertisement is paid for by the cooperating lawyers;**

(2) **names each of the cooperating lawyers;**

(3) **sets forth conspicuously the special competency requirements required by Rule 7.04(b) of lawyers who advertise in the public media;**

(4) **does not state or imply that the lawyers participating in the advertising cooperative or venture possess professional superiority, are able to perform services in a superior manner, or possess special competence in any area of law advertised, except that the advertisement may contain the information permitted by Rule 7.04(b)(2); and**

(5) **does not otherwise violate the Texas Disciplinary Rules of Professional Conduct.**

(p) **Each lawyer who advertises in the public media as part of an advertising cooperative or venture shall be individually responsible for:**

(1) **ensuring that each advertisement does not violate this Rule; and**

(2) **complying with the filing requirements of Rule 7.07.**

(Adopted to be eff. April 1, 1995; on March 31, 1995, the Texas Supreme Court extended the effective date 120 days after the date of judgment of the U.S. District Court in Texans Against Censorship, Inc. v. State Bar of Texas, 888 F.Supp. 1328 (E.D.Tex. 1995).)

COMMENT

1. Neither Rule 7.04 nor Rule 7.05 prohibits communications authorized by law, such as notice to members of a class in class action litigation.

Advertising Areas of Practice and Special Competence

2. Paragraphs (a) and (b) permit a lawyer, under the restrictions set forth, to indicate areas of practice in advertisements about the lawyer's services. See also paragraph (d). The restrictions are designed primarily to require that accurate information be conveyed. These restrictions recognize that a lawyer has a right protected by the United

States Constitution to advertise publicly, but that the right may be regulated by reasonable restrictions designed to protect the public from false or misleading information. The restrictions contained in Rule 7.04 are based on the experience of the legal profession in the State of Texas and are designed to curtail what experience has shown to be misleading and deceptive advertising. To ensure accountability, sub-paragraph (b)(1) requires identification of at least one lawyer responsible for the content of the advertisement.

3. Because of long-standing tradition a lawyer admitted to practice before the United States Patent Office may use the designation "patents," "patent attorney" or "patent lawyer" or any combination of those terms. As recognized by paragraph (a)(1), a lawyer engaged in patent and trademark practice may hold himself or herself out as concentrating in "intellectual property law," "patents, or trademarks and related matters," or "patent, trademark, copyright law and unfair competition" or any of those terms.

4. Paragraph (a)(2) recognizes the propriety of listing a lawyer's name in legal directories according to the areas of law in which the lawyer will accept new matters. The same right is given with respect to lawyer referral service offices, but only if those services comply with statutory guidelines. The restriction in paragraph (a)(2) does not prevent a legal aid agency or prepaid legal services plan from advertising legal services provided under its auspices.

5. Paragraph (a)(3) permits advertisements by lawyers to other lawyers in legal directories and legal newspapers, subject to the same requirements of truthfulness that apply to all other forms of lawyer advertising. Such advertisements traditionally contain information about the name, location, telephone numbers, and general availability of a lawyer to work on particular legal matters. Other information may be included so long as it is not false or misleading. Because advertisements in these publications are not available to the general public, lawyers who list various areas of practice are not required to comply with paragraph (b).

6. Some advertisements, sometimes known as tombstone advertisements, mention only such matters as the name of the lawyer or law firm, a listing of lawyers associated with the firm, office addresses and telephone numbers, office and telephone service hours, dates of admission to bars, the acceptance of credit cards, and fees. The content of such advertisements is not the kind of information intended to be regulated by Rule 7.04(b). However, if the advertisement in the public media mentions any area of the law in which the lawyer practices, then, because of the likelihood of misleading material, the lawyer must comply with paragraph (b).

7. Sometimes lawyers choose to advertise in the public media the fact that they have been certified or designated by a particular organization or that they are members of a particular organization. Such statements naturally lead the public to believe that the lawyer possesses

special competence in the area of law mentioned. Consequently, in order to ensure that the public will not be misled by such statements, sub-paragraph (b)(2) and paragraph (c) place limited but necessary restrictions upon a lawyer's basic right to advertise those affiliations.

8. Rule 7.04(b)(2) gives lawyers who possess certificates of specialization from the Texas Board of Legal Specialization or other meritorious credentials from organizations approved by the Board the option of stating that fact. If a lawyer mentions in an advertisement in the public media an area of the law in which the lawyer practices and that lawyer has not been awarded a Certificate in the area advertised, then the lawyer must disclaim or, where applicable, state that no certification is available. See sub-paragraph (b)(3). Sub-paragraphs (b)(2) and (b)(3) require that the restrictions set forth be complied with as to each area of law advertised.

9. Paragraph (c) is intended to ensure against misleading or material variations from the statements required by paragraph (b).

10. Paragraphs (e) and (f) provide the advertising lawyer, the Bar, and the public with requisite records should questions arise regarding the propriety of a public media advertisement. Paragraph (e), like paragraph (b)(1), ensures that a particular attorney accepts responsibility for the advertisement. It is in the public interest and in the interest of the legal profession that the records of those advertisements and approvals be maintained.

Examples of Prohibited Advertising

11. Paragraphs (g) through (*o*) regulate conduct that has been found to mislead or be likely to mislead the public. Each paragraph is designed to protect the public and to guard the legal profession against these documented misleading practices while at the same time respecting the constitutional rights of any lawyer to advertise.

12. Paragraph (g) is a limited regulation of video and audio forms of advertising. It prohibits lawyers from misleading the public into believing a nonlawyer portrayor or narrator in the advertisement is one of the lawyers prepared to perform services for the public. It does not prohibit the narration of an advertisement in the third person by an actor, as long as it is clear to those hearing or seeing the advertisement that the actor is not a lawyer prepared to perform services for the public.

13. Contingent fee contracts present unusual opportunities for deception by lawyers or for misunderstanding by the public. By requiring certain disclosures, paragraph (h) safeguards the public from misleading or potentially misleading advertisements that involve representation on a contingent fee basis. The affirmative requirements of paragraph (h) are not triggered solely by the expression of "contingent fee" or "percentage fee" in the advertisement. To the contrary, they encompass advertisements in the public media where the lawyer or firm expresses a mere willingness or potential willingness to render services for a contingent fee. Therefore, statements in an advertise-

ment such as "no fee if no recovery" or "fees in the event of recovery only" are clearly included as a form of advertisement subject to the disclosure requirements of paragraph (h).

14. Paragraphs (i), (j), (k) and (*l*) jointly address the problem of advertising that experience has shown misleads the public concerning the fees that will be charged, the location where services will be provided, or the attorney who will be performing these services. Together they prohibit the same sort of "bait and switch" advertising tactics by lawyers that are universally condemned.

15. Paragraph (i) requires a lawyer who advertises a specific fee or range of fees in the public media to honor those commitments for the period during which the advertisement is reasonably expected to be in circulation or otherwise expected to be effective in attracting clients, unless the advertisement itself specifies a shorter period. In no event, however, is a lawyer required to honor an advertised fee or range of fees for more than one year after publication.

16. Paragraph (j) prohibits advertising the availability of a satellite office that is not staffed by a lawyer at least on a part-time basis. Paragraph (j) does not require, however, that a lawyer or firm identify the particular office as its principal one. Experience has shown that, in the absence of such regulation, members of the public have been misled into employing a lawyer in a distant city who advertises that there is a nearby satellite office, only to learn later that the lawyer is rarely available to the client because the nearby office is seldom open or is staffed only by lay personnel. Paragraph (k) is not intended to restrict the ability of legal services programs to advertise satellite offices in remote parts of the program's service area even if those satellite offices are staffed irregularly by attorneys. Otherwise low-income individuals in and near such communities might be denied access to the only legal services truly available to them.

17. When a lawyer or firm advertises, the public has a right to expect that lawyer or firm will perform the legal services. Experience has shown that attorneys not in the same firm may create a relationship wherein one will finance advertising for the other in return for referrals. Nondisclosure of such a referral relationship is misleading to the public. Accordingly, paragraph (k) prohibits such a relationship between an advertising lawyer and a lawyer who finances the advertising unless the advertisement discloses the nature of the financial relationship between the two lawyers. Paragraph (*l*) addresses the same problem from a different perspective, requiring a lawyer who advertises the availability of legal services and who knows or should know at the time that the advertisement is placed in the media that business will likely be referred to another lawyer or firm, to include a conspicuous statement of that fact in any such advertising. This requirement applies whether or not the lawyer to whom the business is referred is financing the advertisements of the referring lawyer. It does not, however, require disclosure of all possible scenarios under which a referral could occur, such as an

unforeseen need to associate with a specialist in accordance with Rule 1.01(a) or the possibility of a referral if a prospective client turns out to have a conflict of interest precluding representation by the advertising lawyer.

18.   Paragraph (m) protects the public by forbidding mottos, slogans, and jingles that are false or misleading.   There are, however, mottos, slogans, and jingles that are informative rather than false or misleading.   Accordingly, paragraph (m) recognizes an advertising lawyer's constitutional right to include appropriate mottos, slogans, and jingles in advertising.

19.   Some lawyers choose to band together in a cooperative or joint venture to advertise.   Although those arrangements are lawful, the fact that several independent lawyers have joined together in a single advertisement increases the risk of misrepresentation or other forms of inappropriate expression.   Special care must be taken to ensure that cooperative advertisements identify each cooperating lawyer, state that each cooperating lawyer is paying for the advertisement, and accurately describe the professional qualifications of each cooperating lawyer.   See paragraph (o).   Furthermore, each cooperating lawyer must comply with the filing requirements of Rule 7.07.   See paragraph (p).

(Comment adopted by State Bar Board of Directors Jan. 20, 1995.)

RULE 7.05   Prohibited Written Solicitations

(a) A lawyer shall not send or deliver, or knowingly permit or cause another to send, deliver, on the lawyer's behalf, a written communication to a prospective client for the purpose of obtaining professional employment if:

(1) the communication involves coercion, duress, fraud, overreaching, intimidation, undue influence, or harassment;

(2) the communication contains information prohibited by Rule 7.02 or fails to satisfy each of the requirements of Rule 7.04(a) through (c), and (h) through (o) that would be applicable to the communication if it were an advertisement in the public media; or

(3) the communication contains a false, fraudulent, misleading, deceptive, or unfair statement or claim.

(b) Except as provided in paragraph (e) of this Rule, a written solicitation communication to prospective clients for the purpose of obtaining professional employment:

(1) shall conform to the provisions of Rule 7.04(a) through (c);

(2) shall be plainly marked "ADVERTISEMENT" on the first page of the written communication, and the face of the envelope also shall be plainly marked "ADVERTISEMENT," however, if the written communication is in the form of the

self mailing brochure or pamphlet, the word "ADVERTISE-MENT," shall be: (i) in a color that contrasts sharply with the background color; and (ii) in a size of at least 3/8″ vertically or three times the vertical height of the letters used in the body of such communication, whichever is larger.

(3) shall not be made to resemble legal pleadings or other legal documents;

*(4) shall not contain a statement or implication that the written communication has received any kind of authorization or approval from the State Bar of Texas or from the Law Advertisement and Solicitation Review Committee;

*(5) shall not be sent in a manner, such as by registered mail, that requires personal delivery to a particular individual;

* **Publisher's Note**: In Texans Against Censorship, Inc. v. State Bar of Texas, 888 F. Supp. 1328 (E.D.Tex. 1995), the U.S. District Court for the Eastern District of Texas held that Rules 7.05(b)(4) and 7.05(b)(5) are unconstitutional. Affirmed, Texans v. State Bar of Texas, 100 F.3d 953 (5th Cir. 1996).

(6) shall not reveal on the envelope used for the communication, or on the outside of a self-mailing brochure or pamphlet, the nature of the legal problem of the prospective client or non-client; and

(7) shall disclose how the lawyer obtained the information prompting such written communication to solicit professional employment, if such contact was prompted by a specific occurrence involving the recipient of the communication or a family member of such person(s);

(c) All written communications to a prospective client for the purpose of obtaining professional employment must be reviewed and either signed by or approved in writing by the lawyer or a lawyer in the firm.

(d) A copy of each written communication, the name and address, to which each such communication was sent; and the means by which each such communication was sent shall be kept by the lawyer or firm for four years after its dissemination.

(e) The provisions of paragraph (b) of this Rule do not apply to a written solicitation communication:

(1) directed to a family member or a person with whom the lawyer had or has an attorney-client relationship;

(2) that is not motivated by or concerned with a particular past occurrence or event or a particular series of past occurrences or events, and also is not motivated by or concerned with the prospective client's specific existing legal problem of which the lawyer is aware;

(3) if the lawyer's use of the communication to secure professional employment was not significantly motivated by a desire for, or by the possibility of obtaining, pecuniary gain; or

(4) that is requested by the prospective client.

(Adopted to be eff. April 1, 1995; on March 31, 1995, the Texas Supreme Court extended the effective date 120 days after the date of judgment of the U.S. District Court in Texans Against Censorship, Inc. v. State Bar of Texas, 888 F.Supp. 1328 (E.D.Tex. 1995).)

COMMENT

1. Rule 7.03 deals with in-person or telephone contact between a lawyer and a prospective client wherein the lawyer seeks professional employment. Rule 7.04 deals with advertisements in the public media by a lawyer seeking professional employment. This Rule deals with written solicitations between a lawyer and a prospective client. Typical examples are letters or other forms of correspondence addressed to a prospective client.

2. Written solicitations raise more concerns than do comparable written advertisements. Being private, they are more difficult to monitor, and for that reason paragraph (d) requires retention for four years of certain information regarding written solicitations. See also Rule 7.07(a). Paragraph (a) addresses such concerns as well as problems stemming from exceptionally outrageous communications such as written solicitations involving fraud, intimidation, or deceptive and misleading claims. Because receipt of multiple solicitations appears to be most pronounced and vexatious in situations involving accident victims, paragraph (b)(7) requires disclosure of the source of information if the solicitation was prompted by a specific occurrence.

3. Because experience has shown that many written solicitations have been intrusive or misleading by reason of being personalized or being disguised as some form of official communication special prohibitions against such practices are necessary. The requirements of paragraph (b) greatly lessen those dangers of deception and harassment.

4. Newsletters or other works published by a lawyer that are not circulated for the purpose of obtaining professional employment are not within the ambit of paragraph (b).

5. In addition to addressing these special problems posed by written solicitations, Rule 7.05 regulates the content of those communications. It does so by incorporating the standards of Rule 7.02 and those of Rule 7.04 that would apply to the written solicitation were it instead a written advertisement in the public media. See paragraphs (a)(2), (3), and (b)(1). In brief, this approach means that, a lawyer may not include or omit anything from a written solicitation unless the lawyer could do so were the communication a written advertisement in the public media, except for those statements or disclaimers required by Rule 7.04(a)–(c). See sub-paragraph (b)(1).

6. Paragraph (e) provides that none of the restrictions in paragraph (b) apply in certain situations because the dangers of deception, harassment, vexation and overreaching are quite low. For example, a written solicitation may be directed to a family member or a present or a former client, or in response to a request by a prospective client. Similarly, a written solicitation may be used in seeking general employment in commercial matters from a bank or other corporation, when there is neither concern with specific existing legal problems nor concern with a particular past event or series of events. All such communications, however, remain subject to Rule 7.02 and paragraphs (h) through (*o*) of Rule 7.04. See sub-paragraph (a)(2).

7. In addition, paragraph (e) allows such communications in situations not involving the lawyer's pecuniary gain. For purposes of these rules, it is presumed that communications made on behalf of a nonprofit legal aid agency, union, or other qualified nonprofit organization are not motivated by a desire for, or by the possibility of obtaining, pecuniary gain, but that presumption may be rebutted.

(Comment adopted by State Bar Board of Directors Jan. 20, 1995.)

RULE 7.06 Prohibited Employment

A lawyer shall not accept or continue employment when the lawyer knows or reasonably should know that that the person who seeks the lawyer's services does so as a result of conduct prohibited by these rules.

(Former Rule 7.03 adopted eff. Jan. 1, 1990; redesignated and amended to be eff. April 1, 1995; on March 31, 1995, the Texas Supreme Court extended the effective date 120 days after the date of judgment of the U.S. District Court in Texans Against Censorship, Inc. v. State Bar of Texas, 888 F.Supp. 1328 (E.D.Tex. 1995).)

COMMENT

Selection of a lawyer by a client often is a result of the advice and recommendation of third parties—relatives, friends, acquaintances, business associates and other lawyers. Although that method of referral is perfectly legitimate, the client is best served if the recommendation is disinterested and informed. All lawyers must guard against creating situations where referral from others is the consequence of some form of prohibited compensation or from some form of false or misleading communication, or by virtue of some other violation of these rules. This prohibition on accepting or continuing employment applies even if the lawyer whose services are involved had no direct or indirect involvement with the underlying violation of these Rules, provided that lawyer knows of the violation. See also Rule 7.03(d), forbidding a lawyer to charge or collect a fee where the misconduct involves violations of Rule 7.03(a), (b), or (c).

(Comment amended by State Bar Board of Directors Jan. 20, 1995.)

RULE 7.07   Filing Requirements for Public Advertisements and Written Solicitations

(a) Except as provided in paragraph (d)of this Rule, a lawyer shall file with the Lawyer Advertisement and Solicitation Review Committee of the State Bar of Texas, either before or concurrently with the mailing or sending of a written solicitation communication:

(1) a copy of the written solicitation communication being sent or to be sent to one or more prospective clients for the purpose of obtaining professional employment, together with a representative sample of the envelopes in which the communications are enclosed; and

(2) a check or money order payable to the State Bar of Texas for the fee set by the Board of Directors. Such fee shall be for the sole purpose of defraying the expense of enforcing the rules related to such solicitations.

(b) Except as provided in paragraph (d) of this Rule, a lawyer shall file with the Lawyer Advertisement and Solicitation Review Committee of the State Bar of Texas, either before or concurrently with the first dissemination of an advertisement in the public media, a copy of that advertisement. The filing shall include:

(1) a copy of the advertisement in the form in which it appears or is or will be disseminated, such as a videotape, an audiotape, a print copy, or a photograph of outdoor advertising;

(2) a production script of the advertisement setting forth all words used and describing in detail the actions, events, scenes, and background sounds used in such advertisement together with a listing of the names and addresses of persons portrayed or heard to speak, if the advertisement is in or will be in a form in which the advertised message is not fully revealed by a print copy or photograph;

(3) a statement of when and where the advertisement has been, is, or will be used; and

(4) a check or money order payable to the State Bar of Texas for the fee set by the Board of Directors. Such fee shall be for the sole purpose of defraying the expense of enforcing the rules related to such advertisements.

(c) A lawyer who desires to secure an advance advisory opinion, concerning compliance of a contemplated written solicitation communication or advertisement may submit to the Lawyer Advertisement and Solicitation Review Committee, not less than thirty (30) days prior to the date of first dissemination, the material specified in paragraph (a) or (b) of this Rule, including the required fee; provided however, it shall not be necessary to submit a videotape if the videotape has not then been prepared and the production script submitted reflects in detail and accurately the actions, events, scenes, and background sounds that will be depicted or contained on such videotapes, when prepared, as well as the narrative transcript of the verbal and printed portions of such advertisement. An advisory opinion of the Lawyer Advertisement and Solicitation Review Committee of noncompliance is not binding in a disciplinary proceeding or disciplinary action but a finding of compliance is binding in favor of the submitting lawyer if the representations, statements, materials, facts and written assurances received in connection therewith are true and are not misleading. The finding constitutes admissible evidence if offered by a party.

(d) The filing requirements of paragraphs (a) and (b) do not extend to any of the following materials

(1) an advertisement in the public media that contains only part or all of the following information, provided the information is not false or misleading:

(i) the name of a lawyer or firm and lawyers associated with the firm, with office addresses, telephone numbers, office and telephone service hours, telecopier numbers, and a designation of the profession such as "attorney," "lawyer," "law office," or "firm";

(ii) the fields of law in which the lawyer or firm specialization and the statements required by Rule 7.04(a) through (c);

(iii) the date of admission of the lawyer or lawyers to the State Bar of Texas, to particular federal courts, and to the bars of other jurisdictions;

(iv) technical and professional licenses granted by this state and other recognized licensing authorities;

(v) foreign language ability;

(vi) fields of law in which one or more lawyers are certified or designated, provided the statement of this information is in compliance with Rule 7.02(a) through (c);

(vii) identification of prepaid or group legal service plans in which the lawyer participates;

(viii) the acceptance or nonacceptance of credit cards;

(ix) any fee for initial consultation and fee schedule;

(x) that the lawyer or firm is a sponsor of a charitable, civic, or community program or event, or is a sponsor of a public service announcement;

(xi) any disclosure or statement required by these rules; and

(xii) any other information specified from time to time in orders promulgated by the Supreme Court of Texas:

(2) an advertisement in the public media that:

(i) identifies one or more lawyers or a firm as a contributor to a specified charity or as a sponsor of a specified charitable, community, or public interest program, activity, or event; and

(ii) contains no information about the lawyers or firm other than name* of the lawyers or firm or both, location of the law offices, and the fact of the sponsorship or contribution;

* So in February 23, 1995 Order.

(3) a listing or entry in a regularly published law list;

(4) an announcement card stating new or changed associations, new offices, or similar changes relating to a lawyer or firm, or a tombstone professional card;

(5) a newsletter mailed only to:

(i) existing or former clients;

(ii) other lawyers or professionals; and

(iii) members of a nonprofit organization that meets the following conditions: the primary purposes of the organization do not include the rendition of legal services; the recommending, furnishing, paying for, or educating persons regarding legal services is incidental and reasonably related the primary purposes of the organization; the organization does not derive a financial benefit from the rendition of legal services by a lawyer; and the person for whom the legal services are rendered, and not the organization, is recognized as the client of the lawyer who is recommended, furnished, or paid by the organization;

(6) a written solicitation communication that is not motivated by or concerned with a particular past occurrence or event or a particular series of past occurrences or events, and also is not motivated by or concerned with the prospective client's specific existing legal problem of which the lawyer is aware;

(7) a written solicitation communication if the lawyer's use of the communication to secure professional employment was not significantly motivated by a desire for, or by the possibility of obtaining, pecuniary gain; or

(8) a written solicitation communication that is requested by the prospective client.

(e) If requested by the Lawyer Advertisement and Solicitation Review Committee, a lawyer shall promptly submit information to substantiate statements or representations made or implied in any advertisement in the public media and/or written solicitation.

(Adopted to be eff. April 1, 1995; on March 31, 1995, the Texas Supreme Court extended the effective date 120 days after the date of judgment of the U.S. District Court in Texans Against Censorship, Inc. v. State Bar of Texas, 888 F.Supp. 1328 (E.D.Tex. 1995).)

COMMENT

1. Rule 7.07 covers the filing requirements for public media advertisements (see Rule 7.04) and written solicitations (see Rule 7.05). Rule 7.07(a) deals with those written solicitations sent by a lawyer to one or more specified prospective clients. Rule 7.07(b) deals with advertisements in the public media. Each provision allows the Bar to charge a fee for reviewing submitted materials, but requires that fee be set solely to defray the expenses of enforcing those provisions.

2. Copies of non-exempt written solicitations or advertisements in the public media must be provided to the Advertising Review Committee of the State Bar of Texas either in advance or concurrently with dissemination, together with the fee required by the State Bar of Texas Board of Directors. Presumably, the Advertising Review Committee will report to the appropriate grievance committee any lawyer whom it finds from the reviewed products has disseminated an advertisement in the public media or written solicitation that violates Rules 7.02, 7.03, 7.04, or 7.05, or, at a minimum, any lawyer whose violation raises a substantial question as to that lawyer's honesty, trustworthiness, or fitness as a lawyer in other respects. See Rule 8.03(a).

3. Paragraphs (a) and (b) do not require that a lawyer submit a copy of each and every written solicitation letter a lawyer sends. If the same form letter is sent to several people, only a representative sample of each form letter, along with a representative sample of the envelopes used to mail the letters, need be filed.

4. A lawyer wishing to do so may secure an advisory opinion from the Advertising Review Committee concerning any proposed advertisement in the public media or any written solicitation in advance of its first use or mailing by complying with Rule 7.07(c). This procedure is intended as a service to those lawyers who want to resolve any possible doubts about their proposed advertisements' or written solicitations' compliance with these Rules before utilizing them. Its use is purely

397

optional. No lawyer is required to obtain advance clearance of any advertisement or written solicitation communication from the State Bar. Although a finding of noncompliance by the Advertising Review Committee is not binding in a disciplinary proceeding, a finding of compliance is binding in favor of the submitting lawyer, as long as the lawyer's presentation to the Advertising Review Committee in connection with that advisory opinion is true and not misleading.

5. Under its Internal Rules and Operating Procedures, the Advertising Review Committee is to complete its evaluations no later than 25 days after the date of receipt of a filing. The only way that the Committee can extend that review period is to: (1) determine that there is reasonable doubt whether the advertisement or written solicitation communication complies with these Rules; (2) conclude that further examination is warranted but cannot be completed within the 25-day period; and (3) advise the lawyer of those determinations in writing within that 25-day period. The Committee's Internal Rules and Operating Procedures also provide that a failure to send such a communication to the lawyer within the 25-day period constitutes approval of the advertisement or written solicitation communication. Consequently, if an attorney submits an advertisement in the public media or written solicitation communication to the Committee for advance approval not less than 30 days prior to the date of first dissemination as required by these Rules, the attorney will receive an assessment of that advertisement or communication before the date of its first intended use.

6. Consistent with the effort to protect the first amendment rights of lawyers while ensuring the right of the public to be free from misleading advertising and the right of the Texas legal profession to maintain its integrity, paragraph (d) exempts certain types of advertisements and written solicitations prepared for the purpose of seeking paid professional employment from the filing requirements of paragraphs (a) and (b). Those types of communications need not be filed at all if they were not prepared to secure paid professional employment.

7. For the most part, the types of exempted advertising listed in subparagraphs (d)(1)–(5) are objective and less likely to result in false, misleading or fraudulent content. Similarly the types of exempted written solicitations listed in subparagraphs (d)(6)–(8) are those found least likely to result in harm to the public. See Rule 7.05(e), and comment 5 to Rule 7.05. The fact that a particular advertisement or written solicitation made by a lawyer is exempted from the filing requirements of this Rule does not exempt a lawyer from the other applicable obligations of these Rules. See generally Rules 7.01 through 7.06.

8. Paragraph (e) does not empower the Advertising Review Committee to seek information from a lawyer to substantiate statements or representations made or implied in advertisements or written communications that do not seek to obtain paid professional employment for that lawyer.

STATE MODIFICATIONS **Fla.Rule 8.4(d)**

(Comment adopted by State Bar Board of Directors Jan. 20, 1995.)

MAINTAINING THE INTEGRITY OF THE PROFESSION

Kansas Rule 8.3

[Kansas amended Model Rule 8.3 as follows:]

RULE 8.3 Reporting Professional Misconduct

(a) **A lawyer having knowledge, of any action, inaction, or conduct which in his or her opinion constitutes misconduct of an attorney under these rules shall inform the appropriate professional authority.**

(b) **A lawyer having knowledge that a judge has committed a violation of applicable rules of judicial conduct that raises a substantial question as to the judge's fitness for office shall inform the appropriate authority.**

(c) **This rule does not require disclosure of information otherwise protected by Rule 1.6. In addition, a lawyer is not required to disclose information concerning any such violation which is discovered through participation in a Substance Abuse Committee, Service to the Bar Committee or similar committee sponsored by a state or local bar association, or by participation in a self-help organization such as Alcoholics Anonymous, through which aid is rendered to another lawyer who may be impaired in the practice of law.**

* * *

KANSAS COMMENT:

Substance Abuse Committees have earned an important position in the organization of bar association activities and render a valuable and important service to the profession and the public. As such, these committees and other recognized self-help organizations, and the lawyers who serve on them should be allowed to function without fear of the requirement to report every violation which might be uncovered during the course of their service. To provide otherwise might inhibit free and open communication by the incapacitated lawyer and result in neglected matters remaining so. In this instance, the Kansas Committee feels that the public is better served by providing a measure of confidentiality to the incapacitated lawyer's communications with those who would help the lawyer in serving clients.

Florida Rule 8.4(d)

[Florida has modified Model Rule 8.4 to read as follows:]

RULE 4–8.4 Misconduct

A lawyer shall not:

* * *

(d) engage in conduct in connection with the practice of law that is prejudicial to the administration of justice, including to knowingly, or through callous indifference, disparage, humiliate, or discriminate against litigants, jurors, witnesses, court personnel, or other lawyers on any basis, including, but not limited to, on account of race, ethnicity, gender, religion, national origin, disability, marital status, sexual orientation, age, socioeconomic status, employment, or physical characteristic;

    * * *

(h) willfully refuse, as determined by a court of competent jurisdiction, to timely pay a child support obligation; or

(i) engage in sexual conduct with a client that exploits the lawyer-client relationship.

Louisiana Rule 8.4

[Louisiana has amended Model Rule 8.4 to add the following:]

RULE 8.4 Misconduct

It is professional misconduct for a lawyer to:

    * * *

(g) Except upon the expressed assertion of a constitutional privilege, to fail to cooperate with the Committee on Professional Responsibility in its investigation of alleged misconduct.

(h) Present, participate in presenting, or threaten to present criminal charges solely to obtain an advantage in a civil matter.

Minnesota Rule 8.4

[Minnesota, one of the first states to include a prohibition against discriminatory conduct by lawyers, has amended Model Rule 8.4 to add the following:]

RULE 8.4 Misconduct

It is professional misconduct for a lawyer to:

* * *

(g) harass a person on the basis of sex, race, age, creed, religion, color, national origin, disability, sexual preference or marital status in connection with a lawyer's professional activities;

(h) commit a discriminatory act, prohibited by federal, state or local statute or ordinance, that reflects adversely on the lawyer's fitness as a lawyer. Whether a discriminatory act reflects adversely on a lawyer's fitness as a lawyer shall be deter-

400

mined after consideration of all the circumstances, including (1) the seriousness of the act, (2) whether the lawyer knew that it was prohibited by statute or ordinance, (3) whether it was part of a pattern of prohibited conduct, and (4) whether it was committed in connection with the lawyer's professional activities.

COMMENT–1991

* * *

Paragraph (g) specifies a particularly egregious type of discriminatory act—harassment on the basis of sex, race, age, creed, religion, color, national origin, disability, sexual preference, or marital status. What constitutes harassment in this context may be determined with reference to antidiscrimination legislation and case law thereunder. This harassment ordinarily involves the active burdening of another, rather than mere passive failure to act properly.

Harassment on the basis of sex, race, age, creed, religion, color, national origin, disability, sexual preference, or marital status may violate either paragraph (g) or paragraph (h). The harassment violates paragraph (g) if the lawyer committed it in connection with the lawyer's professional activities. Harassment, even if not committed in connection with the lawyer's professional activities, violates paragraph (h) if the harassment (1) is prohibited by antidiscrimination legislation and (2) reflects adversely on the lawyer's fitness as a lawyer, determined as specified in paragraph (h).

Paragraph (h) reflects the premise that the concept of human equality lies at the very heart of our legal system. A lawyer whose behavior demonstrates hostility toward or indifference to the policy of equal justice under the law may thereby manifest a lack of character required of members of the legal profession. Therefore, a lawyer's discriminatory act prohibited by statute or ordinance may reflect adversely on his or her fitness as a lawyer even if the unlawful discriminatory act was not committed in connection with the lawyer's professional activities.

Whether an unlawful discriminatory act reflects adversely on fitness as a lawyer is determined after consideration of all relevant circumstances, including the four factors listed in paragraph (h). It is not required that the listed factors be considered equally, nor is the list intended to be exclusive. For example, it would also be relevant that the lawyer reasonably believed that his or her conduct was protected under the state or federal constitution or that the lawyer was acting in a capacity for which the law provides an exemption from civil liability. See, e.g., Minn.Stat. Section 317A.257 (unpaid director or officer of nonprofit organization acting in good faith and not willfully or recklessly).

A lawyer may refuse to comply with an obligation imposed by law upon a good faith belief that no valid obligation exists. The provisions of Rule 1.2(c)(d) concerning a good faith challenge to the validity, scope, meaning or application of the law apply to challenges of legal regulation of the practice of law.

New Jersey Rule 8.4(g)

[New Jersey has modified Model Rule 8.4 to read as follows:]

RULE 8.4 Misconduct

It is professional misconduct for a lawyer to:

* * *

(g) engage, in a professional capacity, in conduct involving discrimination (except employment discrimination unless resulting in a final agency or judicial determination) because of race, color, religion, age, sex, sexual orientation, national origin, marital status, socioeconomic status, or handicap, where the conduct is intended or likely to cause harm.

COMMENT BY SUPREME COURT:

This rule amendment (the addition of paragraph g) is intended to make discriminatory conduct unethical when engaged in by lawyers in their professional capacity. It would, for example, cover activities in the court house, such as a lawyer's treatment of court support staff, as well as conduct more directly related to litigation; activities related to practice outside of the court house, whether or not related to litigation, such as treatment of other attorneys and their staff; bar association and similar activities; and activities in the lawyer's office and firm. Except to the extent that they are closely related to the foregoing, purely private activities are not intended to be covered by this rule amendment, although they may possibly constitute a violation of some other ethical rule. Nor is employment discrimination in hiring, firing, promotion, or partnership status intended to be covered unless it has resulted in either an agency or judicial determination of discriminatory conduct. The Supreme Court believes that existing agencies and courts are better able to deal with such matters, that the disciplinary resources required to investigate and prosecute discrimination in the employment area would be disproportionate to the benefits to the system given remedies available elsewhere, and that limiting ethics proceedings in this area to cases where there has been an adjudication represents a practical resolution of conflicting needs.

"Discrimination" is intended to be construed broadly. It includes sexual harassment, derogatory or demeaning language, and, generally, any conduct towards the named groups that is both harmful and discriminatory.

Case law has already suggested both the area covered by this amendment and the possible direction of future cases. *In re Vincenti,* 114 N.J. 275 (554 A.2d 470) (1989). The Court believes the administration of justice would be better served, however, by the adoption of this general rule than by a case by case development of the scope of the professional obligation.

While the origin of this rule was a recommendation of the Supreme Court's Task Force on Women in the Courts, the Court concluded that the protection, limited to women and minorities in that recommendation, should be expanded. The groups covered in the initial proposed amendment to the rule are the same as those named in Canon 3A(4) of the Code of Judicial Conduct.

Following the initial publication of this proposed subsection (g) and receipt of various comments and suggestions, the Court revised the proposed amendment by making explicit its intent to limit the rule to conduct by attorneys in a professional capacity, to exclude employment discrimination unless adjudicated, to restrict the scope to conduct intended or likely to cause harm, and to include discrimination because of sexual orientation or socioeconomic status, these categories having been proposed by the ABA's Standing Committee on Ethics and Professional Responsibility as additions to the groups now covered in Canon 3A(4) of the New Jersey Code of Judicial Conduct. That Committee has also proposed that judges require attorneys, in proceedings before a judge, refrain from manifesting by words or conduct any bias or prejudice based on any of these categories. See proposed Canon 3A(6). This revision to the RPC further reflects the Court's intent to cover all discrimination where the attorney intends to cause harm such as inflicting emotional distress or obtaining a tactical advantage and not to cover instances when no harm is intended unless its occurrence is likely regardless of intent, e.g., where discriminatory comments or behavior is repetitive. While obviously the language of the rule cannot explicitly cover every instance of possible discriminatory conduct, the Court believes that, along with existing case law, it sufficiently narrows the breadth of the rule to avoid any suggestion that it is overly broad. See, e.g., *In re Vincenti,* 114 N.J. 275 (554 A.2d 470) (1989).

District of Columbia Rule 9.1

[The District of Columbia has added the following provision which has no counterpart in the Model Rules]

NONDISCRIMINATION BY MEMBERS OF THE BAR

RULE 9.1 Discrimination in Employment

A lawyer shall not discriminate against any individual in conditions of employment because of the individual's race, col-

or, religion, national origin, sex, age, marital status, sexual orientation, family responsibility, or physical handicap.

COMMENT:

[1] This provision is modeled after the D.C. Human Rights Act, D.C. Code § 1–2512 (1981), though in some respects more limited in scope. There are also provisions of federal law that contain certain prohibitions on discrimination in employment. The rule is not intended to create ethical obligations that exceed those imposed on a lawyer by applicable law.

* * *

[3] The investigation and adjudication of discrimination claims may involve particular expertise of the kind found within the D.C. Office of Human Rights and the federal Equal Employment Opportunity Commission. Such experience may involve, among other things, methods of analysis of statistical data regarding discrimination claims. These agencies also have, in appropriate circumstances, the power to award remedies to the victims of discrimination, such as reinstatement or back pay, which extend beyond the remedies that are available through the disciplinary process. Remedies available through the disciplinary process include such sanctions as disbarment, suspension, censure, and admonition, but do not extend to monetary awards or other remedies that could alter the employment status to take into account the impact of prior acts of discrimination.

[4] If proceedings are pending before other organizations, such as the D.C. Office of Human Rights or the Equal Employment Opportunity Commission, the processing of complaints by Bar Counsel may be deferred or abated where there is substantial similarity between the complaint filed with Bar Counsel and material allegations involved in such other proceedings. See § 19(d) of Rule XI of the Rules Governing the Bar of the District of Columbia.

STATE MODIFICATIONS

Appendix:

States That Have Adopted a Version of the Model Rules*

Alabama

Alaska

Arizona

Arkansas

Colorado

Connecticut

Delaware

District of Columbia

Florida

Hawaii

Idaho

Illinois

Indiana

Kansas

Kentucky

Louisiana

Maryland

Massachusetts

Michigan

Minnesota

Mississippi

Missouri

Montana

Nevada

New Hampshire

New Jersey

New Mexico

New York (Amended version of code to include many Model Rules provisions)

North Carolina (structure of Rules and Comment but organized under the Canons of the Model Code)

* Source: ABA/BNA Manual on Professional Conduct 01:3 (2000) (State Ethics Rules).

North Dakota
Oklahoma
Pennsylvania
Rhode Island
South Carolina
South Dakota
Texas
Utah
Washington
West Virginia
Wisconsin
Wyoming

OTHER SELECTED STATE STANDARDS, RULES, AND STATUTES

TABLE OF CONTENTS

Introduction

This section presents a more in depth perspective on how two states have chosen to regulate lawyers. The California Rules of Professional Conduct for governing lawyers' conduct differ substantially from the ABA codes of ethics. The California approach to regulating lawyer must also consider the legislature's control over lawyers. This form of regulation is contained in the California Business and Professions Code. Selected sections are reproduced below. We include the Disciplinary Rules of the New York Code of Professional Responsibility as an example of a state that continues to retain a code based upon the ABA Model Code of Professional Responsibility. New York in 1999 extensively modified its code of ethics to include many Model Rules provisions.

CALIFORNIA RULES OF PROFESSIONAL CONDUCT

Approved by Supreme Court August 13, 1992

Effective September 14, 1992

CHAPTER 1. PROFESSIONAL INTEGRITY IN GENERAL

CHAPTER 2. RELATIONSHIP AMONG MEMBERS

CHAPTER 3. PROFESSIONAL RELATIONSHIP WITH CLIENTS

CHAPTER 4. FINANCIAL RELATIONSHIP WITH CLIENTS

CHAPTER 1. PROFESSIONAL INTEGRITY IN GENERAL

Rule 1–100. Rules of Professional Conduct, in General

(A) Purpose and Function.

The following rules are intended to regulate professional conduct of members of the State Bar through discipline. They have been adopted by the Board of Governors of the State Bar of California and approved by the Supreme Court of California pursuant to Business and Professions Code sections 6076 and 6077 to protect the public and to promote respect and confidence in the legal profession. These rules together with any standards adopted by the Board of Governors pursuant to these rules shall be binding upon all members of the State Bar.

For a willful breach of any of these rules, the Board of Governors has the power to discipline members as provided by law.

The prohibition of certain conduct in these rules is not exclusive. Members are also bound by applicable law including the State Bar Act (Bus. & Prof. Code, § 6000 et seq.) and opinions of California courts. Although not binding, opinions of ethics committees in California should be consulted by members for guidance on proper professional conduct. Ethics opinions and rules and standards promulgated by other jurisdictions and bar associations may also be considered.

These rules are not intended to create new civil causes of action. Nothing in these rules shall be deemed to create, augment, diminish, or eliminate any substantive legal duty of lawyers or the non-disciplinary consequences of violating such a duty.

(B) Definitions.

    (1) "Law Firm" means:

(a) two or more lawyers whose activities constitute the practice of law, and who share its profits, expenses, and liabilities; or

(b) a law corporation which employs more than one lawyer; or

(c) a division, department, office, or group within a business entity, which includes more than one lawyer who performs legal services for the business entity; or

(d) a publicly funded entity which employs more than one lawyer to perform legal services.

(2) "Member" means a member of the State Bar of California.

(3) "Lawyer" means a member of the State Bar of California or a person who is admitted in good standing of and eligible to practice before the bar of any United States court or the highest court of the District of Columbia or any state, territory, or insular possession of the United States or is licensed to practice law is, or is admitted in good standing and is eligible to practice before the bar of the highest court of a foreign country or any political subdivision thereof.

(4) "Associate" means an employee or fellow employee who is employed as a lawyer.

(5) "Shareholder" means a shareholder in a professional corporation pursuant to Business and Professions Code section 6160 et seq.

(C) Purpose of Discussions.

Because it is a practical impossibility to convey in black letter form all of the nuances of these disciplinary rules, the comments contained in the Discussions of the rules, while they do not add independent basis for imposing discipline, are intended to provide guidance for interpreting the rules and practicing in compliance with them.

(D) Geographic Scope of Rules.

(1) As to members:

These rules shall govern the activities of members in and outside this state, except as members lawfully practicing outside this state may be specifically required by a jurisdiction in which they are practicing to follow rules of professional conduct different from these rules.

(2) As to lawyers from other jurisdictions who are not members:

These rules shall also govern the activities of lawyers while engaged in the performance of lawyer functions in this state; but nothing contained in these rules shall be deemed to authorize the performance of such functions by such persons in this state except as otherwise permitted by law.

(E) These rules may be cited and referred to as "Rules of Professional Conduct of the State Bar of California."

Discussion:

The Rules of Professional Conduct are intended to establish the standards for members for purposes of discipline. (See *Ames v. State Bar* (1973) 8 Cal.3d 910 [106 Cal.Rptr. 489].) The fact that a member has engaged in conduct that may be contrary to these rules does not automatically give rise to a civil cause of action. (See *Noble v. Sears, Roebuck & Co.* (1973) 33 Cal.App.3d 654 [109 Cal.Rptr. 269]; *Wilhelm v. Pray, Price, Williams & Russell* (1986) 186 Cal.App.3d 1324 [231 Cal. Rptr. 355].) These rules are not intended to supercede existing law relating to members in non-disciplinary contexts. (See, e.g., *Klemm v. Superior Court* (1977) 75 Cal.App.3d 893 [142 Cal.Rptr. 509] (motion for disqualification of counsel due to a conflict of interest); *Academy of California Optometrists, Inc. v. Superior Court* (1975) 51 Cal.App.3d 999 [124 Cal.Rptr. 668] (duty to return client files); *Chronometrics, Inc. v. Sysgen, Inc.* (1980) 110 Cal.App.3d 597 [168 Cal.Rptr. 196] (disqualification of member appropriate remedy for improper communication with adverse party).

Law firm, as defined by subparagraph (B)(1), is not intended to include an association of lawyers who do not share profits, expenses, and liabilities. The subparagraph is not intended to imply that a law firm may include a person who is not a member in violation of the law governing the unauthorized practice of law.

Rule 1–110. Disciplinary Authority of the State Bar

A member shall comply with conditions attached to public or private reprovals or other discipline administered by the State Bar pursuant to Business and Professions Code sections 6077 and 6078 and rule 956, California Rules of Court.

Rule 1–120. Assisting, Soliciting, or Inducing Violations

A member shall not knowingly assist in, solicit, or induce any violation of these rules or the State Bar Act.

Rule 1–200. False Statement Regarding Admission to the State Bar

(A) A member shall not knowingly make a false statement regarding a material fact or knowingly fail to disclose a material fact in connection with an application for admission to the State Bar.

(B) A member shall not further an application for admission to the State Bar of a person whom the member knows to be unqualified in respect to character, education, or other relevant attributes.

(C) This rule shall not prevent a member from serving as counsel of record for an applicant for admission to practice in proceedings related to such admission.

Discussion:

For purposes of rule 1–200 "admission" includes readmission.

Rule 1–300.   Unauthorized Practice of Law

(A) A member shall not aid any person or entity in the unauthorized practice of law.

(B) A member shall not practice law in a jurisdiction where to do so would be in violation of regulations of the profession in that jurisdiction.

Rule 1–310.   Forming a Partnership With a Non-lawyer

A member shall not form a partnership with a person who is not a lawyer if any of the activities of that partnership consist of the practice of law.

Discussion:

Rule 1–310 is not intended to govern members' activities which cannot be considered to constitute the practice of law. It is intended solely to preclude a member from being involved in the practice of law with a person who is not lawyer.

Rule 1–311.   Employment of Disbarred, Suspended, Resigned, or Involuntarily Inactive Member

(A) For purposes of this rule:

  (1) "Employ" means to engage the services of another, including employees, agents, independent contractors and consultants, regardless of whether any compensation is paid;

  (2) "Involuntarily inactive member" means a member who is ineligible to practice law as a result of action taken pursuant to Business and Professions Code sections 6007, 6203(c), or California Rule of Court 958(d); and

  (3) "Resigned member" means a member who has resigned from the State Bar while disciplinary charges are pending.

(B) A member shall not employ, associate professionally with, or aid a person the member knows or reasonably should know is a disbarred, suspended, resigned, or involuntarily inactive member to perform the following on behalf of the member's client:

  (1) Render legal consultation or advice to the client;

  (2) Appear on behalf of a client in any hearing or proceeding or before any judicial officer, arbitrator, mediator, court, public agency, referee, magistrate, commissioner, or hearing officer;

  (3) Appear as a representative of the client at a deposition or other discovery matter;

(4) Negotiate or transact any matter for or on behalf of the client with third parties;

(5) Receive, disburse or otherwise handle the client's funds; or

(6) Engage in activities which constitute the practice of law.

(C) A member may employ, associate professionally with, or aid a disbarred, suspended, resigned, or involuntarily inactive member to perform research, drafting or clerical activities, including but not limited to:

(1) Legal work of a preparatory nature, such as legal research, the assemblage of data and other necessary information, drafting of pleadings, briefs, and other similar documents;

(2) Direct communication with the client or third parties regarding matters such as scheduling, billing, updates, confirmation of receipt or sending of correspondence and messages; or

(3) Accompanying an active member in attending a deposition or other discovery matter for the limited purpose of providing clerical assistance to the active member who will appear as the representative of the client.

(D) Prior to or at the time of employing a person the member knows or reasonably should know is a disbarred, suspended, resigned, or involuntarily inactive member, the member shall serve upon the State Bar written notice of the employment, including a full description of such person's current bar status. The written notice shall also list the activities prohibited in paragraph (B) and state that the disbarred, suspended, resigned, or involuntarily inactive member will not perform such activities. The member shall serve similar written notice upon each client on whose specific matter such person will work, prior to or at the time of employing such person to work on the client's specific matter. The member shall obtain proof of service of the client's written notice and shall retain such proof and a true and correct copy of the client's written notice for two years following termination of the member's employment with the client.

(E) A member may, without client or State Bar notification, employ a disbarred, suspended, resigned or involuntarily inactive member whose sole function is to perform office physical plant or equipment maintenance, courier or delivery services, catering, reception, typing or transcription, or other similar support activities.

(F) Upon termination of the disbarred, suspended, resigned, or involuntarily inactive member, the member shall promptly serve upon the State Bar written notice of the termination.

Discussion

For discussion of the activities that constitute the practice of law, see *Farnham v. State Bar* (1976) 17 Cal.3d 605 [131 Cal.Rptr. 611];

Bluestein v. State Bar (1974) 13 Cal.3d 162 [118 Cal.Rptr. 175]; *Baron v. City of Los Angeles* (1970) 2 Cal.3d 535 [86 Cal.Rptr. 673]; *Crawford v. State Bar* (1960) 54 Cal.2d 659 [7 Cal.Rptr. 746]; *People v. Merchants Protective Corporation* (1922) 189 Cal. 531, 535 [209 P. 363]; *People v. Landlords Professional Services* (1989) 215 Cal.App.3d 1599 [264 Cal. Rptr. 548]; and *People v. Sipper* (1943) 61 Cal.App.2d Supp. 844 [142 P.2d 960].)

Paragraph (D) is not intended to prevent or discourage a member from fully discussing with the client the activities that will be performed by the disbarred, suspended, resigned, or involuntarily inactive member on the client's matter. If a member's client is an organization, then the written notice required by paragraph (D) shall be served upon the highest authorized officer, employee, or constituent overseeing the particular engagement. (See rule 3–600.)

Nothing in rule 1–311 shall be deemed to limit or preclude any activity engaged in pursuant to rules 983, 983.1, 983.2, and 988 of the California Rules of Court, or any local rule of a federal district court concerning admission pro hac vice.

Rule 1–320. Financial Arrangements With Non-lawyers

(A) Neither a member nor a law firm shall directly or indirectly share legal fees with a person who is not a lawyer, except that:

(1) An agreement between a member and a law firm, partner, or associate may provide for the payment of money after the member's death to the member's estate or to one or more specified persons over a reasonable period of time; or

(2) A member or law firm undertaking to complete unfinished legal business of a deceased member may pay to the estate of the deceased member or other person legally entitled thereto that proportion of the total compensation which fairly represents the services rendered by the deceased member;

(3) A member or law firm may include non-member employees in a compensation, profit-sharing, or retirement plan even though the plan is based in whole or in part on a profit-sharing arrangement, if such plan does not circumvent these rules or Business and Professions Code section 6000 et seq.; or

(4) A member may pay a prescribed registration, referral, or participation fee to a lawyer referral service established, sponsored, and operated in accordance with the State Bar of California's Minimum Standards for a Lawyer Referral Service in California.

(B) A member shall not compensate, give, or promise anything of value to any person or entity for the purpose of recommending or securing employment of the member or the member's law firm by a client, or as a reward for having made a recommendation resulting in employment of the member or the member's law firm by a client. A member's offering of or giving a gift or gratuity to any person or entity having made a recommendation resulting in the employment of the member or the member's law firm shall not of itself violate this rule, provided that the gift or gratuity was not offered or given in consideration of any promise, agreement, or understanding that such a gift or gratuity would be forthcoming or that referrals would be made or encouraged in the future.

(C) A member shall not compensate, give, or promise anything of value to any representative of the press, radio, television, or other communication medium in anticipation of or in return for publicity of the member, the law firm, or any other member as such in a news item, but the incidental provision of food or beverage shall not of itself violate this rule.

Discussion:

Rule 1–320(C) is not intended to preclude compensation to the communications media in exchange for advertising the member's or law firm's availability for professional employment.

Rule 1–400. Advertising and Solicitation

(A) For purposes of this rule, "communication" means any message or offer made by or on behalf of a member concerning the availability for professional employment of a member or a law firm directed to any former, present, or prospective client, including but not limited to the following:

(1) Any use of firm name, trade name, fictitious name, or other professional designation of such member or law firm; or

(2) Any stationery, letterhead, business card, sign, brochure, or other comparable written material describing such member, law firm, or lawyers; or

(3) Any advertisement (regardless of medium) of such member or law firm directed to the general public or any substantial portion thereof; or

(4) Any unsolicited correspondence from a member or law firm directed to any person or entity.

(B) For purposes of this rule, a "solicitation" means any communication:

(1) Concerning the availability for professional employment of a member or a law firm in which a significant motive is pecuniary gain; and

(2) Which is;

(a) delivered in person or by telephone, or

(b) directed by any means to a person known to the sender to be represented by counsel in a matter which is a subject of the communication.

(C) A solicitation shall not be made by or on behalf of a member or law firm to a prospective client with whom the member or law firm has no family or prior professional relationship, unless the solicitation is protected from abridgment by the Constitution of the United States or by the Constitution of the State of California. A solicitation to a former or present client in the discharge of a member's or law firm's professional duties is not prohibited.

(D) A communication or a solicitation (as defined herein) shall not:

    (1) Contain any untrue statement; or

    (2) Contain any matter, or present or arrange any matter in a manner or format which is false, deceptive, or which tends to confuse, deceive, or mislead the public; or

    (3) Omit to state any fact necessary to make the statements made, in the light of circumstances under which they are made, not misleading to the public; or

    (4) Fail to indicate clearly, expressly, or by context, that it is a communication or solicitation, as the case may be; or

    (5) Be transmitted in any manner which involves intrusion, coercion, duress, compulsion, intimidation, threats, or vexatious or harassing conduct.

    (6) State that a member is a "certified specialist" unless the member holds a current certificate as a specialist issued by the Board of Legal Specialization, or any other entity accredited by the State Bar to designate specialists pursuant to standards adopted by the Board of Governors, and states the complete name of the entity which granted certification.

(E) The Board of Governors of the State Bar shall formulate and adopt standards as to communications which will be presumed to violate this rule 1–400. The standards shall only be used as presumptions affecting the burden of proof in disciplinary proceedings involving alleged violations of these rules. "Presumption affecting the burden of proof" means that presumption defined in Evidence Code sections 605 and 606. Such standards formulated and adopted by the Board, as from time to time amended, shall be effective and binding on all members.

(F) A member shall retain for two years a true and correct copy or recording of any communication made by written or electronic media. Upon written request, the member shall make any such copy or recording available to the State Bar, and, if requested, shall provide to the State Bar evidence to support any factual or objective claim contained in the communication.

Standards:

Pursuant to Rule 1–400(E) the Board of Governors of the State Bar has adopted the following standards effective May 27, 1989 as forms of "communication" defined in rule 1–400(A) which are presumed to be in violation of Rule 1–400:

    (1) A "communication" which contains guarantees, warranties, or predictions regarding the result of the representation.

    (2) A "communication" which contains testimonials about or endorsements of a member unless such communication also con-

tains an express disclaimer such as "this testimonial or endorsement does not constitute a guarantee, warranty, or prediction regarding the outcome of your legal matter."

(3) A "communication" which is delivered to a potential client whom the member knows or should reasonably know is in such a physical, emotional, or mental state that he or she would not be expected to exercise reasonable judgment as to the retention of counsel.

(4) A "communication" which is transmitted at the scene of an accident or at or en route to a hospital, emergency care center, or other health care facility.

(5) A "communication," except professional announcements, seeking professional employment for pecuniary gain, which is transmitted by mail or equivalent means which does not bear the word "Advertisement," "Newsletter" or words of similar import in 12 point print on the first page. If such communication, including firm brochures, newsletters, recent legal development advisories, and similar materials, is transmitted in an envelope, the envelope shall bear the word "Advertisement," "Newsletter" or words of similar import on the outside thereof.*

* Amended, effective May 11, 1994.

(6) A "communication" in the form of a firm name, trade name, fictitious name, or other professional designation which states or implies a relationship between any member in private practice and a government agency or instrumentality or a public or non-profit legal services organization.

(7) A "communication" in the form of a firm name, trade name, fictitious name, or other professional designation which states or implies that a member has a relationship to any other lawyer or a law firm as a partner or associate, or officer or shareholder pursuant to Business and Professions Code sections 6160–6172 unless such relationship in fact exists.

(8) A "communication" which states or implies that a member or law firm is "of counsel" to another lawyer or a law firm unless the former has a relationship with the latter (other than as a partner or associate, or officer or shareholder pursuant to Business and Professions Code sections 6160–6172) which is close, personal, continuous, and regular.

(9) A "communication" in the form of a firm name, trade name, fictitious name, or other professional designation used by a member or law firm in private practice which differs materially from any other such designation used by such member or law firm at the same time in the same community.

(10) A "communication" which implies that the member or law firm is participating in a lawyer referral service which has been certified by the State Bar of California or as having satisfied the Minimum Standards for Lawyer Referral Services in California, when that is not the case.

(11) [Repealed eff. June 1, 1997.] A "communication" which states or implies that a member is a "certified specialist" unless such communication also states the complete name of the entity which granted the certification as a specialist.

(12) A "communication," except professional announcements, in the form of an advertisement primarily directed to seeking professional employment primarily for pecuniary gain transmitted to the general public or any substantial portion thereof by mail or equivalent means or by means of television, radio, newspaper, magazine or other form of commercial mass media which does not state the name of the member responsible for the communication. When the communication is made on behalf of a law firm, the communication shall state the name of at least one member responsible for it.**

** Added, effective May 11, 1994.

(13) A "communication" which contains a dramatization unless such communication contains a disclaimer which states "this is a dramatization" or words of similar import.*

(14) A "communication" which states or implies "no fee without recovery" unless such communication also expressly discloses whether or not the client will be liable for costs.*

(15) A "communication" which states or implies that a member is able to provide legal services in a language other than English unless the member can actually provide legal services in such language or the communication also states in the language of the communication (a) the employment title of the person who speaks such language and (b) that the person is not a member of the State Bar of California, if that is the case.*

(16) An unsolicited "communication" transmitted to the general public or any substantial portion thereof primarily directed to seeking professional employment primarily for pecuniary gain which sets forth a specific fee or range of fees for a particular service where, in fact, the member charges a greater fee than advertised in such communication within a period of 90 days following dissemination of such communication, unless such communication expressly specifies a shorter period of time regarding the advertised fee. Where the communication is published in the classified or "yellow pages" section of telephone, business or legal directories or in other media not published more frequently than once a year, the member shall conform to the advertised fee for a period of one year from initial publication, unless such communication expressly specifies a shorter period of time regarding the advertised fee.*

Rule 1–500. Agreements Restricting a Member's Practice

(A) A member shall not be a party to or participate in offering or making an agreement, whether in connection with the settlement of a lawsuit or otherwise, if the agreement restricts the right of a member to practice law, except that this rule shall not prohibit such an agreement which:

(1) Is a part of an employment, shareholders' or partnership agreement among members provided the restrictive agreement does not survive the termination of the employment, shareholder, or partnership relationship; or

(2) Requires payments to a member upon the member's retirement from the practice of law.

(3) Is authorized by Business and Professions Code Sections 6092.5, subdivision (i) on 6093.

(B) A member shall not be a party to or participate in offering or making an agreement which precludes the reporting of a violation of these rules.

Discussion:

Paragraph (A) makes it clear that the practice, in connection with settlement agreements, of proposing that a member refrain from representing other clients in similar litigation, is prohibited. Neither counsel may demand or suggest such provisions nor may opposing counsel accede or agree to such provisions.

Paragraph (A) permits a restrictive covenant in a law corporation, partnership, or employment agreement. The law corporation shareholder, partner, or associate may agree not to have a separate practice during the existence of the relationship; however, upon termination of the relationship (whether voluntary or involuntary), the member is free to practice law without any contractual restriction except in the case of retirement from the active practice of law.

Rule 1–600. Legal Service Programs

(A) A member shall not participate in a nongovernmental program activity, or organization furnishing, recommending, or paying for legal services, which allows any third person or organization to interfere with the member's independence of professional judgment, or with the client-lawyer relationship, or allows unlicensed persons to practice law, or allows any third person or organization to receive directly or indirectly any part of the consideration paid to the member except as permitted by these rules, or otherwise violates the State Bar Act or these rules.

(B) The Board of Governors of the State Bar shall formulate and adopt Minimum Standards for Lawyer Referral Services, which, as from time to time amended, shall be binding on members.

Discussion:

The participation of a member in a lawyer referral service established, sponsored, supervised, and operated in conformity with the

Minimum Standards for a Lawyer Referral Service in California is encouraged and is not, of itself, a violation of these rules.

Rule 1–600 is not intended to override any contractual agreement or relationship between insurers and insureds regarding the provision of legal services.

Rule 1–600 is not intended to apply to the activities of a public agency responsible for providing legal services to a government or to the public.

For purposes of paragraph (A), "a nongovernmental program, activity, or organization" includes, but is not limited to group, prepaid, and voluntary legal service programs, activities, or organizations.

Rule 1–700. Member as Candidate for Judicial Office

(A) A member who is a candidate for judicial office in California shall comply with Canon 5 of the Code of Judicial Ethics.

(B) For purposes of this rule, "candidate for judicial office" means a member seeking judicial office by election. The determination of when a member is a candidate for judicial office is defined in the terminology section of the California Code of Judicial Ethics. A member's duty to comply with paragraph (A) shall end when the member announces withdrawal of the member's candidacy or when the results of the election are final, whichever occurs first.

Discussion

Nothing in rule 1–700 shall be deemed to limit the applicability of any rule or law.

(Approved by order of the Supreme Court, effective November 21, 1997.)

CHAPTER 2. RELATIONSHIP AMONG MEMBERS

Rule 2–100. Communication With a Represented Party

(A) While representing a client, a member shall not communicate directly or indirectly about the subject of the representation with a party the member knows to be represented by another lawyer in the matter, unless the member has the consent of the other lawyer.

(B) For purposes of this rule, a "party" includes:

(1) An officer, director, or managing agent of a corporation or association, and a partner or managing agent of a partnership; or

(2) An association member or an employee of an association, corporation, or partnership, if the subject of the communication is any act or omission of such person in connection with the matter which may be binding upon or imputed to the organization for purposes of civil or criminal liability or whose statement may constitute an admission on the part of the organization.

(C) This rule shall not prohibit:

(1) Communications with a public officer, board, committee, or body;

(2) Communications initiated by a party seeking advice or representation from an independent lawyer of the party's choice; or

(3) Communications otherwise authorized by law.

Discussion:

Rule 2–100 is intended to control communications between a member and persons the member knows to be represented by counsel unless a statutory scheme or case law will override the rule. There are a number of express statutory schemes which authorize communications between a member and person who would otherwise be subject to this rule. These statutes protect a variety of other rights such as the right of employees to organize and to engage in collective bargaining, employee health and safety, or equal employment opportunity. Other applicable law also includes the authority of government prosecutors and investigators to conduct criminal investigations, as limited by the relevant decisional law.

Rule 2–100 is not intended to prevent the parties themselves from communicating with respect to the subject matter of the representation, and nothing in the rule prevents a member from advising the client that such communication can be made. Moreover, the rule does not prohibit a member who is also a party to a legal matter from directly or indirectly communicating on his or her own behalf with a represented party. Such a member has independent rights as a party which should not be abrogated because of his or her professional status. To prevent any possible abuse in such situations, the counsel for the opposing party may advise that party (1) about the risks and benefits of communications with a lawyer-party, and (2) not to accept or engage in communications with the lawyer-party.

Rule 2–100 also addresses the situation in which member A is contacted by an opposing party who is represented and, because of dissatisfaction with that party's counsel, seeks A's independent advice. Since A is employed by the opposition, the member cannot give independent advice.

As used in paragraph (A), "the subject of the representation," "matter," and "party" are not limited to a litigation context.

Paragraph (B) is intended to apply only to persons employed at the time of the communication. See *Triple A Machine Shop, Inc. v. State of California* (1989) 213 Cal.App.3d 131 [261 Cal.Rptr. 493].

Subparagraph (C)(2) is intended to permit a member to communicate with a party seeking to hire new counsel or to obtain a second opinion. A member contacted by such a party continues to be bound by other Rules of Professional Conduct. (See, e.g., rules 1–400 and 3–310.)

Rule 2–200. Financial Arrangements Among Lawyers

(A) A member shall not divide a fee for legal services with a lawyer who is not a partner of, associate of, or shareholder with the member unless:

   (1) The client has consented in writing thereto after a full disclosure has been made in writing that a division of fees will be made and the terms of such division; and

   (2) The total fee charged by all lawyers is not increased solely by reason of the provision for division of fees and is not unconscionable as that term is defined in rule 4–200.

(B) Except as permitted in paragraph (A) of this rule or rule 2–300, a member shall not compensate, give, or promise anything of value to any lawyer for the purpose of recommending or securing employment of the member or the member's law firm by a client, or as a reward for having made a recommendation resulting in employment of the member or the member's law firm by a client. A member's offering of or giving a gift or gratuity to any lawyer who has made a recommendation resulting in the employment of the member or the member's law firm shall not of itself violate this rule, provided that the gift or gratuity was not offered in consideration of any promise, agreement, or understanding that such a gift or gratuity would be forthcoming or that referrals would be made or encouraged in the future.

Rule 2–300. Sale or Purchase of a Law Practice of a Member, Living or Deceased

All or substantially all of the law practice of a member, living or deceased, including goodwill, may be sold to another member or law firm subject to all the following conditions:

(A) Fees charged to clients shall not be increased solely by reason of such sale.

(B) If the sale contemplates the transfer of responsibility for work not yet completed or responsibility for client files or information protected by Business and Professions Code section 6068, subdivision (e), then;

   (1) if the seller is deceased, has a conservator or other person acting in a representative capacity, and no member has been appointed to act for the seller pursuant to Business and Professions Code section 6180.5, then prior to the transfer;

      (a) the purchaser shall cause a written notice to be given to the client stating that the interest in the law practice is being transferred to the purchaser; that the client has the right to retain other counsel; that the client may take possession of any client papers and property, as required by rule 3–700(D); and that if no response is received to the notification within 90 days of the sending of such notice, or in the event the client's rights would be prejudiced by a failure to act during that time, the purchaser may act on behalf of the client until otherwise notified by the client. Such notice shall comply with the requirements as set forth in rule 1–400(D) and any provisions relating to attorney-client fee arrangements, and

(b) the purchaser shall obtain the written consent of the client provided that such consent shall be presumed until otherwise notified by the client if no response is received to the notification specified in subparagraph (a) within 90 days of the date of the sending of such notification to the client's last address as shown on the records of the seller, or the client's rights would be prejudiced by a failure to act during during such 90-day period.

(2) in all other circumstances, not less than 90 days prior to the transfer;

(a) the seller, or the member appointed to act for the seller pursuant to Business and Professions Code section 6180.5 shall cause a written notice to be given to the client stating that the interest in the law practice is being transferred to the purchaser; that the client has the right to retain other counsel; that the client may take possession of any client papers and property, as required by rule 3–700(D); and that if no response is received to the notification within 90 days of the sending of such notice, the purchaser may act on behalf of the client until otherwise notified by the client. Such notice shall comply with the requirements as set forth in rule 1–400(D) and any provisions relating to attorney-client fee arrangements, and

(b) the seller, or the member appointed to act for the seller pursuant to Business and Professions Code section 6180.5 shall obtain the written consent of the client prior to the transfer provided that such consent shall be presumed until otherwise notified by the client if no response is received to the notification specified in subparagraph (a) within 90 days of the date of the sending of such notification to the client's last address as shown on the records of the seller.

(C) If substitution is required by the rules of a tribunal in which a matter is pending, all steps necessary to substitute a member shall be taken.

(D) All activity of a purchaser or potential purchaser under this rule shall be subject to compliance with rules 3–300 and 3–310 where applicable.

(E) Confidential information shall not be disclosed to a nonmember in connection with a sale under this rule.

(F) Admission to or retirement from a law partnership or law corporation, retirement plans and similar arrangements, or sale of tangible assets of a law practice shall not be deemed a sale or purchase under this rule.

Discussion:

Paragraph (A) is intended to prohibit the purchaser from charging the former clients of the seller a higher fee than the purchaser is charging his or her existing clients.

"All or substantially all of the law practice of a member" means, for purposes of rule 2–300, that, for example, a member may retain one or two clients who have such a longstanding personal and professional relationship with the member that transfer of those clients' files is not feasible. Conversely, rule 2–300 is not intended to authorize the sale of a law practice in a piecemeal fashion except as may be required by subparagraph (B)(1)(a) or paragraph (D).

Transfer of individual client matters, where permitted, is governed by rule 2–200. Payment of a fee to a non-lawyer broker for arranging the sale or purchase of a law practice is governed by rule 1–320.

Rule 2–400. Prohibited Discriminatory Conduct in a Law Practice

(A) For purposes of this rule:

    (1) "law practice" includes sole practices, law partnerships, law corporations, corporate and governmental legal departments, and other entities which employ members to practice law;

    (2) "knowingly permit" means a failure to advocate corrective action where the member knows of a discriminatory policy or practice which results in the unlawful discrimination prohibited in paragraph (B); and

    (3) "unlawfully" and "unlawful" shall be determined by reference to applicable state or federal statutes or decisions making unlawful discrimination in employment and in offering goods and services to the public.

(B) In the management or operation of a law practice, a member shall not unlawfully discriminate or knowingly permit unlawful discrimination on the basis of race, national origin, sex, sexual orientation, religion, age or disability in:

    (1) hiring, promoting, discharging or otherwise determining the conditions of employment of any person; or

    (2) accepting or terminating representation of any client.

(C) No disciplinary investigation or proceeding may be initiated by the State Bar against a member under this rule unless and until a tribunal of competent jurisdiction, other than a disciplinary tribunal, shall have first adjudicated a complaint of alleged discrimination and found that unlawful conduct occurred. Upon such adjudication, the tribunal finding or verdict shall then be admissible evidence of the occurrence or non-occurrence of the alleged discrimination in any disciplinary proceeding initiated under this rule. In order for discipline to be imposed under this rule, however, the finding of unlawfulness must be upheld and final after appeal, the time for filing an appeal must have expired, or the appeal must have been dismissed.

Discussion:

In order for discriminatory conduct to be actionable under this rule, it must first be found to be unlawful by an appropriate civil administrative or judicial tribunal under applicable state or federal law. Until there is a finding of civil unlawfulness, there is no basis for disciplinary action under this rule.

A complaint of misconduct based on this rule may be filed with the State Bar following a finding of unlawfulness in the first instance even though that finding is thereafter appealed.

A disciplinary investigation or proceeding for conduct coming within this rule may be initiated and maintained, however, if such conduct warrants discipline under California Business and Professions Code sections 6106 and 6068, the California Supreme Court's inherent authority to impose discipline, or other disciplinary standard.
Adopted, eff. March 1, 1994.

CHAPTER 3. PROFESSIONAL RELATIONSHIP WITH CLIENTS

Rule 3–110. Failing to Act Competently

(A) A member shall not intentionally, recklessly, or repeatedly fail to perform legal services with competence.

(B) For purposes of this rule, "competence" in any legal service shall mean to apply the 1) diligence, 2) learning and skill, and 3) mental, emotional, and physical ability reasonably necessary for the performance of such service.

(C) If a member does not have sufficient learning and skill when the legal service is undertaken, the member may nonetheless perform such services competently by 1) associating with or, where appropriate, professionally consulting another lawyer reasonably believed to be competent, or 2) by acquiring sufficient learning and skill before performance is required.

Discussion:

The duties set forth in rule 3–110 include the duty to supervise the work of subordinate attorney and non-attorney employees or agents. (See, e.g., *Waysman v. State Bar* (1986) 41 Cal.3d 452; *Trousil v. State Bar* (1985) 38 Cal.3d 337, 342 [211 Cal.Rptr. 525]; *Palomo v. State Bar*

(1984) 36 Cal.3d 785 [205 Cal.Rptr. 834]; *Crane v. State Bar* (1981) 30 Cal.3d 117, 122; *Black v. State Bar* (1972) 7 Cal.3d 676, 692 [103 Cal.Rptr. 288; 499 P.2d 968]; *Vaughn v. State Bar* (1972) 6 Cal.3d 847, 857–858 [100 Cal.Rptr. 713; 494 P.2d 1257]; *Moore v. State Bar* (1964) 62 Cal.2d 74, 81 [41 Cal.Rptr. 161; 396 P.2d 577].)

In an emergency a lawyer may give advice or assistance in a matter in which the lawyer does not have the skill ordinarily required where referral to or consultation with another lawyer would be impractical. Even in an emergency, however, assistance should be limited to that reasonably necessary in the circumstances.

Rule 3–120. Sexual Relations With Client

(A) For purposes of this rule, "sexual relations" means sexual intercourse or the touching of an intimate part of another person for the purpose of sexual arousal, gratification, or abuse.

(B) A member shall not:

    (1) Require or demand sexual relations with a client incident to or as a condition of any professional representation; or

    (2) Employ coercion, intimidation, or undue influence in entering into sexual relations with a client; or

    (3) Continue representation of a client with whom the member has sexual relations if such sexual relations cause the member to perform legal services incompetently in violation of rule 3–110.

(C) Paragraph (B) shall not apply to sexual relations between members and their spouses or to ongoing consensual sexual relationships which predate the initiation of the lawyer-client relationship.

(D) Where a lawyer in a firm has sexual relations with a client but does not participate in the representation of that client, the lawyers in the firm shall not be subject to discipline under this rule solely because of the occurrence of such sexual relations.

Discussion:

Rule 3–120 is intended to prohibit sexual exploitation by a lawyer in the course of a professional representation. Often, based upon the nature of the underlying representation, a client exhibits great emotional vulnerability and dependence upon the advice and guidance of counsel. Attorneys owe the utmost duty of good faith and fidelity to clients. (See, e.g., Greenbaum v. State Bar (1976) 15 Cal.3d 893, 903 [126 Cal.Rptr. 785]; Alkow v. State Bar (1971) 3 Cal.3d 924, 935 [92 Cal.Rptr. 279]; Cutler v. State Bar (1969) 71 Cal.2d 241, 251 [78 Cal.Rptr. 172]; Clancy v. State Bar (1969) 71 Cal.2d 140, 146 [77 Cal.Rptr. 657].) The relationship between an attorney and client is a fiduciary relationship of the very highest character and all dealings between an attorney and client that are beneficial to the attorney will be closely scrutinized with the utmost strictness for unfairness. (See, e.g., Giovanazzi v. State Bar

(1980) 28 Cal.3d 465, 472 [169 Cal.Rptr. 581]; Benson v. State Bar (1975) 13 Cal.3d 581, 586 [119 Cal.Rptr. 297]; Lee v. State Bar (1970) 2 Cal.3d 927, 939 [88 Cal.Rptr. 361]; Clancy v. State Bar (1969) 71 Cal.2d 140, 146 [77 Cal.Rptr. 657].) Where attorneys exercise undue influence over clients or take unfair advantage of clients, discipline is appropriate. (See, e.g., Magee v. State Bar (1962) 58 Cal.2d 423 [24 Cal.Rptr. 839]; Lantz v. State Bar (1931) 212 Cal. 213 [298 P. 497].) In all client matters, a member is advised to keep clients' interests paramount in the course of the member's representation.

For purposes of this rule, if the client is an organization, any individual overseeing the representation shall be deemed to be the client. (See rule 3–600.)

Although paragraph (C) excludes representation of certain clients from the scope of rule 3–120, such exclusion is not intended to preclude the applicability of other Rules of Professional Conduct, including rule 3–110.

Rule 3–200. Prohibited Objectives of Employment

A member shall not seek, accept, or continue employment if the member knows or should know that the objective of such employment is:
(A) To bring an action, conduct a defense, assert a position in litigation, or take an appeal, without probable cause and for the purpose of harassing or maliciously injuring any person; or

(B) To present a claim or defense in litigation that is not warranted under existing law, unless it can be supported by a good faith argument for an extension, modification, or reversal of such existing law.

Rule 3–210. Advising the Violation of Law

A member shall not advise the violation of any law, rule, or ruling of a tribunal unless the member believes in good faith that such law, rule, or ruling is invalid. A member may take appropriate steps in good faith to test the validity of any law, rule, or ruling of a tribunal.

Discussion:

Rule 3–210 is intended to apply not only to the prospective conduct of a client but also to the interaction between the member and client and to the specific legal service sought by the client from the member. An example of the former is the handling of physical evidence of a crime in the possession of the client and offered to the member. (See *People v. Meredith* (1981) 29 Cal.3d 682 [175 Cal.Rptr. 612].) An example of the latter is a request that the member negotiate the return of stolen property in exchange for the owner's agreement not to report the theft to the police or prosecutorial authorities. (See *People v. Pic'l* (1982) 31 Cal.3d 731 [183 Cal.Rptr. 685].)

Rule 3-300. Avoiding Interests Adverse to a Client

A member shall not enter into a business transaction with a client; or knowingly acquire an ownership, possessory, security, or other pecuniary interest adverse to a client, unless each of the following requirements has been satisfied:

(A) The transaction or acquisition and its terms are fair and reasonable to the client and are fully disclosed and transmitted in writing to the client in a manner which should reasonably have been understood by the client; and

(B) The client is advised in writing that the client may seek the advice of an independent lawyer of the client's choice and is given a reasonable opportunity to seek that advice; and

(C) The client thereafter consents in writing to the terms of the transaction or the terms of the acquisition.

Discussion:

Rule 3-300 is not intended to apply to the agreement by which the member is retained by the client, unless the agreement confers on the member an ownership, possessory, security, or other pecuniary interest adverse to the client. Such an agreement is governed, in part, by rule 4-200.

Rule 3-300 is not intended to apply where the member and client each make an investment on terms offered to the general public or a significant portion thereof. For example, rule 3-300 is not intended to apply where A, a member, invests in a limited partnership syndicated by a third party. B, A's client, makes the same investment. Although A and B are each investing in the same business, A did not enter into the transaction "with" B for the purposes of the rule.

Rule 3-300 is intended to apply where the member wishes to obtain an interest in client's property in order to secure the amount of the member's past due or future fees.

Rule 3-310. Avoiding the Representation of Adverse Interests

(A) For purposes of this rule:

    (1) "Disclosure" means informing the client or former client of the relevant circumstances and of the actual and reasonably foreseeable adverse consequences to the client or former client;

    (2) "Informed written consent" means the client's or former client's written agreement to the representation following written disclosure;

    (3) "Written" means any writing as defined in Evidence Code section 250.

(B) A member shall not accept or continue representation of a client without providing written disclosure to the client where:

(1) The member has a legal, business, financial, professional, or personal relationship with a party or witness in the same matter; or

(2) The member knows or reasonably should know that:

    (a) the member previously had a legal, business, financial, professional, or personal relationship with a party or witness in the same matter; and

    (b) the previous relationship would substantially affect the member's representation; or

(3) The member has or had a legal, business, financial, professional, or personal relationship with another person or entity the member knows or reasonably should know would be affected substantially by resolution of the matter; or

(4) The member has or had a legal, business, financial, or professional interest in the subject matter of the representation.

(C) A member shall not, without the informed written consent of each client:

    (1) Accept representation of more than one client in a matter in which the interests of the clients potentially conflict; or

    (2) Accept or continue, representation of more than one client in a matter in which the interests of the clients actually conflict; or

    (3) Represent a client in a matter and at the same time in a separate matter accept as a client a person or entity whose interest in the first matter is adverse to the client in the first matter.

(D) A member who represents two or more clients shall not enter into an aggregate settlement of the claims of or against the clients without the informed written consent of each client.

(E) A member shall not, without the informed written consent of the client or former client, accept employment adverse to the client or former client where, by reason of the representation of the client or former client, the member has obtained confidential information material to the employment.

(F) A member shall not accept compensation for representing a client from one other than the client unless:

    (1) There is no interference with the member's independence of professional judgment or with the client-lawyer relationship; and

    (2) Information relating to representation of the client is protected as required by Business and Professions Code section 6068, subdivision (e); and

    (3) The member obtains the client's informed written consent, provided that no disclosure or consent is required if:

        (a) such nondisclosure is otherwise authorized by law; or

        (b) the member is rendering legal services on behalf of any public agency which provides legal services to other public agencies or the public.

Discussion:

Rule 3–310 is not intended to prohibit a member from representing parties having antagonistic positions on the same legal question that has arisen in different cases, unless representation of either client would be adversely affected.

Other rules and laws may preclude making adequate disclosure under this rule. If such disclosure is precluded, informed written consent is likewise precluded. (See, e.g., Business and Professions Code section 6068, subsection (e).)

Paragraph (B) is not intended to apply to the relationship of a member to another party's lawyer. Such relationships are governed by rule 3–320.

Paragraph (B) is not intended to require either the disclosure of the new engagement to a former client or the consent of the former client to the new engagement. However, such disclosure or consent is required if paragraph (E) applies.

While paragraph (B) deals with the issues of adequate disclosure to the present client or clients of the member's present or past relationships to other parties or witnesses or present interest in the subject matter of the representation, paragraph (E) is intended to protect the confidences of another present or former client. These two paragraphs are to apply as complementary provisions.

Paragraph (B) is intended to apply only to a member's own relationships or interests, unless the member knows that a partner or associate in the same firm as the member has or had a relationship with another party or witness or has or had an interest in the subject matter of the representation.

Subparagraphs (C)(1) and (C)(2) are intended to apply to all types of legal employment, including the concurrent representation of multiple parties in litigation or in a single transaction or in some other common enterprise or legal relationship. Examples of the latter include the formation of a partnership for several partners or a corporation for several shareholders, the preparation of an ante-nuptial agreement, or joint or reciprocal wills for a husband and wife, or the resolution of an "uncontested" marital dissolution. In such situations, for the sake of convenience or economy, the parties may well prefer to employ a single counsel, but a member must disclose the potential adverse aspects of such multiple representation (e.g., Evid.Code, § 962) and must obtain the informed written consent of the clients thereto pursuant to subparagraph (C)(1). Moreover, if the potential adversity should become actual, the member must obtain the further informed written consent of the clients pursuant to subparagraph (C)(2).

Subparagraph (C)(3) is intended to apply to representations of clients in both litigation and transactional matters.

There are some matters in which the conflicts are such that written consent may not suffice for non-disciplinary purposes. (See Woods v. Superior Court (1983) 149 Cal.App.3d 931 [197 Cal.Rptr. 185]; Klemm v. Superior Court (1977) 75 Cal.App.3d 893 [142 Cal.Rptr. 509]; Ishmael v. Millington (1966) 241 Cal.App.2d 520 [50 Cal.Rptr. 592].)

Paragraph (D) is not intended to apply to class action settlements subject to court approval.

Paragraph (F) is not intended to abrogate existing relationships between insurers and insureds whereby the insurer has the contractual right to unilaterally select counsel for the insured, where there is no conflict of interest. (See San Diego Navy Federal Credit Union v. Cumis Insurance Society (1984) 162 Cal.App.3d 358 [208 Cal.Rptr. 494].)

Rule 3–320. Relationship With Other Party's Lawyer

A member shall not represent a client in a matter in which another party's lawyer is a spouse, parent, child, or sibling of the member, lives with the member, is a client of the member, or has an intimate personal relationship with the member, unless the member informs the client in writing of the relationship.

Discussion:

Rule 3–320 is not intended to apply to circumstances in which a member fails to advise the client of a relationship with another lawyer who is merely a partner or associate in the same law firm as the adverse party's counsel, and who has no direct involvement in the matter.

Rule 3–400. Limiting Liability to Client

A member shall not:

(A) Contract with a client prospectively limiting the member's liability to the client for the member's professional malpractice; or

(B) Settle a claim or potential claim for the member's liability to the client for the member's professional malpractice unless the client is informed in writing that the client may seek the advice of an independent lawyer of the client's choice regarding the settlement and is given a reasonable opportunity to seek that advice.

Discussion:

Rule 3–400 is not intended to apply to customary qualifications and limitations in legal opinions and memoranda, nor is it intended to prevent a member from reasonably limiting the scope of the member's employment or representation.

Rule 3–500. Communication

A member shall keep a client reasonably informed about significant developments relating to the employment or representation, including

431

promptly complying with reasonable requests for information and copies of significant documents when necessary to keep the client so informed.

Discussion:

Rule 3-500 is not intended to change a member's duties to his or her clients. It is intended to make clear that, while a client must be informed of significant developments in the matter, a member will not be disciplined for failing to communicate insignificant or irrelevant information. (See Bus. & Prof.Code, § 6068, subd. (m).)

A member may contract with the client in their employment agreement that the client assumes responsibility for the cost of copying significant documents. This rule is not intended to prohibit a claim for the recovery of the member's expense in any subsequent legal proceeding.

Rule 3-500 is not intended to create. augment, diminish, or eliminate any application of the work product rule. The obligation of the member to provide work product to the client shall be governed by relevant statutory and decisional law. Additionally, this rule is not intended to apply any document or correspondence that is subject to a protective order or non-disclosure agreement, or to override applicable statutory or decisional law requiring that certain information not be provided to criminal defendants who are clients of the member.

(Amended by order of the Supreme Court, operative June 5, 1997.)

Rule 3-510. Communication of Settlement Offer

(A) A member shall promptly communicate to the member's client:

    (1) All terms and conditions of any offer made to the client in a criminal matter; and

    (2) All amounts, terms, and conditions of any written offer of settlement made to the client in all other matters.

(B) As used in this rule, "client" includes a person who possesses the authority to accept an offer of settlement or plea, or, in a class action, all the named representatives of the class.

Discussion:

Rule 3-510 is intended to require that counsel in a criminal matter convey all offers, whether written or oral, to the client, as give and take negotiations are less common in criminal matters, and, even were they to occur, such negotiations should require the participation of the accused.

Any oral offers of settlement made to the client in a civil matter should also be communicated if they are "significant" for the purposes of rule 3-500.

Rule 3–600. Organization as Client

(A) In representing an organization, a member shall conform his or her representation to the concept that the client is the organization itself, acting through its highest authorized officer, employee, body, or constituent overseeing the particular engagement.

(B) If a member acting on behalf of an organization knows that an actual or apparent agent of the organization acts or intends or refuses to act in a manner that is or may be a violation of law reasonably imputable to the organization, or in a manner which is likely to result in substantial injury to the organization, the member shall not violate his or her duty of protecting all confidential information as provided in Business and Professions Code section 6068, subdivision (e). Subject to Business and Professions Code section 6068, subdivision (e), the member may take such actions as appear to the member to be in the best lawful interest of the organization. Such actions may include among others:

 (1) Urging reconsideration of the matter while explaining its likely consequences to the organization; or

 (2) Referring the matter to the next higher authority in the organization, including, if warranted by the seriousness of the matter, referral to the highest internal authority that can act on behalf of the organization.

(C) If, despite the member's actions in accordance with paragraph (B), the highest authority that can act on behalf of the organization insists upon action or a refusal to act that is a violation of law and is likely to result in substantial injury to the organization, the member's response is limited to the member's right, and, where appropriate, duty to resign in accordance with rule 3–700.

(D) In dealing with an organization's directors, officers, employees, members, shareholders, or other constituents, a member shall explain the identity of the client for whom the member acts, whenever it is or becomes apparent that the organization's interests are or may become adverse to those of the constituent(s) with whom the member is dealing. The member shall not mislead such a constituent into believing that the constituent may communicate confidential information to the member in a way that will not be used in the organization's interest if that is or becomes adverse to the constituent.

(E) A member representing an organization may also represent any of its directors, officers, employees, members, shareholders, or other constituents, subject to the provisions of rule 3–310. If the organization's consent to the dual representation is required by rule 3–310, the consent shall be given by an appropriate constituent of the organization other than the individual or constituent who is to be represented, or by the shareholder(s) or organization members.

Discussion:

 Rule 3–600 is not intended to enmesh members in the intricacies of the entity and aggregate theories of partnership.

Rule 3–600 is not intended to prohibit members from representing both an organization and other parties connected with it, as for instance (as simply one example) in establishing employee benefit packages for closely held corporations or professional partnerships.

Rule 3–600 is not intended to create or to validate artificial distinctions between entities and their officers, employees, or members, nor is it the purpose of the rule to deny the existence or importance of such formal distinctions. In dealing with a close corporation or small association, members commonly perform professional engagements for both the organization and its major constituents. When a change in control occurs or is threatened, members are faced with complex decisions involving personal and institutional relationships and loyalties and have frequently had difficulty in perceiving their correct duty. (See *People ex rel. Deukmejian v. Brown* (1981) 29 Cal.3d 150 [172 Cal.Rptr. 478]; *Goldstein v. Lees* (1975) 46 Cal.App.3d 614 [120 Cal.Rptr. 253]; *Woods v. Superior Court* (1983) 149 Cal.App.3d 931 [197 Cal.Rptr. 185]; *In re Banks* (1978) 283 Ore. 459 [584 P.2d 284]; 1 A.L.R.4th 1105.) In resolving such multiple relationships, members must rely on case law.

Rule 3–700. Termination of Employment

(A) In General.

    (1) If permission for termination of employment is required by the rules of a tribunal, a member shall not withdraw from employment in a proceeding before that tribunal without its permission.

    (2) A member shall not withdraw from employment until the member has taken reasonable steps to avoid reasonably foreseeable prejudice to the rights of the client, including giving due notice to the client, allowing time for employment of other counsel, complying with rule 3–700(D), and complying with applicable laws and rules.

(B) Mandatory Withdrawal.

A member representing a client before a tribunal shall withdraw from employment with the permission of the tribunal, if required by its rules, and a member representing a client in other matters shall withdraw from employment, if:

    (1) The member knows or should know that the client is bringing an action, conducting a defense, asserting a position in litigation, or taking an appeal, without probable cause and for the purpose of harassing or maliciously injuring any person; or

    (2) The member knows or should know that continued employment will result in violation of these rules or of the State Bar Act; or

    (3) The member's mental or physical condition renders it unreasonably difficult to carry out the employment effectively.

(C) Permissive Withdrawal.

If rule 3–700(B) is not applicable, a member may not request permission to withdraw in matters pending before a tribunal, and may not withdraw in other matters, unless such request or such withdrawal is because:

(1) The client

   (a) insists upon presenting a claim or defense that is not warranted under existing law and cannot be supported by good faith argument for an extension, modification, or reversal of existing law, or

   (b) seeks to pursue an illegal course of conduct, or

   (c) insists that the member pursue a course of conduct that is illegal or that is prohibited under these rules or the State Bar Act, or

   (d) by other conduct renders it unreasonably difficult for the member to carry out the employment effectively, or

   (e) insists, in a matter not pending before a tribunal, that the member engage in conduct that is contrary to the judgment and advice of the member but not prohibited under these rules or the State Bar Act, or

   (f) breaches an agreement or obligation to the member as to expenses or fees.

(2) The continued employment is likely to result in a violation of these rules or of the State Bar Act; or

(3) The inability to work with co-counsel indicates that the best interests of the client likely will be served by withdrawal; or

(4) The member's mental or physical condition renders it difficult for the member to carry out the employment effectively; or

(5) The client knowingly and freely assents to termination of the employment; or

(6) The member believes in good faith, in a proceeding pending before a tribunal, that the tribunal will find the existence of other good cause for withdrawal.

(D) Papers, Property and Fees.

A member whose employment has terminated shall:

(1) Subject to any protective order or non-disclosure agreement, promptly release to the client, at the request of the client, all the client papers and property. "Client papers and property" includes correspondence, pleadings, deposition transcripts, exhibits, physical evidence, expert's reports, and other items reasonably necessary to the client's representation, whether the client has paid for them or not; and

(2) Promptly refund any part of a fee paid in advance that has not been earned. This provision is not applicable to a true retainer fee which is paid solely for the purpose of ensuring the availability of the member for the matter.

Discussion:

Subparagraph (A)(2) provides that "a member shall not withdraw from employment until the member has taken reasonable steps to avoid reasonably foreseeable prejudice to the rights of the clients." What such steps would include, of course, will vary according to the circumstances. Absent special circumstances, "reasonable steps" do not include providing additional services to the client once the successor counsel has been employed and rule 3–700(D) has been satisfied.

Paragraph (D) makes clear the member's duties in the recurring situation in which new counsel seeks to obtain client files from a member discharged by the client. It codifies existing case law. (See *Academy of California Optometrists v. Superior .Court* (1975) 51 Cal. App.3d 999 [124 Cal.Rptr. 668]; *Weiss v. Marcus* (1975) 51 Cal.App.3d 590 [124 Cal.Rptr. 297].) Paragraph (D) also requires that the member "promptly" return unearned fees paid in advance. If a client disputes the amount to be returned, the member shall comply with rule 4–100(A)(2).

Paragraph (D) is not intended to prohibit a member from making, at the member's own expense, and retaining copies of papers released to the client, nor to prohibit a claim for the recovery of the member's expense in any subsequent legal proceeding.

CHAPTER 4. FINANCIAL RELATIONSHIP WITH CLIENTS

Rule 4–100. Preserving Identity of Funds and Property of a Client

(A) All funds received or held for the benefit of clients by a member or law firm, including advances for costs and expenses, shall be deposited in one or more identifiable bank accounts labelled "Trust Account," "Client's Funds Account" or words of similar import, maintained in the State of California, or, with written consent of the client, in any other jurisdiction where there is a substantial relationship between the client or the client's business and the other jurisdiction. No funds belonging to the member or the law firm shall be deposited therein or otherwise commingled therewith except as follows:

(1) Funds reasonably sufficient to pay bank charges.

(2) In the case of funds belonging in part to a client and in part presently or potentially to the member or the law firm, the portion belonging to the member or law firm must be withdrawn at the earliest reasonable time after the member's interest in that portion becomes fixed. However, when the right of the member or law firm to receive a portion of trust funds is disputed by the client, the disputed portion shall not be withdrawn until the dispute is finally resolved.

(B) A member shall:

(1) Promptly notify a client of the receipt of the client's funds, securities, or other properties.

(2) Identify and label securities and properties of a client promptly upon receipt and place them in a safe deposit box or other place of safekeeping as soon as practicable.

(3) Maintain complete records of all funds, securities, and other properties of a client coming into the possession of the member or law firm and render appropriate accounts to the client regarding them; preserve such records for a period of no less than five years after final appropriate distribution of such funds or properties; and comply with any order for an audit of such records issued pursuant to the Rules of Procedure of the State Bar.

(4) Promptly pay or deliver, as requested by the client, any funds, securities, or other properties in the possession of the member which the client is entitled to receive.

(C) The Board of Governors of the State Bar shall have the authority to formulate and adopt standards as to what "records" shall be maintained by members and law firms in accordance with subparagraph (B)(3). The standards formulated and adopted by the Board, as from time to time amended, shall be effective and binding on all members.

Standards:

Pursuant to rule 4-100(C) the Board of Governors of the State Bar adopted the following standards as to what "records" shall be maintained by members and law firms in accordance with subparagraph (B)(3).

(1) A member shall, from the date of receipt of client funds through the period ending five years from the date of appropriate disbursement of such funds, maintain:

(a) a written ledger for each client on whose behalf funds are held that sets forth:

    (i) the name of such client,

    (ii) the date, amount and source of all funds received on behalf of such client,

    (iii) the date, amount, payee and purpose of each disbursement made on behalf of such client, and

    (iv) the current balance for such client;

(b) a written journal for each bank account that sets forth:

    (i) the name of such account,

    (ii) the date, amount and client affected by each debit and credit, and

    (iii) the current balance in such account;

(c) all bank statements and cancelled checks for each bank account; and

(d) each monthly reconciliation (balancing) of (a), (b), and (c).

(2) A member shall, from the date of receipt of all securities and other properties held for the benefit of client through the period ending five years from the date of appropriate disbursement of such securities and other properties, maintain a written journal that specifies:

   (a) each item of security and property held;

   (b) the person on whose behalf the security or property is held;

   (c) the date of receipt of the security or property;

   (d) the date of distribution of the security or property; and

   (e) person to whom the security or property was distributed.

(Trust Account Record Keeping Standards as Adopted by the Board of Governors on July 11, 1992 Effective on January 1, 1993)

Rule 4–200. Fees for Legal Services

(A) A member shall not enter into an agreement for, charge, or collect an illegal or unconscionable fee.

(B) Unconscionability of a fee shall be determined on the basis of all the facts and circumstances existing at the time the agreement is entered into except where the parties contemplate that the fee will be affected by later events. Among the factors to be considered, where appropriate, in determining the conscionability of a fee are the following:

(1) The amount of the fee in proportion to the value of the services performed.

(2) The relative sophistication of the member and the client.

(3) The novelty and difficulty of the questions involved and the skill requisite to perform the legal service properly.

(4) The likelihood, if apparent to the client, that the acceptance of the particular employment will preclude other employment by the member.

(5) The amount involved and the results obtained.

(6) The time limitations imposed by the client or by the circumstances.

(7) The nature and length of the professional relationship with the client.

(8) The experience, reputation, and ability of the member or members performing the services.

(9) Whether the fee is fixed or contingent.

(10) The time and labor required.

(11) The informed consent of the client to the fee.

Rule 4–210. Payment of Personal or Business Expenses Incurred by or for a Client

(A) A member shall not directly or indirectly pay or agree to pay, guarantee, represent, or sanction a representation that the member or member's law firm will pay the personal or business expenses of a prospective or existing client, except that this rule shall not prohibit a member:

    (1) With the consent of the client, from paying or agreeing to pay such expenses to third persons from funds collected or to be collected for the client as a result of the representation; or

    (2) After employment, from lending money to the client upon the client's promise in writing to repay such loan; or

    (3) From advancing the costs of prosecuting or defending a claim or action or otherwise protecting or promoting the client's interests, the repayment of which may be contingent on the outcome of the matter. Such costs within the meaning of this subparagraph (3) shall be limited to all reasonable expenses of litigation or reasonable expenses in preparation for litigation or in providing any legal services to the client.

(B) Nothing in rule 4–210 shall be deemed to limit rules 3–300, 3–310, and 4–300.

Rule 4–300. Purchasing Property at a Foreclosure or a Sale Subject to Judicial Review

(A) A member shall not directly or indirectly purchase property at a probate, foreclosure, receiver's, trustee's or judicial sale in an action or proceeding in which such member or any lawyer affiliated by reason of personal, business, or professional relationship with that member or with that member's law firm is acting as a lawyer for a party or as executor, receiver, trustee, administrator, guardian, or conservator.

(B) A member shall not represent the seller at a probate, foreclosure, receiver, trustee, or judicial sale in an action or proceeding in which the purchaser is a spouse or relative of the member or of another lawyer in the member's law firm or is an employee of the member or the member's law firm.

Rule 4–400. Gifts From Client

A member shall not induce a client to make a substantial gift, including a testamentary gift, to the member or to the member's parent, child, sibling, or spouse, except where the client is related to the member.

Discussion:

A member may accept a gift from a member's client, subject to general standards of fairness and absence of undue influence. The member who participates in the preparation of an instrument memorializing a gift which is otherwise permissible ought not to be subject to professional discipline. On the other hand, where impermissible influence occurred, discipline is appropriate. (See *Magee v. State Bar* (1962) 58 Cal.2d 423 [24 Cal.Rptr. 839].)

CHAPTER 5.   ADVOCACY AND REPRESENTATION

Rule 5–100.   Threatening Criminal, Administrative, or Disciplinary Charges

(A) A member shall not threaten to present criminal, administrative, or disciplinary charges to obtain an advantage in a civil dispute.

(B) As used in paragraph (A) of this rule, the term "administrative charges" means the filing or lodging of a complaint with a federal, state, or local governmental entity which may order or recommend the loss or suspension of a license, or may impose or recommend the imposition of a fine, pecuniary sanction, or other sanction of a quasi-criminal nature but does not include filing charges with an administrative entity required by law as a condition precedent to maintaining a civil action.

(C) As used in paragraph (A) of this rule, the term "civil dispute" means a controversy or potential controversy over the rights and duties of two or more parties under civil law, whether or not an action has been commenced, and includes an administrative proceeding of a quasi-civil nature pending before a federal, state, or local governmental entity.

Discussion:

Rule 5–100 is not intended to apply to a member's threatening to initiate contempt proceedings against a party for a failure to comply with a court order.

Paragraph (B) is intended to exempt the threat of filing an administrative charge which is a prerequisite to filing a civil complaint on the same transaction or occurrence.

For purposes of paragraph (C), the definition of "civil dispute" makes clear that the rule is applicable prior to the formal filing of a civil action.

Rule 5–110.   Performing the Duty of Member in Government Service

A member in government service shall not institute or cause to be instituted criminal charges when the member knows or should know that the charges are not supported by probable cause. If, after the institution of criminal charges, the member in government service having responsibility for prosecuting the charges becomes aware that those charges are not supported by probable cause, the member shall promptly so advise the court in which the criminal matter is pending.

Rule 5–120. Trial Publicity

(A) A member who is participating or has participated in the investigation or litigation of a matter shall not make an extrajudicial statement that a reasonable person would expect to be disseminated by means of public communication if the member knows or reasonably should know that it will have a substantial likelihood of materially prejudicing an adjudicative proceeding in the matter.

(B) Notwithstanding paragraph (A), a member may state:
   (1) the claim, offense or defense involved and, except when prohibited by law, the identity of the persons involved;
   (2) the information contained in a public record;
   (3) that an investigation of the matter is in progress;
   (4) the scheduling or result of any step in litigation;
   (5) a request for assistance in obtaining evidence and information necessary thereto;
   (6) a warning of danger concerning the behavior of a person involved, when there is reason to believe that there exists the likelihood of substantial harm to an individual or the public interest; and
   (7) in a criminal case, in addition to subparagraphs (1) through (6):
      (a) the identity, residence, occupation, and family status of the accused;
      (b) if the accused has not been apprehended, information necessary to aid in apprehension of that person;
      (c) the fact, time, and place of arrest; and
      (d) the identity of investigating and arresting officers or agencies and the length of the investigation.

(C) Notwithstanding paragraph (A), a member may make a statement that a reasonable member would believe is required to protect a client from the substantial undue prejudicial effect of recent publicity not initiated by the member or the member's client. A statement made pursuant to this paragraph shall be limited to such information as is necessary to mitigate the recent adverse publicity.

Discussion

Rule 5–120 is intended to apply equally to prosecutors and criminal defense counsel. Whether an extrajudicial statement violates rule 5–120 depends on many factors, including:

(1) whether the extrajudicial statement presents information clearly inadmissible as evidence in the matter for the purpose of proving or disproving a material fact in issue;

(2) whether the extrajudicial statement presents information the member knows is false, deceptive, or the use of which would violate Business and Professions Code section 6068(d);

441

(3) whether the extrajudicial statement violates a lawful "gag" order, or protective order, statute, rule of court, or special rule of confidentiality (for example, in juvenile, domestic, mental disability, and certain criminal proceedings); and

(4) the timing of the statement.

Paragraph (A) is intended to apply to statements made by or on behalf of the member. Subparagraph (B)(6) is not intended to create, augment, diminish, or eliminate any application of the lawyer-client privilege or of Business and Professions Code section 6068(e) regarding the member's duty to maintain client confidence and secrets.

Rule 5–200. Trial Conduct

In presenting a matter to a tribunal, a member:

(A) Shall employ, for the purpose of maintaining the causes confided to the member such means only as are consistent with truth;

(B) Shall not seek to mislead the judge, judicial officer, or jury by an artifice or false statement of fact or law;

(C) Shall not intentionally misquote to a tribunal the language of a book, statute, or decision;

(D) Shall not, knowing its invalidity, cite as authority a decision that has been overruled or a statute that has been repealed or declared unconstitutional; and

(E) Shall not assert personal knowledge of the facts at issue, except when testifying as a witness.

Rule 5–210. Member as Witness

A member shall not act as an advocate before a jury which will hear testimony from the member unless:

(A) The testimony relates to an uncontested matter; or

(B) The testimony relates to the nature and value of legal services rendered in the case; or

(C) The member has the informed, written consent of the client. If the member represents the People or a governmental entity, the consent shall be obtained from the head of the office or a designee of the head of the office by which the member is employed and shall be consistent with principles of recusal.

Discussion:

Rule 5–210 is intended to apply to situations in which the member knows or should know that he or she ought to be called as a witness in litigation in which there is a jury. This rule is not intended to encompass situations in which the member is representing the client in an adversarial proceeding and is testifying before a judge. In non-adversarial proceedings, as where the lawyer testifies on behalf of the client, in a hearing before a legislative body, rule 5-210 is not applicable.

Rule 5-210 is not intended to apply to circumstances in which a lawyer in an advocate's firm will be a witness.

Rule 5-220. Suppression of Evidence

A member shall not suppress any evidence that the member or the member's client has a legal obligation to reveal or to produce.

Rule 5-300. Contact With Officials

(A) A member shall not directly or indirectly give or lend anything of value to a judge, official, or employee of a tribunal unless the personal or family relationship between the member and the judge, official, or employee is such that gifts are customarily given and exchanged. Nothing contained in this rule shall prohibit a member from contributing to the campaign fund of a judge running for election or confirmation pursuant to applicable law pertaining to such contributions.

(B) A member shall not directly or indirectly communicate with or argue to a judge or judicial officer upon the merits of a contested matter pending before such judge or judicial officer, except:

    (1) In open court; or

    (2) With the consent of all other counsel in such matter; or

    (3) In the presence of all other counsel in such matter; or

    (4) In writing with a copy thereof furnished to such other counsel; or

    (5) In ex parte matters.

(C) As used in this rule, "judge" and "judicial officer" shall include law clerks, research attorneys, or other court personnel who participate in the decision-making process.

Rule 5-310. Prohibited Contact With Witnesses

A member shall not:

(A) Advise or directly or indirectly cause a person to secrete himself or herself or to leave the jurisdiction of a tribunal for the purpose of making that person unavailable as a witness therein.

(B) Directly or indirectly pay, offer to pay, or acquiesce in the payment of compensation to a witness contingent upon the content of the witness's testimony or the outcome of the case. Except where prohibited by law, a member may advance, guarantee, or acquiesce in the payment of:

    (1) Expenses reasonably incurred by a witness in attending or testifying.

    (2) Reasonable compensation to a witness for loss of time in attending or testifying.

(3) A reasonable fee for the professional services of an expert witness.

Rule 5–320. Contact With Jurors

(A) A member connected with a case shall not communicate directly or indirectly with anyone the member knows to be a member of the venire from which the jury will be selected for trial of that case.

(B) During trial a member connected with the case shall not communicate directly or indirectly with any juror.

(C) During trial a member who is not connected with the case shall not communicate directly or indirectly concerning the case with anyone the member knows is a juror in the case.

(D) After discharge of the jury from further consideration of a case a member shall not ask questions of or make comments to a member of that jury that are intended to harass or embarrass the juror or to influence the juror's actions in future jury service.

(E) A member shall not directly or indirectly conduct an out of court investigation of a person who is either a member of the venire or a juror in a manner likely to influence the state of mind of such person in connection with present or future jury service.

(F) All restrictions imposed by this rule also apply to communications with or investigations of members of the family of a person who is either a member of the venire or a juror.

(G) A member shall reveal promptly to the court improper conduct by a person who is either a member of a venire or a juror, or by another toward a person who is either a member of a venire or a juror or a member of his or her family, of which the member has knowledge.

(H) This Rule does not prohibit a member from communicating with persons who are members of a venire or jurors as a part of the official proceedings.

(I) For purposes of this Rule, "juror" means any empaneled, discharged, or excused juror.

CALIFORNIA BUSINESS AND PROFESSIONS CODE

(Selected Sections)

TABLE OF CONTENTS

CHAPTER 4. ATTORNEYS

ARTICLE 4. ADMISSION TO THE PRACTICE OF LAW

§ 6067. Oath

Every person on his admission shall take an oath to support the Constitution of the United States and the Constitution of the State of California, and faithfully to discharge the duties of any attorney at law to the best of his knowledge and ability. A certificate of the oath shall be indorsed upon his license.

§ 6068. Duties of attorney

It is the duty of an attorney:

(a) To support the Constitution and laws of the United States and of this State.

(b) To maintain the respect due to the courts of justice and judicial officers.

(c) To counsel or maintain such actions, proceedings or defenses only as appear to him legal or just, except the defense of a person charged with a public offense.

(d) To employ, for the purpose of maintaining the causes confided to him such means only as are consistent with truth, and never to seek to mislead the judge or any judicial officer by an artifice or false statement of fact or law.

(e) To maintain inviolate the confidence, and at every peril to himself to preserve the secrets, of his client.

(f) To advance no fact prejudicial to the honor or reputation of a party or witness, unless required by the justice of the cause with which he is charged.

(g) Not to encourage either the commencement or the continuance of an action or proceeding from any corrupt motive of passion or interest.

(h) Never to reject, for any consideration personal to himself, the cause of the defenseless or the oppressed.

(i) To cooperate and participate in any disciplinary investigation or other regulatory or disciplinary proceeding pending against himself or herself. However, this subdivision shall not be construed to deprive an attorney of any privilege guaranteed by the Fifth Amendment to the Constitution of the United States or any other constitutional or statutory privileges. This subdivision shall not be construed to require an attorney to cooperate with a request that requires him or her to waive any constitutional or statutory privilege or to comply with a request for information or other matters within an unreasonable period of time in light of the time constraints of the attorney's practice. Any exercise by an attorney of any constitutional or statutory privilege shall not be used against the attorney in a regulatory or disciplinary proceeding against him or her.

(j) To comply with the requirements of Section 6002.1.

(k) To comply with all conditions attached to any disciplinary probation, including a probation imposed with the concurrence of the attorney.

(*l*) To keep all agreements made in lieu of disciplinary prosecution with the agency charged with attorney discipline.

(m) To respond promptly to reasonable status inquiries of clients and to keep clients reasonably informed of significant developments in matters with regard to which the attorney has agreed to provide legal services.

(n) To provide copies to the client of certain documents under time limits and as prescribed in a rule of professional conduct which the board shall adopt.

(*o*) To report to the agency charged with attorney discipline, in writing, within 30 days of the time the attorney has knowledge of any of the following:

(1) The filing of three or more lawsuits in a 12-month period against the attorney for malpractice or other wrongful conduct committed in a professional capacity.

(2) The entry of judgment against the attorney in any civil action for fraud, misrepresentation, breach of fiduciary duty, or gross negligence committed in a professional capacity.

(3) The imposition of any judicial sanctions against the attorney, except for sanctions for failure to make discovery or monetary sanctions of less than one thousand dollars ($1,000).

(4) The bringing of an indictment or information charging a felony against the attorney.

(5) The conviction of the attorney, including any verdict of guilty, or plea of guilty or no contest, of any felony, or any misdemeanor committed in the course of the practice of law, or in any manner in which a client of the attorney was the victim, or a necessary element of which, as determined by the statutory or common law definition of the misdemeanor, involves improper conduct of an attorney, including dishonesty or other moral turpitude, or an attempt or a conspiracy or solicitation of another to commit a felony or any such misdemeanor.

(6) The imposition of discipline against the attorney by any professional or occupational disciplinary agency or licensing board, whether in California or elsewhere.

(7) Reversal of judgment in a proceeding based in whole or in part upon misconduct, grossly incompetent representation, or wilful misrepresentation by an attorney.

(8) As used in this subdivision, "against the attorney" includes claims and proceedings against any firm of attorneys for the practice

of law in which the attorney was a partner at the time of the conduct complained of and any law corporation in which the attorney was a shareholder at the time of the conduct complained of unless the matter has to the attorney's knowledge already been reported by the law firm or corporation.

(9) The State Bar may develop a prescribed form for the making of reports required by this section, usage of which it may require by rule or regulation.

(10) This subdivision is only intended to provide that the failure to report as required herein may serve as a basis of discipline.

§ 6090.5 Settlements; prohibited agreements

(a) It is cause for suspension, disbarment, or other discipline for any member, whether as a party or as an attorney for a party, to agree or seek agreement, that:

(1) The professional misconduct or the terms of a settlement of a claim for professional misconduct shall not be reported to the disciplinary agency.

(2) The plaintiff shall withdraw a disciplinary complaint or shall not cooperate with the investigation or prosecution conducted by the disciplinary agency.

(3) The record of any civil action for professional misconduct shall be sealed from review by the disciplinary agency.

(b) The section applies to all settlements, whether made before or after the commencement of a civil action.
(Amended by Stats.1996, c. 1104 (A.B.2787), § 4.)

ARTICLE 6. DISCIPLINARY AUTHORITY OF THE COURTS

§ 6100. Disbarment or suspension

For any of the causes provided in this article, arising after an attorney's admission to practice, he or she may be disbarred or suspended by the Supreme Court. Nothing in this article limits the inherent power of the Supreme Court to discipline, including to summarily disbar, any attorney.

§ 6101. Conviction of crime; notice of pendency of action; record of conviction; proceedings

(a) Conviction of a felony or misdemeanor, involving moral turpitude, constitutes a cause for disbarment or suspension.

In any proceeding, whether under this article or otherwise, to disbar or suspend an attorney on account of that conviction, the record of conviction shall be conclusive evidence of guilt of the crime of which he or she has been convicted.

(b) The district attorney, city attorney, or other prosecuting agency shall notify the Office of the State Bar of California of the pendency of an action against an attorney charging a felony or misdemeanor immediately upon obtaining information that the defendant is an attorney. The notice shall identify the attorney and describe the crimes charged and the alleged facts. The prosecuting agency shall also notify the clerk of the court in which the action is pending that the defendant is an attorney, and the clerk shall record prominently in the file that the defendant is an attorney.

(c) The clerk of the court in which an attorney is convicted of a crime shall, within 48 hours after the conviction, transmit a certified copy of the record of conviction to the Office of the State Bar. Within five days of receipt, the Office of the State Bar shall transmit the record of any conviction which involves or may involve moral turpitude to the Supreme Court with such other records and information as may be appropriate to establish the Supreme Court's jurisdiction. The State Bar of California may procure and transmit the record of conviction to the Supreme Court when the clerk has not done so or when the conviction was had in a court other than a court of this state.

(d) The proceedings to disbar or suspend an attorney on account of such a conviction shall be undertaken by the Supreme Court pursuant to the procedure provided in this section and Section 6102, upon the receipt of the certified copy of the record of conviction.

(e) A plea or verdict of guilty, an acceptance of a nolo contendere plea, or a conviction after a plea of nolo contendere is deemed to be a conviction within the meaning of those sections.

§ 6102. Immediate suspension and subsequent disbarment upon conviction of crime; crimes involving moral turpitude or felonies; procedure

(a) Upon the receipt of the certified copy of the record of conviction, if it appears therefrom that the crime of which the attorney was convicted involved or that there is probable cause to believe that it involved moral turpitude or is a felony under the laws of California, the United States, or any state or territory thereof, the Supreme Court shall suspend the attorney until the time for appeal has elapsed, if no appeal has been taken, or until the judgment of conviction has been affirmed on appeal, or has otherwise become final, and until the further order of the court. Upon its own motion or upon good cause shown the court may decline to impose, or may set aside, the suspension when it appears to be in the interest of justice to do so, with due regard being given to maintaining the integrity of and confidence in the profession.

(b) For the purposes of this section, a crime is a felony under the law of California if it is declared to be so specifically or by subdivision (a) of Section 17 of the Penal Code, unless it is charged as a misdemeanor pursuant to paragraph (4) or (5) of subdivision (b) of Section 17 of the Penal Code, irrespective of whether in a particular case the crime may be considered a misdemeanor as a result of postconviction proceedings, including proceedings resulting in punishment or probation set forth in paragraph (1) or (3) of subdivision (b) of Section 17 of the Penal Code.

(c) After the judgment of conviction of an offense specified in subdivision (a) has become final or, irrespective of any subsequent order under Section 1203.4 of the Penal Code or similar statutory provision, an order granting probation has been made suspending the imposition of sentence, the Supreme Court shall summarily disbar the attorney if the offense is a felony under the laws of California, the United States, or any state or territory thereof, and an element of the offense is the specific intent to deceive, defraud, steal, or make or suborn a false statement or involved moral turpitude.

(d) For purposes of this section, a conviction under the laws of another state or territory of the United States shall be deemed a felony if:

(1) The judgment or conviction was entered as a felony irrespective of any subsequent order suspending sentence or granting probation and irrespective of whether the crime may be considered a misdemeanor as a result of postconviction proceedings.

(2) The elements of the offense for which the member was convicted would constitute a felony under the laws of the State of California at the time the offense was committed.

(e) Except as provided in subdivision (c), if after adequate notice and opportunity to be heard (which hearing shall not be had until the judgment of conviction has become final or, irrespective of any subsequent order under Section 1203.4 of the Penal Code, an order granting probation has been made suspending the imposition of sentence), the court finds that the crime of which the attorney was convicted, or the circumstances of its commission, involved moral turpitude, it shall enter an order disbarring the attorney or suspending him or her from practice for a limited time, according to the gravity of the crime and the circumstances of the case; otherwise it shall dismiss the proceedings. In determining the extent of the discipline to be imposed in a proceeding pursuant to this article any prior discipline imposed upon the attorney may be considered.

(f) The court may refer the proceedings or any part thereof or issue therein, including the nature or extent of discipline, to the State Bar for hearing, report, and recommendation.

(g) The record of the proceedings resulting in the conviction, including a transcript of the testimony therein, may be received in evidence.

(h) The Supreme Court shall prescribe rules for the practice and procedure in proceedings conducted pursuant to this section and Section 6101.

(i) The other provisions of this article providing a procedure for the disbarment or suspension of an attorney do not apply to proceedings pursuant to this section and Section 6101, unless expressly made applicable.

§ 6103. Disobedience of court order; violation of oath or attorney's duties

A wilful disobedience or violation of an order of the court requiring him to do or forbear an act connected with or in the course of his profession, which he ought in good faith to do or forbear, and any violation of the oath taken by him, or of his duties as such attorney, constitute causes for disbarment or suspension.

§ 6103.5 Written offers of settlement; required communication to client; discovery

(a) A member of the State Bar shall promptly communicate to the member's client all amounts, terms, and conditions of any written offer of settlement made by or on behalf of an opposing party. As used in this section, "client" includes any person employing the member of the State Bar who possesses the authority to accept an offer of settlement, or in a class action, who is a representative of the class.

(b) Any written offer of settlement or any required communication of a settlement offer, as described in subdivision (a), shall be discoverable by either party in any action in which the existence or communication of the offer of settlement is an issue before the trier of fact.

§ 6104. Unauthorized appearance

Corruptly or wilfully and without authority appearing as attorney for a party to an action or proceeding constitutes a cause for disbarment or suspension.

§ 6105. Permitting misuse of name

Lending his name to be used as attorney by another person who is not an attorney constitutes a cause for disbarment or suspension.

§ 6106. Moral turpitude, dishonesty or corruption irrespective of criminal conviction

The commission of any act involving moral turpitude, dishonesty or corruption, whether the act is committed in the course of his relations as an attorney or otherwise, and whether the act is a felony or misdemeanor or not, constitutes a cause for disbarment or suspension.

If the act constitutes a felony or misdemeanor, conviction thereof in a criminal proceeding is not a condition precedent to disbarment or suspension from practice therefor.

§ 6106.1   Advocacy of overthrow of government

Advocating the overthrow of the Government of the United States or of this State by force, violence, or other unconstitutional means, constitutes a cause for disbarment or suspension.

§ 6106.5   Insurance claims; fraud

It shall constitute cause for disbarment or suspension for an attorney to engage in any conduct prohibited under Section 1871.1 or 1871.4 of the Insurance Code.

§ 6106.7   Miller–Ayala Athlete Agents Act; violation of requirements

It shall constitute cause for the imposition of discipline of an attorney within the meaning of this chapter for an attorney to violate any provision of the Miller–Ayala Athlete Agents Act (Chapter 2.5 (commencing with Section 18895) of Division 8), or to violate any provision of Chapter 1 (commencing with Section 1500) of Part 6 of Division 2 of the Labor Code, prior to January 1, 1997, or to violate any provision of the law of any other state regulating athlete agents.

§ 6106.8   Sexual involvement between lawyers and clients; rule of professional conduct

(a) The Legislature hereby finds and declares that there is no rule that governs propriety of sexual relationships between lawyers and clients. The Legislature further finds and declares that it is difficult to separate sound judgment from emotion or bias which may result from sexual involvement between a lawyer and his or her client during the period that an attorney-client relationship exists, and that emotional detachment is essential to the lawyer's ability to render competent legal services. Therefore, in order to ensure that a lawyer acts in the best interest of his or her client, a rule of professional conduct governing sexual relations between attorneys and their clients shall be adopted.

(b) With the approval of the Supreme Court, the State Bar shall adopt a rule of professional conduct governing sexual relations between attorneys and their clients in cases involving, but not limited to, probate matters and domestic relations, including dissolution proceedings, child custody cases, and settlement proceedings.

(c) The State Bar shall submit the proposed rule to the Supreme Court for approval no later than January 1, 1991.

(d) Intentional violation of this rule shall constitute a cause for suspension or disbarment.

§ 6106.9   Sexual relations between attorney and client; cause for discipline; complaints to state bar

(a) It shall constitute cause for the imposition of discipline of an attorney within the meaning of this chapter for an attorney to do any of the following:

(1) Expressly or impliedly condition the performance of legal services for a current or prospective client upon the client's willingness to engage in sexual relations with the attorney.

(2) Employ coercion, intimidation, or undue influence in entering into sexual relations with a client.

(3) Continue representation of a client with whom the attorney has sexual relations if the sexual relations cause the attorney to perform legal services incompetently in violation of Rule 3–110 of the Rules of Professional Conduct of the State Bar of California, or if the sexual relations would, or would be likely to, damage or prejudice the client's case.

(b) Subdivision (a) shall not apply to sexual relations between attorneys and their spouses or persons in an equivalent domestic relationship or to ongoing consensual sexual relationships that predate the initiation of the attorney-client relationship.

(c) Where an attorney in a firm has sexual relations with a client but does not participate in the representation of that client, the attorneys in the firm shall not be subject to discipline under this section solely because of the occurrence of those sexual relations.

(d) For the purposes of this section, "sexual relations" means sexual intercourse or the touching of an intimate part of another person for the purpose of sexual arousal, gratification, or abuse.

(e) Any complaint made to the State Bar alleging a violation of subdivision (a) shall be verified under oath by the person making the complaint.

§ 6107.   Proceedings upon court's own knowledge or upon information

The proceedings to disbar or suspend an attorney, on grounds other than the conviction of a felony or misdemeanor, involving moral turpitude, may be taken by the court for the matters within its knowledge, or may be taken upon the information of another.

§ 6108.   Accusation

If the proceedings are upon the information of another, the accusation shall be in writing and shall state the matters charged, and be verified by the oath of some person, to the effect that the charges therein contained are true.

The verification may be made upon information and belief when the accusation is presented by an organized bar association.

§ 6109.   Order to appear and answer; service

Upon receiving the accusation, the court shall make an order requiring the accused to appear and answer it at a specified time, and shall cause a copy of the order and of the accusation to be served upon the accused at least five days before the day appointed in the order.

§ 6110. Citation

The court or judge may direct the service of a citation to the accused, requiring him to appear and answer the accusation, to be made by publication for thirty days in a newspaper of general circulation published in the county in which the proceeding is pending, if it appears by affidavit to the satisfaction of the court or judge that the accused either:

(a) Resides out of the State.

(b) Has departed from the State.

(c) Can not, after due diligence, be found within the State.

(d) Conceals himself to avoid the service of the order to show cause.

The citation shall be:

(a) Directed to the accused.

(b) Recite the date of the filing of the accusation, the name of the accuser, and the general nature of the charges against him.

(c) Require him to appear and answer the accusation at a specified time.

On proof of the publication of the citation as herein required, the court has jurisdiction to proceed to hear the accusation and render judgment with like effect as if an order to show cause and a copy of the accusation had been personally served on the accused.

§ 6111. Appearance; determination upon default

The accused shall appear at the time appointed in the order, and answer the accusation, unless, for sufficient cause, the court assigns another day for that purpose. If he does not appear, the court may proceed and determine the accusation in his absence.

§ 6112. Answer

The accused may answer to the accusation either by objecting to its sufficiency or by denying it.

If he objects to the sufficiency of the accusation, the objection shall be in writing, but need not be in any specific form. It is sufficient if it presents intelligibly the grounds of the objection.

If he denies the accusation, the denial may be oral and without oath, and shall be entered upon the minutes.

§ 6113. Time for answer after objection

If an objection to the sufficiency of the accusation is not sustained, the accused shall answer within the time designated by the court.

§ 6114. Judgment upon plea of guilty or failure to answer; trial upon denial of charges

If the accused pleads guilty, or refuses to answer the accusation, the court shall proceed to judgment of disbarment or suspension.

If he denies the matters charged, the court shall, at such time as it may appoint, proceed to try the accusation.

§ 6115. Reference to take depositions

The court may, in its discretion, order a reference to a committee to take depositions in the matter.

§ 6116. Judgment

When an attorney has been found guilty of the charges made in proceedings not based upon a record of conviction, judgment shall be rendered disbarring the attorney or suspending him from practice for a limited time, according to the gravity of the offense charged.

§ 6117. Effect of disbarment or suspension

During such disbarment or suspension, the attorney shall be precluded from practicing law.

When disbarred, his name shall be stricken from the roll of attorneys.

ARTICLE 7. UNLAWFUL PRACTICE OF LAW

§ 6125. Necessity of active membership in state bar

No person shall practice law in California unless the person is an active member of the State Bar.

§ 6126. Unauthorized practice, advertising or holding out; penalties

(a) Any person advertising or holding himself or herself out as practicing or entitled to practice law or otherwise practicing law who is not an active member of the State Bar, is guilty of a misdemeanor.

(b) Any person who has been involuntarily enrolled as an inactive member of the State Bar, or has been suspended from membership from the State Bar, or has been disbarred, or has resigned from the State Bar with charges pending, and thereafter advertises or holds himself or herself out as practicing or otherwise entitled to practice law, is guilty of a crime punishable by imprisonment in the state prison or county jail.

However, any person who has been involuntarily enrolled as an inactive member of the State Bar pursuant to paragraph (1) of subdivision (e) of Section 6007 and who knowingly thereafter advertises or holds himself or herself out as practicing or otherwise entitled to practice law, is guilty of a crime punishable by imprisonment in the state prison or county jail.

(c) The willful failure of a member of the State Bar, or one who has resigned or been disbarred, to comply with an order of the Supreme Court to comply with Rule 955, constitutes a crime punishable by imprisonment in the state prison or county jail.

§ 6126.5   Additional remedies and penalties

(a) In addition to any remedies and penalties available in any enforcement action brought in the name of the people of the State of California by the Attorney General, a district attorney, or a city attorney, acting as a public prosecutor, the court shall award relief in the enforcement action for any person who obtained services offered or provided in violation of Section 6125 or 6126 or who purchased any goods, services, or real or personal property in connection with services offered or provided in violation of Section 6125 or 6126 against the person who violated Section 6125 or 6126, or who sold goods, services, or property in connection with that violation. The court shall consider the following relief:

(1) Actual damages.

(2) Restitution of all amounts paid.

(3) The amount of penalties and tax liabilities incurred in connection with the sale or transfer of assets to pay for any goods, services, or property.

(4) Reasonable attorney's fees and costs expended to rectify errors made in the unlawful practice of law.

(5) Prejudgment interest at the legal rate from the date of loss to the date of judgment.

(6) Appropriate equitable relief, including the rescission of sales made in connection with a violation of law.

(b) The relief awarded under paragraphs (1) to (6), inclusive, of subdivision (a) shall be distributed to, or on behalf of, the person for whom it was awarded or, if it is impracticable to do so, shall be distributed as may be directed by the court pursuant to its equitable powers.

(c) The court shall also award the Attorney General, district attorney, or city attorney reasonable attorney's fees and costs and, in the court's discretion, exemplary damages as provided in Section 3294 of the Civil Code.

(d) This section shall not be construed to create, abrogate, or otherwise affect claims, rights, or remedies, if any, that may be held by a person or entity other than those law enforcement agencies described in subdivision (a). The remedies provided in this section are cumulative to each other and to the remedies and penalties provided under other laws.

§ 6127.   Contempt of court

The following acts or omissions in respect to the practice of law are contempts of the authority of the courts:

(a) Assuming to be an officer or attorney of a court and acting as such, without authority.

(b) Advertising or holding oneself out as practicing or as entitled to practice law or otherwise practicing law in any court, without being an active member of the State Bar.

Proceedings to adjudge a person in contempt of court under this section are to be taken in accordance with the provisions of Title V of Part III of the Code of Civil Procedure.

§ 6127.5   Law corporation under professional corporation act

Nothing in Sections 6125, 6126 and 6127 shall be deemed to apply to the acts and practices of a law corporation duly certificated pursuant to the Professional Corporation Act, as contained in Part 4 (commencing with Section 13400) of Division 3 of Title 1 of the Corporations Code, and pursuant to Article 10 (commencing with Section 6160) of Chapter 4 of Division 3 of this code, when the law corporation is in compliance with the requirements of (a) the Professional Corporation Act; (b) Article 10 (commencing with Section 6160) of Chapter 4 of Division 3 of this code; and (c) all other statutes and all rules and regulations now or hereafter enacted or adopted pertaining to such corporation and the conduct of its affairs.

§ 6128.   Deceit, collusion, delay of suit and improper receipt of money as misdemeanors

Every attorney is guilty of a misdemeanor who either:

(a) Is guilty of any deceit or collusion, or consents to any deceit or collusion, with intent to deceive the court or any party.

(b) Wilfully delays his client's suit with a view to his own gain.

(c) Wilfully receives any money or allowance for or on account of any money which he has not laid out or become answerable for.

Any violation of the provisions of this section is punishable by imprisonment in the county jail not exceeding six months, or by a fine not exceeding two thousand five hundred dollars ($2,500), or by both.

§ 6129.   Buying claim as misdemeanor

Every attorney who, either directly or indirectly, buys or is interested in buying any evidence of debt or thing in action, with intent to bring suit thereon, is guilty of a misdemeanor.

Any violation of the provisions of this section is punished by imprisonment in the county jail not exceeding six months, or by a fine not exceeding two thousand five hundred dollars ($2,500), or by both.

§ 6130. Disbarred or suspended attorney suing as assignee

No person, who has been an attorney, shall while a judgment of disbarment or suspension is in force appear on his own behalf as plaintiff in the prosecution of any action where the subject of the action has been assigned to him subsequent to the entry of the judgment of disbarment or suspension and solely for purpose of collection.

§ 6131. Aiding defense where partner or self has acted as public prosecutor; misdemeanor and disbarment

Every attorney is guilty of a misdemeanor and, in addition to the punishment prescribed therefor, shall be disbarred:

(a) Who directly or indirectly advises in relation to, or aids, or promotes the defense of any action or proceeding in any court the prosecution of which is carried on, aided or promoted by any person as district attorney or other public prosecutor with whom such person is directly or indirectly connected as a partner.

(b) Who, having himself prosecuted or in any manner aided or promoted any action or proceeding in any court as district attorney or other public prosecutor, afterwards, directly or indirectly, advises in relation to or takes any part in the defense thereof, as attorney or otherwise, or who takes or receives any valuable consideration from or on behalf of any defendant in any such action upon any understanding or agreement whatever having relation to the defense thereof.

This section does not prohibit an attorney from defending himself in person, as attorney or counsel, when prosecuted, either civilly or criminally.

ARTICLE 8.5   FEE AGREEMENTS

§ 6146. Limitations; periodic payments

(a) An attorney shall not contract for or collect a contingency fee for representing any person seeking damages in connection with an action for injury or damage against a health care provider based upon such person's alleged professional negligence in excess of the following limits:

(1) Forty percent of the first fifty thousand dollars ($50,000) recovered.

(2) Thirty-three and one-third percent of the next fifty thousand dollars ($50,000) recovered.

(3) Twenty-five percent of the next five hundred thousand dollars ($500,000) recovered.

(4) Fifteen percent of any amount on which the recovery exceeds six hundred thousand dollars ($600,000).

The limitations shall apply regardless of whether the recovery is by settlement, arbitration, or judgment, or whether the person for whom the recovery is made is a responsible adult, an infant, or a person of unsound mind.

(b) If periodic payments are awarded to the plaintiff pursuant to Section 667.7 of the Code of Civil Procedure, the court shall place a total value on these payments based upon the projected life expectancy of the plaintiff and include this amount in computing the total award from which attorney's fees are calculated under this section.

(c) For purposes of this section:

(1) "Recovered" means the net sum recovered after deducting any disbursements or costs incurred in connection with prosecution or settlement of the claim.   Costs of medical care incurred by the plaintiff and the attorney's office-overhead costs or charges are not deductible disbursements or costs for such purpose.

(2) "Health care provider" means any person licensed or certified pursuant to Division 2 (commencing with Section 500), or licensed pursuant to the Osteopathic Initiative Act, or the Chiropractic Initiative Act, or licensed pursuant to Chapter 2.5 (commencing with Section 1440) of Division 2 of the Health and Safety Code; and any clinic, health dispensary, or health facility, licensed pursuant to Division 2 (commencing with Section 1200) of the Health and Safety Code.   "Health care provider" includes the legal representatives of a health care provider.

(3) "Professional negligence" is a negligent act or omission to act by a health care provider in the rendering of professional services, which act or omission is the proximate cause of a personal injury or wrongful death, provided that the services are within the scope of services for which the provider is licensed and which are not within any restriction imposed by the licensing agency or licensed hospital.

§ 6147.   Contingency fee contracts; duplicate copy; contents; effect of noncompliance; recovery of workers' compensation benefits

(a) An attorney who contracts to represent a client on a contingency fee basis shall, at the time the contract is entered into, provide a duplicate copy of the contract, signed by both the attorney and the client, or the client's guardian or representative, to the client, or to the client's guardian or representative.   The contract shall be in writing and shall include, but is not limited to, all of the following:

(1) A statement of the contingency fee rate that the client and attorney have agreed upon.

(2) A statement as to how disbursements and costs incurred in connection with the prosecution or settlement of the claim will affect the contingency fee and the client's recovery.

(3) A statement as to what extent, if any, the client could be required to pay any compensation to the attorney for related matters that arise out of their relationship not covered by their contingency fee contract. This may include any amounts collected for the plaintiff by the attorney.

(4) Unless the claim is subject to the provisions of Section 6146, a statement that the fee is not set by law but is negotiable between attorney and client.

(5) If the claim is subject to the provisions of Section 6146, a statement that the rates set forth in that section are the maximum limits for the contingency fee agreement, and that the attorney and client may negotiate a lower rate.

(b) Failure to comply with any provision of this section renders the agreement voidable at the option of the plaintiff, and the attorney shall thereupon be entitled to collect a reasonable fee.

(c) This section shall not apply to contingency fee contracts for the recovery of workers' compensation benefits.

(d) This section shall become operative on January 1, 2000.

§ 6147.5 Contingency fee contracts; recovery of claims between merchants

(a) Sections 6147 and 6148 shall not apply to contingency fee contracts for the recovery of claims between merchants as defined in Section 2104 of the Commercial Code, arising from the sale or lease of goods or services rendered, or money loaned for use, in the conduct of a business or profession if the merchant contracting for legal services employs 10 or more individuals.

(b)(1) In the instances in which no written contract for legal services exists as permitted by subdivision (a), an attorney shall not contract for or collect a contingency fee in excess of the following limits:

(A) Twenty percent of the first three hundred dollars ($300) collected.

(B) Eighteen percent of the next one thousand seven hundred dollars ($1,700) collected.

(C) Thirteen percent of sums collected in excess of two thousand dollars ($2,000).

(2) However, the following minimum charges may be charged and collected:

(A) Twenty-five dollars ($25) in collections of seventy-five dollars ($75) to one hundred twenty-five dollars ($125).

(B) Thirty-three and one-third percent of collections less than seventy-five dollars ($75).

§ 6148. Contracts for services in cases not coming within § 6147; bills rendered by attorney; contents; failure to comply

(a) In any case not coming within Section 6147 in which it is reasonably foreseeable that total expense to a client, including attorney fees will exceed one thousand dollars ($1,000), the contract for services in the case shall be in writing. At the time the contract is entered into, the attorney shall provide a duplicate copy of the contract signed by both the attorney and the client, or the client's guardian or representative, to the client or the client's guardian or representative. The written contract shall contain all of the following:

(1) Any basis of compensation including, but not limited to, hourly rates, statutory fees or flat fees, and other standard rates, fees, and charges applicable to the case.

(2) The general nature of the legal services to be provided to the client.

(3) The respective responsibilities of the attorney and the client as to the performance of the contract.

(b) All bills rendered by an attorney to a client shall clearly state the basis thereof. Bills for the fee portion of the bill shall include the amount, rate, basis for calculation, or other method of determination of the attorney's fees and costs. Bills for the cost and expense portion of the bill shall clearly identify the costs and expenses incurred and the amount of the costs and expenses. Upon request by the client, the attorney shall provide a bill to the client no later than 10 days following the request unless the attorney has provided a bill to the client within 31 days prior to the request, in which case the attorney may provide a bill to the client no later than 31 days following the date the most recent bill was provided. The client is entitled to make similar requests at intervals of no less than 30 days following the initial request. In providing responses to client requests for billing information, the attorney may use billing data that is currently effective on the date of the request, or, if any fees or costs to that date cannot be accurately determined, they shall be described and estimated.

(c) Failure to comply with any provision of this section renders the agreement voidable at the option of the client, and the attorney shall, upon the agreement being voided, be entitled to collect a reasonable fee.

(d) This section shall not apply to any of the following:

(1) Services rendered in an emergency to avoid foreseeable prejudice to the rights or interests of the client or where a writing is otherwise impractical.

(2) An arrangement as to the fee implied by the fact that the attorney's services are of the same general kind as previously rendered to and paid for by the client.

(3) If the client knowingly states in writing, after full disclosure of this section, that a writing concerning fees is not required.

(4) If the client is a corporation.

(e) This section applies prospectively only to fee agreements following its operative date.

(f) This section shall become operative on January 1, 2000.

§ 6149.   Written fee contract as confidential communication

A written fee contract shall be deemed to be a confidential communication within the meaning of subdivision (e) of Section 6068 and of Section 952 of the Evidence Code.

§ 6149.5   Third-party liability claim; settlement by insurer; notice to claimant; effect on action or defense

(a) Upon the payment of one hundred dollars ($100) or more in settlement of any third-party liability claim the insurer shall provide written notice to the claimant if both of the following apply:

(1) The claimant is a natural person.

(2) The payment is delivered to the claimant's lawyer or other representative by draft, check, or otherwise.

(b) For purposes of this section, "written notice" includes providing to the claimant a copy of the cover letter sent to the claimant's attorney or other representative that accompanied the settlement payment.

(c) This section shall not create any cause of action for any person against the insurer based upon the insurer's failure to provide the notice to a claimant required by this section. This section shall not create a defense for any party to any cause of action based upon the insurer's failure to provide this notice.

ARTICLE 9.   UNLAWFUL SOLICITATION

§ 6150.   Relation of article to chapter

This article is a part of Chapter 4 of this division of the Business and Professions Code, but the phrase "this chapter" as used in Chapter 4 does not apply to the provisions of this article unless expressly made applicable.

§ 6151.   Definitions

As used in this article:

(a) A runner or capper is any person, firm, association or corporation acting for consideration in any manner or in any capacity as an agent for an attorney at law or law firm, whether the attorney or any member of the law firm is admitted in California or any other jurisdiction, in the solicitation or procurement of business for the attorney at law or law firm as provided in this article.

(b) An agent is one who represents another in dealings with one or more third persons.

§ 6152. Prohibition of solicitation

(a) It is unlawful for:

(1) Any person, in an individual capacity or in a capacity as a public or private employee, or for any firm, corporation, partnership or association to act as a runner or capper for any attorneys or to solicit any business for any attorneys in and about the state prisons, county jails, city jails, city prisons, or other places of detention of persons, city receiving hospitals, city and county receiving hospitals, county hospitals, municipal courts, superior courts, or in any public institution or in any public place or upon any public street or highway or in and about private hospitals, sanitariums or in and about any private institution or upon private property of any character whatsoever.

(2) Any person to solicit another person to commit or join in the commission of a violation of subdivision (a).

(b) A general release from a liability claim obtained from any person during the period of the first physical confinement, whether as an inpatient or outpatient, in a clinic or health facility, as defined in Sections 1203 and 1250 of the Health and Safety Code, as a result of the injury alleged to have given rise to the claim and primarily of treatment of the injury, is presumed fraudulent if the release is executed within 15 days after the commencement of confinement or prior to release from confinement, which ever occurs first.

(c) Nothing in this section shall be construed to prevent the recommendation of professional employment where that recommendation is not prohibited by the Rules of Professional Conduct of the State Bar of California.

(d) Nothing in this section shall be construed to mean that a public defender or assigned counsel may not make known his or her services as a criminal defense attorney to persons unable to afford legal counsel whether those persons are in custody or otherwise.

§ 6153. Violation; penalty

Any person, firm, partnership, association, or corporation violating subdivision (a) of Section 6152 is punishable, upon a first conviction by imprisonment in a county jail for not more than one year or by a fine not exceeding fifteen thousand dollars ($15,000), or by both that imprisonment and fine. Upon a second or subsequent conviction, a person, firm, partnership, association, or corporation is punishable by imprisonment in a county jail for not more than one year, or by imprisonment in the state prison for 2, 3 or 4 years, or by a fine not exceeding fifteen thousand dollars ($15,000), or by both that imprisonment and fine.

Any person employed either as an officer, director, trustee, clerk, servant or agent of this State or of any county or other municipal corporation or subdivision thereof, who is found guilty of violating any of the provisions of this article, shall forfeit the right to his office and employment in addition to any other penalty provided in this article.

§ 6154. Runner or capper used to procure business's void contract; divesting of fees and other compensation; fees recovered from workers' compensation actions

(a) Any contract for professional services secured by any attorney at law or law firm in this state through the services of a runner or capper is void. In any action against any attorney or law firm under the Unfair Practices Act, Chapter 4 (commencing with Section 17000) of Division 7, or Chapter 5 (commencing with Section 17200) of Division 7, any judgment shall include an order divesting the attorney or law firm of any fees and other compensation received pursuant to any such void contract. Those fees and compensation shall be recoverable as additional civil penalties under Chapter 4 (commencing with Section 17000) or Chapter 5 (commencing with Section 17200) of Division 7.

(b) Notwithstanding Section 17206 or any other provision of law, any fees recovered pursuant to subdivision (a) in an action involving professional services related to the provision of workers' compensation shall be allocated as follows: if the action is brought by the Attorney General, one-half of the penalty collected shall be paid to the State General Fund, and one-half of the penalty collected shall be paid to the Workers' Compensation Fraud Account in the Insurance Fund; if the action is brought by a district attorney, one-half of the penalty collected shall be paid to the treasurer of the county in which the judgment was entered, and one-half of the penalty collected shall be paid to the Workers' Compensation Fraud Account in the Insurance Fund; if the action is brought by a city attorney or city prosecutor, one-half of the penalty collected shall be paid to the Workers' Compensation Fraud Account in the Insurance Fund. Moneys deposited into the Workers' Compensation Fraud Account pursuant to this subdivision shall be used in the investigation and prosecution of workers' compensation fraud, as appropriated by the Legislature.

§ 6155. Referral services; conflicts of interest; enforcement; rules and regulations; duration of section

(a) An individual, partnership, corporation, association, or any other entity shall not operate for the direct or indirect purpose, in whole or in part, of referring potential clients to attorneys, and no attorney shall accept a referral of such potential clients, unless all of the following requirements are met:

(1) The service is registered with the State Bar of California and (a) on July 1, 1988, is operated in conformity with minimum standards for a lawyer referral service established by the State Bar, or (b) upon approval by the Supreme Court of minimum standards for a lawyer referral service, is operated in conformity with those standards.

(2) The combined charges to the potential client by the referral service and the attorney to whom the potential client is referred do not exceed the total cost that the client would normally pay if no referral service were involved.

(b) A referral service shall not be owned or operated, in whole or in part, directly or indirectly, by those lawyers to whom, individually or collectively, more than 20 percent of referrals are made. For purposes of this subdivision, a referral service that is owned or operated by a bar association, as defined in the minimum standards, shall be deemed to be owned or operated by its governing committee so long as the governing committee is constituted and functions in the manner prescribed by the minimum standards.

(c) None of the following is a lawyer referral service:

(1) A plan of legal insurance as defined in Section 119.6 of the Insurance Code.

(2) A group or prepaid legal plan, whether operated by a union, trust, mutual benefit or aid association, public or private corporation, or other entity or person, which meets both of the following conditions:

(A) It recommends, furnishes, or pays for legal services to its members or beneficiaries.

(B) It provides telephone advice or personal consultation.

(3) A program having as its purpose the referral of clients to attorneys for representation on a pro bono basis.

(d) The following are in the public interest and do not constitute an unlawful restraint of trade or commerce:

(1) An agreement between a referral service and a participating attorney to eliminate or restrict the attorney's fee for an initial office consultation for each potential client or to provide free or reduced fee services.

(2) Requirements by a referral service that attorneys meet reasonable participation requirements, including experience, education, and training requirements.

(3) Provisions of the minimum standards as approved by the Supreme Court.

(4) Requirements that the application and renewal fees for certification as a lawyer referral service be determined, in whole or in part, by a consideration of any combination of the following factors: a referral service's gross annual revenues, number of panels, number of panel members, amount of fees charged to panel members, or for-profit or nonprofit status; provided that the application and renewal fees do not exceed ten thousand dollars ($10,000) or 1 percent of the gross annual revenues, whichever is less.

(5) Requirements that, to increase access to the justice system for all Californians, lawyer referral services establish separate ongoing activities or arrangements that serve persons of limited means.

(e) A violation or threatened violation of this section may be enjoined by any person.

(f) With the approval of the Supreme Court, the State Bar shall formulate and enforce rules and regulations for carrying out this section, including rules and regulations which do the following:

(1) Establish minimum standards for lawyer referral services. The minimum standards shall include provisions ensuring that panel membership shall be open to all attorneys practicing in the geographical area served who are qualified by virtue of suitable experience, and limiting attorney registration and membership fees to reasonable sums which do not discourage widespread attorney membership.

(2) Require that an entity seeking to qualify as a lawyer referral service register with the State Bar and obtain from the State Bar a certificate of compliance with the minimum standards for lawyer referral services.

(3) Require that the certificate may be obtained, maintained, suspended, or revoked pursuant to procedures set forth in the rules and regulations.

(4) Require the lawyer referral service to pay an application and renewal fee for the certificate in such reasonable amounts as may be determined by the State Bar. The State Bar shall adopt rules authorizing the waiver or reduction of the fees upon a demonstration of financial necessity. The State Bar may require that the application and renewal fees for certification as a lawyer referral service be determined, in whole or in part, by a consideration of any combination of the following factors: a referral service's gross annual revenues, number of panels, number of panel members, amount of fees charged to panel members, or for-profit or nonprofit status; provided that the application and renewal fees do not exceed ten thousand dollars ($10,000) or 1 percent of the gross annual revenues, whichever is less.

(5) Require that, to increase access to the justice system for all Californians, lawyer referral services establish separate ongoing activities or arrangements that serve persons of limited means.

(6) Require each lawyer who is a member of a certified lawyer referral service to comply with all applicable professional standards, rules, and regulations, and to possess a policy of errors and omissions insurance in an amount not less than one hundred thousand dollars ($100,000) for each occurrence and three hundred thousand dollars ($300,000) aggregate, per year. By rule, the State Bar may provide for alternative proof of financial responsibility to meet this requirement.

(g) Provide that cause for denial of certification or recertification or revocation of certification of a lawyer referral service shall include, but not be limited to:

(1) Noncompliance with the statutes or minimum standards governing lawyer referral services as adopted and from time to time amended.

(2) Sharing common or cross ownership, interests, or operations with any entity which engages in referrals to licensed or unlicensed health care providers.

(3) Direct or indirect consideration regarding referrals between an owner, operator, or member of a lawyer referral service and any licensed or unlicensed health care provider.

(4) Advertising on behalf of attorneys in violation of the Rules of Professional Conduct or the Business and Professions Code.

(h) This section shall not be construed to prohibit attorneys from jointly advertising their services.

(1) Permissible joint advertising, among other things, identifies by name the advertising attorneys or law firms whom the consumer of legal services may select and initiate contact with.

(2) Certifiable referral activity involves, among other things, some person or entity other than the consumer and advertising attorney or law firms which, in person, electronically, or otherwise, refers the consumer to an attorney or law firm not identified in the advertising.

(i) A lawyer referral service certified under this section and operating in full compliance with this section, and in full compliance with the minimum standards and the rules and regulations of the State Bar governing lawyer referral services, shall not be deemed to be in violation of Section 3215 of the Labor Code or Section 750 of the Insurance Code.

(j) The payment by an attorney or law firm member of a certified referral service of the normal fees of that service shall not be deemed to be in violation of Section 3215 of the Labor Code or Section 750 of the Insurance Code, provided that the attorney or law firm member is in full compliance with the minimum standards and the rules and regulations of the State Bar governing lawyer referral services.

(k) Certifications of lawyer referral services issued by the State Bar shall not be transferable.

[Ed. Note: The California Bar has prepared two documents relating to referral services: (1) Minimum Standards for a Lawyer Referral Service in California, and (2) Certification and Renewal Fees for Lawyer Referral Services. These documents are omitted from this publication.]

ARTICLE 9.5   LEGAL ADVERTISING

§ 6157. Definitions

As used in this article, the following definitions apply:

(a) "Member" means a member in good standing of the State Bar and includes the terms "lawyer" and "attorney" and includes any agent of the member and any law firm or law corporation doing business in the State of California.

(b) "Lawyer" means a member of the State Bar or a person who is admitted in good standing and eligible to practice before the bar of any United States court or the highest court of the District of Columbia or any state, territory, or insular possession of the United States, or is licensed to practice law in, or is admitted in good standing and eligible to practice before the bar of the highest court of, a foreign country or any political subdivision thereof, and includes any agent of the lawyer or law firm or law corporation doing business in the this state.

(c) "Advertise" or "advertisement" means any communication, disseminated by television or radio, by any print medium including, but not limited to, newspapers and billboards, or by means of a mailing directed generally to members of the public and not to a specific person, that solicits employment of legal services provided by a member, and is directed to the general public and is paid for by, or on the behalf of, an attorney.

(d) "Electronic medium" means television, radio, or computer networks.

§ 6157.1 False, misleading or deceptive statements; prohibition

No advertisement shall contain any false, misleading, or deceptive statement or omit to state any fact necessary to make the statements made, in light of circumstances under which they are made, not false, misleading, or deceptive.

§ 6157.2 Prohibited statements regarding outcome; dramatizations; contingent fee basis representations

No advertisement shall contain or refer to any of the following:

(a) Any guarantee or warranty regarding the outcome of a legal matter as a result of representation by the member.

(b) Statements or symbols stating that the member featured in the advertisement can generally obtain immediate cash or quick settlements.

(c)(1) An impersonation of the name, voice, photograph, or electronic image of any person other than the lawyer, directly or implicitly purporting to be that of a lawyer.

(2) An impersonation of the name, voice, photograph, or electronic image of any person directly or implicitly purporting to be a client of the member featured in the advertisement, or a dramatization of events, unless disclosure of the impersonation or dramatization is made in the advertisement.

(3) A spokesperson, including a celebrity spokesperson, unless there is a disclosure of the spokesperson's title.

(d) A statement that a member offers representation on a contingent basis unless the statement also advises whether a client will be held responsible for any costs advanced by the member when no recovery is obtained on behalf of the client. If the client will not be held responsible for costs, no disclosure is required.

§ 6157.3 Advertisements made on behalf of member; required representations

Any advertisement made on behalf of a member, which is not paid for by the member, shall disclose any business relationship, past or present, between the member and the person paying for the advertisement.

§ 6157.4 Lawyer referral service advertising

Any advertisement that is created or disseminated by a lawyer referral service shall disclose whether the attorneys on the organization's referral list, panel, or system, paid any consideration, other than a proportional share of actual cost, to be included on that list, panel, or system.

§ 6157.5 Immigration and naturalization services advertising; member seeking professional employment; application of section

(a) All advertisements published, distributed, or broadcasted by or on behalf of a member seeking professional employment for the member in providing services relating to immigration or naturalization shall include a statement that he or she is an active member of the State Bar, licensed to practice law in this state. If the advertisement seeks employment for a law firm or law corporation employing more than one attorney, the advertisement shall include a statement that all the services relating to immigration and naturalization provided by the firm or corporation shall be provided by an active member of the State Bar or by a person under the supervision of an active member of the State Bar. This subdivision shall not apply to classified or "yellow pages" listings in a telephone or business directory of three lines or less that state only the name, address, and telephone number of the listed entity.

(b) If the advertisement is in a language other than English, the statement required by subdivision (a) shall be in the same language as the advertisement.

(c) This section shall not apply to members employed by public agencies or by nonprofit entities registered with the Secretary of State.

(d) A violation of this section by a member shall be cause for discipline by the State Bar.

§ 6158. Electronic media advertising; false, misleading or deceptive message; factual substantiation

In advertising by electronic media, to comply with Sections 6157.1 and 6157.2, the message as a whole may not be false, misleading, or deceptive, and the message as a whole must be factually substantiated. The message means the effect in combination of the spoken word, sound, background, action, symbols, visual image, or any other technique employed to create the message. Factually substantiated means capable of verification by a credible source.

§ 6158.1. False, misleading or deceptive messages; rebuttable presumption

There shall be a rebuttable presumption affecting the burden of producing evidence that the following messages are false, misleading, or deceptive within the meaning of Section 6158:

(a) A message as to the ultimate result of a specific case or cases presented out of context without adequately providing information as to the facts or law giving rise to the result.

(b) The depiction of an event through methods such as the use of displays of injuries, accident scenes, or portrayals of other injurious events which may or may not be accompanied by sound effects and which may give rise to a claim for compensation.

(c) A message referring to or implying money received by or for a client in a particular case or cases, or to potential monetary recovery for a prospective client. A reference to money or monetary recovery includes, but is not limited to, a specific dollar amount, characterization of a sum of money, monetary symbols, or the implication of wealth.

§ 6158.2. Information presumed to be in compliance with article

The following information shall be presumed to be in compliance with this article for purposes of advertising by electronic media, provided the message as a whole is not false, misleading, or deceptive:

(a) Name, including name of law firm, names of professional associates, addresses, telephone numbers, and the designation "lawyer," "attorney," "law firm," or the like.

(b) Fields of practice, limitation of practice, or specialization.

(c) Fees for routine legal services, subject to the requirements of subdivision (d) of Section 6157.2 and the Rules of Professional Conduct.

(d) Date and place of birth.

(e) Date and place of admission to the bar of state and federal courts.

(f) Schools attended, with dates of graduation, degrees, and other scholastic distinctions.

(g) Public or quasi-public offices.

(h) Military service.

(i) Legal authorship.

(j) Legal teaching positions.

(k) Memberships, offices, and committee assignments in bar associations.

(l) Memberships and offices in legal fraternities and legal societies.

(m) Technical and professional licenses.

(n) Memberships in scientific, technical, and professional associations and societies.

(o) Foreign language ability of the advertising lawyer or a member of lawyer's firm.

§ 6158.3. Electronic media advertising; required disclosures

In addition to any disclosure required by Section 6157.2, Section 6157.3, and the Rules of Professional Conduct, the following disclosure shall appear in advertising by electronic media. Use of the following disclosure alone may not rebut any presumption created in Section 6158.1. If an advertisement in the electronic media conveys a message portraying a result in a particular case or cases, the advertisement must state, in either an oral or printed communication, either of the following disclosures: The advertisement must adequately disclose the factual and legal circumstances that justify the result portrayed in the message, including the basis for liability and the nature of injury or damage sustained, or the advertisement must state that the result portrayed in the advertisement was dependent on the facts of that case, and that the results will differ if based on different facts.

§ 6158.4. Violation; complaint; contents; procedure

(a) Any person claiming a violation of Section 6158, 6158.1, or 6158.3 may file a complaint with the State Bar that states the name of the advertiser, a description of the advertisement claimed to violate these sections, and that specifically identifies the alleged violation. A copy of the complaint shall be served simultaneously upon the advertiser. The advertiser shall have nine days from the date of service of the complaint to voluntarily withdraw from broadcast the advertisement that is the subject of the complaint. If the advertiser elects to withdraw the advertisement, the advertiser shall notify the State Bar of that fact, and no further action may be taken by the complainant. The advertiser shall provide a copy of the complained of advertisement to the State Bar for review within seven days of service of the complaint. Within 21 days of the delivery of the complained of advertisement, the State Bar shall determine whether substantial evidence of a violation of these sections exists. The review shall be conducted by a State Bar attorney who has expertise in the area of lawyer advertising.

(b)(1) Upon a State Bar determination that substantial evidence of a violation exists, if the member or certified lawyer referral service withdraws that advertisement from broadcast within 72 hours, no further action may be taken by the complainant.

(2) Upon a State Bar determination that substantial evidence of a violation exists, if the member or certified lawyer referral service fails to withdraw the advertisement within 72 hours, a civil enforcement action brought pursuant to subdivision (e) may be commenced within one year of the State Bar decision. If the member or certified lawyer referral service withdraws an advertisement upon a State Bar determination that substantial evidence of a violation exists and subsequently rebroadcasts the same advertisement without a finding by the trier of fact in an action brought pursuant to subdivision (c) or (e) that the advertisement does not violate Section 6158, 6158.1, or 6158.3, a civil enforcement action may be commenced within one year of the rebroadcast.

(3) Upon a determination that substantial evidence of a violation does not exist, the complainant is barred from bringing a civil enforcement action pursuant to subdivision (e), but may bring an action for declaratory relief pursuant to subdivision (c).

(c) Any member or certified lawyer referral service who was the subject of a complaint and any complainant affected by the decision of the State Bar may bring an action for declaratory relief in the superior court to obtain a judicial declaration of whether Section 6158, 6158.1, or 6158.3 has been violated, and, if applicable, may also request injunctive relief. Any defense otherwise available at law may be raised for the first time in the declaratory relief action, including any constitutional challenge. Any civil enforcement action filed pursuant to subdivision (e) shall be stayed pending the resolution of the declaratory relief action. The action shall be defended by the real party in interest. The State Bar shall not be considered a party to the action unless it elects to intervene in the action.

(1) Upon a State Bar determination that substantial evidence of a violation exists, if the complainant or the member or certified lawyer referral service brings an action for declaratory relief to obtain a judicial declaration of whether the advertisement violates Section 6158, 6158.1, or 6158.3, and the court declares that the advertisement violates one or more of the sections, a civil enforcement action pursuant to subdivision

(e) may be filed or maintained if the member or certified lawyer referral service failed to withdraw the advertisement within 72 hours of the State Bar determination. The decision of the court that an advertisement violates Section 6158, 6158.1, or 6158.3 shall be binding on the issue of whether the advertisement is unlawful in any pending or prospective civil enforcement action brought pursuant to subdivision (e) if that binding effect is supported by the doctrine of collateral estoppel or res judicata.

If, in that declaratory relief action, the court declares that the advertisement does not violate Section 6158, 6158.1, or 6158.3, the member or lawyer referral service may broadcast the advertisement. The decision of the court that an advertisement does not violate Section 6158, 6158.1, or 6158.3 shall bar any pending or prospective civil enforcement action brought pursuant to subdivision (e) if that prohibitive effect is supported by the doctrine of collateral estoppel or res judicata.

(2) If, following a State Bar determination that does not find substantial evidence that an advertisement violates Section 6158, 6158.1, or 6158.3, the complainant or the member or certified lawyer referral service brings an action for declaratory relief to obtain a judicial declaration of whether the advertisement violates Section 6158, 6158.1, or 6158.3, and the court declares that the advertisement violates one or more of the sections, a civil enforcement action pursuant to subdivision (e) may be filed or maintained if the member or certified lawyer referral service broadcasts the same advertisement following the decision in the declaratory relief action. The decision of the court that an advertisement violates Section 6158, 6158.1, or 6158.3 shall be binding on the issue of whether the advertisement is unlawful in any pending or prospective civil enforcement action brought pursuant to subdivision (e) if that binding effect is supported by the doctrine of collateral estoppel or res judicata.

If, in that declaratory relief action, the court declares that the advertisement does not violate Section 6158, 6158.1, or 6158.3, the member or lawyer referral service may continue broadcast of the advertisement. The decision of the court that an advertisement does not violate Section 6158, 6158.1, or 6158.3 shall bar any pending or prospective civil enforcement action brought pursuant to subdivision (e) if that prohibitive effect is supported by the doctrine of collateral estoppel or res judicata.

(d) The State Bar review procedure shall apply only to members and certified referral services. A direct civil enforcement action for a violation of Section 6158, 6158.1, or 6158.3 may be maintained against any other advertiser after first giving 14 days' notice to the advertiser of the alleged violation. If the advertiser does not withdraw from broadcast the advertisement that is the subject of the notice within 14 days of service of the notice, a civil enforcement action pursuant to subdivision (e) may be commenced. The civil enforcement action shall be commenced within one year of the date of the last publication or broadcast of the advertisement that is the subject of the action.

(e) Subject to Section 6158.5, a violation of Section 6158, 6158.1, or 6158.3 shall be cause for a civil enforcement action brought by any person residing within the State of California for an amount up to five thousand dollars ($5,000) for each individual broadcast that violates Section 6158, 6158.1, or 6158.3. Venue shall be in a county where the advertisement was broadcast.

(f) In any civil action brought pursuant to this section, the matter shall be determined according to the law and procedure relating to the trial of civil actions, including trial by jury, if demanded.

(g) The decision of the State Bar pursuant to subdivision (a) shall be admissible in the civil enforcement action brought pursuant to subdivision (e). However, the State Bar shall not be a party or a witness in either a declaratory relief proceeding brought pursuant to subdivision (c) or the civil enforcement action brought pursuant to subdivision (e). Additionally, no direct action may be filed against the State Bar challenging the State Bar's decision pursuant to subdivision (a).

(h) Amounts recovered pursuant to this section shall be paid into the Client Security Fund maintained by the State Bar.

(i) In any civil action brought pursuant to this section, the court shall award attorney's fees pursuant to Section 1021.5 of the Code of Civil Procedure if the court finds that the action has resulted in the enforcement of an important public interest or that a significant benefit has been conferred on the public.

(j) The State Bar shall maintain records of all complainants and complaints filed pursuant to subdivision (a) for a period of seven years. If a complainant files five or more unfounded complaints within seven years, the complainant shall be considered a vexatious litigant for purposes of this section. The State Bar shall require any person deemed a vexatious litigant to post security in the minimum amount of twenty-five thousand dollars ($25,000) prior to considering any complaint filed by that person and shall refrain from taking any action until the security is posted. In any civil action arising from this section brought by a person deemed a vexatious litigant, the defendant may advise the court and trier of fact that the plaintiff is deemed to be a vexatious litigant under the provisions of this section and disclose the basis for this determination.

(k) Nothing in this section shall restrict any other right available under existing law or otherwise available to a citizen seeking redress for false, misleading, or deceptive advertisements.

§ 6158.5. Application of article

This article applies to all lawyers, members, law partnerships, law corporations, entities subject to regulation under Section 6155, advertising collectives, cooperatives, or other individuals, including nonlawyers, or groups advertising the availability of legal services. Subdivisions (a) to (k), inclusive, of Section 6158.4 do not apply to qualified legal services projects as defined in Article 14 (commencing with Section 6210) and nonprofit lawyer referral services certified under Section 6155. Sections 6157 to 6158.5, inclusive, do not apply to the media in which the advertising is displayed or to an advertising agency that prepares the contents of an advertisement and is not directly involved in the formation or operation of lawyer advertising collectives or cooperatives, referral services, or other groups existing primarily for the purpose of advertising the availability of legal services or making referrals to attorneys.

§ 6158.7. Violation as cause for discipline by state bar

A violation of Section 6158, 6158.1, or 6158.3 by a member shall be cause for discipline by the State Bar. In addition to the existing grounds for initiating a disciplinary proceeding set forth in a statute or in the Rules of Professional Conduct, the State Bar may commence an investigation based upon a complaint filed by a person pursuant to Section 6158.4. The State Bar's decision pursuant to subdivision (a) of Section 6158.4 shall be admissible, but shall not be determinative, in any disciplinary proceeding brought as a result of that complaint.

§ 6159. Report by court of article violators

The court shall report the name, address, and professional license number of any person found in violation of this article to the appropriate professional licensing agency for review and possible disciplinary action.

§ 6159.1 Retention of advertising copy by payor

A true and correct copy of any advertisement made by a person or member shall be retained for one year by the person or member who pays for an advertisement soliciting employment of legal services.

§ 6159.2 Rights and duties under other laws

(a) Nothing in this article shall be deemed to limit or preclude enforcement of any other provision of law, or of any court rule, or of the State Bar Rules of Professional Conduct.

(b) Nothing in this article shall limit the right of advertising protected under the Constitution of the State of California or of the United States. If any provision of this article is found to violate either Constitution, that provision is severable and the remaining provisions shall be enforceable without the severed provision.

ARTICLE 13.   ARBITRATION OF ATTORNEYS' FEES

§ 6200.   Establishment of system and procedure; applicability of article; voluntary or mandatory nature; rules; immunity of arbitrator; powers of arbitrator; confidentiality of mediation

(a) The board of governors shall, by rule, establish, maintain, and administer a system and procedure for the arbitration, and may establish, maintain, and administer a system and procedure for mediation of disputes concerning fees, costs, or both, charged for professional services by members of the State Bar or by members of the bar of other jurisdictions.   The rules may include provision for a filing fee in such amount as the board may, from time to time, determine.

(b) This article shall not apply to any of the following:

(1) Disputes where a member of the State Bar of California is also admitted to practice in another jurisdiction or where an attorney is only admitted to practice in another jurisdiction, and he or she maintains no office in the State of California, and no material portion of the services were rendered in the State of California.

(2) Claims for affirmative relief against the attorney for damages or otherwise based upon alleged malpractice or professional misconduct, except as provided in subdivision (a) of Section 6203.

(3) Disputes where the fee or cost to be paid by the client or on his or her behalf has been determined pursuant to statute or court order.

(c) Unless the client has agreed in writing to arbitration under this article of all disputes concerning fees, costs, or both, arbitration under this article shall be voluntary for a client and shall be mandatory for an attorney if commenced by a client.   Mediation under this article shall be voluntary for an attorney and a client.

(d) The board of governors shall adopt rules to allow arbitration and mediation of attorney fee and cost disputes under this article to proceed under arbitration and mediation systems sponsored by local bar associations in this state.   Rules of procedure promulgated by local bar associations are subject to review by the board to insure that they provide for a fair, impartial, and speedy hearing and award.

(e) In adopting or reviewing rules of arbitration under this section the board shall provide that the panel shall include one attorney member whose area of practice is either, at the option of the client, civil law, if the attorney's representation involved civil law, or criminal law, if the attorney's representation involved criminal law, as follows:

(1) If the panel is composed of three members the panel shall include one attorney member whose area of practice is either, at the

option of the client, civil or criminal law, and shall include one lay member.

(2) If the panel is composed of one member, that member shall be an attorney whose area of practice is either, at the option of the client, civil or criminal law.

(f) In any arbitration or mediation conducted pursuant to this article by the State Bar or by a local bar association, pursuant to rules of procedure approved by the board of governors, an arbitrator or mediator, as well as the arbitrating association and its directors, officers, and employees, shall have the same immunity which attaches in judicial proceedings.

(g) In the conduct of arbitrations under this article the arbitrator or arbitrators may do all of the following:

(1) Take and hear evidence pertaining to the proceeding.

(2) Administer oaths and affirmations.

(3) Compel, by subpoena, the attendance of witnesses and the production of books, papers, and documents pertaining to the proceeding.

(h) Participation in mediation is a voluntary consensual process, based on direct negotiations between the attorney and his or her client, and is an extension of the negotiated settlement process. All discussions and offers of settlement are confidential and may not be disclosed in any subsequent arbitration or other proceedings.

§ 6201. Notice to client and state bar; stay of action; right to arbitration; waiver by client

(a) The rules adopted by the board of governors shall provide that an attorney shall forward a written notice to the client prior to or at the time of service of summons or claim in an action against the client or prior to or at the commencement of any other proceeding against client under a contract between attorney and client which provides for an alternative to arbitration under this article, for recovery of fees, costs, or both. The written notice shall be in the form that the board of governors prescribes, and shall include a statement of the client's right to arbitration under this article. Failure to give this notice shall be a ground for the dismissal of the action or other proceeding. The notice shall not be required, however, prior to initiating mediation of the dispute.

The rules adopted by the board of governors shall provide that the client's failure to request arbitration within 30 days after receipt of notice from the attorney shall be deemed a waiver of the client's right to arbitration under the provisions of this article.

(b) If an attorney, or the attorney's assignee, commences an action in any court or any other proceeding and the client is entitled to maintain arbitration under this article, and the dispute is not one to which subdivision (b) of Section 6200 applies, the client may stay the action or other proceeding by serving and filing a request for arbitration in accordance with the rules established by the board of governors pursuant to subdivision (a) of Section 6200. The request for arbitration shall be served and filed prior to the filing of an answer in the action or equivalent response in the other proceeding; failure to so request arbitration prior to the filing of an answer or equivalent response shall be deemed a waiver of the client's right to arbitration under the provisions of this article if notice of the client's right to arbitration was given pursuant to subdivision (a).

(c) Upon filing and service of the request for arbitration, the action or other proceeding shall be automatically stayed until the award of the arbitrators is issued or the arbitration is otherwise terminated. The stay may be vacated in whole or in part, after a hearing duly noticed by any party or the court, if and to the extent the court finds that the matter is not appropriate for arbitration under the provisions of this article. The action or other proceeding may thereafter proceed subject to the provisions of Section 6204.

(d) A client's right to request or maintain arbitration under the provisions of this article is waived by the client commencing an action or filing any pleading seeking either of the following: (1) Judicial resolution of a fee dispute to which this article applies. (2) Affirmative relief against the attorney for damages or otherwise based upon alleged malpractice or professional misconduct.

(e) If the client waives the right to arbitration under this article, the parties may stipulate to set aside the waiver and to proceed with arbitration.

§ 6203. Award; contents; damages and offset; fees and costs; finality of award; appellate fees and costs; attorney inactive status and penalties

(a) The award shall be in writing and signed by the arbitrators concurring therein. It shall include a determination of all the questions submitted to the arbitrators, the decision of which is necessary in order to determine the controversy. The award shall not include any award to either party for costs or attorney's fees incurred in preparation for or in the course of the fee arbitration proceeding, notwithstanding any contract between the parties providing for such an award or attorney's fees. However, the filing fee paid may be allocated between the parties by the arbitrators. This section shall not preclude an award of costs or attorney's fees to either party by a court pursuant to subdivision (c) of this section or of subdivision (d) of Section 6204. The State Bar, or the local bar association delegated by the State Bar to conduct the arbitration, shall deliver to each of the parties with the award, an original declaration of service of the award.

Evidence relating to claims of malpractice and professional misconduct, shall be admissible only to the extent that those claims bear upon the fees, costs, or both, to which the attorney is entitled. The arbitrators shall not award affirmative relief, in the form of damages or offset or otherwise, for injuries underlying any such claim. Nothing in this section shall be construed to prevent the arbitrators from awarding a refund of unearned prepaid fees.

(b) Even if the parties to the arbitration have not agreed in writing to be bound, the arbitration award shall become binding upon the passage of 30 days after mailing of notice of the award, unless a party has, within the 30 days, sought a trial after arbitration pursuant to Section 6204. If an action has previously been filed in any court, any petition to confirm, correct, or vacate the award shall be to the court in which the action is pending, and may be served by mail on any party who has appeared, as provided in Chapter 4 (commencing with Section 1003) of Title 14 of Part 2 of the Code of Civil Procedure; otherwise it shall be in the same manner as provided in Chapter 4 (commencing with Section 1285) of Title 9 of Part 3 of the Code of Civil Procedure. If no action is pending in any court, the award may be confirmed, corrected, or vacated by petition to the court having jurisdiction over the amount of the arbitration award, but otherwise in the same manner as provided in Chapter 4 (commencing with Section 1285) of Title 9 of Part 3 of the Code of Civil Procedure.

(c) Neither party to the arbitration may recover costs or attorney's fees incurred in preparation for or in the course of the fee arbitration proceeding with the exception of the filing fee paid pursuant to subdivision (a) of this section. However, a court confirming, correcting, or vacating an award under this section may award to the prevailing party reasonable fees and costs including, if applicable, fees or costs on appeal, incurred in obtaining confirmation, correction, or vacation of the award. The party obtaining judgment confirming, correcting, or vacating the award shall be the prevailing party except that, without regard to consideration of who the prevailing party may be, if a party did not appear at the arbitration hearing in the manner provided by the rules adopted by the board of governors, that party shall not be entitled to attorney's fees or costs upon confirmation, correction, or vacation of the award.

(d)(1) In any matter arbitrated under this article in which the award is binding or has become binding by operation of law or has become a judgment either after confirmation under subdivision (c) or after a trial after arbitration under Section 6204, or in any matter mediated under this article, if: (A) the award, judgment, or agreement reached after mediation includes a refund of fees or costs, or both, to the client and (B) the attorney has not complied with that award, judgment, or agreement the State Bar shall enforce the award, judgment, or agreement by placing the attorney on involuntary inactive status until the refund has been paid.

(2) The State Bar shall provide for an administrative procedure to determine whether an award, judgment, or agreement should be enforced pursuant to this subdivision. An award, judgment, or agreement shall be so enforced if either of the following applies:

> (A) The State Bar shows that the attorney has failed to comply with a binding fee arbitration award, judgment, or agreement rendered pursuant to this article.

> (B) The attorney has not proposed a payment plan acceptable to the client or the State Bar.

However, the award, judgment, or agreement shall not be so enforced if the attorney has demonstrated that he or she (i) is not personally responsible for making or ensuring payment of the refund, or (ii) is unable to pay the refund.

(3) An attorney who has failed to comply with a binding award, judgment, or agreement shall pay administrative penalties or reasonable costs, or both, as directed by the State Bar. Penalties imposed shall not exceed 20 percent of the amount to be refunded to the client or one thousand dollars ($1,000), whichever is greater. Any penalties or costs, or both, that are not paid shall be added to the membership fee of the attorney for the next calendar year.

(4) The board shall terminate the inactive enrollment upon proof that the attorney has complied with the award, judgment, or agreement and upon payment of any costs or penalties, or both, assessed as a result of the attorney's failure to comply.

(5) A request for enforcement under this subdivision shall be made within four years from the date (A) the arbitration award was mailed, (B) the judgment was entered, or (C) the date the agreement was signed. In an arbitrated matter, however, in no event shall a request be made prior to 100 days from the date of the service of a signed copy of the award. In cases where the award is appealed, a request shall not be made prior to 100 days from the date the award has become final as set forth in this section.

ARTICLE 14. FUNDS FOR THE PROVISION OF LEGAL SERVICES TO INDIGENT PERSONS

§ 6210. Legislative findings; purpose

The Legislature finds that, due to insufficient funding, existing programs providing free legal services in civil matters to indigent persons, especially underserved client groups, such as the elderly, the disabled, juveniles, and non-English-speaking persons, do not adequately meet the needs of these persons. It is the purpose of this article to expand the availability and improve the quality of existing free legal services in civil matters to indigent persons, and to initiate new programs that will provide services to them. The Legislature finds that the use of funds collected by the State Bar pursuant to this article for these purposes is in the public interest, is a proper use of the funds, and is consistent with essential public and governmental purposes in the judicial branch of government. The Legislature further finds that the expansion, improvement, and initiation of legal services to indigent persons will aid in the advancement of the science of jurisprudence and the improvement of the administration of justice.

§ 6211. Establishment by attorney of demand trust account; interest earned to be paid to state bar; other accounts not prohibited; rules of professional conduct, authority of supreme court or state bar not affected

(a) An attorney or law firm, which in the course of the practice of law receives or disburses trust funds, shall establish and maintain an interest bearing demand trust account and shall deposit therein all client deposits that are nominal in amount or are on deposit for a short period of time. All such client funds may be deposited in a single unsegregated account. The interest earned on all such accounts shall be paid to the State Bar of California to be used for the purposes set forth in this article.

(b) Nothing in this article shall be construed to prohibit an attorney or law firm from establishing one or more interest bearing bank accounts or other trust investments as may be permitted by the Supreme Court, with the interest or dividends earned on the accounts payable to clients for trust funds not deposited in accordance with subdivision (a).

(c) With the approval of the Supreme Court, the State Bar may formulate and enforce rules of professional conduct pertaining to the use by attorneys or law firms of interest bearing trust accounts for unsegregated client funds pursuant to this article.

(d) Nothing in this article shall be construed as affecting or impairing the disciplinary powers and authority of the Supreme Court or of the State Bar or as modifying the statutes and rules governing the conduct of members of the State Bar.

§ 6212. Establishment by attorney of demand trust account; amount of interest; remittance to state bar; statements and reports

An attorney who, or a law firm which, establishes an interest bearing demand trust account pursuant to subdivision (a) of Section 6211 shall comply with all of the following provisions:

(a) The interest bearing trust account shall be established with a bank or such other financial institution as are authorized by the Supreme Court.

(b) The rate of interest payable on any interest bearing demand trust account shall not be less than the rate paid by the depository institution to regular, nonattorney depositors. Higher rates offered by the institution to customers whose deposits exceed certain time or quantity qualifications, such as those offered in the form of certificates of deposit, may be obtained by an attorney or law firm so long as there is no impairment of the right to withdraw or transfer principal immediately (except as accounts generally may be subject to statutory notification requirements), even though interest may be sacrificed thereby.

(c) The depository institution shall be directed to do all of the following:

(1) To remit interest on the average daily balance in the account, less reasonable service charges, to the State Bar, at least quarterly.

(2) To transmit to the State Bar with each remittance a statement showing the name of the attorney or law firm for whom the remittance is sent, the rate of interest applied, and the amount of service charges deducted, if any.

(3) To transmit to the depositing attorney or law firm at the same time a report showing the amount paid to the State Bar for that period, the rate of interest applied, the amount of service charges deducted, if any, and the average daily account balance for each month of the period for which the report is made.

§ 6213. Definitions

As used in this article:

(a) "Qualified legal services project" means either of the following:

(1) A nonprofit project incorporated and operated exclusively in California which provides as its primary purpose and function legal services without charge to indigent persons and which has quality control procedures approved by the State Bar of California.

(2) A program operated exclusively in California by a nonprofit law school accredited by the State Bar of California which meets the requirements of subparagraphs (A) and (B).

(A) The program shall have operated for at least two years at a cost of at least twenty thousand dollars ($20,000) per year as an identifiable law school unit with a primary purpose and function of providing legal services without charge to indigent persons.

(B) The program shall have quality control procedures approved by the State Bar of California.

(b) "Qualified support center" means an incorporated nonprofit legal services center, which has as its primary purpose and function the provision of legal training, legal technical assistance, or advocacy support without charge and which actually provides through an office in California a significant level of legal training, legal technical assistance, or advocacy support without charge to qualified legal services projects on a statewide basis in California.

(c) "Recipient" means a qualified legal services project or support center receiving financial assistance under this article.

(d) "Indigent person" means a person whose income is (1) 125 percent or less of the current poverty threshold established by the United States Office of Management and Budget, or (2) who is eligible for Supplemental Security Income or free services under the Older Americans Act or Developmentally Disabled Assistance Act. With regard to a project which provides free services of attorneys in private practice without compensation, "indigent person" also means a person whose income is 75 percent or less of the maximum levels of income for lower income households as defined in Section 50079.5 of the Health and Safety Code. For the purpose of this subdivision, the income of a person who is disabled shall be determined after deducting the costs of medical and other disability-related special expenses.

(e) "Fee generating case" means any case or matter which, if undertaken on behalf of an indigent person by an attorney in private practice, reasonably may be expected to result in payment of a fee for legal services from an award to a client, from public funds, or from the opposing party. A case shall not be considered fee generating if adequate representation is unavailable and any of the following circumstances exist:

(1) The recipient has determined that free referral is not possible because of any of the following reasons:

(A) The case has been rejected by the local lawyer referral service, or if there is no such service, by two attorneys in private practice who have experience in the subject matter of the case.

(B) Neither the referral service nor any attorney will consider the case without payment of a consultation fee.

(C) The case if of the type that attorneys in private practice in the area ordinarily do not accept, or do not accept without prepayment of a fee.

(D) Emergency circumstances compel immediate action before referral can be made, but the client is advised that, if appropriate and consistent with professional responsibility, referral will be attempted at a later time.

(2) Recovery of damages is not the principal object of the case and a request for damages is merely ancillary to an action for equitable or other nonpecuniary relief, or inclusion of a counterclaim requesting damages is necessary for effective defense or because of applicable rules governing joinder of counterclaims.

(3) A court has appointed a recipient or an employee of a recipient pursuant to a statute or a court rule or practice of equal applicability to all attorneys in the jurisdiction.

(4) The case involves the rights of a claimant under a publicly supported benefit program for which entitlement to benefit is based on need.

(f) "Legal Services Corporation" means the Legal Services Corporation established under the Legal Services Corporation Act of 1974, (Public Law 93–355; 42 U.S.C. Sec. 2996 et seq.).

(g) "Older Americans Act" means the Older Americans Act of 1965, as amended (Public Law 89–73; 42 U.S.C. Sec. 3001 et seq.).

(h) "Developmentally Disabled Assistance Act" means the Developmentally Disabled Assistance and Bill of Rights Act of 1975, as amended (Public Law 94–103; 42 U.S.C. Sec. 6001 et seq.).

(i) "Supplemental security income recipient" means an individual receiving or eligible to receive payments under Title XVI of the federal Social Security Act, or payments under Chapter 3 (commencing with Section 12000) of Part 3 of Division 9 of the Welfare and Institutions Code.

§ 6214. Qualified legal service projects

(a) Projects meeting the requirements of subdivision (a) of Section 6213 which are funded either in whole or part by the Legal Services Corporation or with Older American Act funds shall be presumed qualified legal services projects for the purpose of this article.

(b) Projects meeting the requirements of subdivision (a) of Section 6213 but not qualifying under the presumption specified in subdivision (a) shall qualify for funds under this article if they meet all of the following additional criteria:

(1) They receive cash funds from other sources in the amount of at least twenty thousand dollars ($20,000) per year to support free legal representation to indigent persons.

(2) They have demonstrated community support for the operation of a viable ongoing program.

(3) They provide one or both of the following special services:

(A) The coordination of the recruitment of substantial numbers of attorneys in private practice to provide free legal representation to indigent persons or to qualified legal services projects in California.

(B) The provision of legal representation, training, or technical assistance on matters concerning special client groups, including the elderly, the disabled, juveniles, and non-English-speaking groups, or on matters of specialized substantive law important to the special client groups.

§ 6214.5 Qualified legal services projects; eligibility for distributions of funds

A law school program that meets the definition of a "qualified legal services project" as defined in paragraph (2) of subdivision (a) of Section 6213, and that applied to the State Bar for funding under this article not later than February 17, 1984, shall be deemed eligible for all distributions of funds made under Section 6216.

§ 6215. Qualified support centers

(a) Support centers satisfying the qualifications specified in subdivision (b) of Section 6213 which were operating an office and providing services in California on December 31, 1980, shall be presumed to be qualified support centers for the purposes of this article.

(b) Support centers not qualifying under the presumption specified in subdivision (a) may qualify as a support center by meeting both of the following additional criteria:

(1) Meeting quality control standards established by the State Bar.

(2) Being deemed to be of special need by a majority of the qualified legal services projects.

§ 6216. Distribution of funds

The State Bar shall distribute all moneys received under the program established by this article for the provision of civil legal services to indigent persons. The funds first shall be distributed 18 months from the effective date of this article, or upon such a date, as shall be determined by the State Bar, that adequate funds are available to initiate the program. Thereafter, the funds shall be distributed on an annual basis. All distributions of funds shall be made in the following order and in the following manner:

(a) To pay the actual administrative costs of the program, including any costs incurred after the adoption of this article and a reasonable reserve therefor.

(b) Eighty-five percent of the funds remaining after payment of administrative costs allocated pursuant to this article shall be distributed to qualified legal services projects. Distribution shall be by a pro rata county-by-county formula based upon the number of persons whose income is 125 percent or less of the current poverty threshold per county. For the purposes of this section, the source of data identifying the number of persons per county shall be the latest available figures from the United States Department of Commerce, Bureau of the Census. Projects from more than one county may pool their funds to operate a joint, multicounty legal services project serving each of their respective counties.

(1)(A) In any county which is served by more than one qualified legal services project, the State Bar shall distribute funds for the county to those projects which apply on a pro rata basis, based upon the amount of their total budget expended in the prior year for legal services in that county as compared to the total expended in the prior year for legal services by all qualified legal services projects applying therefor in the county. In determining the amount of funds to be allocated to a qualified legal services project specified in paragraph (2) of subdivision (a) of Section 6213, the State Bar shall recognize only expenditures attributable to the representation of indigent persons as constituting the budget of the program.

(B) The State Bar shall reserve 10 percent of the funds allocated to the county for distribution to programs meeting the standards of subparagraph (A) of paragraph (3) and paragraphs (1) and (2) of subdivision (b) of Section 6214 and which perform the services described in subparagraph (A) of paragraph (3) of Section 6214 as their principal means of delivering legal services. The State Bar shall distribute the funds for that county to those programs which apply on a pro rata basis, based upon the amount of their total budget expended for free legal services in that county as compared to the total expended for free legal services by all programs meeting the standards of subparagraph (A) of paragraph (3) and paragraphs (1) and (2) of subdivision (b) of Section 6214 in that county. The State Bar shall distribute any funds for which no program has qualified pursuant hereto, in accordance with the provisions of subparagraph (A) of paragraph (1) of this subdivision.

(2) In any county in which there is no qualified legal services projects providing services, the State Bar shall reserve for the remainder of the fiscal year for distribution the pro rata share of funds as provided for by this article. Upon application of a qualified legal services project proposing to provide legal services to the indigent of the county, the State Bar shall distribute the funds to the project. Any funds not so distributed shall be added to the funds to be distributed the following year.

(c) Fifteen percent of the funds remaining after payment of administrative costs allocated for the purposes of this article shall be distributed equally by the State Bar to qualified support centers which apply for the funds. The funds provided to support centers shall be used only for the provision of legal services within California. Qualified support centers that receive funds to provide services to qualified legal services projects from sources other than this article, shall submit and shall have approved by the State Bar a plan assuring that the services funded under this article are in addition to those already funded for qualified legal services projects by other sources.

§ 6217. Maintenance of quality services, professional standards, attorney-client privilege; funds to be expended in accordance with article; interference with attorney prohibited

With respect to the provision of legal assistance under this article, each recipient shall ensure all of the following:

(a) The maintenance of quality service and professional standards.

(b) The expenditure of funds received in accordance with the provisions of this article.

(c) The preservation of the attorney-client privilege in any case, and the protection of the integrity of the adversary process from any impairment in furnishing legal assistance to indigent persons.

(d) That no one shall interfere with any attorney funded in whole or in part by this article in carrying out his or her professional responsibility to his or her client as established by the rules of professional responsibility and this chapter.

§ 6218. Eligibility for services; establishment of guidelines; funds to be expended in accordance with article

All legal services projects and support centers receiving funds pursuant to this article shall adopt financial eligibility guidelines for indigent persons.

(a) Qualified legal services programs shall ensure that funds appropriated pursuant to this article shall be used solely to defray the costs of providing legal services to indigent persons or for such other purposes as set forth in this article.

(b) Funds received pursuant to this article by support centers shall only be used to provide services to qualified legal services projects as defined in subdivision (a) of Section 6213 which are used pursuant to a plan as required by subdivision (c) of Section 6216, or as permitted by Section 6219.

§ 6219. Provision of work opportunities and scholarships for disadvantaged law students

Qualified legal services projects and support centers may use funds provided under this article to provide work opportunities with pay, and where feasible, scholarships for disadvantaged law students to help defray their law school expenses.

§ 6220. Private attorneys providing legal services without charge; support center services

Attorneys in private practice who are providing legal services without charge to indigent persons shall not be disqualified from receiving the services of the qualified support centers.

§ 6221. Services for indigent members of disadvantaged and underserved groups

Qualified legal services projects shall make significant efforts to utilize 20 percent of the funds allocated under this article for increasing the availability of services to the elderly, the disabled, juveniles, or other indigent persons who are members of disadvantaged and underserved groups within their service area.

§ 6222. Financial statements; submission to state bar; state bar report

A recipient of funds allocated pursuant to this article annually shall submit a financial statement to the State Bar, including an audit of the funds by a certified public accountant or a fiscal review approved by the State Bar, a report demonstrating the programs on which they were expended, a report on the recipient's compliance with the requirements of Section 6217, and progress in meeting the service expansion requirements of Section 6221.

The Board of Governors of the State Bar shall include a report of receipts of funds under this article, expenditures for administrative costs, and disbursements of the funds, on a county-by-county basis, in the annual report of State Bar receipts and expenditures required pursuant to Section 6145.

§ 6223. Expenditure of funds; prohibitions

No funds allocated by the State Bar pursuant to this article shall be used for any of the following purposes:

(a) The provision of legal assistance with respect to any fee generating case, except in accordance with guidelines which shall be promulgated by the State Bar.

(b) The provision of legal assistance with respect to any criminal proceeding.

(c) The provision of legal assistance, except to indigent persons or except to provide support services to qualified legal services projects as defined by this article.

§ 6224. State bar; powers; determination of qualifications to receive funds; denial of funds; termination; procedures

The State Bar shall have the power to determine that an applicant for funding is not qualified to receive funding, to deny future funding, or to terminate existing funding because the recipient is not operating in compliance with the requirements or restrictions of this article.

A denial of an application for funding or for future funding or an action by the State Bar to terminate an existing grant of funds under this article shall not become final until the applicant or recipient has been afforded reasonable notice and an opportunity for a timely and fair hearing. Pending final determination of any hearing held with reference to termination of funding, financial assistance shall be continued at its existing level on a month-to-month basis. Hearings for denial shall be conducted by an impartial hearing officer whose decision shall be final. The hearing officer shall render a decision no later than 30 days after the conclusion of the hearing. Specific procedures governing the conduct of the hearings of this section shall be determined by the State Bar pursuant to Section 6225.

§ 6225. Implementation of article; adoption of rules and regulations; procedures

The Board of Governors of the State Bar shall adopt the regulations and procedures necessary to implement this article and to ensure that the funds allocated herein are utilized to provide civil legal services to indigent persons, especially underserved client groups such as but not limited to the elderly, the disabled, juveniles, and non-English-speaking persons.

In adopting the regulations the Board of Governors shall comply with the following procedures:

(a) The board shall publish a preliminary draft of the regulations and procedures, which shall be distributed, together with notice of the hearings required by subdivision (b), to commercial banking institutions, to members of the State Bar, and to potential recipients of funds.

(b) The board shall hold at least two public hearings, one in southern California and one in northern California where affected and interested parties shall be afforded an opportunity to present oral and written testimony regarding the proposed regulations and procedures.

§ 6226. Implementation of article; resolution

The program authorized by this article shall become operative only upon the adoption of a resolution by the Board of Governors of the State Bar stating that regulations have been adopted pursuant to Section 6225 which conform the program to all applicable tax and banking statutes, regulations, and rulings.

§ 6227. Credit of state not pledged

Nothing in this article shall create an obligation or pledge of the credit of the State of California or of the State Bar of California. Claims arising by reason of acts done pursuant to this article shall be limited to the moneys generated hereunder.

§ 6228. Severability

If any provision of this article or the application thereof to any group or circumstances is held invalid, such invalidity shall not affect the other provisions or applications of this article which can be given effect without the invalid provision or application, and to this end the provisions of this article are severable.

NEW YORK CODE OF PROFESSIONAL RESPONSIBILITY: CANONS AND DISCIPLINARY RULES

[In 1990, the Appellate Divisions of the Supreme Court promulgated the following Code of Professional Responsibility. In 1999, the New York Code was significantly amended to include many provisions of the Model Rules. The New York Code continues to retain the Canons and the Ethical Considerations; however, the ethical considerations are not reprinted below. Ed.]

TABLE OF CONTENTS

PREAMBLE AND PRELIMINARY STATEMENT

Preamble

The continued existence of a free and democratic society depends upon recognition of the concept that justice is based upon the rule of law grounded in respect for the dignity of the individual and his capacity through reason for enlightened self-government. Law so grounded makes justice possible, for only through such law does the dignity of the individual attain respect and protection. Without it, individual rights become subject to unrestrained power, respect for law is destroyed, and rational self-government is impossible.

Lawyers, as guardians of the law, play a vital role in the preservation of society. The fulfillment of this role requires an understanding by lawyers of their relationship with and function in our legal system. A consequent obligation of lawyers is to maintain the highest standards of ethical conduct.

In fulfilling his professional responsibilities, a lawyer necessarily assumes various roles that require the performance of many difficult tasks. Not every situation which he may encounter can be foreseen, but fundamental ethical principles are always present to guide him. Within the framework of these principles, a lawyer must with courage and foresight be able and ready to shape the body of the law to the ever-changing relationships of society.

The Code of Professional Responsibility points the way to the aspiring and provides standards by which to judge the transgressor. Each lawyer must find within his own conscience the touchstone against which to test the extent to which his actions should rise above minimum standards. But in the last analysis it is the desire for the respect and confidence of the members of his profession and of the society which he serves that should provide to a lawyer the incentive for the highest possible degree of ethical conduct. The possible loss of that respect and confidence is the ultimate sanction. So long as its practitioners are guided by these principles, the law will continue to be a noble profession. This is its greatness and its strength, which permit of no compromise.

Preliminary Statement

In furtherance of the principles stated in the Preamble, the American Bar Association has promulgated this Code of Professional Responsibility, consisting of three separate but interrelated parts: Canons, Ethical Considerations, and Disciplinary Rules. The Code is designed to be adopted by appropriate agencies both as an inspirational guide to the members of the profession and as a basis for disciplinary action when the conduct of a lawyer falls below the required minimum standards stated in the Disciplinary Rules.

Obviously the Canons, Ethical Considerations, and Disciplinary Rules cannot apply to non-lawyers; however, they do define the type of ethical conduct that the public has a right to expect not only of lawyers but also of their non-professional employees and associates in all matters pertaining to professional employment. A lawyer should ultimately be responsible for the conduct of his employees and associates in the course of the professional representation of the client.

The Canons are statements of axiomatic norms, expressing in general terms the standards of professional conduct expected of lawyers in their relationships with the public, with the legal system, and with the legal profession. They embody the general concepts from which the Ethical Considerations and the Disciplinary Rules are derived.

The Ethical Considerations are aspirational in character and represent the objectives toward which every member of the profession should strive. They constitute a body of principles upon which the lawyer can rely for guidance in many specific situations.

PROFESSIONAL RESPONSIBILITY

The Disciplinary Rules, unlike the Ethical Considerations, are mandatory in character. The Disciplinary Rules state the minimum level of conduct below which no lawyer can fall without being subject to disciplinary action. Within the framework of fair trial, the Disciplinary Rules should be uniformly applied to all lawyers, regardless of the nature of their professional activities. The Code makes no attempt to prescribe either disciplinary procedures or penalties for violation of a Disciplinary Rule, nor does it undertake to define standards for civil liability of lawyers for professional conduct. The severity of judgment against one found guilty of violating a Disciplinary Rule should be determined by the character of the offense and the attendant circumstances. An enforcing agency, in applying the Disciplinary Rules, may find interpretive guidance in the basic principles embodied in the Canons and in the objectives reflected in the Ethical Considerations.

DEFINITIONS*

(a) "Differing interests" include every interest that will adversely affect either the judgment or the loyalty of a lawyer to a client, whether it be a conflicting, inconsistent, diverse, or other interest.

(b) "Law firm" includes, but is not limited to, a professional legal corporation, a limited liability company or partnership engaged in the practice of law, the legal department of a corporation or other organization and a qualified legal assistance organization.

(c) "Person" includes a corporation, an association, a trust, a partnership, and any other organization or legal entity.

(d) "Professional legal corporation" means a corporation, or an association treated as a corporation, authorized by law to practice law for profit.

(e) "State" includes the District of Columbia, Puerto Rico, and other federal territories and possessions.

(f) "Tribunal" includes all courts and all other adjudicatory bodies. A tribunal shall be deemed "available" when it would have jurisdiction to hear a complaint, if timely brought.

(g) (Repealed)

(h) "Qualified legal assistance organization" means an office or organization of one of the four types listed in section 1200.8(d)(1) through (4), inclusive, that meets all the requirements thereof.

(i) "Fraud" does not include conduct, although characterized as fraudulent by statute or administrative rule, which lacks an element of scienter deceit, intent to mislead, or knowing failure to correct misrepresentations which can be reasonably expected to induce detrimental reliance by another.

---

* "Confidence" and "Secret" are defined in section 1200.19(a) of this Part. "Sexual relations" is defined in section 1200.29–(a) of this Part. "Copy" is defined in section 1200.41(d)(10) of this Part.

(j) "Domestic Relations matters" means representation of a client in a claim, action or proceeding, or preliminary to the filing of a claim, action or proceeding, in either Supreme Court or Family Court, or in any court of appellate jurisdiction, for divorce, separation, annulment, custody, visitation, maintenance, child support, or alimony, or to enforce or modify a judgment or order in connection with any such claims, actions or proceedings.

CANON 1

A Lawyer Should Assist in Maintaining the Integrity and Competence of the Legal Profession

DR 1-101. [22 NYCRR 1200.2] Maintaining Integrity and Competence of the Legal Profession

(a) A lawyer is subject to discipline if the lawyer has made a materially false statement in, or has deliberately failed to disclose a material fact requested in connection with, the lawyer's application for admission to the bar.

(b) A lawyer shall not further the application for admission to the bar of another person that the lawyer knows to be unqualified in respect to character, education, or other relevant attribute.

DR 1-102. [22 NYCRR 1200.3] Misconduct

(a)[1] A lawyer or law firm shall not:

(1) Violate a Disciplinary Rule.

(2) Circumvent a Disciplinary Rule through actions of another.

(3) Engage in illegal conduct that adversely reflects on the lawyer's honesty, trustworthiness or fitness as a lawyer.

(4) Engage in conduct involving dishonesty, fraud, deceit, or misrepresentation.

(5) Engage in conduct that is prejudicial to the administration of justice.

(6) Unlawfully discriminate in the practice of law, including in hiring, promoting or otherwise determining conditions of employment, on the basis of age, race, creed, color, national origin, sex, disability, marital status, or sexual orientation. Where there is a tribunal with jurisdiction to hear a complaint, if timely brought, other than a Departmental Disciplinary Committee, a complaint based on unlawful discrimination shall be brought before such tribunal in the first instance. A certified copy of a determination by such a tribunal, which has become final and enforceable, and as to which the right to judicial or appellate review has been exhausted,

---

1. So in original. No par. (b) has been enacted.

finding that the lawyer has engaged in an unlawful discriminatory practice shall constitute prima facie evidence of professional misconduct in a disciplinary proceeding.

(7) Engage in any other conduct that adversely reflects on the lawyer's fitness as a lawyer.

DR 1–103. [22 NYCRR 1200.4] Disclosure of Information to Authorities

(a) A lawyer possessing knowledge, (1) not protected as a confidence or secret, or (2) not gained in the lawyer's capacity as a member of a bona fide lawyer assistance or similar program or committee, of a violation of section 1200.3 of this Part that raises a substantial question as to another lawyer's honesty, trustworthiness or fitness as a lawyer shall report such knowledge to a tribunal or other authority empowered to investigate or act upon such violation.

(b) A lawyer possessing knowledge or evidence, not protected as a confidence or secret, concerning another lawyer or a judge shall reveal fully such knowledge or evidence upon proper request of a tribunal or other authority empowered to investigate or act upon the conduct of lawyers or judges.

DR 1–104. [22 NYCRR 1200.5] Responsibilities of a Partner or Supervisory Lawyer and Subordinate Lawyers

(a) A law firm shall make reasonable efforts to ensure that all lawyers in the firm conform to the disciplinary rules.

(b) A lawyer with management responsibility in the law firm or direct supervisory authority over another lawyer shall make reasonable efforts to ensure that the other lawyer conforms to the disciplinary rules.

(c) A law firm shall adequately supervise, as appropriate, the work of partners, associates and non-lawyers who work at the firm. The degree of supervision required is that which is reasonable under the circumstances, taking into account factors such as the experience of the person whose work is being supervised, the amount of work involved in a particular matter, and the likelihood that ethical problems might arise in the course of working on the matter.

(d) A lawyer shall be responsible for a violation of the Disciplinary Rules by another lawyer or for conduct of a non-lawyer employed or retained by or associated with the lawyer that would be a violation of the Disciplinary Rules if engaged in by a lawyer if:

(1) The lawyer orders, or directs the specific conduct, or, with knowledge of the specific conduct, ratifies it; or

(2) The lawyer is a partner in the law firm in which the other lawyer practices or the non-lawyer is employed, or has supervisory authority over the other lawyer or the non-lawyer, and knows of such conduct, or in the exercise of reasonable management or

supervisory authority should have known of the conduct so that reasonable remedial action could be or could have been taken at a time when its consequences could be or could have been avoided or mitigated.

(e) A lawyer shall comply with these Disciplinary Rules notwithstanding that the lawyer acted at the direction of another person.

(f) A subordinate lawyer does not violate these Rules of Professional Conduct if that lawyer acts in accordance with a supervisory lawyer's reasonable resolution of an arguable question of professional duty.

DR 1-105. [22 NYCRR 1200.5-a] Disciplinary Authority and Choice of Law

(a) A lawyer admitted to practice in this state is subject to the disciplinary authority of this state, regardless of where the lawyer's conduct occurs. A lawyer may be subject to the disciplinary authority of both this state and another jurisdiction where the lawyer is admitted for the same conduct.

(b) In any exercise of the disciplinary authority of this state, the rules of professional conduct to be applied shall be as follows:

(1) For conduct in connection with a proceeding in a court before which a lawyer has been admitted to practice (either generally or for purposes of that proceeding), the rules to be applied shall be the rules of the jurisdiction in which the court sits, unless the rules of the court provide otherwise; and

(2) For any other conduct:

(i) If the lawyer is licensed to practice only in this state, the rules to be applied shall be the rules of this state, and

(ii) If the lawyer is licensed to practice in this state and another jurisdiction, the rules to be applied shall be the rules of the admitting jurisdiction in which the lawyer principally practices; provided, however, that if particular conduct clearly has its predominant effect in another jurisdiction in which the lawyer is licensed to practice, the rules of that jurisdiction shall be applied to that conduct.

DR 1-106. [22 NYCRR § 1200.5] Responsibilities Regarding Nonlegal Services

(a) With respect to lawyers or law firms providing nonlegal services to clients or other persons:

(1) A lawyer or law firm that provides nonlegal services to a person that are not distinct from legal services being provided to that person by the lawyer or law firm is subject to these Disciplinary Rules with respect to the provision of both legal and nonlegal services.

(2) A lawyer or law firm that provides nonlegal services to a person that are distinct from legal services being provided to that person by the

lawyer or law firm is subject to these Disciplinary Rules with respect to the nonlegal services if the person receiving the services could reasonably believe that the nonlegal services are the subject of an attorney-client relationship.

(3) A lawyer or law firm that is an owner, controlling party or agent of, or that is otherwise affiliated with, an entity that the lawyer of law firm knows to be providing nonlegal services to a person is subject to these Disciplinary Rules with respect to the nonlegal services if the person receiving the services could reasonably believe that the nonlegal services are the subject of an attorney-client relationship.

(4) For purposes of DR 1–106 [1200.5–b] (A)(2) and (A)(3), it will be presumed that the person receiving nonlegal services believes the services to be the subject of an attorney-client relationship unless the lawyer or law firm has advised the person receiving the services in writing that the services are not legal services and that the protection of an attorney-client relationship does not exist with respect to the nonlegal services, or if the interest of the lawyer or law firm in the entity providing nonlegal services is de minimis.

(b) Notwithstanding the provisions of DR 1–106 [1200.5–b] (A), a lawyer or law firm that is an owner, controlling party, agent, or is otherwise affiliated with an entity that the lawyer or law firm knows is providing nonlegal services to a person shall not permit any nonlawyer providing such services or affiliated with that entity to direct or regulate the professional judgment of the lawyer or law firm in rendering legal services to any person, or to cause the lawyer or law firm to compromise its duty under DR 4–101 [1200.19] (B) and (D) with respect to the confidences and secrets of a client receiving legal services.

(c) For purposes of this Disciplinary Rule, "nonlegal services" shall mean those services that lawyers may lawfully provide and that are not prohibited as an unauthorized practice of law when provided by a nonlawyer.

DR 1–107. [22 NYCRR § 1200.5–c] Contractual Relationships Between Lawyers and Nonlegal Professionals

(a) The practice of law has an essential tradition of complete independence and uncompromised loyalty to those it serves. Recognizing this tradition, clients of lawyers practicing in New York State are guaranteed "independent professional judgment and undivided loyalty uncompromised by conflicts of interest." Indeed, these guarantees represent the very foundation of the profession and allow and foster its continued role as a protector of the system of law. Therefore, a lawyer must remain completely responsible for his or her own independent professional judgment, maintain the confidences and secrets of clients, preserve funds of clients and third parties in his or her control, and otherwise comply with the legal and ethical principles governing lawyers in New York State.

Multi-disciplinary practice between lawyers and nonlawyers is incompatible with the core values of the legal profession and therefore, a strict division between services provided by lawyers and those provided by nonlawyers is essential to protect those values. However, a lawyer or law firm may enter into and maintain a contractual relationship with a nonlegal professional or nonlegal professional service firm for the purpose of offering to the public, on a systematic and continuing basis, legal services performed by the lawyer or law firm, as well as other nonlegal professional services, notwithstanding the provisions of DR 5–101 [1200.20](A), provided that:

(1) The profession of the nonlegal professional or nonlegal professional service firm is included in a list jointly established and maintained by the Appellate Divisions pursuant to Section 1205.3 of the Joint Appellate Division rules.

(2) The lawyer or law firm neither grants to the nonlegal professional or nonlegal professional service firm, nor permits such person or firm to obtain, hold or exercise, directly or indirectly, any ownership or investment interest in, or managerial or supervisory right, power or position in connection with the practice of law by the lawyer or law firm, nor, as provided in DR 2–103 [1200.8](B)(1), shares legal fees with a nonlawyer or receives or gives any monetary or other tangible benefit for giving or receiving a referral; and

(3) The fact that the contractual relationship exists is disclosed by the lawyer or law firm to any client of the lawyer or law firm before the client is referred to the nonlegal professional service firm, or to any client of the nonlegal professional service firm before that client receives legal services from the lawyer or law firm; and the client has given informed written consent and has been provided with a copy of the "Statement of Client's Rights In Cooperative Business Arrangements" pursuant to section 1205.4 of the Joint Appellate Divisions rules.

(b) For purposes of DR 1–107 [1205–c](A):

(1) Each profession on the list maintained pursuant to a joint rule of the Appellate Divisions shall have been designated sua sponte, or approved by the Appellate Divisions upon application of a member of a nonlegal profession or nonlegal professional service firm, upon a determination that the profession is composed of individuals who, with respect to their profession:

(i) have been awarded a Bachelor's Degree or its equivalent from an accredited college or university;

(ii) are licensed to practice the profession by an agency of the State of New York or the United States Government; and

(iii) are required under penalty of suspension or revocation of license to adhere to a code of ethical conduct that is reasonably comparable to that of the legal profession.

(2) The term "ownership or investment interest" shall mean any such interest in any form of debt or equity, and shall include any

501

interest commonly considered to be an interest accruing to or enjoyed by an owner or investor.

(c) DR 1–107 [1200.5–c](A)(1) shall not apply to relationships consisting solely of reciprocal referral agreements or understandings between a lawyer or law firm and a nonlegal professional or nonlegal professional service firm.

(d) Notwithstanding DR 3–102 [1200.17] (A), a lawyer or law firm may allocate costs and expenses with a nonlegal professional or nonlegal professional service firm pursuant to a contractual relationship permitted by DR 1–107 [1200.5–c] (A), provided the allocation reasonably reflects only the costs and expenses incurred or expected to be incurred by each.

CANON 2

A Lawyer Should Assist the Legal Profession in Fulfilling Its Duty to Make Legal Counsel Available

DR 2–101.   [22 NYCRR 1200.6] Publicity and Advertising

(a) A lawyer on behalf of himself or herself or partners or associates, shall not use or disseminate or participate in the preparation or dissemination of any public communication or communication to a prospective client containing statements or claims that are false, deceptive or misleading.

(b) (Repealed)

(c) It is proper to include information, provided its dissemination does not violate the provisions of section 1200.6(a) and (b), as to:

(1) education, degrees and other scholastic distinctions, dates of admission to any bar; areas of the law in which the lawyer or law firm practices, as authorized by the Code of Professional Responsibility; public offices and teaching positions held; memberships in bar associations or other professional societies or organizations, including offices and committee assignments therein; foreign language fluency;

(2) names of clients regularly represented, provided that the client has given prior written consent;

(3) bank references; credit arrangements accepted; prepaid or group legal services programs in which the attorney or firm participates; and

(4) legal fees for initial consultation; contingent fee rates in civil matters when accompanied by a statement disclosing the information required by section 1200.6(*l*), range of fees for services, provided that there be available to the public free of charge a written statement clearly describing the scope of each advertised service; hourly rates; and fixed fees for specified legal services.

(d) Advertising and publicity shall be designed to educate the public to an awareness of legal needs and to provide information relevant to the selection of the most appropriate counsel. Information other than that specifically authorized in section 1200.6(c) that is consistent with these purposes may be disseminated providing that it does not violate any other provisions of this Rule.

(e) A lawyer or law firm advertising any fixed fee for specified legal services shall, at the time of fee publication, have available to the public a written statement clearly describing the scope of each advertised service, which statement shall be delivered to the client at the time of retainer for any such service. Such legal services shall include all those services which are recognized as reasonable and necessary under local custom in the area of practice in the community where the services are performed.

(f) If the advertisement is broadcast, it shall be prerecorded or taped and approved for broadcast by the lawyer, and a recording or videotape of the actual transmission shall be retained by the lawyer for a period of not less than one year following such transmission. All advertisements of legal services that are mailed, or are distributed other than by radio, television, directory, newspaper, magazine or other periodical, by a lawyer or law firm that practices law in this state, shall also be subject to the following provisions:

(1) A copy of each advertisement shall at the time of its initial mailing or distribution be filed with the Departmental Disciplinary Committee of the appropriate judicial department.

(2) Such advertisement shall contain no reference to the fact of filing.

(3) If such advertisement is directed to a predetermined address, a list, containing the names and addresses of all persons to whom the advertisement is being or will thereafter be mailed or distributed, shall be retained by the lawyer or law firm for a period of not less than one year following the last date of mailing or distribution.

(4) The advertisements filed pursuant to this subdivision shall be open to public inspection.

(5) The requirements of this subdivision shall not apply to such professional cards or other announcements the distribution of which is authorized by section 1200.7(a) of this Part.

(g) If a lawyer or law firm advertises a range of fees or an hourly rate for services, the lawyer or law firm may not charge more than the fee advertised for such services. If a lawyer or law firm advertises a fixed fee for specified legal services, or performs services described in a fee schedule, the lawyer or law firm may not charge more than the fixed fee for such stated legal service as set forth in the advertisement or fee schedule, unless the client agrees in writing that the services performed or to be performed were not legal services referred to or implied in the advertisement or in the fee schedule and, further, that a different fee arrangement shall apply to the transaction.

(h) Unless otherwise specified in the advertisement, if a lawyer publishes any fee information authorized under this Disciplinary Rule in a publication which is published more frequently than once per month, the lawyer shall be bound by any representation made therein for a period of not less than 30 days after such publication. If a lawyer publishes any fee information authorized under this Rule in a publication which is published once per month or less frequently, the lawyer shall be bound by any representation made therein until the publication of the succeeding issue. If a lawyer publishes any fee information authorized under this Rule in a publication which has no fixed date for publication of a succeeding issue, the lawyer shall be bound by any representation made therein for a reasonable period of time after publication, but in no event less than 90 days.

(i) Unless otherwise specified, if a lawyer broadcasts any fee information authorized under this Rule, the lawyer shall be bound by any representation made therein for a period of not less than 30 days after such broadcast.

(j) A lawyer shall not compensate or give any thing of value to representatives of the press, radio, television or other communication medium in anticipation of or in return for professional publicity in a news item.

(k) All advertisements of legal services shall include the name, office address and telephone number of the attorney or law firm whose services are being offered.

(l) A lawyer or law firm advertising any contingent fee rates shall, at the time of the fee publication, disclose:

(1) Whether percentages are computed before or after deduction of costs, disbursements and other expenses of litigation;

(2) That, in the event there is no recovery, the client shall remain liable for the expenses of litigation, including court costs and disbursements.

DR 2–102. [22 NYCRR 1200.7] Professional Notices, Letterheads, and Signs

(a) A lawyer or law firm may use professional cards, professional announcement cards, office signs, letterheads or similar professional notices or devices, provided the same do not violate any statute or court rule, and are in accordance with section 1200.6 of this Part, including the following:

(1) A professional card of a lawyer identifying the lawyer by name and as a lawyer, and giving addresses, telephone numbers, the name of the law firm, and any information permitted under section

1200.10 of this Part. A professional card of a law firm may also give the names of members and associates.

(2) A professional announcement card stating new or changed associations or addresses, change of firm name, or similar matters pertaining to the professional offices of a lawyer or law firm. It may state biographical data, the names of members of the firm and associates and the names and dates of predecessor firms in a continuing line of succession. It may state the nature of the practice if permitted under section 1200.10 of this Part.

(3) A sign in or near the office and in the building directory identifying the law office. The sign may state the nature of the practice if permitted under section 1200.10 of this Part.

(4) A letterhead identifying the lawyer by name and as a lawyer, and giving addresses, telephone numbers, the name of the law firm, associates and any information permitted under section 1200.10 of this Part. A letterhead of a law firm may also give the names of members and associates, and names and dates relating to deceased and retired members. A lawyer or law firm may be designated "Of Counsel" on a letterhead if there is a continuing relationship with a lawyer or law firm, other than as a partner or associate. A lawyer or law firm may be designated as "General Counsel" or by similar professional reference on stationery of a client if the lawyer or the firm devotes a substantial amount of professional time in the representation of that client. The letterhead of a law firm may give the names and dates of predecessor firms in a continuing line of succession.

(b) A lawyer in private practice shall not practice under a trade name, a name that is misleading as to the identity of the lawyer or lawyers practicing under such name, or a firm name containing names other than those of one or more of the lawyers in the firm, except that the name of a professional corporation shall contain "P.C." or such symbols permitted by law, the name of a limited liability company or partnership shall contain "L.L.C.," "L.L.P." or such symbols permitted by law, and, if otherwise lawful, a firm may use as, or continue to include in its name the name or names of one or more deceased or retired members of the firm or of a predecessor firm in a continuing line of succession. Such terms as "legal clinic," "legal aid," "legal service office," "legal assistance office," "defender office" and the like, may be used only by qualified legal assistance organizations, except that the term "legal clinic" may be used by any lawyer or law firm provided the name of a participating lawyer or firm is incorporated therein. A lawyer who assumes a judicial, legislative or public executive or administrative post or office shall not permit his or her name to remain in the name of a law firm or to be used in professional notices of the firm during any significant period in which the lawyer is not actively and regularly practicing law as a member of the firm and, during such period, other members of the firm shall not use the lawyer's name in the firm name or in professional notices of the firm.

(c) A lawyer shall not hold himself or herself out as having a partnership with one or more other lawyers unless they are in fact partners.

(d) A partnership shall not be formed or continued between or among lawyers licensed in different jurisdictions unless all enumerations of the members and associates of the firm on its letterhead and in other permissible listings make clear the jurisdictional limitations on those members and associates of the firm not licensed to practice in all listed jurisdictions; however, the same firm name may be used in each jurisdiction.

DR 2–103. [22 NYCRR 1200.8] Solicitation and Recommendation of Professional Employment

(a) A lawyer shall not solicit professional employment from a prospective client:

(1) By in-person or telephone contact, except that a lawyer may solicit professional employment from a close friend, relative, former client or current client;

(2) By written or recorded communication if;

(i) The communication or contact violates section 1200.6(a);

(ii) The prospective client has made known to the lawyer a desire not to be solicited by the lawyer;

(iii) The solicitation involves coercion, duress or harassment;

(iv) The lawyer knows or reasonably should know that the age or the physical, emotional or mental state of the recipient make it unlikely that the recipient will be able to exercise reasonable judgment in retaining an attorney; or

(v) The lawyer intends or expects, but does not disclose, that the legal services necessary to handle the matter competently will be performed primarily by another lawyer who is not affiliated with the soliciting lawyer as a partner, associate or of counsel.

(b) A lawyer shall not compensate or give anything of value to a person or organization to recommend or obtain employment by a client, or as a reward for having made a recommendation resulting in employment by a client, except that a lawyer may pay the usual and reasonable fees or dues charged by a qualified legal assistance organization or referral fees to another lawyer as permitted by section 1200.12 of this Part.

(c) No written solicitation shall be sent by a method that requires the recipient to travel to a location other than that at which the recipient ordinarily receives business or personal mail.

(d) A lawyer or the lawyer's partner or associate or any other affiliated lawyer may be recommended, employed or paid by, or may cooperate with one of the following offices or organizations which promote the use of the lawyer's services or those of a partner or associate or any other affiliated lawyer, or request one of the following offices or organizations to recommend or promote the use of the lawyer's services or those of the lawyer's partner or associate, or any other affiliated lawyer as a private practitioner, if there is no interference with the exercise of independent professional judgment on behalf of the client:

(1) A legal aid office or public defender office:

(i) Operated or sponsored by a duly accredited law school;

(ii) Operated or sponsored by a bona fide, non-profit community organization;

(iii) Operated or sponsored by a governmental agency; or

(iv) Operated, sponsored, or approved by a bar association;

(2) A military legal assistance office;

(3) A lawyer referral service operated, sponsored or approved by a bar association or authorized by law or court rule;

(4) Any bona fide organization which recommends, furnishes or pays for legal services to its members or beneficiaries provided the following conditions are satisfied:

(i) Neither the lawyer, not the lawyer's partner, nor associate, nor any other affiliated lawyer nor any non-lawyer, shall have initiated or promoted such organization for the primary purpose of providing financial or other benefit to such lawyer, partner, associate or affiliated lawyer.

(ii) Such organization is not operated for the purpose of procuring legal work or financial benefit for any lawyer as a private practitioner outside of the legal services program of the organization.

(iii) The member or beneficiary to whom the legal services are furnished, and not such organization, is recognized as the client of the lawyer in the matter.

(iv) The legal service plan of such organization provides appropriate relief for any member or beneficiary who asserts a claim that representation by counsel furnished, selected or approved by the organization for the particular matter involved would be unethical, improper or inadequate under the circumstances of the matter involved; and the plan provides an appropriate procedure for seeking such relief.

(v) The lawyer does not know or have cause to know that such organization is in violation of applicable laws, rules of court or other legal requirements that govern its legal service operations.

(vi) Such organization has filed with the appropriate disciplinary authority, to the extent required by such authority, at least annually a report with respect to its legal service plan, if any, showing its terms, its schedule of benefits, its subscription charges, agreements with counsel and financial results of its legal service activities or, if it has failed to do so, the lawyer does not know or have cause to know of such failure.

(e) A lawyer shall not accept employment when the lawyer knows or it is obvious that the person who seeks services does so as a result of conduct prohibited under this Disciplinary Rule.

(f) Advertising not proscribed under section 1200.6 of this Part shall not be deemed in violation of any provision of this Disciplinary Rule.

DR 2–104. [22 NYCRR 1200.9] Suggestion of Need of Legal Services

(a) (Repealed)

(b) (Repealed)

(c) A lawyer may accept employment which results from participation in activities designed to educate the public to recognize legal problems, to make intelligent selection of counsel or to utilize available legal services.

(d) A lawyer who is recommended, furnished or paid by a qualified legal assistance organization may represent a member or beneficiary thereof, to the extent and under the conditions prescribed therein.

(e) Without affecting the right to accept employment, a lawyer may speak publicly or write for publication on legal topics so long as the lawyer does not undertake to give individual advice.

(f) If success in asserting rights or defenses of a client in litigation in the nature of a class action is dependent upon the joinder of others, a lawyer may accept employment from those contacted for the purpose of obtaining their joinder, provided such acceptance does not violate any statute or court rule in the judicial department in which the lawyer practices.

DR 2–105. [22 NYCRR 1200.10] Identification of Practice and Specialty

(a) A lawyer or law firm may publicly identify one or more areas of law in which the lawyer or the law firm practices, or may state that the practice of the lawyer or law firm is limited to one or more areas of law, provided that the lawyer or law firm shall not state that the lawyer or law firm is a specialist or specializes in a particular field of law, except as provided in section 1200.10(b), (c) or (d) of this Part.

(b) A lawyer admitted to engage in patent practice before the United States Patent and Trademark Office may use the designation "Patent Attorney" or a substantially similar designation.

(c) A lawyer may state that the lawyer has been recognized or certified as a specialist only as follows:

(1) A lawyer who is certified as a specialist in a particular area of law or law practice by a private organization approved for that purpose by the American Bar Association may state the fact of certification if, in conjunction therewith, the certifying organization is identified and the following statement is prominently made: "The [name of the private certifying organization] is not affiliated with any governmental authority. Certification is not a requirement for the practice of law in the State of New York and does not necessarily indicate greater competence than other attorneys experienced in this field of law."

(2) A lawyer who is certified as a specialist in a particular area of law or law practice by the authority having jurisdiction over specialization under the laws of another state or territory may state the fact of certification if, in conjunction therewith, the certifying state or territory is identified and the following statement is prominently made: "Certification granted by the [identify state or territory] is not recognized by any governmental authority within the State of New York. Certification is not a requirement for the practice of law in the State of New York and does not necessarily indicate greater competence than other attorneys experienced in this field of law."

DR 2-106.   [22 NYCRR 1200.11] Fee for Legal Services

(a) A lawyer shall not enter into an agreement for, charge or collect an illegal or excessive fee.

(b) A fee is excessive when, after a review of the facts, a lawyer of ordinary prudence would be left with a definite and firm conviction that the fee is in excess of a reasonable fee. Factors to be considered as guides in determining the reasonableness of a fee may include the following:

(1) The time and labor required, the novelty and difficulty of the questions involved and the skill requisite to perform the legal service properly.

(2) The likelihood, if apparent or made known to the client, that the acceptance of the particular employment will preclude other employment by the lawyer.

(3) The fee customarily charged in the locality for similar legal services.

(4) The amount involved and the results obtained.

(5) The time limitations imposed by the client or by circumstances.

(6) The nature and length of the professional relationship with the client.

(7) The experience, reputation and ability of the lawyer or lawyers performing the services.

(8) Whether the fee is fixed or contingent.

(c) A lawyer shall not enter into an arrangement for, charge or collect:

(1) A contingent fee for representing a defendant in a criminal case.

(2) Any fee in a domestic relations matter:

(i) The payment or amount of which is contingent upon the securing of a divorce or in any way determined by reference to the amount of maintenance, support, equitable distribution, or property settlement;

(ii) Unless a written retainer agreement is signed by the lawyer and client setting forth in plain language the nature of the relationship and the details of the fee arrangement. A lawyer shall not include in the written retainer agreement a nonrefundable fee clause; or

(iii) Based on a security interest, confession of judgment or other lien, without prior notice to the client in a signed retainer agreement and approval from a tribunal after notice to the adversary. A lawyer shall not foreclose on a mortgage placed on the marital residence while the spouse who consents to the mortgage remains the titleholder and the residence remains the spouse's primary residence.

(3) A fee proscribed by law or rule of court.

(d) Promptly after a lawyer has been employed in a contingent fee matter, the lawyer shall provide the client with a writing stating the method by which the fee is to be determined, including the percentage or percentages that shall accrue to the lawyer in the event of settlement, trial or appeal, litigation and other expenses to be deducted from the recovery and whether such expenses are to be deducted before or, if not prohibited by statute or court rule, after the contingent fee is calculated. Upon conclusion of a contingent fee matter, the lawyer shall provide the client with a written statement stating the outcome of the matter, and if there is a recovery, showing the remittance to § the client and the method of its determination.

(e) In domestic relations matters, a lawyer shall resolve fee disputes by arbitration at the election of the client.

(f) In domestic relations matters, a lawyer shall provide a prospective client with a statement of client's rights and responsibilities at the initial conference and prior to the signing of a written retainer agreement.

DR 2–107. [22 NYCRR 1200.12] Division of Fees Among Lawyers

(a) A lawyer shall not divide a fee for legal services with another lawyer who is not a partner in or associate of the lawyer's law firm, unless:

(1) The client consents to employment of the other lawyer after a full disclosure that a division of fees will be made.

(2) The division is in proportion to the services performed by each lawyer or, by a writing given the client, each lawyer assumes joint responsibility for the representation.

(3) The total fee of the lawyers does not exceed reasonable compensation for all legal services they rendered the client.

(b) This Disciplinary Rule does not prohibit payment to a former partner or associate pursuant to a separation or retirement agreement.

DR 2–108. [22 NYCRR 1200.13] Agreements Restricting the Practice of a Lawyer

(a) A lawyer shall not be a party to or participate in a partnership or employment agreement with another lawyer that restricts the right of a lawyer to practice law after the termination of a relationship created by the agreement, except as a condition to payment of retirement benefits.

(b) In connection with the settlement of a controversy or suit, a lawyer shall not enter into an agreement that restricts the right of a lawyer to practice law.

DR 2–109. [22 NYCRR 1200.14] Obligation to Decline Employment

(a)[1] A lawyer shall not accept employment on behalf of a person if the lawyer knows or it is obvious that such person wishes to:

(1) Bring a legal action, conduct a defense, or assert a position in litigation, or otherwise have steps taken for such person, merely for the purpose of harassing or maliciously injuring any person.

(2) Present a claim or defense in litigation that is not warranted under existing law, unless it can be supported by a good faith argument for an extension, modification, or reversal of existing law.

---

1. So in original. No par. (b) has been enacted.

DR 2–110.   [22 NYCRR 1200.15] Withdrawal from Employment

(a) In General.

(1) If permission for withdrawal from employment is required by the rules of a tribunal, a lawyer shall not withdraw from employment in a proceeding before that tribunal without its permission.

(2) Even when withdrawal is otherwise permitted or required under section 1200.15(a)(1), (b) or (c) of this Part, a lawyer shall not withdraw from employment until the lawyer has taken steps to the extent reasonably practicable to avoid foreseeable prejudice to the rights of the client, including giving due notice to the client, allowing time for employment of other counsel, delivering to the client all papers and property to which the client is entitled and complying with applicable laws and rules.

(3) A lawyer who withdraws from employment shall refund promptly any part of a fee paid in advance that has not been earned.

(b) Mandatory Withdrawal. A lawyer representing a client before a tribunal, with its permission if required by its rules, shall withdraw from employment, and a lawyer representing a client in other matters shall withdraw from employment, if:

(1) The lawyer knows or it is obvious that the client is bringing the legal action, conducting the defense, or asserting a position in the litigation, or is otherwise having steps taken, merely for the purpose of harassing or maliciously injuring any person.

(2) The lawyer knows or it is obvious that continued employment will result in violation of a Disciplinary Rule.

(3) The lawyer's mental or physical condition renders it unreasonably difficult to carry out the employment effectively.

(4) The lawyer is discharged by his or her client.

(c) Permissive Withdrawal. Except as stated in section 1200.15(a) of this Part, a lawyer may withdraw from representing a client if withdrawal can be accomplished without material adverse effect on the interests of the client, or if:

(1) The client:

(i) Insists upon presenting a claim or defense that is not warranted under existing law and cannot be supported by good faith argument for an extension, modification, or reversal of existing law.

(ii) Persists in a course of action involving the lawyer's services that the lawyer reasonably believes is criminal or fraudulent.

(iii) Insists that the lawyer pursue a course of conduct which is illegal or prohibited under the Disciplinary Rules.

(iv) By other conduct renders it unreasonably difficult for the lawyer to carry out employment effectively.

(v) Insists, in a matter not pending before a tribunal, that the lawyer engage in conduct which is contrary to the judgment and advice of the lawyer but not prohibited under the Disciplinary Rules.

(vi) Deliberately disregards an agreement or obligation to the lawyer as to expenses or fees.

(vii) Has used the lawyer's services to perpetrate a crime or fraud.

(2) The lawyer's continued employment is likely to result in a violation of a Disciplinary Rule.

(3) The lawyer's inability to work with co-counsel indicates that the best interests of the client likely will be served by withdrawal.

(4) The lawyer's mental or physical condition renders it difficult for the lawyer to carry out the employment effectively.

(5) The lawyer's client knowingly and freely assents to termination of the employment.

(6) The lawyer believes in good faith, in a proceeding pending before a tribunal, that the tribunal will find the existence of other good cause for withdrawal.

DR 2-111. [22 NYCRR 1200.15-a] Sale of Law Practice

(a) A lawyer retiring from a private practice of law, a law firm one or more members of which are retiring from the private practice of law with the firm, or the personal representative of a deceased, disabled or missing lawyer, may sell a law practice, including good will, to one or more lawyers or law firms, who may purchase the practice. The seller and the buyer may agree on reasonable restrictions on the seller's private practice of law, notwithstanding any other provision of this Code. Retirement shall include the cessation of the private practice of law in the geographic area, that is, the county and city and any county or city contiguous thereto, in which the practice to be sold has been conducted.

(b) Confidences and Secrets.

(1) With respect to each matter subject to the contemplated sale, the seller may provide prospective buyers with any information not protected as a confidence or secret under section 1200.19 of this Part.

(2) Notwithstanding section 1200.19, the seller may provide the prospective buyer with information as to individual clients:

(i) concerning the identity of the client, except as provided in section 1200.15-a(b)(6) of this Part;

(ii) concerning the status and general nature of the matter;

(iii) available in public court files; and

(iv) concerning the financial terms of the attorney-client relationship and the payment status of the client's account.

(3) Prior to making any disclosure of confidences or secrets that may be permitted under section 1200.15–a (b)(2) of this Part, the seller shall provide the prospective buyer with information regarding the matters involved in the proposed sale sufficient to enable the prospective buyer to determine whether any conflicts of interest exist. Where sufficient information cannot be disclosed without revealing client confidences or secrets, the seller may make the disclosures necessary for the prospective buyer to determine whether any conflict of interest exists, subject to section 1200.15–a (b)(6) of this Part. If the prospective buyer determines that conflicts of interest exist prior to reviewing the information, or determines during the course of review that a conflict of interest exists, the prospective buyer shall not review or continue to review the information unless seller shall have obtained the consent of the client in accordance with section 1200.19(c)(1) of this Part.

(4) Prospective buyers shall maintain the confidentiality of and shall not use any client information received in connection with the proposed sale in the same manner and to the same extent as if the prospective buyers represented the client.

(5) Absent the consent of the client after full disclosure, a seller shall not provide a prospective buyer with information if doing so would cause a violation of the attorney-client privilege.

(6) If the seller has reason to believe that the identity of the client or the fact of the representation itself constitutes a confidence or secret in the circumstances, the seller may not provide such information to a prospective buyer without first advising the client of the identity of the prospective buyer and obtaining the client's consent to the proposed disclosure.

(c) Written notice of the sale shall be given jointly by the seller and the buyer to each of the seller's clients and shall include information regarding:

(1) The client's right to retain other counsel or to take possession of the file;

(2) The fact that the client's consent to the transfer of the client's file or matter to the buyer will be presumed if the client does not take any action or otherwise object within 90 days of the sending of the notice, subject to any court rule or statute requiring express approval by the client or a court;

(3) The fact that agreements between the seller and the seller's clients as to fees will be honored by the buyer;

(4) Proposed fee increases, if any, permitted under section 1200.15–a(e) of this Part; and

(5) The identity and background of the buyer or buyers, including principal office address, bar admissions, number of years in practice in the state, whether the buyer has ever been disciplined for professional misconduct or convicted of a crime, and whether the buyer currently intends to re-sell the practice.

(d) When the buyer's representation of a client of the seller would give rise to a waivable conflict of interest, the buyer shall not undertake such representation unless the necessary waiver or waivers have been obtained in writing.

(e) The fee charged a client by the buyer shall not be increased by reason of the sale, unless permitted by a retainer agreement with the client or otherwise specifically agreed to by the client.

CANON 3

A Lawyer Should Assist in Preventing the Unauthorized Practice of Law

DR 3–101.   [22 NYCRR 1200.16] Aiding Unauthorized Practice of Law

(a) A lawyer shall not aid a non-lawyer in the unauthorized practice of law.

(b) A lawyer shall not practice law in a jurisdiction where to do so would be in violation of regulations of the profession in that jurisdiction.

DR 3–102.   [22 NYCRR 1200.17] Dividing Legal Fees with a Non–Lawyer

(a)[1] A lawyer or law firm shall not share legal fees with a non-lawyer, except that:

(1) An agreement by a lawyer with his or her firm, partner, or associate may provide for the payment of money, over a reasonable period of time after the lawyer's death, to the lawyer's estate or to one or more specified persons.

(2) A lawyer who undertakes to complete unfinished legal business of a deceased lawyer may pay to the estate of the deceased lawyer that proportion of § the total compensation which fairly represents the services rendered by the deceased lawyer.

(3) A lawyer or law firm may compensate a non-lawyer employee, or include a non-lawyer employee in a retirement plan, based in whole or in part on a profit-sharing arrangement.

---

1. So in original. No par. (b) has been enacted.

DR 3–103. [22 NYCRR 1200.18] Forming a Partnership with a Non–Lawyer

(a)[1] A lawyer shall not form a partnership with a non-lawyer if any of the activities of the partnership consist of the practice of law.

*

CANON 4

A Lawyer Should Preserve the Confidences and Secrets of a Client

DR 4–101. [22 NYCRR 1200.19] Preservation of Confidences and Secrets of a Client

(a) "Confidence" refers to information protected by the attorney-client privilege under applicable law, and "secret" refers to other information gained in the professional relationship that the client has requested be held inviolate or the disclosure of which would be embarrassing or would be likely to be detrimental to the client.

(b) Except when permitted under section 1200.19(c) of this Part, a lawyer shall not knowingly:

(1) Reveal a confidence or secret of a client.

(2) Use a confidence or secret of a client to the disadvantage of the client.

(3) Use a confidence or secret of a client for the advantage of the lawyer or of a third person, unless the client consents after full disclosure.

(c) A lawyer may reveal:

(1) Confidences or secrets with the consent of the client or clients affected, but only after a full disclosure to them.

(2) Confidences or secrets when permitted under Disciplinary Rules or required by law or court order.

(3) The intention of a client to commit a crime and the information necessary to prevent the crime.

(4) Confidences or secrets necessary to establish or collect the lawyer's fee or to defend the lawyer or his or her employees or associates against an accusation of wrongful conduct.

(5) Confidences or secrets to the extent implicit in withdrawing a written or oral opinion or representation previously given by the lawyer and believed by the lawyer still to be relied upon by a third person where the lawyer has discovered that the opinion or representation was based on materially inaccurate information or is being used to further a crime or fraud.

(d) A lawyer shall exercise reasonable care to prevent his or her employees, associates, and others whose services are utilized by the lawyer from disclosing or using confidences or secrets of a client, except that a lawyer may reveal the information allowed by subdivision (c) of this section through an employee.

CANON 5

A Lawyer Should Exercise Independent Professional Judgment on Behalf of a Client

DR 5-101. [22 NYCRR 1200.20] Conflicts of Interest—Lawyer's Own Interests

(a)[1] A lawyer shall not accept or continue employment if the exercise of professional judgment on behalf of the client will be or reasonably may be affected by the lawyer's own financial, business, property, or personal interests, unless a disinterested lawyer would believe that the representation of the client will not be adversely affected thereby and the client consents to the representation after full disclosure of the implications of the lawyer's interest.

DR 5-102. [22 NYCRR 1200.21] Lawyers as Witnesses

(a) A lawyer shall not act, or accept employment that contemplates the lawyer's acting, as an advocate on issues of fact before any tribunal if the lawyer knows or it is obvious that the lawyer ought to be called as a witness on a significant issue on behalf of the client, except that the lawyer may act as an advocate and also testify:

(1) If the testimony will relate solely to an uncontested issue.

(2) If the testimony will relate solely to a matter of formality and there is no reason to believe that substantial evidence will be offered in opposition to the testimony.

(3) If the testimony will relate solely to the nature and value of legal services rendered in the case by the lawyer or the lawyer's firm to the client.

(4) As to any matter, if disqualification as an advocate would work a substantial hardship on the client because of the distinctive value of the lawyer as counsel in the particular case.

(b) Neither a lawyer nor the lawyer's firm shall accept employment in contemplated or pending litigation if the lawyer knows or it is obvious that the lawyer or another lawyer in the lawyer's firm may be called as a witness on a significant issue other than on behalf of the client, and it is apparent that the testimony would or might be prejudicial to the client.

(c) If, after undertaking employment in contemplated or pending litigation, a lawyer learns or it is obvious that the lawyer ought to be called as a witness on a significant issue on behalf of the client, the lawyer shall not serve as § an advocate on issues of fact before the

----

1. So in original. No par. (b) was enacted.

tribunal, except that the lawyer may continue as an advocate on issues of fact and may testify in the circumstances enumerated in 1200.21(b)(1) through (4) of this Part.

(d) If, after undertaking employment in contemplated or pending litigation, a lawyer learns or it is obvious that the lawyer or a lawyer in his or her firm may be called as a witness on a significant issue other than on behalf of the client, the lawyer may continue the representation until it is apparent that the testimony is or may be prejudicial to the client at which point the lawyer and the firm must withdraw from acting as an advocate before the tribunal.

DR 5–103.   [22 NYCRR 1200.22] Avoiding Acquisition of Interest in Litigation

(a) A lawyer shall not acquire a proprietary interest in the cause of action or subject matter of litigation he or she is conducting for a client, except that the lawyer may:

(1) Acquire a lien granted by law to secure the lawyer's fee or expenses.

(2) Except as provided in section 1200.11(c)(2) or (3) of this Part, contract with a client for a reasonable contingent fee in a civil case.

(b) While representing a client in connection with contemplated or pending litigation, a lawyer shall not advance or guarantee financial assistance to the client, except that:

(1) A lawyer may advance or guarantee the expenses of litigation, including court costs, expenses of investigation, expenses of medical examination, and costs of obtaining and presenting evidence, provided the client remains ultimately liable for such expenses.

(2) Unless prohibited by law or rule of court, a lawyer representing an indigent client on a pro bono basis may pay court costs and reasonable expenses of litigation on behalf of the client.

DR 5–104.   [22 NYCRR 1200.23] Transactions Between Lawyer and Client

(a) A lawyer shall not enter into a business transaction with a client if they have differing interests therein and if the client expects the lawyer to exercise professional judgment therein for the protection of the client, unless:

(1) The transaction and terms on which the lawyer acquires the interest are fair and reasonable to the client and are fully disclosed and transmitted in writing to the client in a manner that can be reasonably understood by the client;

(2) The lawyer advises the client to seek the advice of independent counsel in the transaction; and

(3) The client consents in writing, after full disclosure, to the terms of the transaction and to the lawyer's inherent conflict of interest in the transaction.

(b) Prior to conclusion of all aspects of the matter giving rise to employment, a lawyer shall not negotiate or enter into any arrangement or understanding:

(1) With a client or a prospective client by which the lawyer acquires an interest in literary or media rights with respect to the subject matter of the employment or proposed employment.

(2) With any person by which the lawyer transfers or assigns any interest in literary or media rights with respect to the subject matter of employment by a client or prospective client.

DR 5-105. [22 NYCRR 1200.24] Conflict of Interest; Simultaneous Representation

(a) A lawyer shall decline proffered employment if the exercise of independent professional judgment in behalf of a client will be or is likely to be adversely affected by the acceptance of the proffered employment, or if it would be likely to involve the lawyer in representing differing interests, except to the extent permitted under subdivision (c) of this section.

(b) A lawyer shall not continue multiple employment if the exercise of independent professional judgment in behalf of a client will be or is likely to be adversely affected by the lawyer's representation of another client, or if it would be likely to involve the lawyer in representing differing interests, except to the extent permitted under subdivision (c) of this section.

(c) In the situations covered by subdivisions (a) and (b) of this section, a lawyer may represent multiple clients if a disinterested lawyer would believe that the lawyer can competently represent the interest of each and if each consents to the representation after full disclosure of the implications of the simultaneous representation and the advantages and risks involved.

(d) While lawyers are associated in a law firm, none of them shall knowingly accept or continue employment when any one of them practicing alone would be prohibited from doing so under section 1200.20(a), 1200.24(a) or (b), 1200.27(a) or (b), or 1200.45(b) of this Part except as otherwise provided therein.

(e) A law firm shall keep records of prior engagements, which records shall be made at or near the time of such engagements and shall have a policy implementing a system by which proposed engagements are checked against current and previous engagements, so as to render effective assistance to lawyers § within the firm in complying with section 1200.24(d) of this Part. Failure to keep records or to have a policy which complies with this subdivision, whether or not a violation of section 1200.24(d) of this Part occurs, shall be a violation by the firm. In cases in which a violation of this subdivision by the firm is a substantial factor in causing a violation of section 1200.24(d) of this Part by a lawyer, the firm, as well as the individual lawyer, shall also be responsible for the violation of section 1200.24(d) of this Part.

DR 5–106. [22 NYCRR 1200.25] Settling Similar Claims of Clients

(a)[1] A lawyer who represents two or more clients shall not make or participate in the making of an aggregate settlement of the claims of or against the clients, unless each client has consented after full disclosure of the implications of the aggregate settlement and the advantages and risks involved, including the existence and nature of all the claims involved and the participation of each person in the settlement.

DR 5–107. [22 NYCRR 1200.26] Avoiding Influence by Others than the Client

(a) Except with the consent of the client after full disclosure a lawyer shall not:

(1) Accept compensation for legal services from one other than the client.

(2) Accept from one other than the client anything of value related to his or her representation of or employment by the client.

(b) Unless authorized by law, a lawyer shall not permit a person who recommends, employs, or pays the lawyer to render legal service for another to direct or regulate his or her professional judgment in rendering such legal services, or to cause the lawyer to compromise the lawyer's duty to maintain the confidences and secrets of the client under section 1200.19(b) of this Part.

(c) A lawyer shall not practice with or in the form of a limited liability company, limited liability partnership or professional corporation authorized to practice law for a profit, if:

(1) A non-lawyer owns any interest therein, except that a fiduciary representative of the estate of a lawyer may hold the stock or interest of the lawyer for a reasonable time during administration;

(2) A non-lawyer is a member, corporate director or officer thereof; or

(3) A non-lawyer has the right to direct or control the professional judgment of a lawyer.

DR 5–108. [22 NYCRR 1200.27] Conflict of Interest; Former Client

(a) Except as provided in section 1200.45(b) with respect to current or former government lawyers, a lawyer who has represented a client in

---

1. So in original. No par. (b) has been enacted.

a matter shall not, without the consent of the former client after full disclosure:

(1) Thereafter represent another person in the same or a substantially related matter in which that person's interests are materially adverse to the interests of the former client.

(2) Use any confidences or secrets of the former client except as permitted by section 1200.19(c) of this Part or when the confidence or secret has become generally known.

(b) Except with the consent of the affected client after full disclosure, a lawyer shall not knowingly represent a person in the same or a substantially related matter in which a firm with which the lawyer formerly was associated had previously represented a client:

(1) Whose interests are materially adverse to that person; and

(2) About whom the lawyer had acquired information protected by section 1200.19(b) of this Part that is material to the matter.

(c) Notwithstanding the provisions of section 1200.24(d) of this Part, when a lawyer has terminated an association with a firm, the firm is prohibited from thereafter representing a person with interests that are materially adverse to those of a client represented by the formerly associated lawyer and not currently represented by the firm only if the law firm or any lawyer remaining in the firm has information protected by section 1200.19(b) of this Part that is material to the matter, unless the affected client consents after full disclosure.

DR 5–109. [22 NYCRR 1200.28] Organization as Client

(a) When a lawyer employed or retained by an organization is dealing with the organization's directors, officers, employees, members, shareholders or other constituents, and it appears that the organization's interests may differ from those of the constituents with whom the lawyer is dealing, the lawyer shall explain that the lawyer is the lawyer for the organization and not for any of the constituents.

(b) If a lawyer for an organization knows that an officer, employee or other person associated with the organization is engaged in action, intends to act or refuses to act in a matter related to the representation that is a violation of a legal obligation to the organization, or a violation of law that reasonably might be imputed to the organization, and is likely to result in substantial injury to the organization, the lawyer shall proceed as is reasonably necessary in the best interest of the organization. In determining how to proceed, the lawyer shall give due consideration to the seriousness of the violation and its consequences, the scope and nature of the lawyer's representation, the responsibility in the organization and the apparent motivation of the person involved, the policies of the organization concerning such matters and any other relevant considerations. Any measures taken shall be designed to minimize disruption of the organization and the risk of revealing information relating to the representation to persons outside the organization, Such measures may include, among others:

(1) Asking reconsideration of the matter;

(2) Advising that a separate legal opinion on the matter be sought for presentation to appropriate authority in the organization; and

(3) Referring the matter to higher authority in the organization, including, if warranted by the seriousness of the matter, referral to the highest authority that can act in behalf of the organization as determined by applicable law.

(c) If, despite the lawyer's efforts in accordance with section 1200.28(b) of this Part, the highest authority that can act on behalf of the organization insists upon action, or a refusal to act, that is clearly a violation of law and is likely to result in a substantial injury to the organization, the lawyer may resign in accordance with section 1200.15 of this Part.

DR 5–110. [22 NYCRR 1200.29] Membership in Legal Service Organization

(a)[1] A lawyer may serve as a director, officer or member of a not-for-profit legal services organization, apart from the law firm in which the lawyer practices, notwithstanding that the organization serves persons having interests that differ from those of a client of the lawyer or the lawyer's firm, provided that the lawyer shall not knowingly participate in a decision or action of the organization:

(1) If participating in the decision or action would be incompatible with the lawyer's duty of loyalty to a client under section 1200.20 through 1200.29 of this Part; or

(2) Where the decision or action could have a material adverse effect on the representation of a client of the organization whose interests differ from those of a client of the lawyer or the lawyer's firm.

DR 5–111. [22 NYCRR 1200.29–a] Sexual Relations With Clients

(a) "Sexual relations" means sexual intercourse or the touching of an intimate part of another person for the purpose of sexual arousal, sexual gratification, or sexual abuse.

(b) A lawyer shall not:

(1) Require or demand sexual relations with a client or third party incident to or as a condition of any professional representation.

(2) Employ coercion, intimidation, or undue influence in entering into sexual relations with a client.

---

1. So in original. No par. (b) has been enacted.

(3) In domestic relations matters, enter into sexual relations with a client during the course of the lawyer's representation of the client.

(c) Section 1200.29–a (b) shall not apply to sexual relations between lawyers and their spouses or to ongoing consensual sexual relationships that predate the initiation of the lawyer-client relationship.

(d) Where a lawyer in a firm has sexual relations with a client but does not participate in the representation of that client, the lawyers in the firm shall not be subject to discipline under this rule solely because of the occurrence of such sexual relations.

CANON 6

A Lawyer Should Represent a Client Competently

DR 6–101. [22 NYCRR 1200.30] Failing to Act Competently

(a)[1] A lawyer shall not:

(1) Handle a legal matter which the lawyer knows or should know that he or she is not competent to handle, without associating with a lawyer who is competent to handle it.

(2) Handle a legal matter without preparation adequate in the circumstances.

(3) Neglect a legal matter entrusted to the lawyer.

DR 6–102. [22 NYCRR 1200.31] Limiting Liability to Client

(a)[1] A lawyer shall not seek, by contract or other means, to limit prospectively the lawyer's individual liability to a client for malpractice, or, without first advising that person that independent representation is appropriate in connection therewith, to settle a claim for such liability with an unrepresented client or former client.

CANON 7

A Lawyer Should Represent a Client Zealously Within the Bounds of the Law

DR 7–101. [22 NYCRR 1200.32] Representing a Client Zealously

(a) A lawyer shall not intentionally:

(1) Fail to seek the lawful objectives of the client through reasonably available means permitted by law and the Disciplinary Rules, except as provided by subdivision (b) of this section. A lawyer does not violate this Disciplinary Rule, however, by acceding to

1. So in original. No par. (b) has been enacted.

1. So in original. No par. (b) has been enacted.

reasonable requests of opposing counsel which do not prejudice the rights of the client, by being punctual in § fulfilling all professional commitments, by avoiding offensive tactics, or by treating with courtesy and consideration all persons involved in the legal process.

(2) Fail to carry out a contract of employment entered into with a client for professional services, but the lawyer may withdraw as permitted under section 1200.15, 1200.21 and 1200.24 of this Part.

(3) Prejudice or damage the client during the course of the professional relationship, except as required under section 1200.33(b) or as authorized by section 1200.15 of this Part.

(b) In the representation of a client, a lawyer may:

(1) Where permissible, exercise professional judgment to waive or fail to assert a right or position of the client.

(2) Refuse to aid or participate in conduct that the lawyer believes to be unlawful, even though there is some support for an argument that the conduct is legal.

DR 7-102. [22 NYCRR 1200.33] Representing a Client Within the Bounds of the Law

(a) In the representation of a client, a lawyer shall not:

(1) File a suit, assert a position, conduct a defense, delay a trial, or take other action on behalf of the client when the lawyer knows or when it is obvious that such action would serve merely to harass or maliciously injure another.

(2) Knowingly advance a claim or defense that is unwarranted under existing law, except that the lawyer may advance such claim or defense if it can be supported by good faith argument for an extension, modification, or reversal of existing law.

(3) Conceal or knowingly fail to disclose that which the lawyer is required by law to reveal.

(4) Knowingly use perjured testimony or false evidence.

(5) Knowingly make a false statement of law or fact.

(6) Participate in the creation or preservation of evidence when the lawyer knows or it is obvious that the evidence is false.

(7) Counsel or assist the client in conduct that the lawyer knows to be illegal or fraudulent.

(8) Knowingly engage in other illegal conduct or conduct contrary to a Disciplinary Rule.

(b) A lawyer who receives information clearly establishing that:

(1) The client has, in the course of the representation, perpetrated a fraud upon a person or tribunal shall promptly call upon the client to rectify the same, and if the client refuses or is unable to

do so, the lawyer shall reveal the fraud to the affected person or tribunal, except when the information is protected as a confidence or secret.

(2) A person other than the client has perpetrated a fraud upon a tribunal shall reveal the fraud to the tribunal.

DR 7–103.   [22 NYCRR 1200.34] Performing the Duty of Public Prosecutor or Other Government Lawyer

(a) A public prosecutor or other government lawyer shall not institute or cause to be instituted criminal charges when he or she knows or it is obvious that the charges are not supported by probable cause.

(b) A public prosecutor or other government lawyer in criminal litigation shall make timely disclosure to counsel for the defendant, or to a defendant who has no counsel, of the existence of evidence, known to the prosecutor or other government lawyer, that tends to negate the guilt of the accused, mitigate the degree of the offense or reduce the punishment.

DR 7–104.   [22 NYCRR 1200.35] Communicating with Represented and Unrepresented Persons

(a) During the course of the representation of a client a lawyer shall not:

(1) Communicate or cause another to communicate on the subject of the representation with a party the lawyer knows to be represented by a lawyer in that matter unless the lawyer has the prior consent of the lawyer representing such other party or is authorized by law to do so.

(2) Give advice to a person who is not represented by a lawyer, other than the advice to secure counsel, if the interests of such person are or have a reasonable possibility of being in conflict with the interests of the lawyer's client.

(b) Notwithstanding the prohibitions of section 1200.35 (a) of this Part, and unless prohibited by law, a lawyer may cause a client to communicate with a represented person, if that person is legally competent, and counsel the client with respect to those communications, provided the lawyer gives reasonable advance notice to the represented person's counsel that such communications will be taking place.

DR 7–105.   [22 NYCRR 1200.36] Threatening Criminal Prosecution

(a)[1] A lawyer shall not present, participate in presenting, or threaten to present criminal charges solely to obtain an advantage in a civil matter.

---

1. So in original. No par. (b) has been enacted.

DR 7–106.   [22 NYCRR 1200.37] Trial Conduct

(a) A lawyer shall not disregard or advise the client to disregard a standing rule of a tribunal or a ruling of a tribunal made in the course of a proceeding, but the lawyer may take appropriate steps in good faith to test the validity of such rule or ruling.

(b) In presenting a matter to a tribunal, a lawyer shall disclose:

(1) Controlling legal authority known to the lawyer to be directly adverse to the position of the client and which is not disclosed by opposing counsel.

(2) Unless privileged or irrelevant, the identities of the clients the lawyer represents and of the persons who employed the lawyer.

(c) In appearing as a lawyer before a tribunal, a lawyer shall not:

(1) State or allude to any matter that he or she has no reasonable basis to believe is relevant to the case or that will not be supported by admissible evidence.

(2) Ask any question that he or she has no reasonable basis to believe is relevant to the case and that is intended to degrade a witness or other person.

(3) Assert personal knowledge of the facts in issue, except when testifying as a witness.

(4) Assert a personal opinion as to the justness of a cause, as to the credibility of a witness, as to the culpability of a civil litigant, or as to the guilt or innocence of an accused; but the lawyer may argue, upon analysis of the evidence, for any position or conclusion with respect to the matters stated herein.

(5) Fail to comply with known local customs of courtesy or practice of the bar or a particular tribunal without giving to opposing counsel timely notice of the intent not to comply.

(6) Engage in undignified or discourteous conduct which is degrading to a tribunal.

(7) Intentionally or habitually violate any established rule of procedure or of evidence.

DR 7–107.   [22 NYCRR 1200.38] Trial Publicity

(a) A lawyer participating in or associated with a criminal or civil matter,or associated in a law firm or government agency with a lawyer participating in or associated with a criminal or civil matter, shall not make an extrajudicial statement that a reasonable person would expect to be disseminated by means of public communication if the lawyer knows or reasonably should know that it will have a substantial likelihood of materially prejudicing an adjudicative proceeding in that matter. Notwithstanding the foregoing, a lawyer may make a statement that a reasonable lawyer would believe is required to protect a client from the substantial prejudicial effect of recent publicity not initiated by the lawyer or the lawyer's client. A statement so made shall be limited to such information as is necessary to mitigate the recent adverse publicity.

(b) A statement ordinarily is likely to prejudice materially an adjudicative proceeding when it refers to a civil matter triable to a jury, a criminal matter, or any other proceeding that could result in incarceration, and the statement relates to:

(1) The character, credibility, reputation or criminal record of a party, suspect in a criminal investigation or witness, or the identity of a witness, or the expected testimony of a party or witness.

(2) In a criminal case or proceeding that could result in incarceration, the possibility of a plea of guilty to the offense or the existence or contents of any confession, admission, or statement given by a defendant or suspect or that person's refusal or failure to make a statement.

(3) The performance or results of any examination or test or the refusal or failure of a person to submit to an examination or test, or the identity or § nature of physical evidence expected to be presented.

(4) Any opinion as to the guilt or innocence of a defendant or suspect in a criminal case or proceeding that could result in incarceration.

(5) Information the lawyer knows or reasonably should know is likely to be inadmissible as evidence in a trial and would if disclosed create a substantial risk of prejudicing an impartial trial.

(6) The fact that a defendant has been charged with a crime, unless there is included therein a statement explaining that the charge is merely an accusation and that the defendant is presumed innocent until and unless proven guilty.

(c) Provided that the statement complies with section 1200.39(a) of this Part, a lawyer involved with the investigation or litigation of a matter may state the following without elaboration:

(1) The general nature of the claim or defense.

(2) The information contained in a public record.

(3) That an investigation of the matter is in progress.

(4) The scheduling or result of any step in litigation.

(5) A request for assistance in obtaining evidence and information necessary thereto.

(6) A warning of danger concerning the behavior of a person involved, when there is reason to believe that there exists the likelihood of substantial harm to an individual or to the public interest.

(7) In a criminal case:

(i) The identity, age, residence, occupation and family status of the accused.

(ii) If the accused has not been apprehended, information necessary to aid in apprehension of that person.

(iii) The fact, time and place of arrest, resistance, pursuit, use of weapons, and a description of physical evidence seized, other than as contained only in a confession, admission, or statement.

(iv) The identity of investigating and arresting officers or agencies and the length of the investigation.

DR 7–108. [22 NYCRR 1200.39] Communication With or Investigation of Jurors

(a) Before the trial of a case a lawyer connected therewith shall not communicate with or cause another to communicate with anyone the lawyer knows to be a member of the venire from which the jury will be selected for the trial of the case.

(b) During the trial of a case:

(1) A lawyer connected therewith shall not communicate with or cause another to communicate with any member of the jury.

(2) A lawyer who is not connected therewith shall not communicate with or cause another to communicate with a juror concerning the case.

(c) Subdivisions (a) and (b) of this section do not prohibit a lawyer from communicating with members of the venire or jurors in the course of official proceedings.

(d) After discharge of the jury from further consideration of a case with which the lawyer was connected, the lawyer shall not ask questions of or make comments to a member of that jury that are calculated merely to harass or embarrass the juror or to influence the juror's actions in future jury service.

(e) A lawyer shall not conduct or cause, by financial support or otherwise, another to conduct a vexatious or harassing investigation of either a member of the venire or a juror.

(f) All restrictions imposed by this section upon a lawyer also apply to communications with or investigations of members of a family of a member of the venire or a juror.

(g) A lawyer shall reveal promptly to the court improper conduct by a member of the venire or a juror, or by another toward a member of the venire or a juror or a member of his or her family of which the lawyer has knowledge.

DR 7–109. [22 NYCRR 1200.40] Contact With Witnesses

(a) A lawyer shall not suppress any evidence that the lawyer or the client has a legal obligation to reveal or produce.

(b) A lawyer shall not advise or cause a person to hide or to leave the jurisdiction of a tribunal for the purpose of making the person unavailable as a witness therein.

(c) A lawyer shall not pay, offer to pay, or acquiesce in the payment of compensation to a witness contingent upon the content of his or her testimony or the outcome of the case. But a lawyer may advance, guarantee, or acquiesce in the payment of:

(1) Expenses reasonably incurred by a witness in attending or testifying.

(2) Reasonable compensation to a witness for the loss of time in attending, testifying, preparing to testify or otherwise assisting counsel.

(3) A reasonable fee for the professional services of an expert witness.

DR 7-110. [22 NYCRR 1200.41] Contact With Officials

(a) A lawyer shall not give or lend anything of value to a judge, official, or employee of a tribunal except as permitted by the Code of Judicial Conduct, but a lawyer may make a contribution to the campaign fund of a candidate for judicial office in conformity with the Code of Judicial Conduct.

(b) In an adversary proceeding, a lawyer shall not communicate, or cause another to communicate, as to the merits of the cause with a judge or an official before whom the proceeding is pending, except:

(1) In the course of official proceedings in the cause.

(2) In writing if the lawyer promptly delivers a copy of the writing to opposing counsel or to an adverse party who is not represented by a lawyer.

(3) Orally upon adequate notice to opposing counsel or to an adverse party who is not represented by a lawyer.

(4) As otherwise authorized by law, or by the Code of Judicial Conduct.

CANON 8

A Lawyer Should Assist in Improving the Legal System

DR 8-101. [22 NYCRR 1200.42] Action as a Public Official

(a)[1] A lawyer who holds public office shall not:

(1) Use the public position to obtain, or attempt to obtain, a special advantage in legislative matters for the lawyer or for a client under circumstances where the lawyer knows or it is obvious that such action is not in the public interest.

---

1. So in original. No par. (b) has been enacted.

(2) Use the public position to influence, or attempt to influence, a tribunal to act in favor of the lawyer or of a client.

(3) Accept anything of value from any person when the lawyer knows or it is obvious that the offer is for the purpose of influencing the lawyer's action as a public official.

DR 8-102. [22 NYCRR 1200.43] Statements Concerning Judges and Other Adjudicatory Officers

(a) A lawyer shall not knowingly make false statements of fact concerning the qualifications of a candidate for election or appointment to a judicial office.

(b) A lawyer shall not knowingly make false accusations against a judge or other adjudicatory officer.

DR 8-103. [22 NYCRR 1200.44] Lawyer Candidate for Judicial Office

(a)[1] A lawyer who is a candidate for judicial office shall comply with the applicable provisions of the Code of Judicial Conduct.

CANON 9

A Lawyer Should Avoid Even the Appearance of Professional Impropriety

DR 9-101. [22 NYCRR 1200.45] Avoiding Even the Appearance of Impropriety

(a) A lawyer shall not accept private employment in a matter upon the merits of which the lawyer has acted in a judicial capacity.

(b) Except as law may otherwise expressly permit:

(1) A lawyer shall not represent a private client in connection with a matter in which the lawyer participated personally and substantially as a public officer or employee, and no lawyer in a firm with which that lawyer is associated may knowingly undertake or continue representation in such a matter unless:

(i) The disqualified lawyer is effectively screened from any participation, direct or indirect, including discussion, in the matter and is apportioned no part of the fee therefrom; and

(ii) There are no other circumstances in the particular representation that create an appearance of impropriety.

(2) A lawyer having information that the lawyer knows is confidential government information about a person, acquired when the lawyer was a public officer or employee, may not represent a private client whose interests are adverse to that person in a matter

---

1. So in original. No par. (b) has been enacted.

in which the information could be used to the material disadvantage of that person. A firm with which that lawyer is associated may knowingly undertake or continue representation in the matter only if the disqualified lawyer is effectively screened from any participation, direct or indirect, including discussion, in the matter and is apportioned no part of the fee therefrom.

(3) A lawyer serving as a public officer or employee shall not:

(i) Participate in a matter in which the lawyer participated personally and substantially while in private practice or non-governmental employment, unless under applicable law no one is, or by lawful delegation may be, authorized to act in the lawyer's stead in the matter; or

(ii) Negotiate for private employment with any person who is involved as a party or as attorney for a party in a matter in which the lawyer is participating personally and substantially.

(c) A lawyer shall not state or imply that the lawyer is able to influence improperly or upon irrelevant grounds any tribunal, legislative body, or public official.

(d) A lawyer related to another lawyer as parent, child, sibling or spouse shall not represent in any matter a client whose interests differ from those of another party to the matter who the lawyer knows is represented by the other lawyer unless the client consents to the representation after full disclosure and the lawyer concludes that the lawyer can adequately represent the interests of the client.

DR 9-102. [22 NYCRR 1200.46] Preserving Identity of Funds and Property of Others; Fiduciary Responsibility; Commingling and Misappropriation of Client Funds or Property; Maintenance of Bank Accounts; Recordkeeping; Examination of Records

(a) Prohibition Against Commingling and Misappropriation of Client Funds or Property. A lawyer in possession of any funds or other property belonging to another person, where such possession is incident to his or her practice of law, is a fiduciary, and must not misappropriate such funds or property or commingle such funds or property with his or her own.

(c) Separate Accounts.

(1) A lawyer who is in possession of funds belonging to another person incident to the lawyer's practice of law, shall maintain such funds in a banking institution within the State of New York which agrees to provide dishonored check reports in accordance with the provisions of Part 1300 of the joint rules of the Appellate Divisions. "Banking institution" means a state or national bank, trust company, savings bank, savings and loan association or credit union. Such funds shall be maintained, in the lawyer's own name, or in the name

of a firm of lawyers of which he or she is a member, or in the name of the lawyer or firm of lawyers by whom he or she is employed, in a special account or accounts, separate from any business or personal accounts of the lawyer or lawyer's firm, and separate from any accounts which the lawyer may maintain as executor, guardian, trustee or receiver, or in any other fiduciary capacity, into which special account or accounts all funds held in escrow or otherwise entrusted to the lawyer or firm shall be deposited; provided, however, that such funds may be maintained in a banking institution located outside the State of New York if such banking institution complies with such Part 1300, and the lawyer has obtained the prior written approval of the person to whom such funds belong which specifies the name and address of the office or branch of the banking institution where such funds are to be maintained.

(2) A lawyer or the lawyer's firm shall identify the special bank account or accounts required by section 1200.46 (b)(1) of this Part as an "Attorney Special Account," or "Attorney Trust Account," or "Attorney Escrow Account," and shall obtain checks and deposit slips that bear such title. Such title may be accompanied by such other descriptive language as the lawyer may deem appropriate provided that such additional language distinguishes such special account or accounts from other bank accounts that are maintained by the lawyer or lawyer's firm.

(3) Funds reasonably sufficient to maintain the account or to pay account charges may be deposited therein.

(4) Funds belonging in part to a client or third person and in part presently or potentially to the lawyer or law firm shall be kept in such special account or accounts, but the portion belonging to the lawyer or law firm may be withdrawn when due unless the right of the lawyer or law firm to receive it is disputed by the client or third person, in which event the disputed portion shall not be withdrawn until the dispute is finally resolved.

(c) Notification of Receipt of Property; Safekeeping; Rendering Accounts; Payment or Delivery of Property. A lawyer shall:

(1) Promptly notify a client or third person of the receipt of funds, securities, or other properties in which the client or third person has an interest.

(2) Identify and label securities and properties of a client or third person promptly upon receipt and place them in a safe deposit box or other place of safekeeping as soon as practicable.

(3) Maintain complete records of all funds, securities, and other properties of a client or third person coming into the possession of the lawyer and render appropriate accounts to the client or third person regarding them.

(4) Promptly pay or deliver to the client or third person as requested by the client or third person the funds, securities, or other properties in the possession of the lawyer which the client or third person is entitled to receive.

(d) Required Bookkeeping Records. A lawyer shall maintain for seven years after the events which they record:

(1) The records of all deposits in and withdrawals from the accounts specified in section 1200.46(b) of this Part and of any other bank account which concerns or affects the lawyer's practice of law. These records shall specifically identify the date, source and description of each item deposited, as well as the date, payee and purpose of each withdrawal or disbursement.

(2) A record for special accounts, showing the source of all funds deposited in such accounts, the names of all persons for whom the funds are or were held, the amount of such funds, the description and amounts, and the names of all persons to whom such funds were disbursed.

(3) Copies of all retainer and compensation agreements with clients.

(4) Copies of all statements to clients or other persons showing the disbursement of funds to them or on their behalf or on their behalf.

(5) Copies of all bills rendered to clients.

(6) Copies of all records showing payments to lawyers, investigators or other persons, not in the lawyer's regular employ, for services rendered or performed.

(7) Copies of all retainer and closing statements filed with the Office of Court Administration.

(8) All checkbooks and check stubs, bank statements, prenumbered canceled checks and duplicated deposit slips.

(9) Lawyers shall make accurate entries of all financial transactions in their records of receipts and disbursements, in their special accounts, in their ledger books or similar records, and in any other books of account kept by them in the regular course of their practice, which entries shall be made at or near the time of the act, condition or event recorded.

(10) For Purposes of section 1200.46(d) of this Part, a lawyer may satisfy the requirements of maintaining "copies" by maintaining any of the following items; original records, photocopies, microfilm, optical imaging, and any other medium that preserves an image of the document that cannot be altered without detection.

(e) Authorized Signatories. All special account withdrawals shall be made only to a named payee and not to cash. Such withdrawals shall be made by check or, with the prior written approval of the party entitled to the proceeds, by bank transfer. Only an attorney admitted to practice law in New York State shall be an authorized signatory of a special account.

(f) Missing Clients. Whenever any sum of money is payable to a client and the lawyer is unable to locate the client, the lawyer shall apply to the court in which the action was brought if in the unified court system, or, if no action was commenced in the unified court system, to the Supreme Court in the county in which the lawyer maintains an office for the practice of law, for an order directing payment to the lawyer of any fees and disbursements that are owed by the client and the balance, if any, to the Lawyer's Fund for Client Protection for safeguarding and disbursement to persons who are entitled thereto.

(g) Designation of Successor Signatories.

(1) Upon the death of a lawyer who was the sole signatory on an attorney trust, escrow or special account, an application may be made to the Supreme Court for an order designating a successor signatory for such trust, escrow or special account who shall be a member of the bar in good standing and admitted to the practice of law in New York State.

(2) An application to designate a successor signatory shall be made to the Supreme Court in the judicial district in which the deceased lawyer maintained an office for the practice of law. The application may be made by the legal representative of the deceased lawyer's estate; a lawyer who was affiliated with the deceased lawyer in the practice of law; any person who has a beneficial interest in such trust, escrow or special account; an officer of a city or county bar association; or counsel for an attorney disciplinary committee. No lawyer may charge a legal fee for assisting with an application to designate a successor signatory pursuant to this rule.

(3) The Supreme Court may designate a successor signatory and may direct the safeguarding of funds from such trust, escrow or special account, and the disbursement of such funds to persons who are entitled thereto, and may order that funds in such account be deposited with the Lawyers' Fund for Client Protection for safeguarding and disbursement to persons who are entitled thereto.

(h) Dissolution of a Firm. Upon the dissolution of any firm of lawyers, the former partners or members shall make appropriate arrangements for the maintenance by one of them or by a successor firm of the records specified in section 1200.46 (d) of this Part.

(i) Availability of Bookkeeping Records; Records Subject to Production in Disciplinary Investigations and Proceedings. The financial records required by this Disciplinary Rule shall be located, or made available, at the principal New York State office of the lawyers subject hereto and any such records shall be produced in response to a notice or subpoena duces tecum issued in connection with a complaint before or any investigation by the appropriate grievance or departmental disciplinary committee, or shall be produced at the direction of the appropriate Appellate Division before any person designated by it. All books and records produced pursuant to this subdivision shall be kept confidential, except for the purpose of the particular proceeding, and their § contents shall not be disclosed by anyone in violation of the lawyer-client privilege.

(j) Disciplinary Action. A lawyer who does not maintain and keep the accounts and records as specified and required by this Disciplinary Rule, or who does not produce any such records pursuant to this Rule, shall be deemed in violation of these Rules and shall be subject to disciplinary proceedings.

AMERICAN BAR ASSOCIATION MODEL CODE OF PROFESSIONAL RESPONSIBILITY

As Amended and in Effect as of 1983.

[The Model Code of Professional Responsibility was the product of the Wright Committee's efforts to replace the Canons of Professional Ethics, which had grown from 32 canons in 1908 to 47 canons in 1964. The Model Code was enacted by the ABA in 1969, and subsequently, most states adopted codes of professional responsibility based upon the Model Code. The distinctive feature of the Model Code is its organization into canons, ethical considerations, and disciplinary rules. The canons provided the Model Code with a theoretical structure. Each canon was a general directive to lawyers about the law of professional responsibility. The ethical considerations were more detailed in that they discussed actual fact situations that arose under each canon. Each ethical consideration, however, was only aspirational in nature. Lawyers were supposed to strive to follow the ethical considerations, but they were not considered binding. The disciplinary rules were the provisions that lawyers needed to follow to avoid disciplinary liability. These rules established minimum standards that lawyers were required to follow and standards that were enforced by the disciplinary committees. The ABA replaced the Model Code with the Model Rules of Professional Conduct in 1983. Ed.]

TABLE OF CONTENTS *

* Prepared by Editor.

PROFESSIONAL RESPONSIBILITY

Canon
8. **A Lawyer Should Assist in Improving the Legal System.**
   EC 8–1 to 8–9
   DR 8–101. Action as a Public Official.
   DR 8–102. Statements Concerning Judges and Other Adjudicatory Officers.
   DR 8–103. Lawyer Candidate of Judicial Office.
9. **A Lawyer Should Avoid Even the Appearance of Professional Impropriety.**
   EC 9–1 to 9–7
   DR 9–101. Avoiding Even the Appearance of Impropriety.
   DR 9–102. Preserving Identity of Funds and Property of a Client.
   Definitions.

PREAMBLE AND PRELIMINARY STATEMENT

Preamble [1]

The continued existence of a free and democratic society depends upon recognition of the concept that justice is based upon the rule of law grounded in respect for the dignity of the individual and his capacity through reason for enlightened self-government.[2] Law so grounded makes justice possible, for only through such law does the dignity of the individual attain respect and protection. Without it, individual rights become subject to unrestrained power, respect for law is destroyed, and rational self-government is impossible.

Lawyers as guardians of the law, play a vital role in the preservation of society. The fulfillment of this role requires an understanding by lawyers of their relationship with and function in our legal system.[3] A consequent obligation of lawyers is to maintain the highest standards of ethical conduct.

In fulfilling his professional responsibilities, a lawyer necessarily assumes various roles that require the performance of many difficult tasks. Not every situation which he may encounter can be foreseen,[4] but fundamental ethical principles are always present to guide him. Within the framework of these principles, a lawyer must with courage

---

1. The footnotes are intended merely to enable the reader to relate the provisions of this Code to the ABA Canons of Professional Ethics adopted in 1908, as amended, the Opinions of the ABA Committee on Professional Ethics, and a limited number of other sources; they are not intended to be an annotation of the views taken by the ABA Special Committee on Evaluation of Ethical Standards. Footnotes citing ABA Canons refer to the ABA Canons of Professional Ethics, adopted in 1908, as amended.

2. Cf. ABA Canons, Preamble.

3. "[T]he lawyer stands today in special need of a clear understanding of his obligations and of the vital connection between these obligations and the role his profession plays in society." *Professional Responsibility: Report of the Joint Conference,* 44 A.B.A.J. 1159, 1160 (1958).

4. "No general statement of the responsibilities of the legal profession can encompass all the situations in which the lawyer may be placed. Each position held by him makes its own peculiar demands. These demands the lawyer must clarify for himself in the light of the particular role in which he serves." *Professional Responsibility: Report of the Joint Conference,* 44 A.B.A.J. 1159, 1218 (1958).

and foresight be able and ready to shape the body of the law to the ever-changing relationships of society.[5]

The Code of Professional Responsibility points the way to the aspiring and provides standards by which to judge the transgressor. Each lawyer must find within his own conscience the touchstone against which to test the extent to which his actions should rise above minimum standards. But in the last analysis it is the desire for the respect and confidence of the members of his profession and of the society which he serves that should provide to a lawyer the incentive for the highest possible degree of ethical conduct. The possible loss of that respect and confidence is the ultimate sanction. So long as its practitioners are guided by these principles, the law will continue to be a noble profession. This is its greatness and its strength, which permit of no compromise.

Preliminary Statement

In furtherance of the principles stated in the Preamble, the American Bar Association has promulgated this Code of Professional Responsibility, consisting of three separate but interrelated parts: Canons, Ethical Considerations, and Disciplinary Rules.[6] The Code is designed to be adopted by appropriate agencies both as an inspirational guide to the members of the profession and as a basis for disciplinary action when the conduct of a lawyer falls below the required minimum standards stated in the Disciplinary Rules.

Obviously the Canons, Ethical Considerations, and Disciplinary Rules cannot apply to non-lawyers; however, they do define the type of ethical conduct that the public has a right to expect not only of lawyers but also of their non-professional employees and associates in all matters pertaining to professional employment. A lawyer should ultimately be responsible for the conduct of his employees and associates in the course of the professional representation of the client.

---

5. "The law and its institutions change as social conditions change. They must change if they are to preserve, much less advance, the political and social values from which they derive their purposes and their life. This is true of the most important of legal institutions, the profession of law. The profession, too, must change when conditions change in order to preserve and advance the social values that are its reasons for being." Cheatham, *Availability of Legal Services: The Responsibility of the Individual Lawyer and the Organized Bar,* 12 U.C.L.A.L.Rev. 438, 440 (1965).

6. The Supreme Court of Wisconsin adopted a Code of Judicial Ethics in 1967. "The code is divided into standards and rules, the standards being statements of what the general desirable level of conduct should be, the rules being particular canons, the violation of which shall subject an individual judge to sanctions." In re Promulgation of a Code of Judicial Ethics, 36 Wis.2d 252, 255, 153 N.W.2d 873, 874 (1967).

The portion of the Wisconsin Code of Judicial Ethics entitled "Standards" states that "[t]he following standards set forth the significant qualities of the ideal judge...." Id., 36 Wis.2d at 256, 153 N.W.2d at 875. The portion entitled "Rules" states that "[t]he court promulgates the following rules because the requirements of judicial conduct embodied therein are of sufficient gravity to warrant sanctions if they are not obeyed...." Id., 36 Wis.2d at 259, 153 N.W.2d at 876.

The Canons are statements of axiomatic norms, expressing in general terms the standards of professional conduct expected of lawyers in their relationships with the public, with the legal system, and with the legal profession. They embody the general concepts from which the Ethical Considerations and the Disciplinary Rules are derived.

The Ethical Considerations are aspirational in character and represent the objectives toward which every member of the profession should strive. They constitute a body of principles upon which the lawyer can rely for guidance in many specific situations.[7]

The Disciplinary Rules, unlike the Ethical Considerations, are mandatory in character. The Disciplinary Rules state the minimum level of conduct below which no lawyer can fall without being subject to disciplinary action. Within the framework of fair trial,[8] the Disciplinary Rules should be uniformly applied to all lawyers,[9] regardless of the

7. "Under the conditions of modern practice is it peculiarly necessary that the lawyer should understand, not merely the established standards of professional conduct, but the reasons underlying these standards. Today the lawyer plays a changing and increasingly varied role. In many developing fields the precise contribution of the legal profession is as yet undefined." *Professional Responsibility: Report of the Joint Conference,* 44 A.B.A.J. 1159 (1958).

"A true sense of professional responsibility must derive from an understanding of the reasons that lie back of specific restraints, such as those embodied in the Canons. The grounds for the lawyer's peculiar obligations are to be found in the nature of his calling. The lawyer who seeks a clear understanding of his duties will be led to reflect on the special services his profession renders to society and the services it might render if its full capacities were realized. When the lawyer fully understands the nature of his office, he will then discern what restraints are necessary to keep that office wholesome and effective." *Id.*

8. "Disbarment, designed to protect the public, is a punishment or penalty imposed on the lawyer. * * * He is accordingly entitled to procedural due process, which includes fair notice of the charge." In re Ruffalo, 390 U.S. 544, 550, 20 L.Ed.2d 117, 122, 88 S.Ct. 1222, 1226 (1968), rehearing denied, 391 U.S. 961, 20 L.Ed.2d 874, 88 S.Ct. 1833 (1968).

"A State cannot exclude a person from the practice of law or from any other occupation in a manner or for reasons that contravene the Due Process or Equal Protection Clause of the Fourteenth Amendment.... A State can require high standards of qualification ... but any qualification must have a rational connection with the applicant's fitness or capacity to practice law." Schware v. Bd. of Bar Examiners, 353 U.S. 232, 239, 1 L.Ed.2d 796, 801–02, 77 S.Ct. 752, 756 (1957).

"[A]n accused lawyer may expect that he will not be condemned out of a capricious self-righteousness or denied the essentials of a fair hearing." Kingsland v. Dorsey, 338 U.S. 318, 320, 94 L.Ed. 123, 126, 70 S.Ct. 123, 124–25 (1949).

"The attorney and counsellor being, by the solemn judicial act of the court, clothed with his office, does not hold it as a matter of grace and favor. The right which it confers upon him to appear for suitors, and to argue causes is something more than a mere indulgence, revocable at the pleasure of the court, or at the command of the legislature. It is a right of which he can only be deprived by the judgment of the court, for moral or professional delinquency." Ex parte Garland, 71 U.S. (4 Wall.) 333, 378–79, 18 L.Ed. 366, 370 (1866).

See generally Comment, *Procedural Due Process and Character Hearings for Bar Applicants,* 15 Stan.L.Rev. 500 (1963).

9. "The canons of professional ethics must be enforced by the Courts and must nature of their professional activities.[10] The Code makes no attempt to prescribe either disciplinary procedures or penalties [11] for violation of a Disciplinary Rule,[12] nor does it undertake to define standards for civil liability of lawyers for professional conduct. The severity of judgment against one found guilty of violating a Disciplinary Rule should be determined by the character of the offense and the attendant circumstances.[13] An enforcing agency, in applying the Disciplinary Rules, may find interpretive guidance in the basic principles embodied in the Canons and in the objectives reflected in the Ethical Considerations.

CANON 1

A Lawyer Should Assist in Maintaining the Integrity and Competence of the Legal Profession

ETHICAL CONSIDERATIONS

EC 1–1 A basic tenet of the professional responsibility of lawyers is that every person in our society should have ready access to the independent professional services of a lawyer of integrity and competence.

be respected by members of the Bar if we are to maintain public confidence in the integrity and impartiality of the administration of justice." In re Meeker, 76 N.M. 354, 357, 414 P.2d 862, 864 (1966), appeal dismissed, 385 U.S. 449 (1967).

10. See ABA Canon 45.

"The Canons of this Association govern all its members, irrespective of the nature of their practice, and the application of the Canons is not affected by statutes or regulations governing certain activities of lawyers which may prescribe less stringent standards." ABA Comm. on Professional Ethics, Opinions, No. 203 (1940) [hereinafter each Opinion is cited as "ABA Opinion"].

Cf. *ABA Opinion* 152 (1936).

11. "There is generally no prescribed discipline for any particular type of improper conduct. The disciplinary measures taken are discretionary with the courts, which may disbar, suspend, or merely censure the attorney as the nature of the offense and past indicia of character may warrant." Note, 43 Cornell L.Q. 489, 495 (1958).

12. The Code seeks only to specify conduct for which a lawyer should be disciplined. Recommendations as to the procedures to be used in disciplinary actions and the gravity of disciplinary measures appro-

priate for violations of the Code are within the jurisdiction of the American Bar Association Special Committee on Evaluation of Disciplinary Enforcement.

13. "The severity of the judgment of this court should be in proportion to the gravity of the offenses, the moral turpitude involved, and the extent that the defendant's acts and conduct affect his professional qualifications to practice law." Louisiana State Bar Ass'n v. Steiner, 204 La. 1073, 1092–93, 16 So.2d 843, 850 (1944) (Higgins, J., concurring in decree).

"Certainly an erring lawyer who has been disciplined and who having paid the penalty has given satisfactory evidence of repentance and has been rehabilitated and restored to his place at the bar by the court which knows him best ought not to have what amounts to an order of permanent disbarment entered against him by a federal court solely on the basis of an earlier criminal record and without regard to his subsequent rehabilitation and present good character.... We think, therefore, that the district court should reconsider the appellant's application for admission and grant it unless the court finds it to be a fact that the appellant is not presently of good moral or professional character." In re Dreier, 258 F.2d 68, 69–70 (3d Cir.1958).

Maintaining the integrity and improving the competence of the bar to meet the highest standards is the ethical responsibility of every lawyer.

EC 1–2 The public should be protected from those who are not qualified to be lawyers by reason of a deficiency in education [1] or moral standards [2] or of other relevant factors [3] but who nevertheless seek to practice law. To assure the maintenance of high moral and educational standards of the legal profession, lawyers should affirmatively assist courts and other appropriate bodies in promulgating, enforcing, and improving requirements for admission to the bar.[4] In like manner, the

1. "[W]e cannot conclude that all educational restrictions [on bar admission] are unlawful. We assume that few would deny that a grammar school education requirement, before taking the bar examination, was reasonable. Or that an applicant had to be able to read or write. Once we conclude that *some* restriction is proper, then it becomes a matter of degree—the problem of drawing the line.

. . .

"We conclude the fundamental question here is whether Rule IV, Section 6 of the Rules Pertaining to Admission of Applicants to the State Bar of Arizona is 'arbitrary, capricious and unreasonable.' We conclude an educational requirement of graduation from an accredited law school is not." Hackin v. Lockwood, 361 F.2d 499, 503–04 (9th Cir.1966), cert. denied, 385 U.S. 960, 17 L.Ed.2d 305, 87 S.Ct. 396 (1966).

2. "Every state in the United States, as a prerequisite for admission to the practice of law, requires that applicants possess 'good moral character.' Although the requirement is of judicial origin, it is now embodied in legislation in most states." Comment, *Procedural Due Process and Character Hearings for Bar Applicants,* 15 Stan.L.Rev. 500 (1963).

"Good character in the members of the bar is essential to the preservation of the integrity of the courts. The duty and power of the court to guard its portals against intrusion by men and women who are mentally and morally dishonest, unfit because of bad character, evidenced by their course of conduct, to participate in the administrative law, would seem to be unquestioned in the matter of preservation of judicial dignity and integrity." In re Monaghan, 126 Vt. 53, 222 A.2d 665, 670 (1966).

"Fundamentally, the question involved in both situations [i.e. admission and disciplinary proceedings] is the same—is the applicant for admission or the attorney sought to be disciplined a fit and proper person to be permitted to practice law, and that usually turns upon whether he has committed or is likely to continue to commit acts of moral turpitude. At the time of oral argument the attorney for respondent frankly conceded that the test for admission and for discipline is and should be the same. We agree with this concession." Hallinan v. Comm. of Bar Examiners, 65 Cal.2d 447, 453, 421 P.2d 76, 81, 55 Cal.Rptr. 228, 233 (1966).

3. "Proceedings to gain admission to the bar are for the purpose of protecting the public and the courts from the ministrations of persons unfit to practice the profession. Attorneys are officers of the court appointed to assist the court in the administration of justice. Into their hands are committed the property, the liberty and sometimes the lives of their clients. This commitment demands a high degree of intelligence, knowledge of the law, respect for its function in society, sound and faithful judgment and, above all else, integrity of character in private and professional conduct." In re Monaghan, 126 Vt. 53, 222 A.2d 665, 676 (1966) (Holden, C.J., dissenting).

4. "A bar composed of lawyers of good moral character is a worthy objective but it is unnecessary to sacrifice vital freedoms in order to obtain that goal. It is also important both to society and the bar itself that lawyers be unintimidated—free to think, speak, and act as members of an Independent Bar." Konigsberg v. State Bar, 353 U.S. 252, 273, 1 L.Ed.2d 810, 825, 77 S.Ct. 722, 733 (1957).

bar has a positive obligation to aid in the continued improvement of all phases of pre-admission and post-admission legal education.

EC 1-3 Before recommending an applicant for admission, a lawyer should satisfy himself that the applicant is of good moral character. Although a lawyer should not become a self-appointed investigator or judge of applicants for admission, he should report to proper officials all unfavorable information he possesses relating to the character or other qualifications of an applicant.[5]

EC 1-4 The integrity of the profession can be maintained only if conduct of lawyers in violation of the Disciplinary Rules is brought to the attention of the proper officials. A lawyer should reveal voluntarily to those officials all unprivileged knowledge of conduct of lawyers which he believes clearly to be in violation of the Disciplinary Rules.[6] A lawyer should, upon request, serve on and assist committees and boards having responsibility for the administration of the Disciplinary Rules.[7]

EC 1-5 A lawyer should maintain high standards of professional conduct and should encourage fellow lawyers to do likewise. He should be temperate and dignified, and he should refrain from all illegal and morally reprehensible conduct.[8] Because of his position in society, even minor violations of law by a lawyer may tend to lessen public confidence in the legal profession. Obedience to law exemplifies respect for law. To lawyers especially, respect for the law should be more than a platitude.

EC 1-6 An applicant for admission to the bar or a lawyer may be unqualified, temporarily or permanently, for other than moral and educational reasons, such as mental or emotional instability. Lawyers should be diligent in taking steps to see that during a period of disqualification such person is not granted a license or, if licensed, is not permitted to practice.[9] In like manner, when the disqualification has

---

5. *See* ABA Canon 29.

6. ABA Canon 28 designates certain conduct as unprofessional and then states that: "A duty to the public and to the profession devolves upon every member of the Bar having knowledge of such practices upon the part of any practitioner immediately to inform thereof, to the end that the offender may be disbarred." ABA Canon 29 states a broader admonition: "Lawyers should expose without fear or favor before the proper tribunals corrupt or dishonest conduct in the profession."

7. "It is the obligation of the organized Bar and the individual lawyer to give unstinted cooperation and assistance to the highest court of the state in discharging its function and duty with respect to discipline

and in purging the profession of the unworthy." *Report of the Special Committee on Disciplinary Procedures*, 80 A.B.A.Rep. 463, 470 (1955).

8. Cf. ABA Canon 32.

9. "We decline, on the present record, to disbar Mr. Sherman or to reprimand him—not because we condone his actions, but because, as heretofore indicated, we are concerned with whether he is mentally responsible for what he has done.

"The logic of the situation would seem to dictate the conclusion that, if he was mentally responsible for the conduct we have outlined, he should be disbarred; and, if he was not mentally responsible, he should not be permitted to practice law.

terminated, members of the bar should assist such person in being licensed, or, if licensed, in being restored to his full right to practice.

DISCIPLINARY RULES

DR 1–101 Maintaining Integrity and Competence of the Legal Profession.

(A) A lawyer is subject to discipline if he has made a materially false statement in, or if he has deliberately failed to disclose a material fact requested in connection with, his application for admission to the bar.[10]

(B) A lawyer shall not further the application for admission to the bar of another person known by him to be unqualified in respect to character, education, or other relevant attribute.[11]

DR 1–102 Misconduct.

(A) A lawyer shall not:
(1) Violate a Disciplinary Rule.
(2) Circumvent a Disciplinary Rule through actions of another.[12]

"However, the flaw in the logic is that he may have been mentally irresponsible [at the time of his offensive conduct] ..., and, yet, have sufficiently improved in the almost two and one-half years intervening to be able to capably and competently represent his clients....

. . .

"We would make clear that we are satisfied that a case has been made against Mr. Sherman, warranting a refusal to permit him to further practice law in this state unless he can establish his mental irresponsibility at the time of the offenses charged. The burden of proof is upon him.

"If he establishes such mental irresponsibility, the burden is then upon him to establish his present capability to practice law." In re Sherman, 58 Wash.2d 1, 6–7, 354 P.2d 888, 890 (1960), cert. denied, 371 U.S. 951, 9 L.Ed.2d 499, 83 S.Ct. 506 (1963).

10. "This Court has the inherent power to revoke a license to practice law in this State, where such license was issued by this Court, and its issuance was procured by the fraudulent concealment, or by the false and fraudulent representation by the applicant of a fact which was manifestly material to the issuance of the license." North Carolina ex rel. Attorney General v. Gorson, 209 N.C. 320, 326, 183 S.E. 392, 395 (1936), cert. denied, 298 U.S. 662, 80 L.Ed. 1387, 56 S.Ct. 752 (1936).

See also Application of Patterson, 318 P.2d 907, 913 (Or.1957), cert. denied, 356 U.S. 947, 2 L.Ed.2d 822, 78 S.Ct. 795 (1958).

11. See ABA Canon 29.

12. In *ABA Opinion* 95 (1933), which held that a municipal attorney could not permit police officers to interview persons with claims against the municipality when the attorney knew the claimants to be represented by counsel, the Committee on Professional Ethics said:

"The law officer is, of course, responsible for the acts of those in his department who are under his supervision and control." *Opinion 85.* In re Robinson, 136 N.Y.S. 548 (affirmed 209 N.Y. 354–1912) held that it was a matter of disbarment for an attorney to adopt a general course of approving the unethical conduct of employees of his client, even though he did not actively participate therein.

(3) **Engage in illegal conduct involving moral turpitude.**[13]
(4) **Engage in conduct involving dishonesty, fraud, deceit, or misrepresentation.**
(5) **Engage in conduct that is prejudicial to the administration of justice.**
(6) **Engage in any other conduct that adversely reflects on his fitness to practice law.**[14]

" '. . . The attorney should not advise or sanction acts by his client which he himself should not do.' *Opinion 75."*

13. "The most obvious non-professional ground for disbarment is conviction for a felony. Most states make conviction for a felony grounds for automatic disbarment. Some of these states, including New York, make disbarment mandatory upon conviction for *any* felony, while others require disbarment only for those felonies which involve moral turpitude. There are strong arguments that some felonies, such as involuntary manslaughter, reflect neither on an attorney's fitness, trustworthiness, nor competence and, therefore, should not be grounds for disbarment, but most states tend to disregard these arguments and, following the common law rule, make disbarment mandatory on conviction for any felony." Note, 43 Cornell L.Q. 489, 490 (1958).

"Some states treat conviction for misdemeanors as grounds for automatic disbarment. . . . However, the vast majority, accepting the common law rule, require that the misdemeanor involve moral turpitude. While the definition of moral turpitude may prove difficult, it seems only proper that those minor offenses which do not affect the attorney's fitness to continue in the profession should not be grounds for disbarment. A good example is an assault and battery conviction which would not involve moral turpitude unless done with malice and deliberation." Id. at 491.

"The term 'moral turpitude' has been used in the law for centuries. It has been the subject of many decisions by the courts but has never been clearly defined because of the nature of the term. Perhaps the best general definition of the term 'moral turpitude' is that it imports an act of baseness, vileness or depravity in the duties which one person owes to another or to society in general, which is contrary to the usual, accepted and customary rule of right and

duty which a person should follow. 58 C.J.S. at page 1201. Although offenses against revenue laws have been held to be crimes of moral turpitude, it has also been held that the attempt to evade the payment of taxes due to the government or any subdivision thereof, while wrong and unlawful, does not involve moral turpitude. 58 C.J.S. at page 1205." Comm. on Legal Ethics v. Scheer, 149 W.Va. 721, 726–27, 143 S.E.2d 141, 145 (1965).

"The right and power to discipline an attorney, as one of its officers, is inherent in the court. . . . This power is not limited to those instances of misconduct wherein he has been employed, or has acted, in a professional capacity; but, on the contrary, this power may be exercised where his misconduct outside the scope of his professional relations shows him to be an unfit person to practice law." In re Wilson, 391 S.W.2d 914, 917–18 (Mo.1965).

14. "It is a fair characterization of the lawyer's responsibility in our society that he stands 'as a shield,' to quote Devlin, J., in defense of right and to ward off wrong. From a profession charged with these responsibilities there must be exacted those qualities of truth-speaking, of a high sense of honor, of granite discretion, of the strictest observance of fiduciary responsibility, that have, throughout the centuries, been compendiously described as 'moral character.' " Schware v. Bd. of Bar Examiners, 353 U.S. 232, 247 L.Ed.2d 796, 806, 77 S.Ct. 752, 761 (1957) (Frankfurter, J., concurring).

"Particularly applicable here is Rule 4.47 providing that 'A lawyer should always maintain his integrity; and shall not willfully commit any act against the interest of the public; nor shall he violate his duty to the courts or his clients; *nor shall he, by any misconduct, commit any offense against the laws of Missouri or the United States of*

DR 1-103   Disclosure of Information to Authorities.

(A) A lawyer possessing unprivileged knowledge of a violation of DR 1-102 shall report such knowledge to a tribunal or other authority empowered to investigate or act upon such violation.[15]

(B) A lawyer possessing unprivileged knowledge or evidence concerning another lawyer or a judge shall reveal fully such knowledge or evidence upon proper request of a tribunal or other authority empowered to investigate or act upon the conduct of lawyers or judges.[16]

CANON 2

A Lawyer Should Assist the Legal Profession in Fulfilling Its Duty to Make Legal Counsel Available

ETHICAL CONSIDERATIONS

EC 2-1   The need of members of the public for legal services [1] is met only if they recognize their legal problems, appreciate the importance of seeking assistance,[2] and are able to obtain the services of acceptable legal counsel.[3]   Hence, important functions of the legal profession are to educate laymen to recognize their problems, to facilitate the process of

---

America, which amounts to a crime involving acts done by him contrary to justice, honesty, modesty or good morals; nor shall he be guilty of any other misconduct whereby, for the protection of the public and those charged with the administration of justice, he should no longer be entrusted with the duties and responsibilities belonging to the office of an attorney.' " In re Wilson, 391 S.W.2d 914, 917 (Mo.1965).

15.   See ABA Canon 29; cf. ABA Canon 28.

16.   Cf. ABA Canons 28 and 29.

1.   "Men have need for more than a system of law; they have need for a system of law which functions, and that means they have need for lawyers." Cheatham, *The Lawyer's Role and Surroundings,* 25 Rocky Mt.L.Rev. 405 (1953).

2.   "Law is not self-applying; men must apply and utilize it in concrete cases. But the ordinary man is incapable. He cannot know the principles of law or the rules guiding the machinery of law administration; he does not know how to formulate his desires with precision and to put them into writing; he is ineffective in the presen-

tation of his claims." Cheatham, *The Lawyer's Role and Surroundings,* 25 Rocky Mt. L.Rev. 405 (1953).

3.   "This need [to provide legal services] was recognized by . . . Mr. [Lewis F.] Powell [Jr., President, American Bar Association, 1963-64], who said: 'Looking at contemporary America realistically, we must admit that despite all our efforts to date (and these have not been insignificant), far too many persons are not able to obtain equal justice under law. This usually results because their poverty or their ignorance has prevented them from obtaining legal counsel.' "   Address by E. Clinton Bamberger, Association of American Law Schools 1965 Annual Meeting, Dec. 28, 1965, in Proceedings, Part II, 1965, 61, 63-64 (1965).

"A wide gap separates the need for legal services and its satisfaction, as numerous studies reveal. Looked at from the side of the layman, one reason for the gap is poverty and the consequent inability to pay legal fees. Another set of reasons is ignorance of the need for and the value of legal services, and ignorance of where to find a dependable lawyer. There is fear of the mysterious intelligent selection of lawyers, and to assist in making legal services fully available.[4]

Recognition of Legal Problems

EC 2–2 The legal profession should assist lay-persons to recognize legal problems because such problems may not be self-revealing and often are not timely noticed. Therefore, lawyers should encourage and participate in educational and public relations programs concerning our legal system with particular reference to legal problems that frequently arise. Preparation of advertisements and professional articles for lay publications [5] and participation in seminars, lectures, and civic programs should be motivated by a desire to educate the public to an awareness of legal needs and to provide information relevant to the selection of the most appropriate counsel rather than to obtain publicity for particular lawyers. The problems of advertising on television require special consideration, due to the style, cost, and transitory nature of such media. If the interests of laypersons in receiving relevant lawyer advertising are not adequately served by print media and radio advertising, and if adequate safeguards to protect the public can reasonably be formulated, television advertising may serve a public interest.

As amended in 1977.

EC 2–3 Whether a lawyer acts properly in volunteering in-person advice to a layperson to seek legal services depends upon the circumstances.[6] The giving of advice that one should take legal action could well be in fulfillment of the duty of the legal profession to assist laypersons in recognizing legal problems.[7] The advice is proper only if

processes and delays of the law, and there is fear of overreaching and overcharging by lawyers, a fear stimulated by the occasional exposure of shysters." Cheatham, *Availability of Legal Services: The Responsibility of the Individual Lawyer and of the Organized Bar,* 12 U.C.L.A.L.Rev. 438 (1965).

4. "It is not only the right but the duty of the profession as a whole to utilize such methods as may be developed to bring the services of its members to those who need them, so long as this can be done ethically and with dignity." *ABA Opinion* 320 (1968).

"[T]here is a responsibility on the bar to make legal services available to those who need them. The maxim, 'privilege brings responsibilities,' can be expanded to read, exclusive privilege to render public service brings responsibility to assure that the service is available to those in need of it." Cheatham, *Availability of Legal Services: The Responsibility of the Individual Lawyer*

and of the Organized Bar, 12 U.C.L.A.L.Rev. 438, 443 (1965).

"The obligation to provide legal services for those actually caught up in litigation carries with it the obligation to make preventive legal advice accessible to all. It is among those unaccustomed to business affairs and fearful of the ways of the law that such advice is often most needed. If it is not received in time, the most valiant and skillful representation in court may come too late." *Professional Responsibility: Report of the Joint Conference,* 44 A.B.A.J. 1159, 1216 (1958).

5. "A lawyer may with propriety write articles for publications in which he gives information upon the law...." A.B.A. Canon 40.

6. See ABA Canon 28.

7. This question can assume constitutional dimensions: "We meet at the outset the contention that 'solicitation' is wholly motivated by a desire to protect one who does not recognize that he may have legal problems or who is ignorant of his legal rights or obligations. It is improper if motivated by a desire to obtain personal benefit, secure personal publicity, or cause legal action to be taken merely to harass or injure another. A lawyer should not initiate an in-person contact with a non-client, personally or through a representative, for the purpose of being retained to represent him for compensation.

As amended in 1977.

EC 2–4 Since motivation is subjective and often difficult to judge, the motives of a lawyer who volunteers in-person advice likely to produce legal controversy may well be suspect if he receives professional employment or other benefits as a result.[8] A lawyer who volunteers in-person advice that one should obtain the services of a lawyer generally should not himself accept employment, compensation, or other benefit in connection with that matter. However, it is not improper for a lawyer to volunteer such advice and render resulting legal services to close friends, relatives, former clients (in regard to matters germane to former employment), and regular clients.[9]

As amended in 1977.

EC 2–5 A lawyer who writes or speaks for the purpose of educating members of the public to recognize their legal problems should carefully refrain from giving or appearing to give a general solution applicable to

outside the area of freedoms protected by the First Amendment. To this contention there are two answers. The first is that a State cannot foreclose the exercise of constitutional rights by mere labels. The second is that abstract discussion is not the only species of communication which the Constitution protects; the First Amendment also protects vigorous advocacy, certainly of lawful ends, against governmental intrusion....

.   .   .

"However valid may be Virginia's interest in regulating the traditionally illegal practice of barratry, maintenance and champerty, that interest does not justify the prohibition of the NAACP activities disclosed by this record. Malicious intent was of the essence of the common-law offenses of fomenting or stirring up litigation. And whatever may be or may have been true of suits against governments in other countries, the exercise in our own, as in this case of First Amendment rights to enforce Constitutional rights through litigation, as a matter of law, cannot be deemed malicious." NAACP v. Button, 371 U.S. 415,

429, 439–40, 9 L.Ed.2d 405, 415–16, 422, 83 S.Ct. 328, 336, 341 (1963).

8. "It is disreputable for an attorney to breed litigation by seeking out those who have claims for personal injuries or other grounds of action in order to secure them as clients, or to employ agents or runners, or to reward those who bring or influence the bringing of business to his office.... Moreover, it tends quite easily to the institution of baseless litigation and the manufacture of perjured testimony. From early times, this danger has been recognized in the law by the condemnation of the crime of common barratry, or the stirring up of suits or quarrels between individuals at law or otherwise." In re Ades, 6 F.Supp. 467, 474–75 (D.Mary.1934).

9. "*Rule 2.*

"§ a.   . . .

"[A] member of the State Bar shall not solicit professional employment by

"(1) Volunteering counsel or advice except where ties of blood relationship or trust make it appropriate." Cal.Business and Professions Code § 6076 (West 1962).

all apparently similar individual problems,[10] since slight changes in fact situations may require a material variance in the applicable advice; otherwise, the public may be mislead and misadvised. Talks and writings by lawyers for laypersons should caution them not to attempt to solve individual problems upon the basis of the information contained therein.[11]

As amended in 1977.

Selection of a Lawyer

EC 2–6 Formerly a potential client usually knew the reputations of local lawyers for competency and integrity and therefore could select a practitioner in whom he had confidence. This traditional selection process worked well because it was initiated by the client and the choice was an informed one.

EC 2–7 Changed conditions, however, have seriously restricted the effectiveness of the traditional selection process. Often the reputations of lawyers are not sufficiently known to enable laypersons to make intelligent choices.[12] The law has become increasingly complex and specialized. Few lawyers are willing and competent to deal with every kind of legal matter, and many laypersons have difficulty in determining the competence of lawyers to render different types of legal services. The selection of legal counsel is particularly difficult for transients, persons moving into new areas, persons of limited education or means, and others who have little or no contact with lawyers.[13] Lack of information about the availability of lawyers, the qualifications of particular lawyers, and the expense of legal representation leads laypersons to avoid seeking legal advice.

As amended in 1977.

10. *"Rule 18* ... A member of the State Bar shall not advise inquirers or render opinions to them through or in connection with a newspaper, radio or other publicity medium of any kind in respect to their specific legal problems, whether or not such attorney shall be compensated for his services." Cal.Business and Professions Code § 6076 (West 1962).

11. "In any case where a member might well apply the advice given in the opinion to his individual affairs, the lawyer rendering the opinion [concerning problems common to members of an association and distributed to the members through a periodic bulletin] should specifically state that this opinion should not be relied on by any member as a basis for handling his individual affairs, but that in every case he should con-sult his counsel. In the publication of the opinion the association should make a similar statement." *ABA Opinion* 273 (1946).

12. "A group of recent interrelated changes bears directly on the availability of legal services.... [One] change is the constantly accelerating urbanization of the country and the decline of personal and neighborhood knowledge of whom to retain as a professional man." Cheatham, *Availability of Legal Services: The Responsibility of the Individual Lawyer and of the Organized Bar,* 12 U.C.L.A.L.Rev. 438, 440 (1965).

13. Cf. Cheatham, *A Lawyer When Needed: Legal Services for the Middle Classes,* 63 Colum.L.Rev. 973, 974 (1963).

EC 2–8 Selection of a lawyer by a layperson should be made on an informed basis. Advice and recommendation of third parties—relatives, friends, acquaintances, business associates, or other lawyers—and disclosure of relevant information about the lawyer and his practice may be helpful. A layperson is best served if the recommendation is disinterested and informed. In order that the recommendation be disinterested, a lawyer should not seek to influence another to recommend his employment. A lawyer should not compensate another person for recommending him, for influencing a prospective client to employ him, or to encourage future recommendations.[14] Advertisements and public communications, whether in law lists, telephone directories, newspapers, other forms of print media, television or radio, should be formulated to convey only information that is necessary to make an appropriate selection. Such information includes: (1) office information, such as, name, including name of law firm and names of professional associates; addresses; telephone numbers; credit card acceptability; fluency in foreign languages; and office hours; (2) relevant biographical information; (3) description of the practice, but only by using designations and definitions authorized by [the agency having jurisdiction of the subject under state law], for example, one or more fields of law in which the lawyer or law firm practices; a statement that practice is limited to one or more fields of law; and/or a statement that the lawyer or law firm specializes in a particular field of law practice, but only by using designations, definitions and standards authorized by [the agency having jurisdiction of the subject under state law]; and (4) permitted fee information. Self-laudation should be avoided.

As amended in 1978.

Selection of a Lawyer: Lawyer Advertising

EC 2–9 The lack of sophistication on the part of many members of the public concerning legal services, the importance of the interests affected by the choice of a lawyer and prior experience with unrestricted lawyer advertising, require that special care be taken by lawyers to avoid misleading the public and to assure that the information set forth in any advertising is relevant to the selection of a lawyer. The lawyer must be mindful that the benefits of lawyer advertising depend upon its reliability and accuracy. Examples of information in lawyer advertising that would be deceptive include misstatements of fact, suggestions that the ingenuity or prior record of a lawyer rather than the justice of the claim are the principal factors likely to determine the result, inclusion of information irrelevant to selecting a lawyer, and representations concerning the quality of service, which cannot be measured or verified. Since lawyer advertising is calculated and not spontaneous, reasonable regulation of lawyer advertising designed to foster compliance with

14. See ABA Canon 28.

appropriate standards serves the public interest without impeding the flow of useful, meaningful, and relevant information to the public.

As amended in 1977.

EC 2–10 A lawyer should ensure that the information contained in any advertising which the lawyer publishes, broadcasts or causes to be published or broadcast is relevant, is disseminated in an objective and understandable fashion, and would facilitate the prospective client's ability to compare the qualifications of the lawyers available to represent him. A lawyer should strive to communicate such information without undue emphasis upon style and advertising stratagems which serve to hinder rather than to facilitate intelligent selection of counsel. Because technological change is a recurrent feature of communications forms, and because perceptions of what is relevant in lawyer selection may change, lawyer advertising regulations should not be cast in rigid, unchangeable terms. Machinery is therefore available to advertisers and consumers for prompt consideration of proposals to change the rules governing lawyer advertising. The determination of any request for such change should depend upon whether the proposal is necessary in light of existing Code provisions, whether the proposal accords with standards of accuracy, reliability and truthfulness, and whether the proposal would facilitate informed selection of lawyers by potential consumers of legal services. Representatives of lawyers and consumers should be heard in addition to the applicant concerning any proposed change. Any change which is approved should be promulgated in the form of an amendment to the Code so that all lawyers practicing in the jurisdiction may avail themselves of its provisions.

As amended in 1977.

EC 2–11 The name under which a lawyer conducts his practice may be a factor in the selection process.[15] The use of a trade name or an assumed name could mislead laypersons concerning the identity, responsibility, and status of those practicing thereunder.[16] Accordingly, a lawyer in private practice should practice only under a designation containing his own name, the name of a lawyer employing him, the name of one or more of the lawyers practicing in a partnership, or, if permitted by law, the name of a professional legal corporation, which should be clearly designated as such. For many years some law firms have used a firm name retaining one or more names of deceased or retired partners and such practice is not improper if the firm is a bona fide successor of a firm in which the deceased or retired person was a member, if the use of the name is authorized by law or by contract, and if the public is not misled thereby.[17] However, the name of a partner who withdraws from

---

15. *Cf. ABA Opinion* 303 (1961).

16. *See* ABA Canon 33.

17. Id.

"The continued use of a firm name by one or more surviving partners after the death of a member of the firm whose name is in the firm title is expressly permitted by the Canons of Ethics. The reason for this a firm but continues to practice law should be omitted from the firm name in order to avoid misleading the public.

As amended in 1977.

EC 2–12 A lawyer occupying a judicial, legislative, or public executive or administrative position who has the right to practice law concurrently may allow his name to remain in the name of the firm if he actively continues to practice law as a member thereof. Otherwise, his name should be removed from the firm name,[18] and he should not be identified as a past or present member of the firm; and he should not hold himself out as being a practicing lawyer.

EC 2–13 In order to avoid the possibility of misleading persons with whom he deals, a lawyer should be scrupulous in the representation of his professional status.[19] He should not hold himself out as being a partner or associate of a law firm if he is not one in fact,[20] and thus should not hold himself out as partner or associate if he only shares offices with another lawyer.[21]

EC 2–14 In some instances a lawyer confines his practice to a particular field of law.[22] In the absence of state controls to insure the existence

---

is that all of the partners have by their joint and several efforts over a period of years contributed to the good will attached to the firm name. In the case of a firm having widespread connections, this good will is disturbed by a change in firm name every time a name partner dies, and that reflects a loss in some degree of the good will to the building up of which the surviving partners have contributed their time, skill and labor through a period of years. To avoid this loss the firm name is continued, and to meet the requirements of the Canon the individuals constituting the firm from time to time are listed." *ABA Opinion* 267 (1945).

"Accepted local custom in New York recognizes that the name of a law firm does not necessarily identify the individual members of the firm, and hence the continued use of a firm name after the death of one or more partners is not a deception and is permissible. . . . The continued use of a deceased partner's name in the firm title is not affected by the fact that another partner withdraws from the firm and his name is dropped, or the name of the new partner is added to the firm name." *Opinion* No. 45, Committee on Professional Ethics, New York State Bar Ass'n, 39 N.Y.St.B.J. 455 (1967).

18. Cf. ABA Canon 33 and *ABA Opinion* 315 (1965).

19. Cf. *ABA Opinions* 283 (1950) and 81 (1932).

20. See *ABA Opinion* 316 (1967).

21. "The word 'associates' has a variety of meanings. Principally through custom the word when used on the letterheads of law firms has come to be regarded as describing those who are employees of the firm. Because the word has acquired this special significance in connection with the practice of the law the use of the word to describe lawyer relationships other than employer-employee is likely to be misleading." In re Sussman and Tanner, 241 Ore. 246, 248, 405 P.2d 355, 356 (1965).

According to *ABA Opinion* 310 (1963), use of the term "associates" would be misleading in two situations: (1) where two lawyers are partners and they share both responsibility and liability for the partnership; and (2) where two lawyers practice separately, sharing no responsibility or liability, and only share a suite of offices and some costs.

22. "For a long time, many lawyers have, of necessity, limited their practice to certain branches of law. The increasing complexity of the law and the demand of of special competence, a lawyer should not be permitted to hold himself out as a specialist or as having official recognition as a specialist, other than in the fields of admiralty, trademark, and patent law where a holding out as a specialist historically has been permitted. A lawyer may, however, indicate in permitted advertising, if it is factual, a limitation of his practice or one or more particular areas or fields of law in which he practices using designations and definitions authorized for that purpose by [the state agency having jurisdiction]. A lawyer practicing in a jurisdiction which certifies specialists must also be careful not to confuse laypersons as to his status. If a lawyer discloses areas of law in which he practices or to which he limits his practice, but is not certified in [the jurisdiction], he, and the designation authorized in [the jurisdiction], should avoid any implication that he is in fact certified.

As amended in 1977.

EC 2–15 The legal profession has developed lawyer referral systems designed to aid individuals who are able to pay fees but need assistance in locating lawyers competent to handle their particular problems. Use of a lawyer referral system enables a layman to avoid an uninformed selection of a lawyer because such a system makes possible the employment of competent lawyers who have indicated an interest in the subject matter involved. Lawyers should support the principle of lawyer referral systems and should encourage the evolution of other ethical plans which aid in the selection of qualified counsel.

Financial Ability to Employ Counsel: Generally

EC 2–16 The legal profession cannot remain a viable force in fulfilling its role in our society unless its members receive adequate compensation for services rendered, and reasonable fees [23] should be charged in appropriate cases to clients able to pay them. Nevertheless, persons unable to pay all or a portion of a reasonable fee should be able to obtain necessary legal services,[24] and lawyers should support and participate in ethical activities designed to achieve that objective.[25]

Financial Ability to Employ Counsel: Persons Able to Pay Reasonable Fees

EC 2–17 The determination of a proper fee requires consideration of

the public for more expertness on the part of the lawyer has, in the past few years—particularly in the last ten years—brought about specialization on an increasing scale." *Report of the Special Committee on Specialization and Specialized Legal Services,* 79 A.B.A.Rep. 582, 584 (1954).

23. See ABA Canon 12.

24. Cf. ABA Canon 12.

25. "If there is any fundamental proposition of government on which all would agree, it is that one of the highest goals of society must be to achieve and maintain equality before the law. Yet this ideal remains an empty form of words unless the legal profession is ready to provide adequate representation for those unable to pay the usual fees." *Professional Representation: Report of the Joint Conference,* 44 A.B.A.J. 1159, 1216 (1958).

the interests of both client and lawyer.[26] A lawyer should not charge more than a reasonable fee,[27] for excessive cost of legal service would deter laymen from utilizing the legal system in protection of their rights. Furthermore, an excessive charge abuses the professional relationship between lawyer and client. On the other hand, adequate compensation is necessary in order to enable the lawyer to serve his client effectively and to preserve the integrity and independence of the profession.[28]

EC 2–18 The determination of the reasonableness of a fee requires consideration of all relevant circumstances,[29] including those stated in the Disciplinary Rules. The fees of a lawyer will vary according to many factors, including the time required, his experience, ability, and reputation, the nature of the employment, the responsibility involved, and the results obtained. It is a commendable and long-standing tradition of the bar that special consideration is given in the fixing of any fee for services rendered a brother lawyer or a member of his immediate family.

As amended in 1974.

EC 2–19 As soon as feasible after a lawyer has been employed, it is desirable that he reach a clear agreement with his client as to the basis of the fee charges to be made. Such a course will not only prevent later misunderstanding but will also work for good relations between the lawyer and the client. It is usually beneficial to reduce to writing the understanding of the parties regarding the fee, particularly when it is contingent. A lawyer should be mindful that many persons who desire to employ him may have had little or no experience with fee charges of lawyers, and for this reason he should explain fully to such persons the reasons for the particular fee arrangement he proposes.

EC 2–20 Contingent fee arrangements [30] in civil cases have long been commonly accepted in the United States in proceedings to enforce claims. The historical bases of their acceptance are that (1) they often, and in a variety of circumstances, provide the only practical means by which one having a claim against another can economically afford, finance, and obtain the services of a competent lawyer to prosecute his claim, and (2) a successful prosecution of the claim produces a *res* out of

26. See ABA Canon 12.

27. Cf. ABA Canon 12.

28. "When members of the Bar are induced to render legal services for inadequate compensation as a consequence the quality of the service rendered may be lowered, the welfare of the profession injured and the administration of justice made less efficient." *ABA Opinion* 302 (1961).

Cf. *ABA Opinion* 307 (1962).

29. See ABA Canon 12.

30. See ABA Canon 13; see also MacKinnon, Contingent Fees for Legal Services (1964) (A report of the American Bar Foundation).

"A contract for a reasonable contingent fee where sanctioned by law is permitted by *Canon 13,* but the client must remain responsible to the lawyer for expenses advanced by the latter. 'There is to be no barter of the privilege of prosecuting a cause for gain in exchange for the promise of the attorney to prosecute at his own expense.' (Cardozo, C.J. In Matter of Gilman, 251 N.Y. 265, 270–271.)" *ABA Opinion* 246 (1942).

which the fee can be paid.[31]   Although a lawyer generally should decline to accept employment on a contingent fee basis by one who is able to pay a reasonable fixed fee, it is not necessarily improper for a lawyer, where justified by the particular circumstances of a case, to enter into a contingent fee contract in a civil case with any client who, after being fully informed of all relevant factors, desires that arrangement.   Because of the human relationships involved and the unique character of the proceedings, contingent fee arrangements in domestic relation cases are rarely justified.   In administrative agency proceedings contingent fee contracts should be governed by the same consideration as in other civil cases.   Public policy properly condemns contingent fee arrangements in criminal cases, largely on the ground that legal services in criminal cases do not produce a *res* with which to pay the fee.

EC 2–21 A lawyer should not accept compensation or any thing of value incident to his employment or services from one other than his client without the knowledge and consent of his client after full disclosure.[32]

EC 2–22 Without the consent of his client, a lawyer should not associate in a particular matter another lawyer outside his firm.   A fee may properly be divided between lawyers [33] properly associated if the division is in proportion to the services performed and the responsibility assumed by each lawyer [34] and if the total fee is reasonable.

EC 2–23 A lawyer should be zealous in his efforts to avoid controversies over fees with clients [35] and should attempt to resolve amicably any differences on the subject.[36]   He should not sue a client for a fee unless

---

31. See Comment, *Providing Legal Services for the Middle Class in Civil Matters: The Problem, the Duty and a Solution,* 26 U.Pitt.L.Rev. 811, 829 (1965).

32. See ABA Canon 38.

"Of course, as ... [Informal Opinion 679] points out, there must be full disclosure of the arrangement [that an entity other than the client pays the attorney's fee] by the attorney to the client...." *ABA Opinion* 320 (1968).

33. "Only lawyers may share in ... a division of fees, but ... it is not necessary that both lawyers be admitted to practice in the same state, so long as the division was based on the division of services or responsibility." *ABA Opinion* 316 (1967).

34. See ABA Canon 34.

"We adhere to our previous rulings that where a lawyer merely brings about the employment of another lawyer *but renders*

no service and assumes no responsibility in the matter, a division of the latter's fee is improper. *(Opinions 18 and 153).*

"It is assumed that the bar, generally, understands what acts or conduct of a lawyer may constitute 'services' to a client within the intendment of *Canon 12.* Such acts or conduct invariably, if not always involve 'responsibility' on the part of the lawyer, whether the word 'responsibility' be construed to denote the possible resultant legal or moral liability on the part of the lawyer to the client or to others, or the onus of deciding what should or should not be done in behalf of the client. The word 'services' in *Canon 12* must be construed in this broad sense and may apply to the selection and retainer of associate counsel as well as to others acts or conduct in the client's behalf." *ABA Opinion* 204 (1940).

35. See ABA Canon 14.

36. Cf. *ABA Opinion* 320 (1968).

necessary to prevent fraud or gross imposition by the client.[37]

Financial Ability to Employ Counsel: Persons Unable to Pay Reasonable Fees

EC 2–24 A layman whose financial ability is not sufficient to permit payment of any fee cannot obtain legal services, other than in cases where a contingent fee is appropriate, unless the services are provided for him. Even a person of moderate means may be unable to pay a reasonable fee which is large because of the complexity, novelty, or difficulty of the problem or similar factors.[38]

EC 2–25 Historically, the need for legal services of those unable to pay reasonable fees has been met in part by lawyers who donated their services or accepted court appointments on behalf of such individuals. The basic responsibility for providing legal services for those unable to pay ultimately rests upon the individual lawyer, and personal involvement in the problems of the disadvantaged can be one of the most rewarding experiences in the life of a lawyer. Every lawyer, regardless of professional prominence or professional workload, should find time to participate in serving the disadvantaged. The rendition of free legal services to those unable to pay reasonable fees continues to be an obligation of each lawyer, but the efforts of individual lawyers are often

---

37. See ABA Canon 14.

"Ours is a learned profession, not a mere money-getting trade.... Suits to collect fees should be avoided. Only where the circumstances imperatively require, should resort be had to a suit to compel payment. And where a lawyer does resort to a suit to enforce payment of fees which involves a disclosure, he should carefully avoid any disclosure not clearly necessary to obtaining or defending his rights." *ABA Opinion* 250 (1943).

But cf. *ABA Opinion* 320 (1968).

38. "As a society increases in size, sophistication and technology, the body of laws which is required to control that society also increases in size, scope and complexity. With this growth, the law directly affects more and more facets of individual behavior, creating an expanding need for legal services on the part of the individual members of the society.... As legal guidance in social and commercial behavior increasingly becomes necessary, there will come a concurrent demand from the layman that such guidance be made available to him. This demand will not come from those who are able to employ the best legal talent, nor from those who can obtain legal assistance at little or no cost. It will come from the large 'forgotten middle income class,' who can neither afford to pay proportionately large fees nor qualify for ultra-low-cost services. The legal profession must recognize this inevitable demand and consider methods whereby it can be satisfied. If the profession fails to provide such methods, the laity will." Comment, *Providing Legal Services for the Middle Class in Civil Matters: The Problem, the Duty and a Solution,* 26 U.Pitt.L.Rev. 811, 811–12 (1965).

"The issue is not whether we shall do something or do nothing. The demand for ordinary everyday legal justice is so great and the moral nature of the demand is so strong that the issue has become whether we devise, maintain, and support suitable agencies able to satisfy the demand, or by our own default, force the government to take over the job, supplant us, and ultimately dominate us." Smith, *Legal Service Offices for Persons of Moderate Means,* 1949 Wis.L.Rev. 416, 418 (1949).

not enough to meet the need.[39] Thus it has been necessary for the profession to institute additional programs to provide legal services.[40] Accordingly, legal aid offices,[41] lawyer referral services, and other related programs have been developed, and others will be developed, by the profession.[42] Every lawyer should support all proper efforts to meet this need for legal services.[43]

Acceptance and Retention of Employment

EC 2–26 A lawyer is under no obligation to act as advisor or advocate for every person who may wish to become his client; but in furtherance of the objective of the bar to make legal services fully available, a lawyer should not lightly decline proffered employment. The fulfillment of this objective requires acceptance by a lawyer of his share of tendered employment which may be unattractive both to him and the bar general-

39. "Lawyers have peculiar responsibilities for the just administration of the law, and these responsibilities include providing advice and representation for needy persons. To a degree not always appreciated by the public at large, the bar has performed these obligations with zeal and devotion. The Committee is persuaded, however, that a system of justice that attempts, in mid-twentieth century America, to meet the needs of the financially incapacitated accused through primary or exclusive reliance on the uncompensated services of counsel will prove unsuccessful and inadequate.... A system of adequate representation, therefore, should be structured and financed in a manner reflecting its public importance.... We believe that fees for private appointed counsel should be set by the court within maximum limits established by the statute." Report of the Att'y Gen's Comm. on Poverty and the Administration of Criminal Justice 41–43 (1963).

40. "At present this representation [of those unable to pay usual fees] is being supplied in some measure through the spontaneous generosity of individual lawyers, through legal aid societies, and—increasingly—through the organized efforts of the Bar. If those who stand in need of this service know of its availability and their need is in fact adequately met, the precise mechanism by which this service is provided becomes of secondary importance. It is of great importance, however, that both the impulse to render this service and the plan for making that impulse effective, should arise within the legal profession itself."

Professional Responsibility: Report of the Joint Conference, 44 A.B.A.J. 1159, 1216 (1958).

41. "Free legal clinics carried on by the organized bar are not ethically objectionable. On the contrary, they serve a very worthwhile purpose and should be encouraged." *ABA Opinion* 191 (1939).

42. "Whereas the American Bar Association believes that it is a fundamental duty of the bar to see to it that all persons requiring legal advice be able to attain it, irrespective of their economic status....

"Resolved, that the Association approves and sponsors the setting up by state and local bar associations of lawyer referral plans and low-cost legal service methods for the purpose of dealing with cases of persons who might not otherwise have the benefit of legal advice...." *Proceedings of the House of Delegates of the American Bar Association,* Oct. 30, 1946, 71 A.B.A.Rep. 103, 109–10 (1946).

43. "The defense of indigent citizens, without compensation, is carried on throughout the country by lawyers representing legal aid societies, not only with the approval, but with the commendation of those acquainted with the work. Not infrequently services are rendered out of sympathy or for other philanthropic reasons, by individual lawyers who do not represent legal aid societies. There is nothing whatever in the Canons to prevent a lawyer from performing such an act, nor should there be." *ABA Opinion* 148 (1935).

ly.[44]

EC 2–27   History is replete with instances of distinguished and sacrificial services by lawyers who have represented unpopular clients and causes. Regardless of his personal feelings, a lawyer should not decline representation because a client or a cause is unpopular or community reaction is adverse.[45]

EC 2–28   The personal preference of a lawyer to avoid adversary alignment against judges, other lawyers,[46] public officials, or influential members of the community does not justify his rejection of tendered employment.

EC 2–29   When a lawyer is appointed by a court or requested by a bar association to undertake representation of a person unable to obtain counsel, whether for financial or other reasons, he should not seek to be excused from undertaking the representation except for compelling reasons.[47]   Compelling reasons do not include such factors as the repugnance of the subject matter of the proceeding, the identity [48] or position of a person involved in the case, the belief of the lawyer that the defendant in a criminal proceeding is guilty,[49] or the belief of the lawyer

44.   But cf. ABA Canon 31.

45.   "One of the highest services the lawyer can render to society is to appear in court on behalf of clients whose causes are in disfavor with the general public." *Professional Responsibility: Report of the Joint Conference*, 44 A.B.A.J. 1159, 1216 (1958).

One author proposes the following proposition to be included in "A Proper Oath for Advocates": "I recognize that it is sometimes difficult for clients with unpopular causes to obtain proper legal representation. I will do all that I can to assure that the client with the unpopular cause is properly represented, and that the lawyer representing such a client receives credit from and support of the bar for handling such a matter." Thode, *The Ethical Standard for the Advocate*, 39 Texas L.Rev. 575, 592 (1961).

"§ 6068. . . .   It is the duty of an attorney.

. . .

"(h) Never to reject, for any consideration personal to himself, the cause of the defenseless or the oppressed." Cal.Business and Professions Code § 6068 (West 1962).   Virtually the same language is found in the Oregon statutes at Ore.Rev. Stats. Ch. 9, § 9.460(8).

See Rostow, *The Lawyer and His Client*, 48 A.B.A.J. 25 and 146 (1962).

46.   See ABA Canons 7 and 29.

"We are of the opinion that it is not professionally improper for a lawyer to accept employment to compel another lawyer to honor the just claim of a layman. On the contrary, it is highly proper that he do so. Unfortunately, there appears to be a widespread feeling among laymen that it is difficult, if not impossible, to obtain justice when they have claims against members of the Bar because other lawyers will not accept employment to proceed against them. The honor of the profession, whose members proudly style themselves officers of the court, must surely be sullied if its members bind themselves by custom to refrain from enforcing just claims of laymen against lawyers." *ABA Opinion* 144 (1935).

47.   ABA Canon 4 uses a slightly different test, saying, "A lawyer assigned as counsel for an indigent prisoner ought not to ask to be excused for any trivial reason. . . ."

48.   Cf. ABA Canon 7.

49.   See ABA Canon 5.

regarding the merits of the civil case.[50]

EC 2–30 Employment should not be accepted by a lawyer when he is unable to render competent service[51] or when he knows or it is obvious that the person seeking to employ him desires to institute or maintain an action merely for the purpose of harassing or maliciously injuring another.[52] Likewise, a lawyer should decline employment if the intensity of his personal feeling, as distinguished from a community attitude, may impair his effective representation of a prospective client. If a lawyer knows a client has previously obtained counsel, he should not accept employment in the matter unless the other counsel approves[53] or withdraws, or the client terminates the prior employment.[54]

EC 2–31 Full availability of legal counsel requires both that persons be able to obtain counsel and that lawyers who undertake representation complete the work involved. Trial counsel for a convicted defendant should continue to represent his client by advising whether to take an appeal and, if the appeal is prosecuted, by representing him through the appeal unless new counsel is substituted or withdrawal is permitted by the appropriate court.

EC 2–32 A decision by a lawyer to withdraw should be made only on the basis of compelling circumstances,[55] and in a matter pending before a tribunal he must comply with the rules of the tribunal regarding withdrawal. A lawyer should not withdraw without considering carefully and endeavoring to minimize the possible adverse effect on the rights

---

50. Dr. Johnson's reply to Boswell upon being asked what he thought of "supporting a cause which you know to be bad" was: "Sir, you do not know it to be good or bad till the Judge determines it. I have said that you are to state facts fairly; so that your thinking, or what you call knowing, a cause to be bad, must be from reasoning, must be from supposing your arguments to be weak and inconclusive. But, Sir, that is not enough. An argument which does not convince yourself, may convince the Judge to whom you urge it; and if it does convince him, why, then, Sir, you are wrong, and he is right." 2 Boswell, The Life of Johnson 47–48 (Hill ed. 1887).

51. "The lawyer deciding whether to undertake a case must be able to judge objectively whether he is capable of handling it and whether he can assume its burdens without prejudice to previous commitments...." *Professional Responsibility: Report of the Joint Conference,* 44 A.B.A.J. 1158, 1218 (1958).

52. "The lawyer must decline to conduct a civil cause or to make a defense when convinced that it is intended merely to harass or to injure the opposite party or to work oppression or wrong." ABA Canon 30.

53. See ABA Canon 7.

54. Id.

"From the facts stated we assume that the client has discharged the first attorney and given notice of the discharge. Such being the case, the second attorney may properly accept employment. *Canon 7; Opinions 10, 130, 149.*" ABA Opinion 209 (1941).

55. See ABA Canon 44.

"I will carefully consider, before taking a case, whether it appears that I can fully represent the client within the framework of law. If the decision is in the affirmative, then it will take extreme circumstances to cause me to decide later that I cannot so represent him." Thode, *The Ethical Standard for the Advocate,* 39 Texas L.Rev. 575, 592 (1961) (from "A Proper Oath for Advocates").

of his client and the possibility of prejudice to his client [56] as a result of his withdrawal. Even when he justifiably withdraws, a lawyer should protect the welfare of his client by giving due notice of his withdrawal,[57] suggesting employment of other counsel, delivering to the client all papers and property to which the client is entitled, cooperating with counsel subsequently employed, and otherwise endeavoring to minimize the possibility of harm. Further, he should refund to the client any compensation not earned during the employment.[58]

EC 2–33 As a part of the legal profession's commitment to the principle that high quality legal services should be available to all, attorneys are encouraged to cooperate with qualified legal assistance organizations providing prepaid legal services. Such participation should at all times be in accordance with the basic tenets of the profession: independence, integrity, competence and devotion to the interests of individual clients. An attorney so participating should make certain that his relationship with a qualified legal assistance organization in no way interferes with his independent, professional representation of the interests of the individual client. An attorney should avoid situations in which officials of the organization who are not lawyers attempt to direct attorneys concerning the manner in which legal services are performed for individual members, and should also avoid situations in which considerations of economy are given undue weight in determining the attorneys employed by an organization or the legal services to be performed for the member or beneficiary rather than competence and quality of service. An attorney interested in maintaining the historic traditions of the profession and preserving the function of a lawyer as a trusted and independent advisor to individual members of society should carefully assess such factors when accepting employment by, or otherwise participating in, a particular qualified legal assistance organization, and while so participating should adhere to the highest professional standards of effort and competence.

Added in 1974; amended in 1975.

DISCIPLINARY RULES

DR 2–101 Publicity.

(A) A lawyer shall not, on behalf of himself, his partner, associate or any other lawyer affiliated with him or his firm, use or participate in the use of any form of public communication contain-

---

56. *ABA Opinion* 314 (1965) held that a lawyer should not disassociate himself from a cause when "it is obvious that the very act of disassociation would have the effect of violating *Canon 37*."

57. ABA Canon 44 enumerates instances in which "... the lawyer may be warranted in withdrawing on due notice to the client, allowing him time to employ another lawyer."

58. *See* ABA Canon 44.

ing a false, fraudulent, misleading, deceptive, self-laudatory or unfair statement or claim.

(B) In order to facilitate the process of informed selection of a lawyer by potential consumers of legal services, a lawyer may publish or broadcast, subject to DR 2–103, the following information in print media distributed or over television or radio broadcast in the geographic area or areas in which the lawyer resides or maintains offices or in which a significant part of the lawyer's clientele resides, provided that the information disclosed by the lawyer in such publication or broadcast complies with DR 2–101(A), and is presented in a dignified manner:

(1) Name, including name of law firm and names of professional associates; addresses and telephone numbers;

(2) One or more fields of law in which the lawyer or law firm practices, a statement that practice is limited to one or more fields of law, or a statement that the lawyer or law firm specializes in a particular field of law practice, to the extent authorized under DR 2–105;

(3) Date and place of birth;

(4) Date and place of admission to the bar of state and federal courts;

(5) Schools attended, with dates of graduation, degrees and other scholastic distinctions;

(6) Public or quasi-public offices;

(7) Military service;

(8) Legal authorships;

(9) Legal teaching positions;

(10) Memberships, offices, and committee assignments, in bar associations;

(11) Membership and offices in legal fraternities and legal societies;

(12) Technical and professional licenses;

(13) Memberships in scientific, technical and professional associations and societies;

(14) Foreign language ability;

(15) Names and addresses of bank references;

(16) With their written consent, names of clients regularly represented;

(17) Prepaid or group legal services programs in which the lawyer participates;

(18) Whether credit cards or other credit arrangements are accepted;

(19) Office and telephone answering service hours;

(20) Fee for an initial consultation;

(21) Availability upon request of a written schedule of fees and/or an estimate of the fee to be charged for specific services;

(22) Contingent fee rates subject to DR 2–106(C), provided that the statement discloses whether percentages are computed before or after deduction of costs;

(23) Range of fees for services, provided that the statement discloses that the specific fee within the range which will be charged will vary depending upon the particular matter to be handled for each client and the client is entitled without obligation to an estimate of the fee within the range likely to be charged. In print size equivalent to the largest print used in setting forth the fee information;

(24) Hourly rate, provided that the statement discloses that the total fee charged will depend upon the number of hours which must be devoted to the particular matter to be handled for each client and the client is entitled to without obligation an estimate of the fee likely to be charged, in print size at least equivalent to the largest print used in setting forth the fee information;

(25) Fixed fees for specific legal services,* the description of which would not be misunderstood or be deceptive, provided that the statement discloses that the quoted fee will be available only to clients whose matters fall into the services described and that the client is entitled without obligation to a specific estimate of the fee likely to be charged in print size at least equivalent to the largest print used in setting forth the fee information.

(C) Any person desiring to expand the information authorized for disclosure in DR 2–101(B), or to provide for its dissemination through other forums may apply to [the agency having jurisdiction under state law]. Any such application shall be served upon [the agencies having jurisdiction under state law over the regulation of the legal profession and consumer matters] who shall be heard, together with the applicant, on the issue of whether the proposal is necessary in light of the existing provisions of the Code, accords with standards of accuracy, reliability and truthfulness, and would facilitate the process of informed selection of lawyers by potential consumers of legal services. The relief granted in response to any such application shall be promulgated as an amendment to DR 2–101(B), universally applicable to all lawyers.*

* The agency having jurisdiction under state law may desire to issue appropriate guidelines defining "specific legal services."

* The agency having jurisdiction under state law should establish orderly and expeditious procedures for ruling on such applications.

(D) If the advertisement is communicated to the public over television or radio, it shall be prerecorded, approved for broadcast by the lawyer, and a recording of the actual transmission shall be retained by the lawyer.

(E) If a lawyer advertises a fee for a service, the lawyer must render that service for no more than the fee advertised.

(F) Unless otherwise specified in the advertisement if a lawyer publishes any fee information authorized under DR 2-101(B) in a publication that is published more frequently than one time per month, the lawyer shall be bound by any representation made therein for a period of not less than 30 days after such publication. If a lawyer publishes any fee information authorized under DR 2-101(B) in a publication that is published once a month or less frequently, he shall be bound by any representation made therein until the publication of the succeeding issue. If a lawyer publishes any fee information authorized under DR 2-101(B) in a publication which has no fixed date for publication of a succeeding issue, the lawyer shall be bound by any representation made therein for a reasonable period of time after publication but in no event less than one year.

(G) Unless otherwise specified, if a lawyer broadcasts any fee information authorized under DR 2-101(B), the lawyer shall be bound by any representation made therein for a period of not less than 30 days after such broadcast.

(H) This rule does not prohibit limited and dignified identification of a lawyer as a lawyer as well as by name:

    (1) In political advertisements when his professional status is germane to the political campaign or to a political issue.

    (2) In public notices when the name and profession of a lawyer are required or authorized by law or are reasonably pertinent for a purpose other than the attraction of potential clients.

    (3) In routine reports and announcements of a bona fide business, civic, professional, or political organization in which he serves as a director or officer.

    (4) In and on legal documents prepared by him.

    (5) In and on legal textbooks, treatises, and other legal publications, and in dignified advertisements thereof.

(I) A lawyer shall not compensate or give any thing of value to representatives of the press, radio, television, or other communication medium in anticipation of or in return for professional publicity in a news item.

As amended in 1974, 1975, 1977 and 1978.

DR 2–102 Professional Notices, Letterheads and Offices.

(A) A lawyer or law firm shall not use or participate in the use of professional cards, professional announcement cards, office signs, letterheads, or similar professional notices or devices, except that the following may be used if they are in dignified form:

(1) A professional card of a lawyer identifying him by name and as a lawyer, and giving his addresses, telephone numbers, the name of his law firm, and any information permitted under DR 2–105. A professional card of a law firm may also give the names of members and associates. Such cards may be used for identification.

(2) A brief professional announcement card stating new or changed associations or addresses, change of firm name, or similar matters pertaining to the professional offices of a lawyer or law firm, which may be mailed to lawyers, clients, former clients, personal friends, and relatives.[59] It shall not state biographical data except to the extent reasonably necessary to identify the lawyer or to explain the change in his association, but it may state the immediate past position of the lawyer.[60] It may give the names and dates of predecessor firms in a continuing line of succession. It shall not state the nature of the practice except as permitted under DR 2–105.[61]

(3) A sign on or near the door of the office and in the building directory identifying the law office. The sign shall not state the nature of the practice, except as permitted under DR 2–105.

(4) A letter head of a lawyer identifying him by name and as a lawyer, and giving his addresses, telephone numbers, the name of his law firm, associates and any information permitted under DR 2–105. A letterhead of a law firm may also give the names of members and associates,[62] and names and dates relating to deceased and retired mem-

---

59. See *ABA Opinion* 301 (1961).

60. "[I]t has become commonplace for many lawyers to participate in government service; to deny them the right, upon their return to private practice, to refer to their prior employment in a brief and dignified manner, would place an undue limitation upon a large element of our profession. It is entirely proper for a member of the profession to explain his absence from private practice, where such is the primary purpose of the announcement, by a brief and dignified reference to the prior employment.

"... [A]ny such announcement should be limited to the immediate past connection of the lawyer with the government, made upon his leaving that position to enter private practice." *ABA Opinion* 301 (1961).

61. See *ABA Opinion* 251 (1943).

62. "Those lawyers who are working for an individual lawyer or a law firm may be designated on the letterhead and in other appropriate places as 'associates'." *ABA Opinion* 310 (1963).

bers.[63] A lawyer may be designated "Of Counsel" on a letterhead if he has a continuing relationship with a lawyer or law firm, other than as a partner or associate. A lawyer or law firm may be designated as "General Counsel" or by similar professional reference on stationary of a client if he or the firm devotes a substantial amount of professional time in the representation of that client.[64] The letterhead of a law firm may give the names and dates of predecessor firms in a continuing line of succession.

(B) A lawyer in private practice shall not practice under a trade name, a name that is misleading as to the identity of the lawyer or lawyers practicing under such name, or a firm name containing names other than those of one or more of the lawyers in the firm, except that the name of a professional corporation or professional association may contain "P.C." or "P.A." or similar symbols indicating the nature of the organization, and if otherwise lawful a firm may use as, or continue to include in, its name the name or names of one or more deceased or retired members of the firm or of a predecessor firm in a continuing line of succession.[65] A lawyer who assumes a judicial, legislative, or public executive or administrative post or office shall not permit his name to remain in the name of a law firm or to be used in professional notices of the firm during any significant period in which he is not actively and regularly practicing law as a member of the firm,[66] and during such period other members of the firm shall not use his name in the firm name or in professional notices of the firm.[67]

(C) A lawyer shall not hold himself out as having a partnership with one or more other lawyers or professional corporations unless they are in fact partners.[68]

---

63. See ABA Canon 33.

64. But see *ABA Opinion* 285 (1951).

65. See ABA Canon 33; cf. *ABA Opinions* 318 (1967), 267 (1945), 219 (1941), 208 (1940), 192 (1939), 97 (1933), and 6 (1925).

66. *ABA Opinion* 318 (1967) held, anything to the contrary in Formal Opinion 315 or in the other opinions cited notwithstanding that: Where a partner whose name appears in the name of a law firm is elected or appointed to high local, state or federal office, which office he intends to occupy only temporarily, at the end of which time he intends to return to his position with the firm, and provided that he is not precluded by holding such office from engaging in the practice of law and does not in fact sever his relationship with the firm

but only takes a leave of absence, and provided that there is no local law, statute or custom to the contrary, his name may be retained in the firm name during his term or terms of office, but only if proper precautions are taken not to mislead the public as to his degree of participation in the firm's affairs.

Cf. *ABA Opinion* 143 (1935). New York County Opinion 67, and New York City Opinions 36 and 798; but cf. *ABA Opinion* 192 (1939) and Michigan Opinion 164.

67. Cf. ABA Canon 33.

68. See *ABA Opinion* 277 (1948); cf. ABA Canon 33 and *ABA Opinions* 318 (1967), 126 (1935), 115 (1934), and 106 (1934).

(D) A partnership shall not be formed or continued between or among lawyers licensed in different jurisdictions unless all enumerations of the members and associates of the firm on its letterhead and in other permissible listings make clear the jurisdictional limitations on those members and associates of the firm not licensed to practice in all listed jurisdictions;[69] however, the same firm name may be used in each jurisdiction.

(E) Nothing contained herein shall prohibit a lawyer from using or permitting the use of, in connection with his name, an earned degree or title derived therefrom indicating his training in the law.

As amended in 1976, 1977, 1979 and 1980.

DR 2–103   Recommendation of Professional Employment.[70]

(A) A lawyer shall not, except as authorized in DR 2–101(B), recommend employment as a private practitioner,[71] of himself, his partner, or associate to a layperson who has not sought his advice regarding employment of a lawyer.[72]

(B) A lawyer shall not compensate or give anything of value to a person or organization to recommend or secure his employment[73] by a client, or as a reward for having made a recommendation resulting in his employment[74] by a client, except that he may pay the usual and reasonable fees or dues charged by any of the organizations listed in DR 2–103(D).

(C) A lawyer shall not request a person or organization to recommend or promote the use of his services or those of his partner or associate, or any other lawyer affiliated with him or his firm, as a private practitioner,[75] except as authorized in DR 2–101, and except that

---

69. See *ABA Opinions* 318 (1967) and 316 (1967); cf. ABA Canon 33.

70. Cf. ABA Canon 28.

71. "We think it clear that a lawyer's seeking employment in an ordinary law office, or appointment to a civil service position, is not prohibited by . . . [Canon 27]." *ABA Opinion* 197 (1939).

72. "[A] lawyer may not seek from persons not his clients the opportunity to perform . . . a [legal] checkup." *ABA Opinion* 307 (1962).

73. Cf. *ABA Opinion* 78 (1932).

74. " 'No financial connection of any kind between the Brotherhood and any lawyer is permissible. No lawyer can properly pay any amount whatsoever to the Brotherhood or any of its departments, officers or members as compensation, reimbursement of expenses or gratuity in connection with the procurement of a case.' " In re Brotherhood of R.R. Trainmen, 13 Ill.2d 391, 398, 150 N.E.2d 163, 167 (1958), quoted in In re Ratner, 194 Kan. 362, 372, 399 P.2d 865, 873 (1956).

See *ABA Opinion* 147 (1935).

75. "This Court has condemned the practice of ambulance chasing through the media of runners and touters. In similar fashion we have with equal emphasis condemned the practice of direct solicitation by a lawyer. We have classified both offenses as serious breaches of the Canons of Ethics demanding severe treatment of the offending lawyer." State v. Dawson, 111 So.2d 427, 431 (Fla.1959).

(1) **He may request referrals from a lawyer referral service operated, sponsored, or approved by a bar association and may pay its fees incident thereto.**[76]

(2) **He may cooperate with the legal service activities of any of the offices or organizations enumerated in DR 2–103(D)(1) through (4) and may perform legal services for those to whom he was recommended by it to do such work if:**

　(a) **The person to whom the recommendation is made is a member or beneficiary of such office or organization; and**

　(b) **The lawyer remains free to exercise his independent professional judgment on behalf of his client.**

(D) **A lawyer or his partner or associate or any other lawyer affiliated with him or his firm may be recommended, employed or paid by, or may cooperate with, one of the following offices or organizations that promote the use of his services or those of his partner or associate or any other lawyer affiliated with him or his firm if there is no interference with the exercise of independent professional judgment in behalf of his client:**

(1) **A legal aid office or public defender office:**

　(a) **Operated or sponsored by a duly accredited law school.**

　(b) **Operated or sponsored by a bona fide nonprofit community organization.**

　(c) **Operated or sponsored by a governmental agency.**

　(d) **Operated, sponsored, or approved by a bar association.**[77]

(2) **A military legal assistance office.**

(3) **A lawyer referral service operated, sponsored, or approved by a bar association.**

(4) **Any bona fide organization that recommends, furnishes or pays for legal services to its members or beneficiaries**[78] **provided the following conditions are satisfied:**

　(a) **Such organization, including any affiliate, is so organized and operated that no profit is derived by it from the rendition of legal services by lawyers, and that, if the organization is organized for profit, the**

76. "Registrants [of a lawyer referral plan] may be required to contribute to the expense of operating it by a reasonable registration charge or by a reasonable percentage of fees collected by them." *ABA Opinion* 291 (1956).

Cf. *ABA Opinion* 227 (1941).

77. Cf. *ABA Opinion* 148 (1935).

78. United Mine Workers v. Ill. State Bar Ass'n., 389 U.S. 217, 19 L.Ed.2d 426, 88 S.Ct. 353 (1967); Brotherhood of R.R. Trainmen v. Virginia, 371 U.S. 1, 12 L.Ed.2d 89, 84 S.Ct. 1113 (1964); NAACP v. Button, 371 U.S. 415, 9 L.Ed.2d 405, 83 S.Ct. 328 (1963).

legal services are not rendered by lawyers employed, directed, supervised or selected by it except in connection with matters where such organization bears ultimate liability of its member or beneficiary.

(b) Neither the lawyer, nor his partner, nor associate, nor any other lawyer affiliated with him or his firm, nor any non-lawyer, shall have initiated or promoted such organization for the primary purpose of providing financial or other benefit to such lawyer, partner, associate or affiliated lawyer.

(c) Such organization is not operated for the purpose of procuring legal work or financial benefit for any lawyer as a private practitioner outside of the legal services program of the organization.

(d) The member or beneficiary to whom the legal services are furnished, and not such organization, is recognized as the client of the lawyer in the matter.

(e) Any member or beneficiary who is entitled to have legal services furnished or paid for by the organization may, if such member or beneficiary so desires, select counsel other than that furnished, selected or approved by the organization for the particular matter involved; and the legal service plan of such organization provides appropriate relief for any member or beneficiary who asserts a claim that representation by counsel furnished, selected or approved would be unethical, improper or inadequate under the circumstances of the matter involved and the plan provides an appropriate procedure for seeking such relief.

(f) The lawyer does not know or have cause to know that such organization is in violation of applicable laws, rules of court and other legal requirements that govern its legal service operations.

(g) Such organization has filed with the appropriate disciplinary authority at least annually a report with respect to its legal service plan, if any, showing its terms, its schedule of benefits, its subscription charges, agreements with counsel, and financial results of its legal service activities or, if it has failed to do so, the lawyer does not know or have cause to know of such failure.

(E) A lawyer shall not accept employment when he knows or it is obvious that the person who seeks his services does so as a result of conduct prohibited under this Disciplinary Rule.

As amended in 1974, 1975 and 1977.

DR 2-104 Suggestion of Need of Legal Services.[79, 80]

(A) **A lawyer who has given in-person unsolicited advice to a layperson that he should obtain counsel or take legal action shall not accept employment resulting from that advice,[81] except that:**

> **(1) A lawyer may accept employment by a close friend, relative, former client (if the advice is germane to the former employment), or one whom the lawyer reasonably believes to be a client.[82]**
>
> **(2) A lawyer may accept employment that results from his participation in activities designed to educate laypersons to recognize legal problems, to make intelligent selection of counsel, or to utilize available legal services if such activities are conducted or sponsored by a qualified legal assistance organization.**
>
> **(3) A lawyer who is recommended, furnished or paid by a qualified legal assistance organization enumerated in DR 2-103(D)(1) through (4) may represent a member or beneficiary thereof, to the extent and under the conditions prescribed therein.**
>
> **(4) Without affecting his right to accept employment, a lawyer may speak publicly or write for publication on legal topics [83] so long as he does not emphasize his own professional experience or reputation and does not undertake to give individual advice.**
>
> **(5) If success in asserting rights or defenses of his client in litigation in the nature of a class action is dependent**

---

79. "If a bar association has embarked on a program of institutional advertising for an annual legal check-up and provides brochures and reprints, it is not improper to have these available in the lawyer's office for persons to read and take." *ABA Opinion* 307 (1962).

Cf. *ABA Opinion* 121 (1934).

80. ABA Canon 28.

81. Cf. *ABA Opinions* 229 (1941) and 173 (1937).

82. "It certainly is not improper for a lawyer to advise his regular clients of new statutes, court decisions, and administrative rulings, which may affect the client's interests, provided the communication is strictly limited to such information. . . .

"When such communications go to concerns or individuals other than regular clients of the lawyer, they are thinly disguised advertisements for professional employment, and are obviously improper." *ABA Opinion* 213 (1941).

"It is our opinion that where the lawyer has no reason to believe that he has been supplanted by another lawyer, it is not only his right, but it might even be his duty to advise his client of any change of fact or law which might defeat the client's testamentary purpose as expressed in the will.

"Periodic notices might be sent to the client for whom a lawyer has drawn a will, suggesting that it might be wise for the client to reexamine his will to determine whether or not there has been any change in his situation requiring a modification of his will." *ABA Opinion* 210 (1941).

Cf. ABA Canon 28.

83. Cf. *ABA Opinion* 168 (1937).

upon the joinder of others, a lawyer may accept, but shall not seek, employment from those contacted for the purpose of obtaining their joinder.[84]

As amended in 1974, 1975 and 1977.

DR 2–105   Limitation of Practice.[85]

(A) A lawyer shall not hold himself out publicly as a specialist, as practicing in certain areas of law or as limiting his practice permitted under DR 2–101(B), except as follows:

(1) A lawyer admitted to practice before the United States Patent and Trademark Office may use the designation "Patents," "Patent Attorney," "Patent Lawyer," or "Registered Patent Attorney" or any combination of those terms, on his letterhead and office sign.

(2) A lawyer who publicly discloses fields of law in which the lawyer or the law firm practices or states that his practice is limited to one or more fields of law shall do so by using designations and definitions authorized and approved by [the agency having jurisdiction of the subject under state law].

(3) A lawyer who is certified as a specialist in a particular field of law or law practice by [the authority having jurisdiction under state law over the subject of specialization by lawyers] may hold himself out as such, but only in accordance with the rules prescribed by that authority.[86]

As amended in 1977.

DR 2–106   Fees for Legal Services.[87]

(A) A lawyer shall not enter into an agreement for, charge, or collect an illegal or clearly excessive fee.[88]

(B) A fee is clearly excessive when, after a review of the facts, a lawyer of ordinary prudence would be left with a definite -

---

84. But cf. *ABA Opinion* 111 (1934).

85. See ABA Canon 45; cf. ABA Canons 43, and 46.

86. This provision is included to conform to action taken by the ABA House of Delegates at the Mid-Winter Meeting, January, 1969.

87. See ABA Canon 12.

88. The charging of a "clearly excessive fee" is a ground for discipline. State ex rel. Nebraska State Bar Ass'n. v. Richards, 165 Neb. 80, 90, 84 N.W.2d 136, 143 (1957).

"An attorney has the right to contract for any fee he chooses so long as it is not excessive (see Opinion 190), and this Committee is not concerned with the amount of such fees unless so excessive as to constitute a misappropriation of the client's funds (see Opinion 27)." *ABA Opinion* 320 (1968).

Cf. *ABA Opinions* 209 (1940), 190 (1939), and 27 (1930) and State ex rel. Lee v. Buchanan, 191 So.2d 33 (Fla.1966).

and firm conviction that the fee is in excess of a reasonable fee. Factors to be considered as guides in determining the reasonableness of a fee include the following:

(1) The time and labor required, the novelty and difficulty of the questions involved, and the skill requisite to perform the legal service properly.

(2) The likelihood, if apparent to the client, that the acceptance of the particular employment will preclude other employment by the lawyer.

(3) The fee customarily charged in the locality for similar legal services.

(4) The amount involved and the results obtained.

(5) The time limitations imposed by the client or by the circumstances.

(6) The nature and length of the professional relationship with the client.

(7) The experience, reputation, and ability of the lawyer or lawyers performing the services.

(8) Whether the fee is fixed or contingent.[89]

(C) A lawyer shall not enter into an arrangement for, charge, or collect a contingent fee for representing a defendant in a criminal case.[90]

DR 2–107   Division of Fees Among Lawyers.

(A) A lawyer shall not divide a fee for legal services with another lawyer who is not a partner in or associate of his law firm or law office, unless:

(1) The client consents to employment of the other lawyer after a full disclosure that a division of fees will be made.

(2) The division is made in proportion to the services performed and responsibility assumed by each.[91]

(3) The total fee of the lawyers does not clearly exceed reasonable compensation for all legal services they rendered the client.[92]

---

89. Cf. ABA Canon 13; see generally MacKinnon, Contingent Fees for Legal Services (1964) (A Report of the American Bar Foundation).

90. "Contingent fees, whether in civil or criminal cases, are a special concern of the law. . . .

"In criminal cases, the rule is stricter because of the danger of corrupting justice. The second part of Section 542 of the Restatement [of Contracts] reads: 'A bargain to conduct a criminal case . . . in consideration of a promise of a fee contingent on success is illegal. . . .' " Peyton v. Margiotti, 398 Pa. 86, 156 A.2d 865, 967 (1959).

"The third area of practice in which the use of the contingent fee is generally considered to be prohibited is the prosecution and defense of criminal cases. However, there are so few cases, and these are predominantly old, that it is doubtful that there can be said to be any current law on the subject. . . . In the absence of cases on the validity of contingent fees for defense attorneys, it is necessary to rely on the consensus among commentators that such a fee is void as against public policy. The nature of criminal practice itself makes unlikely the use of contingent fee contracts." MacKinnon, Contingent Fees for Legal Services 52 (1964) (A Report of the American Bar Foundation).

(B) This Disciplinary Rule does not prohibit payment to a former partner or associate pursuant to a separation or retirement agreement.

DR 2–108   Agreements Restricting the Practice of a Lawyer.

(A) A lawyer shall not be a party to or participate in a partnership or employment agreement with another lawyer that restricts the right of a lawyer to practice law after the termination of a relationship created by the agreement, except as a condition to payment of retirement benefits.[93]

(B) In connection with the settlement of a controversy or suit, a lawyer shall not enter into an agreement that restricts his right to practice law.

DR 2–109   Acceptance of Employment.

(A) A lawyer shall not accept employment on behalf of a person if he knows or it is obvious that such person wishes to:

  (1) Bring a legal action, conduct a defense, or assert a position in litigation, or otherwise have steps taken for him, merely for the purpose of harassing or maliciously injuring any person.[94]

  (2) Present a claim or defense in litigation that is not warranted under existing law, unless it can be supported by good faith argument for an extension, modification, or reversal of existing law.

---

91. See ABA Canon 34 and *ABA Opinions* 316 (1967) and 294 (1958); see generally *ABA Opinions* 265 (1945), 204 (1940), 190 (1939), 171 (1937), 153 (1936), 97 (1933), 63 (1932), 28 (1930), 27 (1930), and 18 (1930).

92. *"Canon 12* contemplates that a lawyer's fee should not exceed *the value of the services* rendered. . . .

"*Canon 12* applies, whether joint or separate fees are charged [by associate attorneys]. . . ." *ABA Opinion* 204 (1940).

93. "[A] general covenant restricting an employed lawyer, after leaving the employment, from practicing in the community for a stated period, appears to this Committee to be an unwarranted restriction on the right of a lawyer to choose where he will practice and inconsistent with our professional status. Accordingly, the Committee is of the opinion it would be improper for the employing lawyer to require the covenant and likewise for the employed lawyer to agree to it." *ABA Opinion* 300 (1961).

94. See ABA Canon 30.

"*Rule 13.* . . . A member of the State Bar shall not accept employment to prosecute or defend a case solely out of spite, or solely for the purpose of harassing or delaying another. . . ." Cal.Business and Professions Code § 6067 (West 1962).

DR 2–110 Withdrawal From Employment.[95]

(A) In general.

(1) If permission for withdrawal from employment is required by the rules of a tribunal, a lawyer shall not withdraw from employment in a proceeding before that tribunal without its permission.

(2) In any event, a lawyer shall not withdraw from employment until he has taken reasonable steps to avoid foreseeable prejudice to the rights of his client, including giving due notice to his client, allowing time for employment of other counsel, delivering to the client all papers and property to which the client is entitled, and complying with applicable laws and rules.

(3) A lawyer who withdraws from employment shall refund promptly any part of a fee paid in advance that has not been earned.

(B) Mandatory withdrawal.

A lawyer representing a client before a tribunal, with its permission if required by its rules, shall withdraw from employment, and a lawyer representing a client in other matters shall withdraw from employment, if:

(1) He knows or it is obvious that his client is bringing the legal action, conducting the defense, or asserting a position in the litigation, or is otherwise having steps taken for him, merely for the purpose of harassing or maliciously injuring any person.

(2) He knows or it is obvious that his continued employment will result in violation of a Disciplinary Rule.[96]

(3) His mental or physical condition renders it unreasonably difficult for him to carry out the employment effectively.

(4) He is discharged by his client.

(C) Permissive withdrawal.[97]

If DR 2–110(B) is not applicable, a lawyer may not request permission to withdraw in matters pending before a tribunal, and may not withdraw in other matters, unless such request or such withdrawal is because:

(1) His client:

(a) Insists upon presenting a claim or defense that is not warranted under existing law and cannot be sup-

---

95. Cf. ABA Canon 44.

96. See also Code of Professional Responsibility, DR 5–102 and DR 5–105.

97. Cf. ABA Canon 4.

ported by good faith argument for an extension, modification, or reversal of existing law.[98]

(b) Personally seeks to pursue an illegal course of conduct.

(c) Insists that the lawyer pursue a course of conduct that is illegal or that is prohibited under the Disciplinary Rules.

(d) By other conduct renders it unreasonably difficult for the lawyer to carry out his employment effectively.

(e) Insists, in a matter not pending before a tribunal, that the lawyer engage in conduct that is contrary to the judgment and advice of the lawyer but not prohibited under the Disciplinary Rules.

(f) Deliberately disregards an agreement or obligation to the lawyer as to expenses or fees.

(2) His continued employment is likely to result in a violation of a Disciplinary Rule.

(3) His inability to work with co-counsel indicates that the best interests of the client likely will be served by withdrawal.

(4) His mental or physical condition renders it difficult for him to carry out the employment effectively.

(5) His client knowingly and freely assents to termination of his employment.

(6) He believes in good faith, in a proceeding pending before a tribunal, that the tribunal will find the existence of other good cause for withdrawal.

CANON 3

A Lawyer Should Assist in Preventing the Unauthorized Practice of Law

ETHICAL CONSIDERATIONS

EC 3–1 The prohibition against the practice of law by a layman is grounded in the need of the public for integrity and competence of those who undertake to render legal services. Because of the fiduciary and personal character of the lawyer-client relationship and the inherently complex nature of our legal system, the public can better be assured of the requisite responsibility and competence if the practice of law is confined to those who are subject to the requirements and regulations imposed upon members of the legal profession.

EC 3–2 The sensitive variations in the considerations that bear on legal determinations often make it difficult even for a lawyer to exercise

---

98. Cf. Anders v. California, 386 U.S. 738, 18 L.Ed.2d 493, 87 S.Ct. 1396 (1967), rehearing denied, 388 U.S. 924, 18 L.Ed.2d 1377, 87 S.Ct. 2094 (1967).

appropriate professional judgment, and it is therefore essential that the personal nature of the relationship of client and lawyer be preserved. Competent professional judgment is the product of a trained familiarity with law and legal processes, a disciplined, analytical approach to legal problems, and a firm ethical commitment.

EC 3-3 A non-lawyer who undertakes to handle legal matters is not governed as to integrity or legal competence by the same rules that govern the conduct of a lawyer. A lawyer is not only subject to that regulation but also is committed to high standards of ethical conduct. The public interest is best served in legal matters by a regulated profession committed to such standards.[1] The Disciplinary Rules protect the public in that they prohibit a lawyer from seeking employment by improper overtures, from acting in cases of divided loyalties, and from submitting to the control of others in the exercise of his judgment. Moreover, a person who entrusts legal matters to a lawyer is protected by the attorney-client privilege and by the duty of the lawyer to hold inviolate the confidences and secrets of his client.

EC 3-4 A layman who seeks legal services often is not in a position to judge whether he will receive proper professional attention. The entrustment of a legal matter may well involve the confidences, the reputation, the property, the freedom, or even the life of the client. Proper protection of members of the public demands that no person be permitted to act in the confidential and demanding capacity of a lawyer unless he is subject to the regulations of the legal profession.

EC 3-5 It is neither necessary nor desirable to attempt the formulation of a single, specific definition of what constitutes the practice of law.[2] Functionally, the practice of law relates to the rendition of services for others that call for the professional judgment of a lawyer. The essence of the professional judgment of the lawyer is his educated ability to relate the general body and philosophy of law to a specific legal problem of a client; and thus, the public interest will be better served if only lawyers are permitted to act in matters involving professional judgment. Where this professional judgment is not involved, non-

1. "The condemnation of the unauthorized practice of law is designed to protect the public from legal services by persons unskilled in the law. The prohibition of lay intermediaries is intended to insure the loyalty of the lawyer to the client unimpaired by intervening and possibly conflicting interests." Cheatham, *Availability of Legal Services: The Responsibility of the Individual Lawyer and of the Organized Bar,* 12 U.C.L.A.L.Rev. 438, 439 (1965).

2. "What constitutes unauthorized practice of the law in a particular jurisdiction is a matter for determination by the courts of that jurisdiction." *ABA Opinion* 198 (1939).

"In the light of the historical development of the lawyer's functions, it is impossible to lay down an exhaustive definition of 'the practice of law' by attempting to enumerate every conceivable act performed by lawyers in the normal course of their work." State Bar of Arizona v. Arizona Land Title & Trust Co., 90 Ariz. 76, 87, 366 P.2d 1, 8-9 (1961), modified, 91 Ariz. 293, 371 P.2d 1020 (1962).

lawyers, such as court clerks, police officers, abstracters, and many governmental employees, may engage in occupations that require a special knowledge of law in certain areas. But the services of a lawyer are essential in the public interest whenever the exercise of professional legal judgment is required.

EC 3–6 A lawyer often delegates tasks to clerks, secretaries, and other lay persons. Such delegation is proper if the lawyer maintains a direct relationship with his client, supervises the delegated work, and has complete professional responsibility for the work product.[3] This delegation enables a lawyer to render legal service more economically and efficiently.

EC 3–7 The prohibition against a non-lawyer practicing law does not prevent a layman from representing himself, for then he is ordinarily exposing only himself to possible injury. The purpose of the legal profession is to make educated legal representation available to the public; but anyone who does not wish to avail himself of such representation is not required to do so. Even so, the legal profession should help members of the public to recognize legal problems and to understand why it may be unwise for them to act for themselves in matters having legal consequences.

EC 3–8 Since a lawyer should not aid or encourage a layman to practice law, he should not practice law in association with a layman or otherwise share legal fees with a layman.[4] This does not mean, howev-

---

3. "A lawyer can employ lay secretaries, lay investigators, lay detectives, lay researchers, accountants, lay scriveners, nonlawyer draftsmen or nonlawyer researchers. In fact he may employ nonlawyers to do any task for him except counsel clients about law matters, engage directly in the practice of law, appear in court or appear in formal proceedings a part of the judicial process, so long as it is he who takes the work and vouches for it to the client and becomes responsible to the client." *ABA Opinion* 316 (1967).

ABA Opinion 316 (1967) also stated that if a lawyer practices law as part of a law firm which includes lawyers from several states, he may delegate tasks to firm members in other states so long as he "is the person who, on behalf of the firm, vouched for the work of all of the others and, with the client and in the courts, did the legal acts defined by that state as the practice of law."

"A lawyer cannot delegate his professional responsibility to a law student employed in his office. He may avail himself of the assistance of the student in many of the fields of the lawyer's work, such as examination of case law, finding and interviewing witnesses, making collections of claims, examining court records, delivering papers, conveying important messages, and other similar matters. But the student is not permitted, until he is admitted to the Bar, to perform the professional functions of a lawyer, such as conducting court trials, giving professional advice to clients or drawing legal documents for them. The student in all his work must act as agent for the lawyer employing him, who must supervise his work and be responsible for his good conduct." *ABA Opinion* 85 (1932).

4. "No division of fees for legal services is proper, except with another lawyer...." ABA Canon 34. Otherwise, according to *ABA Opinion* 316 (1967), "[t]he Canons of Ethics do not examine into the method by which such persons are remunerated by the lawyer.... They may be paid a salary, a per diem charge, a flat fee, a contract price, etc."

er, that the pecuniary value of the interest of a deceased lawyer in his firm or practice may not be paid to his estate or specified persons such as his widow or heirs.[5] In like manner, profit-sharing retirement plans of a lawyer or law firm which include non-lawyer office employees are not improper.[6] These limited exceptions to the rule against sharing legal fees with laymen are permissible since they do not aid or encourage laymen to practice law.

EC 3–9 Regulation of the practice of law is accomplished principally by the respective states.[7] Authority to engage in the practice of law conferred in any jurisdiction is not per se a grant of the right to practice elsewhere, and it is improper for a lawyer to engage in practice where he is not permitted by law or by court order to do so. However, the demands of business and the mobility of our society pose distinct problems in the regulation of the practice of law by the states.[8] In furtherance of the public interest, the legal profession should discourage regulation that unreasonably imposes territorial limitations upon the right of a lawyer to handle the legal affairs of his client or upon the opportunity of a client to obtain the services of a lawyer of his choice in all matters including the presentation of a contested matter in a tribunal before which the lawyer is not permanently admitted to practice.[9]

See ABA Canons 33 and 47.

5. "Many partnership agreements provide that the active partners, on the death of any one of them, are to make payments to the estate or to the nominee of a deceased partner on a pre-determined formula. It is only where the effect of such an arrangement is to make the estate or nominee a member of the partnership along with the surviving partners that it is prohibited by *Canon 34*. Where the payments are made in accordance with a pre-existing agreement entered into by the deceased partner during his lifetime and providing for a fixed method for determining their amount based upon the value of services rendered during the partner's lifetime and providing for a fixed period over which the payments are to be made, this is not the case. Under these circumstances, whether the payments are considered to be delayed payment of compensation earned but withheld during the partner's lifetime, or whether they are considered to be an approximation of his interest in matters pending at the time of his death, is immaterial. In either event, as Henry S. Drinker says in his book, Legal Ethics, at page 189: 'It would seem, however, that a reasonable agreement to pay the estate a proportion of the receipts for a reasonable period is a proper practical settlement for the lawyer's services to his retirement or death.'" *ABA Opinion* 308 (1963).

6. Cf. ABA Opinion 311 (1964).

7. "That the States have broad power to regulate the practice of law is, of course, beyond question." United Mine Workers v. Ill. State Bar Ass'n, 389 U.S. 217, 222 (1967).

"It is a matter of law, not of ethics, as to where an individual may practice law. Each state has its own rules." *ABA Opinion* 316 (1967).

8. "Much of clients' business crosses state lines. People are mobile, moving from state to state. Many metropolitan areas cross state lines. It is common today to have a single economic and social community involving more than one state. The business of a single client may involve legal problems in several states." *ABA Opinion* 316 (1967).

9. "[W]e reaffirmed the general principle that legal services to New Jersey residents with respect to New Jersey matters may ordinarily be furnished only by New Jersey counsel; but we pointed out that there may be multistate transactions where

DISCIPLINARY RULES

DR 3–101   Aiding Unauthorized Practice of Law.[10]

(A) A lawyer shall not aid a non-lawyer in the unauthorized practice of law.[11]

(B) A lawyer shall not practice law in a jurisdiction where to do so would be in violation of regulations of the profession in that jurisdiction.[12]

DR 3–102   Dividing Legal Fees With a Non-lawyer.

(A) A lawyer or law firm shall not share legal fees with a non-lawyer,[13] except that:

   (1) An agreement by a lawyer with his firm, partner, or associate may provide for the payment of money, over a reasonable period of time after his death, to his estate or to one or more specified persons.[14]

   (2) A lawyer who undertakes to complete unfinished legal business of a deceased lawyer may pay to the estate of the deceased lawyer that proportion of the total compensation which fairly represents the services rendered by the deceased lawyer.

   (3) A lawyer or law firm may include non-lawyer employees in a compensation or retirement plan, even though the plan is based in whole or in part on a profit-sharing arrangement [15] providing such plan does not circumvent another disciplinary rule.[16]

---

strict adherence to this thesis would not be in the public interest and that, under the circumstances, it would have been not only more costly to the client but also 'grossly impractical and inefficient' to have had the settlement negotiations conducted by separate lawyers from different states." In re Estate of Waring, 47 N.J. 367, 376, 221 A.2d 193, 197 (1966).

Cf. ABA Opinion 316 (1967).

10. Conduct permitted by the Disciplinary Rules of Canons 2 and 5 does not violate DR 3–101.

11. See ABA Canon 47.

12. It should be noted, however, that a lawyer may engage in conduct, otherwise prohibited by this Disciplinary Rule, where such conduct is authorized by preemptive federal legislation. See Sperry v. Florida,

373 U.S. 379, 10 L.Ed.2d 428, 83 S.Ct. 1322 (1963).

13. See ABA Canon 34 and *ABA Opinions* 316 (1967), 180 (1938), and 48 (1931).

"The receiving attorney shall not under any guise or form share his fee for legal services with a lay agency, personal or corporate, without prejudice, however, to the right of the lay forwarder to charge and collect from the creditor proper compensation for non-legal services rendered by the law [sic] forwarder which are separate and apart from the services performed by the receiving attorney." *ABA Opinion* 294 (1958).

14. See *ABA Opinion* 266 (1945).

15. Cf. *ABA Opinion* 311 (1964).

16. See ABA Informal Opinion 1440 (1979).

As amended in 1980.

DR 3–103 Forming a Partnership With a Non-lawyer.

(A) A lawyer shall not form a partnership with a non-lawyer if any of the activities of the partnership consist of the practice of law.[17]

CANON 4

A Lawyer Should Preserve the Confidences and Secrets of a Client

ETHICAL CONSIDERATIONS

EC 4–1 Both the fiduciary relationship existing between lawyer and client and the proper functioning of the legal system require the preservation by the lawyer of confidences and secrets of one who has employed or sought to employ him.[1] A client must feel free to discuss whatever he wishes with his lawyer and a lawyer must be equally free to obtain information beyond that volunteered by his client.[2] A lawyer should be

17. See ABA Canon 33; cf. *ABA Opinions* 239 (1942) and 201 (1940).

ABA Opinion 316 (1967) states that lawyers licensed in different jurisdictions may, under certain conditions, enter "into an arrangement for the practice of law" and that a lawyer licensed in State A is not, for such purpose a layman in State B.

1. See ABA Canons 6 and 37 and *ABA Opinions* 287 (1953). "The reason underlying the rule with respect to confidential communications between attorney and client is well stated in Mechem on Agency, 2d Ed., Vol. 2, § 2297, as follows: 'The purposes and necessities of the relation between a client and his attorney require, in many cases on the part of the client, the fullest and freest disclosures to the attorney of the client's objects, motives and acts. This disclosure is made in the strictest confidence, relying upon the attorney's honor and fidelity. To permit the attorney to reveal to others what is so disclosed, would be not only a gross violation of a sacred trust upon his part, but it would utterly destroy and prevent the usefulness and benefits to be derived from professional assistance. Based upon considerations of public policy, therefore, the law wisely declares that all confidential communications and disclosures, made by a client to his legal adviser for the purpose of obtaining his professional aid or advice, shall be strictly privileged:—that the attorney shall not be permitted, without the consent of his client,—and much less will he be compelled—to reveal or disclose communications made to him under such circumstances.' " *ABA Opinion* 250 (1943).

"While it is true that complete revelation of relevant facts should be encouraged for trial purposes, nevertheless an attorney's dealings with his client, if both are sincere, and if the dealings involve more than mere technical matters, should be immune to discovery proceedings. There must be freedom from fear of revealment of matters disclosed to an attorney because of the peculiarly intimate relationship existing." Ellis-Foster Co. v. Union Carbide & Carbon Corp., 159 F.Supp. 917, 919 (D.N.J.1958).

Cf. *ABA Opinions* 314 (1965), 274 (1946) and 268 (1945).

2. "While it is the great purpose of law to ascertain the truth, there is the countervailing necessity of insuring the right of every person to freely and fully confer and confide in one having knowledge of the law, and skilled in its practice, in order that the fully informed of all the facts of the matter he is handling in order for his client to obtain the full advantage of our legal system. It is for the lawyer in the exercise of his independent professional judgment to separate the relevant and important from the irrelevant and unimportant. The observance of the ethical obligation of a lawyer to hold inviolate the confidences and secrets of his client not only facilitates the full development of facts essential to proper representation of the client but also encourages laymen to seek early legal assistance.

EC 4–2 The obligation to protect confidences and secrets obviously does not preclude a lawyer from revealing information when his client consents after full disclosure,[3] when necessary to perform his professional employment, when permitted by a Disciplinary Rule, or when required by law. Unless the client otherwise directs, a lawyer may disclose the affairs of his client to partners or associates of his firm. It is a matter of common knowledge that the normal operation of a law office exposes confidential professional information to non-lawyer employees of the office, particularly secretaries and those having access to the files; and this obligates a lawyer to exercise care in selecting and training his employees so that the sanctity of all confidences and secrets of his clients may be preserved. If the obligation extends to two or more clients as to the same information, a lawyer should obtain the permission of all before revealing the information. A lawyer must always be sensitive to the rights and wishes of his client and act scrupulously in the making of decisions which may involve the disclosure of information obtained in his professional relationship.[4] Thus, in the absence of consent of his client after full disclosure, a lawyer should not associate another lawyer in the handling of a matter; nor should he, in the absence of consent, seek counsel from another lawyer if there is a reasonable possibility that the identity of the client or his confidences or secrets would be revealed to such lawyer. Both social amenities and professional duty should cause a lawyer to shun indiscreet conversations concerning his clients.

EC 4–3 Unless the client otherwise directs, it is not improper for a lawyer to give limited information from his files to an outside agency

former may have adequate advice and a proper defense. This assistance can be made safely and readily available only when the client is free from the consequences of apprehension of disclosure by reason of the subsequent statements of the skilled lawyer." Baird v. Koerner, 279 F.2d 623, 629–30 (9th Cir.1960).

Cf. *ABA Opinion* 150 (1936).

3. "Where ... [a client] knowingly and after full disclosure participates in a [legal fee] financing plan which requires the furnishing of certain information to the bank, clearly by his conduct he has waived any

privilege as to that information." *ABA Opinion* 320 (1968).

4. "The lawyer must decide when he takes a case whether it is a suitable one for him to undertake and after this decision is made, he is not justified in turning against his client by exposing injurious evidence entrusted to him.... [D]oing something intrinsically regrettable, because the only alternative involves worse consequences, is a necessity in every profession." Williston, Life and Law 271 (1940).

Cf. *ABA Opinions* 177 (1938) and 83 (1932).

necessary for statistical, bookkeeping, accounting, data processing, banking, printing, or other legitimate purposes, provided he exercises due care in the selection of the agency and warns the agency that the information must be kept confidential.

EC 4–4 The attorney-client privilege is more limited than the ethical obligation of a lawyer to guard the confidence and secrets of his client. This ethical precept, unlike the evidentiary privilege, exists without regard to the nature or source of information or the fact that others share the knowledge. A lawyer should endeavor to act in a manner which preserves the evidentiary privilege; for example, he should avoid professional discussions in the presence of persons to whom the privilege does not extend. A lawyer owes an obligation to advise the client of the attorney-client privilege and timely to assert the privilege unless it is waived by the client.

EC 4–5 A lawyer should not use information acquired in the course of the representation of a client to the disadvantage of the client and a lawyer should not use, except with the consent of his client after full disclosure, such information for his own purposes.[5] Likewise, a lawyer should be diligent in his efforts to prevent the misuse of such information by his employees and associates.[6] Care should be exercised by a lawyer to prevent the disclosure of the confidences and secrets of one client to another,[7] and no employment should be accepted that might require such disclosure.

EC 4–6 The obligation of a lawyer to preserve the confidences and secrets of his client continues after the termination of his employment.[8] Thus a lawyer should not attempt to sell a law practice as a going business because, among other reasons, to do so would involve the disclosure of confidences and secrets.[9] A lawyer should also provide for the protection of the confidences and secrets of his client following the termination of the practice of the lawyer, whether termination is due to death, disability, or retirement. For example, a lawyer might provide for the personal papers of the client to be returned to him and for the papers of the lawyer to be delivered to another lawyer or to be destroyed. In determining the method of disposition, the instructions and wishes of the client should be a dominant consideration.

---

5. See ABA Canon 11.

6. See ABA Canon 37.

7. See ABA Canons 6 and 37.

"[A]n attorney must not accept professional employment against a client or a former client which will, or even *may* require him to use confidential information obtained by the attorney in the course of his professional relations with such client regarding the subject matter of the employment...." *ABA Opinion* 165 (1936).

8. See ABA Canon 37.

"Confidential communications between an attorney and his client, made because of the relationship and concerning the subject-matter of the attorney's employment, are generally privileged from disclosure without the consent of the client, and this privilege outlasts the attorney's employment. *Canon 37.*" *ABA Opinion* 154 (1936).

9. Cf. *ABA Opinion* 266 (1945).

DISCIPLINARY RULES

DR 4–101 Preservation of Confidences and Secrets of a Client.[10]

(A) "Confidence" refers to information protected by the attorney-client privilege under applicable law, and "secret" refers to other information gained in the professional relationship that the client has requested be held inviolate or the disclosure of which would be embarrassing or would be likely to be detrimental to the client.

(B) Except when permitted under DR 4–101(C), a lawyer shall not knowingly:

(1) Reveal a confidence or secret of his client.[11]

(2) Use a confidence or secret of his client to the disadvantage of the client.

(3) Use a confidence or secret of his client for the advantage of himself [12] or of a third person,[13] unless the client consents after full disclosure.

(C) A lawyer may reveal:

(1) Confidences or secrets with the consent of the client or clients affected, but only after a full disclosure to them.[14]

(2) Confidences or secrets when permitted under Disciplin%-

---

10. See ABA Canon 37; cf. ABA Canon 6.

11. "§ 6068 ... It is the duty of an attorney: ....

"(e) To maintain inviolate the confidence, and at every peril to himself to preserve the secrets, of his client." Cal. Business and Professions Code § 6068 (West 1962). Virtually the same provision is found in the Oregon statutes. Ore.Rev. Stat. ch. 9, § 9.460(5).

"Communications between lawyer and client are privileged (Wigmore on Evidence, 3d Ed., Vol. 8, §§ 2290–2329). The modern theory underlying the privilege is subjective and is to give the client freedom of apprehension in consulting his legal advisor (ibid., § 2290, p. 548). The privilege applies to communications made in seeking legal advice for any purpose (ibid., § 2294, p. 563). The mere circumstance that the advice is given without charge therefore does not nullify the privilege (ibid., § 2303)." *ABA Opinion* 216 (1941).

"It is the duty of an attorney to maintain the confidence and preserve inviolate the secrets of his client...." *ABA Opinion* 155 (1936).

12. See ABA Canon 11.

"The provision respecting employment is in accord with the general rule announced in the adjudicated cases that a lawyer may not make use of knowledge or information acquired by him through his professional relations with his client, or in the conduct of his client's business, to his own advantage or profit (7 C.J.S., § 125, p. 958; Healy v. Gray, 184 Iowa 111, 168 N.W. 222; Baumgardner v. Hudson, D.C.App., 277 F. 552; Goodrum v. Clement, D.C.App., 277 F. 586)." *ABA Opinion* 250 (1943).

13. See *ABA Opinion* 177 (1938).

14. "[A lawyer] may not divulge confidential communications, information, and secrets imparted to him by the client or acquired during their professional relations, unless he is authorized to do so by the client (People v. Gerold, 265 Ill. 448, 107 N.E. 165, 178; Murphy v. Riggs, 238 Mich. 151, 213 N.W. 110, 112; Opinion of this Committee, No. 91)." *ABA Opinion* 202 (1940).

ary Rules or required by law or court order.[15]

(3) The intention of his client to commit a crime [16] **and the information necessary to prevent the crime.**[17]

(4) Confidences or secrets necessary to establish or collect his fee [18] **or to defend himself or his employees or associates against an accusation of wrongful conduct.**[19]

Cf. *ABA Opinion* 91 (1933).

15. "A defendant in a criminal case when admitted to bail is not only regarded as in the custody of his bail, but he is also in the custody of the law, and admission to bail does not deprive the court of its inherent power to deal with the person of the prisoner. Being in lawful custody, the defendant is guilty of an escape when he gains his liberty before he is delivered in due process of law, and is guilty of a separate offense for which he may be punished. In failing to disclose his client's whereabouts as a fugitive under these circumstances the attorney would not only be aiding his client to escape trial on the charge for which he was indicted, but would likewise be aiding him in evading prosecution for the additional offense of escape.

"It is the opinion of the committee that under such circumstances the attorney's knowledge of his client's whereabouts is not privileged, and that he may be disciplined for failing to disclose that information to the proper authorities...." *ABA Opinion* 155 (1936).

"We held in *Opinion* 155 that a communication by a client to his attorney in respect to the future commission of an unlawful act or to a continuing wrong is not privileged from disclosure. Public policy forbids that the relation of attorney and client should be used to conceal wrongdoing on the part of the client.

. . .

"When an attorney representing a defendant in a criminal case applies on his behalf for probation or suspension of sentence, he represents to the court, by implication at least, that his client will abide by the terms and conditions of the court's order. When that attorney is later advised of a violation of that order, it is his duty to advise his client of the consequences of his act, and endeavor to prevent a continuance of the wrongdoing. If his client thereafter per-

sists in violating the terms and conditions of his probation, it is the duty of the attorney as an officer of the court to advise the proper authorities concerning his client's conduct. Such information, even though coming to the attorney from the client in the course of his professional relations with respect to other matters in which he represents the defendant, is not privileged from disclosure...." *ABA Opinion* 156 (1936).

See *ABA Opinion* 155 (1936).

16. *ABA Opinion* 314 (1965) indicates that a lawyer must disclose even the confidences of his clients if "the facts in the attorney's possession indicate beyond reasonable doubt that a crime will be committed."

See *ABA Opinion* 155 (1936).

17. See ABA Canon 37 and *ABA Opinion* 202 (1940).

18. Cf. *ABA Opinion* 250 (1943).

19. See ABA Canon 37 and *ABA Opinions* 202 (1940) and 19 (1930).

"[T]he adjudicated cases recognize an exception to the rule [that a lawyer shall not reveal the confidences of his client], where disclosure is necessary to protect the attorney's interests arising out of the relation of attorney and client in which disclosure was made.

"The exception is stated in Mechem on Agency, 2d Ed., Vol. 2, § 2313, as follows: 'But the attorney may disclose information received from the client when it becomes necessary for his own protection, as if the client should bring an action against the attorney for negligence or misconduct, and it became necessary for the attorney to show what his instructions were, or what was the nature of the duty which the client expected him to perform. So if it became necessary for the attorney to bring an action against the client, the client's privilege could not prevent the attorney from disclos-

(D) A lawyer shall exercise reasonable care to prevent his employees, associates, and others whose services are utilized by him from disclosing or using confidences or secrets of a client, except that a lawyer may reveal the information allowed by DR 4-101(C) through an employee.

CANON 5

A Lawyer Should Exercise Independent Professional Judgment on Behalf of a Client

ETHICAL CONSIDERATIONS

EC 5-1 The professional judgment of a lawyer should be exercised, within the bounds of the law, solely for the benefit of his client and free of compromising influences and loyalties.[1] Neither his personal inter-

ing what was essential as a means of obtaining or defending his own rights.'

"Mr. Jones, in his Commentaries on Evidence, 2d Ed., Vol. 5, § 2165, states the exception thus: 'It has frequently been held that the rule as to privileged communications does not apply when litigation arises between attorney and client to the extent that their communications are relevant to the issue. In such cases, if the disclosure of privileged communications becomes necessary to protect the attorney's rights, he is released from those obligations of secrecy which the law places upon him. He should not, however, disclose more than is necessary for his own protection. It would be a manifest injustice to allow the client to take advantage of the rule of exclusion as to professional confidence to the prejudice of his attorney, or that it should be carried to the extent of depriving the attorney of the means of obtaining or defending his own rights. In such cases the attorney is exempted from the obligations of secrecy.'" *ABA Opinion* 250 (1943).

1. Cf. ABA Canon 35.

"[A lawyer's] fiduciary duty is of the highest order and he must not represent interests adverse to those of the client. It is true that because of his professional responsibility and the confidence and trust which his client may legitimately repose in him, he must adhere to a high standard of honesty, integrity and good faith in dealing with his client. He is not permitted to take advantage of his position or superior knowl-

edge to impose upon the client; nor to conceal facts or law, nor in any way deceive him without being held responsible therefor." Smoot v. Lund, 13 Utah 2d 168, 172, 369 P.2d 933, 936 (1962).

"When a client engages the services of a lawyer in a given piece of business he is entitled to feel that, until that business is finally disposed of in some manner, he has the undivided loyalty of the one upon whom he looks as his advocate and champion. If, as in this case, he is sued and his home attached by his own attorney, who is representing him in another matter, all feeling of loyalty is necessarily destroyed, and the profession is exposed to the charge that it is interested only in money." Grievance Comm. v. Rattner, 152 Conn. 59, 65, 203 A.2d 82, 84 (1964).

"One of the cardinal principles confronting every attorney in the representation of a client is the requirement of complete loyalty and service in good faith to the best of his ability. In a criminal case the client is entitled to a fair trial, but not a perfect one. These are fundamental requirements of due process under the Fourteenth Amendment.... The same principles are applicable in Sixth Amendment cases (not pertinent herein) and suggest that an attorney should have no conflict of interest and that he must devote his full and faithful efforts toward the defense of his client." Johns v. Smyth, 176 F.Supp. 949, 952 (E.D.Va.1959), modified, United States ex rel. Wilkins v.

ests, the interests of other clients, nor the desires of third persons should be permitted to dilute his loyalty to his client.

Interests of a Lawyer That May Affect His Judgment

EC 5–2 A lawyer should not accept proffered employment if his personal interests or desires will, or there is a reasonable probability that they will, affect adversely the advice to be given or services to be rendered the prospective client.[2] After accepting employment, a lawyer carefully should refrain from acquiring a property right or assuming a position that would tend to make his judgment less protective of the interests of his client.

EC 5–3 The self-interest of a lawyer resulting from his ownership of property in which his client also has an interest or which may affect property of his client may interfere with the exercise of free judgment on behalf of his client. If such interference would occur with respect to a prospective client, a lawyer should decline employment proffered by him. After accepting employment, a lawyer should not acquire property rights that would adversely affect his professional judgment in the representation of his client. Even if the property interests of a lawyer do not presently interfere with the exercise of his independent judgment, but the likelihood of interference can reasonably be foreseen by him, a lawyer should explain the situation to his client and should decline employment or withdraw unless the client consents to the continuance of the relationship after full disclosure. A lawyer should not seek to persuade his client to permit him to invest in an undertaking of his client nor make improper use of his professional relationship to influence his client to invest in an enterprise in which the lawyer is interested.

EC 5–4 If, in the course of his representation of a client, a lawyer is permitted to receive from his client a beneficial ownership in publication rights relating to the subject matter of the employment, he may be tempted to subordinate the interests of his client to his own anticipated

Banmiller, 205 F.Supp. 123, 128 n. 5 (E.D.Pa.1962), aff'd 325 F.2d 514 (3d Cir. 1963), cert. denied, 379 U.S. 847, 13 L.Ed.2d 51, 85 S.Ct. 87 (1964).

2. "Attorneys must not allow their private interests to conflict with those of their clients. . . . They owe their entire devotion to the interests of their clients." United States v. Anonymous, 215 F.Supp. 111, 113 (E.D.Tenn.1963).

"[T]he court [below] concluded that a firm may not accept any action against a person whom they are presently representing even though there is no relationship between the two cases. In arriving at this conclusion, the court cites an opinion of the Committee on Professional Ethics of the New York County Lawyers' Association which stated in part: 'While under the circumstances . . . there may be no actual conflict of interest . . . "maintenance of public confidence in the Bar requires an attorney who has accepted representation of a client to decline, while representing such client, any employment from an adverse party in any matter even though wholly unrelated to the original retainer." See Question and Answer No. 350, N.Y. County L. Ass'n, Questions and Answer No. 450 (June 21, 1956).' " Grievance Comm. v. Rattner, 152 Conn. 59, 65, 203 A.2d 82, 84 (1964).

pecuniary gain. For example, a lawyer in a criminal case who obtains from his client television, radio, motion picture, newspaper, magazine, book, or other publication rights with respect to the case may be influenced, consciously or unconsciously, to a course of conduct that will enhance the value of his publication rights to the prejudice of his client. To prevent these potentially differing interests, such arrangements should be scrupulously avoided prior to the termination of all aspects of the matter giving rise to the employment, even though his employment has previously ended.

EC 5–5 A lawyer should not suggest to his client that a gift be made to himself or for his benefit. If a lawyer accepts a gift from his client, he is peculiarly susceptible to the charge that he unduly influenced or over-reached the client. If a client voluntarily offers to make a gift to his lawyer, the lawyer may accept the gift, but before doing so, he should urge that his client secure disinterested advice from an independent, competent person who is cognizant of all the circumstances.[3] Other than in exceptional circumstances, a lawyer should insist that an instrument in which his client desires to name him beneficially be prepared by another lawyer selected by the client.[4]

EC 5–6 A lawyer should not consciously influence a client to name him as executor, trustee, or lawyer in an instrument. In those cases where a client wishes to name his lawyer as such, care should be taken by the lawyer to avoid even the appearance of impropriety.[5]

EC 5–7 The possibility of an adverse effect upon the exercise of free judgment by a lawyer on behalf of his client during litigation generally makes it undesirable for the lawyer to acquire a proprietary interest in the cause of his client or otherwise to become financially interested in the outcome of the litigation.[6] However, it is not improper for a lawyer

---

3. "Courts of equity will scrutinize with jealous vigilance transactions between parties occupying fiduciary relations toward each other.... A deed will not be held invalid, however, if made by the grantor with full knowledge of its nature and effect, and because of the deliberate, voluntary and intelligent desire of the grantor.... Where a fiduciary relation exists, the burden of proof is on the grantee or beneficiary of an instrument executed during the existence of such relationship to show the fairness of the transaction, that it was equitable and just and that it did not proceed from undue influence.... The same rule has application where an attorney engages in a transaction with a client during the existence of the relation and is benefited thereby.... Conversely, an attorney is not prohibited from dealing with his client or buying his property, and such contracts, if open, fair and honest, when deliberately made, are as valid as contracts between other parties.... [I]mportant factors in determining whether a transaction is fair include a showing by the fiduciary (1) that he made a full and frank disclosure of all the relevant information that he had: (2) that the consideration was adequate; and (3) that the principal had independent advice before completing the transaction." McFail v. Braden, 19 Ill.2d 108, 117–18, 166 N.E.2d 46, 52 (1960).

4. See State ex rel. Nebraska State Bar Ass'n v. Richards, 165 Neb. 80, 94–95, 84 N.W.2d 136, 146 (1957).

5. See ABA Canon 9.

6. See ABA Canon 10.

to protect his right to collect a fee for his services by the assertion of legally permissible liens, even though by doing so he may acquire an interest in the outcome of litigation. Although a contingent fee arrangement [7] gives a lawyer a financial interest in the outcome of litigation, a reasonable contingent fee is permissible in civil cases because it may be the only means by which a layman can obtain the services of a lawyer of his choice. But a lawyer, because he is in a better position to evaluate a cause of action, should enter into a continent fee arrangement only in those instances where the arrangement will be beneficial to the client.

EC 5–8 A financial interest in the outcome of litigation also results if monetary advances are made by the lawyer to his client.[8] Although this assistance generally is not encouraged, there are instances when it is not improper to make loans to a client. For example, the advancing or guaranteeing of payment of the costs and expenses of litigation by a lawyer may be the only way a client can enforce his cause of action,[9] but the ultimate liability for such costs and expenses must be that of the client.

EC 5–9 Occasionally a lawyer is called upon to decide in a particular case whether he will be a witness or an advocate. If a lawyer is both counsel and witness, he becomes more easily impeachable for interest and thus may be a less effective witness. Conversely, the opposing counsel may be handicapped in challenging the credibility of the lawyer when the lawyer also appears as an advocate in the case. An advocate who becomes a witness is in the unseemly and ineffective position of arguing his own credibility. The roles of an advocate and of a witness are inconsistent; the function of an advocate is to advance or argue the cause of another, while that of a witness is to state facts objectively.

EC 5–10 Problems incident to the lawyer-witness relationship arise at different stages; they relate either to whether a lawyer should accept employment or should withdraw from employment.[10] Regardless of

---

7. See Code of Professional Responsibility, EC 2–20.

8. See ABA Canon 42.

9. "*Rule 3a.* . . . A member of the State Bar shall not directly or indirectly pay or agree to pay, or represent or sanction the representation that he will pay, medical, hospital or nursing bills or other personal expenses incurred by or for a client, prospective or existing; provided this rule shall not prohibit a member:

"(1) with the consent of the client, from paying or agreeing to pay to third persons such expenses from funds collected or to be collected for the client; or

"(2) after he has been employed, from lending money to his client upon the

client's promise in writing to repay such loan; or

"(3) from advancing the costs of prosecuting or defending a claim or action. Such costs within the meaning of this subparagraph (3) include all taxable costs or disbursements, costs or investigation and costs of obtaining and presenting evidence." Cal. Business and Professions Code § 6076 (West Supp.1967).

10. "When a lawyer knows, prior to trial, that he will be a necessary witness, except as to merely formal matters such as identification or custody of a document or the like, neither he nor his firm or associates should conduct the trial. If, during the trial, he discovers that the ends of juswhen the problem arises, his decision is to be governed by the same basic considerations. It is not objectionable for a lawyer who is a potential witness to be an advocate if it is unlikely that he will be called as a witness because his testimony would be merely cumulative or if his testimony will relate only to an uncontested issue.[11] In the exceptional situation where it will be manifestly unfair to the client for the lawyer to refuse employment or to withdraw when he will likely be a witness on a contested issue, he may serve as advocate even though he may be a witness.[12] In making such decision, he should determine the personal or financial sacrifice of the client that may result from his refusal of employment or withdrawal therefrom, the materiality of his testimony, and the effectiveness of his representation in view of his personal involvement. In weighing these factors, it should be clear that refusal or withdrawal will impose an unreasonable hardship upon the client before the lawyer accepts or continues the employment.[13] Where the question arises, doubts should be resolved in favor of the lawyer testifying and against his becoming or continuing as an advocate.[14]

EC 5–11 A lawyer should not permit his personal interests to influence his advice relative to a suggestion by his client that additional counsel be employed.[15] In like manner, his personal interests should not deter him from suggesting that additional counsel be employed; on the

tice require his testimony, he should, from that point on, if feasible and not prejudicial to his client's case, leave further conduct of the trial to other counsel. If circumstances do not permit withdrawal from the conduct of the trial, the lawyer should not argue the credibility of his own testimony." *A Code of Trial Conduct: Promulgated by the American College of Trial Lawyers,* 43 A.B.A.J. 223, 224–25 (1957).

11. Cf. Canon 19: "When a lawyer is a witness for his client, except as to merely formal matters, such as the attestation or custody of an instrument and the like, he should leave the trial of the case to other counsel."

12. "It is the general rule that a lawyer may not testify in litigation in which he is an advocate unless circumstances arise which could not be anticipated and it is necessary to prevent a miscarriage of justice. In those rare cases where the testimony of an attorney is needed to protect his client's interests, it is not only proper but mandatory that it be forthcoming." Schwartz v. Wenger, 267 Minn. 40, 43–44, 124 N.W.2d 489, 492 (1963).

13. "The great weight of authority in this country holds that the attorney who acts as counsel and witness, in behalf of his

client, in the same cause on a material matter, not of a merely formal character, and not in an emergency, but having knowledge that he would be required to be a witness in ample time to have secured other counsel and given up his service in the case, violates a highly important provision of the Code of Ethics and a rule of professional conduct, but does not commit a legal error in so testifying, as a result of which a new trial will be granted." Erwin M. Jennings Co. v. DiGenova, 107 Conn. 491, 499, 141 A. 866, 869 (1928).

14. "[C]ases may arise, and in practice often do arise, in which there would be a failure of justice should the attorney withhold his testimony. In such a case it would be a vicious professional sentiment which would deprive the client of the benefit of his attorney's testimony." Connolly v. Straw, 53 Wis. 645, 649, 11 N.W. 17, 19 (1881).

But see Canon 19. "Except when essential to the ends of justice, a lawyer should avoid testifying in court in behalf of his client."

15. Cf. ABA Canon 7.

contrary, he should be alert to the desirability of recommending additional counsel when, in his judgment, the proper representation of his client requires it. However, a lawyer should advise his client not to employ additional counsel suggested by the client if the lawyer believes that such employment would be a disservice to the client, and he should disclose the reasons for his belief.

EC 5–12 Inability of co-counsel to agree on a matter vital to the representation of their client requires that their disagreement be submitted by them jointly to their client for his resolution, and the decision of the client shall control the action to be taken.[16]

EC 5–13 A lawyer should not maintain membership in or be influenced by any organization of employees that undertakes to prescribe, direct, or suggest when or how he should fulfill his professional obligations to a person or organization that employs him as a lawyer. Although it is not necessarily improper for a lawyer employed by a corporation or similar entity to be a member of an organization of employees, he should be vigilant to safeguard his fidelity as a lawyer to his employer, free from outside influences.

Interests of Multiple Clients

EC 5–14 Maintaining the independence of professional judgment required of a lawyer precludes his acceptance or continuation of employment that will adversely affect his judgment on behalf of or dilute his loyalty to a client.[17] This problem arises whenever a lawyer is asked to represent two or more clients who may have differing interests, whether such interests be conflicting, inconsistent, diverse, or otherwise discordant.[18]

EC 5–15 If a lawyer is requested to undertake or to continue representation of multiple clients having potentially differing interests, he must weigh carefully the possibility that his judgment may be impaired or his loyalty divided if he accepts or continues the employment. He should resolve all doubts against the propriety of the representation. A lawyer should never represent in litigation multiple clients with differing interests;[19] and there are few situations in which he would be justified in

16. See ABA Canon 7.

17. See ABA Canon 6; cf. *ABA Opinions* 261 (1944), 242 (1942), 142 (1935), and 30 (1931).

18. The ABA Canons speak of "conflicting interests" rather than "differing interests" but make no attempt to define such other than the statement in Canon 6: "Within the meaning of this canon, a lawyer represents conflicting interests when, in behalf of one client, it is his duty to contend for that which duty to another client requires him to oppose."

19. "Canon 6 of the Canons of Professional Ethics, adopted by the American Bar Association on September 30, 1937, and by the Pennsylvania Bar Association on January 7, 1938, provides in part that 'It is unprofessional to represent conflicting interests, except by express consent of all concerned given after a full disclosure of the facts. Within the meaning of this Canon, a lawyer represents conflicting interests representing in litigation multiple clients with potentially differing interests. If a lawyer accepted such employment and the interests did become actually differing, he would have to withdraw from employment with likelihood of resulting hardship on the clients; and for this reason it is preferable that he refuse the employment initially. On the other hand, there are many instances in which a lawyer may properly serve multiple clients having potentially differing interests in matters not involving litigation. If the interests vary only slightly, it is generally likely that the lawyer will not be subjected to an adverse influence and that he can retain his independent judgment on behalf of each client; and if the interests become differing, withdrawal is less likely to have a disruptive effect upon the causes of his clients.

EC 5–16 In those instances in which a lawyer is justified in representing two or more clients having differing interests, it is nevertheless essential that each client be given the opportunity to evaluate his need for representation free of any potential conflict and to obtain other counsel if he so desires.[20] Thus before a lawyer may represent multiple clients, he should explain fully to each client the implications of the common representation and should accept or continue employment only if the clients consent.[21] If there are present other circumstances that might cause any of the multiple clients to question the undivided loyalty of the lawyer, he should also advise all of the clients of those circumstances.[22]

when, in behalf of one client, it is his duty to contend for that which duty to another client requires him to oppose.' The full disclosure required by this canon contemplates that the possibly adverse effect of the conflict be fully explained by the attorney to the client to be affected and by him thoroughly understood....

"The foregoing canon applies to cases where the circumstances are such that possibly conflicting interests may permissibly be represented by the same attorney. But manifestly, there are instances where the conflicts of interest are so critically adverse as not to admit of one attorney's representing both sides. Such is the situation which this record presents. No one could conscionably contend that the same attorney may represent both the plaintiff and defendant in an adversary action. Yet, that is what is being done in this case." Jedwabny v. Philadelphia Transportation Co., 390 Pa. 231, 235, 135 A.2d 252, 254 (1957), cert. denied, 355 U.S. 966, 2 L.Ed.2d 541, 78 S.Ct. 557 (1958).

20. "Glasser wished the benefit of the undivided assistance of counsel of his own choice. We think that such a desire on the part of an accused should be respected. Irrespective of any conflict of interest, the additional burden of representing another party may conceivably impair counsel's effectiveness.

"To determine the precise degree of prejudice sustained by Glasser as a result of the court's appointment of Stewart as counsel for Kretske is at once difficult and unnecessary. The right to have the assistance of counsel is too fundamental and absolute to allow courts to indulge in nice calculations as to the amount of prejudice arising from its denial." Glasser v. United States, 315 U.S. 60, 75–76, 86 L.Ed. 680, 62 S.Ct. 457, 467 (1942).

21. See ABA Canon 6.

22. Id.

EC 5-17 Typically recurring situations involving potentially differing interests are those in which a lawyer is asked to represent co-defendants in a criminal case, co-plaintiffs in a personal injury case, an insured and his insurer,[23] and beneficiaries of the estate of a decedent. Whether a lawyer can fairly and adequately protect the interests of multiple clients in these and similar situations depends upon an analysis of each case. In certain circumstances, there may exist little chance of the judgment of the lawyer being adversely affected by the slight possibility that the interests will become actually differing; in other circumstances, the chance of adverse effect upon his judgment is not unlikely.

EC 5-18 A lawyer employed or retained by a corporation or similar entity owes his allegiance to the entity and not to a stockholder, director, officer, employee, representative, or other person connected with the entity. In advising the entity, a lawyer should keep paramount its interests and his professional judgment should not be influenced by the personal desires of any person or organization. Occasionally a lawyer for an entity is requested by a stockholder, director, officer, employee, representative, or other person connected with the entity to represent him in an individual capacity; in such case the lawyer may serve the individual only if the lawyer is convinced that differing interests are not present.

EC 5-19 A lawyer may represent several clients whose interests are not actually or potentially differing. Nevertheless, he should explain any circumstances that might cause a client to question his undivided loyalty.[24] Regardless of the belief of a lawyer that he may properly

23. Cf. *ABA Opinion* 282 (1950).

"When counsel, although paid by the casualty company, undertakes to represent the policyholder and files his notice of appearance, he owes to his client, the assured, an undeviating and single allegiance. His fealty embraces the requirement to produce in court all witnesses, fact and expert, who are available and necessary for the proper protection of the rights of his client. . . .

". . . The Canons of Professional Ethics make it pellucid that there are not two standards, one applying to counsel privately retained by a client, and the other to counsel paid by an insurance carrier." American Employers Ins. Co. v. Goble Aircraft Specialties, 205 Misc. 1066, 1075, 131 N.Y.S.2d 393, 401 (1954), motion to withdraw appeal granted, 1 App.Div.2d 1008, 154 N.Y.S.2d 835 (1956).

"[C]ounsel, selected by State Farm to defend Dorothy Walker's suit for $50,000

damages, was apprised by Walker that his earlier version of the accident was untrue and that actually the accident occurred because he lost control of his car in passing a Cadillac just ahead. At that point, Walker's counsel should have refused to participate further in view of the conflict of interest between Walker and State Farm. . . . Instead he participated in the ensuing deposition of the Walkers, even took an *ex parte* sworn statement from Mr. Walker in order to advise State Farm what action it should take, and later used the statement against Walker in the District Court. This action appears to contravene an Indiana attorney's duty 'at every peril to himself, to preserve the secrets of his client'. . . ." State Farm Mut. Auto Ins. Co. v. Walker, 382 F.2d 548, 552 (1967), cert. denied, 389 U.S. 1045, 19 L.Ed.2d 837, 88 S.Ct. 789 (1968).

24. See ABA Canon 6.

represent multiple clients, he must defer to a client who holds the contrary belief and withdraw from representation of that client.

EC 5–20 A lawyer is often asked to serve as an impartial arbitrator or mediator in matters which involve present or former clients. He may serve in either capacity if he first discloses such present or former relationships. After a lawyer has undertaken to act as an impartial arbitrator or mediator, he should not thereafter represent in the dispute any of the parties involved.

Desires of Third Persons

EC 5–21 The obligation of a lawyer to exercise professional judgment solely on behalf of his client requires that he disregard the desires of others that might impair his free judgment.[25] The desires of a third person will seldom adversely affect a lawyer unless that person is in a position to exert strong economic, political, or social pressures upon the lawyer. These influences are often subtle, and a lawyer must be alert to their existence. A lawyer subjected to outside pressures should make full disclosure of them to his client;[26] and if he or his client believes that the effectiveness of his representation has been or will be impaired thereby, the lawyer should take proper steps to withdraw from representation of his client.

EC 5–22 Economic, political, or social pressures by third persons are less likely to impinge upon the independent judgment of a lawyer in a matter in which he is compensated directly by his client and his professional work is exclusively with his client. On the other hand, if a lawyer is compensated from a source other than his client, he may feel a sense of responsibility to someone other than his client.

EC 5–23 A person or organization that pays or furnishes lawyers to represent others possesses a potential power to exert strong pressures against the independent judgment of those lawyers. Some employers may be interested in furthering their own economic, political, or social goals without regard to the professional responsibility of the lawyer to his individual client. Others may be far more concerned with establishment or extension of legal principles than in the immediate protection of

---

25. See ABA Canon 35.

"Objection to the intervention of a lay intermediary, who may control litigation or otherwise interfere with the rendering of legal services in a confidential relationship, ... derives from the element of pecuniary gain. Fearful of dangers thought to arise from that element, the courts of several States have sustained regulations aimed at these activities. We intimate no view one way or the other as to the merits of those decisions with respect to the particular ar-

rangements against which they are directed. It is enough that the superficial resemblance in form between those arrangements and that at bar cannot obscure the vital fact that here the entire arrangement employs constitutionally privileged means of expression to secure constitutionally guaranteed civil rights." NAACP v. Button, 371 U.S. 415, 441–42, 9 L.Ed.2d 405, 423–24, 83 S.Ct. 328, 342–43 (1963).

26. Cf. ABA Canon 38.

the rights of the lawyer's individual client. On some occasions, decisions on priority of work may be made by the employer rather than the lawyer with the result that prosecution of work already undertaken for clients is postponed to their detriment. Similarly, an employer may seek, consciously or unconsciously, to further its own economic interests through the action of the lawyers employed by it. Since a lawyer must always be free to exercise his professional judgment without regard to the interests or motives of a third person, the lawyer who is employed by one to represent another must constantly guard against erosion of his professional freedom.[27]

EC 5–24 To assist a lawyer in preserving his professional independence, a number of courses are available to him. For example, a lawyer should not practice with or in the form of a professional legal corporation, even though the corporate form is permitted by law,[28] if any director, officer, or stockholder of it is a non-lawyer. Although a lawyer may be employed by a business corporation with non-lawyers serving as directors or officers, and they necessarily have the right to make decisions of business policy, a lawyer must decline to accept direction of his professional judgment from any layman. Various types of legal aid offices are administered by boards of directors composed of lawyers and laymen. A lawyer should not accept employment from such an organization unless the board sets only broad policies and there is no interference in the relationship of the lawyer and the individual client he serves. Where a lawyer is employed by an organization, a written agreement that defines the relationship between him and the organization and provides for his independence is desirable since it may serve to prevent misunderstanding as to their respective roles. Although other innovations in the means of supplying legal counsel may develop, the responsibility of the lawyer to maintain his professional independence remains constant, and the legal profession must insure that changing circumstances do not result in loss of the professional independence of the lawyer.

27. "Certainly it is true that 'the professional relationship between an attorney and his client is highly personal, involving an intimate appreciation of each individual client's particular problem.' And this Committee does not condone practices which interfere with that relationship. However, the mere fact the lawyer is actually paid by some entity other than the client does not affect that relationship, so long as the lawyer is selected by and is directly responsible to the client. See Informal Opinions 469 and 679. Of course, as the latter decision points out, there must be full disclosure of the arrangement by the attorney to the client . . . ." *ABA Opinion* 320 (1968).

"[A] third party may pay the cost of legal services as long as control remains in the client and the responsibility of the lawyer is solely to the client. Informal Opinions 469 ad [*sic*] 679. See also *Opinion* 237." Id.

28. *ABA Opinion* 303 (1961) recognized that "[s]tatutory provisions now exist in several states which are designed to make [the practice of law in a form that will be classified as a corporation for federal income tax purposes] legally possible, either as a result of lawyers incorporating or forming associations with various corporate characteristics."

DISCIPLINARY RULES

DR 5–101   Refusing Employment When the Interests of the Lawyer May Impair His Independent Professional Judgment.

(A) Except with the consent of his client after full disclosure, a lawyer shall not accept employment if the exercise of his professional judgment on behalf of his client will be or reasonably may be affected by his own financial, business, property, or personal interests.[29]

(B) A lawyer shall not accept employment in contemplated or pending litigation if he knows or it is obvious that he or a lawyer in his firm ought to be called as a witness, except that he may undertake the employment and he or a lawyer in his firm may testify:

   (1) If the testimony will relate solely to an uncontested matter.

   (2) If the testimony will relate solely to a matter of formality and there is no reason to believe that substantial evidence will be offered in opposition to the testimony.

   (3) If the testimony will relate solely to the nature and value of legal services rendered in the case by the lawyer or his firm to the client.

   (4) As to any matter, if refusal would work a substantial hardship on the client because of the distinctive value of the lawyer or his firm as counsel in the particular case.

DR 5–102   Withdrawal as Counsel When the Lawyer Becomes a Witness.[30]

(A) If, after undertaking employment in contemplated or pending litigation, a lawyer learns or it is obvious that he or a lawyer in his firm ought to be called as a witness on behalf

---

29. Cf. ABA Canon 6 and *ABA Opinions* 181 (1938), 104 (1934), 103 (1933), 72 (1932), 50 (1931), 49 (1931), and 33 (1931).

"New York County [Opinion] 203.... [A lawyer] should not advise a client to employ an investment company in which he is interested, without informing him of this." Drinker, *Legal Ethics* 956 (1953).

"In *Opinions* 72 and 49 this Committee held: The relations of partners in a law firm are such that neither the firm nor any member or associate thereof, may accept any professional employment which any member of the firm cannot properly accept.

"In *Opinion* 16 this Committee held that a member of a law firm could not represent a defendant in a criminal case which was being prosecuted by another member of the firm who was public prosecuting attorney. The Opinion stated that it was clearly unethical for one member of the firm to oppose the interest of the state while another member represented those interests.... Since the prosecutor himself could not represent both the public and the defendant, no member of his law firm could either." *ABA Opinion* 296 (1959).

30. Cf. ABA Canon 19 and *ABA Opinions* 220 (1941), 185 (1938), 50 (1931), and 33 (1931); but cf. Erwin M. Jennings Co. v. DiGenova, 107 Conn. 491, 498–99, 141 A. 866, 868 (1928).

of his client, he shall withdraw from the conduct of the trial and his firm, if any, shall not continue representation in the trial, except that he may continue the representation and he or a lawyer in his firm may testify in the circumstances enumerated in DR 5–101(B)(1) through (4).

(B) If, after undertaking employment in contemplated or pending litigation, a lawyer learns or it is obvious that he or a lawyer in his firm may be called as a witness other than on behalf of his client, he may continue the representation until it is apparent that his testimony is or may be prejudicial to his client.[31]

DR 5–103 Avoiding Acquisition of Interest in Litigation.

(A) A lawyer shall not acquire a proprietary interest in the cause of action or subject matter of litigation he is conducting for a client,[32] except that he may:

(1) Acquire a lien granted by law to secure his fee or expenses.

(2) Contract with a client for a reasonable contingent fee in a civil case.[33]

(B) While representing a client in connection with contemplated or pending litigation, a lawyer shall not advance or guarantee financial assistance to his client,[34] except that a lawyer may advance or guarantee the expenses of litigation, including court costs, expenses of investigation, expenses of medical examination, and costs of obtaining and presenting evidence, provided the client remains ultimately liable for such expenses.

DR 5–104 Limiting Business Relations With a Client

(A) A lawyer shall not enter into a business transaction with a client if they have differing interests therein and if the client expects the lawyer to exercise his professional judgment therein for the protection of the client, unless the client has consented after full disclosure.

(B) Prior to conclusion of all aspects of the matter giving rise to his employment, a lawyer shall not enter into any arrange-

---

31. "This *Canon* [19] *of Ethics* needs no elaboration to be applied to the facts here. Apparently, the object of this precept is to avoid putting a lawyer in the obviously embarrassing predicament of testifying and then having to argue the credibility and effect of his own testimony. It was not designed to permit a lawyer to call opposing counsel as a witness and thereby disqualify him as counsel." Galarowicz v. Ward, 119 Utah 611, 620, 230 P.2d 576, 580 (1951).

32. ABA Canon 10 and *ABA Opinions* 279 (1949), 246 (1942) and 176 (1938).

33. See Code of Professional Responsibility, DR 2–106(C).

34. See ABA Canon 42; cf. *ABA Opinion* 288 (1954).

ment or understanding with a client or a prospective client by which he acquires an interest in publication rights with respect to the subject matter of his employment or proposed employment.

DR 5-105   Refusing to Accept or Continue Employment if the Interests of Another Client May Impair the Independent Professional Judgment of the Lawyer.

(A) A lawyer shall decline proffered employment if the exercise of his independent professional judgment in behalf of a client will be or is likely to be adversely affected by the acceptance of the proffered employment,[35] or if it would be likely to involve him in representing differing interests, except to the extent permitted under DR 5-105(C).[36]

(B) A lawyer shall not continue multiple employment if the exercise of his independent professional judgment in behalf of a client will be or is likely to be adversely affected by his representation of another client, or if it would be likely to involve him in representing differing interests, except to the extent permitted under DR 5-105(C).[37]

(C) In the situations covered by DR 5-105(A) and (B), a lawyer may represent multiple clients if it is obvious that he can adequately represent the interest of each and if each consents to the representation after full disclosure of the possible effect of such representation on the exercise of his independent professional judgment on behalf of each.

(D) If a lawyer is required to decline employment or to withdraw from employment under a Disciplinary Rule, no partner or associate, or any other lawyer affiliated with him or his firm may accept or continue such employment.

As amended in 1974.

DR 5-106   Settling Similar Claims of Clients.[38]

(A) A lawyer who represents two or more clients shall not make or participate in the making of an aggregate settlement of

---

35. See ABA Canon 6; cf. *ABA Opinions* 167 (1937), 60 (1931), and 40 (1931).

36. *ABA Opinion* 247 (1942) held that an attorney could not investigate a night club shooting on behalf of one of the owner's liability insurers, obtaining the cooperation of the owner, and later represent the injured patron in an action against the owner and a different insurance company unless the attorney obtain the "express consent of all concerned given after a full disclosure of the facts," since to do so would be to represent conflicting interests.

See *ABA Opinions* 247 (1942), 224 (1941), 222 (1941), 218 (1941), 112 (1934), 83 (1932), and 86 (1932).

37. Cf. *ABA Opinions* 231 (1941) and 160 (1936).

38. Cf. *ABA Opinions* 243 (1942) and 235 (1941).

the claims of or against his clients, unless each client has consented to the settlement after being advised of the existence and nature of all the claims involved in the proposed settlement, of the total amount of the settlement, and of the participation of each person in the settlement.

DR 5–107 Avoiding Influence by Others Than the Client.

(A) Except with the consent of his client after full disclosure, a lawyer shall not:

(1) Accept compensation for his legal services from one other than his client.

(2) Accept from one other than his client any thing of value related to his representation of or his employment by his client.[39]

(B) A lawyer shall not permit a person who recommends, employs, or pays him to render legal services for another to direct or regulate his professional judgment in rendering such legal services.[40]

(C) A lawyer shall not practice with or in the form of a professional corporation or association authorized to practice law for a profit, if:

(1) A non-lawyer owns any interest therein,[41] except that a fiduciary representative of the estate of a lawyer may hold the stock or interest of the lawyer for a reasonable time during administration;

(2) A non-lawyer is a corporate director or officer thereof;[42] or

---

39. See ABA Canon 38.

"A lawyer who receives a commission (whether delayed or not) from a title insurance company or guaranty fund for recommending or selling the insurance to his client, or for work done for the client or the company, without either fully disclosing to the client his financial interest in the transaction, or crediting the client's bill with the amount thus received, is guilty of unethical conduct." *ABA Opinion* 304 (1962).

40. See ABA Canon 35; cf. *ABA Opinion* 237 (1941).

"When the lay forwarder, as agent for the creditor, forwards a claim to an attorney, the direct relationship of attorney and client shall then exist between the attorney and the creditor, and the forwarder shall not interpose itself as an intermediary to control the activities of the attorney." *ABA Opinion* 294 (1958).

41. "Permanent beneficial and voting rights in the organization set up to practice law, whatever its form, must be restricted to lawyers while the organization is engaged in the practice of law." *ABA Opinion* 303 (1961).

42. "*Canon 33* ... promulgates underlying principles that must be observed no matter in what form of organization lawyers practice law. Its requirement that no person shall be admitted or held out as a practitioner or member who is not a member of the legal profession duly authorized to practice, and amendable to professional discipline, makes it clear that any centralized management must be in lawyers to avoid a violation of this Canon." *ABA Opinion* 303 (1961).

(3) A non-lawyer has the right to direct or control the professional judgment of a lawyer.[43]

CANON 6

A Lawyer Should Represent a Client Competently

ETHICAL CONSIDERATIONS

EC 6–1 Because of his vital role in the legal process, a lawyer should act with competence and proper care in representing clients. He should strive to become and remain proficient in his practice [1] and should accept employment only in matters which he is or intends to become competent to handle.

EC 6–2 A lawyer is aided in attaining and maintaining his competence by keeping abreast of current legal literature and developments, participating in continuing legal education programs,[2] concentrating in particu-

---

43. "There is no intervention of any lay agency between lawyer and client when centralized management provided only by lawyers may give guidance or direction to the services being rendered by a lawyer-member of the organization to a client. The language in *Canon 35* that a lawyer should avoid all relations which direct the performance of his duties by or in the interest of an intermediary refers to lay intermediaries and not lawyer intermediaries with whom he is associated in the practice of law." *ABA Opinion* 303 (1961).

1. "[W]hen a citizen is faced with the need for a lawyer, he wants, and is entitled to, the best informed counsel he can obtain. Changing times produce changes in our laws and legal procedures. The natural complexities of law require continuing intensive study by a lawyer if he is to render his clients a maximum of efficient service. And, in so doing, he maintains the high standards of the legal profession; and he also increases respect and confidence by the general public." Rochelle & Payne, *The Struggle for Public Understanding*, 25 Texas B.J. 109, 160 (1962).

"We have undergone enormous changes in the last fifty years within the lives of most of the adults living today who may be seeking advice. Most of these changes have been accompanied by changes and developments in the law.... Every practicing lawyer encounters these problems and is often perplexed with his own inability to keep up, not only with changes in the law, but also with changes in the lives of his clients and their legal problems.

"To be sure, no client has a right to expect that his lawyer will have all of the answers at the end of his tongue or even in the back of his head at all times. But the client does have the right to expect that the lawyer will have devoted his time and energies to maintaining and improving his competence to know where to look for the answers, to know how to deal with the problems, and to know how to advise to the best of his legal talents and abilities." Levy & Sprague, *Accounting and Law: Is Dual Practice in the Public Interest?*, 52 A.B.A.J. 1110, 1112 (1966).

2. "The whole purpose of continuing legal education, so enthusiastically supported by the ABA, is to make it possible for lawyers to make themselves better lawyers. But there are no nostrums for proficiency in the law; it must come through the hard work of the lawyer himself. To the extent that that work, whether it be in attending institutes or lecture courses, in studying after hours or in the actual day in and day out practice of his profession, can be concentrated within a limited field, the greater the proficiency and expertness that can be developed." *Report of the Special Committee on Specialization and Specialized Legal Education*, 79 A.B.A.Rep. 582, 588 (1954).

lar areas of the law, and by utilizing other available means. He has the additional ethical obligation to assist in improving the legal profession, and he may do so by participating in bar activities intended to advance the quality and standards of members of the profession. Of particular importance is the careful training of his younger associates and the giving of sound guidance to all lawyers who consult him. In short, a lawyer should strive at all levels to aid the legal profession in advancing the highest possible standards of integrity and competence and to meet those standards himself.

EC 6–3 While the licensing of a lawyer is evidence that he has met the standards then prevailing for admission to the bar, a lawyer generally should not accept employment in any area of the law in which he is not qualified.[3] However, he may accept such employment if in good faith he expects to become qualified through study and investigation, as long as such preparation would not result in unreasonable delay or expense to his client. Proper preparation and representation may require the association by the lawyer of professionals in other disciplines. A lawyer offered employment in a matter in which he is not and does not expect to become so qualified should either decline the employment or, with the consent of his client, accept the employment and associate a lawyer who is competent in the matter.

EC 6–4 Having undertaken representation, a lawyer should use proper care to safeguard the interests of his client. If a lawyer has accepted employment in a matter beyond his competence but in which he expected to become competent, he should diligently undertake the work and study necessary to qualify himself. In addition to being qualified to handle a particular matter, his obligation to his client requires him to prepare adequately for and give appropriate attention to his legal work.

EC 6–5 A lawyer should have pride in his professional endeavors. His obligation to act competently calls for higher motivation than that arising from fear of civil liability or disciplinary penalty.

EC 6–6 A lawyer should not seek, by contract or other means, to limit his individual liability to his client for his malpractice. A lawyer who handles the affairs of his client properly has no need to attempt to limit his liability for his professional activities and one who does not handle the affairs of his client properly should not be permitted to do so. A lawyer who is a stockholder in or is associated with a professional legal corporation may, however, limit his liability for malpractice of his associates in the corporation, but only to the extent permitted by law.[4]

---

3. "If the attorney is not competent to skillfully and properly perform the work, he should not undertake the service." Degen v. Steinbrink, 202 App.Div. 477, 481, 195 N.Y.S. 810, 814 (1922), aff'd mem., 236 N.Y. 669, 142 N.E. 328 (1923).

4. See *ABA Opinion* 303 (1961); cf. Code of Professional Responsibility EC 2–11.

DISCIPLINARY RULES

DR 6–101   Failing to Act Competently.

(A) A lawyer shall not:

(1) **Handle a legal matter which he knows or should know that he is not competent to handle, without associating with him a lawyer who is competent to handle it.**

(2) **Handle a legal matter without preparation adequate in the circumstances.**

(3) **Neglect a legal matter entrusted to him.[5]**

DR 6–102   Limiting Liability to Client.

(A) A lawyer shall not attempt to exonerate himself from or limit his liability to his client for his personal malpractice.

CANON 7

A Lawyer Should Represent a Client Zealously Within the Bounds of the Law

ETHICAL CONSIDERATIONS

EC 7–1 The duty of a lawyer, both to his client[1] and to the legal system, is to represent his client zealously[2] within the bounds of the

---

5. The annual report for 1967–1968 of the Committee on Grievances of the Association of the Bar of the City of New York showed a receipt of 2,232 complaints; of the 828 offenses against clients, 76 involved conversion, 49 involved "overreaching," and 452, or more than half of all such offenses, involved neglect. *Annual Report of the Committee on Grievances of the Association of the Bar of the City of New York*, N.Y.L.J., Sept. 12, 1968, at 4, col. 5.

1. "The right to be heard would be, in many cases, of little avail if it did not comprehend the right to be heard by counsel. Even the intelligent and educated layman has small and sometimes no skill in the science of law." Powell v. Alabama, 287 U.S. 45, 68–69, 77 L.Ed. 158, 170, 53 S.Ct. 55, 64 (1932).

2. Cf. ABA Canon 4.

"At times ... [the tax lawyer] will be wise to discard some arguments and he should exercise discretion to emphasize the arguments which in his judgment are most likely to be persuasive. But this process involves legal judgment rather than moral attitudes. The tax lawyer should put aside private disagreements with Congressional and Treasury policies. His own notions of policy, and his personal view of what the law should be, are irrelevant. The job entrusted to him by his client is to use all his learning and ability to protect his client's rights, not to help in the process of promoting a better tax system. The tax lawyer need not accept his client's economic and social opinions, but the client is paying for technical attention and undivided concentration upon his affairs. He is equally entitled to performance unfettered by his attorney's economic and social predilections." Paul, *The Lawyer is a Tax Advisor,* 25 Rocky Mt.L.Rev. 412, 418 (1953).

law,[3] which includes Disciplinary Rules and enforceable professional regulations.[4] The professional responsibility of a lawyer derives from his

3. See ABA Canons 15 and 32.

ABA Canon 5, although only speaking of one accused of crime, imposes a similar obligation on the lawyer: "[T]he lawyer is bound, by all fair and honorable means, to present every defense that the law of the land permits, to the end that no person may be deprived of life or liberty, but by due process of law."

"Any persuasion or pressure on the advocate which deters him from planning and carrying out the litigation on the basis of 'what, within the framework of the law, is best for my client's interest?' interferes with the obligation to represent the client fully within the law.

"This obligation, in its fullest sense, is the heart of the adversary process. Each attorney, as an advocate, acts for and seeks that which in his judgment is best for his client, within the bounds authoritatively established. The advocate does not *decide* what is just in this case—he would be usurping the function of the judge and jury—he acts for and seeks for his client that which he is entitled to under the law. He can do no less and properly represent the client." Thode, *The Ethical Standard for the Advocate,* 39 Texas L.Rev. 575, 584 (1961).

"The [Texas public opinion] survey indicates that distrust of the lawyer can be traced directly to certain factors. Foremost of these is a basic misunderstanding of the function of the lawyer as an advocate in an adversary system.

"Lawyers are accused of taking advantage of 'loopholes' and 'technicalities' to win. Persons who make this charge are unaware, or do not understand, that the lawyer is hired to win, and if he does not exercise every legitimate effort in his client's behalf, then he is betraying a sacred trust." Rochelle & Payne, *The Struggle for Public Understanding,* 25 Texas B.J. 109, 159 (1962).

"The importance of the attorney's undivided allegiance and faithful service to one accused of crime, irrespective of the attorney's personal opinion as to the guilt of his client, lies in Canon 5 of the American Bar Association Canon of Ethics.

"The difficulty lies, of course, in ascertaining whether the attorney has been guilty of an error of judgment, such as an election with respect to trial tactics, or has otherwise been actuated by his conscience or belief that his client should be convicted in any event. All too frequently courts are called upon to review actions of defense counsel which are, at the most, errors of judgment, not properly reviewable on habeas corpus unless the trial is a farce and a mockery of justice which requires the court to intervene.... But when defense counsel, in a truly adverse proceeding, admits that his conscience would not permit him to adopt certain customary trial procedures, this extends beyond the realm of judgment and strongly suggests an invasion of constitutional rights." Johns v. Smyth, 176 F.Supp. 949, 952 (E.D.Va.1959), modified, United States ex rel. Wilkins v. Banmiller, 205 F.Supp. 123, 128, n. 5 (E.D. Pa.1962), aff'd 325 F.2d 514 (3d Cir.1963), cert. denied, 379 U.S. 847, 13 L.Ed.2d 51, 85 S.Ct. 87 (1964).

"The adversary system in law administration bears a striking resemblance to the competitive economic system. In each we assume that the individual through partisanship or through self-interest will strive mightily for his side, and that kind of striving we must have. But neither system would be tolerable without restraints and modifications, and at times without outright departures from the system itself. Since the legal profession is entrusted with the system of law administration, a part of its task is to develop in its members appropriate restraints without impairing the values of partisan striving. An accompanying task is to aid in the modification of the adversary system or departure from it in areas to which the system is unsuited." Cheatham, *The Lawyer's Role and Surroundings,* 25 Rocky Mt.L.Rev. 405, 410 (1953).

4. "Rule 4.15 prohibits, in the pursuit of a client's cause, 'any manner of fraud or chicane'; Rule 4.22 requires 'candor and membership in a profession which has the duty of assisting members of the public to secure and protect available legal rights and benefits. In our government of laws and not of men, each member of our society is entitled to have his conduct judged and regulated in accordance with the law; [5] to seek any lawful objective [6] through legally permissible means; [7] and to present for adjudication any lawful claim, issue, or defense.

EC 7–2 The bounds of the law in a given case are often difficult to ascertain.[8] The language of legislative enactments and judicial opinions may be uncertain as applied to varying factual situations. The limits and specific meaning of apparently relevant law may be made doubtful by changing or developing constitutional interpretations, inadequately expressed statutes or judicial opinions, and changing public and judicial attitudes. Certainty of law ranges from well-settled rules through areas of conflicting authority to areas without precedent.

EC 7–3 Where the bounds of law are uncertain, the action of a lawyer may depend on whether he is serving as advocate or adviser. A lawyer may serve simultaneously as both advocate and adviser, but the two

fairness' in the conduct of the lawyer, and forbids the making of knowing misquotations; Rule 4.47 provides that a lawyer 'should always maintain his integrity,' and generally forbids all misconduct injurious to the interests of the public, the courts, or his clients, and acts contrary to 'justice, honesty, modesty or good morals.' Our Commissioner has accurately paraphrased these rules as follows: 'An attorney does not have the duty to do all and whatever he can that may enable him to win his client's cause or to further his client's interest. His duty and efforts in these respects, although they should be prompted by his "entire devotion" to the interest of his client, must be within and not without the bounds of the law.'" In re Wines, 370 S.W.2d 328, 333 (Mo.1963).

See Note, 38 Texas L.Rev. 107, 110 (1959).

5. "Under our system of government the process of adjudication is surrounded by safeguards evolved from centuries of experience. These safeguards are not designed merely to lend formality and decorum to the trial of causes. They are predicated on the assumption that to secure for any controversy a truly informed and dispassionate decision is a difficult thing, requiring for its achievement a special summoning and orga-nization of human effort and the adoption of measures to exclude the biases and pre-judgments that have free play outside the courtroom. All of this goes for naught if the man with an unpopular cause is unable to find a competent lawyer courageous enough to represent him. His chance to have his day in court loses much of its meaning if his case is handicapped from the outset by the very kind of prejudgment our rules of evidence and procedure are intend-ed to prevent." *Professional Responsibility: Report of the Joint Conference,* 44 A.B.A.J. 1159, 1216 (1958).

6. "[I]t is ... [the tax lawyer's] positive duty to show the client how to avail himself to the full of what the law permits. He is not the keeper of the Congressional con-science." Paul, *The Lawyer as a Tax Adviser,* 25 Rocky Mt.L.Rev. 412, 418 (1953).

7. See ABA Canons 15 and 30.

8. "The fact that it desired to evade the law, as it is called, is immaterial, because the very meaning of a line in the law is that you intentionally may go as close to it as you can if you do not pass it.... It is a matter of proximity and degree as to which minds will differ...." Justice Holmes, in Superior Oil Co. v. Mississippi, 280 U.S. 390, 395–96, 74 L.Ed. 504, 508, 50 S.Ct. 169, 170 (1930).

roles are essentially different.[9] In asserting a position on behalf of his client, an advocate for the most part deals with past conduct and must take the facts as he finds them. By contrast, a lawyer serving as adviser primarily assists his client in determining the course of future conduct and relationships. While serving as advocate, a lawyer should resolve in favor of his client doubts as to the bounds of the law.[10] In serving a client as adviser, a lawyer in appropriate circumstances should give his professional opinion as to what the ultimate decisions of the courts would likely be as to the applicable law.

Duty of the Lawyer to a Client

EC 7–4 The advocate may urge any permissible construction of the law favorable to his client, without regard to his professional opinion as to the likelihood that the construction will ultimately prevail.[11] His

9. "Today's lawyers perform two distinct types of functions, and our ethical standards should, but in the main do not, recognize these two functions. Judge Philbrick McCoy recently reported to the American Bar Association the need for a reappraisal of the Canons in light of the new and distinct function of counselor, as distinguished from advocate, which today predominates in the legal profession. . . .

". . . In the first place, any revision of the canons must take into account and speak to this new and now predominant function of the lawyer. . . . It is beyond the scope of this paper to discuss the ethical standards to be applied to the counselor except to state that in my opinion such standards should require a greater recognition and protection for the interest of the public generally than is presently expressed in the canons. Also, the counselor's obligation should extend to requiring him to inform and to impress upon the client a just solution of the problem, considering all interests involved." Thode, *The Ethical Standard for the Advocate,* 39 Texas L.Rev. 575, 578–79 (1961).

"The man who has been called into court to answer for his own actions is entitled to fair hearing. Partisan advocacy plays its essential part in such a hearing, and the lawyer pleading his client's case may properly present it in the most favorable light. A similar resolution of doubts in one direction becomes inappropriate when the lawyer acts as counselor. The reasons that justify and even require partisan advocacy

in the trial of a cause do not grant any license to the lawyer to participate as legal advisor in a line of conduct that is immoral, unfair, or of doubtful legality. In saving himself from this unworthy involvement, the lawyer cannot be guided solely by an unreflective inner sense of good faith; he must be at pains to preserve a sufficient detachment from his client's interests so that he remains capable of a sound and objective appraisal of the propriety of what his client proposes to do." *Professional Responsibility: Report of the Joint Conference,* 44 A.B.J. 1159, 1161 (1958).

10. "[A] lawyer who is asked to advise his client . . . may freely urge the statement of positions most favorable to the client just as long as there is reasonable basis for those positions." *ABA Opinion* 314 (1965).

11. "The lawyer . . . is not an umpire, but an advocate. He is under no duty to refrain from making every proper argument in support of any legal point because he is not convinced of its inherent soundness. . . . His personal belief in the soundness of his cause or of the authorities supporting it, is irrelevant." *ABA Opinion* 280 (1949).

"Counsel apparently misconceived his role. It was his duty to honorably present his client's contentions in the light most favorable to his client. Instead he presumed to advise the court as to the validity and sufficiency of prisoner's motion, by letter. We therefore conclude that the prisoner had no effective assistance of counsel and remand this case to the District Court with conduct is within the bounds of the law, and therefore permissible, if the position taken is supported by the law or is supportable by a good faith argument for an extension, modification, or reversal of the law. However, a lawyer is not justified in asserting a position in litigation that is frivolous.[12]

EC 7–5 A lawyer as adviser furthers the interest of his client by giving his professional opinion as to what he believes would likely be the ultimate decision of the courts on the matter at hand and by informing his client of the practical effect of such decision.[13] He may continue in the representation of his client even though his client has elected to pursue a course of conduct contrary to the advice of the lawyer so long as he does not thereby knowingly assist the client to engage in illegal conduct or to take a frivolous legal position. A lawyer should never encourage or aid his client to commit criminal acts or counsel his client on how to violate the law and avoid punishment therefor.[14]

instructions to set aside the Judgment, appoint new counsel to represent the prisoner if he makes no objection thereto, and proceed anew." McCartney v. United States, 343 F.2d 471, 472 (9th Cir.1965).

12. "Here the court-appointed counsel had the transcript but refused to proceed with the appeal because he found no merit in it.... We cannot say that there was a finding of frivolity by either of the California courts or that counsel acted in any greater capacity than merely as *amicus curiae* which was condemned in *Ellis,* supra. Hence California's procedure did not furnish petitioner with counsel acting in the role of an advocate nor did it provide that full consideration and resolution of the matter as is obtained when counsel is acting in that capacity....

"The constitutional requirement of substantial equality and fair process can only be attained where counsel acts in the role of an active advocate in behalf of his client, as opposed to that of *amicus curiae.* The no-merit letter and the procedure it triggers do not reach that dignity. Counsel should, and can with honor and without conflict, be of more assistance to his client and to the court. His role as advocate requires that he support his client's appeal to the best of his ability. Of course, if counsel finds his case to be wholly frivolous, after a conscientious examination of it, he should so advise the court and request permission to withdraw. That request must, however, be accompanied by a brief referring to anything in the record that might arguably support the appeal. A copy of counsel's brief should be furnished the indigent and time allowed him to raise any points that he chooses; the court—not counsel—then proceeds, after a full examination of all the proceedings, to decide whether the case is wholly frivolous. If it so finds it may grant counsel's request to withdraw and dismiss the appeal insofar as federal requirements are concerned, or proceed to a decision on the merits, if state law so requires. On the other hand, if it finds any of the legal points arguable on their merits (and therefore not frivolous) it must, prior to decision afford the indigent the assistance of counsel to argue the appeal." *Anders v. California,* 386 U.S. 738, 744, 18 L.Ed.2d 493, 498, 87 S.Ct. 1396, 1399–1400 (1967), rehearing denied, 388 U.S. 924, 18 L.Ed.2d 1377, 87 S.Ct. 2094 (1967).

See Paul, *The Lawyer As a Tax Adviser,* 25 Rocky Mt.L.Rev. 412, 432 (1953).

13. See ABA Canon 32.

14. "For a lawyer to represent a syndicate notoriously engaged in the violation of the law for the purpose of advising the members how to break the law and at the same time escape it, is manifestly improper. While a lawyer may see to it that anyone accused of crime, no matter how serious and flagrant, has a fair trial, and present all available defenses, he may not co-operate in planning violations of the law. There is a sharp distinction, of course, between advis-

EC 7–6 Whether the proposed action of a lawyer is within the bounds of the law may be a perplexing question when his client is contemplating a course of conduct having legal consequences that vary according to the client's intent, motive, or desires at the time of the action. Often a lawyer is asked to assist his client in developing evidence relevant to the state of mind of the client at a particular time. He may properly assist his client in the development and preservation of evidence of existing motive, intent, or desire; obviously, he may not do anything furthering the creation or preservation of false evidence. In many cases a lawyer may not be certain as to the state of mind of his client, and in those situations he should resolve reasonable doubts in favor of his client.

EC 7–7 In certain areas of legal representation not affecting the merits of the cause or substantially prejudicing the rights of a client, a lawyer is entitled to make decisions on his own. But otherwise the authority to make decisions is exclusively that of the client and, if made within the framework of the law, such decisions are binding on his lawyer. As typical examples in civil cases, it is for the client to decide whether he will accept a settlement offer or whether he will waive his right to plead an affirmative defense. A defense lawyer in a criminal case has the duty to advise his client fully on whether a particular plea to a charge appears to be desirable and as to the prospects of success on appeal, but it is for the client to decide what plea should be entered and whether an appeal should be taken.[15]

EC 7–8 A lawyer should exert his best efforts to insure that decisions of his client are made only after the client has been informed of relevant considerations. A lawyer ought to initiate this decision-making process if the client does not do so. Advice of a lawyer to his client need not be confined to purely legal considerations.[16] A lawyer should advise his client of the possible effect of each legal alternative.[17] A lawyer should bring to bear upon this decision-making process the fullness of his experience as well as his objective viewpoint.[18] In assisting his client to

ing what can lawfully be done and advising how unlawful acts can be done in a way to avoid conviction. Where a lawyer accepts a retainer from an organization, known to be unlawful, and agrees in advance to defend its members when from time to time they are accused of crime arising out of its unlawful activities, this is equally improper."

"See also *Opinion* 155." *ABA Opinion* 281 (1952).

15. See ABA Special Committee on Minimum Standards for the Administration of Criminal Justice, *Standards Relating to Pleas of Guilty*, pp. 69–70 (1968).

16. "First of all, a truly great lawyer is a wise counselor to all manner of men in

the varied crises of their lives when they most need disinterested advice. Effective counseling necessarily involves a thoroughgoing knowledge of the principles of the law not merely as they appear in the books but as they actually operate in action." Vanderbilt, *The Five Functions of the Lawyer: Service to Clients and the Public*, 40 A.B.A.J. 31 (1954).

17. "A lawyer should endeavor to obtain full knowledge of his client's cause before advising thereon...." ABA Canon 8.

18. "[I]n devising charters of collaborative effort the lawyer often acts where all of the affected parties are present as particireach a proper decision, it is often desirable for a lawyer to point out those factors which may lead to a decision that is morally just as well as legally permissible.[19] He may emphasize the possibility of harsh consequences that might result from assertion of legally permissible positions. In the final analysis, however, the lawyer should always remember that the decision whether to forego legally available objectives or methods because of non-legal factors is ultimately for the client and not for himself. In the event that the client in a non-adjudicatory matter insists upon a course of conduct that is contrary to the judgment and advice of the lawyer but not prohibited by Disciplinary Rules, the lawyer may withdraw from the employment.[20]

EC 7–9 In the exercise of his professional judgment on those decisions which are for his determination in the handling of a legal matter,[21] a lawyer should always act in a manner consistent with the best interests of his client.[22] However, when an action in the best interest of his client seems to him to be unjust, he may ask his client for permission to forego such action.[23]

EC 7–10 The duty of a lawyer to represent his client with zeal does not militate against his concurrent obligation to treat with consideration

pants. But the lawyer also performs a similar function in situations where this is not so, as, for example, in planning estates and drafting wills. Here the instrument defining the terms of collaboration may affect persons not present and often not born. Yet here, too, the good lawyer does not serve merely as a legal conduit for his client's desires, but as a wise counselor, experienced in the art of devising arrangements that will put in workable order the entangled affairs and interests of human beings." *Professional Responsibility: Report of the Joint Conference,* 44 A.B.A.J. 1159, 1162 (1958).

19. See ABA Canon 8.

"Vital as is the lawyer's role in adjudication, it should not be thought that it is only as an advocate pleading in open court that he contributes to the administration of the law. The most effective realization of the law's aims often takes place in the attorney's office, where litigation is forestalled by anticipating its outcome, where the lawyer's quiet counsel takes the place of public force. Contrary to popular belief, the compliance with the law thus brought about is not generally lip-serving and narrow, for by reminding him of its long-run costs the

lawyer often deters his client from a course of conduct technically permissible under existing law, though inconsistent with its underlying spirit and purpose." *Professional Responsibility: Report of the Joint Conference,* 44 A.B.A.J. 1159, 1161 (1958).

20. "My summation of Judge Sharswood's view of the advocate's duty to the client is that he owes to the client the duty to use all legal means in support of the client's case. However, at the same time Judge Sharswood recognized that many advocates would find this obligation unbearable if applicable without exception. Therefore, the individual lawyer is given the choice of representing his client fully within the bounds set by the law *or of telling his client that he cannot do so,* so that the client may obtain another attorney if he wishes." Thode, *The Ethical Standard for the Advocate,* 39 Texas L.Rev. 575, 582 (1961).

Cf. Code of Professional Responsibility, DR 2–110(C).

21. See ABA Canon 24.

22. Thode, *The Ethical Standard for the Advocate,* 39 Texas L.Rev. 575, 592 (1961).

23. Cf. *ABA Opinions* 253 (1946) and 178 (1938).

all persons involved in the legal process and to avoid the infliction of needless harm.

EC 7–11 The responsibilities of a lawyer may vary according to the intelligence, experience, mental condition or age of a client, the obligation of a public officer, or the nature of a particular proceeding. Examples include the representation of an illiterate or an incompetent, service as a public prosecutor or other government lawyer, and appearances before administrative and legislative bodies.

EC 7–12 Any mental or physical condition of a client that renders him incapable of making a considered judgment on his own behalf casts additional responsibilities upon his lawyer. Where an incompetent is acting through a guardian or other legal representative, a lawyer must look to such representative for those decisions which are normally the prerogative of the client to make. If a client under disability has no legal representative, his lawyer may be compelled in court proceedings to make decisions on behalf of the client. If the client is capable of understanding the matter in question or of contributing to the advancement of his interests, regardless of whether he is legally disqualified from performing certain acts, the lawyer should obtain from him all possible aid. If the disability of a client and the lack of a legal representative compel the lawyer to make decisions for his client, the lawyer should consider all circumstances then prevailing and act with care to safeguard and advance the interests of his client. But obviously a lawyer cannot perform any act or make any decision which the law requires his client to perform or make, either acting for himself if competent, or by a duly constituted representative if legally incompetent.

EC 7–13 The responsibility of a public prosecutor differs from that of the usual advocate; his duty is to seek justice, not merely to convict.[24] This special duty exists because: (1) the prosecutor represents the sovereign and therefore should use restraint in the discretionary exercise of governmental powers, such as in the selection of cases to prosecute; (2) during trial the prosecutor is not only an advocate but he also may

---

24. See ABA Canon 5 and Berger v. United States, 295 U.S. 78, 79 L.Ed. 1314, 55 S.Ct. 629 (1935).

"The public prosecutor cannot take as a guide for the conduct of his office the standards of an attorney appearing on behalf of an individual client. The freedom elsewhere wisely granted to a partisan advocate must be severely curtailed if the prosecutor's duties are to be properly discharged. The public prosecutor must recall that he occupies a dual role, being obligated, on the one hand, to furnish that adversary element essential to the informed decision of any controversy, but being possessed, on the

other, of important governmental powers that are pledged to the accomplishment of one objective only, that of impartial justice. Where the prosecutor is recreant to the trust implicit in his office, he undermines confidence, not only in his profession, but in government and the very ideal of justice itself." *Professional Responsibility: Report of the Joint Conference,* 44 A.B.A.J. 1159, 1218 (1958).

"The prosecuting attorney is the attorney for the state, and it is his primary duty not to convict but to see that justice is done." *ABA Opinion* 150 (1936).

make decisions normally made by an individual client, and those affecting the public interest should be fair to all; and (3) in our system of criminal justice the accused is to be given the benefit of all reasonable doubts. With respect to evidence and witnesses, the prosecutor has responsibilities different from those of a lawyer in private practice: the prosecutor should make timely disclosure to the defense of available evidence, known to him, that tends to negate the guilt of the accused, mitigate the degree of the offense, or reduce the punishment. Further, a prosecutor should not intentionally avoid pursuit of evidence merely because he believes it will damage the prosecutor's case or aid the accused.

EC 7–14 A government lawyer who has discretionary power relative to litigation should refrain from instituting or continuing litigation that is obviously unfair. A government lawyer not having such discretionary power who believes there is lack of merit in a controversy submitted to him should so advise his superiors and recommend the avoidance of unfair litigation. A government lawyer in a civil action or administrative proceeding has the responsibility to seek justice and to develop a full and fair record, and he should not use his position or the economic power of the government to harass parties or to bring about unjust settlements or results.

EC 7–15 The nature and purpose of proceedings before administrative agencies vary widely. The proceedings may be legislative or quasi-judicial, or a combination of both. They may be *ex parte* in character, in which event they may originate either at the instance of the agency or upon motion of an interested party. The scope of an inquiry may be purely investigative or it may be truly adversary looking toward the adjudication of specific rights of a party or of classes of parties. The foregoing are but examples of some of the types of proceedings conducted by administrative agencies. A lawyer appearing before an administrative agency,[25] regardless of the nature of the proceeding it is conducting, has the continuing duty to advance the cause of his client within the bounds of the law.[26] Where the applicable rules of the agency impose specific obligations upon a lawyer, it is his duty to comply therewith, unless the lawyer has a legitimate basis for challenging the validity thereof. In all appearances before administrative agencies, a lawyer should identify himself, his client if identity of his client is not privi-

---

25. As to appearances before a department of government, Canon 26 provides: "A lawyer openly ... may render professional services ... in advocacy of claims before departments of government, upon the same principles of ethics which justify his appearance before the Courts...."

26. "But as an advocate before a service which itself represents the adversary point of view, where his client's case is fairly arguable, a lawyer is under no duty to disclose its weaknesses, any more than he would be to make such a disclosure to a brother lawyer. The limitations within which he must operate are best expressed in Canon 22...." *ABA Opinion* 314 (1965).

leged,[27] and the representative nature of his appearance. It is not improper, however, for a lawyer to seek from an agency information available to the public without identifying his client.

EC 7–16 The primary business of a legislative body is to enact laws rather than to adjudicate controversies, although on occasion the activities of a legislative body may take on the characteristics of an adversary proceeding, particularly in investigative and impeachment matters. The role of a lawyer supporting or opposing proposed legislation normally is quite different from his role in representing a person under investigation or on trial by a legislative body. When a lawyer appears in connection with proposed legislation, he seeks to affect the lawmaking process, but when he appears on behalf of a client in investigatory or impeachment proceedings, he is concerned with the protection of the rights of his client. In either event, he should identify himself and his client, if identity of his client is not privileged, and should comply with applicable laws and legislative rules.[28]

EC 7–17 The obligation of loyalty to his client applies only to a lawyer in the discharge of his professional duties and implies no obligation to adopt a personal viewpoint favorable to the interests or desires of his client.[29] While a lawyer must act always with circumspection in order that his conduct will not adversely affect the rights of a client in a matter he is then handling, he may take positions on public issues and espouse legal reforms he favors without regard to the individual views of any client.

EC 7–18 The legal system in its broadest sense functions best when persons in need of legal advice or assistance are represented by their own counsel. For this reason a lawyer should not communicate on the subject matter of the representation of his client with a person he knows to be represented in the matter by a lawyer, unless pursuant to law or rule of court or unless he has the consent of the lawyer for that person.[30] If one is not represented by counsel, a lawyer representing another may

27. See Baird v. Koerner, 279 F.2d 623 (9th Cir.1960).

28. See ABA Canon 26.

29. "Law should be so practiced that the lawyer remains free to make up his own mind how he will vote, what causes he will support, what economic and political philosophy he will espouse. It is one of the glories of the profession that it admits of this freedom. Distinguished examples can be cited of lawyers whose views were at variance from those of their clients, lawyers whose skill and wisdom make them valued advisers to those who had little sympathy with their views as citizens." *Professional*

Responsibility: Report of the Joint Conference, 44 A.B.A.J. 1159, 1217 (1958).

"No doubt some tax lawyers feel constrained to abstain from activities on behalf of a better tax system because they think that their clients may object. Clients have no right to object if the tax adviser handles their affairs competently and faithfully and independently of his private views as to tax policy. They buy his expert services, not his private opinions or his silence on issues that gravely affect the public interest." Paul, *The Lawyer as a Tax Adviser*, 25 Rocky Mt.L.Rev. 412, 434 (1953).

30. See ABA Canon 9.

have to deal directly with the unrepresented person; in such an instance, a lawyer should not undertake to give advice to the person who is attempting to represent himself,[31] except that he may advise him to obtain a lawyer.

Duty of the Lawyer to the Adversary System of Justice

EC 7–19 Our legal system provides for the adjudication of disputes governed by the rules of substantive, evidentiary, and procedural law. An adversary presentation counters the natural human tendency to judge too swiftly in terms of the familiar that which is not yet fully known;[32] the advocate, by his zealous preparation and presentation of facts and law, enables the tribunal to come to the hearing with an open and neutral mind and to render impartial judgments.[33] The duty of a lawyer to his client and his duty to the legal system are the same: to represent his client zealously within the bounds of the law.[34]

EC 7–20 In order to function properly, our adjudicative process requires an informed, impartial tribunal capable of administering justice promptly and efficiently[35] according to procedures that command public confidence and respect.[36] Not only must there be competent, adverse presentation of evidence and issues, but a tribunal must be aided by rules appropriate to an effective and dignified process. The procedures under which tribunals operate in our adversary system have been prescribed largely by legislative enactments, court rules and decisions, and administrative rules. Through the years certain concepts of proper professional conduct have become rules of law applicable to the adversary adjudicative process. Many of these concepts are the bases for standards of professional conduct set forth in the Disciplinary Rules.

EC 7–21 The civil adjudicative process is primarily designed for the settlement of disputes between parties, while the criminal process is

---

31. Id.

32. See *Professional Responsibility: Report of the Joint Conference,* 44 A.B.A.J. 1159, 1160 (1958).

33. "Without the participation of someone who can act responsibly for each of the parties, this essential narrowing of the issues [by exchange of written pleadings or stipulations of counsel] becomes impossible. But here again the true significance of partisan advocacy lies deeper, touching once more the integrity of the adjudicative process itself. It is only through the advocate's participation that the hearing may remain in fact what it purports to be in theory: a public trial of the facts and issues. Each advocate comes to the hearing prepared to present his proofs and arguments, knowing at the same time that his arguments may fail to persuade and that his proof may be rejected as inadequate.... The deciding tribunal, on the other hand, comes to the hearing uncommitted. It has not represented to the public that any fact can be proved, that any argument is sound, or that any particular way of stating a litigant's case is the most effective expression of its merits." *Professional Responsibility: Report of the Joint Conference,* 44 A.B.A.J. 1159, 1160–61 (1958).

34. Cf. ABA Canons 15 and 32.

35. Cf. ABA Canon 21.

36. See *Professional Responsibility: Report of the Joint Conference,* 44 A.B.A.J. 1159, 1216 (1958).

designed for the protection of society as a whole. Threatening to use, or using, the criminal process to coerce adjustment of private civil claims or controversies is a subversion of that process;[37] further, the person against whom the criminal process is so misused may be deterred from asserting his legal rights and thus the usefulness of the civil process in settling private disputes is impaired. As in all cases of abuse of judicial process, the improper use of criminal process tends to diminish public confidence in our legal system.

EC 7–22 Respect for judicial rulings is essential to the proper administration of justice; however, a litigant or his lawyer may, in good faith and within the framework of the law, take steps to test the correctness of a ruling of a tribunal.[38]

EC 7–23 The complexity of law often makes it difficult for a tribunal to be fully informed unless the pertinent law is presented by the lawyers in the cause. A tribunal that is fully informed on the applicable law is better able to make a fair and accurate determination of the matter before it. The adversary system contemplates that each lawyer will present and argue the existing law in the light most favorable to his client.[39] Where a lawyer knows of legal authority in the controlling jurisdiction directly adverse to the position of his client, he should inform the tribunal of its existence unless his adversary has done so; but, having made such disclosure, he may challenge its soundness in whole or in part.[40]

37. "We are of the opinion that the letter in question was improper, and that in writing and sending it respondent was guilty of unprofessional conduct. This court has heretofore expressed its disapproval of using threats of criminal prosecution as a means of forcing settlement of civil claims. . . .

"Respondent has been guilty of a violation of a principle which condemns any confusion of threats of criminal prosecution with the enforcement of civil claims. For this misconduct he should be severely censured." Matter of Gelman, 230 App.Div. 524, 527, 245 N.Y.S. 416, 419 (1930).

38. "An attorney has the duty to protect the interests of his client. He has a right to press legitimate argument and to protest an erroneous ruling." Gallagher v. Municipal Court, 31 Cal.2d 784, 796, 192 P 2d 905, 913 (1948).

"There must be protection, however, in the far more frequent case of the attorney who stands on his rights and combats the order in good faith and without disrespect believing with good cause that it is void, for it is here that the independence of the bar becomes valuable." Note, 39 Colum.L.Rev. 433, 438 (1939).

39. "Too many do not understand that accomplishment of the layman's abstract ideas of justice is the function of the judge and jury, and that it is the lawyer's sworn duty to portray his client's case in its most favorable light." Rochelle and Payne, *The Struggle for Public Understanding*, 25 Texas B.J. 109, 159 (1962).

40. "We are of the opinion that this Canon requires the lawyer to disclose such decisions [that are adverse to his client's contentions] to the court. He may, of course, after doing so, challenge the soundness of the decisions or present reasons which he believes would warrant the court in not following them in the pending case." *ABA Opinion* 146 (1935).

Cf. *ABA Opinion* 280 (1949) and Thode, *The Ethical Standard for the Advocate*, 39 Texas L.Rev. 575, 585–86 (1961).

EC 7–24 In order to bring about just and informed decisions, evidentiary and procedural rules have been established by tribunals to permit the inclusion of relevant evidence and argument and the exclusion of all other considerations. The expression by a lawyer of his personal opinion as to the justness of a cause, as to the credibility of a witness, as to the culpability of a civil litigant, or as to the guilt or innocence of an accused is not a proper subject for argument to the trier of fact.[41] It is improper as to factual matters because admissible evidence possessed by a lawyer should be presented only as sworn testimony. It is improper as to all other matters because, were the rule otherwise, the silence of a lawyer on a given occasion could be construed unfavorably to his client. However, a lawyer may argue, on his analysis of the evidence, for any position or conclusion with respect to any of the foregoing matters.

EC 7–25 Rules of evidence and procedure are designed to lead to just decisions and are part of the framework of the law. Thus while a lawyer may take steps in good faith and within the framework of the law to test the validity of rules, he is not justified in consciously violating such rules and he should be diligent in his efforts to guard against his unintentional violation of them.[42] As examples, a lawyer should subscribe to or verify only those pleadings that he believes are in compliance with applicable law and rules; a lawyer should not make any prefatory statement before a tribunal in regard to the purported facts of the case on trial unless he believes that his statement will be supported by admissible evidence; a lawyer should not ask a witness a question solely for the purpose of harassing or embarrassing him; and a lawyer should not by subterfuge put before a jury matters which it cannot properly consider.

EC 7–26 The law and Disciplinary Rules prohibit the use of fraudulent, false, or perjured testimony or evidence.[43] A lawyer who knowingly [44] participates in introduction of such testimony or evidence is subject to discipline. A lawyer should, however, present any admissible evidence his client desires to have presented unless he knows, or from facts within his knowledge should know, that such testimony or evidence is false, fraudulent, or perjured.[45]

---

41. See ABA Canon 15.

"The traditional duty of an advocate is that he honorably uphold the contentions of his client. He should not voluntarily undermine them." Harders v. State of California, 373 F.2d 839, 842 (9th Cir.1967).

42. See ABA Canon 22.

43. Id. Cf. ABA Canon 41.

44. See generally *ABA Opinion* 287 (1953) as to a lawyer's duty when he unknowingly participates in introducing perjured testimony.

45. "Under any standard of proper ethical conduct an attorney should not sit by silently and permit his client to commit what may have been perjury, and which certainly would mislead the court and the opposing party on a matter vital to the issue under consideration. . . .

. . . .

"Respondent next urges that it was his duty to observe the utmost good faith toward his client, and therefore he could not divulge any confidential information. This duty to the client of course does not extend

EC 7–27 Because it interferes with the proper administration of justice, a lawyer should not suppress evidence that he or his client has a legal obligation to reveal or produce. In like manner, a lawyer should not advise or cause a person to secrete himself or to leave the jurisdiction of a tribunal for the purpose of making him unavailable as a witness therein.[46]

EC 7–28 Witnesses should always testify truthfully [47] and should be free from any financial inducements that might tempt them to do otherwise.[48] A lawyer should not pay or agree to pay a non-expert witness an amount in excess of reimbursement for expenses and financial loss incident to his being a witness; however, a lawyer may pay or agree to pay an expert witness a reasonable fee for his services as an expert. But in no event should a lawyer pay or agree to pay a contingent fee to any witness. A lawyer should exercise reasonable diligence to see that his client and lay associates conform to these standards.[49]

EC 7–29 To safeguard the impartiality that is essential to the judicial process, veniremen and jurors should be protected against extraneous influences.[50] When impartiality is present, public confidence in the judicial system is enhanced. There should be no extrajudicial communication with veniremen prior to trial or with jurors during trial by or on behalf of a lawyer connected with the case. Furthermore, a lawyer who is not connected with the case should not communicate with or cause another to communicate with a venireman or a juror about the case. After the trial, communication by a lawyer with jurors is permitted so long as he refrains from asking questions or making comments that tend to harass or embarrass the juror [51] or to influence actions of the juror in

to the point of authorizing collaboration with him in the commission of fraud." In re Carroll, 244 S.W.2d 474, 474–75 (Ky. 1951).

46. See ABA Canon 5; cf. *ABA Opinion* 131 (1935).

47. Cf. ABA Canon 39.

48. "The prevalence of perjury is a serious menace to the administration of justice, to prevent which no means have as yet been satisfactorily devised. But there certainly can be no greater incentive to perjury than to allow a party to make payments to its opponents witnesses under any guise or on any excuse, and at least attorneys who are officers of the court to aid it in the administration of justice, must keep themselves clear of any connection which in the slightest degree tends to induce witnesses to testify in favor of their clients." In re Robinson, 151 App.Div. 589, 600, 136 N.Y.S. 548,

556–57 (1912), aff'd, 209 N.Y. 354, 103 N.E. 160 (1913).

49. "It will not do for an attorney who seeks to justify himself against charges of this kind to show that he has escaped criminal responsibility under the Penal Law, nor can he blindly shut his eyes to a system which tends to suborn witnesses, to produce perjured testimony, and to suppress the truth. He has an active affirmative duty to protect the administration of justice from perjury and fraud, and that duty is not performed by allowing his subordinates and assistants to attempt to subvert justice and procure results for his clients based upon false testimony and perjured witnesses." Id., 151 App.Div. at 592, 136 N.Y.S. at 551.

50. See ABA Canon 23.

51. "[I]t is unfair to jurors to permit a disappointed litigant to pick over their private associations in search of something to future cases. Were a lawyer to be prohibited from communicating after a trial with a juror, he could not ascertain if the verdict might be subject to legal challenge, in which event the invalidity of a verdict might go undetected.[52]   When an extrajudicial communication by a lawyer with a juror is permitted by law, it should be made considerately and with deference to the personal feelings of the juror.

EC 7–30   Vexatious or harassing investigations of veniremen or jurors seriously impair the effectiveness of our jury system.   For this reason, a lawyer or anyone on his behalf who conducts an investigation of veniremen or jurors should act with circumspection and restraint.

EC 7–31   Communications with or investigations of members of families of veniremen or jurors by a lawyer or by anyone on his behalf are subject to the restrictions imposed upon the lawyer with respect to his communications with or investigations of veniremen and jurors.

EC 7–32   Because of his duty to aid in preserving the integrity of the jury system, a lawyer who learns of improper conduct by or towards a venireman, a juror, or a member of the family of either should make a prompt report to the court regarding such conduct.

EC 7–33   A goal of our legal system is that each party shall have his case, criminal or civil, adjudicated by an impartial tribunal.   The attainment of this goal may be defeated by dissemination of news or comments which tend to influence judge or jury.[53]   Such news or comments may

discredit them and their verdict. And it would be unfair to the public too if jurors should understand that they cannot convict a man of means without risking an inquiry of that kind by paid investigators, with, to boot, the distortions an inquiry of that kind can produce." State v. LaFera, 42 N.J. 97, 107, 199 A.2d 630, 636 (1964).

52. *ABA Opinion* 319 (1968) points out that "[m]any courts today, and the trend is in this direction, allow the testimony of jurors as to all irregularities in and out of the courtroom except those irregularities whose existence can be determined only by exploring the consciousness of a single particular juror, New Jersey v. Kociolek, 20 N.J. 92, 118 A.2d 812 (1955). Model Code of Evidence Rule 301.   Certainly as to states in which the testimony and affidavits of jurors may be received in support of or against a motion for new trial, a lawyer, in his obligation to protect his client, must have the tools for ascertaining whether or not grounds for a new trial exist and it is not unethical for him to talk to and question jurors."

53.   Generally see ABA Advisory Committee on Fair Trial and Free Press, Standards Relating to Fair Trial and Free Press (1966).

"[T]he trial court might well have proscribed extrajudicial statements by any lawyer, party, witness, or court official which divulged prejudicial matters.... See State v. Van Dwyne, 43 N.J. 369, 389, 204 A.2d 841, 852 (1964), in which the court interpreted Canon 20 of the American Bar Association's Canons of Professional Ethics to prohibit such statements. Being advised of the great public interest in the case, the mass coverage of the press, and the potential prejudicial impact of publicity, the court could also have requested the appropriate city and county officials to promulgate a regulation with respect to dissemination of information about the case by their employees.   In addition, reporters who wrote or broadcast prejudicial stories, could have been warned as to the impropriety of publishing material not introduced in the proceedings....   In this manner, Sheppard's right to a trial free from outside interferprevent prospective jurors from being impartial at the outset of the trial [54] and may also interfere with the obligation of jurors to base their verdict solely upon the evidence admitted in the trial.[55] The release by a

ence would have been given added protection without corresponding curtailment of the news media. Had the judge, the other officers of the court, and the police placed the interest of justice first, the news media would have soon learned to be content with the task of reporting the case as it unfolded in the courtroom—not pieced together from extrajudicial statements." Sheppard v. Maxwell, 384 U.S. 333, 361–62, 16 L.Ed.2d 600, 619–20, 86 S.Ct. 1507, 1521–22 (1966).

"Court proceedings are held for the solemn purpose of endeavoring to ascertain the truth which is the *sine qua non* of a fair trial. Over the centuries Anglo-American courts have devised careful safeguards by rule and otherwise to protect and facilitate the performance of this high function. As a result, at this time those safeguards do not permit the televising and photographing of a criminal trial, save in two States and there only under restrictions. The federal courts prohibit it by specific rule. This is weighty evidence that our concepts of a fair trial do not tolerate such an indulgence. We have always held that the atmosphere essential to the preservation of a fair trial— the most fundamental of all freedoms— must be maintained at all costs." Estes v. State of Texas, 381 U.S. 532, 540, 14 L.Ed.2d 543, 549, 85 S.Ct. 1628, 1631–32 (1965), rehearing denied, 382 U.S. 875, 15 L.Ed.2d 118, 86 S.Ct. 18 (1965).

54. "Pretrial can create a major problem for the defendant in a criminal case. Indeed, it may be more harmful than publicity during the trial for it may well set the community opinion as to guilt or innocence.... The trial witnesses present at the hearing, as well as the original jury panel, were undoubtedly made aware of the peculiar public importance of the case by the press and television coverage being provided, and by the fact that they themselves were televised live and their pictures rebroadcast on the evening show." Id., 381 U.S. at 536–37, 14 L.Ed.2d at 546–47, 85 S.Ct. at 1629–30.

55. "The undeviating rule of this Court was expressed by Mr. Justice Holmes over

half a century ago in Patterson v. Colorado, 205 U.S. 454, 462 (1907):

"The theory of our system is that the conclusions to be reached in a case will be induced only by evidence and argument in open court, and not by any outside influence, whether of private talk or public print."

Sheppard v. Maxwell, 384 U.S. 333, 351, 16 L.Ed.2d 600, 614, 86 S.Ct. 1507, 1516 (1966).

"The trial judge has a large discretion in ruling on the issue of prejudice resulting from the reading by jurors of news articles concerning the trial.... Generalizations beyond that statement are not profitable, because each case must turn on its special facts. We have here the exposure of jurors to information of a character which the trial judge ruled was so prejudicial it could not be directly offered as evidence. The prejudice to the defendant is almost certain to be as great when that evidence reaches the jury through news accounts as when it is a part of the prosecution's evidence.... It may indeed be greater for it is then not tempered by protective procedures." Marshall v. United States, 360 U.S. 310, 312– 13, 3 L.Ed.2d 1250, 1252, 79 S.Ct. 1171, 1173 (1959).

"The experienced trial lawyer knows that an adverse public opinion is a tremendous disadvantage to the defense of his client. Although grand jurors conduct their deliberations in secret, they are selected from the body of the public. They are likely to know what the general public knows and to reflect the public attitude. Trials are open to the public, and aroused public opinion respecting the merits of a legal controversy creates a court room atmosphere which, without any vocal expression in the presence of the petit jury, makes itself felt and has its effect upon the action of the petit jury. Our fundamental concepts of justice and our American sense of fair play requires that the petit jury shall be composed of persons with fair and impartial minds and without preconceived views as to the lawyer of out-of-court statements regarding an anticipated or pending trial may improperly affect the impartiality of the tribunal.[56] For these reasons, standards for permissible and prohibited conduct of a lawyer with respect to trial publicity have been established.

EC 7–34 The impartiality of a public servant in our legal system may be impaired by the receipt of gifts or loans. A lawyer,[57] therefore, is never justified in making a gift or a loan to a judge, a hearing officer, or an official or employee of a tribunal, except as permitted by Section C(4) of Canon 5 of the Code of Judicial Conduct, but a lawyer may make a contribution to the campaign fund of a candidate for judicial office in conformity with Section B(2) under Canon 7 of the Code of Judicial Conduct.[58]

    As amended in 1974.

EC 7–35 All litigants and lawyers should have access to tribunals on an equal basis. Generally, in adversary proceedings a lawyer should not communicate with a judge relative to a matter pending before, or which is to be brought before, a tribunal over which he presides in circumstances which might have the effect or give the appearance of granting undue advantage to one party.[59] For example, a lawyer should not communicate with a tribunal by a writing unless a copy thereof is promptly delivered to opposing counsel or to the adverse party if he is not represented by a lawyer. Ordinarily an oral communication by a lawyer with a judge or hearing officer should be made only upon adequate notice to opposing counsel, or, if there is none, to the opposing party. A lawyer should not condone or lend himself to private importu-

merits of the controversy, and that it shall determine the issues presented to it solely upon the evidence adduced at the trial and according to the law given in the instructions of the trial judge.

"While we may doubt that the effect of public opinion would sway or bias the judgment of the trial judge in an equity proceeding, the defendant should not be called upon to run that risk and the trial court should not have his work made more difficult by any dissemination of statements to the public that would be calculated to create a public demand for a particular judgment in a prospective or pending case." *ABA Opinion* 199 (1940).

Cf. Estes v. State of Texas, 381 U.S. 532, 544–45, 14 L.Ed.2d 543, 551, 85 S.Ct. 1628, 1634 (1965), rehearing denied, 381 U.S. 875, 15 L.Ed.2d 118, 86 S.Ct. 18 (1965).

56. See ABA Canon 20.

57. Canon 3 observes that a lawyer "deserves rebuke and denunciation for any de-

vice or attempt to gain from a Judge special personal consideration or favor."

See ABA Canon 32.

58. "*Judicial Canon 32 provides:*

" 'A judge should not accept any presents or favors from litigants, or from lawyers practicing before him or from others whose interests are likely to be submitted to him for judgment.'

"The language of this Canon is perhaps broad enough to prohibit campaign contributions by lawyers, practicing before the court upon which the candidate hopes to sit. However, we do not think it was intended to prohibit such contributions when the candidate is obligated, by force of circumstances over which he has no control, to conduct a campaign, the expense of which exceeds that which he should reasonably be expected to personally bear!" *ABA Opinion* 226 (1941).

59. See ABA Canons 3 and 32.

nities by another with a judge or hearing officer on behalf of himself or his client.

EC 7-36 Judicial hearings ought to be conducted through dignified and orderly procedures designed to protect the rights of all parties. Although a lawyer has the duty to represent his client zealously, he should not engage in any conduct that offends the dignity and decorum of proceedings.[60] While maintaining his independence, a lawyer should be respectful, courteous, and above-board in his relations with a judge or hearing officer before whom he appears.[61] He should avoid undue solicitude for the comfort or convenience of judge or jury and should avoid any other conduct calculated to gain special consideration.

EC 7-37 In adversary proceedings, clients are litigants and though ill feeling may exist between clients, such ill feeling should not influence a lawyer in his conduct, attitude, and demeanor towards opposing lawyers.[62] A lawyer should not make unfair or derogatory personal reference to opposing counsel. Haranguing and offensive tactics by lawyers interfere with the orderly administration of justice and have no proper place in our legal system.

EC 7-38 A lawyer should be courteous to opposing counsel and should accede to reasonable requests regarding court proceedings, settings, continuances, waiver of procedural formalities, and similar matters which do not prejudice the rights of his client.[63] He should follow local customs of courtesy or practice, unless he gives timely notice to opposing counsel of his intention not to do so.[64] A lawyer should be punctual in fulfilling all professional commitments.[65]

EC 7-39 In the final analysis, proper functioning of the adversary system depends upon cooperation between lawyers and tribunals in utilizing procedures which will preserve the impartiality of tribunals and make their decisional processes prompt and just, without impinging upon the obligation of lawyers to represent their clients zealously within the framework of the law.

DISCIPLINARY RULES

DR 7-101 Representing a Client Zealously.

(A) A lawyer shall not intentionally: [66]

    (1) Fail to seek the lawful objectives of his client through reasonably available means [67] **permitted by law and the Disciplinary Rules, except as provided by DR 7-101(B). A**

---

60. Cf. ABA Canon 18.

61. See ABA Canons 1 and 3.

62. See ABA Canon 17.

63. See ABA Canon 24.

64. See ABA Canon 25.

65. See ABA Canon 21.

66. See ABA Canon 15.

67. See ABA Canons 5 and 15; cf. ABA Canons 4 and 32.

lawyer does not violate this Disciplinary Rule, however, by acceding to reasonable requests of opposing counsel which do not prejudice the rights of his client, by being punctual in fulfilling all professional commitments, by avoiding offensive tactics, or by treating with courtesy and consideration all persons involved in the legal process.

(2) Fail to carry out a contract of employment entered into with a client for professional services, but he may withdraw as permitted under DR 2-110, DR 5-102, and DR 5-105.

(3) Prejudice or damage his client during the course of the professional relationship [68] except as required under DR 7-102(B).

(B) In his representation of a client, a lawyer may:

(1) Where permissible, exercise his professional judgment to waive or fail to assert a right or position of his client.

(2) Refuse to aid or participate in conduct that he believes to be unlawful, even though there is some support for an argument that the conduct is legal.

DR 7-102   Representing a Client Within the Bounds of the Law.

(A) In his representation of a client, a lawyer shall not:

(1) File a suit, assert a position, conduct a defense, delay a trial, or take other action on behalf of his client when he knows or when it is obvious that such action would serve merely to harass or maliciously injure another.[69]

(2) Knowingly advance a claim or defense that is unwarranted under existing law, except that he may advance such claim or defense it if can be supported by good faith argument for an extension, modification, or reversal of existing law.

(3) Conceal or knowingly fail to disclose that which he is required by law to reveal.

(4) Knowingly use perjured testimony or false evidence.[70]

(5) Knowingly make a false statement of law or fact.

(6) Participate in the creation or preservation of evidence when he knows or it is obvious that the evidence is false.

(7) Counsel or assist his client in conduct that the lawyer knows to be illegal or fraudulent.

(8) Knowingly engage in other illegal conduct or conduct contrary to a Disciplinary Rule.

(B) A lawyer who receives information clearly establishing that:

---

68. Cf. ABA Canon 24.

69. See ABA Canon 30.

70. Cf. ABA Canons 22 and 29.

(1) **His client has, in the course of the representation, perpetrated a fraud upon a person or tribunal shall promptly call upon his client to rectify the same, and if his client refuses or is unable to do so, he shall reveal the fraud to the affected person or tribunal, except when the information is protected as a privileged communication.**[71]

(2) **A person other than his client has perpetrated a fraud upon a tribunal shall promptly reveal the fraud to the tribunal.**[72]

As amended in 1974.

DR 7–103   Performing the Duty of Public Prosecutor or Other Government Lawyer.[73]

(A) **A public prosecutor or other government lawyer shall not institute or cause to be instituted criminal charges when he knows or it is obvious that the charges are not supported by probable cause.**

(B) **A public prosecutor or other government lawyer in criminal litigation shall make timely disclosure to counsel for the defendant, or to the defendant if he has no counsel, of the existence of evidence, known to the prosecutor or other government lawyer, that tends to negate the guilt of the accused, mitigate the degree of the offense, or reduce the punishment.**

DR 7–104   Communicating With One of Adverse Interest.[74]

(A) **During the course of his representation of a client a lawyer shall not:**

(1) **Communicate or cause another to communicate on the subject of the representation with a party he knows to be represented by a lawyer in that matter unless he has the prior consent of the lawyer representing such other party**[75] **or is authorized by law to do so.**

---

71. See ABA Canon 41; cf. Hinds v. State Bar, 19 Cal.2d 87, 92–93, 119 P.2d 134, 137 (1941); but see *ABA Opinion* 287 (1953) and Texas Canon 38. Also see Code of Professional Responsibility. DR 4–101(C)(2).

72. See Precision Inst. Mfg. Co. v. Automotive M.M. Co., 324 U.S. 806, 89 L.Ed. 1381, 65 S.Ct. 993 (1945).

73. Cf. ABA Canon 5.

74. "*Rule 12.* ... A member of the State Bar shall not communicate with a party represented by counsel upon a subject of controversy, in the absence and without the consent of such counsel. This rule shall not apply to communications with a public officer, board, committee or body." Cal. Business and Professions Code § 6076 (West 1962).

75. See ABA Canon 9; cf. *ABA Opinions* 124 (1934), 108 (1934), 95 (1933), and 75 (1932); also see In re Schwabe, 242 Or. 169, 174–75, 408 P.2d 922, 924 (1965).

(2) Give advice to a person who is not represented by a lawyer, other than the advice to secure counsel,[76] if the interests of such person are or have a reasonable possibility of being in conflict with the interests of his client.[77]

DR 7–105   Threatening Criminal Prosecution.

(A) A lawyer shall not present, participate in presenting, or threaten to present criminal charges solely to obtain an advantage in a civil matter.

DR 7–106   Trial Conduct.

(A) A lawyer shall not disregard or advise his client to disregard a standing rule of a tribunal or a ruling of a tribunal made in the course of a proceeding, but he may take appropriate steps in good faith to test the validity of such rule or ruling.

(B) In presenting a matter to a tribunal, a lawyer shall disclose:[78]

(1) Legal authority in the controlling jurisdiction known to him to be directly adverse to the position of his client and which is not disclosed by opposing counsel.[79]

(2) Unless privileged or irrelevant, the identities of the clients he represents and of the persons who employed him.[80]

"It is clear from the earlier opinions of this committee that *Canon 9* is to be construed literally and does not allow a communication with an opposing party, without the consent of his counsel, though the purpose merely be to investigate the facts. *Opinions 117, 55, 66*," *ABA Opinion* 187 (1938).

76. Cf. *ABA Opinion* 102 (1933).

77. Cf. ABA Canon 9 and *ABA Opinion* 58 (1931).

78. Cf. Note, 38 Texas L.Rev. 107, 108–09 (1959).

79. "In the brief summary in the 1947 edition of the Committee's decisions (p. 17), *Opinion 146* was thus summarized: *Opinion 146*—A lawyer should disclose to the court a decision directly adverse to his client's case that is unknown to his adversary.

. . . .

"We would not confine the Opinion to 'controlling authorities'—i.e., those decisive of the pending case—but, in accordance with the tests hereafter suggested, would apply it to a decision directly adverse to any proposition of law on which the lawyer expressly relies, which would reasonably be considered important by the judge sitting on the case.

* * *

". . . The test in every case should be: Is the decision which opposing counsel has overlooked one which the court should clearly consider in deciding the case? Would a reasonable judge properly feel that a lawyer who advanced, as the law, a proposition adverse to the undisclosed decision, was lacking in candor and fairness to him? Might the judge consider himself misled by an implied representation that the lawyer knew of no adverse authority?" *ABA Opinion* 280 (1949).

80. "The authorities are substantially uniform against any privilege as applied to the fact of retainer or identity of the client. The privilege is limited to confidential communications, and a retainer is not a confidential communication, although it cannot come into existence without some commu-

620

(C) In appearing in his professional capacity before a tribunal, a lawyer shall not:

(1) State or allude to any matter that he has no reasonable basis to believe is relevant to the case or that will not be supported by admissible evidence.[81]

(2) Ask any question that he has no reasonable basis to believe is relevant to the case and that is intended to degrade a witness or other person.[82]

(3) Assert his personal knowledge of the facts in issue, except when testifying as a witness.

(4) Assert his personal opinion as to the justness of a cause, as to the credibility of a witness, as to the culpability of a civil litigant, or as to the guilt or innocence of an accused;[83] but he may argue, on his analysis of the evidence, for any position or conclusion with respect to the matters stated herein.

(5) Fail to comply with known local customs of courtesy or practice of the bar or a particular tribunal without giving to opposing counsel timely notice of his intent not to comply.[84]

nication between the attorney and the—at that stage prospective—client." United States v. Pape, 144 F.2d 778, 782 (2d Cir. 1944), cert. denied, 323 U.S. 752 89 L.Ed.2d 602, 65 S.Ct. 86 (1944).

"To be sure, there may be circumstances under which the identification of a client may amount to the prejudicial disclosure of a confidential communication, as where the substance of a disclosure has already been revealed but not its source." Colton v. United States, 306 F.2d 633, 637 (2d Cir. 1962).

81. See ABA Canon 22; cf. ABA Canon 17.

"The rule allowing counsel when addressing the jury the widest latitude in discussing the evidence and presenting the client's theories falls far short of authorizing the statement by counsel of matter not in evidence, or indulging in argument founded on no proof, or demanding verdicts for purposes other than the just settlement of the matters at issue between the litigants, or appealing to prejudice or passion. The rule confining counsel to legitimate argument is not based on etiquette, but on justice. Its violation is not merely an overstepping of the bounds of propriety, but a violation of a party's rights. The jurors must determine the issues upon the evidence. Counsel's

address should help them do this, not tend to lead them astray." Cherry Creek Nat. Bank v. Fidelity & Cas. Co., 207 App.Div. 787, 790–91, 202 N.Y.S. 611, 614 (1924).

82. Cf. ABA Canon 18.

§ 6068. ... It is the duty of an attorney:

* * *

"(f) To abstain from all offensive personality, and to advance no fact prejudicial to the honor or reputation of a party or witness, unless required by the justice of the cause with which he is charged." Cal.Business and Professions Code § 6068 (West 1962).

83. "The record in the case at bar was silent concerning the qualities and character of the deceased. It is especially improper, in addressing the jury in a murder case, for the prosecuting attorney to make reference to his knowledge of the good qualities of the deceased where there is no evidence in the record bearing upon his character.... A prosecutor should never inject into his argument evidence not introduced at the trial." People v. Dukes, 12 Ill.2d 334, 341, 146 N.E.2d 14, 17–18 (1957).

84. "A lawyer should not ignore known customs or practice of the Bar or of a particular Court, even when the law permits,

(6) Engage in undignified or discourteous conduct which is degrading to a tribunal.

(7) Intentionally or habitually violate any established rule of procedure or of evidence.

DR 7-107   Trial Publicity.[85]

(A) A lawyer participating in or associated with the investigation of a criminal matter shall not make or participate in making an extrajudicial statement that a reasonable person would expect to be disseminated by means of public communication and that does more than state without elaboration:

(1) Information contained in a public record.

(2) That the investigation is in progress.

(3) The general scope of the investigation including a description of the offense and, if permitted by law, the identity of the victim.

(4) A request for assistance in apprehending a suspect or assistance in other matters and the information necessary thereto.

(5) A warning to the public of any dangers.

(B) A lawyer or law firm associated with the prosecution or defense of a criminal matter shall not, from the time of the

without giving timely notice to the opposing counsel." ABA Canon 25.

85. The provisions of Sections (A), (B), (C), and (D) of this Disciplinary Rule incorporate the fair trial-free press standards which apply to lawyers as adopted by the ABA House of Delegates, Feb. 19, 1968, upon the recommendation of the Fair Trial and Free Press Advisory Committee of the ABA Special Committee on Minimum Standards for the Administration of Criminal Justice.

Cf. ABA Canon 20; see generally ABA Advisory Committee on Fair Trial and Free Press, Standards Relating to Fair Trial and Free Press (1966).

"From the cases coming here we note that unfair and prejudicial news comment on pending trials has become increasingly prevalent. Due process requires that the accused receive a trial by an impartial jury free from outside influences. Given the pervasiveness of modern communications and the difficulty of effacing prejudicial publicity from the minds of the jurors, the trial courts must take strong measures to ensure that the balance is never weighed against the accused. And appellate tribunals have the duty to make an independent evaluation of the circumstances. Of course, there is nothing that prescribes the press from reporting events that transpire in the courtroom. But where there is a reasonable likelihood that prejudicial news prior to trial will prevent a fair trial, the judge should continue the case until the threat abates, or transfer it to another county not so permeated with publicity.... The courts must take such steps by rule and regulation that will protect their processes from prejudicial outside interferences. Neither prosecutors, counsel for defense, the accused, witnesses, court staff nor enforcement officers coming under the jurisdiction of the court should be permitted to frustrate its function. Collaboration between counsel and the press as to information affecting the fairness of a criminal trial is not only subject to regulation, but is highly censurable and worthy of disciplinary measures." Sheppard v. Maxwell, 384 U.S. 333, 362–63, 16 L.Ed.2d 600, 620, 86 S.Ct. 1507, 1522 (1966).

filing of a complaint, information, or indictment, the issuance of an arrest warrant, or arrest until the commencement of the trial or disposition without trial, make or participate in making an extrajudicial statement that a reasonable person would expect to be disseminated by means of public communication and that relates to:

(1) The character, reputation, or prior criminal record (including arrests, indictments, or other charges of crime) of the accused.

(2) The possibility of a plea of guilty to the offense charged or to a lesser offense.

(3) The existence or contents of any confession, admission, or statement given by the accused or his refusal or failure to make a statement.

(4) The performance or results of any examinations or tests or the refusal or failure of the accused to submit to examinations or tests.

(5) The identity, testimony, or credibility of a prospective witness.

(6) Any opinion as to the guilt or innocence of the accused, the evidence, or the merits of the case.

(C) DR 7-107(B) does not preclude a lawyer during such period from announcing:

(1) The name, age, residence, occupation, and family status of the accused.

(2) If the accused has not been apprehended, any information necessary to aid in his apprehension or to warn the public of any dangers he may present.

(3) A request for assistance in obtaining evidence.

(4) The identity of the victim of the crime.

(5) The fact, time, and place of arrest, resistance, pursuit, and use of weapons.

(6) The identity of investigating and arresting officers or agencies and the length of the investigation.

(7) At the time of seizure, a description of the physical evidence seized, other than a confession, admission, or statement.

(8) The nature, substance, or text of the charge.

(9) Quotations from or references to public records of the court in the case.

(10) The scheduling or result of any step in the judicial proceedings.

(11) That the accused denies the charges made against him.

(D) During the selection of a jury or the trial of a criminal matter, a lawyer or law firm associated with the prosecution or defense of a criminal matter shall not make or participate

623

in making an extra-judicial statement that a reasonable person would expect to be disseminated by means of public communication and that relates to the trial, parties, or issues in the trial or other matters that are reasonably likely to interfere with a fair trial, except that he may quote from or refer without comment to public records of the court in the case.

(E) After the completion of a trial or disposition without trial of a criminal matter and prior to the imposition of sentence, a lawyer or law firm associated with the prosecution or defense shall not make or participate in making an extra-judicial statement that a reasonable person would expect to be disseminated by public communication and that is reasonably likely to affect the imposition of sentence.

(F) The foregoing provisions of DR 7-107 also apply to professional disciplinary proceedings and juvenile disciplinary proceedings when pertinent and consistent with other law applicable to such proceedings.

(G) A lawyer or law firm associated with a civil action shall not during its investigation or litigation make or participate in making an extra-judicial statement, other than a quotation from or reference to public records, that a reasonable person would expect to be disseminated by means of public communication and that relates to:

(1) Evidence regarding the occurrence or transaction involved.

(2) The character, credibility, or criminal record of a party, witness, or prospective witness.

(3) The performance or results of any examinations or tests or the refusal or failure of a party to submit to such.

(4) His opinion as to the merits of the claims or defenses of a party, except as required by law or administrative rule.

(5) Any other matter reasonably likely to interfere with a fair trial of the action.

(H) During the pendency of an administrative proceeding, a lawyer or law firm associated therewith shall not make or participate in making a statement, other than a quotation from or reference to public records, that a reasonable person would expect to be disseminated by means of public communication if it is made outside the official course of the proceeding and relates to:

(1) Evidence regarding the occurrence or transaction involved.

(2) The character, credibility, or criminal record of a party, witness, or prospective witness.

(3) Physical evidence or the performance or results of any examinations or tests or the refusal or failure of a party to submit to such.

(4) His opinion as to the merits of the claims, defenses, or positions of an interested person.

(5) Any other matter reasonably likely to interfere with a fair hearing.

(I) The foregoing provisions of DR 7-107 do not preclude a lawyer from replying to charges of misconduct publicly made against him or from participating in the proceedings of legislative, administrative, or other investigative bodies.

(J) A lawyer shall exercise reasonable care to prevent his employees and associates from making an extra-judicial statement that he would be prohibited from making under DR 7-107.

DR 7-108 Communication With or Investigation of Jurors.

(A) Before the trial of a case a lawyer connected therewith shall not communicate with or cause another to communicate with anyone he knows to be a member of the venire from which the jury will be selected for the trial of the case.

(B) During the trial of a case:

(1) A lawyer connected therewith shall not communicate with or cause another to communicate with any member of the jury.[86]

(2) A lawyer who is not connected therewith shall not communicate with or cause another to communicate with a juror concerning the case.

(C) DR 7-108(A) and (B) do not prohibit a lawyer from communicating with veniremen or jurors in the course of official proceedings.

(D) After discharge of the jury from further consideration of a case with which the lawyer was connected, the lawyer shall not ask questions of or make comments to a member of that jury that are calculated merely to harass or embarrass the juror or to influence his actions in future jury service.[87]

(E) A lawyer shall not conduct or cause, by financial support or otherwise, another to conduct a vexatious or harassing investigation of either a venireman or a juror.

(F) All restrictions imposed by DR 7-108 upon a lawyer also apply to communications with or investigations of members of a family of a venireman or a juror.

(G) A lawyer shall reveal promptly to the court improper conduct by a venireman or a juror, or by another toward a

---

86. See ABA Canon 23.

87. "[I]t would be unethical for a lawyer to harass, entice, induce or exert influence on a juror to obtain his testimony." *ABA Opinion* 319 (1968).

venireman or a juror or a member of his family, of which the lawyer has knowledge.

DR 7-109   Contact With Witnesses.

(A) A lawyer shall not suppress any evidence that he or his client has a legal obligation to reveal or produce.[88]

(B) A lawyer shall not advise or cause a person to secrete himself or to leave the jurisdiction of a tribunal for the purpose of making him unavailable as a witness therein.[89]

(C) A lawyer shall not pay, offer to pay, or acquiesce in the payment of compensation to a witness contingent upon the content of his testimony or the outcome of the case.[90] But a lawyer may advance, guarantee, or acquiesce in the payment of:

  (1) Expenses reasonably incurred by a witness in attending or testifying.

  (2) Reasonable compensation to a witness for his loss of time in attending or testifying.

  (3) A reasonable fee for the professional services of an expert witness.

DR 7-110   Contact With Officials.[91]

(A) A lawyer shall not give or lend any thing of value to a judge, official, or employee of a tribunal, except as permitted by Section C(4) of Canon 5 of the Code of Judicial Conduct, but a lawyer may make a contribution to the campaign fund of a candidate for judicial office in conformity with Section B(2) under Canon 7 of the Code of Judicial Conduct.

(B) In an adversary proceeding, a lawyer shall not communicate, or cause another to communicate, as to the merits of the cause with a judge or an official before whom the proceeding is pending, except:

  (1) In the course of official proceedings in the cause.

  (2) In writing if he promptly delivers a copy of the writing to opposing counsel or to the adverse party if he is not represented by a lawyer.

  (3) Orally upon adequate notice to opposing counsel or to the adverse party if he is not represented by a lawyer.

---

88. See ABA Canon 5.

89. Cf. ABA Canon 5.

"*Rule 15.* . . . A member of the State Bar shall not advise a person, whose testimony could establish or tend to establish a material fact, to avoid service of process, or secrete himself, or otherwise to make his testimony unavailable." Cal.Business and Professions Code § 6076 (West 1962).

90. See In re O'Keefe, 49 Mont. 369, 142 P. 638 (1914).

91. Cf. ABA Canon 3.

(4) As otherwise authorized by law, or by Section A(4) under Canon 3 of the Code of Judicial Conduct.[92]

As amended in 1974.

CANON 8

A Lawyer Should Assist in Improving the Legal System

ETHICAL CONSIDERATIONS

EC 8–1 Changes in human affairs and imperfections in human institutions make necessary constant efforts to maintain and improve our legal system.[1] This system should function in a manner that commands public respect and fosters the use of legal remedies to achieve redress of grievances. By reason of education and experience, lawyers are especially qualified to recognize deficiencies in the legal system and to initiate corrective measures therein. Thus they should participate in proposing and supporting legislation and programs to improve the system,[2] without regard to the general interests or desires of clients or former clients.[3]

---

92. "*Rule 16. ...* A member of the State Bar shall not, in the absence of opposing counsel, communicate with or argue to a judge or judicial officer except in open court upon the merits of a contested matter pending before such judge or judicial officer; nor shall he, without furnishing opposing counsel with a copy thereof, address a written communication to a judge or judicial officer concerning the merits of a contested matter pending before such judge or judicial officer. This rule shall not apply to ex parte matters." Cal.Business and Professions Code § 6076 (West 1962).

1. "... [Another] task of the great lawyer is to do his part individually and as a member of the organized bar to improve his profession, the courts, and the law. As President Theodore Roosevelt aptly put it, 'Every man owes some of his time to the upbuilding of the profession to which he belongs.' Indeed, this obligation is one of the great things which distinguishes a profession from a business. The soundness and the necessity of President Roosevelt's admonition insofar as it relates to the legal profession cannot be doubted. The advances in natural science and technology are so startling and the velocity of change in business and in social life is so great that the law along with the other social sciences, and even human life itself, is in grave dan-

ger of being extinguished by new gods of its own invention if it does not awake from its lethargy." Vanderbilt, *The Five Functions of the Lawyer: Service to Clients and the Public,* 40 A.B.A.J. 31, 31–32 (1954).

2. See ABA Cannon 29; Cf. Cheatham, *The Lawyer's Role and Surroundings,* 25 Rocky Mt.L.Rev. 405, 406–07 (1953).

"The lawyer tempted by repose should recall the heavy costs paid by his profession when needed legal reform has to be accomplished through the initiative of public-spirited laymen. Where change must be thrust from without upon an unwilling Bar, the public's least flattering picture of the lawyer seems confirmed. The lawyer concerned for the standing of his profession will, therefore, interest himself actively in the improvement of the law. In doing so he will not only help to maintain confidence in the Bar, but will have the satisfaction of meeting a responsibility inhering in the nature of his calling." *Professional Responsibility: Report of the Joint Conference,* 44 A.B.A.J. 1159, 1217 (1958).

3. See Stayton, *Cum Honore Officium,* 19 Tex.B.J. 765, 766 (1956); *Professional Responsibility: Report of the Joint Conference,* 44 A.B.A.J. 1159, 1162 (1958); and Paul, *The Lawyer as a Tax Adviser,* 25 Rocky Mt.L.Rev. 412, 433–34 (1953).

EC 8–2 Rules of law are deficient if they are not just, understandable, and responsive to the needs of society. If a lawyer believes that the existence or absence of a rule of law, substantive or procedural, causes or contributes to an unjust result, he should endeavor by lawful means to obtain appropriate change in the law. He should encourage the simplification of laws and the repeal or amendment of laws that are outmoded.[4] Likewise, legal procedures should be improved whenever experience indicates a change is needed.

EC 8–3 The fair administration of justice requires the availability of competent lawyers. Members of the public should be educated to recognize the existence of legal problems and the resultant need for legal services, and should be provided methods for intelligent selection of counsel. Those persons unable to pay for legal services should be provided needed services. Clients and lawyers should not be penalized by undue geographical restraints upon representation in legal matters, and the bar should address itself to improvements in licensing, reciprocity, and admission procedures consistent with the needs of modern commerce.

EC 8–4 Whenever a lawyer seeks legislative or administrative changes, he should identify the capacity in which he appears, whether on behalf of himself, a client, or the public.[5] A lawyer may advocate such changes on behalf of a client even though he does not agree with them. But when a lawyer purports to act on behalf of the public, he should espouse only those changes which he conscientiously believes to be in the public interest.

EC 8–5 Fraudulent, deceptive, or otherwise illegal conduct by a participant in a proceeding before a tribunal or legislative body is inconsistent with fair administration of justice, and it should never be participated in or condoned by lawyers. Unless constrained by his obligation to preserve the confidences and secrets of his client, a lawyer should reveal to appropriate authorities any knowledge he may have of such improper conduct.

EC 8–6 Judges and administrative officials having adjudicatory powers ought to be persons of integrity, competence, and suitable temperament. Generally, lawyers are qualified, by personal observation or investiga-

---

4. "There are few great figures in the history of the Bar who have not concerned themselves with the reform and improvement of the law. The special obligation of the profession with respect to legal reform rests on considerations too obvious to require enumeration. Certainly it is the lawyer who has both the best chance to know when the law is working badly and the special competence to put it in order." *Professional Responsibility: Report of the Joint Conference,* 44 A.B.A.J. 1159, 1217 (1958).

5. "*Rule 14.* ... A member of the State Bar shall not communicate with, or appear before, a public officer, board, committee or body, in his professional capacity, without first disclosing that he is an attorney representing interests that may be affected by action of such officer, board, committee or body." Cal.Business and Professions Code § 6076 (West 1962).

tion, to evaluate the qualifications of persons seeking or being considered for such public offices, and for this reason they have a special responsibility to aid in the selection of only those who are qualified.[6] It is the duty of lawyers to endeavor to prevent political considerations from outweighing judicial fitness in the selection of judges. Lawyers should protest earnestly against the appointment or election of those who are unsuited for the bench and should strive to have elected [7] or appointed thereto only those who are willing to forego pursuits, whether of a business, political, or other nature, that may interfere with the free and fair consideration of questions presented for adjudication. Adjudicatory officials, not being wholly free to defend themselves, are entitled to receive the support of the bar against unjust criticism.[8] While a lawyer as a citizen has a right to criticize such officials publicly,[9] he should be certain of the merit of his complaint, use appropriate language, and avoid petty criticisms, for unrestrained and intemperate statements tend to lessen public confidence in our legal system.[10] Criticisms motivated

6. See ABA Canon 2.

"Lawyers are better able than laymen to appraise accurately the qualifications of candidates for judicial office. It is proper that they should make that appraisal known to the voters in a proper and dignified manner. A lawyer may with propriety endorse a candidate for judicial office and seek like endorsement from other lawyers. But the lawyer who endorses a judicial candidate or seeks that endorsement from other lawyers should be actuated by a sincere belief in the superior qualifications of the candidate for judicial service and not by personal or selfish motives; and a lawyer should not use or attempt to use the power or prestige of the judicial office to secure such endorsement. On the other hand, the lawyer whose endorsement is sought, if he believes the candidate lacks the essential qualifications for the office or believes the opposing candidate is better qualified, should have the courage and moral stamina to refuse the request for endorsement." *ABA Opinion* 189 (1938).

7. "[W]e are of the opinion that, whenever a candidate for judicial office merits the endorsement and support of lawyers, the lawyers may make financial contributions toward the campaign if its cost, when reasonably conducted, exceeds that which the candidate would be expected to bear personally." *ABA Opinion* 226 (1941).

8. See ABA Canon 1.

9. "Citizens have a right under our constitutional system to criticize governmental officials and agencies. Courts are not, and should not be, immune to such criticism." Konigsberg v. State Bar of California, 353 U.S. 252, 269 (1957).

10. "[E]very lawyer, worthy of respect, realizes that public confidence in our courts is the cornerstone of our governmental structure, and will refrain from unjustified attack on the character of the judges, while recognizing the duty to denounce and expose a corrupt or dishonest judge." Kentucky State Bar Ass'n v. Lewis, 282 S.W.2d 321, 326 (Ky.1955).

"We should be the last to deny that Mr. Meeker has the right to uphold the honor of the profession and to expose without fear or favor corrupt or dishonest conduct in the profession, whether the conduct be that of a judge or not.... However, this Canon [29] does not permit one to make charges which are false and untrue and unfounded in fact. When one's fancy leads him to make false charges, attacking the character and integrity of others, he does so at his peril. He should not do so without adequate proof of his charges and he is certainly not authorized to make careless, untruthful and vile charges against his professional brethren." In re Meeker, 76 N.M. 354, 364–65, 414 P.2d 862, 869 (1966), appeal dismissed, 385 U.S. 449, 17 L.Ed.2d 510, 87 S.Ct. 613 (1967).

by reasons other than a desire to improve the legal system are not justified.

EC 8–7 Since lawyers are a vital part of the legal system, they should be persons of integrity, of professional skill, and of dedication to the improvement of the system. Thus a lawyer should aid in establishing, as well as enforcing, standards of conduct adequate to protect the public by insuring that those who practice law are qualified to do so.

EC 8–8 Lawyers often serve as legislators or as holders of other public offices. This is highly desirable, as lawyers are uniquely qualified to make significant contributions to the improvement of the legal system. A lawyer who is a public officer, whether full or part-time, should not engage in activities in which his personal or professional interests are or foreseeably may be in conflict with his official duties.[11]

EC 8–9 The advancement of our legal system is of vital importance in maintaining the rule of law and in facilitating orderly changes; therefore, lawyers should encourage, and should aid in making, needed changes and improvements.

DISCIPLINARY RULES

DR 8–101   Action as a Public Official.

(A) A lawyer who holds public office shall not:

    (1) Use his public position to obtain, or attempt to obtain, a special advantage in legislative matters for himself or for a client under circumstances where he knows or it is obvious that such action is not in the public interest.

---

11. *"Opinions 16, 30, 34, 77, 118* and *134* relate to *Canon 6,* and pass on questions concerning the propriety of the conduct of an attorney who is a public officer, in representing private interests adverse to those of the public body which he represents. The principle applied in those opinions is that an attorney holding public office should avoid all conduct which might lead the layman to conclude that the attorney is utilizing his public position to further his professional success or personal interests." *ABA Opinion* 192 (1939).

"The next question is whether a lawyer-member of a legislative body may appear as counsel or co-counsel at hearings before a zoning board of appeals, or similar tribunal, created by the legislative group of which he is a member. We are of the opinion that he may practice before fact-finding officers, hearing bodies and commissioners, since under our views he may appear as counsel

in the courts where his municipality is a party. Decisions made at such hearings are usually subject to administrative review by the courts upon the record there made. It would be inconsistent to say that a lawyer-member of a legislative body could not participate in a hearing at which the record is made, but could appear thereafter when the cause is heard by the courts on administrative review. This is subject to an important exception. He should not appear as counsel where the matter is subject to review by the legislative body of which he is a member.... We are of the opinion that where a lawyer does so appear there would be conflict of interests between his duty as an advocate for his client on the one hand and the obligation to his governmental unit on the other." In re Becker, 16 Ill.2d 488, 494–95, 158 N.E.2d 753, 756–57 (1959).

Cf. *ABA Opinions* 186 (1938), 136 (1935), 118 (1934), and 77 (1932).

(2) Use his public position to influence, or attempt to influence, a tribunal to act in favor of himself or of a client.

(3) Accept any thing of value from any person when the lawyer knows or it is obvious that the offer is for the purpose of influencing his action as a public official.

DR 8–102   Statements Concerning Judges and Other Adjudicatory Officers.[12]

(A) A lawyer shall not knowingly make false statements of fact concerning the qualifications of a candidate for election or appointment to a judicial office.

(B) A lawyer shall not knowingly make false accusations against a judge or other adjudicatory officer.

DR 8–103   Lawyer Candidate for Judicial Office.

(A) A lawyer who is a candidate for judicial office shall comply with the applicable provisions of Canon 7 of the Code of Judicial Conduct.

Added in 1974.

CANON 9

A Lawyer Should Avoid Even the Appearance of Professional Impropriety

ETHICAL CONSIDERATIONS

EC 9–1 Continuation of the American concept that we are to be governed by rules of law requires that the people have faith that justice can be obtained through our legal system.[1] A lawyer should promote public confidence in our system and in the legal profession.[2]

EC 9–2 Public confidence in law and lawyers may be eroded by irresponsible or improper conduct of a lawyer. On occasion, ethical conduct of a lawyer may appear to laymen to be unethical. In order to avoid misunderstandings and hence to maintain confidence, a lawyer should fully and promptly inform his client of material developments in the

---

12.   Cf. ABA Canons 1 and 2.

1.   "Integrity is the very breath of justice. Confidence in our law, our courts, and in the administration of justice is our supreme interest. No practice must be permitted to prevail which invites towards the administration of justice a doubt or distrust of its integrity." Erwin M. Jennings Co. v. DiGenova, 107 Conn. 491, 499, 141 A. 866, 868 (1928).

2.   "A lawyer should never be reluctant or too proud to answer unjustified criticism of his profession, of himself, or of his brother lawyer. He should guard the reputation of his profession and of his brothers as zealously as he guards his own." Rochelle and Payne, *The Struggle for Public Understanding*, 25 Texas B.J. 109, 162 (1962).

matters being handled for the client. While a lawyer should guard against otherwise proper conduct that has a tendency to diminish public confidence in the legal system or in the legal profession, his duty to clients or to the public should never be subordinate merely because the full discharge of his obligation may be misunderstood or may tend to subject him or the legal profession to criticism. When explicit ethical guidance does not exist, a lawyer should determine his conduct by acting in a manner that promotes public confidence in the integrity and efficiency of the legal system and the legal profession.[3]

EC 9–3 After a lawyer leaves judicial office or other public employment, he should not accept employment in connection with any matter in which he had substantial responsibility prior to his leaving, since to accept employment would give the appearance of impropriety even if none exists.[4]

EC 9–4 Because the very essence of the legal system is to provide procedures by which matters can be presented in an impartial manner so that they may be decided solely upon the merits, any statement or suggestion by a lawyer that he can or would attempt to circumvent those procedures is detrimental to the legal system and tends to undermine public confidence in it.

EC 9–5 Separation of the funds of a client from those of his lawyer not only serves to protect the client but also avoids even the appearance of impropriety, and therefore commingling of such funds should be avoided.

EC 9–6 Every lawyer owes a solemn duty to uphold the integrity and honor of his profession; to encourage respect for the law and for the courts and the judges thereof; to observe the Code of Professional Responsibility; to act as a member of a learned profession, one dedicated to public service; to cooperate with his brother lawyers in supporting the organized bar through the devoting of his time, efforts, and financial support as his professional standing and ability reasonably permit; to conduct himself so as to reflect credit on the legal profession and to inspire the confidence, respect, and trust of his clients and of the public; and to strive to avoid not only professional impropriety but also the appearance of impropriety.[5]

3. See ABA Canon 29.

4. See ABA Canon 36.

5. "As said in Opinion 49 of the Committee on Professional Ethics and Grievances of the American Bar Association, page 134: 'An attorney should not only avoid impropriety but should avoid the appearance of impropriety.' " State ex rel. Nebraska State Bar Ass'n v. Richards, 165 Neb. 80, 93, 84 N.W.2d 136, 145 (1957).

"It would also be preferable that such contribution [to the campaign of a candidate for judicial office] be made to a campaign committee rather than to the candidate personally. In so doing, possible appearances of impropriety would be reduced to a minimum." *ABA Opinion* 226 (1941).

"The lawyer assumes high duties, and has imposed upon him grave responsibilities. He may be the means of much good or much mischief. Interests of vast magnitude are entrusted to him; confidence is reposed in him; life, liberty, character and

EC 9-7 A lawyer has an obligation to the public to participate in collective efforts of the bar to reimburse persons who have lost money or property as a result of the misappropriation or defalcation of another lawyer, and contribution to a clients' security fund is an acceptable method of meeting this obligation.

DISCIPLINARY RULES

DR 9-101   Avoiding Even the Appearance of Impropriety.[6]

(A) A lawyer shall not accept private employment in a matter upon the merits of which he has acted in a judicial capacity.[7]

(B) A lawyer shall not accept private employment in a matter in which he had substantial responsibility while he was a public employee.[8]

property should be protected by him. He should guard, with jealous watchfulness, his own reputation, as well as that of his profession." People ex rel. Cutler v. Ford, 54 Ill. 520, 522 (1870), and also quoted in State Board of Law Examiners v. Sheldon, 43 Wyo. 522, 526, 7 P.2d 226, 227 (1932).

See *ABA Opinion* 150 (1936).

6. Cf. Code of Professional Responsibility, EC 5-6.

7. See *ABA* Canon 36.

"It is the duty of the judge to rule on questions of law and evidence in misdemeanor cases and examinations in felony cases. That duty calls for impartial and uninfluenced judgment, regardless of the effect on those immediately involved or others who may, directly or indirectly, be affected. Discharge of that duty might be greatly interfered with if the judge, in another capacity, were permitted to hold himself out to employment by those who are to be, or who may be, brought to trial in felony cases, even though he did not conduct the examination. His private interests as a lawyer in building up his clientele, his duty as such zealously to espouse the cause of his private clients and to defend against charges of crime brought by law-enforcement agencies of which he is a part, might prevent, or even destroy, that unbiased judicial judgment which is so essential in the administration of justice.

"In our opinion, acceptance of a judgeship with the duties of conducting misdemeanor trials, and examinations in felony cases to determine whether those accused should be bound over for trial in a higher court, ethically bars the judge from acting as attorney for the defendants upon such trial, whether they were examined by him or by some other judge. Such a practice would not only diminish public confidence in the administration of justice in both courts, but would produce serious conflict between the private interests of the judge as a lawyer, and of his clients, and his duties as a judge in adjudicating important phases of criminal processes in other cases. The public and private duties would be incompatible. The prestige of the judicial office would be diverted to private benefit, and the judicial office would be demeaned thereby." *ABA Opinion* 242 (1942).

"A lawyer, who has previously occupied a judicial position or acted in a judicial capacity, should refrain from accepting employment in any matter involving the same facts as were involved in any specific question which he acted upon in a judicial capacity and, for the same reasons, should also refrain from accepting any employment which might reasonably appear to involve the same facts." *ABA Opinion* 49 (1931).

See *ABA Opinion* 110 (1934).

8. See *ABA Opinions* 135 (1935) and 134 (1935); cf. ABA Canon 36 and *ABA Opinions* 39 (1931) and 26 (1930). But see *ABA Opinion* 37 (1931).

(C) A lawyer shall not state or imply that he is able to influence improperly or upon irrelevant grounds any tribunal, legislative body,[9] or public official.

DR 9–102   Preserving Identity of Funds and Property of a Client.[10]

(A) All funds of clients paid to a lawyer or law firm, other than advances for costs and expenses, shall be deposited in one or more identifiable bank accounts maintained in the state in which the law office is situated and no funds belonging to the lawyer or law firm shall be deposited therein except as follows:

> **(1) Funds reasonably sufficient to pay bank charges may be deposited therein.**

> **(2) Funds belonging in part to a client and in part presently or potentially to the lawyer or law firm must be deposited therein, but the portion belonging to the lawyer or law firm may be withdrawn when due unless the right of the lawyer or law firm to receive it is disputed by the client, in which event the disputed portion shall not be withdrawn until the dispute is finally resolved.**

(B) A lawyer shall:

> **(1) Promptly notify a client of the receipt of his funds, securities, or other properties.**

---

9. "[A statement by a governmental department or agency with regard to a lawyer resigning from its staff that includes a laudation of his legal ability] carries implications, probably not founded in fact, that the lawyer's acquaintance and previous relations with the personnel of the administrative agencies of the government place him in an advantageous position in practicing before such agencies. So to imply would not only represent what probably is untrue, but would be highly reprehensible." *ABA Opinion* 184 (1938).

10. See ABA Canon 11.

"*Rule 9.* . . . A member of the State Bar shall not commingle the money or other property of a client with his own; and he shall promptly report to the client the receipt by him of all money and other property belonging to such client. Unless the client otherwise directs in writing, he shall promptly deposit his client's funds in a bank or trust company . . . in a bank account separate from his own account and clearly designated as 'Clients' Funds Account' or 'Trust Funds Account' or words of similar import. Unless the client otherwise directs in writing, securities of a client in bearer form shall be kept by the attorney in a safe deposit box at a bank or trust company, . . . which safe deposit box shall be clearly designated as 'Client's Account' or 'Trust Account' or words of similar import, and be separate from the attorney's own safe deposit box." Cal.Business and Professions Code § 6076 (West 1962).

"[C]ommingling is committed when a client's money is intermingled with that of his attorney and its separate identity lost so that it may be used for the attorney's personal expenses or subjected to claims of his creditors.... The rule against commingling was adopted to provide against the probability in some cases, the possibility in many cases, and the danger in all cases that such commingling will result in the loss of clients' money." Black v. State Bar, 57 Cal.2d 219, 225–26, 368 P.2d 118, 122, 18 Cal.Rptr. 518, 522 (1962).

(2) Identify and label securities and properties of a client promptly upon receipt and place them in a safe deposit box or other place of safekeeping as soon as practicable.

(3) Maintain complete records of all funds, securities, and other properties of a client coming into the possession of the lawyer and render appropriate accounts to his client regarding them.

(4) Promptly pay or deliver to the client as requested by a client the funds, securities, or other properties in the possession of the lawyer which the client is entitled to receive.

DEFINITIONS *

As used in the Disciplinary Rules of the Code of Professional Responsibility:

(1) "Differing interests" include every interest that will adversely affect either the judgment or the loyalty of a lawyer to a client, whether it be a conflicting, inconsistent, diverse, or other interest.

(2) "Law firm" includes a professional legal corporation.

(3) "Person" includes a corporation, an association, a trust, a partnership, and any other organization or legal entity.

(4) "Professional legal corporation" means a corporation, or an association treated as a corporation, authorized by law to practice law for profit.

(5) "State" includes the District of Columbia, Puerto Rico, and other federal territories and possessions.

(6) "Tribunal" includes all courts and all other adjudicatory bodies.

(7) "A Bar association" includes a bar association of specialists as referred to in DR 2-105(A)(1) or (3).

(8) "Qualified legal assistance organization" means an office or organization of one of the four types listed in DR 2-103(D)(1)-(4), inclusive that meets all the requirements thereof.

As amended in 1974.

* "Confidence" and "secret" are defined in DR 4-101(A).

INDEX TO ABA MODEL CODE

A

Acceptance of Employment. *See* Employment, acceptance of.

Acquiring interest in litigation. *See* Adverse effect on professional judgment, interests of lawyer.

Address change, notification of, DR 2–102 (A) (2)

Administrative agencies and tribunals,
  former employee, rejection of employment by, DR 9–101 (B)
  improper influences on, EC 5–13, EC 5–21, EC 5–24, DR 5–107 (A), (B), EC 8–5, EC 8–6, DR 8–101 (A)
  representation of client, generally, Canon 7, EC 7–15, EC 7–16, EC 8–4, EC 8–8, DR 8–101 (A)

Admiralty practitioners, EC 2–14

Admission to practice,
  duty of lawyers as to applicants, EC 1–3, DR 1–101 (B)
  requirements for, EC 1–2, EC 1–3, EC 1–6, DR 1–101 (A)

Advancing funds to clients, EC 5–8, DR 5–103 (B)
  court costs, EC 5–8, DR 5–103 (B)
  investigation expenses, EC 5–8, DR 5–103 (B)
  litigation expenses, EC 5–7, EC 5–8, DR 5–103 (B)
  medical examination, EC 5–8, DR 5–103 (B)
  personal expenses, EC 5–8, DR 5–103 (B)

Adversary system, duty of lawyer to, Canon 7

Adverse effect on professional judgment of lawyer, Canon 5
  desires of third persons, EC 5–21 – EC 5–24, DR 5–107
  interests of lawyer, EC 5–2 – EC 5–13, DR 5–101, DR 5–104
  interests of other clients, EC 5–14 – EC 5–20, DR 5–105, DR 5–106

Adverse legal authority, duty to reveal, EC 7–23, DR 7–106 (B) (1)

Advertising,
  See also Name, use of. EC 2–6 – EC 2–15, DR 2–101, DR 2–102
  announcement of change of association, DR 2–102 (A) (2)

Advertising—Cont'd
  announcement of change of firm name, DR 2–102 (A) (2)
  announcement of change of office address, DR 2–102 (A) (2)
  announcement of establishment of law office, DR 2–102 (A) (2)
  announcement of office opening, DR 2–102 (A) (2)
  books written by lawyer, DR 2–101 (H) (5)
  building directory, DR 2–102 (A) (3)
  cards, professional announcement, DR 2–102 (A) (1), (2)
  commercial publicity, EC 2–8 – EC 2–10, DR 2–101
  compensation for, EC 2–8, DR 2–101 (B), DR 2–101 (I)
  jurisdictional limitations of members of firm, required, notice of, DR 2–102 (D)
  legal documents, DR 2–101 (H) (4)
  letterheads,
    of clients, DR 2–102 (A) (4)
    of law firm, DR 2–102 (A) (4), DR 2–102 (B)
    of lawyer, DR 2–102 (A) (4), DR 2–102 (B)
  limited practice, EC 2–14, DR 2–101 (B) (2), DR 2–105
  magazine, DR 2–101 (B), DR 2–101 (I)
  name, *See* Name, use of newspaper, DR 2–101 (B), DR 2–101 (I)
  office, identification of, DR 2–101 (B) (1), DR 2–102 (A)
  office address change, DR 2–102 (A) (2)
  office building directory, DR 2–102 (A) (3)
  office establishment, DR 2–102 (A) (2)
  office sign, DR 2–102 (A) (3)
  political, DR 2–101 (H) (1)
  public notices, DR 2–101 (H) (2)
  radio, DR 2–101 (B), DR 2–101 (D), DR 2–101 (I)
  reasons for regulating, EC 2–6 – EC 2–10
  sign, DR 2–102 (A) (3)
  specialization, EC 2–14, DR 2–101 (B) (2), DR 2–105
  television, EC 2–8, DR 2–101 (B), (D)
  textbook, DR 2–101 (H) (5)
  treatises, DR 2–101 (H) (5)

Advice by lawyer to secure legal services, EC 24 – EC 2-5, DR 2-104
> client, former or regular, EC 2-4, DR 2-104 (A) (1)
> close friend, EC 2-4, DR 2-104 (A) (1)
> employment resulting from, EC 2-4, DR 2-104
> motivation, effect of, EC 2-4
> other laymen parties to class action, DR 2-104 (A) (5)
> relative, EC 2-4, DR 2-104 (A) (1)
> volunteered, EC 2-4, DR 2-104
> within permissible legal service programs, DR 2-104 (A) (3)

Advocacy, professional, Canon 7

Aiding unauthorized practice of law, Canon 3

Ambulance chasing. *See* Recommendation of professional employment.

Announcement card. *See* Advertising, cards, professional announcement.

Appearance of impropriety, avoiding, EC 5-6, Canon 9

Appearance of lawyer. *See* Administrative agencies, representation of client before; Courts, representation of client before; Legislature, representation of client before; Witness, lawyer acting as.

Applicant for bar admission. *See* Admission to practice.

Arbitrator, lawyer acting as, EC 5-20

Argument,
> before administrative agency, EC 7-15
> before jury, EC 7-24, EC 7-25, DR 7-106 (C)
> before legislature, EC 7-16
> before tribunal, EC 7-19 – EC 7-25, DR 7-102, DR 7-106

Associates of lawyer, duty to control, EC 1-4, DR 2-103, EC 3-8, EC 3-9, EC 4-2, DR 4-101 (D), DR 7-107

Association of counsel,
> *See also* Co-counsel; Division of legal fees.
> client's suggestion of, EC 5-10, EC 5-11
> lawyer's suggestion of, EC 5-10, EC 5-11, EC 6-3, DR 6-101 (1)

Assumed name. *See* Name, use of, assumed name.

Attempts to exert personal influence on tribunal, EC 7-24, EC 7-29 – EC 7-33, EC 7-36, DR 7-106 (C), DR 7-108, DR 7-110

Attorney-client privilege. *See also* Confidences of client; Secrets of client. EC 4-4, DR 4-101 (A), DR 7-102 (B) (1)

Attorney's lien. *See* Fee for legal services, collection of. Availability of counsel, EC 2-1, EC 2-7, EC 2-24 – EC 2-33

B

Bank accounts for clients' funds, EC 9-5, DR 9-102

Bank charges on clients' accounts, EC 9-5, DR 9-102

Bar applicant. *See* Admission to practice. bar examiners, assisting, EC 1-2

Bar associations,
> disciplinary authority, assisting, EC 1-4, DR 1-103
> educational activities, EC 6-2
> lawyer referral service, DR 2-103 (C) (1), DR 2-103 (D) (3)
> legal aid office, DR 2-103 (D) (1) (d)

Barratry. *See* Advice by lawyer to secure legal services; Recommendation of professional employment.

Bequest by client to lawyer, EC 5-5

Best efforts. *See* Zeal.

Bounds of law,
> difficulty of ascertaining, EC 7-2, EC 7-3, EC 7-4, EC 7-6
> duty to observe, EC 7-1, DR 7-102
> generally, Canon 7

Bribes. *See* Gifts to tribunal officer or employee by lawyer.

Building directory. *See* Advertising, building directory.

Business card. *See* Advertising, cards, professional.

C

Calling card. *See* Advertising, cards, professional.

Candidate. *See* Political activity.

Canons, purpose and function of, Preamble & Preliminary Statement

Cards. *See* Advertising, cards.

Change of association. *See* Advertising, announcement of change of association.

Change of firm name. *See* Advertising, announcement of change of firm name.

Change of office address. *See* Advertising, announcement of change of office address.

Character requirements, EC 1-3

Class action. *See* Advice by lawyer to secure legal services, parties to legal action.

Clients,
> *See also* Employment; Adverse effect on professional judgment of lawyer; Fee for legal services; Indigent parties, representation of; Unpopular party, representation of.
> appearance as witness for, EC 5-9, EC 5-10, DR 5-101 (B), DR 5-102
> attorney-client privilege, Canon 4

Fee for legal services—Cont'd
determination of, factors to consider,
ability of lawyer, EC 2–18, DR 2–106
(B) (7)
amount involved, DR 2–106 (B) (4)
customary, DR 2–106 (B) (3)
effort required, DR 2–106 (B) (1)
employment, likelihood of preclusion
of other, DR 2–106 (B) (2)
experience of lawyer, EC 2–18, DR
2–106 (B) (7)
fee customarily charged in locality,
DR 2–106 (B) (3)
interests of client and lawyer, EC
2–17
labor required, DR 2–106 (B) (1)
nature of employment, EC 2–18
question involved, difficulty and novelty of, DR 2–106 (B) (1)
relationship with client, professional,
EC 2–17, DR 2–106 (B) (6)
reputation of lawyer, EC 2–18, DR
2–106 (7)
responsibility assumed by lawyer, EC
2–18
results obtained, EC 2–18, DR 2–106
(B) (4)
skill requisite to services, EC 2–18
time required, EC 2–18, DR 2–106
(B) (1)
type of fee, fixed or contingent, EC
2–18, DR 2–106 (B) (8)
division of, EC 2–22, DR 2–107, DR
3–102
establishment of fee, use of client's confidences and secrets, DR 4–101
(C) (4)
excessive fee, EC 2–17, DR 2–106 (A)
explanation of, EC 2–17, EC 2–18
illegal fee, prohibition against, DR 2–106
(A)
persons able to pay reasonable fee, EC
2–17, EC 2–18
persons only able to pay a partial fee,
EC 2–16
persons without means to pay a fee, EC
2–24, EC 2–25
reasonable fee, rational against overcharging, EC 2–17
refund of unearned portion to client, DR
2–110 (A) (3)
Felony. See Discipline of lawyer, grounds
for, illegal conduct.
Firm name. See Name, use of, firm name.
Framework of law. See Bounds of law.
Frivolous position, avoiding, EC 7–4, DR
7–102 (A) (1)
Funds of client, protection of, EC 9–5, DR
9–102
Future conduct of client, counseling as to.
See Clients, counseling.

G

"General counsel" designation, DR 2–102
(A) (4)
Gift to lawyer by client, EC 5–5
Gifts to tribunal officer or employee by lawyer, DR 7–110 (A)
Government legal assistance agencies,
working with, DR 2–103 (C) (2), DR
2–103 (D) (1) (C)
Grievance committee. See Bar associations, disciplinary authority, assisting.
Guaranteeing payment of client's cost and
expenses, EC 5–8, DR 5–103 (B)

H

Harassment, duty to avoid litigation involving, EC 2–30, DR 2–109 (A) (1), DR
7–102 (A) (1)
as limiting practice, EC 2–8, EC 2–14,
DR 2–101 (B) (2), DR 2–105
as partnership, EC 2–13, DR 2–102 (C)
as specialist, EC 2–8, EC 2–14, DR
2–101 (B) (2), DR 2–105

I

Identity of client, duty to reveal, EC 7–16,
EC 8–5
Illegal conduct, as cause for discipline, EC
1–5, DR 1–102 (A) (3), DR 7–102 (A)
(7)
Impartiality of tribunal, aiding in the, Canon 7
Improper influences,
gift or loan to judicial officer, EC 7–34,
DR 7–110 (A)
on judgment of lawyer. See Adverse
effect on professional judgment of
lawyer.
Improvement of legal system, EC 8–1, EC
8–2, EC 8–9
Incompetence, mental. See Instability,
mental or emotional; Mental competence of client.
Incompetence, professional. See Competence, professional.
Independent professional judgment, duty to
preserve, Canon 5
Indigent parties,
provision of legal services to, EC 2–24,
EC 2–25
representation of, EC 2–25
Instability, mental or emotional,
of bar applicant, EC 1–6
of lawyer, EC 1–6, DR 2–110 (B) (3), DR
2–110 (C) (4)
recognition of rehabilitation, EC 1–6

M

N

O

Rebate, propriety of accepting, EC 2–24, EC 2–25

Recognition of legal problems, aiding laymen in, EC 2–1, EC 2–5

Recommendation of bar applicant, duty of lawyer to satisfy himself that applicant is qualified, EC 1–3, DR 1–101 (B)

Recommendation of professional employment, EC 2–8, EC 2–15, DR 2–103

Records of funds, securities, and properties of clients, EC 9–5, DR 9–102 (B)

Referral service. *See* Lawyer referral services.

Refund of unearned fee when withdrawing, duty to give to client, EC 2–32, DR 2–110

Regulation of legal profession, Canons 3 and 8, EC 3–1, EC 3–3, EC 3–9, EC 8–7

Rehabilitation of bar applicant or lawyer, recognition of, EC 1–6

Representation of multiple clients. *See* Adverse effect on professional judgment of lawyer, interest of other clients.

Reputation of lawyer, EC 2–6, EC 2–7

Requests for recommendation for employment, EC 2–8, DR 2–103 (C)

Requirements for bar admission, EC 1–2, EC 1–6, DR 1–101 (B)

Respect for law, EC 1–5

Restrictive covenant, DR 2–108

Retention of employment. *See* Employment.

Retirement,
See also Name, use of, retired partner.
from judicial office, EC 9–3, DR 9–101 (A)
from public employment, EC 9–3, DR 9–101 (B)
plan for laymen employees, EC 3–8, DR 3–102 (3)

Revealing of confidences, EC 4–1, EC 4–2, EC 4–6, DR 4–101 (B) (1), (C), (D)

Revealing of secrets, EC 4–1, EC 4–2, EC 4–6, DR 4–101 (B) (1), (C), (D)

Revealing to tribunal jury misconduct, EC 7–32, DR 7–108 (G)

Runner, prohibition against use of, EC 2–8, DR 2–103 (B)

S

Sanction for violating disciplinary rules, Preliminary Statement

Secrets of client, Canon 4

Selection of judges, duty of lawyers, EC 8–6, DR 8–102 (A)

Selection of lawyer, EC 2–6, EC 2–7, EC 2–8, EC 2–9, EC 2–11, EC 2–14, EC 2–15, DR 2–101

Self-interest of lawyer. *See* Adverse effect on professional judgment of lawyer, interests of lawyer.

Self-representation, privilege of, EC 3–7

Settlement agreement, DR 5–106

Solicitation of business. *See* Advertising: Recommendation of professional employment.

Specialist, holding out as, EC 2–14, DR 2–105

Specialization,
admiralty, EC 2–14
holding out as having, EC 2–14, DR 2–105
patents, EC 2–14, DR 2–105 (A) (1)
trademark, EC 2–14, DR 2–105 (A) (1)

Speeches to lay groups, EC 2–2, EC 2–5

State of mind of client, effect of in advising him, EC 7–11, EC 7–12

State's attorney. *See* Prosecuting attorney.

"Stirring up litigation." *See* Advertising: Advice by lawyer to secure legal services; Recommendation of professional employment.

Stockholders of corporation, corporate counsel's allegiance to, EC 5–18

Suit to harass another, duty to avoid, EC 2–30, DR 2–109 (A) (1), EC 7–10, EC 7–14, DR 7–102 (A) (1)

Suit to maliciously harm another, duty to avoid, EC 2–30, DR 2–109 (A) (1), EC 7–10, EC 7–14, DR 7–102 (A) (1)

Suggested fee schedule. *See* Fees for legal services, determination of minimum fee schedule.

Suggestion of need for legal services. *See* Advice by lawyer to secure legal services.

Suppression of evidence, EC 7–27, DR 7–102 (A) (2), DR 7–103 (B), DR 7–106 (C) (7)

T

Technical and professional licenses, DR 2–101 (B) (12), DR 2–102 (E)

Termination of employment. *See* Confidences of client; Employment, withdrawal from.

Third persons, desires of. *See* Adverse effect on professional judgment of lawyer, desires of third persons.

Threatening criminal process, EC 7–21, DR 7–105 (A)

Trademark practitioner, EC 2–14, DR 2–105 (A) (1)

Trade name. *See* Name, use of, trade name.

AMERICAN BAR ASSOCIATION CANONS OF PROFESSIONAL ETHICS

As amended until 1969.

[The ABA adopted 32 Canons of Professional Ethics at its thirty-first annual meeting on August 27, 1908. Between 1908 and 1969, the ABA added Canons 33 through 47. Although the Canons were in effect for 61 years, the general aspirational approach of the Canons proved to be outmoded to regulate the conduct of lawyers in the 1950s and 1960s. The Canons were superseded in 1969 by the Model Code of Professional Responsibility. Ed.]

CANONS OF PROFESSIONAL ETHICS

Preamble.

In America, where the stability of Courts and of all departments of government rests upon the approval of the people, it is peculiarly essential that the system for establishing and dispensing Justice be developed to a high point of efficiency and so maintained that the public shall have absolute confidence in the integrity and impartiality of its administration. The future of the Republic, to a great extent, depends upon our maintenance of Justice pure and unsullied. It cannot be so maintained unless the conduct and the motives of the members of our profession are such as to merit the approval of all just men.

No code or set of rules can be framed, which will particularize all the duties of the lawyer in the varying phases of litigation or in all the relations of professional life. The following canons of ethics are adopted by the American Bar Association as a general guide, yet the enumeration of particular duties should not be construed as a denial of the existence of others equally imperative, though not specifically mentioned.

CANON 1

The Duty of the Lawyer to the Courts

It is the duty of the lawyer to maintain towards the Courts a respectful attitude, not for the sake of the temporary incumbent of the judicial office, but for the maintenance of its supreme importance. Judges, not being wholly free to defend themselves, are peculiarly entitled to receive the support of the Bar against unjust criticism and clamor. Whenever there is proper ground for serious complaint of a judicial officer, it is the right and duty of the lawyer to submit his grievances to the proper authorities. In such cases, but not otherwise, such charges should be encouraged and the person making them should be protected.

CANON 2

The Selection of Judges

It is the duty of the Bar to endeavor to prevent political considerations from outweighing judicial fitness in the selections of Judges. It should protest earnestly and actively against the appointment or election of those who are unsuitable for the Bench; and it should strive to have elevated thereto only those willing to forego other employments, whether of a business, political or other character, which may embarrass their free and fair consideration of questions before them for decision. The aspiration of lawyers for judicial position should be governed by an impartial estimate of their ability to add honor to the office and not by a desire for the distinction the position may bring to themselves.

CANON 3

Attempts to Exert Personal Influence on the Court

Marked attention and unusual hospitality on the part of a lawyer to a Judge, uncalled for by the personal relations of the parties, subject both the Judge and the lawyer to misconstructions of motive and should be avoided. A lawyer should not communicate or argue privately with the Judge as to the merits of a pending cause, and he deserves rebuke and denunciation for any device or attempt to gain from a Judge special personal consideration or favor. A self-respecting independence in the discharge of professional duty, without denial or diminution of the courtesy and respect due the Judge's station, is the only proper foundation for cordial personal and official relations between Bench and Bar.

CANON 4

When Counsel for an Indigent Prisoner

A lawyer assigned as counsel for an indigent prisoner ought not to ask to be excused for any trivial reason, and should always exert his best efforts on his behalf.

CANON 5

The Defense or Prosecution of Those Accused of Crime

It is the right of the lawyer to undertake the defense of a person accused of crime, regardless of his personal opinion as to the guilt of the accused; otherwise innocent persons, victims only of suspicious circumstances, might be denied proper defense. Having undertaken such defense, the lawyer is bound, by all fair and honorable means, to present every defense that the law of the land permits, to the end that no person may be deprived of life or liberty, but by due process of law.

The primary duty of a lawyer engaged in public prosecution is not to convict, but to see that justice is done. The suppression of facts or the secreting of witnesses capable of establishing the innocence of the accused is highly reprehensible.

CANON 6

Adverse Influences and Conflicting Interests

It is the duty of a lawyer at the time of retainer to disclose to the client all the circumstances of his relations to the parties, and any interest in or connection with the controversy, which might influence the client in the selection of counsel.

It is unprofessional to represent conflicting interests, except by express consent of all concerned given after a full disclosure of the facts. Within the meaning of this canon, a lawyer represents conflicting interests when, in behalf of one client, it is his duty to contend for that which duty to another client requires him to oppose.

The obligation to represent the client with undivided fidelity and not to divulge his secrets or confidences forbids also the subsequent acceptance of retainers or employment from others in matters adversely affecting any interest of the client with respect to which confidence has been reposed.

CANON 7

Professional Colleagues and Conflicts of Opinion

A client's proffer of assistance of additional counsel should not be regarded as evidence of want of confidence, but the matter should be left to the determination of the client. A lawyer should decline association as colleague if it is objectionable to the original counsel, but if the lawyer first retained is relieved, another may come into the case.

When lawyers jointly associated in a cause cannot agree as to any matter vital to the interest of the client, the conflict of opinion should be frankly stated to him for his final determination. His decision should be accepted unless the nature of the difference makes it impracticable for the lawyer whose judgment has been overruled to cooperate effectively. In this event it is his duty to ask the client to relieve him.

Efforts, direct or indirect, in any way to encroach upon the professional employment of another lawyer, are unworthy of those who should be brethren at the Bar; but, nevertheless, it is the right of any lawyer, without fear or favor, to give proper advice to those seeking relief against unfaithful or neglectful counsel, generally after communication with the lawyer of whom the complaint is made.

CANON 8

Advising Upon the Merits of a Client's Cause

A lawyer should endeavor to obtain full knowledge of his client's cause before advising thereon, and he is bound to give a candid opinion of the merits and probable result of pending or contemplated litigation. The miscarriages to which justice is subject, by reason of surprises and disappointments in evidence and witnesses, and through mistakes of juries and errors of Courts, even though only occasional, admonish lawyers to beware of bold and confident assurances to clients, especially where the employment may depend upon such assurance. Whenever the controversy will admit of fair adjustment, the client should be advised to avoid or to end the litigation.

CANON 9

Negotiations With Opposite Party

A lawyer should not in any way communicate upon the subject of controversy with a party represented by counsel; much less should he undertake to negotiate or compromise the matter with him, but should deal only with his counsel. It is incumbent upon the lawyer most particularly to avoid everything that may tend to mislead a party not represented by counsel, and he should not undertake to advise him as to the law.

CANON 10

Acquiring Interest in Litigation

The lawyer should not purchase any interest in the subject matter of the litigation which he is conducting.

CANON 11

Dealing With Trust Property

The lawyer should refrain from any action whereby for his personal benefit or gain he abuses or takes advantage of the confidence reposed in him by his client.

Money of the client or collected for the client or other trust property coming into the possession of the lawyer should be reported and accounted for promptly, and should not under any circumstances be commingled with his own or be used by him.

CANON 12

Fixing the Amount of the Fee

In fixing fees, lawyers should avoid charges which overestimate their advice and services, as well as those which undervalue them. A client's ability to pay cannot justify a charge in excess of the value of the service, though his poverty may require a less charge, or even none at all. The reasonable requests of brother lawyers, and of their widows and orphans without ample means, should receive special and kindly consideration.

In determining the amount of the fee, it is proper to consider: (1) the time and labor required, the novelty and difficulty of the questions involved and the skill requisite properly to conduct the cause; (2) whether the acceptance of employment in the particular case will preclude the lawyer's appearance for others in cases likely to arise out of the transaction, and in which there is a reasonable expectation that otherwise he would be employed, or will involve the loss of other employment while employed in the particular case or antagonisms with other clients; (3) the customary charges of the Bar for similar services; (4) the amount involved in the controversy and the benefits resulting to the client from the services; (5) the contingency or the certainty of the compensation; and (6) the character of the employment, whether casual or for an established and constant client. No one of these considerations in itself is controlling. They are mere guides in ascertaining the real value of the service.

In determining the customary charges of the Bar for similar services, it is proper for a lawyer to consider a schedule of minimum fees adopted by a Bar Association, but no lawyer should permit himself to be controlled thereby or to follow it as his sole guide in determining the amount of his fee.

In fixing fees it should never be forgotten that the profession is a branch of the administration of justice and not a mere money-getting trade.

CANON 13

Contingent Fees

A contract for a contingent fee, where sanctioned by law, should be reasonable under all the circumstances of the case, including the risk and uncertainty of the compensation, but should always be subject to the supervision of a court, as to its reasonableness.

CANON 14

Suing a Client for a Fee

Controversies with clients concerning compensation are to be avoided by the lawyer so far as shall be compatible with his self-respect and with his right to receive reasonable recompense for his services; and lawsuits with clients should be resorted to only to prevent injustice, imposition or fraud.

CANON 15

How Far a Lawyer May Go in Supporting a Client's Cause

Nothing operates more certainly to create or to foster popular prejudice against lawyers as a class, and to deprive the profession of that full measure of public esteem and confidence which belongs to the proper discharge of its duties than does the false claim, often set up by the unscrupulous in defense of questionable transactions, that it is the duty of the lawyer to do whatever may enable him to succeed in winning his client's cause.

It is improper for a lawyer to assert in argument his personal belief in his client's innocence or in the justice of his cause.

The lawyer owes "entire devotion to the interest of the client, warm zeal in the maintenance and defense of his rights and the exertion of his utmost learning and ability," to the end that nothing be taken or be withheld from him, save by the rules of law, legally applied. No fear of judicial disfavor or public unpopularity should restrain him from the full discharge of his duty. In the judicial forum the client is entitled to the benefit of any and every remedy and defense that is authorized by the law of the land, and he may expect his lawyer to assert every such remedy or defense. But it is steadfastly to be borne in mind that the great trust of the lawyer is to be performed within and not without the bounds of the law. The office of attorney does not permit, much less does it demand of him for any client, violation of law or any manner of fraud or chicane. He must obey his own conscience and not that of his client.

CANON 16

Restraining Clients From Improprieties

A lawyer should use his best efforts to restrain and to prevent his clients from doing those things which the lawyer himself ought not to do, particularly with reference to their conduct towards Courts, judicial officers, jurors, witnesses and suitors. If a client persists in such wrongdoing the lawyer should terminate their relation.

CANON 17

Ill–Feeling and Personalities Between Advocates

Clients, not lawyers, are the litigants. Whatever may be the ill-feeling existing between clients, it should not be allowed to influence counsel in their conduct and demeanor toward each other or toward suitors in the case. All personalities between counsel should be scrupulously avoided. In the trial of a cause it is indecent to allude to the personal history or the personal peculiarities and idiosyncrasies of counsel on the other side. Personal colloquies between counsel which cause delay and promote unseemly wrangling should also be carefully avoided.

CANON 18

Treatment of Witnesses and Litigants

A lawyer should always treat adverse witnesses and suitors with fairness and due consideration, and he should never minister to the malevolence or prejudices of a client in the trial or conduct of a cause. The client cannot be made the keeper of the lawyer's conscience in professional matters. He has no right to demand that his counsel shall abuse the opposite party or indulge in offensive personalities. Improper speech is not excusable on the ground that it is what the client would say if speaking in his own behalf.

CANON 19

Appearance of Lawyer as Witness for His Client

When a lawyer is a witness for his client, except as to merely formal matters, such as the attestation or custody of an instrument and the like, he should leave the trial of the case to other counsel. Except when essential to the ends of justice, a lawyer should avoid testifying in court in behalf of his client.

CANON 20

Newspaper Discussion of Pending Litigation

Newspaper publications by a lawyer as to pending or anticipated litigation may interfere with a fair trial in the Courts and otherwise prejudice the due administration of justice.   Generally they are to be condemned.   If the extreme circumstances of a particular case justify a statement to the public, it is unprofessional to make it anonymously. An *ex parte* reference to the facts should not go beyond quotation from the records and papers on file in the court; but even in extreme cases it is better to avoid any *ex parte* statement.

CANON 21

Punctuality and Expedition

It is the duty of the lawyer not only to his client, but also to the Courts and to the public to be punctual in attendance, and to be concise and direct in the trial and disposition of causes.

CANON 22

Candor and Fairness

The conduct of the lawyer before the Court and with other lawyers should be characterized by candor and fairness.

It is not candid or fair for the lawyer knowingly to misquote the contents of a paper, the testimony of a witness, the language or the argument of opposing counsel, or the language of a decision of a textbook; or with knowledge of its invalidity, to cite as authority a decision that has been overruled, or a statute that has been repealed; or in argument to assert as a fact that which has not been proved, or in those jurisdictions where a side has the opening and closing arguments to mislead his opponent by concealing or withholding positions in his opening argument upon which his side then intends to rely.

It is unprofessional and dishonorable to deal other than candidly with the facts in taking the statements of witnesses, in drawing affidavits and other documents, and in the presentation of causes.

A lawyer should not offer evidence which he knows the Court should reject, in order to get the same before the jury by argument for its admissibility, nor should he address to the Judge arguments upon any point not properly calling for determination by him.   Neither should he introduce into an argument, addressed to the court, remarks or statements intended to influence the jury or bystanders.

These and all kindred practices are unprofessional and unworthy of an officer of the law charged, as is the lawyer, with the duty of aiding in the administration of justice.

CANON 23

Attitude Toward Jury

All attempts to curry favor with juries by fawning, flattery or pretended solicitude for their personal comfort are unprofessional. Suggestions of counsel, looking to the comfort or convenience of jurors, and propositions to dispense with argument, should be made to the Court out of the jury's hearing. A lawyer must never converse privately with jurors about the case; and both before and during the trial he should avoid communicating with them, even as to matters foreign to the cause.

CANON 24

Right of Lawyer to Control the Incidents of the Trial

As to incidental matters pending the trial, not affecting the merits of the cause, or working substantial prejudice to the rights of the client, such as forcing the opposite lawyer to trial when he is under affliction or bereavement; forcing the trial on a particular day to the injury of the opposite lawyer when no harm will result from a trial at a different time; agreeing to an extension of time for signing a bill of exceptions, cross interrogatories and the like, the lawyer must be allowed to judge. In such matters no client has a right to demand that his counsel shall be illiberal, or that he do anything therein repugnant to his own sense of honor and propriety.

CANON 25

Taking Technical Advantage of Opposite Counsel; Agreements With Him

A lawyer should not ignore known customs or practice of the Bar or of a particular Court, even when the law permits, without giving timely notice to the opposing counsel. As far as possible, important agreements, affecting the rights of clients, should be reduced to writing; but it is dishonorable to avoid performance of an agreement fairly made because it is not reduced to writing, as required by rules of Court.

CANON 26

Professional Advocacy Other Than Before Courts

A lawyer openly, and in his true character may render professional services before legislative or other bodies, regarding proposed legislation and in advocacy of claims before departments of government, upon the same principles of ethics which justify his appearance before the Courts; but it is unprofessional for a lawyer so engaged to conceal his attorneyship, or to employ secret personal solicitations, or to use means other than those addressed to the reason and understanding, to influence action.

CANON 27

Advertising, Direct or Indirect

It is unprofessional to solicit professional employment by circulars, advertisements, through toutors or by personal communications or interviews not warranted by personal relations. Indirect advertisements for professional employment such as furnishing or inspiring newspaper comments, or procuring his photograph to be published in connection with causes in which the lawyer has been or is engaged or concerning the manner of their conduct, the magnitude of the interest involved, the importance of the lawyer's position, and all other like self-laudation, offend the traditions and lower the tone of our profession and are reprehensible; but the customary use of simple professional cards is not improper.

Publication in reputable law lists in a manner consistent with the standards of conduct imposed by these canons of brief biographical and informative data is permissible. Such data must not be misleading and may include only a statement of the lawyer's name and the names of his professional associates; addresses, telephone numbers, cable addresses; branches of the profession practiced; date and place of birth and admission to the bar; schools attended; with dates of graduation, degrees and other educational distinctions; public or quasi-public offices; posts of honor; legal authorships; legal teaching positions; memberships and offices in bar associations and committees thereof, in legal and scientific societies and legal fraternities; foreign language ability; the fact of listings in other reputable law lists; the names and addresses of references; and, with their written consent, the names of clients regularly represented. A certificate of compliance with the Rules and Standards issued by the Standing Committee on Law Lists may be treated as evidence that such list is reputable.

It is not improper for a lawyer who is admitted to practice as a proctor in admiralty to use that designation on his letterhead or shingle or for a lawyer who has complied with the statutory requirements of admission to practice before the patent office, to so use the designation "patent attorney" or "patent lawyer" or "trademark attorney" or "trademark lawyer" or any combination of those terms.

CANON 28

Stirring Up Litigation, Directly or Through Agents

It is unprofessional for a lawyer to volunteer advice to bring a lawsuit, except in rare cases where ties of blood, relationship or trust make it his duty to do so. Stirring up strife and litigation is not only unprofessional, but it is indictable at common law. It is disreputable to hunt up defects in titles or other causes of action and inform thereof in order to be employed to bring suit or collect judgment, or to breed litigation by seeking out those with claims for personal injuries or those having any other grounds of action in order to secure them as clients, or to employ agents or runners for like purposes, or to pay or reward, directly or indirectly, those who bring or influence the bringing of such cases to his office, or to remunerate policemen, court or prison officials, physicians, hospital *attachés* or others who may succeed, under the guise of giving disinterested friendly advice, in influencing the criminal, the sick and the injured, the ignorant or others, to seek his professional services. A duty to the public and to the profession devolves upon every member of the Bar having knowledge of such practices upon the part of any practitioner immediately to inform thereof, to the end that the offender may be disbarred.

CANON 29

Upholding the Honor of the Profession

Lawyers should expose without fear or favor before the proper tribunals corrupt or dishonest conduct in the profession, and should accept without hesitation employment against a member of the Bar who has wronged his client. The counsel upon the trial of a cause in which perjury has been committed owe it to the profession and to the public to bring the matter to the knowledge of the prosecuting authorities. The lawyer should aid in guarding the Bar against the admission to the profession of candidates unfit or unqualified because deficient in either moral character or education. He should strive at all times to uphold the honor and to maintain the dignity of the profession and to improve not only the law but the administration of justice.

CANON 30

Justifiable and Unjustifiable Litigations

The lawyer must decline to conduct a civil cause or to make a defense when convinced that it is intended merely to harass or to injure the opposite party or to work oppression or wrong. But otherwise it is his right, and, having accepted retainer, it becomes his duty to insist upon the judgment of the Court as to the legal merits of his client's claim. His appearance in Court should be deemed equivalent to an assertion on his honor that in his opinion his client's case is one proper for judicial determination.

CANON 31

Responsibility for Litigation

No lawyer is obliged to act either as adviser or advocate for every person who may wish to become his client. He has the right to decline employment. Every lawyer upon his own responsibility must decide what employment he will accept as counsel, what causes he will bring into Court for plaintiffs, what cases he will contest in Court for defendants. The responsibility for advising as to questionable transactions, for bringing questionable suits, for urging questionable defenses, is the lawyer's responsibility. He cannot escape it by urging as an excuse that he is only following his client's instructions.

CANON 32

The Lawyer's Duty in Its Last Analysis

No client, corporate or individual, however powerful, nor any cause, civil or political, however important, is entitled to receive nor should any lawyer render any service or advice involving disloyalty to the law whose ministers we are, or disrespect of the judicial office, which we are bound to uphold, or corruption of any person or persons exercising a public office or private trust, or deception or betrayal of the public. When rendering any such improper service or advice, the lawyer invites and merits stern and just condemnation. Correspondingly, he advances the honor of his profession and the best interests of his client when he renders service or gives advice tending to impress upon the client and his undertaking exact compliance with the strictest principles of moral law. He must also observe and advise his client to observe the statute law, though until a statute shall have been construed and interpreted by competent adjudication, he is free and is entitled to advise as to its validity and as to what he conscientiously believes to be its just meaning and extent. But above all a lawyer will find his highest honor in a deserved reputation for fidelity to private trust and to public duty, as an honest man and as a patriotic and loyal citizen.

CANON 33

Partnerships—Names

Partnerships among lawyers for the practice of their profession are very common and are not to be condemned. In the formation of partnerships and the use of partnership names care should be taken not to violate any law, custom, or rule of court locally applicable. Where partnerships are formed between lawyers who are not all admitted to practice in the courts of the state, care should be taken to avoid any misleading name or representation which would create a false impression as to the professional position or privileges of the member not locally admitted. In the formation of partnerships for the practice of law, no person should be admitted or held out as a practitioner or member who is not a member of the legal profession duly authorized to practice, and amenable to professional discipline. In the selection and use of a firm name, no false, misleading, assumed or trade name should be used. The continued use of the name of a deceased or former partner, when permissible by local custom, is not unethical, but care should be taken that no imposition or deception is practiced through this use. When a member of the firm, on becoming a judge, is precluded from practicing law, his name should not be continued in the firm name.

Partnerships between lawyers and members of other professions or non-professional persons should not be formed or permitted where any part of the partnership's employment consists of the practice of law.

CANON 34

Division of Fees

No division of fees for legal services is proper, except with another lawyer, based upon a division of service or responsibility.

CANON 35

Intermediaries

The professional services of a lawyer should not be controlled or exploited by any lay agency, personal or corporate, which intervenes between client and lawyer. A lawyer's responsibilities and qualifications are individual. He should avoid all relations which direct the performance of his duties by or in the interest of such intermediary. A lawyer's relation to his client should be personal, and the responsibility should be direct to the client. Charitable societies rendering aid to the indigents are not deemed such intermediaries.

A lawyer may accept employment from any organization, such as an association, club or trade organization, to render legal services in any matter in which the organization, as an entity, is interested, but this employment should not include the rendering of legal services to the members of such an organization in respect to their individual affairs.

CANON 36

Retirement From Judicial Position or Public Employment

A lawyer should not accept employment as an advocate in any matter upon the merits of which he has previously acted in a judicial capacity.

A lawyer, having once held public office or having been in the public employ, should not after his retirement accept employment in connection with any matter which he has investigated or passed upon while in such office or employ.

CANON 37

Confidences of a Client

It is the duty of a lawyer to preserve his client's confidences. This duty outlasts the lawyer's employment, and extends as well to his employees; and neither of them should accept employment which involves or may involve the disclosure or use of these confidences, either for the private advantage of the lawyer or his employees or to the disadvantage of the client, without his knowledge and consent, and even though there are other available sources of such information. A lawyer should not continue employment when he discovers that this obligation prevents the performance of his full duty to his former or to his new client.

If a lawyer is accused by his client, he is not precluded from disclosing the truth in respect to the accusation. The announced intention of a client to commit a crime is not included within the confidences which he is bound to respect. He may properly make such disclosures as may be necessary to prevent the act or protect those against whom it is threatened.

CANON 38

Compensation, Commissions and Rebates

A lawyer should accept no compensation, commissions, rebates or other advantages from others without the knowledge and consent of his client after full disclosure.

CANON 39

Witnesses

A lawyer may properly interview any witness or prospective witness for the opposing side in any civil or criminal action without the consent of opposing counsel or party. In doing so, however, he should scrupulously avoid any suggestion calculated to induce the witness to suppress or deviate from the truth, or in any degree to affect his free and untrammeled conduct when appearing at the trial or on the witness stand.

CANON 40

Newspapers

A lawyer may with propriety write articles for publications in which he gives information upon the law; but he should not accept employment from such publications to advise inquirers in respect to their individual rights.

CANON 41

Discovery of Imposition and Deception

When a lawyer discovers that some fraud or deception has been practiced, which has unjustly imposed upon the court or a party, he should endeavor to rectify it; at first by advising his client, and if his client refuses to forego the advantage thus unjustly gained, he should promptly inform the injured person or his counsel, so that they may take appropriate steps.

CANON 42

Expenses of Litigation

A lawyer may not properly agree with a client that the lawyer shall pay or bear the expenses of litigation; he may in good faith advance expenses as a matter of convenience, but subject to reimbursement.

CANON 43

Approved Law Lists

It shall be improper for a lawyer to permit his name to be published in a law list the conduct, management or contents of which are calculated or likely to deceive or injure the public or the profession, or to lower the dignity or standing of the profession.

CANON 44

Withdrawal From Employment as Attorney or Counsel

The right of an attorney or counsel to withdraw from employment, once assumed, arises only from good cause. Even the desire or consent of the client is not always sufficient. The lawyer should not throw up the unfinished task to the detriment of his client except for reasons of honor or self-respect. If the client insists upon an unjust or immoral course in the conduct of his case, or if he persists over the attorney's remonstrance in presenting frivolous defenses, or if he deliberately disregards an agreement or obligation as to fees or expenses, the lawyer

663

may be warranted in withdrawing on due notice to the client, allowing him time to employ another lawyer. So also when a lawyer discovers that his client has no case and the client is determined to continue it; or even if the lawyer finds himself incapable of conducting the case effectively. Sundry other instances may arise in which withdrawal is to be justified. Upon withdrawing from a case after a retainer has been paid, the attorney should refund such part of the retainer as has not been clearly earned.

CANON 45

Specialists

The canons of the American Bar Association apply to all branches of the legal profession; specialists in particular branches are not to be considered as exempt from the application of these principles.

CANON 46

Notice to Local Lawyers

A lawyer available to act as an associate of other lawyers in a particular branch of the law or legal service may send to local lawyers only and publish in his local legal journal, a brief and dignified announcement of his availability to serve other lawyers in connection therewith. The announcement should be in a form which does not constitute a statement or representation of special experience or expertise.

CANON 47

Aiding the Unauthorized Practice of Law

No lawyer shall permit his professional services, or his name, to be used in aid of, or to make possible, the unauthorized practice of law by any lay agency, personal or corporate.

PARALLEL TABLES BETWEEN THE ABA CANONS OF PROFESSIONAL ETHICS AND THE ABA MODEL CODE OF PROFESSIONAL RESPONSIBILITY *

CANONS OF PROFESSIONAL ETHICS TO CODE OF PROFESSIONAL RESPONSIBILITY

Preamble
Preamble
DR 1–102(A)(5)
EC 7–20
EC 7–39
EC 8–1
EC 9–1
EC 9–2

Canon 1
DR 1–103(B)
EC 7–36
EC 8–6
DR 7–106(C)(6)
DR 8–102(B)

Canon 2
EC 8–6
DR 8–102(A)

Canon 3
EC 7–34
EC 7–35
EC 7–36
DR 7–110

Canon 4
EC 2–29
EC 7–1
EC 7–19
DR 2–110(C)
DR 7–101(A)(1)

Canon 5
EC 1–5
DR 1–102(A)(4)
EC 2–29
EC 7–1
EC 7–4
EC 7–13
EC 7–19
EC 7–27
DR 7–101(A)(1)
DR 7–102(A)(3)–(7)
DR 7–103
DR 7–109(A)–(B)
EC 8–5

Canon 6
EC 4–1

EC 4–5
DR 4–101(B)
EC 5–1
EC 5–3
EC 5–14
EC 5–15
EC 5–16
EC 5–17
EC 5–19
DR 5–101(A)
DR 5–105
DR 5–106
EC 8–8

Canon 7
EC 2–28
EC 2–29
EC 2–30
EC 2–32
DR 2–108
DR 2–110(C)(3)
EC 4–2
EC 5–11
EC 5–12
DR 7–101(A)(2)

Canon 8
EC 2–9
EC 7–5
EC 7–8

Canon 9
EC 7–18
DR 7–104

Canon 10
EC 5–7
DR 5–103(A)

Canon 11
EC 4–5
DR 4–101(B)(3)
EC 9–5
DR 9–102

Canon 12
EC 2–16
EC 2–17
EC 2–18
EC 2–25

DR 2–106

Canon 13
EC 2–20
DR 2–106
EC 5–7
DR 5–103(A)(2)

Canon 14
EC 2–23
EC 5–7
DR 5–103(A)(1)

Canon 15
EC 1–5
DR 1–102(A)(4)
EC 7–1
EC 7–2
EC 7–3
EC 7–4
EC 7–5
EC 7–6
EC 7–19
EC 7–24
EC 7–26
DR 7–101(A)(1)
DR 7–101(B)(2)
DR 7–102(A)(2)
DR 7–102(A)(3)–(7)
DR 7–106(C)(4)
EC 9–2

Canon 16
EC 2–32
DR 2–110(C)(1)(b)
EC 7–28
DR 7–101(A)(2)
EC 8–5

Canon 17
EC 1–5
EC 7–10
EC 7–37
EC 7–38
DR 7–101(A)(1)

Canon 18
EC 1–5
EC 7–10
EC 7–25

EC 7–36
DR 7–101(A)(1)
DR 7–106(C)(2)

Canon 19
EC 5–9
EC 5–10
DR 5–101(B)
DR 5–102

Canon 20
EC 7–33
DR 7–107

Canon 21
EC 6–4
DR 6–101(A)(3)
EC 7–20
EC 7–38
DR 7–101(A)(1)

Canon 22
EC 1–5
DR 1–102(A)(4)
EC 7–6
EC 7–25
EC 7–26
EC 7–27
DR 7–102(A)(3)–(7)
DR 7–106(C)(1)
EC 8–5

Canon 23
EC 7–29
EC 7–31
EC 7–36
DR 7–108

Canon 24
EC 7–7
EC 7–9
EC 7–10
EC 7–38
DR 7–101(A)(1)
DR 7–101(B)(1)

Canon 25

* Compiled by Olavi Maru, Reference Librarian, William Nelson Cromwell Library, American Bar Foundation.

EC 7–38
DR 7–101(A)(1)
DR 7–106(C)(5)

Canon 26
EC 7–15
EC 7–16
EC 7–36
DR 7–106(B)(2)
DR 7–107(F)
DR 7–107(H)
DR 7–107(I)
DR 7–110(B)
EC 8–4

Canon 27
EC 2–21
EC 2–3
EC 2–4
EC 2–8
EC 2–9
EC 2–10
EC 2–14
DR 2–101
DR 2–102(A)
DR 2–102(E)
DR 2–103(A)
DR 2–105(A)

Canon 28
EC 1–4
EC 1–5
EC 2–1
EC 2–2
EC 2–3
EC 2–4
EC 2–8
DR 1–103(A)–(B)
DR 2–103(A)
DR 2–104(A)

Canon 29
EC 1–2
EC 1–3
EC 1–4
DR 1–101(B)
DR 1–103(A)
DR 1–103(B)
EC 2–28

DR 7–102(A)(3)–(7)
DR 7–102(B)(2)
EC 8–1
EC 8–2
EC 8–5
EC 8–7
EC 8–9
EC 9–2
EC 9–6

Canon 30
EC 1–5
DR 1–102(A)(4)
EC 2–3
EC 2–30
DR 2–109(A)(1)
EC 7–1
EC 7–4
EC 7–19
DR 7–101(A)(1)
DR 7–102(A)(1)

Canon 31
EC 2–26
EC 2–27
EC 2–28
EC 2–29
DR 2–109(A)(2)
EC 7–1
EC 7–4
EC 7–5
EC 7–14
EC 7–19
DR 7–101(B)(2)
DR 7–102(A)(2)

Canon 32
EC 1–5
DR 1–102(A)(5)
EC 7–1
EC 7–5
EC 7–19
DR 7–102(A)(3)–(7)
EC 8–5

Canon 33
EC 2–11
EC 2–12
EC 2–13

DR 2–102(B)
DR 2–102(C)
DR 2–102(D)
EC 3–8
DR 3–103
DR 5–107(C)

Canon 34
EC 2–22
DR 2–103(B)
DR 2–107(A)
EC 3–8
DR 3–102

Canon 35
DR 2–103(D)
DR 2–104(A)(2)
DR 2–104(A)(3)
EC 5–1
EC 5–13
EC 5–21
EC 5–22
EC 5–23
EC 5–24
DR 5–107(B)
DR 5–107(C)(3)

Canon 36
EC 9–3
DR 9–101

Canon 37
Canon 4 generally
EC 2–32
DR 2–110
DR 4–101(B)
DR 4–101(B)(2)–(3)
DR 4–101(C)
DR 4–101(D)
DR 7–101(A)(2)

Canon 38
EC 2–21
EC 5–21
DR 5–107(A)(2)

Canon 39
EC 1–5
DR 1–102(A)(4)

EC 7–28
DR 7–102(A)(3)–(7)
DR 7–109(C)

Canon 40
EC 2–2
EC 2–5
DR 2–104(A)(4)

Canon 41
DR 7–102(B)(1)
EC 8–5

Canon 42
EC 5–8
DR 5–103(B)

Canon 43
DR 2–102(A)(6)

Canon 44
EC 1–5
DR 1–102(A)(5)
EC 2–31
EC 2–32
DR 2–110
EC 5–15
EC 5–19
EC 5–21
DR 5–102
DR 5–105(B)
DR 5–105(D)
EC 7–8
DR 7–101(A)(2)

Canon 45
Preliminary statement

Canon 46
EC 2–14
DR 2–105(A)(3)

Canon 47
EC 1–5
DR 1–102(A)(5)
EC 3–1 through
EC 3–9
DR 3–101

PARALLEL TABLES BETWEEN THE ABA MODEL CODE OF PROFESSIONAL RESPONSIBILITY AND THE ABA CANONS OF PROFESSIONAL ETHICS

Code	Canons	Code	Canons
Preamble	Preamble	EC 2–14	27
Preliminary			46
Statement	45	EC 2–16	12
		EC 2–17	12
Canon 1		EC 2–18	12
EC 1–2	29	EC 2–20	13
EC 1–3	29	EC 2–21	38
EC 1–4	28	EC 2–22	34
	29	EC 2–23	14
EC 1–5	5	EC 2–25	12
	15	EC 2–26	31
	17	EC 2–27	31
	18	EC 2–28	7
	22		29
	28		31
	30	EC 2–29	4
	32		5
	39		7
	44		31
	47	EC 2–30	7
DR 1–101			30
(B)	29	EC 2–31	44
DR 1–102		EC 2–32	7
(A)(4)	5		16
	15		37
	22		44
	30	DR 2–101	27
	39	DR 2–102	
(A)(5)	Preamble	(A)	27
	32	(A)(6)	43
	44	(B)	33
	47	(C)	33
DR 1–103		(D)	33
(A)	28	(E)	27
	29	DR 2–103	
(B)	1	(A)	27
	28		28
	29	(B)	34
Canon 2		(D)	35
EC 2–1	28	DR 2–104	
EC 2–2	27	(A)	28
	28	(A)(2)	35
	40	(A)(3)	35
EC 2–3	27	DR 2–104	
	28	(A)(4)	40
	30	DR 2–105	
EC 2–4	27	(A)	27
	28	(A)(3)	46
EC 2–5	40	DR 2–106	12
EC 2–8	27		13
	28	DR 2–107	
EC 2–9	8	(A)	34
	27	DR 2–108	7
EC 2–10	27	DR 2–109	
EC 2–11	33	(A)(1)	30
EC 2–12	33	(A)(2)	31
EC 2–13	33	DR 2–110	37

667

SELECTED STANDARDS ON PROFESSIONALISM AND COURTESY

TABLE OF CONTENTS

AMERICAN BAR ASSOCIATION REPORT OF COMMISSION ON PROFESSIONALISM (1986)

(Selected sections)

[The report has been approved for distribution by the House of Delegates of the American Bar Association. However, the views expressed are those of the Commission on Professionalism. They have not been approved by the House of Delegates or the Board of Governors and, accordingly, should not be construed as representing the policy of the Association. Ed.]

* * *

III. THE MEANING OF PROFESSIONALISM

"Professionalism" is an elastic concept the meaning and application of which are hard to pin down. That is perhaps as it should be. The term has a rich, long-standing heritage, and any single definition runs the risk of being too confining.

Yet the term is so important to lawyers that at least a working definition seems essential. Lawyers are proud of being part of one of the "historic" or "learned" professions, along with medicine and the clergy, which have been seen as professions through many centuries.

When he was asked to define a profession, Dean Roscoe Pound of Harvard Law School said:

> The term refers to a group ... pursuing a learned art as a common calling in the spirit of public service—no less a public service

because it may incidentally be a means of livelihood. Pursuit of the learned art in the spirit of a public service is the primary purpose.

The rhetoric may be dated, but the Commission believes the spirit of Dean Pound's definition stands the test of time. The practice of law "in the spirit of a public service" can and ought to be the hallmark of the legal profession.

More recently, others have identified some common elements which distinguish a profession from other occupations. Commission member Professor Eliot Freidson of New York University defines our profession as:

An occupation whose members have special privileges, such as exclusive licensing, that are justified by the following assumptions:

1. That its practice requires substantial intellectual training and the use of complex judgments.

2. That since clients cannot adequately evaluate the quality of the service, they must trust those they consult.

3. That the client's trust presupposes that the practitioner's self-interest is overbalanced by devotion to serving both the client's interest and the public good, and

4. That the occupation is self-regulating—that is, organized in such a way as to assure the public and the courts that its members are competent, do not violate their client's trust, and transcend their own self-interest.

Again, the Commission suggests that this list of elements is useful in thinking through the issues which follow.

Some may argue on the basis of the cases previously discussed that the legal profession is no longer "special." They might say that lawyers should treat their ideals as archaic, construe the rules of professional conduct as narrowly as possible, and try only to maximize their incomes. The Commission disagrees. Moreover, the testimony we have heard and the surveys we have examined indicate that the public wants the legal profession to maintain its long-held professional ideals. Indeed, the public should expect no less.

We have earlier described the diversity of the Bar, both in terms of demographics and areas of practice. One can properly ask whether any common ideas of professionalism can suffice for such a varied institution. We believe they can. While one must always be conscious of the variety within the legal profession, more unites than separates us.

* * *

The suggestions and conclusions which follow are grouped by the role to be played by each segment of the Bar. In discussing the practicing Bar, we want it to be clear that we are including in that category all lawyers—whether litigators or non-litigators, whether sole practitioners, members or employees of firms, government lawyers or lawyers employed by corporations, educational institutions or other entities.

It is our hope that the recommendations which follow will not be unobserved aspirations, but will represent concrete ways in which lawyers can inspire a rebirth of respect and confidence in themselves, in the services they provide and in the legal system itself. We believe that much can be done. Taken individually, the proposals may not appear substantial, but in the aggregate we believe they can have a significant impact. However, to be effective, they must have the support not only of every part of the legal community, but also of the citizens of this country—the public whose interests lawyers are to serve.

We first present a summary of our recommendations, and then a discussion of each.

IV. SUMMARY OF RECOMMENDATIONS

A. LAW SCHOOLS

1. Law schools should give continuing attention to the form and content of their courses in ethics and professionalism. They should weave ethical and professional issues into courses in both substantive and procedural fields. They should give serious consideration to supplementing courses in ethics and professionalism with a required summer reading list for entering students and with a film or videotape on ethics, along the lines discussed later in this report.

2. Law schools should expose students to promising new methods of dealing with legal problems. Thus, for example, consideration should be given to instruction in such matters as alternative methods of dispute resolution and processes of negotiation.

3. Deans and faculties of law schools should keep in mind that the law school experience provides a student's first exposure to the profession, and that professors inevitably serve as important role models for students. Therefore, the highest standards of ethics and professionalism should be adhered to within law schools.

4. Law schools should adopt codes of student conduct, possibly based on the Model Rules of Professional Conduct. They should report convictions of serious infractions of law school rules to the Character and Fitness Committees, or their equivalent, of states in which the student applies for admission to the Bar.

5. Law schools should retain high admission standards in the face of declining applications and should not lower their standards for graduation.

B. PRACTICING BAR AND BAR ASSOCIATIONS

1. Law firms should help their newly-admitted associates to face the practical and ethical issues which inevitably arise in practice. This can be done in a variety of ways, and small firms or sole practitioners should work together to sponsor programs to facilitate such training. Local bar associations and law schools should assist in such efforts.

2. In order to assure greater competence of practicing lawyers, continuing legal education courses should be strengthened and made mandatory. Where practical, some form of examination in courses taken should be required.

3. The Commission recommends that the American Bar Association prepare a series of six to eight films or videotapes dealing with ethical and professional issues. The tapes should effectively present a wide range of such issues and should use the Socratic approach so effectively used in the Columbia University Media & Society Seminar programs. If feasible, at least one such tape should be designed especially for use in law schools. The tapes also should be made available to state and local bar associations for use in mandatory continuing legal education programs.

4. False, fraudulent or misleading advertising is not constitutionally protected and should be referred to disciplinary authorities for action against offending lawyers. Appropriate measures short of disciplinary action should be considered. Such measures could include requiring an advertisement to contain warnings or disclaimers.

5. The Bar should place increasing emphasis on the role of lawyers as officers of the court, or more broadly, as officers of the system of justice. Lawyers should exercise independent judgment as to how to pursue legal matters. They have a duty to make the system of justice work properly. Ideally, clients should recognize this duty and appreciate the importance to society of maintaining the system of justice.

6. The Bar should study the issue of the participation of law firms and individual lawyers in business activities, certainly where either actual or potential conflicts of interest may be involved.

7. When not representing clients before legislative bodies, lawyers should put aside self-interest and should support legislation that is in the public interest. In addition, the Bar should urge legislative bodies to consider the consequences of proposed legislation on the courts. All too frequently, such legislation, when enacted, inundates the courts with cases never contemplated by the drafters.

8. Fees are a source of misunderstanding between many lawyers and their clients. Further, the amount of fees charged by lawyers in some instances results in bitter criticism of the Bar. The Commission suggests:

    a. Fee arrangements between lawyers and their clients should be in writing, where feasible.

b. If, at the end of a lawyer's services in any matter, the client believes that the fee charged was inappropriate, the client should be able to have the matter reviewed by an impartial fee review committee, possibly appointed by the state Supreme Court. All such committees or entities should include lay members.

9. Lawyers and judges should report to the appropriate disciplinary committee or prosecuting attorney any serious misconduct on the part of other lawyers and judges which they believe would support a complaint for discipline or criminal charges.

10. Bar associations should be constantly alert to seek improvements in the system of justice. This should embrace such activities as supporting an expanded use of alternative methods of dispute resolution.

C. JUDGES

1. Trial judges should take a more active role in the conduct of litigation. They should see that cases advance promptly, fairly and without abuse. Granting increased authority to judges runs the risk of arbitrary behavior on their part, but reviewing courts should provide whatever counterbalance is needed.

2. Judges should impose sanctions for abuse of the litigation process. Currently, the Federal Rules of Civil Procedure permit the imposition of sanctions for such abuses, and increasing use is being made of the sanctions to penalize the lawyer or the client, or both. In many state systems, the Supreme Courts have not promulgated such rules. State Supreme Courts should adopt rules similar to Rule 11 of the Federal Rules, so that authority to act is clearly given to trial judges.

3. Merit selection should be the means by which judges are chosen. The Commission believes that a bench of the quality that merit selection can provide is essential to improve our system of justice.

4. State disciplinary agencies under the control of state supreme courts are, in general, insufficiently funded and staffed. They now cannot do much more than deal with charges of theft, neglect or the commission of a felony. Adequate funding should be made available to the disciplinary agencies, enabling them to do a thorough and competent job in pursuing the full range of offenses which occur.

5. State supreme courts control admission to the Bar. They often charge character and fitness committees or their equivalent with the responsibility of reviewing the qualifications of applicants. Adequate funding and authority should be provided to such committees so that they can do a thorough job of investigation.

D. IN GENERAL

All segments of the Bar should:

1. Preserve and develop within the profession integrity, competence, fairness, independence, courage and a devotion to the public interest.

2. Resolve to abide by higher standards of conduct than the minimum required by the Code of Professional Responsibility and the Model Rules of Professional Conduct.

3. Increase the participation of lawyers in *pro bono* activities and help lawyers recognize their obligation to participate.

4. Resist the temptation to make the acquisition of wealth a primary goal of law practice.

5. Encourage innovative methods which simplify and make less expensive the rendering of legal services.

6. Educate the public about legal processes and the legal system.

7. Resolve to employ all the organizational resources necessary in order to assure that the legal profession is effectively self-regulating.

* * *

AMERICAN BAR ASSOCIATION
A LAWYER'S CREED OF PROFESSIONALISM

Copyright © American Bar Association. All Rights Reserved. Reprinted with permission.

On August 9th, 1988, the American Bar Association House of Delegates adopted the following resolutions regarding so-called "Codes of Courtesy."

BE IT RESOLVED that the American Bar Association recommends to state and local bar associations that they encourage their members to accept as a guide for their individual conduct, and to comply with, a lawyer's creed of professionalism.

BE IT FURTHER RESOLVED that nothing contained in such a creed shall be deemed to supersede or in any way amend the Model Rules of Professional Conduct or other disciplinary codes, alter existing standards of conduct against which lawyer negligence might be judged or become a basis for the imposition of civil penalty of any kind.

Following is a proposed example of "A Lawyer's Creed of Professionalism."

Preamble

As a lawyer I must strive to make our system of justice work fairly and efficiently. In order to carry out that responsibility, not only will I comply with the letter and spirit of the disciplinary standards applicable to all lawyers, but I will also conduct myself in accordance with the following Creed of Professionalism when dealing with my client, opposing parties, their counsel, the courts and the general public.

A. With respect to my client:

1. I will be loyal and committed to my client's cause, but I will not permit that loyalty and commitment to interfere with my ability to provide my client with objective and independent advice;

2. I will endeavor to achieve my client's lawful objectives in business transactions and in litigation as expeditiously and economically as possible;

3. In appropriate cases, I will counsel my client with respect to mediation, arbitration and other alternative methods of resolving disputes;

4. I will advise my client against pursuing litigation (or any other course of action) that is without merit and against insisting on tactics which are intended to delay resolution of the matter or to harass or drain the financial resources of the opposing party;

5. I will advise my client that civility and courtesy are not to be equated with weakness;

6. While I must abide by my client's decision concerning the objectives of the representation, I nevertheless will counsel my client that a willingness to initiate or engage in settlement discussions is consistent with zealous and effective representation.

B. With respect to opposing parties and their counsel:

1. I will endeavor to be courteous and civil, both in oral and in written communications;

2. I will not knowingly make statements of fact or of law that are untrue;

3. In litigation proceedings I will agree to reasonable requests for extensions of time or for waiver of procedural formalities when the legitimate interests of my client will not be adversely affected;

4. I will endeavor to consult with opposing counsel before scheduling depositions and meetings and before re-scheduling hearings, and I will cooperate with opposing counsel when scheduling changes are requested;

5. I will refrain from utilizing litigation or any other course of conduct to harass the opposing party;

6. I will refrain from engaging in excessive and abusive discovery, and I will comply with all reasonable discovery requests;

7. I will refrain from utilizing delaying tactics;

8. In depositions and other proceedings, and in negotiations, I will conduct myself with dignity, avoid making groundless objections and refrain from engaging in acts of rudeness or disrespect;

9. I will not serve motions and pleadings on the other party, or his counsel, at such a time or in such a manner as will unfairly limit the other party's opportunity to respond;

10. In business transactions I will not quarrel over matters of form or style, but will concentrate on matters of substance and content;

11. I will clearly identify, for other counsel or parties, all changes that I have made in documents submitted to me for review.

C. With respect to the courts and other tribunals:

1. I will be a vigorous and zealous advocate on behalf of my client, while recognizing, as an officer of the court, that excessive zeal may be detrimental to my client's interests as well as to the proper functioning of our system of justice;

2. Where consistent with my client's interests, I will communicate with opposing counsel in an effort to avoid litigation and to resolve litigation that has actually commenced;

3. I will voluntarily withdraw claims or defenses when it becomes apparent that they do not have merit or are superfluous;

4. I will refrain from filing frivolous motions;

5. I will make every effort to agree with other counsel, as early as possible, on a voluntary exchange of information and on a plan for discovery;

6. I will attempt to resolve, by agreement, my objections to matters contained in my opponent's pleadings and discovery requests;

7. When scheduled hearings or depositions have to be cancelled, I will notify opposing counsel, and, if appropriate, the court (or other tribunal) as early as possible;

8. Before dates for hearings or trials are set—or, if that is not feasible, immediately after such dates have been set—I will attempt to verify the availability of key participants and witnesses so that I can promptly notify the court (or other tribunal) and opposing counsel of any likely problem in that regard;

9. In civil matters, I will stipulate to facts as to which there is no genuine dispute;

10. I will endeavor to be punctual in attending court hearings, conferences and depositions;

11. I will at all times be candid with the court.

D. With respect to the public and to our system of justice:

1. I will remember that, in addition to commitment to my client's cause, my responsibilities as a lawyer include a devotion to the public good;

2. I will endeavor to keep myself current in the areas in which I practice and, when necessary, will associate with, or refer my client to, counsel knowledgeable in another field of practice;

3. I will be mindful of the fact that, as a member of a self-regulating profession, it is incumbent on me to report violations by fellow lawyers of any disciplinary rule;

4. I will be mindful of the need to protect the image of the legal profession in the eyes of the public and will be so guided when considering methods and contents of advertising;

5. I will be mindful that the law is a learned profession and that among its desirable goals are devotion to public service, improvement of administration of justice, and the contribution of uncompensated time and civic influence on behalf of those persons who cannot afford adequate legal assistance.

AMERICAN BAR ASSOCIATION
LAWYER'S PLEDGE OF PROFESSIONALISM

I will remember that the practice of law is first and foremost a profession, and I will subordinate business concerns to professionalism concerns.

I will encourage respect for the law and our legal system through my words and actions.

I will remember my responsibilities to serve as an officer of the court and protector of individual rights.

I will contribute time and resources to public service, public education, charitable, and *pro bono* activities in my community.

I will work with the other participants in the legal system, including judges, opposing counsel and those whose practices are different from mine, to make our legal system more accessible and responsive.

I will resolve matters expeditiously and without unnecessary expense.

I will resolve disputes through negotiation whenever possible.

I will keep my clients well-informed and involved in making the decisions that affect them.

I will continue to expand my knowledge of the law.

I will achieve and maintain proficiency in my practice.

I will be courteous to those with whom I come into contact during the course of my work.

I will honor the spirit and intent, as well as the requirements, of the applicable rules or code of professional conduct for my jurisdiction, and will encourage others to do the same.

AMERICAN BAR ASSOCIATION ASPIRATIONAL GOALS ON LAWYER ADVERTISING

Preamble

During the past decade, the courts have sought to define the nature and extent of permissible advertising by lawyers. In a series of decisions, the U.S. Supreme Court has held that lawyer advertising which is not false or misleading is commercial speech entitled to protection under the First Amendment of the U.S. Constitution.

Pending further clarification by the courts, some advertising practices exist which may be detrimental. Some forms of advertising may adversely affect public perceptions about the justice system itself. For example, empirical evidence suggests that undignified advertising can detract from the public's confidence in the legal profession and respect for the justice system.

Under present case law, the matter of dignity is widely believed to be so subjective as to be beyond the scope of constitutionally permitted regulation. Nevertheless, it seems entirely proper for the organized bar to suggest non-binding aspirational goals urging lawyers who wish to advertise to do so in a dignified manner. Although only aspirational, such goals must be scrupulously sensitive to fundamental constitutional rights of lawyers and the needs of the public.

It is the role and responsibility of lawyers to provide legal services to the public. It has been demonstrated by responsible studies that people sometimes do not receive needed legal services, either because they are unaware of available services, don't understand how they can benefit from those services or don't understand how to obtain them. Therefore, it is also the legal profession's responsibility to inform the public about the availability of legal services and how to obtain and use them.

Advertising is one of many methods by which lawyers can inform the public about legal services. Although most people find a lawyer through word-of-mouth networks of family, friends and work associates, when properly done, advertising can help people to better understand the legal services available to them and how to obtain those services.

When properly done, advertising can also be a productive way for lawyers to build and maintain their client bases. Advertising and other forms of marketing can enable lawyers to attain efficiencies of scale which may help make legal services more affordable. As the Supreme Court pointed out in *Bates v. State Bar of Arizona,* 433 U.S. 350, 377 (1977), it is "entirely possible that advertising will serve to reduce, not advance, the cost of legal services to the consumer."

Lawyers are at all times officers of the court, and as such, they have a special obligation to assure that their conduct conforms to the highest ideals of the legal profession. Thus, lawyers who advertise should be mindful not only of the effect their advertising may have on their own professional image but also of the effect it may have on the public's overall perception of the judicial system.

If lawyer advertising avoids false, misleading or deceptive representations, or coercive or misleading solicitation, it advances the goal of bringing needed legal services to more people than are now being served.

However, when advertising though not false, misleading or deceptive degenerates into undignified and unprofessional presentations, the public is not served, the lawyer who advertised does not benefit and the image of the judicial system may be harmed.

Accordingly, lawyer advertising should exemplify the inherent dignity and professionalism of the legal community. Dignified lawyer advertising tends to inspire public confidence in the professional competence and ability of lawyers and portrays the commitment of lawyers to serve clients' legal needs in accordance with the ethics and public service tradition of a learned profession.

Lawyer advertising is a key facet of the marketing and delivery of legal services to the public. The professional conduct rules for lawyers adopted by the states regulate some aspects of lawyer advertising, but they also leave lawyers much latitude to decide how to advertise. The following Aspirational Goals are presented in an effort to suggest how lawyers can achieve the beneficial goals of advertising while minimizing or eliminating altogether its negative implications.

These aspirational goals are not intended to establish mandatory requirements which might form the basis for disciplinary enforcement. Rules of Professional Conduct and Disciplinary Rules of Codes of Professional Responsibility in effect in all jurisdictions establish the standards which all lawyers who advertise must meet. Rather, these aspirational goals are intended to provide suggested objectives which all lawyers who engage in advertising their services should be encouraged to achieve in order that lawyer advertising may be more effective and reflect the professionalism of the legal community.

Aspirational Goals

1. Lawyer advertising should encourage and support the public's confidence in the individual lawyer's competence and integrity as well as the commitment of the legal profession to serve the public's legal needs in the tradition of the law as a learned profession.

2. Since advertising may be the only contact many people have with lawyers, advertising by lawyers should help the public understand its legal rights and the judicial process and should uphold the dignity of the legal profession.

3. While "dignity" and "good taste" are terms open to subjective interpretation, lawyers should consider that advertising which reflects the ideals stated in these Aspirational Goals is likely to be dignified and suitable to the profession.

4. Since advertising must be truthful and accurate, and not false or misleading, lawyers should realize that ambiguous or confusing advertising can be misleading.

5. Particular care should be taken in describing fees and costs in advertisements. If an advertisement states a specific fee for a particular service, it should make clear whether or not all problems of that type can be handled for that specific fee. Similar care should be taken in describing the lawyer's areas of practice.

6. Lawyers should consider that the use of inappropriately dramatic music, unseemly slogans, hawkish spokespersons, premium offers, slapstick routines or outlandish settings in advertising does not instill confidence in the lawyer or the legal profession and undermines the serious purpose of legal services and the judicial system.

7. Advertising developed with a clear identification of its potential audience is more likely to be understandable, respectful and appropriate to that audience, and, therefore, more effective. Lawyers should consider using advertising and marketing professionals to assist in identifying and reaching an appropriate audience.

8. How advertising conveys its message is as important as the message itself. Again, lawyers should consider using professional consultants to help them develop and present a clear message to the audience in an effective and appropriate way.

9. Lawyers should design their advertising to attract legal matters which they are competent to handle.

10. Lawyers should be concerned with making legal services more affordable to the public. Lawyer advertising may be designed to build up client bases so that efficiencies of scale may be achieved that will translate into more affordable legal services.

THE TEXAS LAWYER'S CREED—
A MANDATE FOR PROFESSIONALISM

Promulgated by the Supreme Court of Texas and the Texas Court of Criminal Appeals (1989)

I am a lawyer; I am entrusted by the People of Texas to preserve and improve our legal system. I am licensed by the Supreme Court of Texas. I must therefore abide by the Texas Disciplinary Rules of Professional Conduct, but I know that Professionalism requires more than merely avoiding the violation of laws and rules. I am committed to this Creed for no other reason than it is right.

I. OUR LEGAL SYSTEM

A lawyer owes to the administration of justice personal dignity, integrity, and independence. A lawyer should always adhere to the highest principles of professionalism.

1. I am passionately proud of my profession. Therefore, "My word is my bond."

2. I am responsible to assure that all persons have access to competent representation regardless of wealth or position in life.

3. I commit myself to an adequate and effective pro bono program.

4. I am obligated to educate my clients, the public, and other lawyers regarding the spirit and letter of this Creed.

5. I will always be conscious of my duty to the judicial system.

II. LAWYER TO CLIENT

A lawyer owes to a client allegiance, learning, skill, and industry. A lawyer shall employ all appropriate means to protect and advance the client's legitimate rights, claims, and objectives. A lawyer shall not be deterred by any real or imagined fear of judicial disfavor or public unpopularity, nor be influenced by mere self-interest.

1. I will advise my client of the contents of this Creed when undertaking representation.

2. I will endeavor to achieve my client's lawful objectives in legal transactions and in litigation as quickly and economically as possible.

3. I will be loyal and committed to my client's lawful objectives, but I will not permit that loyalty and commitment to interfere with my duty to provide objective and independent advice.

4. I will advise my client that civility and courtesy are expected and are not a sign of weakness.

5. I will advise my client of proper and expected behavior.

6. I will treat adverse parties and witnesses with fairness and due consideration. A client has no right to demand that I abuse anyone or indulge in any offensive conduct.

7. I will advise my client that we will not pursue conduct which is intended primarily to harass or drain the financial resources of the opposing party.

8. I will advise my client that we will not pursue tactics which are intended primarily for delay.

9.   I will advise my client that we will not pursue any course of action which is without merit.

10.   I will advise my client that I reserve the right to determine whether to grant accommodations to opposing counsel in all matters that do not adversely affect my client's lawful objectives. A client has no right to instruct me to refuse reasonable requests made by other counsel.

11.   I will advise my client regarding the availability of mediation, arbitration, and other alternative methods of resolving and settling disputes.

III.   LAWYER TO LAWYER

A lawyer owes to opposing counsel, in the conduct of legal transactions and the pursuit of litigation, courtesy, candor, cooperation, and scrupulous observance of all agreements and mutual understandings. Ill feelings between clients shall not influence a lawyer's conduct, attitude, or demeanor toward opposing counsel. A lawyer shall not engage in unprofessional conduct in retaliation against other unprofessional conduct.

1.   I will be courteous, civil, and prompt in oral and written communications.

2.   I will not quarrel over matters of form or style, but I will concentrate on matters of substance.

3.   I will identify for other counsel or parties all changes I have made in documents submitted for review.

4.   I will attempt to prepare documents which correctly reflect the agreement of the parties. I will not include provisions which have not been agreed upon or omit provisions which are necessary to reflect the agreement of the parties.

5.   I will notify opposing counsel, and, if appropriate, the Court or other persons, as soon as practicable, when hearings, depositions, meetings, conferences or closings are cancelled.

6.   I will agree to reasonable requests for extensions of time and for waiver of procedural formalities, provided legitimate objectives of my client will not be adversely affected.

7.   I will not serve motions or pleadings in any manner that unfairly limits another party's opportunity to respond.

8.   I will attempt to resolve by agreement my objections to matters contained in pleadings and discovery requests and responses.

9.   I can disagree without being disagreeable. I recognize that effective representation does not require antagonistic or obnoxious behavior. I will neither encourage nor knowingly permit my client

or anyone under my control to do anything which would be unethical or improper if done by me.

10. I will not, without good cause, attribute bad motives or unethical conduct to opposing counsel nor bring the profession into disrepute by unfounded accusations of impropriety. I will avoid disparaging personal remarks or acrimony towards opposing counsel, parties and witnesses. I will not be influenced by any ill feeling between clients. I will abstain from any allusion to personal peculiarities or idiosyncrasies of opposing counsel.

11. I will not take advantage, by causing any default or dismissal to be rendered, when I know the identity of an opposing counsel, without first inquiring about that counsel's intention to proceed.

12. I will promptly submit orders to the Court. I will deliver copies to opposing counsel before or contemporaneously with submission to the Court. I will promptly approve the form of orders which accurately reflect the substance of the rulings of the Court.

13. I will not attempt to gain an unfair advantage by sending the Court or its staff correspondence or copies of correspondence.

14. I will not arbitrarily schedule a deposition, Court appearance, or hearing until a good faith effort has been made to schedule it by agreement.

15. I will readily stipulate to undisputed facts in order to avoid needless costs or inconvenience for any party.

16. I will refrain from excessive and abusive discovery.

17. I will comply with all reasonable discovery requests. I will not resist discovery requests which are not objectionable. I will not make objections nor give instructions to a witness for the purpose of delaying or obstructing the discovery process. I will encourage witnesses to respond to all deposition questions which are reasonably understandable. I will neither encourage nor permit my witness to quibble about words where their meaning is reasonably clear.

18. I will not seek Court intervention to obtain discovery which is clearly improper and not discoverable.

19. I will not seek sanctions or disqualification unless it is necessary for protection of my client's lawful objectives or is fully justified by the circumstances.

IV. LAWYER AND JUDGE

Lawyers and judges owe each other respect, diligence, candor, punctuality, and protection against unjust and improper criticism and attack.

PROFESSIONALISM AND COURTESY

Lawyers and judges are equally responsible to protect the dignity and independence of the Court and the profession.

1. I will always recognize that the position of judge is the symbol of both the judicial system and administration of justice. I will refrain from conduct that degrades this symbol.

2. I will conduct myself in Court in a professional manner and demonstrate my respect for the Court and the law.

3. I will treat counsel, opposing parties, the Court, and members of the Court staff with courtesy and civility.

4. I will be punctual.

5. I will not engage in any conduct which offends the dignity and decorum of proceedings.

6. I will not knowingly misrepresent, mischaracterize, misquote or miscite facts or authorities to gain an advantage.

7. I will respect the rulings of the Court.

8. I will give the issues in controversy deliberate, impartial and studied analysis and consideration.

9. I will be considerate of the time constraints and pressures imposed upon the Court, Court staff and counsel in efforts to administer justice and resolve disputes.

PART TWO

CODES OF JUDICIAL CONDUCT

TABLE OF CONTENTS

Introduction

As in the case of regulating lawyers' conduct, the ABA has sought to provide standards for regulating judicial conduct. In 1924, the ABA adopted the Canons of Judicial Ethics. During the 1960s, the federal Judicial Conference of the United States developed standards for federal judges. Soon after the ABA adopted the Model Code of Professional Responsibility, the ABA appointed a commission to produce a revised code of conduct for judges. The resulting document is the 1972 Code of Judicial Conduct. In 1990, the ABA replaced the 1972 Code with a new Code of Judicial Conduct. By 1999, twenty state supreme courts had adopted new standards of judicial conduct based in whole or in part on the 1990 Model Code of Judicial Conduct.

In 1999, the ABA amended the Code of Judicial Conduct to add Canons 3C(5), 3E(1)(e), and 5C(3), (4) & (5).

ABA MODEL CODE OF JUDICIAL CONDUCT (2002) [†]

TABLE OF CONTENTS

PREAMBLE

[1] Our legal system is based on the principle that an independent, fair and competent judiciary will interpret and apply the laws that govern us. The role of the judiciary is central to American concepts of justice and the rule of law. Intrinsic to all sections of this Code are the precepts that judges, individually and collectively, must respect and honor the judicial office as a public trust and strive to enhance and maintain confidence in our legal system. The judge is an arbiter of facts and law for the resolution of disputes and a highly visible symbol of government under the rule of law.

[2] The Code of Judicial Conduct is intended to establish standards for ethical conduct of judges. It consists of broad statements called Canons, specific rules set forth in Sections under each Canon, a Terminology Section, an Application Section and Commentary. The text of the Canons and the Sections, including the Terminology and Application Sections, is authoritative. The Commentary, by explanation and example, provides guidance with respect to the purpose and meaning of the Canons and Sections. The Commentary is not intended as a statement of additional rules. When the text uses "shall" or "shall not," it is intended to impose binding obligations the violation of which can result

---

† Model Code of Judicial Conduct (August 1990) was adopted by the House of Delegates of the American Bar Association on August 7, 1990.

in disciplinary action. When "should" or "should not" is used, the text is intended as hortatory and as a statement of what is or is not appropriate conduct but not as a binding rule under which a judge may be disciplined. When "may" is used, it denotes permissible discretion or, depending on the context, it refers to action that is not covered by specific proscriptions.

[3] The Canons and Sections are rules of reason. They should be applied consistent with constitutional requirements, statutes, other court rules and decisional law and in the context of all relevant circumstances. The Code is to be construed so as not to impinge on the essential independence of judges in making judicial decisions.

[4] The Code is designed to provide guidance to judges and candidates for judicial office and to provide a structure for regulating conduct through disciplinary agencies. It is not designed or intended as a basis for civil liability or criminal prosecution. Furthermore, the purpose of the Code would be subverted if the Code were invoked by lawyers for mere tactical advantage in a proceeding.

[5] The text of the Canons and Sections is intended to govern conduct of judges and to be binding upon them. It is not intended, however, that every transgression will result in disciplinary action. Whether disciplinary action is appropriate, and the degree of discipline to be imposed, should be determined through a reasonable and reasoned application of the text and should depend on such factors as the seriousness of the transgression, whether there is a pattern of improper activity and the effect of the improper activity on others or on the judicial system. See ABA Standards Relating to Judicial Discipline and Disability Retirement.[1]

[6] The Code of Judicial Conduct is not intended as an exhaustive guide for the conduct of judges. They should also be governed in their judicial and personal conduct by general ethical standards. The Code is intended, however, to state basic standards which should govern the conduct of all judges and to provide guidance to assist judges in establishing and maintaining high standards of judicial and personal conduct.

TERMINOLOGY

Terms explained below are noted with an asterisk (*) in the Sections where they appear. In addition, the Sections where terms appear are referred to after the explanation of each term below.

"Appropriate authority" denotes the authority with responsibility for initiation of disciplinary process with respect to the violation to be reported. See Sections 3D(1) and 3D(2).

---

1. Judicial disciplinary procedures adopted in the jurisdictions should comport with the requirements of due process. The ABA Standards Relating to Judicial Discipline and Disability Retirement are cited as an example of how these due process requirements may be satisfied.

"Candidate." A candidate is a person seeking selection for or retention in judicial office by election or appointment. A person becomes a candidate for judicial office as soon as he or she makes a public announcement of candidacy, declares or files as a candidate with the election or appointment authority, or authorizes solicitation or acceptance of contributions or support. The term "candidate" has the same meaning when applied to a judge seeking election or appointment to non-judicial office. See Preamble and Sections 5A, 5B, 5C and 5E.

"Continuing part-time judge." A continuing part-time judge is a judge who serves repeatedly on a part-time basis by election or under a continuing appointment, including a retired judge subject to recall who is permitted to practice law. See Application Section C.

"Court personnel" does not include the lawyers in a proceeding before a judge. See Sections 3B(7)(c) and 3B(9).

"De minimis" denotes an insignificant interest that could not raise reasonable question as to a judge's impartiality. See Sections 3E(1)(c) and 3E(1)(d).

"Economic interest" denotes ownership of a more than de minimis legal or equitable interest, or a relationship as officer, director, advisor or other active participant in the affairs of a party, except that:

(i) ownership of an interest in a mutual or common investment fund that holds securities is not an economic interest in such securities unless the judge participates in the management of the fund or a proceeding pending or impending before the judge could substantially affect the value of the interest;

(ii) service by a judge as an officer, director, advisor or other active participant in an educational, religious, charitable, fraternal or civic organization, or service by a judge's spouse, parent or child as an officer, director, advisor or other active participant in any organization does not create an economic interest in securities held by that organization;

(iii) a deposit in a financial institution, the proprietary interest of a policy holder in a mutual insurance company, of a depositor in a mutual savings association or of a member in a credit union, or a similar proprietary interest, is not an economic interest in the organization unless a proceeding pending or impending before the judge could substantially affect the value of the interest;

(iv) ownership of government securities is not an economic interest in the issuer unless a proceeding pending or impending before the judge could substantially affect the value of the securities.

690

See Sections 3E(1)(c) and 3E(2).

"Fiduciary" includes such relationships as executor, administrator, trustee, and guardian. See Sections 3E(2) and 4E.

"Knowingly," "knowledge," "known" or "knows" denotes actual knowledge of the fact in question. A person's knowledge may be inferred from circumstances. See Sections 3D, 3E(1), and 5A(3).

"Law" denotes court rules as well as statutes, constitutional provisions and decisional law. See Sections 2A, 3A, 3B(2), 3B(6), 4B, 4C, 4D(5), 4F, 4I, 5A(2), 5A(3), 5B(2), 5C(1), 5C(3) and 5D.

"Member of the candidate's family" denotes a spouse, child, grandchild, parent, grandparent or other relative or person with whom the candidate maintains a close familial relationship. See Section 5A(3)(a).

"Member of the judge's family" denotes a spouse, child, grandchild, parent, grandparent, or other relative or person with whom the judge maintains a close familial relationship. See Sections 4D(3), 4E and 4G.

"Member of the judge's family residing in the judge's household" denotes any relative of a judge by blood or marriage, or a person treated by a judge as a member of the judge's family, who resides in the judge's household. See Sections 3E(1) and 4D(5).

"Nonpublic information" denotes information that, by law, is not available to the public. Nonpublic information may include but is not limited to: information that is sealed by statute or court order, impounded or communicated in camera; and information offered in grand jury proceedings, presentencing reports, dependency cases or psychiatric reports. See Section 3B(11).

"Periodic part-time judge." A periodic part-time judge is a judge who serves or expects to serve repeatedly on a part-time basis but under a separate appointment for each limited period of service or for each matter. See Application Section D.

"Political organization" denotes a political party or other group, the principal purpose of which is to further the election or appointment of candidates to political office. See Sections 5A(1), 5B(2) and 5C(1).

"Pro tempore part-time judge." A pro tempore part-time judge is a judge who serves or expects to serve once or only sporadically on a part-time basis under a separate appointment for each period of service or for each case heard. See Application Section E.

"Public election." This term includes primary and general elections; it includes partisan elections, nonpartisan elections and retention elections. See Section 5C.

"Require." The rules prescribing that a judge "require" certain conduct of others are, like all of the rules in this Code, rules of reason. The use of the term "require" in that context means a judge is to exercise reasonable direction and control over the conduct of those persons subject to the judge's direction and control. See Sections 3B(3), 3B(4), 3B(6), 3B(9) and 3C(2).

"Third degree of relationship." The following persons are relatives within the third degree of relationship: great-grandparent, grandparent, parent, uncle, aunt, brother, sister, child, grandchild, great-grandchild, nephew or niece. See Section 3E(1)(d).

CANON 1

A Judge Shall Uphold the Integrity and Independence of the Judiciary

A. An independent and honorable judiciary is indispensable to justice in our society. A judge should participate in establishing, maintaining and enforcing high standards of conduct, and shall personally observe those standards so that the integrity and independence of the judiciary will be preserved. The provisions of this Code are to be construed and applied to further that objective.

Commentary

[1] Deference to the judgments and rulings of courts depends upon public confidence in the integrity and independence of judges. The integrity and independence of judges depends in turn upon their acting without fear or favor. Although judges should be independent, they must comply with the law, including the provisions of this Code. Public confidence in the impartiality of the judiciary is maintained by the adherence of each judge to this responsibility. Conversely, violation of this Code diminishes public confidence in the judiciary and thereby does injury to the system of government under law.

CANON 2

A Judge Shall Avoid Impropriety and the Appearance of Impropriety in All of the Judge's Activities

A. A judge shall respect and comply with the law * and shall act at all times in a manner that promotes public confidence in the integrity and impartiality of the judiciary.

Commentary

[1] Public confidence in the judiciary is eroded by irresponsible or improper conduct by judges. A judge must avoid all impropriety and

---

* See Terminology, "law."

appearance of impropriety. A judge must expect to be the subject of constant public scrutiny. A judge must therefore accept restrictions on the judge's conduct that might be viewed as burdensome by the ordinary citizen and should do so freely and willingly.

[2] The prohibition against behaving with impropriety or the appearance of impropriety applies to both the professional and personal conduct of a judge. Because it is not practicable to list all prohibited acts, the proscription is necessarily cast in general terms that extend to conduct by judges that is harmful although not specifically mentioned in the Code. Actual improprieties under this standard include violations of law, court rules or other specific provisions of this Code. The test for appearance of impropriety is whether the conduct would create in reasonable minds a perception that the judge's ability to carry out judicial responsibilities with integrity, impartiality and competence is impaired.

See also Commentary under Section 2C.

B. A judge shall not allow family, social, political or other relationships to influence the judge's judicial conduct or judgment. A judge shall not lend the prestige of judicial office to advance the private interests of the judge or others; nor shall a judge convey or permit others to convey the impression that they are in a special position to influence the judge. A judge shall not testify voluntarily as a character witness.

Commentary

[1] Maintaining the prestige of judicial office is essential to a system of government in which the judiciary functions independently of the executive and legislative branches. Respect for the judicial office facilitates the orderly conduct of legitimate judicial functions. Judges should distinguish between proper and improper use of the prestige of office in all of their activities. For example, it would be improper for a judge to allude to his or her judgeship to gain a personal advantage such as deferential treatment when stopped by a police officer for a traffic offense. Similarly, judicial letterhead must not be used for conducting a judge's personal business.

[2] A judge must avoid lending the prestige of judicial office for the advancement of the private interests of others. For example, a judge must not use the judge's judicial position to gain advantage in a civil suit involving a member of the judge's family. In contracts for publication of a judge's writings, a judge should retain control over the advertising to avoid exploitation of the judge's office. As to the acceptance of awards, see Section 4D(5)(a) and Commentary.

[3] Although a judge should be sensitive to possible abuse of the prestige of office, a judge may, based on the judge's personal knowledge, serve as a reference or provide a letter of recommendation. However, a judge must not initiate the communication of information to a sentenc-

ing judge or a probation or corrections officer but may provide to such persons information for the record in response to a formal request.

[4] Judges may participate in the process of judicial selection by cooperating with appointing authorities and screening committees seeking names for consideration, and by responding to official inquiries concerning a person being considered for a judgeship. See also Canon 5 regarding use of a judge's name in political activities.

[5] A judge must not testify voluntarily as a character witness because to do so may lend the prestige of the judicial office in support of the party for whom the judge testifies. Moreover, when a judge testifies as a witness, a lawyer who regularly appears before the judge may be placed in the awkward position of cross-examining the judge. A judge may, however, testify when properly summoned. Except in unusual circumstances where the demands of justice require, a judge should discourage a party from requiring the judge to testify as a character witness.

C. A judge shall not hold membership in any organization that practices invidious discrimination on the basis of race, sex, religion or national origin.

Commentary

[1] Membership of a judge in an organization that practices invidious discrimination gives rise to perceptions that the judge's impartiality is impaired. Section 2C refers to the current practices of the organization. Whether an organization practices invidious discrimination is often a complex question to which judges should be sensitive. The answer cannot be determined from a mere examination of an organization's current membership rolls but rather depends on how the organization selects members and other relevant factors, such as that the organization is dedicated to the preservation of religious, ethnic or cultural values of legitimate common interest to its members, or that it is in fact and effect an intimate, purely private organization whose membership limitations could not be constitutionally prohibited. Absent such factors, an organization is generally said to discriminate invidiously if it arbitrarily excludes from membership on the basis of race, religion, sex or national origin persons who would otherwise be admitted to membership. *See New York State Club Ass'n. Inc. v. City of New York,* 108 S.Ct. 2225, 101 L.Ed.2d 1 (1988); *Board of Directors of Rotary International v. Rotary Club of Duarte,* 481 U.S. 537, 107 S.Ct. 1940, 95 L.Ed.2d 474 (1987); *Roberts v. United States Jaycees,* 468 U.S. 609, 104 S.Ct. 3244, 82 L.Ed.2d 462 (1984).

[2] Although Section 2C relates only to membership in organizations that invidiously discriminate on the basis of race, sex, religion or national origin, a judge's membership in an organization that engages in any discriminatory membership practices prohibited by the law of the jurisdiction also violates Canon 2 and Section 2A and gives the appear-

ance of impropriety. In addition, it would be a violation of Canon 2 and Section 2A for a judge to arrange a meeting at a club that the judge knows practices invidious discrimination on the basis of race, sex, religion or national origin in its membership or other policies, or for the judge to regularly use such a club. Moreover, public manifestation by a judge of the judge's knowing approval of invidious discrimination on any basis gives the appearance of impropriety under Canon 2 and diminishes public confidence in the integrity and impartiality of the judiciary, in violation of Section 2A.

[3] When a person who is a judge on the date this Code becomes effective [in the jurisdiction in which the person is a judge] [2] learns that an organization to which the judge belongs engages in invidious discrimination that would preclude membership under Section 2C or under Canon 2 and Section 2A, the judge is permitted, in lieu of resigning, to make immediate efforts to have the organization discontinue its invidiously discriminatory practices, but is required to suspend participation in any other activities of the organization. If the organization fails to discontinue its invidiously discriminatory practices as promptly as possible (and in all events within a year of the judge's first learning of the practices), the judge is required to resign immediately from the organization.

CANON 3

A Judge Shall Perform the Duties of Judicial Office Impartially and Diligently

A. Judicial Duties in General. The judicial duties of a judge take precedence over all the judge's other activities. The judge's judicial duties include all the duties of the judge's office prescribed by law.* In the performance of these duties, the following standards apply.

B. Adjudicative Responsibilities.

(1) A judge shall hear and decide matters assigned to the judge except those in which disqualification is required.

(2) A judge shall be faithful to the law * and maintain professional competence in it. A judge shall not be swayed by partisan interests, public clamor or fear of criticism.

(3) A judge shall require * order and decorum in proceedings before the judge.

(4) A judge shall be patient, dignified and courteous to litigants, jurors, witnesses, lawyers and others with whom the judge deals in an official capacity, and shall require * similar

---

2. The language within the brackets should be deleted when the jurisdiction adopts this provision.

* See Terminology.

conduct of lawyers, and of staff, court officials and others subject to the judge's direction and control.

Commentary

[1] The duty to hear all proceedings fairly and with patience is not inconsistent with the duty to dispose promptly of the business of the court. Judges can be efficient and businesslike while being patient and deliberate.

(5) A judge shall perform judicial duties without bias or prejudice. A judge shall not, in the performance of judicial duties, by words or conduct manifest bias or prejudice, including but not limited to bias or prejudice based upon race, sex, religion, national origin, disability, age, sexual orientation or socioeconomic status, and shall not permit staff, court officials and others subject to the judge's direction and control to do so.

Commentary

[1] A judge must refrain from speech, gestures or other conduct that could reasonably be perceived as sexual harassment and must require the same standard of conduct of others subject to the judge's direction and control.

[2] A judge must perform judicial duties impartially and fairly. A judge who manifests bias on any basis in a proceeding impairs the fairness of the proceeding and brings the judiciary into disrepute. Facial expression and body language, in addition to oral communication, can give to parties or lawyers in the proceeding, jurors, the media and others an appearance of judicial bias. A judge must be alert to avoid behavior that may be perceived as prejudicial.

(6) A judge shall require * lawyers in proceedings before the judge to refrain from manifesting, by words or conduct, bias or prejudice based upon race, sex, religion, national origin, disability, age, sexual orientation or socioeconomic status, against parties, witnesses, counsel or others. This Section 3B(6) does not preclude legitimate advocacy when race, sex, religion, national origin, disability, age, sexual orientation or socioeconomic status, or other similar factors, are issues in the proceeding.

(7) A judge shall accord to every person who has a legal interest in a proceeding, or that person's lawyer, the right to be heard according to law.* A judge shall not initiate, permit, or consider ex parte communications, or consider other communications made to the judge outside the presence of the parties concerning a pending or impending proceeding except that:

* See Terminology.

(a) Where circumstances require, ex parte communications for scheduling, administrative purposes or emergencies that do not deal with substantive matters or issues on the merits are authorized; provided:

(i) the judge reasonably believes that no party will gain a procedural or tactical advantage as a result of the ex parte communication, and

(ii) the judge makes provision promptly to notify all other parties of the substance of the ex parte communication and allows an opportunity to respond.

(b) A judge may obtain the advice of a disinterested expert on the law * applicable to a proceeding before the judge if the judge gives notice to the parties of the person consulted and the substance of the advice, and affords the parties reasonable opportunity to respond.

(c) A judge may consult with court personnel * whose function is to aid the judge in carrying out the judge's adjudicative responsibilities or with other judges.

(d) A judge may, with the consent of the parties, confer separately with the parties and their lawyers in an effort to mediate or settle matters pending before the judge.

(e) A judge may initiate or consider any ex parte communications when expressly authorized by law * to do so.

Commentary

[1] The proscription against communications concerning a proceeding includes communications from lawyers, law teachers, and other persons who are not participants in the proceeding, except to the limited extent permitted.

[2] To the extent reasonably possible, all parties or their lawyers shall be included in communications with a judge.

[3] Whenever presence of a party or notice to a party is required by Section 3B(7), it is the party's lawyer, or if the party is unrepresented the party, who is to be present or to whom notice is to be given.

[4] An appropriate and often desirable procedure for a court to obtain the advice of a disinterested expert on legal issues is to invite the expert to file a brief amicus curiae.

[5] Certain ex parte communication is approved by Section 3B(7) to facilitate scheduling and other administrative purposes and to accommodate emergencies. In general, however, a judge must discourage ex parte communication and allow it only if all the criteria stated in Section 3B(7) are clearly met. A judge must disclose to all parties all ex parte

* See Terminology.

communications described in Sections 3B(7)(a) and 3B(7)(b) regarding a proceeding pending or impending before the judge.

[6] A judge must not independently investigate facts in a case and must consider only the evidence presented.

[7] A judge may request a party to submit proposed findings of fact and conclusions of law, so long as the other parties are apprised of the request and are given an opportunity to respond to the proposed findings and conclusions.

[8] A judge must make reasonable efforts, including the provision of appropriate supervision, to ensure that Section 3B(7) is not violated through law clerks or other personnel on the judge's staff.

[9] If communication between the trial judge and the appellate court with respect to a proceeding is permitted, a copy of any written communication or the substance of any oral communication should be provided to all parties.

(8) A judge shall dispose of all judicial matters promptly, efficiently and fairly.

Commentary

[1] In disposing of matters promptly, efficiently and fairly, a judge must demonstrate due regard for the rights of the parties to be heard and to have issues resolved without unnecessary cost or delay. Containing costs while preserving fundamental rights of parties also protects the interests of witnesses and the general public. A judge should monitor and supervise cases so as to reduce or eliminate dilatory practices, avoidable delays and unnecessary costs. A judge should encourage and seek to facilitate settlement, but parties should not feel coerced into surrendering the right to have their controversy resolved by the courts.

[2] Prompt disposition of the court's business requires a judge to devote adequate time to judicial duties, to be punctual in attending court and expeditious in determining matters under submission, and to insist that court officials, litigants and their lawyers cooperate with the judge to that end.

(9) A judge shall not, while a proceeding is pending or impending in any court, make any public comment that might reasonably be expected to affect its outcome or impair its fairness or make any nonpublic comment that might substantially interfere with a fair trial or hearing. The judge shall require * similar abstention on the part of court personnel * subject to the judge's direction and control. This Section does not prohibit judges from making public statements in the course of their official duties or from explaining for public information the

* See Terminology.

procedures of the court. **This Section does not apply to proceedings in which the judge is a litigant in a personal capacity.**

Commentary

[1] The requirement that judges abstain from public comment regarding a pending or impending proceeding continues during any appellate process and until final disposition. This Section does not prohibit a judge from commenting on proceedings in which the judge is a litigant in a personal capacity, but in cases such as a writ of mandamus where the judge is a litigant in an official capacity, the judge must not comment publicly. The conduct of lawyers relating to trial publicity is governed by [Rule 3.6 of the ABA Model Rules of Professional Conduct]. (Each jurisdiction should substitute an appropriate reference to its rule.)

(10) A judge shall not commend or criticize jurors for their verdict other than in a court order or opinion in a proceeding, but may express appreciation to jurors for their service to the judicial system and the community.

Commentary

[1] Commending or criticizing jurors for their verdict may imply a judicial expectation in future cases and may impair a juror's ability to be fair and impartial in a subsequent case.

(11) A judge shall not disclose or use, for any purpose unrelated to judicial duties, nonpublic information * acquired in a judicial capacity.

C. Administrative Responsibilities.

(1) A judge shall diligently discharge the judge's administrative responsibilities without bias or prejudice and maintain professional competence in judicial administration, and should cooperate with other judges and court officials in the administration of court business.

(2) A judge shall require staff, court officials and others subject to the judge's direction and control to observe the standards of fidelity and diligence that apply to the judge and to refrain from manifesting bias or prejudice in the performance of their official duties.

(3) A judge with supervisory authority for the judicial performance of other judges shall take reasonable measures to assure the prompt disposition of matters before them and the proper performance of their other judicial responsibilities.

(4) A judge shall not make unnecessary appointments. A judge shall exercise the power of appointment impartially and on the basis of merit. A judge shall avoid nepotism and favorit-

* See Terminology.

699

ism. **A judge shall not approve compensation of appointees beyond the fair value of services rendered.**

Commentary

[1] Appointees of a judge include assigned counsel, officials such as referees, commissioners, special masters, receivers and guardians and personnel such as clerks, secretaries and bailiffs. Consent by the parties to an appointment or an award of compensation does not relieve the judge of the obligation prescribed by Section 3C(4).

(5)[†] A judge shall not appoint a lawyer to a position if the judge either knows that the lawyer has contributed more than [$] within the prior [ ] years to the judges's election campaign,[3] or learns of such a contribution by means of a timely motion by a party or other person properly interested in the matter, unless

(a) the position is substantially uncompensated;

(b) the lawyer has been selected in rotation from a list of a qualified and available lawyers compiled without regard to their having made political contributions; or

(c) the judge or another presiding or administrative judge affirmatively finds that no other lawyer is willing, competent and able to accept the position.

D. Disciplinary Responsibilities.

(1) A judge who receives information indicating a substantial likelihood that another judge has committed a violation of this Code should take appropriate action. A judge having knowledge * that another judge has committed a violation of this Code that raises a substantial question as to the other judge's fitness for office shall inform the appropriate authority.*

(2) A judge who receives information indicating a substantial likelihood that a lawyer has committed a violation of the Rules of Professional Conduct [substitute correct title if the applicable rules of lawyer conduct have a different title] should take appropriate action. A judge having knowledge * that a lawyer has committed a violation of the Rules of Professional Conduct [substitute correct title if the applicable rules of lawyer conduct have a different title] that raises a substantial question as to the lawyer's honesty, trustworthiness or fitness as a lawyer in other respects shall inform the appropriate authority.*

(3) Acts of a judge, in the discharge of disciplinary responsibilities, required or permitted by Sections 3D(1) and 3D(2) are part of a judge's judicial duties and shall be absolutely privi-

---

† [Editor's Note: This language was added by the ABA House of Delegates in 1999.]

3. This provision is meant to be applicable wherever judges are subject to public election; specific amount and time limita-

tions, to be determined based on circumstances within the jurisdiction, should be inserted in the brackets.

* See Terminology.

leged, and no civil action predicated thereon may be instituted against the judge.

Commentary

[1] Appropriate action may include direct communication with the judge or lawyer who has committed the violation, other direct action if available, and reporting the violation to the appropriate authority or other agency or body.

E. Disqualification.

(1) A judge shall disqualify himself or herself in a proceeding in which the judge's impartiality might reasonably be questioned, including but not limited to instances where:

Commentary

[1] Under this rule, a judge is disqualified whenever the judge's impartiality might reasonably be questioned, regardless whether any of the specific rules in Section 3E(1) apply. For example, if a judge were in the process of negotiating for employment with a law firm, the judge would be disqualified from any matters in which that law firm appeared, unless the disqualification was waived by the parties after disclosure by the judge.

[2] A judge should disclose on the record information that the judge believes the parties or their lawyers might consider relevant to the question of disqualification, even if the judge believes there is no real basis for disqualification.

[3] By decisional law, the rule of necessity may override the rule of disqualification. For example, a judge might be required to participate in judicial review of a judicial salary statute, or might be the only judge available in a matter requiring immediate judicial action, such as a hearing on probable cause or a temporary restraining order. In the latter case, the judge must disclose on the record the basis for possible disqualification and use reasonable efforts to transfer the matter to another judge as soon as practicable.

> **(a) the judge has a personal bias or prejudice concerning a party or a party's lawyer, or personal knowledge * of disputed evidentiary facts concerning the proceeding;**
>
> **(b) the judge served as a lawyer in the matter in controversy, or a lawyer with whom the judge previously practiced law served during such association as a lawyer concerning the matter, or the judge has been a material witness concerning it;**

* See Terminology.

Commentary

[1] A lawyer in a government agency does not ordinarily have an association with other lawyers employed by that agency within the meaning of Section 3E(1)(b); a judge formerly employed by a government agency, however, should disqualify himself or herself in a proceeding if the judge's impartiality might reasonably be questioned because of such association.

> **(c) the judge knows * that he or she, individually or as a fiduciary, or the judge's spouse, parent or child wherever residing, or any other member of the judge's family residing in the judge's household,* has an economic interest * in the subject matter in controversy or in a party to the proceeding or has any other more than de minimis * interest that could be substantially affected by the proceeding;**
>
> **(d) the judge or the judge's spouse, or a person within the third degree of relationship * to either of them, or the spouse of such a person:**
>
> > **(i) is a party to the proceeding, or an officer, director or trustee of a party;**
> >
> > **(ii) is acting as a lawyer in the proceeding;**
> >
> > **(iii) is known * by the judge to have a more than de minimis * interest that could be substantially affected by the proceeding;**
> >
> > **(iv) is to the judge's knowledge * likely to be a material witness in the proceeding.**

(e)† the judge knows or learns by means of a timely motion that a party or a party's lawyer has within the previous [ ] year[s] made aggregate* contributions to the judge's campaign in an amount that is greater than [[[$] for an individual or [$] for an entity]] [[is reasonable and appropriate for an individual or an entity]].⁴]

Commentary

[1] The fact that a lawyer in a proceeding is affiliated with a law firm with which a relative of the judge is affiliated does not of itself disqualify the judge. Under appropriate circumstances, the fact that "the judge's impartiality might reasonably be questioned" under Section 3E(1), or that the relative is known by the judge to have an interest in the law firm that could be "substantially affected by the outcome of the

---

* See Terminology

† [Editor's Note: This language was added by the ABA House of Delegates in 1999.]

4. This provision is meant to be applicable wherever judges are subject to public

election. Where specific dollar amounts determined by local circumstances are not used, the "reasonable and appropriate" language should be used.

proceeding'' under Section 3E(1)(d)(iii) may require the judge's disqualification.

(2) A judge shall keep informed about the judge's personal and fiduciary * economic interests,* and make a reasonable effort to keep informed about the personal economic interests of the judge's spouse and minor children residing in the judge's household.

F. Remittal of Disqualification. A judge disqualified by the terms of Section 3E may disclose on the record the basis of the judge's disqualification and may ask the parties and their lawyers to consider, out of the presence of the judge, whether to waive disqualification. If following disclosure of any basis for disqualification other than personal bias or prejudice concerning a party, the parties and lawyers, without participation by the judge, all agree that the judge should not be disqualified, and the judge is then willing to participate, the judge may participate in the proceeding. The agreement shall be incorporated in the record of the proceeding.

Commentary

[1] A remittal procedure provides the parties an opportunity to proceed without delay if they wish to waive the disqualification. To assure that consideration of the question of remittal is made independently of the judge, a judge must not solicit, seek or hear comment on possible remittal or waiver of the disqualification unless the lawyers jointly propose remittal after consultation as provided in the rule. A party may act through counsel if counsel represents on the record that the party has been consulted and consents. As a practical matter, a judge may wish to have all parties and their lawyers sign the remittal agreement.

CANON 4

A Judge Shall So Conduct the Judge's Extra–Judicial Activities as to Minimize the Risk of Conflict With Judicial Obligations

A. Extra-judicial Activities in General. A judge shall conduct all of the judge's extra-judicial activities so that they do not:

(1) cast reasonable doubt on the judge's capacity to act impartially as a judge;

(2) demean the judicial office; or

(3) interfere with the proper performance of judicial duties.

* See Terminology.

Commentary

[1] Complete separation of a judge from extra-judicial activities is neither possible nor wise; a judge should not become isolated from the community in which the judge lives.

[2] Expressions of bias or prejudice by a judge, even outside the judge's judicial activities, may cast reasonable doubt on the judge's capacity to act impartially as a judge. Expressions which may do so include jokes or other remarks demeaning individuals on the basis of their race, sex, religion, national origin, disability, age, sexual orientation or socioeconomic status. See Section 2C and accompanying Commentary.

B. Avocational Activities. A judge may speak, write, lecture, teach and participate in other extra-judicial activities concerning the law,* the legal system, the administration of justice and non-legal subjects, subject to the requirements of this Code.

Commentary

[1] As a judicial officer and person specially learned in the law, a judge is in a unique position to contribute to the improvement of the law, the legal system, and the administration of justice, including revision of substantive and procedural law and improvement of criminal and juvenile justice. To the extent that time permits, a judge is encouraged to do so, either independently or through a bar association, judicial conference or other organization dedicated to the improvement of the law. Judges may participate in efforts to promote the fair administration of justice, the independence of the judiciary and the integrity of the legal profession and may express opposition to the persecution of lawyers and judges in other countries because of their professional activities.

[2] In this and other Sections of Canon 4, the phrase "subject to the requirements of this Code" is used, notably in connection with a judge's governmental, civic or charitable activities. This phrase is included to remind judges that the use of permissive language in various Sections of the Code does not relieve a judge from the other requirements of the Code that apply to the specific conduct.

C. Governmental, Civic or Charitable Activities.

(1) A judge shall not appear at a public hearing before, or otherwise consult with, an executive or legislative body or official except on matters concerning the law,* the legal system or the administration of justice or except when acting pro se in a matter involving the judge or the judge's interests.

* See Terminology.

704

Commentary

[1] See Section 2B regarding the obligation to avoid improper influence.

(2) A judge shall not accept appointment to a governmental committee or commission or other governmental position that is concerned with issues of fact or policy on matters other than the improvement of the law,* the legal system or the administration of justice. A judge may, however, represent a country, state or locality on ceremonial occasions or in connection with historical, educational or cultural activities.

Commentary

[1] Section 4C(2) prohibits a judge from accepting any governmental position except one relating to the law, legal system or administration of justice as authorized by Section 4C(3). The appropriateness of accepting extra-judicial assignments must be assessed in light of the demands on judicial resources created by crowded dockets and the need to protect the courts from involvement in extra-judicial matters that may prove to be controversial. Judges should not accept governmental appointments that are likely to interfere with the effectiveness and independence of the judiciary.

[2] Section 4C(2) does not govern a judge's service in a nongovernmental position. See Section 4C(3) permitting service by a judge with organizations devoted to the improvement of the law, the legal system or the administration of justice and with educational, religious, charitable, fraternal or civic organizations not conducted for profit. For example, service on the board of a public educational institution, unless it were a law school, would be prohibited under Section 4C(2), but service on the board of a public law school or any private educational institution would generally be permitted under Section 4C(3).

(3) A judge may serve as an officer, director, trustee or nonlegal advisor of an organization or governmental agency devoted to the improvement of the law,* the legal system or the administration of justice or of an educational, religious, charitable, fraternal or civic organization not conducted for profit, subject to the following limitations and the other requirements of this Code.

Commentary

[1] Section 4C(3) does not apply to a judge's service in a governmental position unconnected with the improvement of the law, the legal system or the administration of justice; see Section 4C(2).

* See Terminology.

[2] See Commentary to Section 4B regarding use of the phrase "subject to the following limitations and the other requirements of this Code." As an example of the meaning of the phrase, a judge permitted by Section 4C(3) to serve on the board of a fraternal institution may be prohibited from such service by Sections 2C or 4A if the institution practices invidious discrimination or if service on the board otherwise casts reasonable doubt on the judge's capacity to act impartially as a judge.

[3] Service by a judge on behalf of a civic or charitable organization may be governed by other provisions of Canon 4 in addition to Section 4C. For example, a judge is prohibited by Section 4G from serving as a legal advisor to a civic or charitable organization.

(a) A judge shall not serve as an officer, director, trustee or non-legal advisor if it is likely that the organization

(i) will be engaged in proceedings that would ordinarily come before the judge, or

(ii) will be engaged frequently in adversary proceedings in the court of which the judge is a member or in any court subject to the appellate jurisdiction of the court of which the judge is a member.

Commentary

[1] The changing nature of some organizations and of their relationship to the law makes it necessary for a judge regularly to reexamine the activities of each organization with which the judge is affiliated to determine if it is proper for the judge to continue the affiliation. For example, in many jurisdictions charitable hospitals are now more frequently in court than in the past. Similarly, the boards of some legal aid organizations now make policy decisions that may have political significance or imply commitment to causes that may come before the courts for adjudication.

(b) A judge as an officer, director, trustee or non-legal advisor, or as a member or otherwise:

(i) may assist such an organization in planning fund-raising and may participate in the management and investment of the organization's funds, but shall not personally participate in the solicitation of funds or other fund-raising activities, except that a judge may solicit funds from other judges over whom the judge does not exercise supervisory or appellate authority;

(ii) may make recommendations to public and private fund-granting organizations on projects and pro-

706

grams concerning the law,* the legal system or the administration of justice;

(iii) shall not personally participate in membership solicitation if the solicitation might reasonably be perceived as coercive or, except as permitted in Section 4C(3)(b)(i), if the membership solicitation is essentially a fund-raising mechanism;

(iv) shall not use or permit the use of the prestige of judicial office for fund-raising or membership solicitation.

Commentary

[1] A judge may solicit membership or endorse or encourage membership efforts for an organization devoted to the improvement of the law, the legal system or the administration of justice or a nonprofit educational, religious, charitable, fraternal or civic organization as long as the solicitation cannot reasonably be perceived as coercive and is not essentially a fund-raising mechanism. Solicitation of funds for an organization and solicitation of memberships similarly involve the danger that the person solicited will feel obligated to respond favorably to the solicitor if the solicitor is in a position of influence or control. A judge must not engage in direct, individual solicitation of funds or memberships in person, in writing or by telephone except in the following cases: 1) a judge may solicit for funds or memberships other judges over whom the judge does not exercise supervisory or appellate authority, 2) a judge may solicit other persons for membership in the organizations described above if neither those persons nor persons with whom they are affiliated are likely ever to appear before the court on which the judge serves and 3) a judge who is an officer of such an organization may send a general membership solicitation mailing over the judge's signature.

[2] Use of an organization letterhead for fund-raising or membership solicitation does not violate Section 4C(3)(b) provided the letterhead lists only the judge's name and office or other position in the organization, and, if comparable designations are listed for other persons, the judge's judicial designation. In addition, a judge must also make reasonable efforts to ensure that the judge's staff, court officials and others subject to the judge's direction and control do not solicit funds on the judge's behalf for any purpose, charitable or otherwise.

[3] A judge must not be a speaker or guest of honor at an organization's fund-raising event, but mere attendance at such an event is permissible if otherwise consistent with this Code.

D. Financial Activities.

* See Terminology.

(1) A judge shall not engage in financial and business dealings that:

(a) may reasonably be perceived to exploit the judge's judicial position, or

(b) involve the judge in frequent transactions or continuing business relationships with those lawyers or other persons likely to come before the court on which the judge serves.

Commentary

[1] The Time for Compliance provision of this Code (Application, Section F) postpones the time for compliance with certain provisions of this Section in some cases.

[2] When a judge acquires in a judicial capacity information, such as material contained in filings with the court, that is not yet generally known, the judge must not use the information for private gain. See Section 2B; see also Section 3B(11).

[3] A judge must avoid financial and business dealings that involve the judge in frequent transactions or continuing business relationships with persons likely to come either before the judge personally or before other judges on the judge's court. In addition, a judge should discourage members of the judge's family from engaging in dealings that would reasonably appear to exploit the judge's judicial position. This rule is necessary to avoid creating an appearance of exploitation of office or favoritism and to minimize the potential for disqualification. With respect to affiliation of relatives of judge with law firms appearing before the judge, see Commentary to Section 3E(1) relating to disqualification.

[4] Participation by a judge in financial and business dealings is subject to the general prohibitions in Section 4A against activities that tend to reflect adversely on impartiality, demean the judicial office, or interfere with the proper performance of judicial duties. Such participation is also subject to the general prohibition in Canon 2 against activities involving impropriety or the appearance of impropriety and the prohibition in Section 2B against the misuse of the prestige of judicial office. In addition, a judge must maintain high standards of conduct in all of the judge's activities, as set forth in Canon 1. See Commentary for Section 4B regarding use of the phrase "subject to the requirements of this Code."

(2) A judge may, subject to the requirements of this Code, hold and manage investments of the judge and members of the judge's family,* including real estate, and engage in other remunerative activity.

* See Terminology.

Commentary

[1] This Section provides that, subject to the requirements of this Code, a judge may hold and manage investments owned solely by the judge, investments owned solely by a member or members of the judge's family, and investments owned jointly by the judge and members of the judge's family.

(3) A judge shall not serve as an officer, director, manager, general partner, advisor or employee of any business entity except that a judge may, subject to the requirements of this Code, manage and participate in:

(a) a business closely held by the judge or members of the judge's family,* or

(b) a business entity primarily engaged in investment of the financial resources of the judge or members of the judge's family.

Commentary

[1] Subject to the requirements of this Code, a judge may participate in a business that is closely held either by the judge alone, by members of the judge's family, or by the judge and members of the judge's family.

[2] Although participation by a judge in a closely-held family business might otherwise be permitted by Section 4D(3), a judge may be prohibited from participation by other provisions of this Code when, for example, the business entity frequently appears before the judge's court or the participation requires significant time away from judicial duties. Similarly, a judge must avoid participating in a closely-held family business if the judge's participation would involve misuse of the prestige of judicial office.

(4) A judge shall manage the judge's investments and other financial interests to minimize the number of cases in which the judge is disqualified. As soon as the judge can do so without serious financial detriment, the judge shall divest himself or herself of investments and other financial interests that might require frequent disqualification.

(5) A judge shall not accept, and shall urge members of the judge's family residing in the judge's household,* not to accept, a gift, bequest, favor or loan from anyone except for:

Commentary

[1] Section 4D(5) does not apply to contributions to a judge's campaign for judicial office, a matter governed by Canon 5.

* See Terminology.

[2] Because a gift, bequest, favor or loan to a member of the judge's family residing in the judge's household might be viewed as intended to influence the judge, a judge must inform those family members of the relevant ethical constraints upon the judge in this regard and discourage those family members from violating them. A judge cannot, however, reasonably be expected to know or control all of the financial or business activities of all family members residing in the judge's household.

(a) a gift incident to a public testimonial, books, tapes and other resource materials supplied by publishers on a complimentary basis for official use, or an invitation to the judge and the judge's spouse or guest to attend a bar-related function or an activity devoted to the improvement of the law,* the legal system or the administration of justice;

Commentary

[1] Acceptance of an invitation to a law-related function is governed by Section 4D(5)(a); acceptance of an invitation paid for by an individual lawyer or group of lawyers is governed by Section 4D(5)(h).

[2] A judge may accept a public testimonial or a gift incident thereto only if the donor organization is not an organization whose members comprise or frequently represent the same side in litigation, and the testimonial and gift are otherwise in compliance with other provisions of this Code. See Sections 4A(1) and 2B.

(b) a gift, award or benefit incident to the business, profession or other separate activity of a spouse or other family member of a judge residing in the judge's household, including gifts, awards and benefits for the use of both the spouse or other family member and the judge (as spouse or family member), provided the gift, award or benefit could not reasonably be perceived as intended to influence the judge in the performance of judicial duties;

(c) ordinary social hospitality;

(d) a gift from a relative or friend, for a special occasion, such as a wedding, anniversary or birthday, if the gift is fairly commensurate with the occasion and the relationship;

Commentary

[1] A gift to a judge, or to a member of the judge's family living in the judge's household, that is excessive in value raises questions about the judge's impartiality and the integrity of the judicial office and might

* See Terminology.

require disqualification of the judge where disqualification would not otherwise be required. See, however, Section 4D(5)(e).

(e) a gift, bequest, favor or loan from a relative or close personal friend whose appearance or interest in a case would in any event require disqualification under Section 3E;

(f) a loan from a lending institution in its regular course of business on the same terms generally available to persons who are not judges;

(g) a scholarship or fellowship awarded on the same terms and based on the same criteria applied to other applicants; or

(h) any other gift, bequest, favor or loan, only if: the donor is not a party or other person who has come or is likely to come or whose interests have come or are likely to come before the judge; and, if its value exceeds $150.00, the judge reports it in the same manner as the judge reports compensation in Section 4H.

Commentary

[1] Section 4D(5)(h) prohibits judges from accepting gifts, favors, bequests or loans from lawyers or their firms if they have come or are likely to come before the judge; it also prohibits gifts, favors, bequests or loans from clients of lawyers or their firms when the clients' interests have come or are likely to come before the judge.

E.   Fiduciary Activities.

(1) A judge shall not serve as executor, administrator or other personal representative, trustee, guardian, attorney in fact or other fiduciary,* except for the estate, trust or person of a member of the judge's family,* and then only if such service will not interfere with the proper performance of judicial duties.

(2) A judge shall not serve as a fiduciary * if it is likely that the judge as a fiduciary will be engaged in proceedings that would ordinarily come before the judge, or if the estate, trust or ward becomes involved in adversary proceedings in the court on which the judge serves or one under its appellate jurisdiction.

(3) The same restrictions on financial activities that apply to a judge personally also apply to the judge while acting in a fiduciary * capacity.

* See Terminology.

711

Commentary

[1] The Time for Compliance provision of this Code (Application, Section F) postpones the time for compliance with certain provisions of this Section in some cases.

[2] The restrictions imposed by this Canon may conflict with the judge's obligation as a fiduciary. For example, a judge should resign as trustee if detriment to the trust would result from divestiture of holdings the retention of which would place the judge in violation of Section 4D(4).

F. Service as Arbitrator or Mediator. A judge shall not act as an arbitrator or mediator or otherwise perform judicial functions in a private capacity unless expressly authorized by law.*

Commentary

[1] Section 4F does not prohibit a judge from participating in arbitration, mediation or settlement conferences performed as part of judicial duties.

G. Practice of Law. A judge shall not practice law. Notwithstanding this prohibition, a judge may act pro se and may, without compensation, give legal advice to and draft or review documents for a member of the judge's family.*

Commentary

[1] This prohibition refers to the practice of law in a representative capacity and not in a pro se capacity. A judge may act for himself or herself in all legal matters, including matters involving litigation and matters involving appearances before or other dealings with legislative and other governmental bodies. However, in so doing, a judge must not abuse the prestige of office to advance the interests of the judge or the judge's family. See Section 2(B).

[2] The Code allows a judge to give legal advice to and draft legal documents for members of the judge's family, so long as the judge receives no compensation. A judge must not, however, act as an advocate or negotiator for a member of the judge's family in a legal matter.

* * *

[3] Canon 6, new in the 1972 Code, reflected concerns about conflicts of interest and appearances of impropriety arising from compensation for off-the-bench activities. Since 1972, however, reporting requirements that are much more comprehensive with respect to what must be reported and with whom reports must be filed have been adopted by

* See Terminology.

many jurisdictions. The Committee believes that although reports of compensation for extra-judicial activities should be required, reporting requirements preferably should be developed to suit the respective jurisdictions, not simply adopted as set forth in a national model code of judicial conduct. Because of the Committee's concern that deletion of this Canon might lead to the misconception that reporting compensation for extra-judicial activities is no longer important, the substance of Canon 6 is carried forward as Section 4H in this Code for adoption in those jurisdictions that do not have other reporting requirements. In jurisdictions that have separately established reporting requirements, Section 4H(2) (Public Reporting) may be deleted and the caption for Section 4H modified appropriately.

* * *

H. Compensation, Reimbursement and Reporting.

(1) Compensation and Reimbursement. A judge may receive compensation and reimbursement of expenses for the extra-judicial activities permitted by this Code, if the source of such payments does not give the appearance of influencing the judge's performance of judicial duties or otherwise give the appearance of impropriety.

> **(a) Compensation shall not exceed a reasonable amount nor shall it exceed what a person who is not a judge would receive for the same activity.**

> **(b) Expense reimbursement shall be limited to the actual cost of travel, food and lodging reasonably incurred by the judge and, where appropriate to the occasion, by the judge's spouse or guest. Any payment in excess of such an amount is compensation.**

(2) Public Reports. A judge shall report the date, place and nature of any activity for which the judge received compensation, and the name of the payor and the amount of compensation so received. Compensation or income of a spouse attributed to the judge by operation of a community property law is not extra-judicial compensation to the judge. The judge's report shall be made at least annually and shall be filed as a public document in the office of the clerk of the court on which the judge serves or other office designated by law.*

Commentary

[1] See Section 4D(5) regarding reporting of gifts, bequests and loans.

[2] The Code does not prohibit a judge from accepting honoraria or speaking fees provided that the compensation is reasonable and commen-

* See Terminology.

surate with the task performed. A judge should ensure, however, that no conflicts are created by the arrangement. A judge must not appear to trade on the judicial position for personal advantage. Nor should a judge spend significant time away from court duties to meet speaking or writing commitments for compensation. In addition, the source of the payment must not raise any question of undue influence or the judge's ability or willingness to be impartial.

I. Disclosure of a judge's income, debts, investments or other assets is required only to the extent provided in this Canon and in Sections 3E and 3F, or as otherwise required by law.*

Commentary

[1] Section 3E requires a judge to disqualify himself or herself in any proceeding in which the judge has an economic interest. See "economic interest" as explained in the Terminology Section. Section 4D requires a judge to refrain from engaging in business and from financial activities that might interfere with the impartial performance of judicial duties; Section 4H requires a judge to report all compensation the judge received for activities outside judicial office. A judge has the rights of any other citizen, including the right to privacy of the judge's financial affairs, except to the extent that limitations established by law are required to safeguard the proper performance of the judge's duties.

CANON 5 [5]

A Judge or Judicial Candidate Shall Refrain From Inappropriate Political Activity

A. All Judges and Candidates.

5. Introductory Note to Canon 5: There is wide variation in the methods of judicial selection used, both among jurisdictions and within the jurisdictions themselves. In a given state, judges may be selected by one method initially, retained by a different method, and selected by still another method to fill interim vacancies.

According to figures compiled in 1987 by the National Center for State Courts, 32 states and the District of Columbia use a merit selection method (in which an executive such as a governor appoints a judge from a group of nominees selected by a judicial nominating commission) to select judges in the state either initially or to fill an interim vacancy. Of those 33 jurisdictions, a merit selection method is used in 18

jurisdictions to choose judges of courts of last resort, in 13 jurisdictions to choose judges of intermediate appellate courts, in 12 jurisdictions to choose judges of general jurisdiction courts and in 5 jurisdictions to choose judges of limited jurisdiction courts.

Methods of judicial selection other than merit selection include nonpartisan election (10 states use it for initial selection at all court levels, another 10 states use it for initial selection for at least one court level) and partisan election (8 states use it for initial selection at all court levels, another 7 states use it for initial selection for at least one level). In a small minority of the states, judicial selection methods include executive or legislative appointment (without

714

(1) Except as authorized in Sections 5B(2), 5C(1) and 5C(3), a judge or a candidate* for election or appointment to judicial office shall not:

(a) act as a leader or hold an office in a political organization *;

(b) publicly endorse or publicly oppose another candidate for public office;

(c) make speeches on behalf of a political organization;

(d) attend political gatherings; or

(e) solicit funds for, pay an assessment to or make a contribution to a political organization or candidate, or purchase tickets for political party dinners or other functions.

Commentary

[1] A judge or candidate for judicial office retains the right to participate in the political process as a voter.

[2] Where false information concerning a judicial candidate is made public, a judge or another judicial candidate having knowledge of the facts is not prohibited by Section 5A(1) from making the facts public.

[3] Section 5A(1)(a) does not prohibit a candidate for elective judicial office from retaining during candidacy a public office such as county prosecutor, which is not "an office in a political organization."

[4] Section 5A(1)(b) does not prohibit a judge or judicial candidate from privately expressing his or her views on judicial candidates or other candidates for public office.

[5] A candidate does not publicly endorse another candidate for public office by having that candidate's name on the same ticket.

(2) A judge shall resign from judicial office upon becoming a candidate * for a non-judicial office either in a primary or in a general election, except that the judge may continue to hold judicial office while being a candidate for election to or serving as a delegate in a state constitutional convention if the judge is otherwise permitted by law * to do so.

(3) A candidate * for a judicial office:

(a) shall maintain the dignity appropriate to judicial office and act in a manner consistent with the integrity and independence of the judiciary, and shall encourage members of the candidate's family * to adhere to the same standards

nomination of a group of potential appointees by a judicial nominating commission) and court selection. In addition, the federal judicial system utilizes an executive appointment method. See State Court Organization 1987 (National Center for State Courts, 1988).

* See Terminology

of political conduct in support of the candidate as apply to the candidate;

Commentary

[1] Although a judicial candidate must encourage members of his or her family to adhere to the same standards of political conduct in support of the candidate that apply to the candidate, family members are free to participate in other political activity.

(b) shall prohibit employees and officials who serve at the pleasure of the candidate,* and shall discourage other employees and officials subject to the candidate's direction and control from doing on the candidate's behalf what the candidate is prohibited from doing under the Sections of this Canon;

(c) except to the extent permitted by Section 5C(2), shall not authorize or knowingly * permit any other person to do for the candidate * what the candidate is prohibited from doing under the Sections of this Canon;

(d) shall not:

(i) make pledges or promises of conduct in office other than the faithful and impartial performance of the duties of the office;

(ii) make statements that commit or appear to commit the candidate with respect to cases, controversies or issues that are likely to come before the court; or

(iii) knowingly * misrepresent the identity, qualifications, present position or other fact concerning the candidate or an opponent;

Commentary

[1] Section 5A(3)(d) prohibits a candidate for judicial office from making statements that appear to commit the candidate regarding cases, controversies or issues likely to come before the court. As a corollary, a candidate should emphasize in any public statement the candidate's duty to uphold the law regardless of his or her personal views. See also Section 3B(9), the general rule on public comment by judges. Section 5A(3)(d) does not prohibit a candidate from making pledges or promises respecting improvements in court administration. Nor does this Section prohibit an incumbent judge from making private statements to other judges or court personnel in the performance of judicial duties. This Section applies to any statement made in the process of securing judicial office, such as statements to commissions charged with judicial selection

* See Terminology.   * See Terminology.

and tenure and legislative bodies confirming appointment. See also Rule 8.2 of the ABA Model Rules of Professional Conduct.

(e) may respond to personal attacks or attacks on the candidate's record as long as the response does not violate Section 5A(3)(d).

B. Candidates Seeking Appointment to Judicial or Other Governmental Office.

(1) A candidate * for appointment to judicial office or a judge seeking other governmental office shall not solicit or accept funds, personally or through a committee or otherwise, to support his or her candidacy.

(2) A candidate * for appointment to judicial office or a judge seeking other governmental office shall not engage in any political activity to secure the appointment except that:

(a) such persons may:

(i) communicate with the appointing authority, including any selection or nominating commission or other agency designated to screen candidates;

(ii) seek support or endorsement for the appointment from organizations that regularly make recommendations for reappointment or appointment to the office, and from individuals to the extent requested or required by those specified in Section 5B(2)(a); and

(iii) provide to those specified in Sections 5B(2)(a)(i) and 5B(2)(a)(ii) information as to his or her qualifications for the office;

(b) a non-judge candidate * for appointment to judicial office may, in addition, unless otherwise prohibited by law *;

(i) retain an office in a political organization,*

(ii) attend political gatherings, and

(iii) continue to pay ordinary assessments and ordinary contributions to a political organization or candidate and purchase tickets for political party dinners or other functions.

Commentary

[1] Section 5B(2) provides a limited exception to the restrictions imposed by Sections 5A(1) and 5D. Under Section 5B(2), candidates seeking reappointment to the same judicial office or appointment to another judicial office or other governmental office may apply for the appointment and seek appropriate support.

[2] Although under Section 5B(2) non-judge candidates seeking appointment to judicial office are permitted during candidacy to retain

office in a political organization, attend political gatherings and pay ordinary dues and assessments, they remain subject to other provisions of this Code during candidacy. See Sections 5B(1), 5B(2)(a), 5E and Application Section.

   C. Judges and Candidates Subject to Public Election.
   (1) A judge or a candidate * subject to public election * may, except as prohibited by law:*
    (a) at any time

        (i) purchase tickets for and attend political gatherings;

        (ii) identify himself or herself as a member of a political party; and

        (iii) contribute to a political organization *;

    (b) when a candidate for election

        (i) speak to gatherings on his or her own behalf;

        (ii) appear in newspaper, television and other media advertisements supporting his or her candidacy;

        (iii) distribute pamphlets and other promotional campaign literature supporting his or her candidacy; and

        (iv) publicly endorse or publicly oppose other candidates for the same judicial office in a public election in which the judge or judicial candidate is running.

Commentary
   [1] Section 5C(1) permits judges subject to election at any time to be involved in limited political activity. Section 5D, applicable solely to incumbent judges, would otherwise bar this activity.
   (2) A candidate * shall not personally solicit or accept campaign contributions or personally solicit publicly stated support. A candidate may, however, establish committees of responsible persons to conduct campaigns for the candidate through media advertisements, brochures, mailings, candidate forums and other means not prohibited by law. Such committees may solicit and accept reasonable campaign contributions, manage the expenditure of funds for the candidate's campaign and obtain public statements of support for his or her candidacy. Such committees are not prohibited from soliciting and accepting reasonable campaign contributions and public support from lawyers. A candidate's committees may solicit contributions and public support for the candidate's campaign no earlier than

* See Terminology.   * See Terminology.

[one year] before an election and no later than [90] days after the last election in which the candidate participates during the election year. A candidate shall not use or permit the use of campaign contributions for the private benefit of the candidate or others.

Commentary[†]

[1] There is legitimate concern about a judge's impartiality when parties whose interests may come before a judge, or the lawyers who represent such parties, are known to have made contributions to the election campaigns of judicial candidates. This is among the reasons that merit selection of judges is a preferable manner in which to select the judiciary. Notwithstanding that preference, Section 5C(2) recognizes that in many jurisdictions judicial candidates must raise funds to support their candidates for election to judicial office. It therefore permits a candidate, other than a candidate for appointment, to establish campaign committees to solicit and accept public support and reasonable financial contributions. In order to guard against the possibility that conflicts of interest will arise, the candidate must instruct his or her campaign committees at the start of the campaign to solicit or accept only contributions that are reasonable and appropriate under the circumstances. Though not prohibited, campaign contributions of which a judge has knowledge, made by lawyers or others who appear before the judge may, by virtue of their size or source, raise questions about a judge's impartiality and be cause for ~~relevant to~~ disqualification as provided under Section 3(E).

[2] Campaign committees established under Section 5C(2) should manage campaign finances responsibly, avoiding deficits that might necessitate post-election fund-raising, to the extent possible. Such committees must at all times comply with applicable statutory provisions governing their conduct.

[3] Section 5C(2) does not prohibit a candidate from initiating an evaluation by a judicial selection commission or bar association, or, subject to the requirements of this Code, from responding to a request for information from any organization.

(3)[††] A candidate shall instruct his or her campaign committees(s) at the start of the campaign not to accept campaign contributions for any election that exceed, in the aggregate*, $[ ] from an individual or $[ ] from an entity. This limitations is in addition to the limitations provided in Section 5C(2).[6]

---

† In 1997, the ABA amended the Commentary to Canon 5C(2).

†† [Editor's Note: The language in (3) and (4) was added in 1999 by the ABA House of Delegates. The language in (5) was originally numbered as (3) and moved down when the two prior sections were added.]

* See Terminology.

6. Jurisdictions wishing to adopt campaign contribution limits that are lower than generally applicable campaign finance

(4)[††] In addition to complying with all applicable statutory requirements for disclosure of campaign contributions, campaign committees established by a candidate shall file with [ ][7] a report stating the name, address, occupation and employer of each person who has made campaign contributions to the committee whose value in the aggregate* exceed [$].[8] The report must be filed within [ ][9] days following the election.

(5) Except as prohibited by law,* a candidate * for judicial office in a public election * may permit the candidate's name: (a) to be listed on election materials along with the names of other candidates for elective public office, and (b) to appear in promotions of the ticket.

Commentary

[1] Section 5C(5) provides a limited exception to the restrictions imposed by Section 5A(1).

D.   Incumbent Judges.   A judge shall not engage in any political activity except (i) as authorized under any other Section of this Code, (ii) on behalf of measures to improve the law,* the legal system or the administration of justice, or (iii) as expressly authorized by law.

Commentary

[1] Neither Section 5D nor any other section of the Code prohibits a judge in the exercise of administrative functions from engaging in planning and other official activities with members of the executive and legislative branches of government. With respect to a judge's activity on behalf of measures to improve the law, the legal system and the administration of justice, see Commentary to Section 4B and Section 4C(1) and its Commentary.

E.   Applicability. Canon 5 generally applies to all incumbent judges and judicial candidates.* A successful candidate, whether or not an incumbent, is subject to judicial discipline for his or her campaign conduct; an unsuccessful candidate who is a lawyer is subject to lawyer discipline for his or her campaign

regulations provide should adopt this provision, inserting appropriate dollar amounts where brackets appear.

7. Each jurisdiction should identify an appropriate depository for the information required under this provision, giving consideration to this public's need for convenient and timely access to the information. Electronic filing is to be preferred.

8. Jurisdictions wishing to adopt campaign contribution disclosure levels lower than those set in generally applicable campaign finance regulations should adopt this provision, inserting appropriate dollar amounts where brackets appear.

9. A time period chosen by the adopting jurisdiction should appear in the bracketed space.

* See Terminology.

conduct. A lawyer who is a candidate for judicial office is subject to [Rule 8.2(b) of the ABA Model Rules of Professional Conduct]. (An adopting jurisdiction should substitute a reference to its applicable rule.)

APPLICATION OF THE CODE OF JUDICIAL CONDUCT

A. Anyone, whether or not a lawyer, who is an officer of a judicial system[10] and who performs judicial functions, including an officer such as a magistrate, court commissioner, special master or referee, is a judge within the meaning of this Code. All judges shall comply with this Code except as provided below.

Commentary

[1] The four categories of judicial service in other than a full-time capacity are necessarily defined in general terms because of the widely varying forms of judicial service. For the purposes of this Section, as long as a retired judge is subject to recall the judge is considered to "perform judicial functions." The determination of which category and, accordingly, which specific Code provisions apply to an individual judicial officer, depend upon the facts of the particular judicial service.

B. Retired Judge Subject to Recall. A retired judge subject to recall who by law is not permitted to practice law is not required to comply:

(1) except while serving as a judge, with Section 4F; and

(2) at any time with Section 4E.

C. Continuing Part-time Judge. A continuing part-time judge *:

(1) is not required to comply:

(a) except while serving as a judge, with Section 3B(9); and

(b) at any time with Sections 4C(2), 4D(3), 4E(1), 4F, 4G, 4H, 5A(1), 5B(2) and 5D.

(2) shall not practice law in the court on which the judge serves or in any court subject to the appellate jurisdiction of the court on which the judge serves, and shall not act as a lawyer in a proceeding in which the judge has served as a judge or in any other proceeding related thereto.

---

10. Applicability of this Code to administrative law judges should be determined by each adopting jurisdiction. Administrative law judges generally are affiliated with the executive branch of government rather than the judicial branch and each adopting jurisdiction should consider the unique characteristics of particular administrative law judge positions in adopting and adapting the Code for administrative law judges. See, e.g., Model Code of Judicial Conduct for Federal Administrative Law Judges, endorsed by the National Conference of Administrative Law Judges in February 1989.

Commentary

[1] When a person who has been a continuing part-time judge is no longer a continuing part-time judge, including a retired judge no longer subject to recall, that person may act as a lawyer in a proceeding in which he or she has served as a judge or in any other proceeding related thereto only with the express consent of all parties pursuant to [Rule 1.12(a) of the ABA Model Rules of Professional Conduct]. (An adopting jurisdiction should substitute a reference to its applicable rule).

D. Periodic Part-time Judge. A periodic part-time judge *:
(1) is not required to comply
    (a) except while serving as a judge, with Section 3B(9);

    (b) at any time, with Sections 4C(2), 4C(3)(a), 4D(1)(b), 4D(3), 4D(4), 4D(5), 4E, 4F, 4G, 4H, 5A(1), 5B(2) and 5D.

(2) shall not practice law in the court on which the judge serves or in any court subject to the appellate jurisdiction of the court on which the judge serves, and shall not act as a lawyer in a proceeding in which the judge has served as a judge or in any other proceeding related thereto.

Commentary

[1] When a person who has been a periodic part-time judge is no longer a periodic part-time judge (no longer accepts appointments), that person may act as a lawyer in a proceeding in which he or she has served as a judge or in any other proceeding related thereto only with the express consent of all parties pursuant to [Rule 1.12(a) of the ABA Model Rules of Professional Conduct]. (An adopting jurisdiction should substitute a reference to its applicable rule).

E. Pro Tempore Part–Time Judge. A pro tempore part-time judge *:
(1) is not required to comply:
    (a) except while serving as a judge, with Sections 2A, 2B, 3B(9) and 4C(1);

    (b) at any time with Sections 2C, 4C(2), 4C(3)(a), 4C(3)(b), 4D(1)(b), 4D(3), 4D(4), 4D(5), 4E, 4F, 4G, 4H, 5A(1), 5A(2), 5B(2) and 5D.

(2) A person who has been a pro tempore part-time judge * shall not act as a lawyer in a proceeding in which the judge has served as a judge or in any other proceeding related thereto except as otherwise permitted by [Rule 1.12(a) of the ABA Model Rules of Professional Conduct]. (An adopting jurisdiction should substitute a reference to its applicable rule.)

* See Terminology.   * See Terminology.

F. Time for Compliance. A person to whom this Code becomes applicable shall comply immediately with all provisions of this Code except Sections 4D(2), 4D(3) and 4E and shall comply with these Sections as soon as reasonably possible and shall do so in any event within the period of one year.

Commentary

[1] If serving as a fiduciary when selected as judge, a new judge may, notwithstanding the prohibitions in Section 4E, continue to serve as fiduciary but only for that period of time necessary to avoid serious adverse consequences to the beneficiary of the fiduciary relationship and in no event longer than one year. Similarly, if engaged at the time of judicial selection in a business activity, a new judge may, notwithstanding the prohibitions in Section 4D(3), continue in that activity for a reasonable period but in no event longer than one year.

PART THREE

RULES OF EVIDENCE AND PROCEDURE THAT AFFECT THE LEGAL PROFESSION

TABLE OF CONTENTS

Introduction

Until recently, most courses and casebooks in professional responsibility focused solely on the ABA's model codes of conduct. However, the law which governs and regulates the conduct of lawyers must go far beyond the ABA's pronouncements. One other source of law which affects lawyers' conduct must include rules of evidence, procedure, and court. This part includes rules of evidence and procedure which affect the practice of law.

SELECTED RULES OF EVIDENCE
AND PROCEDURE

Federal Rules of Evidence for United States Courts and Magistrates

Appendix of Deleted Rules of Evidence

Federal Rules of Civil Procedure

Federal Rules of Criminal Procedure

Federal Rules of Appellate Procedure

Rules of The Supreme Court of The United States

Draft Federal Rules of Attorney Conduct

FEDERAL RULES OF EVIDENCE FOR UNITED STATES COURTS AND MAGISTRATES

Rule 501. General Rule

Except as otherwise required by the Constitution of the United States or provided by Act of Congress or in rules prescribed by the Supreme Court pursuant to statutory authority, the privilege of a witness, person, government, State, or political subdivision thereof shall be governed by the principles of common law as they may be interpreted by the courts of the United States in the light of reason and experience. However, in civil actions and proceedings, with respect to an element of a claim or defense as to which State law supplies the rule of decision, the privilege of a witness, person, government, State, or political subdivision thereof shall be determined in accordance with State law.

Rule 605. Competency of Judge as Witness

The judge presiding at the trial may not testify in that trial as a witness. No objection need be made in order to preserve the point.

APPENDIX OF DELETED RULES OF EVIDENCE

Rule 503. Lawyer-Client Privilege [Not enacted.]

(a) Definitions. As used in this rule:

(1) A "client" is a person, public officer, or corporation, association, or other organization or entity, either public or private, who is rendered professional legal services by a lawyer, or who consults a lawyer with a view to obtaining professional legal services from him.

(2) A "lawyer" is a person authorized, or reasonably believed by the client to be authorized, to practice law in any state or nation.

(3) A "representative of the lawyer" is one employed to assist the lawyer in the rendition of professional services.

(4) A communication is "confidential" if not intended to be disclosed to third persons other than those to whom disclosure is in furtherance of the rendition of professional legal services to the client or those reasonably necessary for the transmission of the communication.

(b) General rule of privilege. A client has a privilege to refuse to disclose and to prevent any other person from disclosing confidential communications made for the purpose of facilitating the rendition of professional legal services to the client, (1) between himself or his representative and his lawyer or his lawyer's representative, or (2) between his lawyer and the lawyer's representative, or (3) by him or his lawyer to a lawyer representing another in a matter of common interest, or (4) between representatives of the client or between the client and a representative of the client, or (5) between lawyers representing the client.

(c) Who may claim the privilege. The privilege may be claimed by the client, his guardian or conservator, the personal representative of a deceased client, or the successor, trustee, or similar representative of a corporation, association, or other organization, whether or not in existence. The person who was the lawyer at the time of the communication may claim the privilege but only on behalf of the client. His authority to do so is presumed in the absence of evidence to the contrary.

(d) Exceptions. There is no privilege under this rule:

(1) Furtherance of crime or fraud. If the services of the lawyer were sought or obtained to enable or aid anyone to commit or plan to commit what the client knew or reasonably should have known to be a crime or fraud; or

(2) Claimants through same deceased client. As to a communication relevant to an issue between parties who claim through the same deceased client, regardless of whether the claims are by testate or intestate succession or by *inter vivos* transaction; or

(3) Breach of duty by lawyer or client. As to a communication relevant to an issue of breach of duty by the lawyer to his client or by the client to his lawyer; or

(4) Document attested by lawyer. As to a communication relevant to an issue concerning an attested document to which the lawyer is an attesting witness; or

(5) Joint clients. As to a communication relevant to a matter of common interest between two or more clients if the communication was made by any of them to a lawyer retained or consulted in common, when offered in an action between any of the clients.

FEDERAL RULES OF CIVIL PROCEDURE
(as amended to Jan. 1, 1999)

Rule 11. Signing of Pleadings, Motions, and Other Papers; Representations to Court; Sanctions *

(a) Signature. Every pleading, written motion, and other paper shall be signed by at least one attorney of record in the attorney's

---

* [Ed.] This footnote contains the text of Rule 11 after its 1983 Amendment.

Every pleading, motion, and other paper of a party represented by an attorney shall be signed by at least one attorney of record in the attorney's individual name, whose address shall be stated. A party who is not represented by an attorney shall sign the party's pleading, motion, or other paper and state the party's address. Except when otherwise specifically provided by rule or statute, pleadings need not be verified or accompanied by affidavit. The rule in equity that the averments of an answer under oath must be overcome by the testimony of two wit-individual name, or, if the party is not represented by an attorney, shall be signed by the party. Each paper shall state the signer's address and telephone number, if any. Except when otherwise specifically provided by rule or statute, pleadings need not be verified or accompanied by affidavit. An unsigned paper shall be stricken unless omission of the signature is corrected promptly after being called to the attention of the attorney or party.

(b) Representations to Court. By presenting to the court (whether by signing, filing, submitting, or later advocating) a pleading, written motion, or other paper, an attorney or unrepresented party is certifying that to the best of the person's knowledge, information, and belief, formed after an inquiry reasonable under the circumstances,—

(1) it is not being presented for any improper purpose, such as to harass or to cause unnecessary delay or needless increase in the cost of litigation;

(2) the claims, defenses, and other legal contentions therein are warranted by existing law or by a nonfrivolous argument for the extension, modification, or reversal of existing law or the establishment of new law;

(3) the allegations and other factual contentions have evidentiary support or, if specifically so identified, are likely to have evidentiary support after a reasonable opportunity for further investigation or discovery; and

(4) the denials of factual contentions are warranted on the evidence or, if specifically so identified, are reasonably based on a lack of information or belief.

(c) Sanctions. If, after notice and a reasonable opportunity to respond, the court determines that subdivision (b) has been violated, the court may, subject to the conditions stated below, impose an appropriate sanction upon the attorneys, law firms, or parties that have violated subdivision (b) or are responsible for the violation.

nesses or of one witness sustained by corroborating circumstances is abolished. The signature of an attorney or party constitutes a certificate by the signer that the signer has read the pleading, motion, or other paper; that to the best of the signer's knowledge, information, and belief formed after reasonable inquiry it is well grounded in fact and is warranted by existing law or a good faith argument for the extension, modification, or reversal of existing law, and that it is not interposed for any improper purpose, such as to harass or to cause unnecessary delay or needless increase in the cost of litigation.

If a pleading, motion, or other paper is not signed, it shall be stricken unless it is signed promptly after the omission is called to the attention of the pleader or movant. If a pleading, motion, or other paper is signed in violation of this rule, the court, upon motion or upon its own initiative, shall impose upon the person who signed it, a represented party, or both, an appropriate sanction, which may include an order to pay to the other party or parties the amount of the reasonable expenses incurred because of the filing of the pleading, motion, or other paper, including a reasonable attorney's fee.

(1) How Initiated.

(A) By Motion. A motion for sanctions under this rule shall be made separately from other motions or requests and shall describe the specific conduct alleged to violate subdivision (b). It shall be served as provided in Rule 5, but shall not be filed with or presented to the court unless, within 21 days after service of the motion (or such other period as the court may prescribe), the challenged paper, claim, defense, contention, allegation, or denial is not withdrawn or appropriately corrected. If warranted, the court may award to the party prevailing on the motion the reasonable expenses and attorney's fees incurred in presenting or opposing the motion. Absent exceptional circumstances, a law firm shall be held jointly responsible for violations committed by its partners, associates, and employees.

(B) On Court's Initiative. On its own initiative, the court may enter an order describing the specific conduct that appears to violate subdivision (b) and directing an attorney, law firm, or party to show cause why it has not violated subdivision (b) with respect thereto.

(2) Nature of Sanction; Limitations. A sanction imposed for violation of this rule shall be limited to what is sufficient to deter repetition of such conduct or comparable conduct by others similarly situated. Subject to the limitations in subparagraphs (A) and (B), the sanction may consist of, or include, directives of a nonmonetary nature, an order to pay a penalty into court, or, if imposed on motion and warranted for effective deterrence, an order directing payment to the movant of some or all of the reasonable attorneys' fees and other expenses incurred as a direct result of the violation.

(A) Monetary sanctions may not be awarded against a represented party for a violation of subdivision (b)(2).

(B) Monetary sanctions may not be awarded on the court's initiative unless the court issues its order to show cause before a voluntary dismissal or settlement of the claims made by or against the party which is, or whose attorneys are, to be sanctioned.

(3) Order. When imposing sanctions, the court shall describe the conduct determined to constitute a violation of this rule and explain the basis for the sanction imposed.

(d) Inapplicability to Discovery. Subdivisions (a) through (c) of this rule do not apply to disclosures and discovery requests, responses, objections, and motions that are subject to the provisions of Rules 26 through 37.

(As amended Apr. 22, 1993, eff. Dec. 1, 1993.)

ADVISORY COMMITTEE NOTES
1993 Amendments

Purpose of revision. This revision is intended to remedy problems that have arisen in the interpretation and application of the 1983 revision of the rule. * * *

The rule retains the principle that attorneys and pro se litigants have an obligation to the court to refrain from conduct that frustrates the aims of Rule 1. The revision broadens the scope of this obligation, but places greater constraints on the imposition of sanctions and should reduce the number of motions for sanctions presented to the court. New subdivision (d) removes from the ambit of this rule all discovery requests, responses, objections, and motions subject to the provisions of Rule 26 through 37.

Subdivision (a). Retained in this subdivision are the provisions requiring signatures on pleadings, written motions, and other papers. Unsigned papers are to be received by the Clerk, but then are to be stricken if the omission of the signature is not corrected promptly after being called to the attention of the attorney or pro se litigant. Correction can be made by signing the paper on file or by submitting a duplicate that contains the signature. A court may require by local rule that papers contain additional identifying information regarding the parties or attorneys, such as telephone numbers to facilitate facsimile transmissions, though, as for omission of a signature, the paper should not be rejected for failure to provide such information.

The sentence in the former rule relating to the effect of answers under oath is no longer needed and has been eliminated. The provision in the former rule that signing a paper constitutes a certificate that it has been read by the signer also has been eliminated as unnecessary. The obligations imposed under subdivision (b) obviously require that a pleading, written motion, or other paper be read before it is filed or submitted to the court.

Subdivisions (b) and (c). These subdivisions restate the provisions requiring attorneys and pro se litigants to conduct a reasonable inquiry into the law and facts before signing pleadings, written motions, and other documents, and prescribing sanctions for violation of these obligations. The revision in part expands the responsibilities of litigants to the court, while providing greater constraints and flexibility in dealing with infractions of the rule. The rule continues to require litigants to "stop-and-think" before initially making legal or factual contentions. It also, however, emphasizes the duty of candor by subjecting litigants to potential sanctions for insisting upon a position after it is no longer tenable and by generally providing protection against sanctions if they withdraw or correct contentions after a potential violation is called to their attention.

The rule applies only to assertions contained in papers filed with or submitted to the court. It does not cover matters arising for the first time during oral presentations to the court, when counsel may make statements that would not have been made if there had been more time for study and reflection. However, a litigant's obligations with respect to the contents of these papers are not measured solely as of the time they are filed with or submitted to the court, but include reaffirming to the court and advocating positions contained in those pleadings and motions after learning that they cease to have any merit. For example, an attorney who during a pretrial conference insists on a claim or defense should be viewed as "presenting to the court" that contention and would be subject to the obligations of subdivision (b) measured as of that time. Similarly, if after a notice of removal is filed, a party urges in federal court the allegations of a pleading filed in state court (whether as claims, defenses, or in disputes regarding removal or remand), it would be viewed as "presenting"—and hence certifying to the district court under Rule 11—those allegations.

The certification with respect to allegations and other factual contentions is revised in recognition that sometimes a litigant may have good reason to believe that a fact is true or false but may need discovery, formal or informal, from opposing parties or third persons to gather and confirm the evidentiary basis for the allegation. Tolerance of factual contentions in initial pleadings by plaintiffs or defendants when specifically identified as made on information and belief does not relieve litigants from the obligation to conduct an appropriate investigation into the facts that is reasonable under the circumstances; it is not a license to join parties, make claims, or present defenses without any factual basis or justification. Moreover, if evidentiary support is not obtained after a reasonable opportunity for further investigation or discovery, the party has a duty under the rule not to persist with that contention. Subdivision (b) does not require a formal amendment to pleadings for which evidentiary support is not obtained, but rather calls upon a litigant not thereafter to advocate such claims or defenses.

The certification is that there is (or likely will be) "evidentiary support" for the allegation, not that the party will prevail with respect to its contention regarding the fact. That summary judgment is rendered against a party does not necessarily mean, for purposes of this certification, that it had no evidentiary support for its position. On the other hand, if a party has evidence with respect to a contention that would suffice to defeat a motion for summary judgment based thereon, it would have sufficient "evidentiary support" for purposes of Rule 11.

Denials of factual contentions involve somewhat different considerations. Often, of course, a denial is premised upon the existence of evidence contradicting the alleged fact. At other times a denial is permissible because, after an appropriate investigation, a party has no information concerning the matter or, indeed, has a reasonable basis for doubting the credibility of the only evidence relevant to the matter. A party should not deny an allegation it knows to be true; but it is not required, simply because it lacks contradictory evidence, to admit an allegation that it believes is not true.

The changes in subdivisions (b)(3) and (b)(4) will serve to equalize the burden of the rule upon plaintiffs and defendants, who under Rule 8(b) are in effect allowed to deny allegations by stating that from their initial investigation they lack sufficient information to form a belief as to the truth of the allegation. If, after further investigation or discovery, a denial is no longer warranted, the defendant should not continue to insist on that denial. While sometimes helpful, formal amendment of the pleadings to withdraw an allegation or denial is not required by subdivision (b).

Arguments for extensions, modifications, or reversals of existing law or for creation of new law do not violate subdivision (b)(2) provided they are "nonfrivolous." This establishes an objective standard, intended to eliminate any "empty-head pure-heart" justification for patently frivolous arguments. However, the extent to which a litigant has researched the issues and found some support for its theories even in minority opinions, in law review articles, or through consultation with other attorneys should certainly be taken into account in determining whether paragraph (2) has been violated. Although arguments for a change of law are not required to be specifically so identified, a contention that is so identified should be viewed with greater tolerance under the rule.

The court has available a variety of possible sanctions to impose for violations, such as striking the offending paper; issuing an admonition, reprimand, or censure; requiring participation in seminars or other educational programs; ordering a fine payable to the court; referring the matter to disciplinary authorities (or, in the case of government attorneys, to the Attorney General, Inspector General, or agency head), etc. See Manual for Complex Litigation, Second, § 42.3. The rule does not attempt to enumerate the factors a court should consider in deciding whether to impose a sanction or what sanctions would be appropriate in the circumstances; but, for emphasis, it does specifically note that a sanction may be nonmonetary as well as monetary. Whether the improper conduct was willful, or negligent; whether it was part of a pattern of activity, or an isolated event; whether it infected the entire pleading, or only one particular count or defense; whether the person has engaged in similar conduct in other litigation; whether it was intended to injure; what effect it had on the litigation process in time or expense; whether the responsible person is trained in the law; what amount, given the financial resources of the responsible person, is needed to deter that person from repetition in the same case; what amount is needed to deter similar activity by other litigants: all of these may in a particular case be proper considerations. The court has significant discretion in determining what sanctions, if any, should be imposed for a violation, subject to the principle that the sanctions should not be more severe than reasonably necessary to deter repetition of the conduct by the offending person or comparable conduct by similarly situated persons.

Since the purpose of Rule 11 sanctions is to deter rather than to compensate, the rule provides that, if a monetary sanction is imposed, it should ordinarily be paid into court as a penalty. However, under unusual circumstances, particularly for (b)(1) violations, deterrence may be ineffective unless the sanction not only requires the person violating the rule to make a monetary payment, but also directs that some or all of this payment be made to those injured by the violation. Accordingly, the rule authorizes the court, if requested in a motion and if so warranted, to award attorney's fees to another party. Any such award to another party, however, should not exceed the expenses and attorneys' fees for the services directly and unavoidably caused by the violation of the certification requirement. If, for example, a wholly unsupportable count were included in a multi-count complaint or counterclaim for the purpose of needlessly increasing the cost of litigation to an impecunious adversary, any award of expenses should be limited to those directly caused by inclusion of the improper count, and not those resulting from the filing of the complaint or answer itself. The award should not provide compensation for services that could have been avoided by an earlier disclosure of evidence or an earlier challenge to the groundless claims or defenses. Moreover, partial reimbursement of fees may constitute a sufficient deterrent with respect to violations by persons having modest financial resources. In cases brought under statutes providing for fees to be awarded to prevailing parties, the court should not employ cost-shifting under this rule in a manner that would be inconsistent with the standards that govern the statutory award of fees, such as stated in Christiansburg Garment Co. v. EEOC, 434 U.S. 412 (1978).

The sanction should be imposed on the persons—whether attorneys, law firms, or parties—who have violated the rule or who may be determined to be responsible for the violation. The person signing, filing, submitting, or advocating a document has a nondelegable responsibility to the court, and in most situations is the person to be sanctioned for a violation. Absent exceptional circumstances, a law firm is to be held also responsible when, as a result of a motion under subdivision (c)(1)(A), one of its partners, associates, or employees is determined to have violated the rule. Since such a motion may be filed only if the offending paper is not withdrawn or corrected within 21 days after service of the motion, it is appropriate that the law firm ordinarily be viewed as jointly responsible under established principles of agency. This provision is designed to remove the restrictions of the former rule. Cf. Pavelic & LeFlore v. Marvel Entertainment Group, 493 U.S. 120 (1989) (1983 version of Rule 11 does not permit sanctions against law firm of attorney signing groundless complaint).

The revision permits the court to consider whether other attorneys in the firm, co-counsel, other law firms, or the party itself should be held accountable for their part in causing a violation. When appropriate, the court can make an additional inquiry in order to determine whether the sanction should be imposed on such persons, firms, or parties either in addition to or, in unusual circumstances, instead of the person actually making the presentation to the court. For example, such an inquiry may be appropriate in cases involving governmental agencies or other institutional parties that frequently impose substantial restrictions on the discretion of individual attorneys employed by it.

Sanctions that involve monetary awards (such as a fine or an award of attorney's fees) may not be imposed on a represented party for causing a violation of subdivision (b)(2), involving frivolous contentions of law. Monetary responsibility for such violations is more properly placed solely on the party's attorneys. With this limitation, the rule should not be subject to attack under the Rules Enabling Act. See Willy v. Coastal Corp., ___ U.S. ___ (1992); Business Guides, Inc. v. Chromatic Communications Enter. Inc., ___ U.S. ___ (1991). This restriction does not limit the court's power to impose sanctions or remedial orders that may have collateral financial consequences upon a party, such as dismissal of a claim, preclusion of a defense, or preparation of amended pleadings.

Explicit provision is made for litigants to be provided notice of the alleged violation and an opportunity to respond before sanctions are imposed. Whether the matter should be decided solely on the basis of written submissions or should be scheduled for oral argument (or, indeed, for evidentiary presentation) will depend on the circumstances. If the court imposes a sanction, it must, unless waived, indicate its reasons in a written order or on the record; the court should not ordinarily have to explain its denial of a motion for sanctions. Whether a violation has occurred and what sanctions, if any, to impose for a violation are matters committed to the discretion of the trial court; accordingly, as under current law, the standard for appellate review of these decisions will be for abuse of discretion. See Cooter & Gell v. Hartmarx Corp., 496 U.S. 384 (1990) (noting, however, that an abuse would be established if the court based its ruling on an erroneous view of the law or on a clearly erroneous assessment of the evidence).

The revision leaves for resolution on a case-by-case basis, considering the particular circumstances involved, the question as to when a motion for violation of Rule 11 should be served and when, if filed, it should be decided. Ordinarily the motion should be served promptly after the inappropriate paper is filed, and, if delayed too long, may be viewed as untimely. In other circumstances, it should not be served until the other party has had a reasonable opportunity for discovery. Given the "safe harbor" provisions discussed below, a party cannot delay serving its Rule 11 motion until conclusion of the case (or judicial rejection of the offending contention).

Rule 11 motions should not be made or threatened for minor, inconsequential violations of the standards prescribed by subdivision (b). They should not be employed as a discovery device or to test the legal sufficiency or efficacy of allegations in the pleadings; other motions are available for those purposes. Nor should Rule 11 motions be prepared to emphasize the merits of a party's position, to exact an unjust settlement, to intimidate an adversary into withdrawing contentions that are fairly debatable, to increase the costs of litigation, to create a conflict of interest between attorney and client, or to seek disclosure of matters otherwise protected by the attorney-client privilege or the work-product doctrine. As under the prior rule, the court may defer its ruling (or its decision as to the identity of the persons to be sanctioned) until final resolution of the case in order to avoid immediate conflicts of interest and to reduce the disruption created if a disclosure of attorney-client communications is needed to determine whether a violation occurred or to identify the person responsible for the violation.

The rule provides that requests for sanctions must be made as a separate motion, i.e., not simply included as an additional prayer for relief contained in another motion. The motion for sanctions is not, however, to be filed until at least 21 days (or such other period as the court may set) after being served. If, during this period, the alleged violation is corrected, as by withdrawing (whether formally or informally) some allegation or contention, the motion should not be filed with the court. These provisions are intended to provide a type of "safe harbor" against motions under Rule 11 in that a party will not be subject to sanctions on the basis of another party's motion unless, after receiving the motion, it refuses to withdraw that position or to acknowledge candidly that it does not currently have evidence to support a specified allegation. Under the former rule, parties were sometimes reluctant to abandon a questionable contention lest that be viewed as evidence of a violation of Rule 11; under the revision, the timely withdrawal of a contention will protect a party against a motion for sanctions.

To stress the seriousness of a motion for sanctions and to define precisely the conduct claimed to violate the rule, the revision provides that the "safe harbor" period begins to run only upon service of the motion. In most cases, however, counsel should be expected to give informal notice to the other party, whether in person or by a telephone call or letter, of a potential violation before proceeding to prepare and serve a Rule 11 motion.

As under former Rule 11, the filing of a motion for sanctions is itself subject to the requirements of the rule and can lead to sanctions. However, service of a cross motion under Rule 11 should rarely be needed since under the revision the court may award to the person who prevails on a motion under Rule 11—whether the movant or the target of the motion—reasonable expenses, including attorney's fees, incurred in presenting or opposing the motion.

The power of the court to act on its own initiative is retained, but with the condition that this be done through a show cause order. This procedure provides the person with notice and an opportunity to respond. The revision provides that a monetary sanction imposed after a court-initiated show cause order be limited to a penalty payable to the court and that it be imposed only if the show cause order is issued before any voluntary dismissal or an agreement of the parties to settle the claims made by or against the litigant. Parties settling a case should not be subsequently faced with an unexpected order from the court leading to monetary sanctions that might have affected their willingness to settle or voluntarily dismiss a case. Since show cause orders will ordinarily be issued only in situations that are akin to a contempt of court, the rule does not provide a "safe harbor" to a litigant for withdrawing a claim, defense, etc., after a show cause order has been issued on the court's own initiative. Such corrective action, however, should be taken into account in deciding what—if any—sanction to impose if, after consideration of the litigant's response, the court concludes that a violation has occurred.

Subdivision (d). Rules 26(g) and 37 establish certification standards and sanctions that apply to discovery disclosures, requests, responses, objections, and motions. It is appropriate that Rules 26 through 37, which are specially designed for the discovery process, govern such documents and conduct rather than the more general provisions of Rule 11. Subdivision (d) has been added to accomplish this result.

Rule 11 is not the exclusive source for control of improper presentations of claims, defenses, or contentions. It does not supplant statutes permitting awards of attorney's fees to prevailing parties or alter the principles governing such awards. It does not inhibit the court in punishing for contempt, in exercising its inherent powers, or in imposing sanctions, awarding expenses, or directing remedial action authorized under other rules or under 28 U.S.C. § 1927. See Chambers v. NASCO, ___ U.S. ___ (1991). Chambers cautions, however, against reliance upon inherent powers if appropriate sanctions can be imposed under provisions such as Rule 11, and the procedures specified in Rule 11—notice, opportunity to respond, and findings—should ordinarily be employed when imposing a sanction under the court's inherent powers. Finally, it should be noted that Rule 11 does not preclude a party from initiating an independent action for malicious prosecution or abuse of process.

Rule 16. Pretrial Conferences; Scheduling; Management

(a) Pretrial Conferences; Objectives. In any action, the court may in its discretion direct the attorneys for the parties and any unrepresented parties to appear before it for a conference or conferences before trial for such purposes as

(1) expediting the disposition of the action;

(2) establishing early and continuing control so that the case will not be protracted because of lack of management;

(3) discouraging wasteful pretrial activities;

(4) improving the quality of the trial through more thorough preparation, and;

(5) facilitating the settlement of the case.

(b) Scheduling and Planning. Except in categories of actions exempted by district court rule as inappropriate, the district judge, or a magistrate judge when authorized by district court rule, shall, after receiving the report from the parties under Rule 26(f) or after consulting with the attorneys for the parties and any unrepresented parties by a scheduling conference, telephone, mail, or other suitable means, enter a scheduling order that limits the time

(1) to join other parties and to amend the pleadings;

(2) to file motions; and

(3) to complete discovery.

The scheduling order may also include

(4) modifications of the times for disclosures under Rules 26(a) and 26(e)(1) and of the extent of discovery to be permitted;

(5) the date or dates for conferences before trial, a final pretrial conference, and trial; and

(6) any other matters appropriate in the circumstances of the case.

The order shall issue as soon as practicable but in any event within 90 days after the appearance of a defendant and within 120 days after the complaint has been served on a defendant. A schedule shall not be modified except upon a showing of good cause and by leave of the district judge or, when authorized by local rule, by a magistrate judge.

(c) Subjects for Consideration at Pretrial Conferences. At any conference under this rule consideration may be given, and the court may take appropriate action, with respect to

   (1) the formulation and simplification of the issues, including the elimination of frivolous claims or defenses;

   (2) the necessity or desirability of amendments to the pleadings;

   (3) the possibility of obtaining admissions of fact and of documents which will avoid unnecessary proof, stipulations regarding the authenticity of documents, and advance rulings from the court on the admissibility of evidence;

   (4) the avoidance of unnecessary proof and of cumulative evidence, and limitations or restrictions on the use of testimony under Rule 702 of the Federal Rules of Evidence;

   (5) the appropriateness and timing of summary adjudication under Rule 56;

   (6) the control and scheduling of discovery, including orders affecting disclosures and discovery pursuant to Rule 26 and Rules 29 through 37;

   (7) the identification of witnesses and documents, the need and schedule for filing and exchanging pretrial briefs, and the date or dates for further conferences and for trial;

   (8) the advisability of referring matters to a magistrate judge or master;

   (9) settlement and the use of special procedures to assist in resolving the dispute when authorized by statute or local rule;

   (10) the form and substance of the pretrial order;

   (11) the disposition of pending motions;

   (12) the need for adopting special procedures for managing potentially difficult or protracted actions that may involve complex issues, multiple parties, difficult legal questions, or unusual proof problems;

   (13) an order for a separate trial pursuant to Rule 42(b) with respect to a claim, counterclaim, cross-claim, or third-party claim, or with respect to any particular issue in the case;

   (14) an order directing a party or parties to present evidence early in the trial with respect to a manageable issue that could, on the evidence, be the basis for a judgment as a matter of law under Rule 50(a) or a judgment on partial findings under Rule 52(c);

   (15) an order establishing a reasonable limit on the time allowed for presenting evidence; and

(16) such other matters as may facilitate the just, speedy, and inexpensive disposition of the action.

At least one of the attorneys for each party participating in any conference before trial shall have authority to enter into stipulations and to make admissions regarding all matters that the participants may reasonably anticipate may be discussed. If appropriate, the court may require that a party or its representative be present or reasonably available by telephone in order to consider possible settlement of the dispute.

(d) Final Pretrial Conference. Any final pretrial conference shall be held as close to the time of trial as reasonable under the circumstances. The participants at any such conference shall formulate a plan for trial, including a program for facilitating the admission of evidence. The conference shall be attended by at least one of the attorneys who will conduct the trial for each of the parties and by any unrepresented parties.

(e) Pretrial Orders. After any conference held pursuant to this rule, an order shall be entered reciting the action taken. This order shall control the subsequent course of the action unless modified by a subsequent order. The order following a final pretrial conference shall be modified only to prevent manifest injustice.

(f) Sanctions. If a party or party's attorney fails to obey a scheduling or pretrial order, or if no appearance is made on behalf of a party at a scheduling or pretrial conference, or if a party or party's attorney is substantially unprepared to participate in the conference, or if a party or party's attorney fails to participate in good faith, the judge, upon motion or the judge's own initiative, may make such orders with regard hereto as are just, and among others any of the orders provided in Rule 37(b)(2)(B), (C), (D). In lieu of or in addition to any other sanction, the judge shall require the party or the attorney representing the party or both to pay the reasonable expenses incurred because of any noncompliance with this rule, including attorney's fees, unless the judge finds that the noncompliance was substantially justified or that other circumstances make an award of expenses unjust.
(As amended Apr. 22, 1993, eff. Dec. 1, 1993).

1993 Amendments

Subdivision (b). One purpose of this amendment is to provide a more appropriate deadline for the initial scheduling order required by the rule. The former rule directed that the order be entered within 120 days from the filing of the complaint. This requirement has created problems because Rule 4(m) allows 120 days for service and ordinarily at least one defendant should be available to participate in the process of formulating the scheduling order. The revision provides that the order is to be entered within 90 days after the date a defendant first appears (whether by answer or by a motion under Rule 12) or, if earlier (as may occur in some actions against the United States or if service is waived under Rule 4), within 120 days after service of the complaint on a defendant. The longer time provided by the revision is not intended to encourage unnecessary delays in entering the scheduling order. Indeed, in most cases the order can and should be entered at a much earlier date. Rather, the additional time is intended to alleviate problems in multi-defendant cases and should ordinarily be adequate to enable participation by all defendants initially named in the action.

In many cases the scheduling order can and should be entered before this deadline. However, when setting a scheduling conference, the court should take into account the effect this setting will have in establishing deadlines for the parties to meet under revised Rule 26(f) and to exchange information under revised Rule 26(a)(1). While the parties are expected to stipulate to additional time for making their disclosures when warranted by the circumstances, a scheduling conference held before defendants have had time to learn much about the case may result in diminishing the value of the Rule 26(f) meeting, the parties' proposed discovery plan, and indeed the conference itself.

New paragraph (4) has been added to highlight that it will frequently be desirable for the scheduling order to include provisions relating to the timing of disclosures under Rule 26(a). While the initial disclosures required by Rule 26(a)(1) will ordinarily have been made before entry of the scheduling order, the timing and sequence for disclosure of expert testimony and of the witnesses and exhibits to be used at trial should be tailored to the circumstances of the case and is a matter that should be considered at the initial scheduling conference. Similarly, the scheduling order might contain provisions modifying the extent of discovery (e.g., number and length of depositions) otherwise permitted under these rules or by a local rule.

The report from the attorneys concerning their meeting and proposed discovery plan, as required by revised Rule 26(f), should be submitted to the court before the scheduling order is entered. Their proposals, particularly regarding matters on which they agree, should be of substantial value to the court in setting the timing and limitations on discovery and should reduce the time of the court needed to conduct a meaningful conference under Rule 16(b). As under the prior rule, while a scheduling order is mandated, a scheduling conference is not. However, in view of the benefits to be derived from the litigants and a judicial officer meeting in person, a Rule 16(b) conference should, to the extent practicable, be held in all cases that will involve discovery.

This subdivision, as well as subdivision (c)(8), also is revised to reflect the new title of United States Magistrate Judges pursuant to the Judicial Improvements Act of 1990.

Subdivision (c). The primary purposes of the changes in subdivision (c) are to call attention to the opportunities for structuring of trial under Rules 42, 50, and 52 and to eliminate questions that have occasionally been raised regarding the authority of the court to make appropriate orders designed either to facilitate settlement or to provide for an efficient and economical trial. The prefatory language of this subdivision is revised to clarify the court's power to enter appropriate orders at a conference notwithstanding the objection of a party. Of course settlement is dependent upon agreement by the parties and, indeed, a conference is most effective and productive when the parties participate in a spirit of cooperation and mindful of their responsibilities under Rule 1.

Paragraph (4) is revised to clarify that in advance of trial the court may address the need for, and possible limitations on, the use of expert testimony under Rule 702 of the Federal Rules of Evidence. Even when proposed expert testimony might be admissible under the standards of Rules 403 and 702 of the evidence rules, the court may preclude or limit such testimony if the cost to the litigants—which may include the cost to adversaries of securing testimony on the same subjects by other experts—would be unduly expensive given the needs of the case and the other evidence available at trial.

Paragraph (5) is added (and the remaining paragraphs renumbered) in recognition that use of Rule 56 to avoid or reduce the scope of trial is a topic that can, and often should, be considered at a pretrial conference. Renumbered paragraph (11) enables the court to rule on pending motions for summary adjudication that are ripe for decision at the time of the conference. Often, however, the potential use of Rule 56 is a matter that arises from discussions during a conference. The court may then call for motions to be filed.

Paragraph (6) is added to emphasize that a major objective of pretrial conferences should be to consider appropriate controls on the extent and timing of discovery. In many cases the court should also specify the times and sequence for disclosure of written reports from experts under revised Rule 26(a)(2)(B) and perhaps direct changes in the types of experts from whom written reports are required. Consideration should also be given to possible changes in the timing or form of the disclosure of trial witnesses and documents under Rule 26(a)(3).

Paragraph (9) is revised to describe more accurately the various procedures that, in addition to traditional settlement conferences, may be helpful in settling litigation. Even if a case cannot immediately be settled, the judge and attorneys can explore possible use of alternative procedures such as mini-trials, summary jury trials, mediation, neutral evaluation, and nonbinding arbitration that can lead to consensual resolution of the dispute without a full trial on the merits. The rule acknowledges the presence of statutes and local rules or plans that may authorize use of some of these procedures even when not agreed to by the parties. See 28 U.S.C. §§ 473(a)(6), 473(b)(4), 651–58; Section 104(b)(2), Pub.L. 101–650. The rule does not attempt to resolve questions as to the extent a court would be authorized to require such proceedings as an exercise of its inherent powers.

The amendment of paragraph (9) should be read in conjunction with the sentence added to the end of subdivision (c), authorizing the court to direct that, in appropriate cases, a responsible representative of the parties be present or available by telephone during a conference in order to discuss possible settlement of the case. The sentence refers to participation by a party or its representative. Whether this would be the individual party, an officer of a corporate party, a representative from an insurance carrier, or someone else would depend on the circumstances. Particularly in litigation in which governmental agencies or large amounts of money are involved, there may be no one with on-the-spot settlement authority, and the most that should be expected is access to a person who would have a major role in submitting a recommendation to the body or board with ultimate decision-making responsibility. The selection of the appropriate representative should ordinarily be left to the party and its counsel. Finally, it should be noted that the unwillingness of a party to be available, even by telephone, for a settlement conference may be a clear signal that the time and expense involved in pursuing settlement is likely to be unproductive and that personal participation by the parties should not be required.

The explicit authorization in the rule to require personal participation in the manner stated is not intended to limit the reasonable exercise of the court's inherent powers, e.g., G. Heileman Brewing Co. v. Joseph Oat Corp., 871 F.2d 648 (7th Cir.1989), or its power to require party participation under the Civil Justice Reform Act of 1990. See 28 U.S.C. § 473(b)(5) (civil justice expense and delay reduction plans adopted by district courts may include requirement that representatives "with authority to bind [parties] in settlement discussions" be available during settlement conferences).

New paragraphs (13) and (14) are added to call attention to the opportunities for structuring of trial under Rule 42 and under revised Rules 50 and 52.

Paragraph (15) is also new. It supplements the power of the court to limit the extent of evidence under Rules 403 and 611(a) of the Federal Rules of Evidence, which typically would be invoked as a result of developments during trial. Limits on the length of trial established at a conference in advance of trial can provide the parties with a better opportunity to determine priorities and exercise selectivity in presenting evidence than when limits are imposed during trial. Any such limits must be reasonable under the circumstances, and ordinarily the court should impose them only after receiving appropriate submissions from the parties outlining the nature of the testimony expected to be presented through various witnesses, and the expected duration of direct and cross-examination.

1983 Amendment

. . .

Subdivision (f); Sanctions. Original Rule 16 did not mention the sanctions that might be imposed for failing to comply with the rule. However, courts have not hesitated to enforce it by appropriate measures. See, *e.g., Link v. Wabash R. Co.,* 370 U.S. 626 (1962) (district court's dismissal under Rule 41(b) after plaintiff's attorney failed to appear at a pretrial conference upheld); *Admiral Theatre Corp. v. Douglas Theatre,* 585 F.2d 877 (8th Cir.1978) (district court has discretion to exclude exhibits or refuse to permit the testimony of a witness not listed prior to trial in contravention of its pretrial order).

To reflect that existing practice, and to obviate dependence upon Rule 41(b) or the court's inherent power to regulate litigation, *cf. Societe Internationale Pour Participations Industrielles et Commerciales, S.A. v. Rogers,* 357 U.S. 197 (1958), Rule 16(f) expressly provides for imposing sanctions on disobedient or recalcitrant parties, their attorneys, or both in four types of situations. Rodes, Ripple & Mooney, *Sanctions Imposable for Violations of the Federal Rules of Civil Procedure* 65–67, 80–84, Federal Judicial Center (1981). Furthermore, explicit reference to sanctions reenforces the rule's intention to encourage forceful judicial management.

Rule 16(f) incorporates portions of Rule 37(b)(2), which prescribes sanctions for failing to make discovery. This should facilitate application of Rule 16(f), since courts and lawyers already are familiar with the Rule 37 standards. Among the sanctions authorized by the new subdivision are: preclusion order, striking a pleading, staying the proceeding, default judgment, contempt, and charging a party, his attorney, or both with the expenses, including attorney's fees, caused by noncompliance. The contempt sanction, however, is only available for a violation of a court order. The references in Rule 16(f) are not exhaustive.

As is true under Rule 37(b)(2), the imposition of sanctions may be sought by either the court or a party. In addition, the court has discretion to impose whichever sanction it feels is appropriate under the circumstances. Its action is reviewable under the abuse-of-discretion standard. See *National Hockey League v. Metropolitan Hockey Club, Inc.*, 427 U.S. 639 (1976).

Rule 26. General Provisions Governing Discovery; Duty of Disclosure

(a) Required Disclosures; Methods to Discover Additional Matter.

(1) Initial Disclosures. Except in categories of proceedings specified in Rule 26 (a)(1)(E), or to the extent otherwise stipulated or directed by order, a party must, without awaiting a discovery request, provide to other parties:

(A) the name and, if known, the address and telephone number of each individual likely to have discoverable information that the disclosing party may use to support its claims or defenses, unless solely for impeachment, identifying the subjects of the information;

(B) a copy of, or a description by category and location of, all documents, data compilations, and tangible things that are in the possession, custody, or control of the party and that the disclosing party may use to support its claims or defenses, unless solely for impeachment;

(C) a computation of any category of damages claimed by the disclosing party, making available for inspection and copying as under Rule 34 the documents or other evidentiary material, not privileged or protected from disclosure, on which such computation is based, including materials bearing on the nature and extent of injuries suffered; and

(D) for inspection and copying as under Rule 34 any insurance agreement under which any person carrying on an insurance business may be liable to satisfy part or all of a judgment which may be entered in the action or to indemnify or reimburse for payments made to satisfy the judgment.

(E) The following categories of proceedings are exempt from initial disclosure under Rule 26 (a)(1):

(i) an action for review on an administrative record;

(ii) a petition for habeas corpus or other proceeding to challenge a criminal conviction or sentence;

(iii) an action brought without counsel by a person in custody of the United States, a state, or a state subdivision;

(iv) an action to enforce or quash an administrative summons or subpoena;

(v) an action by the United States to recover benefit payments;

(vi) an action by the United States to collect on a student loan guaranteed by the United States;

(vii) a proceeding ancillary to proceedings in other courts; and

(viii) an action to enforce an arbitration award.

These disclosures must be made at or within 14 days after the Rule 26 (f) conference unless a different time is set by stipulation or court order, or unless a party objects during the conference that initial disclosures are not appropriate in the circumstances of the action and states the objection in the Rule 26 (f) discovery plan. In ruling on the objection, the court must determine what disclosures—if any—are to be made, and set the time for disclosure. Any party first served or otherwise joined after the Rule 26 (f) conference must make these disclosures within 30 days after being served or joined unless a different time is set by stipulation or court order. A party must make its initial disclosures based on the information then reasonably available to it and is not excused from making its disclosures because it has not fully completed its investigation of the case or because it challenges the sufficiency of another party's disclosures or because another party has not made its disclosures.

(2) Disclosure of Expert Testimony.

(A) In addition to the disclosures required by paragraph (1), a party shall disclose to other parties the identity of any person who may be used at trial to present evidence under Rules 702, 703, or 705 of the Federal Rules of Evidence.

(B) Except as otherwise stipulated or directed by the court, this disclosure shall, with respect to a witness who is retained or specially employed to provide expert testimony in the case or whose duties as an employee of the party regularly involve giving expert testimony, be accompanied by a written report prepared and signed by the witness. The report shall contain a complete statement of all opinions to be expressed and the basis and reasons therefor; the data or other information considered by the witness in forming the opinions; any exhibits to be used as a summary of or support for the opinions; the qualifications of the witness, including a list of all publications authored by the witness within the preceding ten years; the compensation to be paid for the study and testimony; and a listing of any other cases in which the witness has testified as an expert at trial or by deposition within the preceding four years.

(C) These disclosures shall be made at the times and in the sequence directed by the court. In the absence of other directions from the court or stipulation by the parties, the disclosures shall be made at least 90 days before the trial date or the date the case is to be ready for trial or, if the evidence is intended solely to contradict or rebut evidence on the same subject matter identified by another party under paragraph (2)(B), within 30 days after the disclosure made by the other party. The parties shall supplement these disclosures when required under subdivision (e)(1).

(3) Pretrial Disclosures. In addition to the disclosures required by Rule 26 (a)(1) and (2), a party must provide to other parties and promptly file with the court the following information regarding the evidence that it may present at trial other than solely for impeachment:

(A) the name and, if not previously provided, the address and telephone number of each witness, separately identifying those whom the party expects to present and those whom the party may call if the need arises;

(B) the designation of those witnesses whose testimony is expected to be presented by means of a deposition and, if not taken stenographically, a transcript of the pertinent portions of the deposition testimony; and (C) an appropriate identification of each document or other exhibit, including summaries of other evidence, separately identifying those which the party expects to offer and those which the party may offer if the need arises. Unless otherwise directed by the court, these disclosures must be made at least 30 days before trial. Within 14 days thereafter, unless a different time is specified by the court, a party may serve and promptly file a list disclosing (i) any objections to the use under Rule 32(a) of a deposition designated by another party under Rule 26 (a)(3)(B), and (ii) any objection, together with the grounds therefor, that may be made to the admissibility of materials identified under Rule 26 (a)(3)(C). Objections not so disclosed, other than objections under Rules 402 and 403 of the Federal Rules of Evidence, are waived unless excused by the court for good cause.

(4) Form of Disclosures. Unless the court orders otherwise, all disclosures under Rules 26 (a)(1) through (3) must be made in writing, signed, and served.

(5) Methods to Discover Additional Matter. Parties may obtain discovery by one or more of the following methods: depositions upon

oral examination or written questions; written interrogatories; production of documents or things or permission to enter upon land or other property under Rule 34 or 45(a)(1)(C), for inspection and other purposes; physical and mental examinations; and requests for admission.

(b) Discovery Scope and Limits. Unless otherwise limited by order of the court in accordance with these rules, the scope of discovery is as follows:

(1) In General. Parties may obtain discovery regarding any matter, not privileged, that is relevant to the claim or defense of any party, including the existence, description, nature, custody, condition, and location of any books, documents, or other tangible things and the identity and location of persons having knowledge of any discoverable matter. For good cause, the court may order discovery of any matter relevant to the subject matter involved in the action. Relevant information need not be admissible at the trial if the discovery appears reasonably calculated to lead to the discovery of admissible evidence. All discovery is subject to the limitations imposed by Rule 26 (b)(2)(i), (ii), and (iii).

(2) Limitations. By order, the court may alter the limits in these rules on the number of depositions and interrogatories or the length of depositions under Rule 30. By order or local rule, the court may also limit the number of requests under Rule 36. The frequency or extent of use of the discovery methods otherwise permitted under these rules and by any local rule shall be limited by the court if it determines that: (i) the discovery sought is unreasonably cumulative or duplicative, or is obtainable from some other source that is more convenient, less burdensome, or less expensive; (ii) the party seeking discovery has had ample opportunity by discovery in the action to obtain the information sought; or (iii) the burden or expense of the proposed discovery outweighs its likely benefit, taking into account the needs of the case, the amount in controversy, the parties' resources, the importance of the issues at stake in the litigation, and the importance of the proposed discovery in resolving the issues. The court may act upon its own initiative after reasonable notice or pursuant to a motion under Rule 26 (c).

(3) Trial Preparation: Materials. Subject to the provisions of subdivision (b)(4) of this rule, a party may obtain discovery of documents and tangible things otherwise discoverable under subdivision (b)(1) of this rule and prepared in anticipation of litigation or for trial by or for another party or by or for that other party's representative (including the other party's attorney, consultant, surety, indemnitor, insurer, or agent) only upon a showing that the party seeking discovery has substantial need of the materials in the preparation of the party's case and that the party is unable without undue hardship to obtain the substantial equivalent of the materials

by other means. In ordering discovery of such materials when the required showing has been made, the court shall protect against disclosure of the mental impressions, conclusions, opinions, or legal theories of an attorney or other representative of a party concerning the litigation.

A party may obtain without the required showing a statement concerning the action or its subject matter previously made by that party. Upon request, a person not a party may obtain without the required showing a statement concerning the action or its subject matter previously made by that person. If the request is refused, the person may move for a court order. The provisions of Rule 37(a)(4) apply to the award of expenses incurred in relation to the motion. For purposes of this paragraph, a statement previously made is (A) a written statement signed or otherwise adopted or approved by the person making it, or (B) a stenographic, mechanical, electrical, or other recording, or a transcription thereof, which is a substantially verbatim recital of an oral statement by the person making it and contemporaneously recorded.

(4) Trial Preparation: Experts.

(A) A party may depose any person who has been identified as an expert whose opinions may be presented at trial. If a report from the expert is required under subdivision (a)(2)(B), the deposition shall not be conducted until after the report is provided.

(B) A party may, through interrogatories or by deposition, discover facts known or opinions held by an expert who has been retained or specially employed by another party in anticipation of litigation or preparation for trial and who is not expected to be called as a witness at trial, only as provided in Rule 35(b) or upon a showing of exceptional circumstances under which it is impracticable for the party seeking discovery to obtain facts or opinions on the same subject by other means.

(C) Unless manifest injustice would result, (i) the court shall require that the party seeking discovery pay the expert a reasonable fee for time spent in responding to discovery under this subdivision; and (ii) with respect to discovery obtained under subdivision (b)(4)(B) of this rule the court shall require the party seeking discovery to pay the other party a fair portion of the fees and expenses reasonably incurred by the latter party in obtaining facts and opinions from the expert.

(5) Claims of Privilege or Protection of Trial Preparation Materials. When a party withholds information otherwise discoverable under these rules by claiming that it is privileged or subject to protection as trial preparation material, the party shall make the claim expressly and shall describe the nature of the documents,

communications, or things not produced or disclosed in a manner that, without revealing information itself privileged or protected, will enable other parties to assess the applicability of the privilege or protection.

(c) Protective Orders. Upon motion by a party or by the person from whom discovery is sought, accompanied by a certification that the movant has in good faith conferred or attempted to confer with other affected parties in an effort to resolve the dispute without court action, and for good cause shown, the court in which the action is pending or alternatively, on matters relating to a deposition, the court in the district where the deposition is to be taken may make any order which justice requires to protect a party or person from annoyance, embarrassment, oppression, or undue burden or expense, including one or more of the following:

(1) that the disclosure or discovery not be had;

(2) that the disclosure or discovery may be had only on specified terms and conditions, including a designation of the time or place;

(3) that the discovery may be had only by a method of discovery other than that selected by the party seeking discovery;

(4) that certain matters not be inquired into, or that the scope of the disclosure or discovery be limited to certain matters;

(5) that discovery be conducted with no one present except persons designated by the court;

(6) that a deposition, after being sealed, be opened only by order of the court;

(7) that a trade secret or other confidential research, development, or commercial information not be revealed or be revealed only in a designated way; and

(8) that the parties simultaneously file specified documents or information enclosed in sealed envelopes to be opened as directed by the court. If the motion for a protective order is denied in whole or in part, the court may, on such terms and conditions as are just, order that any party or other person provide or permit discovery. The provisions of Rule 37(a)(4) apply to the award of expenses incurred in relation to the motion.

(d) Timing and Sequence of Discovery. Except in categories of proceedings exempted from initial disclosure under Rule 26 (a)(1)(E), or when authorized under these rules or by order or agreement of the parties, a party may not seek discovery from any source before the parties have conferred as required by Rule 26 (f). Unless the court upon motion, for the convenience of parties and witnesses and in the interests of justice, orders otherwise, methods of discovery may be used in any sequence, and the fact that a party is conducting discovery, whether by deposition or otherwise, does not operate to delay any other party's discovery.

(e) Supplementation of Disclosures and Responses.A party who has made a disclosure under subdivision (a) or responded to a request for discovery with a disclosure or response is under a duty to supplement or correct the disclosure or response to include information thereafter acquired if ordered by the court or in the following circumstances:

(1) A party is under a duty to supplement at appropriate intervals its disclosures under subdivision (a) if the party learns that in some material respect the information disclosed is incomplete or incorrect and if the additional or corrective information has not otherwise been made known to the other parties during the discovery process or in writing. With respect to testimony of an expert from whom a report is required under subdivision (a)(2)(B) the duty extends both to information contained in the report and to information provided through a deposition of the expert, and any additions or other changes to this information shall be disclosed by the time the party's disclosures under Rule 26 (a)(3) are due.

(2) A party is under a duty seasonably to amend a prior response to an interrogatory, request for production, or request for admission if the party learns that the response is in some material respect incomplete or incorrect and if the additional or corrective information has not otherwise been made known to the other parties during the discovery process or in writing.

(f) Conference of Parties; Planning for Discovery.Except in categories of proceedings exempted from initial disclosure under Rule 26 (a)(1)(E) or when otherwise ordered, the parties must, as soon as practicable and in any event at least 21 days before a scheduling conference is held or a scheduling order is due under Rule 16(b), confer to consider the nature and basis of their claims and defenses and the possibilities for a prompt settlement or resolution of the case, to make or arrange for the disclosures required by Rule 26 (a)(1), and to develop a proposed discovery plan that indicates the parties' views and proposals concerning:

(1) what changes should be made in the timing, form, or requirement for disclosures under Rule 26 (a), including a statement as to when disclosures under Rule 26 (a)(1) were made or will be made;

(2) the subjects on which discovery may be needed, when discovery should be completed, and whether discovery should be conducted in phases or be limited to or focused upon particular issues;

(3) what changes should be made in the limitations on discovery imposed under these rules or by local rule, and what other limitations should be imposed; and

(4) any other orders that should be entered by the court under Rule 26 (c) or under Rule 16(b) and (c).

The attorneys of record and all unrepresented parties that have appeared in the case are jointly responsible for arranging the conference, for attempting in good faith to agree on the proposed discovery plan, and for submitting to the court within 14 days after the conference a written report outlining the plan. A court may order that the parties or attorneys attend the conference in person. If necessary to comply with its expedited schedule for Rule 16(b) conferences, a court may by local rule (i) require that the conference between the parties occur fewer than 21 days before the scheduling conference is held or a scheduling order is due under Rule 16(b), and (ii) require that the written report outlining the discovery plan be filed fewer than 14 days after the conference between the parties, or excuse the parties from submitting a written report and permit them to report orally on their discovery plan at the Rule 16(b) conference.

(g) Signing of Disclosures, Discovery Requests, Responses, and Objections.

(1) Every disclosure made pursuant to subdivision (a)(1) or subdivision (a)(3) shall be signed by at least one attorney of record in the attorney's individual name, whose address shall be stated. An unrepresented party shall sign the disclosure and state the party's address. The signature of the attorney or party constitutes a certification that to the best of the signer's knowledge, information, and belief, formed after a reasonable inquiry, the disclosure is complete and correct as of the time it is made.

(2) Every discovery request, response, or objection made by a party represented by an attorney shall be signed by at least one attorney of record in the attorney's individual name, whose address shall be stated. An unrepresented party shall sign the request, response, or objection and state the party's address. The signature of the attorney or party constitutes a certification that to the best of the signer's knowledge, information, and belief, formed after a reasonable inquiry, the request, response, or objection is:

(A) consistent with these rules and warranted by existing law or a good faith argument for the extension, modification, or reversal of existing law;

(B) not interposed for any improper purpose, such as to harass or to cause unnecessary delay or needless increase in the cost of litigation; and

(C) not unreasonable or unduly burdensome or expensive, given the needs of the case, the discovery already had in the case, the amount in controversy, and the importance of the issues at stake in the litigation.

If a request, response, or objection is not signed, it shall be stricken unless it is signed promptly after the omission is called to the attention of the party making the request, response, or objection, and a party shall not be obligated to take any action with respect to it until it is signed.

(3) If without substantial justification a certification is made in violation of the rule, the court, upon motion or upon its own initiative, shall impose upon the person who made the certification, the party on whose behalf the disclosure, request, response, or objection is made, or both, an appropriate sanction, which may include an order to pay the amount of the reasonable expenses incurred because of the violation, including a reasonable attorney's fee.

HISTORY: (Amended March 19, 1948; July 1, 1963; July 1, 1966; July 1, 1970; Aug. 1, 1980; Aug. 1, 1983; Aug. 1, 1987; Dec. 1, 1993.)

(As amended Dec. 1, 2000.)

Rule 37.   Failure to Make or Cooperate in Discovery; Sanctions

(a) Motion for Order Compelling Disclosure or Discovery. A party, upon reasonable notice to other parties and all persons affected thereby, may apply for an order compelling disclosure or discovery as follows:

(1) Appropriate Court. An application for an order to a party shall be made to the court in which the action is pending. An application for an order to a person who is not a party shall be made to the court in the district where the discovery is being, or is to be, taken.

(2) Motion.

(A) If a party fails to make a disclosure required by Rule 26 (a), any other party may move to compel disclosure and for appropriate sanctions. The motion must include a certification that the movant has in good faith conferred or attempted to confer with the party not making the disclosure in an effort to secure the disclosure without court action.

(B) If a deponent fails to answer a question propounded or submitted under Rules 30 or 31, or a corporation or other entity fails to make a designation under Rule 30(b)(6) or 31(a), or a party fails to answer an interrogatory submitted under Rule 33, or if a party, in response to a request for inspection submitted under Rule 34, fails to respond that inspection will be permitted as requested or fails to permit inspection as requested, the discovering party may move for an order compelling answer, or a designation, or an order compelling inspection in accordance with the request. The motion must include a certification that the movant has in good faith conferred or attempted to confer with the person or party failing to make the discovery in an effort to secure the information or material without court action. When taking a deposition on oral examination, the proponent of the question may complete or adjourn the examination before applying for an order.

(3) Evasive or Incomplete Disclosure, Answer, or Response. For purposes of this subdivision an evasive or incomplete disclosure, answer, or response is to be treated as a failure to disclose, answer, or respond.

(4) Expenses and Sanctions.

(A) If the motion is granted or if the disclosure or requested discovery is provided after the motion was filed, the court shall, after affording an opportunity to be heard, require the party or deponent whose conduct necessitated the motion or the party or attorney advising such conduct or both of them to pay to the moving party the reasonable expenses incurred in making the motion, including attorney's fees, unless the court finds that the motion was filed without the movant's first making a good faith effort to obtain the disclosure or discovery without court action, or that the opposing party's nondisclosure, response, or objection was substantially justified, or that other circumstances make an award of expenses unjust.

(B) If the motion is denied, the court may enter any protective order authorized under Rule 26 (c) and shall, after affording an opportunity to be heard, require the moving party or the attorney filing the motion or both of them to pay to the party or deponent who opposed the motion the reasonable expenses incurred in opposing the motion, including attorney's fees, unless the court finds that the making of the motion was substantially justified or that other circumstances make an award of expenses unjust.

(C) If the motion is granted in part and denied in part, the court may enter any protective order authorized under Rule 26 (c) and may, after affording an opportunity to be heard, apportion the reasonable expenses incurred in relation to the motion among the parties and persons in a just manner.

(b) Failure to comply with order.

(1) Sanctions by Court in District Where Deposition is Taken. If a deponent fails to be sworn or to answer a question after being directed to do so by the court in the district in which the deposition is being taken, the failure may be considered a contempt of that court.

(2) Sanctions by Court in Which Action Is Pending. If a party or an officer, director, or managing agent of a party or a person designated under Rule 30(b)(6) or 31(a) to testify on behalf of a

party fails to obey an order to provide or permit discovery, including an order made under subdivision (a) of this rule or Rule 35, or if a party fails to obey an order entered under Rule 26 (f), the court in which the action is pending may make such orders in regard to the failure as are just, and among others the following:

(A) An order that the matters regarding which the order was made or any other designated facts shall be taken to be established for the purposes of the action in accordance with the claim of the party obtaining the order;

(B) An order refusing to allow the disobedient party to support or oppose designated claims or defenses, or prohibiting that party from introducing designated matters in evidence;

(C) An order striking out pleadings or parts thereof, or staying further proceedings until the order is obeyed, or dismissing the action or proceeding or any part thereof, or rendering a judgment by default against the disobedient party;

(D) In lieu of any of the foregoing orders or in addition thereto, an order treating as a contempt of court the failure to obey any orders except an order to submit to a physical or mental examination;

(E) Where a party has failed to comply with an order under Rule 35(a) requiring that party to produce another for examination, such orders as are listed in paragraphs (A), (B), and (C) of this subdivision, unless the party failing to comply shows that that party is unable to produce such person for examination.

In lieu of any of the foregoing orders or in addition thereto, the court shall require the party failing to obey the order or the attorney advising that party or both to pay the reasonable expenses, including attorney's fees,caused by the failure, unless the court finds that the failure was substantially justified or that other circumstances make an award of expenses unjust.

(c) Failure to Disclose; False or Misleading Disclosure; Refusal to Admit.

(1) A party that without substantial justification fails to disclose information required by Rule 26 (a) or 26(e)(1), or to amend a prior response to discovery as required by Rule 26 (e)(2), is not, unless such failure is harmless, permitted to use as evidence at a trial, at a hearing, or on a motion any witness or information not so disclosed. In addition to or in lieu of this sanction, the court, on motion and after affording an opportunity to be heard, may impose other appropriate sanctions. In addition to requiring payment of reasonable expenses, including attorney's fees, caused by the failure, these sanctions may include any of the actions authorized under

Rule37(b)(2)(A), (B), and (C) and may include informing the jury of the failure to make the disclosure.

(2) If a party fails to admit the genuineness of any document or the truth of any matter as requested under Rule 36, and if the party requesting the admissions thereafter proves the genuineness of the document or the truth of the matter, the requesting party may apply to the court for an order requiring the other party to pay the reasonable expenses incurred in making that proof, including reasonable attorney's fees. The court shall make the order unless it finds that (A) the request was held objectionable pursuant to Rule 36(a), or (B) the admission sought was of no substantial importance, or (C) the party failing to admit had reasonable ground to believe that the party might prevail on the matter, or (D) there was other good reason for the failure to admit.

(d) Failure of Party to Attend at Own Deposition or Serve Answers to Interrogatories or Respond to Request for Inspection. If a party or an officer, director, or managing agent of a party or a person designated under Rule 30(b)(6) or 31(a) to testify on behalf of a party fails (1) to appear before the officer who is to take the deposition, after being served with a proper notice, or (2) to serve answers or objections to interrogatories submitted under Rule 33, after proper service of the interrogatories, or (3) to serve a written response to a request for inspection submitted under Rule 34, after proper service of the request, the court in which the action is pending on motion may make such orders in regard to the failure as are just, and among others it may take any action authorized under subparagraphs (A), (B), and (C) of subdivision (b)(2) of this rule. Any motion specifying a failure under clause (2) or (3) of this subdivision shall include a certification that the movant has in good faith conferred or attempted to confer with the party failing to answer or respond in an effort to obtain such answer or response without court action. In lieu of any order or in addition thereto, the court shall require the party failing to act or the attorney advising that party or both to pay the reasonable expenses, including attorney's fees, caused by the failure unless the court finds that the failure was substantially justified or that other circumstances make an award of expenses unjust.

The failure to act described in this subdivision may not be excused on the ground that the discovery sought is objectionable unless the party failing to act has a pending motion for a protective order as provided by Rule 26 (c).

(e) [Abrogated]

(f) [Repealed]

(g) Failure to Participate in the Framing of a Discovery Plan. If a party or a party's attorney fails to participate in the development and submission of a proposed discovery plan as required by Rule 26 (f), the court may, after opportunity for hearing, require such party or attorney

751

to pay to any other party the reasonable expenses, including attorney's fees, caused by the failure.

HISTORY: (Amended Oct. 20, 1949; July 1, 1970; Aug. 1, 1980; Oct. 21, 1980; Aug. 1, 1987.)

(As amended Dec. 1, 1993; Dec. 1, 2000.)

Rule 60.   Relief From Judgment or Order

(a) Clerical Mistakes.   Clerical mistakes in judgments, orders or other parts of the record and errors therein arising from oversight or omission may be corrected by the court at any time of its own initiative or on the motion of any party and after such notice, if any, as the court orders.   During the pendency of an appeal, such mistakes may be so corrected before the appeal is docketed in the appellate court, and thereafter while the appeal is pending may be so corrected with leave of the appellate court.

(b) Mistakes; Inadvertence; Excusable Neglect; Newly Discovered Evidence; Fraud, etc.   On motion and upon such terms as are just, the court may relieve a party or a party's legal representative from a final judgment, order, or proceeding for the following reasons: (1) mistake, inadvertence, surprise, or excusable neglect; (2) newly discovered evidence which by due diligence could not have been discovered in time to move for a new trial under Rule 59(b); (3) fraud (whether heretofore denominated intrinsic or extrinsic), misrepresentation, or other misconduct of an adverse party; (4) the judgment is void; (5) the judgment has been satisfied, released, or discharged, or a prior judgment upon which it is based has been reversed or otherwise vacated, or it is no longer equitable that the judgment should have prospective application; or (6) any other reason justifying relief from the operation of the judgment.   The motion shall be made within a reasonable time, and for reasons (1), (2), and (3) not more than one year after the judgment, order, or proceeding was entered or taken.   A motion under this subdivision (b) does not affect the finality of a judgment or suspend its operation.   This rule does not limit the power of a court to entertain an independent action to relieve a party from a judgment, order, or proceeding, or to grant relief to a defendant not actually personally notified as provided in Title 28, U.S.C. § 1655, or to set aside a judgment for fraud upon the court.   Writs of coram nobis, coram vobis, audita querela, and bills of review and bills in the nature of a bill of review, are abolished, and the procedure for obtaining any relief from a judgment shall be by motion as prescribed in these rules or by an independent action.

(As amended Dec. 27, 1946, eff. Mar. 19, 1948; Dec. 29, 1948, eff. Oct. 20, 1949; Mar. 2, 1987, eff. Aug. 1, 1987.)

Rule 63.   Disability of a Judge

If a trial or hearing has been commenced and the judge is unable to proceed, any other judge may proceed with it upon certifying familiarity

with the record and determining that the proceedings in the case may be completed without prejudice to the parties. In a hearing or trial without a jury, the successor judge shall at the request of a party recall any witness whose testimony is material and disputed and who is available to testify again without undue burden. The successor judge may also recall any other witness.
(As amended Mar. 2, 1987, eff. Aug. 1, 1987; Apr. 30, 1991, eff. Dec. 1, 1991.)

Rule 68. Offer of Judgment

At any time more than 10 days before the trial begins, a party defending against a claim may serve upon the adverse party an offer to allow judgment to be taken against the defending party for the money or property or to the effect specified in the offer, with costs then accrued. If within 10 days after the service of the offer the adverse party serves written notice that the offer is accepted, either party may then file the offer and notice of acceptance together with proof of service thereof and thereupon the clerk shall enter judgment. An offer not accepted shall be deemed withdrawn and evidence thereof is not admissible except in a proceeding to determine costs. If the judgment finally obtained by the offeree is not more favorable than the offer, the offeree must pay the costs incurred after the making of the offer. The fact that an offer is made but not accepted does not preclude a subsequent offer. When the liability of one party to another has been determined by verdict or order or judgment, but the amount or extent of the liability remains to be determined by further proceedings, the party adjudged liable may make an offer of judgment, which shall have the same effect as an offer made before trial if it is served within a reasonable time not less than 10 days prior to the commencement of hearings to determine the amount or extent of liability.
(As amended Dec. 27, 1946, eff. Mar. 19, 1948; Feb. 28, 1966, eff. July 1, 1966; Mar. 2, 1987, eff. Aug. 1, 1987.)

FEDERAL RULES OF CRIMINAL PROCEDURE

Rule 44. Right to and Assignment of Counsel

(a) Right to Assigned Counsel. Every defendant who is unable to obtain counsel shall be entitled to have counsel assigned to represent that defendant at every stage of the proceedings from initial appearance before the federal magistrate judge or the court through appeal, unless that defendant waives such appointment.

(b) Assignment Procedure. The procedures for implementing the right set out in subdivision (a) shall be those provided by law and by local rules of court established pursuant thereto.

(c) Joint Representation. Whenever two or more defendants have been jointly charged pursuant to Rule 8(b) or have been joined for trial pursuant to Rule 13, and are represented by the same retained or assigned counsel or by retained or assigned counsel who are associated in the practice of law, the court shall promptly inquire with respect to such joint representation and shall personally advise each defendant of the right to the effective assistance of counsel, including separate representation.   Unless it appears that there is good cause to believe no conflict of interest is likely to arise, the court shall take such measures as may be appropriate to protect each defendant's right to counsel.

(As amended Apr. 30, 1979, eff. Dec. 1, 1980; Mar. 9, 1987, eff. Aug. 1, 1987; Apr. 22, 1993, eff. Dec. 1, 1993.)

1979 Amendment

Rule 44(c) establishes a procedure for avoiding the occurrence of events which might otherwise give rise to a plausible post-conviction claim that because of joint representation the defendants in a criminal case were deprived of their Sixth Amendment right to the effective assistance of counsel.   Although "courts have differed with respect to the scope and nature of the affirmative duty of the trial judge to assure that criminal defendants are not deprived of their right to the effective assistance of counsel by joint representation of conflicting interests."   *Holloway v. Arkansas,* 98 S.Ct. 1173 (1978) (where the Court found it unnecessary to reach this issue), this amendment is generally consistent with the current state of the law in several circuits.   As held in *United States v. Carrigan,* 543 F.2d 1053 (2d Cir.1976):

> When a potential conflict of interest arises, either where a court has assigned the same counsel to represent several defendants or where the same counsel has been retained by co-defendants in a criminal case, the proper course of action for the trial judge is to conduct a hearing to determine whether a conflict exists to the degree that a defendant may be prevented from receiving advice and assistance sufficient to afford him the quality of representation guaranteed by the Sixth Amendment.   The defendant should be fully advised by the trial court of the facts underlying the potential conflict and be given the opportunity to express his views.

See also *United States v. Lawriw,* 568 F.2d 98 (8th Cir.1977) (duty on trial judge to make inquiry where joint representation by appointed or retained counsel, and "without such an inquiry a finding of knowing and intelligent waiver will seldom, if ever, be sustained by this Court"); *Abraham v. United States,* 549 F.2d 236 (2d Cir.1977); *United States v. Mari,* 526 F.2d 117 (2d Cir.1975); *United States v. Truglio,* 493 F.2d 574 (4th Cir.1974) (joint representation should cause trial judge "to inquire whether the defenses to be presented in any way conflict"); *United States v. DeBerry,* 487 F.2d 488 (2d Cir.1973); *United States ex rel. Hart v. Davenport,* 478 F.2d 203 (3d Cir.1973) (noting there "is much to be said for the rule ... which assumes prejudice and nonwaiver if there has been no on-the-record inquiry by the court as to the hazards to defendants from joint representation"); *United States v. Alberti,* 470 F.2d 878 (2d Cir.1973); *United States v. Foster,* 469 F.2d 1 (1st Cir.1972) (lack of sufficient inquiry shifts the burden of proof on the question of prejudice to the government); *Campbell v. United States,* 352 F.2d 359 (D.C.Cir.1965) (where joint representation, court "has a duty to ascertain whether each defendant has an awareness of the potential risks of that course and nevertheless has knowingly chosen it").   Some states have taken a like position; see, e.g., *State v. Olsen,* Minn.1977, 258 N.W.2d 898.

This procedure is also consistent with that recommended in the ABA Standards Relating to the Function of the Trial Judge (Approved Draft, 1972), which provide in § 3.4(b):

> Whenever two or more defendants who have been jointly charged, or whose cases have been consolidated, are represented by the same attorney, the trial judge should inquire into potential conflicts with may jeopardize the right of each defendant to the fidelity of his counsel.

Avoiding a conflict-of-interest situation is in the first instance a responsibility of the attorney.   If a lawyer represents "multiple clients having potentially differing interests, he must weigh carefully the possibility that his judgment may be impaired or his loyalty divided if he accepts or continues the employment," and he is to "resolve all doubts against the propriety of the representation." Code of Professional Responsibility, Ethical Consideration 5–15. See also ABA Standards Relating to the Defense Function § 3.5(b) (Approved Draft, 1971) concluding that the "potential for conflict of interest in representing multiple defendants is so grave that ordinarily a lawyer should decline to act for more than one of several co-defendants except in unusual situations when, after careful investigation, it is clear that no conflict is likely to develop and when the several defendants give an informed consent to such multiple representation."

It by no means follows that the inquiry provided for by rule 44(c) is unnecessary. For one thing, even the most diligent attorney may be unaware of facts giving rise to a potential conflict. Often "counsel must operate somewhat in the dark and feel their way uncertainly to an understanding of what their clients may be called upon to meet upon a trial" and consequently "are frequently unable to foresee developments which may require changes in strategy." *United States v. Carrigan*, supra (concurring opinion). "Because the conflicts are often subtle it is not enough to rely upon counsel, who may not be totally disinterested, to make sure that each of his joint clients has made an effective waiver." *United States v. Lawriw*, supra.

Moreover, it is important that the trial judge ascertain whether the effective and fair administration of justice would be adversely affected by continued joint representation, even when an actual conflict is not then apparent. As noted in *United States v. Mari*, supra (concurring opinion):

> Trial court insistence that, except in extraordinary circumstances, codefendants retain separate counsel will in the long run ... prove salutary not only to the administration of justice and the appearance of justice but the cost of justice; habeas corpus petitions, petitions for new trials, appeals and occasionally retrials ... can be avoided. Issues as to whether there is an actual conflict of interest, whether the conflict has resulted in prejudice, whether there has been a waiver, whether the waiver is intelligent and knowledgeable, for example, can all be avoided. Where a conflict that first did not appear subsequently arises in or before trial, ... continuances or mistrials can be saved. Essentially by the time a case ... gets to the appellate level the harm to the appearance of justice has already been done, whether or not reversal occurs; at the trial level it is a matter which is so easy to avoid.

A rule 44(c) inquiry is required whether counsel is assigned or retained. It "makes no difference whether counsel is appointed by the court or selected by the defendants; even where selected by the defendants the same dangers of potential conflict exist, and it is also possible that the rights of the public to the proper administration of justice may be affected adversely." *United States v. Mari*, supra (concurring opinion). See also *United States v. Lawriw*, supra. When there has been "no discussion as to possible conflict initiated by the court," it cannot be assumed that the choice of counsel by the defendants "was intelligently made with knowledge of any possible conflict." *United States v. Carrigan*, supra. As for assigned counsel, it is provided by statute that "the court shall appoint separate counsel for defendants having interests that cannot properly be represented by the same counsel, or when other good cause is shown." 18 U.S.C. § 3006(A)(b). Rule 44(c) is not intended to prohibit the automatic appointment of separate counsel in the first instance, see *Ford v. United States*, 379 F.2d 123 (D.C.Cir.1967); *Lollar v. United States*, 376 F.2d 243 (D.C.Cir.1967), which would obviate the necessity for an inquiry.

Under rule 44(c), an inquiry is called for when the joined defendants are represented by the same attorney and also when they are represented by attorneys "associated in the practice of law." This is consistent with Code of Professional Responsibility, Disciplinary Rule 5–105(D) (providing that if "a lawyer is required to decline employment or to withdraw from employment" because of a potential conflict, "no partner or associate of his or his firm may accept or continue such employment"); and ABA Standards Relating to the Defense Function § 3.5(b) (Approved Draft, 1971) (applicable to "a lawyer or lawyers who are associated in practice"). Attorneys representing joined defendants should so advise the court if they are associated in the practice of law.

The rule 44(c) procedure is not limited to cases expected to go to trial. Although the more dramatic conflict situations, such as when the question arises as to whether the several defendants should take the stand, *Morgan v. United States*, 396 F.2d 110 (2d Cir.1968), tend to occur in a trial context, serious conflicts may also arise when one or more of the jointly represented defendants pleads guilty.

The problem is that even where as here both codefendants pleaded guilty there are frequently potential conflicts of interest.... [T]he prosecutor may be inclined to accept a guilty plea from one codefendant which may harm the interests of the other. The contrast in the dispositions of the cases may have a harmful impact on the codefendant who does not initially plead guilty; he may be pressured into pleading guilty himself rather than face his codefendant's bargained-for testimony at a trial. And it will be his own counsel's recommendation to the initially pleading codefendant which will have contributed to this harmful impact upon him.... [I]n a given instance it would be at least conceivable that the prosecutor would be willing to accept pleas to lesser offenses from two defendants in preference to a plea of guilty by one defendant to a greater offense.

United States v. Mari, supra (concurring opinion).   To the same effect is ABA Standards Relating to the Defense Function at 213–14.

It is contemplated that under rule 44(c) the court will make appropriate inquiry of the defendants and of counsel regarding the possibility of a conflict of interest developing. Whenever it is necessary to make a more particularized inquiry into the nature of the contemplated defense, the court should "pursue the inquiry with defendants and their counsel on the record but in chambers" so as "to avoid the possibility of prejudicial disclosures to the prosecution." *United States v. Foster,* supra.   It is important that each defendant be "fully advised of the facts underlying the potential conflict and is given an opportunity to express his or her views." *United States v. Alberti,* supra.   The rule specifically requires that the court personally advise each defendant of his right to effective assistance of counsel, including separate representation.   See *United States v. Foster,* supra, requiring that the court make a determination that jointly represented defendants "understand that they may retain separate counsel, or if qualified, may have such counsel appointed by the court and paid for by the government."

Under rule 44(c), the court is to take appropriate measures to protect each defendant's right to counsel unless it appears "there is good cause to believe no conflict of interest is likely to arise" as a consequence of the continuation of such joint representation.   A less demanding standard would not adequately protect the Sixth Amendment right to effective assistance of counsel or the effective administration of criminal justice.   Although joint representation "is not per se violative of constitutional guarantees of effective assistance of counsel," *Holloway v. Arkansas,* supra, it would not suffice to require the court to act only when a conflict of interest is then apparent, for it is not possible to "anticipate with complete accuracy the course that a criminal trial may take." *Fryar v. United States,* 404 F.2d 1071 (10th Cir.1968).   This is particularly so in light of the fact that if a conflict later arises and a defendant thereafter raises a Sixth Amendment objection, a court must grant relief without indulging "in nice calculations as to the amount of prejudice arising from its denial." *Glasser v. United States,* 315 U.S. 60 (1942).   This is because, as the Supreme Court more recently noted in *Holloway v. Arkansas,* supra, "in a case of joint representation of conflicting interests the evil ... is in what the advocate finds himself compelled to refrain from doing," and this makes it "virtually impossible" to assess the impact of the conflict.

Rule 44(c) does not specify what particular measures must be taken.   It is appropriate to leave this within the court's discretion, for the measures which will best protect each defendant's right to counsel may well vary from case to case.   One possible course of action is for the court to obtain a knowing, intelligent and voluntary waiver of the right to separate representation, for, as noted in *Holloway v. Arkansas,* supra, "a defendant may waive his right to the assistance of an attorney unhindered by a conflict of interests."   See *United States v. DeBerry,* supra, holding that defendants should be jointly represented only if "the court has ascertained that ... each understands clearly the possibilities of a conflict of interest and waives any rights in connection with it."   It must be emphasized that a "waiver of the right to separate representation should not be accepted by the court unless the defendants have each been informed of the probable hazards; and the voluntary character of their waiver is apparent."   ABA Standards Relating to the Function of the Trial Judge at 45.   *United States v. Garcia,* supra, spells out in significant detail what should be done to assure an adequate waiver:

As in Rule 11 procedures, the district court should address each defendant personally and forthrightly advise him of the potential dangers of representation by counsel with a conflict of interest.   The defendant must be at liberty to question the district court as to the nature and consequences of his legal representation.   Most significantly, the court should seek to elicit a narrative response from each defendant that he has been advised of his right to effective representation, that he understands the details of his attorney's possible conflict of interest and the potential perils of such a conflict, that he has discussed the matter with his attorney or if he wishes with outside counsel, and that he voluntarily waives his Sixth Amendment protections. It is, of course, vital that the waiver be established by "clear, unequivocal, and unambiguous language." ... Mere assent in response to a series of questions from the bench may in some circumstances constitute an adequate waiver, but the court should nonetheless endeavor to have each defendant personally articulate in detail his intent to forego this significant constitutional protection. Recordation of the waiver colloque between defendant and judge, will also serve the government's interest by assisting in shielding any potential conviction from collateral attack, either on Sixth Amendment grounds or on a Fifth or Fourteenth Amendment "fundamental fairness" basis.

See also Hyman, Joint Representation of Multiple Defendants in a Criminal Trial: The Court's Headache, 5 Hofstra L.Rev. 315, 334 (1977).

Another possibility is that the court will order that the defendants be separately represented in subsequent proceedings in the case.

Though the court must remain alert to and take account of the fact that "certain advantages might accrue from joint representation," *Holloway v. Arkansas,* supra, it need not permit the joint representation to continue merely because the defendants express a willingness to so proceed. That is, there will be cases where the court should require separate counsel to represent certain defendants despite the expressed wishes of such defendants. Indeed, failure of the trial court to require separate representation may ... require a new trial, even though the defendants have expressed a desire to continue with the same counsel. The right to effective representation by counsel whose loyalty is undivided is so paramount in the proper administration of criminal justice that it must in some cases take precedence over all other considerations, including the expressed preference of the defendants concerned and their attorney.

United States v. Carrigan, supra (concurring opinion). See also *United States v. Lawriw,* supra; *Abraham v. United States,* supra; ABA Standards Relating to the Defense Function at 213, concluding that in some circumstances "even full disclosure and consent of the client may not be an adequate protection." As noted in *United States v. Dolan,* 570 F.2d 1177 (3d Cir.1978), such an order may be necessary where the trial judge is

not satisfied that the waiver is proper. For example, a defendant may be competent enough to stand trial, but not competent enough to understand the complex, subtle, and sometimes unforeseeable dangers inherent in multiple representation. More importantly, the judge may find that the waiver cannot be intelligently made simply because he is not in a position to inform the defendant of the foreseeable prejudices multiple representation might entail for him.

As concluded in *Dolan,* "exercise of the court's supervisory powers by disqualifying an attorney representing multiple criminal defendants in spite of the defendants' express desire to retain that attorney does not necessarily abrogate defendant's sixth amendment rights". It does not follow from the absolute right of self-representation recognized in *Faretta v. California,* 422 U.S. 806 (1975), that there is an *absolute* right to counsel of one's own choice. Thus,

when a trial court finds an actual conflict of interest which impairs the ability of a criminal defendant's chosen counsel to conform with the ABA Code of Professional Responsibility, the court should not be required to tolerate an inadequate representation of a defendant. Such representation not only constitutes a breach of professional ethics and invites disrespect for the integrity of the court, but it is also detrimental to the independent interest of the trial judge to be free from future attacks over the adequacy of the waiver or the fairness of the proceedings in his own court and the subtle problems implicating the defendant's comprehension of the waiver. Under such circumstances, the court can elect to exercise its supervisory authority over members of the bar to enforce the ethical standard requiring an attorney to decline multiple representation.

United States v. Dolan, supra. See also Geer, Conflict of Interest and Multiple Defendants in a Criminal Case: Professional Responsibilities of the Defense Attorney, 62 Minn.L.Rev. 119 (1978); Note, Conflict of Interests in Multiple Representation of Criminal Co-Defendants, 68 J.Crim.L. & C. 226 (1977).

The failure in a particular case to conduct a rule 44(c) inquiry would not, standing alone, necessitate the reversal of a conviction of a jointly represented defendant. However, as is currently the case, a reviewing court is more likely to assume a conflict resulted from the joint representation when no inquiry or an inadequate inquiry was conducted. *United States v. Carrigan,* supra; *United States v. DeBerry,* supra. On the other hand, the mere fact that a rule 44(c) inquiry was conducted in the early stages of the case does not relieve the court of all responsibility in this regard thereafter. The obligation placed upon the court by rule 44(c) is a continuing one, and thus in a particular case further inquiry may be necessary on a later occasion because of new developments suggesting a potential conflict of interest.

FEDERAL RULES OF APPELLATE PROCEDURE

Rule 38. Damages and Costs for Frivolous Appeals

If a court of appeals determines that an appeal is frivolous, it may, after a separately filed motion or notice from the court and reasonable opportunity to respond, award just damages and single or double costs to the appellee.

(As amended Apr. 29, 1994, eff. Dec. 1, 1994; April 24, 1998, effective December 1, 1998.)

ADVISORY COMMITTEE NOTES
1994 Amendments

The amendment requires that before a court of appeals may impose sanctions, the person to be sanctioned must have notice and an opportunity to respond. The amendment reflects the basic principle enunciated in the Supreme Court's opinion in Roadway Express, Inc. v. Piper, 447 U.S. 752, 767 (1980), that notice and opportunity to respond must precede the imposition of sanctions. A separately filed motion requesting sanctions constitutes notice. A statement inserted in a party's brief that the party moves for sanctions is not sufficient notice. Requests in briefs for sanctions have become so commonplace that it is unrealistic to expect careful responses to such requests without any indication that the court is actually contemplating such measures. Only a motion, the purpose of which is to request sanctions, is sufficient. If there is no such motion filed, notice must come from the court. The form of notice from the court and of the opportunity for comment purposely are left to the court's discretion.

Rule 46. Attorneys

(a) Admission to the Bar.

(1) *Eligibility.* An attorney is eligible for admission to the bar of a court of appeals if that attorney is of good moral and professional character and is admitted to practice before the Supreme Court of the United States, the highest court of a state, another United States court of appeals, or a United States district court (including the district courts for Guam, the Northern Mariana Islands, and the Virgin Islands).

(2) *Application.* An applicant must file an application for admission, on a form approved by the court that contains the applicant's personal statement showing eligibility for membership. The applicant must subscribe to the following oath or affirmation:

"I, _____, do solemnly swear (or affirm) that I will conduct myself as an attorney and counselor of this court, uprightly and according to law; and that I will support the Constitution of the United States.

(3) *Admission Procedures.* On written or oral motion of a member of the court's bar, the court will act on the application. An applicant may be admitted by oral motion in open court. But, unless the court orders otherwise, an applicant need not appear before the court to be admitted. Upon admission, an applicant must pay the clerk the fee prescribed by local rule or court order.

(b) Suspension or Disbarment.

(1) *Standard.* A member of the court's bar is subject to suspension or disbarment by the court if the member:

(A) has been suspended or disbarred from practice in any other court; or

(B) is guilty of conduct unbecoming a member of the court's bar.

(2) *Procedure.* The member must be given an opportunity to show good cause, within the time prescribed by the court, why the member should not be suspended or disbarred.

(3) *Order.* The court must enter an appropriate order after the member responds and a hearing is held, if requested, or after the time prescribed for a response expires, if no response is made.

(c) Discipline. A court of appeals may discipline an attorney who practices before it for conduct unbecoming a member of the bar or for failure to comply with any court rule. First, however, the court must afford the attorney reasonable notice, an opportunity to show cause to the contrary, and, if requested, a hearing.

(Amended March 10, 1986, effective July 1, 1986; April 24, 1998, effective December 1, 1998.)

RULES OF THE SUPREME COURT OF THE UNITED STATES

PART II. ATTORNEYS AND COUNSELORS

Rule 5. Admission to the Bar

1. To qualify for admission to the Bar of this Court, an applicant must have been admitted to practice in the highest court of a State, Commonwealth, Territory or Possession, or of the District of Columbia for a period of at least three years immediately before the date of application; must not have been the subject of any adverse disciplinary action pronounced or in effect during that 3–year period; and must appear to the Court to be of good moral and professional character.

2. Each applicant shall file with the Clerk (1) a certificate from the presiding judge, clerk, or other authorized official of that court evidencing the applicant's admission to practice there and the applicant's current good standing, and (2) a completely executed copy of the form

approved by this Court and furnished by the Clerk containing (a) the applicant's personal statement, and (b) the statement of two sponsors endorsing the correctness of the applicant's statement, stating that the applicant possesses all the qualifications required for admission, and affirming that the applicant is of good moral and professional character. Both sponsors must be members of the Bar of this Court who personally know, but are not related to, the applicant.

3. If the documents submitted demonstrate that the applicant possesses the necessary qualifications, and if the applicant has signed the oath or affirmation and paid the required fee, the Clerk will notify the applicant of acceptance by the Court as a member of the Bar and issue a certificate of admission. An applicant who so wishes may be admitted in open court on oral motion by a member of the Bar of this Court, provided that all other requirements for admission have been satisfied.

4. Each applicant shall take or subscribe to the following oath or affirmation: I, _____, do solemnly swear (or affirm) that as an attorney and as a counselor of this Court, I will conduct myself uprightly and according to law, and that I will support the Constitution of the United States.

5. The fee for admission to the Bar and a certificate bearing the seal of the Court is $100, payable to the United States Supreme Court. The Marshal will deposit such fees in a separate fund to be disbursed by the Marshal at the direction of the Chief Justice for the costs of admissions, for the benefit of the Court and its Bar, and for related purposes.

6. The fee for a duplicate certificate of admission to the Bar bearing the seal of the Court is $15, payable to the United States Supreme Court. The proceeds will be maintained by the Marshal as provided in paragraph 5 of this rule.

* * *

Rule 6. Argument Pro Hac Vice

1. An attorney not admitted to practice in the highest court of a State, Commonwealth, Territory or Possession, or of the District of Columbia for the requisite three years, but who is otherwise eligible for admission to practice in this Court under Rule 5.1, may be permitted to argue *pro hac vice.*

2. An attorney, barrister, or advocate who is qualified to practice in the courts of a foreign state may be permitted to argue *pro hac vice.*

3. Oral argument *pro hac vice* will be allowed only on motion of the attorney of record for the party on whose behalf leave is requested. The motion must briefly and distinctly state the appropriate qualifications of the attorney who is to argue *pro hac vice.* It must be filed with the Clerk, in the form prescribed by Rule 21, no later than the date on which the respondent's or appellee's brief on the merits is due to be filed and must be accompanied by proof of service pursuant to Rule 29.

Rule 7. Prohibition Against Practice

No employee of this Court shall practice as an attorney or counselor in any court or before any agency of government while employed by the Court; nor shall any person after leaving such employment participate in any professional capacity in any case pending before this Court or in any case being considered for filing in this Court, until two years have elapsed after separation; nor shall a former employee ever participate in any professional capacity in any case that was pending in this Court during the employee's tenure.

Rule 8. Disbarment and Disciplinary Action

1. Whenever a member of the Bar of this Court has been disbarred or suspended from practice in any court of record, or has engaged in conduct unbecoming a member of the Bar of this Court, the Court will enter an order suspending that member from practice before this Court and affording the member an opportunity to show cause, within 40 days, why a disbarment order should not be entered. Upon response, or if no response is timely filed, the Court will enter an appropriate order.

2. After reasonable notice and an opportunity to show cause why disciplinary action should not be taken, and after a hearing if material facts are not in dispute, the Court may take any appropriate disciplinary action against any attorney who is admitted to practice before it for conduct unbecoming a member of the Bar or for failure to comply with these Rules or any Rule or order of the Court.

PART FOUR

RESTATEMENT (THIRD) OF LAW
THE LAW GOVERNING LAWYERS

TABLE OF CONTENTS

Introduction

This part includes the text of the sections of the Restatement (Third) of the Law Governing Lawyers and selected comments and illustrations.

RESTATEMENT (THIRD) OF LAW GOVERNING LAWYERS (2000)

[In 1986, the American Law Institute began the process of writing the Restatement of Law Governing Lawyers. This long and difficult task has culminated in the publication of the Restatement (Third) of Law Governing Lawyers in 2000. From the language of the first tentative drafts, courts, commentators, and bar personnel have taken account of the research brought together on this project. Due to space considerations, the entire comments or reporters notes cannot be reprinted. However, selected reporters' comments are reprinted below to the sections which are most pertinent to the courses in professional responsibility. Of course, those who research problems of professional responsibility should consult the two volume work published by the ALI. Ed.]

TABLE OF CONTENTS

RESTATEMENT OF LAW GOVERNING LAWYERS

CHAPTER 1: REGULATION OF THE LEGAL PROFESSION

TOPIC 1. REGULATION OF LAWYERS—IN GENERAL

§ 1. Regulation of Lawyers—In General

Upon admission to the bar of any jurisdiction, a person becomes a lawyer and is subject to applicable law governing such matters as professional discipline, procedure and evidence, civil remedies, and criminal sanctions.

Comment:

* * *

b. Lawyer codes and background law. Today, as for the last quarter-century, professional discipline of a lawyer in the United States is conducted pursuant to regulations contained in regulatory codes that have been approved in most states by the highest court in the jurisdiction in which the lawyer has been admitted. Such codes are referred to in this Restatement as lawyer codes. Those codes are more or less patterned on model codes published by the American Bar Association, but only the version of the code officially adopted and in force in a jurisdiction regulates the activities of lawyers subject to it. While in most jurisdictions the lawyer code is adopted and subject to revision only through action of the highest court in the state (see Comment c hereto), in all jurisdictions at least some legislation is applicable to lawyers and law practice. See, e.g., § 56, Comments i and j (federal legislation and state consumer-protection laws applicable to lawyers); § 58(3) and Comment b thereto (statutes authorizing lawyers to practice in the form of limited-liability partnerships and similar types of law firms); § 68 and following (attorney-client privilege). Federal district courts generally have adopted the lawyer code of the jurisdiction in which the court sits, and all federal courts exercise the power to regulate lawyers appearing before them. Some administrative agencies, primarily within the federal government, have also regulated lawyers practicing before the agency, sometimes through lawyer codes adopted by the agency and specifically applicable to those practitioners. Although uniformity is desirable for many purposes, lawyer codes in fact differ markedly in certain respects from one jurisdiction to another, and no state follows any nationally promulgated bar-association model in all respects.

The legal effect of officially adopted lawyer codes is fundamental and diverse. Lawyer codes are promulgated and applied primarily for the purpose of establishing mandatory standards for the assessment of a lawyer's conduct in the course of a professional-discipline proceeding brought against the lawyer (see Topic 2). Such lawyer codes also typically include commentary containing, among other things, nonbinding advice on how a lawyer may address particular issues or, in general, better practice law. Lawyer-code provisions may also be relevant with respect to the definition of substantive rights or the articulation of factors relevant in granting remedies in other areas. For example, courts have held that lawyer-code provisions may be relevant in determining the reasonableness of a lawyer's fee (see § 34, Comment d), in determining questions of fee forfeiture (see § 37, Comment c), in defining the appropriate standard of care in legal malpractice (see § 52, Comment f), in determining a lawyer's fiduciary duty to a client (see § 48) in determining whether a conflict of interest exists (see § 121, Comment c) or has appropriately been consented to by affected clients (see generally § 122), or for the purpose of a motion to disqualify the lawyer. Lawyer-code provisions may also be relevant as an expression of the public policy of the jurisdiction with respect to such issues as the enforceability of transactions entered into in violation of them (e.g. § 47 & Comment i thereto).

Lawyer codes in turn reflect other law. Prior to the adoption by states of versions of the 1969 ABA Model Code of Professional Responsibility, many states had no officially adopted lawyer code, although most state bar associations considered the 1908 ABA Canons of Ethics as relevant to guide lawyers. (Some few states had adopted the Canons as explicitly disciplinary rules, although they were not designed for that purpose and in certain respects ill-served it.) There was, however, no regulatory vacuum, for courts had historically asserted plenary power to regulate lawyers (see Comment *c*) and did so through the common-law process. For example, most of the core concepts of lawyer conflicts of interest (see Chapter 8) were already well developed and applied through common-law decisions in disciplinary, disqualification, and legal-malpractice proceedings long before jurisdictions officially adopted lawyer codes stating rules about the same concepts. The drafters of lawyer codes, in turn, have drawn heavily on such decisions in articulating lawyer obligations.

The lawyer codes and much general law remain complementary. The lawyer codes draw much of their moral force and, in many particulars, the detailed description of their rules from preexisting legal requirements and concepts found in the law of torts, contracts, agency, trusts, property, remedies, procedure, evidence, and crimes. Thus, lawyer codes particularize some general legal rules in the particular occupational situation of lawyers but are not exhaustive of those rules. By the same token, lawyer codes often establish the same rules as would apply in a comparable situation involving a nonlawyer professional providing a related service or a rule very like it. The lawyer codes presuppose the general legal background thus referred to and its applicability to lawyers and the rules that make up that background, and they do not preclude application of remedies prescribed by other law. Particular lawyer conduct may violate a lawyer code, tort law, and a criminal statute, or it may have less than all those legal effects. Lawyer codes sometimes differ from other legal provisions with respect to such factors as the following: the specified mental state of the lawyer-actor defined in the standard of conduct; the required presence and kind or degree of harm on the part of the claimant or injured victim of the lawyer's action or nonaction; the possible relevance of reliance by others; and the extent of imputed knowledge, duty, and liability (see Topic 3, Introductory Note)

c. The inherent powers of courts. The highest courts in most states have ruled as a matter of state constitutional law that their power to regulate lawyers is inherent in the judicial function. Thus, the grant of judicial power in a state constitution devolves upon the courts the concomitant regulatory power. The power is said to derive both from the historical role of courts in the United States in regulating lawyers through admission and disbarment and from the traditional practice of courts in England. Admitting lawyers to practice (see § 2), formulating and amending lawyer codes (see Comment *b*), and regulating the system of lawyer discipline (see § 5, Comment *b*) are functions reserved in most states to the highest court of the state. Nonetheless, other tribunals, such as hearing bodies in administrative agencies, perform the important role of implementing the lawyer codes in adjudicating disputes when and to the extent their provisions are relevant (see Comment *b* hereto & Topic 3, Introductory Note).

Beyond affirmative empowerment, some state courts have further held that their constitutional power to regulate lawyers is exclusive of other branches of state government with respect to some matters. On that basis, those courts have held that an attempt by another branch of state government to regulate lawyers is an interference with that judicial power and a violation of the state's constitutionally mandated separation of powers. Some decisions have given effect to an otherwise-invalid statute or regulation on a notion of comity, when the court is persuaded of the wisdom of the enactment and convinced that it does not pose a threat to the court's overall regulation of lawyers.

Federal courts have also affirmed an inherent role in regulating lawyers. That is reflected in enactment of disciplinary rules in each federal court and, often, in creation of a disciplinary apparatus. It is also implicated when federal courts apply provisions of lawyer codes in deciding cases, as in ruling on disqualification motions or requests for fees. There is, however, no body of federal decisional law broadly asserting that federal courts have inherent power to regulate lawyers to the exclusion of the federal legislative and executive branches. Similarly, the regulatory power of federal courts over lawyers practicing before them does not extend into judicial regulation of activities of lawyers appearing before or otherwise dealing with the other branches of the federal government or the public.

d. The role of bar associations. Beginning in the early decades of the 20th century, bar associations have played an increasingly active role in regulating the conduct of lawyers. Together with lawyers who work on disciplinary and similar committees within state-and federal-court systems, bar associations have become the chief embodiment of the concept that lawyers are a self-regulated profession. Self-regulation provides protection of lawyers against political control by the state. However, self-regulation also carries its own risk of under-regulation of lawyers as a whole, regulation (however strict) that is in the interest of lawyers as a group and not the public, or regulation that focuses disproportionately on groups of lawyers disfavored within the controlling bar association or committee.

The three lawyer codes promulgated in this century by the American Bar Association have served as models for regulations adopted in most of the states and the federal courts (see Comment *b*). Even in states—such as California and, to a lesser extent, Texas—in which the form of the lawyer code is markedly different from the ABA models, examination of the code shows significant borrowing in many rules. (By the same token, the two most recent ABA model rules often borrowed from preexisting state codes, such as the code then in effect in California. The 1908 ABA Canons were copied with little change from a preexisting state code.)

In a number of states, membership in the state's bar association is compulsory, in the sense that a lawyer otherwise appropriately admitted to practice must maintain active membership in the bar association as a condition of retention of a valid license to practice law within the jurisdiction. (Such mandatory bars are sometimes called "integrated" bars.) Decisions of the United States Supreme Court have limited the extent to which a member of such a mandatory bar association can be required to pay any portion of dues that supports activities not germane to the organization's functions in providing self-regulation. Those generally include activities of a political or ideological nature not directly connected to the regulation of lawyers and maintenance of the system of justice. Under those decisions, the bar must maintain a system for allocating dues payments for permissible and noncovered purposes and a process to permit lawyers to regain the portion of dues collected for noncovered purposes.

TOPIC 2. PROCESS OF PROFESSIONAL REGULATION

TITLE A.   ADMISSION TO PRACTICE LAW

§ 2.   Admission to Practice Law

In order to become a lawyer and qualify to practice law in a jurisdiction of admission, a prospective lawyer must comply with requirements of the jurisdiction relating to such matters as education, other demonstration of competence such as success in a bar examination, and character.

TITLE B. AUTHORIZED AND UNAUTHORIZED PRACTICE

§ 3.   Jurisdictional Scope of the Practice of Law by a Lawyer

A lawyer currently admitted to practice in a jurisdiction may provide legal services to a client:

    (1) at any place within the admitting jurisdiction;

    (2) before a tribunal or administrative agency of another jurisdiction or the federal government in compliance with requirements for temporary or regular admission to practice before that tribunal or agency; and

    (3) at a place within a jurisdiction in which the lawyer is not admitted to the extent that the lawyer's activities arise out of or are otherwise reasonably related to the lawyer's practice under Subsection (1) or (2).

Comment:

a.   Scope and cross-references. This Section concerns jurisdictional limits on permissible practice by a lawyer. On choice-of-law issues generally involved in the regulation of lawyers, see § 1, Comment *e*. On jurisdictional and choice-of-law issues involved in lawyer discipline, see § 5, Comment *h*. On unauthorized practice by a nonlawyer or on a lawyer's aiding such unauthorized practice, see § 4.

The state in which a lawyer is admitted is referred to herein as the lawyer's home state. A lawyer who practices law in violation of the rules stated in the Section is susceptible to a variety of sanctions, including professional discipline, injunction, and denial of recovery of fees otherwise earned (see § 49).

b. Rationale. As reflected in this Section, jurisdictional limitations on practice applicable to lawyers are primarily a function of state lines (see Introductory Note). For many purposes, lawyers must respect those lines—limiting their general practice to the territory of the one or more jurisdictions in which the lawyer is admitted—although pro hac vice admission (see Comment *e* hereto) and admission to practice in federal courts and before federal agencies (see Comment *e* hereto) authorize extraterritorial practice. Occasionally, proposals are put forward for removal of state-line limitations on practice, as by means of a national bar-admission process. However, local interest in maintaining regulatory control of lawyers practicing locally is strong and historically has prevented adoption of such proposals. Nonetheless, the need to provide effective and efficient legal services to persons and businesses with interstate legal concerns requires that jurisdictions not erect unnecessary barriers to interstate law practice (see Comment *e*).

c. Required maintenance of a lawyer's admitted status. In general, only a lawyer who is in current compliance with applicable legal requirements in the admitting jurisdiction (see § 2) for maintaining the lawyer's law license in a currently effective status is qualified to practice law there. Those conditions vary by jurisdiction and can be technical in nature. In some few jurisdictions, for example, maintenance of a valid license is conditioned on maintaining an office within the jurisdiction for the practice of law (see § 2, Comment *f*). Many jurisdictions now require a minimum number of hours per year of qualifying continuing legal education.

A lawyer who was once admitted to practice in a state violates the prohibition against unauthorized practice by continuing to practice law in the state notwithstanding disbarment or suspension, lapse of the lawyer's license to practice in the state (for example, for failure to pay mandatory bar dues or, as indicated above, to comply with applicable continuing-legal-education requirements), resignation, or assumption of nonactive status (as when the lawyer retires or moves to another state). Lapse can occur for failure to file an annual renewal application with self-certification of compliance with the indicated requirements. Any such unauthorized practice by a lawyer is a violation of the state's lawyer code and thus subjects the lawyer to discipline. It may also violate a statutory prohibition in the state against unauthorized practice of law. Such impermissible practice by a lawyer may also lead, among other remedies, to forfeiture of an otherwise valid claim for legal fees (see § 37). When lapse of license for such reasons is not directly related to continuing competence to practice, it does not by itself indicate either legal malpractice or incompetent representation in a criminal-defense representation.

d. Definition of practice by a lawyer. What constitutes the practice of law for the purposes of defining unauthorized practice by a lawyer varies with the reason for which the lawyer is no longer authorized to practice. Either by rule, decisional law, or specific order, a jurisdiction may, for example, prohibit a disbarred or suspended lawyer from functioning as a paralegal in a law firm (compare § 4, Comment *g*), even beyond the prohibition against practicing as a lawyer or holding oneself out as such. The concern is not only that a disbarred lawyer functioning as a paralegal will harm the interests of clients by performing services incompetently, but also that a lawyer who has committed a violation sufficiently serious to warrant substantial discipline and who as a result has been deprived of a law license and the income that it represents is in a position and may be motivated to use such a role as a subterfuge to continue law practice.

e. Extra-jurisdictional law practice by a lawyer. Admission in a state permits a lawyer to maintain an office and otherwise practice law anywhere within its borders. No state today continues the restrictions of former centuries that limited practice to a particular judicial district or county in which a lawyer was admitted.

The rules governing interstate practice by nonlocal lawyers were formed at a time when lawyers conducted very little practice of that nature. Thus, the limitation on legal services threatened by such rules imposed little actual inconvenience. However, as interstate and international commerce, transportation, and communications have expanded, clients have increasingly required a truly interstate and international range of practice by their lawyers. (To a limited extent, many states recognize such needs in the international realm by providing for limited practice in the state by foreign legal consultants. See § 2, Comment *g*.) Applied literally, the old restrictions on practice of law in a state by a lawyer admitted elsewhere could seriously inconvenience clients who have need of such services within the state. Retaining locally admitted counsel would often cause serious delay and expense and could require the client to deal with unfamiliar counsel. Modern communications, including ready electronic connection to much of the law of every state, makes concern about a competent analysis of a distant state's law unfounded. Accordingly, there is much to be said for a rule permitting a lawyer to practice in any state, except for litigation matters or for the purpose of establishing a permanent in-state branch office. Results approaching that rule may arguably be required under the federal interstate commerce clause and the privileges and immunities clause. The approach of the Section is more guarded. However, its primary focus is appropriately on the needs of clients.

The extent to which a lawyer may practice beyond the borders of the lawyer's home state depends on the circumstances in which the lawyer acts in both the lawyer's home state and the other state. At one extreme, it is clear that a lawyer's admission to practice in one jurisdiction does not authorize the lawyer to practice generally in another jurisdiction as if the lawyer were also fully admitted there. Thus, a lawyer admitted in State A may not open an office in State B for the general practice of law there or otherwise engage in the continuous, regular, or repeated representation of clients within the other state.

Certainty is provided in litigated matters by procedures for securing the right to practice elsewhere, although the arrangement is limited to appearances as counsel in individual litigated matters. Apparently all states provide such a procedure for temporary admission of an unadmitted lawyer, usually termed admission pro hac vice. (Compare admission on-motion to the right to practice generally within a jurisdiction as described in § 2, Comment *b*.) Although the decision is sometimes described as discretionary, a court will grant admission pro hac vice if the lawyer applying for admission is in good standing in the bar of another jurisdiction and has complied with applicable requirements (sometimes requiring the association of local counsel), and if no reason is shown why the lawyer cannot be relied upon to provide competent representation to the lawyer's client in conformance with the local lawyer code. Such temporary admission is recognized in Subsection (2). Courts are particularly apt to grant such applications in criminal-defense representations. Some jurisdictions impose limitations, such as a maximum number of such admissions in a specified period. Admission pro hac vice normally permits the lawyer to engage within the jurisdiction in all customary and appropriate activities in conducting the litigation, including appropriate office practice. Activities in contemplation of such admission are also authorized, such as investigating facts or consulting with the client within the jurisdiction prior to drafting a complaint and filing the action.

A lawyer who is properly admitted to practice in a state with respect to litigation pending there, either generally or pro hac vice, may need to conduct proceedings and activities ancillary to the litigation in other states, such as counseling clients, dealing with co-counsel or opposing counsel, conducting depositions, examining documents, interviewing witnesses, negotiating settlements, and the like. Such activities incidental to permissible practice are appropriate and permissible.

Transactional and similar out-of-court representation of clients may raise similar issues, yet there is no equivalent of temporary admission pro hac vice for such representation, as there is in litigation. Even activities that bear close resemblance to in-court litigation, such as representation of clients in arbitration or in administrative hearings, may not include measures for pro hac vice appearance. Some activities are clearly permissible. Thus, a lawyer conducting activities in the lawyer's home state may advise a client about the law of another state, a proceeding in another state, or a transaction there, including conducting research in the law of the other state, advising the client about the application of that law, and drafting legal documents intended to have legal effect there. There is no per se bar against such a lawyer giving a formal opinion based in whole or in part on the law of another jurisdiction, but a lawyer should do so only if the lawyer has adequate familiarity with the relevant law. It is also clearly permissible for a lawyer from a home-state office to direct communications to persons and organizations in other states (in which the lawyer is not separately admitted), by letter, telephone, telecopier, or other forms of electronic communication. On the other hand, as with litigation, it would be impermissible for a lawyer to set up an office for the general practice of nonlitigation law in a jurisdiction in which the lawyer is not admitted as described in § 2.

When other activities of a lawyer in a non-home state are challenged as impermissible for lack of admission to the state's bar, the context in which and purposes for which the lawyer acts should be carefully assessed. Beyond home-state activities, proper representation of clients often requires a lawyer to conduct activities while physically present in one or more other states. Such practice is customary in many areas of legal representation. As stated in Subsection (3), such activities should be recognized as permissible so long as they arise out of or otherwise reasonably relate to the lawyer's practice in a state of admission. In determining that issue, several factors are relevant, including the following: whether the lawyer's client is a regular client of the lawyer or, if a new client, is from the lawyer's home state, has extensive contacts with that state, or contacted the lawyer there; whether a multistate transaction has other significant connections with the lawyer's home state; whether significant aspects of the lawyer's activities are conducted in the lawyer's home state; whether a significant aspect of the matter involves the law of the lawyer's home state; and whether either the activities of the client involve multiple jurisdictions or the legal issues involved are primarily either multistate or federal in nature. Because lawyers in a firm often practice collectively, the activities of all lawyers in the representation of a client are relevant. The customary practices of lawyers who engage in interstate law practice is one appropriate measure of the reasonableness of a lawyer's activities out of state. Association with local counsel may permit a lawyer to conduct in-state activities not otherwise permissible, but such association is not required in most instances of in-state practice. Among other things, the additional expense for the lawyer's client of retaining additional counsel and educating that lawyer about the client's affairs would make such required retention unduly burdensome.

Particularly in the situation of a lawyer representing a multistate or multinational organization, the question of geographical connection may be difficult to assess or establish. Thus, a multinational corporation wishing to select a location in the United States to build a new facility may engage a lawyer to accompany officers of the corporation to survey possible sites in several states, perhaps holding discussions with local governmental officers about such topics as zoning, taxation, environmental requirements, and the like. Such occasional, temporary in-state services, when reasonable and appropriate in performing the lawyer's functions for the client, are a proper aspect of practice and do not constitute impermissible practice in the other state.

Illustrations:

1.   Lawyer has an office and is duly licensed to practice law in State A. Lawyer's office is in a community near State B, where Lawyer is not admitted to practice. In the past, several of Lawyer's clients have been residents of State B, and their legal issues sometimes involve research into issues of State B law. In order to provide better service to those clients and to attract business of other clients there, Lawyer rents space, hires nonlawyer assistants, and otherwise prepares premises for the general practice of law at a branch-office location in State B. While representation of residents of State B in Lawyer's office in State A is permissible, Lawyer may not open an office for the general practice of law in State B without obtaining general admission to practice there (see § 2).

2.   Same facts as in Illustration 1, except that Lawyer represents a regulated Utility, which operates a power plant in State A near the border with State B. Lawyer's work for Utility principally relates to environmental issues, such as providing advice, obtaining permits, and otherwise complying with federal law and the law of State A. Utility also has occasional issues relating to compliance with the environmental laws of State B because of those same activities. It is permissible for Lawyer to travel to State B to deal with governmental officials with respect to environmental issues arising out of Utility's activities.

3.   Same facts as in Illustration 2, except that Lawyer's original work for Utility in State A related to rate-setting proceedings before a utility commission in that state and before the Federal Energy Regulatory Commission. Under recent legislation, Utility may now be able to make retail sales of electricity to consumers in many states. Because of Lawyer's extensive knowledge of Utility's rate-related financial information, Utility has asked Lawyer to take charge of new rate applications in 15 other states, all being states in which Lawyer is not admitted to practice. Lawyer's work in those matters would involve extensive presence and activities in each of the other states until the necessary rates have been established. Although local counsel would often be retained in such matters, Lawyer and other lawyers in Lawyer's firm may permissibly conduct those activities in the other states on behalf of Utility.

4.   Lawyer, who practices with a law firm in California, is a nationally known expert in corporate mergers and acquisitions. Utility is a major electricity generator and distributor in the southeastern United States. Under the new legislation referred to in Illustration 3, Utility is considering a hostile takeover of Old Company, an established regional electricity generator and distributor in

the northeastern United States. Legal work on the acquisition would require the physical presence of Utility's mergers-and-acquisitions counsel in a number of states in addition to the West Coast state in which Lawyer is admitted, in addition to representation before at least one federal agency in Washington, D.C. Given the multistate and federal nature of the legal work, Lawyer and other members of Lawyer's firm may represent Utility as requested.

5. Lawyer is admitted to practice and has an office in Illinois, where Lawyer practices in the area of trusts and estates, an area involving, among other things, both the law of wills, property, taxation, and trusts of a particular state and federal income, estate, and gift tax law. Client A, whom Lawyer has represented in estate-planning matters, has recently moved to Florida and calls Lawyer from there with a request that leads to Lawyer's preparation of a codicil to A's will, which Lawyer takes to Florida to obtain the necessary signatures. While there, A introduces Lawyer to B, a friend of A, who, after learning of A's estate-planning arrangements from A, wishes Lawyer to prepare a similar estate arrangement for B. Lawyer prepares the necessary documents and conducts legal research in Lawyer's office in Illinois, frequently conferring by telephone and letter with B in Florida. Lawyer then takes the documents to Florida for execution by B and necessary witnesses. Lawyer's activities in Florida on behalf of both A and B were permissible.

f. Multistate practice by inside legal counsel. States have permitted practice within the jurisdiction by inside legal counsel for a corporation or similar organization, even if the lawyer is not locally admitted and even if the lawyer's work consists entirely of in-state activities, when all of the lawyer's work is for the employer-client (compare § 4, Comment *e*) and does not involve appearance in court. Leniency is appropriate because the only concern is with the client-employer, who is presumably in a good position to assess the quality and fitness of the lawyer's work. In the course of such work, the lawyer may deal with outsiders, such as by negotiating with others in settling litigation or directing the activities of lawyers who do enter an appearance for the organization in litigation.

g. Authorized practice in a federal agency or court. A lawyer properly admitted to practice before a federal agency or in a federal court (see § 2, Comment *b*) may practice federal law for a client either at the physical location of the agency or court or in an office in any state, so long as the lawyer's practice arises out of or is reasonably related to the agency's or court's business. Such a basis for authorized practice is recognized in Subsection (2). Thus, a lawyer registered with the United States Patent and Trademark Office could counsel a client from an office anywhere about filing a patent or about assigning the ensuing patent right, matters reasonably related to the lawyer's admission to the agency. (The permissible scope of practice of a nonlawyer patent agent may be less, since admission to the agency does not suggest competence to deal with matters, such as the assignment of patents, beyond the jurisdiction of the agency.)

A lawyer admitted in one state who is admitted to practice in a United States district court located in another state, but who is not otherwise admitted in the second state, can practice law in the state so long as the practice is limited to cases filed in that federal court. Local rules in some few federal district courts additionally require admission to the bar of the sitting state as a condition of admission to the federal court. The requirement is inconsistent with the federal nature of the court's business.

A lawyer or law firm similarly may employ a lawyer or nonlawyer who practices pursuant to such a limited license from a federal agency or court to perform services permissible under the license. Because the person's practice is authorized, the employing lawyer is not engaged in assisting unauthorized practice (compare § 4, Comments *f* & *g*). On the other hand, the employing lawyer or law firm would be so engaged if the unadmitted lawyer or nonlawyer engaged in practice not reasonably related to the work the person is authorized to conduct.

§ 4. Unauthorized Practice by a Nonlawyer

A person not admitted to practice as a lawyer (see § 2) may not engage in the unauthorized practice of law, and a lawyer may not assist a person to do so.

Comment:

a. Scope and cross-references. This Section addresses legal restrictions on the practice of law by a person not admitted to practice as described in § 2. On somewhat similar restrictions on disbarred or suspended lawyers or on lawyers practicing in a jurisdiction in which the lawyer is not admitted, see § 3.

To some, the expression "unauthorized practice of law" by a non-lawyer is incongruous, because it can be taken to imply that nonlawyers may engage in some aspects of law practice, but not others. The phrase has gained near-universal usage in the courts, ethics-committee opinions, and scholarly writing, and it is well understood not to imply any necessary area of permissible practice by a nonlawyer. Moreover, a nonlawyer undoubtedly may engage in some limited forms of law practice, such as self-representation in a civil or criminal matter (see Comment *d*). See also, e.g., § 3, Comment *g*; Comments *c*, *e*, and *g* hereof. It thus would not be accurate for the black letter to state flatly that a nonlawyer may not engage in law practice. On defining unauthorized practice, see Comment *c* hereto.

A nonlawyer who impermissibly engages in the practice of law may be subject to several sanctions, including injunction, contempt, and conviction for crime.

781

b.   Unauthorized practice by a nonlawyer—in general. Courts, typically as the result of lawsuits brought by bar associations, began in the early part of the 20th century to adapt common-law rules to permit bar associations and lawyer-competitors to seek injunctions against some forms of unauthorized practice by nonlawyers. The courts also played a large role in attempting to define and delineate such practice. The primary justification given for unauthorized practice limitations was that of consumer protection—to protect consumers of unauthorized practitioner services against the significant risk of harm believed to be threatened by the nonlawyer practitioner's incompetence or lack of ethical constraints. Delineating the respective areas of permissible and impermissible activities has often been controversial. Some consumer groups and governmental agencies have criticized some restrictions as over-protective, anti-competitive, and costly to consumers.

In the latter part of the 20th century, unauthorized practice restrictions have lessened, to a greater or lesser extent, in most jurisdictions. In some few jurisdictions traditional restraints are apparently still enforced through active programs. In other jurisdictions, enforcement has effectively ceased, and large numbers of lay practitioners perform many traditional legal services. Debate continues about the broad public-policy elements of unauthorized-practice restrictions, including the delineation of lawyer-only practice areas. On areas of nonlawyer practice officially permitted, see Comment *c* hereof.

c.   Delineation of unauthorized practice. The definitions and tests employed by courts to delineate unauthorized practice by nonlawyers have been vague or conclusory, while jurisdictions have differed significantly in describing what constitutes unauthorized practice in particular areas.

Certain activities, such as the representation of another person in litigation, are generally proscribed. Even in that area, many jurisdictions recognize exceptions for such matters as small-claims and landlord-tenant tribunals and certain proceedings in administrative agencies. Moreover, many jurisdictions have authorized law students and others not admitted in the state to represent indigent persons or others as part of clinical legal-education programs.

Controversy has surrounded many out-of-court activities such as advising on estate planning by bank trust officers, advising on estate planning by insurance agents, stock brokers, or benefit-plan and similar consultants, filling out or providing guidance on forms for property transactions by real-estate agents, title companies, and closing-service companies, and selling books or individual forms containing instructions on self-help legal services or accompanied by personal, nonlawyer assistance on filling them out in connection with legal procedures such as obtaining a marriage dissolution. The position of bar associations has traditionally been that nonlawyer provision of such services denies the person served the benefit of such legal measures as the attorney-client privilege, the benefits of such extraordinary duties as that of confidentiality of client information and the protection against conflicts of interest, and the protection of such measures as those regulating lawyer trust accounts and requiring lawyers to supervise nonlawyer personnel. Several jurisdictions recognize that many such services can be provided by nonlawyers without significant risk of incompetent service, that actual experience in several states with extensive nonlawyer provision of traditional legal services indicates no significant risk of harm to consumers of such services, that persons in need of legal services may be significantly aided in obtaining assistance at a much lower price than would be entailed by segregating out a portion of a transaction to be handled by a lawyer for a fee, and that many persons can ill afford, and most persons are at least inconvenienced by, the typically higher cost of lawyer services. In addition, traditional common-law and statutory consumer-protection measures offer significant protection to consumers of such nonlawyer services.

d. Pro se appearance. Every jurisdiction recognizes the right of an individual to proceed "pro se" by providing his or her own representation in any matter, whether or not the person is a lawyer. Because the appearance is personal only, it does not involve an issue of unauthorized practice. The right extends to self-preparation of legal documents and other kinds of out-of-court legal work as well as to in-court representation. In some jurisdictions, tribunals have inaugurated programs to assist persons without counsel in filing necessary papers, with appropriate cautions that court personnel assisting the person do not thereby undertake to provide legal assistance. The United States Supreme Court has held that a person accused of crime in a federal or state prosecution has, as an aspect of the right to the assistance of counsel, the constitutional right to waive counsel and to proceed pro se. In general, however, a person appearing pro se cannot represent any other person or entity, no matter how close the degree of kinship, ownership, or other relationship.

e. Unauthorized practice for and by entities. A limitation on pro se representation (see Comment *d*) found in many jurisdictions is that a corporation cannot represent itself in litigation and must accordingly always be represented by counsel. The rule applies, apparently, only to appearances in litigated matters. Thus a nonlawyer officer of a corporation may permissibly draft legal documents, negotiate complex transactions, and perform other tasks for the employing organization, even if the task is typically performed by lawyers for organizations. With respect to litigation, several jurisdictions except representation in certain tribunals, such as landlord-tenant and small-claims courts and in certain administrative proceedings (see Comment *c* hereto), where incorporation (typically of a small owner-operated business) has little bearing on the prerogative of the person to provide self-representation.

Under traditional concepts of unauthorized practice, a lawyer employed by an organization may provide legal services only to the organization as an entity with respect to its own interests and not, for example, to customers of the entity with respect to their own legal matters. Included within the powers of a lawyer retained by an organization (see § 3, Comment *f*) should be the capacity to perform legal services for all entities within the same organizational family. It has proved controversial whether a lawyer employed full time by an insurance company (see § 134) may represent policyholders of the company in covered matters.

f. Lawyer assistance to nonlawyer unauthorized practice. The lawyer codes have traditionally prohibited lawyers from assisting nonlawyers in activities that constitute the unauthorized practice of law. That prohibition is stated in the Section. The limitation supplements requirements that lawyers provide adequate supervision to nonlawyer employees and agents (see Comment *g* hereto; § 11, Comment *e*). By the same token, it has prevented lawyers from sponsoring non-law-firm enterprises in which legal services are provided mainly or entirely by nonlawyers and in which the lawyer gains the profits (see generally § 10).

g. Nonlawyer employees of law firms. For obvious reasons of convenience and better service to clients, lawyers and law firms are empowered to retain nonlawyer personnel to assist firm lawyers in providing legal services to clients. In the course of that work, a nonlawyer may conduct activities that, if conducted by that person alone in representing a client, would constitute unauthorized practice. Those activities are permissible and do not constitute unauthorized practice, so long as the responsible lawyer or law firm provides appropriate supervision (see § 11, Comment *e*), and so long as the nonlawyer is not permitted to own an interest in the law firm, split fees, or exercise management powers with respect to a law-practice aspect of the firm (see § 10).

TITLE C. PROFESSIONAL DISCIPLINE

§ 5. Professional Discipline

(1) A lawyer is subject to professional discipline for violating any provision of an applicable lawyer code.

(2) A lawyer is also subject to professional discipline under Subsection (1) for attempting to commit a violation, knowingly assisting or inducing another to do so, or knowingly doing so through the acts of another.

(3) A lawyer who knows of another lawyer's violation of applicable rules of professional conduct raising a substantial question of the lawyer's honesty or trustworthiness or the lawyer's fitness as a lawyer in some other respect must report that information to appropriate disciplinary authorities.

TOPIC 3.   CIVIL JUDICIAL REMEDIES IN GENERAL

§ 6.   Jurisdictional Remedies Available to a Client or Nonclient for Lawyer Wrongs

For a lawyer's breach of a duty owed to the lawyer's client or to a nonclient, judicial remedies may be available through judgment or order entered in accordance with the standards applicable to the remedy awarded, including standards concerning limitation of remedies. Judicial remedies include the following:

(1) awarding a sum of money as damages;

(2) providing injunctive relief, including requiring specific performance of a contract or enjoining its nonperformance;

(3) requiring restoration of a specific thing or awarding a sum of money to prevent unjust enrichment;

(4) ordering cancellation or reformation of a contract, deed, or similar instrument;

(5) declaring the rights of the parties, such as determining that an obligation claimed by the lawyer to be owed to the lawyer is not enforceable;

(6) punishing the lawyer for contempt;

(7) enforcing an arbitration award;

(8) disqualifying a lawyer from a representation;

(9) forfeiting a lawyer's fee (see § 37);

(10) denying the admission of evidence wrongfully obtained;

(11) dismissing the claim or defense of a litigant represented by the lawyer;

(12) granting a new trial; and

(13) entering a procedural or other sanction.

Comment:

a. Scope and cross-references. This Section describes judicial relief available to a client or nonclient whose legal rights have been violated by actions of a lawyer. This Restatement does not purport to describe in detail such remedies and rules regarding their implementation (see Introductory Note). Instead, the Section and the following Comments note in general terms the most familiar, applicable remedies and certain circumstances involved in their application to lawyers. This list is not exhaustive, and the availability of one remedy does not necessarily foreclose others. For example, a court awarding a sum of money to prevent unjust enrichment (Subsection (3)) may also impose a constructive trust and order an accounting (see Restatement of Restitution § 160 and Restatement Second, Restitution § 30 (Tentative Draft No. 2, 1984)).

Availability of a particular remedy is subject to customary rules applicable to the remedy, including the general principle that duplicative remedies not be awarded. With respect to limitation of remedies, see Comment *n*.

Generally applicable law defines the elements that must be proved by a party seeking a remedy or seeking to defend against a claim for such a remedy. When the conduct of a lawyer is drawn into question, the provisions of lawyer codes regulating the lawyer with respect to such conduct may be relevant in determining the propriety of the conduct (see § 1, Comment *b*, & § 52, Comment *f*).

b. Damages. The most common kind of case in which damages are allowed is a claim of malpractice by a client against a lawyer. See generally Chapter 4. On the extent of damage remedies available to a nonclient against a lawyer, see generally §§ 51 and 56.

c. Specific performance and other injunctive relief. A lawyer's general undertaking to provide legal services to a client is not specifically enforceable. On the doctrine that a personal-services contract, including a contract to provide legal services, will not be specifically enforced, see Restatement Second, Contracts § 367(1). On the other hand, in litigation matters a court generally has discretion to refuse to permit a lawyer to withdraw to the extent stated in § 32(4) and Comment *d* thereto. The general rule providing limited injunctive relief against a lawyer's breach of a contract to provide personal services exclusively to one client (see id. § 367(2)) would not normally be relevant due to the unenforceability on grounds of public policy of a purported promise by a lawyer not to provide legal services to another client (see § 13). A lawyer employed in a full-time position as employee, such as inside legal counsel to a corporation, government agency, or similar entity, will often function under an agreement or rule requiring the lawyer not to practice law in outside employment. The typical remedy for breach of such an agreement is internal discipline or termination, rather than injunctive relief.

A lawyer may contract with a client to provide nonlegal services, such as when a lawyer and client enter into a business contract that the client seeks to enforce (see § 126). Such a contract is enforceable in accordance with the customary rules governing contracts, including remedies available for breach of such a contract.

Injunctive relief may also be appropriate for a lawyer's violation of noncontractual duties to a client. Thus, a lawyer who fails or refuses to turn over to a client or the client's successor files or other property to which the client is entitled (see § 33(1) & Comment *b* thereto) may be required to do so by injunctive order.

With respect to a nonclient, the instances in which injunctive relief against an opposing lawyer would be appropriate are limited. Nonetheless, when no other suitable remedy is available, it may be appropriate, for example, to enter an injunction against an opposing lawyer's violation of the prohibition against contact with employees of a nonclient (see §§ 99–102).

d. Preventing unjust enrichment. A court in a civil action may order a lawyer to return specific property, such as client property wrongfully retained by a lawyer (see § 45). See also § 60(2) (accounting for profits from improper use of confidential information). Disciplinary authorities are also sometimes empowered to order restitution as a disciplinary sanction (see § 5, Comment *j*). On forfeiture of a lawyer's fees, see § 37.

e. Rescission or reformation of a transaction. Cancellation of an instrument with otherwise legal effect would be appropriate when, for example, a lawyer obtains a deed to a client's property through undue influence in violation of limitations on business dealings with a client (see § 126) or on client gifts to lawyers (see § 127) or when the instrument was prepared by a lawyer representing clients with substantial conflicts of interests (see § 130). The remedy implements substantive standards applicable to lawyers as an expression of the strong public policy of the jurisdiction.

f. Declaratory relief. Under standards otherwise governing the availability of declaratory relief, it may be appropriate for a court to enter an order declaring the respective rights of lawyer and client with respect to a disputed issue or the responsibilities of a lawyer with respect to a nonclient.

g. Contempt. An order providing a sanction for civil or criminal contempt may be appropriate for a lawyer's violation of a court injunction or similar order. See Comment *c*; see also § 105. In addition, a lawyer functioning as advocate in a proceeding may be subject to remedies through contempt orders without issuance of a prior judicial order where necessary and appropriate to maintain order in the courtroom or otherwise to prevent significant impairment of the proceedings (see § 105, Comment *e*). Included in such relief may be an appropriate sanction directed toward repairing or punishing harm that the lawyer's contemptuous conduct caused to the lawyer's own client.

h. Enforcing an arbitration award. As indicated in § 42, Comment *b*, a lawyer and client may agree to submit a dispute to binding arbitration, and a jurisdiction may require a lawyer to submit to fee arbitration when a client so elects. See also § 54, Comment *b* (malpractice arbitration). As with arbitration awards generally, a court may in an appropriate case enter an order enforcing such an award or denying it enforcement on appropriate grounds. On arbitration awards in a lawyer's favor and against a client or former client, see § 7, Comment *c*.

i. Disqualification from a representation. Disqualification of a lawyer and those affiliated with the lawyer from further participation in a pending matter has become the most common remedy for conflicts of interest in litigation (see Chapter 8). Disqualification draws on the inherent power of courts to regulate the conduct of lawyers (see § 1, Comment c) as well as the related inherent power of judges to regulate the course of proceedings before them and to issue injunctive and similar directive orders (see Comment c hereto). Disqualification, where appropriate, ensures that the case is well presented in court, that confidential information of present or former clients is not misused, and that a client's substantial interest in a lawyer's loyalty is protected. In most instances, determining whether a lawyer should be disqualified involves a balancing of several interests and is appropriate only when less-intrusive remedies are not reasonably available.

The costs imposed on a client deprived of a lawyer's services by disqualification can be substantial. At a minimum, the client is forced to incur the cost of finding a new lawyer not burdened by conflict in whom the client has confidence and educating that lawyer about the facts and issues. The costs of delay in the proceeding are borne by that client in part, but also by the tribunal and society. Disqualification is often the most effective sanction for a conflict of interest and will likely continue to be vigorously applied where necessary to protect the integrity of a proceeding or an important interest of the moving party. In applying it, however, tribunals should be vigilant to prevent its use as a tactic by which one party may impose unwarranted delay, costs, and other burdens on another. In an appropriate case, additional or other remedies may be appropriate, such as professional discipline (see § 5), legal-malpractice recovery (see Chapter 4), fee forfeiture (see § 37 & Comment d hereto), rescission or reformation of an instrument (see Comment d hereto), various procedural remedies (see Comments j-m hereto), or possible criminal sanctions (see § 8). Injunctive relief (see Comment c hereto) may be appropriate in a matter not before a tribunal, so that disqualification in a proceeding already underway cannot be sought.

The costs associated with disqualification require that standing to seek disqualification ordinarily be limited to present or former clients who would be adversely affected by the continuing representation, whether or not they are parties to the present litigation. Tribunals should not ordinarily permit parties who are not directly affected to invoke the putative interests of an absent client with whom they are not in privity. However, concerns about the fairness of the processes of tribunals may require that tribunals in some cases raise conflicts issues on their own motion or permit a party who otherwise lacks standing to raise the issue. Particularly in criminal prosecutions (see § 129, Comment c), a court may intervene where necessary to protect a defendant against the ineffective assistance of counsel that may result from a conflict of interest.

Concern that motions to disqualify might be used to delay proceedings and harass opposing parties also requires that the motion to disqualify be timely. If a present or former client with knowledge of the conflict fails to take reasonably prompt steps to object or to seek a remedy, disqualification may be precluded. Whether an objection is timely depends on such circumstances as the length of delay from the time when the conflict was reasonably apparent, whether the movant was represented by counsel at relevant times, why the delay occurred, and whether acting now would result in prejudice to the responding party.

A file of the work done on a matter before disqualification by a disqualified lawyer may be provided to a successor lawyer in circumstances in which doing so does not threaten confidential information (see generally § 59) of the successful moving client. The party seeking to justify such a transfer may be required to show both that no impermissible confidential client information is contained in the material transferred, and that the former and new lawyers exchange none in the process of transferring responsibilities for the matter.

Illustration:

> 1. Lawyer was retained by Defendant to defend a claim for breach of warranty. Lawyer prepared a memorandum of legal research on the question of proper venue and made notes of interviews with three of Defendant's employees who had substantial knowledge of the processes used in manufacture of the product. Shortly thereafter, Lawyer's firm hired New Lawyer, who had been actively working on the case on behalf of Plaintiff at a former firm. Even if Lawyer would be disqualified from continuing to represent Defendant in the case (compare §§ 123–124), the interview notes and memorandum of law could be made available to successor counsel for Defendant because Defendant can show that they were not enhanced or otherwise based on confidential information of Plaintiff revealed by New Lawyer to Lawyer.

When a lawyer undertakes a representation that is later determined to involve a conflict of interest that could not reasonably have been and in fact was not identified at an earlier point (see § 121, Comment *g*), the lawyer is not liable for damages or subject to professional discipline. In such a situation, disqualification may or may not be appropriate (see § 49, Illustration 2).

j. Denying the admissibility of evidence. If the admission of evidence on behalf of a party would violate the obligation owed by a lawyer to a client or former client (see generally § 60) or was obtained by a lawyer in violation of the lawyer's obligation not to mislead a nonclient (see § 98), the tribunal may exercise discretion to exclude the evidence, even if the evidence is not otherwise subject to exclusion because of the attorney-client privilege (see § 68 and following) or the work-product immunity (see § 87 and following). Exclusion is proper where it would place the parties in the position they would have occupied if the lawyer had not obtained the confidential information in the first place.

k. Dismissing a claim or defense. When a litigant bases an essential element of a claim or defense entirely on confidential client information improperly disclosed by a lawyer (see generally § 60), the tribunal may exercise discretion to dismiss the claim or defense. Such extreme relief is appropriate when no less drastic relief would adequately remedy the disclosure. If, on the other hand, the tribunal finds that the claim or defense would have been made notwithstanding the disclosure, a more appropriate remedy may be disqualification of the revealing lawyer if the lawyer presently represents the responding party and suppression of only such evidence (see Comment *j*) as would not be properly discoverable.

l. New trial. Where the determination in a case was affected prejudicially and substantially by a conflict of interest, by a lawyer misuse of confidential information of an objecting client, by a breach of rules governing admissibility of evidence or conduct of the proceeding, or by similarly wrongful conduct of a lawyer, the determination may be reversed and the matter retried. Tribunals are properly reluctant to grant such a remedy. On the other hand, it may be the only effective remedy in a particular case, for example in a criminal case in which a lawyer representing the defendant labored under an impermissible conflict of interest (see § 129). When the complaining party is the client of the offending lawyer in a civil case, tribunals generally relegate the client to such remedies as the client may have directly against the lawyer, concluding that reversal of a determination in favor of an otherwise uninvolved opposing party would be inappropriate (see § 26, Comment *d*).

m. Procedural or other sanctions. Most tribunals possess the power to provide sanctions against participants in litigation, including lawyers, who engage in seriously harassing or other sanctionable activities. See generally § 1; see also § 110. Such sanctions include an award of attorney fees to a party injured by the lawyer's conduct, a fine, or a reprimand. In appropriate circumstances, the court may determine that the client was blameless and the lawyer fully blameworthy and accordingly direct that the full weight of a sanction entered against a party be borne only by the lawyer and not by the lawyer's client (see § 110, Comment *g*). Rarely will such relief entail an award from the offending lawyer to that lawyer's own client. However, such an order may be appropriate, for example, when, due to the lawyer's offensive activities, the lawyer's client has retained another lawyer and the court retains jurisdiction to award such a sanction against the predecessor lawyer.

n. Limitation of remedies. Applicable rules of the law of remedies may limit relief that otherwise would be available, such as the limitation on recovery of damages for failure to avoid preventable loss. See Restatement Second, Contracts § 350; see also id. §§ 351 (unforeseeability and related limitations), 352 (uncertainty), 353 (losses due to emotional disturbance), and 356 (limitation on liquidated damages and penalties).

Similarly, certain remedies may be withheld because precluded by election or affirmance (see id., Ch. 16, Topic 5; see also § 54).

§ 7. Jurisdictional Remedies Available to a Lawyer for or Client Wrongs

A lawyer may obtain a remedy based on a present or former client's breach of a duty to the lawyer if the remedy:

(1) is appropriate under applicable law governing the remedy; and

(2) does not put the lawyer in a position prohibited by an applicable lawyer code.

Comment:

a. Scope and cross-references. This Section states the general availability of remedies to a lawyer (Subsection (1)), subject to Subsection (2), which recognizes that special limitations on such remedies may be appropriate in view of what the tribunal may properly determine to be overriding considerations arising from appropriate enforcement of a lawyer-code provision applicable to the lawyer. While the discussion herein is limited to remedies, similar considerations may apply to defenses that a lawyer asserts against claims of a client or former client.

b. Rationale. A lawyer seeking relief from a present or former client is not in the same position as are most other claimants with respect to responding parties. The relationship between lawyer and client is one in which the lawyer generally owes the client rigorously enforced fiduciary duties, including duties of the utmost good faith and fair dealing (see § 16). Those duties are diminished, but not entirely extinguished, at the end of the representation. While those duties inform many of the substantive rights that a lawyer might assert against a client, it may also be appropriate to take account of the lawyer's fiduciary duties when assessing the suitability of an otherwise-available remedy (e.g., § 41) (fee-collection methods). In view of the predominant role of courts in regulating lawyers (see § 2, Comment *c*), such concepts will be particularly relevant when the remedy in question is discretionary with the court or when a tribunal deals with a novel common-law question of remedy.

Illustrations:

1. In a written contract by which Client retained Lawyer to provide legal services in a personal-injury case, Client agreed to give Lawyer at least 30 days' notice of discharge. Client was a person not experienced in dealings with lawyers, and the representation was a routine personal-injury action. Client later discharged Lawyer without giving prior notice. Lawyer filed suit against Client, seeking damages for Client's violation of the 30-day-notice agreement. Due to Client's right to discharge Lawyer at any time (see § 32), the

tribunal should refuse to enforce the 30–day limitation restricting that right.

2. Same facts as in Illustration 1, except that Client is a large organization represented in the negotiations with Lawyer by inside legal counsel. The matter involves an unusual time and capital commitment by Lawyer, necessitating that Lawyer hire additional professional and clerical assistance, terminate representation of other clients, and train office staff to deal with a complex set of technical issues entailed in representing Client. In the circumstances, the 30–day-notice requirement is not unreasonable, as it protects clear and legitimate interests of Lawyer and does not in the circumstances unduly burden Client's right of discharge.

On the right of a discharged inside legal counsel to maintain a suit against a client organization for wrongful dismissal, see § 32, Comment *b*; cf. § 37, Comment *e*.

c. Public-policy limitations on remedies to lawyer. As with other considerations of public policy, a tribunal will accord respect to the special rules regulating lawyers, including applicable provisions of a lawyer code, in adjudicating a dispute between a lawyer and a client or former client. Such attention is appropriate both in determining applicable remedial and substantive rules and when dealing with particular defenses, such as defenses of public policy in contract law (see, e.g., Restatement Second, Contracts § 197 et seq.) (unavailability of restitution on public-policy grounds). See § 1, Comment *b*; see, e.g., § 37 (fee forfeiture).

TOPIC 4. LAWYER CRIMINAL OFFENSES

§ 8. Lawyer Criminal Offenses

The traditional and appropriate activities of a lawyer in representing a client in accordance with the requirements of the applicable lawyer code are relevant factors for the tribunal in assessing the propriety of the lawyer's conduct under the criminal law. In other respects, a lawyer is guilty of an offense for an act committed in the course of representing a client to the same extent and on the same basis as would a nonlawyer acting similarly.

TITLE A. ASSOCIATION OF LAWYERS IN LAW ORGANIZATIONS

§ 9. Law Practice Organizations—In General

(1) A lawyer may practice as a solo practitioner, as an employee of another lawyer or law firm, or as a member of a law firm constituted as a partnership, professional corporation, or similar entity.

(2) A lawyer employed by an entity described in Subsection (1) is subject to applicable law governing the creation, operation, management, and dissolution of the entity.

(3) Absent an agreement with the firm providing a more permissive rule, a lawyer leaving a law firm may solicit firm clients:

>   (a) prior to leaving the firm:

>>   (i) only with respect to firm clients on whose matters the lawyer is actively and substantially working; and

>>   (ii) only after the lawyer has adequately and timely informed the firm of the lawyer's intent to contact firm clients for that purpose; and

>   (b) after ceasing employment in the firm, to the same extent as any other nonfirm lawyer.

TITLE B. LIMITATIONS ON NONLAWYER INVOLVEMENT IN A LAW FIRM

§ 10. Limitations on Nonlawyer Involvement in a Law Firm

(1) A nonlawyer may not own any interest in a law firm, and a nonlawyer may not be empowered to or actually direct or control the professional activities of a lawyer in the firm.

(2) A lawyer may not form a partnership or other business enterprise with a nonlawyer if any of the activities of the enterprise consist of the practice of law.

(3) A lawyer or law firm may not share legal fees with a person not admitted to practice as a lawyer, except that:

>   (a) an agreement by a lawyer with the lawyer's firm or another lawyer in the firm may provide for payment, over a reasonable period of time after the lawyer's death, to the lawyer's estate or to one or more specified persons;

>   (b) a lawyer who undertakes to complete unfinished legal business of a deceased lawyer may pay to the estate of the deceased lawyer a portion of the total compensation that fairly represents services rendered by the deceased lawyer; and

>   (c) a lawyer or law firm may include nonlawyer employees in a compensation or retirement plan, even though the plan is based in whole or in part on a profit-sharing arrangement.

Comment:

a. Scope and cross-references. This Section states several interrelated limitations on the extent to which nonlawyers may own or exercise managerial responsibility in a law firm or share in its fee income and on the correlative extent to which a lawyer may be involved in non-law-firm endeavors, including endeavors some of the activities of which consist of the practice of law. On limitations on the extent to which a nonclient may direct a lawyer's provision of legal services to a client, see § 134. On limitations on fee-splitting among lawyers, see § 47.

b.   Rationale. This Section is based on lawyer-code limitations on law-firm structure and practices. Those limitations are prophylactic and are designed to safeguard the professional independence of lawyers. A person entitled to share a lawyer's fees is likely to attempt to influence the lawyer's activities so as to maximize those fees. That could lead to inadequate legal services. The Section should be construed so as to prevent nonlawyer control over lawyers' services, not to implement other goals such as preventing new and useful ways of providing legal services or making sure that nonlawyers do not profit indirectly from legal services in circumstances and under arrangements presenting no significant risk of harm to clients or third persons.

The prohibition of Subsection (3) has no application when a person, such as a spouse, advances an otherwise valid claim on the lawyer's income, net worth, including good will in a law practice, or other wealth (see Principles of the Law of Family Dissolution: Analysis and Recommendations § 4.07) (Proposed Final Draft, Part I, 1997). Jurisdictions disagree as to the permissibility of a sale of the practice of a deceased or retired lawyer and, if permitted, how it may be accomplished.

As indicated in Subsection (3)(a), postdeath distributions to nonlawyers, such as a deceased firm member's spouse or estate, are permissible. Such a distribution may be based on the firm agreement, but it may also be made gratuitously.

c.   Nonlawyer ownership or management power in a law firm. As reflected in Subsection (1), the lawyer codes have traditionally prohibited arrangements under which a nonlawyer owns an interest in a law firm or exercises managerial responsibility in a law firm on how legal services are provided. In applying that prohibition, certain areas of nonapplication are recognized. Plainly, a nonlawyer may direct the activities of lawyers when the nonlawyer is a client or an agent of a client in the matter (see § 21(2)), such as a nonlawyer officer of a corporation who directs the activities of a lawyer in the office of inside legal counsel of the organization (see § 96, Comment *d*). A lawyer undertaking to complete unfinished business of a deceased lawyer may agree to pay to the deceased lawyer's estate total compensation that fairly represents the services rendered by that lawyer (see Subsection (3)(b)). Under pension-plan and similar retirement arrangements, it is permissible for nonlawyer personnel of a law firm to share in firm profits (see Subsection (3)(c)).

As with other instances of fee-splitting with a nonlawyer (see Comment *b*), the traditional set of restrictions is intended to protect the professional independence of lawyers. Here also the concern is that permitting such ownership or direction would induce or require lawyers to violate the mandates of the lawyer codes, such as by subjecting the lawyer to the goals and interests of the nonlawyer in ways adverse to the lawyer's duties to a client. As a result, for example, statutes and court rules providing for establishing a law firm as a partnership or professional corporation commonly provide that no principal or partner may be admitted to the partnership or own stock in the corporation who is not a lawyer.

Such restrictions, however, impose costs. One cost is that any kind of capital infusion that would entail granting an ownership or security interest in the law firm itself (as distinguished from its assets) to a nonlawyer investor is prohibited. Perhaps as much as any other constraint, such practical barriers to infusion of capital into law firms significantly limit the ability of law firms to attain what its lawyers may consider to be a more optimal size at which to provide higher-quality and lower-price services to clients. They may also deter law firms from more effectively competing with established law firms and with nonlawyer organizations, such as consulting companies, investment bankers, and accounting firms, to whom clients may turn for more cost-effective law-related services. Further, unlike other persons in many (but not all) occupations, lawyers are unable to realize the present economic value of their reputations, which otherwise could be obtained through sale to investors of stock or other ownership interest.

d. Referral arrangements. Under the rule of Subsection (3), a lawyer may not pay or agree to pay a nonlawyer for referring a client to the lawyer. Such arrangements would give the nonlawyer an incentive to refer to lawyers who will pay the highest referral fee, rather than to lawyers who can provide the most effective services. They also would give the nonlawyer referring person the power and an incentive to influence the lawyer's representation by an explicit or implicit threat to refer no additional clients or by appealing to the lawyer's sense of gratitude for the referral already made. That incentive is not present when the referral comes from a nonprofit referral service. Moreover, a lawyer may pay an advertising, marketing, or similar service for providing professional services in connection with the lawyer's own permissible efforts to advertise for clients. Fee-splitting with a lawyer admitted only in another jurisdiction is subject to § 47 but not to Subsection (3) hereof.

e. Compensation of nonlawyer employees. This Section, of course, does not prohibit a lawyer from providing compensation to secretaries, nonlawyer professionals, and other permanent or temporary employees. That is so even though their compensation indirectly comes from the lawyer's fees and the employees hence have some interest in maximizing the lawyer's fee income. Compare § 47, Comment *b;* on the duty to supervise all such nonlawyer personnel, see § 11. Such compensation may be a percentage of or otherwise contingent on the lawyer's income, so long as the compensation is not contingent on the lawyer's revenue in an individual matter. Thus, under Subsection (3)(c), nonlawyer employees may join in a profit-sharing plan for compensation or retirement. Under tax regulations certain kinds of retirement and similar plans must often be made available to all employees on specified terms of equality.

A lawyer may have business relationships with nonlawyers in non-law practice matters. Thus, a lawyer may serve as co-trustee of a trust or co-executor of an estate and share fees earned for such functions with a nonlawyer co-fiduciary.

f. Nontraditional forms of law practice. The rule against splitting fees with nonlawyers has been one ground for the prohibition of partnerships between lawyers and nonlawyers when the practice of law is an activity of the partnership and for the prohibition of profit-making professional law corporations with stock owned by nonlawyers. This Section does not prohibit a law firm from cooperating with a legally separate partnership or other organization of nonlawyers in providing multi-disciplinary services to clients. The Section allows a lawyer employed and compensated by a nonprofit public-interest organization or a union to remit court-awarded fees to the employing organization, provided that the organization uses the funds only for legal services.

g. Lawyer involvement in ancillary business activities. Ancillary business activities of lawyers can be conducted consistent with the Section and with other applicable requirements. A lawyer may, for example, operate a real-estate agency, insurance agency, title-insurance company, consulting enterprise, or similar business, along with a law practice. So long as each enterprise bills separately and so long as the ancillary enterprise does not engage in the practice of law, involvement of both the lawyer's law practice and the lawyer's ancillary business enterprise in the same matter does not constitute impermissible fee-splitting with a nonlawyer, even if nonlawyers have ownership interests or exercise management powers in the ancillary enterprise.

However, a lawyer's dual practice of law and the ancillary enterprise must be conducted in accordance with applicable legal restrictions, including those of the lawyer codes. Among other things, the lawyer's self-interest in promoting the enterprise must not distort the lawyer's judgment in the provision of legal services to a client, including in making recommendations of the lawyer's own ancillary service. To avoid misleading the client, a lawyer must reveal the lawyer's interest in the ancillary enterprise when it should be reasonably apparent that the client would wish to or should assess that information in determining whether to engage the services of the other business. The lawyer must also, of course, avoid representing a client (or do so only with informed client consent) in a matter in which the ancillary enterprise has an adverse interest of such a kind that it would materially and adversely affect the lawyer's representation of the client (see § 125). The lawyer must also disclose to the client, unless the client is already sufficiently aware, that the client will not have a client-lawyer relationship with the ancillary business and the significance of that fact. Other disclosures may be required in the course of the matter. For example, when circumstances indicate the need to do so to protect an important interest of the client, the lawyer must disclose to the client that the client's communications with personnel of the ancillary enterprise—unlike communications with personnel in the lawyer's law office (see § 70, Comment *g*)—are not protected under the attorney-client privilege. If relevant, the lawyer should also disclose to the client that the ancillary business is not subject to conflict-of-interest rules (see generally Chapter 8) similar to those applicable to law practice.

A lawyer's provision of services to a client through an ancillary business may in some circumstances constitute the rendition of legal services under an applicable lawyer code. As a consequence, the possibly more stringent requirements of the code may control the provision of the ancillary services, such as with respect to the reasonableness of fee charges (§ 34) or confidentiality obligations (§ 60 and following). When those services are distinct and the client understands the significance of the distinction, the ancillary service should not be considered as the rendition of legal services. When those conditions are not met, the lawyer is subject to the lawyer code with respect to all services provided. Whether the services are distinct depends on the client's reasonably apparent understanding concerning such considerations as the nature of the respective ancillary-business and legal services, the physical location at which the services are provided, and the identities and affiliations of lawyer and nonlawyer personnel working on the matter.

h. Sanctions; enforceability of improper agreements. A lawyer who enters a fee-splitting arrangement violating this Section is subject to professional discipline (see § 5) and fee forfeiture (see § 37). Tribunals will not assist such a lawyer to enforce such an arrangement. Whether a nonlawyer may enforce a fee-splitting agreement with a lawyer depends on whether the jurisdiction limits its regulation to lawyers or subjects nonlawyers who enter such agreements to criminal or civil sanctions. With respect to the nonlawyer, a violation of the prohibition of Subsection (2) may constitute unauthorized practice of law, incurring the sanctions applicable to such activity (see § 4).

TITLE C. SUPERVISION OF LAWYERS AND NONLAWYERS WITHIN AN ORGANIZATION

§ 11. A Lawyer's Duty of Supervision

(1) A lawyer who is a partner in a law-firm partnership or a principal in a law firm organized as a corporation or similar entity is subject to professional discipline for failing to make reasonable efforts to ensure that the firm has in effect measures giving reasonable assurance that all lawyers in the firm conform to applicable lawyer-code requirements.

(2) A lawyer who has direct supervisory authority over another lawyer is subject to professional discipline for failing to

make reasonable efforts to ensure that the other lawyer conforms to applicable lawyer-code requirements.

(3) A lawyer is subject to professional discipline for another lawyer's violation of the rules of professional conduct if:

(a) the lawyer orders or, with knowledge of the specific conduct, ratifies the conduct involved; or

(b) the lawyer is a partner or principal in the law firm, or has direct supervisory authority over the other lawyer, and knows of the conduct at a time when its consequences can be avoided or mitigated but fails to take reasonable remedial measures.

(4) With respect to a nonlawyer employee of a law firm, the lawyer is subject to professional discipline if either:

(a) the lawyer fails to make reasonable efforts to ensure:

(i) that the firm in which the lawyer practices has in effect measures giving reasonable assurance that the nonlawyer's conduct is compatible with the professional obligations of the lawyer; and

(ii) that conduct of a nonlawyer over whom the lawyer has direct supervisory authority is compatible with the professional obligations of the lawyer; or

(b) the nonlawyer's conduct would be a violation of the applicable lawyer code if engaged in by a lawyer, and

(i) the lawyer orders or, with knowledge of the specific conduct, ratifies the conduct; or

(ii) the lawyer is a partner or principal in the law firm, or has direct supervisory authority over the nonlawyer, and knows of the conduct at a time when its consequences can be avoided or mitigated but fails to take reasonable remedial measures.

§ 12. Duty of a Lawyer Subject to Supervision

(1) For purposes of professional discipline, a lawyer must conform to the requirements of an applicable lawyer code even if the lawyer acted at the direction of another lawyer or other person.

(2) For purposes of professional discipline, a lawyer under the direct supervisory authority of another lawyer does not violate an applicable lawyer code by acting in accordance with the supervisory lawyer's direction based on a reasonable resolution of an arguable question of professional duty.

TITLE D.   RESTRICTIONS ON THE RIGHT TO PRACTICE LAW

§ 13.   Restrictions on the Right to Practice Law

(1) A lawyer may not offer or enter into a law-firm agreement that restricts the right of the lawyer to practice law after terminating the relationship, except for a restriction incident to the lawyer's retirement from the practice of law.

(2) In settling a client claim, a lawyer may not offer or enter into an agreement that restricts the right of the lawyer to practice law, including the right to represent or take particular action on behalf of other clients.

CHAPTER 2:   THE CLIENT LAWYER RELATIONSHIP

TOPIC 1.   CREATING A CLIENT–LAWYER RELATIONSHIP

§ 14.   Formation of Client–Lawyer Relationship

A relationship of client and lawyer arises when:

(1) a person manifests to a lawyer the person's intent that the lawyer provide legal services for the person; and either

(a) the lawyer manifests to the person consent to do so; or

(b) the lawyer fails to manifest lack of consent to do so, and the lawyer knows or reasonably should know that the person reasonably relies on the lawyer to provide the services; or

(2) a tribunal with power to do so appoints the lawyer to provide the services.

§ 15.   A Lawyer's Duties to a Prospective Client

(1) When a person discusses with a lawyer the possibility of their forming a client-lawyer relationship for a matter and no such relationship ensues, the lawyer must:

(a) not subsequently use or disclose confidential information learned in the consultation, except to the extent permitted with respect to confidential information of a client or former client as stated in §§ 61–67;

(b) protect the person's property in the lawyer's custody as stated in §§ 44–46; and

(c) use reasonable care to the extent the lawyer provides the person legal services.

(2) A lawyer subject to Subsection (1) may not represent a client whose interests are materially adverse to those of a former prospective client in the same or a substantially related

matter when the lawyer or another lawyer whose disqualification is imputed to the lawyer under §§ 123 and 124 has received from the prospective client confidential information that could be significantly harmful to the prospective client in the matter, except that such a representation is permissible if:

(a)(i) any personally prohibited lawyer takes reasonable steps to avoid exposure to confidential information other than information appropriate to determine whether to represent the prospective client, and (ii) such lawyer is screened as stated in § 124(2)(b) and (c); or

(b) both the affected client and the prospective client give informed consent to the representation under the limitations and conditions provided in § 122.

Comment:

* * *

b. Rationale. Prospective clients are like clients in that they often disclose confidential information to a lawyer, place documents or other property in the lawyer's custody, and rely on the lawyer's advice. But a lawyer's discussions with a prospective client often are limited in time and depth of exploration, do not reflect full consideration of the prospective client's problems, and leave both prospective client and lawyer free (and sometimes required) to proceed no further. Hence, prospective clients should receive some but not all of the protection afforded clients, as indicated in the Section and following Comments.

c. Confidential information of a prospective client. It is often necessary for a prospective client to reveal and for the lawyer to learn confidential information (see § 59) during an initial consultation prior to their decision about formation of a client-lawyer relationship. For that reason, the attorney-client privilege attaches to communications of a prospective client (see § 70, Comment *c*). The lawyer must often learn such information to determine whether a conflict of interest exists with an existing client of the lawyer or the lawyer's firm and whether the matter is one that the lawyer is willing to undertake. In all instances, the lawyer must treat that information as confidential in the interest of the prospective client, even if the client or lawyer decides not to proceed with the representation (see Subsection (1)(a); see also § 60(2)). The duty exists regardless of how brief the initial conference may be and regardless of whether screening is instituted under Subsection (2)(a)(ii). The exceptions to the principles of confidentiality and privilege apply to such communications (see §§ 61–67).

Subsection (2) states rules parallel to those governing former-client conflicts under § 132, but it relaxes two analogous former-client rules. First, personal disqualification of a lawyer who deals with a prospective client occurs only when the subsequent matter presents the opportunity to use information obtained from the former prospective client that would be "significantly harmful." In contrast, § 132 applies whenever there is a "substantial risk" of adverse use of the former client's confidential information, regardless of the degree of threatened harm. Second, screening is permitted under Subsection (2)(a) so long as the lawyer takes reasonable steps to limit his or her exposure to confidential information during the initial consultation. In contrast, screening under § 124(2)(a) is permissible only when information obtained in the earlier representation would not likely be of significance in the subsequent representation.

In order to avoid acquiring disqualifying information, a lawyer considering whether or not to undertake a new matter may limit the initial interview to such confidential information as reasonably appears necessary for that purpose. Where that information indicates that a conflict of interest or other reasons for nonrepresentation exists, the lawyer should so inform the prospective client or simply decline the representation. If the prospective client still wishes to retain the lawyer, and if consent is possible under § 122(1), consent from any other affected present or former client should be obtained before further confidential information is elicited. The lawyer may also condition conversations with the prospective client on the person's consent to the lawyer's representation of other clients (see § 122, Comment *d*) or on the prospective client's agreement that any information disclosed during the consultation is not to be treated as confidential (see § 62). The prospective client's informed consent to such an agreement frees the lawyer to represent a client in a matter and to use in that matter, but only if the agreement so provides, confidential information received from the prospective client. A prospective client may also consent to a representation in other ways applicable to a client under § 122.

Even in the absence of such an agreement, when a consultation with a prospective client does not lead to a lawyer's retention the lawyer is not always prohibited from representing a client with interests adverse to those of the prospective client in the same or a substantially related matter. A prospective client's assurance of confidentiality through prophylactic prohibition as broad as that required in the case of a former client under § 132 must yield to a reasonable degree to the need of the legal system and to the interests of the lawyer and of other clients, including the need of a lawyer to obtain information needed to determine whether the lawyer may properly accept the representation without undue risk of prohibitions if no representation ensues. Thus, under Subsection (2), prohibition exists only when the lawyer has received from the prospective client information that could be significantly harmful to the prospective client in the matter. In such an instance and absent the prospective client's consent, the lawyer must withdraw from a substantially related representation commenced before the prospective client communicated with the lawyer and must not represent a client in such a matter in the future, including a client the lawyer ordinarily represents on a continuing basis.

When a tribunal is asked to disqualify a lawyer based on prior dealings with a former prospective client, that person bears the burden of persuading the tribunal that the lawyer received such information. The prohibition is imputed to other lawyers as provided in § 123, but may be avoided if all personally prohibited lawyers are screened as stated in § 124(2)(b) and (2)(c) (see Subsection (2)(a)). In that situation, screening avoids imputation even when the requirements of § 124(2)(a) have not been met. In deciding whether to exercise discretion to require disqualification, a tribunal may consider whether the prospective client disclosed confidential information to the lawyer for the purpose of preventing the lawyer or the lawyer's firm from representing an adverse party rather than in a good-faith endeavor to determine whether to retain the lawyer. The tribunal may also consider whether the disclosure of significantly harmful confidential information resulted from the failure of the lawyer or the prospective client to take precautions reasonable in the circumstances. In addition to screening, Subsection (2)(b) permits representation if both the former prospective client and any affected present client consent.

Illustrations:

1. Person makes an appointment with Lawyer to discuss obtaining a divorce from Person's Spouse. During the initial consultation, Lawyer makes no effort to limit the conversation or obtain any agreement on Person's part to nonconfidentiality. During the course of the one-hour discussion, Person discusses his reasons for seeking a divorce and the nature and extent of his and Spouse's property interests. Because Person considers Lawyer's suggested fee too high, Person retains other counsel. Thereafter, Spouse seeks Lawyer's assistance in defending against Person's divorce action. Lawyer may not accept the representation of Spouse. If Lawyer is screened as provided in§ 124(2)(b) and (c), Lawyer's disqualification is not imputed to other members of Lawyer's firm (see Subsection (2)(a)).

2. The President of Company A makes an appointment with Lawyer, who had not formerly had dealings with Company A. At the outset of the meeting, Lawyer informs President that it will first be necessary to obtain information about Company A and its affiliates and about the general nature of the legal matter to perform a conflicts check pursuant to procedures followed in Lawyer's firm. President supplies that information in a 15–minute meeting, including the information that the matter involves a contract dispute with Company B. The ensuing conflicts check reveals a conflict of interest with another Client of the firm (other than Company B), and Lawyer accordingly declines the representation. Lawyer and the other firm lawyers may continue representing Client (see Subsection (2)(a)).

3. Same facts as Illustration 2, except that Lawyer is later approached by Company B to represent it in its contract dispute with Company A. Both Lawyer and other firm lawyers may accept the representation unless Company A had disclosed to Lawyer confidential information that could be significantly harmful to Company A in the contract dispute. Even if such a disclosure had been made, if Lawyer is screened as provided in § 124(2)(b) and (c), Lawyer's disqualification is not imputed to other members of Lawyer's firm (see Subsection (2)(a)).

4. Same facts as Illustration 2, except that President wishes their first meeting both to discuss conflicts facts and to review Lawyer's preliminary thoughts on the merits of the contract dispute. Lawyer states willingness to do so only if Company A agrees that Lawyer would not be required to keep confidential information revealed during the preliminary discussion. President agrees, and the preliminary discussion ranges over several aspects of the dispute. Lawyer later declines the representation because of a conflict involving another firm client. Thereafter, Lawyer is approached by Company B to represent it in its contract dispute with Company A. Lawyer may accept the representation. Because of President's agreement, Lawyer is not required to keep confidential from Company B information learned during the initial consultation.

d. Protecting a prospective client's property. When prospective clients confide valuables or papers to a lawyer's care, the lawyer is under a duty to safeguard them in the same way as valuables or papers of any person that are in the lawyer's possession as the result of a professional relationship (see §§ 44–46). Ordinarily, if no client-lawyer relationship ensues, the lawyer must promptly return all material received from the prospective client.

e. A lawyer's duty of reasonable care to a prospective client. When a prospective client and a lawyer discuss the possibility of representation, the lawyer might comment on such matters as whether the person has a promising claim or defense, whether the lawyer is appropriate for the matter in question, whether conflicts of interest exist and if so how they might be dealt with, the time within which action must be taken and, if the representation does not proceed, what other lawyer might represent the prospective client. Prospective clients might rely on such advice, and lawyers therefore must use reasonable care in rendering it. The lawyer must also not harm a prospective client through unreasonable delay after indicating that the lawyer might undertake the representation. What care is reasonable depends on the circumstances, including the lawyer's expertise and the time available for consideration (see § 52).

If a lawyer provides advice that is intended to be only tentative or preliminary, the lawyer should so inform the prospective client. Depending on the circumstances, the burden of removing ambiguities rests with the lawyer, particularly as to disclaiming conclusions that the client reasonably assumed from their discussion, for example whether the client has a good claim.

f. Other duties to a prospective client. In addition to duties of confidentiality and care, the lawyer is subject to general law in dealing with a prospective client. The lawyer, for example, may not give the prospective client harmful advice calculated to benefit another client (see §§ 51(2) & 56).

g. Compensation of a lawyer for consultation with a prospective client. In the absence of circumstances indicating otherwise, prospective clients would ordinarily not expect to pay for preliminary discussions with a lawyer. When a client-lawyer relationship does not result, a lawyer is not entitled to be compensated unless that has been expressly agreed or it is otherwise clear from the circumstances that payment will be required.

TOPIC 2. SUMMARY OF THE DUTIES UNDER A CLIENT–LAWYER RELATIONSHIP

§ 16. A Lawyer's Duties to a Client—In General

To the extent consistent with the lawyer's other legal duties and subject to the other provisions of this Restatement, a lawyer must, in matters within the scope of the representation:

(1) proceed in a manner reasonably calculated to advance a client's lawful objectives, as defined by the client after consultation;

(2) act with reasonable competence and diligence;

(3) comply with obligations concerning the client's confidences and property, avoid impermissible conflicting interests, deal honestly with the client, and not employ advantages arising from the client-lawyer relationship in a manner adverse to the client; and

(4) fulfill valid contractual obligations to the client.

Comment:

* * *

b. Rationale. A lawyer is a fiduciary, that is, a person to whom another person's affairs are entrusted in circumstances that often make it difficult or undesirable for that other person to supervise closely the performance of the fiduciary. Assurances of the lawyer's competence, diligence, and loyalty are therefore vital. Lawyers often deal with matters most confidential and vital to the client. A lawyer's work is sometimes complex and technical, often is performed in the client's absence, and often cannot properly be evaluated simply by observing the results. Special safeguards are therefore necessary.

Correlatively, adequate representation is often essential to secure persons their legal rights. Persons are often unable either to know or to secure their rights without a lawyer's help. The law encourages clients to consult lawyers and limits the liability to third persons of lawyers who act vigorously for their clients (see §§ 51 & 56). Requiring lawyers to protect their clients' interests with competence, diligence, and loyalty furthers those goals.

A lawyer is not required to accept a client, to undertake representation without pay (except when a court has appointed the lawyer), or to remain in a representation when withdrawal is permissible (see §§ 14, 32, 34, & 35). By undertaking a representation, a lawyer does not guarantee success in it, unless the lawyer makes extraordinary representations or warranties or unless the matter is routine and any reasonably competent lawyer could achieve the client's objectives (for example, drafting a deed or setting up a corporation). Lawyers may have duties to others that limit those owed to a client (see Comment *c* hereto).

c. Goals of a representation. The lawyer's efforts in a representation must be for the benefit of the client (see Restatement Second, Agency § 387). A client-lawyer relationship is thus different from a partnership entered into for mutual profit; the lawyer may hope to further the lawyer's professional reputation and income through a representation, but may do so only as a by-product of promoting the client's success.

Individual clients define their objectives differently. One litigant might seek the greatest possible personal recovery, another an amicable or speedy resolution of the case, and a third a precedent implementing the client's view of the public interest. The client, not the lawyer, determines the goals to be pursued, subject to the lawyer's duty not to do or assist an unlawful act (see § 94). The lawyer must keep the client informed and consult with the client as is reasonably appropriate to learn the client's decisions (see § 20) and must follow a client's instructions (see § 21(2)). On a lawyer's decisions in the representation, see §§ 22–24.

The lawyer's duties are ordinarily limited to matters covered by the representation. A lawyer who has agreed to write a contract is not required to litigate its validity, even though the client's general objectives may ultimately be aided by resort to litigation (see §§ 14 & 19). Ordinarily the lawyer may not act beyond the scope of contemplated representation without additional authorization from the client (see § 27, Comment *e*). Nevertheless, some of the lawyer's duties survive termination of the representation (see § 33).

The lawyer's legal duties to other persons also limit duties to the client. On the rules governing conflicts of interest, see Chapter 8. A lawyer owes duties to the court or legal system and to an opposing party in litigation (see Chapters 6 & 7) and may owe duties to certain nonclients who might be injured by the lawyer's acts (see § 51). Sometimes a client's duties to other persons, for example as a trustee or class representative, may impose on the lawyer similar consequential duties (see § 14, Comment *f*). A lawyer may not do or assist an unlawful act on behalf of a client (see §§ 23, 32, & 94). Circumstances also exist in which a lawyer may refrain from pursuing the client's goals through means that the lawyer considers lawful but repugnant (see § 23, Comment *c*; § 32).

d. Duties of competence and diligence. In pursuing a client's objectives, a lawyer must use reasonable care (see § 52; see also Restatement Second, Agency § 379). The lawyer must be competent to handle the matter, having the appropriate knowledge, skills, time, and professional qualifications. The lawyer must use those capacities diligently, not letting the matter languish but proceeding to perform the services called for by the client's objectives, including appropriate factual research, legal analysis, and exercise of professional judgment. On delay in litigated matters, see § 110. The law seeks to elicit competent and diligent representation through civil liability (see Chapter 4), disciplinary sanctions (see § 5), and such other means as educational and examination requirements for admission to the bar and programs of continued legal education and peer review. Other remedies may be available, such as a new trial in a criminal prosecution because of ineffective assistance of counsel (see § 6).

The Preamble to the ABA Model Rules of Professional Conduct (1983) (see id. § [2]) and EC 7–1 of the ABA Model Code of Professional Responsibility (1969) refer to a lawyer's duty to act "zealously" for a client. The term sets forth a traditional aspiration, but it should not be misunderstood to suggest that lawyers are legally required to function with a certain emotion or style of litigating, negotiating, or counseling. For legal purposes, the term encompasses the duties of competence and diligence.

e. Duties of loyalty. The responsibilities entailed in promoting the objectives of the client may be broadly classified as duties of loyalty, but their fulfillment also requires skill in gathering and analyzing information and acting appropriately. In general, they prohibit the lawyer from harming the client. Those duties are enforceable in appropriate circumstances by remedies, such as disqualification, to enforce rules governing conflicts of interest (see § 121, Comment *f*), civil liability (see §§ 50 & 55), and professional discipline (§ 5).

A lawyer may not use or disclose sensitive information about the client, except in appropriate circumstances (see Chapter 5). Likewise, the lawyer must take reasonable measures to safeguard the client's property and papers that come into the lawyer's possession (see §§ 44–46). The rules forbidding conflicts of interest (see Chapter 8) likewise protect against the abuse of client information.

A lawyer must be honest with a client. A lawyer may not obtain unfair contracts or gifts (see §§ 126 & 127) or enter a sexual relationship with a client when that would undermine the client's case, abuse the client's dependence on the lawyer, or create risk to the lawyer's independent judgment, for example when the lawyer represents the client in divorce proceedings (see also, e.g., § 41 (abusive fee-collection methods); see generally Restatement Second, Agency §§ 387–398). A lawyer may not knowingly make false statements to a client and must make disclosures to a client necessary to avoid misleading the client. However, a lawyer's duty of confidentiality to another client may prohibit some disclosures. On the general duty voluntarily to disclose facts to a client, see § 20.

The duties of loyalty are subject to exceptions described elsewhere in this Restatement. Those exceptions typically protect the concerns of third persons and the public or satisfy the practical necessities of the legal system.

f.   Duties defined by contract. Contracts generally create or define the duties the lawyer owes the client (see Restatement Second, Agency § 376). One or more contracts between client and lawyer may specify the services the lawyer is being retained to provide, the services the lawyer is not obliged to provide, and the goals of the representation. They may address such matters as which lawyers in a law firm will provide the services; what reports are to be provided to the client; whether the lawyer will present a detailed budget for the representation; what arrangements will be made for billing statements for legal services and disbursements; what decisions will be made by the lawyer and what matters decided by the client; and what alternative-dispute-resolution methods the lawyer will explore. Such matters may also be handled by client instructions during the representation (see Topic 3). Various requirements govern client-lawyer contracts (e.g., §§ 18, 19, 22–23, 34–46, 121, & 126–127). A lawyer's intentional failure to fulfill a valid contract may in appropriate circumstances subject the lawyer to professional discipline as well as to contractual remedies.

With respect to contracts between lawyer and client involving business other than fees and disbursements for professional services, see § 126.

§ 17.   A Client's Duty to a Lawyer

Subject to the other provisions of this Restatement, in matters covered by the representation a client must:

(1) compensate a lawyer for services and expenses as stated in Chapter 3;

(2) indemnify the lawyer for liability to which the client has exposed the lawyer without the lawyer's fault; and

(3) fulfill any valid contractual obligations to the lawyer.

§ 18.   Client–Lawyer Contacts

(1) A contract between a lawyer and client concerning the client-lawyer relationship, including a contract modifying an

existing contract, may be enforced by either party if the contract meets other applicable requirements, except that:

(a) if the contract or modification is made beyond a reasonable time after the lawyer has begun to represent the client in the matter (see § 38(1)), the client may avoid it unless the lawyer shows that the contract and the circumstances of its formation were fair and reasonable to the client; and

(b) if the contract is made after the lawyer has finished providing services, the client may avoid it if the client was not informed of facts needed to evaluate the appropriateness of the lawyer's compensation or other benefits conferred on the lawyer by the contract.

(2) A tribunal should construe a contract between client and lawyer as a reasonable person in the circumstances of the client would have construed it.

§ 19. Agreements Limiting Client or Lawyer Duties

(1) Subject to other requirements stated in this Restatement, a client and lawyer may agree to limit a duty that a lawyer would otherwise owe to the client if:

(a) the client is adequately informed and consents; and

(b) the terms of the limitation are reasonable in the circumstances.

(2) A lawyer may agree to waive a client's duty to pay or other duty owed to the lawyer.

Comment:

* * *

b. Rationale. Restrictions on the power of a client to redefine a lawyer's duties are classified as paternalism by some and as necessary protection by others. On the one hand, for some clients the costs of more extensive services may outweigh their benefits. A client might reasonably choose to forgo some of the protection against conflicts of interest, for example, in order to get the help of an especially able or inexpensive lawyer or a lawyer already familiar to the client. The scope of a representation may properly change during a representation, and the lawyer may sometimes be obligated to bring changes of scope to a client's notice (see § 20). In some instances, such as an emergency, a restricted representation may be the only practical way to provide legal services (see Comments *c* and *d* hereto).

On the other hand, there are strong reasons for protecting those who entrust vital concerns and confidential information to lawyers (see § 16, Comment *b*). Clients inexperienced in such limitations may well have difficulty understanding important implications of limiting a lawyer's duty. Not every lawyer who will benefit from the limitation can be trusted to explain its costs and benefits fairly. Also, any attempt to assess the basis of a client's consent could force disclosure of the client's confidences. In the long run, moreover, a restriction could become a standard practice that constricts the rights of clients without compensating benefits. The administration of justice may suffer from distrust of the legal system that may result from such a practice. Those reasons support special scrutiny of noncustomary contracts limiting a lawyer's duties, particularly when the lawyer requests the limitation.

c. Limiting a representation. Clients and lawyers may define in reasonable ways the services a lawyer is to provide (see § 16), for example to handle a trial but not any appeal, counsel a client on the tax aspects of a transaction but not other aspects, or advise a client about a representation in which the primary role has been entrusted to another lawyer. Such arrangements are not waivers of a client's right to more extensive services but a definition of the services to be performed. They are therefore treated separately under many lawyer codes as contracts limiting the objectives of the representation. Clients ordinarily understand the implications and possible costs of such arrangements. The scope of many such representations requires no explanation or disclaimer of broader involvement.

Some contracts limiting the scope or objectives of a representation may harm the client, for example if a lawyer insists on agreement that a proposed suit will not include a substantial claim that reasonably should be joined. Section 19(1) hence qualifies the power of client and lawyer to limit the representation. Taken together with requirements stated in other Sections, five safeguards apply.

First, a client must be informed of any significant problems a limitation might entail, and the client must consent (see § 19(1)(a)). For example, if the lawyer is to provide only tax advice, the client must be aware that the transaction may pose non-tax issues as well as being informed of any disadvantages involved in dividing the representation among several lawyers (see also §§ 15 & 20).

Second, any contract limiting the representation is construed from the standpoint of a reasonable client (see § 18(2)).

Third, the fee charged by the lawyer must remain reasonable in view of the limited representation (see § 34).

Fourth, any change made an unreasonably long time after the representation begins must meet the more stringent tests of § 18(1) for postinception contracts or modifications.

Fifth, the terms of the limitation must in all events be reasonable in the circumstances (§ 19(1)(b)). When the client is sophisticated in such waivers, informed consent ordinarily permits the inference that the waiver is reasonable. For other clients, the requirement is met if, in addition to informed consent, the benefits supposedly obtained by the waiver—typically, a reduced legal fee or the ability to retain a particularly able lawyer—could reasonably be considered to outweigh the potential risk posed by the limitation. It is also relevant whether there were special circumstances warranting the limitation and whether it was the client or the lawyer who sought it. Also relevant is the choice available to clients; for example, if most local lawyers, but not lawyers in other communities, insist on the same limitation, client acceptance of the limitation is subject to special scrutiny.

The extent to which alternatives are constrained by circumstances might bear on reasonableness. For example, a client who seeks assistance on a matter on which the statute of limitations is about to run would not reasonably expect extensive investigation and research before the case must be filed. A lawyer may be asked to assist a client concerning an unfamiliar area because other counsel are unavailable. If the lawyer knows or should know that the lawyer lacks competence necessary for the representation, the lawyer must limit assistance to that which the lawyer believes reasonably necessary to deal with the situation.

Reasonableness also requires that limits on a lawyer's work agreed to by client and lawyer not infringe on legal rights of third persons or legal institutions. Hence, a contract limiting a lawyer's role during trial may require the tribunal's approval.

Illustrations:

1. Corporation wishes to hire Law Firm to litigate a substantial suit, proposing a litigation budget. Law Firm explains to Corporation's inside legal counsel that it can litigate the case within that budget but only by conducting limited discovery, which could materially lessen the likelihood of success. Corporation may waive its right to more thorough representation. Corporation will benefit by gaining representation by counsel of its choice at limited expense and could readily have bargained for more thorough and expensive representation.

2. A legal clinic offers for a small fee to have one of its lawyers (a tax specialist) conduct a half-hour review of a client's income-tax return, telling the client of the dangers or opportunities that the review reveals. The tax lawyer makes clear at the outset that the review may fail to find important tax matters and that clients can have a more complete consideration of their returns only if they arrange for a second appointment and agree to pay more. The arrangement is reasonable and permissible. The clients' consent is free and adequately informed, and clients gain the benefit of an inexpensive but expert tax review of a matter that otherwise might well receive no expert review at all.

3. Lawyer offers to provide tax-law advice for an hourly fee lower than most tax lawyers charge. Lawyer has little knowledge of tax law and asks Lawyer's occasional tax clients to agree to waive the requirement of reasonable competence. Such a waiver is invalid,

even if clients benefit to some extent from the low price and consent freely and on the basis of adequate information. Moreover, allowing such general waivers would seriously undermine competence requirements essential for protection of the public, with little compensating gain. On prohibitions against limitations of a lawyer's liability, see § 54.

* * *

TOPIC 3. AUTHORITY TO MAKE DECISIONS

§ 20. A Lawyer's Duty to Inform and Consult with a Client

(1) A lawyer must keep a client reasonably informed about the matter and must consult with a client to a reasonable extent concerning decisions to be made by the lawyer under §§ 21–23.

(2) A lawyer must promptly comply with a client's reasonable requests for information.

(3) A lawyer must notify a client of decisions to be made by the client under §§ 21–23 and must explain a matter to the extent reasonably necessary to permit the client to make informed decisions regarding the representation.

§ 21. Allocating the Authority to Decide Between a Client and a Lawyer

As between client and lawyer:

(1) A client and lawyer may agree which of them will make specified decisions, subject to the requirements stated in §§ 18, 19, 22, 23, and other provisions of this Restatement. The agreement may be superseded by another valid agreement.

(2) A client may instruct a lawyer during the representation, subject to the requirements stated in §§ 22, 23, and other provisions of this Restatement.

(3) Subject to Subsections (1) and (2) a lawyer may take any lawful measure within the scope of representation that is reasonably calculated to advance a client's objectives as defined by the client, consulting with the client as required by § 20.

(4) A client may ratify an act of a lawyer that was not previously authorized.

§ 22. Authority Reserved to a Client

(1) As between client and lawyer, subject to Subsection (2) and § 23, the following and comparable decisions are reserved to the client except when the client has validly authorized the

811

lawyer to make the particular decision: whether and on what terms to settle a claim; how a criminal defendant should plead; whether a criminal defendant should waive jury trial; whether a criminal defendant should testify; and whether to appeal in a civil proceeding or criminal prosecution.

(2) A client may not validly authorize a lawyer to make the decisions described in Subsection (1) when other law (such as criminal-procedure rules governing pleas, jury-trial waiver, and defendant testimony) requires the client's personal participation or approval.

(3) Regardless of any contrary contract with a lawyer, a client may revoke a lawyer's authority to make the decisions described in Subsection (1).

§ 23. Authority Reserved to a Lawyer

As between client and lawyer, a lawyer retains authority that may not be overridden by a contract with or an instruction from the client:

(1) to refuse to perform, counsel, or assist future or ongoing acts in the representation that the lawyer reasonably believes to be unlawful;

(2) to make decisions or take actions in the representation that the lawyer reasonably believes to be required by law or an order of a tribunal.

§ 24. A Client with Diminished Capacity

(1) When a client's capacity to make adequately considered decisions in connection with the representation is diminished, whether because of minority, physical illness, mental disability, or other cause, the lawyer must, as far as reasonably possible, maintain a normal client-lawyer relationship with the client and act in the best interests of the client as stated in Subsection (2).

(2) A lawyer representing a client with diminished capacity as described in Subsection (1) and for whom no guardian or other representative is available to act, must, with respect to a matter within the scope of the representation, pursue the lawyer's reasonable view of the client's objectives or interests as the client would define them if able to make adequately considered decisions on the matter, even if the client expresses no wishes or gives contrary instructions.

(3) If a client with diminished capacity as described in Subsection (1) has a guardian or other person legally entitled to act for the client, the client's lawyer must treat that person as entitled to act with respect to the client's interests in the matter, unless:

(a) the lawyer represents the client in a matter against the interests of that person; or

(b) that person instructs the lawyer to act in a manner that the lawyer knows will violate the person's legal duties toward the client.

(4) A lawyer representing a client with diminished capacity as described in Subsection (1) may seek the appointment of a guardian or take other protective action within the scope of the representation when doing so is practical and will advance the client's objectives or interests, determined as stated in Subsection (2).

Comment:

> * * *

b. Rationale. An unimpaired client can define the client's own objectives (see § 19), confer with counsel (see § 20), and make important decisions (see §§ 21 & 22). To the extent a client is incapable of doing so and no other person is empowered to make such decisions, the lawyer's role in making decisions will increase. An alternative is to appoint a guardian for the client, but that may be expensive, not feasible under the circumstances, and embarrassing for the client. In some cases, different views about the client's welfare may be presented by opposing counsel for a tribunal's decision. This Section recognizes that a lawyer must often exercise an informed professional judgment in choosing among those imperfect alternatives. Accordingly, each Subsection applies based on the reasonable belief of the lawyer at the time the lawyer acts on behalf of a client described in Subsection (1).

c. Maintaining a normal client-lawyer relationship so far as possible. Disabilities in making decisions vary from mild to totally incapacitating; they may impair a client's ability to decide matters generally or only with respect to some decisions at some times; and they may be caused by childhood, old age, physical illness, retardation, chemical dependency, mental illness, or other factors. Clients should not be unnecessarily deprived of their right to control their own affairs on account of such disabilities. Lawyers, moreover, should be careful not to construe as proof of disability a client's insistence on a view of the client's welfare that a lawyer considers unwise or otherwise at variance with the lawyer's own views.

When a client with diminished capacity is capable of understanding and communicating, the lawyer should maintain the flow of information and consultation as much as circumstances allow (see § 20). The lawyer should take reasonable steps to elicit the client's own views on decisions necessary to the representation. Sometimes the use of a relative, therapist, or other intermediary may facilitate communication (see §§ 70 & 71). Even when the lawyer is empowered to make decisions for the client (see Comment *d*), the lawyer should, if practical, communicate the proposed decision to the client so that the client will have a chance to comment, remonstrate, or seek help elsewhere. A lawyer may properly withhold from a disabled client information that would harm the client, for example when showing a psychiatric report to a mentally-ill client would be likely to cause the client to attempt suicide, harm another person, or otherwise act unlawfully (see § 20, Comment *b*, & § 46, Comment *c*).

A lawyer for a client with diminished capacity may be retained by a parent, spouse, or other relative of the client. Even when that person is not also a co-client, the lawyer may provide confidential client information to the person to the extent appropriate in providing representation to the client (see § 61). If the disclosure is to be made to a nonclient and there is a significant risk that the information may be used adversely to the client, the lawyer should consult with the client concerning such disclosure.

A client with diminished capacity is entitled to make decisions normally made by clients to the extent that the client is able to do so. The lawyer should adhere, to the extent reasonably possible, to the lawyer's usual function as advocate and agent of the client, not judge or guardian, unless the lawyer's role in the situation is modified by other law. The lawyer should, for example, help the client oppose confinement as a juvenile delinquent even though the lawyer believes that confinement would be in the long-term interests of the client and has unsuccessfully urged the client to accept confinement. Advancing the latter position should be left to opposing counsel.

If a client with diminished capacity owes fiduciary duties to others, the lawyer should be careful to avoid assisting in a violation of those duties (cf. § 51(4)).

d. Deciding for a client with diminished capacity. When a client's disability prevents maintaining a normal client-lawyer relationship and there is no guardian or other legal representative to make decisions for the client, the lawyer may be justified in making decisions with respect to questions within the scope of the representation that would normally be made by the client. A lawyer should act only on a reasonable belief, based on appropriate investigation, that the client is unable to make an adequately considered decision rather than simply being confused or misguided. Because a disability might vary from time to time, the lawyer must reasonably believe that the client is unable to make an adequately considered decision without prejudicial delay.

A lawyer's reasonable belief depends on the circumstances known to the lawyer and discoverable by reasonable investigation. Where practicable and reasonably available, independent professional evaluation of the client's capacity may be sought. If a conflict of interest between client and lawyer is involved (see § 125), disinterested evaluation by another lawyer may be appropriate. Careful consideration is required of the client's circumstances, problems, needs, character, and values, including interests of the client beyond the matter in which the lawyer represents the client. If the client, when able to decide, had expressed views relevant to the decision, the lawyer should follow them unless there is reason to believe that changed circumstances would change those views. The lawyer should also give appropriate weight to the client's presently expressed views.

A lawyer may bring the client's diminished capacity before a tribunal when doing so is reasonably calculated to advance the client's objectives or interests as the client would define them if able to do so rationally. A proceeding seeking appointment of a guardian for the client is one example (see Comment *e*). A lawyer may also raise the issue of the client's incompetence to stand trial in a criminal prosecution or, when a client is incompetent to stand trial, interpose the insanity defense. In such situations, the court and the adversary process provide some check on the lawyer's decision.

In some jurisdictions, if a criminal defendant's competence to stand trial is reasonably arguable, the defendant's lawyer must bring the issue to the court's attention, whether or not the lawyer reasonably believes this to be for the client's benefit. That should not be considered a duty to the client flowing from the representation and is not provided for by this Section.

A lawyer must also make necessary decisions for an incompetent client when it is impractical or undesirable to have a guardian appointed or to take other similar protective measures. For example, when a court appoints a lawyer to represent a young child, it may consider the lawyer to be in effect the child's guardian ad litem. When a client already has a guardian but retains counsel to proceed against that guardian, a court often will not appoint a second guardian to make litigation decisions for the client. Other situations exist in which appointment of a guardian would be too expensive, traumatic, or otherwise undesirable or impractical in the circumstances.

It is often difficult to decide whether the conditions of this Section have been met. A lawyer who acts reasonably and in good faith in perplexing circumstances is not subject to professional discipline or malpractice or similar liability (see Chapter 4). In some situations (for example, when a lawyer discloses a client's diminished capacity to a tribunal against a client's wishes), the lawyer might be required to attempt to withdraw as counsel if the disclosure causes the client effectively to discharge the lawyer (see § 32(2)(c)).

e. Seeking appointment of a guardian. When a client's diminished capacity is severe and no other practical method of protecting the client's best interests is available, a lawyer may petition an appointment of a guardian or other representative to make decisions for the client. A general or limited power of attorney may sometimes be used to avoid the expense and possible embarrassment of a guardianship.

The client might instruct the lawyer to seek appointment of a guardian or take other protective measures. On the use of confidential client information in a guardianship proceeding, see § 61 and § 69, Comment *f*.

A lawyer is not required to seek a guardian for a client whenever the conditions of Subsection (4) are satisfied. For example, it may be clear that the courts will not appoint a guardian or that doing so is not in the client's best interests (see § 16 & Comment *d* hereto).

f.   Representing a client for whom a guardian or similar person may act. When a guardian has been appointed, the guardian normally speaks for the client as to matters covered by the guardianship. (When under the law of the jurisdiction a client's power of attorney remains in effect during a disability, the appointee has such authority.) The lawyer therefore should normally follow the decisions of the guardian as if they were those of the client. That principle does not apply when the lawyer is representing the client in proceedings against the guardian, for example, in an attempt to have the guardianship terminated or its terms altered. The law sometimes authorizes the client to bypass a guardian— for example, when a mature minor seeks a court order authorizing her to have an abortion without having to disclose her pregnancy to her parents or guardians. The lawyer may also believe that the guardian is violating fiduciary duties owed to the client and may then seek relief setting aside the guardian's decision or replacing the guardian (see also § 51(4)). If the lawyer believes the guardian to be acting lawfully but inconsistently with the best interests of the client, the lawyer may remonstrate with the guardian or withdraw under § 32(3)(d) (see § 23, Comment *c*).

When a guardian retains a lawyer to represent the guardian, the guardian is the client.

TOPIC 4.   A LAWYER'S AUTHORITY TO ACT FOR A CLIENT

§ 25.   Appearance Before a Tribunal

A lawyer who enters an appearance before a tribunal on behalf of a person is presumed to represent that person as a client. The presumption may be rebutted.

§ 26.   A Lawyer's Actual Authority

A lawyer's act is considered to be that of a client in proceedings before a tribunal or in dealings with third persons when:

> **(1) the client has expressly or impliedly authorized the act;**

> **(2) authority concerning the act is reserved to the lawyer as stated in § 23; or**

> **(3) the client ratifies the act.**

Comment:

a.   Scope, cross-references, and terminology. In general, a client is bound by a lawyer's acts in dealings with third persons discussed in this

Section or, under § 27, by giving the lawyer an appearance of authority. For situations in which a client may avoid responsibility for authorized acts because of a lawyer's misconduct, see § 29. The word "act" includes failures to act, for example when a lawyer does not object to something done in court.

Although the forms of client approval set forth in this Section might be described as instances of actual authority, agency law has often used finer distinctions. Specific authorization, for example to sell an automobile to a stated person for a stated price, is sometimes called express authority, as opposed to implied authority arising out of a more general delegation of power to act (see Restatement Second, Agency § 7, Comment c). An authorization required by law, regardless of the wishes of the principal, is sometimes called inherent authority (see Restatement Second Agency, § 8A); the authority of a lawyer stated in § 26(2) may be so classified. A principal's approval following an agent's act, as provided in § 26(3), is referred to in agency law as ratification (see Restatement Second, Agency § 82). Those terminological matters and other aspects of the authority of an agent are set forth in Restatement Second, Agency, Chapters 1, 3, and 4.

On waiver of the attorney-client privilege by a client who disclaims a lawyer's authority, see § 80(1)(b).

b. *Rationale*. Legal representation saves the client's time and effort and enables legal work to be delegated to an expert. Lawyers therefore are recognized as agents for their clients in litigation and other legal matters. Indeed, courts commonly will not allow a corporation to participate in litigation through an agent other than a lawyer.

Allowing clients to act through lawyers also subjects clients to obligations and disabilities. With respect to the rights of a third person, the client is bound when a case is lost or a negotiation handled disadvantageously by a lawyer. Attributing the acts of lawyers to their clients is warranted by the fact that, in an important sense, they really are acts authorized by the principal. Much serious activity in business and personal affairs is done through lawyers. The same considerations apply, with qualifications, in holding the client liable for certain wrongs committed by the lawyer (see Comment d hereto).

Binding clients to the acts of their lawyers can be unfair in some circumstances. A client might have authorized a lawyer's conduct only in general terms, without contemplating the particular acts that lead to liability. However, it has been regarded as more appropriate for costs flowing from a lawyer's misconduct generally to be borne by the client rather than by an innocent third person. Where the lawyer rather than the client is directly to blame, the client may be able to recover any losses by suing the lawyer, a right not generally accorded to nonclients (see Chapter 4). In practice, however, clients are sometimes unable to control their lawyer's conduct and accordingly may sometimes be excused from the consequences of their lawyer's behavior when that can be done without seriously harming others (see § 29).

c.   Forms of client authorization. A client has authorized the act within the meaning of this Section in the circumstances described in §§ 21 and 23. A person dealing with the lawyer might require the lawyer to provide express authority from the lawyer's client. Courts likewise may require such authority, for example ordering a lawyer attending a pretrial conference either to secure settlement authority or to bring the client to the conference.

d.   Effects of attributing authorized acts to a client. When a lawyer's act is attributed to a client various legal consequences might follow for the client. If the act consisted of assenting to a contract, the client is bound by the contract (see Restatement Second, Agency, Chapter 6). If the lawyer was authorized to bring or defend a lawsuit, the client is bound by the result. Likewise, the client is bound by authorized lawyer action or inaction during litigation, for example when the lawyer asks a question that elicits an answer harmful to the client or files a frivolous motion.

When a lawyer's act is wrongful and causes injury to a third person, the client as principal is liable as provided by agency law (see Restatement Second, Agency, Chapter 7; see also § 27, Comment *e*).

Illustrations:

1.   Seller authorizes Lawyer to negotiate the sale of Seller's factory to Buyer. Lawyer states to Buyer that the factory's foundations are in good condition, knowing that they are not. Because making representations about the factory was within the scope of authority for one authorized to negotiate, Seller is liable to Buyer for misrepresentation and can be required to rescind the sale if the other conditions for rescission have been satisfied. That is so even if Seller did not know about Lawyer's statements or the condition of the foundations (see Restatement Second, Agency §§ 257–259).

2.   Same facts as in Illustration 1, except that Lawyer negligently collides with Buyer's automobile while arriving for a negotiating session. Client is not liable to Buyer, unless Lawyer was Seller's employee (for example, because Seller is a corporation and Lawyer is its inside legal counsel) (see Restatement Second, Agency §§ 250 & 251).

A lawyer's conduct may be attributed to a client to determine the client's criminal responsibility. Attribution depends on the criminal law. A client who asks a lawyer to perform a criminal act or assists in its performance is guilty of the lawyer's act as an accomplice (see Model Penal Code § 2.06). A client would be liable as a co-conspirator for crimes committed by a lawyer in pursuit of a criminal conspiracy in which both were engaged. In general, however, criminal liability for another's act is significantly more limited than civil liability.

This Section deals only with the effect of a lawyer's authorized acts on the client, not with their effects on the lawyer. Whether the lawyer can be held liable for contract breaches, torts, and sanctionable litigation behavior is considered in § 30.

e. Ratification by a client. A client may later ratify a lawyer's act for which the lawyer lacked actual authority when it occurred. A client who has ratified a lawyer's act is bound by it. For more detailed consideration, see § 21, Comment *f*, and Restatement Second, Agency, Chapter 4.

§ 27. A Lawyer's Apparent Authority

A lawyer's act is considered to be that of the client in proceedings before a tribunal or in dealings with a third person if the tribunal or third person reasonably assumes that the lawyer is authorized to do the act on the basis of the client's (and not the lawyer's) manifestations of such authorization.

Comment:

a. Scope and cross-references. This Section addresses apparent authority. The concept is employed in this Restatement as defined in Restatement Second, Agency § 8. Because lawyers ordinarily have broad actual authority (see §§ 21 & 23), simply retaining a lawyer confers broad apparent authority on the lawyer unless other facts apparent to the third person show that the lawyer's authority is narrower (see Comment *c*). Such authority arising from the act of retention alone does not extend to matters, such as approving a settlement, reserved for client decision (see § 22). To create apparent authority in such matters, the client must do more than simply retain the lawyer (see Comment *d*). For the effect of a lawyer's discharge or withdrawal on apparent authority, see § 31(3) and Comments *c* and *i* thereto.

b. Rationale. Under the law of agency, a client is bound by the lawyer's act or failure to act when the client has vested the lawyer with apparent authority—an appearance of authority arising from and in accordance with the client's manifestations to third persons (see Restatement Second, Agency § 8). Apparent authority can be identical to, greater, or less than a lawyer's actual authority (see id. Comment *a*). The concepts of actual and apparent authority often lead to similar results. The same acts or statements of a client that confer actual authority can serve to manifest authority to a third person and vice versa. Apparent authority extends beyond actual authority in a lawyer's transactions with third persons when the client has limited the lawyer's actual authority but the limitation has not been disclosed to that person and, instead, the client has manifested to the third person that the lawyer has authority to act in the matter.

Apparent authority exists when and to the extent a client causes a third person to form a reasonable belief that a lawyer is authorized to act for the client. Permitting disavowal would allow clients at their convenience to ratify or disavow their lawyer's acts despite the client's inconsistent manifestation of the lawyer's authority. It would also impose on the third person the burden of proving a fact better known to the client. A client usually can make clear to third persons the limited scope of a lawyer's authority or take care to act in ways that do not manifest authority that the client does not intend.

Recognizing a lawyer as agent creates a risk that a client will be bound by an act the client never intended to authorize. Several safeguards are therefore included in the apparent-authority principle. First, the client must in fact have retained the lawyer or given the third party reason to believe that the client has done so. Second, the client's own acts (including the act of retaining the lawyer) must have warranted a reasonable observer in believing that the client authorized the lawyer to act. Third, the third person must in fact have such a belief. The test thus includes both an objective and a subjective element (see Restatement Second, Agency § 27). In some circumstances courts will take into account the lawyer's lack of actual authority in deciding whether to vacate a default (see § 29). If the client suffers detriment from a lawyer's act performed with apparent but not actual authority, the client can recover from the lawyer for acting beyond the scope of the lawyer's authority (see Comment *f* hereto & § 30; Restatement Second, Agency § 383).

c. Apparent authority created by retention of a lawyer. By retaining a lawyer, a client implies that the lawyer is authorized to act for the client in matters relating to the representation and reasonably appropriate in the circumstances to carry it out. Circumstances known to the third person can narrow the scope of apparent authority thus conferred, for example statements by the client or lawyer that the lawyer is to handle only specified matters (see § 21(2) & Comment *d* thereto). The client can also enlarge the lawyer's apparent authority, for example by acquiescing, to the outsider's knowledge, in the lawyer's taking certain action. In the absence of such variations, a lawyer has apparent authority to do acts that reasonably appear to be calculated to advance the client's objectives in the representation, except for matters reserved to the client under § 22. (For apparent authority with respect to matters reserved to the client, see Comment *d* hereto.)

When a lawyer's apparent authority is in question, what reasonably appears calculated to advance the client's objectives must be determined from the third person's viewpoint. The third person's belief in the lawyer's authority must be reasonable. The same standard applies in a proceeding before a tribunal. However, because of the lawyer's broad actual authority in litigation (see §§ 21 & 23), it will often be unnecessary to conduct a factual inquiry into whether a lawyer had apparent authority in the eyes of either the opposing party or the tribunal.

Illustrations:

1. At Judge's suggestion, Lawyer agrees that both parties to a civil action will waive further discovery and that the trial will begin

the next week. Judge does not know, but opposing counsel does, that Lawyer's Client (which has many similar cases) instructs its lawyers in writing not to bring cases to trial without specified discovery, some of which Lawyer has not yet accomplished. Although Lawyer lacked actual authority to waive discovery, Lawyer had apparent authority from Judge's reasonable point of view, and Judge may hold Client to the trial date. Client's remedies are to seek discretionary release from the waiver (see § 29) and to seek to recover any damages from Lawyer for acting beyond authority (see Comment f hereto & § 30).

2. At a pretrial conference in a medical-malpractice case, Lawyer agrees with opposing counsel that neither party will call more than one expert witness at the trial. Opposing counsel is not aware that Lawyer's client (which has many similar cases) instructs its lawyers to present expert testimony from at least two witnesses in every medical-malpractice case involving more than a certain amount in claimed damages. Judge knows of the client's practice but does not inform opposing counsel. The opposing party can hold Lawyer's client to the contract, which Lawyer had apparent authority to make, unless the court releases the parties from the contract (see § 29).

d. *Lawyer's apparent authority to settle and perform other acts reserved to a client.* Generally a client is not bound by a settlement that the client has not authorized a lawyer to make by express, implied, or apparent authority (and that is not validated by later ratification under § 26(3)). Merely retaining a lawyer does not create apparent authority in the lawyer to perform acts governed by § 22. When a lawyer purports to enter a settlement binding on the client but lacks authority to do so, the burden of inconvenience resulting if the client repudiates the settlement is properly left with the opposing party, who should know that settlements are normally subject to approval by the client and who has no manifested contrary indication from the client. The opposing party can protect itself by obtaining clarification of the lawyer's authority. Refusing to uphold a settlement reached without the client's authority means that the case remains open, while upholding such a settlement deprives the client of the right to have the claim resolved on other terms.

Illustrations:

3. Lawyer represents Client in a civil action in which the court orders counsel either to appear at a pretrial conference with authority to settle the case or to arrange for the presence of a person so authorized. Client has not been informed of the order and has not authorized Lawyer to approve a settlement. Lawyer, without disclosing that lack of authority, attends the conference and agrees to a settlement. Client is not bound by the settlement. Lawyer can be

subject to disciplinary sanctions, including contempt of court, and liability for damages or sanctions to the opposing party.

4. The same facts as in Illustration 3, except that the opposing party observes that Client is in the courtroom and hears the court's order but leaves as the settlement conference begins without further comment to the court or opposing party. Client's acts create apparent authority in Lawyer to enter the settlement on Client's behalf, and Client is bound by the settlement agreed to by Lawyer.

e. Effects of attributing to clients acts performed with apparent authority. A client is liable in tort to a third person when apparent authority manifested by the client aids a lawyer to perform a tortious act injurious to the third person. A client is liable, for example, for misrepresentations and defamatory statements made by a lawyer with apparent authority to make the statements in representing the client (see Restatement Second, Agency § 265, compare § 57(1) (immunity for defamatory statements in the course of litigation)). The lawyer of the client is not considered an employee (servant) of the client unless employed full-or part-time as such an employee (see generally Restatement Second, Agency § 2(2)). The client is therefore not liable for tortious acts committed while the lawyer is acting within the scope of employment but outside the lawyer's actual or apparent authority (see § 26, Comment *d*).

The concept of apparent authority is of little utility in assessing criminal liability of the client. A client who manifested to third persons the lawyer's authority to act for the client might be convicted as an accessory, but only if the client knowingly advanced the criminal enterprise. Similar requirements apply for a client to be convicted as a co-conspirator in crimes committed by a lawyer (see § 26, Comment *d*).

f. Recovery against a lawyer. When a client is bound by an act of a lawyer with apparent but not actual authority, a lawyer is subject to liability to the client for any resulting damages to the client, unless the lawyer reasonably believed that the act was authorized by the client (see Restatement Second, Agency § 383, §§ 16, 21, & 22 hereto). The lawyer can also be subject to professional discipline (see § 5) or procedural sanctions (see § 110) for harming the interests of a client through action taken without the client's consent.

If a lawyer's act does not bind the client, the lawyer can be subject to liability to a third person who dealt with the lawyer in good faith. Liability can be based on implied warranty of actual authority or on misrepresentation of the lawyer's authority (see § 30; Restatement Second, Agency §§ 329 & 330). The lawyer is also subject to liability for damages to the client, for example the client's expenses of having the act declared not to be binding (see § 53, Comment *f* (client's recovery of legal fees in such an instance)).

§ 28. A Lawyer's Knowledge; Notification to a Lawyer; and Statements of a Lawyer

(1) Information imparted to a lawyer during and relating to the representation of a client is attributed to the client for the purpose of determining the client's rights and liabilities in matters in which the lawyer represents the client, unless those rights or liabilities require proof of the client's personal knowledge or intentions or the lawyer's legal duties preclude disclosure of the information to the client.

(2) Unless applicable law otherwise provides, a third person may give notification to a client, in a matter in which the client is represented by a lawyer, by giving notification to the client's lawyer, unless the third person knows of circumstances reasonably indicating that the lawyer's authority to receive notification has been abrogated.

(3) A lawyer's unprivileged statement is admissible in evidence against a client as if it were the client's statement if either:

(a) the client authorized the lawyer to make a statement concerning the subject; or

(b) the statement concerns a matter within the scope of the representation and was made by the lawyer during it.

§ 29. A Lawyer's Act or Advice as Mitigating or Avoiding a Client's Responsibility

(1) When a client's intent or mental state is in issue, a tribunal may consider otherwise admissible evidence of a lawyer's advice to the client.

(2) In deciding whether to impose a sanction on a person or to relieve a person from a criminal or civil ruling, default, or judgment, a tribunal may consider otherwise admissible evidence to prove or disprove that the lawyer who represented the person did so inadequately or contrary to the client's instructions.

§ 30 A Lawyer's Liability to a Third Person for Conduct on Behalf of a Client

(1) For improper conduct while representing a client, a lawyer is subject to professional discipline as stated in § 5, to civil liability as stated in Chapter 4, and to prosecution as provided in the criminal law (see § 7).

(2) Unless at the time of contracting the lawyer or third person disclaimed such liability, a lawyer is subject to liability to third persons on contracts the lawyer entered into on behalf of a client if:

(a) the client's existence or identity was not disclosed to the third person; or

(b) the contract is between the lawyer and a third person who provides goods or services used by lawyers and who, as the lawyer knows or reasonably should know, relies on the lawyer's credit.

(3) A lawyer is subject to liability to a third person for damages for loss proximately caused by the lawyer's acting without authority from a client under § 26 if:

(a) the lawyer tortiously misrepresents to the third person that the lawyer has authority to make a contract, conveyance, or affirmation on behalf of the client and the third person reasonably relies on the misrepresentation; or

(b) the lawyer purports to make a contract, conveyance, or affirmation on behalf of the client, unless the lawyer manifests that the lawyer does not warrant that the lawyer is authorized to act or the other party knows that the lawyer is not authorized to act.

TOPIC 5. ENDING A CLIENT–LAWYER RELATIONSHIP

§ 31. Termination of Lawyer's Authority

(1) A lawyer must comply with applicable law requiring notice to or permission of a tribunal when terminating a representation and with an order of a tribunal requiring the representation to continue.

(2) Subject to Subsection (1) and § 33, a lawyer's actual authority to represent a client ends when:

(a) the client discharges the lawyer;

(b) the client dies or, in the case of a corporation or similar organization, loses its capacity to function as such;

(c) the lawyer withdraws;

(d) the lawyer dies or becomes physically or mentally incapable of providing representation, is disbarred or suspended from practicing law, or is ordered by a tribunal to cease representing a client; or

(e) the representation ends as provided by contract or because the lawyer has completed the contemplated services.

(3) A lawyer's apparent authority to act for a client with respect to another person ends when the other person knows or should know of facts from which it can be reasonably inferred that the lawyer lacks actual authority, including knowledge of any event described in Subsection (2).

§ 32 **Discharge by a Client and Withdrawal by a Lawyer**

(1) Subject to Subsection (5), a client may discharge a lawyer at any time

(2) Subject to Subsection (5), a lawyer may not represent a client or, where representation has commenced, must withdraw from the representation of a client if:

(a) the representation will result in the lawyer's violating rules of professional conduct or other law;

(b) the lawyer's physical or mental condition materially impairs the lawyer's ability to represent the client; or

(c) the client discharges the lawyer.

(3) Subject to Subsections (4) and (5), a lawyer may withdraw from representing a client if:

(a) withdrawal can be accomplished without material adverse effect on the interests of the client;

(b) the lawyer reasonably believes withdrawal is required in circumstances stated in Subsection (2);

(c) the client gives informed consent;

(d) the client persists in a course of action involving the lawyer's services that the lawyer reasonably believes is criminal, fraudulent, or in breach of the client's fiduciary duty;

(e) the lawyer reasonably believes the client has used or threatens to use the lawyer's services to perpetrate a crime or fraud;

(f) the client insists on taking action that the lawyer considers repugnant or imprudent;

(g) the client fails to fulfill a substantial financial or other obligation to the lawyer regarding the lawyer's services and the lawyer has given the client reasonable warning that the lawyer will withdraw unless the client fulfills the obligation;

(h) the representation has been rendered unreasonably difficult by the client or by the irreparable breakdown of the client-lawyer relationship; or

(i) other good cause for withdrawal exists.

(4) In the case of permissive withdrawal under Subsections (3)(f)-(i), a lawyer may not withdraw if the harm that withdrawal would cause significantly exceeds the harm to the lawyer or others in not withdrawing.

(5) Notwithstanding Subsections (1)-(4), a lawyer must comply with applicable law requiring notice to or permission of a

tribunal when terminating a representation and with a valid order of a tribunal requiring the representation to continue.

§ 33. A Lawyer's Duties When Representation Terminates

(1) In terminating a representation, a lawyer must take steps to the extent reasonably practicable to protect the client's interests, such as giving notice to the client of the termination, allowing time for employment of other counsel, surrendering papers and property to which the client is entitled, and refunding any advance payment of fee the lawyer has not earned.

(2) Following termination of a representation, a lawyer must:

(a) observe obligations to a former client such as those dealing with client confidences (see Chapter 5), conflicts of interest (see Chapter 8), client property and documents (see §§ 44–46), and fee collection (see § 41);

(b) take no action on behalf of a former client without new authorization and give reasonable notice, to those who might otherwise be misled, that the lawyer lacks authority to act for the client;

(c) take reasonable steps to convey to the former client any material communication the lawyer receives relating to the matter involved in the representation; and

(d) take no unfair advantage of a former client by abusing knowledge or trust acquired by means of the representation.

Comment:

a. Scope and cross-references. This Section describes the duties of a lawyer during (see § 33(1)) and after (see § 33(2)) the termination of a client-lawyer relationship. The Section applies regardless of whether client or lawyer initiates the termination or whether termination occurs prematurely or when contemplated. Grounds for termination are set forth in §§ 31 and 32. Former clients owe the duty discussed in Chapter 3 to compensate for services rendered.

b. Protecting a client's interests when a representation ends. Ending a representation before a lawyer has completed a matter usually poses special problems for a client. Beyond consultation required before withdrawal (see § 32, Comment *n*), in the process of withdrawal itself a lawyer might be required to consult with the client and engage in other protective measures. New counsel must be found, papers and property retrieved or transferred, imminent deadlines extended, and tribunals and opposing parties notified to deal with new counsel. Lawyers must therefore take reasonably appropriate and practicable measures to protect clients when representation terminates.

What efforts are appropriate and practicable depends on the circumstances, including the subsisting relationship between client and lawyer. The lawyer must ordinarily advise the client of the implications of termination, assist in finding a new lawyer, and devote reasonable efforts to transferring responsibility for the matter. The lawyer must make the client's property and papers available to the client or the client's new lawyer, except to the extent that the lawyer is entitled to retain them. If the client is threatened with an imminent deadline that will expire before new counsel can act, the lawyer must take reasonable steps either to extend the deadline or comply with it (see § 31, Comment *e*). Failure to take such steps can give rise to disciplinary sanctions and malpractice liability. In some situations, the lawyer will be considered still to be the client's representative. Fewer measures usually are required when other lawyers representing the client in the same matter continue to do so (see § 32, Comment *h*(*ii*)).

c. Client confidences. A lawyer's obligation to protect the confidences of a client, addressed in detail in Chapter 5, continues after the representation ends.

d. Former-client conflicts of interest. Following termination, the former-client conflict-of-interest rules apply (see § 132). On consent, see Comment *i* hereto and § 122. On a former government lawyer, see § 133.

e. A former client's property and documents. The duties of a lawyer to protect and deliver a client's property and documents (see §§ 44–46) continue after the representation ends. Termination entails special duties to deliver to the client property (see § 45, Comment *b*) and documents or copies (see § 46(2)). The lawyer may not keep the client's property or documents in order to secure payment of compensation, except when the lawyer has a valid lien (see § 43) or when the client has not paid for the lawyer's work product (see § 46(3)).

f. Collecting compensation and returning unearned fees. The lawyer's efforts to collect compensation are governed by the requirements stated in Chapter 3.

g. The duty not to act for a former client. When representation ends a lawyer loses actual authority to act on behalf of the client (see § 31). Purporting to do so subjects the lawyer to discipline and can make the lawyer liable to the former client (see § 27, Comment *f*, & Chapter 4; Restatement Second, Agency § 386) or to third persons who have relied on the lawyer's claimed authority (see § 30(4) & Comment *e* thereto). However the lawyer retains authority to take steps protecting the client's interests (see Comment *b* hereto). The former client can also authorize the lawyer to act, for example by asking the lawyer to convey a request for additional time to opposing counsel.

h. Conveying communications to a former client. After termination a lawyer might receive a notice, letter, or other communication intended for a former client. The lawyer must use reasonable efforts to forward the communication. The lawyer ordinarily must also inform the source of the communication that the lawyer no longer represents the former client (see Comment *g* hereto). The lawyer must likewise notify a former client if a third person seeks to obtain material relating to the representation that is still in the lawyer's custody.

A lawyer has no general continuing obligation to pass on to a former client information relating to the former representation. The lawyer might, however, have such an obligation if the lawyer continues to represent the client in other matters or under a continuing relationship. Whether such an obligation exists regarding particular information depends on such factors as the client's reasonable expectations; the scope, magnitude, and duration of the client-lawyer relationship; the evident significance of the information to the client; the burden on the lawyer in making disclosure; and the likelihood that the client will receive the information from another source.

i. The duty not to take unfair advantage of a former client. A lawyer may not take unfair advantage of a former client by abusing knowledge or trust acquired through the representation (see §§ 41 & 43; Restatement Second, Agency § 396(d)). For example, a lawyer seeking a former client's consent to a conflict of interest (see § 132) must make adequate disclosure of facts that the former client should know in order to consider whether to consent (see § 122, Comment *c(i)*).

CHAPTER 3: CLIENT AND LAWYER: THE FINANCIAL AND PROPERTY RELATIONSHIP

TOPIC 1. LEGAL CONTROLS ON ATTORNEY FEES

§ 34. Reasonable and Lawful Fees

A lawyer may not charge a fee larger than is reasonable in the circumstances or that is prohibited by law.

Comment:

a. Scope and cross-references. This Section forbids unlawful fees and unreasonably large fees, while leaving clients and lawyers free to negotiate a broad range of compensation terms. It does not forbid lawyers to serve for low fees or without charge; such service is often in the public interest (see § 38, Comment *c*). Nor does the Section render unenforceable all fee arrangements that might be considered objectionable by some persons, for example, a lawyer's insistence that a needy client pay for the lawyer's services at the lawyer's usual rates. The prohibition on unreasonable payment arrangements is not limited to fees in a narrow sense. It applies also to excessive disbursement or interest charges or improper security interests (see § 43).

The Section applies in two different contexts. First, in fee disputes between lawyer and client, a fee will not be approved to the extent that it violates this Section even though the parties had agreed to the fee. This Section thus applies in proceedings such as suits by lawyers for fees, suits by clients to recover fees already paid, and fee-arbitration proceedings (see § 42). If the parties have not agreed (whether before, during, or after the representation; see § 18) to the basis or amount of the fee, the tribunal will set a fee compensating the lawyer for the fair value of services rendered (see § 39). The fair-value fee will usually be at the lower range of reasonable fees and thus less than a fee for the same services that would be upheld as reasonable if the parties had agreed upon it.

Second, this Section applies when courts or other disciplinary authorities seek to discipline a lawyer for charging unreasonably high fees (see Comment f hereto & § 5). In many jurisdictions, authorities have been reluctant to discipline lawyers on such grounds. For a variety of reasons, discipline might be withheld for charging a fee that would nevertheless be set aside as unreasonable in a fee-dispute proceeding. It is therefore important to distinguish between applying this Section in fee disputes (see Comments b through e hereto) and applying it in disciplinary proceedings (see Comment f hereto).

A contract otherwise in compliance with this Section will nevertheless be unenforceable if it violates other restrictions (see §§ 35, 36, & 47), or if the lawyer's misconduct leads to forfeiture of the contractual fee (see §§ 37, 40, & 41). On the lawyer's duty to inform a client of the basis or rate of the fee, see § 38(1).

b. *Rationale.* In general, clients and lawyers are free to contract for the fee that client is to pay (see §§ 18 & 38). Many client-lawyer fee arrangements operate entirely without official scrutiny. A client-lawyer fee arrangement will be set aside when its provisions are unreasonable as to the client (compare Restatement Second, Contracts § 208 (unconscionable contracts)). Courts are concerned to protect clients, particularly those who are unsophisticated in matters of lawyers' compensation, when a lawyer has overreached. Information about fees for legal services is often difficult for prospective clients to obtain. Many clients do not bargain effectively because of their need and inexperience. The services required are often unclear beforehand and difficult to monitor as a lawyer provides them. Lawyers usually encourage their clients to trust them. Lawyers, therefore, owe their clients greater duties than are owed under the general law of contracts.

Moreover, the availability of legal services is often essential if people of limited means are to enjoy legal rights. Those seeking to vindicate their rights through the private bar should not be deterred by the risk of unwarranted fee burdens.

c. *Unenforceable fee contracts.* This Section is typically applied in cases where a client and lawyer agreed on a fee before the lawyer's service began, and the client later challenges that fee. If a fee contract was reached after the lawyer began to serve, it will be enforceable only if it satisfies the standards of § 18. If a tribunal agrees that the fee satisfies those standards, the fee will fall within the range of reasonableness allowed by this Section. If the contract was reached after the services were complete, its validity depends primarily on the circumstances in which the contract was reached (see § 18(1)(b)). In the absence of a fee contract, the tribunal will apply § 39 (see Comment *a* hereto). When a court awards to a prevailing litigant attorney fees payable by an opposing party or out of a common fund, different standards might be used for determining the amount of the fee.

The lawyer codes state factors bearing on the reasonableness of fee arrangements. ABA Model Rules of Professional Conduct, Rule 1.5(a) (1983), and ABA Model Code of Professional Responsibility, DR 2–106(B) (1969), enumerate the following factors: "(1) the time and labor required, the novelty and difficulty of the questions involved, and the skill requisite to perform the legal service properly; (2) the likelihood, if apparent to the client, that the acceptance of the particular employment will preclude other employment by the lawyer; (3) the fee customarily charged in the locality for similar legal services; (4) the amount involved and the results obtained; (5) the time limitations imposed by the client or by the circumstances; (6) the nature and length of the professional relationship with the client; (7) the experience, reputation, and ability of the lawyer or lawyers performing the services; and (8) whether the fee is fixed or contingent." Other factors might also be relevant, such as the client's sophistication, the disclosures made to the client, and the client's ability to pay.

Those factors might be viewed as responding to three questions. First, when the contract was made, did the lawyer afford the client a free and informed choice? Relevant circumstances include whether the client was sophisticated in entering into such arrangements, whether the client was a fiduciary whose beneficiary deserves special protection, whether the client had a reasonable opportunity to seek another lawyer, whether the lawyer adequately explained the probable cost and other implications of the proposed fee contract (see § 38), whether the client understood the alternatives available from this lawyer and others, and whether the lawyer explained the benefits and drawbacks of the proposed legal services without misleading intimations. Fees agreed to by clients sophisticated in entering into such arrangements (such as a fee contract made by inside legal counsel in behalf of a corporation) should almost invariably be found reasonable.

Second, does the contract provide for a fee within the range commonly charged by other lawyers in similar representations? To the extent competition for legal services exists among lawyers in the relevant community, a tribunal can assume that the competition has produced an appropriate level of fee charges. A stated hourly rate, for example, should be compared with the hourly rates charged by lawyers of comparable qualifications for comparable services, and the number of hours claimed should be compared with those commonly invested in similar representations. The percentage in a contingent-fee contract should be compared to percentages commonly used in similar representations for similar services (for example, preparing and trying a novel products-liability claim).

Whatever the fee basis, it is also relevant whether accepting the case was likely to foreclose other work or to attract it and whether pursuing the matter at the usual fee was reasonable in light of the client's needs and resources. See § 39, Comment *b*, which discusses the fair-value standard applied in quantum meruit cases and possible defects of a market standard.

Third, was there a subsequent change in circumstances that made the fee contract unreasonable? Although reasonableness is usually assessed as of the time the contract was entered into, later events might be relevant. Some fee contracts make the fee turn on later events. Accordingly, the reasonableness of a fee due under an hourly rate contract, for example, depends on whether the number of hours the lawyer worked was reasonable in light of the matter and client. It is also relevant whether the lawyer provided poor service, such as might make unreasonable a fee that would be appropriate for better services, or services that were better or more successful than normally would have been expected (compare §§ 37 & 40 concerning forfeiture of fees). Finally, events not known or contemplated when the contract was made can render the contract unreasonably favorable to the lawyer or, occasionally, to the client. Compare Restatement Second, Contracts §§ 152–154 and 261–265 (doctrines of mistake, supervening impracticality, supervening frustration). To determine what events client and lawyer contemplated, their contract must be construed in light of its goals and circumstances and in light of the possibilities discussed with the client (see id. §§ 294 & 50). A contingent-fee contract, for example, allocates to the lawyer the risk that the case will require much time and produce no recovery and to the client the risk that the case will require little time and produce a substantial fee. Events within that range of risks, such as a high recovery, do not make unreasonable a contract that was reasonable when made.

Illustration:

1. Bank Clerk is charged with criminal embezzlement and retains Lawyer to defend against the charges for a $15,000 flat fee. The next day another employee confesses to having taken the money, and the prosecutor (not knowing of Lawyer's retention by Bank Clerk) immediately drops the charges against Bank Clerk. Lawyer has done nothing on the case beyond speaking with Bank Clerk. In the absence of special circumstances, such as prior discussion of this possibility or the lawyer having rejected another representation offering a comparable fee in reliance on this engagement, it would be unreasonable for Lawyer to be paid $15,000 for doing so little. Client must pay the fair value of Lawyer's services (see § 39), but more than that is not due and the lawyer must refund the excess if already paid (see § 42). If, however, the prosecutor dropped the charges as the result of a plea bargain negotiated by Lawyer, the rapid disposition would not render unreasonable an otherwise prop-

er $15,000 flat fee. A negotiated disposition without trial is a common event that parties are assumed to contemplate when they agree that the lawyer will receive a flat fee.

d.   Reasonable contingent fees; percentage fees. On reasonable contingent fees, see § 35. Fees based on a percentage of the value of the property involved in a decedent's estate or in a real-estate transaction often are predicated on an assumption by the lawyer of the risk that more work than usual will be required. The same might be true of a lump-sum fee. Such fees should therefore be judged in light of the range of lawyer time that matters of the sort and size in question are likely to take. However, unlike contingent fees, percentage fees in such matters usually do not require the lawyer to forgo compensation when the result is unfavorable to the client. If the lawyer does not bear the risk of not being paid, compensation for such a risk is irrelevant in assessing the reasonableness of the fee.

e.   Retainer fees. The term "retainer" has been employed to describe different fee arrangements. As used in this Restatement, an "engagement retainer fee" is a fee paid, apart from any other compensation, to ensure that a lawyer will be available for the client if required. An engagement retainer must be distinguished from a lump-sum fee constituting the entire payment for a lawyer's service in a matter and from an advance payment from which fees will be subtracted (see § 38, Comment *g*). A fee is an engagement retainer only if the lawyer is to be additionally compensated for actual work, if any, performed. In some jurisdictions, an engagement retainer is referred to as a "general" or "special" retainer. On the effect of premature termination of the representation on an engagement-retainer fee, see § 40.

An engagement-retainer fee satisfies the requirements of this Section if it bears a reasonable relationship to the income the lawyer sacrifices or expense the lawyer incurs by accepting it, including such costs as turning away other clients (for reasons of time or due to conflicts of interest), hiring new associates so as to be able to take the client's matter, keeping up with the relevant field, and the like. When a client experienced in retaining and compensating lawyers agrees to pay an engagement-retainer fee, the fee will almost invariably be found to fall within the range of reasonableness. Engagement-retainer fees agreed to by clients not so experienced should be more closely scrutinized to ensure that they are no greater than is reasonable and that the engagement-retainer fee is not being used to evade the rules requiring a lawyer to return unearned fees (see § 38, Comment *g*, & § 40, Illustrations 2A & 2B). In some circumstances, large engagement-retainer fees constitute unenforceable liquidated-damage clauses (see Restatement Second, Contracts § 356(1)) or are subject to challenge in the client's bankruptcy proceeding.

f.   The standard for lawyer discipline. The standards that apply when fees are challenged as unreasonable in fee disputes are also relevant in the discipline of lawyers for charging unreasonably high fees. If a fee would not be set aside in a fee dispute, disciplinary authorities can be expected to find that receiving or charging such a fee does not warrant sanctions for unreasonableness. Disciplinary authorities likewise rely on the list of factors (see Comment *d* hereto) that tribunals refer to in fee disputes. Discipline is also appropriate if the lawyer overreached by deceiving the client, failed to provide all the services in question, or unjustifiably demanded a fee larger than the contract provided. Discipline may also be appropriate if the clear unreasonableness of the fee is demonstrated by other circumstances, including what other lawyers handling such matters charge, the facial unreasonableness of any express fee agreement, limits imposed by statutes, rules, and judicial precedents, previous warnings to the lawyer, evidence that the fee is uniformly deemed to be clearly excessive by responsible practitioners, or other evidence demonstrating the lawyer's gross insensitivity to broadly accepted billing standards.

A lawyer can be disciplined for unreasonably making a large fee claim even though the fee was not collected. In a fee dispute, however, the tribunal is concerned primarily with the reasonableness of the fee the lawyer actually seeks before the tribunal rather than the reasonableness of earlier fee claims made between the parties. On the extent to which a lawyer's abusive fee-collection methods affects the lawyer's entitlement to a fee, see § 41.

g. Unlawful fees. A fee that violates a statute or rule regulating the size of fees is impermissible under this Section. General principles governing the enforceability of contracts that violate legal requirements are set forth in Restatement Second, Contracts §§ 178–185. Statutes or rules in some jurisdictions control the percentage of a contingent fee, generally or in particular categories such as worker-compensation claims or medical-malpractice litigation. Other common legislation limits the fees chargeable in proceedings against the government, forbids contingent fees for legislative lobbying, prohibits public defenders or defense counsel paid by the government from accepting payment from their clients, and prohibits lawyers representing wards of the court from accepting payments not approved by the court. A fee for a service a lawyer may not lawfully perform, such as questioning jurors after a trial where that is forbidden (see § 115), is likewise unlawful regardless of the size of the fee (see Restatement Second, Contract §§ 192 & 193). A lawyer may not require a client to pay a fee larger than that contracted for, unless the client validly agrees to the increase.

That a fee contract violates some legal requirement does not necessarily render it unenforceable. The requirement might be one not meant to protect clients or one for which refusal to enforce is an inappropriate sanction. For example, when a lawyer violates a lawyer-code requirement that a fee contract be in writing but the client does not dispute the amount owed under it, that violation alone should not make the contract unenforceable. When only certain parts of a contract between client and lawyer contravene the law, moreover, the lawful parts remain enforceable, except where the lawyer should forfeit the whole fee (see § 37).

§ 35. Contingent–Fee Arrangements

(1) A lawyer may contract with a client for a fee the size or payment of which is contingent on the outcome of a matter, unless the contract violates § 34 or another provision of this Restatement or the size or payment of the fee is:

> **(a) contingent on success in prosecuting or defending a criminal proceeding; or**

> **(b) contingent on a specified result in a divorce proceeding or a proceeding concerning custody of a child.**

(2) Unless the contract construed in the circumstances indicates otherwise, when a lawyer has contracted for a contingent fee, the lawyer is entitled to receive the specified fee only when and to the extent the client receives payment.

Comment:

a. Scope and cross-references. This Section complements the general prohibition of unlawful and unreasonably high fees set forth in § 34 and the restrictions on certain other financial arrangements between clients and lawyers set forth in § 36. On a lawyer's duty to inform a client concerning the basis and rate of a fee, see § 38, Comment *b*.

A contingent-fee contract is one providing for a fee the size or payment of which is conditioned on some measure of the client's success. Examples include a contract that a lawyer will receive one-third of a client's recovery and a contract that the lawyer will be paid by the hour but receive a bonus should a stated favorable result occur (see § 34, Comment *a*, & § 35).

b. Rationale. Contingent-fee arrangements perform three valuable functions. First, they enable persons who could not otherwise afford counsel to assert their rights, paying their lawyers only if the assertion succeeds. Second, contingent fees give lawyers an additional incentive to seek their clients' success and to encourage only those clients with claims having a substantial likelihood of succeeding. Third, such fees enable a client to share the risk of losing with a lawyer, who is usually better able to assess the risk and to bear it by undertaking similar arrangements in other cases (cf. Restatement Second, Agency § 445).

Although contingent fees were formerly prohibited in the United States and are still prohibited in many other nations, the prohibition reflects circumstances not present in the contemporary United States. Many other nations routinely award attorney fees to the winning party and often have relatively low, standardized and regulated attorney fees, thus providing an alternative means of access to the legal system, which is not generally available here. Those nations might also regard civil litigation as more of an evil and less of an opportunity for the protection of rights than do lawmakers here. Contingent fees are thus criticized there as stirring up litigation and fostering overzealous advocacy.

While many of those criticisms of contingent fees are inapposite in the United States, it remains true that contingent-fee clients are often unsophisticated and inexperienced users of legal services, and their financial position might leave them little choice but to accept whatever contingent-fee arrangements prevail in the locality. It is often difficult even for a careful client or lawyer to estimate in advance how likely it is that a claim will prevail, what the recovery will be, and how much lawyer time will be needed. Finally, standardized contingent-fee arrangements might not take proper account of cases with low risks or high recoveries. Accordingly, courts scrutinize contingent fees with care in determining whether they are reasonable.

The Section forbids contingent-fee arrangements creating certain conflicts of interest that might induce the lawyer to disserve the client's interest or certain public interests. Some such conflicts exist in all fee arrangements. However, some arrangements have been prohibited because their dangers are thought to outweigh their benefits.

 c. Reasonable contingent fees. A contingent fee may permissibly be greater than what an hourly fee lawyer of similar qualifications would receive for the same representation. A contingent-fee lawyer bears the risk of receiving no pay if the client loses and is entitled to compensation for bearing that risk. Nor is a contingent fee necessarily unreasonable because the lawyer devoted relatively little time to a representation, for the customary terms of such arrangements commit the lawyer to provide necessary effort without extra pay if a relatively large expenditure of the lawyer's time were entailed. However, large fees unearned by either effort or a significant period of risk are unreasonable (see § 34, Comment *c*, & Illustration 1 thereto).

A tribunal will find a contingent fee unreasonable due to a defect in the calculation of risk in two kinds of cases in particular: those in which there was a high likelihood of substantial recovery by trial or settlement, so that the lawyer bore little risk of nonpayment; and those in which the client's recovery was likely to be so large that the lawyer's fee would clearly exceed the sum appropriate to pay for services performed and risks assumed. A lawyer's failure to disclose to the client the general likelihood of recovery, the approximate probable size of any recovery, or the availability of alternative fee systems can also bear upon whether the fee is reasonable.

Illustration:

 1. Client seeks Lawyer's help in collecting life-insurance benefits under a $15,000 policy on Client's spouse and agrees to pay a one-third contingent fee. There is no reasonable ground to contest that the benefits are due, the claim has not been contested by the insurer, and when Lawyer presents it the insurer pays without

dispute. The $5,000 fee provided by the client-lawyer contract is not reasonable.

d.   Reasonable rate and basis of a contingent fee. In addition to unreasonableness due to lack of risk, a contingent fee can also be unreasonable because either the percentage rate is excessive or the base against which the percentage is applied is excessive or otherwise unreasonable. If different from the customary base—the plaintiff's recovery—a contingent base will be unreasonable if it is an inappropriate measure of the lawyer's work and risk and the benefit the client derived from the lawyer's services. Contingent-fee contracts typically contemplate that the client, if successful, will receive a lump-sum award, a stated percentage of which will constitute the lawyer's fees. A client entering a contingent-fee contract reasonably expects that the lawyer will be paid only if and to the extent that the client recovers. For example, when a judgment for the client is entered but not collected, no fee is due unless the contract so provides.

The rule stated in Subsection (2) also requires that, unless the contract indicates otherwise, a contingent-fee lawyer is to receive the specified share of the client's actual-damages recovery. For that purpose, recovery includes damages, restitution, back pay, similar equitable payments, and amounts received in settlement. Unless the contract with the client indicates otherwise, the lawyer is not entitled to the specified percentage of items such as costs and attorney fees that are not usually considered damages. In the absence of prior agreement to the contrary, the amount of the client's recovery is computed net of any offset, such as a recovery by an opposing party on a counterclaim.

Illustrations:

2.   Client agrees to pay Lawyer "35 percent of the recovery" in a suit. The court awards Client $20,000 in damages, $500 in costs for disbursements, and $1,000 in attorney fees because of the defendant's discovery abuses. Lawyer is entitled to receive a contingent fee of $7,000 (35% of $20,000), but not 35 percent of the costs' payments. If Lawyer advanced the $500 costs in question, Client must reimburse Lawyer unless their contract validly provides to the contrary (see § 38, Comment e). Whether Lawyer is entitled to recover a portion of the $1,000 attorney-fee award requires both interpretation of the fee contract and consideration of the nature of the fee-shifting award (see § 38(3)(b) & Comment f thereto).

3.   Same facts as in Illustration 2, except that Lawyer has also expended $1,500 in disbursements not recoverable from the opposing party as costs but recoverable from Client (see § 38(3)(a) & Comment e thereto). Unless their contract construed in its circumstances provides otherwise, Lawyer is entitled to reimbursement of the $1,500 out of the $20,000 award and to a contingent fee of $6,475, that is, 35 percent of $18,500, the balance of the award.

e. Contingent fees in structured settlements. Under "structured settlements" and some legislation, a claimant will receive regular payments over the claimant's lifetime or some other period rather than receiving a lump sum. If so, under the rule of this Section the lawyer is entitled to receive the stated share of each such payment if and when it is made to the client or (when so provided) for the client's benefit, unless the client-lawyer contract provides otherwise. When a contingent-fee contract provides that the fee is to be paid at once if there is a structured settlement and provides no other method of calculation, the fee should be calculated only on the present value of the settlement.

Illustration:

4. Lawyer brings a personal-injury suit for Client against Defendant under a fee contract stating that, if the suit is settled before trial, Lawyer is to receive a fee equaling "thirty percent of the recovery." Client and Defendant enter a structured settlement under which Defendant is to pay Client $100,000 at once and to buy an annuity (which will in fact cost Defendant $200,000) entitling Client to monthly payments of $1,500 until Client dies. In the absence of a contrary agreement, lawyer is entitled to receive $30,000 when the $100,000 payment is made and $450 (30% of $1,500) if and when each $1,500 payment is made.

f(i). Contingent fees in criminal cases—defense counsel. Contingent fees for defending criminal cases have traditionally been prohibited. The prohibition applies only to representations in a criminal proceeding. It does not forbid a contingent fee for legal work that forestalls a criminal proceeding or work that partly relates to a criminal matter and partly to a noncriminal matter. A lawyer may thus contract for a contingent fee to persuade an administrative agency to terminate an investigation that might have led to civil as well as criminal proceedings or to bring a police-brutality damages suit in which the settlement includes dismissal of criminal charges against the plaintiff.

f(ii). Contingent fees in criminal cases—prosecuting counsel. Fees contingent on success in prosecuting a criminal case violate public policy. Thus, for example, a lawyer in private practice retained to prosecute a criminal contempt should not be compensated contingent on success in the prosecution. A prosecutor whose pay depends on securing a conviction might be tempted to seek convictions more than justice (see § 97). The government does not generally need contingent fees to afford counsel or to transfer to counsel the risk of loss.

g. Contingent fees in divorce or custody cases. Most jurisdictions continue to prohibit fees contingent on securing divorce or child custody. The traditional grounds of the prohibition in divorce cases are that such a fee creates incentives inducing lawyers to discourage reconciliation and encourages bitter and wounding court battles (cf. Restatement Second, Contracts § 190(2)). Since the passage of no-fault divorce legislation, however, public policy does not clearly favor the continuation of a marriage that one spouse wishes to end. Furthermore, in practice, once one spouse retains a lawyer to seek a divorce, a divorce will follow in most cases regardless of the basis of the fee. The principal dispute is likely to be a financial one. The prohibition might hence make it more difficult for the poorer spouse to secure vigorous representation, at least in the relatively rare instances in which law does not provide fee-shifting for the benefit of that client.

The other argument for the prohibition in divorce cases, and the ground for prohibition in custody cases, is that such a fee arrangement is usually unnecessary in order to secure an attorney in a divorce proceeding or custody dispute. The issue usually arises when one or the other spouse has assets, because otherwise there would be no means of paying a contingent fee. If the spouse retaining counsel has assets, no contingent fee is necessary. If it is the other spouse that has assets, the courts will usually require that spouse to pay the first spouse reasonable attorney fees. Again, no contingent fee is necessary.

When either of the two policies supporting the prohibition is inapplicable, the Section should not apply. If, for example, a divorce or custody order has already been finally approved when the fee contract is entered into, there can be little concern that a contingent fee based on the size of the property settlement or child-support payments will discourage reconciliation or custody compromises. (On limitations on post-inception fee contracts, see § 18(1)(a).) In such a situation, the fee is not contingent upon the securing of a divorce or custody order, and this Section does not apply, just as it does not apply to a contingent fee in a property dispute between nondivorcing or already divorced spouses. The prohibition would, however, apply to a contract with a client who is then married that provides for a fee contingent on the amount of the alimony, property disposition, or child-support award but that does not explicitly condition the fee on the grant of a divorce.

§ 36. Forbidden Client Lawyer Financial Arrangements

(1) A lawyer may not acquire a proprietary interest in the cause of action or subject matter of litigation that the lawyer is conducting for a client, except that the lawyer may:

(a) acquire a lien as provided by § 43 to secure the lawyer's fee or expenses; and

(b) contract with a client for a contingent fee in a civil case except when prohibited as stated in § 35.

(2) A lawyer may not make or guarantee a loan to a client in connection with pending or contemplated litigation that the lawyer is conducting for the client, except that the lawyer may make or guarantee a loan covering court costs and expenses of litigation, the repayment of which to the lawyer may be contingent on the outcome of the matter.

(3) A lawyer may not, before the lawyer ceases to represent a client, make an agreement giving the lawyer literary or media rights to a portrayal or account based in substantial part on information relating to the representation.

§ 37. Forbidden Client Lawyer Financial Arrangements

A lawyer engaging in clear and serious violation of duty to a client may be required to forfeit some or all of the lawyer's compensation for the matter. Considerations relevant to the question of forfeiture include the gravity and timing of the violation, its willfulness, its effect on the value of the lawyer's work for the client, any other threatened or actual harm to the client, and the adequacy of other remedies.

Comment:

a. Scope and cross-references; relation to other doctrines. Even if a fee is otherwise reasonable (see § 34) and complies with the other requirements of this Chapter, this Section can in some circumstances lead to forfeiture. See also § 41, on abusive fee-collection methods, and § 43, Comments *f* and *g*, discussing the discharge of attorney liens. A client who has already paid a fee subject to forfeiture can sue to recover it (see §§ 33(1) & 42).

A lawyer's improper conduct can reduce or eliminate the fee that the lawyer may reasonably charge under § 34 (see Comment *c* thereof). A lawyer is not entitled to be paid for services rendered in violation of the lawyer's duty to a client or for services needed to alleviate the consequences of the lawyer's misconduct. See Reinstatement Second, Agency § 469 (agent entitled to no compensation for conduct which is disobedient or breach of duty of loyalty to principal). A tribunal will also consider misconduct more broadly, as evidence of the lawyer's lack of competence and loyalty, and hence of the value of the lawyer's services.

Illustration:

1. Lawyer has been retained at an hourly rate to negotiate a contract for Client. Lawyer assures the other parties that Client has consented to a given term, knowing this to be incorrect. Lawyer devotes five hours to working out the details of the term. When Client insists that the term be stricken (see § 22), Lawyer devotes four more hours to explaining to the other parties that Lawyer's lack of authority and Client's rejection of the term requires further negotiations. Lawyer is not entitled to compensation for any of those nine hours of time under either § 34 or § 39. The tribunal, moreover, may properly consider the incident if it bears on the value of such of Lawyer's other time as is otherwise reasonably compensable.

Second, under contract law a lawyer's conduct can render unenforceable the lawyer's fee contract with a client. Thus under contract law the misconduct could constitute a material breach of contract (see § 40) or vitiate the formation of the contract (as in the case of misrepresentations concerning the lawyer's credentials). Alternatively, the contract can be unenforceable because it contains an unlawful provision (see Restatement Second, Contracts §§ 163, 164, 184, 237, 241, & 374; Restatement Second, Agency § 467). In some cases, although the contract is unenforceable on its own terms, the lawyer will still be able to recover the fair value of services rendered (see § 39, Comment *e*).

Third, a lawyer's misconduct can constitute malpractice rendering the lawyer liable for any resulting damage to the client under the common law or, in some jurisdictions, a consumer-protection statute (see § 41, Comment *b*). Malpractice damages can be greater or smaller than the forfeited fees. Conduct constituting malpractice is not always the same as conduct warranting fee forfeiture. A lawyer's negligent legal research, for example, might constitute malpractice, but will not necessarily lead to fee forfeiture. On malpractice liability and measures of damages generally, see § 53. On the duty of an agent to recompense a principal for loss caused by the agent's breach of duty, see Restatement Second, Agency § 401.

b. Rationale. The remedy of fee forfeiture presupposes that a lawyer's clear and serious violation of a duty to a client destroys or severely impairs the client-lawyer relationship and thereby the justification of the lawyer's claim to compensation. See Restatement Second, Agency § Second, Trusts § 243 (court has discretion to deny or reduce compensation of trustee who commits breach of trust); cf. Restatement Second, Agency § 456(b) (willful and deliberate breach disentitles agent to recover in quantum meruit when agency contract does not apportion compensation). Forfeiture is also a deterrent. The damage that misconduct causes is often difficult to assess. In addition, a tribunal often can determine a forfeiture sanction more easily than a right to compensating damages.

Forfeiture of fees, however, is not justified in each instance in which a lawyer violates a legal duty, nor is total forfeiture always appropriate. Some violations are inadvertent or do not significantly harm the client. Some can be adequately dealt with by the remedies described in Comment *a* or by a partial forfeiture (see Comment *e*). Denying the lawyer all compensation would sometimes be an excessive sanction, giving a windfall to a client. The remedy of this Section should hence be applied with discretion.

c. Violation of a duty to a client. This Section provides for forfeiture when a lawyer engages in a clear and serious violation (see Comment *d* hereto) of a duty to the client. The source of the duty can be civil or criminal law, including, for example, the requirements of an applicable lawyer code or the law of malpractice. The misconduct might have occurred when the lawyer was retained, during the representation, or during attempts to collect a fee (see § 41). On improper withdrawal as a ground for forfeiture, see § 40, Comment *e*.

The Section refers only to duties that a lawyer owes to a client, not to those owed to other persons. That a lawyer, for example, harassed an opponent in litigation without harming the client does not warrant relieving the client of any duty to pay the lawyer. On other remedies in such situations, see § 110. But sometimes harassing a nonclient will also violate the lawyer's duty to the client, perhaps exposing the client to demands for sanctions or making the client's cause less likely to prevail. Forfeiture will then be appropriate unless the client is primarily responsible for the breach of duty to a nonclient.

d. *A clear and serious violation—relevant factors.* A lawyer's violation of duty to a client warrants fee forfeiture only if the lawyer's violation was clear. A violation is clear if a reasonable lawyer, knowing the relevant facts and law reasonably accessible to the lawyer, would have known that the conduct was wrongful. The sanction of fee forfeiture should not be applied to a lawyer who could not have been expected to know that conduct was forbidden, for example when the lawyer followed one reasonable interpretation of a client-lawyer contract and another interpretation was later held correct.

To warrant fee forfeiture a lawyer's violation must also be serious. Minor violations do not justify leaving the lawyer entirely unpaid for valuable services rendered to a client, although some such violations will reduce the size of the fee or render the lawyer liable to the client for any harm caused (see Comment a hereto).

In approaching the ultimate issue of whether violation of duty warrants fee forfeiture, several factors are relevant. The extent of the misconduct is one factor. Normally, forfeiture is more appropriate for repeated or continuing violations than for a single incident. Whether the breach involved knowing violation or conscious disloyalty to a client is also relevant. See Restatement Second, Agency § 469 (forfeiture for willful and deliberate breach). Forfeiture is generally inappropriate when the lawyer has not done anything willfully blameworthy, for example, when a conflict of interest arises during a representation because of the unexpected act of a client or third person.

Forfeiture should be proportionate to the seriousness of the offense. For example, a lawyer's failure to keep a client's funds segregated in a separate account (see § 44) should not result in forfeiture if the funds are preserved undiminished for the client. But forfeiture is justified for a flagrant violation even though no harm can be proved.

The adequacy of other remedies is also relevant. If, for example, a lawyer improperly withdraws from a representation and is consequently limited to a quantum meruit recovery significantly smaller than the fee contract provided (see § 40), it might be unnecessary to forfeit the quantum meruit recovery as well.

e. *Extent of forfeiture.* Ordinarily, forfeiture extends to all fees for the matter for which the lawyer was retained, such as defending a criminal prosecution or incorporating a corporation. (For a possibly more limited loss of fees under other rules, see Comment a hereto.) See § 42 (client's suit for refund of fees already paid). Forfeiture does not extend to a disbursement made by the lawyer to the extent it has conferred a benefit on the client (see § 40, Comment *d*).

Sometimes forfeiture for the entire matter is inappropriate, for example when a lawyer performed valuable services before the misconduct began, and the misconduct was not so grave as to require forfeiture of the fee for all services. Ultimately the question is one of fairness in view of the seriousness of the lawyer's violation and considering the special duties imposed on lawyers, the gravity, timing, and likely consequences to the client of the lawyer's misbehavior, and the connection between the various services performed by the lawyer.

When a lawyer-employee of a client is discharged for misconduct, except in an extreme instance this Section does not warrant forfeiture of all earned salary and pension entitlements otherwise due. The lawyer's loss of employment will itself often be a penalty graver than would be the loss of a fee for a single matter for a nonemployee lawyer. Employers, moreover, are often in a better position to protect themselves against misconduct of their lawyer-employees through supervision and other means. See Comment *a* hereto; Restatement Second, Agency § 401. For an employer's liability for unjust discharge of a lawyer employee, see § 32, Comment *b*.

TOPIC 2.   A LAWYER'S CLAIM TO COMPENSATION

§ 38.   Client–Lawyer Fee Contracts

(1) Before or within a reasonable time after beginning to represent a client in a matter, a lawyer must communicate to the client, in writing when applicable rules so provide, the basis or rate of the fee, unless the communication is unnecessary for the client because the lawyer has previously represented that client on the same basis or at the same rate.

(2) The validity and construction of a contract between a client and a lawyer concerning the lawyer's fees are governed by § 18.

(3) Unless a contract construed in the circumstances indicates otherwise:

(a) a lawyer may not charge separately for the lawyer's general office and overhead expenses;

(b) payments that the law requires an opposing party or that party's lawyer to pay as attorney-fee awards or sanctions are credited to the client, not the client's lawyer, absent a contrary statute or court order; and

(c) when a lawyer requests and receives a fee payment that is not for services already rendered, that payment is to be credited against whatever fee the lawyer is entitled to collect.

§ 39. A Lawyer's Fee in the Absence of a Contract

If a client and lawyer have not made a valid contract providing for another measure of compensation, a client owes a lawyer who has performed legal services for the client the fair value of the lawyer's services.

Comment:

a. Scope and cross-references. This Section sets forth a lawyer's right to recover a fair fee in quantum meruit for legal services provided to a client when a lawyer and client have not agreed upon another fee. It assumes that a client-lawyer relationship has been created (see § 14). Section 18 specifies requirements for a fee contract (see also § 38). The circumstances might also show that the lawyer was to serve without charge (see § 38, Comment *c*). A fee in quantum meruit may not exceed the applicable legal limits described in Topic 1 of this Chapter. Topic 3 discusses fee-collection procedures, including the various proceedings in which fee disputes can be resolved (see § 42); this Section applies to those proceedings.

A contract gives a client notice of what the fee will be, as required by § 38. A lawyer who fails to give such notice has a weaker claim to a fee whose amount the client might not have anticipated. The reasonableness requirement of § 34 is relevant (a) when a fee contract is challenged as unenforceable because the fee is too large or (b) when disciplinary authorities seek to discipline for a fee that is unreasonably large. The provisions of this Section are relevant but not conclusive when a lawyer faces such charges. However, discipline is inappropriate simply because a lawyer in good faith seeks a larger fee than a tribunal later determines to be due under this Section. If there is no valid fee contract, this Section measures the fee that is due, and a lawyer may then not seek a fee plainly improper under this Section.

The "fair value" fee recoverable under this Section is not measured by the standards applied when a party recovers a reasonable attorney fee from an opposing party under a fee-award statute or doctrine. The latter kind of fee often implicates factors—such as a legislative intent to encourage such suits or to limit fee awards to less than full compensation (for example, when the main purpose of the fee award is to deter misconduct by the fee-paying party)—not present in quantum meruit recovery under this Section.

b. Rationale. The fair-value standard of this Section persists (see Restatement Second, Agency § 443(b)), largely because of the defects of other standards.

b(i). The extent of a right to recover in the absence of a contract. The law permits a lawyer who has not agreed on a fee to recover one. Although both lawyers and clients might be reluctant to discuss fees in advance, both usually expect that some payment will be due. Denying compensation would be unfair to the lawyer and a windfall to the client.

Moreover, the parties might have agreed on a measure of compensation, but in a contract unenforceable because it does not meet an applicable legal standard (see Comment *e* hereto)—for example, because it is a contingent-fee contract but is not in writing as a court rule requires. Quantum meruit recovery then provides compensation in circumstances in which it would be contrary to the parties' expectation to deprive the lawyer of all compensation.

b(ii). Measuring fair value. The market value of a lawyer's services is relevant in determining fair value but is not as such the measure of restitutionary recovery. Market value is the basis on which quantum meruit recoveries for other services or goods are often computed (see Restatement of Restitution § 152). When applicable, it assists the tribunal's inquiry, because those active in the market will know the going price and can give evidence about it.

However, some measures of price from a competitive market might be inappropriate. For example, the market price of services for the vigorous litigation of a claim for specific performance of a land-purchase contract might be disproportionate to the value of a particular claim. For some clients, particularly those of small means, paying that price might be a foolish investment. Moreover, a strictly economic calculation of market value presupposes an informed client. But market prices might reflect client ignorance rather than fair bargaining. Where there has been no prior contract as to fee, the lawyer presumably did not adequately explain the cost of pursuing the claim and is thus the proper party to bear the risk of indeterminacy. Hence, the fair-value standard assesses additional considerations and starts with an assumption that the lawyer is entitled to recovery only at the lower range of what otherwise would be a reasonable negotiated fee.

c. Applying the fair-value standard. Assessing the fair value of a lawyer's services might require answers to three questions. What fees are customarily charged by comparable lawyers in the community for similar legal services? What would a fully informed and properly advised client in the client's situation agree to pay for such services? In light of those and other relevant circumstances, what is a fair fee (see Comment *b* hereto)?

In some cases, a standard market rate for a legal service might in fact exist. A lawyer who proves that a standard fee exists in the area should ordinarily be entitled to receive it, unless the client shows that a sophisticated, informed, and properly advised client in the client's situation would have refused to pay the standard fee—for example, because such a client would have decided not to proceed (see Comment *b(ii)* hereto). Similarly, a client should not be required to pay more than the standard fee unless the lawyer shows that, because of the circumstances of the case, a sophisticated, informed, and properly advised client would have agreed to pay a higher fee.

Calculation of an hourly fee might provide guidance. Except in certain areas such as criminal-defense or tort-plaintiff representation, hourly fees are a common contractual basis of payment for legal services. The hourly fee would be that charged by lawyers of similar experience and other credentials in comparable cases, but not more than the standard rate of the lawyer in question for that type of work. The lawyer must show, by records or otherwise, the hours actually and reasonably devoted to the case in view of the importance of the case to the client, the client's financial situation and instructions, and the time that a comparable lawyer would have needed.

The standard rate or hourly fee might be modified by other factors bearing on fairness, including success in the representation and whether the lawyer assumed part of the risk of the client's loss, as in a contingent-fee contract (see § 35). Reference can be made to the factors in § 34, Comment *c*. Concerning expenses and disbursements paid by the lawyer and attorney-fee awards and sanctions collected from an opposing party, the principles of § 38(3)(a) and (b) apply.

A conservative evaluation is usually appropriate in assessing fees under this Section. When a lawyer fails to agree with the client in advance on the fee to be charged, the client should not have to pay as much as some clients might have agreed to pay. A fair-value fee under this Section is thus less than the highest contractual fee that would be upheld as reasonable under § 34.

* * *

§ 40. Fees on Termination

If a client-lawyer relationship ends before the lawyer has completed the services due for a matter and the lawyer's fee has not been forfeited under § 37:

(1) a lawyer who has been discharged or withdraws may recover the lesser of the fair value of the lawyer's services as determined under § 39 and the ratable proportion of the compensation provided by any otherwise enforceable contract between lawyer and client for the services performed; except that

(2) the tribunal may allow such a lawyer to recover the ratable proportion of the compensation provided by such a contract if:

(a) the discharge or withdrawal is not attributable to misconduct of the lawyer;

(b) the lawyer has performed severable services; and

(c) allowing contractual compensation would not burden the client's choice of counsel or the client's ability to replace counsel.

845

TOPIC 3. FEE–COLLECTION PROCEDURES

§ 41. Fee–Collection Methods

In seeking compensation claimed from a client or former client, a lawyer may not employ collection methods forbidden by law, use confidential information (as defined in Chapter 5) when not permitted under § 65, or harass the client.

§ 42. Remedies and the Burden of Persuasion

(1) A fee dispute between a lawyer and a client may be adjudicated in any appropriate proceeding, including a suit by the lawyer to recover an unpaid fee, a suit for a refund by a client, an arbitration to which both parties consent unless applicable law renders the lawyer's consent unnecessary, or in the court's discretion a proceeding ancillary to a pending suit in which the lawyer performed the services in question.

(2) In any such proceeding the lawyer has the burden of persuading the trier of fact, when relevant, of the existence and terms of any fee contract, the making of any disclosures to the client required to render a contract enforceable, and the extent and value of the lawyer's services.

§ 43. Lawyer Liens

(1) Except as provided in Subsection (2) or by statute or rule, a lawyer does not acquire a lien entitling the lawyer to retain the client's property in the lawyer's possession in order to secure payment of the lawyer's fees and disbursements. A lawyer may decline to deliver to a client or former client an original or copy of any document prepared by the lawyer or at the lawyer's expense if the client or former client has not paid all fees and disbursements due for the lawyer's work in preparing the document and nondelivery would not unreasonably harm the client or former client.

(2) Unless otherwise provided by statute or rule, client and lawyer may agree that the lawyer shall have a security interest in property of the client recovered for the client through the lawyer's efforts, as follows:

(a) the lawyer may contract in writing with the client for a lien on the proceeds of the representation to secure payment for the lawyer's services and disbursements in that matter;

(b) the lien becomes binding on a third party when the party has notice of the lien;

(c) the lien applies only to the amount of fees and disbursements claimed reasonably and in good faith for the lawyer's services performed in the representation; and

(d) the lawyer may not unreasonably impede the speedy and inexpensive resolution of any dispute concerning those fees and disbursements or the lien.

(3) A tribunal where an action is pending may in its discretion adjudicate any fee or other dispute concerning a lien asserted by a lawyer on property of a party to the action, provide for custody of the property, release all or part of the property to the client or lawyer, and grant such other relief as justice may require.

(4) With respect to property neither in the lawyer's possession nor recovered by the client through the lawyer's efforts, the lawyer may obtain a security interest on property of a client only as provided by other law and consistent with §§ 18 and 126. Acquisition of such a security interest is a business or financial transaction with a client within the meaning of § 126.

TOPIC 4. PROPERTY AND DOCUMENTS OF CLIENTS AND OTHERS

§ 44. Safeguarding and Segregating Property

(1) A lawyer holding funds or other property of a client in connection with a representation, or such funds or other property in which a client claims an interest, must take reasonable steps to safeguard the funds or property. A similar obligation may be imposed by law on funds or other property so held and owned or claimed by a third person. In particular, the lawyer must hold such property separate from the lawyer's property, keep records of it, deposit funds in an account separate from the lawyer's own funds, identify tangible objects, and comply with related requirements imposed by regulatory authorities.

(2) Upon receiving funds or other property in a professional capacity and in which a client or third person owns or claims an interest, a lawyer must promptly notify the client or third person. The lawyer must promptly render a full accounting regarding such property upon request by the client or third person.

§ 45. Surrendering Possession of Property

(1) Except as provided in Subsection (2), a lawyer must promptly deliver, to the client or nonclient so entitled, funds or other property in the lawyer's possession belonging to a client or nonclient.

(2) A lawyer may retain possession of funds or other property of a client or nonclient if:

(a) the client or nonclient consents;

(b) the lawyer's client is entitled to the property, the lawyer appropriately possesses the property for purposes of the representation, and the client has not asked for delivery of the property;

(c) the lawyer has a valid lien on the property (see § 43);

(d) there are substantial grounds for dispute as to the person entitled to the property; or

(e) delivering the property to the client or nonclient would violate a court order or other legal obligation of the lawyer.

§ 46. Documents Relating to a Representation

(1) A lawyer must take reasonable steps to safeguard documents in the lawyer's possession relating to the representation of a client or former client.

(2) On request, a lawyer must allow a client or former client to inspect and copy any document possessed by the lawyer relating to the representation, unless substantial grounds exist to refuse.

(3) Unless a client or former client consents to nondelivery or substantial grounds exist for refusing to make delivery, a lawyer must deliver to the client or former client, at an appropriate time and in any event promptly after the representation ends, such originals and copies of other documents possessed by the lawyer relating to the representation as the client or former client reasonably needs.

(4) Notwithstanding Subsections (2) and (3), a lawyer may decline to deliver to a client or former client an original or copy of any document under circumstances permitted by § 43(1).

TOPIC 5.   FEE–SPLITTING WITH A LAWYER NOT IN THE SAME FIRM

§ 47.   Fee-Splitting with a Lawyer Not in the Same Firm

A division of fees between lawyers who are not in the same firm may be made only if:

(1) (a) the division is in proportion to the services performed by each lawyer or (b) by agreement with the client, the lawyers assume joint responsibility for the representation;

(2) the client is informed of and does not object to the fact of division, the terms of the division, and the participation of the lawyers involved; and

(3) the total fee is reasonable (see § 34).

CHAPTER 4: LAWYER CIVIL LIABILITY

TOPIC 1. LIABILITY FOR PROFESSIONAL NEGLIGENCE AND BREACH OF FIDUCIARY DUTY

§ 48. Professional Negligence—Elements and Defenses Generally

In addition to the other possible bases of civil liability described in §§ 49, 55, and 56, a lawyer is civilly liable for professional negligence to a person to whom the lawyer owes a duty of care within the meaning of § 50 or § 51, if the lawyer fails to exercise care within the meaning of § 52 and if that failure is a legal cause of injury within the meaning of § 53, unless the lawyer has a defense within the meaning of § 54.

§ 49. Breach of Fiduciary Duty—Generally

In addition to the other possible bases of civil liability described in §§ 48, 55, and 56, a lawyer is civilly liable to a client if the lawyer breaches a fiduciary duty to the client set forth in § 16(3) and if that failure is a legal cause of injury within the meaning of § 53, unless the lawyer has a defense within the meaning of § 54.

§ 50. Duty of Care to a Client

For purposes of liability under § 48, a lawyer owes a client the duty to exercise care within the meaning of § 52 in pursuing the client's lawful objectives in matters covered by the representation.

§ 51. Duty of Care to Certain Nonclients

For purposes of liability under § 48, a lawyer owes a duty to use care within the meaning of § 52 in each of the following circumstances:

(1) to a prospective client, as stated in § 15;

(2) to a nonclient when and to the extent that:

(a) the lawyer or (with the lawyer's acquiescence) the lawyer's client invites the nonclient to rely on the lawyer's opinion or provision of other legal services, and the nonclient so relies; and

(b) the nonclient is not, under applicable tort law, too remote from the lawyer to be entitled to protection;

(3) to a nonclient when and to the extent that:

849

(a) the lawyer knows that a client intends as one of the primary objectives of the representation that the lawyer's services benefit the nonclient;

(b) such a duty would not significantly impair the lawyer's performance of obligations to the client; and

(c) the absence of such a duty would make enforcement of those obligations to the client unlikely; and

(4) to a nonclient when and to the extent that:

(a) the lawyer's client is a trustee, guardian, executor, or fiduciary acting primarily to perform similar functions for the nonclient;

(b) the lawyer knows that appropriate action by the lawyer is necessary with respect to a matter within the scope of the representation to prevent or rectify the breach of a fiduciary duty owed by the client to the nonclient, where (i) the breach is a crime or fraud or (ii) the lawyer has assisted or is assisting the breach;

(c) the nonclient is not reasonably able to protect its rights; and

(d) such a duty would not significantly impair the performance of the lawyer's obligations to the client.

Comment:

a. Scope and cross-references. This Section sets forth the limited circumstances in which a lawyer owes a duty of care to a nonclient. Compare § 14, describing when one becomes a client, and § 50, which sets forth a lawyer's duty to a client. On the meaning of the term "duty," see § 50, Comment *a.* Even when a duty exists, a lawyer is liable for negligence only if the lawyer violates the duty (see § 52), the violation is the legal cause of damages (see § 53), and no defense is established (see § 54).

As stated in § 54(1), a lawyer is not liable under this Section for any action or inaction the lawyer reasonably believed to be required by law, including a professional rule. As stated in §§ 66(3) and 67(4), a lawyer who takes action or decides not to take action permitted under those Sections is not, solely by reason of such action or inaction, liable for damages.

In appropriate circumstances, a lawyer is also subject to liability to a nonclient on grounds other than negligence (see §§ 48 & 56), for litigation sanctions (see § 110), and for acting without authority (see § 30). On indemnity and contribution, see § 53, Comment *i.* This Section does not consider those liabilities, such as liabilities arising under securities or similar legislation. Nor does the Section consider when a lawyer found liable to a nonclient may recover from a client under such theories as indemnity, contribution, or subrogation. On a client's liability to a nonclient arising out of a lawyer's conduct, see § 26, Comment *d*.

b.   Rationale. Lawyers regularly act in disputes and transactions involving nonclients who will foreseeably be harmed by inappropriate acts of the lawyers. Holding lawyers liable for such harm is sometimes warranted. Yet it is often difficult to distinguish between harm resulting from inappropriate lawyer conduct on the one hand and, on the other hand, detriment to a nonclient resulting from a lawyer's fulfilling the proper function of helping a client through lawful means. Making lawyers liable to nonclients, moreover, could tend to discourage lawyers from vigorous representation. Hence, a duty of care to nonclients arises only in the limited circumstances described in the Section. Such a duty must be applied in light of those conflicting concerns.

c.   Opposing parties. A lawyer representing a party in litigation has no duty of care to the opposing party under this Section, and hence no liability for lack of care, except in unusual situations such as when a litigant is provided an opinion letter from opposing counsel as part of a settlement (see Subsection (2) and Comment *e* hereto). Imposing such a duty could discourage vigorous representation of the lawyer's own client through fear of liability to the opponent. Moreover, the opposing party is protected by the rules and procedures of the adversary system and, usually, by counsel. In some circumstances, a lawyer's negligence will entitle an opposing party to relief other than damages, such as vacating a settlement induced by negligent misrepresentation. For a lawyer's liability to sanctions, which may include payments to an opposing party, based on certain litigation misconduct, see § 110. See also § 56, on liability for intentional torts.

Similarly, a lawyer representing a client in an arm's-length business transaction does not owe a duty of care to opposing nonclients, except in the exceptional circumstances described in this Section. On liability for aiding a client's unlawful conduct, see § 56.

Illustration:

1. Lawyer represents Plaintiff in a personal-injury action against Defendant. Because Lawyer fails to conduct an appropriate factual investigation, Lawyer includes a groundless claim in the complaint. Defendant incurs legal expenses in obtaining dismissal of this claim. Lawyer is not liable for negligence to Defendant. Lawyer may, however, be subject to litigation sanctions for having asserted a claim without proper investigation (see § 110). On claims against lawyers for wrongful use of civil proceedings and the like, see § 57(2) and Comment d thereto.

d.   Prospective clients (Subsection (1)). When a person discusses with a lawyer the possibility of their forming a client-lawyer relationship, and even if no such relationship arises, the lawyer may be liable for failure to use reasonable care to the extent the lawyer advises or provides other legal services for the person (see § 15(2) and the Comments thereto). On duties to a former client, see § 50, Comment *c*.

e. Inviting reliance of a nonclient (Subsection (2)). When a lawyer or that lawyer's client (with the lawyer's acquiescence) invites a nonclient to rely on the lawyer's opinion or other legal services, and the nonclient reasonably does so, the lawyer owes a duty to the nonclient to use care (see § 52), unless the jurisdiction's general tort law excludes liability on the ground of remoteness. Accordingly, the nonclient has a claim against the lawyer if the lawyer's negligence with respect to the opinion or other legal services causes injury to the nonclient (see § 95). The lawyer's client typically benefits from the nonclient's reliance, for example, when providing the opinion was called for as a condition to closing under a loan agreement, and recognition of such a claim does not conflict with duties the lawyer properly owed to the client. Allowing the claim tends to benefit future clients in similar situations by giving nonclients reason to rely on similar invitations. See Restatement Second, Torts § 552. If a client is injured by a lawyer's negligence in providing opinions or services to a nonclient, for example because that renders the client liable to the nonclient as the lawyer's principal, the lawyer may have corresponding liability to the client (see § 50).

Clients or lawyers may invite nonclients to rely on a lawyer's legal opinion or services in various circumstances (see § 95). For example, a sales contract for personal property may provide that as a condition to closing the seller's lawyer will provide the buyer with an opinion letter regarding the absence of liens on the property being sold (see id., Illustrations 1 & 2; § 52, Illustration 2). A nonclient may require such an opinion letter as a condition for engaging in a transaction with a lawyer's client. A lawyer's opinion may state the results of a lawyer's investigation and analysis of facts as well as the lawyer's legal conclusions (see § 95). On when a lawyer may properly decline to provide an opinion and on a lawyer's duty when a client insists on nondisclosure, see § 95, Comment *d*. A lawyer's acquiescence in use of the lawyer's opinion may be manifested either before or after the lawyer renders it.

In some circumstances, reliance by unspecified persons may be expected, as when a lawyer for a borrower writes an opinion letter to the original lender in a bank credit transaction knowing that the letter will be used to solicit other lenders to become participants in syndication of the loan. Whether a subsequent syndication participant can recover for the lawyer's negligence in providing such an opinion letter depends on what, if anything, the letter says about reliance and whether the jurisdiction in question, as a matter of general tort law, adheres to the limitations on duty of Restatement Second, Torts § 552(2) or those of Ultramares Corp v. Touche, 174 N.E. 441 (N.Y.1931), or has rejected such limitations. To account for such differences in general tort law, Subsection (2) refers to applicable law excluding liability to persons too remote from the lawyer.

When a lawyer owes a duty to a nonclient under this Section, whether the nonclient's cause of action may be asserted in contract or in tort should be determined by reference to the applicable law of professional liability generally. The cause of action ordinarily is in substance identical to a claim for negligent misrepresentation and is subject to rules such as those concerning proof of materiality and reliance (see Restatement Second, Torts §§ 552–554). For liability under securities legislation, see § 56, Comment *i*. Whether the representations are actionable may be affected by the duties of disclosure, if any, that the client owes the nonclient (see § 98, Comment *e*). In the absence of such duties of disclosure, the duty of a lawyer providing an opinion is ordinarily limited to using care to avoid making or adopting misrepresentations. On a lawyer's obligations in furnishing an opinion, see § 95, Comment *c*. On intentionally making or assisting misrepresentations, see § 56, Comment *f*, and § 98.

A lawyer may avoid liability to nonclients under Subsection (2) by making clear that an opinion or representation is directed only to a client and should not be relied on by others. Likewise, a lawyer may limit or avoid liability under Subsection (2) by qualifying a representation, for example by making clear through limiting or disclaiming language in an opinion letter that the lawyer is relying on facts provided by the client without independent investigation by the lawyer (assuming that the lawyer does not know the facts provided by the client to be false, in which case the lawyer would be liable for misrepresentation). The effectiveness of a limitation or disclaimer depends on whether it was reasonable in the circumstances to conclude that those provided with the opinion would receive the limitation or disclaimer and understand its import. The relevant circumstances include customary practices known to the recipient concerning the construction of opinions and whether the recipient is represented by counsel or a similarly experienced agent.

When a nonclient is invited to rely on a lawyer's legal services, other than the lawyer's opinion, the analysis is similar. For example, if the seller's lawyer at a real-estate closing offers to record the deed for the buyer, the lawyer is subject to liability to the buyer for negligence in doing so, even if the buyer did not thereby become a client of the lawyer. When a nonclient is invited to rely on a lawyer's nonlegal services, the lawyer's duty of care is determined by the law applicable to providers of the services in question.

f. A nonclient enforcing a lawyer's duties to a client (Subsection (3)). When a lawyer knows (see Comment *h* hereto) that a client intends a lawyer's services to benefit a third person who is not a client, allowing the nonclient to recover from the lawyer for negligence in performing those services may promote the lawyer's loyal and effective pursuit of the client's objectives. The nonclient, moreover, may be the only person likely to enforce the lawyer's duty to the client, for example because the client has died.

A nonclient's claim under Subsection (3) is recognized only when doing so will both implement the client's intent and serve to fulfill the lawyer's obligations to the client without impairing performance of those obligations in the circumstances of the representation. A duty to a third person hence exists only when the client intends to benefit the third person as one of the primary objectives of the representation, as in the Illustrations below and in Comment *g* hereto. Without adequate evidence of such an intent, upholding a third person's claim could expose lawyers to liability for following a client's instructions in circumstances where it would be difficult to prove what those instructions had been. Threat of such liability would tend to discourage lawyers from following client instructions adversely affecting third persons. When the claim is that the lawyer failed to exercise care in preparing a document, such as a will, for which the law imposes formal or evidentiary requirements, the third person must prove the client's intent by evidence that would satisfy the burden of proof applicable to construction or reformation (as the case may be) of the document. See Restatement Third, Property (Donative Transfers) §§ 11.2 and 12.1 (Tentative Draft No. 1, 1995) (preponderance of evidence to resolve ambiguity in donative instruments; clear and convincing evidence to reform such instruments).

Subsections (3) and (4), although related in their justifications, differ in application. In situations falling under Subsection (3), the client need not owe any preexisting duty to the intended beneficiary. The scope of the intended benefit depends on the client's intent and the lawyer's undertaking. On the other hand, the duty under Subsection (4) typically arises when a lawyer helps a client-fiduciary to carry out a duty of the fiduciary to a beneficiary recognized and defined by trust or other law.

Illustrations:

2.   Client retains Lawyer to prepare and help in the drafting and execution of a will leaving Client's estate to Nonclient. Lawyer prepares the will naming Nonclient as the sole beneficiary, but negligently arranges for Client to sign it before an inadequate number of witnesses. Client's intent to benefit Nonclient thus appears on the face of the will executed by Client. After Client dies, the will is held ineffective due to the lack of witnesses, and Nonclient is thereby harmed. Lawyer is subject to liability to Nonclient for negligence in drafting and supervising execution of the will.

3.   Same facts as in Illustration 2, except that Lawyer arranges for Client to sign the will before the proper number of witnesses, but Nonclient later alleges that Lawyer negligently wrote the will to name someone other than Nonclient as the legatee. Client's intent to benefit Nonclient thus does not appear on the face of the will. Nonclient can establish the existence of a duty from Lawyer to Nonclient only by producing clear and convincing evidence that Client communicated to Lawyer Client's intent that Nonclient be

the legatee. If Lawyer is held liable to Nonclient in situations such as this and the preceding Illustration, applicable principles of law may provide that Lawyer may recover from their unintended recipients the estate assets that should have gone to Nonclient.

4. Same facts as in Illustration 2, except that Lawyer arranges for Client to sign the will before the proper number of witnesses. After Client's death, Heir has the will set aside on the ground that Client was incompetent and then sues Lawyer for expenses imposed on Heir by the will, alleging that Lawyer negligently assisted Client to execute a will despite Client's incompetence. Lawyer is not subject to liability to Heir for negligence. Recognizing a duty by lawyers to heirs to use care in not assisting incompetent clients to execute wills would impair performance of lawyers' duty to assist clients even when the clients' competence might later be challenged. Whether Lawyer is liable to Client's estate or personal representative (due to privity with the lawyer) is beyond the scope of this Restatement. On a lawyer's obligations to a client with diminished capacity, see § 24.

g. A liability insurer's claim for professional negligence. Under Subsection (3), a lawyer designated by an insurer to defend an insured owes a duty of care to the insurer with respect to matters as to which the interests of the insurer and insured are not in conflict, whether or not the insurer is held to be a co-client of the lawyer (see § 134, Comment *f*). For example, if the lawyer negligently fails to oppose a motion for summary judgment against the insured and the insurer must pay the resulting adverse judgment, the insurer has a claim against the lawyer for any proximately caused loss. In such circumstances, the insured and insurer, under the insurance contract, both have a reasonable expectation that the lawyer's services will benefit both insured and insurer. Recognizing that the lawyer owes a duty to the insurer promotes enforcement of the lawyer's obligations to the insured. However, such a duty does not arise when it would significantly impair, in the circumstances of the representation, the lawyer's performance of obligations to the insured. For example, if the lawyer recommends acceptance of a settlement offer just below the policy limits and the insurer accepts the offer, the insurer may not later seek to recover from the lawyer on a claim that a competent lawyer in the circumstances would have advised that the offer be rejected. Allowing recovery in such circumstances would give the lawyer an interest in recommending rejection of a settlement offer beneficial to the insured in order to escape possible liability to the insurer.

h. Duty based on knowledge of a breach of fiduciary duty owed by a client (Subsection (4)). A lawyer representing a client in the client's capacity as a fiduciary (as opposed to the client's personal capacity) may in some circumstances be liable to a beneficiary for a failure to use care to protect the beneficiary. The duty should be recognized only when the requirements of Subsection (4) are met and when action by the lawyer would not violate applicable professional rules (see § 54(1)). The duty arises from the fact that a fiduciary has obligations to the beneficiary that go beyond fair dealing at arm's length. A lawyer is usually so situated as to have special opportunity to observe whether the fiduciary is complying with those obligations. Because fiduciaries are generally obliged to pursue the interests of their beneficiaries, the duty does not subject the lawyer to conflicting or inconsistent duties. A lawyer who knowingly assists a client to violate the client's fiduciary duties is civilly liable, as would be a nonlawyer (see Restatement Second, Trusts § 326). Moreover, to the extent that the lawyer has assisted in creating a risk of injury, it is appropriate to impose a preventive and corrective duty on the lawyer (cf. Restatement Second, Torts § 321).

The duty recognized by Subsection (4) is limited to lawyers representing only a limited category of the persons described as fiduciaries—trustees, executors, guardians, and other fiduciaries acting primarily to fulfill similar functions. Fiduciary responsibility, imposing strict duties to protect specific property for the benefit of specific, designated persons, is the chief end of such relationships. The lawyer is hence less likely to encounter conflicting considerations arising from other responsibilities of the fiduciary-client than are entailed in other relationships in which fiduciary duty is only a part of a broader role. Thus, Subsection (4) does not apply when the client is a partner in a business partnership, a corporate officer or director, or a controlling stockholder.

The scope of a client's fiduciary duties is delimited by the law governing the relationship in question (see, e.g., Restatement Second, Trusts §§ 169–185). Whether and when such law allows a beneficiary to assert derivatively the claim of a trust or other entity against a lawyer is beyond the scope of this Restatement (see Restatement Second, Trusts § 282). Even when a relationship is fiduciary, not all the attendant duties are fiduciary. Thus, violations of duties of loyalty by a fiduciary are ordinarily considered breaches of fiduciary duty, while violations of duties of care are not.

Sometimes a lawyer represents both a fiduciary and the fiduciary's beneficiary and thus may be liable to the beneficiary as a client under § 50 and may incur obligations concerning conflict of interests (see §§ 130–131). A lawyer who represents only the fiduciary may avoid such liability by making clear to the beneficiary that the lawyer represents the fiduciary rather than the beneficiary (compare § 103, Comment *e*).

The duty recognized by Subsection (4) arises only when the lawyer knows that appropriate action by the lawyer is necessary to prevent or mitigate a breach of the client's fiduciary duty. As used in this Subsection and Subsection (3) (see Comment *f*), "know" is the equivalent of the same term defined in ABA Model Rules of Professional Conduct, Terminology § [5] (1983) (" ... 'Knows' denotes actual knowledge of the fact in question. A person's knowledge may be inferred from circumstances."). The concept is functionally the same as the terminology "has reason to know" as defined in Restatement Second, Torts § 12(1) (actor has reason to know when actor "has information from which a person of reasonable intelligence or of the superior intelligence of the actor would infer that the fact in question exists, or that such person would govern his conduct upon the assumption that such facts exists."). The "know" terminology should not be confused with "should know" (see id. § 12(2)). As used in Subsection (3) and (4) "knows" neither assumes nor requires a duty of inquiry.

Generally, a lawyer must follow instruction of the client-fiduciary (see § 21(2) hereto) and may assume in the absence of contrary information that the fiduciary is complying with the law. The duty stated in Subsection (4) applies only to breaches constituting crime or fraud, as determined by applicable law and subject to the limitations set out in § 67, Comment *d*, and § 82, Comment *d*, or those in which the lawyer has assisted or is assisting the fiduciary. A lawyer assists fiduciary breaches, for example, by preparing documents needed to accomplish the fiduciary's wrongful conduct or assisting the fiduciary to conceal such conduct. On the other hand, a lawyer subsequently consulted by a fiduciary to deal with the consequences of a breach of fiduciary duty committed before the consultation began is under no duty to inform the beneficiary of the breach or otherwise to act to rectify it. Such a duty would prevent a person serving as fiduciary from obtaining the effective assistance of counsel with respect to such a past breach.

Liability under Subsection (4) exists only when the beneficiary of the client's fiduciary duty is not reasonably able to protect its rights. That would be so, for example, when the fiduciary client is a guardian for a beneficiary unable (for reasons of youth or incapacity) to manage his or her own affairs. By contrast, for example, a beneficiary of a family voting trust who is in business and has access to the relevant information has no similar need of protection by the trustee's lawyer. In any event, whether or not there is liability under this Section, a lawyer may be liable to a nonclient as stated in § 56.

A lawyer owes no duty to a beneficiary if recognizing such duty would create conflicting or inconsistent duties that might significantly impair the lawyer's performance of obligations to the lawyer's client in the circumstances of the representation. Such impairment might occur, for example, if the lawyer were subject to liability for assisting the fiduciary in an open dispute with a beneficiary or for assisting the fiduciary in exercise of its judgment that would benefit one beneficiary at the expense of another. For similar reasons, a lawyer is not subject to liability to a beneficiary under Subsection (4) for representing the fiduciary in a dispute or negotiation with the beneficiary with respect to a matter affecting the fiduciary's interests.

Under Subsection (4) a lawyer is not liable for failing to take action that the lawyer reasonably believes to be forbidden by professional rules (see § 54(1)). Thus, a lawyer is not liable for failing to disclose confidences when the lawyer reasonably believes that disclosure is forbidden.

For example, a lawyer is under no duty to disclose a prospective breach in a jurisdiction that allows disclosure only regarding a crime or fraud threatening imminent death or substantial bodily harm. However, liability could result from failing to attempt to prevent the breach of fiduciary duty through means that do not entail disclosure. In any event, a lawyer's duty under this Section requires only the care set forth in § 52.

Illustrations:

5. Lawyer represents Client in Client's capacity as trustee of an express trust for the benefit of Beneficiary. Client tells Lawyer that Client proposes to transfer trust funds into Client's own account, in circumstances that would constitute embezzlement. Lawyer informs Client that the transfer would be criminal, but Client nevertheless makes the transfer, as Lawyer then knows. Lawyer takes no steps to prevent or rectify the consequences, for example by warning Beneficiary or informing the court to which Client as trustee must make an annual accounting. The jurisdiction's professional rules do not forbid such disclosures (see § 67). Client likewise makes no disclosure. The funds are lost, to the harm of Beneficiary. Lawyer is subject to liability to Beneficiary under this Section.

6. Same facts as in Illustration 5, except that Client asserts to Lawyer that the account to which Client proposes to transfer trust funds is the trust's account. Even though lawyer could have exercised diligence and thereby discovered this to be false, Lawyer does not do so. Lawyer is not liable to the harmed Beneficiary. Lawyer did not owe Beneficiary a duty to use care because Lawyer did not know (although further investigation would have revealed) that appropriate action was necessary to prevent a breach of fiduciary duty by Client.

7. Same facts as in Illustration 5, except that Client proposes to invest trust funds in a way that would be unlawful, but would not constitute a crime or fraud under applicable law. Lawyer's services are not used in consummating the investment. Lawyer does nothing to discourage the investment. Lawyer is not subject to liability to Beneficiary under this Section.

§ 52. Standard of Care

(1) For purposes of liability under §§ 48 and 49, a lawyer who owes a duty of care must exercise the competence and diligence normally exercised by lawyers in similar circumstances.

(2) Proof of a violation of a rule or statute regulating the conduct of lawyers:

(a) does not give rise to an implied cause of action for professional negligence or breach of fiduciary duty;

(b) does not preclude other proof concerning the duty of care in Subsection (1) or the fiduciary duty; and

(c) may be considered by a trier of fact as an aid in understanding and applying the standard of Subsection (1) or § 49 to the extent that (i) the rule or statute was designed for the protection of persons in the position of the claimant and (ii) proof of the content and construction of such a rule or statute is relevant to the claimant's claim.

Comment:

a. Scope and cross-references. This Section defines the duty of care a lawyer owes to clients and to nonclients to whom a duty of care is owed under § 51. A lawyer must exercise such care in pursuing a client's objectives and in fulfilling fiduciary duties owed to a client (see § 50). On the application of the duty to nonclients, see Comment *e* hereto. For a lawyer to be liable for malpractice, the lawyer's violation of this duty must be a legal cause of injury (see § 53) to a person to whom the lawyer owes a duty of care (see §§ 50 & 51), and the lawyer must have established no defense (see § 54). Whether a lawyer has failed to exercise the care required by this Section is not necessarily the same issue as whether the lawyer is subject to professional discipline, litigation sanctions, or other remedies other than legal-malpractice liability. On a lawyer's liability to a client for breach of contract, see § 55. On the applicability of this Section in a client's action for breach of a lawyer's fiduciary duty, see § 49, Comment *d*. On the use of confidential client information by a lawyer defending against a former client's claim of malpractice, see §§ 64 and 80.

b. Competence. The duty of competence set forth in this Section is that generally applicable to practitioners of a profession, that is, "the skill and knowledge normally possessed by members of that profession or trade in good standing ... " (Restatement Second, Torts § 299A). Informed clients expect services of this kind; it is practical for lawyers to provide them; and the practice of the profession will most often be evidence of what clients need. As is generally true for professions, the legal duty refers to normal professional practice to define the ordinary standard of care for lawyers, rather than referring to that standard as simply evidence of reasonableness.

The competence duty, like that for diligence, does not make the lawyer a guarantor of a successful outcome in the representation (see § 55(1)). It does not expose the lawyer to liability to a client for acting only within the scope of the representation (see § 19 & § 54, Comment *b*) or following the client's instructions (see § 21(2) & § 54, Comment *h*). It does not require a lawyer, in a situation involving the exercise of professional judgment, to employ the same means or select the same options as would other competent lawyers in the many situations in which competent lawyers reasonably exercise professional judgment in different ways. The duty also does not require "average" performance, which would imply that the less skillful part of the profession would automatically be committing malpractice. The duty is one of reasonableness in the circumstances.

A trier of fact applying the standard may consider such circumstances as time pressures, uncertainty about facts or law, the varying means by which different competent lawyers seek to accomplish the same client goal, and the impossibility that all clients will reach their goals. Such factors are especially prevalent in litigation. They warrant caution in evaluating lawyers' decisions, although they do not warrant the view, still occasionally asserted, that all decisions taken in good faith are exempt from malpractice liability. Expert testimony by those knowledgeable about the legal subject matter in question is relevant in applying the standard (see Comment *g* hereto). In appropriate circumstances, a tribunal passing on a motion for summary judgment or directed verdict may determine whether a lawyer has satisfied the duty.

The professional community whose practices and standards are relevant in applying this duty of competence is ordinarily that of lawyers undertaking similar matters in the relevant jurisdiction (typically, a state). (On conflict-of-laws problems, see § 5, Comment *h* (lawyer discipline); § 48, Comment *f*.) The narrower "locality test," under which the standards of a local community governed, has seldom been recognized for lawyers. Restatement Second, Torts § 299A, Comment *g*. The locality test is now generally rejected for all professions, because all professionals can normally obtain access to standard information and facilities, because clients no longer limit themselves to local professionals, and because of the practicalities of proof in malpractice cases (see Comment *g* hereto). In many fields of legal practice, for example the preparation of securities-registration statements or the representation of clients in federal court in litigation under federal legislation, there exists a national practice with national standards. In applying the competence duty, however, it may be appropriate to consider factors such as the unavailability of particular research sources in the community where a lawyer practices in light of the difficulty and probable value in the circumstances of having done further research.

c. Diligence. A lawyer must devote reasonable diligence to a representation. The lawyer must perform tasks reasonably appropriate to the representation, including, where appropriate, inquiry into facts, analysis of law, exercise of professional judgment, communication with the client, rendering of practical and ethical advice, and drafting of documents. What kind and extent of effort is appropriate depends on factors such as the scope of the representation (see § 19(1)), the client's instructions (see § 21(2)), the importance of the matter to the client (which may be indicated by the client's own assertions as well as by the matter's probable impact on the client's affairs), the cost of the effort, customary practice, and the time available. A lawyer who informs a client that the lawyer will undertake a specifically described activity is required to do so, as is one properly instructed by a client to take a particular step (see § 21(2)). Circumstances might make it necessary to provide more than one lawyer for a client's matter or to provide appropriate supervision of subordinate lawyers (see § 11) or certain corresponding counsel (see § 58, Comment *e*). When paralegals or other nonlawyers are used, they must be properly supervised. See Restatement Second, Torts § 231, § 58 (vicarious liability of firm and partners); § 11(4) (duty to supervise). Even when a lawyer has been inadequately diligent, the lawyer's breach of duty might not be the legal cause of compensable damage (see § 53), for example if without required investigation the lawyer recommended that the client accept a settlement offer that was in fact a good one.

* * *

§ 53. Causation and Damages

A lawyer is liable under § 48 or § 49 only if the lawyer's breach of a duty of care or breach of fiduciary duty was a legal cause of injury, as determined under generally applicable principles of causation and damages.

Comment:

* * *

b. Action by a civil litigant: loss of a judgment. In a lawyer-negligence or fiduciary-breach action brought by one who was the plaintiff in a former and unsuccessful civil action, the plaintiff usually seeks to recover as damages the damages that would have been recovered in the previous action or the additional amount that would have been recovered but for the defendant's misconduct. To do so, the plaintiff must prove by a preponderance of the evidence that, but for the defendant lawyer's misconduct, the plaintiff would have obtained a more favorable judgment in the previous action. The plaintiff must thus prevail in a "trial within a trial." All the issues that would have been litigated in the previous action are litigated between the plaintiff and the plaintiff's former lawyer, with the latter taking the place and bearing the burdens that properly would have fallen on the defendant in the original action. Similarly, the plaintiff bears the burden the plaintiff would have borne in the original trial; in considering whether the plaintiff has carried that burden, however, the trier of fact may consider whether the defendant lawyer's misconduct has made it more difficult for the plaintiff to prove what would have been the result in the original trial. (On a lawyer's right to disclose client confidences when reasonably necessary in defending against a claim, see §§ 64 and 80.) Similar principles apply when a former civil defendant contends that, but for the misconduct of the defendant's former lawyer, the defendant would have secured a better result at trial.

What would have been the result of a previous trial presenting issues of fact normally is an issue for the factfinder in the negligence or fiduciary-breach action. What would have been the result of an appeal in the previous action is, however, an issue of law to be decided by the judge in the negligence or fiduciary-breach action. The judges or jurors who heard or would have heard the original trial or appeal may not be called as witnesses to testify as to how they would have ruled. That would constitute an inappropriate burden on the judiciary and jurors and an unwise personalization of the issue of how a reasonable judge or jury would have ruled.

A plaintiff may show that the defendant's negligence or fiduciary breach caused injury other than the loss of a judgment. For example, a plaintiff may contend that, in a previous action, the plaintiff would have obtained a settlement but for the malpractice of the lawyer who then represented the plaintiff. A plaintiff might contend that the defendant in the previous action made a settlement offer, that the plaintiff's then lawyer negligently failed to inform plaintiff of the offer (see § 20(3)), and that, if informed, plaintiff would have accepted the offer. If the plaintiff can prove this, the plaintiff can recover the difference between what the claimant would have received under the settlement offer and the amount, if any, the claimant in fact received through later settlement or judgment. Similarly, in appropriate circumstances, a plaintiff who can establish that the negligence or fiduciary breach of the plaintiff's former lawyer deprived the plaintiff of a substantial chance of prevailing and that, due to that misconduct, the results of a previous trial cannot be reconstructed, may recover for the loss of that chance in jurisdictions recognizing such a theory of recovery in professional-malpractice cases generally.

The plaintiff in a previous civil action may recover without proving the results of a trial if the party claims damages other than loss of a judgment. For example, a lawyer who negligently discloses a client's trade secret during litigation might be liable for harm to the client's business caused by the disclosure.

Even when a plaintiff would have recovered through trial or settlement in a previous civil action, recovery in the negligence or fiduciary-breach action of what would have been the judgment or settlement in the previous action is precluded in some circumstances. Thus, the lawyer's misconduct will not be the legal cause of loss to the extent that the defendant lawyer can show that the judgment or settlement would have been uncollectible, for example because the previous defendant was insolvent and uninsured. The defendant lawyer bears the burden of coming forward with evidence that this was so. Placement of this burden on the defending lawyer is appropriate because most civil judgments are collectible and because the defendant lawyer was the one who undertook to seek the judgment that the lawyer now calls worthless. The burden of persuading the jury as to collectibility remains upon the plaintiff.

c. Action by a civil litigant: attorney fees that would have been due. When it is shown that a plaintiff would have prevailed in the former civil action but for the lawyer's legal fault, it might be thought that—

applying strict causation principles—the damages to be recovered in the legal-malpractice action should be reduced by the fee due the lawyer in the former matter. That is, the plaintiff has lost the net amount recovered after paying that attorney fee. Yet if the net amount were all the plaintiff could recover in the malpractice action, the defendant lawyer would in effect be credited with a fee that the lawyer never earned, and the plaintiff would have to pay two lawyers (the defendant lawyer and the plaintiff's lawyer in the malpractice action) to recover one judgment.

Denial of a fee deduction hence may be an appropriate sanction for the defendant lawyer's misconduct: to the extent that the lawyer defendant did not earn a fee due to the lawyer's misconduct, no such fee may be deducted in calculating the recovery in the malpractice action. The same principles apply to a legal-malpractice plaintiff who was a defendant in a previous civil action. The appropriateness and extent of disallowing deduction of the fee are determined under the standards of § 37 governing fee forfeiture. In some circumstances, those standards allow the lawyer to be credited with fees for services that benefited the client. See § 37, Comment e.

Illustration:

1. Plaintiff retains Lawyer to bring a contract action seeking to recover $40,000, at a fee of $150 per hour. After working 10 hours, Lawyer withdraws without cause just before the trial. As a result, Plaintiff's case is dismissed with prejudice. When Plaintiff then sues Lawyer for malpractice and shows that Plaintiff would have prevailed in the contract action but for Lawyer's withdrawal, Plaintiff is entitled to recover $40,000. Lawyer is not entitled to deduct either attorney fees for hours devoted to the case before the withdrawal or hours that would have been devoted to the trial, for both were forfeited by Lawyer's improper and harmful withdrawal (see §§ 37 & 40, Comment e).

d. Action by a criminal defendant. A convicted criminal defendant suing for malpractice must prove both that the lawyer failed to act properly and that, but for that failure, the result would have been different, for example because a double-jeopardy defense would have prevented conviction. Although most jurisdictions addressing the issue have stricter rules, under this Section it is not necessary to prove that the convicted defendant was in fact innocent. As required by most jurisdictions addressing the issue, a convicted defendant seeking damages for malpractice causing a conviction must have had that conviction set aside when process for that relief on the grounds asserted in the malpractice action is available.

A judgment in a postconviction proceeding is binding in the malpractice action to the extent provided by the law of judgments. That law prevents a convicted defendant from relitigating an issue decided in a postconviction proceeding after a full and fair opportunity to litigate, even though the lawyer sued was not a party to that proceeding and is hence not bound by any decision favorable to the defendant. See Restatement Second, Judgements §§ 27–29. Some jurisdictions hold public defenders immune from malpractice suits.

e. Nonlitigated matters. Generally applicable principles of causation and damages apply in malpractice actions arising out of a nonlitigated matter. When a lawyer is subject to liability to a nonclient under § 51(2) for negligence in preparing an opinion letter on which the nonclient reasonably relied, recovery is ordinarily governed by the causation and damages rules applicable to negligent misrepresentation actions, unless the lawyer has undertaken greater responsibility to the nonclient (see Restatement Second, Torts § 552B).

f. Attorney fees as damages. Like other civil litigants, the winning party in a malpractice action ordinarily cannot recover its attorney fees and other expenses in the malpractice action itself, except to the limited extent that the jurisdiction allows the recovery of court costs. The rule barring fee recovery has exceptions, which may be applicable in a malpractice action in appropriate circumstances. For example, many jurisdictions allow recovery of attorney fees against a plaintiff or defendant that litigates in bad faith (see also § 110, Comment *g* (litigation sanctions)).

The rule barring recovery of fees does not prevent a successful legal-malpractice plaintiff from recovering as damages additional legal expenses reasonably incurred outside the malpractice action itself as a result of a lawyer's misconduct. For example, if a lawyer's negligent title search causes a client to buy land with an unclear title and as a result to incur legal expenses defending the title against a challenger, the client may recover those expenses from the negligent lawyer.

g. Damages for emotional distress. General principles applicable to the recovery of damages for emotional distress apply to legal-malpractice actions. In general, such damages are inappropriate in types of cases in which emotional distress is unforeseeable. Thus, emotional-distress damages are ordinarily not recoverable when a lawyer's misconduct causes the client to lose profits from a commercial transaction, but are ordinarily recoverable when misconduct causes a client's imprisonment. The law in some jurisdictions permits recovery for emotional-distress damages only when the defendant lawyer's conduct was clearly culpable (see also § 56, Comment *g*).

h. Punitive damages. Whether punitive damages are recoverable in a legal-malpractice action depends on the jurisdiction's generally applicable law. Punitive damages are generally permitted only on a showing of intentional or reckless misconduct by a defendant.

A few decisions allow a plaintiff to recover from a lawyer punitive damages that would have been recovered from the defendant in an underlying action but for the lawyer's misconduct. However, such recovery is not required by the punitive and deterrent purposes of punitive damages. Collecting punitive damages from the lawyer will neither punish nor deter the original tortfeasor and calls for a speculative reconstruction of a hypothetical jury's reaction.

i. Joint and several liability; contribution; claims against successor counsel. The principles of joint and several or several liability generally applicable to negligence actions apply to professional-negligence and fiduciary-breach actions (see Chapter 4, Introductory Note). If, for example, a seller and the seller's lawyer both participate in negligent misrepresentations to a buyer, and if the lawyer owes a duty of care to the buyer under § 51(2), general principles of law make the seller and lawyer jointly and severally liable for resulting damages. See also § 56, Comment *d* (liability for advising and assisting clients); Restatement Second, Torts §§ 875–886B. Generally applicable law also governs whether one tortfeasor who has been held liable can obtain contribution or indemnity from another. On a client's obligation to indemnify a lawyer for liabilities to which the client has exposed the lawyer without the lawyer's fault, see § 17(2). On vicarious liability of law firms and their partners for certain torts of firm lawyers, see § 58.

When the damage caused by the negligence or fiduciary breach of a lawyer is increased by the negligence or fiduciary breach of successor counsel retained by the client, the first lawyer is liable to the client for the whole damage if the conditions set forth in Restatement Second, Torts § 447 are satisfied. The successor lawyer is also directly liable to the client for damage caused by that lawyer's negligence or fiduciary breach. The first lawyer, however, may not seek contribution or indemnity from the successor lawyer in the same action in which the successor lawyer represents the client, for that would allow the first lawyer to create or exacerbate a conflict of interest for the second lawyer and force withdrawal of the second lawyer from the action. The first lawyer may, however, dispute liability in the negligence or fiduciary breach action for the portion of the damages caused by the second lawyer on the ground that the conditions of in Restatement Second, Torts § 447 are not satisfied. The client may then choose whether to accept the possibility of such a reduction in damages or to assert a second claim against successor counsel, with the resultant necessity of retaining a third lawyer to proceed against the first two. Regardless of whether the client asserts a second claim, such three-sided disputes may raise problems involving client confidences (see § 52, Comment *h*), conflicts of interest (see § 125), lawyer duties of disclosure (see § 20, Comment *c*), and lawyer witnesses (see § 108) that require lawyers and judges to act carefully to protect the rights of clients and lawyers.

§ 54. Defenses; Prospective Liability Waiver; Settlement with a Client

(1) Except as otherwise provided in this Section, liability under §§ 48 and 49 is subject to the defenses available under

generally applicable principles of law governing respectively actions for professional negligence and breach of fiduciary duty. A lawyer is not liable under § 48 or § 49 for any action or inaction the lawyer reasonably believed to be required by law, including a professional rule.

(2) An agreement prospectively limiting a lawyer's liability to a client for malpractice is unenforceable.

(3) The client or former client may rescind an agreement settling a claim by the client or former client against the person's lawyer if:

(a) the client or former client was subjected to improper pressure by the lawyer in reaching the settlement; or

(b) (i) the client or former client was not independently represented in negotiating the settlement, and (ii) the settlement was not fair and reasonable to the client or former client.

(4) For purposes of professional discipline, a lawyer may not:

(a) make an agreement prospectively limiting the lawyer's liability to a client for malpractice; or

(b) settle a claim for such liability with an unrepresented client or former client without first advising that person in writing that independent representation is appropriate in connection therewith.

TOPIC 2.   OTHER CIVIL LIABILITY

§ 55.   Civil Remedies of a Client Other Than for Malpractice

(1) A lawyer is subject to liability to a client for injury caused by breach of contract in the circumstances and to the extent provided by contract law.

(2) A client is entitled to restitutionary, injunctive, or declaratory remedies against a lawyer in the circumstances and to the extent provided by generally applicable law governing such remedies.

§ 56.   Liability to a Client or Nonclient Under General Law

Except as provided in § 57 and in addition to liability under §§ 48–55, a lawyer is subject to liability to a client or nonclient when a nonlawyer would be in similar circumstances.

§ 57.   Nonclient Claims—Certain Defenses and Exceptions to Liability

(1) In addition to other absolute or conditional privileges, a lawyer is absolutely privileged to publish matter concerning a nonclient if:

(a) the publication occurs in communications preliminary to a reasonably anticipated proceeding before a tribunal or in the institution or during the course and as a part of such a proceeding;

(b) the lawyer participates as counsel in that proceeding; and

(c) the matter is published to a person who may be involved in the proceeding, and the publication has some relation to the proceeding.

(2) A lawyer representing a client in a civil proceeding or procuring the institution of criminal proceedings by a client is not liable to a nonclient for wrongful use of civil proceedings or for malicious prosecution if the lawyer has probable cause for acting, or if the lawyer acts primarily to help the client obtain a proper adjudication of the client's claim in that proceeding.

(3) A lawyer who advises or assists a client to make or break a contract, to enter or dissolve a legal relationship, or to enter or not enter a contractual relation, is not liable to a nonclient for interference with contract or with prospective contractual relations or with a legal relationship, if the lawyer acts to advance the client's objectives without using wrongful means.

TOPIC 3. VICARIOUS LIABILITY

§ 58. Nonclient Claims—Certain Defenses and Exceptions to Liability

(1) A law firm is subject to civil liability for injury legally caused to a person by any wrongful act or omission of any principal or employee of the firm who was acting in the ordinary course of the firm's business or with actual or apparent authority.

(2) Each of the principals of a law firm organized as a general partnership without limited liability is liable jointly and severally with the firm.

(3) A principal of a law firm organized other than as a general partnership without limited liability as authorized by law is vicariously liable for the acts of another principal or employee of the firm to the extent provided by law.

CHAPTER 5:   CONFIDENTIAL CLIENT INFORMATION

TOPIC 1.   CONFIDENTIALITY RESPONSIBILITIES
OF LAWYERS

TITLE A.   A LAWYER'S CONFIDENTIALITY DUTIES

§ 59.   Definition of "Confidential Client Information"

Confidential client information consists of information relating to representation of a client, other than information that is generally known.

Comment:

a. Scope and cross-references. This Section defines information concerning the representation of a client governed by the confidentiality rule stated in § 60 and for which exceptions are stated in other Sections in this Topic. For the most part, the definition of this Section is relevant to applications of the general duty of confidentiality (see § 60) owed to a current client and to former clients. On the relevance of the definition of confidential information to a determination whether a former matter is "substantially related" to a current matter, see § 132, Comment *d(ii).*

b. Kinds of confidential client information. A client's approach to a lawyer for legal assistance implies that the client trusts the lawyer to advance and protect the interests of the client (see § 16(1)). The resulting duty of loyalty is the predicate of the duty of confidentiality. The information that a lawyer is obliged to protect and safeguard is called confidential client information in this Restatement.

This definition covers all information relating to representation of a client, whether in oral, documentary, electronic, photographic, or other forms. It covers information gathered from any source, including sources such as third persons whose communications are not protected by the attorney-client privilege (see § 70). It includes work product that the lawyer develops in representing the client, such as the lawyer's notes to a personal file, whether or not the information is immune from discovery as lawyer work product (see Topic 3). It includes information acquired by a lawyer in all client-lawyer relationships (see § 14), including functioning as inside or outside legal counsel, government or private-practice lawyer, counselor or litigator, advocate or intermediary. It applies whether or not the client paid a fee, and whether a lawyer learns the information personally or through an agent, for example information acquired by a lawyer's partners or associate lawyers or by an investigator, paralegal, or secretary. Information acquired by an agent is protected even if it was not thereafter communicated to the lawyer, such as material acquired by an investigator and kept in the investigator's files.

The definition includes information that becomes known by others, so long as the information does not become generally known. See

Comment *d* hereto; compare § 71 (condition of attorney-client privilege that communication be made with reasonable expectation of confidentiality); § 79 (waiver of the attorney-client privilege by subsequent disclosure). The fact that information falls outside the attorney-client privilege or work-product immunity does not determine its confidentiality under this Section.

A lawyer may learn information relevant to representation of a client in the course of representing another client, from casual reading or in other accidental ways. On the use of information learned from representation of another client, see § 60, Comment *l*. In the course of representation, a lawyer may learn confidential information about the client that is not necessary for the representation but which is of a personal or proprietary nature or other character such that the client evidently would not wish it disclosed. Such information is confidential under this Section.

c. The time at which information is acquired. Information acquired during the representation or before or after the representation is confidential so long as it is not generally known (see Comment *d* hereto) and relates to the representation. Such information, for example, might be acquired by the lawyer in considering whether to undertake a representation. On the duties of a lawyer with respect to confidential information of a prospective client, see § 15, Comment *c*. Post-representation confidential client information might be acquired, for example, in the form of information on subsequent developments.

Illustrations:

1. Lawyer represents Employer in defending against a claim of employment discrimination by Plaintiff. Plaintiff has joined both Employer and Personnel Director as defending parties. Lawyer extensively confers with Inside Legal Counsel, general counsel of Employer, who provides information about the claim as it relates to Personnel Director. Subsequently, Inside Legal Counsel authorizes Lawyer to represent Personnel Director as a co-client. Information acquired by Lawyer relating to representation of Personnel Director prior to forming the client-lawyer relationship is confidential client information under this Section. On application of the attorney-client privilege, compare § 76 (common-interest arrangements).

2. Lawyer represented Defendant in civil litigation, in which Defendant prevailed. Two years after the representation ended, a Juror in the case writes a letter to Lawyer stating that Defendant approached Juror and several other jurors in a recess during their deliberations and improperly provided them with new evidence that persuaded the jury to find for Defendant. Juror states in the letter that Juror wishes Lawyer to show the letter to the Judge who presided at the trial. Although not subject to the attorney-client privilege (see §§ 70 & 71), the letter relates to Lawyer's representa-

tion of Defendant and is thus confidential under this Section. Whether Lawyer may disclose the information is governed by §§ 61–67.

d. Generally known information. Confidential client information does not include information that is generally known. Such information may be employed by lawyer who possesses it in permissibly representing other clients (see § 60, Comments *g* & *h*) and in other contexts where there is a specific justification for doing so (compare Comment *e* hereto). Information might be generally known at the time it is conveyed to the lawyer or might become generally known thereafter. At the same time, the fact that information has become known to some others does not deprive it of protection if it has not become generally known in the relevant sector of the public.

Whether information is generally known depends on all circumstances relevant in obtaining the information. Information contained in books or records in public libraries, public-record depositaries such as government offices, or in publicly accessible electronic-data storage is generally known if the particular information is obtainable through publicly available indexes and similar methods of access. Information is not generally known when a person interested in knowing the information could obtain it only by means of special knowledge or substantial difficulty or expense. Special knowledge includes information about the whereabouts or identity of a person or other source from which the information can be acquired, if those facts are not themselves generally known.

A lawyer may not justify adverse use or disclosure of client information simply because the information has become known to third persons, if it is not otherwise generally known. Moreover, if a current client specifically requests that information of any kind not be used or disclosed in ways otherwise permissible, the lawyer must either honor that request or withdraw from the representation (see § 32; see also §§ 16(2) & 21(2)).

e. Information concerning law, legal institutions, and similar matters. Confidential client information does not include what a lawyer learns about the law, legal institutions such as courts and administrative agencies, and similar public matters in the course of representing clients. Such information is part of the general fund of information available to the lawyer. During legal research of an issue while representing a client, a lawyer may discover a particularly important precedent or devise a novel legal approach that is useful both in the immediate matter and in other representations. The lawyer and other members of the lawyer's firm may use and disclose that information in other representations, so long as they thereby disclose no confidential client information except as permitted by § 60. A lawyer may use such information—about the state of the law, the best way to approach an administrative agency, the preferable way to frame an argument before a particular judge—in a future, otherwise unrelated representation that is adverse to the former client. On the otherwise general prohibition against adverse use or disclosure of confidential information of a former client, see § 132, Comment *f*.

§ 60. A Lawyer's Duty to Safeguard Confidential Client Information

(1) Except as provided in §§ 61–67, during and after representation of a client:

(a) the lawyer may not use or disclose confidential client information as defined in § 59 if there is a reasonable prospect that doing so will adversely affect a material interest of the client or if the client has instructed the lawyer not to use or disclose such information;

(b) the lawyer must take steps reasonable in the circumstances to protect confidential client information against impermissible use or disclosure by the lawyer's associates or agents that may adversely affect a material interest of the client or otherwise than as instructed by the client.

(2) Except as stated in § 62, a lawyer who uses confidential information of a client for the lawyer's pecuniary gain other than in the practice of law must account to the client for any profits made.

Comment:

a. Scope and cross-references. This Section states the principal duties of a lawyer with respect to confidential client information. The first duty is negative—not to use or disclose the information. The second is positive—to safeguard confidential client information in the client's interests. The third duty protects clients against lawyer use or disclosure of confidential information for self-profit (see Comment *j* hereto). The duty not to use or disclose confidential client information is subject to the exceptions provided in §§ 61–67. The duty to safeguard entails the corollary duties to provide adequate supervision of nonlawyer personnel (see § 11) and to assert privileges and other legal protection applicable to confidential client information such as the attorney-client privilege (see § 86(1)(b)) and the work-product immunity (see § 87). See Comment *c* hereto. The duty to safeguard such information is also a principal basis for the rules prohibiting former client conflicts of interest (see Chapter 8, Topic 4). On a lawyer's duty to safeguard confidential information of a prospective client, see § 15.

Remedies for a lawyer's breach of the obligation of § 60 may depend upon the kind of information involved and the nature of the improper use or disclosure. Remedies include exclusion or suppression of the lawyer's attempted testimony in violation of the attorney-client privilege (see § 86), the protection of lawyer work-product against intrusion by third parties (see Topic 3), a client's right to recover damages for negligent (see § 48) or intentional (see § 56) breach of an obligation of confidentiality, professional discipline (see § 5), and the remedies relating to conflicts of interest (see § 6, Comment *i*).

b. Conflicts between protection of confidential client information and other values. The broad prohibition against divulging confidential client information comes at a cost to both lawyers and society. Lawyers sometimes learn information that cannot be disclosed because of the rule of confidentiality but that would be highly useful to other persons. Those may include persons whose personal plight and character are much more sympathetic than those of the lawyer's client or who could accomplish great public good or avoid great public detriment if the information were disclosed. Moreover, the free-speech interests of lawyers is impinged by a broad rule of confidentiality. Nonetheless, despite those costs, the confidentiality rule reflects a considered judgment that high net social value justifies it. It is recognized that the rule better protects legitimate client expectations about communications to their lawyers and that permitting divulgence would be inconsistent with the goal of furthering the lawful objectives of clients (see § 16(1)).

Illustration:

1. Lawyer is appointed to represent Client, a person who has been accused of murder. During confidential conferences between them, Client informs Lawyer that Client in fact committed not only the murder charged but two others as well. Client gives Lawyer sufficient detail to confirm beyond question that Client's story is true. The two other murders involve victims whose bodies have not yet been discovered. Because of similarities between the circumstances of the murders, parents of one of the victims approach Lawyer and beg for any information about their child. Lawyer realizes the personal anguish of the victim's parents and the peace the information that he knows could bring them. Unless Client consents to disclosure (see § 62), Lawyer must respond that Lawyer has no information to give them.

c. Impermissible use or disclosure—in general. A lawyer is prohibited from using or disclosing confidential client information if either of two conditions exists—risk of harm to the client or client instruction.

c(i). Impermissible use or disclosure—a reasonable prospect of adverse effect on a material client interest. The duty of confidentiality is defined in terms of the risk of harm. Subject to exceptions provided in §§ 61–67, use or disclosure of confidential client information is generally prohibited if there is a reasonable prospect that doing so will adversely affect a material interest of the client or prospective client. Although the lawyer codes do not express this limitation, such is the accepted interpretation. For example, under a literal reading of ABA Model Rules of Professional Conduct, Rule 1.6(a) (1983), a lawyer would commit a disciplinary violation by telling an unassociated lawyer in casual conversation the identity of a firm client, even if mention of the client's identity creates no possible risk of harm. Such a strict interpretation goes beyond the proper interpretation of the rule.

What constitutes a reasonable prospect of adverse effect on a material client interest depends on the circumstances. Whether such a prospect exists must be judged from the perspective of a reasonable lawyer based on the specific context of the client matter. Some representations involve highly secret client information; others involve routine information as to which secrecy has little or no material importance. In most representations, some information will be more sensitive than other information. In all representations, the relevant inquiry is whether a lawyer of reasonable caution, considering only the client's objectives, would regard use or disclosure in the circumstances as creating an unreasonable risk of adverse effect either to those objectives or to other interests of the client. For example, a lawyer advising a client on tax planning for a gift that the client intends to keep anonymous from the donee would violate this Section if the lawyer revealed the client's purpose to the donee. If there is a reasonable ground to doubt whether use or disclosure of a client's confidential information would have the described effect, the lawyer should take reasonable steps to ascertain whether adverse effect would result, including consultation with the client when appropriate. Alternatively, the lawyer in such circumstances may obtain client consent to the use or disclosure (see § 62).

Adverse effects include all consequences that a lawyer of reasonable prudence would recognize as risking material frustration of the client's objectives in the representation or material misfortune, disadvantage, or other prejudice to a client in other respects, either during the course of the present representation or in the future. It includes consequences such as financial or physical harm and personal embarrassment that could be caused to a person of normal susceptibility and a normal interest in privacy.

Both use and disclosure adverse to a client are prohibited. As the term is employed in the Section, use of information includes taking the information significantly into account in framing a course of action, such as in making decisions when representing another client or in deciding whether to make a personal investment. Disclosure of information is revealing the information to a person not authorized to receive it and in a form that identifies the client or client matter either expressly or through reasonably ascertainable inference. Revealing information in a way that cannot be linked to the client involved is not a disclosure prohibited by the Section if there is no reasonable likelihood of adverse effect on a material interest of the client. Use of confidential client information can be adverse without disclosure. For example, in representing a subsequent client against the interests of a former client in a related matter, a lawyer who shapes the subsequent representation by employing confidential client information gained about the original client violates the duty of § 60(1) not to use that information, even if the lawyer does not disclose the information to anyone else (see § 132).

c(ii). Impermissible use or disclosure—specific client instructions. Even in the absence of a reasonable prospect of risk of harm to a client, use or disclosure is also prohibited if the affected client instructs the lawyer (see § 21(2)) not to use or disclose information. Such a direction is the client's definition of the client's interests (see § 16(1)), which controls (see § 21(2)). Such an instruction may also limit a lawyer's implied authority to use or disclose confidential client information to advance a client's interests. On the ability of a lawyer to withdraw, see § 32. However, client limitations on a lawyer's authority do not alter a lawyer's obligations under § 63 (using or disclosing confidential client information when required by law or court order) (see § 23). With respect to communications with a third person such as a relative of a client with diminished capacity, see § 24, Comment *c*.

When a fee for a client is paid by a third person (see § 134(1)) and in the absence of different client agreement or instructions, the client and not the third person directs the lawyer with respect to such matters as the treatment of files or other confidential client information. For the special instance of liability insurers, compare § 134, Comment *f*.

d. A lawyer's duty to safeguard confidential client information. A lawyer who acquires confidential client information has a duty to take reasonable steps to secure the information against misuse or inappropriate disclosure, both by the lawyer and by the lawyer's associates or agents to whom the lawyer may permissibly divulge it (see Comment *e*). This requires that client confidential information be acquired, stored, retrieved, and transmitted under systems and controls that are reasonably designed and managed to maintain confidentiality. In responding to a discovery request, for example, a lawyer must exercise reasonable care against the risk that confidential client information not subject to the request is inadvertently disclosed (see § 79). A lawyer should so conduct interviews with clients and others that the benefit of the attorney-client privilege and work-product immunity are preserved (see § 70, Comment *f*). On the release of information to further a client's objectives, including the waiver of claims of privilege or immunity, see § 61, Comment *d*. On asserting objections to attempts to obtain the client's confidential information, see § 63, Comment *b*.

A lawyer must take reasonable steps so that law-office personnel and other agents such as independent investigators properly handle confidential client information. That includes devising and enforcing appropriate policies and practices concerning confidentiality and supervising such personnel in performing those duties (see § 11). A lawyer may act reasonably in relying on other responsible persons in the office or on reputable independent contractors to provide that instruction and supervision (see id.). The reasonableness of specific protective measures depends on such factors as the duties of the agent or other person, the extent to which disclosure would adversely affect the client, the extent of prior training or experience of the person, the existence of other assurances such as adequate supervision by senior employees, and the customs and reputation of independent contractors.

Greater precautions may be necessary when use or disclosure is not directed toward representation of the client (see Comment *f* hereto) or facilitating the lawyer's law practice (see Comment *g*), for example when information is provided to a lawyer outside the firm to assist that lawyer's own representations. A lawyer must not engage in casual or frivolous conversation about a client's matters that creates an unreasonable risk of harm to the interests of the client.

e. Postrepresentation safeguarding. The duty of confidentiality continues so long as the lawyer possesses confidential client information. It extends beyond the end of the representation and beyond the death of the client. Accordingly, a lawyer must take reasonable steps for the future safekeeping of client files, including files in closed matters, or the systematic destruction of nonessential closed files. A lawyer must also take reasonably appropriate steps to provide for return, destruction, or continued safekeeping of client files in the event of the lawyer's retirement, ill health, death, discipline, or other interruption of the lawyer's practice.

f. Divulgence to persons assisting a lawyer in representing a client. A lawyer generally has authority to use or disclose confidential client information to persons assisting the lawyer in representing the client. Those include other lawyers in the same firm and employees such as secretaries and paralegals. A lawyer also may disclose information to independent contractors who assist in the representation, such as investigators, lawyers in other firms, prospective expert witnesses, and public courier companies and photocopy shops, to the extent reasonably appropriate in the client's behalf (see also § 70, Comment *h*). Such disclosures are not permitted contrary to a client's instructions, even within the lawyer's firm (see Comment *c(ii)* hereto), or when screening is required to avoid imputed disqualification of the lawyer's firm (see § 124, Comment *d*, & § 133, Comment *g*).

A lawyer's authority to disclose information for purposes of carrying out the representation is implied and therefore does not require express client consent (see § 21(3)). Agents of a lawyer assisting in representing a client serve as subagents and as such independently owe a duty of confidentiality to the client. See generally Restatement Second, Agency § 428(1) (subagent's general duties to known principals); id.§ 395 (agent's general duty of confidentiality).

g. Divulgence to facilitate law practice. A lawyer may disclose confidential client information for the purpose of facilitating the lawyer's law practice, where no reasonable prospect of harm to the client is thereby created and where appropriate safeguards against impermissible use or disclosure are taken. Thus, disclosure is permitted to other lawyers in the same firm and to employees and agents such as accountants, file clerks, office managers, secretaries, and similar office assistants in the lawyer's firm, and with confidential, independent consultants, such as computer technicians, accountants, bookkeepers, lawpractice consultants, and others who assist in furthering the law-practice business of the lawyer or the lawyer's firm. Use or disclosure of confidential client information, if prohibited under § 60, is not permitted for other business purposes, such as aiding investment or business, including one in which the lawyer owns an interest.

h. Divulgence for purpose of professional assistance and development; historical research. When no material risk to a client is entailed, a lawyer may disclose information derived from representing clients for purposes of providing professional assistance to other lawyers, whether informally, as in educational conversations among lawyers, or more formally, as in continuing-legal-education lectures. Thus, a lawyer may confer with another lawyer (whether or not in the same firm) concerning an issue in which the disclosing lawyer has gained experience through representing a client in order to assist the other lawyer in representing that lawyer's own clients.

A lawyer may cooperate with reasonable efforts to obtain information about clients and law practice for public purposes, such as historical research, when no material risk to a client is entailed, such as financial or reputational harm. A lawyer thereby cooperates in furthering public understanding of the law and law practice.

i. Divulgence concerning property dispositions by a deceased client. The attorney-client privilege does not apply to communications relevant to an issue between parties who claim an interest through the same decedent (see § 81). As a corollary, the lawyer may reveal confidential client information to contending heirs or other claimants to an interest through a deceased client, in advance of testifying, if there is a reasonable prospect that doing so would advance the interests of the client-decedent (see § 61). Authority to instruct the lawyer (see Comment *c(ii)* hereto) with respect to such divulgence is determined under the law of succession.

j. A lawyer's self-dealing in confidential client information. Subsection (2) prohibits a lawyer from using or disclosing confidential client information for the lawyer's personal enrichment, regardless of lack of risk of prejudice to the affected client. The duty is removed by client consent (see § 62). The sole remedy of the client for breach of the duty is restitutionary relief in the form of disgorgement of profit (see Restatement Second, Agency § 388, Comment *c*). The lawyer codes differ over whether such self-enriching use or disclosure constitutes a disciplinary violation in the absence of prejudice to the client.

The strict confidentiality duty of the Subsection is warranted for prophylactic purposes. A lawyer who acquires confidential client information as the result of a representation should not be tempted by expectation of profit to risk a possibly incorrect assessment of future harm to a client. There is no important social interest in permitting lawyers to make unconsented use or revelation of confidential client information for self-enrichment in personal transactions.

On limitations on business transactions between a lawyer and client, see § 126.

It is not inconsistent with Subsection (2) for a lawyer to use one client's confidential information for the benefit of another client in the course of representing the other client, even if doing so might also redound to the lawyer's gain, such as by enhancing a contingent-fee recovery. In all such instances, of course, the lawyer may not do so when it would create a material risk of harm to the original client. Thus, if otherwise permissible, a lawyer representing a plaintiff who has acquired extensive confidential information about the manner in which a defendant manufactured a product may employ that information for the benefit of another client with a claim against the same defendant arising out of a defect in the same product.

k. Confidentiality duties to a prospective client. See § 15, Comment *c.*

l. Use or disclosure of confidential information of co-clients. A lawyer may represent two or more clients in the same matter as co-clients either when there is no conflict of interest between them (see § 121) or when a conflict exists but the co-clients have adequately consented (see § 122). When a conflict of interest exists, as part of the process of obtaining consent, the lawyer is required to inform each co-client of the effect of joint representation upon disclosure of confidential information (see § 122, Comment *c(i)*), including both that all material information will be shared with each co-client during the course of the representation and that a communicating co-client will be unable to assert the attorney-client privilege against the other in the event of later adverse proceedings between them (see § 75).

Sharing of information among the co-clients with respect to the matter involved in the representation is normal and typically expected. As between the co-clients, in many such relationships each co-client is under a fiduciary duty to share all information material to the co-clients' joint enterprise. Such is the law, for example, with respect to members of a partnership. Limitation of the attorney-client privilege as applied to communications of co-clients is based on an assumption that each intends that his or her communications with the lawyer will be shared with the other co-clients but otherwise kept in confidence (see § 75, Comment *d*). Moreover, the common lawyer is required to keep each of the co-clients informed of all information reasonably necessary for the co-client to make decisions in connection with the matter (see § 20). The lawyer's duty extends to communicating information to other co-clients that is adverse to a co-client, whether learned from the lawyer's own investigation or learned in confidence from that co-client.

Co-clients may understand from the circumstances those obligations on the part of the lawyer and their own obligations, or they may explicitly agree to share information. Co-clients can also explicitly agree that the lawyer is not to share certain information, such as described categories of proprietary, financial, or similar information with one or more other co-clients (see § 75, Comment *d*). A lawyer must honor such agreements. If one co-client threatens physical harm or other types of crimes or fraud against the other, an exception to the lawyer's duty of confidentiality may apply (see §§ 66–67).

There is little case authority on the responsibilities of a lawyer when, in the absence of an agreement among the co-clients to restrict sharing of information, one co-client provides to the lawyer material information with the direction that it not be communicated to another co-client. The communicating co-client's expectation that the information be withheld from the other co-client may be manifest from the circumstances, particularly when the communication is clearly antagonistic to the interests of the affected co-client. The lawyer thus confronts a dilemma. If the information is material to the other co-client, failure to communicate it would compromise the lawyer's duties of loyalty, diligence (see § 16(1) & (2)), and communication (see § 20) to that client. On the other hand, sharing the communication with the affected co-client would compromise the communicating client's hope of confidentiality and risks impairing that client's trust in the lawyer.

Such circumstances create a conflict of interest among the co-clients (see § 121 & § 122, Comment *h*). The lawyer cannot continue in the representation without compromising either the duty of communication to the affected co-client or the expectation of confidentiality on the part of the communicating co-client. Moreover, continuing the joint representation without making disclosure may mislead the affected client or otherwise involve the lawyer in assisting the communicating client in a breach of fiduciary duty or other misconduct. Accordingly, the lawyer is required to withdraw unless the communicating client can be persuaded to permit sharing of the communication (see § 32(2)(a)). Following withdrawal, the lawyer may not, without consent of both, represent either co-client adversely to the other with respect to the same or a substantially related matter (see § 121, Comment *e(i)*).

In the course of withdrawal, the lawyer has discretion to warn the affected co-client that a matter seriously and adversely affecting that person's interests has come to light, which the other co-client refuses to permit the lawyer to disclose. Beyond such a limited warning, the lawyer, after consideration of all relevant circumstances, has the further discretion to inform the affected co-client of the specific communication if, in the lawyer's reasonable judgment, the immediacy and magnitude of the risk to the affected co-client outweigh the interest of the communicating client in continued secrecy. In making such determinations, the lawyer may take into account superior legal interests of the lawyer or of affected third persons, such as an interest implicated by a threat of physical harm to the lawyer or another person. See also § 66.

Illustration:

2. Lawyer has been retained by Husband and Wife to prepare wills pursuant to an arrangement under which each spouse agrees to leave most of their property to the other (compare § 130, Comment c, Illustrations 1–3). Shortly after the wills are executed, Husband (unknown to Wife) asks Lawyer to prepare an inter vivos trust for an illegitimate child whose existence Husband has kept secret from Wife for many years and about whom Husband had not previously informed Lawyer. Husband states that Wife would be distraught at learning of Husband's infidelity and of Husband's years of silence and that disclosure of the information could destroy their marriage. Husband directs Lawyer not to inform Wife. The inter vivos trust that Husband proposes to create would not materially affect Wife's own estate plan or her expected receipt of property under Husband's will, because Husband proposes to use property designated in Husband's will for a personally favored charity. In view of the lack of material effect on Wife, Lawyer may assist Husband to establish and fund the inter vivos trust and refrain from disclosing Husband's information to Wife.

3. Same facts as Illustration 2, except that Husband's proposed inter vivos trust would significantly deplete Husband's estate, to Wife's material detriment and in frustration of the Spouses' intended testamentary arrangements. If Husband refuses to inform Wife or to permit Lawyer to do so, Lawyer must withdraw from representing both Husband and Wife. In the light of all relevant circumstances, Lawyer may exercise discretion whether to inform Wife either that circumstances, which Lawyer has been asked not to reveal, indicate that she should revoke her recent will or to inform Wife of some or all the details of the information that Husband has recently provided so that Wife may protect her interests. Alternatively, Lawyer may inform Wife only that Lawyer is withdrawing because Husband will not permit disclosure of relevant information.

4. Lawyer represents both A and B in forming a business. Before the business is completely formed, A discloses to Lawyer that he has been convicted of defrauding business associates on two recent occasions. The circumstances of the communication from A are such that Lawyer reasonably infers that A believes that B is unaware of that information and does not want it provided to B. Lawyer reasonably believes that B would call off the arrangement with A if B were made aware of the information. Lawyer must first attempt to persuade A either to inform B directly or to permit Lawyer to inform B of the information. Failing that, Lawyer must withdraw from representing both A and B. In doing so, Lawyer has discretion to warn B that Lawyer has learned in confidence information indicating that B is at significant risk in carrying through with the business arrangement, but that A will not permit Lawyer to disclose that information to B. On the other hand, even if the

circumstances do not warrant invoking § 67, Lawyer has the further discretion to inform B of the specific nature of A's communication to B if Lawyer reasonably believes this necessary to protect B's interests in view of the immediacy and magnitude of the threat that Lawyer perceives posed to B.

Even if the co-clients have agreed that the lawyer will keep certain categories of information confidential from one or more other co-clients, in some circumstances it might be evident to the lawyer that the uninformed co-client would not have agreed to nondisclosure had that co-client been aware of the nature of the adverse information. For example, a lawyer's examination of confidential financial information, agreed not to be shown to another co-client to reduce antitrust concerns, could show in fact, contrary to all exterior indications, that the disclosing co-client is insolvent. In view of the co-client's agreement, the lawyer must honor the commitment of confidentiality and not inform the other client, subject to the exceptions described in § 67. The lawyer must, however, withdraw if failure to reveal would mislead the affected client, involve the lawyer in assisting the communicating client in a course of fraud, breach of fiduciary duty, or other unlawful activity, or, as would be true in most such instances, involve the lawyer in representing conflicting interests.

m.   Use or disclosure of confidential information of a nonclient. A lawyer may come into possession of confidential information of a nonclient, such as that of an opposing party in litigation or in negotiations. Such information may come from the other person or the lawyer or other agent of the person. When the receiving lawyer reasonably concludes that the transmission was authorized, the lawyer may use the information for the client's benefit, for example, where an opposing lawyer has conveyed the information apparently to advance representation (see § 61). Otherwise, the receiving lawyer's responsibilities depend on the circumstances. If the disclosure operates to end legal protection for the information, the lawyer may use it for the benefit of the lawyer's own client and may be required to do so if that would advance the client's lawful objectives (see § 16(1)). That would follow, for example, when an opposing lawyer failed to object to privileged or immune testimony (compare §§ 78, 86(1)(b), & 91(3)). The same legal result may follow when divulgence occurs inadvertently outside of court (see §§ 79 & 91). The receiving lawyer may be required to consult with that lawyer's client (see § 20) about whether to take advantage of the lapse.

If the person whose information was disclosed is entitled to have it suppressed or excluded (see § 79, Comment *c*), the receiving lawyer must either return the information or hold it for disposition after appropriate notification to the opposing person or that person's counsel. A court may suppress material after an inadvertent disclosure that did not amount to a waiver of the attorney-client privilege (see § 79, Comment *h*).

Where deceitful or illegal means were used to obtain the information, the receiving lawyer and that lawyer's client may be liable, among other remedies, for damages for harm caused or for injunctive relief against use or disclosure. The receiving lawyer must take steps to return such confidential client information and to keep it confidential from the lawyer's own client in the interim.

Similarly, if the receiving lawyer is aware that disclosure is being made in breach of trust by a lawyer or other agent of the opposing person, the receiving lawyer must not accept the information. An offending lawyer may be disqualified from further representation in a matter to which the information is relevant if the lawyer's own client would otherwise gain a substantial advantage (see § 6, Comment *i*). A tribunal may also order suppression or exclusion of such information.

TITLE B.   USING OR DISCLOSING CONFIDENTIAL CLIENT INFORMATION

§ 61.   Using or Disclosing Information to Advance Client Interests

A lawyer may use or disclose confidential client information when the lawyer reasonably believes that doing so will advance the interests of the client in the representation.

§ 62.   Using or Disclosing Information with Client Consent

A lawyer may use or disclose confidential client information when the client consents after being adequately informed concerning the use or disclosure

§ 63.   Using or Disclosing Information When Required by Law

A lawyer may use or disclose confidential client information when required by law, after the lawyer takes reasonably appropriate steps to assert that the information is privileged or otherwise protected against disclosure

§ 64.   Using or Disclosing Information in a Lawyer's Self-Defense

A lawyer may use or disclose confidential client information when and to the extent that the lawyer reasonably believes necessary to defend the lawyer or the lawyer's associate or agent against a charge or threatened charge by any person that the lawyer or such associate or agent acted wrongfully in the course of representing a client.

§ 65.   Using or Disclosing Information in a Compensation Dispute

A lawyer may use or disclose confidential client information when and to the extent that the lawyer reasonably believes

necessary to permit the lawyer to resolve a dispute with the client concerning compensation or reimbursement that the lawyer reasonably claims the client owes the lawyer

§ 66. Using or Disclosing Information to Prevent Death or Serious Bodily Harm

(1) A lawyer may use or disclose confidential client information when the lawyer reasonably believes that its use or disclosure is necessary to prevent reasonably certain death or serious bodily harm to a person.

(2) Before using or disclosing information under this Section, the lawyer must, if feasible, make a good-faith effort to persuade the client not to act. If the client or another person has already acted, the lawyer must, if feasible, advise the client to warn the victim or to take other action to prevent the harm and advise the client of the lawyer's ability to use or disclose information as provided in this Section and the consequences thereof.

(3) A lawyer who takes action or decides not to take action permitted under this Section is not, solely by reason of such action or inaction, subject to professional discipline, liable for damages to the lawyer's client or any third person, or barred from recovery against a client or third person.

Comment:

a. Scope and cross-references. This Section states an exception to the general duty of confidentiality in § 60(1), recognizing discretion in a lawyer to prevent the consequences of threats to life or personal safety. The rule stated in this Section is distinguishable from financial-harm disclosure under § 67 in three principal ways. First, the threat here need not be the product of a client act (see Comment *c* hereto). Second, the threat need not be created by a criminal or otherwise unlawful act (see id.). Third, the lawyer's services need not have been used to bring about the threatened death or serious bodily harm. As with § 67, a lawyer has discretion under this Section even if the use or disclosure threatens harm to the lawyer's client (see id.).

On cross-references to other Sections, see § 67, Comment *a*.

b. Rationale. The exception recognized by this Section is based on the overriding value of life and physical integrity. Threats to life or body encompassed within this Section may be the product of an act of the client or a nonclient and may be created by wrongful acts, by accident, or by circumstances. See Comment *c*. In all such events, the ultimate threat is the same, and its existence suffices to warrant a lawyer's taking corrective steps to prevent the threatened death or serious bodily harm.

No lawyer code explicitly permits disclosure, as broadly as permitted by Subsection (1), solely on the justification that death or serious bodily harm is threatened, such as where a lawyer becomes aware that a person's life is at risk because of a noncriminal act of a client. There are no reported judicial decisions on the issue. On the other hand, it seems highly unlikely that a court would impose discipline or other liability on a lawyer in an instance within Subsection (1), should the lawyer act reasonably, even in a way that prejudices the client, to remove the threat to life or body. Moreover, seven states do permit (indeed require) disclosure of a client's wrongful violent act to prevent harm.

  c. Use or disclosure to prevent death or serious bodily harm. Subsection (1) applies whenever a lawyer has a reasonable basis for believing that use or disclosure of a client's confidential information is necessary to prevent reasonably certain death or serious bodily harm to a person. On what constitutes reasonable belief, see § 67, Comment *h.* A threat within Subsection (1) need not be the product of a client act; an act of a nonclient threatening life or personal safety is also included, as is a threat created through accident or natural causes. It follows that if such a threat is created by a person, whether a client or a nonclient, there is no requirement that the act be criminal or otherwise unlawful.

Illustration:

  1. Lawyer is representing Defendant, a responding party in a suit by Plaintiff seeking damages for personal injuries arising out of a vehicle accident. Lawyer asks Doctor, as a consulting expert, to conduct an evaluation of medical evidence submitted by Plaintiff in support of a claim of personal injury. Following the examination, Doctor reports to Lawyer that Plaintiff has an undiagnosed aortal aneurism, which is serious and life-threatening but which can readily be repaired through surgery. Lawyer knows from work on the case that Plaintiff, as well as Plaintiff's treating physician, lawyer, and medical experts, are unaware of the condition. Lawyer is also aware that, if notified of the condition, Plaintiff will likely claim significant additional damages following corrective surgery. Despite Lawyer's urging, Defendant refuses to permit revelation of the condition to Plaintiff. Under this Section, Lawyer has discretion under Subsection (1) to reveal the condition to Plaintiff.

  So long as the predicate threat to life or body exists, discretion under Subsection (1) exists notwithstanding that the threat is created by the completed act of a person (including a client) or that the lawyer's information comes from otherwise privileged conversations.

Illustrations:

  2. Client seeks legal advice from Lawyer about his dismissal from a maintenance position by Landlord and eviction from his apartment. In expressing his anger about Landlord, Client reveals that Client has set a mechanical device to ignite and burn down the building. Lawyer has reason to believe that there are people living in

the building. Despite Lawyer's remonstration, Client refuses to take any action to prevent the fire or to warn others. Despite the risk that calling the fire department or police may result in serious criminal charges against Client, Lawyer has discretion under Subsection (1) to do so.

3. As the result of confidential disclosures at a meeting with engineers employed by Client Corporation, Lawyer reasonably believes that one of the engineers released a toxic substance into a city's water-supply system. Lawyer reasonably believes that the discharge will cause reasonably certain death or serious bodily harm to elderly or ill persons within a short period and that Lawyer's disclosure of the discharge is necessary to permit authorities to remove that threat or lessen the number of its victims. Lawyer's efforts to persuade responsible Client Corporation personnel to take corrective action have been unavailing. Although the act creating the threat has already occurred, Lawyer has discretion to disclose under Subsection (1) for the purpose of preventing the consequences of the act.

In circumstances such as those in Illustration 3, the Section applies even if the act creating the threat of death or serious bodily harm was not a crime or fraud. In other situations, the likelihood that other actors know about and will eliminate the risk may be relevant. Most situations will be intensely fact-sensitive. For example, the character of a threatened act as a crime or fraud suggests a state of mind on the part of the perpetrator that is more threatening to the intended victim than an act that is merely negligent or not wrongful, and thus may more readily warrant the lawyer's conclusion that the risk of harm is great.

Serious bodily harm within the meaning of the Section includes life-threatening illness and injuries and the consequences of events such as imprisonment for a substantial period and child sexual abuse. It also includes a client's threat of suicide.

Illustration:

4. Lawyer advises Manufacturer on product-liability matters. Lawyer had previously advised Manufacturer that use of Component A in a consumer product did not create an unreasonable risk of harm and was in compliance with consumer-protection and other law. Lawyer has now learned that Supplier, unknown to Manufacturer, provided Component A in a form not in compliance with Manufacturer's specifications. Manufacturer promptly altered its production methods so as to avoid any significant risk of harm in products manufactured in the future. There is a slight statistical chance that a consumer using the prior version of the product containing the noncomplying version of Component A might suffer serious bodily harm, but only in a highly unlikely combination of circumstances. Manufacturer's responsible officers have decided not

to issue a public notice of the slightly increased risk of harm. Lawyer does not have discretion under this Section to use or disclose Manufacturer's confidential information to make a public warning of the slightly increased risk of harm.

d. A lawyer's reasonable belief. A lawyer's discretion to take appropriate action to prevent death or serious bodily harm under this Section is predicated on the lawyer's reasonable belief that the action is necessary to prevent reasonably certain death or serious bodily harm to a person. Some factors stated in Comment *f* as relevant to a lawyer's choice of appropriate action will also be relevant to the lawyer in assessing whether a situation warranting action exists. Some facts, particularly concerning future acts and probabilities and a client's or third person's subjective state of mind, may be unlikely or difficult for the lawyer to ascertain. Before making disclosure where such facts are ambiguous, the lawyer must make a reasonable effort to determine the relevant facts, taking into account the risks inherent in either action or inaction by the lawyer. As with other matters affecting a lawyer's responsibilities that may arise in the course of representing a client, a lawyer may consult with another lawyer about whether to proceed under this Section.

The Section refers (as does § 67) to a lawyer's reasonable belief that use or disclosure is "necessary" to prevent "reasonably certain" death or serious bodily harm, while ABA Model Rules of Professional Conduct, Rule 1.6(b)(1) (1983) (in its exception dealing with threats of death or bodily harm) refers to "imminent" death or serious bodily harm. The concept of imminence is included in the meaning of the terms "necessary" and "reasonably certain" death or bodily harm in that the need to act must be reasonably believed to exist in view of a present threat of probable death or bodily harm. The concept of imminence is susceptible of an overly narrow interpretation, under which use or disclosure would be precluded until immediately before the threatened death or bodily harm would occur. While such occasions are included within the Section, a lawyer is also permitted to act under the Section whenever the lawyer reasonably believes that intervention is necessary in response to a present threat, even if the death or serious bodily harm appears likely to occur some time in the future. ABA Model Rules of Professional Conduct, Rule 1.6(b)(1) (1983) can be similarly interpreted.

e. Counseling a client. As does § 67(3), Subsection (2) requires counseling with the client, if feasible. The interest protected by such counseling is the client's interest in limiting use or disclosure of confidential information and in taking responsible action to deal with situations that may be of the client's own making or attributable to the client. If a client, whether in response to a lawyer's counseling or otherwise, takes corrective action—such as by ceasing the threatened act before harm is caused—use or disclosure by the lawyer would not be necessary and therefore would not be permissible under this Section. Particularly when the actor is a nonclient or when the act is deliberate or malicious, a lawyer making adverse use or disclosure under this Section may, in the circumstances, reasonably conclude that superior interests of the lawyer or others in their own personal safety preclude personal contact with the actor.

f. Appropriate action. A lawyer's use or disclosure under this Section is a last resort when no other available action is reasonably likely to prevent the threatened death or serious bodily harm. Use or disclosure, when made, should be no more extensive than the lawyer reasonably believes necessary to accomplish the relevant purpose.

Preventive steps that a lawyer may appropriately take include consulting with relatives or friends of the person likely to cause the death or serious bodily harm and with other advisers to that person. (The lawyer may also seek the assistance of such persons in efforts to persuade the person not to act or to warn the threatened victim (see Comment *e* hereto).) A lawyer may also consult with law-enforcement authorities or agencies with jurisdiction over the type of conduct involved in order to prevent it and warn a threatened victim.

What particular measures are reasonable depends on the circumstances known to the lawyer. Relevant circumstances include the degree to which it appears likely that the threatened death or serious bodily harm will actually result, the irreversibility of its consequences once the act has taken place, the time available, whether victims might be unaware of the threat or might rely on the lawyer to protect them, the lawyer's prior course of dealings with the client, and the extent of adverse effect on the client that may result from disclosure contemplated by the lawyer. The lawyer must reasonably believe that the measures are appropriate and that they will entail no more adverse consequences to the client than necessary (see also § 64, Comment *e*).

When a lawyer has taken action under the Section, in all but extraordinary cases the relationship between lawyer and client would have so far deteriorated as to make the lawyer's effective representation of the client impossible. Generally, therefore, the lawyer is required to withdraw from the representation (see § 32(2)(a) & Comment *f* thereto), unless the client gives informed consent to the lawyer's continued representation notwithstanding the lawyer's adverse use or disclosure of information. In any event, the lawyer generally must inform the client of the fact of the lawyer's use or disclosure (see § 20(1)), unless the lawyer has a superior interest in not informing the client, such as to protect the lawyer from wrongful retaliation by the client, to effectuate permissible measures that are not yet complete, or to prevent the client from inflicting further harms on third persons.

g. Effects of a lawyer taking or not taking discretionary remedial action. A lawyer's decision to take action to disclose or not to disclose under this Section is discretionary with the lawyer (compare § 63 (disclosure required by law)). Such action would inevitably conflict to a significant degree with the lawyer's customary role of protecting client interests. Critical facts may be unclear, emotions may be high, and little time may be available in which the lawyer must decide on an appropriate course of action. Subsequent re-examination of the reasonableness of a lawyer's action in the light of later developments would be unwarranted; reasonableness of the lawyer's belief at the time and in the circumstances in which the lawyer acts is alone controlling.

As stated in Subsection (3) and in the corresponding § 67(4), a lawyer who takes action or decides not to take action in a situation described in and consistent with the rule of the Section and § 67 is not, by reason of such action or inaction alone, liable for professional discipline or liable for damages to the client or any third person injured by the client's action. Similarly, a client may not assert as an affirmative defense in a fee or similar suit that the lawyer has or has not taken steps permitted under the Section (see § 37). The same results apply with respect to questions of the vicarious liability (see § 58) of the firm in which the lawyer practices. That is precluded both because of the absence of any violation of duty by the individual lawyer (see § 58(1)) and because vicarious liability would be equally inconsistent with the reasons, stated above, for treating the lawyer's action or inaction as discretionary. Apart from this Section or § 67(4), a lawyer would of course remain liable for otherwise actionable wrongs, such as by participating with a client as a co-principal or accessory in the client's wrongful act (see § 8, Comment *e*).

Because the interests protected by the rule are those of the public and third persons, the discretion of a lawyer to take action consistent with the Section may not be contracted away by agreement between the lawyer and the client or the lawyer and a third person (compare § 23(1)).

§ 67. Using or Disclosing Information to Prevent, Rectify, or Mitigate Substantial Financial Loss

(1) A lawyer may use or disclose confidential client information when the lawyer reasonably believes that its use or disclosure is necessary to prevent a crime or fraud, and:

(a) the crime or fraud threatens substantial financial loss;

(b) the loss has not yet occurred;

(c) the lawyer's client intends to commit the crime or fraud either personally or through a third person; and

(d) the client has employed or is employing the lawyer's services in the matter in which the crime or fraud is committed.

(2) If a crime or fraud described in Subsection (1) has already occurred, a lawyer may use or disclose confidential client information when the lawyer reasonably believes its use or disclosure is necessary to prevent, rectify, or mitigate the loss.

(3) Before using or disclosing information under this Section, the lawyer must, if feasible, make a good-faith effort to persuade the client not to act. If the client or another person has already acted, the lawyer must, if feasible, advise the client to warn the victim or to take other action to prevent, rectify, or mitigate the loss. The lawyer must, if feasible, also advise the client of the lawyer's ability to use or disclose information as provided in this Section and the consequences thereof.

(4) A lawyer who takes action or decides not to take action permitted under this Section is not, solely by reason of such action or inaction, subject to professional discipline, liable for damages to the lawyer's client or any third person, or barred from recovery against a client or third person.

Comment:

a. Scope and cross-references. This Section states exceptions to the general confidentiality rule of § 60(1) and recognizes discretion in a lawyer to prevent, mitigate, or rectify the described types of financial loss to another person even if the use or disclosure threatens risk to the lawyer's client. The exception applies when a client intends to commit a criminal or fraudulent act and permits a lawyer, in taking reasonable preventive or corrective measures, to use or disclose confidential client information to prevent the act or to rectify or mitigate it.

Unless this Section or § 66 applies, a lawyer may use or disclose confidential client information only if the client consents (see § 62), if other law so requires (see § 63), or if reasonably necessary in a lawyer's self-defense (see § 64) or in a compensation dispute (see § 65).

On the crime-fraud exception to the attorney-client privilege, see § 82. For a comparison of the Sections, see Comment *c* hereto. On the rule that disclosure under this Section (or § 66) does not constitute waiver by subsequent disclosure for purposes of the attorney-client privilege, see Comment *c* hereto and § 79, Comment *c*.

On a lawyer's nonliability for action or inaction under this Section, see Comment *k* hereto. On a lawyer's liability for certain client harms to described third persons, see §§ 51 and 56.

On a lawyer's general responsibilities with respect to counseling or assisting a client concerning illegal acts, see § 94. See also Comment *i* hereto. On providing information to a client, see generally § 20. On advising an organizational client, see § 96; on advising a governmental client, see § 97. With respect to a lawyer's duties and discretion when dealing with perjury by a client or other witness or with other false evidence, see § 120. A lawyer has the right to withdraw when the lawyer reasonably believes the client is employing the lawyer's assistance to aid wrongful acts, including breaches of fiduciary duty (see § 32(3)(d) & (e)). On a lawyer's duty to withdraw after using or disclosing confidential client information under the Section, see Comment *j* hereto.

b. Rationale. The exceptions recognized in this Section reflect a balance between the competing considerations of protecting interests in client confidentiality and lawyer loyalty to clients, on the one hand, and protecting the interests of society and third persons in avoiding substantial financial consequences of crimes or frauds, on the other. The integrity, professional reputation, and financial interests of the lawyer can also be implicated under Subsections (1) and (2) in view of the requirement that the lawyer's services have been employed in commission of the crime or fraud. The exceptions are also justified on the ground that the client is not entitled to the protection of confidentiality when the client knowingly causes substantial financial harm through a crime or fraud and when, as required under Subsections (1) and (2), the client has in effect misused the client-lawyer relationship for that purpose. In most instances of unlawful client acts that threaten such consequences to others, it may be hoped that the client's own sober reflection and the lawyer's counseling (see Comment *i* hereto) will lead the client to refrain from the act or to prevent or mitigate its consequences.

The issues addressed in this Section are variously treated in American jurisdictions. The 1983 ABA Model Rules of Professional Conduct (1983), in Rule 1.6(b), recommended a narrow rule that would permit use or disclosure only in the case of a client's "criminal act that the lawyer believes is likely to result in imminent death or substantial bodily harm … "(compare § 66). Some sponsors of that formulation asserted that, despite the absence of explicit permission to act to prevent client fraud, Rule 1.6(b) nonetheless permitted a lawyer to act to prevent a client's crime or fraud as long as the lawyer did not disclose as such the explicit content of communications from the client. In any event, only a small minority of jurisdictions have adopted the apparently restrictive formulation of ABA Model Rule 1.6(b). As indicated in the Reporter's Note, over 40 jurisdictions have rejected the recommended model rule and have broadened the rule so as to permit use or disclosure to prevent substantial financial injury. Seventeen states also permit use or disclosure to rectify past and completed client fraud, which Subsection (2) also permits (see Comment *f* hereto). Lawyer codes in seven states mandate disclosure in at least some circumstances of client fraud; there is no similar requirement in this Section.

The exceptions stated in this Section permit a lawyer to exercise discretion to prevent the described loss to third persons, even though adverse effects might befall the client as a result. The exceptions are extraordinary. The only acts covered under the Section are the described crimes or frauds that threaten substantial financial loss to others. Clients remain protected in consulting a lawyer concerning the legal consequences of any such act in which the lawyer's services were not employed, including acts constituting crimes or frauds.

The discretion recognized in this Section may to an unknowable extent lessen some clients' willingness to consult freely with their lawyers. In this respect, the Section has an effect similar to that of the crime-fraud exception to the attorney-client privilege (see § 82; see also Comment *d* hereto). The social benefits of allowing a lawyer to prevent, mitigate, or rectify substantial financial loss to intended victims of criminal or fraudulent client acts under the described circumstances warrant incurring that additional risk.

Not all crimes and frauds are covered by this Section, but only those that involve a risk of substantial financial loss. The Section applies when a client intends to commit a crime or fraud either personally or through a third person (see Subsection (1)(c)). What constitutes a crime or a fraud is determined under otherwise applicable law. The distinction between acts entailing risks of such loss and other acts that may also be criminal or fraudulent reflects a balance between client confidentiality (see § 60, Comment *b*) and protection of third persons. It could be argued that a lawyer's discretion should be constrained in another manner, for example through case-by-case balancing of those competing interests, perhaps including as a factor the extent to which exercise of the lawyer's discretion would harm the client. Lawyers can be expected to take into account that and other relevant considerations in determining whether to exercise the professional discretion that the Section recognizes. However, the Section does not require that the lawyer exercise discretion only after explicitly making such an evaluation or in any other particular manner.

c.   Comparison with the crime-fraud exception to the attorney-client privilege. This Section generally corresponds to the crime-fraud exception to the attorney-client privilege (see § 82, Comment *d*). Somewhat different considerations underlie the two rules and they operate in different settings, testimonial and nontestimonial. This Section § 82 both apply to client crimes or frauds. Both apply to acts that a client intends to commit and to acts by a third person whom the client intends to aid.

This Section applies only when the likelihood of financial loss is great and the lawyer reasonably believes that use or revelation is necessary to prevent the crime or fraud or to prevent, rectify, or mitigate the loss it causes (see Comment *f* hereto). In contrast, the crime-fraud exception to the attorney-client privilege stated in § 82 applies without regard to the consequences of the intended act so long as the act itself is a crime or fraud. That exception to the attorney-client privilege applies only when a client consults a lawyer with intention to obtain assistance to commit a crime or fraud or so uses the lawyer's services, whereas the Section applies regardless of the client's intention at the time of consultation (see Comment *g* hereto). The crime-fraud exception to the attorney-client privilege is administered by a tribunal and applies only when a lawyer or another person is called upon to give evidence, whereas the Section concerns action that a lawyer may take on the basis of a reasonable belief and outside of any proceeding and thus without direction from a judicial officer. Finally, this Section is limited to client acts in which a lawyer's services are employed; the crime-fraud exception applies whether or not the lawyer's services are so employed. Due to the several differences in the requirements for this Section and § 82, a finding that a lawyer permissibly used or disclosed confidential client information under this Section and a determination whether § 82 applies must be made independently.

Lawyer disclosure under this Section is taken in the lawyer's personal capacity and not as agent. Accordingly, such disclosure would not constitute disclosure by an agent of the client for purposes of subject-matter waiver of other confidential communications under § 79 (see § 79, Comment c).

d. Client crime or fraud. As with the corresponding crime-fraud exception to the attorney-client privilege (see § 82), this Section is limited to acts that under applicable law constitute crimes and frauds. "Fraud" as employed in this Section has the same limited meaning stated in § 82, Comment *d*. As there stated, inaction (through nondisclosure) as well as action may constitute fraud under applicable law. Many acts that will have seriously harmful financial consequences are denominated as crimes or frauds in the law. However, some acts causing financial loss to third persons constitute breaches of other legal obligations, such as intentional torts, breaches of contract, violation of property rights, or violations of statutory, regulatory, or other legal duties that are not crimes or frauds. Some of those acts may be particularly opprobrious in specific instances. However, society has traditionally defined seriously wrongful conduct in terms of crime and fraud. Limiting the exceptions in this Section to crime and fraud is also a matter of practicality, because no other categorical description of harmful acts provides an equally definite limitation on these exceptions to a lawyer's duty of confidentiality.

e. Employment of the lawyer's services in the client's act. Use or disclosure under either Subsection (1) or (2) requires that the lawyer's services are being or were employed in commission of a criminal or fraudulent act. The lawyer's involvement need not be known to or discoverable by the victim or other person. Subsections (1) and (2) apply without regard either to the lawyer's prior knowledge of the client's intended use of the lawyer's services or to when the lawyer forms a reasonable basis for a belief concerning the nature of the client's act. Such employment may occur, for example, when a client has a document prepared by the lawyer for use in a criminal or fraudulent scheme, receives the lawyer's advice concerning the act to assist in carrying it out, asks the lawyer to appear before a court or administrative agency as part of a transaction, or obtains advice that will assist the client in avoiding detection or apprehension for the crime or fraud. It is not necessary that the lawyer's services have been critical to success of the client's act or that the services were specifically requested by the client. It suffices if the services were or are being employed in the commission of the act.

Illustrations:

1. As part of a business transaction, Lawyer on behalf of Client prepares and sends to Victim an opinion letter helpful to Client in completing an aspect of the transaction. At the time of preparing and sending the opinion letter, Lawyer had no reason to believe that the transaction was other than proper, but Lawyer thereafter receives information giving reason to believe the transaction constitutes a crime or fraud by Client within this Section. If the other conditions of the Section are present, Lawyer's opinion letter will have been employed in commission of Client's act, and Lawyer accordingly has discretion to use or disclose confidential information of Client as provided in the Section.

2. Client has put in place a scheme to defraud Victim of substantial funds. After doing so, but before Victim has actually lost any funds, Client seeks Lawyer's assistance in meeting regulatory action and a suit by Victim seeking restitution that might ensue. Despite Lawyer's counseling, Client refuses to warn Victim, return the funds, or take other corrective action. Because Lawyer's services have not been employed in the commission of Client's fraud, Lawyer may not use or disclose Client's confidential information under this Section.

Legal assistance provided only after the client's crime or fraud has already been committed is not within this Section, whether or not loss to the victim has already occurred, if the lawyer's services are not employed for the purposes of a further crime or fraud, such as the crime of obstruction of justice or other unlawful attempt to cover up the prior wrongful act. While applicable law may provide that a completed act is regarded for some purposes as a continuing offense, the limitation of Subsection (1)(d) applies with attention to the time at which the client's acts actually occurred.

Illustrations:

3. Client has been charged by a regulatory agency with participation in a scheme to defraud Victim. Client seeks the assistance of Lawyer in defending against the charges. The loss to Victim has already occurred. During the initial interview and thereafter, Lawyer is provided with ample reason to believe that Client's acts were fraudulent and caused substantial financial loss to Victim. Because Lawyer's services were not employed by Client in committing the fraud, Lawyer does not have discretion under this Section to use or disclose Client's confidential information.

4. The same facts as in Illustration 3, except that the law of the applicable jurisdiction provides that each day during which a wrongdoer in the position of Client fails to make restitution to Victim constitutes a separate offense of the same type as the original

wrong. Notwithstanding the continuing-offense law, commission of the fraudulent act of Client has already occurred without use of Lawyer's services. As in Illustration 3, Lawyer does not have discretion under this Section to use or disclose Client's confidential information.

f. Use or disclosure to prevent (Subsection (1)) or to rectify or mitigate (Subsection (2)) a client wrongful act. A lawyer has discretion to use or disclose under this Section when necessary to achieve either of two different purposes—to prevent the act from occurring (Subsection (1)) or to prevent, rectify, or mitigate loss caused by the act (Subsection (2)). Under Subsection (1), a lawyer may take preventive measures even though some act has already occurred, if some material part of the crime or fraud has not yet occurred or has not yet been inflicted on a victim. For example, in a criminal or fraudulent transaction involving more than one step, a lawyer would have discretion to take preventive action under Subsection (1) if some acts remained to be accomplished. Further, if all steps in a transaction to be taken by the client have already occurred, but the intended victim has not taken a final step, such as dispatching funds to the client, action to warn the victim not to take final steps is permissible preventive action within Subsection (1).

Action by the lawyer to prevent, rectify, or mitigate loss under Subsection (2) is in addition to and goes beyond that permitted for preventive purposes under Subsection (1). Actions to prevent, rectify, or mitigate the loss caused by the client's act include correcting or preventing the effects of the client's criminal or fraudulent act, even if the client's crime or fraud has already occurred and regardless of whether its impact has been visited upon the victim. Thus, a lawyer who acquires information from which the lawyer reasonably believes that a client has already defrauded a victim in a scheme in which the lawyer's services were employed may disclose the fraud to the victim when necessary to permit the victim to take possible corrective action, such as to initiate proceedings promptly in order to seize or recover assets fraudulently obtained by the client.

Once use or disclosure of information has been made to prevent, rectify, or mitigate loss under Subsection (2), the lawyer is not further warranted in actively assisting the victim on an ongoing basis in pursuing a remedy against the lawyer's client or in any similar manner aiding the victim or harming the client. Thus, a lawyer is not warranted under this Section in serving as legal counsel for a victim (see also § 132), volunteering to serve as witness in a proceeding by the victim, or cooperating with an administrative agency in obtaining compensation for victims. The lawyer also may not use or disclose information for the purpose of voluntarily assisting a law-enforcement agency to apprehend and prosecute the client, unless the lawyer reasonably believes that such disclosure would be necessary to prevent, rectify, or mitigate the victim's loss. On the rule that disclosure of confidential client information does not constitute waiver of the client's privilege due to subsequent disclosure by an agent, see Comment *c* hereto.

Illustrations:

> 5. Lawyer has assisted Client in preparing documents by means of which Client will obtain a $5,000,000 loan from Bank. The loan closing occurred on Monday and Bank will make the funds available for Client's use on Wednesday. On Tuesday Client reveals to Lawyer for the first time that Client knowingly obtained the loan by means of a materially false statement of Client's assets. Assuming that the other conditions for application of Subsection (2) are present, while Client's fraudulent act of obtaining the loan has, in large part, already occurred, Lawyer has discretion under the Subsection to use or disclose Client's confidential information to prevent the consequences of the fraud (final release of the funds from Bank) from occurring.

> 6. The same facts as in Illustration 5, except that Lawyer learned of the fraud on Wednesday after Bank had already released the funds to Client. Under Subsection (2), Lawyer's use or disclosure would be permissible if necessary for the purpose, for example, of enabling Bank to seize assets of Client in its possession or control as an offset against the fraudulently obtained loan or to prevent Client from sending the funds overseas and thereby making it difficult or impossible to trace them.

g. Client's intent. It is not required that the client's requisite intent existed at the time the client consulted the lawyer. For example, the client may form a plan to employ the lawyer's former services in drafting documents in a scheme that the client devises after the lawyer's services have ended. The client need not be aware specifically that the contemplated act was a crime or fraud (see also § 82, Comment *c*). As stated in Subsection (1)(c), the client may act either directly or through a third person. The Section does not apply if the lawyer is aware that the client's purpose had been abandoned, because in that situation disclosure is no longer necessary as required by the Section.

h. A lawyer's reasonable belief. A lawyer's discretion to take appropriate measures to prevent financial loss under this Section or to rectify or mitigate it is predicated on the lawyer's reasonable belief that the client intends to engage in the described crime or fraud and that the lawyer's use or disclosure is necessary to prevent the loss or to rectify or mitigate it. Some facts, particularly concerning future acts and probabilities and a client's subjective state of mind, may be difficult to ascertain. Before making disclosure in such circumstances, the lawyer must make a reasonable effort to determine the relevant facts. As with other matters affecting a lawyer's responsibilities that may arise in the course of representing a client, a lawyer may consult with another lawyer about whether to proceed under the Section. See also § 66, Comment *d*.

i. Counseling a client. When a lawyer becomes aware of a client's intent to pursue a course of action that is criminal or fraudulent, the lawyer may be able, through appeal to the good judgment and moral sense of the client, to persuade the client to abandon the intended course or to make whole any victim of a fraudulent or criminal act (see § 94). Such counseling may avoid difficulties for the client and others. Accordingly, before a lawyer may take remedial action under the Section, the lawyer must consult with the affected client as stated in Subsection (3), if consultation is feasible in view of the imminence of the threatened loss and similar time considerations, the likelihood of the threatened activity and its consequences and the apparent firmness of the client's intentions, any risk to the lawyer or others that may be reasonably apprehended, and other constraints. In the course of consulting with the client, the lawyer must ordinarily inform the client of the lawyer's ability to act pursuant to this Section if the client fails to take corrective action (see § 20), unless the lawyer has a superior interest in not informing the client, such as to protect the lawyer from reasonably apprehended and wrongful retaliation by the client, to effectuate permissible measures that are not yet complete, or to prevent the client from inflicting further financial loss on third persons. If a client, whether in response to a lawyer's counseling or otherwise, takes corrective action—such as by ceasing the threatened act before loss is caused—use or disclosure by the lawyer would not be necessary and therefore would not be permissible under this Section.

j. Appropriate action. A lawyer's use or disclosure of information under the Section is a last resort when no other available action is reasonably likely to prevent the threatened financial loss or to rectify or mitigate it. Use or disclosure, when made, should be no more extensive than the lawyer reasonably believes necessary to accomplish the relevant purpose. On consulting with suitable advisers to a client, the importance of the circumstances known to the lawyer in determining the reasonableness of measures taken, withdrawal by the lawyer, and informing the client after use or disclosure, see § 66, Comment *f.*

In using or disclosing under this Section, the lawyer may also withdraw or disaffirm opinion letters, affidavits, and other legal documents that had been prepared for the client or others that might be employed or that might have been employed in furthering the crime or fraud or contributed to its consequences. In addition, under § 64, a lawyer may take steps that are justified as reasonably appropriate to defend the lawyer and the lawyer's associates against a charge of wrongdoing arising from the representation. Other law may require a lawyer to use or disclose confidential client information in such circumstances (see § 63).

Comment k. Effects of a lawyer taking or not taking discretionary remedial action. The rule of Subsection (4) corresponds to that of § 66(3). See also § 66, Comment *g.*

TOPIC 2.   THE ATTORNEY–CLIENT PRIVILEGE

TITLE A.   THE SCOPE OF THE PRIVILEGE

§ 68.   Attorney–Client Privilege

Except as otherwise provided in this Restatement, the attorney-client privilege may be invoked as provided in § 86 with respect to:

(1) a communication

(2) made between privileged persons

(3) in confidence

(4) for the purpose of obtaining or providing legal assistance for the client.

Comment:

a. Scope and cross-references. This Section states the general formulation of the attorney-client testimonial privilege. It must be read in the context of succeeding Sections that elaborate its four elements: § 69, defining types of communications protected by the privilege; § 70, delineating the privileged persons who may be the source of or receive privileged communications; § 71, defining the requirements of "in confidence"; and § 72, specifying that legal assistance be the purpose of the communication. Applications of the rule with respect to organizational and multiple clients are set out in Title B. The privilege is subject to a number of important waivers, exceptions, and extensions set out in Title C. On invoking the protection of the privilege, see § 86. The legal duty of a lawyer to keep client information confidential is examined in Topic 1.

b. Relationship to other confidentiality principles. The attorney-client privilege and its underlying policies have influenced such related rules as the work-product immunity (see Topic 3), the lawyer's duties respecting confidential client information (see Topic 1), and the immunities of lawyers and clients for injurious statements made in the course of a judicial proceeding (see § 57(1)).

c. Rationale supporting the privilege. The modern attorney-client privilege evolved from an earlier reluctance of English courts to require lawyers to breach the code of a gentleman by being compelled to reveal in court what they had been told by clients. The privilege, such as it was then, belonged to the lawyer. It was a rule congenial with the law, which prevailed in England until the mid–19th century, that made parties to litigation themselves incompetent to testify, whether called as witnesses in their own behalf or by their adversaries. The modern conception of the privilege, reflected in this Restatement, protects clients, not lawyers, and clients have primary authority to determine whether to assert the privilege (see § 86) or waive it (see §§ 78–80).

The rationale for the privilege is that confidentiality enhances the value of client-lawyer communications and hence the efficacy of legal services. The rationale is founded on three related assumptions. First, vindicating rights and complying with obligations under the law and under modern legal processes are matters often too complex and uncertain for a person untrained in the law, so that clients need to consult lawyers. The second assumption is that a client who consults a lawyer needs to disclose all of the facts to the lawyer and must be able to receive in return communications from the lawyer reflecting those facts. It is assumed that, in the absence of such frank and full discussion between client and lawyer, adequate legal assistance cannot be realized. Many legal rules are complex and most are fact-specific in their application. Lawyers are much better situated than nonlawyers to appreciate the effect of legal rules and to identify facts that determine whether a legal rule is applicable. Full disclosure by clients facilitates efficient presentation at trials and other proceedings and in a lawyer's advising functions.

The third assumption supporting the privilege is controversial—that clients would be unwilling to disclose personal, embarrassing, or unpleasant facts unless they could be assured that neither they nor their lawyers could be called later to testify to the communication. Relatedly, it is assumed that lawyers would not feel free in probing client's stories and giving advice unless assured that they would not thereby expose the client to adverse evidentiary risk. Those assumptions cannot be tested but are widely believed by lawyers to be sound. The privilege implies an impairment of the search for truth in some instances. Recognition of the privilege reflects a judgment that this impairment is outweighed by the social and moral values of confidential consultations. The privilege provides a zone of privacy within which a client may more effectively exercise the full autonomy that the law and legal institutions allow.

The evidentiary consequences of the privilege are indeterminate. If the behavioral assumptions supporting the privilege are well-founded, perhaps the evidence excluded by the privilege would not have come into existence save for the privilege. In any event, testimony concerning out-of-court communications often would be excluded as hearsay, although some of it could come in under exceptions such as that for statements against interest. The privilege also precludes an abusive litigation practice of calling an opposing lawyer as a witness.

Some judicial fact findings undoubtedly have been erroneous because the privilege excluded relevant evidence. The privilege creates tension with the right to confront and cross-examine opposing witnesses. It excuses lawyers from giving relevant testimony and precludes full examination of clients. The privilege no doubt protects wrongdoing in some instances. To that extent the privilege may facilitate serious social harms. The crime-fraud exception to the privilege (see § 82) results in forced disclosure of some such confidential conversations, but certainly not all.

Suggestions have been made that the privilege be conditional, not absolute, and thus inapplicable in cases where extreme need can be shown for admitting evidence of attorney-client communications. The privilege, however, is not subject to ad hoc exceptions. The predictability of a definite rule encourages forthright discussions between client and lawyer. The law accepts the risks of factual error and injustice in individual cases in deference to the values that the privilege vindicates.

d.   Source of the law concerning the privilege. In most of the states, the privilege is defined by statute or rule, typically in an evidence code; in a few states, the privilege is common law. In the federal system, the definition of the privilege is left to the common-law process with respect to issues on which federal law applies. Federal Rule of Evidence 501 provides generally that questions of privilege "shall be governed by the principles of the common law as they may be interpreted by the courts of the United States in the light of reason and experience." On elements of a claim or defense as to which state law supplies the rule of decision, however, Rule 501 provides that the federal courts are to apply the attorney-client privilege of the relevant state.

§ 69   Attorney–Client Privilege—"Communication"

A communication within the meaning of § 68 is any expression through which a privileged person, as defined in § 70, undertakes to convey information to another privileged person and any document or other record revealing such an expression.

Comment:

a.   Scope and cross-references. This Section defines the concept of "communication" stated in § 68(1). The elements of § 68(2)-(3) are considered in §§ 70–72. On invoking the privilege, see § 86. On the confidentiality responsibilities of lawyers, see §§ 59–67.

b.   Communications qualifying for the privilege. A communication can be in any form. Most confidential client communications to a lawyer are written or spoken words, but the privilege applies to communication through technologically enhanced methods such as telephone and telegraph, audio or video tape recording, film, telecopier, and other electronic means. However, communications through a public mode may suggest the absence of a reasonable expectation of confidentiality (see § 71, Comment *e*).

c.   Intercepted communications. The communication need not in fact succeed; for example, an intercepted communication is within this Section (see § 71, Comment *c* (eavesdroppers)).

Illustration:

1.   Lawyer represents Client in a pending criminal investigation. Lawyer directs Client to make a tape recording detailing everything that Client knows about an unlawful enterprise for

Lawyer's review. Client makes the tape recording in secret. A cell mate, after learning of the tape recording, informs the prosecutor who causes the tape to be seized under a subpoena. The attorney-client privilege covers the tape recording.

For the rule where a communication is disclosed to nonprivileged persons, see § 79.

d. *Distinction between the content of a communication and knowledge of facts.* The attorney-client privilege protects only the content of the communication between privileged persons, not the knowledge of privileged persons about the facts themselves. Although a client cannot be required to testify about communications with a lawyer about a subject, the client may be required to testify about what the client knows concerning the same subject. The client thus may invoke the privilege with respect to the question "Did you tell your lawyer the light was red?" but not with respect to the question "Did you see that the light was red?" Similarly, the privilege does not apply to preexisting documents or other tangible evidence (see Comment *j*), even if they concern the same subject as a privileged communication.

Illustration:

> 2. Client, a defendant in a breach-of-contract suit, confidentially informs Lawyer about Client's recollection of a course of dealings between Client and a subcontractor, Plaintiff in the pending contract suit. The attorney-client privilege does not prevent Plaintiff from requiring Client to testify at a deposition or trial concerning Client's present recollection of the course of dealings between Client and Plaintiff. Plaintiff may not, however, require Lawyer or Client to testify concerning what Client told Lawyer about those same facts.

e. *Communicative client acts.* The privilege extends to nonverbal communicative acts intended to convey information. For example, a client may communicate with a lawyer through facial expressions or other communicative bodily motions or gestures (nodding or shaking the head or holding up a certain number of fingers to indicate number) or acting out a recalled incident. On the other hand, the privilege does not extend to a client act simply because the client performed the act in the lawyer's presence. The privilege applies when the purpose in performing the act is to convey information to the lawyer.

Illustrations:

> 3. Client, charged with a crime, retains Lawyer as defense counsel. Lawyer obtains a police report stating that the perpetrator of the crime had a tattooed right forearm. Lawyer asks Client whether Client's right arm is tattooed. In answer, Client rolls up his right sleeve revealing his forearm. The information that the lawyer thereby acquires derives from a protected communication.

4.   The same facts as in Illustration 3, except that, shortly after the crime, Client appears at Lawyer's office wearing a short-sleeved shirt. The observation by Lawyer that Client had a tattoo on his arm is not a communication protected by the privilege.

5.   Lawyer represents Client in a divorce and child-custody proceeding. While accompanying Client in a visit to the residence of Client's child, Lawyer observes Client physically break into the premises. Lawyer's knowledge is not protected as a communication from Client.

f.   A lawyer's testimony on a client's mental state. A lawyer may have knowledge about a client's mental state based on the client's communications with the lawyer. That knowledge may be relevant, for example, in the context of determining whether an accused is competent to stand trial. The lawyer in such cases is uniquely competent to testify concerning the client's ability to assist in presenting a defense. Testimony may be elicited that concerns the client's mode of thought but not if it would disclose particulars that would tend to incriminate the client. On representing a client with diminished capacity, see § 24.

g.   Client identity, the fact of consultation, fee payment, and similar matters. Courts have sometimes asserted that the attorney-client privilege categorically does not apply to such matters as the following: the identity of a client; the fact that the client consulted the lawyer and the general subject matter of the consultation; the identity of a nonclient who retained or paid the lawyer to represent the client; the details of any retainer agreement; the amount of the agreed-upon fee; and the client's whereabouts. Testimony about such matters normally does not reveal the content of communications from the client. However, admissibility of such testimony should be based on the extent to which it reveals the content of a privileged communication. The privilege applies if the testimony directly or by reasonable inference would reveal the content of a confidential communication. But the privilege does not protect clients or lawyers against revealing a lawyer's knowledge about a client solely on the ground that doing so would incriminate the client or otherwise prejudice the client's interests.

Illustration:

6.   Client consults Lawyer about Client's taxes. In the consultation, Client communicates to Lawyer Client's name and information indicating that Client owes substantial amounts in back taxes. The fact that Client owes back taxes is not known to the taxing authorities. Lawyer sends a letter to the taxing authorities and encloses a bank draft to cover the back taxes of Client. Lawyer does so to gain an advantage for Client under the tax laws by providing a basis for arguing against the accrual of penalties for continued nonpayment of taxes. Neither Lawyer's letter nor the bank draft reveals the identity of Client. (For the purpose of the Illustration, it is assumed

that the client-lawyer communication occurred for the purpose of obtaining legal assistance (see § 72)). In a grand-jury proceeding investigating Client's past failure to pay taxes, Lawyer cannot be required to testify concerning the identity of Client because, on the facts of the Illustration, that testimony would by reasonable inference reveal a confidential communication from Client, Client's communication concerning Client's nonpayment of taxes.

A client also enjoys the constitutional protection against self-incrimination. But this right does not provide a basis on which the client's lawyer can refuse to reveal incriminating information about the client that is not protected by the attorney-client privilege. The precise interaction of the attorney-client and self-incrimination privileges is beyond the scope of this Restatement. Protection may also be provided by the constitutional guarantee of the right to counsel. On the application of the attorney-client privilege to a lawyer's testimony about how the lawyer came into the possession of instrumentalities of crime or the fruits of crime, see § 119.

h. A record of a privileged communication. The privilege applies both to communications when made and to confidential records of such communications, such as a lawyer's note of the conversation. The privilege applies to a record when a communication embodied in the record can be traced to a privileged person as its expressive source (see § 70) and the record was created (see § 71) and preserved (see § 79) in a confidential state.

i. Lawyer communications to a client. Confidential communications by a lawyer to a client are also protected, including a record of a privileged communication such as a memorandum to a confidential file or to another lawyer or other person privileged to receive such a communication under § 71. Some decisions have protected a lawyer communication only if it contains or expressly refers to a client communication. That limitation is rejected here in favor of a broader rule more likely to assure full and frank communication (see § 68, Comment *c*). Moreover, the broader rule avoids difficult questions in determining whether a lawyer's communication itself discloses a client communication. A lawyer communication may also be protected by the work-product immunity (see Topic 3).

Illustration:

7. Lawyer writes a confidential letter to Client offering legal advice on a tax matter on which Client had sought Lawyer's professional assistance. Lawyer's letter is based in part on information that Client supplied to Lawyer, in part on information gathered by Lawyer from third persons, and in part on Lawyer's legal research. Even if each such portion of the letter could be separated from the others, the letter is a communication under this Section, and neither

Lawyer nor Client can be made to disclose or testify about any of its contents.

A lawyer may serve as the conduit for information to be conveyed from third persons to the lawyer's client. For most purposes, notice to a lawyer constitutes notice to the lawyer's client (see § 28(1)). In any event, both lawyer and client can be required to testify to the message for which the lawyer served as conduit. Lawyers in such situations serve, not as confidants, but as a communicative link between their clients and opposing parties, courts, and other legal institutions. Were such communications privileged, an opposing party would be required to communicate directly with the client, in derogation of the rule that communications with represented parties must be conducted through their lawyers (see § 99).

j. Preexisting documents and records. A client may communicate information to a lawyer by sending writings or other kinds of documentary or electronic recordings that came into existence prior to the time that the client communicates with the lawyer. The privilege protects the information that the client so communicated but not the preexisting document or record itself. A client-authored document that is not a privileged document when originally composed does not become privileged simply because the client has placed it in the lawyer's hands. However, if a document was a privileged preexisting document and was delivered to the lawyer under circumstances that otherwise would make its communication privileged, it remains privileged in the hands of the lawyer.

Illustrations:

8. Client confidentially delivers Client's business records to Lawyer, who specializes in tax matters, in order to obtain Lawyer's legal advice about taxes. As business records, the documents were not themselves prepared for the purpose of obtaining legal advice and are not protected by another testimonial privilege. They gain no privileged status by the fact that Client delivers them to Lawyer in seeking legal advice.

9. Client possesses a memorandum prepared by Client to communicate with Lawyer A during an earlier representation by Lawyer A. Client takes the memorandum to Lawyer B in confidence to obtain legal services on a different matter. The memorandum qualified as a privileged communication in the earlier matter. While in the hands of Lawyer B, the memorandum remains protected by the attorney-client privilege due to its originally privileged nature.

§ 70. Attorney–Client Privilege—"Privileged Persons"

Privileged persons within the meaning of § 68 are the client (including a prospective client), the client's lawyer, agents of

either who facilitate communications between them, and agents of the lawyer who facilitate the representation.

Comment:

   a. Scope and cross-references. This Section addresses the requirement of § 68(2) that a confidential communication be "made between privileged persons." On determining which persons in a corporate or other organization qualify as agents for communication, see § 73, Comment *d*. On invoking the privilege, see § 86. See also § 75 (co-client communication) and § 76 (communication in common-interest arrangement).

   b. A privileged person as the expressive source. To qualify as privileged, a communication must originate from a person who may make privileged communications and be addressed to persons who may receive them. Those persons are referred to in this Restatement as privileged persons. Client and lawyer are, of course, included. Other privileged persons are those who serve to facilitate communication between client and lawyer and persons who aid the lawyer in representing the client.

   The privilege does not extend to communications from nonprivileged persons, even if the client transmits such a person's communication to the lawyer, for example by carrying to the lawyer a document written by a nonprivileged person. Such information may, however, be given a qualified immunity from discovery under the work-product immunity (see § 87). Moreover, if the communication from a nonprivileged person is incorporated in a protected communication from which it cannot be separated, the entire communication is privileged. For example, a lawyer may not be required to testify to what a client had communicated concerning the client's memory of a conversation with a nonprivileged third person.

   c. An initial consultation. The privilege protects prospective clients—persons who communicate with a lawyer in an initial consultation but whom the lawyer does not thereafter represent—as well as persons with whom a client-lawyer relationship is established (see § 72(1) & Comment *d* thereof; see also § 15).

   d. Third-party payment of a fee. A person who pays a lawyer's fee is not necessarily a client. The relevant question is whether the lawyer undertook to give legal advice or provide other legal assistance to that person (see § 14; see also § 134).

   e. Privileged agents for a client or lawyer: in general. The privilege normally applies to communications involving persons who on their own behalf seek legal assistance from a lawyer (see § 72). However, a client need not personally seek legal assistance, but may appoint a third person to do so as the client's agent (e.g., § 134, Comment *f*). Whether a third person is an agent of the client or lawyer or a nonprivileged "stranger" is critical in determining application of the attorney-client privilege. If the third person is an agent for the purpose of the privilege, communications through or in the presence of that person are privileged; if the third person is not an agent, then the communications are not in confidence (see § 71) and are not privileged. Accordingly, a lawyer should allow a nonclient to participate only upon clarifying that person's role and when it reasonably appears that the benefit of that person's presence offsets the risk of a later claim that the presence of a third person forfeited the privilege.

f. A client's agent for communication. A person is a confidential agent for communication if the person's participation is reasonably necessary to facilitate the client's communication with a lawyer or another privileged person and if the client reasonably believes that the person will hold the communication in confidence. Factors that may be relevant in determining whether a third person is an agent for communication include the customary relationship between the client and the asserted agent, the nature of the communication, and the client's need for the third person's presence to communicate effectively with the lawyer or to understand and act upon the lawyer's advice.

Illustrations:

> 1. The police arrest Client and do not permit Client to communicate directly with Client's regular legal counsel, Lawyer. Client asks Friend, a person whom Client trusts to keep information confidential, to convey to Lawyer the message that Lawyer should not permit the police to search Client's home. Friend is an agent for communication.

> 2. Client and Lawyer do not speak a language known by the other. Client uses Translator to communicate an otherwise privileged message to Lawyer. Translator is an acquaintance of Client. Translator is an agent for communication.

> 3. Client regularly employs Secretary to record and transcribe Client's important business letters, including confidential correspondence. Client uses the services of Secretary to prepare a letter to Lawyer. Secretary is an agent for communication.

An agent for communication need not take a direct part in client-lawyer communications, but may be present because of the Client's psychological or other need. A business person may be accompanied by a business associate or expert consultant who can assist the client in interpreting the legal situation.

Illustrations:

> 4. Client, 16 years old, is represented by Lawyer. Client's parents accompany Client at a meeting with Lawyer concerning a property interest of Client. Client's parents are appropriate agents for communication.

5.   Client is advised by Accountant to consult a lawyer about a legal problem involving complex questions of tax accounting. Client, who does not fully understand the nature of the accounting questions, asks Accountant to accompany Client to a consultation with Lawyer so that Accountant can explain the nature of Client's legal matter to Lawyer. Accountant is Client's agent for communication. That would also be true if Accountant were to explain Lawyer's legal advice in business or accounting terms more understandable to Client.

The privilege applies to communications to and from the client disclosed to persons who hire the lawyer as an incident of the lawyer's engagement. Thus, the privilege covers communications by a client-insured to an insurance-company investigator who is to convey the facts to the client's lawyer designated by the insurer, as well as communications from the lawyer for the insured to the insurer in providing a progress report or discussing litigation strategy or settlement (see § 134, Comment *f*). Such situations must be distinguished from communications by an insured to an insurance investigator who will report to the company, to which the privilege does not apply.

g.   A lawyer's agent. A lawyer may disclose privileged communications to other office lawyers and with appropriate nonlawyer staff— secretaries, file clerks, computer operators, investigators, office managers, paralegal assistants, telecommunications personnel, and similar law-office assistants. On the duty of a lawyer to protect client information being handled by nonlawyer personnel, see § 60(1)(b). The privilege also extends to communications to and from the client that are disclosed to independent contractors retained by a lawyer, such as an accountant or physician retained by the lawyer to assist in providing legal services to the client and not for the purpose of testifying.

h.   An incompetent person as a client. When a client is mentally or physically incapacitated from effectively consulting with a lawyer, a representative may communicate with the incompetent person's lawyer under the protection of the privilege. The privilege also extends to any communications between the incompetent person and the representative relating to the communication with the lawyer.

Illustration:

6.   Client is mentally incapacitated, and a court has appointed Guardian as the guardian of the person and property of Client. A question has arisen concerning a right of Client in certain property, and Lawyer is retained to represent the interests of Client in the property. Guardian serves as the agent for communication of Client in discussing the matter with Lawyer.

§ 71.   Attorney–Client Privilege—"In Confidence"

A communication is in confidence within the meaning of § 68 if, at the time and in the circumstances of the communica-

tion, the communicating person reasonably believes that no one will learn the contents of the communication except a privileged person as defined in § 70 or another person with whom communications are protected under a similar privilege.

Comment:

a. Scope and cross-references. This Section considers the requirement of § 68(3) that a communication must be "in confidence." The elements of § 68(1)-(2) and § 68(4) are explained in §§ 69–70 and § 72. Even if the initial communication is in confidence and otherwise qualifies for protection as a privileged communication, its privileged status may be lost by subsequent revelation of the communication (see § 79). On the agency power of a lawyer to waive a privilege by disclosure to a nonprivileged person, see § 79. On the legal responsibilities of lawyers with respect to confidential client information, see generally §§ 60–67. With respect to communications between co-clients, see § 75, and with respect to a communication in a common-interest arrangement, see § 76.

b. Rationale. Given the objectives of the attorney-client privilege (see § 68, Comment *c*), a communication must be made in circumstances reasonably indicating that it will be learned only by the lawyer, client, or another privileged person (see § 70). The matter communicated need not itself be secret. For example, a privileged person receiving the communication may have known the same information from another source. The intent of the communicating person to communicate in confidence is relevant but not determinative. Thus, communication in a nonconfidential setting evidences that secrecy was not a consideration even if it is later protested that confidentiality was intended. Extending the privilege to a nonconfidential communication would not further the policy of the privilege and would result in excluding otherwise admissible and relevant evidence (see § 68, Comment *d*). If the communicating person did not intend that the communication be confidential, it is not privileged regardless of the circumstances otherwise attending its transmission.

The presence of a stranger to the lawyer-client relationship does not destroy confidentiality if another privilege protects the communications in the same way as the attorney-client privilege. Thus, in a jurisdiction that recognizes an absolute husband-wife privilege, the presence of a wife at an otherwise confidential meeting between the husband and the husband's lawyer does not destroy the confidentiality required for the attorney-client privilege.

c. Confidential and nonconfidential communications. The circumstances must indicate that the communicating persons reasonably believed that the communication would be confidential. Thus, a conversation between lawyer and client in the lawyer's offices is privileged. The same will not necessarily apply to a communication in offices of the client, inasmuch as not all agents of the client are privileged persons within the meaning of § 70 (compare Illustration 1 hereto & Comment *d*). For the delineation of privileged persons in the case of a client that is an organization, see § 73.

The circumstances may indicate that the communicating person knows that a nonprivileged person will learn of it, thus impairing its confidentiality. For example, a client may talk with a lawyer in a loud voice in a public place where nonprivileged persons could readily overhear. Communication over a medium from which it is impossible to exclude other listeners, such as radio, strongly suggests that secrecy is not reasonably expected. Whether the client or other communicating person knew that nonprivileged persons would learn of the communication depends on the specific circumstances. The relevant circumstances are those reasonably evident to the communicating person, not the auditor. Thus, the presence of a surreptitious eavesdropper does not destroy confidentiality.

Illustrations:

1. Client and Lawyer confer in Client's office about a legal matter. Client realizes that occupants of nearby offices can normally hear the sound of voices coming from Client's office but reasonably supposes they cannot intelligibly detect individual words. An occupant of an adjoining office secretly records the conference between Client and Lawyer and is able to make out the contents of their communications. Even if it violates no law in the jurisdiction, the secret recording ordinarily would not be anticipated by persons wishing to confer in confidence. Accordingly, the fact that the eavesdropper overheard the Client–Lawyer communications does not impair their confidential status.

2. During a recess in a trial, Client and Lawyer walk into a courthouse corridor crowded with other persons attending the trial and discuss Client's intended testimony in tones loud enough to be readily overheard by bystanders. As Lawyer knows, the courthouse premises include several areas more appropriate for a confidential conversation than the corridor. The corridor conversation is not in confidence for the purposes of the privilege, and the privilege does not bar examining either Client or Lawyer concerning it.

Confidentiality is a practical requirement. Exigent circumstances may require communications under conditions where ordinary precautions for confidentiality are impossible. The privilege applies if the communicating person has taken reasonable precautions in the circumstances.

Illustration:

3. A jailer requires Client, an incarcerated person, and Lawyer to confer only in a conference area that, as Client and Lawyer know, is sometimes secretly subjected to recorded video surveillance by the jailer. If Client and Lawyer take reasonable precautions to avoid

being overheard, the fact that the jailer secretly records their conversation does not deprive it of its confidential character.

d. A communication intended for a nonprivileged person. A client may disclose information to a lawyer intending that it be conveyed to a nonprivileged third person and not intending that the lawyer determine the suitability of thus publishing it. Such a communication is not confidential for purposes of the privilege. Willingness to disclose a communication to nonprivileged persons (compare § 70) without prior review by the lawyer indicates that assurance of confidentiality did not importantly motivate communication.

The critical element is whether the privileged person's evident purpose is that the contents of the communication be made available to a nonprivileged person. Clients do not typically have such a purpose. Rather, a client ordinarily expects the lawyer to release information to nonprivileged persons only after exercising judgment about whether to do so and about the form in which it should be released. In ascertaining purpose, the nature of the legal assistance that the lawyer is providing and the nature of the communication asserted to be confidential are relevant.

A common instance of nonconfidential client-lawyer communications is where a lawyer functions as an attesting witness on a document signed by the lawyer's client. Those circumstances plainly warrant the inference that the lawyer may testify to facts relevant to the attestation, including communications from the client relating to that function.

e. Random dissemination of a communication. Communicating randomly to many auditors indicates that the communicating person was oblivious to secrecy.

Illustration:

4. Client makes an audiotape recording in which Client confesses to committing a crime, remorse for which, Client says on the tape, has led Client to attempt suicide. Client addresses the audio tape to business associates of Client. On the tape, Client mentions that the business associates might wish to provide the tape to Client's Lawyer. Client fails in the suicide attempt and is charged with the crime confessed on the tape. The business associates to whom the tape is addressed give the tape to Lawyer. Client did not intend the message as a confidential communication. It is immaterial whether or not nonprivileged persons in fact listened to the tape and thus actually learned of the communication.

In many circumstances, including the foregoing Illustration, when a communication is addressed to an audience that includes nonprivileged persons, an additional reason the privilege does not apply is that the client did not communicate to obtain legal assistance (see § 72(2)).

908

§ 72 Attorney–Client Privilege—Legal Assistance as the Object of Privileged Communication

A communication is made for the purpose of obtaining or providing legal assistance within the meaning of § 68 if it is made to or to assist a person:

(1) who is a lawyer or who the client or prospective client reasonably believes to be a lawyer; and

(2) whom the client or prospective client consults for the purpose of obtaining legal assistance.

TITLE B. THE ATTORNEY–CLIENT PRIVILEGE FOR ORGANIZATIONAL AND MULTIPLE CLIENTS

§ 73. The Privilege for an Organizational Client

When a client is a corporation, unincorporated association, partnership, trust, estate, sole proprietorship, or other for-profit or not-for-profit organization, the attorney-client privilege extends to a communication that:

(1) otherwise qualifies as privileged under §§ 68–72;

(2) is between an agent of the organization and a privileged person as defined in § 70;

(3) concerns a legal matter of interest to the organization; and

(4) is disclosed only to:

(a) privileged persons as defined in § 70; and

(b) other agents of the organization who reasonably need to know of the communication in order to act for the organization.

Comment:

a. Scope and cross-references. This Section states the conditions under which an organization can claim the attorney-client privilege. The requirements of §§ 68–72 must be satisfied, except that this Section recognizes a special class of agents who communicate in behalf of the organizational client (see Comment *d*). The Section also requires that the communication relate to a matter of interest to the organization as such (see Subsection (3) & Comment *f* hereto) and that it be disclosed within the organization only to persons having a reasonable need to know of it (see Subsection (4)(b) & Comment *g* hereto).

Conflicts of interest between an organizational client and its officers and other agents are considered in § 131, Comment *e*. On the application of the privilege to governmental organizations and officers, see § 74.

b. Rationale. The attorney-client privilege encourages organizational clients to have their agents confide in lawyers in order to realize the

909

organization's legal rights and to achieve compliance with law (Comment *d* hereto). Extending the privilege to corporations and other organizations was formerly a matter of doubt but is no longer questioned. However, two pivotal questions must be resolved.

The first is defining the group of persons who can make privileged communications on behalf of an organization. Balance is required. The privilege should cover a sufficiently broad number of organizational communications to realize the organization's policy objectives, but not insulate ordinary intraorganizational communications that may later have importance as evidence. Concern has been expressed, for example, that the privilege would afford organizations "zones of silence" that would be free of evidentiary scrutiny. A subsidiary problem is whether persons who would be nonprivileged occurrence witnesses with respect to communications to a lawyer representing a natural person can be conduits of privileged communications when the client is an organization. That problem has been addressed in terms of the "subject-matter" and "control-group" tests for the privilege (see Comment *d*).

Second is the problem of defining the types of organizations treated as clients for purposes of the privilege. It is now accepted that the privilege applies to corporations, but some decisions have questioned whether the privilege should apply to unincorporated associations, partnerships, or sole proprietorships. Neither logic nor principle supports limiting the organizational privilege to the corporate form (see Comment *c* hereto).

c. Application of the privilege to an organization. As stated in the Section, the privilege applies to all forms of organizations. A corporation with hundreds of employees could as well be a sole proprietorship if its assets were owned by a single person rather than its shares being owned by the same person. It would be anomalous to accord the privilege to a business in corporate form but not if it were organized as a sole proprietorship. In general, an organization under this Section is a group having a recognizable identity as such and some permanency. Thus, an organization under this Section ordinarily would include a law firm, however it may be structured (as a professional corporation, a partnership, a sole proprietorship, or otherwise). The organization need not necessarily be treated as a legal entity for any other legal purpose. The privilege extends as well to charitable, social, fraternal, and other nonprofit organizations such as labor unions and chambers of commerce.

d. An agent of an organizational client. As stated in Subsection (2), the communication must involve an agent of the organization, on one hand, and, on the other, a privileged person within the meaning of § 70, such as the lawyer for the organization. Persons described in Subsection (4)(b) may disclose the communication under a need-to-know limitation (see Comment *g* hereto). The existence of a relationship of principal and agent between the organizational client and the privileged agent is determined according to agency law (see generally Restatement Second, Agency §§ 1–139).

Some decisions apply a "control group" test for determining the scope of the privilege for an organization. That test limits the privilege to communications from persons in the organization who have authority to mold organizational policy or to take action in accordance with the lawyer's advice. The control-group circle excludes many persons within an organization who normally would cooperate with an organization's lawyer. Such a limitation overlooks that the division of functions within an organization often separates decisionmakers from those knowing relevant facts. Such a limitation is unnecessary to prevent abuse of the privilege (see Comment g) and significantly frustrates its purpose.

Other decisions apply a "subject matter" test. That test extends the privilege to communications with any lower-echelon employee or agent so long as the communication relates to the subject matter of the representation. In substance, those decisions comport with the need-to-know formulation in this Section (see Comment g).

It is not necessary that the agent receive specific direction from the organization to make or receive the communication (see Comment h).

Agents of the organization who may make privileged communications under this Section include the organization's officers and employees. For example, a communication by any employee of a corporation to the corporation's lawyer concerning the matter as to which the lawyer was retained to represent the corporation would be privileged, if other conditions of the privilege are satisfied. The concept of agent also includes independent contractors with whom the corporation has a principal-agent relationship and extends to agents of such persons when acting as subagents of the organizational client. For example, a foreign-based corporation may retain a general agency (perhaps a separate corporation) in an American city for the purpose of retaining counsel to represent the interests of the foreign-based corporation. Communications by the general agency would be by an agent for the purpose of this Section.

For purpose of the privilege, when a parent corporation owns controlling interest in a corporate subsidiary, the parent corporation's agents who are responsible for legal matters of the subsidiary are considered agents of the subsidiary. The subsidiary corporation's agents who are responsible for affairs of the parent are also considered agents of the parent for the purpose of the privilege. Directors of a corporation are not its agents for many legal purposes, because they are not subject to the control of the corporation (see Restatement Second, Agency § 14C). However, in communications with the organization's counsel, a director who communicates in the interests and for the benefit of the corporation is its agent for the purposes of this Section. Depending on the circumstances, a director acts in that capacity both when participating in a meeting of directors and when communicating individually with a lawyer for the corporation about the corporation's affairs. Communications to and from nonagent constituents of a corporation, such as shareholders and creditors, are not privileged.

In the case of a partnership, general partners and employees and other agents and subagents of the partnership may serve as agents of the organization for the purpose of making privileged communications (see generally Restatement Second, Agency § 14A). Limited partners who have no other relationship (such as employee) with the limited partnership are analogous to shareholders of a corporation and are not such agents.

In the case of an unincorporated association, agents whose communications may be privileged under this Section include officers and employees and other contractual agents and subagents. Members of an unincorporated association, for example members of a labor union, are not, solely by reason of their status as members, agents of the association for the purposes of this Section. In some situations, for example, involving a small unincorporated association with very active members, the members might be considered agents for the purpose of this Section on the ground that the association functionally is a partnership whose members are like partners.

In the case of an enterprise operated as a sole proprietorship, agents who may make communications privileged under this Section with respect to the proprietorship include employees or contractual agents and subagents of the proprietor.

Communications of a nonagent constituent of the organization may be independently privileged under § 75 where the person is a co-client along with the organization. If the agent of the organization has a conflict of interest with the organization, the lawyer for the organization must not purport to represent both the organization and the agent without consent (see § 131, Comment c). The lawyer may not mislead the agent about the nature of the lawyer's loyalty to the organization (see § 103). If a lawyer fails to clarify the lawyer's role as representative solely of the organization and the organization's agent reasonably believes that the lawyer represents the agent, the agent may assert the privilege personally with respect to the agent's own communications (compare § 72(2), Comment f; see also § 131, Comment e).

The lawyer must also observe limitations on the extent to which a lawyer may communicate with a person of conflicting interests who is not represented by counsel (see § 103) and limitations on communications with persons who are so represented (see § 99 and following).

e. The temporal relationship of principal-agent. Under Subsection (2), a person making a privileged communication to a lawyer for an organization must then be acting as agent of the principal-organization. The objective of the organizational privilege is to encourage the organization to have its agents communicate with its lawyer (see Comment d hereto). Generally, that premise implies that persons be agents of the organization at the time of communicating. The privilege may also extend, however, to communications with a person with whom the organization has terminated, for most other purposes, an agency relationship. A former agent is a privileged person under Subsection (2) if, at the time of communicating, the former agent has a continuing legal obligation to the principal-organization to furnish the information to the organization's lawyer. The scope of such a continuing obligation is determined by the law of agency and the terms of the employment contract (see Restatement Second, Agency § 275, Comment *e*, & § 381, Comment *f*). The privilege covers communications with a lawyer for an organization by a retired officer of the organization concerning a matter within the officer's prior responsibilities that is of legal importance to the organization.

Subsection (2) does not include a person with whom the organization established a principal-agent relationship predominantly for the purpose of providing the protection of the privilege to the person's communications, if the person was not an agent at the time of learning the information. For example, communications between the lawyer for an organization and an eyewitness to an event whose communications would not otherwise be privileged cannot be made privileged simply through the organization hiring the person to consult with the organization's lawyer. (As to experts and similar persons employed by a lawyer, see § 70, Comment *g*).

Ordinarily, an agent communicating with an organization's lawyer within this Section will have acquired the information in the course of the agent's work for the organization. However, it is not necessary that the communicated information be so acquired. Thus, a person may communicate under this Section with respect to information learned prior to the relationship or learned outside the person's functions as an agent, so long as the person bears an agency relationship to the principal-organization at the time of the communication and the communication concerns a matter of interest to the organization (see Comment *f*). For example, a chemist for an organization who communicates to the organization's lawyer information about a process that the chemist learned prior to being employed by the organization makes a privileged communication if the other conditions of this Section are satisfied.

f. Limitation to communications relating to the interests of the organization. Subsection (3) requires that the communication relate to a legal matter of interest to the organization. The lawyer must be representing the organization as opposed to the agent who communicates with the lawyer, such as its individual officer or employee. A lawyer representing such an officer or employee, of course, can have privileged communications with that client. But the privilege will not be that of the organization. When a lawyer represents as co-clients both the organization and one of its officers or employees, the privileged nature of communications is determined under § 75. On the conflicts of interest involved in such representations, see § 131, Comment *e*.

g. The need-to-know limitation on disclosing privileged communications. Communications are privileged only if made for the purpose of obtaining legal services (see § 72), and they remain privileged only if neither the client nor an agent of the client subsequently discloses the communication to a nonprivileged person (see § 79; see also § 71, Comment *d*). Those limitations apply to organizational clients as provided in Subsection (4). Communications become, and remain, so protected by the privilege only if the organization does not permit their dissemination to persons other than to privileged persons. Agents of a client to whom confidential communications may be disclosed are generally defined in § 70, Comment *f*, and agents of a lawyer are defined in § 70, Comment *g*. Included among an organizational client's agents for communication are, for example, a secretary who prepares a letter to the organization's lawyer on behalf of a communicating employee.

The need-to-know limitation of Subsection (4)(b) permits disclosing privileged communications to other agents of the organization who reasonably need to know of the privileged communication in order to act for the organization in the matter. Those agents include persons who are responsible for accepting or rejecting a lawyer's advice on behalf of the organization or for acting on legal assistance, such as general legal advice, provided by the lawyer. Access of such persons to privileged communications is not limited to direct exchange with the lawyer. A lawyer may be required to take steps assuring that attorney-client communications will be disseminated only among privileged persons who have a need to know. Persons defined in Subsection (4)(b) may be apprised of privileged communications after they have been made, as by examining records of privileged communications previously made, in order to conduct the affairs of the organization in light of the legal services provided.

Illustration:

1. Lawyer for Organization makes a confidential report to President of Organization, describing Organization's contractual relationship with Supplier, and advising that Organization's contract with Supplier could be terminated without liability. President sends a confidential memorandum to Manager, Organization's purchasing manager, asking whether termination of the contract would nonetheless be inappropriate for business reasons. Because Manager's response would reasonably depend on several aspects of Lawyer's advice, Manager would have need to know the justifying reason for Lawyer's advice that the contract could be terminated. Lawyer's report to President remains privileged notwithstanding that President shared it with Manager.

The need-to-know concept properly extends to all agents of the organization who would be personally held financially or criminally liable for conduct in the matter in question or who would personally benefit from it, such as general partners of a partnership with respect to a claim for or against the partnership. It extends to persons, such as members of a board of directors and senior officers of an organization, whose general management and supervisory responsibilities include wide areas of organizational activities and to lower-echelon agents of the organization whose area of activity is relevant to the legal advice or service rendered.

Dissemination of a communication to persons outside those described in Subsection (4)(b) implies that the protection of confidentiality was not significant (see § 71, Comment *b*). An organization may not immunize documents and other communications generated or circulated for a business or other nonlegal purpose (see § 72).

h.   Directed and volunteered agent communications. It is not necessary that a superior organizational authority specifically direct an agent to communicate with the organization's lawyer. Unless instructed to the contrary, an agent has authority to volunteer information to a lawyer when reasonably related to the interests of the organization. An agent has similar authority to respond to a request for information from a lawyer for the organization. And the lawyer for the organization ordinarily may seek relevant information directly from employees and other agents without prior direction from superior authorities in the organization.

i.   Inside legal counsel and outside legal counsel. The privilege under this Section applies without distinction to lawyers who are inside legal counsel or outside legal counsel for an organization (see § 72, Comment *c*). Communications predominantly for a purpose other than obtaining or providing legal services for the organization are not within the privilege (see § 72, Comment *c*). On the credentials of a lawyer for the purposes of the privilege, see § 72(1), Comment *e*.

j.   Invoking and waiving the privilege of an organizational client. The privilege for organizational clients can be asserted and waived only by a responsible person acting for the organization for this purpose. On waiver, see §§ 78–80. Communications involving an organization's director, officer, or employee may qualify as privileged, but it is a separate question whether such a person has authority to invoke or waive the privilege on behalf of the organization. If the lawyer was representing both the organization and the individual as co-clients, the question of invoking and waiving the privilege is determined under the rule for co-clients (see § 75, Comment *e*). Whether a lawyer has formed a client-lawyer relationship with a person affiliated with the organization, as well as with the organization, is determined under § 14. Communications of such a person who approaches a lawyer for the organization as a prospective client are privileged as provided in § 72. Unless the person's contrary intent is reasonably manifest to a lawyer for the organization, the lawyer acts properly in assuming that a communication from any such person is on behalf and in the interest of the organization and, as such, is privileged in the interest of the organization and not of the individual making the communication. When the person manifests an intention to make a communication privileged against the organization, the lawyer must resist entering into such a client-lawyer relationship

915

and receiving such a communication if doing so would constitute an impermissible conflict of interest (see § 131, Comment *e*).

An agent or former agent may have need for a communication as to which the organization has authority to waive the privilege, for example, when the agent is sued personally. A tribunal may exercise discretion to order production of such a communication for benefit of the agent if the agent establishes three conditions. First, the agent must show that the agent properly came to know the contents of the communication. Second, the agent must show substantial need of the communication. Third, the agent must show that production would create no material risk of prejudice or embarrassment to the organization beyond such evidentiary use as the agent may make of the communication. Such a risk may be controlled by protective orders, redaction, or other measures.

Illustration:

2.   Lawyer, representing only Corporation, interviews Employee by electronic mail in connection with reported unlawful activities in Corporation's purchasing department in circumstances providing Corporation with a privilege with respect to their communications. Corporation later dismisses Employee, who sues Corporation, alleging wrongful discharge. Employee files a discovery request seeking all copies of communications between Employee and Lawyer. The tribunal has discretion to order discovery under the conditions stated in the preceding paragraph. In view of the apparent relationship of Employee's statements to possible illegal activities, it is doubtful that Employee could persuade the tribunal that access by Employee would create no material risk that third persons, such as a government agency, would thereby learn of the communication and thus gain a litigation or other advantage with respect to Corporation.

k.   Succession in legal control of an organization. When ownership of a corporation or other organization as an entity passes to successors, the transaction carries with it authority concerning asserting or waiving the privilege. After legal control passes in such a transaction, communications from directors, officers, or employees of the acquired organization to lawyers who represent only the predecessor organization, if it maintains a separate existence from the acquiring organization, may no longer be covered by the privilege. When a corporation or other organization has ceased to have a legal existence such that no person can act in its behalf, ordinarily the attorney-client privilege terminates (see generally § 77, Comment *c*).

Illustration:

3.   X, an officer of Ajax Corporation, communicates in confidence with Lawyer, who represents Ajax, concerning dealings between Ajax and one of its creditors, Vendor Corporation. Ajax later

is declared bankrupt and a bankruptcy court appoints Trustee as the trustee in bankruptcy for Ajax. Thereafter, Lawyer is called to the witness stand in litigation between Vendor Corporation and Trustee. Trustee has authority to determine whether the attorney-client privilege should be asserted or waived on behalf of the bankrupt Ajax Corporation with respect to testimony by Lawyer about statements by X. X cannot assert a privilege because X was not a client of Lawyer in the representation. Former officers and directors of Ajax cannot assert the privilege because control of the corporation has passed to Trustee.

A lawyer for an organization is ordinarily authorized to waive the privilege in advancing the interests of the client (see § 61 & § 79, Comment *c*). Otherwise, when called to testify, a lawyer is required to invoke the privilege on behalf of the client (see § 86(1)(b)). On waiver, see §§ 78–80.

§ 74. The Privilege for a Governmental Client

Unless applicable law otherwise provides, the attorney-client privilege extends to a communication of a governmental organization as stated in § 73 and of an individual employee or other agent of a governmental organization as a client with respect to his or her personal interest as stated in §§ 68–72.

Comment:

a. Scope and cross-references. This Section provides that the attorney-client privilege ordinarily applies to governmental agencies as to other organizations as provided in § 73 and to individual governmental employees and other agents who are individually represented as it would for individuals under §§ 68–72.

b. Rationale. The objectives of the attorney-client privilege (see § 68, Comment *c*), including the special objectives relevant to organizational clients (see § 73, Comment *b*), apply in general to governmental clients. The privilege aids government entities and employees in obtaining legal advice founded on a complete and accurate factual picture. Communications from such persons should be correspondingly privileged.

A narrower privilege for governmental clients may be warranted by particular statutory formulations. Open-meeting and open-files statutes reflect a public policy against secrecy in many areas of governmental activity. Moreover, unlike persons in private life, a public agency or employee has no autonomous right of confidentiality in communications relating to governmental business.

Nonetheless, the legal system has recognized the strategic concerns of a public agency or officer in establishing and asserting public legal rights. Even public legal rights are contingent at their boundaries and subject to argumentation and dispute as to their precise extent. Members

917

of the public who assert legal interests against a public agency or officer act not in the general public interest but in their private interest or in what they assert is the public interest. The public acting through its public agencies is entitled to resist claims and contentions that the agency considers legally or factually unwarranted. To that end, a public agency or employee is entitled to engage in confidential communications with counsel to establish and maintain legal positions. Accordingly, courts generally have construed open-meeting, open-files, whistle-blower, and similar statutes as subject to the attorney-client privilege, recognizing that otherwise governments would be at unfair disadvantage in litigation, in handling claims and in negotiations.

A privilege that would cover only litigation, including claims or investigations, would be a plausible alternative. Rule 502(d)(6) of the Revised Uniform Rules of Evidence proposed a governmental-client privilege thus limited, but most states rejected that limitation. Another alternative would be a general but qualified privilege protecting confidential communications unless a tribunal found good cause to require disclosure. The privilege for the government could also be limited to a stated period of time (compare § 77, Reporter's Note to Comment *c*). More particularized rules may be necessary where one agency of government claims the privilege in resisting a demand for information by another. Such rules should take account of the complex considerations of governmental structure, tradition, and regulation that are involved.

This Section, however, states the generally prevailing rule that governmental agencies and employees enjoy the same privilege as nongovernmental counterparts. In any event, information covered by the privilege would, in some situations, be protected from disclosure by such rules as executive privilege or state secrets. Of course, a legislative determination of a need for less confidentiality, for example in a statute that limits attorney-client confidentiality in areas outside of litigation, would prevail over the common-law rule stated in this Section.

c. Application of the general attorney-client-privilege rules to a governmental client. The general requirements of the attorney-client privilege apply with respect to assertedly privileged communications of a governmental client. For example, the privilege extends only to communication for the purpose of obtaining or giving legal assistance (see § 72).

The privilege does not apply to a document that has an independent legal effect as an operative statement of governmental policy. For example, a memorandum by a government lawyer that directs, rather than advises, a governmental officer to act in a certain way is not protected by the privilege. Such a document is a necessarily public statement of public policy and as such is meant to be publicly disseminated (see § 71, Comment *e*).

Communications between a lawyer representing one governmental agency and an employee of another governmental agency are privileged only if the lawyer represents both agencies (see § 75) or if the communication is pursuant to a common-interest arrangement (see § 76).

d. Individual government employees and agents. Employees and agents of a governmental agency may have both official and personal interests in a matter. A police officer sued for damages for the alleged use of excessive force, for example, may be both officially and personally interested in the lawsuit. The officer has the right to consult counsel of the officer's choice with respect to the officer's personal interests. If the officer consults a lawyer retained by the officer's agency or department, the principles of § 73, Comment *j*, determine whether the officer is a co-client with the agency or department (see § 75) or is not a client of the lawyer. Government lawyers may be prohibited from the private practice of law or accepting a matter adverse to the government. Thus, the fact that the common employer of both lawyer and officer is a government agency may affect the reasonableness of the officer's claim of expectation that the lawyer could function as personal counsel for the officer. On the conflict-of-interest limitations on such joint representations, see § 131, Comment *e*. If a lawyer is retained by the agency as separate counsel to represent the personal interests of the employee, for purposes of the privilege the employee is the sole client. As with agents of nongovernmental organizations, the status of a governmental employee or agent as co-client (see § 75), individual client, or nonrepresented communicating agent of the agency sometimes may be difficult to determine. Inquiry in such cases should focus upon the employment relationship of the lawyer and the reasonable belief of the agent at the time of communicating.

e. Invoking and waiving the privilege of a governmental client. The privilege for governmental entities may be asserted or waived by the responsible public official or body. The identity of that responsible person or body is a question of local governmental law. In some states, for example, the state's attorney general decides matters of litigation policy for state agencies, including decisions about the privilege. In other states, such decisions are made by another executive officer or agency in suits in which the attorney general otherwise conducts the litigation. As a general proposition, the official or body that is empowered to assert or forego a claim or defense is entitled to assert or forego the privilege for communications relating to the claim or defense. Waiver of the privilege is determined according to the standards set forth in § 73, Comment *j*. See also Comment *d* hereto.

§ 75. The Privilege of Co–Clients

(1) If two or more persons are jointly represented by the same lawyer in a matter, a communication of either co-client that otherwise qualifies as privileged under §§ 68–72 and relates to matters of common interest is privileged as against third persons, and any co-client may invoke the privilege, unless it has been waived by the client who made the communication.

(2) Unless the co-clients have agreed otherwise, a communication described in Subsection (1) is not privileged as between the co-clients in a subsequent adverse proceeding between them.

Comment:

a. Scope and cross-references. This Section states the attorney-client-privilege rules that apply when co-clients have communications with the same lawyer. The privilege applies only if the other conditions of §§ 68–72 are met, except that Subsection (1) qualifies the requirement of § 71 that the communication be in confidence and Subsection (2) qualifies the rule of § 79 concerning waiver. On invoking the privilege, see § 86. Subsection (2) modifies the normally applicable rules of waiver (see §§ 78–80) in the case of a subsequent proceeding in which the co-clients are adverse. On the duration of the privilege, see § 77. On representation of multiple clients with conflicts of interest, see §§ 121–122 and §§ 128–131. On confidentiality obligations when representing co-clients, see § 60, Comment *l.*

A communication subject to the privilege for co-clients may be made through a client's agents for communication and a lawyer's agents for communication and other agents (see § 70).

b. The co-client privilege. Under Subsection (1), communications by co-clients with their common lawyer retain confidential characteristics as against third persons. The rule recognizes that it may be desirable to have multiple clients represented by the same lawyer.

c. Delimiting co-client situations. Whether a client-lawyer relationship exists between each client and the common lawyer is determined under § 14, specifically whether they have expressly or impliedly agreed to common representation in which confidential information will be shared. A co-client representation can begin with a joint approach to a lawyer or by agreement after separate representations had begun. However, clients of the same lawyer who share a common interest are not necessarily co-clients. Whether individuals have jointly consulted a lawyer or have merely entered concurrent but separate representations is determined by the understanding of the parties and the lawyer in light of the circumstances (see § 14).

Co-client representations must also be distinguished from situations in which a lawyer represents a single client, but another person with allied interests cooperates with the client and the client's lawyer (see § 76).

The scope of the co-client relationship is determined by the extent of the legal matter of common interest. For example, a lawyer might also represent one co-client on other matters separate from the common one. On whether, following the end of a co-client relationship, the lawyer may continue to represent one former co-client adversely to the interests of another, see § 121, Comment *e.* On the confidentiality of communications during a co-client representation, see Comment *d* hereto.

d. The subsequent-proceeding exception to the co-client privilege. As stated in Subsection (2), in a subsequent proceeding in which former co-clients are adverse, one of them may not invoke the attorney-client privilege against the other with respect to communications involving either of them during the co-client relationship. That rule applies whether or not the co-client's communication had been disclosed to the other during the co-client representation, unless they had otherwise agreed.

Rules governing the co-client privilege are premised on an assumption that co-clients usually understand that all information is to be disclosed to all of them. Courts sometimes refer to this as a presumed intent that there should be no confidentiality between co-clients. Fairness and candor between the co-clients and with the lawyer generally precludes the lawyer from keeping information secret from any one of them, unless they have agreed otherwise (see § 60, Comment *l*).

Illustration:

1. Client X and Client Y jointly consult Lawyer about establishing a business, without coming to any agreement about the confidentiality of their communications to Lawyer. X sends a confidential memorandum to Lawyer in which X outlines the proposed business arrangement as X understands it. The joint representation then terminates, and Y knows that X sent the memorandum but not its contents. Subsequently, Y files suit against X to recover damages arising out of the business venture. Although X's memorandum would be privileged against a third person, in the litigation between X and Y the memorandum is not privileged. That result follows although Y never knew the contents of the letter during the joint representation.

Whether communications between the lawyer and a client that occurred before formation of a joint representation are subject to examination depends on the understanding at the time that the new person was joined as a co-client.

Co-clients may agree that the lawyer will not disclose certain confidential communications of one co-client to other co-clients. If the co-clients have so agreed and the co-clients are subsequently involved in adverse proceedings, the communicating client can invoke the privilege with respect to such communications not in fact disclosed to the former co-client seeking to introduce it. In the absence of such an agreement, the lawyer ordinarily is required to convey communications to all interested co-clients (see § 60, Comment *l*). A co-client may also retain additional, separate counsel on the matter of the common representation; communications with such counsel are not subject to this Section.

e. Standing to assert the co-client privilege; waiver. If a third person attempts to gain access to or to introduce a co-client communication, each co-client has standing to assert the privilege. The objecting client need not have been the source of the communication or previously have known about it.

The normal rules of waiver (see §§ 78–80) apply to a co-client's own communications to the common lawyer. Thus, in the absence of an agreement with co-clients to the contrary, each co-client may waive the privilege with respect to that co-client's own communications with the lawyer, so long as the communication relates only to the communicating and waiving client.

One co-client does not have authority to waive the privilege with respect to another co-client's communications to their common lawyer. If a document or other recording embodies communications from two or more co-clients, all those co-clients must join in a waiver, unless a nonwaiving co-client's communication can be redacted from the document.

Disclosure of a co-client communication in the course of subsequent adverse proceeding between co-clients operates as waiver by subsequent disclosure under § 79 with respect to third persons.

§ 76. The Privilege in Common–Interest Arrangements

(1) If two or more clients with a common interest in a litigated or nonlitigated matter are represented by separate lawyers and they agree to exchange information concerning the matter, a communication of any such client that otherwise qualifies as privileged under §§ 68–72 that relates to the matter is privileged as against third persons. Any such client may invoke the privilege, unless it has been waived by the client who made the communication.

(2) Unless the clients have agreed otherwise, a communication described in Subsection (1) is not privileged as between clients described in Subsection (1) in a subsequent adverse proceeding between them.

Comment:

a. Scope and cross-references. This Section states the common-interest attorney-client privilege. The rule differs from the co-client rule of § 75 in that the clients are represented by separate lawyers. Subsection (1) applies only if the other conditions of §§ 68–72 are satisfied, except it qualifies the requirement of § 71 that the communication be in confidence. Subsection (2) modifies the normal rules of waiver (see §§ 78–85) with respect to subsequent adverse proceedings between the clients.

b. Rationale. The rule in this Section permits persons who have common interests to coordinate their positions without destroying the privileged status of their communications with their lawyers. For example, where conflict of interest disqualifies a lawyer from representing two co-defendants in a criminal case (see § 129), the separate lawyers representing them may exchange confidential communications to prepare their defense without loss of the privilege. Clients thus can elect separate representation while maintaining the privilege in cooperating on common elements of interest.

c. Confidentiality and common-interest rules. The common-interest privilege somewhat relaxes the requirement of confidentiality (see § 71) by defining a widened circle of persons to whom clients may disclose privileged communications. As a corollary, the rule also limits what would otherwise be instances of waiver by disclosing a communication (compare § 79). Communications of several commonly interested clients remain confidential against the rest of the world, no matter how many clients are involved. However, the known presence of a stranger negates the privilege for communications made in the stranger's presence.

Exchanging communications may be predicated on an express agreement, but formality is not required. It may pertain to litigation or to other matters. Separately represented clients do not, by the mere fact of cooperation under this Section, impliedly undertake to exchange all information concerning the matter of common interest.

d. The permissible extent of common-interest disclosures. Under the privilege, any member of a client set—a client, the client's agent for communication, the client's lawyer, and the lawyer's agent (see § 70)—can exchange communications with members of a similar client set. However, a communication directly among the clients is not privileged unless made for the purpose of communicating with a privileged person as defined in § 70. A person who is not represented by a lawyer and who is not himself or herself a lawyer cannot participate in a common-interest arrangement within this Section.

e. Extent of common interests. The communication must relate to the common interest, which may be either legal, factual, or strategic in character. The interests of the separately represented clients need not be entirely congruent.

Illustration:

1. Lawyer One separately represents Corporation A and Lawyer Two represents Corporation B in defending a products-liability action brought by a common adversary, Plaintiff X. The two lawyers agree to exchange otherwise privileged communications of their respective clients concerning settlement strategies. Plaintiff Y later sues Corporation A and Corporation B for damages for alleged defects involving the same products and attempts to obtain discovery of the communications between Lawyer One and Lawyer Two. The communications exchanged between the lawyers for Corporation A and Corporation B are privileged and cannot be discovered.

Unlike the relationship between co-clients, the common-interest relationship does not imply an undertaking to disclose all relevant information (compare § 75, Comment *d*). Confidential communications

923

disclosed to only some members of the arrangement remain privileged against other members as well as against the rest of the world.

f. Subsequent adverse proceedings. Disclosing privileged communications to members of a common-interest arrangement waives the privilege as against other members in subsequent adverse proceedings between them, unless they have agreed otherwise. In that respect, the common-interest exception operates in the same way as the exception for subsequent adverse proceedings as between co-clients (see § 75, Comment *d*). Disclosing information does not waive the privilege with respect to other communications that might also be germane to the matter of common interest but that were not in fact disclosed.

There is no waiver between the members exchanging a communication if they have agreed that it will remain privileged as against each other in subsequent adverse proceedings.

g. Standing to assert the privilege; waiver. Any member of a common-interest arrangement may invoke the privilege against third persons, even if the communication in question was not originally made by or addressed to the objecting member.

In the absence of an agreement to the contrary, any member may waive the privilege with respect to that person's own communications. Correlatively, a member is not authorized to waive the privilege for another member's communication. If a document or other recording embodies communications from two or more members, a waiver is effective only if concurred in by all members whose communications are involved, unless an objecting member's communication can be redacted.

TITLE C.   DURATION OF THE ATTORNEY–CLIENT PRIVILEGE; WAIVERS AND EXCEPTIONS

§ 77. Duration of the Privilege

Unless waived (see §§ 78–80) or subject to exception (see §§ 81–85), the attorney-client privilege may be invoked as provided in § 86 at any time during or after termination of the relationship between client or prospective client and lawyer.

Comment:

a. Scope and cross-references. For limitations on the privilege in subsequent adverse proceedings between co-clients, see § 75(2), and in common-interest arrangements, see § 76(2). The right of the personal representative of a deceased client to assert or waive the privilege is stated in § 86(1)(a).

b. Termination of the client-lawyer relationship. The attorney-client privilege continues indefinitely. Termination of the client-lawyer relationship, even for cause, does not terminate the privilege.

c. Death of a client or cessation of existence of an organization. The privilege survives the death of the client. A lawyer for a client who has died has a continuing obligation to assert the privilege (see § 63, Comment *b*). On standing to assert the privilege, see § 86, Comments *c* and *d*.

The privilege is subject to exception in a controversy concerning a deceased client's disposition of property (see § 81). When ownership or control of an organizational client is transferred or when the organization ceases to exist, the right to invoke the privilege in behalf of the organization may also shift to others or terminate (see § 73, Comment *k*).

d. Situations of need and hardship. The law recognizes no exception to the rule of this Section. Set out below are considerations that may support such an exception, although no court or legislature has adopted it.

It would be desirable that a tribunal be empowered to withhold the privilege of a person then deceased as to a communication that bears on a litigated issue of pivotal significance. The tribunal could balance the interest in confidentiality against any exceptional need for the communication. The tribunal also could consider limiting the proof or sealing the record to limit disclosure. Permitting such disclosure would do little to inhibit clients from confiding in their lawyers. The fortuity of death prevents waiver of the privilege by the client. Appointing a personal representative to consider waiving the privilege simply transforms the issue into one before a probate court. It would be more direct to permit the judge in the proceeding in which the evidence is offered to make a determination based on the relevant factors.

§ 78. Agreement, Disclaimer, or Failure to Object

The attorney-client privilege is waived if the client, the client's lawyer, or another authorized agent of the client:

(1) agrees to waive the privilege;

(2) disclaims protection of the privilege and

(a) another person reasonably relies on the disclaimer to that person's detriment; or

(b) reasons of judicial administration require that the client not be permitted to revoke the disclaimer; or

(3) in a proceeding before a tribunal, fails to object properly to an attempt by another person to give or exact testimony or other evidence of a privileged communication.

Comment:

a. Scope and cross-references. This Section defines the circumstances under which a client loses the protection of the privilege by consent or through conduct inconsistent with maintaining the privilege. On assertion of the privilege, see § 86. On a lawyer's obligation to raise the objection, see § 63, Comment *b*. On the effect of partial disclosure on other communications, see § 79, Comment *c*. See also § 79, Comment *c* (waiver through disclosure by authorized agent). On the effect of waiver on a client's power to raise the privilege on another occasion, see § 79, Comment *i*. On waiver of the lawyer's work-product immunity, see §§ 91–92.

b. Rationale. The attorney-client privilege is personal to the client whose interests it protects. A client can relinquish its protection.

Waiver of the privilege must be contrasted with a lawyer's use or disclosure of confidential client information with client consent under § 62. Under that Section, client consent is effective only if the client is adequately informed (see § 62, Comment *c*). However, because of the interests of third persons and of judicial administration, under this Section the privilege can be lost even though the client is unaware of the privilege or the consequences of waiver (see particularly Comment *e* hereto).

c. Client agreement. Subsection (1) recognizes that the privilege can be waived by consent of a client, the client's lawyer, or another authorized agent. A lawyer generally has implied authority to waive a client's confidentiality rights in the course of representing the client (see § 61). That authority is especially important in litigation, where the lawyer is empowered to deal with evidentiary issues (see § 16(3) & § 26). A lawyer may be required in some circumstances to advise a client concerning waiver (see § 22). Whether a client can contract away the privilege by consent to a conflict of interest is considered in § 122.

Illustration:

1.   A and B were partners in a business enterprise experiencing financial difficulties. Each retained a lawyer. A agreed to send B communications that he had received from his lawyer analyzing financial arrangements between them if B would forbear from filing suit against A. B delayed filing suit, but A refused to honor his agreement. In subsequent litigation, B seeks discovery of the information communicated to A by A's lawyer. A's agreement waives the protection of the attorney-client privilege.

The power of an agent, such as an employee of an organization, to waive the privilege is determined under the law of agency.

d. Client disclaimer. An announced intention to waive the privilege, not part of an enforceable promise, does not itself waive the privilege. The client ordinarily may rescind the intention, but, as stated in Subsection (2), not if another person reasonably and detrimentally relies on the announcement (see generally Restatement Second, Contracts § 90). So also, a tribunal has discretion to hold a litigant to an announced intention to waive the privilege, even without detrimental reliance.

e. Failure to object to evidence. Failure to object properly to another party's attempt to offer privileged evidence during a proceeding waives the privilege. Reasonable efforts must be exerted to maintain the secrecy of confidential communications, including making timely objection (see § 86) to their disclosure. Waiver by failing to make proper objection is an application of the general rule requiring parties to object contemporaneously to inadmissible evidence. E.g., Federal Rules of Evidence, Rule 103(a)(1).

In pretrial discovery, excessive concern with avoiding waiver can unduly delay and encumber the proceeding. Accordingly, procedural rules commonly permit parties to stipulate that privilege is not waived by failure to object during pretrial discovery (see Federal Rules of Civil Procedure, Rule 29).

§ 79. Subsequent Disclosure

The attorney-client privilege is waived if the client, the client's lawyer, or another authorized agent of the client voluntarily discloses the communication in a nonprivileged communication.

Comment:

a. Scope and cross-references. This Section becomes relevant only if the requirements for the privilege (see §§ 68–72) have been satisfied. On waiver in the case of co-clients, see § 75, Comment *c*. Concerning separately represented clients who exchange confidential communications in a common-interest arrangement, see § 76, Comment *f*.

b. Subsequent disclosure. Voluntary disclosure of a privileged communication is inconsistent with a later claim that the communication is to be protected. When the disclosure has been made voluntarily, it is unnecessary that there have been detrimental reliance (compare § 78(2)).

c. Authorized disclosure by a lawyer or other agent. The privilege is waived if the client's lawyer or another authorized agent of the client discloses the communication acting under actual or apparent authority. A lawyer generally has implied authority to disclose confidential client communications in the course of representing a client (see § 27, Comment *c*; see also § 61). Ratification of the agent's authority has the same effect (see § 26, Comment *e*). Whether a subagent of the client or lawyer has authority to waive is governed by agency law. A file clerk in a law firm, for example, does not have implied authority.

Unauthorized disclosure by a lawyer not in pursuit of the client's interests does not constitute waiver under this Section. For example, disclosure of a client's confidential information to prevent a threat to the life or safety of another (§ 66) or to prevent a client crime or fraud (§ 67) does not constitute waiver within the meaning of this Section, although another basis for finding the privilege inapplicable may apply.

Because of the lawyer's apparent authority to act for the client, a lawyer's failure to consult the client about disclosing privileged information generally will not affect the rights of third persons. A third person may not, however, reasonably rely on acts of an opposing lawyer or other agent constituting manifest disregard of responsibility for the client's interests (see also § 60, Comment *l*, & § 71, Comment *c* (eavesdroppers)). Upon discovery of an agent's wrongful disclosure, the client must promptly take reasonable steps to suppress or recover the wrongfully disclosed communication in order to preserve the privilege.

Illustration:

1. Lawyer sends a confidential memorandum containing privileged communications to Client for Client's review. Lawyer sends it by a reputable document-courier service. An employee of the document-courier service opens the sealed envelope, makes copies, and gives the copies to a government agency. As soon as the existence of the copies is discovered, Lawyer takes reasonable steps to recover them and demands that the document-courier service and the government agency return all communications taken or information gained from them. Even if the document-courier service is considered an agent of Lawyer for some purposes, its employee's actions do not waive Client's privilege in the communications.

d. A privileged subsequent disclosure. A subsequent disclosure that is itself privileged does not result in waiver. Thus, a client who discloses a communication protected by the attorney-client privilege to a second lawyer does not waive the privilege if the attorney-client privilege or work-product immunity protects the second communication. So also, showing a confidential letter from the client's lawyer to the client's spouse under circumstances covered by the marital privilege preserves the attorney-client privilege.

e. Extent of disclosure. Waiver results only when a nonprivileged person learns the substance of a privileged communication. Knowledge by the nonprivileged person that the client consulted a lawyer does not result in waiver, nor does disclosure of nonprivileged portions of a communication or its general subject matter. Public disclosure of facts that were discussed in confidence with a lawyer does not waive the privilege if the disclosure does not also reveal that they were communicated to the lawyer. See § 69, Comment *d* (distinction between communications and facts).

Illustrations:

2. Client, a defendant in a personal-injury action, makes a privileged communication to Lawyer concerning the circumstances of the accident. In a later judicial proceeding, Client, under questioning by Lawyer, testifies about the occurrence but not about what Client told Lawyer about the same matter. On cross-examination, the lawyer for Plaintiff inquires whether the Client's testimony is

consistent with the account Client gave to Lawyer in confidence. Client's testimony did not waive the privilege.

3.   The same facts as in Illustration 2, except that Client states that "I've testified exactly as I told Lawyer just a week after the accident happened. I told Lawyer that the skid marks made by Plaintiff's car were 200 feet long. And I've said the same things here." Such testimony waives the privilege by subsequent disclosure. On the extent of waiver, see Comment f hereto.

In the circumstances of Illustration 3, if the client merely testifies that the subject of skid marks was discussed with the client's lawyer, the privilege is not waived.

   f.   Partial subsequent disclosure and "subject matter" waiver. An initial disclosure resulting in waiver under this Section may consist of disclosure of fewer than all communications between lawyer and client on the subject. The question then arises whether an inquiring party is entitled to access to other relevant communications beyond those actually disclosed. (Similar questions can arise with respect to waiver under § 78 (waiver by agreement, disclaimer, or failure to object) and § 80 (waiver by putting assistance or communication in issue).)

General waiver of all related communications is warranted when a party has selectively offered in evidence before a factfinder only part of a more extensive communication or one of several related communications, and the opposing party seeks to test whether the partial disclosure distorted the context or meaning of the part offered. All authorities agree that in such a situation waiver extends to all otherwise-privileged communications on the same subject matter that are reasonably necessary to make a complete and balanced presentation (compare Federal Rules of Evidence, Rule 106). That breadth of waiver is required by considerations of forensic fairness, to prevent a partial disclosure that would otherwise mislead the factfinder because selectively incomplete. Similar considerations generally apply when the privilege holder makes a partial disclosure in pretrial proceedings, as in support of a motion for summary judgment or during a pretrial hearing on a request for provisional relief.

   If partial disclosure occurs in a nontestimonial setting or in the context of pretrial discovery, a clear majority of decisions indicates that a similar broad waiver will be found, even though the disclosure is not intended to obtain advantage as a possibly misleading half-truth in testimony. Although arguably different considerations might apply (because of the absence of opportunity to mislead a factfinder by partial disclosure), courts insist in effect that a party who wishes to assert the privilege take effective steps to protect against even partial disclosure, regardless of the nontestimonial setting. In an appropriate factual setting, waiver may also be supportable on the ground that the partial disclosure was designed to mislead an opposing party in negotiations or was inconsistent with a candid exchange of information in pretrial discovery.

Parties may agree that disclosure of one privileged communication will not be regarded as waiver as to others, and a tribunal may so order, for example in a discovery protective order. Such an agreement or order governs questions of waiver both in the proceeding involved and, with respect to the parties to the agreement, in other proceedings.

g. Voluntary subsequent disclosure. To constitute waiver, a disclosure must be voluntary. The disclosing person need not be aware that the communication was privileged, nor specifically intend to waive the privilege. A disclosure in obedience to legal compulsion or as the product of deception does not constitute waiver.

Illustrations:

> 4. A burglar ransacks Client's confidential files and carries away copies of communications from Client to Lawyer protected by the attorney-client privilege. The police apprehend the burglar, recover the copies, and examine them in order to identify their owner. Client's right to invoke the privilege is not lost.

> 5. At a hearing before a tribunal, the presiding officer erroneously overrules Lawyer's objection to a question put to Client that calls for a communication protected by the attorney-client privilege. Client then testifies. By testifying, Client has not waived objection to efforts to elicit additional privileged communications in the litigation nor to claim on appeal that the hearing officer incorrectly overruled Lawyer's objection. Client also can seek protection of the attorney-client privilege in subsequent litigation.

On resisting disclosure by legal compulsion, see § 86.

h. Inadvertent disclosure. A subsequent disclosure through a voluntary act constitutes a waiver even though not intended to have that effect. It is important to distinguish between inadvertent waiver and a change of heart after voluntary waiver. Waiver does not result if the client or other disclosing person took precautions reasonable in the circumstances to guard against such disclosure. What is reasonable depends on circumstances, including: the relative importance of the communication (the more sensitive the communication, the greater the necessary protective measures); the efficacy of precautions taken and of additional precautions that might have been taken; whether there were externally imposed pressures of time or in the volume of required disclosure; whether disclosure was by act of the client or lawyer or by a third person; and the degree of disclosure to nonprivileged persons.

Once the client knows or reasonably should know that the communication has been disclosed, the client must take prompt and reasonable steps to recover the communication, to reestablish its confidential nature, and to reassert the privilege. Otherwise, apparent acceptance of the disclosure may reflect indifference to confidentiality. Even if fully successful retrieval is impracticable, the client must nonetheless take feasible steps to prevent further distribution.

Illustration:

> 6. Plaintiff has threatened Client with suit unless Client is able to persuade Plaintiff's lawyers that Client is free from fault. Plaintiff imposes a stringent deadline for Client's showing. Client authorizes Lawyer to produce a large mass of documents. Although reviewed by Lawyer, the documents include a confidential memorandum by Client to Lawyer. The standard procedure of lawyers in the circumstances would not have included reexamining the copies prior to submission. Lawyer's inadvertent disclosure did not waive the privilege. After discovering the mistake, Client must promptly reassert the privilege and demand return of the document.

i. Consequences of client waiver of the privilege. Waiver ordinarily extends to the litigation in or in anticipation of which a disclosure was made and future proceedings as well, whether or not related to the original proceeding. However, if no actual disclosure resulted from the waiver, a client might be in a position to reassert the privilege. For example, inadvertent disclosure of a privileged document in discovery should not preclude subsequent assertion of the privilege against a different opponent in different litigation if the disclosure does not result in the document becoming known to anyone other than the party who received it.

§ 80. Putting Assistance or a Communication in Issue

(1) The attorney-client privilege is waived for any relevant communication if the client asserts as to a material issue in a proceeding that:

> **(a) the client acted upon the advice of a lawyer or that the advice was otherwise relevant to the legal significance of the client's conduct; or**

> **(b) a lawyer's assistance was ineffective, negligent, or otherwise wrongful.**

(2) The attorney-client privilege is waived for a recorded communication if a witness:

> **(a) employs the communication to aid the witness while testifying; or**

> **(b) employed the communication in preparing to testify, and the tribunal finds that disclosure is required in the interests of justice.**

Comment:

a. Scope and cross-references. This Section addresses waiver by interjecting the contents of a confidential communication into litigation.

On the exception to the attorney-client privilege in fee suits and for lawyer self-defense, see § 83. On the circumstances in which a client can limit liability or justify an action by relying on legal advice, see § 29.

b. Putting a privileged communication into issue. The exceptions stated in Subsection (1) are based on considerations of forensic fairness (compare § 79). If the communication could not be introduced, a client could present the justification of legal advice in an inaccurate, incomplete, and self-serving way. The issue of reliance on legal advice can be interjected through pleadings or testimony. Waiver extends to all communications relevant to the issue asserted by the client. A tribunal may control discovery to postpone or pretermit the issue. For example, if legal advice is presented as an alternative defense, discovery with respect to that issue may be postponed to allow the client opportunity to determine whether to withdraw that defense.

c. A client attack on a lawyer's services. A client who contends that a lawyer's assistance was defective waives the privilege with respect to communications relevant to that contention. Waiver affords to interested parties fair opportunity to establish the facts underlying the claim. When the lawyer is a party, the privilege is waived under § 83. Proceedings not involving the lawyer as a party include attacks on a criminal conviction on the ground of ineffective assistance of counsel or on a settlement on the ground that the lawyer lacked authority to bind the client (see §§ 26 & 27).

d. Using a privileged communication while testifying or preparing to testify. A witness with consent of or authorized by the client entitled to obtain the privilege might use a privileged communication while testifying or in preparing to testify. An opposing party is permitted to test whether the privileged communication has shaped the testimony. Waiver is automatic when the witness uses the communication in testifying. The standard of permitting review when the presiding officer determines that to be necessary "in the interest of justice" is the formulation employed in the Federal Rules of Evidence (Rule 612(2)). When the witness used the communication to prepare, waiver depends on a determination by the tribunal of whether the witness can recall and testify independent of the communication. Mere review of a privileged communication by a prospective witness does not constitute waiver. The exception should be applied with caution to avoid interfering with legitimate efforts to prepare witnesses for testimony.

If waiver is found, it applies whether the testimony follows or departs from the communication.

§ 81. A Dispute Concerning a Decedent's Disposition of Property

The attorney-client privilege does not apply to a communication from or to a decedent relevant to an issue between parties who claim an interest through the same deceased client, either

by testate or intestate succession or by an inter vivos transaction.

§ 82. Client Crime or Fraud

The attorney-client privilege does not apply to a communication occurring when a client:

(a) consults a lawyer for the purpose, later accomplished, of obtaining assistance to engage in a crime or fraud or aiding a third person to do so, or

(b) regardless of the client's purpose at the time of consultation, uses the lawyer's advice or other services to engage in or assist a crime or fraud.

Comment:

a. Scope and cross-references. The attorney-client privilege is defined in §§ 68–72. The exception applies to all communications from or to privileged persons (see § 70), if the client's purpose in or use of the consultation is as described. The burden of establishing the elements of the exception is upon a person seeking to overcome the privilege (see § 86(3)).

On a lawyer's responsibilities with respect to counseling a client concerning illegal acts, see § 94. On a lawyer's responsibilities with respect to perjurious or other false evidence, see § 120. A lawyer's duty to safeguard confidential client information (see § 60(1)(b)) is subject to §§ 66–67, permitting a lawyer to use or disclose information as reasonably necessary to prevent (or in some instances to mitigate) certain illegal acts of a client.

b. Rationale. When a client consults a lawyer intending to violate elemental legal obligations, there is less social interest in protecting the communication. Correlatively, there is a public interest in preventing clients from attempting to misuse the client-lawyer relationship for seriously harmful ends. Denying protection of the privilege can be founded on the additional moral ground that the client's wrongful intent forfeits the protection. The client can choose whether or not to commit or aid the act after consulting the lawyer and thus is able to avoid exposing secret communications. The exception does not apply to communications about client crimes or frauds that occurred prior to the consultation. Whether a communication relates to past or ongoing or future acts can be a close question. See Comment *e* hereto.

c. Intent of the client and lawyer. The client need not specifically understand that the contemplated act is a crime or fraud. The client's purpose in consulting the lawyer or using the lawyer's services may be inferred from the circumstances. It is irrelevant that the legal service sought by the client (such as drafting an instrument) was itself lawful.

Illustrations:

1. Client is a member of a group engaged in the ongoing enterprise of importing and distributing illegal drugs. Client has agreed with confederates, as part of the consideration for participating in the enterprise, that Client will provide legal representation for the confederates when necessary. Client and Lawyer agree that, for a substantial monthly retainer, Lawyer will stand ready to provide legal services in the event that Client or Client's associates encounter legal difficulties during the operation of the enterprise. In a communication that otherwise qualifies as privileged under § 68, Client informs Lawyer of the identities of confederates in the enterprise. Client continues to engage in the criminal enterprise following the communication. The crime-fraud exception renders nonprivileged the communications between Client and Lawyer, including identification of Client's confederates.

2. Client, who is in financial difficulty, consults Lawyer A concerning the sale of a parcel of real estate owned by Client. Lawyer A provides legal services in connection with the sale. Client then asks Lawyer A to represent Client in petitioning for bankruptcy. Lawyer A advises Client that the bankruptcy petition must list the sale of the real estate because it occurred within the year previous to the date of filing the petition. Client ends the representation. Client shortly thereafter hires Lawyer B. Omitting to tell Lawyer B about the land sale, Client directs Lawyer B to file a bankruptcy petition that does not disclose the proceeds of the sale. In a subsequent proceeding in which Client's fraud in filing the petition is in issue, a tribunal would be warranted in inferring that Client consulted Lawyer A with the purpose of obtaining assistance to defraud creditors in bankruptcy and thus that the communications between Client and Lawyer A concerning report of the land sale in the bankruptcy petition are not privileged. It would also suffice should the tribunal find that Client attempted to use Lawyer A's advice about the required contents of a bankruptcy petition to defraud creditors by withholding information about the land sale from Lawyer B.

A client could intend criminal or fraudulent conduct but not carry through the intended act. The exception should not apply in such circumstances, for it would penalize a client for doing what the privilege is designed to encourage—consulting a lawyer for the purpose of achieving law compliance. By the same token, lawyers might be discouraged from giving full and candid advice to clients about legally questionable courses of action. On the other hand, a client may consult a lawyer about a matter that constitutes a criminal conspiracy but that is later frustrated—and, in that sense, not later accomplished (cf. Subsection (a))—or, similarly, about a criminal attempt. Such a crime is within the exception stated in the Section if its elements are established.

The crime-fraud exception applies regardless of the fact that the client's lawyer is unaware of the client's intent. The exception also applies if the lawyer actively participates in the crime or fraud. However, if a client does not intend to commit a criminal or fraudulent act, the privilege protects the client's communication even if the client's lawyer acts with a criminal or fraudulent intent in giving advice.

Illustration:

3. Lawyer, in complicity with confederates who are not clients, is furthering a scheme to defraud purchasers in a public offering of shares of stock. Client, believing that the stock offering is legitimate and ignorant of facts indicating its wrongful nature, seeks to participate in the offering as an underwriter. In the course of obtaining legal advice from Lawyer, Client conveys communications to Lawyer that are privileged under § 68. The crime-fraud exception does not prevent Client from asserting the attorney-client privilege, despite Lawyer's complicity in the fraud.

Compare Illustration 1 to this Comment.

d. Kinds of illegal acts included within the exception. The authorities agree that the exception stated in this Section applies to client conduct defined as a crime or fraud. Fraud, for the purpose of the exception, requires a knowing or reckless misrepresentation (or nondisclosure when applicable law requires disclosure) likely to injure another (see Restatement Second, Torts §§ 525–530 (defining elements of fraudulent misrepresentation)).

The evidence codes and judicial decisions are divided on the question of extending the exception to other wrongs such as intentional torts, which, although not criminal or fraudulent, have hallmarks of clear illegality and the threat of serious harm. Legislatures and courts classify illegal acts as crimes and frauds for purposes and policies different from those defining the scope of the privilege. Thus, limiting the exception to crimes and frauds produces an exception narrower than principle and policy would otherwise indicate. Nonetheless, the prevailing view limits the exception to crimes and frauds. The actual instances in which a broader exception might apply are probably few and isolated, and it would be difficult to formulate a broader exception that is not objectionably vague.

Consultation about some acts of civil disobedience is privileged under the Section, for example violations of a law based on a nonfrivolous claim that the law is unconstitutional. The same is true of a communication concerning a contempt sanction necessary to obtain immediate appellate review of an order whose validity is challenged in good faith. (See § 94, Comment *e*, & § 105, Comment *e*.) If, however, the client's position is that the law is valid but there is a superior moral justification for violating it, this Section applies if its conditions are otherwise satisfied.

e. Continuing crimes and frauds. The crime-fraud exception depends on a distinction between past client wrongs and acts that are continuing or will occur in the future. The exception does not apply to communications about client criminal or fraudulent acts that occurred in the past. Communications about past acts are necessary in defending against charges concerning such conduct and, for example, providing background for legal advice concerning a present transaction that is neither criminal nor fraudulent. The possible social costs of denying access to relevant evidence of past acts is accepted in order to realize the enhanced legality and fairness that confidentiality fosters (see § 68, Comment *c*).

The exception does apply to client crimes or frauds that are ongoing or continuing. With respect to past acts that have present consequences, such as the possession of stolen goods, consultation of lawyer and client is privileged if it addresses how the client can rectify the effects of the illegal act—such as by returning the goods to their rightful owner—or defending the client against criminal charges arising out of the offense.

Illustration:

4. Client consults Lawyer about Client's indictment for the crimes of theft and of unlawfully possessing stolen goods. Applicable law treats possession of stolen goods as a continuing offense. Client is hiding the goods in a secret place, knowing that they are stolen. Confidential communications between Client and Lawyer concerning the indictment for theft and possession and the facts underlying those offenses are privileged. Confidential communications concerning ways in which Client can continue to possess the stolen goods, including information supplied by Client about their present location, are not protected by the privilege because of the crime-fraud exception. Confidential communications about ways in which Client might lawfully return the stolen goods to their owner are privileged.

Strict limitation of the exception to ongoing or future crimes and frauds would prohibit a lawyer from testifying that a client confessed to a crime for which an innocent person is on trial. The law of the United Kingdom recognizes an exception in such cases. At least in capital cases, the argument for so extending the exception seems compelling. Compare also § 66 (disclosure to prevent loss of life or serious bodily injury, whether or not risk is created by wrongful client act).

f. Invoking the crime-fraud exception. The crime-fraud exception is relevant only after the attorney-client privilege is successfully invoked. The person seeking access to the communication then must present a prima facie case for the exception. A prima facie case need show only a reasonable basis for concluding that the elements of the exception (see Comment *d*) exist. The showing must be made by evidence other than the contested communication itself. Once a prima facie showing is made, the tribunal has discretion to examine the communication or hear testimony about it in camera, that is, without requiring that the communications be revealed to the party seeking to invoke the exception (see § 86, Comment *f*).

Unless the crime-fraud exception plainly applies to a client-lawyer communication, a lawyer has an obligation to assert the privilege (see § 63, Comment *b*).

g. Effects of the crime-fraud exception. A communication to which the crime-fraud exception applies is not privileged under § 68 for any purpose. Evidence of the communication is admissible in the proceeding in which that determination is made or in another proceeding. The privilege still applies, however, to communications that were not for a purpose included within this Section. For example, a client who consulted a lawyer about several different matters on several different occasions could invoke the privilege with respect to consultations concerning matters unrelated to the illegal acts (compare § 79, Comment *e*). With respect to a lawyer's duty not to use or disclose client information even if not privileged, see § 60; compare §§ 66–67.

§ 83. Lawyer Self–Protection

The attorney-client privilege does not apply to a communication that is relevant and reasonably necessary for a lawyer to employ in a proceeding:

> **(1) to resolve a dispute with a client concerning compensation or reimbursement that the lawyer reasonably claims the client owes the lawyer; or**

> **(2) to defend the lawyer or the lawyer's associate or agent against a charge by any person that the lawyer, associate, or agent acted wrongfully during the course of representing a client.**

§ 84. Fiduciary–Lawyer Communications

In a proceeding in which a trustee of an express trust or similar fiduciary is charged with breach of fiduciary duties by a beneficiary, a communication otherwise within § 68 is nonetheless not privileged if the communication:

> **(a) is relevant to the claimed breach; and**

> **(b) was between the trustee and a lawyer (or other privileged person within the meaning of § 70) who was retained to advise the trustee concerning the administration of the trust.**

§ 85. Communications Involving a Fiduciary Within an Organization

In a proceeding involving a dispute between an organizational client and shareholders, members, or other constituents

of the organization toward whom the directors, officers, or similar persons managing the organization bear fiduciary responsibilities, the attorney-client privilege of the organization may be withheld from a communication otherwise within § 68 if the tribunal finds that:

(a) those managing the organization are charged with breach of their obligations toward the shareholders, members, or other constituents or toward the organization itself;

(b) the communication occurred prior to the assertion of the charges and relates directly to those charges; and

(c) the need of the requesting party to discover or introduce the communication is sufficiently compelling and the threat to confidentiality sufficiently confined to justify setting the privilege aside.

TITLE D.   INVOKING THE PRIVILEGE AND ITS EXCEPTIONS

§ 86.   Invoking the Privilege and Its Exceptions

(1) When an attempt is made to introduce in evidence or obtain discovery of a communication privileged under § 68:

(a) A client, a personal representative of an incompetent or deceased client, or a person succeeding to the interest of a client may invoke or waive the privilege, either personally or through counsel or another authorized agent.

(b) A lawyer, an agent of the lawyer, or an agent of a client from whom a privileged communication is sought must invoke the privilege when doing so appears reasonably appropriate, unless the client:

(i) has waived the privilege; or

(ii) has authorized the lawyer or agent to waive it.

(c) Notwithstanding failure to invoke the privilege as specified in Subsections (1)(a) and (1)(b), the tribunal has discretion to invoke the privilege.

(2) A person invoking the privilege must ordinarily object contemporaneously to an attempt to disclose the communication and, if the objection is contested, demonstrate each element of the privilege under § 68.

(3) A person invoking a waiver of or exception to the privilege (§§ 78–85) must assert it and, if the assertion is contested, demonstrate each element of the waiver or exception.

TOPIC 3. THE LAWYER WORK–PRODUCT IMMUNITY

TITLE A. THE SCOPE OF THE LAWYER WORK–PRODUCT IMMUNITY

§ 87. Lawyer Work–Product Immunity

(1) Work product consists of tangible material or its intangible equivalent in unwritten or oral form, other than underlying facts, prepared by a lawyer for litigation then in progress or in reasonable anticipation of future litigation.

(2) Opinion work product consists of the opinions or mental impressions of a lawyer; all other work product is ordinary work product.

(3) Except for material which by applicable law is not so protected, work product is immune from discovery or other compelled disclosure to the extent stated in §§ 88 (ordinary work product) and 89 (opinion work product) when the immunity is invoked as described in § 90.

Comment:

a. Scope and cross-references. This Section defines the work-product immunity as it applies to lawyers. Federal and state discovery rules accord work-product protection to others, including personnel who assist a lawyer, and to litigation preparation of a party and the party's representatives. Application of the immunity with respect to such other persons is beyond the scope of this Restatement.

Section 88 sets forth the standard for overcoming ordinary work-product immunity. The broader protection afforded opinion work product is considered in § 89. Procedures for invoking the immunity and its exceptions are considered in Title B. Title C discusses exceptions to that rule.

b. Rationale. The Federal Rules of Civil Procedure in 1938 provided for notice pleading supplemented by expanded discovery. The Rules sought to eliminate the "sporting" concept of litigation in favor of more accurate factfinding and open truth-seeking. However, the discovery rules presupposed that counsel should be able to work within an area of professional confidentiality, described by the work-product rule. A companion assumption has been that the truth emerges from the adversary presentation of information by opposing sides, in which opposing lawyers competitively develop their own sources of factual and legal information. The work-product doctrine also protects client interests in obtaining diligent assistance from lawyers. A lawyer whose work product would be open to the other side might forgo useful preparatory procedures, for example, note-taking. The immunity also reduces the possibility that a

939

lawyer would have to testify concerning witness statements (compare § 108).

Nonetheless, the work-product immunity is in tension with the purposes of modern discovery by impeding the pretrial exchange of information. The immunity also entails duplication of investigative efforts, perhaps increasing litigation costs. Enforcement of the immunity causes satellite litigation and additional expense.

Protection of lawyer thought processes (see § 89) is at the core of work-product rationale; accordingly, those are accorded the broadest protection. A lawyer's analysis can readily be replicated by an opposing lawyer and, in any event, would usually be inadmissible in evidence. Factual information gathered by a lawyer usually relates directly to controverted issues and generally is discoverable in forms that do not reveal the lawyer's thought processes.

Beyond that, the work-product rules are a set of compromises between openness and secrecy. Thus, under Federal Rule 26(b), the identity of witnesses must be disclosed even if ascertaining their identity has been burdensome or involved confidential consultations with a client. Similarly, under Rule 26(b) statements given by a party to an opposing lawyer are subject to discovery, even though such a statement necessarily reflects the lawyer's thought process in some degree. So also are the opinions of an expert who is expected to testify at trial. A nonparty witness's statement must be produced upon demand by that witness. A party's documents and other records are generally discoverable even if they have been reviewed by counsel. On the other hand, the identity of an expert consulted but who will not testify is protected against discovery, even if that expert's opinion is highly material. So also, the classification systems employed by a lawyer in reviewing a client's documents are not subject to discovery.

c. Applications of the work-product immunity. The work-product immunity operates primarily as a limitation on pretrial discovery, but it can apply to evidence at a trial or hearing. Work-product immunity is also recognized in criminal and administrative proceedings and is incorporated as a limitation on other types of disclosure, for example in the federal Freedom of Information Act. The scope of those applications of the work-product rule is generally beyond the scope of this Restatement.

d. The relationship of the work-product immunity to the attorney-client privilege. The attorney-client privilege is limited to communications between a client and lawyer and certain of their agents (see § 70); in contrast, work product includes many other kinds of materials (see Comment *f*), even when obtained from sources other than the client. Application of the attorney-client privilege absolutely bars discovery or testimonial use; in contrast, the work-product immunity is a qualified protection that, in various circumstances, can be overcome on a proper showing (see §§ 88 & 89). The attorney-client privilege protects communications between client and lawyer regarding all kinds of legal services (see § 72); in contrast, the work-product immunity is limited to materials prepared for or in anticipation of litigation (see Comments *h-j*).

Work-product immunity is also similar to the rule recognized in some jurisdictions that a self-evaluation study and report is immune from discovery. The self-evaluation immunity is not limited to work performed in anticipation of litigation. The scope of self-evaluation and similar immunities is beyond the scope of this Restatement.

e. The source of the law concerning work-product immunity. In the federal system, work-product immunity is recognized both under Rule 26(b)(3) of the Federal Rules of Civil Procedure and as a common-law rule following the decision in *Hickman v. Taylor*. In a few states work-product immunity is established by common law, but in most states it is defined by statute or court rule. Some state statutes mirror Federal Rule of Civil Procedure 26(b)(3), others codify the principles of *Hickman v. Taylor* more broadly; and others codify pre-*Hickman* rules that were not adopted for the federal courts. State courts, in construing their statutes, often look to federal case law in applying work-product immunity.

f. Types of work-product materials. Work product includes tangible materials and intangible equivalents prepared, collected, or assembled by a lawyer. Tangible materials include documents, photographs, diagrams, sketches, questionnaires and surveys, financial and economic analyses, hand-written notes, and material in electronic and other technologically advanced forms, such as stenographic, mechanical, or electronic recordings or transmissions, computer data bases, tapes, and printouts. Intangible work product is equivalent work product in unwritten, oral or remembered form. For example, intangible work product can come into question by a discovery request for a lawyer's recollections derived from oral communications.

A compilation or distillation of non-work-product materials can itself be work product. For example, a lawyer's memorandum analyzing publicly available information constitutes work product. The selection or arrangement of documents that are not themselves protected might reflect mental impressions and legal opinions inherent in making a selection or arrangement. Thus, a lawyer's index of a client's preexisting and discoverable business files will itself be work product if prepared in anticipation of litigation. So also, the manner in which a lawyer has selected certain client files, organized them in pretrial work, and plans to present them at trial is work product.

g. The distinction between protected materials and nonprotected underlying facts. Work-product immunity does not apply to underlying facts of the incident or transaction involved in the litigation, even if the same information is contained in work product. For a comparison to the nonprivileged status accorded to facts under the attorney-client privilege, see § 69, Comment *d*.

The distinction between discoverable underlying facts and nondiscoverable work product can be difficult to draw. Relevant are the form of the question or request, the identity of the person who is to respond, and the form of a responsive answer. Immunity does not attach merely because the underlying fact was discovered through a lawyer's effort or is recorded only in otherwise protected work product, for example, in a lawyer's file memorandum. Immunity does not apply to an interrogatory seeking names of witnesses to the occurrence in question or whether a witness recounts a particular version of events, for example that a traffic light was red or green. On the other hand, an interrogatory seeking the substantially verbatim contents of the witness's unrecorded statement would be objectionable.

h. Anticipation of litigation: kinds of proceedings. The limitation of the work-product immunity to litigation activities is best explained by the origin of the rule in the context of litigation. "Litigation" includes civil and criminal trial proceedings, as well as adversarial proceedings before an administrative agency, an arbitration panel or a claims commission, and alternative-dispute-resolution proceedings such as mediation or mini-trial. It also includes a proceeding such as a grand jury or a coroner's inquiry or an investigative legislative hearing. In general, a proceeding is adversarial when evidence or legal argument is presented by parties contending against each other with respect to legally significant factual issues. Thus, an adversarial rulemaking proceeding is litigation for purposes of the immunity.

i. Anticipation of litigation: the reasonableness standard. Work-product immunity attaches when litigation is then in progress or there is reasonable anticipation of litigation by the lawyer at the time the material was prepared. On what constitutes litigation, see Comment *h* hereto. The fact that litigation did not actually ensue does not affect the immunity.

In one sense, almost all of a lawyer's work anticipates litigation to some degree, because preparing documents or arranging transactions is aimed at avoiding future litigation or enhancing a client's position should litigation occur. However, the immunity covers only material produced when apprehension of litigation was reasonable in the circumstances. The reasonableness of anticipation is determined objectively by considering the factual context in which materials are prepared, the nature of the materials, and the expected role of the lawyer in ensuing litigation.

Illustrations:

1. Employer's Lawyer writes to Physician, setting out circumstances of an employee's death and asking for Physician's opinion as to the cause, stating that Lawyer is preparing for a "possible claim" by the employee's executor for worker-compensation benefits. Lawyer's letter is protected work product.

2. Informed that agents of the Justice Department are questioning Publisher's customers, Lawyer for Publisher prepared a memorandum analyzing the antitrust implications of Publisher's

standard contract form with commercial purchasers. Publisher's employees testify before a grand jury investigating antitrust issues in the publishing industry. Lawyer, reasonably believing there is a risk that the grand jury will indict Publisher, interviews the employees and prepares a debriefing memorandum. Both Lawyer's memorandum analyzing the contract form and Lawyer's debriefing memorandum were prepared in anticipation of litigation. The grand-jury proceeding is itself litigation for this purpose (see Comment *h*).

j. Future litigation. If litigation was reasonably anticipated, the immunity is afforded even if litigation occurs in an unanticipated way. For example, work product prepared during or in anticipation of a lawsuit remains immune in a subsequent suit for indemnification, whether or not the indemnification claim could have been anticipated. Work product prepared in anticipation of litigation remains protected in all future litigation.

§ 88. Ordinary Work Product

When work product protection is invoked as described in § 90, ordinary work product (§ 87(2)) is immune from discovery or other compelled disclosure unless either an exception recognized in §§ 91–93 applies or the inquiring party:

(1) has a substantial need for the material in order to prepare for trial; and

(2) is unable without undue hardship to obtain the substantial equivalent of the material by other means.

Comment:

a. Scope and cross-references. This Section states the limited immunity of ordinary work product from involuntary disclosure and the need-and-hardship exception. On the much narrower exception for opinion work product, see § 89.

b. The need-and-hardship exception—in general. The demonstration of need and hardship operates only when it is first established (see § 90, Comment *b*) that the requested material constitutes protected work product (see § 87). The exception does not provide access if other privileges apply, for example, the attorney-client privilege (see §§ 68–86), the privilege against self-incrimination, or a privilege for proprietary information.

Demonstrating the requisite need and hardship requires the inquiring party to show that the material is relevant to the party's claim or defense, and that the inquiring party will likely be prejudiced in the absence of discovery. As a corollary, it must be shown that substantially equivalent material is not available or, if available, only through cost and effort substantially disproportionate to the amount at stake in the litigation and the value of the information to the inquiring party. The necessary showing is more easily made after other discovery has been completed.

The most common situation involves a prior statement by a witness who is absent, seriously ill, or deceased and thus now unavailable. See Federal Rule of Evidence 804(a). Another common situation concerns statements made contemporaneously with an event. Such statements are often the most reliable recording of recollections of that event and in that sense unique. A third situation is where the passage of time has dulled the memory of the witness.

Illustration:

> 1. Several witnesses testify before a grand jury investigating the publishing industry. Shortly afterward, Lawyer for Publisher debriefs the witnesses and writes memoranda of those interviews in anticipation of the possible indictment of Publisher and later civil suits. Six years later, Plaintiffs, representing a class of consumers, file an antitrust class action against Publisher and seek discovery of the non-opinion work-product portions of Lawyer's debriefing memoranda. Plaintiffs have been diligent in preparing their case and gathering evidence through other means and demonstrate that the witnesses now are unable to recall the events to which they testified. The court may order the memorandum produced. If the memorandum contains both ordinary and opinion work product, see § 89, Comment *c*.

Substantial need also exists when the material consists of tests performed nearly contemporaneously with a litigated event and substantially equivalent testing is no longer possible.

c. Material for impeachment. Need is shown when a requesting party demonstrates that there is likely to be a material discrepancy between a prior statement of a witness reflected in a lawyer's notes and a statement of the same person made later during discovery, such as during a deposition. The discrepancy must be of an impeaching quality. A clear case exists when the witness admits to such a discrepancy. However, the inquiring party may demonstrate a reasonable basis by inference from circumstances. In camera inspection of the statement may be appropriate to determine whether the material should be produced.

d. Witness statements. A statement given to a lawyer by a witness is work product. Being ordinary work product, a witness statement may be obtained by an opposing party only upon an appropriate showing of need and hardship. Under the Federal Rules and the law of many states, the person who gives a substantially verbatim statement has the right to obtain a copy of it.

§ 89 Opinion Work Product

When work product protection is invoked as described in § 90, opinion work product (§ 87(2)) is immune from discovery

or other compelled disclosure unless either the immunity is waived or an exception applies (§§ 91–93) or extraordinary circumstances justify disclosure.

Comment:

a. Scope and cross-references. Opinion work product of a lawyer is defined in § 87(2). Ordinary work product is subject to a general exception for need and hardship (see § 88).

b. Rationale. Mental impressions, opinions, conclusions, and legal theories form the core of work product. As impressions formed after the event or transaction in issue, they are also not of the same evidentiary value as percipient witness observation or contemporaneous recording of the event. Disclosure of ordinary work product in cases of need and hardship facilitates trial preparation, but no comparable utility ordinarily attends discovery of a lawyer's theories, conclusions, and other opinions. Strict protection for opinion work product effectuates functioning of the adversary system (see § 87, Comment *b*). Moreover, analysis expressed in opinion work product can be carried out by the requesting party's lawyer.

The protection for opinion work product is qualified by discovery rules requiring disclosure of legal contentions on which a party intends to rely (see Federal Rules of Civil Procedure 33(b) and 36(a), cf. id., Rule 16 (pretrial conference)). Also, an advocate is required under certain circumstances to inform a tribunal of adverse legal authority (see § 111).

c. Material combining opinion and ordinary work product. The material sought might contain both ordinary and opinion work product, for example, notes of an interview containing both the recollections of the witness and the thoughts of the lawyer who made the notes. If the tribunal finds that the ordinary work-product material should be produced, it may order production of the notes in redacted form. The tribunal may conduct an in camera inspection to determine whether redaction is appropriate and feasible. If opinion work product is so intertwined in the material that it cannot be redacted without destroying the value of the ordinary work product, the tribunal must balance the need for disclosure against the need for privacy.

d. The extraordinary-circumstances exception. The concept of "extraordinary circumstances" has never been intelligibly defined (see Reporter's Note). It apparently signifies unwillingness on the part of tribunals to put the work-product immunity on quite the same footing as the attorney-client privilege.

TITLE B. PROCEDURAL ADMINISTRATION OF THE LAWYER WORK–PRODUCT IMMUNITY

§ 90. Involving the Lawyer Work–Product Immunity and Its Exceptions

(1) Work-product immunity may be invoked by or for a person on whose behalf the work product was prepared.

(2) The person invoking work-product immunity must object and, if the objection is contested, demonstrate each element of the immunity.

(3) Once a claim of work product has been adequately supported, a person entitled to invoke a waiver or exception must assert it and, if the assertion is contested, demonstrate each element of the waiver or exception.

TITLE C. WAIVERS AND EXCEPTIONS TO THE LAWYER WORK–PRODUCT IMMUNITY

§ 91. Voluntary Acts

Work-product immunity is waived if the client, the client's lawyer, or another authorized agent of the client:

(1) agrees to waive the immunity;

(2) disclaims protection of the immunity and:

(a) another person reasonably relies on the disclaimer to that person's detriment; or

(b) reasons of judicial administration require that the client not be permitted to revoke the disclaimer; or

(3) in a proceeding before a tribunal, fails to object properly to an attempt by another person to give or exact testimony or other evidence of work product; or

(4) discloses the material to third persons in circumstances in which there is a significant likelihood that an adversary or potential adversary in anticipated litigation will obtain it.

§ 92. Use of Lawyer Work Product in Litigation

(1) Work-product immunity is waived for any relevant material if the client asserts as to a material issue in a proceeding that:

(a) the client acted upon the advice of a lawyer or that the advice was otherwise relevant to the legal significance of the client's conduct; or

(b) a lawyer's assistance was ineffective, negligent, or otherwise wrongful.

(2) The work-product immunity is waived for recorded material if a witness

(a) employs the material to aid the witness while testifying, or

(b) employed the material in preparing to testify, and the tribunal finds that disclosure is required in the interests of justice.

Comment:

a. Scope and cross-references. This Section parallels the analogous rules governing waiver of the attorney-client privilege by putting legal assistance or privileged communications into issue (see § 80(1)) or using work-product material or privileged communications to assist a witness (see § 80(2)).

b. Putting work product into issue. A party waives work-product protection by putting the protected material into issue, including claims of reliance on counsel and of good faith evidenced by consultation with counsel, or where determining the truth of the party's allegation requires examination of work product. Such waivers, like the analogous waivers of the attorney-client privilege, are based on considerations of fairness (see § 80, Comment *b*). The immunity is not lost if the proceeding in which the claim or defense is asserted, for example in a pleading, ends without other disclosure of the work product (see Comment *f* hereto).

Although discovery of opinion work product is more restricted (see § 89), when the advice or other service of counsel is directly in issue and is evidenced by the lawyer's opinion work product, the balance is struck in favor of disclosure.

c. A client's attack on a lawyer's services. A party who asserts that a lawyer's assistance was defective may not invoke work-product immunity to prevent an opposing party's access to information concerning the claim. See § 80, Comment *c* (analogous waiver of attorney-client privilege). Where the interests of the lawyer and the client conflict (see § 83 & § 90, Comment *c*), the lawyer may not use the work-product protection to deny the client access to relevant work-product materials (see § 90, Comment *c*).

d. Use of work product at a hearing. When a witness has relied on work-product material in testimony, the rules of evidence afford an opposing party the opportunity to examine the relevant portions of the work product. Portions not relevant to the witness's direct examination may be ordered to be redacted.

§ 93. Client Crime or Fraud

Work-product immunity does not apply to materials prepared when a client consults a lawyer for the purpose, later accomplished, of obtaining assistance to engage in a crime or fraud or to aid a third person to do so or uses the materials for such a purpose.

Comment:

a. Scope and cross-references. For the crime-fraud exception to be relevant, the requested materials must qualify as work product under § 87. The crime-fraud exception overcomes protection for both ordinary (see § 88) and opinion (see § 89) work product. The party seeking production need not show need or hardship (compare § 88). On invoking the crime-fraud exception, see § 90, Comment *b*.

For the analogous crime-fraud exception to the attorney-client privilege, see § 82, including the element of accomplishment of the wrongful objective (see § 82, Comment *c*). On the limited circumstances in which a lawyer may disclose a client's intended crime or fraud, see §§ 66–67. On a lawyer's responsibilities with respect to counseling a client concerning illegal acts, see § 94. On a lawyer's responsibilities with respect to false evidence, see § 120.

b.   Rationale. Like the crime-fraud exception to the attorney-client privilege (see § 82, Comment *b*), the crime-fraud exception for work-product immunity recognizes that crime and fraud do not warrant such protection. The exception applies to ongoing or future crimes or frauds but not to work product prepared in a representation concerning completed client acts. Whether work product relates to past acts or future or ongoing acts requires close analysis (see § 82, Comment *e*).

c.   The intents of the client and the lawyer. To overcome the immunity by use of the crime-fraud exception, the inquiring party must make a sufficient showing that the client's ongoing or future conduct was criminal or fraudulent. The particulars of that showing are the same as for the corresponding exception to the attorney-client privilege (see § 82).

If the client alone has the requisite criminal or fraudulent intent, work-product immunity is lost despite the innocence of the lawyer (see § 82, Comment *c*). The public interest in deterring wrongful acts outweighs the innocent lawyer's interest in privacy. The rule also prevents a client from advancing an illegal scheme through a noncomplicit lawyer. Once the required showing is made, opinion work product of an innocent lawyer is subject to disclosure along with opinion work product of the client and ordinary work product of both client and lawyer. Conversely, the exception does not apply when a lawyer representing an innocent client commits or is complicit in another's crime or fraud (see § 82, Comment *c*, Illustration 3).

d.   Invoking the crime-fraud exception. The crime-fraud exception applies only after a client or lawyer establishes the elements of work-product immunity, as provided in § 90, Comment *b*. The party seeking access to the work product then has the burden of establishing that it falls within the exception (id.; see also § 82, Comment *f*).

CHAPTER 6: REPRESENTING CLIENTS—IN GENERAL

TOPIC 1.   LAWYERS FUNCTIONS IN REPRESENTING CLIENTS—IN GENERAL

§ 94.   Advising and Assisting a Client—In General

(1) A lawyer who counsels or assists a client to engage in conduct that violates the rights of a third person is subject to liability:

(a) to the third person to the extent stated in §§ 51 and 56–57; and

(b) to the client to the extent stated in §§ 50, 55, and 56.

(2) For purposes of professional discipline, a lawyer may not counsel or assist a client in conduct that the lawyer knows to be criminal or fraudulent or in violation of a court order with the intent of facilitating or encouraging the conduct, but the lawyer may counsel or assist a client in conduct when the lawyer reasonably believes:

(a) that the client's conduct constitutes a good-faith effort to determine the validity, scope, meaning, or application of a law or court order; or

(b) that the client can assert a nonfrivolous argument that the client's conduct will not constitute a crime or fraud or violate a court order.

(3) In counseling a client, a lawyer may address nonlegal aspects of a proposed course of conduct, including moral, reputational, economic, social, political, and business aspects.

§ 95. An Evaluation Undertaken for a Third Person

(1) In furtherance of the objectives of a client in a representation, a lawyer may provide to a nonclient the results of the lawyer's investigation and analysis of facts or the lawyer's professional evaluation or opinion on the matter.

(2) When providing the information, evaluation, or opinion under Subsection (1) is reasonably likely to affect the client's interests materially and adversely, the lawyer must first obtain the client's consent after the client is adequately informed concerning important possible effects on the client's interests.

(3) In providing the information, evaluation, or opinion under Subsection (1), the lawyer must exercise care with respect to the nonclient to the extent stated in § 51(2) and not make false statements prohibited under § 98.

TOPIC 2. REPRESENTING ORGANIZATIONAL CLIENTS—IN GENERAL

§ 96. Representing an Organization as Client

(1) When a lawyer is employed or retained to represent an organization:

(a) the lawyer represents the interests of the organization as defined by its responsible agents acting pursuant to the organization's decision-making procedures; and

(b) subject to Subsection (2), the lawyer must follow instructions in the representation, as stated in § 21(2), given

949

by persons authorized so to act on behalf of the organization.

(2) If a lawyer representing an organization knows of circumstances indicating that a constituent of the organization has engaged in action or intends to act in a way that violates a legal obligation to the organization that will likely cause substantial injury to it, or that reasonably can be foreseen to be imputable to the organization and likely to result in substantial injury to it, the lawyer must proceed in what the lawyer reasonably believes to be the best interests of the organization.

(3) In the circumstances described in Subsection (2), the lawyer may, in circumstances warranting such steps, ask the constituent to reconsider the matter, recommend that a second legal opinion be sought, and seek review by appropriate supervisory authority within the organization, including referring the matter to the highest authority that can act in behalf of the organization.

Comment:

a. Scope and cross-references. This Section concerns the duties of a lawyer who represents an organization as client and in doing so deals with constituents of the organization. On the definition of organization, see Comment *c*; on the definition of constituent, see Comment *b*. To the extent not inconsistent with § 97, this Section applies to counseling governmental clients.

On forming a client-lawyer relationship with an organizational client, see § 14, Comment *f*. On conflicts of interest involved generally in representing an organization, see § 131; on conflicts involved in representing an organization concurrently with one or more constituents, see § 131, Comments *e* and *f*; on conflicting interests of affiliated organizations, see § 131, Comment *d*. On conflicts of interest that may be involved in providing legal services to an organization while also serving as an officer or director of the organization, see § 135, Comment *d*.

On limitations on advising and assisting a client, see § 94. The attorney-client privilege as applied to corporate and similar clients is considered in § 73.

On disclosing confidential client information with respect to certain unlawful acts of a client, see §§ 66–67. Disclosure under §§ 66–67 differs from action permissible for a lawyer to take under this Section in several respects. First, the purpose of allowing disclosure under §§ 66–67 is to protect third persons or the lawyer, while the purpose of action within the organization under Subsection (2) (see Comments *e* & *f* hereof) is to protect the interests of the organizational client. Second, the crime or fraud warranting disclosure to prevent financial loss under § 67 is that of the client. In situations arising under Subsection (2), a nonclient constituent commits the wrongful act and the client organization is either the victim of the act or is vicariously responsible as a result of the wrongful act of the constituent. Third, permissible disclosure under §§ 66–67 is limited to a future or continuing act of the client (except for disclosure under § 67(2)), and under § 67 is limited to client acts in which the lawyer's legal services were employed by the client. Under Subsection (2), a lawyer may be required to protect the organizational client from past as well as ongoing and future wrongful acts of a constituent (see Comment *e*) and from acts in which the lawyer's services were not employed.

b. Rationale: an organization as client. A lawyer who has been employed or retained to represent an organization as a client owes professional duties of loyalty and competence to the organization. By representing the organization, a lawyer does not thereby also form a client-lawyer relationship with all or any individuals employed by it or who direct its operations or who have an ownership or other beneficial interest in it, such as its shareholders. However additional circumstances may result in a client-lawyer relationship with constituents while the lawyer concurrently represents the organization (see Comment *h* hereto).

A lawyer representing only an organization does not owe duties of care (see § 52), diligence (see § 16), or confidentiality (see § 60) to constituents of the organization. Compare § 132, Comment *g(ii)* (duties of confidentiality to persons about whom lawyer learned confidential information in prior representation of client). Correspondingly, although a lawyer for the organization acts at the direction of its officers, the lawyer for an organization does not possess, solely in that capacity, power to act for officers as their lawyer. Thus, third persons may not reasonably conclude, solely from that capacity, that a lawyer for the organization represents officers individually (compare §§ 26 & 27). Similarly, a lawyer representing only a constituent does not, by virtue of that representation, owe either to the organization employing the constituent or to other constituents obligations that would arise only from a client-lawyer relationship with the organization.

The so-called "entity" theory of organizational representation, stated in Subsection (1), is now universally recognized in American law, for purposes of determining the identity of the direct beneficiary of legal representation of corporations and other forms of organizations. On the definition of organizations within the meaning of this Section, see Comment *c*. Pursuant to the entity theory, the rights and responsibilities of the client-lawyer relationship described in Chapter 2 obtain between the organization and the lawyer.

A lawyer representing an organization deals with individuals such as its officers, directors, and employees, who serve as constituents of the organization. Such individuals acting under the organization's authority retain and direct the lawyer to act on behalf of the organization (see Comment *d* hereto). Nonetheless, personal dealings with such persons do not lessen the lawyer's responsibilities to the organization as client, and the lawyer may not let such dealings hinder the lawyer in the performance of those responsibilities.

A "constituent" of an organization within the meaning of the Section has the same meaning as in Rule 1.13 of the ABA Model Rules of Professional Conduct (1983). A constituent includes an officer, director, or employee of the organization. A shareholder of a stock corporation or a member of a membership corporation is also a constituent within the meaning of this Section, as under Rule 1.13.

A lawyer may represent an organization either as an employee of the organization (inside legal counsel) or as a lawyer in private practice retained by the organization (outside legal counsel). In general, a lawyer's responsibilities to a client organization are the same in both capacities. Special rules for inside legal counsel are stated in § 32, Comment *b*; § 37, Comment *e*; § 58, Comment *c*; and § 123, Comment *d(i)*. However, the nature of the lawyer's work and greater or less access to an organization's channels of information can affect the lawyer's knowledge and thus, for example, the reasonableness of the lawyer's reliance on a constituent of the organization for information and direction.

c. Forms of client organizations. In general, this Section applies to representation of formally constituted organizations. In all events, whether a client-lawyer relationship is formed is to be determined in light of the considerations stated in § 14. Such organizations include for-profit and nonprofit corporations, limited-liability companies, unincorporated associations (such as trade associations and labor unions), general and limited partnerships, professional corporations, business trusts, joint ventures, and similar organizations. An organization client may also be an informal entity such as a social club or an informal group that has established an investment pool. For the purposes of this Section, whether the organization is a formal legal entity is relevant but not determinative. For example, while a sole proprietorship is not treated as an entity for many legal purposes, such an organization may be of sufficient size and complexity to warrant treatment as an organizational client under this Section.

d. The direction of a lawyer's work for a client organization. Persons authorized to act for the organization make decisions about retaining or discharging a lawyer for the organization, determine the scope of the representation, and create an obligation for the organization to compensate the lawyer. As stated in Subsection (1)(b), such persons also direct the activities of the lawyer during the course of the representation (see generally §§ 14, 21, & 38). Unless the lawyer withdraws, the lawyer must follow instructions and implement decisions of those persons, as the lawyer would follow instructions and decisions of an individual client. On advising a client respecting nonlegal considerations, see § 94(3) and Comment *h* thereto. A constituent of the organization authorized to do so may discharge the lawyer. On client discharge generally, see § 32; on withdrawal generally, see § 32(2) and (3). As stated in § 23(1), a lawyer is not bound by a constituent's instruction to a lawyer to perform, counsel, or assist future or ongoing acts that the lawyer reasonably believes to be unlawful. Such an instruction also does not remove the lawyer's duty to protect the best interests of the organizational client as stated in Subsection (2) (see Comments *e* & *f* hereto).

Who within an organization or among related organizations is authorized to direct the activities of a lawyer representing an organization is a question of organizational law beyond the scope of this Restatement. Such law determines whether, for example, an officer of a parent corporation is authorized to direct the activities of a lawyer representing a subsidiary corporation.

e. A constituent's breach of a legal obligation to the client organization. A lawyer representing an organization is required to act with reasonable competence and diligence in the representation (see § 16(2)) and to use care in representing the organizational client (see § 50). The lawyer thus must not knowingly or negligently assist any constituent to breach a legal duty to the organization. However, a lawyer's duty of care to the organization is not limited to avoidance of assisting acts that threaten injury to a client. A lawyer is also required to act diligently and to exercise care by taking steps to prevent reasonably foreseeable harm to a client. Thus, Subsection (2) requires a lawyer to take action to protect the interests of the client organization with respect to certain breaches of legal duty to the organization by a constituent.

The lawyer is not prevented by rules of confidentiality from acting to protect the interests of the organization by disclosing within the organization communications gained from constituents who are not themselves clients. That follows even if disclosure is against the interests of the communicating person, of another constituent whose breach of duty is in issue, or of other constituents (see § 131, Comment *e*). Such disclosure within the organization is subject to direction of a constituent who is authorized to act for the organization in the matter and who is not complicit in the breach (see Comment *d*). The lawyer may withdraw any support that the lawyer may earlier have provided the intended act, such as by withdrawing an opinion letter or draft transaction documents prepared by the lawyer.

Illustration:

1. Lawyer represents Charity, a not-for-profit corporation. Charity promotes medical research through tax-deductible contributions made to it. President as chief executive officer of Charity retained Lawyer to represent Charity as outside general counsel and has extensively communicated in confidence with Lawyer on a variety of matters concerning Charity. President asks Lawyer to draft documents by which Charity would make a gift of a new luxury automobile to a social friend of President. In that and all other work, Lawyer represents only Charity and not President as a client.

Lawyer concludes that such a gift would cause financial harm to Charity in violation of President's legal duties to it. Lawyer may not draft the documents. If unable to dissuade President from effecting the gift, Lawyer must take action to protect the interests of Charity (see Subsection (2) & Comment *f*). Lawyer may, for example, communicate with members of Charity's board of directors in endeavoring to prevent the gift from being effectuated.

f. Proceeding in the best interests of the client organization. Within the meaning of Subsection (2), a wrongful act of a constituent threatening substantial injury to a client organization may be of two types. One is an act or failure to act that violates a legal obligation to the organization and that would directly harm the organization, such as by unlawfully converting its assets. The other is an act or failure to act by the constituent that, although perhaps intended to serve an interest of the organization, will foreseeably cause injury to the client, such as by exposing the organization to criminal or civil liability.

In either circumstance, as stated in Subsection (2), if the threatened injury is substantial the lawyer must proceed in what the lawyer reasonably believes to be the best interests of the organization. Those interests are normally defined by appropriate managers of the organization in the exercise of the business and managerial judgment that would be exercised by a person of ordinary prudence in a similar position. The lawyer's duty of care is that of an ordinarily prudent lawyer in such a position (see ALI Principles of Corporate Governance: Analysis and Recommendations § 4.01, at 148–149 (1994)). In the face of threats of substantial injury to the organization of the kind described in Subsection (2), the lawyer must assess the following: the degree and imminence of threatened financial, reputational, and other harms to the organization; the probable results of litigation that might ensue against the organization or for which it would be financially responsible; the costs of taking measures within the organization to prevent or correct the harm; the likely efficaciousness of measures that might be taken; and similar considerations.

The measures that a lawyer may take are those described in Subsection (3), among others. Whether a lawyer has proceeded in the best interests of the organization is determined objectively, on the basis of the circumstances reasonably apparent to the lawyer at the time. Not all lawyers would attempt to resolve a problem defined in Subsection (2) in the same manner. Not all threats to an organization are of the same degree of imminence or substantiality. In some instances the constituent may be acting solely for reasons of self-interest. In others, the constituent may act on the basis of a business judgment whose utility or prudence may be doubtful but that is within the authority of the constituent. The lawyer's assessment of those factors may depend on the constituent's credibility and intentions, based on prior dealings between them and other information available to the lawyer.

The appropriate measures to take are ordinarily a matter for the reasonable judgment of the lawyer, with due regard for the circumstances in which the lawyer must function. Those circumstances include such matters as time and budgetary limitations and limitations of access to additional information and to persons who may otherwise be able to act. If one measure fails, the lawyer must, if the nature of the threat warrants and circumstances permit, take other reasonably available measures. With respect to the lawyer's possible liability to the organizational client, failure to take a particular remedial step is tested under the general standard of § 50. When the lawyer reasonably concludes that any particular step would not likely advance the best interests of the client, the step need not be taken.

Several options are described in Subsection (3). The lawyer may be able to prevent the wrongful act or its harmful consequences by urging reconsideration by the constituent who intends to commit the act. The lawyer may also suggest that the organization obtain a second legal or other expert opinion concerning the questioned activity. It may be appropriate to refer the matter to someone within the organization having authority to prevent the prospective harm, such as an official in the organization senior in authority to the constituent threatening to act. In appropriate circumstances, the lawyer may request intervention by the highest executive authority in the organization or by its governing body, such as a board of directors or the independent directors on the board, or by an owner of a majority of the stock in the organization. In determining how to proceed, the lawyer may be guided by the organization's internal policies and lines of authority or channels of communication.

In a situation arising under Subsection (2), a lawyer does not fulfill the lawyer's duties to the organizational client by withdrawing from the representation without attempting to prevent the constituent's wrongful act. However, the lawyer's threat to withdraw unless corrective action is taken may constitute an effective step in such an attempt.

If a lawyer has attempted appropriately but unsuccessfully to protect the best interests of the organizational client, the lawyer may withdraw if permissible under § 32. Particularly when the lawyer has unsuccessfully sought to enlist assistance from the highest authority within the organization, the lawyer will be warranted in withdrawing either because the client persists in a course of action involving the lawyer's services that the lawyer reasonably believes is criminal or fraudulent (see § 32(3)(d)) or because the client insists on taking action that the lawyer considers repugnant or imprudent (see § 32(3)(f)). On proportionality between certain grounds for withdrawal and possible harm to the organizational client that would be caused by withdrawal, see § 32, Comment h(i). On the circumstances in which a lawyer is required to withdraw, see § 32(2). Following withdrawal, if the lawyer had fulfilled applicable duties prior to withdrawal, the lawyer has no further duty to initiate action to protect the interests of the client organization with respect to the matter. The lawyer continues to be subject to the duties owed to any former client, such as the duty not to become involved in subsequent adverse representations (see § 132) or otherwise to use or disclose the former client's confidential information adversely to the former client (see § 60).

Whether the lawyer may disclose a constituent's breach of legal duty to persons outside the organization is determined primarily under §§ 66–67 (see also §§ 61–64). In limited circumstances, it may clearly appear that limited disclosure to prevent or limit harm would be in the interests of the organizational client and that constituents who purport to forbid disclosure are not authorized to act for the organization. Whether disclosure in such circumstances is warranted is a difficult and rarely encountered issue, on which this Restatement does not take a position.

g. A constituent's breach of fiduciary duty to another constituent. One constituent of an organization may owe fiduciary duties to another such constituent, for example in some instances a majority stockholder to a minority holder. A lawyer representing only the organization has no duty to protect one constituent from another, including from a breach by one constituent of such fiduciary duties, unless the interests of the lawyer's client organization are at risk. On communicating with a nonclient constituent, see § 103, Comment *e*. However, if the lawyer represents as a client either the entity or the constituent owing fiduciary duties, the lawyer may not counsel or assist a breach of any fiduciary obligation owed by the constituent to the organization.

Illustrations:

2. Lawyer represents Client, a closely held corporation, and not any constituent of Client. Under law applicable to the corporation, a majority shareholder owes a fiduciary duty of fair dealing to a minority shareholder in a transaction caused by action of a board of directors whose members have been designated by the majority stockholder. The law provides that the duty is breached if the action detrimentally and substantially affects the value of the minority shareholder's stock. Majority Shareholder has asked the board of directors of Client, consisting of Majority Shareholder's designees, to adopt a plan for buying back stock of the majority's shareholders in Client. A minority shareholder has protested the plan as unfair to the minority shareholder. Lawyer may advise the board about the position taken by the minority shareholder, but is not obliged to advise against or otherwise seek to prevent action that is consistent with the board's duty to Client.

3. The same facts as in Illustration 2, except that Lawyer has reason to know that the plan violates applicable corporate law and will likely be successfully challenged by minority shareholders in a suit against Client and that Client will likely incur substantial

expense as a result. Lawyer owes a duty to Client to take action to protect Client, such as by advising Client's board about the risks of adopting the plan.

On conflicts of interest in cases of intra-organization disagreement, see § 131, Comment *h*.

The foregoing discussion assumes an entity of substantial size and significant degree of organization. On the other hand, in the case of a closely held organization, some decisions have held that a lawyer may owe duties to a nonclient constituent, such as one who owns a minority interest.

h. Relationships with constituent and affiliated organization. Subject to conflict-of-interest considerations addressed in § 131, a lawyer representing a client organization may also represent one or more constituents of the organization, such as an officer or director of the organization (§ 131, Comment *e*) or an organization affiliated with the client (see § 131, Comment *d*). On whether a lawyer has entered into a client-lawyer relationship with a constituent person or an organization affiliated with a client organization, see § 14, Comment *f*. On avoiding misleading a corporate constituent about the role of a lawyer for the organization, see § 103, Comment *e*.

§ 97. Representing a Governmental Client

A lawyer representing a governmental client must proceed in the representation as stated in § 96, except that the lawyer:

(1) possesses such rights and responsibilities as may be defined by law to make decisions on behalf of the governmental client that are within the authority of a client under §§ 22 and 21(2);

(2) except as otherwise provided by law, must proceed as stated in §§ 96(2) and 96(3) with respect to an act of a constituent of the governmental client that violates a legal obligation that will likely cause substantial public or private injury or that reasonably can be foreseen to be imputable to and thus likely result in substantial injury to the client;

(3) if a prosecutor or similar lawyer determining whether to file criminal proceedings or take other steps in such proceedings, must do so only when based on probable cause and the lawyer's belief, formed after due investigation, that there are good factual and legal grounds to support the step taken; and

(4) must observe other applicable restrictions imposed by law on those similarly functioning for the governmental client.

Comment:

a. Scope and cross-references. This Section addresses government lawyers' relationship with their clients. To the extent not inconsistent with this Section, the provisions of § 96 on representing client organizations apply to representing governmental clients. On identifying a lawyer's governmental client, see Comment *c.* Law applicable to governmental organizations determines the appropriate authority of different legal offices of the same government—a matter beyond the scope of this Restatement. On prosecutors and similar government lawyers, see Comment *h.*

This Section covers a lawyer employed full time by a governmental client as well as a lawyer in private practice who provides legal services to a governmental client. With respect to such governmental-representation matters, see Comment *i* hereto.

Many legal rules beyond those stated in the Section apply to a lawyer representing a governmental client. Such a lawyer is required to act in a manner reasonably calculated to advance the lawful objectives of the client entity as defined by persons authorized to instruct the lawyer on behalf of the client. See §§ 16 and 96; see also §§ 16(3) and 112 (duty to protect confidential information of a governmental client); §§ 16(3) and 121 (duty to comply with conflict-of-interest requirements); § 16(2) and Comment *d* thereto (duty to act with reasonable competence and diligence). On the application of the attorney-client privilege to governmental clients, see § 74.

On the civil remedies available to a governmental or any other client with respect to a governmental lawyer's legal malpractice and similar defaults, see § 48 et seq. With respect to some civil remedies, governmental lawyers may be immune from liability with respect to persons other than the lawyer's client (see § 57, Comment *e*).

b. Rationale. Although similar in many respects to representation of a client in private practice (see Comment *a* hereto), representation of a governmental client may significantly differ in three principal respects. First, the goals of a governmental client necessarily include pursuit of the public interest, as identified by law and as determined by decisions of government officials in the course of their duties. Second, both government lawyers and governmental officials directing the activities of government lawyers are often subject to greater legal constraint (for example, under state and federal constitutions) than is true of lawyers representing nongovernmental persons or entities. Third, and conversely, a government lawyer may possess powers beyond those possessed by a lawyer representing a nongovernmental client, such as the power to select those persons who will be charged with serious crimes (see Comment *h*). Some government lawyers, such as an elected state attorney general or similar officer, have discretionary powers under law that have no parallel in representation of nongovernmental clients (see Comment *g*).

A lawyer representing a governmental client may also enjoy legal rights with respect to the client that are not possessed by lawyers representing nongovernmental clients. For example, a governmental lawyer in a position for which partisan affiliation is not an appropriate requirement is protected under the federal Constitution against promotion, transfer, recall, and hiring decisions made solely for reasons of political affiliation or support (compare § 32(1) (client may discharge lawyer without cause)).

  c. Identity of a governmental client. No universal definition of the client of a governmental lawyer is possible. For example, it has been asserted that government lawyers represent the public, or the public interest. However, determining what individual or individuals personify the government requires reference to the need to sustain political and organizational responsibility of governmental officials, as well as the organizational arrangements structured by law within which governmental lawyers work. Those who speak for the governmental client may differ from one representation to another. The identity of the client may also vary depending on the purpose for which the question of identity is posed. For example, when government lawyers negotiate a disputed question of departmental jurisdiction between two federal agencies, it is not helpful to refer to the client of each of the lawyers as "the federal government" or "the public" when considering who is empowered to direct the lawyers' activities. For many purposes, the preferable approach on the question presented is to regard the respective agencies as the clients and to regard the lawyers working for the agencies as subject to the direction of those officers authorized to act in the matter involved in the representation (see Subsection (3)).

  Government agencies exist in various forms, ranging from departments or governmental corporations that may sue and be sued in their own names, to divisions of government without such separate legal status, to legislatures or committees of legislatures. If a question arises concerning which of several possible governmental entities a government lawyer represents, the identity of the lawyer's governmental client depends on the circumstances. Relevant are such factors as the terms of retention or other manifestations of the reasonable understanding of the lawyer and the hiring authority involved, the anticipated scope and nature of the lawyer's services, particular regulatory arrangements relevant to the lawyer's work, and the history and traditions of the office (see also § 96, Comment *h*).

  A lawyer employed by a governmental agency to represent persons accused of offenses in military court-martial proceedings, in a state-operated public-defender office, or in similar arrangements is properly regarded as representing the individual and not any governmental entity. That would be true despite the fact that for other legal purposes the lawyer is an officer or employee of the government. On the requirement that a lawyer not permit his or her exercise of independent professional judgment to be directed by a nonclient source of the lawyer's fee, see § 134(2) and Comment *d*.

Some litigation involving governmental policy is brought by or against individual governmental officials in their capacity as such, such as is commonly done in mandamus proceedings, habeas corpus proceedings, and agency proceedings brought in the name of the head of the agency or other officer. Proceeding in that form remains the required method of much federal-court litigation against state governmental officials because of the Eleventh Amendment prohibition against suits against a state as such. A lawyer representing a governmental official in such a proceeding is subject to this Section.

When a lawyer is retained to represent a specific individual, either in that person's public (see Comment *b*) or private (nongovernmental) capacity, the person (in the appropriate capacity) is the client, unless the use of the individual's name is merely nominal and the government is the interested party. As described above with respect to multiple agencies, the identity and the specification of the capacity of the person represented by the lawyer is determined by the undertaking and reasonable expectations of both the lawyer and individual (see § 14). A lawyer who represents a governmental official in the person's public capacity must conduct the representation to advance public interests as determined by appropriate governmental officers and not, if different, the personal interests of the occupant of the office (see generally Comment *f*).

* * *

TOPIC 3.   LAWYER DEALINGS WITH A NONCLIENT

TITLE A.   DEALINGS WITH A NONCLIENT—GENERALLY

§ 98.   Statements to a Nonclient

A lawyer communicating on behalf of a client with a nonclient may not:

> **(1) knowingly make a false statement of material fact or law to the nonclient,**
>
> **(2) make other statements prohibited by law; or**
>
> **(3) fail to make a disclosure of information required by law.**

Comment:

a.   Scope and cross-references. This Section considers misrepresentations by a lawyer in the course of representing a client. Its rules may apply in representing a client in litigation, such as when negotiating a settlement, as well as in nonlitigation situations. On remedies, see Comment *g* hereto and § 51 and § 56, Comment *f*; see also generally

§ 6. For liability with respect to erroneous statements in an opinion letter or similar evaluation, see § 51(2) and Comment *e* thereto and § 95. On more stringent requirements for statements in some representations of a client before a legislative or administrative body, see § 104. The Section does not purport to state rules of liability under state and federal securities legislation.

On the standard of truthfulness for statements to clients, see §§ 16, 20, and 56. On the standard for communications with a tribunal, see § 120(1)(b). See also § 112 (ex parte and similar proceedings).

On warning a potential victim of certain criminal or fraudulent activities of a client, see §§ 66–67. On a lawyer's right to withdraw when the client engages in criminal or fraudulent conduct, see § 32(3)(d). On a lawyer's duty to protect confidential information of a client, see § 60. A lawyer's obligation not to make statements that mislead an unrepresented nonclient is addressed in § 103.

b. Rationale. A lawyer communicating with a nonclient on behalf of a client is not privileged to make a material misrepresentation of fact or law to the nonclient. See generally Restatement Second, Agency §§ 343 and 348. The law governing misrepresentation by a lawyer includes the criminal law (theft by deception), the law of misrepresentation in tort law and of mistake and fraud in contract law, and procedural law governing statements by an advocate (see § 120, Comment *f*). Compliance with those obligations meets social expectations of honesty and fair dealing and facilitates negotiation and adjudication, which are important professional functions of lawyers. Corresponding duties are stated in lawyer codes, which are generally based on the requirements of criminal and civil law.

This Section applies equally to statements made to a sophisticated person, such as to a lawyer representing another client, as well as to an unsophisticated person. However, the sophistication in similar transactions of a person to whom a representation is made is relevant in determining such issues as the reasonableness of the person's reliance on the representation.

c. Knowing misrepresentation. The law of misrepresentation applies to lawyers. See generally Restatement Second, Contracts § 159 and following; Restatement Second, Torts § 525 and following. For purposes of common-law damage recovery, reckless as well as knowing misrepresentation by a lawyer may be actionable. On negligent misrepresentation, see also § 51(2). A misrepresentation can occur through direct statement or through affirmation of a misrepresentation of another, as when a lawyer knowingly affirms a client's false or misleading statement. A statement can also be false because only partially true. If constrained from conveying specific information to a nonclient, for example due to confidentiality obligations to the lawyer's client, the lawyer must either make no representation or make a representation that is not false.

For purposes of professional discipline, the lawyer codes generally incorporate the definition of misrepresentation employed in the civil law of tort damage liability for knowing misrepresentation, including the elements of falsity, scienter, and materiality. However, for disciplinary purposes, reliance by and injury to another person are not required. The lawyer codes of many jurisdictions also prohibit a lawyer from engaging in "conduct involving dishonesty, fraud, deceit, or misrepresentation" (see § 5, Comment *c*). Some courts have interpreted these provisions to impose a more exacting standard of disclosure than the prohibition against knowing misrepresentation (compare id.).

A knowing misrepresentation may relate to a proposition of fact or law. Certain statements, such as some statements relating to price or value, are considered nonactionable hyperbole or a reflection of the state of mind of the speaker and not misstatements of fact or law (see Restatement Second, Contracts § 168, Restatement Third, Unfair Competition § 3, Comment *d*). Whether a misstatement should be so characterized depends on whether it is reasonably apparent that the person to whom the statement is addressed would regard the statement as one of fact or based on the speaker's knowledge of facts reasonably implied by the statement or as merely an expression of the speaker's state of mind. Assessment depends on the circumstances in which the statement is made, including the past relationship of the negotiating persons, their apparent sophistication, the plausibility of the statement on its face, the phrasing of the statement, related communication between the persons involved, the known negotiating practices of the community in which both are negotiating, and similar circumstances. In general, a lawyer who is known to represent a person in a negotiation will be understood by nonclients to be making nonimpartial statements, in the same manner as would the lawyer's client. Subject to such an understanding, the lawyer is not privileged to make misrepresentations described in this Section.

A lawyer may also be liable under civil or criminal law for aiding and abetting a client's misrepresentation (see § 8). A lawyer representing a client in a transaction with respect to which the client has made a misrepresentation is not free, after the lawyer learns of the misrepresentation, to continue providing assistance to the client as if the misrepresentation had not been made when the lawyer's continued representation of the client would induce the nonclient reasonably to believe that no such misrepresentation has occurred.

Illustration:

1.   Client has contracted to sell interests in Client's business to Buyer. As part of the arrangement, Lawyer for Client prepares an offering statement to be presented to Buyer. Lawyer knows that information in the statement, provided by Client, is materially misleading; the information shows Client's business as profitable and growing, but Lawyer knows that its assets are heavily encum-

bered, business is declining and unprofitable, and the company has substantial debts. Lawyer's knowing actions assisted Client's fraud.

d. Subsequently discovered falsity. A lawyer who has made a representation on behalf of a client reasonably believing it true when made may subsequently come to know of its falsity. An obligation to disclose before consummation of the transaction ordinarily arises, unless the lawyer takes other corrective action. See Restatement Second, Agency § 348, Comment *c*; Restatement Second, Contracts § 161(a) (nondisclosure as equivalent to assertion when person "knows that disclosure of the fact is necessary to prevent some previous assertion from being a misrepresentation or from being fraudulent or material"). Disclosure, being required by law (see § 63), is not prohibited by the general rule of confidentiality (see § 60). Disclosure should not exceed what is required to comply with the disclosure obligation, for example by indicating to recipients that they should not rely on the lawyer's statement. On permissive disclosure to prevent or rectify a client's wrongful act, see §§ 66–67.

e. Affirmative disclosure. In general, a lawyer has no legal duty to make an affirmative disclosure of fact or law when dealing with a nonclient. Applicable statutes, regulations, or common-law rules may require affirmative disclosure in some circumstances, for example disciplinary rules in some states requiring lawyers to disclose a client's intent to commit life-threatening crimes or other wrongful conduct (see § 66, Comment *b*, and Reporter's Note thereto; on permissive disclosure, see §§ 66–67).

On the duty to disclose the lawyer's role as representative of a client to avoid misleading an unrepresented nonclient, see § 103. With respect to a duty to disclose legal authority to a tribunal, see § 111. On the absence of a general duty to disclose facts to a tribunal, see § 120, Comment *b*. See also § 112 on disclosure requirements in ex parte and similar proceedings. On the duty to disclose false evidence to a tribunal, see § 120(2) and Comment *i*.

f. Other wrongful statements. Beyond the law of misrepresentation, other civil or criminal law may constrain a lawyer's statements, for example, the criminal law of extortion. In some jurisdictions, lawyer codes prohibit a lawyer negotiating a civil claim from referring to the prospect of filing criminal charges against the opposing party. On the extent of lawyer liability for defamatory statements concerning nonclients, see § 57(1).

g. Remedies. In general, a lawyer who makes a fraudulent misrepresentation is subject to liability to the injured person when the other elements of the tort are established (see Restatement Second, Agency § 348, see generally § 56). On remedies for nonnegligent misrepresentation, see Restatement Second, Torts § 552C (difference in values represented and those in fact existing). A lawyer's misrepresentation may also be a basis for setting aside or reforming a contract, as well as other contractual remedies (see Restatement Second, Contracts § 345).

The types of misstatements prohibited in the lawyer codes are different in certain important respects from the definitions of false statement for the purposes of many kinds of civil actions, for example because the disciplinary standard does not require third-party reliance or actual harm (see Comment *c* hereto). Conversely, a lawyer's merely negligent misrepresentation (see § 51(2)) may constitute grounds for liability to an injured party but not for discipline for fraud.

TITLE B.   CONTACT WITH A REPRESENTED NONCLIENT

§ 99.   A Represented Nonclient—The General Anti–Contact Rule

(1) A lawyer representing a client in a matter may not communicate about the subject of the representation with a nonclient whom the lawyer knows to be represented in the matter by another lawyer or with a representative of an organizational nonclient so represented as defined in § 100, unless:

(a) the communication is with a public officer or agency to the extent stated in § 101;

(b) the lawyer is a party and represents no other client in the matter;

(c) the communication is authorized by law;

(d) the communication reasonably responds to an emergency; or

(e) the other lawyer consents.

(2) Subsection (1) does not prohibit the lawyer from assisting the client in otherwise proper communication by the lawyer's client with a represented nonclient.

§ 100.   Definition of a Represented Nonclient

Within the meaning of § 99, a represented nonclient includes:

(1) a natural person represented by a lawyer; and:

(2) a current employee or other agent of an organization represented by a lawyer:

(a) if the employee or other agent supervises, directs, or regularly consults with the lawyer concerning the matter or if the agent has power to compromise or settle the matter;

(b) if the acts or omissions of the employee or other agent may be imputed to the organization for purposes of civil or criminal liability in the matter; or

964

(c) if a statement of the employee or other agent, under applicable rules of evidence, would have the effect of binding the organization with respect to proof of the matter.

§ 101. A Represented Governmental Agency or Officer

(1) Unless otherwise provided by law (see § 99(1)(c)) and except as provided in Subsection (2), the prohibition stated in § 99 against contact with a represented nonclient does not apply to communications with employees of a represented governmental agency or with a governmental officer being represented in the officer's official capacity.

(2) In negotiation or litigation by a lawyer of a specific claim of a client against a governmental agency or against a governmental officer in the officer's official capacity, the prohibition stated in § 99 applies, except that the lawyer may contact any officer of the government if permitted by the agency or with respect to an issue of general policy

§ 102. Information of a Nonclient Known to Be Legally Protected

A lawyer communicating with a nonclient in a situation permitted under § 99 may not seek to obtain information that the lawyer reasonably should know the nonclient may not reveal without violating a duty of confidentiality to another imposed by law.

TITLE C. DEALINGS WITH A UNREPRESENTED NONCLIENT

§ 103. Dealings with an Unrepresented Nonclient

In the course of representing a client and dealing with a nonclient who is not represented by a lawyer:

(1) the lawyer may not mislead the nonclient, to the prejudice of the nonclient, concerning the identity and interests of the person the lawyer represents; and

(2) when the lawyer knows or reasonably should know that the unrepresented nonclient misunderstands the lawyer's role in the matter, the lawyer must make reasonable efforts to correct the misunderstanding when failure to do so would materially prejudice the nonclient.

TOPIC 4. LEGISLATIVE AND ADMINISTRATIVE MATTERS

§ 104. Representing a Client in Legislative and Administrative Matters

A lawyer representing a client before a legislature or administrative agency:

(1) must disclose that the appearance is in a representative capacity and not misrepresent the capacity in which the lawyer appears;

(2) must comply with applicable law and regulations governing such representations; and

(3) except as applicable law otherwise provides:

(a) in an adjudicative proceeding before a government agency or involving such an agency as a participant, has the legal rights and responsibilities of an advocate in a proceeding before a judicial tribunal; and

(b) in other types of proceedings and matters, has the legal rights and responsibilities applicable in the lawyer's dealings with a private person.

CHAPTER 7: REPRESENTING CLIENTS IN LITIGATION

TOPIC 1.   ADVOCACY IN GENERAL

§ 105.   Complying with Law and Tribunal Rulings

In representing a client in a matter before a tribunal, a lawyer must comply with applicable law, including rules of procedure and evidence and specific tribunal rulings.

§ 106.   Dealing with Other Participants in Proceedings

In representing a client in a matter before a tribunal, a lawyer may not use means that have no substantial purpose other than to embarrass, delay, or burden a third person or use methods of obtaining evidence that are prohibited by law.

Comment:

a. Scope and cross-references. This Section states the general duty of an advocate to avoid harassing other participants in the proceeding or using means prohibited by law in dealing with them. The rule stated is taken from ABA Model Rules of Professional Conduct, Rule 4.4 (1983). On possible remedies in addition to lawyer discipline, see the Comments hereto and § 57(2) and Comments *d* and *e* thereto (malicious prosecution and similar torts). On the general duties of a lawyer not to file frivolous litigation or take frivolous positions in litigation, see § 110. For restrictions on presenting testimony and other evidence, including dealing with witnesses, see §§ 114–118. On a lawyer's general duty to comply with law and court rulings, see § 105. On the role of a criminal-defense lawyer, see § 110(2) and Comment *f* thereto. On the more-exacting duties of prosecutors, see § 97, Comment *h*. On obligations of candor in dealing with third persons in nonlitigated matters, see § 98. For general restrictions on contacting represented or nonrepresented persons, see §§ 99–103.

b. Investigating and tape recording witnesses. A lawyer may conduct an investigation of a witness to gather information from or about the witness. Such an investigation may legitimately address potentially relevant aspects of the finances, associations, and personal life of the witness. In conducting such investigations personally or through others, however, a lawyer must observe legal constraints on intrusion on privacy. The law of some jurisdictions, for example, prohibits recording conversations with another person without the latter's consent. When secret recording is not prohibited by law, doing so is permissible for lawyers conducting investigations on behalf of their clients, but should be done only when compelling need exists to obtain evidence otherwise unavailable in an equally reliable form. Such a need may exist more readily in a criminal-defense representation. In conducting such an investigation, a lawyer must comply with the limitations of § 99 prohibiting contact with represented person, of § 102 restricting communication with persons who owe certain duties of confidentiality to others, and of § 103 prohibiting misleading an unrepresented person.

c. Calling and examining witness. In general, lawyers make the initial decision concerning which witnesses to call to testify at a deposition or trial. On consultation with a client, see § 20; on interviewing and preparing a witness prior to testimony, see § 116.

Wide latitude is extended to advocates in examining an adverse witness. Limitations are imposed by the rules of evidence, such as the rules of relevance and privilege and through the authority of presiding officers to maintain order and prevent abusive examination. A further restraint on aggressive cross-examination is the risk of incurring antipathy on the part of the presiding officer or jury. A lawyer may also be subject to professional discipline (see § 5) for intimidating or demeaning witnesses in violation of the rule of this Section.

Distinguishing between permissible and impermissible examination is normally left to the discretion of the officer presiding at the hearing. A client may instruct a lawyer how to proceed in examining witnesses, subject to the lawyer's obligations to the tribunal (see § 21(2) & Comment *d* thereto & § 23). A particularly difficult problem is presented when a lawyer has an opportunity to cross-examine a witness with respect to testimony that the lawyer knows to be truthful, including harsh implied criticism of the witness's testimony, character, or capacity for truth-telling. Even if legally permissible, a lawyer would presumably do so only where that would not cause the lawyer to lose credibility with the tribunal or alienate the factfinder. Moreover, a lawyer is never required to conduct such examination, and the lawyer may withdraw if the lawyer's client insists on such a course of action in a setting in which the lawyer considers it imprudent or repugnant (see § 32(3)(f) & Comment *j* thereto).

A lawyer who asks irrelevant or otherwise objectionable questions or employs other means that have no purpose other than to harass the witness may be subjected to judicial sanctions or professional discipline. Rules of permissible questioning under the evidence law applied in a particular tribunal regulate such questions and appropriate judicial responses to them.

A lawyer other than a prosecutor (see § 97, Comment *h*) is not required to inform any nonclient witness or prospective witness of the right to invoke privileges against answering, including the privilege against self-incrimination. On the prohibition against misleading a nonclient witness or other person, see § 99; see also § 103.

d. Opposing counsel and other participants. The professional ideal for the relationship between opposing advocates is that they bear toward each other a respectful and cooperative attitude marked by civility, consistent with their primary responsibilities to their clients. Similar respect and cooperativeness should characterize a lawyer's interactions with all participants in a proceeding. Certain conduct toward other participants, including opposing lawyers, is prohibited, including unlawful physical force or its threat, racial or gender or similar slurs, and charges of wrongdoing made recklessly or knowing them to be without foundation. Also prohibited are legally impermissible forms of partisanship, such as misrepresenting the record (see § 120, Comment *f*). However, a lawyer is permitted to make vigorous argument and to attack an opposing position on all legally available grounds (see § 110). On limitations on calling opposing counsel as a witness, see § 108(4).

e. Embarrassment, delay, or burdening of a third person. Some measure of embarrassment, delay, and burden is inherent in litigation. However, when an advocate lacks a substantial purpose for conduct having those consequences, a disciplinary offense occurs (see § 110). A ruling of a tribunal officer or a standing rule may impose specific time limitations within which prescribed action must be taken; a lawyer ordinarily must comply with them (see § 105). For example, seeking delay in a trial date in order to gather additional relevant evidence is nonfrivolous. On the other hand, delaying a trial solely to permit a client to extract a nuisance-value settlement is an improper purpose. In seeking delay, a lawyer must assert positions only if nonfrivolous under § 110(1), must avoid misstating facts (see § 120(1)(b)) or using evidence known to be false (see § 120(3)), and must comply with court rules and orders (see § 105).

§ 107. Prohibited Forensic Tactics

In representing a client in a matter before a tribunal, a lawyer may not, in the presence of the trier of fact:

(1) state a personal opinion about the justness of a cause, the credibility of a witness, the culpability of a civil litigant, or the guilt or innocence of an accused, but the

lawyer may argue any position or conclusion adequately supported by the lawyer's analysis of the evidence; or

(2) allude to any matter that the lawyer does not reasonably believe is relevant or that will not be supported by admissible evidence.

§ 108. An Advocate as a Witness

(1) Except as provided in Subsection (2), a lawyer may not represent a client in a contested hearing or trial of a matter in which:

(a) the lawyer is expected to testify for the lawyer's client; or

(b) the lawyer does not intend to testify but (i) the lawyer's testimony would be material to establishing a claim or defense of the client, and (ii) the client has not consented as stated in § 122 to the lawyer's intention not to testify.

(2) A lawyer may represent a client when the lawyer will testify as stated in Subsection (1)(a) if:

(a) the lawyer's testimony relates to an issue that the lawyer reasonably believes will not be contested or to the nature and value of legal services rendered in the proceeding;

(b) deprivation of the lawyer's services as advocate would work a substantial hardship on the client; or

(c) consent has been given by (i) opposing parties who would be adversely affected by the lawyer's testimony and, (ii) if relevant, the lawyer's client, as stated in § 122 with respect to any conflict of interest between lawyer and client (see § 125) that the lawyer's testimony would create.

(3) A lawyer may not represent a client in a litigated matter pending before a tribunal when the lawyer or a lawyer in the lawyer's firm will give testimony materially adverse to the position of the lawyer's client or materially adverse to a former client of any such lawyer with respect to a matter substantially related to the earlier representation, unless the affected client has consented as stated in § 122 with respect to any conflict of interest between lawyer and client (see § 125) that the testimony would create.

(4) A tribunal should not permit a lawyer to call opposing trial counsel as a witness unless there is a compelling need for the lawyer's testimony.

§ 109. An Advocate's Public Comment on Pending Litigation

(1) In representing a client in a matter before a tribunal, a lawyer may not make a statement outside the proceeding that a

969

reasonable person would expect to be disseminated by means of public communication when the lawyer knows or reasonably should know that the statement will have a substantial likelihood of materially prejudicing a juror or influencing or intimidating a prospective witness in the proceeding. However, a lawyer may in any event make a statement that is reasonably necessary to mitigate the impact on the lawyer's client of substantial, undue, and prejudicial publicity recently initiated by one other than the lawyer or the lawyer's client.

(2) A prosecutor must, except for statements necessary to inform the public of the nature and extent of the prosecutor's action and that serve a legitimate law-enforcement purpose, refrain from making extrajudicial comments that have a substantial likelihood of heightening public condemnation of the accused.

TOPIC 2.   LIMITS ON ADVOCACY

§ 110.   Frivolous Advocacy

(1) A lawyer may not bring or defend a proceeding or assert or controvert an issue therein, unless there is a basis for doing so that is not frivolous, which includes a good-faith argument for an extension, modification, or reversal of existing law.

(2) Notwithstanding Subsection (1), a lawyer for the defendant in a criminal proceeding or the respondent in a proceeding that could result in incarceration may so defend the proceeding as to require that the prosecutor establish every necessary element.

(3) A lawyer may not make a frivolous discovery request, fail to make a reasonably diligent effort to comply with a proper discovery request of another party, or intentionally fail otherwise to comply with applicable procedural requirements concerning discovery.

Comment:

a. Scope and cross-references. Subsection (1) states the rule of professional codes requiring that a lawyer have a nonfrivolous basis for steps taken in advocacy for a client. On procedural rules found in most jurisdictions that impose a more exacting requirement, see Comment *c.* Subsection (2) states the more permissive requirement for advocacy in criminal-defense representations. On the requirements that a lawyer not misrepresent the law to a tribunal and that a lawyer cite controlling authority, see § 111. Several Sections in Topic 4 state additional duties in an advocate's dealings with witnesses and evidence. See also § 106 (prohibition against harassing third persons).

b.   Rationale. Frivolous advocacy inflicts distress, wastes time, and causes increased expense to the tribunal and adversaries and may achieve results for a client that are unjust. Nonetheless, disciplinary enforcement against frivolous litigation is rare. Most bar disciplinary agencies rely on the courts in which litigation occurs to deal with abuse. Tribunals usually sanction only extreme abuse. Administration and interpretation of prohibitions against frivolous litigation should be tempered by concern to avoid overenforcement.

c.   Procedural sanction against unfounded assertions in litigation. Procedural rules modeled on Rule 11 of the Federal Rules of Civil Procedure impose affirmative obligations going beyond a requirement of minimally plausible position. In addition, courts have inherent power to impose sanctions against frivolous or otherwise abusive litigation tactics (see generally § 1, Comment *b*).

Such procedural rules generally have four elements, although jurisdictions differ on particulars. First, a lawyer may file a pleading, motion, or other paper only after making an inquiry about facts and law that is reasonable in the circumstances. Second, the lawyer's conclusions as to the facts and law must meet an objective, minimal standard of supportability. Third, litigation measures may not be taken for an improper purpose, even in instances in which they are otherwise minimally supportable. Finally, remedies provided for violations may include sanctions such as fee shifting, which in appropriate cases may be imposed directly on an offending lawyer (see Comment *g*).

Federal Rule 11 and corresponding state procedural rules generally are applicable only to positions asserted in writings signed by a lawyer, such as a pleading or motion. Other sources of law may extend a court's power to other activities of an advocate. For example, in the federal system, § 1927 of Title 28 of the United States Code prohibits actions of a lawyer, not limited to writings, that unduly multiply proceedings. A similar authority is conferred on federal appellate courts under Federal Rule of Appellate Procedure 38. Many courts also recognize a residual inherent power to impose sanctions on lawyers for bad-faith litigation. Detailed consideration of Federal Rule 11 and similar procedural rules is beyond the scope of this Restatement.

d.   Frivolous positions in litigation. A frivolous position is one that a lawyer of ordinary competence would recognize as so lacking in merit that there is no substantial possibility that the tribunal would accept it. A nonfrivolous argument includes a good-faith argument for an extension, modification, or reversal of existing law. Whether good faith exists depends on such factors as whether the lawyer in question or another lawyer established a precedent adverse to the position being argued (and, if so, whether the lawyer disclosed that precedent), whether new legal grounds of plausible weight can be advanced, whether new or additional authority supports the lawyer's position, or whether for other reasons, such as a change in the composition of a multi-member court, arguments can be advanced that have a substantially greater chance of success.

Illustrations:

1. The supreme court of a jurisdiction held 10 years ago that only the state legislature could set aside the employment-at-will rule of the state's common law. In a subsequent decision, the same court again referred to the employment-at-will doctrine, stating that "whatever the justice or defects of that rule, we feel presently bound to continue to follow it." In the time since the subsequent decision, the employment-at-will doctrine has been extensively discussed, often critically, in the legal literature, and courts in some jurisdictions have overturned or limited the older decisions. Lawyer now represents an employee at will. Notwithstanding the earlier rulings of the state supreme court, intervening events indicate that a candid attempt to obtain reversal of the employment-at-will doctrine is a nonfrivolous legal position in the jurisdiction. On the other hand, if the state supreme court had unanimously reaffirmed the doctrine in recent months, the action would be frivolous in the absence of reason to believe that there is a substantial possibility that, notwithstanding the recent adverse precedent, the court would reconsider altering its stance.

2. Following unsuccessful litigation in a state court, Lawyer, representing the unsuccessful Claimant in the state-court litigation, filed an action in federal court seeking damages under a federal civil-rights statute, 42 U.S.C. § 1983, against the state-court trial judge, alleging that the judge had denied due process to Claimant in rulings made in the state-court action. The complaint was evidently based on the legal position that the doctrine of absolute judicial immunity should not apply to a case in which a judge has made an egregious error. Although some scholars have criticized the rule, the law is and continues to be well settled that absolute judicial immunity under § 1983 extends to such errors and precludes an action such as that asserted by Claimant. No intervening legal event suggests that any federal court would alter that interpretation. Given the absence of any basis for believing that a substantial possibility exists that an argument against the immunity would be accepted in a federal court, the claim is frivolous.

It may be reasonably doubtful to a lawyer whether existing precedent supports a legal position or whether the lawyer should instead ask a court to extend, modify, or reverse existing law. When an advocate has adequately referred to the relevant authority (see § 111) the rule of this Section is not violated if the lawyer argues that existing precedent supports a legal position even though the tribunal concludes that the argument should more appropriately have been couched as an effort to modify existing law. In any event, a lawyer may not make a false statement of a material proposition of law to the tribunal (see § 111(1)).

e. Abusive discovery practice. As stated in Subsection (3), a lawyer may not, in pretrial procedure, make a frivolous discovery request or fail to make reasonably diligent effort to comply with a proper discovery request of another party. Frivolousness is determined under the standard stated in Comment *d*. Whether a lawyer complying with a discovery request has made a reasonably diligent effort is determined by an objective standard. In any response, the Section permits a lawyer to assert on behalf of the client any nonfrivolous basis for noncompliance. A lawyer must not, for example, delay a discovery response beyond the time permitted by law without adequate justification, provide answers to discovery requests that the lawyer knows to be false and misleading, or knowingly withhold discoverable information in responding to proper requests for such material. Procedural rules (see generally Comment *c*) may impose more stringent standards for making or responding to discovery requests.

f. Advocacy in a criminal-defense representation. The rules in this Section apply generally to criminal-defense lawyers. However, as stated in Subsection (2), a lawyer defending a person accused of crime, even if convinced that the guilt of the offense charged can be proved beyond a reasonable doubt, may require the prosecution to prove every element of the offense, including those facts as to which the lawyer knows the accused can present no effective defense. A criminal-defense lawyer may take any step required or permitted by the constitutional guarantee of the effective assistance of counsel. With respect to propositions of law, a criminal-defense lawyer may make any nonfrivolous argument. Under decisions of the United States Supreme Court, a lawyer representing a convicted person on appeal may be required to file a so-called *Anders* brief in the event the lawyer concludes that there is no nonfrivolous ground on which the appeal can be maintained.

g. Remedies. This Section restates requirements of the lawyer codes, violations of which are sanctioned through professional discipline. Many jurisdictions by legislation or rule provide for fee shifting as a sanction for frivolous advocacy, including sanctions against an advocate, a party, or both and often under standards stricter than those stated in the Section (see Comment *c*). In relatively rare instances, damages may be recovered in an independent action (see generally § 57, Comments *d* & *e*). Under some legislation or rules, an offending lawyer may be fined, reprimanded, otherwise sanctioned, or referred to a disciplinary agency.

Courts generally attempt to impose sanctions for unwarranted litigation on the lawyer or client (see § 29, Comment *d*) in proportion to their relative responsibility. In appropriate circumstances, when a sanction is focused upon a lawyer for deterrence purposes, a tribunal may order that the lawyer not seek reimbursement from a client. Allocating responsibility may be difficult. Achieving precise allocation may entail inquiry into matters that are generally protected by the attorney-client privilege (see § 68 and following) or the work-product immunity (see § 87 and following). In addition, such an inquiry may interject conflicts of interest between lawyer and client with respect to the burdens of the sanction (see Comment *b*). Particularly when the representation is not at an end

973

and the relative fault of lawyer and client is doubtful, the preferable approach is to leave questions of ultimate responsibility between them to resolution after the proceedings are concluded.

§ 111.   Disclosure of Legal Authority

In representing a client in a matter before a tribunal, a lawyer may not knowingly:

(1) make a false statement of a material proposition of law to the tribunal; or

(2) fail to disclose to the tribunal legal authority in the controlling jurisdiction known to the lawyer to be directly adverse to the position asserted by the client and not disclosed by opposing counsel.

§ 112.   Advocacy in Ex Parte and Other Proceedings

In representing a client in a matter before a tribunal, a lawyer applying for ex parte relief or appearing in another proceeding in which similar special requirements of candor apply must comply with the requirements of § 110 and §§ 118–120 and further:

(1) must not present evidence the lawyer reasonably believes is false;

(2) must disclose all material and relevant facts known to the lawyer that will enable the tribunal to reach an informed decision; and

(3) must comply with any other applicable special requirements of candor imposed by law.

TOPIC 3.   ADVOCATES AND TRIBUNALS

§ 113.   Improperly Influencing a Judicial Officer

(1) A lawyer may not knowingly communicate ex parte with a judicial officer before whom a proceeding is pending concerning the matter, except as authorized by law.

(2) A lawyer may not make a gift or loan prohibited by law to a judicial officer, attempt to influence the officer otherwise than by legally proper procedures, or state or imply an ability so to influence a judicial officer.

§ 114.   A Lawyer's Statements Concerning a Judicial Officer

A lawyer may not knowingly or recklessly make publicly a false statement of fact concerning the qualifications or integrity of an incumbent of a judicial office or a candidate for election to such an office.

§ 115. Lawyer Contact with a Juror

A lawyer may not:

(1) except as allowed by law, communicate with or seek to influence a person known by the lawyer to be a member of a jury pool from which the jury will be drawn;

(2) except as allowed by law, communicate with or seek to influence a member of a jury; or

(3) communicate with a juror who has been excused from further service:

(a) when that would harass the juror or constitute an attempt to influence the juror's actions as a juror in future cases; or

(b) when otherwise prohibited by law.

TOPIC 4. ADVOCATES AND EVIDENCE

§ 116. Interviewing and Preparing a Prospective Witness

(1) A lawyer may interview a witness for the purpose of preparing the witness to testify.

(2) A lawyer may not unlawfully obstruct another party's access to a witness.

(3) A lawyer may not unlawfully induce or assist a prospective witness to evade or ignore process obliging the witness to appear to testify.

(4) A lawyer may not request a person to refrain from voluntarily giving relevant testimony or information to another party, unless:

(a) the person is the lawyer's client in the matter; or

(b) (i) the person is not the lawyer's client but is a relative or employee or other agent of the lawyer or the lawyer's client, and (ii) the lawyer reasonably believes compliance will not materially and adversely affect the person's interests.

Comments:

* * *

b. Preparing a witness to testify. Under litigation practice uniformly followed in the United States, a lawyer may interview prospective witnesses prior to their testifying. A prospective witness is generally under no obligation to submit to such an interview. As a practical matter, rules requiring inquiry to support factual allegations in a complaint or other document (see § 110, Comment *c*) may require a lawyer to interview witnesses to gain the necessary factual foundation. Competent preparation for trial (see generally § 52(1)) (general negligence standard might also require pre-testimonial interviews with witnesses).

The work-product immunity (see Chapter 5, Topic 3) and the obligation of confidentiality regarding trial-preparation material (see § 60(1)), result in the process of witness preparation normally being confidential. Compare § 80(2)(b) (loss of confidentiality of material otherwise protected by attorney-client privilege); § 92(1) (same for work-product immunity).

Attempting to induce a witness to testify falsely as to a material fact is a crime, either subornation of perjury or obstruction of justice, and is ground for professional discipline and other remedies (see § 120, Comment *l*). It may also constitute fraud, warranting denial of the attorney-client privilege to client-lawyer communications relating to preparation of the witness (see § 82).

In preparing a witness to testify, a lawyer may invite the witness to provide truthful testimony favorable to the lawyer's client. Preparation consistent with the rule of this Section may include the following: discussing the role of the witness and effective courtroom demeanor; discussing the witness's recollection and probable testimony; revealing to the witness other testimony or evidence that will be presented and asking the witness to reconsider the witness's recollection or recounting of events in that light; discussing the applicability of law to the events in issue; reviewing the factual context into which the witness's observations or opinions will fit; reviewing documents or other physical evidence that may be introduced; and discussing probable lines of hostile cross-examination that the witness should be prepared to meet. Witness preparation may include rehearsal of testimony. A lawyer may suggest choice of words that might be employed to make the witness's meaning clear. However, a lawyer may not assist the witness to testify falsely as to a material fact (see § 120(1)(a)).

* * *

§ 117. Compensating a Witness

A lawyer may not offer or pay to a witness any consideration:

> **(1) in excess of the reasonable expenses of the witness incurred and the reasonable value of the witness's time spent in providing evidence, except that an expert witness may be offered and paid a noncontingent fee;**

> **(2) contingent on the content of the witness's testimony or the outcome of the litigation; or**

> **(3) otherwise prohibited by law.**

§ 118. Falsifying or Destroying Evidence

> **(1) A lawyer may not falsify documentary or other evidence.**

(2) A lawyer may not destroy or obstruct another party's access to documentary or other evidence when doing so would violate a court order or other legal requirements, or counsel or assist a client to do so.

Comment:

a. Scope and cross-references. This Section states rules derived from the lawyer code, which in turn are based primarily on criminal-law prohibitions against tampering with evidence. See also § 94(2) (prohibition against counseling or assisting a client to violate a court order) and § 120 (prohibitions against presenting false evidence). On dealing with stolen property, see § 45, Comment *f.* On dealing with evidence of crimes, see § 119. With respect to dealings with a witness, see § 116.

For purposes of Subsection (2), "evidence" is usually defined as documentary or other physical material (including material stored in electronically retrievable form) that a reasonable lawyer would understand may be relevant to an official proceeding. It does not include exhibits and the like that an advocate or client constructs for illustrative purposes at a proceeding, even if the exhibit would be regarded as evidence for some other purpose.

b. Falsifying documentary and other evidence. Advocates in the adversary system are primarily responsible for assembling documentary and other evidence to be presented. A lawyer thereby may serve as custodian of evidentiary material, which ordinarily should reach the proceeding in its original condition. A lawyer may not alter such material in any way that impairs its evidentiary value for other parties. Rules of procedure may permit alteration of evidence in the course of reasonable scientific tests by experts.

A lawyer may not forge a document or alter a document with the purpose of misleading another, such as by back-dating the document, removing the document to another file to create a false impression of its provenance, deleting or adding language or other characters to the document so as to alter its effect, or materially changing its physical appearance.

A document, such as an affidavit or declaration, prepared by a lawyer for verification by another person must include only factual statements that the lawyer reasonably believes the person would make if testifying in person before the factfinder. On a submission to a tribunal based on the lawyer's personal knowledge, such as the lawyer's own affidavit or declaration, see § 120.

c. Destroying documentary or other physical evidence. Unlawful destruction or concealment of documents or other evidence during or in anticipation of litigation may subvert fair and full exposition of the facts. On the other hand, it would be intolerable to require retention of all documents and other evidence against the possibility that an adversary in future litigation would wish to examine them. Accordingly, it is presumptively lawful to act pursuant to an established document retention-destruction program that conforms to existing law and is consistently followed, absent a supervening obligation such as a subpoena or other lawful demand for or order relating to the material. On a lawyer's advice to a client on such matters as document retention or suppression, see generally § 94. If the client informs the lawyer that the client intends to destroy a document unlawfully or in violation of a court order, the lawyer must not advise or assist the client to do so (id.).

It may be difficult under applicable criminal law to define the point at which legitimate destruction becomes unlawful obstruction of justice. Under criminal law, a lawyer generally is subject to constraints no different from those imposed on others. Obstruction of justice and similar statutes generally apply only when an official proceeding is ongoing or imminent. For example, The American Law Institute Model Penal Code § 241.7 (1985) provides that the offense of tampering with or fabricating physical evidence occurs only if "an official proceeding or investigation is pending or about to be instituted. . . ."

A lawyer may not destroy evidence or conceal or alter it when a discovery demand, subpoena, or court order has directed the lawyer or the lawyer's client to turn over the evidence. Difficult questions of interpretation can arise with respect to destruction of documents in anticipation of a subpoena or similar process that has not yet issued at the time of destruction. For example, a company manufacturing a product that may cause injuries in the future is not, in the absence of specific prohibition, prohibited from destroying all manufacturing records after a period of time; but difficult questions of interpretation of obstruction-of-justice statutes may arise concerning such practices as culling incriminating documents while leaving others in place. No general statement can accurately describe the legality of record destruction; statutes and decisions in the particular jurisdiction must be consulted. In many jurisdictions, there is no applicable precedent. Legality may turn on such factual questions as the state of mind of the client or a lawyer.

Particular statutes and regulations may impose special obligations to retain records and files and to make them accessible to governmental officials. Procedural law or a tribunal ruling may impose other or additional obligations. For example, a lawyer may not knowingly withhold a document that has been properly requested in discovery unless the lawyer does so in procedurally proper form (see § 110, Comment *e*). Conversely, a lawyer responding to a request for discovery of documents may not mix responsive and nonresponsive documents together in a way designed to obstruct detection of responsive documents (see id.).

Some jurisdictions have recognized an action for damages by a litigant who suffers loss from "spoliation"—an opposing party's or lawyer's unwarranted and injurious suppression of evidence. In some jurisdictions, an unfavorable evidentiary inference may be drawn from failure to produce material that was at one time in the possession and under the control of a party to litigation. The inference may be invoked even in circumstances in which destruction is otherwise lawful. Section

51 does not provide for a lawyer's liability to a nonclient for negligence in such a situation. Falsification or unlawful destruction of evidence may also constitute contempt or may be subject to the tribunal's inherent power to impose a suitable sanction (see § 1, Comment c).

§ 119. Physical Evidence of a Client Crime

With respect to physical evidence of a client crime, a lawyer:

(1) may, when reasonably necessary for purposes of the representation, take possession of the evidence and retain it for the time reasonably necessary to examine it and subject it to tests that do not alter or destroy material characteristics of the evidence; but

(2) following possession under Subsection (1), the lawyer must notify prosecuting authorities of the lawyer's possession of the evidence or turn the evidence over to them.

Comment:

a. Scope and cross-references. This Section states general rules applicable to a lawyer's possession of evidence of client crimes. The rules are derived primarily from scattered decisions dealing with the question and reflect the Institute's view of how a lawyer might appropriately proceed. A lawyer confronted with an issue under the Section should be aware that local law on such questions as a lawyer's ability to remove physical evidence from a site for the purpose of examination may not yet be recognized by applicable decisions. On the obligations of lawyers in dealing with evidence other than evidence of client crime, see § 118. On a lawyer's dealing with stolen property belonging to a third person, see § 45, Comment f. On dealing with witnesses, see § 116.

This Section applies to evidence of a client crime, contraband, weapons, and similar implements used in an offense. It also includes such material as documents and material in electronically retrievable form used by the client to plan the offense, documents used in the course of a mail-fraud violation, or transaction documents evidencing a crime.

Witness statements, photographs of the scene of a crime, trial exhibits, and the like prepared by a lawyer or the lawyer's assistants constitute work product and thus are not subject to the Section, even if such material could constitute evidence of a client crime for some purposes, such as if waived. See § 87, Comment f, and § 92, Comment e; see also § 87, Comment b, on the distinction between work-product materials and preexisting documents, such as client files or financial records.

b. Physical evidence of a client crime; retention for reasonably necessary examination. As stated in Subsection (1), a lawyer may legitimately need to possess evidence relating to a crime for the purpose of examining it to prepare a defense. A lawyer has the same privilege as prosecutors to possess and examine such material for the lawful purpose of assisting in the trial of criminal cases. Such an examination may include scientific tests, so long as they do not alter or destroy the value of the evidence for possible use by the prosecution. So long as the lawyer's possession is for that purpose, criminal laws that generally prohibit possession of contraband or other evidence of crimes are inapplicable to the lawyer. Nonetheless, possession of such material otherwise than in strict compliance with the requirements stated in this Section may subject the lawyer to risk of prosecution as an accessory after the fact for accepting evidence that might otherwise be found. A lawyer's office may also thereby be subject to search. In dealing with such evidence, a lawyer may not unlawfully alter, destroy, or conceal it (see § 118). On the prohibition against advising or assisting another person, including the client, to do so, see § 94.

   c.   Disposition of evidence of a client crime. Once a lawyer's reasonable need for examination of evidence of a client crime has been satisfied, a lawyer's responsibilities with respect to further possession of the evidence are determined under the criminal law and the law affecting confidentiality of client information (see generally Chapter 5). Under the general criminal law, physical evidence of a client crime in possession of the lawyer may not be retained to a point at which its utility as evidence for the prosecution is significantly impaired, such as by waiting until after the trial.

   Some decisions have alluded to an additional option—returning the evidence to the site from which it was taken, when that can be accomplished without destroying or altering material characteristics of the evidence. That will often be impossible. The option would also be unavailable when the lawyer reasonably should know that the client or another person will intentionally alter or destroy the evidence.

   Evidence subject to this Section will come to the attention of the authorities either through being turned over by the lawyer to them or through notification by the lawyer or another. In the latter case, the authorities may obtain the evidence from the lawyer by proper process. The prosecution and defense should make appropriate arrangements for introduction and authentication of the evidence at trial. Because of the risk of prejudice to the client, that should be done without improperly revealing the source of the evidence to the finder of fact. The parties may also agree that the tribunal may instruct the jury, without revealing the lawyer's involvement, that an appropriate chain of possession links the evidence to the place where it was located before coming into the lawyer's possession. In the absence of agreement to such an instruction by the defense, the prosecutor may offer evidence of the lawyer's possession if necessary to establish the chain of possession.

§ 120.   False Testimony or Evidence

   (1) A lawyer may not:

(a) knowingly counsel or assist a witness to testify falsely or otherwise to offer false evidence;

(b) knowingly make a false statement of fact to the tribunal;

(c) offer testimony or other evidence as to an issue of fact known by the lawyer to be false.

(2) If a lawyer has offered testimony or other evidence as to a material issue of fact and comes to know of its falsity, the lawyer must take reasonable remedial measures and may disclose confidential client information when necessary to take such a measure.

(3) A lawyer may refuse to offer testimony or other evidence that the lawyer reasonably believes is false, even if the lawyer does not know it to be false.

Comment:

a. Scope and cross-references. Subsections (1) and (2) state limitations on testimony or other evidence that a lawyer may offer (see Comment *d*) before a tribunal, including measures that a lawyer must take on discovering that testimony or other evidence previously offered by the lawyer is false. Under Subsection (3), a lawyer has discretion to offer or to refuse to offer evidence believed to be false, a lesser standard of knowledge than that under Subsections (1) and (2). The rules are drawn from the lawyer codes, although nondisciplinary remedies may also be available. See Comment *l* hereto. With respect to other limitations on a lawyer's advocacy, see Topics 1–4 of this Chapter.

On special duties of candor in ex parte and similar proceedings, see § 112. On the prohibition against false statements of law, see § 111. On special duties of candor applicable to prosecutors in criminal cases, see § 97, Comment *h*.

b. Rationale. An advocate seeks to achieve the client's objectives (see § 16(1)) but in doing so may not distort factfinding by the tribunal by knowingly offering false testimony or other evidence.

A lawyer's discovery that testimony or other evidence is false may occur in circumstances suggesting complicity by the client in preparing or offering it, thus presenting the risk that remedial action by the lawyer can lead to criminal investigation or other adverse consequences for the client. At the very least, remedial action will deprive the client of whatever evidentiary advantage the false evidence would otherwise provide. It has therefore been asserted that remedial action by the lawyer is inconsistent with the requirements of loyalty and confidentiality (see § 60 and following). However, preservation of the integrity of the forum is a superior interest, which would be disserved by a lawyer's knowing offer of false evidence. Moreover, a client has no right to the assistance of counsel in offering such evidence. As indicated in Subsection (2), taking remedial measures required to correct false evidence may necessitate the disclosure of confidential client information otherwise protected under Chapter 5 (see Comment *h* hereto).

The procedural rules concerning burden of proof allocate responsibility for bringing forward evidence. A lawyer might know of testimony or other evidence vital to the other party, but unknown to that party or their advocate. The advocate who knows of the evidence, and who has complied with applicable rules concerning pretrial discovery and other applicable disclosure requirements (see, e.g, § 118), has no legal obligation to reveal the evidence, even though the proceeding thereby may fail to ascertain the facts as the lawyer knows them.

c. A lawyer's knowledge. A lawyer's obligations under Subsection (2) depend on what the lawyer knows and, in the case of Subsection (3), on what the lawyer reasonably believes (see Comment *j*). A lawyer's knowledge may be inferred from the circumstances. Actual knowledge does not include unknown information, even if a reasonable lawyer would have discovered it through inquiry. However, a lawyer may not ignore what is plainly apparent, for example, by refusing to read a document (see § 94, Comment *g*). A lawyer should not conclude that testimony is or will be false unless there is a firm factual basis for doing so. Such a basis exists when facts known to the lawyer or the client's own statements indicate to the lawyer that the testimony or other evidence is false.

d. Offer of false testimony or other false evidence. False testimony includes testimony that a lawyer knows to be false and testimony from a witness who the lawyer knows is only guessing or reciting what the witness has been instructed to say. This Section employs the terms "false testimony" and "false evidence" rather than "perjury" because the latter term defines a crime, which may require elements not relevant for application of the requirements of the Section in other contexts. For example, although a witness who testifies in good faith but contrary to fact lacks the mental state necessary for the crime of perjury, the rule of the Section nevertheless applies to a lawyer who knows that such testimony is false. When a lawyer is charged with the criminal offense of suborning perjury, the more limited definition appropriate to the criminal offense applies.

A lawyer's responsibility for false evidence extends to testimony or other evidence in aid of the lawyer's client offered or similarly sponsored by the lawyer. The responsibility extends to any false testimony elicited by the lawyer, as well as such testimony elicited by another lawyer questioning the lawyer's own client, another witness favorable to the lawyer's client, or a witness whom the lawyer has substantially prepared to testify (see § 116(1)). A lawyer has no responsibility to correct false testimony or other evidence offered by an opposing party or witness. Thus, a plaintiff's lawyer, aware that an adverse witness being examined by the defendant's lawyer is giving false evidence favorable to the plaintiff, is not required to correct it (compare Comment *e*). However, the lawyer may not attempt to reinforce the false evidence, such as by arguing to the factfinder that the false evidence should be accepted as true or otherwise sponsoring or supporting the false evidence (see also Comment *e*).

Illustrations:

1. Lawyer, representing Defendant, knows that a contract between Plaintiff's decedent and Defendant had been superseded by a materially revised version that was executed and retained by Defendant. Plaintiff's Counsel is unaware of the revised contract and has failed to seek information about it in discovery. At trial, Lawyer elicits testimony from Defendant by inquiring about "the contract that you and Plaintiff's decedent signed" and presents Defendant with the original contract, asking, "Is this the contract that you and Plaintiff's decedent signed?" Defendant responds affirmatively. Lawyer has violated Subsection (1)(c).

2. Same facts as in Illustration 1, except that Lawyer does not elicit the testimony there described and Plaintiff's Counsel, mistakenly believing that the revised contract was not in writing, offers an accurate account of its contents through the testimony of a third-party witness. Lawyer successfully objects to the proposed testimony under the jurisdiction's statute of frauds, thereby removing the only evidence known to Plaintiff's Counsel on which the factfinder could find that the original contract was superseded. Defendant offers no additional evidence, and Lawyer does not produce the revised contract. As a result the tribunal enters a directed verdict for Defendant. Lawyer did not violate this Section in making the successful objection, which kept out evidence, or in failing to inform the lawyer for Defendant of the evidence in fact available.

e. Counseling or assisting a witness to offer false testimony or other false evidence. A lawyer may not knowingly counsel or assist a witness to testify falsely or otherwise to offer false evidence as to a material issue of fact (Subsection (1)(a)). With respect to the right of a criminal defendant to testify and application of the rule to criminal-defense counsel, see Comment *i* hereto. If a lawyer knows that a witness will provide truthful evidence as to some matters but false evidence as to others, the lawyer must not elicit the false evidence. On affirmative remedial steps that a lawyer must take when a lawyer knows that a witness has offered false evidence, see Comment *h*.

Illustration:

3. Lawyer, representing as Plaintiffs the officers of a closed financial institution, seeks a preliminary injunction requiring governmental regulators to reopen the institution. Plaintiffs have the burden of establishing that certain documents were executed prior to closure of the institution. Lawyer drafts an affidavit for the signature of the president of the institution, stating that attached as

exhibits are such documents. As Lawyer knows, the exhibits are in fact drafts that were not executed when dated but which have been backdated. Lawyer's offer of the affidavit would violate the rule of Subsection (1)(c).

The prohibitions against false evidence address matters offered in aid of the lawyer's client (see Comment *d*). It is not a violation to elicit from an adversary witness evidence known by the lawyer to be false and apparently adverse to the lawyer's client. The lawyer may have sound tactical reasons for doing so, such as eliciting false testimony for the purpose of later demonstrating its falsity to discredit the witness. Requiring premature disclosure could, under some circumstances, aid the witness in explaining away false testimony or recasting it into a more plausible form.

Illustration:

4. Lawyer, representing Plaintiff, takes the deposition of Witness, who describes the occurrence in question in a way unfavorable to Plaintiff. From other evidence, Lawyer knows that Witness is testifying falsely. Subsequently, the case is settled, and Lawyer never discloses the false nature of Witness's deposition testimony. Lawyer's conduct does not violate this Section.

f. A lawyer's statement of fact to a tribunal. A lawyer may make a submission to a tribunal based on the lawyer's personal knowledge, such as the lawyer's own affidavit or declaration or a representation made on the lawyer's own knowledge. For example, the lawyer may state during a scheduling conference that a conflict exists in the lawyer's trial schedule or state on appeal that certain evidence appears of record. In such statements the lawyer purports to convey information based on personal knowledge. A tribunal or another party should be able to rely on such a statement. Such a statement must have a reasonable basis for belief.

Illustration:

5. Lawyer, representing Accused in defending against criminal charges, files a motion to suppress a purported confession. Lawyer attaches to the motion a copy of a document that appears to be the written confession of Accused. Lawyer states in the motion that Lawyer obtained the document from a police file, but Lawyer takes the position in the motion that other evidence accompanying the motion indicates that the document is a forgery. Because Lawyer purports to be asserting as a personally known fact that the document was obtained from the police file, Lawyer must know from Lawyer's own knowledge that the document is what Lawyer asserts it to be. On the other hand, Lawyer may characterize the document as a forgery based on other evidence so long as Lawyer has a nonfrivolous basis for that position (see § 110(1), Subsection (2) &

Comment *d* hereto), even if Lawyer does not personally believe that the document is a forgery.

For the purpose of Subsection (1)(b) a knowing false statement of fact includes a statement on which the lawyer then has insufficient information from which reasonably to conclude that the statement is accurate. A lawyer may make conditional or suppositional statements so long as they are so identified and are neither known to be false nor made without a reasonable basis in fact for their conditional or suppositional character.

Illustration:

6. Lawyer represents A Corporation as defendant in an action seeking damages. Lawyer has filed A Corporation's motion to dismiss for lack of personal jurisdiction. In support of the motion, Lawyer's affidavit states that an attached certificate of a governmental agency of State X is genuine. The certificate states the jurisdiction in which A Corporation is incorporated, a material issue on the motion. Lawyer sought such a certificate from the relevant agency, but the certificate had not arrived by the time for filing the affidavit. Lawyer accordingly prepares what Lawyer reasonably believes is an accurate copy of the certificate and signs it in the name of a governmental official, having seen a telecopied facsimile of the certificate transmitted from the state agency. The certificate arrives the day following the filing of the motion and corresponds to the document attached to Lawyer's affidavit. Lawyer has violated this Section, as well as § 118. Lawyer would not have violated this Section if Lawyer had stated in the affidavit that the attached document was a copy of a document the original of which would be supplied by supplemental submission.

For purposes of professional discipline, the lawyer codes prohibit a lawyer from making only a false statement of "material" fact. A similar condition attaches to the crime of perjury (although often not to the related crime of false swearing or false statements.) However, other procedural or substantive rules may contain no such qualification.

g. Remonstrating with a client or witness. Before taking other steps, a lawyer ordinarily must confidentially remonstrate with the client or witness not to present false evidence or to correct false evidence already presented. Doing so protects against possibly harsher consequences. The form and content of such a remonstration is a matter of judgment. The lawyer must attempt to be persuasive while maintaining the client's trust in the lawyer's loyalty and diligence. If the client insists on offering false evidence, the lawyer must inform the client of the lawyer's duty not to offer false evidence and, if it is offered, to take appropriate remedial action (see Comment *h*).

h. Reasonable remedial measures. A lawyer who has taken appropriate steps to avoid offering false evidence (see Comment *g*) may be required to take additional measures. A lawyer may be surprised by unexpected false evidence given by a witness or may come to know of its falsity only after it has been offered.

If the lawyer's client or the witness refuses to correct the false testimony (see Comment *g*), the lawyer must take steps reasonably calculated to remove the false impression that the evidence may have made on the finder of fact (Subsection (2)). Alternatively, a lawyer could seek a recess and attempt to persuade the witness to correct the false evidence (see Comment *g*). If such steps are unsuccessful, the lawyer must take other steps, such as by moving or stipulating to have the evidence stricken or otherwise withdrawn, or recalling the witness if the witness had already left the stand when the lawyer comes to know of the falsity. Once the false evidence is before the finder of fact, it is not a reasonable remedial measure for the lawyer simply to withdraw from the representation, even if the presiding officer permits withdrawal (see Comment *k* hereto). If no other remedial measure corrects the falsity, the lawyer must inform the opposing party or tribunal of the falsity so that they may take corrective steps.

To the extent necessary in taking reasonable remedial measures under Subsection (2), a lawyer may use or reveal otherwise confidential client information (see § 63). However, the lawyer must proceed so that, consistent with carrying out the measures (including, if necessary, disclosure to the opposing party or tribunal), the lawyer causes the client minimal adverse effects. The lawyer has discretion as to which measures to adopt, so long as they are reasonably calculated to correct the false evidence. If the lawyer makes disclosure to the opposing party or tribunal, thereafter the lawyer must leave further steps to the opposing party or tribunal. Whether testimony concerning client-lawyer communications with respect to the false evidence can be elicited is determined under § 82 (crime-fraud exception to attorney-client privilege). The lawyer's disclosure may give rise to a conflict between the lawyer and client requiring the lawyer to withdraw from the representation (see Comment *k* hereto).

Responsibilities of a lawyer under this Section extend to the end of the proceeding in which the question of false evidence arises. Thus, a lawyer representing a client on appeal from a verdict in a trial continues to carry responsibilities with respect to false evidence offered at trial, particularly evidence discovered to be false after trial (see Comment *i*). If a lawyer is discharged by a client or withdraws, whether or not for reasons associated with the false evidence, the lawyer's obligations under this Section are not thereby terminated. In such an instance, a reasonable remedial measure may consist of disclosing the matter to successor counsel.

Even after the proceeding concludes, the rule stated in other Sections of this Restatement may permit corrective or self-protective action, such as through notification of others of the fact of withdrawal (see §§ 66–67 & 64).

i. False evidence in a criminal-defense representation. The rules stated in the Section generally govern defense counsel in criminal cases. The requirement stated in Comment *g* with respect to remonstrating with a client may often be relevant. However, because of the right to the effective assistance of counsel, withdrawal (see Comment *k*) may be inappropriate in response to threatened client perjury in a criminal case. If defense counsel withdraws, normally it will be necessary for the accused to retain another lawyer or for the court to appoint one, unless the accused proceeds without counsel. Replacement counsel also may have to deal with the same client demand to take the stand to testify falsely. A tribunal may also be concerned that controversy over false evidence may be contrived to delay the proceeding. In criminal cases many courts thus are strongly inclined not to permit withdrawal of defense counsel, particularly if trial is underway or imminent. Withdrawal may be required, however, if the accused denies defense counsel's assertion that presentation of false evidence is threatened.

Some courts permit an accused in such circumstances to give "open narrative" testimony, without requiring defense counsel to take affirmative remedial action as required under Subsection (2). Defense counsel asks only a general question about the events, provides no guidance through additional questions, and does not refer to the false evidence in subsequent argument to the factfinder. Counsel does not otherwise indicate to the presiding officer or opposing counsel that the testimony or other evidence is false, although such indication may be necessary to deal with a prosecutor's objection to use of the open-narrative form of testimony. From the unusual format of examination, prosecutor and presiding officer are likely to understand that the accused is offering false testimony, but an unguided jury may be unaware of or confused about its significance. That solution is not consistent with the rule stated in Subsection (2) or with the requirements of the lawyer codes in most jurisdictions.

However, the defendant may still insist on giving false testimony despite defense counsel's efforts to persuade the defendant not to testify or to testify accurately (see Comment *g*). The accused has the constitutional rights to take the witness stand and to offer evidence in self-defense (see § 22). Unlike counsel in a civil case, who can refuse to call a witness (including a client) who will offer false evidence (see Comment *e*), defense counsel in a criminal case has no authority (beyond persuasion) to prevent a client-accused from taking the witness stand. (Defense counsel does possess that authority with respect to nonclient witnesses and must exercise it consistent with this Section (see § 23).) If the client nonetheless insists on the right to take the stand, defense counsel must accede to the demand of the accused to testify. Thereafter defense counsel may not ask the accused any question if counsel knows that the response would be false. Counsel must also be prepared to take remedial measures, including disclosure, in the event that the accused indeed testifies falsely (see Comment *h*).

In one situation, disclosure of client perjury to the tribunal may not be feasible. When a criminal case is being tried without a jury, informing the judge of perjury by an accused might be tantamount to informing the factfinder of the guilt of the accused. In such an instance, disclosure to the prosecutor might suffice as a remedial measure. The prosecutor may not refer in the judge's presence to the information provided by defense counsel under this Section.

j. An advocate's discretion to refuse to offer testimony or other evidence reasonably believed to be false. The rule of Subsection (3) protects a lawyer from forced complicity in violations of the law and protects the tribunal and third persons from erroneous decisions. It also protects the lawyer's reputation as an honest person and as an advocate capable of discriminating between reliable and unreliable evidence. A lawyer may not by agreement with a client surrender the discretion stated in Subsection (3) (see § 23(1)).

The rule of Subsection (3) consists of two elements. First, the lawyer's knowledge is assessed objectively according to a standard of reasonable belief. (In contrast, a firm factual basis is necessary before the mandatory rules stated in Subsections (1) and (2) are applicable (see Comment *c*).) Second, a lawyer who reasonably believes (but does not know) that evidence is false, has discretion to offer or to refuse to offer it.

k. False evidence and the client-lawyer relationship. A lawyer's actions in accordance with this Section may impair the trust and respect that otherwise would exist between lawyer and client. A lawyer may be discharged by the client or withdraw from the representation (see § 32).

If a difference between lawyer and client over falsity occurs just before or during trial, a tribunal may refuse to permit a lawyer to withdraw when withdrawal would require the client to proceed without counsel (see § 32(4)).

l. Remedies. Violation of Subsections (1) and (2) may be sanctioned through professional discipline. Certain violations may also be remedied through appropriate sanctions in the proceeding (see § 110, Comment *g*). Criminal liability exists for perjury or subornation of perjury. A court may have discretion to disqualify a lawyer who violates a rule of the Section from further representation in the proceeding. Knowing use of perjured testimony may be a basis for granting a new trial or for vacating a judgment or setting aside a settlement based on the false evidence. A litigant has no damage remedy against an opposing lawyer for an alleged perjurious client based solely on violation of this Section. Compare § 57, Comments *d* and *e* (lawyer liability for abuse of process and similar intentional torts).

CHAPTER 8: CONFLICTS OF INTEREST

TOPIC 1. CONFLICTS OF INTERESTS—IN GENERAL

§121. The Basic Prohibition of Conflicts of Interests

Unless all affected clients and other necessary persons consent to the representation under the limitations and conditions provided in §122, a lawyer may not represent a client if the representation would involve a conflict of interest. A conflict of interest is involved if there is a substantial risk that the lawyer's representation of the client would be materially and adversely affected by the lawyer's own interests or by the lawyer's duties to another current client, a former client, or a third person.

Comment:

* * *

b. Rationale. The prohibition against lawyer conflicts of interest reflects several competing concerns. First, the law seeks to assure clients that their lawyers will represent them with undivided loyalty. A client is entitled to be represented by a lawyer whom the client can trust. Instilling such confidence is an objective important in itself. For example, the principle underlying the prohibition against a lawyer's filing suit against a present client in an unrelated matter (see §128, Comment *e*) may also extend to situations, not involving litigation, in which significant impairment of a client's expectation of the lawyer's loyalty would be similarly likely. Contentious dealings, for example involving charges of bad faith against the client whom the lawyer represents in another matter would raise such a concern. So also would negotiating on behalf of one client when a large proportion of the lawyer's other client's net worth is at risk.

Second, the prohibition against conflicts of interest seeks to enhance the effectiveness of legal representation. To the extent that a conflict of interest undermines the independence of the lawyer's professional judgment or inhibits a lawyer from working with appropriate vigor in the client's behalf, the client's expectation of effective representation (see §16) could be compromised.

Third, a client has a legal right to have the lawyer safeguard the client's confidential information (see §60). Preventing use of confidential client information against the interests of the client, either to benefit the lawyer's personal interest, in aid of some other client, or to foster an assumed public purpose is facilitated through conflicts rules that reduce the opportunity for such abuse.

Fourth, conflicts rules help ensure that lawyers will not exploit clients, such as by inducing a client to make a gift to the lawyer (see §127).

Finally, some conflict-of-interest rules protect interests of the legal system in obtaining adequate presentations to tribunals. In the absence of such rules, for example, a lawyer might appear on both sides of the litigation, complicating the process of taking proof and compromising adversary argumentation (see § 128).

On the other hand, avoiding conflicts of interest can impose significant costs on lawyers and clients. Prohibition of conflicts of interest should therefore be no broader than necessary. First, conflict avoidance can make representation more expensive. To the extent that conflict-of-interest rules prevent multiple clients from being represented by a single lawyer, one or both clients will be required to find other lawyers. That might entail uncertainty concerning the successor lawyers' qualifications, usually additional cost, and the inconvenience of separate representation. In matters in which individual claims are small, representation of multiple claimants might be required if the claims are effectively to be considered at all. Second, limitations imposed by conflicts rules can interfere with client expectations. At the very least, one of the clients might be deprived of the services of a lawyer whom the client had a particular reason to retain, perhaps on the basis of a long-time association with the lawyer. In some communities or fields of practice there might be no lawyer who is perfectly conflict-free. Third, obtaining informed consent to conflicted representation itself might compromise important interests. As discussed in § 122, consent to a conflict of interest requires that each affected client give consent based on adequate information. The process of obtaining informed consent is not only potentially time-consuming; it might also be impractical because it would require the disclosure of information that the clients would prefer not to have disclosed, for example, the subject matter about which they have consulted the lawyer. Fourth, conflicts prohibitions interfere with lawyers' own freedom to practice according to their own best judgment of appropriate professional behavior. It is appropriate to give significant weight to the freedom and professionalism of lawyers in the formulation of legal rules governing conflicts.

c. The general conflict-of-interest standard. The standard adopted in this Chapter answers the four questions to which any conflicts-of-interest standard must respond. Those are (i) What kind of effect is prohibited? (ii) How significant must the effect be? (iii) What probability must there be that the effect will occur? (iv) From whose perspective are conflicts of interest to be determined? The standard adopted here incorporates elements common to all three of the major lawyer codes developed in this century. It casts the answer to each question in terms of factual predicates and practical consequences that are reasonably susceptible of objective assessment by lawyers subject to the rules, by clients whom the rules affect, and by tribunals.

c(i). Prohibited effects. Unless there is risk that the lawyer's representation would be affected "adversely," there is no conflict of interest. The 1969 Code of Professional Responsibility uses the term "differing interests" to define situations that a lawyer must treat as an actual or potential conflict. However, this standard can be interpreted over-inclusively. Two clients rarely have interests that are entirely identical. If the term "differing" interests were given its broadest meaning, a lawyer might almost never be able to represent two clients without the client's consent.

"Adverse" effect relates to the quality of the representation, not necessarily the quality of the result obtained in a given case. The standard refers to the incentives faced by the lawyer before or during the representation because it often cannot be foretold what the actual result would have been if the representation had been conflict-free.

Illustration:

1. Lawyer has been retained by A and B, each a competitor for a single broadcast license, to assist each of them in obtaining the license from Agency. Such work often requires advocacy by the lawyer for an applicant before Agency. Lawyer's representation will have an adverse effect on both A and B as that term is used in this Section. Even though either A or B might obtain the license and thus arguably not have been adversely affected by the joint representation, Lawyer will have duties to A that restrict Lawyer's ability to urge B's application and vice versa. In most instances, informed consent of both A and B would not suffice to allow the dual representation (see § 122).

c(ii). "Materially" adverse effect. Materiality of a possible conflict is determined by reference to obligations necessarily assumed by the lawyer (see § 16), or assumed by agreement with the client either in the retainer agreement (see § 19) or in the course of the representation (see § 21). An otherwise immaterial conflict could be considered material if, for example, a client had made clear that the client considered the possible conflict a serious and substantial matter.

Illustration:

2. Lawyer is asked by Client A to represent Client A in an aspect of the hostile takeover by Client A of Lawyer's corporate Client B. Success in such a venture would have a material adverse effect on Client B and hence involves a conflict of interest within the meaning of this Section. Whether informed consent of both A and B would be sufficient to allow the dual representation in this situation is considered in § 122.

c(iii). Likelihood of effect. There is no conflict of interest within the meaning of this Section unless there is a "substantial risk" that a material adverse effect will occur. In many cases the material adverse effect on the representation will be immediate, actual, and apparent. Other situations, however, might present a risk that is only potential or contingent. In this context, "substantial risk" means that in the circumstances the risk is significant and plausible, even if it is not certain or even probable that it will occur. The standard requires more than a mere possibility of adverse effect.

Illustration:

>   3.   Clients A and B have come to Lawyer for help in organizing a new business. Lawyer is satisfied that both clients are committed to forming the enterprise and that an agreement can be prepared that will embody their common undertaking. Nonetheless, because a substantial risk of future conflict exists in any such arrangement, Lawyer must explain to the clients that because of future economic uncertainties inherent in any such undertaking, the clients' interests could differ in material ways in the future. Lawyer must obtain informed consent pursuant to § 122 before undertaking the common representation.

Some conflicts can be eliminated by an agreement limiting the scope of the lawyer's representation if the limitation can be given effect without rendering the remaining representation objectively inadequate (see § 19 & § 122, Comment *g(iv)*).

Illustration:

>   4.   Lawyer has been retained by Client to represent Client in general business matters. Client has a distribution contract with Manufacturer, and there is a chance that disputes could arise under the contract. Lawyer represents Manufacturer in local real-estate matters completely unrelated to Client's business. An agreement between Lawyer and Client that the scope of Lawyer's representation of Client will not extend to dealing with disputes with Manufacturer would eliminate the conflict posed by the chance otherwise of representing Client in matters adverse to Manufacturer (see § 128). Such an agreement would not require the consent of Manufacturer.

General antagonism between clients does not necessarily mean that a lawyer would be engaged in conflicted representations by representing the clients in separate, unrelated matters. A conflict for a lawyer ordinarily exists only when there is conflict in the interests of the clients that are involved in the matters being handled by the lawyer or when unrelated representations are of such a nature that the lawyer's relationship with one or both clients likely would be adversely affected.

Illustration:

>   5.   For many years Law Firm has represented Bank in mortgage foreclosures and does so currently. Other lawyers in Law Firm have continuously represented Manufacturer as outside general counsel and do so currently. Bank and Manufacturer entered into an agreement under which Bank would loan a sum of money to Manufacturer. Lawyers from Law Firm did not represent either client in

negotiating the loan agreement. A dispute arose between the parties to the agreement, and Manufacturer announced that it would file suit against Bank for breach of the loan contract. Absent client consent as provided in § 122, Law Firm lawyers may not represent either Bank or Manufacturer in the litigation (see § 128(2)). Law Firm may not withdraw from representing either client in order to file or defend a suit on the loan agreement against the other (see § 132, Comment c). Law Firm may, however, continue to provide legal services to both clients in matters unrelated to the litigation because as to those matters the clients' interests are not in conflict.

c(iv). The perspective for determining conflict of interest. This Section employs an objective standard by which to assess the adverseness, materiality, and substantiality of the risk of the effect on representation. The standard of this Section is not the "appearance of impropriety" standard formerly used by some courts to define the scope of impermissible conflicts. That standard could prohibit not only conflicts as defined in this Section, but also situations that might appear improper to an uninformed observer or even an interested party.

The propriety of the lawyer's action should be determined based only on facts and circumstances that the lawyer knew or should have known at the time of undertaking or continuing a representation. It should not be evaluated in light of information that became known only later and that could not reasonably have been anticipated.

The standard of this Section allows consideration in a given situation of the social value of the lawyer's behavior alleged to constitute the conflict. For example, a lawyer's statement about a matter of public importance might conflict with a client's objectives, but the public importance of free expression is a factor to be considered in limiting the possible reach of the relevant conflicts rule (see § 125, Comment e).

Whether there is adverseness, materiality, and substantiality in a given circumstance is often dependent on specific circumstances that are ambiguous and the subject of conflicting evidence. Accordingly, there are necessarily circumstances in which the lawyer's avoidance of a representation is permissible but not obligatory. A lawyer also would be justified in withdrawing from some representations in circumstances in which it would be improper to disqualify the lawyer or the lawyer's firm.

d. Representation of a client. The prohibition of conflicts of interest ordinarily restricts a lawyer's activities only where those activities materially and adversely affect the lawyer's ability to represent a client including such an effect on a client's reasonable expectation of the lawyer's loyalty. The formation of a client-lawyer relationship is considered in § 14. Obligations to nonclients might be imposed on a lawyer by other principles of law, see § 135. That a formal client-lawyer relationship has come to an end does not terminate all conflict-of-interest restrictions, such as the prohibition against a lawyer accepting representation contrary to the interest of a former client (see § 132).

For purposes of identifying conflicts of interest, a lawyer's client is ordinarily the person or entity that consents to the formation of the client-lawyer relationship, see § 14. For example, when a lawyer is retained by Corporation A, Corporation A is ordinarily the lawyer's client; neither individual officers of Corporation A nor other corporations in which Corporation A has an ownership interest, that hold an ownership interest in Corporation A, or in which a major shareholder in Corporation A has an ownership interest, are thereby considered to be the lawyer's client.

In some situations, however, the financial or personal relationship between the lawyer's client and other persons or entities might be such that the lawyer's obligations to the client will extend to those other persons or entities as well. That will be true, for example, where financial loss or benefit to the nonclient person or entity will have a direct, adverse impact on the client.

Illustrations:

6.   Lawyer represents Corporation A in local real-estate transactions. Lawyer has been asked to represent Plaintiff in a products-liability action against Corporation B claiming substantial damages. Corporation B is a wholly owned subsidiary of Corporation A; any judgment obtained against Corporation B will have a material adverse impact on the value of Corporation B's assets and on the value of the assets of Corporation A. Just as Lawyer could not file suit against Corporation A on behalf of another client, even in a matter unrelated to the subject of Lawyer's representation of Corporation A (see § 128, Comment e), Lawyer may not represent Plaintiff in the suit against Corporation B without the consent of both Plaintiff and Corporation A under the limitations and conditions provided in § 122.

7.   The same facts as in Illustration 6, except that Corporation B is not a subsidiary of Corporation A. Instead, 51 percent of the stock of Corporation A and 60 percent of the stock of Corporation B are owned by X Corporation. The remainder of the stock in both Corporation A and Corporation B is held by the public. Lawyer does not represent X Corporation. The circumstances are such that an adverse judgment against Corporation B will have no material adverse impact on the financial position of Corporation A. No conflict of interest is presented; Lawyer may represent Plaintiff in the suit against Corporation B.

Similar problems could arise where the client and nonclient are individuals and representation adverse to the nonclient could have direct material effect on the client's interest. Such a situation would exist, for example, where a lawyer representing one spouse was asked to bring suit against the other, or where a lawyer representing one holder of an interest in property was asked by someone else to bring suit against the other holder in circumstances where the suit could materially and adversely affect the interest of the lawyer's client.

In yet other situations, the conflict of interest arises because the circumstances indicate that the confidence that a client reasonably reposes in the loyalty of a lawyer would be compromised due to the lawyer's relationship with another client or person whose interests would be adversely affected by the representation.

Illustration:

8.   The same facts as in Illustration 7, except that one-half of Lawyer's practice consists of work for Corporation A. Plaintiff could reasonably believe that Lawyer's concern about a possible adverse reaction by Corporation A to the suit against Corporation B will inhibit Lawyer's pursuit of Plaintiff's case against Corporation B (see §§ 125 & 128). Lawyer may not represent Plaintiff in the suit against Corporation B unless Plaintiff consents to the representation under the limitations and conditions provided in § 122. Because Lawyer's representation of Corporation A is assumed in Illustration 7 not to be adversely affected by the representation of Plaintiff, the consent of Corporation A to the representation is not required.

Significant control of the nonclient by the client also might suffice to require a lawyer to treat the nonclient as if it were a client in determining whether a conflict of interest exists in a lawyer's representation of another client with interests adverse to the nonclient.

Illustration:

9.   The same facts as in Illustration 7, except that X Corporation has elected a majority of the Directors of Corporation B and has approved its key officers. Officers of X Corporation regularly supervise decisions made by Corporation B, and Lawyer has regularly advised X Corporation on products-liability issues affecting all of the corporations in which X Corporation owns an interest. X Corporation has used that advice to give direction about minimizing claims exposure to Corporation B. Although Lawyer does not represent Corporation B, Lawyer's earlier assistance to X Corporation on products-liability matters was substantially related to the suit that Plaintiff has asked Lawyer to file against Corporation B (see § 132). Lawyer may not represent Plaintiff in the suit against Corporation B unless Plaintiff, X Corporation, and Corporation B consent to the representation under the limitations and conditions provided in § 122. In the circumstances, informed consent on behalf of Corporation B may be provided by officers of X Corporation who direct the legal affairs of Corporation B pursuant to applicable corporate law.

A conflict of interest can also arise because of specific obligations, such as the obligation to hold information confidential, that the lawyer has assumed to a nonclient.

Illustration:

10. Lawyer represents Association, a trade association in which Corporation C is a member, in supporting legislation to protect Association's industry against foreign imports. Lawyer does not represent any individual members of Association, including Corporation C, but at the request of Association and Lawyer, Corporation C has given Lawyer confidential information about Corporation C's cost of production. Plaintiff has asked Lawyer to sue Corporation C for unfair competition based on Corporation C's alleged pricing below the cost of production. Although Corporation C is not Lawyer's client, unless both Plaintiff and Corporation C consent to the representation under the limitations and conditions provided in § 122, Lawyer may not represent Plaintiff against Corporation C in the matter because of the serious risk of material adverse use of Corporation C's confidential information against Corporation C.

e. Withdrawal from conflicting representations—in general. A conflict can be avoided by declining to represent a new client or, when appropriate, by obtaining effective consent (see § 122). However, a lawyer might undertake representation before realizing that a conflict exists. In addition, subsequent events might create conflicts. For example, a merger of law firms or a merger of a corporate client with a nonclient enterprise might create conflicts after the representation begins (see Comment *e(v)* hereto). The appropriate course of action in such situations might vary with the circumstances, as indicated in the following Comments.

e(i). Withdrawal or consent in typical cases of postrepresentation conflict. If a lawyer withdraws from representation of multiple clients because of a conflict of interest (or for any other reason), the rule stated in § 132 prohibits representation in the same or a substantially related matter of a remaining client whose interests in the matter are materially adverse to the interests of a now-former client. For example, two clients previously represented by lawyers in a firm in the same transaction pursuant to effective consent might thereafter have a falling out such that litigation is in prospect (see §§ 130 & 128). The firm may not withdraw from representing one client and take an adversary position against that client in behalf of the other in the subsequent litigation (see § 132, Comment *c*). The firm must obtain informed consent from both clients (see § 122) or withdraw entirely. Consent in advance to such continued representation may also be provided as stated in § 122, Comment *d*. The fact that neither joint client could assert the attorney-client privilege in subsequent litigation between them (see § 75) does not by itself negate the lawyer's more extensive obligations of confidentiality under § 60 and loyalty under § 16(1).

e(ii). Successive representations involving no conflict. A lawyer or firm might be in a position to withdraw from fewer than all the representations in a joint-client representation and thereby remove a conflict if it is possible after withdrawal for the lawyer to continue representation only with respect to matters not substantially related to the former representation (compare § 132) or with respect to related matters for clients that are not adverse to the now-former client.

Illustration:

11. The same facts as in Illustration 5, except that Law Firm represented Bank in negotiating the loan agreement. That was done after Law Firm obtained the effective consent of Manufacturer, although the consent did not extend to representation of Bank in possible future litigation concerning the agreement (see § 122, Comments *d-f*). The clients have now reached a point of serious difference over the agreement. Law Firm must cure the resulting conflict by renewed informed consents or by withdrawal. If either Bank or Manufacturer is unwilling to consent, Law Firm must withdraw from further representing Bank in the dispute over the agreement. However, Law Firm may continue to represent Bank and Manufacturer in their unrelated, separate matters because in those matters, as in Illustration 5, there is no conflict of interest between the clients.

e(iii). *Withdrawal due to revocation of consent.* On the effect of one client's revocation of consent on a lawyer's ability to continue representing other clients, see § 122, Comment *f*.

e(iv). *Withdrawal from representing an "accommodation" client.* On representing a regular client after withdrawal from representation of another client undertaken for a limited purpose and as an accommodation to the clients, see § 132, Comment *i*.

e(v). *Withdrawal to cure a conflict created by a business transaction of a client.* On continuing to represent a client after that client's opponent in litigation has been acquired by another of the lawyer's clients, see § 132, Comment *j*.

f. *Sanctions and remedies for conflicts of interest.* In addition to the sanction of professional discipline, disqualifying a lawyer from further participation in a pending matter is a common remedy for conflicts of interest in litigation (§ 6, Comment *i*). For matters not before a tribunal where disqualification can be sought, an injunction against a lawyer's further participation in the matter is a comparable remedy (§ 6, Comment *c*).

When a conflict of interest has caused injury to a client, the remedy of legal malpractice is available (§§ 48 and following). Availability of the sanction of fee forfeiture is considered in § 37. If the result in a matter was affected prejudicially by conflicting loyalties or misuse of confidential information by the lawyer, the result will sometimes be reversed or set aside. Some conflicts of interest subject a lawyer to criminal sanctions.

In general, whether a particular sanction or remedy is appropriate in a specific instance depends on the relationship between the lawyer and client or clients involved, the nature and seriousness of the conflict, the circumstances giving rise to the conflict and its avoidability, and the consequences of the particular remedy sought. In some situations, even an appropriate process for determining conflicts of interest could result in a conflict going undetected for a period of time. For example, the fact that someone in a law firm possesses confidential information that would be material in a pending matter (see § 132) might be difficult to ascertain in some cases. When a lawyer undertakes a representation that is later determined to involve a conflict of interest that could not reasonably have been and in fact was not identified at an earlier point (see Comment *g*), the lawyer is not liable for damages or subject to discipline.

g. Detecting conflicts. For the purpose of identifying conflicts of interest, a lawyer should have reasonable procedures, appropriate for the size and type of firm and practice, to detect conflicts of interest, including procedures to determine in both litigation and nonlitigation matters the parties and interests involved in each representation.

Based on concern about a conflict of interest under self-imposed standards more exacting than those of this Section, a lawyer ordinarily may decline a representation (see § 14) or withdraw as provided in § 32. A client may urge a lawyer to limit practice in conformance with the client's own more-exacting concepts of conflict, but the lawyer is not required to comply. The lawyer must not misrepresent the lawyer's standards to the client, for example by purporting to limit the lawyer's other representations but evading the restriction in secret. Moreover, the lawyer may not agree to such a limitation when doing so would violate applicable professional prohibitions against restricting by agreement a lawyer's right to practice law.

The reasonableness of a lawyer's initial determination concerning a conflict is subject to later review by a tribunal to the extent indicated in Comment *f*. When a lawyer is or should reasonably be aware that there is a substantial risk that the lawyer's representation of the client will be challenged on conflicts grounds and thus delay the representation to the client's material disadvantage or make it otherwise more expensive or burdensome for the client, the lawyer must either decline representation or consult with the client concerning the risk (see § 20) and proceed only with the informed consent of the client. If the representation has already commenced when an issue of conflict arises, the lawyer must consult with the client (see § 20) and proceed in the best interests of the client. On withdrawal, see § 32.

§ 122. Client Consent to a Conflict of Interest

(1) A lawyer may represent a client notwithstanding a conflict of interest prohibited by § 121 if each affected client or

former client gives informed consent to the lawyer's representation. Informed consent requires that the client or former client have reasonably adequate information about the material risks of such representation to that client or former client.

(2) Notwithstanding the informed consent of each affected client or former client, a lawyer may not represent a client if:

(a) the representation is prohibited by law;

(b) one client will assert a claim against the other in the same litigation; or

(c) in the circumstances, it is not reasonably likely that the lawyer will be able to provide adequate representation to one or more of the clients.

Comment:

* * *

b. Rationale. The prohibition against lawyer conflicts of interest is intended to assure clients that a lawyer's work will be characterized by loyalty, vigor, and confidentiality (see § 121, Comment *b*). The conflict rules are subject to waiver through informed consent by a client who elects less than the full measure of protection that the law otherwise provides. For example, a client in a multiple representation might wish to avoid the added costs that separate representation often entails. Similarly, a client might consent to a conflict where that is necessary in order to obtain the services of a particular law firm.

Other considerations, however, limit the scope of a client's power to consent to a conflicted representation. A client's consent will not be effective if it is based on an inadequate understanding of the nature and severity of the lawyer's conflict (Comment *c* hereto), violates law (Comment *g(i)*), or if the client lacks capacity to consent (Comment *c*). Client consent must also, of course, be free of coercion. Consent will also be insufficient to permit conflicted representation if it is not reasonably likely that the lawyer will be able to provide adequate representation to the affected clients, or when a lawyer undertakes to represent clients who oppose each other in the same litigation (Comment *g(iii)*).

In effect, the consent requirement means that each affected client or former client has the power to preclude the representation by withholding consent. When a client withholds consent, a lawyer's power to withdraw from representation of that client and proceed with the representation of the other client is determined under § 121, Comment *e*.

While a lawyer may elect to proceed with a conflicted representation after effective client consent as stated in this Section, a lawyer is not required to do so (compare § 14, Comment *g* (required representation by order of court)). A lawyer might be unwilling to accept the risk that a consenting client will later become disappointed with the representation and contend that the consent was defective, or the lawyer might conclude for other reasons that the lawyer's own interests do not warrant proceeding. In such an instance, the lawyer also may elect to withdraw if grounds permitting withdrawal are present under § 32. After withdrawal, a lawyer's ability to represent other clients is as described in § 121, Comment *e*.

c(i).   The requirement of informed consent—adequate information. Informed consent requires that each affected client be aware of the material respects in which the representation could have adverse effects on the interests of that client. The information required depends on the nature of the conflict and the nature of the risks of the conflicted representation. The client must be aware of information reasonably adequate to make an informed decision.

Information relevant to particular kinds of conflicts is considered in several of the Sections hereafter. In a multiple-client situation, the information normally should address the interests of the lawyer and other client giving rise to the conflict; contingent, optional, and tactical considerations and alternative courses of action that would be foreclosed or made less readily available by the conflict; the effect of the representation or the process of obtaining other clients' informed consent upon confidential information of the client; any material reservations that a disinterested lawyer might reasonably harbor about the arrangement if such a lawyer were representing only the client being advised; and the consequences and effects of a future withdrawal of consent by any client, including, if relevant, the fact that the lawyer would withdraw from representing all clients (see § 121, Comment *e*). Where the conflict arises solely because a proposed representation will be adverse to an existing client in an unrelated matter, knowledge of the general nature and scope of the work being performed for each client normally suffices to enable the clients to decide whether or not to consent.

When the consent relates to a former-client conflict (see § 132), it is necessary that the former client be aware that the consent will allow the former lawyer to proceed adversely to the former client. Beyond that, the former client must have adequate information about the implications (if not readily apparent) of the adverse representation, the fact that the lawyer possesses the former client's confidential information, the measures that the former lawyer might undertake to protect against unwarranted disclosures, and the right of the former client to refuse consent. The former client will often be independently represented by counsel. If so, communication with the former client ordinarily must be through successor counsel (see § 99 and following).

The lawyer is responsible for assuring that each client has the necessary information. A lawyer who does not personally inform the client assumes the risk that the client is inadequately informed and that the consent is invalid. A lawyer's failure to inform the clients might also bear on the motives and good faith of the lawyer. On the other hand, clients differ as to their sophistication and experience, and situations differ in terms of their complexity and the subtlety of the conflicts presented. The requirements of this Section are satisfied if the client already knows the necessary information or learns it from other sources. A client independently represented—for example by inside legal counsel or by other outside counsel—will need less information about the consequences of a conflict but nevertheless may have need of information adequate to reveal its scope and severity. When several lawyers represent the same client, responsibility to make disclosure and obtain informed consent may be delegated to one or more of the lawyers who appears reasonably capable of providing adequate information.

Disclosing information about one client or prospective client to another is precluded if information necessary to be conveyed is confidential (see § 60). The affected clients may consent to disclosure (see § 62), but it also might be possible for the lawyer to explain the nature of undisclosed information in a manner that nonetheless provides an adequate basis for informed consent. If means of adequate disclosure are unavailable, consent to the conflict may not be obtained.

The requirement of consent generally requires an affirmative response by each client. Ambiguities in a client's purported expression of consent should be construed against the lawyer seeking the protection of the consent (cf. § 18). In general, a lawyer may not assume consent from a client's silent acquiescence. However, consent may be inferred from active participation in a representation by a client who has reasonably adequate information about the material risks of the representation after a lawyer's request for consent. Even in the absence of consent, a tribunal applying remedies such as disqualification (see § 121, Comment *f*) will apply concepts of estoppel and waiver when an objecting party has either induced reasonable reliance on the absence of objection or delayed an unreasonable period of time in making objection.

Effective client consent to one conflict is not necessarily effective with respect to other conflicts or other matters. A client's informed consent to simultaneous representation of another client in the same matter despite a conflict of interest (see Topic 3) does not constitute consent to the lawyer's later representation of the other client in a manner that would violate the former-client conflict rule (see § 132; see also § 121, Comment *e(i)*).

Illustration:

    1. Client A and Client B give informed consent to a joint representation by Lawyer to prepare a commercial contract. Lawyer's bill for legal services is paid by both clients and the matter is terminated. Client B then retains Lawyer to file a lawsuit against former Client A on the asserted ground that A breached the contract. Lawyer may not represent Client B against Client A in the lawsuit without A's informed consent (see § 132). Client A's earlier consent to Lawyer's joint representation to draft the contract does not itself permit Lawyer's later adversarial representation.

c(ii).   The requirement of informed consent—the capacity of the consenting person. Each client whose consent is required must have the legal capacity to give informed consent. Consent purportedly given by a client who lacks legal capacity to do so is ineffective. Consent of a person under a legal disability normally must be obtained from a guardian or conservator appointed for the person. Consent of a minor normally is effective when given by a parent or guardian of the minor. In class actions certification of the class, determination that the interests of its members are congruent, and assessment of the adequacy of representation are typically made by a tribunal.

In some jurisdictions, a governmental unit might lack legal authority under applicable law to give consent to some conflicts of interest (see Comment *g(ii)* below).

When the person who normally would make the decision whether or not to give consent—members of a corporate board of directors, for example—is another interested client of the lawyer, or is otherwise self-interested in the decision whether to consent, special requirements apply to consent (see §§ 131 & 135, Comment *d*). Similarly, an officer of a government agency capable of consenting might be disabled from giving consent when that officer is a lawyer personally interested in consenting to the conflict.

d.   Consent to future conflicts. Client consent to conflicts that might arise in the future is subject to special scrutiny, particularly if the consent is general. A client's open-ended agreement to consent to all conflicts normally should be ineffective unless the client possesses sophistication in the matter in question and has had the opportunity to receive independent legal advice about the consent. A client's informed consent to a gift to a lawyer (see § 127) ordinarily should be given contemporaneously with the gift.

On the other hand, particularly in a continuing client-lawyer relationship in which the lawyer is expected to act on behalf of the client without a new engagement for each matter, the gains to both lawyer and client from a system of advance consent to defined future conflicts might be substantial. A client might, for example, give informed consent in advance to types of conflicts that are familiar to the client. Such an agreement could effectively protect the client's interest while assuring that the lawyer did not undertake a potentially disqualifying representation.

Illustrations:

2.   Law Firm has represented Client in collecting commercial claims through Law Firm's New York office for many years. Client is a long-established and sizable business corporation that is sophisticated in commercial matters generally and specifically in dealing with lawyers. Law Firm also has a Chicago office that gives tax advice to many companies with which Client has commercial dealings. Law Firm asks for advance consent from Client with respect to

conflicts that otherwise would prevent Law Firm from filing commercial claims on behalf of Client against the tax clients of Law Firm's Chicago office (see § 128). If Client gives informed consent the consent should be held to be proper as to Client. Law Firm would also be required to obtain informed consent from any tax client of its Chicago office against whom Client wishes to file a commercial claim, should Law Firm decide to undertake such a representation.

3. The facts being otherwise as stated in Illustration 2, Law Firm seeks advance consent from each of its Chicago-office corporate-tax clients to its representation of any of its other clients in matters involving collection of commercial claims adverse to such tax clients if the matters do not involve information that Law Firm might have learned in the tax representation. To provide further assurance concerning the protection of confidential information, the consent provides that, should Law Firm represent any client in a collection matter adverse to a tax client, a procedure to protect confidential information of the tax client will be established (compare § 124, Comment *d*). Unless such a tax client is shown to be unsophisticated about legal matters and relationships with lawyers, informed consent to the arrangement should be held to be proper.

If a material change occurs in the reasonable expectations that formed the basis of a client's informed consent, the new conditions must be brought to the attention of the client and new informed consent obtained (see also Comment *f* hereto (client revocation of consent)). If the new conflict is not consentable (see Comment *g* hereto), the lawyer may not proceed.

e. Partial or conditional consent. A client's informed consent to a conflict can be qualified or conditional. A client might consent, for example, to joint representation with one co-party but not another. Similarly, the client might condition consent on particular action being taken by the lawyer or law firm. For example, a former client might consent that the conflict of one individually prohibited lawyer should not be imputed (see § 123) to the rest of the firm, but only if the firm takes steps to assure that the prohibited lawyer is not involved in the representation (see § 124; see also Illustration 3 hereto). Such a partial or conditional consent can be valid even if an unconditional consent in the same situation would be invalid. For example, a client might give informed consent to a lawyer serving only in the role of mediator between clients (see § 130, Comment *d*), but not to the lawyer representing those clients opposing each other in litigation if mediation is unavailing (see Comment *g(iii)* hereto).

f. Revocation of consent through client action or a material change of circumstances. A client who has given informed consent to an otherwise conflicted representation may at any time revoke the consent (see § 21(2)). Revoking consent to the client's own representation, however, does not necessarily prevent the lawyer from continuing to represent other clients who had been jointly represented along with the revoking client. Whether the lawyer may continue the other representation depends on whether the client was justified in revoking the consent (such as because of a material change in the factual basis on which the client originally gave informed consent) and whether material detriment to the other client or lawyer would result. In addition, if the client had reserved the prerogative of revoking consent, that agreement controls the lawyer's subsequent ability to continue representation of other clients.

A material change in the factual basis on which the client originally gave informed consent can justify a client in withdrawing consent. For example, in the absence of an agreement to the contrary, the consent of a client to be represented concurrently with another (see Topic 3) normally presupposes that the co-clients will not develop seriously antagonistic positions. If such antagonism develops, it might warrant revoking consent. If the conflict is subject to informed consent (see Comment *(g)(iii)* hereto), the lawyer must thereupon obtain renewed informed consent of the clients, now adequately informed of the change of circumstances. If the conflict is not consentable, or the lawyer cannot obtain informed consent from the other client or decides not to proceed with the representation, the lawyer must withdraw from representing all affected clients adverse to any former client in the matter (see § 121, Comment *e*).

A client who has given informed consent to be represented as a joint client with another would be justified in revoking the consent if the common lawyer failed to represent that client with reasonable loyalty (see Comment *h* hereto). The client would also be justified in revoking consent if a co-client materially violated the express or implied terms of the consent, such as by abusing the first client's confidential information through disclosing important information to third persons without justification. Improper behavior of the other client or the lawyer might indicate that one or both of them cannot be trusted to respect the legitimate interests of the consenting client.

Illustration:

4. Client A and Client B validly consent to be represented by Lawyer in operating a restaurant in a city. After a period of amicable and profitable collaboration, Client A reasonably concludes that Lawyer has begun to take positions against Client A and consistently favoring the interests of Client B in the business. Reasonably concerned that Lawyer is no longer properly serving the interests of both clients, Client A withdraws consent. Withdrawal of consent is effective and justified (see Comment *h* hereto). Lawyer may not thereafter continue representing either Client A or Client B in a matter adverse to the other and substantially related to Lawyer's former representation of the clients (see § 121, Comment *e(i)*).

In the absence of valid reasons for a client's revocation of consent, the ability of the lawyer to continue representing other clients depends on whether material detriment to the other client or lawyer would result and, accordingly, whether the reasonable expectations of those persons would be defeated. Once the client or former client has given informed consent to a lawyer's representing another client, that other client as well as the lawyer might have acted in reliance on the consent. For example, the other client and the lawyer might already have invested time, money, and effort in the representation. The other client might already have disclosed confidential information and developed a relationship of trust and confidence with the lawyer. Or, a client relying on the consent might reasonably have elected to forgo opportunities to take other action.

Illustrations:

5. On Monday, Client A and Client B validly consent to being represented by Lawyer in the same matter despite a conflict of interest. On Wednesday, before either Client B or Lawyer has taken or forgone any significant action in reliance, Client A withdraws consent. Lawyer is no longer justified in continuing with the joint representation. Lawyer also may not continue to represent Client B alone without A's renewed informed consent to Lawyer's representation of B if doing so would violate other Sections of this Chapter, for example because A's and B's interests in the matter would be antagonistic or because Lawyer had learned confidential information from A relevant in the matter (see § 132; see also § 15, Comment c, & § 121, Comment e(i)). Similarly, if Client A on Wednesday did not unequivocally withdraw consent but stated to Lawyer that on further reflection Client A now had serious doubts about the wisdom of the joint representation, Lawyer could not reasonably take material steps in reliance on the consent. Before proceeding, Lawyer must clarify with Client A whether A indeed gives informed consent and whether the joint representation may thereby continue.

6. Clients A and B validly consent to Lawyer representing them jointly as co-defendants in a breach-of-contract action. On the eve of trial and after months of pretrial discovery on the part of all parties, Client A withdraws consent to the joint representation for reasons not justified by the conduct of Lawyer or Client B and insists that Lawyer cease representing Client B. At this point it would be difficult and expensive for Client B to find separate representation for the impending trial. Client A's withdrawal of consent is ineffective to prevent the continuing representation of B in the absence of compelling considerations such as harmful disloyalty by Lawyer.

7. Client A, who consulted Lawyer about a tax question, gave informed advance consent to Lawyer's representing any of Lawyer's

other clients against Client A in matters unrelated to Client A's tax question. Client B, who had not theretofore been a client of Lawyer, wishes to retain Lawyer to file suit against Client A for personal injuries suffered in an automobile accident. After Lawyer informs Client B of the nature of Lawyer's work for Client A, and the nature and risks presented by any conflict that might be produced, Client B consents to the conflict of interest. After Lawyer has undertaken substantial work in preparation of Client B's case, Client A seeks to withdraw the advance consent for reasons not justified by the conduct of Lawyer or Client B. Even though Client A was Lawyer's client before Client B was a client, the material detriment to both Lawyer and Client B would render Client A's attempt to withdraw consent ineffective.

The terms of the consent itself can control the effects of revocation of consent. A client's consent could state that it is conditioned on the client's right to revoke consent at any time for any reason. If so conditioned, the consent would cease to be effective if the client exercised that right.

g.   Nonconsentable conflicts. Some conflicts of interest preclude adverse representation even if informed consent is obtained.

g(i).   Representations prohibited by law. As stated in Subsection (2)(a), informed consent is unavailing when prohibited by applicable law. In some states, for example, the law provides that the same lawyer may not represent more than one defendant in a capital case and that informed consent does not cure the conflict (see § 129, Comment *c*). Under federal criminal statutes, certain representations by a former government lawyer (cf. § 133) are prohibited, and informed consent by the former client is not recognized as a defense.

g(ii).   Consent by governmental clients. Decisional law in a minority of states has limited the extent to which a governmental client may consent to a conflict of interest. Subject to local law on the powers of governmental bodies and the requirement that any consenting governmental officer must be disinterested in the issues giving rise to the question of conflict (see Comment *c(ii)* hereto), such questions should otherwise be decided under the customary rules governing conflicts of interest.

g(iii).   Conflicts between adversaries in litigation. When clients are aligned directly against each other in the same litigation, the institutional interest in vigorous development of each client's position renders the conflict nonconsentable (see § 128, Comment *c*, & § 129). The rule applies even if the parties themselves believe that the common interests are more significant in the matter than the interests dividing them. While the parties might give informed consent to joint representation for purposes of negotiating their differences (see § 130, Comment *d*), the joint representation may not continue if the parties become opposed to each other in litigation.

Illustration:

8. A and B wish to obtain an amicable dissolution of their marriage. State law treats marriage dissolution as a contested judicial proceeding. Lawyer is asked to represent both A and B in negotiation of the property settlement to be submitted to the court in the proceeding. Informed consent can authorize Lawyer to represent both parties in the property-settlement negotiations (subject to exceptions in some jurisdictions, where interests of children are involved, for example), but consent does not authorize Lawyer to represent both A and B if litigation is necessary to obtain the final decree. The parties may agree that Lawyer will represent only one of them in the judicial proceeding. The other party would either be represented by another lawyer or appear pro se (see §§ 128 & 130).

Whether clients are aligned directly against each other within the meaning of this Comment requires examination of the context of the litigation. In multi-party litigation, a single lawyer might, for example, represent members of a class in a class action, multiple creditors or debtors in a bankruptcy proceeding, or multiple interested parties in environmental clean-up litigation (see § 128). Joint representation is appropriate following effective client consent, together with compliance with applicable statutory or rule requirements, which may require court approval of the representation after disclosure of the conflict. Such joint representation is appropriate, notwithstanding that the co-clients may have conflicting claims against each other in other matters as to which the lawyer is not providing representation. The clients may also give informed consent to joint representation while they negotiate any differences they may have in the matter in litigation, perhaps employing the lawyer as appropriate in such negotiations (see § 130, Comments c & d), or prior agreement on such negotiated matters may be a condition of the clients' consent (see Comment e hereto). Where the alignment of parties, clients, and claims is such that the lawyer will not oppose another client with respect to the matters of dispute between them, as indicated in § 122(2)(b), there is no conflict. Thus, in complex litigation, the same lawyer may represent two defendants with largely congruent positions with respect to their defense, if other counsel are representing the two clients with respect to a dispute between them.

g(iv). Other circumstances rendering a lawyer incapable of providing adequate representation. Concern for client autonomy generally warrants respecting a client's informed consent. In some situations, however, joint representation would be objectively inadequate despite a client's voluntary and informed consent. In criminal cases, for example, joint representation of co-defendants with irreconcilable or unreconciled interests might render their representation constitutionally inadequate and thus require a court to prohibit the joint representation (see § 129, Comment c). Similarly, a conflict of interest among class members might render a lawyer's representation in a class action inadequate despite informed consent by the class representatives (see § 128, Comment *d*; see also, e.g., § 131, Comment *f*, Illustration 5).

The general standard stated in Subsection (2)(c) assesses the likelihood that the lawyer will, following consent, be able to provide adequate representation to the clients. The standard includes the requirements both that the consented-to conflict not adversely affect the lawyer's relationship with either client and that it not adversely affect the representation of either client. In general, if a reasonable and disinterested lawyer would conclude that one or more of the affected clients could not consent to the conflicted representation because the representation would likely fall short in either respect, the conflict is nonconsentable.

Decisions holding that a conflict is nonconsentable often involve facts suggesting that the client, who is often unsophisticated in retaining lawyers, was not adequately informed or was incapable of adequately appreciating the risks of the conflict (compare Comments *c(i)* & *c(ii)* hereto). Decisions involving clients sophisticated in the use of lawyers, particularly when advised by independent counsel, such as by inside legal counsel, rarely hold that a conflict is nonconsentable.

The nature of the conflict is also important. The professional rules and court decisions indicate that informed consent will always suffice with respect to a former-client conflict of interest (§ 132). With respect to simultaneous-representation conflicts (Topic 3), when the matters are unrelated it would only be in unusual circumstances that a lawyer could not provide adequate representation with consent of all affected clients. On the other hand, when the representation involves the same matter or the matters are significantly related, it may be more difficult for the lawyer to provide adequate legal assistance to multiple clients (see, e.g., § 131, Comment *e*, Illustration 4).

Illustrations:

9.   Lawyer occasionally represents Bank in collection matters and is doing so currently in one lawsuit. Employee requests Lawyer to file an employment-discrimination charge against Bank. Bank, acting through its inside legal counsel, gives informed consent to Lawyer's representation of Employee against Bank with respect to the matter. Employee, following discussion with Lawyer concerning the nature of Lawyer's collection representations of Bank, freely gives informed consent as well. The circumstances indicate no basis for concluding that Lawyer would be unable to provide adequate representation to Bank in the collection matters and to Employee in the discrimination claim against Bank.

10.   Lawyer has been asked by Buyer and Seller to represent both of them in negotiating and documenting a complex real-estate transaction. The parties are in sharp disagreement on several impor-

tant terms of the transaction. Given such differences, Lawyer would be unable to provide adequate representation to both clients.

11. The facts being otherwise as stated in Illustration 10, the parties are both in agreement on terms and possess comparable knowledge and experience in such transactions, but, viewed objectively, the transaction is such that both parties should receive extensive counseling concerning their rights in the transaction and possible optional arrangements, including security interests, guarantees, and other rights against each other and in resisting the claims of the other party for such rights. Given the scope of legal representation that each prospective client should receive, Lawyer would be unable to provide adequate representation to both clients.

A conflict can be rendered nonconsentable because of personal circumstances affecting the lawyer's ability in fact to provide adequate representation. For example, if the lawyer has such strong feelings of friendship toward one of two prospective joint clients that the lawyer could not provide adequate representation to the other client (compare Comment *h* hereto), the lawyer may not proceed with the joint representation.

h. Duties of a lawyer representing a client subject to a conflict consent. When a lawyer undertakes representation despite a conflict and after required disclosure and informed consent, the lawyer must represent all affected clients diligently and competently (see § 16) and must not regard informed consent as a basis for limiting the scope of the representation or favoring the interests of one client over the interests of another, except as expressly agreed under the informed consent. The lawyer must protect the confidential information of all affected clients (see § 60), subject to whatever modifications are warranted pursuant to the informed consent. On communicating information with each client in the absence of a different agreement among co-clients, see § 60, Comment *l*, and § 75, Comment *d*.

§ 123. Imputation of a Conflict of Interest to an Affiliated Lawyer

Unless all affected clients consent to the representation under the limitations and conditions provided in § 122 or unless imputation hereunder is removed as provided in § 124, the restrictions upon a lawyer imposed by §§ 125–135 also restrict other affiliated lawyers who:

(1) are associated with that lawyer in rendering legal services to others through a law partnership, professional corporation, sole proprietorship, or similar association;

(2) are employed with that lawyer by an organization to render legal services either to that organization or to others to advance the interests or objectives of the organization; or

(3) share office facilities without reasonably adequate measures to protect confidential client information so that it will not be available to other lawyers in the shared office.

§ 124. Removing Imputation

(1) Imputation specified in § 123 does not restrict an affiliated lawyer when the affiliation between the affiliated lawyer and the personally prohibited lawyer that required the imputation has been terminated, and no material confidential information of the client, relevant to the matter, has been communicated by the personally prohibited lawyer to the affiliated lawyer or that lawyer's firm.

(2) Imputation specified in § 123 does not restrict an affiliated lawyer with respect to a former-client conflict under § 132, when there is no substantial risk that confidential information of the former client will be used with material adverse effect on the former client because:

(a) any confidential client information communicated to the personally prohibited lawyer is unlikely to be significant in the subsequent matter;

(b) the personally prohibited lawyer is subject to screening measures adequate to eliminate participation by that lawyer in the representation; and

(c) timely and adequate notice of the screening has been provided to all affected clients.

(3) Imputation specified in § 123 does not restrict a lawyer affiliated with a former government lawyer with respect to a conflict under § 133 if:

(a) the personally prohibited lawyer is subject to screening measures adequate to eliminate involvement by that lawyer in the representation; and

(b) timely and adequate notice of the screening has been provided to the appropriate government agency and to affected clients.

Comment:

a. Scope and cross-references. This Section removes the prohibition of § 123 from affiliated lawyers when the justifications for imputation are insignificant. This Section presupposes that a lawyer in an affiliation is personally prohibited from a representation or action pursuant to §§ 125–135; that the affected client or clients have not consented as provided in § 122 to representation despite the conflict; and that applying § 123 would impute the prohibition to affiliated lawyers but for the operation of this Section.

Subsection (1) removes imputation when a lawyer or firm of lawyers possesses no material confidential information relevant to the matter. Subsection (2) removes imputation under § 132 when the confidential information is unlikely to be significant in the matter and an appropriate screen is erected. Subsection (3) removes, also through effective screening, imputation under § 133; it removes imputation even when the confidential information may be significant in the succeeding representation.

A lawyer's general obligation to preserve confidential client information is considered in § 60 and throughout Chapter 5. On limiting conflicts of interest in the case of prospective clients, see § 15.

b. Rationale. Imputation creates burdens both for clients and lawyers. Some clients who wish to be represented by a trusted or highly recommended lawyer or law firm must forgo the engagement. A single personally prohibited lawyer can conflict out literally hundreds of lawyers in a firm. Prospective imputed prohibition inhibits mobility of lawyers from one firm or employer to another. The burden of prohibition should end when material risks to confidentiality and loyalty resulting from shared income and access to information have been avoided by appropriate measures (see Comment *d* hereto).

c. Imputation after the termination of an affiliation.

c(i). Personally prohibited lawyer terminates the affiliation. During the time that a personally prohibited lawyer is associated with another lawyer, law firm, or other organization to which prohibition is imputed under § 123, the lawyer could reveal confidential information to any other lawyer within the organization. Accordingly, imputed prohibition of all lawyers in the firm is appropriately required by § 123. However, after the personally prohibited lawyer has left the firm, an irrebuttable presumption of continued sharing of client confidences or continued disloyalty induced by the affiliation is no longer justified.

The lawyers remaining in the affiliation may rebut the presumption that confidential information was shared during the period of actual affiliation. They have the burden of persuasion concerning three facts: (1) that no material confidential client information relevant to the matter was revealed to any lawyer remaining in the firm; (2) that the firm does not now possess or have access to sources of client confidential information, particularly client documents or files; and (3) that the personally prohibited lawyer will not share fees in the matter so as to have an interest in the representation.

Illustration:

1. Lawyer A is a partner in ABC law firm, and Lawyer B formerly was a partner. Client X has sought to retain Lawyer A to file suit on behalf of X against Y. Before joining the ABC firm, Lawyer B had represented Y at an earlier stage of the current dispute. Lawyer B has now resigned from the ABC firm, disclosed no confidential information about Y relevant to the matter to other

lawyers in ABC, left no files at ABC that relate to the proposed suit, and will not share in fees derived by the ABC firm from the representation of X. The limitation governing B, resulting from the proposed representation being substantially related to the prior representation of Y by B (see § 132), is no longer imputed to A. Hence A may represent Client X against Y.

A personally prohibited lawyer who enters a new law firm or other affiliation causes imputed prohibition of all affiliated lawyers as stated in § 123. Such imputation is subject to removal under Subsection (2) or (3).

c(ii). A non-personally-prohibited lawyer terminates the affiliation. When a lawyer leaves a firm or other organization whose lawyers were subject to imputed prohibition owing to presence in the firm of another lawyer, the departed lawyer becomes free of imputation so long as that lawyer obtained no material confidential client information relevant to the matter. Similarly, lawyers in the new affiliation are free of imputed prohibition if they can carry the burden of persuading the finder of fact that the arriving lawyer did not obtain confidential client information about a questioned representation by another lawyer in the former affiliation.

Illustration:

> 2. Client X has sought to retain Lawyer A, a partner in the firm of ABC, to represent X in a suit against Y. The suit has not yet been filed. Lawyer A is required to decline the representation because Y is also a client of Lawyer B in ABC. Lawyer A resigns from the ABC firm without having learned material confidential information of Y relevant to X's claim. The imputed disqualification is thereby removed, and Lawyer A may now represent Client X.

d. Screening against the risk of misuse of confidential information.

d(i). Screening—in general. Three situations must be distinguished. First, a lawyer's minor involvement in a matter for a former client might have involved no or so little exposure to confidential information that no conflict should be found (see § 132, Comment *h*). Second, the lawyer's involvement might have been more substantial, rendering the lawyer personally prohibited from the representation by reason of a former-client conflict of interest (see § 132), but screening may be appropriate under Subsection (2). A common instance in which this may be true is that of a junior lawyer in a law firm who provides minimal assistance on a peripheral element of a transaction, thereby gaining little confidential information that would be relevant in the later matter. Third, in the circumstances the lawyer's involvement and the nature and relevance of confidential information in the lawyer's possession might be such that screening will not remove imputation under Subsection (2). Determining which result is appropriate requires careful analysis of the particular facts.

If the requirements of either Subsection (2) or (3) are met, imputation is removed and consent to the representation by the former client is not required. The required screening measures must be imposed in the subsequent representation at the time the conflict is discovered or reasonably should have been discovered, and they must be of sufficient scope, continuity, and duration to assure that there will be no substantial risk to confidential client information.

Lawyer codes generally recognize the screening remedy in cases involving former government lawyers who have returned to private practice (see Comment e hereto). Screening to prevent imputation from former private-client representations has similar justification, giving clients wider choice of counsel and making it easier for lawyers to change employers. The rule in Subsection (2) thus permits screening as a remedy in situations in which the information possessed by a personally prohibited lawyer is not likely to be significant. The lawyer or firm seeking to remove imputation has the burden of persuasion that there is no substantial risk that confidential information of the former client will be used with material adverse effect on the former client.

Significance of the information is determined by its probable utility in the later representation, including such factors as the following: (1) whether the value of the information as proof or for tactical purposes is peripheral or tenuous; (2) whether the information in most material respects is now publicly known; (3) whether the information was of only temporary significance; (4) the scope of the second representation; and (5) the duration and degree of responsibility of the personally prohibited lawyer in the earlier representation.

The lawyer codes in most states impose disciplinary responsibility in a wider range of circumstances of former private-client representations. Specifically, most codes do not recognize that screening can preclude disqualification of a law firm by imputation from a personally prohibited lawyer, even if the screening is timely and effective and the client information involved is innocuous. The issue typically arises under motions to disqualify, not in disciplinary proceedings. A tribunal has discretion whether or not to require disqualification. Subsection (2) states a rule to guide exercise of that discretion.

Illustrations:

3. As can readily be shown from contemporaneous time records, when Lawyer was an associate in Law Firm ABC, Lawyer spent one-half hour in conversation with another associate about research strategies involving a narrow issue of venue in federal court in the case of Developer v. Bank, in which the firm represented Bank. The conversation was based entirely on facts pleaded in the complaint and answer, and Lawyer learned no confidential information about the matter. Lawyer then left Firm ABC and became an associate in Firm DEF. Two years later, Lawyer was asked to represent Developer against Bank in a matter substantially

related to the matter in which Firm ABC represented Bank. In the circumstances, due to the proven lack of exposure of Lawyer to confidential information of Bank, Bank should not be regarded as the former client of Lawyer for the purpose of applying § 132 (see § 132, Comment *h*). Alternatively, a tribunal may require that Lawyer be screened from participation in the matter as provided in this Section and, on that basis, permit other lawyers affiliated with Lawyer in Firm DEF to represent the client against Bank.

4. The same facts as Illustration 3, except that Lawyer while representing Bank in Firm ABC was principally in charge of developing factual information about the underlying dispute. The dispute involved a loan Bank made to Developer on Tract A in the city in which both conduct business. The dispute was resolved after extensive discovery and a full trial before Lawyer left Firm ABC. An affiliated lawyer in Lawyer's new firm, Firm DEF, has been asked to represent Developer in a dispute with Bank over a loan on Tract B. Because of the similarity of facts in the two disputes—involving both tracts, both loans, and both parties to them—a tribunal finds the matters are substantially related and accordingly that Lawyer is personally prohibited from representing Developer against Bank with respect to Tract B (see § 132). However, the tribunal also finds that, despite that factual overlap, the information Lawyer might have acquired about Bank would have little significance in the later dispute because it concerned only an earlier period of time so that any importance it might have had was significantly diminished by the time of the second dispute, because it mainly involves information already a matter of public record in the earlier trial, and because all factual information will be largely irrelevant in view of the fact that the pleadings indicate that the only contested issue in the second dispute involves a matter of contract interpretation. In the circumstances, the tribunal should further find that Firm DEF may represent Developer against Bank if Lawyer has been screened as provided in Subsection (2).

5. The same facts as Illustration 4, except that the earlier dispute was settled after Lawyer had conducted extensive examination of Bank's files but without any discovery by Developer's then counsel or trial. Little time has passed since Lawyer acquired the information from Bank, and the information remains highly relevant in the later dispute. The pleadings in the second dispute indicate that a large number of important factual issues similar to those in the earlier dispute remain open. In the circumstances, the likelihood that the information possessed by Lawyer will be significant in the second matter renders screening under this Section inappropriate.

d(ii). Screening—adequacy of measures. Screening must assure that confidential client information will not pass from the personally prohibited lawyer to any other lawyer in the firm. The screened lawyer should be prohibited from talking to other persons in the firm about the matter as to which the lawyer is prohibited, and from sharing documents about the matter and the like. Further, the screened lawyer should receive no direct financial benefit from the firm's representation, based upon the outcome of the matter, such as a financial bonus or a larger share of firm income directly attributable to the matter. However, it is not impermissible that the lawyer receives compensation and benefits under standing arrangements established prior to the representation. An adequate showing of screening ordinarily requires affidavits by the personally prohibited lawyer and by a lawyer responsible for the screening measures. A tribunal can require that other appropriate steps be taken.

If a lawyer in a law firm assertedly observing screening measures in fact breaches the screen and shares confidential information with lawyers proceeding adversely to the former client, the tribunal should take appropriate corrective measures. The screen should no longer be considered adequate to prevent disqualification of affiliated lawyers. Contempt might be an appropriate remedy to the extent that breach of the screen was knowing and deliberate and in violation of direct undertakings to the tribunal. In circumstances involving lesser culpability, lesser sanctions within the court's inherent power may be appropriate.

d(iii). Screening—timely and adequate notice of screening to all affected clients. An affected client will usually have difficulty demonstrating whether screening measures have been honored. Timely and adequate notice of the screening must therefore be given to the affected clients, including description of the screening measures reasonably sufficient to inform the affected client of their adequacy. Notice will give opportunity to protest and to allow arrangements to be made for monitoring compliance.

Notice should ordinarily be given as soon as practical after the lawyer or firm realizes or should realize the need for screening. Obligations of confidentiality to a current client, however, might justify reasonable delay. A firm advising about a possible takeover of a former client of a lawyer now in the firm, for example, need not provide notice until the attempt becomes known to the target client.

e. Screening a former government lawyer. As stated in Comment *d* hereto, avoidance of imputation by screening of former government lawyers is permitted in most lawyer codes. If hiring a former government lawyer would disqualify an entire firm from cases arising before that lawyer's agency, the lawyer would not likely be hired. That, in turn, would make it more difficult for the government to hire able lawyers at the outset.

The personally prohibited lawyer must be screened from any participation in the matter and should receive no direct financial benefit from the firm's representation as stated in Comment *d(ii).* Written notice must be given to the appropriate government agency so that it can ascertain compliance with the screening requirement. Those precautions prevent imputation even if the confidential information communicated to the lawyer in the prior matter is significant (see § 74 & § 133, Comment *b*).

In appropriate cases, the government may challenge screening as inadequate to protect the government's interest. For example, where a former prosecutor who personally knows the strengths and weaknesses of a criminal case has become affiliated with defense counsel, disqualification of defense counsel may be required despite screening. Similarly, where the lawyer acquires while in the government highly confidential information about a person whom an affiliated lawyer's client now opposes in a substantially related matter, a court has discretion to disqualify the entire firm to protect the confidentiality of the information.

TOPIC 2.   CONFLICTS OF INTEREST BETWEEN A LAWYER AND A CLIENT

§ 125. A Lawyer's Personal Interest Affecting the Representation of a Client

Unless the affected client consents to the representation under the limitations and conditions provided in § 122, a lawyer may not represent a client if there is a substantial risk that the lawyer's representation of the client would be materially and adversely affected by the lawyer's financial or other personal interests.

Comment:

a. Scope and cross-references. This Section is a specific application of the general conflicts standard expressed in § 121. Conflicts arising under this Section are imputed to affiliated lawyers pursuant to § 123, except as provided in Comment *g* hereto. Economic incentives created by particular forms of fee agreements are analogous to the conflicts raised in this Section, but they are separately considered. See, e.g., § 38 (agreements for contingent fee, hourly rates, and fixed fees); § 36(1) (lawyer acquisition of an interest in the subject matter of litigation); and § 36(3) (arrangements to secure media rights to a client's story). Issues presented when a third person pays a client's fee are considered in § 134. Section 135 addresses conflicts created by a lawyer's fiduciary or similar obligations to a nonclient.

Conflicts arising under this Section are subject to client consent to the extent and in the manner stated in § 122. Often only one client will be affected by a conflict under this Section, and only that client's informed consent is required.

Sanctions and remedies for violation of this Section are outlined in § 121, Comment *f*. Disqualification is ordinarily not a relevant remedy because the harm is suffered by the lawyer's client who may terminate the lawyer at any time (see § 32(1)). If the lawyer's personal interest is the proximate cause of harm to the client, the remedy of professional malpractice is available (see § 48 and following). If the breach of the lawyer's duty to the client is sufficiently serious, the lawyer can be required to forfeit the fee otherwise due (see § 37).

b. Rationale. Personal interests of a lawyer that are inconsistent with those of a client might significantly limit the lawyer's ability to pursue the client's interest. Even if a lawyer could subordinate significant personal interests to the interests of clients, it is difficult to determine after the fact whether a lawyer had succeeded in keeping a client's interests foremost.

c. A lawyer with a personal or financial interest adverse to an interest of a client. Client interests include all those that a reasonable lawyer, unaffected by a conflicting personal interest, would protect or advance. Perhaps the clearest case of a conflict is where the lawyer has a significant adverse financial interest in the object of the representation. Such a financial interest, other than one so insignificant that a person of normal sensibility would be unaffected by it, ordinarily constitutes a conflict of interest. A lawyer having such an interest is prohibited from accepting or continuing the representation unless the affected client gives informed consent.

A conflict under this Section need not be created by a financial interest. Included are interests that might be altruistic, such as an interest in furthering a charity favored by the lawyer, and matters of personal relationship, for example where the opposing party is the lawyer's spouse or a long-time friend or an institution with which the lawyer has a special relationship of loyalty. Such a conflict may also result from a lawyer's deeply held religious, philosophical, political, or public-policy beliefs. (On the limited imputation of such conflicts, see Comment *g* hereto.) A conflict exists if such an interest would materially impair the lawyer's ability to consider alternative courses of action that otherwise might be available to a client, to discuss all relevant aspects of the subject matter of the representation with the client, or otherwise to provide effective representation to the client. In some cases, a conflict between the personal or financial interests of a lawyer and those of a client will be so substantial that client consent will not suffice to remove the disability (see § 122, Comment *g*).

Illustrations:

1. Lawyer owns a 25 percent interest in a restaurant. Client was a customer at the restaurant and suffered severe food poisoning. Client has asked Lawyer to file suit against the restaurant for damages substantially in excess of insurance coverage. Lawyer's interest as investor in the restaurant might materially and adversely affect Lawyer's representation of Client. Because Client's recovery could significantly affect the value of Lawyer's investment interest,

Lawyer may not represent Client even if Client were to give informed consent (see § 122(2)).

2.   Same facts as in Illustration 1, except that Lawyer's child owns a five percent interest in the restaurant. Even though Lawyer owns no interest personally, concern about injuring the financial position or reputation of Lawyer's child might materially and adversely affect Lawyer's representation of Client. If Lawyer concludes that Lawyer can overcome the personal concerns involved and represent Client effectively, the representation may proceed if Client gives informed consent to the representation (see § 122).

3.   Lawyer owns stock in a publicly held mutual fund that, in turn, carries in its diversified portfolio an interest of less than one percent in the common stock of Ajax Corporation, a publicly held corporation that produces frozen foods. The value of Lawyer's indirect interest in Ajax Corporation is less than $25.00. Client developed food poisoning after eating frozen peas that had been processed by Ajax Corporation and has asked Lawyer to file suit for damages against it. The described interest is so small, and the possibility of an effect on Lawyer's representation is so remote, that Lawyer need not raise the possibility of a conflict of interest with Client.

A representation that commences with no prospect of a conflict might, because of a change of circumstances, require the lawyer thereupon to cease the representation or to obtain the client's informed consent. A lawyer who becomes aware of such a change must call the circumstances to the attention of the client and permit the client to determine whether the lawyer may continue the representation after client provides informed consent (see § 121, Comment *e(i)*)..

d.   A lawyer seeking employment with an opposing party or law firm. This Section applies when a lawyer seeks to discuss the possibility of the lawyer's future employment with an adversary or an adversary's law firm. The conflict arises whether the discussions about future employment are initiated by the lawyer or by the other side. If discussion of employment has become concrete and the interest in such employment is mutual, the lawyer must promptly inform the client. Without effective client consent (see § 122), the lawyer must terminate all further discussions concerning the employment, or withdraw from representing the client (see § 32(2) & (3)). The same protocol is required with respect to a merger of law firms or similar change (see § 123).

Illustration:

4.   Lawyer has been employed by Law Firm ABC for three years. For the last two of those years, Lawyer has worked on a case on behalf of Client against a company represented by Law Firm DEF. Lawyer decided to explore leaving Law Firm ABC. Lawyer wrote letters to 10 firms, including Law Firm DEF, to determine if they had any openings. Law Firm DEF indicated that it has an

opening and encouraged Lawyer to come for an interview. This Section does not require Lawyer, at the time of sending the initial letters, to inform Client of the possible relationship to Law Firm DEF. However, when Firm DEF responded favorably, the possibility of employment became both concrete and mutual. At that point, Lawyer must promptly notify Client, fully inform Client of the nature and consequences of the conflict, and obtain Client's voluntary consent before continuing the representation.

e. *A lawyer openly expressing public-policy views inconsistent with a client's position.* In general, a lawyer may publicly take personal positions on controversial issues without regard to whether the positions are consistent with those of some or all of the lawyer's clients. Consent of the lawyer's clients is not required. Lawyers usually represent many clients, and professional detachment is one of the qualities a lawyer brings to each client. Moreover, it is a tradition that a lawyer's advocacy for a client should not be construed as an expression of the lawyer's personal views. Resolution of many public questions is benefited when independent legal minds are brought to bear on them. For example, if tax lawyers advocating positions about tax reform were obliged to advocate only positions that would serve the positions of their present clients, the public would lose the objective contributions to policy making of some persons most able to help.

However, a lawyer's right to freedom of expression is modified by the lawyer's duties to clients. Thus, a lawyer may not publicly take a policy position that is adverse to the position of a client that the lawyer is currently representing if doing so would materially and adversely affect the lawyer's representation of the client in the matter. The requirement that a lawyer not misuse a client's confidential information (see § 60) similarly applies to discussion of public issues. On the right of a lawyer to withdraw from a representation because of disagreement with a client's views, see § 32.

Illustrations:

5. Lawyer currently represents Client, a large mining company with mining operations in Lawyer's state. Lawyer's work for Client includes lobbying before government agencies concerning restoration of strip-mined land. Lawyer has also been a long-time member of Seed, an organization with an interest in preserving the environment. Seed has proposed legislation that would require mining companies to restore strip-mined land to a fertile condition, legislation that Lawyer's work for Client will require Lawyer to oppose. Unless Lawyer obtains Client's informed consent (see § 122), Lawyer may not personally take a public position supporting the legislation.

6. Lawyer represents Corporation in negotiating with the Internal Revenue Service to permit Corporation to employ accelerated

depreciation methods for machinery purchased in a prior tax year. At the same time, Lawyer believes that the accelerated depreciation laws for manufacturing equipment reflect unwise public policy. Lawyer has been working with a bar-association committee to develop a policy statement against the allowance, and the committee chair has requested Lawyer to testify in favor of the report and its proposal to repeal all such depreciation allowances. Any new legislation, as is true generally of such tax enactments, would apply only for current and future tax years, thus not directly affecting Corporation's matter before the IRS. Although the proposed legislation would be against Corporation's economic interests, Lawyer may, without Corporation's consent, continue the representation of Corporation while working to repeal the allowance.

Whether a lawyer's interest in furthering the objectives of a client requires the lawyer to abstain from participating in professional forums is to be determined by the rules of those forums or the groups sponsoring them and is beyond the scope of the Restatement.

f. Initiation and settlement of class actions and other multiple-client representations. Class actions and similar proceedings can raise a number of personal-interest conflict-of-interest questions. A class action can transform a modest claim into a set of claims of large consequence and often has potential for magnifying attorney's fees. An individual plaintiff usually begins with a concern about an individual wrong, and prompt and complete redress of that wrong is often the client's goal. A class action might be the only practical means of vindicating the client interest. However, a class action can substitute a longer, more complex proceeding for one more beneficial for the client's individual interests. Where bringing a claim as a class action might materially and adversely affect the interests of the individual client, that possibility must be disclosed to that client. On the determination of client-lawyer relationships in class actions, see § 14, Comment *f.*

Settlement of a class action or similar suit can also create a conflict concerning the lawyer's fee. The defendant, for example, might offer to settle the matter for an amount or kind of relief that is relatively generous to the lawyer's client if the lawyer will agree to accept a low fee award. Conversely, the defendant might acquiesce in a generous award of attorney's fees in exchange for relatively modest relief for the client's substantive claim. The latter arrangement must be rejected by the class lawyer as subordinating the interests of the lawyer's client to the lawyer's own interest.

The lawyer should make reasonable effort to separate settlement of the substantive claim from determination of the amount of attorney's fees. Some decisions have attempted to effectuate that requirement by forbidding settlement discussions to address the fee that the lawyer is to receive. Some commentators have urged that a court refuse to approve a settlement unless award of reasonable attorney's fees is to be judicially determined rather than negotiated. Neither of those suggestions gives adequate effect to the interests of the client in all cases.

A more appropriate arrangement, where possible, is for the lawyer's fee to be negotiated initially by the client and lawyer at the outset of the relationship, it being understood and disclosed to the client that the ultimate award may be scrutinized by the opposing party and approved by the court (compare § 22, Comment c). On interpretation of agreements between client and lawyer concerning fee awards, see § 38, Comment f. On aggregate settlement of claims involving multiple clients who are not class members, see § 128, Comment d(i).

g. *Effect of personal-interest conflicts of associated lawyers.* The stated rule of the lawyer codes, followed in the Section and in § 123, is that personal-interest conflicts of a lawyer such as those described in this Section are imputed to affiliated lawyers. It may be appropriate not to impose any sanction if the personal-interest conflict was not known to the lawyer handling the matter and could not have been determined by use of a reasonable conflict-checking system. In addition, personal interests of a lawyer may be idiosyncratic or otherwise of such a kind that it is improbable that affiliated lawyers would be impaired in their representation of clients due to such interests. Consequently, one affiliated lawyer's personal interests that produce personal prohibition disable an affiliated lawyer from representing the same client only when there is a significant risk that the interests of the first lawyer would materially and adversely impair the second lawyer's representation. Whether such a risk exists requires examination of such facts as the magnitude of the interest of the personally prohibited lawyer, the extent to which pursuing the client's interests would threaten that interest, and the other circumstances that might indicate the described significant risk.

Illustration:

7.   Lawyer A has a strong philosophical or political aversion to the objectives of Landlord, whom Lawyer B in the same firm represents in eviction proceedings. Lawyer A's feelings are sufficiently strong that they would disable Lawyer A from providing effective representation to Landlord. Lawyer A therefore may not represent Landlord under the rule of this Section (see Comment c hereto). So long as Lawyer A has no part in the representation and no supervisory or other control over Lawyer B, there is no adequate basis for concluding that Lawyer A's personal interests should preclude Lawyer B from the representation.

§ 126. Business Transactions Between a Lawyer and a Client

A lawyer may not participate in a business or financial transaction with a client, except a standard commercial transaction in which the lawyer does not render legal services, unless:

(1) the client has adequate information about the terms of the transaction and the risks presented by the lawyer's involvement in it;

(2) the terms and circumstances of the transaction are fair and reasonable to the client; and

(3) the client consents to the lawyer's role in the transaction under the limitations and conditions provided in § 122 after being encouraged, and given a reasonable opportunity, to seek independent legal advice concerning the transaction.

Comment:

a. Scope and cross-references. This Section is a specific application of the general prohibition of conflicts of interest in § 121. Conduct that violates this Section is presumed to cause the material and adverse effect on representation that creates a conflict of interest under § 121. Accordingly, additional conditions for consent to a conflict are required beyond those specified by § 122, in particular that the transaction be objectively fair and reasonable and that the client have opportunity to obtain independent counsel. In contrast to § 125, there is no requirement that business transactions addressed in this Section have any adverse effect on any aspect of the client's representation aside from the transaction itself.

The prohibition in this Section is imputed to affiliated lawyers pursuant to § 123. Imputation is not provided for under the ABA Model Rules of Professional Conduct (1983) but is provided for in several jurisdictions following the ABA Model Code of Professional Responsibility (1969), which this Section follows. In all jurisdictions, a lawyer who enters into a business transaction—other than a standard commercial transaction in which the lawyer does not render legal services—with a client of an affiliated lawyer without complying with this Section does so at the risk that the transaction is voidable by the client and subject to other appropriate remedies (see § 121, Comment *f*).

The requirements of this Section do not apply to ordinary client-lawyer fee agreements providing, for example, for hourly, lump-sum, or contingent fees. They do apply when a lawyer takes an interest in the client's business as payment of all or part of a legal fee. Other financial arrangements are examined in Chapter 3, including the reasonableness of legal fees (see § 34; see also § 135 (acting as officer or director of a client)). With respect to conflict-of-interest issues that arise out of transactions involving a client and a business in which a lawyer has an interest, see § 125, Comment *c*.

In any civil proceeding between a lawyer and a client or their successors, the lawyer has the burden of persuading the tribunal that requirements stated in this Section have been satisfied. In a disciplinary, criminal, or similar proceeding, the burden of persuasion rests on the prosecution (see § 5 (lawyer discipline)). In a discipline case, once proof has been introduced that the lawyer entered into a business transaction with a client, the burden of persuasion is on the lawyer to show that the transaction was fair and reasonable and that the client was adequately informed.

b. Rationale. A lawyer's legal skill and training, together with the relationship of trust that arises between client and lawyer, create the possibility of overreaching when a lawyer enters into a business transaction with a client. Furthermore, a lawyer who engages in a business transaction with a client is in a position to arrange the form of the transaction or give legal advice to protect the lawyer's interests rather than advancing the client's interests. Proving fraud or actual overreaching might be difficult. Hence, the law does not require such a showing on the part of a client.

Illustration:

> 1. Lawyer, Investor, and Developer agree to form a corporation for the purpose of developing a residential subdivision. At the time, Lawyer represents both Investor and Developer as clients in other matters. Stock allocations are to be based on the agreed value of Investor's contributed land, the value of Developer's design and development services, and the value of Lawyer's legal services in organizing the enterprise and representing it thereafter. The arrangement constitutes a business transaction with a client and is subject to the requirements of this Section throughout the period during which the parties continue the arrangement.

This Section applies only to transactions of a lawyer with a client of the lawyer or of the lawyer's firm (see § 123). Transactions of a lawyer with a nonclient are not covered. While this Section does not apply to a lawyer's transaction with a former client, such a transaction is subject to challenge if the lawyer takes advantage of the lawyer's former position (see Restatement Second, Trusts § 170, Comment *g*).

c. Standard commercial transactions. The requirements of informed consent and objective fairness are satisfied when lawyer and client enter into standard commercial transactions in the regular course of business of the client, involving a product or service as to which the lawyer provides no legal services. This Section therefore does not apply to such transactions. Standard commercial transactions are those regularly entered into between the client and the general public, typically in which the terms and conditions are the same for all customers. In such circumstances, the client's interests in the transaction with the lawyer need no special protection. On the other hand, where a lawyer engages in the sale of goods or services ancillary to the practice of law, for example, the sale of title insurance, the requirements of this Section do apply.

d. A client's knowledge of the terms and the lawyer's role. A lawyer violates the standard of candor by entering into a transaction with a client as undisclosed principal, or without disclosing information or terms that might materially affect the client's bargain (see Restatement Second, Trusts § 170(2)).

Illustrations:

2. Lawyer represents the surviving Spouse of a long-time client. Lawyer advises Spouse that farmland owned by the estate should be sold to pay taxes. Using the name of a business associate as purported buyer, Lawyer purchases the land from Spouse without disclosing Lawyer's involvement in the purchase. Even if the price is objectively fair, Lawyer has violated the requirement that Lawyer's identity be disclosed to the client.

3. Lawyer has been helping Client negotiate the terms for the purchase of a boat. Client has experienced difficulties arranging financing and will lose a substantial deposit on the boat if Client cannot raise $30,000 by the end of the day. Lawyer has $30,000 in available cash. Lawyer agrees to lend the money to Client and, without explaining the agreement, has Client sign a security agreement in favor of Lawyer in properties owned by Client. When Client defaults on the loan, Lawyer files suit against Client to foreclose on the properties. Lawyer has violated this Section by failing to explain to Client the terms of the transaction. Client can, for example, rescind the transaction and prevent the foreclosure (see § 121, Comment *f*).

e. The requirement that the terms of the transaction be fair. The requirement that the transaction be fair from the perspective of an objective observer derives from the general fiduciary requirement of fair dealing with a client (see § 16(3); Restatement Second, Trusts § 170(2) & Comment *w* thereto). Unintended overreaching is a possibility in transactions involving lawyers and their clients. Accordingly a lawyer must overcome a presumption that overreaching occurred by demonstrating the fairness of the transaction. Fairness is determined based on facts that reasonably could be known at the time of the transaction, not as the facts later develop. The relative ability of lawyer and client to foresee how the facts might develop, however, is relevant in determining fairness. An appropriate test is whether a disinterested lawyer would have advised the client not to enter the transaction with some other party.

Illustrations:

4. Lawyer and Client agree to purchase a parcel of land together. Because Client lacks sufficient cash, Client borrows the money from Lawyer at an interest rate of 10 percent. That was the general market rate of interest on the date of the loan, but Lawyer

knew from discussions with another client, Banker, that Client would be able to borrow the same amount from several financial institutions at a lower rate of interest. Lawyer violated Lawyer's obligations to deal fairly with Client. Lawyer had reliable information, relevant to a material element of the transaction, that Lawyer failed to convey to Client.

f.   Consent only after encouragement and opportunity to obtain independent legal advice. The client must be encouraged and have a reasonable opportunity to obtain independent legal advice before entering into the transaction. There is no requirement that the client actually consult another lawyer. A client might determine to consult another trusted adviser, such as an accountant, a tax adviser, or a business person, or to consult no one at all.

An opportunity to obtain competent independent advice tends to assure that the client has time to consider the transaction and that the lawyer is not applying undue pressure on the client. By the same token, evidence that a lawyer has not allowed the client opportunity to obtain independent counsel is evidence of overreaching. An independent adviser also can bring an objective eye to the proposed arrangement.

Illustration:

> 5.   Lawyer helped negotiate for Client a sale of Client's family business for $1 million. Client, who was inexperienced in business or investments, asked Lawyer for help in investing the proceeds. Lawyer offered to borrow the money from Client at an interest rate of 15 percent. Lawyer prepared and signed a note evidencing the loan. Lawyer afforded Client no encouragement or opportunity to obtain independent advice before entering into the transaction. Lawyer has violated this Section.

g.   The requirement of written notice and consent. Lawyer codes commonly require that notice to the client and the client's consent to a business transaction with the client's lawyer be in writing. When required by law, disclosure to the client of the terms of the transaction must also be in writing. Absence of the required writing renders the transaction voidable at the client's option. Written notice focuses the client's attention upon the right to withhold consent and has important evidentiary value if a dispute later arises concerning the client's consent. The notice should provide the client sufficient time to enable the client to study the transaction and obtain independent advice.

§ 127. A Client Gift to a Lawyer

(1) A lawyer may not prepare any instrument effecting any gift from a client to the lawyer, including a testamentary gift, unless the lawyer is a relative or other natural object of the client's generosity and the gift is not significantly disproportionate to those given other donees similarly related to the donor.

(2) A lawyer may not accept a gift from a client, including a testamentary gift, unless:

    (a) the lawyer is a relative or other natural object of the client's generosity;

    (b) the value conferred by the client and the benefit to the lawyer are insubstantial in amount; or

    (c) the client, before making the gift, has received independent advice or has been encouraged, and given a reasonable opportunity, to seek such advice.

TOPIC 3. CONFLICTS OF INTEREST AMONG CURRENT CLIENTS

§ 128. Representing Clients with Conflicting Interests in Civil Litigation

Unless all affected clients consent to the representation under the limitations and conditions provided in § 122, a lawyer in civil litigation may not:

    (1) represent two or more clients in a matter if there is a substantial risk that the lawyer's representation of one client would be materially and adversely affected by the lawyer's duties to another client in the matter; or

    (2) represent one client to assert or defend a claim against or brought by another client currently represented by the lawyer, even if the matters are not related.

Comment:

a. Scope and cross-references. This Section applies the general conflicts standard in § 121 to situations in which a lawyer represents two or more parties in civil litigation. On identifying who is the lawyer's client within the meaning of this rule, see § 121, Comment *d*. Conflicts under this Section are subject to consent under the limitations and conditions provided in § 122. The conflicts are imputed to affiliated lawyers by § 123, and the imputation can be removed as described in § 124. On limiting conflicts of interest in the case of a prospective client, see § 15.

Multiple representation in criminal litigation is considered in § 129 and, in matters not involving litigation, in § 130. Conflicts arising when a lawyer represents both an entity and one or more of its officers, employees, or other associated persons are considered in § 131. Conflicts in filing and settling class actions are examined in § 125, as well as in this Section.

Remedies for violation of this Section include those set forth in § 121, Comment *f*. The most common remedy is the lawyer's disqualification from further representation of one or more clients in a matter (see § 6, Comment *i*). A suit for professional malpractice is available if a client has suffered damage as a result of a lawyer's conflict of interest (see § 48 and following). In appropriate cases, the lawyer is also subject to professional discipline (see § 5) or fee forfeiture (see § 37).

b. Rationale. Dealing with a conflict of interest among current clients requires reconciling four fundamental and sometimes competing values. First, confidential information of one client must not be used, intentionally or inadvertently, on behalf of another client in ways that would have material and adverse consequences for the disadvantaged client. Although such use violates the requirement of § 60(1), the fact of use will often be difficult to detect and therefore requires preventive measures. Second, the client's faith in the lawyer's loyalty to the client's interests will be severely tried whenever the lawyer must be loyal to another client whose interests are materially adverse. Third, a tribunal properly wishes assurance that its own processes not be compromised by less than vigorous advocacy, delayed by a necessary change of counsel in the course of the proceeding, or later reversed because a litigant was inadequately represented. Even if the parties would give informed consent to being represented by one lawyer, in some cases the parties' positions cannot be effectively presented through the same advocate (see § 122(2)(b) & Comment *g(iii)* thereto). Fourth, clients might want to reduce the costs of litigation and achieve the benefits of a coordinated position in their cases. Clients normally are allowed to give informed consent to a representation that otherwise would violate this Section.

c(i). Clients aligned in opposition to each other—in general. Fundamental conflicts of loyalty and threats to client confidentiality would be inevitable if a lawyer were to represent clients opposing each other in the same litigation. Many actions that the lawyer took on behalf of one client would have the potential for being at the expense of the other. Furthermore, the public interest in the orderly management of litigation could be seriously compromised. Thus, the same lawyer may not represent both plaintiff and defendant in a breach-of-contract lawsuit, for example. A similar rule applies, as stated in Subsection (2), when the clients are involved in two or more lawsuits that are otherwise unrelated. The rule of Subsection (2) applies without regard to the specific inquiries relevant in assessing a conflict under Subsection (1). See Comment *e* hereto.

c(ii). Opposing clients in multiparty litigation. Certain types of civil proceedings may involve multiple parties and disputes, such as bankruptcy cases and proceedings involving environmental liability for alleged polluted conditions. In general, in all multiparty situations the lawyer must comply with Subsection (1) and § 121 generally, both before and after the filing of a formal proceeding.

With respect to bankruptcy, there is substantial disagreement whether certain types of cases or proceedings should be considered under the automatic rule of Subsection (2) or under the general rule of § 121 and, in general, whether general conflict-of-interest rules should be changed in some instances. Tribunals must resolve such questions in light of a body of decisions developed in the specific context of bankruptcy, and often the issues are controlled by statute. The Restatement takes no position on the applicability of Subsection (2) in the many situations that may arise in bankruptcy.

d.   Clients nominally aligned on the same side in the litigation. Multiple representation is precluded when the clients, although nominally on the same side of a lawsuit, in fact have such different interests that representation of one will have a material and adverse effect on the lawyer's representation of the other. Such conflicts can occur whether the clients are aligned as co-plaintiffs or co-defendants, as well as in complex and multiparty litigation.

d(i).   Clients aligned as co-plaintiffs. No conflict of interest is ordinarily presented when two or more of a lawyer's clients assert claims against a defendant. However, sometimes two parties aligned on the same side of a case as co-claimants might wish to characterize the facts differently. The client-claimants might also have a potential lawsuit against each other. For example, a passenger in an automobile damage action might be a co-plaintiff with the driver of the car in a suit alleging negligence of the driver of the other car, but also be able to contend that the driver of the passenger's car was negligent as well, a conclusion that the driver would be motivated to deny. Where there are such possible claims, the lawyer must warn clients about the possibilities of such differences and obtain the consent of each before agreeing to represent them as co-claimants (see § 122).

When multiple claimants assert claims against a defendant who lacks sufficient assets to meet all of the damage claims, a conflict of interest might also be presented. Indeed, whether or not the defendant has assets sufficient to pay all claims, a proposed settlement might create conflicts because the plaintiffs differ in their willingness to accept the settlement. Before any settlement is accepted on behalf of multiple clients, their lawyer must inform each of them about all of the terms of the settlement, including the amounts that each of the other claimants will receive if the settlement is accepted. A similar conflict of interest can arise for a lawyer representing multiple defending parties.

Illustrations:

1.   Lawyer represents A and B, pedestrians struck by an automobile as they stood at a street corner. Each has sued C, the owner-driver, for $150,000. C has $100,000 in liability insurance coverage and no other assets with which to satisfy a judgment. Neither A nor B can be paid the full amount of their claims and any sum recovered by one will reduce the assets available to pay the other's claim. Because of the conflict of interest, Lawyer can continue to represent both A and B only with the informed consent of each (see § 122).

2.   The same facts as in Illustration 1, except that C offers to settle A's claim for $60,000 and B's claim for $40,000. Lawyer must inform both A and B of all of the terms of the proposed settlement, including the amounts offered to each client. If one client wishes to accept and the other wishes to reject the proposed settlement, Lawyer may continue to represent both A and B only after a renewal of informed consent by each.

d(ii).   Clients aligned as co-defendants in civil case. Clients aligned as co-defendants also can have conflicting interests. Each would usually prefer to see the plaintiff defeated altogether, but if the plaintiff succeeds, each will often prefer to see liability deflected mainly or entirely upon other defendants. Indeed, a plaintiff often sues multiple defendants in the hope that each of the defendants will take the position that another of them is responsible, thus enhancing the likelihood of the plaintiff's recovering. Such conflicts preclude joint representation, absent each co-defendant's informed consent (see § 122).

A contract between the parties can eliminate the conflict. When an employee injures someone in an incident arising out of the employment, for example, an employer that is capable of paying the judgment might agree in advance to hold the employee harmless in the matter so that only the employer will bear any judgment ultimately entered. If only one of the parties will ultimately be liable to the plaintiff, there is little reason to incur the expense of separate counsel. However, the initial conflict must be understood by both defendants and each must consent, particularly if the clients must negotiate an agreement governing who will bear ultimate liability (see § 130).

d(iii).   Complex and multiparty litigation. Not all possibly differing interests of co-clients in complex and multiparty litigation involve material interests creating conflict. Determination whether a conflict of material interests exists requires careful attention to the context and other circumstances of the representation and in general should be based on whether (1) issues common to the clients' interests predominate, (2) circumstances such as the size of each client's interest make separate representation impracticable, and (3) the extent of active judicial supervision of the representation. For example, a lawyer might represent several unsecured creditors in a bankruptcy proceeding. In addition to general conflict-of-interest rules that may apply, a lawyer representing such multiple clients must also comply with statutory regulations if more stringent.

Similar considerations apply in representing multiple co-parties in class-action proceedings, due to the possible existence of different objectives or other interests of class members (see also § 125 on creation and settlement of class actions). A plaintiff class might agree, for example, that the local school system discriminates against a racial or ethnic minority, but there might be important differences within the class over what remedy is appropriate (see § 14, Comment *f*). As one possible corrective, under procedural law a class may be subdivided. Through that process objecting members of the class may be heard. However, such differences within the class do not necessarily produce conflicts requiring that the lawyer for the class not represent some or all members of the class or necessitate creation of subclasses. The tasks of a lawyer for a class may include monitoring and mediating such differences. In instances of intractable difference, the lawyer may proceed in what the lawyer reasonably concludes to be the best interests of the class as a whole, for example urging the tribunal to accept an appropriate settlement even if it is not accepted by class representatives or members of the class. In such instances, of course, the lawyer must inform the tribunal of the differing views within the class or on the part of a class representative.

e. *Suing a present client in an unrelated matter.* A lawyer's representation of Client A might require the lawyer to file a lawsuit against Client B whom the lawyer represents in an unrelated matter. Because the matters are unrelated, no confidential information is likely to be used improperly, nor will the lawyer take both sides in a single proceeding. However, the lawyer has a duty of loyalty to the client being sued. Moreover, the client on whose behalf suit is filed might fear that the lawyer would pursue that client's case less effectively out of deference to the other client. Thus, a lawyer may not sue a current client on behalf of another client, even in an unrelated matter, unless consent is obtained under the conditions and limitations of § 122. On identifying who is a present client, see § 14 and § 121, Comment *d*. On the possibility of informed consent in advance to such suits in certain cases, see § 122, Comment *d*.

Illustrations:

3. Lawyer represents Client B in seeking a tax refund. Client A wishes to file suit against Client B in a contract action unrelated to the tax claim. Lawyer may not represent Client A in the suit against Client B as long as Lawyer represents Client B in the tax case, unless both clients give informed consent. On withdrawal, see § 121, Comment *e*.

4. The same facts as in Illustration 3, except that Client A's contract action is against corporation C, which is not Lawyer's client. After A's suit has been filed, C is acquired by and merged into Lawyer's client B, thus creating the conflict. Unauthorized use of confidential information would not be an issue in such a case, and any remedy imposed by a tribunal should minimize adverse impact on the parties. Because the action of B created the conflict, Lawyer might be permitted to withdraw from pursuing the tax claim on behalf of B, for example, but continue to pursue the contract action. Compare the discussion at § 132, Comment *e*.

f. Concurrently taking adverse legal positions on behalf of different clients. A lawyer ordinarily may take inconsistent legal positions in different courts at different times. While each client is entitled to the lawyer's effective advocacy of that client's position, if the rule were otherwise law firms would have to specialize in a single side of legal issues.

However, a conflict is presented when there is a substantial risk that a lawyer's action in Case A will materially and adversely affect another of the lawyer's clients in Case B. Factors relevant in determining the risk of such an effect include whether the issue is before a trial court or an appellate court; whether the issue is substantive or procedural; the temporal relationship between the matters; the practical significance of the issue to the immediate and long-run interests of the clients involved; and the clients' reasonable expectations in retaining the lawyer. If a conflict of interest exists, absent informed consent of the affected clients under § 122, the lawyer must withdraw from one or both of the matters. Informed client consent is provided for in § 122. On circumstances in which informed client consent would not allow the lawyer to proceed with representation of both clients, see § 122(2)(c) and Comment *g(iv)* thereto.

Illustrations:

5. Lawyer represents two clients in damage actions pending in different United States District Courts. In one case, representing the plaintiff, Lawyer will attempt to introduce certain evidence at trial and argue there for its admissibility. In the other case, representing a defendant, Lawyer will object to an anticipated attempt by the plaintiff to introduce similar evidence. Even if there is some possibility that one court's ruling might be published and cited as authority in the other proceeding, Lawyer may proceed with both representations without obtaining the consent of the clients involved.

6. The same facts as in Illustration 5, except that the cases have proceeded to the point where certiorari has been granted in each by the United States Supreme Court to consider the common evidentiary question. Any position that Lawyer would assert on behalf of either client on the legal issue common to each case would have a material and adverse impact on the interests of the other client. Thus, a conflict of interest is presented. Even the informed consent of both Client A and Client B would be insufficient to permit Lawyer to represent each before the Supreme Court.

§ 129. Conflicts of Interest in Criminal Litigation

Unless all affected clients consent to the representation under the limitations and conditions provided in § 122, a lawyer in a criminal matter may not represent:

    (1) two or more defendants or potential defendants in the same matter; or

    (2) a single defendant, if the representation would involve a conflict of interest as defined in § 121.

Comment:

    a.   Scope and cross-references. This Section addresses the analogues in criminal litigation to the issues raised in § 128. The Section is a specific application of the conflicts standard expressed in § 121, as interpreted and applied in light of the constitutional issues that arise in criminal cases. It is subject to consent under the limitations and conditions provided in § 122. See Comment *c* hereto. The conflict is imputed to affiliated lawyers under § 123, an imputation that can be removed as described in § 124.

    Section 131 considers conflicts arising when a criminal-defense lawyer represents both an organization and employees or other persons associated with the organization. Conflicts arising from duties that a criminal-defense lawyer owes to a former client are examined in § 132. Conflict issues arising from third-person payment of a criminal-defense lawyer's fee are considered in § 134. Conflicts of a prosecuting attorney are analyzed in § 135. A lawyer's obligation to preserve the confidential information of a client is discussed in § 60 and other Sections in Chapter 5.

    The remedies for conflicts of interest (see § 121, Comment *f*) available in a civil case (see § 128) are also generally available in a criminal case. In addition, courts sometimes exercise judicial supervisory power to disqualify lawyers for prophylactic reasons in instances in which the lawyer is otherwise permissibly representing multiple clients. A lawyer's ability to obtain effective consents (see § 122(2)) to conflicts in criminal representations is, to that extent, less than in comparable civil cases.

    b.   Rationale. The rules in this Section, like those examined in § 128, seek to protect confidential client information, enhance clients' sense of lawyers' loyalty, assist a court's effort to assure fairness and the finality of results, and minimize the cost of legal assistance for clients. In addition, criminal litigation is governed by constitutional protections not applicable in civil litigation. The Sixth Amendment, for example, guarantees that "In all criminal prosecutions, the accused shall enjoy the right . . . to have the Assistance of Counsel for his defense." That guarantee and its implied right to the effective assistance of counsel impose special constraints on the representation of multiple clients in criminal matters. However, the same guarantee cautions that a tribunal not disturb a fully informed selection of counsel absent compelling circumstances.

    This Section applies to all stages of the criminal-justice process from initial investigation, whether or not before a grand jury, through final appeal. In some situations, rules stated in other Sections can also apply because of parallel administrative or other civil proceedings. Whether or not a conflict is presented in any given stage of the process depends in part on what the lawyer has undertaken to do in that particular stage. A lawyer for two or more targets of a grand-jury investigation might be able to represent them jointly, for example, if there were little risk of abuse of confidential information or breach of the duty of loyalty while awaiting the decision of the grand jury whether to indict. On the other hand, if plea negotiations allow the possibility of testimony on behalf of the government, joint representation without informed consent ordinarily would be improper (see Comment c hereto).

c. *Multiple criminal-defense representations.* Subsection (1) recognizes that the representation of co-defendants in criminal cases involves at least the potential for conflicts of interest. For example, if one defendant is offered favorable treatment in return for testimony against a co-defendant, a single lawyer could not give advice favorable to one defendant's interests while adhering to the duty of loyalty to the other. Similarly, individual defendants might have had different motives for and understandings of events, so that establishing a common position among them is difficult. Witnesses who would be favorable to one defendant might be subject to cross-examination that would be unfavorable to another defendant. In closing argument, counsel must choose which facts to stress. For example, stressing the minor role of one defendant might imply the major role of another.

Because of such potential conflicts and the constitutional significance of the issues they raise, joint representation in criminal cases often has a material and adverse effect on the representation of each defendant and thus cannot be undertaken in the absence of client consent under the limitations and conditions stated in § 122.

Criminal defendants might nonetheless consider it in their interest to be represented by a single lawyer even when the financial cost of separate counsel is not a factor. A single lawyer can help assure a common position and increase the likelihood that none of the co-defendants will cooperate with the prosecution against the others. For such reasons, a criminal conviction involving joint representation ordinarily is not impeachable absent a showing of timely objection and actual prejudice. Were the rule otherwise, defendants could avoid raising a conflict issue before trial so as to create an issue for later appeal.

On the other hand, both the prosecutor and the trial judge have a responsibility to assure a fair trial for each defendant. When a defense lawyer would be required to assume an adverse position with respect to one or more of the clients, the conflict is nonconsentable (see § 122(2)(b) & Comment g(iii) thereto). Efficient operation of the judicial system requires that a verdict not be vulnerable to contentions that a defendant was disadvantaged by an undisclosed conflict of interest. A prosecutor might object to joint-representation arrangements to assure that a conflict possibility is resolved before trial. Even without objection by the prosecutor or defendant, the tribunal may raise the issue on its own initiative and refuse to permit joint representation where there is a significant threat to the interest in the finality of judgments.

Illustrations:

1.   A and B are co-defendants charged with a felony offense of armed robbery. They are both represented by Lawyer. The prosecutor believes that A planned the crime and was the only one carrying a weapon. The prosecutor offers to accept B's plea of guilty to a misdemeanor if B will testify against A. Lawyer's loyalty to A causes Lawyer to persuade B that the prosecutor's proposal should be rejected. Following a trial, both A and B are convicted of the felony. When plea negotiations involving B's separate interests began, B should have received independent counsel. In the circumstances, Lawyer could not properly represent A and B even with the informed consent of both clients (see § 122, Comment *g(iii)*).

2.   The same facts as in Illustration 1, except that the evidence at trial is highly damaging to Defendant A but less so to Defendant B. Both defendants were represented by Lawyer, who did not consult with A and B concerning their conflicting interests. Lawyer spent most of the closing argument explaining away A's guilt and did not mention the weak case against B, because doing so would invite the jury to consider the greater likelihood of A's guilt. Lawyer could represent B only with the informed consent of B (see § 122).

d.   A criminal-defense lawyer with conflicting duties to other clients. As required in Subsection (2), a conflict exists when a defense lawyer in a criminal matter has duties to clients in other matters that might conflict. A conflict exists, for example, if the lawyer also represents either a prosecutor or a prosecution witness in an unrelated matter. The conflict could lead the lawyer to be less vigorous in defending the criminal case in order to avoid offending the other client, or the lawyer might be constrained in cross-examining the other client (see § 60(1)). A lawyer who represents a criminal defendant may not represent the state in unrelated civil matters when such representation would have a material and adverse effect on the lawyer's handling of the criminal case.

Ordinarily, these conflicts may be waived by client consent under the limitations and conditions in § 122. Because the defendant's constitutional rights are implicated, court procedures often require that consent be made part of the formal record in the criminal case (see Comment *c* hereto).

§ 130.   Multiple Representation in Nonlitigated Matter

Unless all affected clients consent to the representation under the limitations and conditions provided in § 122, a lawyer may not represent two or more clients in a matter not involving litigation if there is a substantial risk that the lawyer's representation of one or more of the clients would be materially and

adversely affected by the lawyer's duties to one or more of the other clients.

Comment:

a. Scope and cross-references. This Section is a specific application of the general conflicts standard expressed in § 121. Whereas §§ 128 and 129 consider conflicts of interest among current clients in litigation, this Section addresses situations not involving litigation. Representation can progress from one setting to the other or otherwise involve more than one setting, thus making relevant more than one Section. The conflicts identified in this Section are subject to consent under the limitations and conditions provided in § 122. The conflicts are imputed to affiliated lawyers by § 123, and the imputation can be removed as described in § 124. Identification of the lawyer's clients is addressed in § 14 and § 121, Comment *d*.

The conflicts considered in this Section generally arise in two contexts. The multiple clients might seek the lawyer's assistance on achieving a common goal, such as forming a corporation, recognizing that they have common interests with respect to major elements of the relationship but also interests concerning which there might be differences and potential for conflict. Second, multiple clients might seek the lawyer's assistance to resolve a recognized area of difference, such as the settlement outside litigation of a business dispute. The latter conflicts include those considered under the heading of "intermediation" in ABA Model Rules of Professional Conduct, Rule 2.2 (1983). Although its terminology might be thought to imply otherwise, Rule 2.2 addresses a particular setting for applying the general rules governing conflicts. "Intermediation" is a term that has not passed into general professional usage and is not employed here.

Clients represented by the lawyer under the terms of this Section are "co-clients"; the communications of each with the lawyer are not privileged from disclosure to the other co-clients unless the co-clients have agreed otherwise (see § 75). On confidentiality in co-client representations, see § 60, Comment *l*. Counseling clients is considered generally in § 94.

Remedies for a violation of this Section include those set forth for conflicts generally in § 121, Comment *f*. Ordinarily, a remedy for a violation of this Section causing actionable damage to a client is a suit for professional malpractice (see § 48 and following). In appropriate cases, the lawyer is subject to professional discipline (see § 5) or fee forfeiture (see § 37).

b. Rationale. As in litigated cases, multiple representation not involving litigation requires a lawyer to remain loyal to clients and protect their confidential information (see § 60(1)). Providing economical legal services is also a relevant concern (see § 128 & § 129, Comment *b*). The orderly administration of tribunals is, by definition, not a relevant factor for the issues in this Section.

Whether a lawyer can function in a situation of conflict (see § 121) depends on whether the conflict is consentable (see § 122(2)), which in turn depends on whether it is "reasonably likely that the lawyer will be able to provide adequate representation" to all affected clients (see § 122(2)). Conflicted but unconsented representation of multiple clients, for example of the buyer and seller of property, is sometimes defended with the argument that the lawyer was performing the role of mere "scrivener" or a similarly mechanical role. The characterization is usually inappropriate. A lawyer must accept responsibility to give customary advice and customary range of legal services, unless the clients have given their informed consent to a narrower range of the lawyer's responsibilities. On limitations of a lawyer's responsibilities, see § 19(1).

c. Assisting multiple clients with common objectives, but conflicting interests. When multiple clients have generally common interests, the role of the lawyer is to advise on relevant legal considerations, suggest alternative ways of meeting common objectives, and draft instruments necessary to accomplish the desired results. Multiple representations do not always present a conflict of interest requiring client consent (see § 121). For example, in representing spouses jointly in the purchase of property as co-owners, the lawyer would reasonably assume that such a representation does not involve a conflict of interest. A conflict could be involved, however, if the lawyer knew that one spouse's objectives in the acquisition were materially at variance with those of the other spouse.

Illustrations:

1.   Husband and Wife consult Lawyer for estate-planning advice about a will for each of them. Lawyer has had professional dealings with the spouses, both separately and together, on several prior occasions. Lawyer knows them to be knowledgeable about their respective rights and interests, competent to make independent decisions if called for, and in accord on their common and individual objectives. Lawyer may represent both clients in the matter without obtaining consent (see § 121). While each spouse theoretically could make a distribution different from the other's, including a less generous bequest to each other, those possibilities do not create a conflict of interest, and none reasonably appears to exist in the circumstances.

2.   The same facts as in Illustration 1, except that Lawyer has not previously met the spouses. Spouse A does most of the talking in the initial discussions with Lawyer. Spouse B, who owns significantly more property than Spouse A, appears to disagree with important positions of Spouse A but to be uncomfortable in expressing that disagreement and does not pursue them when Spouse A appears impatient and peremptory. Representation of both spouses would involve a conflict of interest. Lawyer may proceed to provide the

requested legal assistance only with consent given under the limitations and conditions provided in § 122.

    3.   The same facts as in Illustration 1, except that Lawyer has not previously met the spouses. But in this instance, unlike in Illustration 2, in discussions with the spouses, Lawyer asks questions and suggests options that reveal both Spouse A and Spouse B to be knowledgeable about their respective rights and interests, competent to make independent decisions if called for, and in accord on their common and individual objectives. Lawyer has adequately verified the absence of a conflict of interest and thus may represent both clients in the matter without obtaining consent (see § 122).

Clients might not fully understand the potential for conflict in their interests as the result of ignorance about their legal rights, about possible alternatives to those that the clients have considered prior to retaining the lawyer, or about the uncommunicated plans or objectives of another client. In other situations, prospective clients might agree on objectives when they first approach the common lawyer, but it should be reasonably apparent that a conflict is likely to develop as the representation proceeds. A client's right to communicate in confidence with the attorney should not be constrained by concern that discord might result (cf. § 75). A lawyer is not required to suggest or assume discord where none exists, but when a conflict is reasonably apparent or foreseeable, the lawyer may proceed with multiple representation only after all affected clients have consented as provided in § 122.

Illustration:

    4.   A, B, and C are interested in forming a partnership in which A is to provide the capital, B the basic patent, and C the management skill. Only C will spend significant amounts of time operating the business. A, B, and C jointly request Lawyer to represent them in creating the partnership. The different contributions to be made to the partnership alone indicate that the prospective partners have conflicts of interest with respect to the structure and governance of the partnership (see § 121). With the informed consent of each (see § 122), Lawyer may represent all three clients in forming the business. Lawyer may assist the clients in valuing their respective contributions and suggest arrangements to protect their respective interests. With respect to conflicts and informed consent in representing the partnership as well as the partners once the business is established, see § 131, Comment e.

    d.   *Clients with known differences to be resolved.* Multiple prospective clients might already be aware that their interests and objectives are antagonistic to some degree. The lawyer must ascertain at the outset what kind of assistance the clients require. Service by the lawyer or another person as an arbitrator or mediator (and not as a lawyer representing clients), for example, might well serve the clients' interests.

When circumstances reasonably indicate that the prospective clients might be able to reach a reasonable reconciliation of their differences by agreement and with the lawyer's assistance, the lawyer may represent them after obtaining informed consent (see § 122). In particular, the lawyer should explain the effect of joint representation on the lawyer's ability to protect each client's confidential information (see § 75). If the joint representation is undertaken, the lawyer should help the clients reach agreement on outstanding issues but should not advance the interests of one of the clients to the detriment of another (see § 122, Comment *h*).

Relations among multiple clients can develop into adversarial, even litigated, matters. Even if the possibility of litigation is substantial and even though the consent does not permit the lawyer to represent one client against the other if litigation does ensue (see § 122(2)(b) & § 128), with informed consent a lawyer could accept multiple representation in an effort to reconcile the differences of the clients short of litigation. The lawyer should inform the clients that the effort to overcome differences might ultimately fail and require the lawyer's complete withdrawal from the matter, unless the clients agreed that the lawyer thereafter could continue to represent less than all clients (see § 121, Comment *e(i)*). The lawyer is not required to encourage each client to obtain independent advice about being jointly represented, but the lawyer should honor any client request for such an opportunity.

Illustrations:

5.   The same facts as in Illustration 4, except that the partnership of A, B, and C is formed and commences business. The business encounters difficulty in securing customers and controlling costs, and it shortly appears that the business will fail unless additional funding is obtained. No outside funds are available, and A announces unwillingness to provide additional capital unless B and C agree to increase A's interest in the business. B and C believe that A is requesting an unreasonably large additional share. A, B, and C seek Lawyer's assistance in resolving their disagreements. A conflict clearly exists between the clients (§ 121). Lawyer may agree to represent the three clients in seeking to arrive at a mutually satisfactory resolution, but only after Lawyer obtains the informed consent of each client and there is a clear definition of the services that Lawyer will provide. In representing the clients, Lawyer may not favor the position of any client over the others (see § 122, Comment *h*).

6.   Husband and Wife have agreed to obtain an uncontested dissolution of their marriage. They have consulted Lawyer to help them reach an agreement on disposition of their property. A conflict of interest clearly exists between the prospective clients (§ 121). If reasonable prospects of an agreement exist, Lawyer may accept the

joint representation with the effective consent of both (see § 122). However, in the later dissolution proceeding, Lawyer may represent only one of the parties (see § 128, Comment *c*), and Lawyer must withdraw from representing both clients if their efforts to reach an agreement fail (see § 121, Comment *e(i)*).

§ 131. Conflicts of Interest in Representing an Organization

Unless all affected clients consent to the representation under the limitations and conditions provided in § 122, a lawyer may not represent both an organization and a director, officer, employee, shareholder, owner, partner, member, or other individual or organization associated with the organization if there is a substantial risk that the lawyer's representation of either would be materially and adversely affected by the lawyer's duties to the other.

Comment:

a. Scope and cross-references. This Section concerns conflict-of-interest issues involving a lawyer for an organization. For the purpose of this Section, an organization includes a corporation (whether for-profit or not-for-profit), limited or general partnership (whether formal or informal), labor union, unincorporated association, joint venture, trust, estate, or similar entity with a recognizable form, internal organization, and relative permanence. Many organizations are recognized as entities for other legal purposes, but such recognition is not invariably required for the purposes of this Section (see, e.g., Comment *f* hereto, Illustration 5).

This Section is a particular application of the general conflicts standard expressed in § 121. The conflict is subject to consent under the limitations and conditions provided in § 122. The conflict is imputed to affiliated lawyers by § 123, an imputation that can be removed as described in § 124. Remedies for violation of the Section include those set forth in § 121, Comment *f*. A lawyer's violation of this Section that injures the organization renders the lawyer liable to the organization for professional malpractice (see § 48 and following).

Issues of who constitutes a lawyer's client are addressed in § 14 and § 121, Comment *d*. This Section presupposes that the lawyer has a client-lawyer relationship with an organization. On the power of authorized agents of the organization to instruct the lawyer on behalf of the client, see § 96, Comment *d*.

The duty to preserve confidential client information of organizational clients is described in § 60 and the attorney-client privilege for organizations in § 73. A lawyer's role in counseling organizational clients is addressed in § 96; on a lawyer's duties when a person associated with an organizational client threatens to harm the organization, see § 96(2). A lawyer's ownership of an interest in an organizational client is considered in § 126. Representation of two or more individuals who are forming an organization is examined in § 130, Comment *c*. Payment by an organization of the legal expenses of one or more directors, officers, employees, or other individuals, is considered in § 134. Conflicts of interest created by a lawyer's duties as a corporate director or officer is discussed in § 135, Comment *d*.

b. Rationale. An organization with more than a single owner-employee is an aggregation of multiple interests, if only because it is made up of multiple persons or entities. Persons initially forming an organization are linked by a common interest that partly transcends their individual interests. The individuals might have separate lawyers for their other activities and for negotiating the question of their shares or other forms of control in the organization. However, a lawyer might be retained for representation relating to the organization separate from that of any individual associated with the enterprise. An organization's lawyer thus is said to represent the entity and not the elements that make it up. A lawyer for an organization serves whatever lawful interest the organization defines as its interest, acting through its responsible agents and in accordance with its decision making procedures (see § 96(1) and Comment *d* thereto).

c. A challenge to the policy of a client organization. Individuals having responsible roles in an organization can disagree about the definition of its interests. However, that does not by itself indicate that a lawyer representing the organization has a conflict of interest within the meaning of § 121. If conduct of the organization is challenged as unlawful, the lawyer for the organization generally may defend at least until it is ruled upon by the tribunal or changed pursuant to the procedures of the organization. Such a change can occur, for example, because the lawyer is directed to settle the controversy as instructed by the agent (see § 21).

Illustration:

1. The Board of Directors of Corporation, acting pursuant to its articles and by-laws, votes not to declare a preferred stock dividend because of a perceived shortage of working capital. This is done contrary to the recommendation of Lawyer for Corporation, who believes that there is a reasonable argument that the dividend can be omitted but that a tribunal would probably order the dividend declared. Thereafter, Lawyer implements the decision of Board, memorializing its decision in a resolution. Several shareholders file suit to compel Corporation to issue a dividend. Neither Lawyer's earlier advice nor the lawsuit itself creates a conflict of interest that would prevent Lawyer from defending against the suit.

On the lawyer's duty if the responsible agent is acting in violation of a duty to the organization, see § 96(2). On the lawyer's duty if the organization engages in a crime or fraud, see § 67. On the lawyer's right to withdraw from representation because of disagreement with the organizational policy, see § 32. On the lawyer's right to take public positions inconsistent with those of the lawyer's client, see § 125, Comment *e*.

d. Conflicting interests of affiliated organizations. Whether a lawyer represents affiliated organizations as clients is a question of fact determined under § 14 (see Comment *f* thereto). When a lawyer represents two or more organizations with some common ownership or membership, whether a conflict exists is determined primarily on the basis of formal organizational distinctions. If a single business corporation has established two divisions within the corporate structure, for example, conflicting interests or objectives of those divisions do not create a conflict of interest for a lawyer representing the corporation. Differences within the organization are to be resolved through the organization's decisionmaking procedures.

If an enterprise consists of two or more organizations and ownership of the organizations is identical, the lawyer's obligation is ordinarily to respond according to the decisionmaking procedures of the enterprise, subject to any special limitations that might be validly imposed by regulatory regimes such as those governing financial institutions and insurance companies.

On the other hand, when ownership or membership of two or more organizations is not identical, the lawyer must respect the organizational boundaries of each and analyze possible conflicts of interest on the basis that the organizations are separate entities. That is true even when a single individual or organization has sufficient ownership or influence to exercise working control of the organizations (cf. § 123, Comment *d(i)*).

Illustration:

> 2.   A Corporation owns 60 percent of the stock of B Corporation. All of the stock of A Corporation is publicly owned, as is the remainder of the stock in B Corporation. Lawyer has been asked by the President of A Corporation to act as attorney for B in causing B to make a proposed transfer of certain real property to A at a price whose fairness cannot readily be determined by reference to the general real-estate market. Lawyer may do so only with effective informed consent of the management of B (as well as that of A). The ownership of A and B is not identical and their interests materially differ in the proposed transaction.

e. Representation of an organization and an individual constituent. Representation of a client organization often is facilitated by a close working relationship between the lawyer and the organization's officers, directors, and employees. However, unless the lawyer and such an individual person enter into a client-lawyer relationship (see § 14, Comment *f*), the individual is not a client of the lawyer (see § 121, Comment *d*). With respect to the attorney-client privilege attaching to communications with a person affiliated with an organization, see § 73, Comment *j*.

When a lawyer proposes to represent both an organization and a person associated with it, such as an officer, director, or employee, whether a conflict exists is determined by an analysis of the interests of the organization as an entity and those of the individuals involved. That is true whether the multiple representation involves civil (see § 128) or criminal (see § 129) litigation or a nonlitigated matter (see § 130). The interests of the organization are those defined by its agents authorized to act in the matter (see § 96, Comment *d*). For example, when an organization is accused of wrongdoing, an individual such as a director, officer, or other agent will sometimes be charged as well, and the lawyer representing the organization might be asked also to represent the individual. Such representation would constitute a conflict of interest when the individual's interests are materially adverse to the interests of the organization (see § 121). When there is no material adversity of interest, such as when the individual owns all of the equity in the organization or played a routine role in the underlying transaction, no conflict exists. In instances of adversity, concurrent representation would be permissible with the consent of all affected clients under the limitations and conditions stated in § 122.

Consent by an organization can be given in any manner consistent with the organization's lawful decision making procedures. Applicable corporate law may provide that an officer who is personally interested in the matter may not provide consent in the matter. In deciding whether to consent to multiple representation by outside counsel, the organization might rely upon the advice of inside legal counsel. Issues concerning informed consent by public organizations to otherwise conflicted representations are discussed in § 122, Comment *c*.

Illustrations:

   3.   President, the chief executive officer of Corporation, has been charged with discussing prices with the president of a competing firm. If found guilty, both President and Corporation will be subject to civil and criminal penalties. Lawyer, who is representing Corporation, has concluded after a thorough investigation that no such pricing discussions occurred. Both Corporation and President plan to defend on that ground. President has asked Lawyer to represent President as well as Corporation in the proceedings. Although the factual and legal defenses of President and Corporation appear to be consistent at the outset, the likelihood of conflicting positions in such matters as plea bargaining requires Lawyer to obtain the informed consent of both clients before proceeding with the representation (see § 129, Comment *c*).

   4.   The same facts as in Illustration 3, except that after further factual investigation both President and Corporation now concede

that the pricing discussions took place. One of President's defenses will be that the former general counsel of Corporation told President that discussion of general pricing practices with a competitor was not illegal. Corporation denies that such was the advice given and asserts that President acted without authority. The conflict between President and Corporation is so great that the same lawyer could not provide adequate legal services to both in the matter. Thus, continued representation of both is not subject to consent (see § 122, Comment *g(iii)*, & §§ 128 & 129).

If a person affiliated with an organization makes an unsolicited disclosure of information to a lawyer who represents only the organization, indicating the person's erroneous expectation that the lawyer will keep the information confidential from the organization, the lawyer must inform the person that the lawyer does not represent the person (see § 103, Comment *e*). The lawyer generally is not prohibited from sharing the communication with the organization. However, the requirements stated in § 15, Comment *c*, with respect to safeguarding confidential information of a prospective client may apply. That would occur when the person reasonably appeared to be consulting the lawyer as present or prospective client with respect to the person's individual interests, and the lawyer failed to warn the associated person that the lawyer represents only the organization and could act against the person's interests as a result (see § 103, Comment *e*). With respect to a lawyer's duties when a person associated with the organization expressed an intent to act wrongfully and thereby threatens harm to the organization client, see § 96(2) and Comment *f* thereto.

Issues considered in this Comment may be particularly acute in the case of close corporations, small partnerships, and similar organizations in which, for example, one person with substantial ownership interests also manages. Such a manager may have a corresponding tendency to treat corporate and similar entity distinctions as mere formalities. In such instances, when ownership is so concentrated that no nonmanaging owner exists and in the absence of material impact on the interests of other nonclients (such as creditors in the case of an insolvent corporation), a lawyer acts reasonably in accepting in good faith a controlling manager's position that the interests of all controlling persons and the entity should be treated as if they were the same. Similar considerations apply when a close corporation or similar organization is owned and managed by a small number of owner-managers whose interests are not materially in conflict.

f. A challenge by a client organization to the action of an associated person. Both Subsections of this Section can be applicable when the organization challenges the action of one or more of its associated persons, such as an officer, director, or employee. The policy of the organization in the matter will be that established according to the organization's decision making procedures (see § 96(1)(a)). Because the interests of the organization and the associated person are necessarily adverse, the conflict of interest ordinarily will not be subject to consent (see § 122(2)(c)). On the lawyer's dealing with threatened wrongdoing by a person associated with an organizational client, see § 96(2); see also §§ 66–67.

Illustration:

5. Treasurer, the chief financial officer of Club, a private investment trust, has been accused of converting $25,000 of Club's assets for personal use. Responsible other officers of Club, acting on Club's behalf, retain Lawyer to recover the money from Treasurer. They direct Lawyer not to reveal the loss or file suit until other collection efforts have been exhausted. Lawyer may properly represent Club and in doing so must proceed in the manner directed. Further, although the matter is not yet in litigation, the interests of Club and Treasurer are so adverse that even informed consent of both would not permit their common representation by Lawyer in the matter (see § 122, Comment *g*).

g. Derivative action. When an organization such as a business corporation is sued in a derivative action, the organization is ordinarily aligned as an involuntary plaintiff. Persons associated with the organization who are accused of breaching a duty to the organization, typically officers and directors of the organization, are ordinarily named as defendants. The theory of a derivative action is that relief is sought from the individuals for the benefit of the organization. Even with informed consent of all affected clients, the lawyer for the organization ordinarily may not represent an individual defendant as well (see § 128, Comment *c*). If, however, the disinterested directors conclude that no basis exists for the claim that the defending officers and directors have acted against the interests of the organization, the lawyer may, with the effective consent of all clients, represent both the organization and the officers and directors in defending the suit (see § 122).

In a derivative action, if the advice of the lawyer acting for the organization was an important factor in the action of the officers and directors that gave rise to the suit, it is appropriate for the lawyer to represent, if anyone, the officers and directors and for the organization to obtain new counsel. Because the lawyer would be representing clients with interests adverse to the corporation, consent of the corporation would be required. That would be true even if the lawyer withdrew from representing the corporation in order to represent the individuals (see § 132, Comment *c*). Whom the lawyer should represent in the matter, if anyone, should be determined by responsible agents of the organization. Ordinarily, those will be persons who are not named and are not likely to be named parties in the case.

If an action challenging an act of an organization is not a derivative action, whether a conflict exists is determined under § 128, Comment *d(ii)*.

h. Proxy fights and takeover attempts. Outsiders or insiders might challenge incumbent management for control of organizations. Incumbent management, shareholders, creditors, and employees will all be affected by such a contest in various ways. When the challenge to incumbent management comes from outside the management group, the role of the lawyer representing the organization must be to follow policies adopted by the organization, in accordance with the organization's decision making procedures. Persons authorized to act on behalf of the organization determine the organization's interest in responding to the challenge (see § 96(1)).

When all or part of incumbent management seeks to obtain control of the organization, typically by restructuring ownership of and authority in the organization, a conflict of interest is presented between the individual interests of those members of management and the holders of ownership and authority. Because of their personal interests, those members of management ordinarily would not be appropriate agents to direct the work of a lawyer for the organization with respect to the takeover attempt. Whether a lawyer's personal interests, for example, those based on longtime association with incumbent management, preclude the lawyer from representing the organization or the managers seeking control depends on whether the lawyer's personal interests create a substantial risk of material and adverse effect on the representation (see § 125).

Illustrations:

6. The Board of Directors of Company A expects soon to receive a letter from Company B offering to purchase a controlling interest in Company A at a price 20 percent above current market value of the stock. The Board of Directors decides to resist the takeover attempt and directs Lawyer, the general counsel of Company A, to prepare a by-law amendment making it more difficult for Company B to gain control. In such circumstances, the Board of Directors, not Lawyer, has the legal responsibility to determine whether or not the by-law change is in the best interests of Company A. Lawyer may advise the Board of Directors concerning the proposed by-law.

7. The same facts as in Illustration 6, except that President and Treasurer of Company A have proposed to transform Company A into a privately held corporation in which they would hold all the shares. Without effective consent, Lawyer's responsibilities to Company A would not permit Lawyer to represent President and Treasurer in the transaction. If Lawyer participates in the matter at all, it should be to represent Company A's interest as defined by the

members of Company A's Board of Directors who are empowered to act.

Similar considerations apply when a contest over ownership or control arises within a closely held corporation or similar small organization such as a two-person partnership. If the lawyer also represents a principal in such an enterprise personally, the possibility of conflict is increased if the lawyer undertakes to represent that person in such a contest. When it reasonably appears that the lawyer can serve effectively in the role of conciliator between contending factions, the lawyer may undertake to do so with effective consent of all affected clients (see § 130, Comment *d*). In other cases, however, the lawyer will be required to withdraw from representing all of the individual interests (see § 132).

TOPIC 4. CONFLICTS OF INTEREST WITH A FORMER CLIENT

§ 132. A Representation Adverse to the Interests of a Former Client

Unless both the affected present and former clients consent to the representation under the limitations and conditions provided in § 122, a lawyer who has represented a client in a matter may not thereafter represent another client in the same or a substantially related matter in which the interests of the former client are materially adverse. The current matter is substantially related to the earlier matter if:

(1) the current matter involves the work the lawyer performed for the former client; or

(2) there is a substantial risk that representation of the present client will involve the use of information acquired in the course of representing the former client, unless that information has become generally known.

Comment:

a. Scope and cross-references. This Section applies the general conflicts principles of § 121 to situations in which a lawyer represents a present client in a matter in which there is a substantial risk of material and adverse effect on the interests of the present or a former client. Such a risk can arise from the threat to that client's confidential information, to the interests of the present client because of the lawyer's continuing duties to a former client, or to the interests of both clients because of confusion of the lawyer's role. A lawyer formerly employed by the government is subject to the similar provisions of § 133. Imputation to affiliated lawyers of a conflict identified by this Section is addressed in § 123. Circumstances under which imputation can be removed are addressed in § 124(1) and (2). Conflicts of interest arising out of dealings with a prospective client are addressed in § 15, Comment *c*.

In light of the confidentiality requirements of Chapter 5, a lawyer representing a client in a matter may not use confidential client information if doing so will adversely affect a material interest of the former client, even though that matter is not substantially related to a former representation (see Comments *f* & *g* hereto).

The conflict described in this Section is subject to consent of the present and former clients under the limitations and conditions provided in § 122. Conditional consent might be especially relevant in situations arising under this Section (see § 122, Comment *e*). For example, a client might give informed consent on the condition that a law firm employ screening measures such as those described in § 124.

Remedies discussed in § 121, Comment *f*, can be invoked for a violation of this Section. Because the issues raised by this Section often arise in litigation against or negotiations with a former client, the remedies of disqualification and injunction are commonly invoked. The sanction of professional discipline is also available (see § 5). If a violation of this Section causes injury to a present or former client, the remedy of professional malpractice might be available (see § 48 and following). When a lawyer has undertaken a representation that is later determined to involve a conflict of interest, but could not reasonably have identified the conflict, that should be given substantial weight in determining what sanction, if any, is appropriate.

b. Rationale. The rule described in this Section accommodates four policies. First, absent the rule, a lawyer's incentive to serve a present client might cause the lawyer to compromise the lawyer's continuing duties to the former client (see § 33). Specifically, the lawyer might use confidential information of the former client contrary to that client's interest and in violation of § 60. The second policy consideration is the converse of the first. The lawyer's obligations to the former client might constrain the lawyer in representing the present client effectively, for example, by limiting the questions the lawyer could ask the former client in testimony. Third, at the time the lawyer represented the former client, the lawyer should have no incentive to lay the basis for subsequent representation against that client, such as by drafting provisions in a contract that could later be construed against the former client. Fourth, and pointing the other way, because much law practice is transactional, clients often retain lawyers for service only on specific cases or issues. A rule that would transform each engagement into a lifetime commitment would make lawyers reluctant to take new, relatively modest matters.

c. The relationship between current-client and former-client conflicts rules. The difference between a former-client conflict under this Section and a present-client conflict considered in Topic 3 (§§ 128–130) is that this Section applies only to representation in the same or a substantially related matter. The present-client conflict rules prohibit adverse representation regardless of the lack of any other relationship between them. If the two representations overlap in time, the rules of §§ 128–130 apply.

Withdrawal is effective to render a representation "former" for the purposes of this Section if it occurs at a point that the client and lawyer had contemplated as the end of the representation (see § 32, Comment *c*). The representation will also be at an end for purposes of this Section if the existing client discharges the lawyer (other than for cause arising from the improper representation) or if other grounds for mandatory or permissive withdrawal by the lawyer exist (see § 32), and the lawyer is not motivated primarily by a desire to represent the new client.

If a lawyer is approached by a prospective client seeking representation in a matter adverse to an existing client, the present-client conflict may not be transformed into a former-client conflict by the lawyer's withdrawal from the representation of the existing client. A premature withdrawal violates the lawyer's obligation of loyalty to the existing client and can constitute a breach of the client-lawyer contract of employment (see § 32, Comment *c*). On withdrawal when a dispute arises between two or more of the lawyer's clients, see § 121, Comment *e(i)*. On advance consent, see id. and § 122, especially Comment *d*.

d. The same or a substantially related matter. As indicated in the Section, three types of former-client conflicts are prohibited.

d(i). Switching sides in the same matter. Representing one side and then switching to represent the other in the same matter clearly implicates loyalty to the first client and protection of that client's confidences. Similar considerations apply in nonlitigated matters. For example, a lawyer negotiating a complex agreement on behalf of Seller could not withdraw and represent Buyer against the interests of Seller in the same transaction. Switching sides in a litigated matter can also risk confusing the trier of fact. Just as a lawyer may not represent both sides concurrently in the same case (see §§ 128–130), the lawyer also may not represent them consecutively.

d(ii). Attacking a lawyer's own former work. Beyond switching sides in the same matter, the concept of substantial relationship applies to later developments out of the original matter. A matter is substantially related if it involves the work the lawyer performed for the former client. For example, a lawyer may not on behalf of a later client attack the validity of a document that the lawyer drafted if doing so would materially and adversely affect the former client. Similarly, a lawyer may not represent a debtor in bankruptcy in seeking to set aside a security interest of a creditor that is embodied in a document that the lawyer previously drafted for the creditor.

Illustration:

1. Lawyer has represented Husband in a successful effort to have Wife removed as beneficiary of his life insurance policy. After Husband's death, Wife seeks to retain Lawyer to negotiate with the insurance company to set aside the change of beneficiary and obtain

the proceeds of the policy for Wife. The subsequent representation would require that Lawyer attack the work Lawyer performed for Husband. Accordingly, Lawyer may not accept Wife as a client in the matter.

d(iii).   The substantial-relationship test and the protection of confidential information of a former client. The substantial-relationship standard is employed most frequently to protect the confidential information of the former client obtained in the course of the representation. A subsequent matter is substantially related to an earlier matter within the meaning of Subsection (2) if there is a substantial risk that the subsequent representation will involve the use of confidential information of the former client obtained in the course of the representation in violation of § 60. "Confidential information" is defined in § 59. Substantial risk exists where it is reasonable to conclude that it would materially advance the client's position in the subsequent matter to use confidential information obtained in the prior representation.

A concern to protect a former client's confidential information would be self-defeating if, in order to obtain its protection, the former client were required to reveal in a public proceeding the particular communication or other confidential information that could be used in the subsequent representation. The interests of subsequent clients also militate against extensive inquiry into the precise nature of the lawyer's representation of the subsequent client and the nature of exchanges between them.

The substantial-relationship test avoids requiring disclosure of confidential information by focusing upon the general features of the matters involved and inferences as to the likelihood that confidences were imparted by the former client that could be used to adverse effect in the subsequent representation. The inquiry into the issues involved in the prior representation should be as specific as possible without thereby revealing the confidential client information itself or confidential information concerning the second client. When the prior matter involved litigation, it will be conclusively presumed that the lawyer obtained confidential information about the issues involved in the litigation. When the prior matter did not involve litigation, its scope is assessed by reference to the work that the lawyer undertook and the array of information that a lawyer ordinarily would have obtained to carry out that work. The information obtained by the lawyer might also be proved by inferences from redacted documents, for example. On the use of in camera procedures to disclose confidential material to the tribunal but not to an opposing party, see § 86, Comment *f*.

Illustrations:

2. Lawyer represented Client A for a period of five years lobbying on environmental issues relating to uranium production. In the course of the representation in one matter, Lawyer learned the

basis for Client A's uranium-production decisions. Lawyer now has been asked to represent Client B, a purchaser of uranium, in an antitrust action against A and others alleging a conspiracy to impose limits on production. It is likely that Client B's claims against A would include addressing the same production decisions about which Lawyer earlier learned. Use of confidential information concerning A's production decisions learned in the earlier representation would materially advance the position of Client B in the antitrust matter. The matters are substantially related, and Lawyer may not represent Client B without effective consent of both A and B (see § 122).

3. Lawyer was general inside legal counsel to Company A for many years, dealing with all aspects of corporate affairs and management. Lawyer was dismissed from that position when Company A hired a new president. Company B has asked Lawyer to represent it in an antitrust suit against Company A based on facts arising after Lawyer left Company A's employ but involving broad charges of anti-competitive practices of Company A that, if true, were occurring at the time that Lawyer represented Company A. Lawyer may not represent Company B in the antitrust action. Because of the breadth of confidential client information of Company A to which Lawyer is likely to have had access during the earlier representation and the breadth of issues open in the antitrust claim of Company B, a substantial risk exists that use of that information would materially advance Company B's position in the later representation.

4. Lawyer represented Client A, a home builder, at the closings of the sales of several homes Client A had built in Tract X. Lawyers performing such work normally might encounter issues relating to marketability of title. A is now represented by other counsel. Client B has asked Lawyer to represent him in a suit against A in connection with B's sale to A of Tract Y, a parcel of land owned by Client B on which A plans to build homes. The present suit involves the marketability of the title to Tract Y. Although both representations involve marketability of title, it is unlikely that Lawyer's knowledge of marketability of Tract X would be relevant to the litigation involving the marketability of title to Tract Y. Accordingly, the matters are not substantially related. Lawyer may represent Client B against A without informed consent of A.

As used in this Section, the term "matter" includes not only representation in a litigated case, but also any representation involving a contract, claim, charge, or other subject of legal advice (compare § 133, Comment *e*). The term "matter" ordinarily does not include a legal position taken on behalf of a former client unless the underlying facts are also related. For example, a lawyer who successfully argued that a statute is constitutional on behalf of a former client may later argue that the statute is unconstitutional on behalf of a present client in a case not involving the former client, even though the lawyer's success on behalf of the present client might adversely affect the former client (compare § 128, Comment *f*).

Information that is confidential for some purposes under § 59 (so that, for example, a lawyer would not be free to discuss it publicly (see § 60)) might nonetheless be so general, readily observable, or of little value in the subsequent representation that it should not by itself result in a substantial relationship. Thus, a lawyer may master a particular substantive area of the law while representing a client, but that does not preclude the lawyer from later representing another client adversely to the first in a matter involving the same legal issues, if the matters factually are not substantially related. A lawyer might also have learned a former client's preferred approach to bargaining in settlement discussions or negotiating business points in a transaction, willingness or unwillingness to be deposed by an adversary, and financial ability to withstand extended litigation or contract negotiations. Only when such information will be directly in issue or of unusual value in the subsequent matter will it be independently relevant in assessing a substantial relationship.

e. A subsequent client with interests "materially adverse" to the interests of a former client. A later representation is prohibited if the second client's interests are materially adverse to those of the former client (see § 121, Comments *c(i)* (adverseness) & *c(ii)* (materiality)). The scope of a client's interests is normally determined by the scope of work that the lawyer undertook in the former representation. Thus, a lawyer who undertakes to represent a corporation with respect to the defense of a personal-injury claim involving only issues of causation and damages does not represent the corporation with respect to other interests. The lawyer may limit the scope of representation specifically for the purpose of avoiding a future conflict (see § 16). Similarly, the lawyer may limit the scope of representation of a later client so as to avoid representation substantially related to that undertaken for a previous client.

Illustration:

> 5. Lawyer formerly represented Client A in obtaining FDA approval to market prescription drug X for treating diseases of the eye. Client B has now asked Lawyer for legal assistance to obtain FDA approval for sale of prescription drug Y for treating diseases of the skin. Client B is also interested in possibly later application for FDA approval to market a different form of drug Y to treat diseases of the eye, thus significantly reducing the profitability of Client A's drug X. Confidential information that Lawyer gained in representing Client A in the earlier matter would be substantially related to work that Lawyer would do with respect to any future application by Client B for use of drug Y for eye diseases (although the information would not relate to the use of drug Y for treating diseases of the skin). Client B and Lawyer agree that Lawyer's work will relate only

to FDA approval for use of drug Y to treat diseases of the skin. Thus limited, Lawyer's work for Client B does not involve representation adverse to former Client A on a substantially related matter.

f.   A lawyer's subsequent use of confidential information. Even if a subsequent representation does not involve the same or a substantially related matter, a lawyer may not disclose or use confidential information of a former client in violation of § 60.

Illustration:

6.   Lawyer, now a prosecutor, had formerly represented Client in defending against a felony charge. During the course of a confidential interview, Client related to Lawyer a willingness to commit perjury. Lawyer is now prosecuting another person, Defendant, for a matter not substantially related to the former prosecution. In the jurisdiction, a defendant is not required to serve notice of defense witnesses that will be called. During the defense case, Defendant's lawyer calls Client as an alibi witness. Lawyer could not reasonably have known previously that Client would be called. Because of the lack of substantial relationship between the matters, Lawyer was not prohibited from undertaking the prosecution. Because Lawyer's knowledge of Client's statement about willingness to lie is confidential client information under § 59, Lawyer may not use that information in cross-examining Client, but otherwise Lawyer may cross-examine Client vigorously.

g.   A lawyer's duties of confidentiality other than to a former client. The principles in this Section presuppose that the lawyer in question has previously represented the person adversely affected by the present representation. Whether a client-lawyer relationship exists is considered in § 14 and § 121, Comment *d*. Two situations present analogous problems—communications with a prospective client and confidential information about a nonclient learned in representing a former client.

g(i).   Duties to a prospective client. A lawyer's obligation of confidentiality with respect to information revealed during an initial consultation prior to the decision about formation of a lawyer-client relationship is considered in § 15, Comment *c*.

g(ii).   Duties to a person about whom a lawyer learned confidential information while representing a former client. A lawyer might have obligations to persons who were not the lawyer's clients but about whom information was revealed to the lawyer under circumstances obligating the lawyer not to use or disclose the information. Those obligations arise under other law, particularly under the law of agency. For example, a lawyer might incur obligations of confidentiality as the subagent of a principal whom the lawyer's client serves as an agent (see Restatement Second, Agency §§ 5, 241, & 396). An important difference between general agency law and the law governing lawyers is that general agency law does not normally impute a restriction to other persons. Thus, when a lawyer's relationship to a nonclient is not that of lawyer-client but that, for example, of subagent-principal, imputation might not be required under the law governing subagents.

Illustrations:

7. Lawyer has represented Hospital in several medical-malpractice cases. In the course of preparing to defend one such case, Lawyer reviewed the confidential medical file of Patient who was not a party in the action. From the file, Lawyer learned that Patient had been convicted of a narcotics offense in another jurisdiction. Patient is now a material witness for the defense in an unrelated case that Lawyer has filed on behalf of Plaintiff. Adequate representation of Plaintiff would require Lawyer to cross-examine Patient about the narcotics conviction in an effort to undermine Patient's credibility. Lawyer may not reveal information about Patient that Hospital has an obligation to keep confidential. That limitation in turn may preclude effective representation of Plaintiff in the pending case. However if, without violating the obligation to Patient, Lawyer can adequately reveal to Plaintiff the nature of the conflict of interest and the likely effect of restricted cross-examination, Lawyer may represent Plaintiff with Plaintiff's informed consent (see § 122, Comment c).

8. Lawyer represents Underwriter in preparing to sell an issue of Company's bonds; Lawyer does not represent Company. Several questions concerning facts have arisen in drafting disclosure documents pertaining to the issue. Under applicable law, Underwriter must be satisfied that the facts are not material. Lawyer obtains confidential information from Company in the course of preparing Lawyer's opinion for Underwriter. Among the information learned is that Company might be liable to A for breach of contract. Unless the information has become generally known (see § 59), Lawyer may not represent A in a breach of contract action against Company because the information was learned from Company in confidence.

In the circumstances described in Illustration 8, standards of agency law or other law might permit the underwriter to provide services to another customer in a subsequent transaction so long as the underwriter takes appropriate steps to screen its employees. A lawyer affiliated with the disqualified lawyer could represent the underwriter in the second transaction after appropriate screening of the disqualified lawyer (compare § 124).

A lawyer's duties as fiduciary to nonclient third persons might create a conflict of interest with clients of the lawyer (see § 135).

A lawyer who learns confidential information from a person represented by another lawyer pursuant to a common-interest sharing arrangement (see § 76) is precluded from a later representation adverse to the former sharing person when information actually shared by that person with the lawyer or the lawyer's client is material and relevant to the later matter (see Illustration 8, above). Such a threatened use of shared information is inconsistent with the undertaking of confidentiality that is part of such an arrangement.

h. A lawyer with only a minor role in a prior representation. The specific tasks in which a lawyer was engaged might make the access to confidential client information insignificant. The lawyer bears the burden of persuasion as to that issue and as to the absence of opportunity to acquire confidential information. When such a burden has been met, the lawyer is not precluded from proceeding adversely to the former client (see § 124, Comment *d*, Illustration 3).

i. Withdrawal from representing an "accommodation" client. With the informed consent of each client as provided in § 122, a lawyer might undertake representation of another client as an accommodation to the lawyer's regular client, typically for a limited purpose in order to avoid duplication of services and consequent higher fees. If adverse interests later develop between the clients, even if the adversity relates to the matter involved in the common representation, circumstances might warrant the inference that the "accommodation" client understood and impliedly consented to the lawyer's continuing to represent the regular client in the matter. Circumstances most likely to evidence such an understanding are that the lawyer has represented the regular client for a long period of time before undertaking representation of the other client, that the representation was to be of limited scope and duration, and that the lawyer was not expected to keep confidential from the regular client any information provided to the lawyer by the other client. On obtaining express consent in advance to later representation of the regular client in such circumstances, see § 122, Comment *d*. The lawyer bears the burden of showing that circumstances exist to warrant an inference of understanding and implied consent. On other situations of withdrawal, see § 121, Comment *e*.

Illustrations:

9. Law Firm has represented Financial Corporation for many years as outside general counsel. Financial Corporation, represented by Law Firm, and Client Two, represented by separate counsel, entered into an agreement to operate a business. A shareholder derivative suit was later filed against both Financial Corporation and Client Two on a claim related to the agreement. Client Two by this point had become hard-pressed financially. Financial Corporation and Client Two had potential claims against each other arising out of the transaction but did not assert them so as to present a united front to the plaintiffs in the shareholder suit. Although separately represented in the shareholder derivative action, Financial Corporation and Client Two exchanged information in that action for the common purpose of defending against it (see § 76). During pretrial, Law Firm, with the informed consent of Financial

Corporation and Client Two, filed motions in the action in behalf of both Financial Corporation and Client Two. Later, Client Two filed for bankruptcy, and the Trustee in bankruptcy brought suit against Financial Corporation, seeking to recover damages based on the same underlying agreement. Notwithstanding Trustee's objection (compare Comment *c* hereto), Law Firm may withdraw from representing Client Two in the derivative action and represent Financial Corporation in defending against Trustee's suit. Circumstances warrant the inference that Client Two understood that Law Firm would continue to represent Financial Corporation in any such action.

10. The same facts as in Illustration 9, except that Law Firm withdraws from representing Financial Corporation and seeks to represent Trustee in the claims filed against Financial Corporation by Client Two. Even if withdrawal is permissible in the circumstances (compare § 32), Law Firm's representation of Trustee without the informed consent of Financial Corporation would violate this Section (see Comment *c* hereto).

j. Cure of conflicts created by transactions of a client. A lawyer may withdraw in order to continue an adverse representation against a theretofore existing client when the matter giving rise to the conflict and requiring withdrawal comes about through initiative of the clients. An example is a client's acquisition of an interest in an enterprise against which the lawyer is proceeding on behalf of another client. However, if the client's acquisition of the other enterprise was reasonably foreseeable by the lawyer when the lawyer undertook representation of the client, withdrawal will not cure the conflict. In any event, continuing the representation must be otherwise consistent with the former-client conflict rules.

Illustration:

11. Law Firm represents Client One in litigation against X Corporation. At the same time, Law Firm represents Client Two in an unrelated matter. Client Two, assisted by other counsel, acquires X Corporation as a wholly owned subsidiary. The circumstances are such that a conflict would exist in Law Firm's continued representation of Client One against the subsidiary (X Corporation) of Client Two (compare § 131, Comment *d*). Law Firm may withdraw from representing Client Two in order to continue representing Client One in the suit against X Corporation, and must do so unless the affected clients provided consent (see § 121). Law Firm may not represent X Corporation in the suit by Client One by withdrawing from representing Client One (see § 121, Comment *e(i)*).

§ 133. A Former Government Lawyer or Officer

(1) A lawyer may not act on behalf of a client with respect to a matter in which the lawyer participated personally and sub-

stantially while acting as a government lawyer or officer unless both the government and the client consent to the representation under the limitations and conditions provided in § 122.

(2) A lawyer who acquires confidential information while acting as a government lawyer or officer may not:

(a) if the information concerns a person, represent a client whose interests are materially adverse to that person in a matter in which the information could be used to the material disadvantage of that person; or

(b) if the information concerns the governmental client or employer, represent another public or private client in circumstances described in § 132(2).

Comment:

a. Scope and cross-references. This Section deals with a lawyer who leaves government employment and then undertakes private representation in the matter on which the lawyer was employed while in government or is otherwise in a position to use confidential information gained while in public employment. This Section applies whether the lawyer was formerly employed by a governmental agency as a lawyer or in some other capacity, such as an officer of the agency. If conflicts involving a government agency are governed by more stringent statutory or regulatory requirements, they also apply.

This Section is a special application of the general prohibition set forth in § 121 and is subject to consent under the limitations and conditions described in § 122. The law in some jurisdictions limits the extent to which governmental officials can waive the rights of the government (see § 122, Comment *g(ii)*). In addition, under 18 U.S.C. § 207, a criminal statute governing, among other kinds of conflicts, the conflicts of a former employee of the federal government, there is no provision for government consent.

The prohibition of this Section is imputed to affiliated lawyers by § 123. Removing the imputed prohibition is governed by § 124(3). The application of the attorney-client privilege to governmental clients is addressed in § 74; a lawyer's general duty of confidentiality, applicable to both governmental and nongovernmental clients, is considered in § 60.

The remedies for violation of this Section are those in § 121, Comment *f*. Criminal penalties are provided for in some statutes on conflicts of interest by former government employees.

b. Rationale. Prohibitions on the activities of former government lawyers are based on concerns similar to those protecting former private clients. Because those concerns apply somewhat differently to government clients, however, the rule of this Section is both broader and narrower than that of § 132.

First, the protection accorded government confidential information is parallel to that for confidential information of private clients. As discussed in § 74, however, statutes requiring openness in government operations might limit the government information that is given protection. Second, since government agencies have special powers to allocate public benefits and burdens, it is reasonable to prohibit a lawyer while in government from taking action designed to improve the lawyer's opportunities upon leaving government service.

On the other hand, government agencies must be able to recruit able lawyers. If the experience gained could not be used after lawyers left government service, recruiting lawyers would be more difficult. There is also a public interest in having lawyers in private practice who have served in government and understand both the substance and rationale of government policy. The experience of such lawyers might sometimes enable clients to achieve higher levels of compliance with law. Thus, this Section protects three government functions, those of client, recruiter of able employees, and law enforcer.

c. Personal and substantial involvement. This Section forbids former government lawyers or officers from taking on matters on which they worked personally and substantially while in government. Former government lawyers are not forbidden to work on matters solely because the matters were pending in the agency during the period of their employment.

The standard of "substantiality" is both formal and functional. A lawyer who signed a complaint on behalf of the government is substantially involved in the matter even if the lawyer knew few of the underlying facts. An action undertaken by a lawyer in the name of a superior is also within the rule.

Illustrations:

1. While acting as special assistant to the Governor of a state, Lawyer participated in negotiation of the purchase of a new computer system for state government. Lawyer is now in the private practice of law. Lawyer may not represent the computer contractor in a dispute arising under the contract.

2. While Lawyer was serving as general counsel of a government agency with many branch offices, a staff attorney in one branch office wrote a letter to X, a private citizen, initiating an official inquiry into a transaction involving X. The letter bore the stamped signature of Lawyer, but Lawyer had no personal involvement in the matter. After leaving government service, Lawyer is asked to represent X in resisting the inquiry. Lawyer may do so under this Section, unless an applicable statute or regulation prohibits the representation.

d. Adverse involvement is not required. The rule of this Section differs from § 132 in that prohibition applies even though the subsequent representation is not adverse to the interests of the former government client. There are three justifications for this distinction. First, prohibiting representation in a matter, even where consistent with the government's interest, diminishes the risk of subsequent misuse of information obtained by the government. If a former government lawyer could make use of confidential reports to an agency, for example, even in a cause that was consistent with the government position, it would go beyond the original purpose for making the reports and make it more difficult for the government to obtain voluntary disclosures from members of the public. Second, the rule removes an incentive to gain later advantages through methods of gathering information that are available only to the government, such as a grand-jury investigation. Third, the rule removes an incentive to begin proceedings as a government agent with a view to obtaining a subsequent advantage in private practice, such as by filing a complementary action for a subsequent private client. Because the rationale for this rule is in part to prevent misconduct by government officials while still in government, in some circumstances the government should not be permitted to consent to the subsequent representation (see § 122(2)(c)).

Illustration:

3. While working for the Securities and Exchange Commission, Lawyer participated in development of a case of securities fraud against a securities dealer. After leaving the Commission, Lawyer may not represent a private person victimized by the fraud in a suit for damages against the dealer, even though the representation is not adverse to the government.

e. *Definition of a "matter."* The term "matter," as applied to former government employees, is often defined as a judicial or other proceeding, application, request for a ruling or other determination, contract, claim, controversy, investigation, charge, accusation, arrest, or other particular matter involving a specific party or parties. Drafting of a statute or regulation of general applicability is not included under that definition, nor is work on a case of the same type (but not the same parties) as the one in which the lawyer seeks to be involved. The definition is narrower than that governing former-client conflicts of interest under § 132 (see id., Comment *d(iii)*).

Illustrations:

4. While serving in the general counsel's office of the state revenue department, Lawyer was involved in the drafting of regulations to implement new amendments to the state tax law. The regulations affected a large number of taxpayers. When Lawyer returns to private practice, Lawyer may advise taxpayers seeking to determine how the regulations apply, suing to have the regulations

construed or challenging the constitutionality of the statute or regulations.

5. In the capacity of city corporation counsel, Lawyer participated in drafting and negotiating the terms of an ordinance to rezone a specific tract of land of a major developer. Now that Lawyer has returned to private practice, the developer has sought to retain Lawyer in a lawsuit to construe the ordinance to permit more housing density than the city asserts the ordinance permits. Lawyer may not accept the case. The work by Lawyer on behalf of city was not of general application and was analogous to representation of the city in a case involving a particular party and parcel of land.

f. Possession of confidential information. Even if a lawyer was not personally and substantially involved in a matter while in government service, there can still be a risk that the lawyer will either misuse governmental authority and power against a citizen or misuse confidential information of the former governmental client against its interests. To protect against such misuse, Subsection (2) imposes two additional prohibitions.

f(i). A risk of misuse of confidential information. Subsection (2)(a), following ABA Model Rules of Professional Conduct, Rule 1.11(b) (1983), imposes limitations on representations after return to private practice of a former government lawyer or officer who learned confidential government information about a person while employed in government service. It prohibits private-practice representation against the interests of that person when the information could be used to the person's material disadvantage. The prohibition reflects two concerns. The first parallels the restriction against use of confidential information of a nonclient that has been obtained in representing a client, in this case the government to whom the third person provided confidential information (see § 132, Comment *g(ii)*). A second concern reflects the government's unique coercive powers to collect information. If a former government lawyer were free to use such information against the provider, the cooperative instincts to provide such information to the government would be chilled, and there would be legitimate indignation at misuse of powers of a public agency to benefit a private client (see Comment *d*). Such confidential information includes all information obtained under governmental authority (whether of the particular governmental employer or some other agency) which, at the time Subsection (2)(a) is applied, either the government is prohibited by law from disclosing to the public or has a privilege not to disclose, and which is not otherwise available to the public (compare § 131 (broader definition of confidential client information for purposes of the prohibitions stated in § 60)).

f(ii). A risk of misuse of information against a former governmental client or employer. Even if not personally and substantially participating in a matter, a government lawyer or employee might overhear or otherwise learn of confidential information of the employing agency. Its subsequent use against the interests of the agency is prohibited to the extent provided in § 132, Comment *f*.

g. Screening a former government lawyer. Screening of a former government lawyer will remove the imputed effects of the personally prohibited former government lawyer as provided in § 124(3) and Comment *e* thereto.

TOPIC 5.   CONFLICTS OF INTEREST DUE TO A LAWYER'S OBLIGATION TO A THIRD PERSON

§ 134.   Compensation or Direction of a Lawyer by a Third Person

(1) A lawyer may not represent a client if someone other than the client will wholly or partly compensate the lawyer for the representation, unless the client consents under the limitations and conditions provided in § 122 and knows of the circumstances and conditions of the payment.

(2) A lawyer's professional conduct on behalf of a client may be directed by someone other than the client if:

(a) the direction does not interfere with the lawyer's independence of professional judgment;

(b) the direction is reasonable in scope and character, such as by reflecting obligations borne by the person directing the lawyer; and

(c) the client consents to the direction under the limitations and conditions provided in § 122.

Comment:

a. Scope and cross-references. This Section applies the general conflicts prohibition of § 121 to the various situations in which a third person pays a lawyer's fee for representing a client or directs a lawyer's work for a client. The third person might be interested as a relative or friend or have obligations to the client because of indemnification or similar arrangements, or be interested directly in the matter because of a co-client, such as a corporation sued along with one or more of its employees (see § 131, Comment *e*). The risk of adverse effect on representation of the client is inherent in any such payment or direction. Accordingly, this Section, following the standard rule of the lawyer codes, requires informed consent of the client and imposes limitations on the control that a third person may exercise over the lawyer's work.

While discussion in the following Comments (see Comment *f*) will consider issues of the law governing a lawyer representing an insured person, the relationship between the insured person and the insurer or indemnitor will be controlled by other law, such as the law of insurance or of contract. Similarly, other law may govern other relationships between a client and a third person who pays or directs the lawyer, such as when the government pays a lawyer to represent a client in a criminal or civil matter (see Comment *g*). Issues relating to all such other relationships are beyond the scope of the Restatement.

The prohibition imposed by this Section applies to all affiliated lawyers (see § 123). Sanctions and remedies listed in § 6, are available for violation of this Section. Where a violation of this Section has caused actionable harm to a client, the remedy of legal malpractice (see Chapter 4) is available.

Issues relating to payment of legal fees generally are considered in Chapter 3. Chapter 5 examines a lawyer's duty to protect confidential information of a client.

b. Initial client consent. As stated in the Section, under § 122 a client must consent to a lawyer's accepting either a third person's payment of the fee for a client or a third person's direction in a matter. In particular, the client must have knowledge of the circumstances and conditions under which the fee payment or direction is to be provided and any substantial risks to the client thereby created (see § 122, Comment *c*). On consent in insurance-defense representations, see Comment *f* hereto. In an emergency situation in which the lawyer must take action to protect the interests of the client, as in filing an answer to avoid default, the lawyer may take such action even if a conflict appears to exist, but must also promptly take action to address the conflict.

c. Third-person fee payment. This Section accommodates two values implicated by third-person payment of legal fees. First, it requires that a lawyer's loyalty to the client not be compromised by the third-person source of payment. The lawyer's duty of loyalty is to the client alone, although it may also extend to any co-client when that relationship is either consistent with the duty owing to each co-client or is consented to in accordance with § 122. Second, however, the Section acknowledges that it is often in the client's interest to have legal representation paid for by another. Most liability-insurance contracts, for example, provide that the insurer will provide legal representation for an insured who is charged with responsibility for harm to another (see also Comment *f* hereto). Lawyers paid by civil-rights organizations have helped citizens pursue their individual rights and establish legal principles of general importance. Similarly, lawyers in private practice or in a legal-services organization may be appointed or otherwise come to represent indigent persons pursuant to arrangements under which their fees will be paid by a governmental body (see Comment *g*).

d. Third-person direction of a representation. The principle that a lawyer must exercise independent professional judgment on behalf of the client (Subsection (2)(a)) is reflected in the requirement of the lawyer codes that no third person control or direct a lawyer's professional judgment on behalf of a client. Consistent with that requirement, a third person may, with the client's consent and otherwise in the circumstances and to the extent stated in Subsection (2), direct the lawyer's representation of the client. When the conditions of the Subsection are satisfied, the client has, in effect, transferred to the designated third person the client's prerogatives of directing the lawyer's activities (see § 21(2)). The third person's directions must allow for effective representation of the client, and the client must give informed consent to the exercise of the power of direction by the third person. The direction must be reasonable in scope and character, such as by reflecting obligations borne by the person directing the lawyer. Such directions are reasonable in scope and character if, for example, the third party will pay any judgment rendered against the client and makes a decision that defense costs beyond those designated by the third party would not significantly change the likely outcome. Informed client consent may be effective with respect to many forms of direction, ranging from informed consent to particular instances of direction, such as in a representation in which the client otherwise directs the lawyer, to informed consent to general direction of the lawyer by another, such as an insurer or indemnitor on whom the client has contractually conferred the power of direction (see Comment *f*).

Illustration:

1. Resettle, a nonprofit organization, works to secure better living conditions for refugees. Resettle's board of directors believes that a case should be filed to test whether a federal policy of detaining certain refugees is legally justified. Client is a refugee who has recently been detained under the federal policy, and Resettle has offered to pay Lawyer to seek Client's release from detention. With the informed consent of Client, Lawyer may accept payment by Resettle and may agree to make contentions that Resettle wishes to have tested by the litigation.

Just as there are limits to client consent in § 122, there are limits to the restrictions on scope of the representation permitted under this Section. See § 122, Comment *g* (nonconsentable conflicts).

Illustrations:

2. Client is charged with the crime of illegally selling securities. Client's employer, Brokerage, has offered to pay Lawyer to defend Client on the condition that Client agree not to implicate Brokerage or any of its other employees in the crimes charged against Client. Lawyer may not accept the representation on those terms. Whether to accept a plea bargain, for example, and whether to implicate others in the wrongdoing are matters about which the client, not the person paying for the defense, must have the authority to make decisions (see § 22).

3. Same facts as stated in Illustration 2, except that there is no substantial factual or legal basis for implicating Brokerage or any of its other employees and Client consents to accept Lawyer's representation on the condition stated by Brokerage under the limitations and conditions provided in § 122, including knowledge that Broker-

age has stated the condition. Under such circumstances, Client's consent authorizes Lawyer to accept payment from Brokerage and adhere to the described conditions.

e. Preserving confidential client information. Although a legal fee may be paid or direction given by a third person, a lawyer must protect the confidential information of the client. Informed client consent to the third-person payment or direction does not by itself constitute informed consent to the lawyer's revealing such information to that person. Consent to reveal confidential client information must meet the separate requirements of § 62.

Illustration:

> 4. Employer has agreed to pay for representation of Employee in defending a claim involving facts arguably arising out of pursuit of Employer's business. Employer asks Lawyer what Employee intends to testify about the circumstances of Employee's actions. Without consent of Employee as provided in § 62, Lawyer may not give Employer that information.

On a lawyer's discretion to disclose confidential information of a client to a co-client in the representation, see § 60, Comment *l*.

f. Representing an insured. A lawyer might be designated by an insurer to represent the insured under a liability-insurance policy in which the insurer undertakes to indemnify the insured and to provide a defense. The law governing the relationship between the insured and the insurer is, as stated in Comment *a*, beyond the scope of the Restatement. Certain practices of designated insurance-defense counsel have become customary and, in any event, involve primarily standardized protection afforded by a regulated entity in recurring situations. Thus a particular practice permissible for counsel representing an insured may not be permissible under this Section for a lawyer in noninsurance arrangements with significantly different characteristics.

It is clear in an insurance situation that a lawyer designated to defend the insured has a client-lawyer relationship with the insured. The insurer is not, simply by the fact that it designates the lawyer, a client of the lawyer. Whether a client-lawyer relationship also exists between the lawyer and the insurer is determined under § 14. Whether or not such a relationship exists, communications between the lawyer and representatives of the insurer concerning such matters as progress reports, case evaluations, and settlement should be regarded as privileged and otherwise immune from discovery by the claimant or another party to the proceeding. Similarly, communications between counsel retained by an insurer to coordinate the efforts of multiple counsel for insureds in multiple suits and such coordinating counsel are subject to the privilege. Because and to the extent that the insurer is directly concerned in the matter financially, the insurer should be accorded standing to assert a claim for appropriate relief from the lawyer for financial loss proximately caused by professional negligence or other wrongful act of the lawyer. Compare § 51, Comment *g*.

The lawyer's acceptance of direction from the insurer is considered in Subsection (2) and Comment *d* hereto. With respect to client consent (see Comment *b* hereto) in insurance representations, when there appears to be no substantial risk that a claim against a client-insured will not be fully covered by an insurance policy pursuant to which the lawyer is appointed and is to be paid, consent in the form of the acquiescence of the client-insured to an informative letter to the client-insured at the outset of the representation should be all that is required. The lawyer should either withdraw or consult with the client-insured (see § 122) when a substantial risk that the client-insured will not be fully covered becomes apparent (see § 121, Comment *c(iii)*).

Illustration:

5.   Insurer, a liability-insurance company, has issued a policy to Policyholder under which Insurer is to provide a defense and otherwise insure Policyholder against claims covered under the insurance policy. A suit filed against Policyholder alleges that Policyholder is liable for a covered act and for an amount within the policy's monetary limits. Pursuant to the policy's terms, Insurer designates Lawyer to defend Policyholder. Lawyer believes that doubling the number of depositions taken, at a cost of $5,000, would somewhat increase Policyholder's chances of prevailing and Lawyer so informs Insurer and Policyholder. If the insurance contract confers authority on Insurer to make such decisions about expense of defense, and Lawyer reasonably believes that the additional depositions can be forgone without violating the duty of competent representation owed by Lawyer to Policyholder (see § 52), Lawyer may comply with Insurer's direction that taking depositions would not be worth the cost.

Material divergence of interest might exist between a liability insurer and an insured, for example, when a claim substantially in excess of policy limits is asserted against an insured. If the lawyer knows or should be aware of such an excess claim, the lawyer may not follow directions of the insurer if doing so would put the insured at significantly increased risk of liability in excess of the policy coverage. Such occasions for conflict may exist at the outset of the representation or may be created by events that occur thereafter. The lawyer must address a conflict whenever presented. To the extent that such a conflict is subject to client consent (see § 122(2)(c)), the lawyer may proceed after obtaining client consent under the limitations and conditions stated in § 122.

When there is a question whether a claim against the insured is within the coverage of the policy, a lawyer designated to defend the insured may not reveal adverse confidential client information of the insured to the insurer concerning that question (see § 60) without explicit informed consent of the insured (see § 62). That follows whether or not the lawyer also represents the insurer as co-client and whether or not the insurer has asserted a "reservation of rights" with respect to its defense of the insured (compare § 60, Comment *l* (confidentiality in representation of co-clients in general)).

With respect to events or information that create a conflict of interest between insured and insurer, the lawyer must proceed in the best interests of the insured, consistent with the lawyer's duty not to assist client fraud (see § 94) and, if applicable, consistent with the lawyer's duties to the insurer as co-client (see § 60, Comment *l*). If the designated lawyer finds it impossible so to proceed, the lawyer must withdraw from representation of both clients as provided in § 32 (see also § 60, Comment *l*). The designated lawyer may be precluded by duties to the insurer from providing advice and other legal services to the insured concerning such matters as coverage under the policy, claims against other persons insured by the same insurer, and the advisability of asserting other claims against the insurer. In such instances, the lawyer must inform the insured in an adequate and timely manner of the limitation on the scope of the lawyer's services and the importance of obtaining assistance of other counsel with respect to such matters. Liability of the insurer with respect to such matters is regulated under statutory and common-law rules such as those governing liability for bad-faith refusal to defend or settle. Those rules are beyond the scope of this Restatement (see Comment *a* hereto).

g. Legal service and similarly funded representations. Lawyers who provide representation to indigent persons may do so pursuant to various arrangements under which their fees or other compensation will be paid by a governmental agency or similar funding organization. For example, a lawyer may represent clients as a staff attorney of a legal aid, military legal assistance, or similar organization, with compensation in the form of a salary paid by the organization. Lawyers in private practice may be appointed by a court, defender or legal-service organization, or bar association to represent a person accused of crime or a person involved in a civil matter (see § 14, Comment *g*), with the lawyer's fee to be paid by the government or organization, often pursuant to a schedule of fees. Certain for-profit legal-service arrangements have also been approved, under which individual private practitioners provide assistance to participants who pay a flat charge to the legal-service organization for limited legal services. Regardless of the method of appointment, the form of compensation, or the nature of the paying organization (for example, whether governmental or private or whether nonprofit or for-profit), the lawyer's representation of and relationship with the individual client must proceed as provided for in this Section.

§ 135. A Lawyer with a Fiduciary or Other Legal Obligation to a Nonclient

Unless the affected client consents to the representation under the limitations and conditions provided in § 122, a lawyer

may not represent a client in any matter with respect to which the lawyer has a fiduciary or other legal obligation to another if there is a substantial risk that the lawyer's representation of the client would be materially and adversely affected by the lawyer's obligation.

PARALLEL TABLES OF RESTATEMENT THIRD SECTION NUMBERS AND OF ANNUAL MEETING DRAFT SECTION NUMBERS

Restatement Third, The Law Governing Lawyers, was developed in the course of eight Tentative Drafts (1988–1994; 1997) and two Proposed Final Drafts (1996 and 1998), all of which were considered at Annual Meetings of The American Law Institute. The order of the Chapters were not changed for the Official Text, but section numbers were renumbered to make them consecutive. Because many sections have been dismissed in cases, articles, and texts under their Annual Meeting Draft section numbers, the following tables are provided to facilitate conversion.

The Tables correlate the final versions with the section numbers found in the last three Annual Meeting Drafts: Proposed Final Draft No. 1 (1996), Tentative Draft No. 8 (1997), and Proposed Final Draft No. 2 (1998). Table I converts from Official Text section numbers to Annual Meeting Draft section numbers, and Table II does the reverse.

TABLE I

SECTION NUMBERS FROM OFFICIAL TEXT TO ANNUAL MEETING DRAFTS

Official Text Section Number	Annual Meeting Draft Section Number	Official Text Section Number	Annual Meeting Draft Section Number
1	1	21	32
2	2	22	33
3	3	23	34
4	4	24	35
5	5	25	37
6	6	26	38
7	7	27	39
8	8	28	40
9	10	29	41
10	11	30	42
11	12	31	43
12	13	32	44
13	14	33	45
14	26	34	46
15	27	35	47
16	28	36	48
17	29	37	49
18	29A	38	50
19	30	39	51
20	31	40	52
		41	53

Official Text Section Number	Annual Meeting Draft Section Number	Official Text Section Number	Annual Meeting Draft Section Number
42	54	89	138
43	55	90	139
44	56	91	140
45	57	92	141
46	58	93	142
47	59	94	151
48	70 (previously 71)	95	152
49	71	96	155
50	72	97	156
51	73	98	157
52	74	99	158
53	75	100	159
54	76	101	161
55	76A	102	162
56	77	103	163
57	78	104	164
58	79	105	165
59	111	106	166
60	112	107	167
61	113	108	168
62	114	109	169
63	115	110	170
64	116	111	171
65	117	112	172
66	117A	113	173
67	117B	114	174
68	118	115	175
69	119	116	176
70	120	117	177
71	121	118	178
72	122	119	179
73	123	120	180
74	124	121	201
75	125	122	202
76	126	123	203
77	127	124	204
78	128	125	206
79	129	126	207
80	130	127	208
81	131	128	209
82	132	129	210
83	133	130	211
84	134A	131	212
85	134B	132	213
86	135	133	214
87	136	134	215
88	137	135	216

TABLE II

SECTION NUMBERS FROM ANNUAL MEETING DRAFTS TO OFFICIAL TEXT

Annual Meeting Draft Section Number	Official Text Section Number	Annual Meeting Draft Section Number	Official Text Section Number
1	1	113	61
2	2	114	62
3	3	115	63
4	74	116	64
5	5	117	65
6	6	117A	66
7	7	117B	67
8	8	118	68
10	9	119	69
11	10	120	70
12	11	121	71
13	12	122	72
14	13	123	73
26	14	124	74
27	15	125	75
28	16	126	76
29	17	127	77
29A	18	128	78
30	19	129	79
31	20	130	80
32	21	131	81
33	22	132	82
34	23	133	83
35	24	134A	84
37	25	134B	85
38	26	135	86
39	27	136	87
40	28	137	88
41	29	138	89
42	30	139	90
43	31	140	91
44	32	141	92
45	33	142	93
46	34	151	94
47	35	152	95
48	36	155	96
49	37	156	97
50	38	157	98
51	39	158	99
52	40	159	100
53	41	161	101
54	42	162	102
55	43	163	103
56	44	164	104
57	45	165	105
58	46	166	106
59	47	167	107
70 (previously 71)	48	168	108
71	49	169	109
72	50	170	110
73	51	171	111
74	52	172	112
75	53	173	113
76	54	174	114
76A	55	175	115
77	56	176	116
78	57	177	117
79	58	178	118
111	59	179	119
112	60	180	120
		201	121

PART FIVE

STATUTES THAT AFFECT THE LEGAL PROFESSION

TABLE OF CONTENTS

Introduction

This part includes several selected federal statutes that affect the legal profession.

SELECTED FEDERAL STATUTES

5 U.S.C.A.

CHAPTER 73. SUITABILITY, SECURITY, AND CONDUCT

18 U.S.C.A.

CHAPTER 11. BRIBERY AND GRAFT

CHAPTER 21. CONTEMPTS

CHAPTER 49. FUGITIVES FROM JUSTICE

CHAPTER 63. MAIL FRAUD

CHAPTER 73. OBSTRUCTION OF JUSTICE

---

5 U.S.C.A.

CHAPTER 73. SUITABILITY, SECURITY, AND CONDUCT

§ 7301. Presidential Regulations

* * *

Executive Order No. 12674: Principles of Ethical Conduct for Government Officers and Employees

"By virtue of the authority vested in me as President by the Constitution and the laws of the United States of America, and in order to establish fair and exacting standards of ethical conduct for all executive branch employees, it is hereby ordered as follows:

Part 1—Principles Of Ethical Conduct

Section 101. Principles of Ethical Conduct. To ensure that every citizen can have complete confidence in the integrity of the Federal Government, each Federal employee shall respect and adhere to the fundamental principles of ethical service as implemented in regulations promulgated under sections 201 and 301 of this order:

"**(a)** Public service is a public trust, requiring employees to place loyalty to the Constitution, the laws, and ethical principles above private gain.

"**(b)** Employees shall not hold financial interests that conflict with the conscientious performance of duty.

"**(c)** Employees shall not engage in financial transactions using nonpublic Government information or allow the improper use of such information to further any private interest.

"**(d)** An employee shall not, except pursuant to such reasonable exceptions as are provided by regulation, solicit or accept any gift or other item of monetary value from any person or entity seeking official action from, doing business with, or conducting activities regulated by the employee's agency, or whose interests may be substantially affected by the performance or nonperformance of the employee's duties.

"**(e)** Employees shall put forth honest effort in the performance of their duties.

"**(f)** Employees shall make no unauthorized commitments or promises of any kind purporting to bind the Government.

"**(g)** Employees shall not use public office for private gain.

"**(h)** Employees shall act impartially and not give preferential treatment to any private organization or individual.

"**(i)** Employees shall protect and conserve Federal property and shall not use it for other than authorized activities.

"**(j)** Employees shall not engage in outside employment or activities, including seeking or negotiating for employment, that conflict with official Government duties and responsibilities.

"**(k)** Employees shall disclose waste, fraud, abuse, and corruption to appropriate authorities.

"**(l)** Employees shall satisfy in good faith their obligations as citizens, including all just financial obligations, especially those—such as Federal, State, or local taxes—that are imposed by law.

"**(m)** Employees shall adhere to all laws and regulations that provide equal opportunity for all Americans regardless of race, color, religion, sex, national origin, age, or handicap.

"**(n)** Employees shall endeavor to avoid any actions creating the appearance that they are violating the law or the ethical standards promulgated pursuant to this order.

"**Sec. 102.   Limitations on Outside Earned Income.**

"**(a)** No employee who is appointed by the President to a full-time noncareer position in the executive branch (including full-time noncareer employees in the White House Office, the Office of Policy Development, and the Office of Cabinet Affairs), shall receive any earned income for any outside employment or activity performed during that Presidential appointment.

"**(b)** The prohibition set forth in subsection (a) shall not apply to any full-time noncareer employees employed pursuant to 3 U.S.C. 105 [section 105 of Title 3, The President] and 3 U.S.C. 107(a) [section 107(a) of Title 3] at salaries below the minimum rate of basic pay then paid for GS–9 of the General Schedule. Any outside employment must comply with relevant agency standards of conduct, including any requirements for approval of outside employment.

"Part II—Office Of Government Ethics Authority

"**Sec. 201. The Office of Government Ethics.** The Office of Government Ethics shall be responsible for administering this order by:

"**(a)** Promulgating, in consultation with the Attorney General and the Office of Personnel Management, regulations that establish a single, comprehensive, and clear set of executive-branch standards of conduct that shall be objective, reasonable, and enforceable.

"**(b)** Developing, disseminating, and periodically updating an ethics manual for employees of the executive branch describing the applicable statutes, rules, decisions, and policies.

"**(c)** Promulgating, with the concurrence of the Attorney General, regulations interpreting the provisions of the post-employment statute, section 207 of title 18, United States Code [section 207 of Title 18, Crimes and Criminal Procedure]; the general conflict-of-interest statute, section 208 of title 18, United States Code [section 208 of Title 18]; and the statute prohibiting supplementation of salaries, section 209 of title 18, United States Code [section 209 of Title 18].

"**(d)** Promulgating, in consultation with the Attorney General and the Office of Personnel Management, regulations establishing a system of nonpublic (confidential) financial disclosure by executive branch employees to complement the system of public disclosure under the Ethics in Government Act of 1978. Such regulations shall include criteria to guide agencies in determining which employees shall submit these reports.

"**(e)** Ensuring that any implementing regulations issued by agencies under this order are consistent with and promulgated in accordance with this order.

"**Sec. 202. Executive Office of the President.** In that the agencies within the Executive Office of the President (EOP) currently exercise functions that are not distinct and separate from each other within the meaning and for the purposes of section 207(e) of title 18, United States Code [section 207(e) of Title 18], those agencies shall be treated as one agency under section 207(c) of title 18, United States Code [section 207(c) of Title 18].

"Part III—Agency Responsibilities

"**Sec. 301. Agency Responsibilities.** Each agency head is directed to:

"**(a)** Supplement, as necessary and appropriate, the comprehensive executive branch-wide regulations of the Office of Government Ethics, with regulations of special applicability to the particular functions and activities of that agency. Any supplementary agency regulations shall be prepared as addenda to the branch-wide regulations and promulgated jointly with the Office of Government Ethics, at the agency's expense, for inclusion in Title 5 of the Code of Federal Regulations.

"**(b)** Ensure the review by all employees of this order and regulations promulgated pursuant to the order.

"**(c)** Coordinate with the Office of Government Ethics in developing annual agency ethics training plans. Such training shall include mandatory annual briefings on ethics and standards of conduct for all employees appointed by the President, all employees in the Executive Office of the President, all officials required to file public or nonpublic financial disclosure reports, all employees who are contracting officers and procurement officials, and any other employees designated by the agency head.

"**(d)** Where practicable, consult formally or informally with the Office of Government Ethics prior to granting any exemption under section 208 of title 18, United States Code [section 208 of Title 18], and provide the Director of the Office of Government Ethics a copy of any exemption granted.

"**(e)** Ensure that the rank, responsibilities, authority, staffing, and resources of the Designated Agency Ethics Official are sufficient to ensure the effectiveness of the agency ethics program. Support should include the provision of a separate budget line item for ethics activities, where practicable.

* * *

18 U.S.C.A.

CHAPTER 11. BRIBERY AND GRAFT

§ 201. Bribery of public officials and witnesses

(a) For the purpose of this section—

(1) the term "public official" means Member of Congress, Delegate, or Resident Commissioner, either before or after such official has qualified, or an officer or employee or person acting for or on behalf of the United States, or any department, agency or branch of Government thereof, including the District of Columbia, in any official function, under or by authority of any such department, agency, or branch of Government, or a juror;

(2) the term "person who has been selected to be a public official" means any person who has been nominated or appointed to be a public official, or has been officially informed that such person will be so nominated or appointed; and

(3) the term "official act" means any decision or action on any question, matter, cause, suit, proceeding or controversy, which may at any time be pending, or which may by law be brought before any public official, in such official's official capacity, or in such official's place of trust or profit.

(b) Whoever—

(1) directly or indirectly, corruptly gives, offers or promises anything of value to any public official or person who has been selected to be a public official, or offers or promises any public official or any person who has been selected to be a public official to give anything of value to any other person or entity, with intent—

(A) to influence any official act; or

(B) to influence such public official or person who has been selected to be a public official to commit or aid in committing, or collude in, or allow, any fraud, or make opportunity for the commission of any fraud, on the United States; or

(C) to induce such public official or such person who has been selected to be a public official to do or omit to do any act in violation of the lawful duty of such official or person;

(2) being a public official or person selected to be a public official, directly or indirectly, corruptly demands, seeks, receives, accepts, or agrees to receive or accept anything of value personally or for any other person or entity, in return for:

(A) being influenced in the performance of any official act;

(B) being influenced to commit or aid in committing, or to collude in, or allow, any fraud, or make opportunity for the commission of any fraud, on the United States; or

(C) being induced to do or omit to do any act in violation of the official duty of such official or person;

(3) directly or indirectly, corruptly gives, offers, or promises anything of value to any person, or offers or promises such person to give anything of value to any other person or entity, with intent to

1077

influence the testimony under oath or affirmation of such first-mentioned person as a witness upon a trial, hearing, or other proceeding, before any court, any committee of either House or both Houses of Congress, or any agency, commission, or officer authorized by the laws of the United States to hear evidence or take testimony, or with intent to influence such person to absent himself therefrom;

(4) directly or indirectly, corruptly demands, seeks, receives, accepts, or agrees to receive or accept anything of value personally or for any other person or entity in return for being influenced in testimony under oath or affirmation as a witness upon any such trial, hearing, or other proceeding, or in return for absenting himself therefrom;

shall be fined under this title or not more than three times the monetary equivalent of the thing of value, whichever is greater, or imprisoned for not more than fifteen years, or both, and may be disqualified from holding any office of honor, trust, or profit under the United States.

(c) Whoever—

(1) otherwise than as provided by law for the proper discharge of official duty—

(A) directly or indirectly gives, offers, or promises anything of value to any public official, former public official, or person selected to be a public official, for or because of any official act performed or to be performed by such public official, former public official, or person selected to be a public official; or

(B) being a public official, former public official, or person selected to be a public official, otherwise than as provided by law for the proper discharge of official duty, directly or indirectly demands, seeks, receives, accepts, or agrees to receive or accept anything of value personally for or because of any official act performed or to be performed by such official or person;

(2) directly or indirectly, gives, offers, or promises anything of value to any person, for or because of the testimony under oath or affirmation given or to be given by such person as a witness upon a trial, hearing, or other proceeding, before any court, any committee of either House or both Houses of Congress, or any agency, commission, or officer authorized by the laws of the United States to hear evidence or take testimony, or for or because of such person's absence therefrom;

(3) directly or indirectly demands, seeks, receives, accepts, or agrees to receive or accept anything of value personally for or because of the testimony under oath or affirmation given or to be given by such person as a witness upon any such trial, hearing, or

other proceeding, or for or because of such person's absence there-from;

shall be fined under this title or imprisoned for not more than two years, or both.

(d) Paragraphs (3) and (4) of subsection (b) and paragraphs (2) and (3) of subsection (c) shall not be construed to prohibit the payment or receipt of witness fees provided by law, or the payment, by the party upon whose behalf a witness is called and receipt by a witness, of the reasonable cost of travel and subsistence incurred and the reasonable value of time lost in attendance at any such trial, hearing, or proceeding, or in the case of expert witnesses, a reasonable fee for time spent in the preparation of such opinion, and in appearing and testifying.

(e) The offenses and penalties prescribed in this section are separate from and in addition to those prescribed in sections 1503, 1504, and 1505 of this title.

§ 202. Definitions

(a) For the purpose of sections 203, 205, 207, 208, and 209 of this title the term "special Government employee" shall mean an officer or employee of the executive or legislative branch of the United States Government, of any independent agency of the United States or of the District of Columbia, who is retained, designated, appointed, or employed to perform, with or without compensation, for not to exceed one hundred and thirty days during any period of three hundred and sixty-five consecutive days, temporary duties either on a full-time or intermittent basis, a part-time United States commissioner, a part-time United States magistrate, or, regardless of the number of days of appointment, an independent counsel appointed under chapter 40 of title 28 and any person appointed by that independent counsel under section 594(c) of title 28. Notwithstanding the next preceding sentence, every person serving as a part-time local representative of a Member of Congress in the Member's home district or State shall be classified as a special Government employee. . . .

(b) For the purposes of sections 205 and 207 of this title, the term "official responsibility" means the direct administrative or operating authority, whether intermediate or final, and either exercisable alone or with others, and either personally or through subordinates, to approve, disapprove, or otherwise direct Government action.

(c) Except as otherwise provided in such sections, the terms "officer" and "employee" in sections 203, 205, 207 through 209 and 218 of this title, mean those individuals defined in sections 2104 and 2105 of title 5. The terms "officer" and "employee" shall not include the President, the Vice President, a Member of Congress, or a Federal judge.

(d) The term "Member of Congress" in sections 204 and 207 means—

(1) a United States Senator; and

(2) a Representative in, or a Delegate or Resident Commissioner to, the House of Representatives.

(e) As used in this chapter, the term—

(1) "executive branch" includes each executive agency as defined in title 5, and any other entity or administrative unit in the executive branch;

(2) "judicial branch" means the Supreme Court of the United States; the United States courts of appeals; the United States district courts; the Court of International Trade; the United States bankruptcy courts; any court created pursuant to article I of the United States Constitution, including the Court of Appeals for the Armed Forces, the United States Claims Court, and the United States Tax Court, but not including a court of a territory or possession of the United States; the Federal Judicial Center; and any other agency, office, or entity in the judicial branch; and

(3) "legislative branch" means—

(A) the Congress; and

(B) the Office of the Architect of the Capitol, the United States Botanic Garden, the General Accounting Office, the Government Printing Office, the Library of Congress, the Office of Technology Assessment, the Congressional Budget Office, the United States Capitol Police, and any other agency, entity, office, or commission established in the legislative branch.

§ 203. Compensation to Members of Congress, officers, and others in matters affecting the Government

(a) Whoever, otherwise than as provided by law for the proper discharge of official duties, directly or indirectly—

(1) demands, seeks, receives, accepts, or agrees to receive or accept any compensation for any representational services, as agent or attorney or otherwise, rendered or to be rendered either personally or by another—

(A) at a time when such person is a Member of Congress, Member of Congress Elect, Delegate, Delegate Elect, Resident Commissioner, or Resident Commissioner Elect; or

(B) at a time when such person is an officer or employee or Federal Judge of the United States in the executive, legislative, or judicial branch of the Government, or

in any agency of the United States, in relation to any proceeding, application, request for a ruling or other determination, contract, claim, controversy, charge, accusation, arrest, or other particular matter in which the United States is a party or has a direct and substantial interest, before any department, agency, court, court-martial, officer, or any civil, military, or naval commission; or

(2) knowingly gives, promises, or offers any compensation for any such representational services rendered or to be rendered at a time when the person to whom the compensation is given, promised, or offered, is or was such a Member, Member Elect, Delegate, Delegate Elect, Commissioner, Commissioner Elect, Federal Judge, officer, or employee;

shall be subject to the penalties set forth in section 216 of this title.

(b) Whoever, otherwise than as provided by law for the proper discharge of official duties, directly or indirectly—

(1) demands, seeks, receives, accepts, or agrees to receive or accept any compensation for any representational services, as agent or attorney or otherwise, rendered or to be rendered either personally or by another, at a time when such person is an officer or employee of the District of Columbia, in relation to any proceeding, application, request for a ruling or other determination, contract, claim, controversy, charge, accusation, arrest, or other particular matter in which the District of Columbia is a party or has a direct and substantial interest, before any department, agency, court, officer, or commission; or

(2) knowingly gives, promises, or offers any compensation for any such representational services rendered or to be rendered at a time when the person to whom the compensation is given, promised, or offered, is or was an officer or employee of the District of Columbia;

shall be subject to the penalties set forth in section 216 of this title; and

(c) A special Government employee shall be subject to subsections (a) and (b) only in relation to a particular matter involving a specific party or parties—

(1) in which such employee has at any time participated personally and substantially as a Government employee or as a special Government employee or as a special Government employee through decision, approval, disapproval, recommendation, the rendering of advice, investigation or otherwise; or

(2) which is pending in the department or agency of the Government in which such employee is serving except that paragraph (2) of this subsection shall not apply in the case of a special Government employee who has served in such department or agency no more than sixty days during the immediately preceding period of three hundred and sixty-five consecutive days.

(d) Nothing in this section prevents an officer or employee, including a special Government employee, from acting, with or without compensation, as agent or attorney for or otherwise representing his parents, spouse, child, or any person for whom, or for any estate for which, he is serving as guardian, executor, administrator, trustee, or other personal fiduciary except—

(1) in those matters in which he has participated personally and substantially as a Government employee or as a special Government employee through decision, approval, disapproval, recommendation, the rendering of advice, investigation, or otherwise; or

(2) in those matters that are the subject of his official responsibility,

subject to approval by the Government official responsible for appointment to his position.

(e) Nothing in this section prevents a special Government employee from acting as agent or attorney for another person in the performance of work under a grant by, or a contract with or for the benefit of, the United States if the head of the department or agency concerned with the grant or contract certifies in writing that the national interest so requires and publishes such certification in the Federal Register.

(f) Nothing in this section prevents an individual from giving testimony under oath or from making statements required to be made under penalty of perjury.

§ 204. Practice in United States Claims Court or the United States Court of Appeals for the Federal Circuit by Members of Congress

Whoever, being a Member of Congress or Member of Congress Elect, practices in the United States Claims Court or the United States Court of Appeals for the Federal Circuit shall be subject to the penalties set forth in section 216 of this title.

§ 205. Activities of officers and employees in claims against and other matters affecting the Government

(a) Whoever, being an officer or employee of the United States in the executive, legislative, or judicial branch of the Government or in any agency of the United States, otherwise than in the proper discharge of his official duties—

(1) acts as agent or attorney for prosecuting any claim against the United States, or receives any gratuity, or any share of or interest in any such claim in consideration of assistance in the prosecution of such claim, or

(2) acts as agent or attorney for anyone before any department, agency, court, court-martial, officer, or civil, military, or naval commission in connection with any covered matter in which the United States is a party or has a direct and substantial interest—

shall be subject to the penalties set forth in section 216 of this title.

(b) Whoever, being an officer or employee of the District of Columbia or an officer or employee of the Office of the United States Attorney for the District of Columbia, otherwise than in the proper discharge of official duties—

   (1) acts as agent or attorney for prosecuting any claim against the District of Columbia, or receives any gratuity, or any share of or interest in any such claim in consideration of assistance in the prosecution of such claim; or

   (2) acts as agent or attorney for anyone before any department, agency, court, officer, or commission in connection with any covered matter in which the District of Columbia is a party or has a direct and substantial interest;

shall be subject to the penalties set forth in section 216 of this title.

(c) A special Government employee shall be subject to subsections (a) and (b) only in relation to a covered matter involving a specific party or parties—

   (1) in which he has at any time participated personally and substantially as a Government employee or special Government employee through decision, approval, disapproval, recommendation, the rendering of advice, investigation, or otherwise; or

   (2) which is pending in the department or agency of the Government in which he is serving.

Paragraph (2) shall not apply in the case of a special Government employee who has served in such department or agency no more than sixty days during the immediately preceding period of three hundred and sixty-five consecutive days.

(d)(1) Nothing in subsection (a) or (b) prevents an officer or employee, if not inconsistent with the faithful performance of that officer's or employee's duties, from acting without compensation as agent or attorney for, or otherwise representing—

   (A) any person who is the subject of disciplinary, loyalty, or other personnel administration proceedings in connection with those proceedings; or

   (B) except as provided in paragraph (2), any cooperative, voluntary, professional, recreational, or similar organization or group not established or operated for profit, if a majority of the organization's or group's members are current officers or employees of the United States or of the District of Columbia, or their spouses or dependent children.

(2) Paragraph (1)(B) does not apply with respect to a covered matter that—

   (A) is a claim under subsection (a)(1) or (b)(1);

   (B) is a judicial or administrative proceeding where the organization or group is a party; or

(C) involves a grant, contract, or other agreement (including a request for any such grant, contract, or agreement) providing for the disbursement of Federal funds to the organization or group.

(e) Nothing in subsection (a) or (b) prevents an officer or employee, including a special Government employee, from acting, with or without compensation, as agent or attorney for, or otherwise representing, his parents, spouse, child, or any person for whom, or for any estate for which, he is serving as guardian, executor, administrator, trustee, or other personal fiduciary except—

(1) in those matters in which he has participated personally and substantially as a Government employee or special Government employee through decision, approval, disapproval, recommendation, the rendering of advice, investigation, or otherwise, or

(2) in those matters which are the subject of his official responsibility,

subject to approval by the Government official responsible for appointment to his position.

(f) Nothing in subsection (a) or (b) prevents a special Government employee from acting as agent or attorney for another person in the performance of work under a grant by, or a contract with or for the benefit of, the United States if the head of the department or agency concerned with the grant or contract certifies in writing that the national interest so requires and publishes such certification in the Federal Register.

(g) Nothing in this section prevents an officer or employee from giving testimony under oath or from making statements required to be made under penalty for perjury or contempt.

(h) For the purpose of this section, the term "covered matter" means any judicial or other proceeding, application, request for a ruling or other determination, contract, claim, controversy, investigation, charge, accusation, arrest, or other particular matter.

(i) Nothing in this section prevents an employee from acting pursuant to—

(1) chapter 71 of title 5;

(2) section 1004 or chapter 12 of title 39;

(3) section 3 of the Tennessee Valley Authority Act of 1933 (16 U.S.C. 831b);

(4) chapter 10 of title I of the Foreign Service Act of 1980 (22 U.S.C. 4104 et seq.); or

(5) any provision of any other Federal or District of Columbia law that authorizes labor-management relations between an agency or instrumentality of the United States or the District of Columbia and any labor organization that represents its employees.

§ 207. Restrictions on former officers, employees, and elected officials of the executive and legislative branches

(a) Restrictions on all officers and employees of the executive branch and certain other agencies.—

(1) Permanent restrictions on representation on particular matters.—Any person who is an officer or employee (including any special Government employee) of the executive branch of the United States (including any independent agency of the United States), or of the District of Columbia, and who, after the termination of his or her service or employment with the United States or the District of Columbia, knowingly makes, with the intent to influence, any communication to or appearance before any officer or employee of any department, agency, court, or court-martial of the United States or the District of Columbia, on behalf of any other person (except the United States or the District of Columbia) in connection with a particular matter—

(A) in which the United States or the District of Columbia is a party or has a direct and substantial interest,

(B) in which the person participated personally and substantially as such officer or employee, and

(C) which involved a specific party or specific parties at the time of such participation,

shall be punished as provided in section 216 of this title.

(2) Two-year restrictions concerning particular matters under official responsibility.—Any person subject to the restrictions contained in paragraph (1) who, within 2 years after the termination of his or her service or employment with the United States or the District of Columbia, knowingly makes, with the intent to influence, any communication to or appearance before any officer or employee of any department, agency, court, or court-martial of the United States or the District of Columbia, on behalf of any other person (except the United States or the District of Columbia), in connection with a particular matter—

(A) in which the United States or the District of Columbia is a party or has a direct and substantial interest,

(B) which such person knows or reasonably should know was actually pending under his or her official responsibility as such officer or employee within a period of 1 year before the termination of his or her service or employment with the United States or the District of Columbia, and

(C) which involved a specific party or specific parties at the time it was so pending,

shall be punished as provided in section 216 of this title.

(3) Clarification of restrictions.—The restrictions contained in paragraphs (1) and (2) shall apply—

    (A) in the case of an officer or employee of the executive branch of the United States (including any independent agency), only with respect to communications to or appearances before any officer or employee of any department, agency, court, or court-martial of the United States on behalf of any other person (except the United States), and only with respect to a matter in which the United States is a party or has a direct and substantial interest; and

    (B) in the case of an officer or employee of the District of Columbia, only with respect to communications to or appearances before any officer or employee of any department, agency, or court of the District of Columbia on behalf of any other person (except the District of Columbia), and only with respect to a matter in which the District of Columbia is a party or has a direct and substantial interest.

(b) One-year restrictions on aiding or advising.—

    (1) In general.—Any person who is a former officer or employee of the executive branch of the United States (including any independent agency) and is subject to the restrictions contained in subsection (a)(1), or any person who is a former officer or employee of the legislative branch or a former Member of Congress, who personally and substantially participated in any ongoing trade or treaty negotiation on behalf of the United States within the 1–year period preceding the date on which his or her service or employment with the United States terminated, and who had access to information concerning such trade or treaty negotiation which is exempt from disclosure under section 552 of title 5, which is so designated by the appropriate department or agency, and which the person knew or should have known was so designated, shall not, on the basis of that information, knowingly represent, aid, or advise any other person (except the United States) concerning such ongoing trade or treaty negotiation for a period of 1 year after his or her service or employment with the United States terminates. Any person who violates this subsection shall be punished as provided in section 216 of this title.

    (2) Definition.—For purposes of this paragraph—

    (A) the term "trade negotiation" means negotiations which the President determines to undertake to enter into a trade agreement pursuant to section 1102 of the Omnibus Trade and Competitiveness Act of 1988, and does not include any action taken before that determination is made; and

(B) the term "treaty" means an international agreement made by the President that requires the advice and consent of the Senate.

(c) One-year restrictions on certain senior personnel of the executive branch and independent agencies.—

(1) Restrictions.—In addition to the restrictions set forth in subsections (a) and (b), any person who is an officer or employee (including any special Government employee) of the executive branch of the United States (including an independent agency), who is referred to in paragraph (2), and who, within 1 year after the termination of his or her service or employment as such officer or employee, knowingly makes, with the intent to influence, any communication to or appearance before any officer or employee of the department or agency in which such person served within 1 year before such termination, on behalf of any other person (except the United States), in connection with any matter on which such person seeks official action by any officer or employee of such department or agency, shall be punished as provided in section 216 of this title.

(2) Persons to whom restrictions apply.—(A) Paragraph (1) shall apply to a person (other than a person subject to the restrictions of subsection (d))—

(i) employed at a rate of pay specified in or fixed according to subchapter II of chapter 53 of title 5,

(ii) employed in a position which is not referred to in clause (i) and for which the basic rate of pay, exclusive of any locality-based pay adjustment under section 5302 of title 5 (or any comparable adjustment pursuant to interim authority of the President), is equal to or greater than the rate of basic pay payable for level 5 of the Senior Executive Service,

(iii) appointed by the President to a position under section 105(a)(2)(B) of title 3 or by the Vice President to a position under section 106(a)(1)(B) of title 3, or

(iv) employed in a position which is held by an active duty commissioned officer of the uniformed services who is serving in a grade or rank for which the pay grade (as specified in section 201 of title 37) is pay grade 0–7 or above.

(B) Paragraph (1) shall not apply to a special Government employee who serves less than 60 days in the 1–year period before his or her service or employment as such employee terminates.

(C) At the request of a department or agency, the Director of the Office of Government Ethics may waive the restrictions contained in paragraph (1) with respect to any position, or category of positions, referred to in clause (ii) or (iv) of subparagraph (A), in such department or agency if the Director determines that—

(i) the imposition of the restrictions with respect to such position or positions would create an undue hardship on the department or agency in obtaining qualified personnel to fill such position or positions, and

(ii) granting the waiver would not create the potential for use of undue influence or unfair advantage.

(d) Restrictions on very senior personnel of the executive branch and independent agencies.—

(1) Restrictions.—In addition to the restrictions set forth in subsections (a) and (b), any person who—

(A) serves in the position of Vice President of the United States,

(B) is employed in a position in the executive branch of the United States (including any independent agency) at a rate of pay payable for level I of the Executive Schedule or employed in a position in the Executive Office of the President at a rate of pay payable for level II of the Executive Schedule, or

(C) is appointed by the President to a position under section 105(a)(2)(A) of title 3 or by the Vice President to a position under section 106(a)(1)(A) of title 3,

and who, within 1 year after the termination of that person's service in that position, knowingly makes, with the intent to influence, any communication to or appearance before any person described in paragraph (2), on behalf of any other person (except the United States), in connection with any matter on which such person seeks official action by any officer or employee of the executive branch of the United States, shall be punished as provided in section 216 of this title.

(2) Persons who may not be contacted.—The persons referred to in paragraph (1) with respect to appearances or communications by a person in a position described in subparagraph (A), (B), or (C) of paragraph (1) are—

(A) any officer or employee of any department or agency in which such person served in such position within a period of 1 year before such person's service or employment with the United States Government terminated, and

(B) any person appointed to a position in the executive branch which is listed in sections 5312, 5313, 5314, 5315, or 5316 of title 5.

(e) Restrictions on members of Congress and officers and employees of the legislative branch.—

(1) Members of congress and elected officers.—(A) Any person who is a Member of Congress or an elected officer of either

House of Congress and who, within 1 year after that person leaves office, knowingly makes, with the intent to influence, any communication to or appearance before any of the persons described in subparagraph (B) or (C), on behalf of any other person (except the United States) in connection with any matter on which such former Member of Congress or elected officer seeks action by a Member, officer, or employee of either House of Congress, in his or her official capacity, shall be punished as provided in section 216 of this title.

(B) The persons referred to in subparagraph (A) with respect to appearances or communications by a former Member of Congress are any Member, officer, or employee of either House of Congress, and any employee of any other legislative office of the Congress.

(C) The persons referred to in subparagraph (A) with respect to appearances or communications by a former elected officer are any Member, officer, or employee of the House of Congress in which the elected officer served.

(2) Personal staff.—**(A)** Any person who is an employee of a Senator or an employee of a Member of the House of Representatives and who, within 1 year after the termination of that employment, knowingly makes, with the intent to influence, any communication to or appearance before any of the persons described in subparagraph (B), on behalf of any other person (except the United States) in connection with any matter on which such former employee seeks action by a Member, officer, or employee of either House of Congress, in his or her official capacity, shall be punished as provided in section 216 of this title.

(B) The persons referred to in subparagraph (A) with respect to appearances or communications by a person who is a former employee are the following:

> **(i)** the Senator or Member of the House of Representatives for whom that person was an employee; and

> **(ii)** any employee of that Senator or Member of the House of Representatives.

(3) Committee staff.—Any person who is an employee of a committee of Congress and who, within 1 year after the termination of that person's employment on such committee, knowingly makes, with the intent to influence, any communication to or appearance before any person who is a Member or an employee of that committee or who was a Member of the committee in the year immediately prior to the termination of such person's employment by the committee, on behalf of any other person (except the United States) in connection with any matter on which such former employee seeks action by a Member, officer, or employee of either House of Congress, in his or her official capacity, shall be punished as provided in section 216 of this title.

(4) Leadership staff.—(A) Any person who is an employee on the leadership staff of the House of Representatives or an employee on the leadership staff of the Senate and who, within 1 year after the termination of that person's employment on such staff, knowingly makes, with the intent to influence, any communication to or appearance before any of the persons described in subparagraph (B), on behalf of any other person (except the United States) in connection with any matter on which such former employee seeks action by a Member, officer, or employee of either House of Congress, in his or her official capacity, shall be punished as provided in section 216 of this title.

(B) The persons referred to in subparagraph (A) with respect to appearances or communications by a former employee are the following:

> **(i)** in the case of a former employee on the leadership staff of the House of Representatives, those persons are any Member of the leadership of the House of Representatives and any employee on the leadership staff of the House of Representatives; and

> **(ii)** in the case of a former employee on the leadership staff of the Senate, those persons are any Member of the leadership of the Senate and any employee on the leadership staff of the Senate.

(5) Other legislative offices.—(A) Any person who is an employee of any other legislative office of the Congress and who, within 1 year after the termination of that person's employment in such office, knowingly makes, with the intent to influence, any communication to or appearance before any of the persons described in subparagraph (B), on behalf of any other person (except the United States) in connection with any matter on which such former employee seeks action by any officer or employee of such office, in his or her official capacity, shall be punished as provided in section 216 of this title.

(B) The persons referred to in subparagraph (A) with respect to appearances or communications by a former employee are the employees and officers of the former legislative office of the Congress of the former employee.

(6) Limitation on restrictions.—(A) The restrictions contained in paragraphs (2), (3), and (4) apply only to acts by a former employee who, for at least 60 days, in the aggregate, during the 1–year period before that former employee's service as such employee terminated, was paid a rate of basic pay equal to or greater than an amount which is 75 percent of the basic rate of pay payable for a Member of the House of Congress in which such employee was employed.

(B) The restrictions contained in paragraph (5) apply only to acts by a former employee who, for at least 60 days, in the aggregate, during the 1–year period before that former employee's service as such employee terminated, was employed in a position for which the rate of basic pay, exclusive of any locality-based pay adjustment under section 5302 of title 5 (or any comparable adjustment pursuant to interim authority of the President), is equal to or greater than the basic rate of pay payable for level V of the Executive Schedule.

(7) Definitions.—As used in this subsection—

(A) the term "committee of Congress" includes standing committees, joint committees, and select committees;

(B) a person is an employee of a House of Congress if that person is an employee of the Senate or an employee of the House of Representatives;

(C) the term "employee of the House of Representatives" means an employee of a Member of the House of Representatives, an employee of a committee of the House of Representatives, an employee of a joint committee of the Congress whose pay is disbursed by the Clerk of the House of Representatives, and an employee on the leadership staff of the House of Representatives;

(D) the term "employee of the Senate" means an employee of a Senator, an employee of a committee of the Senate, an employee of a joint committee of the Congress whose pay is disbursed by the Secretary of the Senate, an employee on the leadership staff of the Senate;

(E) a person is an employee of a Member of the House of Representatives if that person is an employee of a Member of the House of Representatives under the clerk hire allowance;

(F) a person is an employee of a Senator if that person is an employee in a position in the office of a Senator;

(G) the term "employee of any other legislative office of the Congress" means an officer or employee of the Architect of the Capitol, the United States Botanic Garden, the General Accounting Office, the Government Printing Office, the Library of Congress, the Office of Technology Assessment, the Congressional Budget Office, the Copyright Royalty Tribunal, the United States Capitol Police, and any other agency, entity, or office in the legislative branch not covered by paragraph (1), (2), (3), or (4) of this subsection;

(H) the term "employee on the leadership staff of the House of Representatives" means an employee of the office of a Member of the leadership of the House of Representatives described in subparagraph (L), and any elected minority employee of the House of Representatives;

(I) the term "employee on the leadership staff of the Senate" means an employee of the office of a Member of the leadership of the Senate described in subparagraph (M);

(J) the term "Member of Congress" means a Senator or a Member of the House of Representatives;

(K) the term "Member of the House of Representatives" means a Representative in, or a Delegate or Resident Commissioner to, the Congress;

(L) the term "Member of the leadership of the House of Representatives" means the Speaker, majority leader, minority leader, majority whip, minority whip, chief deputy majority whip, chief deputy minority whip, chairman of the Democratic Steering Committee, chairman and vice chairman of the Democratic Caucus, chairman, vice chairman, and secretary of the Republican Conference, chairman of the Republican Research Committee, and chairman of the Republican Policy Committee, of the House of Representatives (or any similar position created on or after the effective date set forth in section 102(a) of the Ethics Reform Act of 1989);

(M) the term "Member of the leadership of the Senate" means the Vice President, and the President pro tempore, Deputy President pro tempore, majority leader, minority leader, majority whip, minority whip, chairman and secretary of the Conference of the Majority, chairman and secretary of the Conference of the Minority, chairman and co-chairman of the Majority Policy Committee, and chairman of the Minority Policy Committee, of the Senate (or any similar position created on or after the effective date set forth in section 102(a) of the Ethics Reform Act of 1989).

(f) Restrictions relating to foreign entities.—

(1) Restrictions.—Any person who is subject to the restrictions contained in subsection (c), (d), or (e) and who knowingly, within 1 year after leaving the position, office, or employment referred to in such subsection—

(A) represents a foreign entity before any officer or employee of any department or agency of the United States with the intent to influence a decision of such officer or employee in carrying out his or her official duties, or

(B) aids or advises a foreign entity with the intent to influence a decision of any officer or employee of any department or agency of the United States, in carrying out his or her official duties,

shall be punished as provided in section 216 of this title.

(2) Special rule for Trade Representative.—With respect to a person who is the United States Trade Representative or Deputy United States Trade Representative, the restrictions described in paragraph (1) shall apply to representing, aiding, or advising foreign entities at any time after the termination of that person's service as the United States Trade Representative.

(3) Definition.—For purposes of this subsection, the term "foreign entity" means the government of a foreign country as defined in section 1(e) of the Foreign Agents Registration Act of 1938, as amended, or a foreign political party as defined in section 1(f) of that Act.

(g) Special rules for detailees.—

For purposes of this section, a person who is detailed from one department, agency, or other entity to another department, agency, or other entity shall, during the period such person is detailed, be deemed to be an officer or employee of both departments, agencies, or such entities.

(h) Designations of separate statutory agencies and bureaus.—

(1) Designations.—For purposes of subsection (c) and except as provided in paragraph (2), whenever the Director of the Office of Government Ethics determines that an agency or bureau within a department or agency in the executive branch exercises functions which are distinct and separate from the remaining functions of the department or agency and that there exists no potential for use of undue influence or unfair advantage based on past Government service, the Director shall by rule designate such agency or bureau as a separate department or agency. On an annual basis the Director of the Office of Government Ethics shall review the designations and determinations made under this subparagraph and, in consultation with the department or agency concerned, make such additions and deletions as are necessary. Departments and agencies shall cooperate to the fullest extent with the Director of the Office of Government Ethics in the exercise of his or her responsibilities under this paragraph.

(2) Inapplicability of designations.—No agency or bureau within the Executive Office of the President may be designated under paragraph (1) as a separate department or agency. No designation under paragraph (1) shall apply to persons referred to in subsection (c)(2)(A)(i) or (iii).

(i) Definitions.—

For purposes of this section—

(1) the term "officer or employee", when used to describe the person to whom a communication is made or before whom an appearance is made, with the intent to influence, shall include—

> **(A)** in subsections (a), (c), and (d), the President and the Vice President; and

> **(B)** in subsection (f), the President, the Vice President, and Members of Congress;

(2) the term "participated" means an action taken as an officer or employee through decision, approval, disapproval, recommendation, the rendering of advice, investigation, or other such action; and

(3) the term "particular matter" includes any investigation, application, request for a ruling or determination, rulemaking, contract, controversy, claim, charge, accusation, arrest, or judicial or other proceeding.

(j) Exceptions.—

(1) Official government duties.—The restrictions contained in this section shall not apply to acts done in carrying out official duties on behalf of the United States or the District of Columbia or as an elected official of a State or local government.

(2) State and local governments and institutions, hospitals, and organizations.—The restrictions contained in subsections (c), (d), and (e) shall not apply to acts done in carrying out official duties as an employee of—

> **(A)** an agency or instrumentality of a State or local government if the appearance, communication, or representation is on behalf of such government, or

> **(B)** an accredited, degree-granting institution of higher education, as defined in section 101 of the Higher Education Act of 1965, or a hospital or medical research organization, exempted and defined under section 501(c)(3) of the Internal Revenue Code of 1986, if the appearance, communication, or representation is on behalf of such institution, hospital, or organization.

(3) International organizations.—The restrictions contained in this section shall not apply to an appearance or communication on behalf of, or advice or aid to, an international organization in which the United States participates, if the Secretary of State certifies in advance that such activity is in the interests of the United States.

(4) Special knowledge.—The restrictions contained in subsections (c), (d), and (e) shall not prevent an individual from making or providing a statement, which is based on the individual's own special knowledge in the particular area that is the subject of the statement, if no compensation is thereby received.

(5) Exception for scientific or technological information.—The restrictions contained in subsections (a), (c), and (d) shall not apply with respect to the making of communications solely for the purpose of furnishing scientific or technological information, if such communications are made under procedures acceptable to the department or agency concerned or if the head of the department or agency concerned with the particular matter, in consultation with the Director of the Office of Government Ethics, makes a certification, published in the Federal Register, that the former officer or employee has outstanding qualifications in a scientific, technological, or other technical discipline, and is acting with respect to a particular matter which requires such qualifications, and that the national interest would be served by the participation of the former officer or employee. For purposes of this paragraph, the term "officer or employee" includes the Vice President.

(6) Exception for testimony.—Nothing in this section shall prevent an individual from giving testimony under oath, or from making statements required to be made under penalty of perjury. Notwithstanding the preceding sentence—

(A) a former officer or employee of the executive branch of the United States (including any independent agency) who is subject to the restrictions contained in subsection (a)(1) with respect to a particular matter may not, except pursuant to court order, serve as an expert witness for any other person (except the United States) in that matter; and

(B) a former officer or employee of the District of Columbia who is subject to the restrictions contained in subsection (a)(1) with respect to a particular matter may not, except pursuant to court order, serve as an expert witness for any other person (except the District of Columbia) in that matter.

(7) Political parties and campaign committees.—(A) Except as provided in subparagraph (B), the restrictions contained in subsections (c), (d), and (e) shall not apply to a communication or appearance made solely on behalf of a candidate in his or her capacity as a candidate, an authorized committee, a national committee, a national Federal campaign committee, a State committee, or a political party.

(B) Subparagraph (A) shall not apply to—

(i) any communication to, or appearance before, the Federal Election Commission by a former officer or employee of the Federal Election Commission; or

(ii) a communication or appearance made by a person who is subject to the restrictions contained in subsections (c), (d), or (e) if, at the time of the communication or appearance, the person is employed by a person or entity other than—

(I) a candidate, an authorized committee, a national committee, a national Federal campaign committee, a State committee, or a political party; or

(II) a person or entity who represents, aids, or advises only persons or entities described in subclause (I).

(C) For purposes of this paragraph—

(i) the term "candidate" means any person who seeks nomination for election, or election, to Federal or State office or who has authorized others to explore on his or her behalf the possibility of seeking nomination for election, or election, to Federal or State office;

(ii) the term "authorized committee" means any political committee designated in writing by a candidate as authorized to receive contributions or make expenditures to promote the nomination for election, or the election, of such candidate, or to explore the possibility of seeking nomination for election, or the election, of such candidate, except that a political committee that receives contributions or makes expenditures to promote more than 1 candidate may not be designated as an authorized committee for purposes of subparagraph (A);

(iii) the term "national committee" means the organization which, by virtue of the bylaws of a political party, is responsible for the day-to-day operation of such political party at the national level;

(iv) the term "national Federal campaign committee" means an organization that, by virtue of the bylaws of a political party, is established primarily for the purpose of providing assistance, at the national level, to candidates nominated by that party for election to the office of Senator or Representative in, or Delegate or Resident Commissioner to, the Congress;

(v) the term "State committee" means the organization which, by virtue of the bylaws of a political party, is responsible for the day-to-day operation of such political party at the State level;

(vi) the term "political party" means an association, committee, or organization that nominates a candidate for election to any Federal or State elected office whose name appears on the election ballot as the candidate of such association, committee, or organization; and

(vii) the term "State" means a State of the United States, the District of Columbia, the Commonwealth of Puerto Rico, and any territory or possession of the United States.

(k)(1)(A) The President may grant a waiver of a restriction imposed by this section to any officer or employee described in paragraph (2) if the President determines and certifies in writing that it is in the public interest to grant the waiver and that the services of the officer or employee are critically needed for the benefit of the Federal Government. Not more than 25 officers and employees currently employed by the Federal Government at any one time may have been granted waivers under this paragraph.

(B)(i) A waiver granted under this paragraph to any person shall apply only with respect to activities engaged in by that person after that person's Federal Government employment is terminated and only to that person's employment at a Government-owned, contractor operated entity with which the person served as an officer or employee immediately before the person's Federal Government employment began.

(ii) Notwithstanding clause (i), a waiver granted under this paragraph to any person who was an officer or employee of Lawrence Livermore National Laboratory, Los Alamos National Laboratory, or Sandia National Laboratory immediately before the person's Federal Government employment began shall apply to that person's employment by any such national laboratory after the person's employment by the Federal Government is terminated.

(2) Waivers under paragraph (1) may be granted only to civilian officers and employees of the executive branch, other than officers and employees in the Executive Office of the President.

(3) A certification under paragraph (1) shall take effect upon its publication in the Federal Register and shall identify—

(A) the officer or employee covered by the waiver by name and by position, and

(B) the reasons for granting the waiver.

A copy of the certification shall also be provided to the Director of the Office of Government Ethics.

(4) The President may not delegate the authority provided by this subsection.

(5)(A) Each person granted a waiver under this subsection shall prepare reports, in accordance with subparagraph (B), stating whether the person has engaged in activities otherwise prohibited by this section for each six-month period described in subparagraph (B), and if so, what those activities were.

(B) A report under subparagraph (A) shall cover each six-month period beginning on the date of the termination of the person's Federal Government employment (with respect to which the waiver under this subsection was granted) and ending two years after that date. Such report shall be filed with the President and the Director of the Office of Government Ethics not later than 60 days after the end of the six-month period covered by the report. All reports filed with the Director under this paragraph shall be made available for public inspection and copying.

(C) If a person fails to file any report in accordance with subparagraphs (A) and (B), the President shall revoke the waiver and shall notify the person of the revocation. The revocation shall take effect upon the person's receipt of the notification and shall remain in effect until the report is filed.

(D) Any person who is granted a waiver under this subsection shall be ineligible for appointment in the civil service unless all reports required of such person by subparagraphs (A) and (B) have been filed.

(E) As used in this subsection, the term "civil service" has the meaning given that term in section 2101 of title 5.

§ 208. Acts affecting a personal financial interest

(a) Except as permitted by subsection (b) hereof, whoever, being an officer or employee of the executive branch of the United States Government, or of any independent agency of the United States, a Federal Reserve bank director, officer, or employee, or an officer or employee of the District of Columbia, including a special Government employee, participates personally and substantially as a Government officer or employee, through decision, approval, disapproval, recommendation, the rendering of advice, investigation, or otherwise, in a judicial or other proceeding, application, request for a ruling or other determination, contract, claim, controversy, charge, accusation, arrest, or other particular matter in which, to his knowledge, he, his spouse, minor child, general partner, organization in which he is serving as officer, director, trustee, general partner or employee, or any person or organization with whom he is negotiating or has any arrangement concerning prospective employment, has a financial interest—

Shall be subject to the penalties set forth in section 216 of this title.

(b) Subsection (a) shall not apply—

(1) if the officer or employee first advises the Government official responsible for appointment to his or her position of the nature and circumstances of the judicial or other proceeding, application, request for a ruling or other determination, contract, claim, controversy, charge, accusation, arrest, or other particular matter and makes full disclosure of the financial interest and receives in

advance a written determination made by such official that the interest is not so substantial as to be deemed likely to affect the integrity of the services which the Government may expect from such officer or employee;

(2) if, by regulation issued by the Director of the Office of Government Ethics, applicable to all or a portion of all officers and employees covered by this section, and published in the Federal Register, the financial interest has been exempted from the requirements of subsection (a) as being too remote or too inconsequential to affect the integrity of the services of the Government officers or employees to which such regulation applies;

(3) in the case of a special Government employee serving on an advisory committee within the meaning of the Federal Advisory Committee Act (including an individual being considered for an appointment to such a position), the official responsible for the employee's appointment, after review of the financial disclosure report filed by the individual pursuant to the Ethics in Government Act of 1978, certifies in writing that the need for the individual's services outweighs the potential for a conflict of interest created by the financial interest involved; or

(4) if the financial interest that would be affected by the particular matter involved is that resulting solely from the interest of the officer or employee, or his or her spouse or minor child, in birthrights—

(A) in an Indian tribe, band, nation, or other organized group or community, including any Alaska Native village corporation as defined in or established pursuant to the Alaska Native Claims Settlement Act, which is recognized as eligible for the special programs and services provided by the United States to Indians because of their status as Indians,

(B) in an Indian allotment the title to which is held in trust by the United States or which is inalienable by the allottee without the consent of the United States, or

(C) in an Indian claims fund held in trust or administered by the United States,

if the particular matter does not involve the Indian allotment or claims fund or the Indian tribe, band, nation, organized group or community, or Alaska Native village corporation as a specific party or parties.

(c)(1) For the purpose of paragraph (1) of subsection (b), in the case of class A and B directors of Federal Reserve Banks, the Board of Governors of the Federal Reserve System shall be deemed to be the Government official responsible for appointment.

(2) The potential availability of an exemption under any particular paragraph of subsection (b) does not preclude an exemption being granted pursuant to another paragraph of subsection (b).

(d)(1) Upon request, a copy of any determination granting an exemption under subsection (b)(1) or (b)(3) shall be made available to the public by the agency granting the exemption pursuant to the procedures set forth in section 105 of the Ethics in Government Act of 1978. In making such determination available, the agency may withhold from disclosure any information contained in the determination that would be exempt from disclosure under section 552 of title 5. For purposes of determinations under subsection (b)(3), the information describing each financial interest shall be no more extensive than that required of the individual in his or her financial disclosure report under the Ethics in Government Act of 1978.

(2) The Office of Government Ethics, after consultation with the Attorney General, shall issue uniform regulations for the issuance of waivers and exemptions under subsection (b) which shall—

(A) list and describe exemptions; and

(B) provide guidance with respect to the types of interests that are not so substantial as to be deemed likely to affect the integrity of the services the Government may expect from the employee.

§ 209. Salary of Government officials and employees payable only by United States

(a) Whoever receives any salary, or any contribution to or supplementation of salary, as compensation for his services as an officer or employee of the executive branch of the United States Government, of any independent agency of the United States, or of the District of Columbia, from any source other than the Government of the United States, except as may be contributed out of the treasury of any State, county, or municipality; or

Whoever, whether an individual, partnership, association, corporation, or other organization pays, or makes any contribution to, or in any way supplements the salary of, any such officer or employee under circumstances which would make its receipt a violation of this subsection—

Shall be subject to the penalties set forth in section 216 of this title.

(b) Nothing herein prevents an officer or employee of the executive branch of the United States Government, or of any independent agency of the United States, or of the District of Columbia, from continuing to participate in a bona fide pension, retirement, group life, health or accident insurance, profit-sharing, stock bonus, or other employee welfare or benefit plan maintained by a former employer.

(c) This section does not apply to a special Government employee or to an officer or employee of the Government serving without compensation, whether or not he is a special Government employee, or to any person paying, contributing to, or supplementing his salary as such.

(d) This section does not prohibit payment or acceptance of contributions, awards, or other expenses under the terms of chapter 41 of title 5.

(e) This section does not prohibit the payment of actual relocation expenses incident to participation, or the acceptance of same by a participant in an executive exchange or fellowship program in an executive agency: *Provided*, That such program has been established by statute or Executive order of the President, offers appointments not to exceed three hundred and sixty-five days, and permits no extensions in excess of ninety additional days or, in the case of participants in overseas assignments, in excess of three hundred and sixty-five days.

(f) This section does not prohibit acceptance or receipt, by any officer or employee injured during the commission of an offense described in section 351 or 1751 of this title, of contributions or payments from an organization which is described in section 501(c)(3) of the Internal Revenue Code of 1954 and which is exempt from taxation under section 501(a) of such Code.

§ 216. Penalties and injunctions

(a) The punishment for an offense under sections 203, 204, 205, 207, 208, or 209 of this title is the following:

(1) Whoever engages in the conduct constituting the offense shall be imprisoned for not more than one year or fined in the amount set forth in this title, or both.

(2) Whoever willfully engages in the conduct constituting the offense shall be imprisoned for not more than five years or fined in the amount set forth in this title, or both.

(b) The Attorney General may bring a civil action in the appropriate United States district court against any person who engages in conduct constituting an offense under sections 203, 204, 205, 207, 208, or 209 of this title and, upon proof of such conduct by a preponderance of the evidence, such person shall be subject to a civil penalty of not more than $50,000 for each violation or the amount of compensation which the person received or offered for the prohibited conduct, whichever amount is greater. The imposition of a civil penalty under this subsection does not preclude any other criminal or civil statutory, common law, or administrative remedy, which is available by law to the United States or any other person.

(c) If the Attorney General has reason to believe that a person is engaging in conduct constituting an offense under section 203, 204, 205, 207, 208, or 209 of this title, the Attorney General may petition an appropriate United States district court for an order prohibiting that person from engaging in such conduct. The court may issue an order prohibiting that person from engaging in such conduct if the court finds that the conduct constitutes such an offense. The filing of a petition under this section does not preclude any other remedy which is available by law to the United States or any other person.

§ 218. Voiding transactions in violation of chapter; recovery by the United States

In addition to any other remedies provided by law the President or, under regulations prescribed by him, the head of any department or agency involved, may declare void and rescind any contract, loan, grant, subsidy, license, right, permit, franchise, use, authority, privilege, benefit, certificate, ruling, decision, opinion, or rate schedule awarded, granted, paid, furnished, or published, or the performance of any service or transfer or delivery of any thing to, by or for any agency of the United States or officer or employee of the United States or person acting on behalf thereof, in relation to which there has been a final conviction for any violation of this chapter, and the United States shall be entitled to recover in addition to any penalty prescribed by law or in a contract the amount expended or the thing transferred or delivered on its behalf, or the reasonable value thereof.

CHAPTER 21. CONTEMPTS

§ 401. Power of court

A court of the United States shall have power to punish by fine or imprisonment, at its discretion, such contempt of its authority, and none other, as—

> (1) Misbehavior of any person in its presence or so near thereto as to obstruct the administration of justice;

> (2) Misbehavior of any of its officers in their official transactions;

> (3) Disobedience or resistance to its lawful writ, process, order, rule, decree, or command.

§ 402. Contempts constituting crimes

Any person, corporation or association willfully disobeying any lawful writ, process, order, rule, decree, or command of any district court of the United States or any court of the District of Columbia, by doing any act or thing therein, or thereby forbidden, if the act or thing so done be of such character as to constitute also a criminal offense under any statute of the United States or under the laws of any State in which the act was committed, shall be prosecuted for such contempt as provided in section 3691 of this title and shall be punished by a fine under this title or imprisonment, or both.

Such fine shall be paid to the United States or to the complainant or other party injured by the act constituting the contempt, or may, where more than one is so damaged, be divided or apportioned among them as the court may direct, but in no case shall the fine to be paid to the United States exceed, in case the accused is a natural person, the sum of $1,000, nor shall such imprisonment exceed the term of six months.

This section shall not be construed to relate to contempts committed in the presence of the court, or so near thereto as to obstruct the administration of justice, nor to contempts committed in disobedience of any lawful writ, process, order, rule, decree, or command entered in any suit or action brought or prosecuted in the name of, or on behalf of, the United States, but the same, and all other cases of contempt not specifically embraced in this section may be punished in conformity to the prevailing usages at law.

For purposes of this section, the term "State" includes a State of the United States, the District of Columbia, and any commonwealth, territory, or possession of the United States.

CHAPTER 49. FUGITIVES FROM JUSTICE

§ 1074. Flight to avoid prosecution for damaging or destroying any building or other real or personal property

(a) Whoever moves or travels in interstate or foreign commerce with intent either (1) to avoid prosecution, or custody, or confinement after conviction, under the laws of the place from which he flees, for willfully attempting to or damaging or destroying by fire or explosive any building, structure, facility, vehicle, dwelling house, synagogue, church, religious center or educational institution, public or private, or (2) to avoid giving testimony in any criminal proceeding relating to any such offense shall be fined under this title or imprisoned not more than five years, or both.

(b) Violations of this section may be prosecuted in the Federal judicial district in which the original crime was alleged to have been committed or in which the person was held in custody or confinement: *Provided, however*, That this section shall not be construed as indicating an intent on the part of Congress to prevent any State, Territory, Commonwealth, or possession of the United States of any jurisdiction over any offense over which they would have jurisdiction in the absence of such section.

CHAPTER 63. MAIL FRAUD

§ 1341. Frauds and swindles

Whoever, having devised or intending to devise any scheme or artifice to defraud, or for obtaining money or property by means of false or fraudulent pretenses, representations, or promises, or to sell, dispose of, loan, exchange, alter, give away, distribute, supply, or furnish or procure for unlawful use any counterfeit or spurious coin, obligation, security, or other article, or anything represented to be or intimated or held out to be such counterfeit or spurious article, for the purpose of executing such scheme or artifice or attempting so to do, places in any post office or authorized depository for mail matter, any matter or thing whatever to be sent or delivered by the Postal Service, or deposits or causes to be deposited any matter or thing whatever to be sent or delivered by any private or commercial interstate carrier, or takes or receives therefrom, any such matter or thing, or knowingly causes to be delivered by mail or such carrier according to the direction thereon, or at the place at which it is directed to be delivered by the person to whom it is addressed, any such matter or thing, shall be fined under this title or imprisoned not more than five years, or both. If the violation affects a financial institution, such person shall be fined not more than $1,000,000 or imprisoned not more than 30 years, or both.

CHAPTER 73. OBSTRUCTION OF JUSTICE

§ 1501. Assault on process server

Whoever knowingly and willfully obstructs, resists, or opposes any officer of the United States, or other person duly authorized, in serving, or attempting to serve or execute, any legal or judicial writ or process of any court of the United States, or United States commissioner; or

Whoever assaults, beats, or wounds any officer or other person duly authorized, knowing him to be such officer, or other person so duly authorized, in serving or executing any such writ, rule, order, process, warrant, or other legal or judicial writ or process—

Shall, except as otherwise provided by law, be fined under this title or imprisoned not more than one year, or both.

§ 1502. Resistance to extradition agent

Whoever knowingly and willfully obstructs, resists, or opposes an extradition agent of the United States in the execution of his duties, shall be fined under this title or imprisoned not more than one year, or both.

§ 1503. Influencing or injuring officer or juror generally

(a) Whoever corruptly, or by threats or force, or by any threatening letter or communication, endeavors to influence, intimidate, or impede any grand or petit juror, or officer in or of any court of the United States, or officer who may be serving at any examination or other proceeding before any United States commissioner or other committing magistrate, in the discharge of his duty, or injures any such grand or petit juror in his person or property on account of any verdict or indictment assented to by him, or on account of his being or having been such juror, or injures any such officer, commissioner, or other committing magistrate in his person or property on account of the performance of his official duties, or corruptly or by threats or force, or by any threatening letter or communication, influences, obstructs, or impedes, or endeavors to influence, obstruct, or impede, the due administration of justice, shall be punished as provided in subsection (b).

(b) The punishment for an offense under this section is—

(1) in the case of a killing, the punishment provided in sections 1111 and 1112;

(2) in the case of an attempted killing, or a case in which the offense was committed against a petit juror and in which a class A or B felony was charged, imprisonment for not more than 20 years, a fine under this title, or both; and

(3) in any other case, imprisonment for not more than 10 years, a fine under this title, or both.

§ 1504. Influencing juror by writing

Whoever attempts to influence the action or decision of any grand or petit juror of any court of the United States upon any issue or matter pending before such juror, or before the jury of which he is a member, or pertaining to his duties, by writing or sending to him any written communication, in relation to such issue or matter, shall be fined under this title or imprisoned not more than six months, or both.

Nothing in this section shall be construed to prohibit the communication of a request to appear before the grand jury.

§ 1505. Obstruction of proceedings before departments, agencies, and committees

Whoever, with intent to avoid, evade, prevent, or obstruct compliance, in whole or in part, with any civil investigative demand duly and properly made under the Antitrust Civil Process Act, willfully withholds, misrepresents, removes from any place, conceals, covers up, destroys, mutilates, alters, or by other means falsifies any documentary material, answers to written interrogatories, or oral testimony, which is the subject of such demand; or attempts to do so or solicits another to do so; or

Whoever corruptly, or by threats or force, or by any threatening letter or communication influences, obstructs, or impedes or endeavors to influence, obstruct, or impede the due and proper administration of the law under which any pending proceeding is being had before any department or agency of the United States, or the due and proper exercise of the power of inquiry under which any inquiry or investigation is being had by either House, or any committee of either House or any joint committee of the Congress—

Shall be fined under this title or imprisoned not more than five years, or both.

§ 1506. Theft or alteration of record or process; false bail

Whoever feloniously steals, takes away, alters, falsifies, or otherwise avoids any record, writ, process, or other proceeding, in any court of the United States, whereby any judgment is reversed, made void, or does not take effect; or

Whoever acknowledges, or procures to be acknowledged in any such court, any recognizance, bail, or judgment, in the name of any other person not privy or consenting to the same—

Shall be fined under this title or imprisoned not more than five years, or both.

§ 1507. Picketing or parading

Whoever, with the intent of interfering with, obstructing, or impeding the administration of justice, or with the intent of influencing any judge, juror, witness, or court officer, in the discharge of his duty, pickets or parades in or near a building housing a court of the United States, or in or near a building or residence occupied or used by such judge, juror, witness, or court officer, or with such intent uses any sound-truck or similar device or resorts to any other demonstration in or near any such building or residence, shall be fined under this title or imprisoned not more than one year, or both.

Nothing in this section shall interfere with or prevent the exercise by any court of the United States of its power to punish for contempt.

§ 1508. Recording, listening to, or observing proceedings of grand or petit juries while deliberating or voting

Whoever knowingly and willfully, by any means or device whatsoever—

 (a) records, or attempts to record, the proceedings of any grand or petit jury in any court of the United States while such jury is deliberating or voting; or

 (b) listens to or observes, or attempts to listen to or observe, the proceedings of any grand or petit jury of which he is not a member in any court of the United States while such jury is deliberating or voting—

shall be fined under this title or imprisoned not more than one year, or both.

Nothing in paragraph (a) of this section shall be construed to prohibit the taking of notes by a grand or petit juror in any court of the United States in connection with and solely for the purpose of assisting him in the performance of his duties as such juror.

§ 1509. Obstruction of court orders

Whoever, by threats or force, willfully prevents, obstructs, impedes, or interferes with, or willfully attempts to prevent, obstruct, impede, or interfere with, the due exercise of rights or the performance of duties under any order, judgment, or decree of a court of the United States, shall be fined under this title or imprisoned not more than one year, or both.

No injunctive or other civil relief against the conduct made criminal by this section shall be denied on the ground that such conduct is a crime.

§ 1510. Obstruction of criminal investigations

(a) Whoever willfully endeavors by means of bribery to obstruct, delay, or prevent the communication of information relating to a violation of any criminal statute of the United States by any person to a criminal investigator shall be fined under this title, or imprisoned not more than five years, or both.

(b)(1) Whoever, being an officer of a financial institution, with the intent to obstruct a judicial proceeding, directly or indirectly notifies any other person about the existence or contents of a subpoena for records of that financial institution, or information that has been furnished to the grand jury in response to that subpoena, shall be fined under this title or imprisoned not more than 5 years, or both.

(2) Whoever, being an officer of a financial institution, directly or indirectly notifies—

(A) a customer of that financial institution whose records are sought by a grand jury subpoena; or

(B) any other person named in that subpoena;

about the existence or contents of that subpoena or information that has been furnished to the grand jury in response to that subpoena, shall be fined under this title or imprisoned not more than one year, or both.

(3) As used in this subsection—

(A) the term "an officer of a financial institution" means an officer, director, partner, employee, agent, or attorney of or for a financial institution; and

(B) the term "subpoena for records" means a Federal grand jury subpoena for customer records that has been served relating to a violation of, or a conspiracy to violate—

(i) section 215, 656, 657, 1005, 1006, 1007, 1014, or 1344, 1956, 1957, or chapter 53 of title 31; or

(ii) section 1341 or 1343 affecting a financial institution.

(c) As used in this section, the term "criminal investigator" means any individual duly authorized by a department, agency, or armed force of the United States to conduct or engage in investigations of or prosecutions for violations of the criminal laws of the United States.

§ 1511. Obstruction of State or local law enforcement

(a) It shall be unlawful for two or more persons to conspire to obstruct the enforcement of the criminal laws of a State or political subdivision thereof, with the intent to facilitate an illegal gambling business if—

(1) one or more of such persons does any act to effect the object of such a conspiracy;

(2) one or more of such persons is an official or employee, elected, appointed, or otherwise, of such State or political subdivision; and

(3) one or more of such persons conducts, finances, manages, supervises, directs, or owns all or part of an illegal gambling business.

(b) As used in this section—

(1) "illegal gambling business" means a gambling business which—

(i) is a violation of the law of a State or political subdivision in which it is conducted;

(ii) involves five or more persons who conduct, finance, manage, supervise, direct, or own all or part of such business; and

(iii) has been or remains in substantially continuous operation for a period in excess of thirty days or has a gross revenue of $2,000 in any single day.

(2) "gambling" includes but is not limited to pool-selling, book-making, maintaining slot machines, roulette wheels, or dice tables, and conducting lotteries, policy, bolita or numbers games, or selling chances therein.

(3) "State" means any State of the United States, the District of Columbia, the Commonwealth of Puerto Rico, and any territory or possession of the United States.

(c) This section shall not apply to any bingo game, lottery, or similar game of chance conducted by an organization exempt from tax under paragraph (3) of subsection (c) of section 501 of the Internal Revenue Code of 1954, as amended, if no part of the gross receipts derived from such activity inures to the benefit of any private shareholder, member, or employee of such organization, except as compensation for actual expenses incurred by him in the conduct of such activity.

(d) Whoever violates this section shall be punished by a fine under this title or imprisonment for not more than five years, or both.

§ 1512. Tampering with a witness, victim, or an informant

(a)(1) Whoever kills or attempts to kill another person, with intent to—

(A) prevent the attendance or testimony of any person in an official proceeding;

(B) prevent the production of a record, document, or other object, in an official proceeding; or

(C) prevent the communication by any person to a law enforcement officer or judge of the United States of information relating to the commission or possible commission of a Federal offense or a violation of conditions of probation, parole, or release pending judicial proceedings;

shall be punished as provided in paragraph (2).

(2) The punishment for an offense under this subsection is—

(A) In the case of murder (as defined in section 1111), the death penalty or imprisonment for life, and in the case of any other killing, the punishment provided in section 1112;

(B) in the case of an attempt, imprisonment for not more than twenty years.

(b) Whoever knowingly uses intimidation or physical force, or threatens another person, or attempts to do so, or engages in misleading conduct toward another person, with intent to—

(1) influence, delay, or prevent the testimony of any person in an official proceeding;

(2) cause or induce any person to—

(A) withhold testimony, or withhold a record, document, or other object, from an official proceeding;

(B) alter, destroy, mutilate, or conceal an object with intent to impair the object's integrity or availability for use in an official proceeding;

(C) evade legal process summoning that person to appear as a witness, or to produce a record, document, or other object, in an official proceeding; or

(D) be absent from an official proceeding to which such person has been summoned by legal process; or

(3) hinder, delay, or prevent the communication to a law enforcement officer or judge of the United States of information relating to the commission or possible commission of a Federal offense or a violation of conditions of probation, parole, or release pending judicial proceedings;

shall be fined under this title or imprisoned not more than ten years, or both.

(c) Whoever intentionally harasses another person and thereby hinders, delays, prevents, or dissuades any person from—

(1) attending or testifying in an official proceeding;

1109

(2) reporting to a law enforcement officer or judge of the United States the commission or possible commission of a Federal offense or a violation of conditions of probation, parole, or release pending judicial proceedings;

(3) arresting or seeking the arrest of another person in connection with a Federal offense; or

(4) causing a criminal prosecution, or a parole or probation revocation proceeding, to be sought or instituted, or assisting in such prosecution or proceeding;

or attempts to do so, shall be fined under this title or imprisoned not more than one year, or both.

(d) In a prosecution for an offense under this section, it is an affirmative defense, as to which the defendant has the burden of proof by a preponderance of the evidence, that the conduct consisted solely of lawful conduct and that the defendant's sole intention was to encourage, induce, or cause the other person to testify truthfully.

(e) For the purposes of this section—

(1) an official proceeding need not be pending or about to be instituted at the time of the offense; and

(2) the testimony, or the record, document, or other object need not be admissible in evidence or free of a claim of privilege.

(f) In a prosecution for an offense under this section, no state of mind need be proved with respect to the circumstance—

(1) that the official proceeding before a judge, court, magistrate, grand jury, or government agency is before a judge or court of the United States, a United States magistrate, a bankruptcy judge, a Federal grand jury, or a Federal Government agency; or

(2) that the judge is a judge of the United States or that the law enforcement officer is an officer or employee of the Federal Government or a person authorized to act for or on behalf of the Federal Government or serving the Federal Government as an adviser or consultant.

(g) There is extraterritorial Federal jurisdiction over an offense under this section.

(h) A prosecution under this section or section 1503 may be brought in the district in which the official proceeding (whether or not pending or about to be instituted) was intended to be affected or in the district in which the conduct constituting the alleged offense occurred.

CHAPTER 93. PUBLIC OFFICERS AND EMPLOYEES

§ 1905. Disclosure of confidential information generally

Whoever, being an officer or employee of the United States or of any department or agency thereof, any person acting on behalf of the Office of Federal Housing Enterprise Oversight, or agent of the Department of Justice as defined in the Antitrust Civil Process Act (15 U.S.C. 1311–1314), publishes, divulges, discloses, or makes known in any manner or to any extent not authorized by law any information coming to him in the course of his employment or official duties or by reason of any examination or investigation made by, or return, report or record made to or filed with, such department or agency or officer or employee thereof, which information concerns or relates to the trade secrets, processes, operations, style of work, or apparatus, or to the identity, confidential statistical data, amount or source of any income, profits, losses, or expenditures of any person, firm, partnership, corporation, or association; or permits any income return or copy thereof or any book containing any abstract or particulars thereof to be seen or examined by any person except as provided by law; shall be fined not more than $1,000, or imprisoned not more than one year, or both; and shall be removed from office or employment.

CHAPTER 201. CRIMINAL PROCEDURE— GENERAL PROVISIONS

§ 3004. Decorum in court room—(Rule)

SEE FEDERAL RULES OF CRIMINAL PROCEDURE

Photographing or radio broadcasting prohibited, Rule 53.

§ 3005. Counsel and witnesses in capital cases

Whoever is indicted for treason or other capital crime shall be allowed to make his full defense by counsel; and the court before which the defendant is to be tried, or a judge thereof, shall promptly, upon the defendant's request, assign 2 such counsel, of whom at least 1 shall be learned in the law applicable to capital cases, and who shall have free access to the accused at all reasonable hours. In assigning counsel under this section, the court shall consider the recommendation of the Federal Public Defender organization, or, if no such organization exists in the district, of the Administrative Office of the United States Courts. The defendant shall be allowed, in his defense to make any proof that he can produce by lawful witnesses, and shall have the like process of the court to compel his witnesses to appear at his trial, as is usually granted to compel witnesses to appear on behalf of the prosecution.

§ 3006. Assignment of counsel—(Rule)

SEE FEDERAL RULES OF CRIMINAL PROCEDURE

Appointment by court, Rule 44.

Accused to be informed of right to counsel, Rules 5 and 44.

§ 3006A. Adequate representation of defendants

(a) Choice of plan.—Each United States district court, with the approval of the judicial council of the circuit, shall place in operation throughout the district a plan for furnishing representation for any person financially unable to obtain adequate representation in accordance with this section. Representation under each plan shall include counsel and investigative, expert, and other services necessary for adequate representation. Each plan shall provide the following:

(1) Representation shall be provided for any financially eligible person who—

(A) is charged with a felony or a Class A misdemeanor;

(B) is a juvenile alleged to have committed an act of juvenile delinquency as defined in section 5031 of this title;

(C) is charged with a violation of probation;

(D) is under arrest, when such representation is required by law;

(E) is charged with a violation of supervised release or faces modification, reduction, or enlargement of a condition, or extension or revocation of a term of supervised release;

(F) is subject to a mental condition hearing under chapter 313 of this title;

(G) is in custody as a material witness;

(H) is entitled to appointment of counsel under the sixth amendment to the Constitution; or

(I) faces loss of liberty in a case, and Federal law requires the appointment of counsel.

(2) Whenever the United States magistrate or the court determines that the interests of justice so require, representation may be provided for any financially eligible person who—

(A) is charged with a Class B or C misdemeanor, or an infraction for which a sentence to confinement is authorized; or

(B) is seeking relief under section 2241, 2254, or 2255 of title 28.

(3) Private attorneys shall be appointed in a substantial proportion of the cases. Each plan may include, in addition to the provisions for private attorneys, either of the following or both:

(A) Attorneys furnished by a bar association or a legal aid agency.

(B) Attorneys furnished by a defender organization established in accordance with the provisions of subsection (g).

Prior to approving the plan for a district, the judicial council of the circuit shall supplement the plan with provisions for representation on appeal. The district court may modify the plan at any time with the approval of the judicial council of the circuit. It shall modify the plan when directed by the judicial council of the circuit. The district court shall notify the Administrative Office of the United States Courts of any modification of its plan.

(b) Appointment of counsel.—Counsel furnishing representation under the plan shall be selected from a panel of attorneys designated or approved by the court, or from a bar association, legal aid agency, or defender organization furnishing representation pursuant to the plan. In every case in which a person entitled to representation under a plan approved under subsection (a) appears without counsel, the United States magistrate or the court shall advise the person that he has the right to be represented by counsel and that counsel will be appointed to represent him if he is financially unable to obtain counsel. Unless the person waives representation by counsel, the United States magistrate or the court, if satisfied after appropriate inquiry that the person is financially unable to obtain counsel, shall appoint counsel to represent him. Such appointment may be made retroactive to include any representation furnished pursuant to the plan prior to appointment. The United States magistrate or the court shall appoint separate counsel for persons having interests that cannot properly be represented by the same counsel, or when other good cause is shown.

(c) Duration and substitution of appointments.—A person for whom counsel is appointed shall be represented at every stage of the proceedings from his initial appearance before the United States magistrate or the court through appeal, including ancillary matters appropriate to the proceedings. If at any time after the appointment of counsel the United States magistrate or the court finds that the person is financially able to obtain counsel or to make partial payment for the representation, it may terminate the appointment of counsel or authorize payment as provided in subsection (f), as the interests of justice may dictate. If at any stage of the proceedings, including an appeal, the United States magistrate or the court finds that the person is financially unable to pay counsel whom he had retained, it may appoint counsel as provided in subsection (b) and authorize payment as provided in subsection (d), as the interests of justice may dictate. The United States magistrate or the court may, in the interests of justice, substitute one appointed counsel for another at any stage of the proceedings.

(d) Payment for representation.—

(1) Hourly rate.—Any attorney appointed pursuant to this section or a bar association or legal aid agency or community defender organization which has provided the appointed attorney shall, at the conclusion of the representation or any segment thereof, be compensated at a rate not exceeding $60 per hour for time expended in court or before a United States magistrate and $40 per hour for time reasonably expended out of court, unless the Judicial Conference determines that a higher rate of not in excess of $75 per hour is justified for a circuit or for particular districts within a circuit, for time expended in court or before a United States magistrate and for time expended out of court. The Judicial Conference shall develop guidelines for determining the maximum hourly rates for each circuit in accordance with the preceding sentence, with variations by district, where appropriate, taking into account such factors as the minimum range of the prevailing hourly rates for qualified attorneys in the district in which the representation is provided and the recommendations of the judicial councils of the circuits. Not less than 3 years after the effective date of the Criminal Justice Act Revision of 1986, the Judicial Conference is authorized to raise the maximum hourly rates specified in this paragraph up to the aggregate of the overall average percentages of the adjustments in the rates of pay under the General Schedule made pursuant to section 5305 of title 5 on or after such effective date. After the rates are raised under the preceding sentence, such maximum hourly rates may be raised at intervals of not less than 1 year each, up to the aggregate of the overall average percentages of such adjustments made since the last raise was made under this paragraph. Attorneys shall be reimbursed for expenses reasonably incurred, including the costs of transcripts authorized by the United States magistrate or the court.

(2) **Maximum amounts.**—For representation of a defendant before the United States magistrate or the district court, or both, the compensation to be paid to an attorney or to a bar association or legal aid agency or community defender organization shall not exceed $3,500 for each attorney in a case in which one or more felonies are charged, and $1,000 for each attorney in a case in which only misdemeanors are charged. For representation of a defendant in an appellate court, the compensation to be paid to an attorney or to a bar association or legal aid agency or community defender organization shall not exceed $2,500 for each attorney in each court. For any other representation required or authorized by this section, the compensation shall not exceed $750 for each attorney in each proceeding.

(3) **Waiving maximum amounts.**—Payment in excess of any maximum amount provided in paragraph (2) of this subsection may be made for extended or complex representation whenever the court in which the representation was rendered, or the United States magistrate if the representation was furnished exclusively before him, certifies that the amount of the excess payment is necessary to provide fair compensation and the payment is approved by the chief

judge of the circuit. The chief judge of the circuit may delegate such approval authority to an active circuit judge.

(4) Disclosure of fees.—

(A) In general.—Subject to subparagraphs (B) through (E), the amounts paid under this subsection for services in any case shall be made available to the public by the court upon the court's approval of the payment.

(B) Pre-trial or trial in progress.—If a trial is in pre-trial status or still in progress and after considering the defendant's interests as set forth in subparagraph (D), the court shall—

    (i) redact any detailed information on the payment voucher provided by defense counsel to justify the expenses to the court; and

    (ii) make public only the amounts approved for payment to defense counsel by dividing those amounts into the following categories:

        (I) Arraignment and or plea.

        (II) Bail and detention hearings.

        (III) Motions.

        (IV) Hearings.

        (V) Interviews and conferences.

        (VI) Obtaining and reviewing records.

        (VII) Legal research and brief writing.

        (VIII) Travel time.

        (IX) Investigative work.

        (X) Experts.

        (XI) Trial and appeals.

        (XII) Other.

(C) Trial completed.—

    (i) In general.—If a request for payment is not submitted until after the completion of the trial and subject to consideration of the defendant's interests as set forth in subparagraph (D), the court shall make available to the public an unredacted copy of the expense voucher.

    (ii) Protection of the rights of the defendant.—If the court determines that defendant's interests as set forth in subparagraph (D) require a limited disclosure, the court shall disclose amounts as provided in subparagraph (B).

(D) Considerations.—The interests referred to in subparagraphs (B) and (C) are—

    (i) to protect any person's 5th amendment right against self-incrimination;

    (ii) to protect the defendant's 6th amendment rights to effective assistance of counsel;

    (iii) the defendant's attorney-client privilege;

    (iv) the work product privilege of the defendant's counsel;

    (v) the safety of any person; and

    (vi) any other interest that justice may require, except that the amount of the fees shall not be considered a reason justifying any limited disclosure under section 3006A(d)(4) of title 18, United States Code.

(E) Notice.—The court shall provide reasonable notice of disclosure to the counsel of the defendant prior to the approval of the payments in order to allow the counsel to request redaction based on the considerations set forth in subparagraph (D). Upon completion of the trial, the court shall release unredacted copies of the vouchers provided by defense counsel to justify the expenses to the court. If there is an appeal, the court shall not release unredacted copies of the vouchers provided by defense counsel to justify the expenses to the court until such time as the appeals process is completed, unless the court determines that none of the defendant's interests set forth in subparagraph (D) will be compromised.

(F) Effective date.—The amendment made by paragraph (4) shall become effective 60 days after enactment of this Act, will apply only to cases filed on or after the effective date, and shall be in effect for no longer than 24 months after the effective date.

(5) Filing claims.—A separate claim for compensation and reimbursement shall be made to the district court for representation before the United States magistrate and the court, and to each appellate court before which the attorney provided representation to the person involved. Each claim shall be supported by a sworn written statement specifying the time expended, services rendered, and expenses incurred while the case was pending before the United States magistrate and the court, and the compensation and reimbursement applied for or received in the same case from any other source. The court shall fix the compensation and reimbursement to be paid to the attorney or to the bar association or legal aid agency or community defender organization which provided the appointed attorney. In cases where representation is furnished exclusively before a United States magistrate, the claim shall be submitted to him and he shall fix the compensation and reimbursement to be paid. In cases where representation is furnished other than before the United States magistrate, the district court, or an appellate court, claims shall be submitted to the district court which shall fix the compensation and reimbursement to be paid.

(6) New trials.—For purposes of compensation and other payments authorized by this section, an order by a court granting a new trial shall be deemed to initiate a new case.

(7) Proceedings before appellate courts.—If a person for whom counsel is appointed under this section appeals to an appellate court or petitions for a writ of certiorari, he may do so without prepayment of fees and costs or security therefor and without filing the affidavit required by section 1915(a) of title 28.

(e) Services other than counsel.—

(1) Upon request.—Counsel for a person who is financially unable to obtain investigative, expert, or other services necessary for adequate representation may request them in an ex parte application. Upon finding, after appropriate inquiry in an ex parte proceeding, that the services are necessary and that the person is financially unable to obtain them, the court, or the United States magistrate if the services are required in connection with a matter over which he has jurisdiction, shall authorize counsel to obtain the services.

(2) Without prior request.—(A) Counsel appointed under this section may obtain, subject to later review, investigative, expert, and other services without prior authorization if necessary for adequate representation. Except as provided in subparagraph (B) of this paragraph, the total cost of services obtained without prior authorization may not exceed $300 and expenses reasonably incurred.

(B) The court, or the United States magistrate (if the services were rendered in a case disposed of entirely before the United States magistrate), may, in the interest of justice, and upon the finding that timely procurement of necessary services could not await prior authorization, approve payment for such services after they have been obtained, even if the cost of such services exceeds $300.

(3) Maximum amounts.—Compensation to be paid to a person for services rendered by him to a person under this subsection, or to be paid to an organization for services rendered by an employee thereof, shall not exceed $1,000, exclusive of reimbursement for expenses reasonably incurred, unless payment in excess of that limit is certified by the court, or by the United States magistrate if the services were rendered in connection with a case disposed of entirely before him, as necessary to provide fair compensation for services of an unusual character or duration, and the amount of the excess payment is approved by the chief judge of the circuit. The chief judge of the circuit may delegate such approval authority to an active circuit judge.

(4) Disclosure of fees.—The amounts paid under this subsection for services in any case shall be made available to the public.

(f) Receipt of other payments.—Whenever the United States magistrate or the court finds that funds are available for payment from or on behalf of a person furnished representation, it may authorize or direct that such funds be paid to the appointed attorney, to the bar association or legal aid agency or community defender organization which provided the appointed attorney, to any person or organization authorized pursuant to subsection (e) to render investigative, expert, or other services, or to the court for deposit in the Treasury as a reimbursement to the appropriation, current at the time of payment, to carry out the provisions of this section. Except as so authorized or directed, no such person or organization may request or accept any payment or promise of payment for representing a defendant.

(g) Defender organization.—

(1) Qualifications.—A district or a part of a district in which at least two hundred persons annually require the appointment of counsel may establish a defender organization as provided for either under subparagraphs (A) or (B) of paragraph (2) of this subsection or both. Two adjacent districts or parts of districts may aggregate the number of persons required to be represented to establish eligibility for a defender organization to serve both areas. In the event that adjacent districts or parts of districts are located in different circuits, the plan for furnishing representation shall be approved by the judicial council of each circuit.

(2) Types of defender organizations.—

(A) Federal Public Defender Organization.—A Federal Public Defender Organization shall consist of one or more full-time salaried attorneys. An organization for a district or part of a district or two adjacent districts or parts of districts shall be supervised by a Federal Public Defender appointed by the court of appeals of the circuit, without regard to the provisions of title 5 governing appointments in the competitive service, after considering recommendations from the district court or courts to be served. Nothing contained herein shall be deemed to authorize more than one Federal Public Defender within a single judicial district. The Federal Public Defender shall be appointed for a term of four years, unless sooner removed by the court of appeals of the circuit for incompetency, misconduct in office, or neglect of duty. Upon the expiration of his term, a Federal Public Defender may, by a majority vote of the judges of the court of appeals, continue to perform the duties of his office until his successor is appointed, or until one year after the expiration of such Defender's term, whichever is earlier. The compensation of the Federal Public Defender shall be fixed by the court of appeals of the circuit at a rate not to exceed the compensation received by the United States attorney for the district where representation is furnished or, if two districts or parts of districts are involved, the compensation of the higher paid United States attorney of the districts. The Federal Public Defender may appoint, without regard to the provisions of title 5 governing appointments in the competitive service, full-time attorneys in such number as may be approved by the court of appeals of the circuit and other personnel in such number as may be approved by the Director of the Administrative Office of the United States Courts. Compensation paid to such attorneys and other personnel of the organization shall be fixed by the Federal Public Defender at a rate not to exceed that paid to attorneys and other personnel of similar qualifications and experience in the Office of the United States attorney in the district where representation is furnished or, if two districts or parts of districts are involved, the higher compensation paid to persons of similar qualifications and experience in the districts. Neither the Federal Public Defender nor any attorney so appointed by him may engage in the private practice of law. Each organization shall submit to the Director of the Administrative Office of the United States Courts, at the time and in the form prescribed by him, reports of its activities and financial position and its proposed budget. The Director of the Administrative Office shall submit, in accordance with section 605 of title 28, a budget for each organization for each fiscal year and shall out of the appropriations therefor make payments to and on behalf of each organization. Payments under this subparagraph to an organization shall be in lieu of payments under subsection (d) or (e).

(B) Community Defender Organization.—A Community Defender Organization shall be a non-profit defense counsel service established and administered by any group authorized by the plan to provide representation. The organization shall be eligible to furnish attorneys and receive payments under this section if its bylaws are set forth in the plan of the district or districts in which it will serve. Each organization shall submit to the Judicial Conference of the United States an annual report setting forth its activities and financial position and the anticipated caseload and expenses for the next fiscal year. Upon application an organization may, to the extent approved by the Judicial Conference of the United States:

(i) receive an initial grant for expenses necessary to establish the organization; and

(ii) in lieu of payments under subsection (d) or (e), receive periodic sustaining grants to provide representation and other expenses pursuant to this section.

(3) Malpractice and negligence suits.—The Director of the Administrative Office of the United States Courts shall, to the extent the Director considers appropriate, provide representation for and hold harmless, or provide liability insurance for, any person who is an officer or employee of a Federal Public Defender Organization established under this subsection, or a Community Defender Organization established under this subsection which is receiving periodic sustaining grants, for money damages for injury, loss of liberty, loss of property, or personal injury or death arising from malpractice or negligence of any such officer or employee in furnishing representational services under this section while acting within the scope of that person's office or employment.

(h) Rules and reports.—Each district court and court of appeals of a circuit shall submit a report on the appointment of counsel within its jurisdiction to the Administrative Office of the United States Courts in such form and at such times as the Judicial Conference of the United States may specify. The Judicial Conference of the United States may, from time to time, issue rules and regulations governing the operation of plans formulated under this section.

(i) Appropriations.—There are authorized to be appropriated to the United States courts, out of any money in the Treasury not otherwise appropriated, sums necessary to carry out the provisions of this section, including funds for the continuing education and training of persons providing representational services under this section. When so specified in appropriation acts, such appropriations shall remain available until expended. Payments from such appropriations shall be made under the supervision of the Director of the Administrative Office of the United States Courts.

(j) Districts included.—As used in this section, the term "district court" means each district court of the United States created by chapter 5 of title 28, the District Court of the Virgin Islands, the District Court for the Northern Mariana Islands, and the District Court of Guam.

(k) Applicability in the District of Columbia.—The provisions of this section shall apply in the United States District Court for the District of Columbia and the United States Court of Appeals for the District of Columbia Circuit. The provisions of this section shall not apply to the Superior Court of the District of Columbia and the District of Columbia Court of Appeals.

28 U.S.C.A.

CHAPTER 5. DISTRICT COURTS

§ 144. Bias or prejudice of judge

Whenever a party to any proceeding in a district court makes and files a timely and sufficient affidavit that the judge before whom the matter is pending has a personal bias or prejudice either against him or in favor of any adverse party, such judge shall proceed no further therein, but another judge shall be assigned to hear such proceeding.

The affidavit shall state the facts and the reasons for the belief that bias or prejudice exists, and shall be filed not less than ten days before the beginning of the term at which the proceeding is to be heard, or good cause shall be shown for failure to file it within such time. A party may file only one such affidavit in any case. It shall be accompanied by a certificate of counsel of record stating that it is made in good faith.

CHAPTER 17. JUDGES—RESIGNATION—RETIREMENT

§ 372. Retirement for disability; substitute judge on failure to retire; judicial discipline

(a) Any justice or judge of the United States appointed to hold office during good behavior who becomes permanently disabled from performing his duties may retire from regular active service, and the President shall, by and with the advice and consent of the Senate, appoint a successor.

Any justice or judge of the United States desiring to retire under this section shall certify to the President his disability in writing.

Whenever an associate justice of the Supreme Court, a chief judge of a circuit or the chief judge of the Court of International Trade, desires to retire under this section, he shall furnish to the President a certificate of disability signed by the Chief Justice of the United States.

A circuit or district judge, desiring to retire under this section, shall furnish to the President a certificate of disability signed by the chief judge of his circuit.

A judge of the Court of International Trade desiring to retire under this section, shall furnish to the President a certificate of disability signed by the chief judge of his court.

Each justice or judge retiring under this section after serving ten years continuously or otherwise shall, during the remainder of his lifetime, receive the salary of the office. A justice or judge retiring under this section who has served less than ten years in all shall, during the remainder of his lifetime, receive one-half the salary of the office.

(b) Whenever any judge of the United States appointed to hold office during good behavior who is eligible to retire under this section does not do so and a certificate of his disability signed by a majority of the members of the Judicial Council of his circuit in the case of a circuit or district judge, or by the Chief Justice of the United States in the case of the Chief Judge of the Court of International Trade, or by the chief judge of his court in the case of a judge of the Court of International Trade, is presented to the President and the President finds that such judge is unable to discharge efficiently all the duties of his office by reason of permanent mental or physical disability and that the appointment of an additional judge is necessary for the efficient dispatch of business, the President may make such appointment by and with the advice and consent of the Senate. Whenever any such additional judge is appointed, the vacancy subsequently caused by the death, resignation, or retirement of the disabled judge shall not be filled. Any judge whose disability causes the appointment of an additional judge shall, for purpose of precedence, service as chief judge, or temporary performance of the duties of that office, be treated as junior in commission to the other judges of the circuit, district, or court.

(c)(1) Any person alleging that a circuit, district, or bankruptcy judge, or a magistrate, has engaged in conduct prejudicial to the effective and expeditious administration of the business of the courts, or alleging that such a judge or magistrate is unable to discharge all the duties of office by reason of mental or physical disability, may file with the clerk of the court of appeals for the circuit a written complaint containing a brief statement of the facts constituting such conduct. In the interests of the effective and expeditious administration of the business of the courts and on the basis of information available to the chief judge of the circuit, the chief judge may, by written order stating reasons therefor, identify a complaint for purposes of this subsection and thereby dispense with filing of a written complaint.

(2) Upon receipt of a complaint filed under paragraph (1) of this subsection, the clerk shall promptly transmit such complaint to the chief judge of the circuit, or, if the conduct complained of is that of the chief judge, to that circuit judge in regular active service next senior in date of commission (hereafter, for purposes of this subsection only, included in the term "chief judge"). The clerk shall simultaneously transmit a copy of the complaint to the judge or magistrate whose conduct is the subject of the complaint.

(3) After expeditiously reviewing a complaint, the chief judge, by written order stating his reasons, may—

> **(A)** dismiss the complaint, if he finds it to be (i) not in conformity with paragraph (1) of this subsection, (ii) directly related to the merits of a decision or procedural ruling, or (iii) frivolous; or

> **(B)** conclude the proceeding if he finds that appropriate corrective action has been taken or that action on the complaint is no longer necessary because of intervening events.

The chief judge shall transmit copies of his written order to the complainant and to the judge or magistrate whose conduct is the subject of the complaint.

(4) If the chief judge does not enter an order under paragraph (3) of this subsection, such judge shall promptly—

> **(A)** appoint himself and equal numbers of circuit and district judges of the circuit to a special committee to investigate the facts and allegations contained in the complaint;

(B) certify the complaint and any other documents pertaining thereto to each member of such committee; and

(C) provide written notice to the complainant and the judge or magistrate whose conduct is the subject of the complaint of the action taken under this paragraph.

A judge appointed to a special committee under this paragraph may continue to serve on that committee after becoming a senior judge or, in the case of the chief judge of the circuit, after his or her term as chief judge terminates under subsection (a)(3) or (c) of section 45 of this title. If a judge appointed to a committee under this paragraph dies, or retires from office under section 371(a) of this title, while serving on the committee, the chief judge of the circuit may appoint another circuit or district judge, as the case may be, to the committee.

(5) Each committee appointed under paragraph (4) of this subsection shall conduct an investigation as extensive as it considers necessary, and shall expeditiously file a comprehensive written report thereon with the judicial council of the circuit. Such report shall present both the findings of the investigation and the committee's recommendations for necessary and appropriate action by the judicial council of the circuit.

(6) Upon receipt of a report filed under paragraph (5) of this subsection, the judicial council—

(A) may conduct any additional investigation which it considers to be necessary;

(B) shall take such action as is appropriate to assure the effective and expeditious administration of the business of the courts within the circuit, including, but not limited to, any of the following actions:

(i) directing the chief judge of the district of the magistrate whose conduct is the subject of the complaint to take such action as the judicial council considers appropriate;

(ii) certifying disability of a judge appointed to hold office during good behavior whose conduct is the subject of the complaint, pursuant to the procedures and standards provided under subsection (b) of this section;

(iii) requesting that any such judge appointed to hold office during good behavior voluntarily retire, with the provision that the length of service requirements under section 371 of this title shall not apply;

(iv) ordering that, on a temporary basis for a time certain, no further cases be assigned to any judge or magistrate whose conduct is the subject of a complaint;

(v) censuring or reprimanding such judge or magistrate by means of private communication;

(**vi**) censuring or reprimanding such judge or magistrate by means of public announcement; or

(**vii**) ordering such other action as it considers appropriate under the circumstances, except that (I) in no circumstances may the council order removal from office of any judge appointed to hold office during good behavior, and (II) any removal of a magistrate shall be in accordance with section 631 of this title and any removal of a bankruptcy judge shall be in accordance with section 152 of this title; and

(**C**) may dismiss the complaint; and

(**D**) shall immediately provide written notice to the complainant and to such judge or magistrate of the action taken under this paragraph.

(**7**)(**A**) In addition to the authority granted under paragraph (6) of this subsection, the judicial council may, in its discretion, refer any complaint under this subsection, together with the record of any associated proceedings and its recommendations for appropriate action, to the Judicial Conference of the United States.

(**B**) In any case in which the judicial council determines, on the basis of a complaint and an investigation under this subsection, or on the basis of information otherwise available to the council, that a judge appointed to hold office during good behavior may have engaged in conduct—

(**i**) which might constitute one or more grounds for impeachment under article I of the Constitution; or

(**ii**) which, in the interest of justice, is not amenable to resolution by the judicial council,

the judicial council shall promptly certify such determination, together with any complaint and a record of any associated proceedings, to the Judicial Conference of the United States.

(**C**) A judicial council acting under authority of this paragraph shall, unless contrary to the interests of justice, immediately submit written notice to the complainant and to the judge or magistrate whose conduct is the subject of the action taken under this paragraph.

(**8**)(**A**) Upon referral or certification of any matter under paragraph (7) of this subsection, the Judicial Conference, after consideration of the prior proceedings and such additional investigation as it considers appropriate, shall by majority vote take such action, as described in paragraph (6)(B) of this subsection, as it considers appropriate. If the Judicial Conference concurs in the determination of the council, or makes its own determination, that consideration of impeachment may be warranted, it shall so certify and transmit the determination and the record of proceedings to the House of Representatives for whatever action the House of Representatives considers to be necessary. Upon receipt of the determination and record of proceedings in the House of Representatives, the Clerk of the House of Representatives shall make available to the public the determination and any reasons for the determination.

(B) If a judge or magistrate has been convicted of a felony and has exhausted all means of obtaining direct review of the conviction, or the time for seeking further direct review of the conviction has passed and no such review has been sought, the Judicial Conference may, by majority vote and without referral or certification under paragraph (7), transmit to the House of Representatives a determination that consideration of impeachment may be warranted, together with appropriate court records, for whatever action the House of Representatives considers to be necessary.

(9)(A) In conducting any investigation under this subsection, the judicial council, or a special committee appointed under paragraph (4) of this subsection, shall have full subpoena powers as provided in section 332(d) of this title.

(B) In conducting any investigation under this subsection, the Judicial Conference, or a standing committee appointed by the Chief Justice under section 331 of this title, shall have full subpoena powers as provided in that section.

(10) A complainant, judge, or magistrate aggrieved by a final order of the chief judge under paragraph (3) of this subsection may petition the judicial council for review thereof. A complainant, judge, or magistrate aggrieved by an action of the judicial council under paragraph (6) of this subsection may petition the Judicial Conference of the United States for review thereof. The Judicial Conference, or the standing committee established under section 331 of this title, may grant a petition filed by a complainant, judge, or magistrate under this paragraph. Except as expressly provided in this paragraph, all orders and determinations, including denials of petitions for review, shall be final and conclusive and shall not be judicially reviewable on appeal or otherwise.

(11) Each judicial council and the Judicial Conference may prescribe such rules for the conduct of proceedings under this subsection, including the processing of petitions for review, as each considers to be appropriate. Such rules shall contain provisions requiring that—

    (A) adequate prior notice of any investigation be given in writing to the judge or magistrate whose conduct is the subject of the complaint;

    (B) the judge or magistrate whose conduct is the subject of the complaint be afforded an opportunity to appear (in person or by counsel) at proceedings conducted by the investigating panel, to present oral and documentary evidence, to compel the attendance of witnesses or the production of documents, to cross-examine witnesses, and to present argument orally or in writing; and

(C) the complainant be afforded an opportunity to appear at proceedings conducted by the investigating panel, if the panel concludes that the complainant could offer substantial information.

Any such rule shall be made or amended only after giving appropriate public notice and an opportunity for comment. Any rule promulgated under this subsection shall be a matter of public record, and any such rule promulgated by a judicial council may be modified by the Judicial Conference. No rule promulgated under this subsection may limit the period of time within which a person may file a complaint under this subsection.

(12) No judge or magistrate whose conduct is the subject of an investigation under this subsection shall serve upon a special committee appointed under paragraph (4) of this subsection, upon a judicial council, upon the Judicial Conference, or upon the standing committee established under section 331 of this title, until all related proceedings under this subsection have been finally terminated.

(13) No person shall be granted the right to intervene or to appear as amicus curiae in any proceeding before a judicial council or the Judicial Conference under this subsection.

(14) Except as provided in paragraph (8), all papers, documents, and records of proceedings related to investigations conducted under this subsection shall be confidential and shall not be disclosed by any person in any proceeding except to the extent that—

    (A) the judicial council of the circuit in its discretion releases a copy of a report of a special investigative committee under paragraph (5) to the complainant whose complaint initiated the investigation by that special committee and to the judge or magistrate whose conduct is the subject of the complaint;

    (B) the judicial council of the circuit, the Judicial Conference of the United States, or the Senate or the House of Representatives by resolution, releases any such material which is believed necessary to an impeachment investigation or trial of a judge under article I of the Constitution; or

    (C) such disclosure is authorized in writing by the judge or magistrate who is the subject of the complaint and by the chief judge of the circuit, the Chief Justice, or the chairman of the standing committee established under section 331 of this title.

(15) Each written order to implement any action under paragraph (6)(B) of this subsection, which is issued by a judicial council, the Judicial Conference, or the standing committee established under section 331 of this title, shall be made available to the public through the appropriate clerk's office of the court of appeals for the circuit. Unless contrary to the interests of justice, each such order issued under this paragraph shall be accompanied by written reasons therefor.

(16) Upon the request of a judge or magistrate whose conduct is the subject of a complaint under this subsection, the judicial council may, if the complaint has been finally dismissed under paragraph (6)(C), recommend that the Director of the Administrative Office of the United States Courts award reimbursement, from funds appropriated to the Federal judiciary, for those reasonable expenses, including attorneys' fees, incurred by that judge or magistrate during the investigation which would not have been incurred but for the requirements of this subsection.

(17) Except as expressly provided in this subsection, nothing in this subsection shall be construed to affect any other provision of this title, the Federal Rules of Civil Procedure, the Federal Rules of Criminal Procedure, the Federal Rules of Appellate Procedure, or the Federal Rules of Evidence.

(18) The United States Court of Federal Claims, the Court of International Trade, and the Court of Appeals for the Federal Circuit shall each prescribe rules, consistent with the foregoing provisions of this subsection, establishing procedures for the filing of complaints with respect to the conduct of any judge of such court and for the investigation and resolution of such complaints. In investigating and taking action with respect to any such complaint, each such court shall have the powers granted to a judicial council under this subsection.

CHAPTER 21. COURTS AND JUDGES

§ 454. Practice of law by justices and judges

Any justice or judge appointed under the authority of the United States who engages in the practice of law is guilty of a high misdemeanor.

§ 455. Disqualification of justice, judge, or magistrate

(a) Any justice, judge, or magistrate of the United States shall disqualify himself in any proceeding in which his impartiality might reasonably be questioned.

(b) He shall also disqualify himself in the following circumstances:

(1) Where he has a personal bias or prejudice concerning a party, or personal knowledge of disputed evidentiary facts concerning the proceeding;

(2) Where in private practice he served as lawyer in the matter in controversy, or a lawyer with whom he previously practiced law served during such association as a lawyer concerning the matter, or the judge or such lawyer has been a material witness concerning it;

(3) Where he has served in governmental employment and in such capacity participated as counsel, adviser or material witness concerning the proceeding or expressed an opinion concerning the merits of the particular case in controversy;

(4) He knows that he, individually or as a fiduciary, or his spouse or minor child residing in his household, has a financial interest in the subject matter in controversy or in a party to the proceeding, or any other interest that could be substantially affected by the outcome of the proceeding;

(5) He or his spouse, or a person within the third degree of relationship to either of them, or the spouse of such a person:

　(i) Is a party to the proceeding, or an officer, director, or trustee of a party;

　(ii) Is acting as a lawyer in the proceeding;

　(iii) Is known by the judge to have an interest that could be substantially affected by the outcome of the proceeding;

　(iv) Is to the judge's knowledge likely to be a material witness in the proceeding.

(c) A judge should inform himself about his personal and fiduciary financial interests, and make a reasonable effort to inform himself about the personal financial interests of his spouse and minor children residing in his household.

(d) For the purposes of this section the following words or phrases shall have the meaning indicated:

(1) "proceeding" includes pretrial, trial, appellate review, or other stages of litigation;

(2) the degree of relationship is calculated according to the civil law system;

(3) "fiduciary" includes such relationships as executor, administrator, trustee, and guardian;

(4) "financial interest" means ownership of a legal or equitable interest, however small, or a relationship as director, adviser, or other active participant in the affairs of a party, except that:

　(i) Ownership in a mutual or common investment fund that holds securities is not a "financial interest" in such securities unless the judge participates in the management of the fund;

　(ii) An office in an educational, religious, charitable, fraternal, or civic organization is not a "financial interest" in securities held by the organization;

　(iii) The proprietary interest of a policyholder in a mutual insurance company, of a depositor in a mutual savings association, or a similar proprietary interest, is a "financial interest" in the organization only if the outcome of the proceeding could substantially affect the value of the interest;

(iv) Ownership of government securities is a "financial interest" in the issuer only if the outcome of the proceeding could substantially affect the value of the securities.

(e) No justice, judge, or magistrate shall accept from the parties to the proceeding a waiver of any ground for disqualification enumerated in subsection (b). Where the ground for disqualification arises only under subsection (a), waiver may be accepted provided it is preceded by a full disclosure on the record of the basis for disqualification.

(f) Notwithstanding the preceding provisions of this section, if any justice, judge, magistrate, or bankruptcy judge to whom a matter has been assigned would be disqualified, after substantial judicial time has been devoted to the matter, because of the appearance or discovery, after the matter was assigned to him or her, that he or she individually or as a fiduciary, or his or her spouse or minor child residing in his or her household, has a financial interest in a party (other than an interest that could be substantially affected by the outcome), disqualification is not required if the justice, judge, magistrate, bankruptcy judge, spouse or minor child, as the case may be, divests himself or herself of the interest that provides the grounds for the disqualification.

PART SIX

STANDARDS FOR SPECIALIZED AREAS OF PRACTICE

TABLE OF CONTENTS

Introduction

Although the ABA has sought to regulate all lawyers' conduct through one general code of conduct, certain groups of lawyers who practice in a specialized area have sought to promulgate their own codes of conduct. On one level, such efforts have been justified on the grounds that their specific area of practice needs its own code of conduct because of unique characteristics that cannot be taken into account in the general code. On another level, such efforts may be viewed as a struggle between the general governing group of the bar and the governing groups of certain specialized areas of practice. By promulgating a special code for an area of practice, lawyers can control conduct and entry in a small area of practice. Although the future of such codes is not entirely clear, one can gain an appreciation for the different attempts to draft rules for a specialized area of practice. Thus, this part examines several standards for specialized areas of practice.

The first two standards, one dealing with criminal law and the other with family law, were drafted by groups within the ABA and are intended as supplements to the general codes of conduct. The third standard illustrates the regulation of one area of practice by a governmental agency, the Treasury of the United States. All lawyers who practice before the Internal Revenue Service must comply with these regulations. The fourth set of standards collects several examples of efforts to control abuse in litigation practice. These codes of professionalism and courtesy in litigation seek to temper the traditional view of the lawyer as a zealous advocate for the client.

AMERICAN BAR ASSOCIATION STANDARDS RELATING TO THE ADMINISTRATION OF CRIMINAL JUSTICE

The Prosecution Function (Chapter 3) was amended in 1992 and is reprinted as approved by the House of Delegates. Copyright © 1992 by American Bar Association. Reprinted with permission. The Defense Function (Chapter 4) was amended in 1991 and is reprinted as approved by the House of Delegates. Copyright © 1991 by American Bar Association. Reprinted with permission. These changes are part of a complete revision of the Standards Relating to the Administration of Criminal Justice, which will be completed over the next several years.

Chapter 3. The Prosecution Function

Chapter 4.   The Defense Function

THE PROSECUTION FUNCTION

PART I.   GENERAL STANDARDS

Standard 3–1.1   The Function of the Standards

These standards are intended to be used as a guide to professional conduct and performance.   They are not intended to be used as criteria for the judicial evaluation of alleged misconduct of the prosecutor to determine the validity of a conviction.   They may or may not be relevant in such judicial evaluation, depending upon all the circumstances.

Standard 3–1.2   The Function of the Prosecutor

(a) The office of prosecutor is charged with responsibility for prosecutions in its jurisdiction.

(b) The prosecutor is both an administrator of justice, and an advocate, and an officer of the court; the prosecutor must exercise sound discretion in the performance of his or her functions.

(c) The duty of the prosecutor is to seek justice, not merely to convict.

(d) It is an important function of the prosecutor to seek to reform and improve the administration of criminal justice.   When inadequacies or injustices in the substantive or procedural law come to the prosecutor's attention, he or she should stimulate efforts for remedial action.

(e) It is the duty of the prosecutor to know and be guided by the standards of professional conduct as defined by applicable professional traditions, ethical codes, and law in the prosecutor's jurisdiction.   The prosecutor should make use of the guidance afforded by an advisory council of the kind described in standard 4–1.5.

Standard 3–1.3   Conflicts of Interest

(a) A prosecutor should avoid a conflict of interest with respect to his or her official duties.

(b) A prosecutor should not represent a defendant in criminal proceedings in a jurisdiction where he or she is also employed as a prosecutor.

(c) A prosecutor should not, except as law may otherwise expressly permit, participate in a matter in which he or she participated personally and substantially while in private practice or non-governmental employment unless under applicable law no one is, or by lawful delegation may be, authorized to act in the prosecutor's stead in the matter.

(d) A prosecutor who has formerly represented a client in a matter in private practice should not thereafter use information obtained from that representation to the disadvantage of the former client unless the rules of attorney-client confidentiality do not apply or the information has become generally known.

(e) A prosecutor should not, except as law may otherwise expressly permit, negotiate for private employment with any person who is involved as an accused or as an attorney or agent for an accused in a matter in which the prosecutor is participating personally and substantially.

(f) A prosecutor should not permit his or her professional judgment or obligations to be affected by his or her own political, financial, business, property, or personal interests.

(g) A prosecutor who is related to another lawyer as parent, child, sibling or spouse should not participate in the prosecution of a person who the prosecutor knows is represented by the other lawyer. Nor should a prosecutor who has a significant personal or financial relationship with another lawyer participate in the prosecution of a person who the prosecutor knows is represented by the other lawyer, unless the prosecutor's supervisor, if any, is informed and approves or unless there is no other prosecutor authorized to act in the prosecutor's stead.

(h) A prosecutor should not recommend the services of particular defense counsel to accused persons or witnesses unless requested by the accused person or witness to make such a recommendation, and should not make a referral that is likely to create a conflict of interest. Nor should a prosecutor comment upon the reputation or abilities of defense counsel to an accused person or witness who is seeking or may seek such counsel's services unless requested by such person.

Standard 3–1.4   Public Statements

(a) A prosecutor should not make or authorize the making of an extrajudicial statement that a reasonable person would expect to be disseminated by means of public communication if the prosecutor knows or reasonably should know that it will have a substantial likelihood of prejudicing a criminal proceeding.

(b) A prosecutor should exercise reasonable care to prevent investigators, law enforcement personnel, employees or other persons assisting or associated with the prosecutor from making an extrajudicial statement that the prosecutor would be prohibited from making under this standard.

Standard 3–1.5   Duty to Respond to Misconduct

(a) Where a prosecutor knows that another person associated with the prosecutor's office is engaged in action, intends to act or refuses to act in a manner that is a violation of a legal obligation to the prosecutor's office or a violation of law, the prosecutor should follow the policies of the prosecutor's office concerning such matters. If such policies are unavailing or do not exist, the prosecutor should ask the person to reconsider the action or inaction which is at issue if such a request is aptly timed to prevent such misconduct and is otherwise feasible. If such a request for reconsideration is unavailing, inapt or otherwise not feasible or if the seriousness of the matter so requires, the prosecutor should refer the matter to higher authority in the prosecutor's office, including, if warranted by the seriousness of the matter, referral to the chief prosecutor.

(b) If, despite the prosecutor's efforts in accordance with section (a), the chief prosecutor insists upon action, or a refusal to act, that is clearly a violation of law, the prosecutor may take further remedial action, including revealing the information necessary to remedy this violation to other appropriate governmental officials not in the prosecutor's office.

PART II. ORGANIZATION OF THE
PROSECUTION FUNCTION

Standard 3–2.1   Prosecution Authority
to Be Vested in a Public Official

The prosecution function should be performed by a public prosecutor who is a lawyer subject to the standards of professional conduct and discipline.

Standard 3–2.2   Interrelationship of Prosecution
Offices Within a State

(a) Local authority and responsibility for prosecution is properly vested in a district, county, or city attorney. Wherever possible, a unit of prosecution should be designed on the basis of population, caseload, and other relevant factors sufficient to warrant at least one full-time prosecutor and the supporting staff necessary to effective prosecution.

(b) In some states, conditions such as geographical area and population may make it appropriate to create a statewide system of prosecution in which the state attorney general is the chief prosecutor and the local prosecutors are deputies.

(c) In all states, there should be coordination of the prosecution policies of local prosecution offices to improve the administration of justice and assure the maximum practicable uniformity in the enforcement of the criminal law throughout the state. A state association of prosecutors should be established in each state.

(d) To the extent needed, a central pool of supporting resources and personnel, including laboratories, investigators, accountants, special counsel, and other experts, should be maintained by the state government and should be available to assist all local prosecutors.

Standard 3–2.3 Assuring High Standards of Professional Skill

(a) The function of public prosecution requires highly developed professional skills. This objective can best be achieved by promoting continuity of service and broad experience in all phases of the prosecution function.

(b) Wherever feasible, the offices of chief prosecutor and staff should be full-time occupations.

(c) Professional competence should be the basis for selection for prosecutorial office. Prosecutors should select their personnel without regard to partisan political influence.

(d) Special efforts should be made to recruit qualified women and members of minority groups for prosecutorial office.

(e) In order to achieve the objective of professionalism and to encourage competent lawyers to accept such offices, compensation for prosecutors and their staffs should be commensurate with the high responsibilities of the office and comparable to the compensation of their peers in the private sector.

Standard 3–2.4 Special Assistants, Investigative Resources, Experts

(a) Funds should be provided to enable a prosecutor to appoint special assistants from among the trial bar experienced in criminal cases, as needed for the prosecution of a particular case or to assist generally.

(b) Funds should be provided to the prosecutor for the employment of a regular staff of professional investigative personnel and other necessary supporting personnel, under the prosecutor's direct control, to the extent warranted by the responsibilities and scope of the office; the prosecutor should also be provided with funds for the employment of qualified experts as needed for particular cases.

Standard 3–2.5 Prosecutor's Handbook; Policy Guidelines and Procedures

(a) Each prosecutor's office should develop a statement of (i) general policies to guide the exercise of prosecutorial discretion and (ii) procedures of the office. The objectives of these policies as to discretion and procedures should be to achieve a fair, efficient, and effective enforcement of the criminal law.

(b) In the interest of continuity and clarity, such statement of policies and procedures should be maintained in an office handbook. This handbook should be available to the public, except for subject matters declared "confidential," when it is reasonably believed that public access to their contents would adversely affect the prosecution function.

Standard 3–2.6 Training Programs

Training programs should be established within the prosecutor's office for new personnel and for continuing education of the staff. Continuing education programs for prosecutors should be substantially expanded and public funds should be provided to enable prosecutors to attend such programs.

Standard 3–2.7 Relations With Police

(a) The prosecutor should provide legal advice to the police concerning police functions and duties in criminal matters.

(b) The prosecutor should cooperate with police in providing the services of the prosecutor's staff to aid in training police in the performance of their function in accordance with law.

Standard 3–2.8 Relations With the Courts and Bar

(a) A prosecutor should not intentionally misrepresent matters of fact or law to the court.

(b) A prosecutor's duties necessarily involve frequent and regular official contacts with the judge or judges of the prosecutor's jurisdiction. In such contacts the prosecutor should carefully strive to preserve the appearance as well as the reality of the correct relationship which professional traditions, ethical codes, and applicable law require between advocates and judges.

(c) A prosecutor should not engage in unauthorized ex parte discussions with or submission of material to a judge relating to a particular case which is or may come before the judge.

(d) A prosecutor should not fail to disclose to the tribunal legal authority in the controlling jurisdiction known to the prosecutor to be directly adverse to the prosecutor's position and not disclosed by defense counsel.

(e) A prosecutor should strive to develop good working relationships with defense counsel in order to facilitate the resolution of ethical problems. In particular, a prosecutor should assure defense counsel that if counsel finds it necessary to deliver physical items which may be relevant to a pending case or investigation to the prosecutor, the prosecutor will not offer the fact of such delivery by defense counsel as evidence before a jury for purposes of establishing defense counsel's client's culpability. However, nothing in this Standard shall prevent a prosecutor from offering evidence of the fact of such delivery in a subsequent proceeding for the purpose of proving a crime or fraud in the delivery of the evidence.

Standard 3–2.9 Prompt Disposition of Criminal Charges

(a) A prosecutor should avoid unnecessary delay in the disposition of cases. A prosecutor should not fail to act with reasonable diligence and promptness in prosecuting an accused.

(b) A prosecutor should not intentionally use procedural devices for delay for which there is no legitimate basis.

(c) The prosecution function should be so organized and supported with staff and facilities as to enable it to dispose of all criminal charges promptly. The prosecutor should be punctual in attendance in court and in the submission of all motions, briefs, and other papers. The prosecutor should emphasize to all witnesses the importance of punctuality in attendance in court.

(d) A prosecutor should not intentionally misrepresent facts or otherwise mislead the court in order to obtain a continuance.

(e) A prosecutor, without attempting to get more funding for additional staff, should not carry a workload that, by reason of its excessive size, interferes with the rendering of quality representation, endangers the interests of justice in the speedy disposition of charges, or may lead to the breach of professional obligations.

Standard 3–2.10 Supersession and Substitution of Prosecutor

(a) Procedures should be established by appropriate legislation to the end that the governor or other elected state official is empowered by law to suspend and supersede a local prosecutor upon making a public finding, after reasonable notice and hearing, that the prosecutor is incapable of fulfilling the duties of office.

(b) The governor or other elected official should be empowered by law to substitute special counsel in the place of the local prosecutor in a particular case, or category of cases, upon making a public finding that this is required for the protection of the public interest.

Standard 3–2.11   Literary or Media Agreements

A prosecutor, prior to conclusion of all aspects of a matter, should not enter into any agreement or understanding by which the prosecutor acquires an interest in literary or media rights to a portrayal or account based in substantial part on information relating to that matter.

PART III.   INVESTIGATION FOR PROSECUTION DECISION

Standard 3–3.1   Investigative Function of Prosecutor

(a) A prosecutor ordinarily relies on police and other investigative agencies for investigation of alleged criminal acts, but the prosecutor has an affirmative responsibility to investigate suspected illegal activity when it is not adequately dealt with by other agencies.

(b) A prosecutor should not invidiously discriminate against or in favor of any person on the basis of race, religion, sex, sexual preference, or ethnicity in exercising discretion to investigate or to prosecute. A prosecutor should not use other improper considerations in exercising such discretion.

(c) A prosecutor should not knowingly use illegal means to obtain evidence or to employ or instruct or encourage others to use such means.

(d) A prosecutor should not discourage or obstruct communication between prospective witnesses and defense counsel. A prosecutor should not advise any person or cause any person to be advised to decline to give to the defense information which such person has the right to give.

(e) A prosecutor should not secure the attendance of persons for interviews by use of any communication which has the appearance or color of a subpoena or similar judicial process unless the prosecutor is authorized by law to do so.

(f) A prosecutor should not promise not to prosecute for prospective criminal activity, except where such activity is part of an officially supervised investigative and enforcement program.

(g) Unless a prosecutor is prepared to forgo impeachment of a witness by the prosecutor's own testimony as to what the witness stated in an interview or to seek leave to withdraw from the case in order to present the impeaching testimony, a prosecutor should avoid interviewing a prospective witness except in the presence of a third person.

Standard 3–3.2   Relations With Victims and Prospective Witnesses

(a) A prosecutor should not compensate a witness, other than an expert, for giving testimony, but it is not improper to reimburse an ordinary witness for the reasonable expenses of attendance upon court, attendance for depositions pursuant to statute or court rule, or attendance for pretrial interviews. Payments to a witness may be for transportation and loss of income, provided there is no attempt to conceal the fact of reimbursement.

(b) A prosecutor should advise a witness who is to be interviewed of his or her rights against self-incrimination and the right to counsel whenever the law so requires. It is also proper for a prosecutor to so advise a witness whenever the prosecutor knows or has reason to believe that the witness may be the subject of a criminal prosecution. However, a prosecutor should not so advise a witness for the purpose of influencing the witness in favor of or against testifying.

(c) The prosecutor should readily provide victims and witnesses who request it information about the status of cases in which they are interested.

(d) The prosecutor should seek to insure that victims and witnesses who may need protections against intimidation are advised of and afforded such protections where feasible.

(e) The prosecutor should insure that victims and witnesses are given notice as soon as practicable of scheduling changes which will affect the victims' or witnesses' required attendance at judicial proceedings.

(f) The prosecutor should not require victims and witnesses to attend judicial proceedings unless their testimony is essential to the prosecution or is required by law. When their attendance is required, the prosecutor should seek to reduce to a minimum the time they must spend at the proceedings.

(g) The prosecutor should seek to insure that victims of serious crimes or their representatives are given timely notice of: (i) judicial proceedings relating to the victims' case; (ii) disposition of the case, including plea bargains, trial and sentencing; and (iii) any decision or action in the case which results in the accused's provisional or final release from custody.

(h) Where practical, the prosecutor should seek to insure that victims of serious crimes or their representatives are given an opportunity to consult with and to provide information to the prosecutor prior to the decision whether or not to prosecute, to pursue a disposition by plea, or to dismiss the charges.

Standard 3–3.3 Relations With Expert Witnesses

(a) A prosecutor who engages an expert for an opinion should respect the independence of the expert and should not seek to dictate the formation of the expert's opinion on the subject. To the extent necessary, the prosecutor should explain to the expert his or her role in the trial as an impartial expert called to aid the fact finders and the manner in which the examination of witnesses is conducted.

(b) A prosecutor should not pay an excessive fee for the purpose of influencing the expert's testimony or to fix the amount of the fee contingent upon the testimony the expert will give or the result in the case.

Standard 3–3.4   Decision to Charge

(a) The decision to institute criminal proceedings should be initially and primarily the responsibility of the prosecutor.

(b) Prosecutors should take reasonable care to ensure that investigators working at their direction or under their authority are adequately trained in the standards governing the issuance of arrest and search warrants and should inform investigators that they should seek the approval of a prosecutor in close or difficult cases.

(c) The prosecutor should establish standards and procedures for evaluating complaints to determine whether criminal proceedings should be instituted.

(d) Where the law permits a citizen to complain directly to a judicial officer or the grand jury, the citizen complainant should be required to present the complaint for prior approval to the prosecutor, and the prosecutor's action or recommendation thereon should be communicated to the judicial officer or grand jury.

Standard 3–3.5   Relations With Grand Jury

(a) Where the prosecutor is authorized to act as legal adviser to the grand jury, the prosecutor may appropriately explain the law and express an opinion on the legal significance of the evidence but should give due deference to its status as an independent legal body.

(b) The prosecutor should not make statements or arguments in an effort to influence grand jury action in a manner which would be impermissible at trial before a petit jury.

(c) The prosecutor's communications and presentations to the grand jury should be on the record.

Standard 3–3.6   Quality and Scope of Evidence Before Grand Jury

(a) A prosecutor should only make statements or arguments to the grand jury and only present evidence to the grand jury which the prosecutor believes is appropriate or authorized under law for presentation to the grand jury. In appropriate cases, the prosecutor may present witnesses to summarize admissible evidence available to the prosecutor which the prosecutor believes he or she will be able to present at trial. The prosecutor should also inform the grand jurors that they have the right to hear any available witnesses, including eyewitnesses.

(b) No prosecutor should knowingly fail to disclose to the grand jury evidence which tends to negate guilt or mitigate the offense.

(c) A prosecutor should recommend that the grand jury not indict if he or she believes the evidence presented does not warrant an indictment under governing law.

(d) If the prosecutor believes that a witness is a potential defendant, the prosecutor should not seek to compel the witness's testimony before the grand jury without informing the witness that he or she may be charged and that the witness should seek independent legal advice concerning his or her rights.

(e) The prosecutor should not compel the appearance of a witness before the grand jury whose activities are the subject of the inquiry if the witness states in advance that if called he or she will exercise the constitutional privilege not to testify, unless the prosecutor intends to judicially challenge the exercise of the privilege or to seek a grant of immunity according to the law.

(f) A prosecutor in presenting a case to a grand jury should not intentionally interfere with the independence of the grand jury, preempt a function of the grand jury, or abuse the processes of the grand jury.

(g) Unless the law of the jurisdiction so permits, a prosecutor should not use the grand jury in order to obtain tangible, documentary or testimonial evidence to assist the prosecutor in preparation for trial of a defendant who has already been charged by indictment or information.

(h) Unless the law of the jurisdiction so permits, a prosecutor should not use the grand jury for the purpose of aiding or assisting in any administrative inquiry.

Standard 3–3.7 Quality and Scope of Evidence for Information

Where the prosecutor is empowered to charge by information, the prosecutor's decisions should be governed by the principles embodied in standards 3–3.6 and 3–3.9, where applicable.

Standard 3–3.8 Discretion as to Noncriminal Disposition

(a) The prosecutor should consider in appropriate cases the availability of noncriminal disposition, formal or informal, in deciding whether to press criminal charges which would otherwise be supported by probable cause; especially in the case of a first offender, the nature of the offense may warrant noncriminal disposition.

(b) Prosecutors should be familiar with the resources of social agencies which can assist in the evaluation of cases for diversion from the criminal process.

Standard 3–3.9 Discretion in the Charging Decision

(a) A prosecutor should not institute, or cause to be instituted, or permit the continued pendency of criminal charges when the prosecutor knows that the charges are not supported by probable cause. A prosecutor should not institute, cause to be instituted, or permit the continued pendency of criminal charges in the absence of sufficient admissible evidence to support a conviction.

(b) The prosecutor is not obliged to present all charges which the evidence might support. The prosecutor may in some circumstances and for good cause consistent with the public interest decline to prosecute, notwithstanding that sufficient evidence may exist which would support a conviction. Illustrative of the factors which the prosecutor may properly consider in exercising his or her discretion are:

(i) the prosecutor's reasonable doubt that the accused is in fact guilty;

(ii) the extent of the harm caused by the offense;

(iii) the disproportion of the authorized punishment in relation to the particular offense or the offender;

(iv) possible improper motives of a complainant;

(v) reluctance of the victim to testify;

(vi) cooperation of the accused in the apprehension or conviction of others; and

(vii) availability and likelihood of prosecution by another jurisdiction.

(c) A prosecutor should not be compelled by his or her supervisor to prosecute a case in which he or she has a reasonable doubt about the guilt of the accused.

(d) In making the decision to prosecute, the prosecutor should give no weight to the personal or political advantages or disadvantages which might be involved or to a desire to enhance his or her record of convictions.

(e) In cases which involve a serious threat to the community, the prosecutor should not be deterred from prosecution by the fact that in the jurisdiction juries have tended to acquit persons accused of the particular kind of criminal act in question.

(f) The prosecutor should not bring or seek charges greater in number or degree than can reasonably be supported with evidence at trial or than are necessary to fairly reflect the gravity of the offense.

(g) The prosecutor should not condition a dismissal of charges, nolle prosequi, or similar action on the accused's relinquishment of the right to seek civil redress unless the accused has agreed to the action knowingly and intelligently, freely and voluntarily, and where such waiver is approved by the court.

Standard 3–3.10   Role in First Appearance and Preliminary Hearing

(a) A prosecutor who is present at the first appearance (however denominated) of the accused before a judicial officer should not communicate with the accused unless a waiver of counsel has been entered, except for the purpose of aiding in obtaining counsel or in arranging for the pretrial release of the accused. A prosecutor should not fail to make reasonable efforts to assure that the accused has been advised of the right to, and the procedure for obtaining, counsel and has been given reasonable opportunity to obtain counsel.

(b) The prosecutor should cooperate in good faith in arrangements for release under the prevailing system for pretrial release.

(c) The prosecutor should not seek to obtain from an unrepresented accused a waiver of important pretrial rights, such as the right to a preliminary hearing.

(d) The prosecutor should not seek a continuance solely for the purpose of mooting the preliminary hearing by securing an indictment.

(e) Except for good cause, the prosecutor should not seek delay in the preliminary hearing after an arrest has been made if the accused is in custody.

(f) The prosecutor should ordinarily be present at a preliminary hearing where such hearing is required by law.

Standard 3–3.11   Disclosure of Evidence by the Prosecutor

(a) A prosecutor should not intentionally fail to make timely disclosure to the defense, at the earliest feasible opportunity, of the existence of all evidence or information which tends to negate the guilt of the accused or mitigate the offense charged or which would tend to reduce the punishment of the accused.

(b) A prosecutor should not fail to make a reasonably diligent effort to comply with a legally proper discovery request.

A prosecutor should not intentionally avoid pursuit of evidence because he or she believes it will damage the prosecution's case or aid the accused.

PART IV.   PLEA DISCUSSIONS

Standard 3–4.1   Availability for Plea Discussions

(a) The prosecutor should have and make known a general policy or willingness to consult with defense counsel concerning disposition of charges by plea.

(b) A prosecutor should not engage in plea discussions directly with an accused who is represented by defense counsel, except with defense counsel's approval. Where the defendant has properly waived counsel, the prosecuting attorney may engage in plea discussions with the defendant, although where feasible, a record of such discussions should be made and preserved.

(c) A prosecutor should not knowingly make false statements or representations as to fact or law in the course of plea discussions with defense counsel or the accused.

Standard 3–4.2 Fulfillment of Plea Discussions

(a) A prosecutor should not make any promise or commitment assuring a defendant or defense counsel that a court will impose a specific sentence or a suspension of sentence; a prosecutor may properly advise the defense what position will be taken concerning disposition.

(b) A prosecutor should not imply a greater power to influence the disposition of a case than is actually possessed.

(c) A prosecutor should not fail to comply with a plea agreement, unless a defendant fails to comply with a plea agreement or other extenuating circumstances are present.

Standard 3–4.3 Record of Reasons
for Nolle Prosequi Disposition

Whenever felony criminal charges are dismissed by way of nolle prosequi (or its equivalent), the prosecutor should make a record of the reasons for the action.

PART V. THE TRIAL

Standard 3–5.1 Calendar Control

Control over the trial calendar should be vested in the court. The prosecuting attorney should advise the court of facts relevant in determining the order of cases on the court's calendar.

Standard 3–5.2 Courtroom Professionalism

(a) As an officer of the court, the prosecutor should support the authority of the court and the dignity of the trial courtroom by strict adherence to codes of professionalism and by manifesting a professional attitude toward the judge, opposing counsel, witnesses, defendants, jurors, and others in the courtroom.

(b) When court is in session, the prosecutor should address the court, not opposing counsel, on all matters relating to the case.

(c) A prosecutor should comply promptly with all orders and directives of the court, but the prosecutor has a duty to have the record reflect adverse rulings or judicial conduct which the prosecutor considers prejudicial. The prosecutor has a right to make respectful requests for reconsideration of adverse rulings.

(d) Prosecutors should cooperate with courts and the organized bar in developing codes of professionalism for each jurisdiction.

Standard 3–5.3   Selection of Jurors

(a) The prosecutor should prepare himself or herself prior to trial to discharge effectively the prosecution function in the selection of the jury and the exercise of challenges for cause and peremptory challenges.

(b) In those cases where it appears necessary to conduct a pretrial investigation of the background of jurors, investigatory methods of the prosecutor should neither harass nor unduly embarrass potential jurors or invade their privacy and, whenever possible, should be restricted to an investigation of records and sources of information already in existence.

(c) The opportunity to question jurors personally should be used solely to obtain information for the intelligent exercise of challenges. A prosecutor should not intentionally use the voir dire to present factual matter which the prosecutor knows will not be admissible at trial or to argue the prosecution's case to the jury.

Standard 3–5.4   Relations With Jury

(a) A prosecutor should not intentionally communicate privately with persons summoned for jury duty or impaneled as jurors prior to or during trial. The prosecutor should avoid the reality or appearance of any such communications.

(b) The prosecutor should treat jurors with deference and respect, avoiding the reality or appearance of currying favor by a show of undue solicitude for their comfort or convenience.

(c) After discharge of the jury from further consideration of a case, a prosecutor should not intentionally make comments to or ask questions of a juror for the purpose of harassing or embarrassing the juror in any way which will tend to influence judgment in future jury service. If the prosecutor believes that the verdict may be subject to legal challenge, he or she may properly, if no statute or rule prohibits such course, communicate with jurors to determine whether such challenge may be available.

Standard 3–5.5   Opening Statement

The prosecutor's opening statement should be confined to a statement of the issues in the case and the evidence the prosecutor intends to offer which the prosecutor believes in good faith will be available and admissible. A prosecutor should not allude to any evidence unless there is a good faith and reasonable basis for believing that such evidence will be tendered and admitted in evidence.

Standard 3–5.6   Presentation of Evidence

(a) A prosecutor should not knowingly offer false evidence, whether by documents, tangible evidence, or the testimony of witnesses, or fail to seek withdrawal thereof upon discovery of its falsity.

(b) A prosecutor should not knowingly and for the purpose of bringing inadmissible matter to the attention of the judge or jury offer inadmissible evidence, ask legally objectionable questions, or make other impermissible comments or arguments in the presence of the judge or jury.

(c) A prosecutor should not permit any tangible evidence to be displayed in the view of the judge or jury which would tend to prejudice fair consideration by the judge or jury until such time as a good faith tender of such evidence is made.

(d) A prosecutor should not tender tangible evidence in the view of the judge or jury if it would tend to prejudice fair consideration by the judge or jury unless there is a reasonable basis for its admission in evidence. When there is any substantial doubt about the admissibility of such evidence, it should be tendered by an offer of proof and a ruling obtained.

Standard 3–5.7   Examination of Witnesses

(a) The interrogation of all witnesses should be conducted fairly, objectively, and with due regard for the dignity and legitimate privacy of the witness, and without seeking to intimidate or humiliate the witness unnecessarily.

(b) The prosecutor's belief that the witness is telling the truth does not preclude cross-examination, but may affect the method and scope of cross-examination. A prosecutor should not use the power of cross-examination to discredit or undermine a witness if the prosecutor knows the witness is testifying truthfully.

(c) A prosecutor should not call a witness in the presence of the jury who the prosecutor knows will claim a valid privilege not to testify.

(d) A prosecutor should not ask a question which implies the existence of a factual predicate for which a good faith belief is lacking.

Standard 3–5.8   Argument to the Jury

(a) In closing argument to the jury, the prosecutor may argue all reasonable inferences from evidence in the record. The prosecutor should not intentionally misstate the evidence or mislead the jury as to the inferences it may draw.

(b) The prosecutor should not express his or her personal belief or opinion as to the truth or falsity of any testimony or evidence or the guilt of the defendant.

(c) The prosecutor should not make arguments calculated to appeal to the prejudices of the jury.

(d) The prosecutor should refrain from argument which would divert the jury from its duty to decide the case on the evidence.

Standard 3–5.9 Facts Outside the Record

The prosecutor should not intentionally refer to or argue on the basis of facts outside the record whether at trial or on appeal, unless such facts are matters of common public knowledge based on ordinary human experience or matters of which the court may take judicial notice.

Standard 3–5.10 Comments by Prosecutor After Verdict

The prosecutor should not make public comments critical of a verdict, whether rendered by judge or jury.

PART VI. SENTENCING

Standard 3–6.1 Role in Sentencing

(a) The prosecutor should not make the severity of sentences the index of his or her effectiveness. To the extent that the prosecutor becomes involved in the sentencing process, he or she should seek to assure that a fair and informed judgment is made on the sentence and avoid unfair sentence disparities.

(b) Where sentence is fixed by the court without jury participation, the prosecutor should be afforded the opportunity to address the court at sentencing and to offer a sentencing recommendation.

(c) Where sentence is fixed by the jury, the prosecutor should present evidence on the issue within the limits permitted in the jurisdiction, but the prosecutor should avoid introducing evidence bearing on sentence which will prejudice the jury's determination of the issue of guilt.

Standard 3–6.2 Information Relevant to Sentencing

(a) The prosecutor should assist the court in basing its sentence on complete and accurate information for use in the presentence report. The prosecutor should disclose to the court any information in the prosecutor's files relevant to the sentence. If incompleteness or inaccurateness in the presentence report comes to the prosecutor's attention, the prosecutor should take steps to present the complete and correct information to the court and to defense counsel.

(b) The prosecutor should disclose to the defense and to the court at or prior to the sentencing proceeding all unprivileged mitigating information known to the prosecutor, except when the prosecutor is relieved of this responsibility by a protective order of the tribunal.

THE DEFENSE FUNCTION

PART I. GENERAL STANDARDS

Standard 4–1.1   The Function of the Standards

These standards are intended to be used as a guide to professional conduct and performance. They are not intended to be used as criteria for the judicial evaluation of alleged misconduct of defense counsel to determine the validity of a conviction. They may or may not be relevant in such judicial evaluation, depending upon all the circumstances.

Standard 4–1.2   The Function of Defense Counsel

(a) Counsel for the accused is an essential component of the administration of criminal justice. A court properly constituted to hear a criminal case must be viewed as a tripartite entity consisting of the judge (and jury, where appropriate), counsel for the prosecution, and counsel for the accused.

(b) The basic duty defense counsel owes to the administration of justice and as an officer of the court is to serve as the accused's counselor and advocate with courage and devotion and to render effective, quality representation.

(c) Since the death penalty differs from other criminal penalties in its finality, defense counsel in a capital case should respond to this difference by making extraordinary efforts on behalf of the accused. Defense counsel should comply with the ABA Guidelines for the Appointment and Performance of Counsel in Death Penalty Cases.

(d) Defense counsel should seek to reform and improve the administration of criminal justice. When inadequacies or injustices in the substantive or procedural law come to defense counsel's attention, he or she should stimulate efforts for remedial action.

(e) Defense counsel, in common with all members of the bar, is subject to standards of conduct stated in statutes, rules, decisions of courts, and codes, canons, or other standards of professional conduct. Defense counsel has no duty to execute any directive of the accused which does not comport with law or such standards. Defense counsel is the professional representative of the accused, not the accused's alter ego.

(f) Defense counsel should not intentionally misrepresent matters of fact or law to the court.

(g) Defense counsel should disclose to the tribunal legal authority in the controlling jurisdiction known to defense counsel to be directly adverse to the position of the accused and not disclosed by the prosecutor.

(h) It is the duty of defense counsel to know and be guided by the standards of professional conduct as defined in codes and canons of the legal profession applicable in defense counsel's jurisdiction. Once representation has been undertaken, the functions and duties of defense counsel are the same whether defense counsel is assigned, privately retained, or serving in a legal aid or defender program.

Standard 4–1.3 Delays; Punctuality; Workload

(a) Defense counsel should act with reasonable diligence and promptness in representing a client.

(b) Defense counsel should avoid unnecessary delay in the disposition of cases. Defense counsel should be punctual in attendance upon court and in the submission of all motions, briefs, and other papers. Defense counsel should emphasize to the client and all witnesses the importance of punctuality in attendance in court.

(c) Defense counsel should not intentionally misrepresent facts or otherwise mislead the court in order to obtain a continuance.

(d) Defense counsel should not intentionally use procedural devices for delay for which there is no legitimate basis.

(e) Defense counsel should not carry a workload that, by reason of its excessive size, interferes with the rendering of quality representation, endangers the client's interest in the speedy disposition of charges, or may lead to the breach of professional obligations. Defense counsel should not accept employment for the purpose of delaying trial.

Standard 4–1.4 Public Statements

Defense counsel should not make or authorize the making of an extrajudicial statement that a reasonable person would expect to be disseminated by means of public communication if defense counsel knows or reasonably should know that it will have a substantial likelihood of prejudicing a criminal proceeding.

Standard 4–1.5 Advisory Councils on Professional Conduct

(a) In every jurisdiction, an advisory body of lawyers selected for their experience, integrity, and standing at the trial bar should be established as an advisory council on problems of professional conduct in criminal cases. This council should provide prompt and confidential guidance and advice to lawyers seeking assistance in the application of standards of professional conduct in criminal cases.

(b) Communications between an inquiring lawyer and an advisory council member have the same attorney-client privilege for protection of the client's confidences as ordinarily exists between any other lawyer and client. The council member should be bound by statute or rule of court in the same manner as a lawyer is ordinarily bound in that jurisdiction not to reveal any disclosure of the client. Confidences may also be revealed, however, to the extent necessary:

(i) if the inquiring lawyer's client challenges the effectiveness of the lawyer's conduct of the case and the lawyer relies on the guidance received from the council member, or

(ii) if the inquiring lawyer's conduct is called into question in an authoritative disciplinary inquiry or proceeding.

Standard 4–1.6   Trial Lawyer's Duty
to Administration of Justice

(a) The bar should encourage through every available means the widest possible participation in the defense of criminal cases by lawyers. Lawyers should be encouraged to qualify themselves for participation in criminal cases both by formal training and through experience as associate counsel.

(b) All such qualified lawyers should stand ready to undertake the defense of an accused regardless of public hostility toward the accused or personal distaste for the offense charged or the person of the defendant.

(c) Such Qualified lawyers should not assert or announce a general unwillingness to appear in criminal cases. Law firms should encourage partners and associates to become qualified and to appear in criminal cases.

(d) Such qualified lawyers should not seek to avoid appointment by a tribunal to represent an accused except for good cause, such as: representing the accused is likely to result in violation of applicable ethical codes or other law, representing the accused is likely to result in an unreasonable financial burden on the lawyer, or the client or crime is so repugnant to the lawyer as to be likely to impair the client-lawyer relationship or the lawyer's ability to represent the client.

PART II.   ACCESS TO COUNSEL

Standard 4–2.1   Communication

Every jurisdiction should guarantee by statute or rule of court the right of an accused person to prompt and effective communication with a lawyer and should require that reasonable access to a telephone or other facilities be provided for that purpose.

Standard 4–2.2   Referral Service for Criminal Cases

(a) To assist persons who wish to retain defense counsel privately and who do not know a lawyer or how to engage one, every jurisdiction should have a referral service for criminal cases. The referral service should maintain a list of defense counsel willing and qualified to undertake the defense of a criminal case; it should be so organized that it can provide prompt service at all times.

(b) The availability of the referral service should be publicized. In addition, notices containing the essential information about the referral service and how to contact it should be posted conspicuously in police stations, jails, and wherever else it is likely to give effective notice.

Standard 4–2.3 Prohibited Referrals

(a) Defense counsel should not give anything of value to a person for recommending the lawyer's services.

(b) Defense counsel should not accept a referral from any source, including prosecutors, law enforcement personnel, victims, bondsmen, or court personnel where the acceptance of such a referral is likely to create a conflict of interest.

PART III. LAWYER–CLIENT RELATIONSHIP

Standard 4–3.1 Establishment of Relationship

(a) Defense counsel should seek to establish a relationship of trust and confidence with the accused and should discuss the objectives of the representation and whether defense counsel will continue to represent the accused if there is an appeal. Defense counsel should explain the necessity of full disclosure of all facts known to the client for an effective defense, and defense counsel should explain the extent to which counsel's obligation of confidentiality makes privileged the accused's disclosures.

(b) To ensure the privacy essential for confidential communication between defense counsel and client, adequate facilities should be available for private discussions between counsel and accused in jails, prisons, courthouses, and other places where accused persons must confer with counsel.

(c) Personnel of jails, prisons, and custodial institutions should be prohibited by law or administrative regulations from examining or otherwise interfering with any communication or correspondence between client and defense counsel relating to legal action arising out of charges or incarceration.

Standard 4–3.2 Interviewing the Client

(a) As soon as practicable, defense counsel should seek to determine all relevant facts known to the accused. In so doing, defense counsel should probe for all legally relevant information without seeking to influence the direction of the client's responses.

(b) Defense counsel should not instruct the client or intimate to the client in any way that the client should not be candid in revealing facts so as to afford defense counsel free rein to take action which would be precluded by counsel's knowing of such facts.

Standard 4–3.3   Fees

(a) Defense counsel should not enter into an agreement for, charge, or collect an illegal or unreasonable fee.

(b) In determining the amount of the fee in a criminal case, it is proper to consider the time and effort required, the responsibility assumed by counsel, the novelty and difficulty of the questions involved, the skill requisite to proper representation, the likelihood that other employment will be precluded, the fee customarily charged in the locality for similar services, the gravity of the charge, the experience, reputation, and ability of defense counsel, and the capacity of the client to pay the fee.

(c) Defense counsel should not imply that his or her compensation is for anything other than professional services rendered by defense counsel or by others for defense counsel.

(d) Defense counsel should not divide a fee with a nonlawyer, except as permitted by applicable ethical codes of conduct.

(e) Defense counsel not in the same firm should not divide fees unless the division is in proportion to the services performed by each counsel or, by written agreement with the client, each counsel assumes joint responsibility for the representation, the client is advised of and does not object to the participation of all counsel involved, and the total fee is reasonable.

(f) Defense counsel should not enter into an arrangement for, charge, or collect a contingent fee for representing a defendant in a criminal case.

(g) When defense counsel has not regularly represented the client, defense counsel should communicate the basis or rate of the fee to the client, preferably in writing, before or within a reasonable time after commencing the representation.

Standard 4–3.4   Obtaining Literary or Media Rights From the Accused

Defense counsel, prior to conclusion of all aspects of the matter giving rise to his or her employment, should not enter into any agreement or understanding with a client or a prospective client by which defense counsel acquires an interest in literary or media rights to a portrayal or account based in substantial part on information relating to the employment or proposed employment.

Standard 4–3.5   Conflicts of Interest

(a) Defense counsel should not permit his or her professional judgment or obligations to be affected by his or her own political, financial, business, property, or personal interests.

(b) Defense counsel should disclose to the defendant at the earliest feasible opportunity any interest in or connection with the case or any other matter that might be relevant to the defendant's selection of counsel to represent him or her or counsel's continuing representation. Such disclosure should include communication of information reasonably sufficient to permit the client to appreciate the significance of any conflict or potential conflict of interest.

(c) Except for preliminary matters such as initial hearings or applications for bail, defense counsel who are associated in practice should not undertake to defend more than one defendant in the same criminal case if the duty to one of the defendants may conflict with the duty to another. The potential for conflict of interest in representing multiple defendants is so grave that ordinarily defense counsel should decline to act for more than one of several codefendants except in unusual situations when, after careful investigation, it is clear either that no conflict is likely to develop at trial, sentencing, or at any other time in the proceeding or that common representation will be advantageous to each of the codefendants represented and, in either case, that:

(i) the several defendants give an informed consent to such multiple representation; and

(ii) the consent of the defendants is made a matter of judicial record. In determining the presence of consent by the defendants, the trial judge should make appropriate inquiries respecting actual or potential conflicts of interest of counsel and whether the defendants fully comprehend the difficulties that defense counsel sometimes encounters in defending multiple clients.

(d) Defense counsel who has formerly represented a defendant should not thereafter use information related to the former representation to the disadvantage of the former client unless the information has become generally known or the ethical obligation of confidentiality otherwise does not apply.

(e) In accepting payment of fees by one person for the defense of another, defense counsel should be careful to determine that he or she will not be confronted with a conflict of loyalty since defense counsel's entire loyalty is due the accused. Defense counsel should not accept such compensation unless:

(i) the accused consents after disclosure;

(ii) there is no interference with defense counsel's independence of professional judgment or with the client-lawyer relationship; and

(iii) information relating to the representation of the accused is protected from disclosure as required by defense counsel's ethical obligation of confidentiality.

Defense counsel should not permit a person who recommends, employs, or pays defense counsel to render legal services for another to direct or regulate counsel's professional judgment in rendering such legal services.

(f) Defense counsel should not defend a criminal case in which counsel's partner or other professional associate is or has been the prosecutor in the same case.

(g) Defense counsel should not represent a criminal defendant in a jurisdiction in which he or she is also a prosecutor.

(h) Defense counsel who formerly participated personally and substantially in the prosecution of a defendant should not thereafter represent any person in the same or a substantially related matter. Defense counsel who was formerly a prosecutor should not use confidential information about a person acquired when defense counsel was a prosecutor in the representation of a client whose interests are adverse to that person in a matter.

(i) Defense counsel who is related to a prosecutor as parent, child, sibling or spouse should not represent a client in a criminal matter where defense counsel knows the government is represented in the matter by such prosecutor. Nor should defense counsel who has a significant personal or financial relationship with a prosecutor represent a client in a criminal matter where defense counsel knows the government is represented in the matter by such prosecutor, except upon consent by the client after consultation regarding the relationship.

(j) Defense counsel should not act as surety on a bond either for the accused represented by counsel or for any other accused in the same or a related case.

(k) Except as law may otherwise expressly permit, defense counsel should not negotiate to employ any person who is significantly involved as an attorney or employee of the government in a matter in which defense counsel is participating personally and substantially.

Standard 4–3.6 Prompt Action to Protect the Accused

Many important rights of the accused can be protected and preserved only by prompt legal action. Defense counsel should inform the accused of his or her rights at the earliest opportunity and take all necessary action to vindicate such rights. Defense counsel should consider all procedural steps which in good faith may be taken, including, for example, motions seeking pretrial release of the accused, obtaining psychiatric examination of the accused when a need appears, moving for change of venue or continuance, moving to suppress illegally obtained evidence, moving for severance from jointly charged defendants, and seeking dismissal of the charges.

Standard 4–3.7 Advice and Service on Anticipated Unlawful Conduct

(a) It is defense counsel's duty to advise a client to comply with the law, but counsel may advise concerning the meaning, scope, and validity of a law.

(b) Defense counsel should not counsel a client in or knowingly assist a client to engage in conduct which defense counsel knows to be illegal or fraudulent but defense counsel may discuss the legal consequences of any proposed course of conduct with a client.

(c) Defense counsel should not agree in advance of the commission of a crime that he or she will serve as counsel for the defendant, except as part of a bona fide effort to determine the validity, scope, meaning, or application of the law, or where the defense is incident to a general retainer for legal services to a person or enterprise engaged in legitimate activity.

(d) Defense counsel should not reveal information relating to representation of a client unless the client consents after consultation, except for disclosures that are impliedly authorized in order to carry out the representation and except that defense counsel may reveal such information to the extent he or she reasonably believes necessary to prevent the client from committing a criminal act that defense counsel believes is likely to result in imminent death or substantial bodily harm.

Standard 4–3.8   Duty to Keep Client Informed

(a) Defense counsel should keep the client informed of the developments in the case and the progress of preparing the defense and should promptly comply with reasonable requests for information.

(b) Defense counsel should explain developments in the case to the extent reasonably necessary to permit the client to make informed decisions regarding the representation.

Standard 4–3.9   Obligations of Hybrid, Standby, and Replacement Counsel

(a) Defense counsel whose duty is to actively assist a pro se accused should permit the accused to make the final decisions on all matters, including strategic and tactical matters relating to the conduct of the case.

(b) Defense counsel whose duty is to assist a pro se accused only when the accused requests assistance may bring to the attention of the accused matters beneficial to him or her, but should not actively participate in the conduct of the defense unless requested by the accused or insofar as directed to do so by the court.

(c) Defense counsel whose duty is to serve as a replacement for the pro se accused when and if the court so orders may bring to the attention of the accused matters beneficial to him or her, but should not actively participate in the conduct of the defense.

PART IV. INVESTIGATION AND PREPARATION

Standard 4–4.1 Duty to Investigate

(a) Defense counsel should conduct a prompt investigation of the circumstances of the case and to explore all avenues leading to facts relevant to the merits of the case and the penalty in the event of conviction. The investigation should include efforts to secure information in the possession of the prosecution and law enforcement authorities. The duty to investigate exists regardless of the accused's admissions or statements to defense counsel of facts constituting guilt or the accused's stated desire to plead guilty.

(b) Defense counsel should not seek to acquire possession of physical evidence personally or through use of an investigator where defense counsel's sole purpose is to obstruct access to such evidence.

Standard 4–4.2 Illegal Investigation

Defense counsel should not knowingly use illegal means to obtain evidence or information or to employ, instruct, or encourage others to do so.

Standard 4–4.3 Relations With Prospective Witnesses

(a) Defense counsel, in representing an accused, should not use means that have no substantial purpose other than to embarrass, delay, or burden a third person, or use methods of obtaining evidence that violate the legal rights of such a person.

(b) Defense counsel should not compensate a witness, other than an expert, for giving testimony, but it is not improper to reimburse a witness for the reasonable expenses of attendance upon court, including transportation and loss of income, attendance for depositions pursuant to statute or court rule, or attendance for pretrial interviews, provided there is no attempt to conceal the fact of reimbursement.

(c) It is not necessary for defense counsel or defense counsel's investigator, in interviewing a prospective witness, to caution the witness concerning possible self-incrimination and the need for counsel.

(d) Defense counsel should not discourage or obstruct communication between prospective witnesses and the prosecutor. It is unprofessional conduct to advise any person other than a client, or cause such person to be advised to decline to give to the prosecutor or defense counsel for codefendants information which such person has a right to give.

(e) Unless defense counsel is prepared to forgo impeachment of a witness by counsel's own testimony as to what the witness stated in an interview or to seek leave to withdraw from the case in order to present such impeaching testimony, defense counsel should avoid interviewing a prospective witness except in the presence of a third person.

Standard 4-4.4 Relations With Expert Witnesses

(a) Defense counsel who engages an expert for an opinion should respect the independence of the expert and should not seek to dictate the formation of the expert's opinion on the subject. To the extent necessary, defense counsel should explain to the expert his or her role in the trial as an impartial witness called to aid the fact finders and the manner in which the examination of witnesses is conducted.

(b) Defense counsel should not pay an excessive fee for the purpose of influencing an expert's testimony or fix the amount of the fee contingent upon the testimony an expert will give or the result in the case.

Standard 4-4.5 Compliance With Discovery Procedure

Defense counsel should make a reasonably diligent effort to comply with a legally proper discovery request.

Standard 4-4.6 Physical Evidence

(a) Defense counsel who receives a physical item under circumstances implicating a client in criminal conduct should disclose the location of or should deliver that item to law enforcement authorities only: (1) if required by law or court order, or (2) as provided in paragraph (d).

(b) Unless required to disclose, defense counsel should return the item to the source from whom defense counsel received it, except as provided in paragraphs (c) and (d). In returning the item to the source, defense counsel should advise the source of the legal consequences pertaining to possession or destruction of the item. Defense counsel should also prepare a written record of these events for his or her file, but should not give the source a copy of such record.

(c) Defense counsel may receive the item for a reasonable period of time during which defense counsel: (1) intends to return it to the owner; (2) reasonably fears that return of the item to the source will result in destruction of the item; (3) reasonably fears that return of the item to the source will result in physical harm to anyone; (4) intends to test, examine, inspect, or use the item in any way as part of defense counsel's representation of the client; or (5) cannot return it to the source. If defense counsel tests or examines the item, he or she should thereafter return it to the source unless there is reason to believe that the evidence might be altered or destroyed or used to harm another or return is otherwise impossible. If defense counsel retains the item, he or she should retain it in his or her law office in a manner that does not impede the lawful ability of law enforcement authorities to obtain the item.

(d) If the item received is contraband, i.e. an item, possession of which is in and of itself a crime, such as narcotics, defense counsel may destroy it where there is no pending case or investigation relating to this evidence and where such destruction is clearly not in violation of any criminal statute. If such destruction is not permitted by law or if in defense counsel's judgment he or she cannot retain the item, whether or not it is contraband, in a way that does not pose an unreasonable risk of physical harm to anyone, defense counsel should disclose the location of or should deliver the item to law enforcement authorities.

(e) If defense counsel discloses the location of or delivers the item to law enforcement authorities under paragraphs (a) or (d), or to a third party under paragraph (c)(1), he or she should do so in the way best designed to protect the client's interests.

PART V. CONTROL AND DIRECTION OF LITIGATION

Standard 4–5.1 Advising the Accused

(a) After informing himself or herself fully on the facts and the law, defense counsel should advise the accused with complete candor concerning all aspects of the case, including a candid estimate of the probable outcome.

(b) Defense counsel should not intentionally understate or overstate the risks, hazards, or prospects of the case to exert undue influence on the accused's decision as to his or her plea.

(c) Defense counsel should caution the client to avoid communication about the case with witnesses, except with the approval of counsel, to avoid any contact with jurors or prospective jurors, and to avoid either the reality or the appearance of any other improper activity.

Standard 4–5.2 Control and Direction of the Case

(a) Certain decisions relating to the conduct of the case are ultimately for the accused and others are ultimately for defense counsel. The decisions which are to be made by the accused after full consultation with counsel include:

    (i) what pleas to enter;

    (ii) whether to accept a plea agreement;

    (iii) whether to waive jury trial;

    (iv) whether to testify in his or her own behalf; and

    (v) whether to appeal.

(b) Strategic and tactical decisions should be made by defense counsel after consultation with the client where feasible and appropriate.

Such decisions include what witnesses to call, whether and how to conduct cross-examination, what jurors to accept or strike, what trial motions should be made, and what evidence should be introduced.

(c) If a disagreement on significant matters of tactics or strategy arises between defense counsel and the client, defense counsel should make a record of the circumstances, counsel's advice and reasons, and the conclusion reached. The record should be made in a manner which protects the confidentiality of the lawyer-client relationship.

PART VI. DISPOSITION WITHOUT TRIAL

Standard 4-6.1 Duty to Explore Disposition Without Trial

(a) Whenever the law, nature, and circumstances of the case permit, defense counsel should explore the possibility of an early diversion of the case from the criminal process through the use of other community agencies.

(b) Defense counsel may engage in plea discussions with the prosecutor. Under no circumstances should defense counsel recommend to a defendant acceptance of a plea unless appropriate investigation and study of the case has been completed, including an analysis of controlling law and the evidence likely to be introduced at trial.

Standard 4-6.2 Plea Discussions

(a) Defense counsel should keep the accused advised of developments arising out of plea discussions conducted with the prosecutor.

(b) Defense counsel should promptly communicate and explain to the accused all significant plea proposals made by the prosecutor.

(c) Defense counsel should not knowingly make false statements concerning the evidence in the course of plea discussions with the prosecutor.

(d) Defense counsel should not seek concessions favorable to one client by any agreement which is detrimental to the legitimate interests of a client in another case.

(e) Defense counsel representing two or more clients in the same or related cases should not participate in making an aggregated agreement as to guilty or nolo contendere pleas, unless each client consents after consultation, including disclosure of the existence and nature of all the claims or pleas involved.

PART VII. TRIAL

Standard 4-7.1 Courtroom Professionalism

(a) As an officer of the court, defense counsel should support the authority of the court and the dignity of the trial courtroom by strict adherence to codes of professionalism and by manifesting a professional attitude toward the judge, opposing counsel, witnesses, jurors, and others in the courtroom.

(b) Defense counsel should not engage in unauthorized ex parte discussions with or submission of material to a judge relating to a particular case which is or may come before the judge.

(c) When court is in session, defense counsel should address the court and should not address the prosecutor directly on all matters relating to the case.

(d) Defense counsel should comply promptly with all orders and directives of the court, but defense counsel has a duty to have the record reflect adverse rulings or judicial conduct which counsel considers prejudicial to his or her client's legitimate interests. Defense counsel has a right to make respectful requests for reconsiderations of adverse rulings.

(e) Defense counsel should cooperate with courts and the organized bar in developing codes of professionalism for each jurisdiction.

Standard 4–7.2 Selection of Jurors

(a) Defense counsel should prepare himself or herself prior to trial to discharge effectively his or her function in the selection of the jury, including the raising of any appropriate issues concerning the method by which the jury panel was selected and the exercise of both challenges for cause and peremptory challenges.

(b) In those cases where it appears necessary to conduct a pretrial investigation of the background of jurors, investigatory methods of defense counsel should neither harass nor unduly embarrass potential jurors or invade their privacy and, whenever possible, should be restricted to an investigation of records and sources of information already in existence.

(c) The opportunity to question jurors personally should be used solely to obtain information for the intelligent exercise of challenges. Defense counsel should not intentionally use the voir dire to present factual matter which defense counsel knows will not be admissible at trial or to argue counsel's case to the jury.

Standard 4–7.3 Relations With Jury

(a) Defense counsel should not intentionally communicate privately with persons summoned for jury duty or impaneled as jurors prior to or during the trial. Defense counsel should avoid the reality or appearance of any such communications.

(b) Defense counsel should treat jurors with deference and respect, avoiding the reality or appearance of currying favor by a show of undue solicitude for their comfort or convenience.

(c) After discharge of the jury from further consideration of a case, defense counsel should not intentionally make comments to or ask questions of a juror for the purpose of harassing or embarrassing the juror in any way which will tend to influence judgment in future jury service. If defense counsel believes that the verdict may be subject to legal challenge, he or she may properly, if no statute or rule prohibits such course, communicate with jurors to determine whether such challenge may be available.

Standard 4–7.4   Opening Statement

Defense counsel's opening statement should be confined to a statement of the issues in the case and the evidence defense counsel believes in good faith will be available and admissible. Defense counsel should not allude to any evidence unless there is a good faith and reasonable basis for believing such evidence will be tendered and admitted in evidence.

Standard 4–7.5   Presentation of Evidence

(a) Defense counsel should not knowingly offer false evidence, whether by documents, tangible evidence, or the testimony of witnesses, or fail to take reasonable remedial measures upon discovery of its falsity.

(b) Defense counsel should not knowingly and for the purpose of bringing inadmissible matter to the attention of the judge or jury to offer inadmissible evidence, ask legally objectionable questions, or make other impermissible comments or arguments in the presence of the judge or jury.

(c) Defense counsel should not permit any tangible evidence to be displayed in the view of the judge or jury which would tend to prejudice fair consideration of the case by the judge or jury until such time as a good faith tender of such evidence is made.

(d) Defense counsel should not tender tangible evidence in the presence of the judge or jury if it would tend to prejudice fair consideration of the case unless there is a reasonable basis for its admission in evidence. When there is any substantial doubt about the admissibility of such evidence, it should be tendered by an offer of proof and a ruling obtained.

Standard 4–7.6   Examination of Witnesses

(a) The interrogation of all witnesses should be conducted fairly, objectively, and with due regard for the dignity and legitimate privacy of the witness, and without seeking to intimidate or humiliate the witness unnecessarily.

(b) Defense counsel's belief or knowledge that the witness is telling the truth does not preclude cross-examination.

(c) Defense counsel should not call a witness in the presence of the jury who the lawyer knows will claim a valid privilege not to testify.

(d) Defense counsel should not ask a question which implies the existence of a factual predicate for which a good faith belief is lacking.

Standard 4–7.7   Argument to the Jury

(a) In closing argument to the jury, defense counsel may argue all reasonable inferences from the evidence in the record. Defense counsel should not intentionally misstate the evidence or mislead the jury as to the inferences it may draw.

(b) Defense counsel should not express a personal belief or opinion in his or her client's innocence or personal belief or opinion in the truth or falsity of any testimony or evidence.

(c) Defense counsel should not make arguments calculated to appeal to the prejudices of the jury.

(d) Defense counsel should refrain from argument which would divert the jury from its duty to decide the case on the evidence.

Standard 4–7.8   Facts Outside the Record

Defense counsel should not intentionally refer to or argue on the basis of facts outside the record whether at trial or on appeal, unless such facts are matters of common public knowledge based on ordinary human experience or matters of which the court can take judicial notice.

Standard 4–7.9   Posttrial Motions

Defense counsel's responsibility includes presenting appropriate posttrial motions to protect the defendant's rights.

PART VIII.   AFTER CONVICTION

Standard 4–8.1   Sentencing

(a) Defense counsel should, at the earliest possible time, be or become familiar with all of the sentencing alternatives available to the court and with community and other facilities which may be of assistance in a plan for meeting the accused's needs. Defense counsel's preparation should also include familiarization with the court's practices in exercising sentencing discretion, the practical consequences of different sentences, and the normal pattern of sentences for the offense involved, including any guidelines applicable at either the sentencing or parole stages. The consequences of the various dispositions available should be explained fully by defense counsel to the accused.

(b) Defense counsel should present to the court any ground which will assist in reaching a proper disposition favorable to the accused. If a presentence report or summary is made available to defense counsel, he or she should seek to verify the information contained in it and should be prepared to supplement or challenge it if necessary. If there is no presentence report or if it is not disclosed, defense counsel should submit to the court and the prosecutor all favorable information relevant to sentencing and in an appropriate case, with the consent of the accused, be prepared to suggest a program of rehabilitation based on defense counsel's exploration of employment, educational, and other opportunities made available by community services.

(c) Defense counsel should also insure that the accused understands the nature of the presentence investigation process, and in particular the significance of statements made by the accused to probation officers and related personnel. Where appropriate, defense counsel should attend the probation officer's interview with the accused.

(d) Defense counsel should alert the accused to the right of allocution, if any, and to the possible dangers of making a statement that might tend to prejudice an appeal.

Standard 4–8.2 Appeal

(a) After conviction, defense counsel should explain to the defendant the meaning and consequences of the court's judgment and defendant's right of appeal. Defense counsel should give the defendant his or her professional judgment as to whether there are meritorious grounds for appeal and as to the probable results of an appeal. Defense counsel should also explain to the defendant the advantages and disadvantages of an appeal. The decision whether to appeal must be the defendant's own choice.

(b) Defense counsel should take whatever steps are necessary to protect the defendant's rights of appeal.

Standard 4–8.3 Counsel on Appeal

(a) Appellate counsel should not seek to withdraw from a case solely on the basis of his or her own determination that the appeal lacks merit.

(b) Appellate counsel should give a client his or her best professional evaluation of the questions that might be presented on appeal. Counsel, when inquiring into the case, should consider all issues that might affect the validity of the judgment of conviction and sentence, including any that might require initial presentation in a postconviction proceeding. Counsel should advise on the probable outcome of a challenge to the conviction or sentence. Counsel should endeavor to persuade the client to abandon a wholly frivolous appeal or to eliminate contentions lacking in substance.

(c) If the client chooses to proceed with an appeal against the advice of counsel, counsel should present the case, so long as such advocacy does not involve deception of the court. When counsel cannot continue without misleading the court, counsel may request permission to withdraw.

(d) Appellate counsel has the ultimate authority to decide which arguments to make on appeal. When appellate counsel decides not to argue all of the issues that his or her client desires to be argued, appellate counsel should inform the client of his or her pro se briefing rights.

(e) In a jurisdiction with an intermediate appellate court, counsel for a defendant-appellant or a defendant-appellee should continue to represent the client if the prosecution seeks review in the highest court, unless new counsel is substituted or unless the court permits counsel to withdraw. Similarly, in any jurisdiction, such appellate counsel should continue to represent the client if the prosecution seeks review in the Supreme Court of the United States.

Standard 4–8.4   Conduct of Appeal

(a) Appellate counsel should be diligent in perfecting appeals and expediting their prompt submission to appellate courts.

(b) Appellate counsel should be accurate in referring to the record and the authorities upon which counsel relies in the presentation to the court of briefs and oral argument.

(c) Appellate counsel should not intentionally refer to or argue on the basis of facts outside the record on appeal, unless such facts are matters of common public knowledge based on ordinary human experience or matters of which the court may take judicial notice.

Standard 4–8.5   Post-conviction Remedies

After a conviction is affirmed on appeal, appellate counsel should determine whether there is any ground for relief under other post-conviction remedies. If there is a reasonable prospect of a favorable result, counsel should explain to the defendant the advantages and disadvantages of taking such action. Appellate counsel is not obligated to represent the defendant in a post-conviction proceeding unless counsel has agreed to do so. In other respects, the responsibility of a lawyer in a post-conviction proceeding should be guided generally by the standards governing the conduct of lawyers in criminal cases.

Standard 4–8.6   Challenges to the Effectiveness of Counsel

(a) If defense counsel, after investigation, is satisfied that another defense counsel who served in an earlier phase of the case did not provide effective assistance, he or she should not hesitate to seek relief for the defendant on that ground.

(b) If defense counsel, after investigation, is satisfied that another defense counsel who served in an earlier phase of the case provided effective assistance, he or she should so advise the client and may decline to proceed further.

(c) If defense counsel concludes that he or she did not provide effective assistance in an earlier phase of the case, defense counsel should explain this conclusion to the defendant and seek to withdraw from representation with an explanation to the court of the reason therefor.

(d) Defense counsel whose conduct of a criminal case is drawn into question is entitled to testify concerning the matters charged and is not precluded from disclosing the truth concerning the accusation to the extent defense counsel reasonably believes necessary, even though this involves revealing matters which were given in confidence.

AMERICAN BAR ASSOCIATION STANDARDS OF PRACTICE FOR LAWYER MEDIATORS IN FAMILY DISPUTES

Preamble

For the purposes of these standards, family mediation is defined as a process in which a lawyer helps family members resolve their disputes in an informative and consensual manner. This process requires that the mediator be qualified by training, experience, and temperament; that the mediator be impartial; that the participants reach decisions voluntarily; that their decisions be based on sufficient factual data; and that each participant understands the information upon which decisions are reached. While family mediation may be viewed as an alternative means of conflict resolution, it is not a substitute for the benefit of independent legal advice.

I. The Mediator Has a Duty to Define and Describe the Process of Mediation and Its Cost Before the Parties Reach an Agreement to Mediate

Specific Considerations

Before the actual mediation sessions begin, the mediator shall conduct an orientation session to give an overview of the process and to assess the appropriateness of mediation for the participants. Among the topics covered, the mediator shall discuss the following:

A. The mediator shall define the process in context so that the participants understand the differences between mediation and other means of conflict resolution available to them. In defining the process, the mediator shall also distinguish it from therapy or marriage counselling.

B. The mediator shall obtain sufficient information from the participants so they can mutually define the issues to be resolved in mediation.

C. It should be emphasized that the mediator may make suggestions for the participants to consider, such as alternative ways of resolving problems and may draft proposals for the participants' consideration, but that all decisions are to be made voluntarily by the participants themselves, and the mediator's views are to be given no independent weight or credence.

1168

D. The duties and responsibilities that the mediator and the participants accept in the mediation process shall be agreed upon. The mediator shall instruct the participants that either of them or the mediator has the right to suspend or terminate the process at any time.

E. The mediator shall assess the ability and willingness of the participants to mediate. The mediator has a continuing duty to assess his or her own ability and willingness to undertake mediation with the particular participants and the issues to be mediated. The mediator shall not continue and shall terminate the process, if in his or her judgment, one of the parties is not able or willing to participate in good faith.

F. The mediator shall explain the fees for mediation. It is inappropriate for a mediator to charge a contingency fee or to base the fee on the outcome of the mediation process.

G. The mediator shall inform the participants of the need to employ independent legal counsel for advice throughout the mediation process. The mediator shall inform the participants that the mediator cannot represent either or both of them in a marital dissolution or in any legal action.

H. The mediator shall discuss the issue of separate sessions. The mediator shall reach an understanding with the participants as to whether and under what circumstances the mediator may meet alone with either of them or with any third party. *Commentary:* The mediator cannot act as lawyer for either party or for them jointly and should make that clear to both parties.

I. It should be brought to the participants' attention that emotions play a part in the decision-making process. The mediator shall attempt to elicit from each of the participants a confirmation that each understands the connection between one's own emotions and the bargaining process.

II. The Mediator Shall Not Voluntarily Disclose Information Obtained Through the Mediation Process Without the Prior Consent of Both Participants

Specific Considerations

A. At the outset of mediation, the parties should agree in writing not to require the mediator to disclose to any third party any statements made in the course of mediation. The mediator shall inform the participants that the mediator will not voluntarily disclose to any third party any of the information obtained through the mediation process, unless such disclosure is required by law, without the prior consent of the participants. The mediator also shall inform the parties of the limitations of confidentiality such as statutory or judicially mandated reporting.

B. If subpoenaed or otherwise noticed to testify, the mediator shall inform the participants immediately so as to afford them an opportunity to quash the process.

C. The mediator shall inform the participants of the mediator's inability to bind third parties to an agreement not to disclose information furnished during the mediation in the absence of any absolute privilege.

III. The Mediator Has a Duty to Be Impartial

Specific Considerations

A. The mediator shall not represent either party during or after the mediation process in any legal matters. In the event the mediator has represented one of the parties beforehand, the mediator shall not undertake the mediation.

B. The mediator shall disclose to the participants any biases or strong views relating to the issues to be mediated, both in the orientation session, and also before these issues are discussed in mediation.

C. The mediator must be impartial as between the mediation participants. The mediator's task is to facilitate the ability of the participants to negotiate their own agreement, while raising questions as to the fairness, equity and feasibility of proposed options for settlement.

D. The mediator has a duty to ensure that the participants consider fully the best interests of the children, that they understand the consequences of any decision they reach concerning the children. The mediator also has a duty to assist parents to examine the separate and individual needs of their children and to consider those needs apart from their own desires for any particular parenting formula. If the mediator believes that any proposed agreement of the parents does not protect the best interests of the children, the mediator has a duty to inform them of this belief and its basis.

E. The mediator shall not communicate with either party alone or with any third party to discuss mediation issues without the prior consent of the mediation participants. The mediator shall obtain an agreement from the participants during the orientation session as to whether and under what circumstances the mediator may speak directly and separately with each of their lawyers during the mediation process.

IV. The Mediator Has a Duty to Assure That the Mediation Participants Make Decisions Based upon Sufficient Information and Knowledge

Specific Considerations

A. The mediator shall assure that there is full financial disclosure, evaluation and development of relevant factual information in the mediation process, such as each would reasonably receive in the discovery process, or that the parties have sufficient information to intelligently waive the right to such disclosure.

B. In addition to requiring this disclosure, evaluation and development of information, the mediator shall promote the equal understanding of such information before any agreement is reached. This consideration may require the mediator to recommend that either or both obtain expert consultation in the event that it appears that additional knowledge or understanding is necessary for balanced negotiations.

C. The mediator may define the legal issues, but shall not direct the decision of the mediation participants based upon the mediator's interpretation of the law as applied to the facts of the situation. The mediator shall endeavor to assure that the participants have a sufficient understanding of appropriate statutory and case law as well as local judicial tradition, before reaching an agreement by recommending to the participants that they obtain independent legal representation during the process.

V. The Mediator Has a Duty to Suspend or Terminate Mediation Whenever Continuation of the Process Would Harm One or More of the Participants

Specific Considerations

A. If the mediator believes that the participants are unable or unwilling to meaningfully participate in the process or that reasonable agreement is unlikely the mediator may suspend or terminate mediation and should encourage the parties to seek appropriate professional help. The mediator shall recognize that the decisions are to be made by the parties on the basis of adequate information. The mediator shall not, however, participate in a process that the mediator believes will result in harm to a participant.

B. The mediator shall assure that each person has had the opportunity to understand fully the implications and ramifications of all options available.

C. The mediator has a duty to assure a balanced dialogue and must attempt to diffuse any manipulative or intimidating negotiation techniques utilized by either of the participants.

D. If the mediator has suspended or terminated the process, the mediator should suggest that the participants obtain additional professional services as may be appropriate.

VI. The Mediator Has a Continuing Duty to Advise Each of the Mediation Participants to Obtain Legal Review Prior to Reaching Any Agreement

Specific Considerations

A. Each of the mediation participants should have independent legal counsel before reaching final agreement. At the beginning of the mediation process, the mediator should inform the participants that each should employ independent legal counsel for advice at the beginning of the process and that the independent legal counsel should be utilized throughout the process and before the participants have reached any accord to which they have made an emotional commitment. In order to promote the integrity of the process, the mediator shall not refer either of the participants to any particular lawyers. When an attorney referral is requested, the parties should be referred to a Bar Association list if available. In the absence of such a list, the mediator may only provide a list of qualified family law attorneys in the community.

B. The mediator shall inform the participants that the mediator cannot represent either or both of them in a marital dissolution.

C. The mediator shall obtain an agreement from the husband and the wife that each lawyer, upon request, shall be entitled to review all the factual documentation provided by the participants in the mediation process.

D. Any memo of understanding or proposed agreement which is prepared in the mediation process should be separately reviewed by independent counsel for each participant before it is signed. While a mediator cannot insist that each participant have separate counsel, they should be discouraged from signing any agreement which has not been so reviewed. If the participants, or either of them, choose to proceed without independent counsel, the mediator shall warn them of any risk involved in not being represented, including where appropriate, the possibility that the agreement they submit to a court may be rejected as unreasonable in light of both parties' legal rights or may not be binding on them.

CIRCULAR 230 REGULATING PRACTICE BEFORE THE TREASURY [†]

31 C.F.R. §§ 10.0–10.97 (1990)

CONTENTS

PART 10. PRACTICE BEFORE THE
INTERNAL REVENUE SERVICE

[†] As this publication was going to print, the Treasury was considering amendments to Circular 230.

[*] Sections 10.1, 10.2, 10.5, 10.6, 10.7 and 10.8 have been omitted. Ed.

PART 10. PRACTICE BEFORE THE
INTERNAL REVENUE SERVICE

Subpart A. Rules Governing Authority to Practice

§ 10.3 Who May Practice

(a) *Attorneys.* Any attorney who is not currently under suspension or disbarment from practice before the Internal Revenue Service may practice before the Service upon filing with the Service a written declaration that he or she is currently qualified as an attorney and is authorized to represent the particular party on whose behalf he or she acts.

(b) *Certified public accountants.* Any certified public accountant who is not currently under suspension or disbarment from practice before the Internal Revenue Service may practice before the Service upon filing with the Service a written declaration that he or she is currently qualified as a certified public accountant and is authorized to represent the particular party on whose behalf he or she acts.

(c) *Enrolled agents.* Any person enrolled as an agent pursuant to this part may practice before the Internal Revenue Service.

(d) *Enrolled actuaries.* (1) Any individual who is enrolled as an actuary by the Joint Board for the Enrollment of Actuaries pursuant to 29 U.S.C. 1242 may practice before the Internal Revenue Service upon filing with the Service a written declaration that he/she is currently qualified as an enrolled actuary and is authorized to represent the particular party on whose behalf he/she acts. Practice as an enrolled actuary is limited to representation with respect to issues involving the following statutory provisions.

Internal Revenue Code (Title 26 U.S.C.) sections: 401 (qualification of employee plans), 403(a) (relating to whether an annuity plan meets the requirements of section 404(a)(2)), 404 (deductibility of employer contributions), 405 (qualification of bond purchase plans), 412 (funding requirements for certain employee plans), 413 (application of qualification requirements to collectively bargained plans and to plans maintained by more than one employer), 414 (containing definitions and special rules relating to the employee plan area), 4971 (relating to excise taxes payable as a result of an accumulated funding deficiency under section 412), 6057 (annual registration of plans), 6058 (information required in connection with certain plans of deferred compensation), 6059 (periodic report of actuary), 6652(e) (failure to file annual registration and other notifications by pension plan), 6652(f) (failure to file information required in connection with certain plans of deferred compensation), 6692 (failure to file actuarial report), 7805(b) (relating to the extent, if any, to which an Internal Revenue Service ruling or determination letter coming under the herein listed statutory provisions shall be applied without retroactive effect); and 29 U.S.C. 1083 (relating to waiver of funding for nonqualified plans).

(2) An individual who practices before the Internal Revenue Service pursuant to this subsection shall be subject to the provisions of this part in the same manner as attorneys, certified public accountants and enrolled agents.

(e) *Others.* Any person qualifying under § 10.5(c) or § 10.7 may practice before Internal Revenue Service to the extent provided in those sections.

(f) *Government officers and employees and others.* An individual, including an officer or employee of the executive, legislative, or judicial branch of the United States Government; officer or employee of the District of Columbia; Member of Congress; or Resident Commissioner, may not practice before the Service if such practice would violate 18 U.S.C. 203 or 205.

(g) *State officers and employees.* No officer or employee of any State, or subdivision thereof, whose duties require him to pass upon, investigate, or deal with tax matters of such State or subdivision, may practice before the Service, if such State employment may disclose facts or information applicable to Federal tax matters.

§ 10.4 Eligibility for Enrollment

(a) *Enrollment upon examination.* The Director of Practice may grant enrollment to an applicant who demonstrates special competence in tax matters by written examination administered by the Internal Revenue Service and who has not engaged in any conduct which would justify the suspension or disbarment of any attorney, certified public accountant, or enrolled agent under the provisions of this part.

(b) *Enrollment of former Internal Revenue Service employees.* The Director of Practice may grant enrollment to an applicant who has not engaged in any conduct which would justify the suspension or disbarment of any attorney, certified public accountant, or enrolled agent under the provisions of this part and who, by virtue of his past service and technical experience in the Internal Revenue Service has qualified for such enrollment, as follows:

(1) Application for enrollment on account of former employment in the Internal Revenue Service shall be made to the Director of Practice. Each applicant will be supplied a form by the Director of Practice, which shall indicate the information required respecting the applicant's qualifications. In addition to the applicant's name, address, citizenship, age, educational experience, etc., such information shall specifically include a detailed account of the applicant's employment in the Internal Revenue Service, which account shall show (i) positions held, (ii) date of each appointment and termination thereof, (iii) nature of services rendered in each position, with particular reference to the degree of technical experience

involved, and (iv) name of supervisor in such positions, together with such other information regarding the experience and training of the applicant as may be relevant.

(2) Upon receipt of each such application, it shall be transmitted to the appropriate officer of the Internal Revenue Service with the request that a detailed report of the nature and rating of the applicant's services in the Internal Revenue Service, accompanied by the recommendation of the superior officer in the particular unit or division of the Internal Revenue Service that such employment does or does not qualify the applicant technically or otherwise for the desired authorization, be furnished to the Director of Practice.

(3) In examining the qualification of an applicant for enrollment on account of employment in the Internal Revenue Service, the Director of Practice will be governed by the following policies:

(i) Enrollment on account of such employment may be of unlimited scope or may be limited to permit the presentation of matters only of the particular class or only before the particular unit or division of the Internal Revenue Service for which his former employment in the Internal Revenue Service has qualified the applicant.

(ii) Application for enrollment on account of employment in the Internal Revenue Service must be made within 3 years from the date of separation from such employment.

(iii) It shall be requisite for enrollment on account of such employment that the applicant shall have had a minimum of 5 years continuous employment in the Service during which he shall have been regularly engaged in applying and interpreting the provisions of the Internal Revenue Code and the regulations thereunder relating to income, estate, gift, employment, or excise taxes.

(iv) For the purposes of paragraph (b)(3)(iii) of this section an aggregate of 10 or more years of employment, at least 3 of which occurred within the 5 years preceding the date of application, shall be deemed the equivalent of 5 years continuous employment.

(c) *Natural persons.* Enrollment to practice may be granted only to natural persons.

Subpart B. Duties and Restrictions Relating to Practice Before the Internal Revenue Service

§ 10.20 Information to Be Furnished

(a) *To the Internal Revenue Service.* No attorney, certified public accountant, enrolled agent, or enrolled actuary shall neglect or refuse promptly to submit records or information in any matter before the Internal Revenue Service, upon proper and lawful request by a duly authorized officer or employee of the Internal Revenue Service, or shall interfere, or attempt to interfere, with any proper and lawful effort by the Internal Revenue Service or its officers or employees to obtain any such record or information, unless he believes in good faith and on reasonable grounds that such record or information is privileged or that the request for, or effort to obtain, such record or information is of doubtful legality.

(b) *To the Director of Practice.* It shall be the duty of an attorney or certified public accountant, who practices before the Internal Revenue Service, or enrolled agent, when requested by the Director of Practice, to provide the Director with any information he may have concerning violation of the regulations in this part by any person, and to testify thereto in any proceeding instituted under this part for the disbarment or suspension of an attorney, certified public accountant, enrolled agent, or enrolled actuary, unless he believes in good faith and on reasonable grounds that such information is privileged or that the request therefor is of doubtful legality.

§ 10.21   Knowledge of Client's Omission

Each attorney, certified public accountant, enrolled agent, or enrolled actuary who, having been retained by a client with respect to a matter administered by the Internal Revenue Service, knows that the client has not complied with the revenue laws of the United States or has made an error in or omission from any return, document, affidavit, or other paper which the client is required by the revenue laws of the United States to execute, shall advise the client promptly of the fact of such noncompliance, error, or omission.

§ 10.22   Diligent as to Accuracy

Each attorney, certified public accountant, enrolled agent, or enrolled actuary shall exercise due diligence:

(a) In preparing or assisting in the preparation of, approving, and filing returns, documents, affidavits, and other papers relating to Internal Revenue Service matters;

(b) In determining the correctness of oral or written representations made by him to the Department of the Treasury; and

(c) In determining the correctness of oral or written representations made by him to clients with reference to any matter administered by the Internal Revenue Service.

§ 10.23   Prompt Disposition of Pending Matters

No attorney, certified public accountant, enrolled agent, or enrolled actuary shall unreasonably delay the prompt disposition of any matter before the Internal Revenue Service.

§ 10.24   Assistance From Disbarred or Suspended Persons and Former Internal Revenue Service Employees

No attorney, certified public accountant, enrolled agent, or enrolled actuary shall, in practice before the Internal Revenue Service, knowingly and directly or indirectly:

(a) Employ or accept assistance from any person who is under disbarment or suspension from practice before the Internal Revenue Service.

(b) Accept employment as associate, correspondent, or subagent from, or share fees with, any such person.

(c) Accept assistance from any former government employee where the provisions of § 10.26 of these regulations or any Federal law would be violated.

§ 10.25   Practice by Partners of Government Employees

No partner of an officer or employee of the executive branch of the U.S. Government, of any independent agency of the United States, or of the District of Columbia, shall represent anyone in any matter administered by the Internal Revenue Service in which such officer or employee of the Government participates or has participated personally and substantially as a Government employee or which is the subject of his official responsibility.

§ 10.26   Practice by Former Government Employees, Their Partners and Their Associates

(a) *Definitions.* For purposes of § 10.26: (1) "Assist" means to act in such a way as to advise, furnish information to or otherwise aid another person, directly or indirectly.

(2) "Government employee" is an officer or employee of the United States or any agency of the United States, including a "special government employee" as defined in 18 U.S.C. 202(a), or of the District of Columbia, or of any State, or a member of Congress or of any State legislature.

(3) "Member of a firm" is a sole practitioner or an employee or associate thereof, or a partner, stockholder, associate, affiliate or employee of a partnership, joint venture, corporation, professional association or other affiliation of two or more practitioners who represent non-Government parties.

(4) Practitioner includes any individual described in § 10.3(e).

(5) "Official responsibility" means the direct administrative or operating authority, whether intermediate or final, and either exercisable alone or with others, and either personally or through subordinates, to approve, disapprove, or otherwise direct Government action, with or without knowledge of the action.

(6) "Participate" or "participation" means substantial involvement as a Government employee by making decisions, or preparing or reviewing documents with or without the right to exercise a judgment of approval or disapproval, or participating in conferences or investigations, or rendering advice of a substantial nature.

(7) "Rule" includes Treasury Regulations, whether issued or under preparation for issuance as Notices of Proposed Rule Making or as Treasury Decisions, and revenue rulings and revenue procedures published in the Internal Revenue bulletin. "Rule" shall not include a "transaction" as defined in paragraph (a)(9) of this section.

(8) "Transaction" means any decision, determination, finding, letter ruling, technical advice, contract or approval or disapproval thereof, relating to a particular factual situation or situations involving a specific party or parties whose rights, privileges, or liabilities under laws or regulations administered by the Internal Revenue Service, or other legal rights, are determined or immediately affected therein and to which the United States is a party or in which it has a direct and substantial interest, whether or not the same taxable periods are involved. "Transaction" does not include "rule" as defined in paragraph (a)(7) of this section.

(b) *General rules.* (1) No former Government employee shall, subsequent to his Government employment, represent anyone in any matter administered by the Internal Revenue Service if the representation would violate 18 U.S.C. 207(a) or (b) or any other laws of the United States.

(2) No former Government employee who participated in a transaction shall, subsequent to his Government employment, represent or knowingly assist, in that transaction, any person who is or was a specific party to that transaction.

(3) No former Government employee who within a period of one year prior to the termination of his Government employment had official responsibility for a transaction shall, within one year after his Government employment is ended, represent or knowingly assist in that transaction any person who is or was a specific party to that transaction.

(4) No former Government employee shall, within one year after his Government employment is ended, appear before any employee of the Treasury Department in connection with the publication, withdrawal, amendment, modification, or interpretation of a rule in the development of which the former Government employee participated or for which, within a period of one year prior to the termination of his Government employment, he had official responsibility. However, this subparagraph

does not preclude such former employee for appearing on his own behalf or from representing a taxpayer before the Internal Revenue Service in connection with a transaction involving the application or interpretation of such a rule with respect to that transaction: *Provided,* That such former employee shall not utilize or disclose any confidential information acquired by the former employee in the development of the rule, and shall not contend that the rule is invalid or illegal. In addition, this subparagraph does not preclude such former employee from otherwise advising or acting for any person.

(c) *Firm representation.* (1) No member of a firm of which a former Government employee is a member may represent or knowingly assist a person who was or is a specific party in any transaction with respect to which the restrictions of paragraph (b)(1) (other than 18 U.S.C. 207(b)) or (b)(2) of this section apply to the former Government employee, in that transaction, unless:

(i) No member of the firm who had knowledge of the participation by the Government employee in the transaction initiated discussions with the Government employee concerning his becoming a member of the firm until his Government employment is ended or six months after the termination of his participation in the transaction, whichever is earlier;

(ii) The former Government employee did not initiate any discussions concerning becoming a member of the firm while participating in the transaction or, if such discussions were initiated, they conformed with the requirements of 18 U.S.C. 208(b); and

(iii) The firm isolates the former Government employee in such a way that he does not assist in the representation.

(2) No member of a firm of which a former Government employee is a member may represent or knowingly assist a person who was or is a specific party in any transaction with respect to which the restrictions of paragraph (b)(3) of this section apply to the former employee, in that transaction unless the firm isolates the former Government employee in such a way that he does not assist in the representation.

(3) When isolation of the former Government employee is required under paragraph (c)(1) or (c)(2) of this section, a statement affirming the fact of such isolation shall be executed under oath by the former Government employee and by a member of the firm acting on behalf of the firm, and shall be filed with the Director of Practice and in such other place and in the manner prescribed by regulation. This statement shall clearly identify the firm, the former Government employee, and the transaction or transactions requiring such isolation.

(d) *Pending representation.* Practice by former Government employees, their partners and associates with respect to representation in specific matters where actual representation commenced before publication of this regulation is governed by the regulations set forth in the June 1972 amendments to the regulations of this part (published at 37

FR 11676): *Provided,* That the burden of showing that representation commenced before publication is with the former Government employees, their partners and associates.

§ 10.27 Notaries

No attorney, certified public accountant, enrolled agent, or enrolled actuary as notary public shall with respect to any matter administered by the Internal Revenue Service take acknowledgments, administer oaths, certify papers, or perform any official act in connection with matters in which he is employed as counsel, attorney, or agent, or in which he may be in any way interested before the Internal Revenue Service (26 Op.Atty.Gen. 236).

§ 10.28 Fees

(a) *Generally.* A practitioner may not charge an unconscionable fee for representing a client in a matter before the Internal Revenue Service.

(b) *Contingent fees for return preparation.* A practitioner may not charge a contingent fee for preparing an original return. A practitioner may charge a contingent fee for preparing an amended return or a claim for refund (other than a claim for refund made on an original return) if the practitioner reasonably anticipates at the time the fee arrangement is entered into that the amended return or claim will receive substantive review by the Service. A contingent fee includes a fee that is based on a percentage of the refund shown on a return or a percentage of the taxes saved, or that otherwise depends on the specific result attained.

§ 10.29 Conflicting Interests

No attorney, certified public accountant, or enrolled agent shall represent conflicting interests in his practice before the Internal Revenue Service, except by express consent of all directly interested parties after full disclosure has been made.

§ 10.30 Solicitation

(a) Advertising and solicitation restrictions. (1) No attorney, certified public accountant, enrolled agent, enrolled actuary, or other individual eligible to practice before the Internal Revenue Service shall, with respect to any Internal Revenue Service matter, in any way use or participate in the use of any form of public communication containing (i) A false, fraudulent, unduly influencing, coercive, or unfair statement or claim; or (ii) a misleading or deceptive statement or claim.

Enrolled agents, in describing their professional designation, may not utilize the term of art "certified" or indicate an employer/employee relationship with the Internal Revenue Service. Examples of acceptable descriptions are "enrolled to represent taxpayers before the Internal Revenue Service," "enrolled to practice before the Internal Revenue Service," and "admitted to practice before the Internal Revenue Service." Enrolled agents and enrolled actuaries may abbreviate such designation to either EA or E.A.

(2) No attorney, certified public accountant, enrolled agent, enrolled actuary, or other individual eligible to practice before the Internal Revenue Service shall make, directly or indirectly, an uninvited solicitation of employment in matters related to the Internal Revenue Service. Solicitation includes, but is not limited to, in-person contacts and telephone communications. This restriction does not apply to (i) Seeking new business from an existing or former client in a related matter; (ii) communications with family members; (iii) making the availability of professional services known to other practitioners, so long as the person or firm contacted is not a potential client; (iv) solicitation by mailings; or (v) non-coercive in-person solicitation by those eligible to practice before the Internal Revenue Service while acting as an employee, member, or officer of an exempt organization listed in sections 501(c)(3) or (4) of the Internal Revenue Code of 1954 (26 U.S.C.).

Any targeted direct mail solicitation, i.e. a mailing to those whose unique circumstances are the basis for the solicitation, distributed by or on behalf of an attorney, certified public accountant, enrolled agency, enrolled actuary, or other individual eligible to practice before the Internal Revenue Service shall be clearly marked as such in capital letters on the envelope and at the top of the first page of such mailing. In addition, all such solicitations must clearly identify the source of the information used in choosing the recipient.

(b) Fee Information. (1) Attorney, certified public accountant, enrolled agent, or enrolled actuary and other individuals eligible to practice before the Internal Revenue Service may disseminate the following fee information:

    (i) Fixed fees for specific routine services.

    (ii) Hourly rates.

    (iii) Range of fees for particular services.

    (iv) Fee charged for an initial consultation.

Any statement of fee information concerning matters in which costs may be incurred shall include a statement disclosing whether clients will be responsible for such costs.

(2) Attorney, certified public accountant, enrolled agent, or enrolled actuary and other individuals eligible to practice before the Internal Revenue Service may also publish the availability of a written schedule of fees.

(3) Attorney, certified public accountant, enrolled agent, or enrolled actuary and other individuals eligible to practice before the Internal

Revenue Service shall be bound to charge the hourly rate, the fixed fee for specific routine services, the range of fees for particular services, or the fee for an initial consultation published for a reasonable period of time, but no less than thirty days from the last publication of such hourly rate or fees.

(c) Communications. Communication, including fee information, may include professional lists, telephone directories, print media, mailings, radio and television, and any other method: Provided, that the method chosen does not cause the communication to become untruthful, deceptive, unduly influencing or otherwise in violation of these regulations. It shall be construed as a violation of these regulations for a practitioner to persist in attempting to contact a prospective client, if such client has made known to the practitioner a desire not to be solicited. In the case of radio and television broadcasting, the broadcast shall be pre-recorded and the practitioner shall retain a recording of the actual audio transmission. In the case of direct mail communications, the practitioner shall retain a copy of the actual mailing, along with a list or other description of persons to whom the communication was mailed or otherwise distributed. Such copy shall be retained by the practitioner for a period of at least 36 months from the date of the last transmission or use.

(d) Improper Associations. An attorney, certified public accountant or enrolled agent, or enrolled actuary may, in matters related to the Internal Revenue Service, employ or accept employment or assistance as an associate, correspondent, or subagent from, or share fees with, any person or entity who, to the knowledge of the practitioner, obtains clients or otherwise practices in a manner forbidden under this section: Provided, That a practitioner does not, directly or indirectly, act or hold himself out as an Internal Revenue Service practitioner in connection with that relationship. Nothing herein shall prohibit an attorney, certified public accountant, or enrolled agent, or enrolled actuary from practice before the Internal Revenue Service in a capacity other than that described above.

§ 10.31 Negotiation of Taxpayer Refund Checks

No attorney, certified public accountant, enrolled agent, or enrolled actuary who is an income tax return preparer shall endorse or otherwise negotiate any check made in respect of income taxes which is issued to a taxpayer other than the attorney, certified public accountant, enrolled agent, or enrolled actuary.

§ 10.32 Practice of Law

Nothing in the regulations in this part shall be construed as authorizing persons not members of the bar to practice law.

§ 10.33　Tax Shelter Opinions

(a) *Tax shelter opinions and offering materials.* A practitioner who provides a tax shelter opinion analyzing the Federal tax effects of a tax shelter investment shall comply with each of the following requirements:

(1) *Factual matters.* (i) The practitioner must make inquiry as to all relevant facts, be satisfied that the material facts are accurately and completely described in the offering materials, and assure that any representations as to future activities are clearly identified, reasonable and complete.

(ii) A practitioner may not accept as true asserted facts pertaining to the tax shelter which he/she should not, based on his/her background and knowledge, reasonably believe to be true. However, a practitioner need not conduct an audit or independent verification of the asserted facts, or assume that a client's statement of the facts cannot be relied upon, unless he/she has reason to believe that any relevant facts asserted to him/her are untrue.

(iii) If the fair market value of property or the expected financial performance of an investment is relevant to the tax shelter, a practitioner may not accept an appraisal or financial projection as support for the matters claimed therein unless:

(A) The appraisal or financial projection makes sense on its face;

(B) The practitioner reasonably believes that the person making the appraisal or financial projection is competent to do so and is not of dubious reputation; and

(C) The appraisal is based on the definition of fair market value prescribed under the relevant Federal tax provisions.

(iv) If the fair market value of purchased property is to be established by reference to its stated purchase price, the practitioner must examine the terms and conditions upon which the property was (or is to be) purchased to determine whether the stated purchase price reasonably may be considered to be its fair market value.

(2) *Relate law to facts.* The practitioner must relate the law to the actual facts and, when addressing issues based on future activities, clearly identify what facts are assumed.

(3) *Identification of material issues.* The practitioner must ascertain that all material Federal tax issues have been considered, and that all of those issues which involve the reasonable possibility of a challenge by the Internal Revenue Service have been fully and fairly addressed in the offering materials.

(4) *Opinion on each material issue.* Where possible, the practitioner must provide an opinion whether it is more likely than not

that an investor will prevail on the merits of each material tax issue presented by the offering which involves a reasonable possibility of a challenge by the Internal Revenue Service. Where such an opinion cannot be given with respect to any material tax issue, the opinion should fully describe the reasons for the practitioner's inability to opine as to the likely outcome.

(5) *Overall evaluation.* (i) Where possible, the practitioner must provide an overall evaluation whether the material tax benefits in the aggregate more likely than not will be realized. Where such an overall evaluation cannot be given, the opinion should fully describe the reasons for the practitioner's inability to make an overall evaluation. Opinions concluding that an overall evaluation cannot be provided will be given special scrutiny to determine if the stated reasons are adequate.

(ii) A favorable overall evaluation may not be rendered unless it is based on a conclusion that substantially more than half of the material tax benefits, in terms of their financial impact on a typical investor, more likely than not will be realized if challenged by the Internal Revenue Service.

(iii) If it is not possible to give an overall evaluation, or if the overall evaluation is that the material tax benefits in the aggregate will not be realized, the fact that the practitioner's opinion does not constitute a favorable overall evaluation, or that it is an unfavorable overall evaluation, must be clearly and prominently disclosed in the offering materials.

(iv) The following examples illustrate the principles of this paragraph:

Example (1). A limited partnership acquires real property in a sale-leaseback transaction. The principal tax benefits offered to investing partners consist of depreciation and interest deductions. Lesser tax benefits are offered to investors by reason of several deductions under Internal Revenue Code section 162 (ordinary and necessary business expenses). If a practitioner concludes that it is more likely than not that the partnership will not be treated as the owner of the property for tax purposes (which is required to allow the interest and depreciation deductions), then he/she may not opine to the effect that it is more likely than not that the material tax benefits in the aggregate will be realized, regardless of whether favorable opinions may be given with respect to the deductions claimed under Code section 162.

Example (2). A corporation electing under subchapter S of the Internal Revenue Code is formed to engage in research and development activities. The offering materials forecast that deductions for research and experimental expenditures equal to

75% of the total investment in the corporation will be available during the first two years of the corporation's operations, other expenses will account for another 15% of the total investment, and that little or no gross income will be received by the corporation during this period. The practitioner concludes that it is more likely than not that deductions for research and experimental expenditures will be allowable. The practitioner may render an opinion to the effect that based on this conclusion, it is more likely than not that the material tax benefits in the aggregate will be realized, regardless of whether he/she can opine that it is more likely than not that any of the other tax benefits will be achieved.

Example (3). An investment program is established to acquire offsetting positions in commodities contracts. The objective of the program is to close the loss positions in year one and to close the profit positions in year two. The principal tax benefit offered by the program is a loss in the first year, coupled with the deferral of offsetting gain until the following year. The practitioner concludes that the losses will not be deductible in year one. Accordingly, he/she may not render an opinion to the effect that it is more likely than not that the material tax benefits in the aggregate will be realized, regardless of the fact that he/she is of the opinion that losses not allowable in year one will be allowable in year two, because the principal tax benefit offered is a one-year deferral of income.

Example (4). A limited partnership is formed to acquire, own and operate residential rental real estate. The offering material forecasts gross income of $2,000,000 and total deductions of $10,000,000, resulting in net losses of $8,000,000 over the first six taxable years. Of the total deductions, depreciation and interest are projected to be $7,000,000, and other deductions $3,000,000. The practitioner concludes that it is more likely than not that all of the depreciation and interest deductions will be allowable, and that it is more likely than not that the other deductions will not be allowed. The practitioner may render an opinion to the effect that it is more likely than not that the material tax benefits in the aggregate will be realized.

(6) *Description of opinion.* The practitioner must assure that the offering materials correctly and fairly represent the nature and extent of the tax shelter opinion.

(b) *Reliance on other opinions—*(1) *In general.* A practitioner may provide an opinion on less than all of the material tax issues only if:

(i) At least one other competent practitioner provides an opinion on the likely outcome with respect to all of the other material tax issues which involve a reasonable possibility of challenge by the

Internal Revenue Service, and an overall evaluation whether the material tax benefits in the aggregate more likely than not will be realized, which is disseminated in the same manner as the practitioner's opinion; and

(ii) The practitioner, upon reviewing such other opinions and any offering materials, has no reason to believe that the standards of paragraph (a) of this section have not been complied with.

Notwithstanding the foregoing, a practitioner who has not been retained to provide an overall evaluation whether the material tax benefits in the aggregate more likely than not will be realized may issue an opinion on less than all the material tax issues only if he/she has no reason to believe, based on his/her knowledge and experience, that the overall evaluation given by the practitioner who furnishes the overall evaluation is incorrect on its face.

(2) *Forecasts and projections.* A practitioner who is associated with forecasts or projections relating to or based upon the tax consequences of the tax shelter offering that are included in the offering materials, or are disseminated to potential investors other than the practitioner's clients, may rely on the opinion of another practitioner as to any or all material tax issues, provided that the practitioner who desires to rely on the other opinion has no reason to believe that the standards of paragraph (a) of this section have not been complied with by the practitioner rendering such other opinion, and the requirements of paragraph (b)(1) of this section are satisfied. The practitioner's report shall disclose any material tax issue not covered by, or incorrectly opined upon, by the other opinion, and shall set forth his/her opinion with respect to each such issue in a manner that satisfies the requirements of paragraph (a) of this section.

(c) *Definitions.* For purposes of this section:

(1) Practitioner includes any individual described in § 10.3(e).

(2) A "tax shelter," as the term is used in this section, is an investment which has as a significant and intended feature for Federal income or excise tax purposes either of the following attributes:

(i) Deductions in excess of income from the investment being available in any year to reduce income from other sources in that year, or

(ii) Credits in excess of the tax attributable to the income from the investment being available in any year to offset taxes on income from other sources in that year. Excluded from the term are municipal bonds; annuities; family trusts (but not including schemes or arrangements that are marketed to the public other than in a direct practitioner-client relationship); qualified retirement plans; individual retirement accounts; stock option plans; securities issued in a corporate reorganization; mineral development ventures, if the only tax benefit would be percentage depletion; and real estate where it is anticipated that in no year is it likely that deductions will exceed gross income from the investment in that year, or that tax credits will exceed the tax attributable to gross income from the investment in that year. Whether an investment is intended to have tax shelter features depends on the objective facts and circumstances of each case. Significant weight will be given to the features described in the offering materials to determine whether the investment is a tax shelter.

(3) A "tax shelter opinion," as the term is used in this section, is advice by a practitioner concerning the Federal tax aspects of a tax shelter either appearing or referred to in the offering materials, or used or referred to in connection with sales promotion efforts, and directed to persons other than the client who engaged the practitioner to give the advice. The term includes the tax aspects or tax risks portion of the offering materials prepared by or at the direction of a practitioner, whether or not a separate opinion letter is issued or whether or not the practitioner's name is referred to in the offering materials or in connection with the sales promotion efforts. In addition, a financial forecast or projection prepared by a practitioner is a tax shelter opinion if it is predicated on assumptions regarding Federal tax aspects of the investment, and it meets the other requirements of the first sentence of this paragraph. The term does not, however, include rendering advice solely to the offeror or reviewing parts of the offering materials, so long as neither the name of the practitioner, nor the fact that a practitioner has rendered advice concerning the tax aspects, is referred to in the offering materials or in connection with the sales promotion efforts.

(4) A "material" tax issue as the term is used in this section is

    (i) Any Federal income or excise tax issue relating to a tax shelter that would make a significant contribution toward sheltering from Federal taxes income from other sources by providing deductions in excess of the income from the tax shelter investment in any year, or tax credits available to offset tax liabilities in excess of the tax attributable to the tax shelter investment in any year;

    (ii) Any other Federal income or excise tax issue relating to a tax shelter that could have a significant impact (either beneficial or adverse) on a tax shelter investor under any reasonably foreseeable circumstances (e.g., depreciation or investment tax credit recapture, availability of long-term capital gain treatment, or realization of taxable income in excess of cash flow, upon sale or other disposition of the tax shelter investment); and

(iii) The potential applicability of penalties, additions to tax, or interest charges that reasonably could be asserted against a tax shelter investor by the Internal Revenue Service with respect to the tax shelter. The determination of what is material is to be made in good faith by the practitioner, based on information available at the time the offering materials are circulated.

(d) For purposes of advising the Director of Practice whether an individual may have violated § 10.33, the Director of Practice is authorized to establish an Advisory Committee, composed of at least five individuals authorized to practice before the Internal Revenue Service. Under procedures established by the Director of Practice, such Advisory Committee shall, at the request of the Director of Practice, review and make recommendations with regard to alleged violations of § 10.33.

Subpart C. Rules Applicable to Disciplinary Proceedings

§ 10.50 Authority to Disbar or Suspend

Pursuant to 31 U.S.C. 330(b), the Secretary of the Treasury after notice and an opportunity for a proceeding, may suspend or disbar any practitioner from practice before the Internal Revenue Service. The Secretary may take such action against any practitioner who is shown to be incompetent or disreputable, who refuses to comply with any regulation in this part, or who, with intent to defraud, willfully and knowingly misleads or threatens a client or prospective client.

§ 10.51 Disreputable Conduct

Disreputable conduct for which an attorney, certified public accountant, enrolled agent, or enrolled actuary may be disbarred or suspended from practice before the Internal Revenue Service includes, but is not limited to:

(a) Conviction of any criminal offense under the revenue laws of the United States, or of any offense involving dishonesty, or breach of trust.

(b) Giving false or misleading information, or participating in any way in the giving of false or misleading information to the Department of the Treasury or any officer or employee thereof, or to any tribunal authorized to pass upon Federal tax matters, in connection with any matter pending or likely to be pending before them, knowing such information to be false or misleading. Facts or other matters contained in testimony, Federal tax returns, financial statements, applications for enrollment, affidavits, declarations, or any other document or statement, written or oral, are included in the term "information."

(c) Solicitation of employment as prohibited under § 10.30, the use of false or misleading representations with intent to deceive a client or prospective client in order to procure employment, or intimating that the practitioner is able improperly to obtain special consideration or action from the Internal Revenue Service or officer or employee thereof.

(d) Willfully failing to make Federal tax return in violation of the revenue laws of the United States, or evading, attempting to evade, or participating in any way in evading or attempting to evade any Federal tax or payment thereof, knowingly counseling or suggesting to a client or prospective client an illegal plan to evade Federal taxes or payment thereof, or concealing assets of himself or another to evade Federal taxes or payment thereof.

(e) Misappropriation of, or failure properly and promptly to remit funds received from a client for the purpose of payment of taxes or other obligations due the United States.

(f) Directly or indirectly attempting to influence, or offering or agreeing to attempt to influence, the official action of any officer or employee of the Internal Revenue Service by the use of threats, false accusations, duress or coercion, by the offer of any special inducement or promise of advantage or by the bestowing of any gift, favor or thing of value.

(g) Disbarment or suspension from practice as an attorney, certified public accountant, public accountant, or actuary by any duly constituted authority of any State, possession, territory, Commonwealth, the District of Columbia, any Federal court of record or any Federal agency, body or board.

(h) Knowingly aiding and abetting another person to practice before the Internal Revenue Service during a period of suspension, disbarment, or ineligibility of such other person. Maintaining a partnership for the practice of law, accountancy, or other related professional service with a person who is under disbarment from practice before the Service shall be presumed to be a violation of this provision.

(i) Contemptuous conduct in connection with practice before the Internal Revenue Service, including the use of abusive language, making false accusations and statements knowing them to be false, or circulating or publishing malicious or libelous matter.

(j) Giving a false opinion, knowingly, recklessly, or through gross incompetence, including an opinion which is intentionally or recklessly misleading, or a pattern of providing incompetent opinions on questions arising under the Federal tax laws. False opinions described in this paragraph include those which reflect or result from a knowing misstatement of fact or law; from an assertion of a position known to be unwarranted under existing law; from counseling or assisting in conduct known to be illegal or fraudulent; from concealment of matters required by law to be revealed; or from conscious disregard of information indicating that material facts expressed in the tax opinion or offering material are false or misleading. For the purpose of this paragraph, reckless conduct is a highly unreasonable omission or misrepresentation, involving an extreme departure from the standards of ordinary care that a practitioner should observe under the circumstances. A pattern of conduct is a factor that will be taken into account in determining whether a practitioner acted knowingly, recklessly, or through gross incompetence. Gross incompetence includes conduct that reflects gross indifference, preparation which is grossly inadequate under the circumstances, and a consistent failure to perform obligations to the client.

§ 10.52 Violation of Regulations

A practitioner may be disbarred or suspended from practice before the Internal Revenue Service for any of the following:

(a) Willfully violating any of the regulations contained in this part.

(b) Recklessly or through gross incompetence (within the meaning of § 10.51(j)) violating § 10.33 or § 10.34 of this part.

§ 10.53 Receipt of Information Concerning Attorneys, Certified Public Accountants and Enrolled Agents

If an officer or employee of the Internal Revenue Service has reason to believe that an attorney, certified public accountant, enrolled agent, or enrolled actuary has violated any provision of this part, or if any such officer or employee receives information to that effect, he shall promptly make a written report thereof, which report or a copy thereof shall be forwarded to the Director of Practice. If any other person has information of such violations, he may make a report thereof to the Director of Practice or to any officer or employee of the Internal Revenue Service.

§ 10.54 Institution of Proceeding

Whenever the Director of Practice has reason to believe that any attorney, certified public accountant, enrolled agent, or enrolled actuary has violated any provision of the laws or regulations governing practice before the Internal Revenue Service, he may reprimand such person or institute a proceeding for disbarment or suspension of such person. The proceeding shall be instituted by a complaint which names the respondent and is signed by the Director of Practice and filed in his office. Except in cases of willfulness, or where time, the nature of the proceeding, or the public interest does not permit, a proceeding will not be instituted under this section until facts or conduct which may warrant such action have been called to the attention of the proposed respondent in writing and he has been accorded opportunity to demonstrate or achieve compliance with all lawful requirements.

[The remaining sections of Circular 230 which deal with the disciplinary process are omitted. Ed.]

SELECTED STANDARDS FOR PROFESSIONALISM AND COURTESY IN LITIGATION

PROFESSIONALISM STANDARDS IN THE NORTHERN DISTRICT OF TEXAS

121 F.R.D. 287, 88 (N.D.Tex.1988) (en banc)

* * *

B.

We next set out the standards to which we expect litigation counsel to adhere.

The Dallas Bar Association recently adopted "Guidelines of Professional Courtesy" and a "Lawyer's Creed" that are both sensible and pertinent to the problems we address here. From them we adopt the following as standards of practice [8] to be observed by attorneys appearing in civil actions in this district:

(A) In fulfilling his or her primary duty to the client, a lawyer must be ever conscious of the broader duty to the judicial system that serves both attorney and client.

(B) A lawyer owes, to the judiciary, candor, diligence and utmost respect.

(C) A lawyer owes, to opposing counsel, a duty of courtesy and cooperation, the observance of which is necessary for the efficient administration of our system of justice and the respect of the public it serves.

(D) A lawyer unquestionably owes, to the administration of justice, the fundamental duties of personal dignity and professional integrity.

(E) Lawyers should treat each other, the opposing party, the court, and members of the court staff with courtesy and civility and conduct themselves in a professional manner at all times.

(F) A client has no right to demand that counsel abuse the opposite party or indulge in offensive conduct. A lawyer shall always treat adverse witnesses and suitors with fairness and due consideration.

---

8. We also commend to counsel the American College of Trial Lawyers' Code of Trial Conduct (rev. 1987). Those portions of the Code that are applicable to our decision today are set out in the appendix.

(G) In adversary proceedings, clients are litigants and though ill feeling may exist between clients, such ill feeling should not influence a lawyer's conduct, attitude, or demeanor towards opposing lawyers.

(H) A lawyer should not use any form of discovery, or the scheduling of discovery, as a means of harassing opposing counsel or counsel's client.

(I) Lawyers will be punctual in communications with others and in honoring scheduled appearances, and will recognize that neglect and tardiness are demeaning to the lawyer and to the judicial system.

(J) If a fellow member of the Bar makes a just request for cooperation, or seeks scheduling accommodation, a lawyer will not arbitrarily or unreasonably withhold consent.

(K) Effective advocacy does not require antagonistic or obnoxious behavior and members of the Bar will adhere to the higher standard of conduct which judges, lawyers, clients, and the public may rightfully expect.

Attorneys who abide faithfully by the standards we adopt should have little difficulty conducting themselves as members of a learned profession whose unswerving duty is to the public they serve and to the system of justice in which they practice. Those litigators who persist in viewing themselves solely as combatants, or who perceive that they are retained to win at all costs without regard to fundamental principles of justice, will find that their conduct does not square with the practices we expect of them. Malfeasant counsel can expect instead that their conduct will prompt an appropriate response from the court, including the range of sanctions the Fifth Circuit suggests in the Rule 11 context: "a warm friendly discussion on the record, a hard-nosed reprimand in open court, compulsory legal education, monetary sanctions, or other measures appropriate to the circumstances." *Thomas*, 836 F.2d at 878.

AMERICAN BAR ASSOCIATION GUIDELINES FOR CONDUCT

August 1998

Preamble

A lawyer's conduct should be characterized at all times by personal courtesy and professional integrity in the fullest sense of those terms. In fulfilling our duty to represent a client vigorously as lawyers, we will be mindful of our obligations to the administration of justice, which is a truth-seeking process designed to resolve human and societal problems in a rational, peaceful, and efficient manner.

A judge's conduct should be characterized at all times by courtesy and patience toward all participants. As judges we owe to all participants in a legal proceeding respect, diligence, punctuality, and protection against unjust and improper criticism or attack.

Conduct that may be characterized as uncivil, abrasive, abusive, hostile, or obstructive impedes the fundamental goal of resolving disputes rationally, peacefully, and efficiently. Such conduct tends to delay and often to deny justice. The following Guidelines are designed to encourage us, judges and lawyers, to meet our obligations to each other, to litigants and to the system of justice, and thereby achieve the twin goals of civility and professionalism, both of which are hallmarks of a learned profession dedicated to public service. We encourage judges, lawyers and clients to make a mutual and firm commitment to these Guidelines. We support the principles espoused in the following Guidelines, but under no circumstances should these Guidelines be used as a basis for litigation or for sanctions or penalties.

Lawyers' Duties to Other Counsel

1.   We will practice our profession with a continuing awareness that our role is to zealously advance the legitimate interests of our clients. In our dealings with others we will not reflect the ill feelings of our clients. We will treat all other counsel, parties, and witnesses in a civil and courteous manner, not only in court, but also in all other written and oral communications.

2.   We will not, even when called upon by a client to do so, abuse or indulge in offensive conduct directed to other counsel, parties, or witnesses. We will abstain from disparaging personal remarks or acrimony toward other counsel, parties, or witnesses. We will treat adverse witnesses and parties with fair consideration.

3.   We will not encourage or knowingly authorize any person under our control to engage in conduct that would be improper if we were to engage in such conduct.

4.   We will not, absent good cause, attribute bad motives or improper conduct to other counsel.

5.   We will not lightly seek court sanctions.

6.   We will in good faith adhere to all express promises and to agreements with other counsel, whether oral or in writing, and to all agreements implied by the circumstances or local customs.

7.   When we reach an oral understanding on a proposed agreement or a stipulation and decide to commit it to writing, the drafter will endeavor in good faith to state the oral understanding accurately and completely. The drafter will provide other counsel the opportunity to review the writing. As drafts are exchanged between or among counsel, changes from prior drafts will be identified in the draft or otherwise explicitly brought to other counsel's attention. We will not include in a draft matters to which there has been no agreement without explicitly advising other counsel in writing of the addition.

8. We will endeavor to confer early with other counsel to assess settlement possibilities. We will not falsely hold out the possibility of settlement to obtain unfair advantage.

9. In civil actions, we will stipulate to relevant matters if they are undisputed and if no good faith advocacy basis exists for not stipulating.

10. We will not use any form of discovery or discovery scheduling as a means of harassment.

11. Whenever circumstances allow, we will make good faith efforts to resolve by agreement objections before presenting them to the court.

12. We will not time the filing or service of motions or pleadings in any way that unfairly limits another party's opportunity to respond.

13. We will not request an extension of time solely for the purpose of unjustified delay or to obtain unfair advantage.

14. We will consult other counsel regarding scheduling matters in a good faith effort to avoid scheduling conflicts.

15. We will endeavor to accommodate previously scheduled dates for hearings, depositions, meetings, conferences, vacations, seminars, or other functions that produce good faith calendar conflicts on the part of other counsel.

16. We will promptly notify other counsel and, if appropriate, the court or other persons, when hearings, depositions, meetings, or conferences are to be canceled or postponed.

17. We will agree to reasonable requests for extensions of time and for waiver of procedural formalities, provided our clients' legitimate rights will not be materially or adversely affected.

18. We will not cause any default or dismissal to be entered without first notifying opposing counsel, when we know his or her identity.

19. We will take depositions only when actually needed. We will not take depositions for the purposes of harassment or other improper purpose.

20. We will not engage in any conduct during a deposition that would not be appropriate in the presence of a judge.

21. We will not obstruct questioning during a deposition or object to deposition questions unless permitted under applicable law.

22. During depositions we will ask only those questions we reasonably believe are necessary, and appropriate, for the prosecution or defense of an action.

23. We will carefully craft document production requests so they are limited to those documents we reasonably believe are necessary, and appropriate, for the prosecution or defense of an action. We will not design production requests to place an undue burden or expense on a party, or for any other improper purpose.

24. We will respond to document requests reasonably and not strain to interpret requests in an artificially restrictive manner to avoid disclosure of relevant and non-privileged documents. We will not produce

documents in a manner designed to hide or obscure the existence of particular documents, or to accomplish any other improper purpose.

25. We will carefully craft interrogatories so they are limited to those matters we reasonably believe are necessary, and appropriate, for the prosecution or defense of an action, and we will not design them to place an undue burden or expense on a party, or for any other improper purpose.

26. We will respond to interrogatories reasonably and will not strain to interpret them in an artificially restrictive manner to avoid disclosure of relevant and non-privileged information, or for any other improper purpose.

27. We will base our discovery objections on a good faith belief in their merit and will not object solely for the purpose of withholding or delaying the disclosure of relevant information, or for any other improper purpose.

28. When a draft order is to be prepared by counsel to reflect a court ruling, we will draft an order that accurately and completely reflects the court's ruling, We will promptly prepare and submit a proposed order to other counsel and attempt to reconcile any differences before the draft order is presented to the court.

29. We will not ascribe a position to another counsel that counsel has not taken.

30. Unless permitted or invited by the court, we will not send copies of correspondence between counsel to the court.

31. Nothing contained in these Guidelines is intended or shall be construed to inhibit vigorous advocacy, including vigorous cross-examination.

Lawyers' Duties to the Court

1. We will speak and write civilly and respectfully in all communications with the court.

2. We will be punctual and prepared for all court appearances so that all hearings, conferences, and trials may commence on time; if delayed, we will notify the court and counsel, if possible.

3. We will be considerate of the time constraints and pressures on the court and court staff inherent in their efforts to administer justice.

4. We will not engage in any conduct that brings disorder or disruption to the courtroom. We will advise our clients and witnesses appearing in court of the proper conduct expected and required there and, to the best of our ability, prevent our clients and witnesses from creating disorder or disruption.

5. We will not knowingly misrepresent, mischaracterize, misquote, or mis-cite facts or authorities in any oral or written communication to the court.

6. We will not write letters to the court in connection with a pending action, unless invited or permitted by the court.

7. Before dates for hearings or trials are set, or if that is not feasible, immediately after such date has been set, we will attempt to verify the availability of necessary participants and witnesses so we can promptly notify the court of any likely problems.

8. We will act and speak civilly to court marshals, clerks, court reporters, secretaries, and law clerks with an awareness that they, too, are an integral part of the judicial system.

Courts' Duties to Lawyers

1. We will be courteous, respectful, and civil to lawyers, parties, and witnesses. We will maintain control of the proceedings, recognizing that judges have both the obligation and the authority to insure that all litigation proceedings are conducted in a civil manner.

2. We will not employ hostile, demeaning, or humiliating words in opinions or in written or oral communications with lawyers, parties, or witnesses.

3. We will be punctual in convening all hearings, meetings, and conferences; if delayed, we will notify counsel, if possible.

4. In scheduling all hearings, meetings and conferences we will be considerate of time schedules of lawyers, parties, and witnesses.

5. We will make all reasonable efforts to decide promptly all matters presented to us for decision.

6. We will give the issues in controversy deliberate, impartial, and studied analysis and consideration.

7. While endeavoring to resolve disputes efficiently, we will be considerate of the time constraints and pressures imposed on lawyers by the exigencies of litigation practice.

8. We recognize that a lawyer has a right and a duty to present a cause fully and properly, and that a litigant has a right to a fair and impartial hearing. Within the practical limits of time, we will allow lawyers to present proper arguments and to make a complete and accurate record.

9. We will not impugn the integrity or professionalism of any lawyer on the basis of the clients whom or the causes which a lawyer represents.

10. We will do our best to insure that court personnel act civilly toward lawyers, parties, and witnesses.

11. We will not adopt procedures that needlessly increase litigation expense.

12. We will bring to lawyers' attention uncivil conduct which we observe.

Judges' Duties to Each Other

1. We will be courteous, respectful, and civil in opinions, ever mindful that a position articulated by another judge is the result of that judge's earnest effort to interpret the law and the facts correctly.

2. In all written and oral communications, we will abstain from disparaging personal remarks or criticisms, or sarcastic or demeaning comments about another judge.

3. We will endeavor to work with other judges in an effort to foster a spirit of cooperation in our mutual goal of enhancing the administration of justice.

PART SEVEN

STANDARDS FOR THE ORGANIZED REGULATION OF LAWYERS

TABLE OF CONTENTS

Although the legal profession has sought to exercise self regulation over its members through the promulgation of codes of conduct, true self regulation will not result unless the profession has implemented a mechanism for enforcing the codes. In other words, violations of the codes of conduct must in some manner be identified and prosecuted with some degree of effectiveness and fairness. Sanctions must be assessed against violators to deter others from violating the rules and to ensure that the violating lawyer does not commit future violations.

Initially, the ABA had not focused its efforts on the disciplinary mechanism and sanctions; instead, its efforts were placed in defining the substantive aspect of the codes of conduct. In 1970, former Justice Tom Clark chaired a commission on evaluating disciplinary enforcement. The Commission's Report concluded that state bars needed model standards on which to base their systems of discipline. In 1979, the ABA adopted Standards for Lawyer Discipline and Disability Proceedings. In 1985, the ABA adopted the Model Rules for Lawyer Disciplinary Enforcement. These early codes for developing disciplinary systems proved to be inadequate and they have been replaced in 1986 by the Standards for Imposing Lawyer Standards and in 1989 by the Model Rules of Disciplinary Enforcement. In 1992, the ABA House of Delegates adopted 21 recommendations for the evaluation of a system of disciplinary enforcement. These standards are reproduced in this part. In 1993, the ABA amended the Model Rules for Lawyer Disciplinary Enforcement to reflect policies in the recommendations adopted in 1992. And, in 1996, the ABA again amended these rules to reflect the use of alternative discipline programs such as mediation and arbitration in cases of lesser misconduct. In 1998, the ABA approved Model Rules for Mediation of Client-Lawyer Disputes to guide the states in the implementation of alternative dispute resolution in disputes between clients and lawyers.

One of the most significant areas for concern in professional discipline has been the area of fee disputes. For several years, the ABA has encouraged the use of alternative dispute resolution techniques in this area. In 1995, the ABA approved the Model Rules for Fee Arbitration.

ABA RECOMMENDATIONS FOR THE EVALUATION OF DISCIPLINARY ENFORCEMENT

[In 1992, the ABA House of Delegates adopted 21 recommendations with respect to the evaluation of systems of disciplinary enforcement. The recommendations were adopted only as suggestions to the various jurisdictions and the determination of whether a suggestion was to be accepted was left up to the individual jurisdictions. Ed.]

Recommendation 1: Regulation of the Profession by the Judiciary

Regulation of the legal profession should remain under the authority of the judicial branch of government.

Recommendation 2: Supporting Judicial Regulation and Professional Responsibility

2.1 The American Bar Association should continue to place the highest priority on promoting, developing, and supporting judicial regulation of the legal profession and professional responsibility.

2.2 The Association should continue to provide adequate funding and staffing for activities to support judicial regulation and professional responsibility.

2.3 To promote the most efficient allocation of resources, the Association should establish written policies to insure that all of its judicial regulation and professional responsibility activities are coordinate, regardless of the Association entity conducting the activity.

Recommendation 3: Expanding the Scope of Public Protection

The Court should establish a system of regulation of the legal profession that consists of:

3.1 component agencies, including but not limited to:
(a) lawyer discipline,
(b) a client protection fund,
(c) mandatory arbitration of fee disputes,
(d) voluntary arbitration of lawyer malpractice claims and other disputes,

(e) mediation,

(f) lawyer practice assistance,

(g) lawyer substance abuse counseling; and

3.2 a central intake office for the receipt of all complaints about lawyers, whose functions should include: (a) providing assistance to complainants in stating their complaints; (b) making a preliminary determination as to the validity of the complaint; (c) dismissing the complaint or determining the appropriate component agency or agencies to which the complaint should be directed and forwarding the complaint; (d) providing information to complainants about available remedies, operations and procedures, and the status of their complaints; and (e) coordinating among agencies and tracking the handling and disposition of each complaint.

Recommendation 4: Lawyer Practice Assistance Committee

4.1 The Court should establish a Lawyer Practice Assistance Committee. At least one third of the members should be nonlawyers. The Lawyer Assistance Committee should consider cases referred to it by the disciplinary counsel and the Court and should assist lawyers voluntarily seeking assistance. The Committee should provide guidance to the lawyer including, when appropriate: (a) review of the lawyer's office and case management practices and recommendations for improvement; and (b) review of the lawyer's substantive knowledge of the law and recommendations for further study.

4.2 In cases in which the lawyer has agreed with disciplinary counsel to submit to practice assistance, the Committee may require the lawyer to attend continuing legal education classes, to attend and successfully complete law school courses or office management courses, to participate in substance abuse recovery programs or in psychological counseling, or to take other actions necessary to improve the lawyer's fitness to practice law.

Recommendation 5: Independence of Disciplinary Officials

All jurisdictions should structure their lawyer disciplinary systems so that disciplinary officials are appointed by the highest court of the jurisdiction or by other disciplinary officials who are appointed by the Court. Disciplinary officials should possess sufficient independent authority to conduct the lawyer discipline function impartially:

5.1 Elected bar officials, their appointees and employees should provide only administrative and other services for the disciplinary system that support the operation of the system without impairing the independence of disciplinary officials.

5.2 Elected bar officials, their appointees and employees should have no investigative, prosecutorial, or adjudicative functions in the disciplinary process.

5.3 The budget for the office of disciplinary counsel should be formulated by disciplinary counsel. The budget for the state-wide disciplinary board should be formulated by the board. Disciplinary budgets should be approved or modified directly by the Court or by an administrative agency of the Court. Disciplinary counsel and the disciplinary board should be accountable for the expenditure of funds only to the Court, except that bar associations may provide accounting and other financial services that do not impair the independence of disciplinary officials.

5.4 Disciplinary counsel and staff, disciplinary adjudicators and staff, and other disciplinary agency personnel should be absolutely immune from civil liability for all actions performed within the scope of their duties, consistent with the American Bar Association's Model Rules for Lawyer Disciplinary Enforcement 12A.

Recommendation 6: Independence of Disciplinary Counsel

6.1 The Court alone should appoint and remove disciplinary counsel and should provide sufficient authority for prosecutorial independence and discretion.

The Court should also promulgate rules providing that disciplinary counsel shall:

(a) have authority to employ and terminate staff, formulate a budget and approve expenditures subject only to the authority of the Court;

(b) have authority, in cases involving allegations of minor incompetence, neglect, or misconduct, to resolve a matter with the consent of the respondent by administrative procedures established by the Court;

(c) have authority to appeal a decision of a hearing committee or the disciplinary board;

(d) be compensated sufficiently to attract competent counsel and retain experienced counsel; and

(e) be prohibited from providing advisory ethics opinions, either orally or in writing.

6.2 The Court should adopt a rule providing that no disciplinary adjudicative official (including hearing committee members, disciplinary board members, or members of the Court) shall communicate ex parte with disciplinary counsel regarding an ongoing investigation or disciplinary matter, except about administrative matters or to report information alleging the misconduct of a lawyer.

Recommendation 7: Access to Disciplinary Information

All records of the lawyer disciplinary agency except the work product of disciplinary counsel should be available to the public after a determination has been made that probable cause exists to believe misconduct occurred, unless the complainant or respondent obtains a protective order from the highest court or its designee for specific testimony, documents or records. All proceedings except adjudicative deliberations should be public after a determination that probable cause exists to believe that misconduct occurred.

Recommendation 8: Complainant's Rights

8.1 Complainants should receive notice of the status of disciplinary proceedings. In general, a complainant should receive, contemporaneously, the same notices and orders the respondent receives as well as copies of respondent's communications to the agency, except information that is subject to another client's privilege.

8.2 Complainants should be permitted a reasonable opportunity to rebut statements of the respondent before a complaint is summarily dismissed.

8.3 Complainants should be notified in writing when the complaint has been dismissed. The notice should include a concise recitation of the specific facts and reasoning upon which the decision to dismiss was made.

8.4 Disciplinary counsel should issue written guidelines for determining which cases will be dismissed for failure to allege facts that, if true, would constitute grounds for disciplinary action. These guidelines should be sent to complainants whose cases are dismissed.

8.5 Complainants should be notified of the date, time, and location of the hearing. Complainants should have the right to personally appear and testify at the hearing.

8.6 All jurisdictions should afford a right of review to complainants whose complaints are dismissed prior to a full hearing on the merits, consistent with the American Bar Association's Model Rules for Lawyer Disciplinary Enforcement 11B(3) and 31.

Recommendation 9: Procedures in Lieu of Discipline for Minor Misconduct

All jurisdictions should adopt procedures in lieu of discipline for matters in which a lawyer's actions constitute minor misconduct, minor incompetence, or minor neglect. The procedures should provide:

9.1 The Court shall define criteria for matters involving minor misconduct, minor incompetence, or minor neglect that may be resolved by non-disciplinary proceedings or dismissal.

9.2 If disciplinary counsel determines that a matter meets the criteria established by the Court, disciplinary counsel may reach agreement with the respondent to submit the matter to non-disciplinary proceedings. Such proceedings may consist of fee arbitration, mediation, lawyer practice assistance, substance abuse recovery programs, psychological counseling, or any other non-disciplinary proceedings authorized by the Court. Disciplinary counsel shall then refer the matter to the agency or agencies authorized by the Court to conduct the proceedings.

9.3 If the lawyer does not comply with the terms of the agreement, disciplinary counsel may resume disciplinary proceedings.

9.4 If the lawyer fulfills the terms of the agreement, the disciplinary counsel shall dismiss the disciplinary proceeding.

Recommendation 10: Expedited Procedures for Minor Misconduct

All jurisdictions should adopt simplified, expedited procedures to adjudicate cases in which the alleged misconduct warrants less than suspension or disbarment or other restriction on the right to practice. Expedited procedures should provide:

10.1 The Court shall define minor violations of the rules of professional conduct that shall subject the respondent to sanctions not constituting restrictions on the right to practice law, consistent with the ABA Standards for Imposing Lawyer Sanctions.

10.2 A hearing shall be held by a single adjudicator (member of a hearing committee).

10.3 The adjudicator shall make concise, written findings of fact and conclusions of law and shall either dismiss the case or impose a sanction that does not constitute a restriction on the respondent's right to practice.

10.4 Respondent and Disciplinary counsel shall have the right to appeal the decision to a second adjudicator (member of the statewide disciplinary board), who shall either adopt the decision below or make written findings. The appellate adjudicator shall either dismiss the case or impose a sanction that does not constitute a restriction on the respondent's right to practice.

10.5 The decision of the appellate adjudicator may be reviewed at the discretion of the Court upon application by respondent or Disciplinary counsel. The Court shall grant review only in cases involving significant issues of law or upon a showing that the decision below constituted an abuse of discretion. The Court shall either adopt the decision below or make written findings. The Court shall either dismiss the case or impose a sanction that does not constitute a restriction on the respondent's right to practice.

10.6 Upon final disposition of the case, the written findings of the final adjudicator shall be published in an appropriate journal or reporter and a copy shall be mailed to the respondent and the complainant and to the ABA National Discipline Data Bank.

Recommendation 11: Disposition of Cases by a Hearing Committee, the Board, or Court

The statewide disciplinary board should not review a determination of the hearing committee except upon a request for review by the disciplinary counsel or respondent or upon the vote of a majority of the Board. The Court should not review a matter except: (a) within its discretion upon a request for review of the determination of the Board by the disciplinary counsel or respondent; or (b) upon the vote of a majority of the Court to review a determination of the hearing committee or Board. Except in unusual cases requiring a de novo hearing by the Court, the Court should exercise its jurisdiction in the capacity of appellate review. The Court should issue and publish full written opinions in all disciplinary cases. In any matter finally determined by a hearing committee or the Board, the Court should, by per curiam order, adopt and publish the findings and conclusions contained in the written report of the committee or Board.

Recommendation 12: Interim Suspension for Threat of Harm

The immediate interim suspension of a lawyer should be ordered upon a finding that the lawyer poses a substantial threat of serious harm to the public.

Recommendation 13: Funding and Staffing

The Court should insure that adequate funding and staffing is provided for the disciplinary agency so that: (a) disciplinary cases are screened, investigated, prosecuted and adjudicated promptly; (b) the work load per staff person permits careful and thorough performance of duties; (c) professional and support staff are compensated at a level sufficient to attract and retain competent personnel; (d) sufficient office and data processing equipment exist to efficiently and quickly process the work load and manage the agency; (e) adequate office space exists to provide a productive working environment; and (f) staff and volunteers are adequately trained in disciplinary law and procedure.

Recommendation 14: Standards for Resources

14.1 Each jurisdiction should keep case load and time statistics to assist in determining the need for additional staff and resources. Case load and time statistics should include, at the minimum:
  (a) time records for all counsel and investigators, tracked by case or other task including time spent on non-disciplinary functions;
  (b) the number of pending cases at each stage in the disciplinary process for each counsel and for the whole agency;
  (c) the number of new cases assigned to each counsel during the year and the total for the agency;
  (d) the number of cases carried over from the prior year for each counsel and the total for the agency;
  (e) the number of cases closed by each counsel during the year and the total for the agency;

(f) the number of cases of special difficulty or complexity at each stage in the proceedings; and

(g) the ratio of staff turnover.

14.2 The American Bar Association, National Organization of Bar Counsel, and disciplinary agencies in each jurisdiction should cooperate to develop standards for: (a) staffing levels and case load per professional and support staff member; (b) case processing time at all stages of disciplinary proceedings; and (c) compensation of professional and support staff.

Recommendation 15: Field Investigations

Disciplinary counsel should have sufficient staff and resources to: (1) fully investigate complaints, by such means as sending investigators into the field to interview witnesses and examine records and evidence; and (2) regularly monitor sources of public information such as news reports and court decisions likely to contain information about lawyer misconduct.

Recommendation 16: Random Audit of Trust Accounts

The Court should adopt a rule providing that lawyer trust accounts selected at random may be audited without having grounds to believe misconduct has occurred and also providing for appropriate procedural safeguards.

Recommendation 17: Burden of Proof in Arbitration of Fee Disputes

The Court should adopt a rule for fee arbitration proceedings to provide that, except where the fee agreement otherwise has been established in a continuing relationship, if there is no written agreement between the lawyer and the client, the lawyer shall bear the burden of proof of all facts, and the lawyer shall be entitled to no more than the reasonable value of services for the work completed or, if the failure to complete the work was caused by the client, for the work performed.

Recommendation 18: Mandatory Malpractice Insurance Study

The American Bar Association should continue studies to determine whether a model program and model rule should be created to: (a) make appropriate levels of malpractice insurance coverage available at a reasonable price; and (b) make coverage mandatory for all lawyers who have clients.

Recommendation 19: Effective Date of Disbarment and Suspension Orders

The Court should adopt a rule providing that orders of disbarment and suspension shall be effective on a date (15) days after the date of the order except where the Court finds that immediate disbarment or suspension is necessary to protect the public, contrary to the provisions of the Model Rules for Lawyer Disciplinary Enforcement 27E.

Recommendation 20: National Discipline Data Bank

The American Bar Association should provide or seek adequate funding to automate the dissemination of reciprocal discipline information by means of electronic data processing and telecommunications, so that:

20.1 appropriate discipline, bar admissions, and other officials in each jurisdiction can directly access and query the National Discipline Data Bank via a computer telecommunications network;

20.2 a uniform data format and software are developed permitting automated cross-checking of jurisdictions' rosters of licensed lawyers against the National Discipline Data Bank's contents;

20.3 a listing of the contents of the National Discipline Data Bank is disseminated to discipline officials quarterly or semi-annually on an electronic data processing medium suitable for automated comparison with a jurisdiction's roster of lawyers.

Recommendation 21: Coordinating Interstate Identification

21.1 The American Bar Association and the appropriate officials in each jurisdiction should establish a system of assigning a universal identification number to each lawyer licensed to practice law.

21.2 The highest court in each jurisdiction should require all lawyers licensed in the jurisdiction to (a) register annually with the agency designated by the Court stating all other jurisdictions in which they are licensed to practice law, and (b) immediately report to the agency designated by the Court changes of law license status in other jurisdictions such as admission to practice, discipline imposed, or resignation.

AMERICAN BAR ASSOCIATION MODEL RULES FOR LAWYER DISCIPLINARY ENFORCEMENT

[The Model Rules for Lawyer Disciplinary Enforcement, adopted by the ABA House of Delegates at its Annual Meeting in August 1989, replace the Standards for Lawyer Discipline and Disability Proceedings (adopted in February 1979) and the Model Rules for Lawyer Disciplinary Enforcement (adopted in July 1985). In 1993, the ABA amended the Model Rules to reflect the policies recommended in 1992. In 1996, the ABA amended several provisions relating to lesser misconduct to encourage the use of alternatives to a discipline program. The new Model Rules for Lawyer Disciplinary Enforcement combine into a single policy document the contents of these two documents which, though formatted in different styles, concerned the same subject matter, i.e., model operating procedures for lawyer disciplinary matters. In 1999, the ABA amended Rules 14, 19, and 25 to reflect comments from bar counsel and other members of the ABA. The Rules are reprinted in full; however, we have omitted some of the commentary due to space considerations. Ed.]

TABLE OF CONTENTS

LAWYER DISCIPLINARY ENFORCEMENT

MODEL RULES

Abatement:

A diminution of conditions in an order of discipline, readmission, or reinstatement pursuant to Rule 26.

Advisory Opinion:

The interpretation of law as applied to an assumed set of facts, whether written or oral.

Central Intake Office:

The office established by Rule 1 that is responsible for the receipt, coordination, processing and disposition of information and complaints regarding the conduct of lawyers.

Expunction or Expungement:

Process by which records or other evidence of the existence of complaints terminated by dismissals are destroyed after a period of time, pursuant to Rule 4(B)(12).

Fraud:

Conduct having a purpose to deceive but not merely negligent misrepresentation.

Interim:

Temporary.

Lesser Misconduct:

Conduct that does not warrant a sanction restricting the respondent's right to practice law, as determined pursuant to Rule 9(B).

Official of the State Bar:

Any person who is elected or appointed to any governing office or board of the state bar, or employed by the state bar.

Respondent:

A lawyer who is subject to a complaint.

Serious Crime:

Any felony or any lesser crime that reflects adversely on the lawyer's honesty, trustworthiness or fitness as a lawyer in other respects or any crime a necessary element of which, as determined by the statutory or common law definition of the crime, involves interference with the administration of justice, false swearing, misrepresentation, fraud, deceit, bribery, extortion, misappropriation, theft, or an attempt, conspiracy, or solicitation of another to commit one of the above.

Substantial:

When used in reference to degree or extent, it denotes a material matter of clear and weighty importance.

PREAMBLE: AUTHORITY OF THE COURT

This court declares that it has exclusive responsibility within this state for the structure and administration of the lawyer discipline and disability system and that it has inherent power to maintain appropriate standards of professional conduct and to dispose of individual cases of lawyer discipline and disability in a manner that does not discriminate by race, creed, color, sex, sexual orientation or national origin. In order to effectuate this declaration, the following rules for lawyer discipline and disability proceedings are hereby promulgated.

I. STRUCTURE AND SCOPE

RULE 1. Comprehensive Lawyer Regulatory System

A. *Component Agencies.* There is hereby established a comprehensive system of regulation of the legal profession that includes, but is not limited to a lawyer discipline and disability system, a client protection fund, mandatory arbitration of fee disputes, voluntary arbitration of lawyer malpractice claims and other disputes, mediation, lawyer practice assistance, and lawyer substance abuse counseling.

B. *Central Intake.* There is hereby established a central intake office, which shall:

(1) receive information and complaints regarding the conduct of lawyers over whom the court has jurisdiction, provided this rule shall not be construed to limit the authority of any authorized agency to institute proceedings;

(2) provide assistance to complainants in stating their complaints;

(3) provide information to complainants about the remedies available under the rules of the court, the operations and procedures of agencies designated by the court under Rule 1(A), and the status of their complaints;

(4) determine whether the facts stated in a complaint or other information regarding the conduct of a lawyer provide grounds for further action by any agency designated by the court under Rule 1(A) and:

(a) dismiss the complaint; or

(b) forward it to the appropriate agency or agencies;

(5) provide to the complainant, if a complaint is dismissed or referred to an agency other than the disciplinary agency:

(a) a copy of the written guidelines for dismissal of complaints;

(b) a concise written statement of the facts and reasons for referral of the complaint to an agency other than the disciplinary agency; and

(c) a notice of complainant's right of appeal pursuant to Rule 31; and

(6) record and, when a complaint involves more than one agency, coordinate the processing and disposition of all complaints by designated agencies.

C. [*Disciplinary Districts.* Disciplinary jurisdiction in this state shall be divided into the following districts: If necessary, provisions dividing the state into two or more disciplinary districts].

Commentary

A simple and direct procedure for making a complaint is needed. Complainants should not be expected to know the distinctions among component agencies. They need a central intake office—one clearly designated agency to which to take any type of complaint regarding lawyer conduct. The skilled lawyers of this office should provide the expertise needed to determine where prima facie valid complaints should be directed. It also emphasizes the importance of accountability.

Providing a regulatory system to deter unethical behavior should remain the highest priority of the judicial branch. The central intake office should screen all complaints for allegations of conduct that is a ground for discipline under Rule 9. It should forward those complaints to the disciplinary agency and to any other relevant agency, so that misconduct is not overlooked.

Lawyer discipline should be directly and exclusively controlled by the highest court in the jurisdiction. However, it may be appropriate for bar associations to administer other components of the system, such as arbitration, mediation, lawyer practice assistance, etc., under the court's authority. Therefore, the disciplinary agency should not be the administrative entity for other component agencies.

A fee dispute arbitration system that is mandatory for the lawyer eliminates the overwhelming advantage lawyers have over the majority of clients who are of modest means and have only the most rudimentary knowledge of the law. These programs can work without being unduly burdensome on the profession. Complaints that do not state legitimate grounds for dispute should be screened out. In cases of valid disputes, mandated fee adjustments can provide the incentive to reform for lawyers who do substandard work.

Providing an additional, voluntary arbitration mechanism for lawyers and clients can greatly benefit both lawyers and clients. Disputes to be considered could include contractual, non-disciplinary, and inadequate representation claims.

Mediation services are useful in preserving ongoing lawyer-client relationships when disputes arise or in matters where a lawyer has placed a lien on a client's file. When handled by a skilled mediator, the process can be simple and efficient, saving time and money for both parties. The lawyer's willingness to have a third party assist in resolving the dispute can demonstrate to the client that the lawyer's intention is to act in the client's best interest.

RULE 2. The Disciplinary Board of the Supreme Court [*State Bar*] of [*State Name*]

A. *Agency.* There is hereby established one permanent statewide agency to administer the lawyer discipline and disability system. The agency consists of a statewide board as provided in this Rule 2, hearing committees as provided for in Rule 3, disciplinary counsel as provided for in Rule 4, and staff appointed by the board and counsel. The agency is a unitary entity. While it performs both prosecutorial and adjudicative functions, these functions shall be separated within the agency insofar as practicable in order to avoid unfairness. The prosecutorial functions shall be directed by a lawyer employed full-time by the agency and performed, insofar as practicable, by employees of the agency. The adjudicative functions shall be performed by practicing lawyers and public members. No official of the [state bar] shall have the right to appoint any members or serve in any ex officio capacity.

B. *Appointment.* A board shall be appointed by the court with the requisite authority and responsibility to administer the lawyer discipline and disability system. The board shall consist of [nine] members to serve for fixed, staggered terms, and to be referred to as the "board," which shall consist of:

(1) [Two] members of the bar of this state and [one] public member appointed for an initial term of three years;

(2) [Two] members of the bar of this state and [one] public member appointed for an initial term of two years; and

(3) [Two] members of the bar of this state and [one] public member appointed for an initial term of one year.

Subsequent terms of all members shall be for three years. No member shall serve more than two consecutive three-year terms. The members of the board shall not be subject to removal by the court during their terms of office except for cause.

C. *Election of Officers.* The members of the board shall annually elect [the Court shall annually appoint] lawyer members as chair and vice-chair. The chair, and in the chair's absence the vice-chair, shall perform the duties normally associated with that office and shall preside over all meetings of the full board, ruling on all motions, objections, and evidence.

D. *Quorum.* [Five] members shall constitute a quorum. The board shall act only with the concurrence of a majority of the whole board except as to administrative matters, which shall only require a majority of those present and voting.

E. *Compensation and Expenses.* Members shall receive no compensation for their services, but may be reimbursed for travel and other expenses incidental to the performance of their duties.

F. *Abstention and Disqualification of Board Members [; Alternate Members].*

(1) Board members shall refrain from taking part in any proceeding in which a judge, similarly situated, would be required to abstain.

(2) In addition to complying with the Rules of Professional Conduct regarding a former judge or arbitrator (Model Rule of Professional Conduct 1.12), a former member of the board shall not personally represent a lawyer in any proceeding as provided in these Rules for a period of one year following completion of the member's service.

(3) [The court shall maintain current rosters of lawyer and nonlawyer alternates. If a board member becomes incapacitated or disqualified, the next alternate on the appropriate roster shall take the place of the board member in the matter.]

G. *Powers and Duties.* The board shall have the following powers and duties:

(1) To propose rules of procedure for lawyer discipline and disability proceedings for promulgation by the court, and to comment on the enforceability of existing and proposed [Rules of Professional Conduct];

(2) To review periodically the operation of the system with the court;

(3) To appoint three or more hearing committees [within each disciplinary district] and

(i) establish the rotation by which they will be assigned formal hearings,

(ii) designate the chair for each, and

(iii) assign the chair to review in rotation dispositions by the central intake office, recommendations of counsel for disposition of disciplinary matters and petitions for transfer to and from disability inactive status pursuant to Rule 3(E)(1); [1]

---

1. See Appendix for alternative provisions.

(4) To perform appellate review functions, consisting of review of the findings of fact, conclusions of law and recommendations of adjudicators in hearings on lesser misconduct pursuant to Rule 18(H) and of hearing committees with respect to formal charges, petitions for transfer to and from disability inactive status, and petitions for reinstatement, and prepare and forward to the court its own findings, if any, and recommendations, together with the record of the proceedings before the hearing committee;[1]

(5) To administer reprimands;

(6) To impose probation for a specified period with the consent of the respondent;

(7) To appoint and supervise its staff, separate from the prosecutorial staff, to assist the board in its functions;

(8) To inform the public about the existence and operation of the system and the disposition of each matter in which public discipline has been imposed, a lawyer has been transferred to or from disability inactive status, or a lawyer has been reinstated or readmitted;

(9) To delegate, in its discretion, to the chair or vice-chair the power to act for the board on administrative and procedural matters.

Commentary

With more than 700,000 lawyers licensed to practice in the United States, the highest courts of the states cannot handle discipline and disability matters directly by themselves. The agency assists the court in the exercise of its inherent power to supervise the bar, inquiring into all matters assigned to its jurisdiction by the court's rules of disciplinary enforcement. The agency performs prosecutorial and adjudicative functions, and reports its findings and recommendations to the court.

A statewide system provides the greatest degree of structural impartiality since it minimizes the adverse effects of local bias. Moreover, a statewide structure provides uniformity, since only a single statewide court and a single statewide agency are involved in the process. In a decentralized structure, complaints in one community may be governed by one set of standards and those in a different community by another. Consequently, lawyers admitted to practice in the same state may receive radically different discipline for the same misconduct.

A single statewide agency avoids these problems by imposing a single standard of conduct throughout the state.

In a unitary system, both prosecution and adjudication are the responsibility of a single agency. Nevertheless, prosecutorial and adjudicative functions should be separated as much as possible within the

---

1. See Appendix for alternative provisions.

unitary system to avoid unfairness and any appearance of unfairness. Persons who perform prosecutorial functions should neither perform nor supervise persons who perform adjudicative functions, and vice versa. In addition, persons who perform adjudicative functions in a particular matter at a preliminary stage should not thereafter perform nor have control over persons who must later perform ultimate adjudicative functions in the same matter.

The disciplinary system should be controlled and managed exclusively by the state's highest court and not by state or local bar associations for these compelling reasons. First, the disciplinary process should be directed solely by the disciplinary policy of the court and its appointees and not influenced by the internal politics of bar associations. Second, the disciplinary system should be free from even the appearance of conflicts of interest or impropriety. When elected bar officials control all or parts of the disciplinary process, these appearances are created, regardless of the actual fairness and impartiality of the system. This is true whether the bar is unified or not.[9]

It is of course desirable, and in the larger states essential, for the board to have available the assistance of staff to carry out its functions. Staff responsible directly to the board, totally separate from counsel, should be hired for that purpose to further the separation of the prosecutorial and adjudicative functions within the unitary agency.

In the appointment process, there should be appropriate representation of all segments of the public and the profession, including minority members, women, and solo or small firm practitioners. A combination of lawyers and nonlawyers on the board results in a more balanced evaluation of complaints. Currently more than two-thirds of all jurisdictions involve public members in their disciplinary structure. Participation by nonlawyers increases the credibility of the discipline and disability process in the eyes of the public. There is a human tendency to suspect the objectivity of a discipline body composed solely of members of the respondent's professional colleagues. Involving public members helps allay that suspicion.

* * *

RULE 3. Hearing Committees [14]

A. *Appointment.* The board shall appoint three or more hearing committees [within each disciplinary district]. Each hearing committee shall consist of two members of the bar of this state and one public member. A lawyer member of each hearing committee shall be appointed chair by the board. No official of the [state bar] shall have the right to appoint any members or serve in an ex officio capacity.

9. Rec. 5.

14. See Appendix for alternative provisions.

B. *Terms of Office.* The chair and other members of the hearing committee shall serve for fixed, staggered terms. One member shall be appointed for an initial term of one year, another member for an initial term of two years and the third member for an initial term of three years. Thereafter all regular terms shall be three years and no member shall serve for more than two consecutive three-year terms. A member whose term has expired may continue to serve on any case that was commenced before the expiration of the member's term. A member who has served two consecutive three-year terms may not be reappointed before the expiration of at least one year. The members shall not be subject to removal by the board during their terms of office except for cause.

C. *Quorum.* Except in hearings alleging lesser misconduct as defined in Rule 9(B) and conduct under Rule 18(H), three members shall constitute a quorum. The committee shall act only with the concurrence of two. The chair of the board may appoint alternate members to a hearing committee as necessary to meet the requirements of this subsection.

D. *Powers and Duties.* Hearing committees shall have the following powers and duties:

(1) To conduct hearings into formal charges of misconduct, petitions for reinstatement or readmission, and petitions for transfer to and from disability inactive status upon assignment; and

(2) To submit to the board written findings of fact, conclusions of law, and recommendations, together with the record of the hearing.

E. *Powers and Duties of Hearing Committee Chair.* Each hearing committee chair shall have the following powers and duties:

(1) To review dispositions by the central intake office or recommendations of disciplinary counsel following investigation for disposition of disciplinary matters, dismissals by disciplinary counsel upon a request for review by complainant, and petitions for transfer to and from disability inactive status. The hearing committee chair may approve, modify, or disapprove the recommendations of disciplinary counsel, or direct that the matter be investigated further. If the hearing committee chair modifies or disapproves the recommendation, or directs that the matter be investigated further, disciplinary counsel may appeal that action to the chair of another hearing committee designated by the board, who shall approve either disciplinary counsel's recommendation or the action of the first hearing committee chair. The decision of the second hearing committee chair shall be final within the agency.

(2) To conduct prehearing conferences regarding formal charges of misconduct, petitions for reinstatement or readmission, and petitions for transfer to and from disability inactive status; and

(3) To consider and decide prehearing motions.

F. *Abstention and Disqualification of Hearing Committee Members.*

(1) Hearing committee members shall refrain from taking part in any proceeding in which a judge, similarly situated, would be required to abstain.

(2) In addition to complying with the Rules of Professional Conduct regarding a former judge or arbitrator (Model Rule of Professional Conduct 1.12), a former member of a hearing committee shall not personally represent a lawyer in any proceeding as provided in these Rules for a period of one year following completion of the member's service.

Commentary

If any member of a hearing committee has a conflict of interest, the entire committee is disqualified and another committee must be appointed in its place. If that is not practicable, the individual member of the committee should be replaced for that particular matter only.

The creation of hearing committees for specific cases should be avoided. Hearing committees should have fixed membership. The committees should sit on a pre-established rotating schedule and cases should be assigned on the basis of which is the next committee to sit. Each committee should have one alternate member scheduled to sit in case of illness, emergency, or conflicts of interest.

* * *

RULE 4. Disciplinary Counsel

A. *Appointment.* The court shall appoint a lawyer admitted to practice in the state to serve as disciplinary counsel. Neither the chief disciplinary counsel nor full-time staff disciplinary counsel shall engage in private practice. No official of the [state bar] shall serve as disciplinary counsel or investigator.

B. *Powers and Duties.* Disciplinary counsel shall perform all prosecutorial functions and have the following powers and duties:

(1) To evaluate all information coming to the attention of the agency to determine whether it concerns a lawyer subject to the jurisdiction of the agency because it relates to misconduct by the lawyer or to the incapacity of the lawyer;

(2) To investigate all information coming to the attention of the agency which, if true, would be grounds for discipline or transfer to disability inactive status and investigate all facts pertaining to petitions for reinstatement or readmission;

(3) To dismiss or recommend probation, informal admonition, a stay, the filing of formal charges, or the petitioning for transfer to

disability inactive status with respect to each matter brought to the attention of the agency;

(4) To prosecute before hearing committees, the board, and the court discipline, reinstatement and readmission proceedings, and proceedings for transfer to or from disability inactive status;

(5) To employ and supervise staff needed for the performance of prosecutorial functions [and, when circumstances necessitate their use, appoint and supervise volunteer assistant counsel];

(6) To notify promptly the complainant and the respondent of the status and the disposition of each matter including but not limited to providing to the complainant:

(a) a copy of any notice, motion, or order sent to respondent;

(b) a copy of any written communication from the respondent to the disciplinary counsel relating to the matter except information that is subject to the privilege of one other than the complainant;

(c) a concise written statement of the facts and reasons a matter has been dismissed prior to a hearing and a copy of the written guidelines for dismissal issued pursuant to Rule 4(B)(7), provided that the complainant shall be given a reasonable opportunity to rebut statements of the respondent before the complaint is dismissed; and

(d) a notice of the date, time, and location of the hearing; [19]

(7) To issue written guidelines for use by the central intake office and disciplinary counsel to determine which matters shall be dismissed for failing to allege facts that, if true, would constitute grounds for disciplinary action.[20]

(8) To notify each jurisdiction in which a lawyer is admitted of a transfer to or from disability inactive status, reinstatement, readmission, or any public discipline imposed in this state;

(9) To seek reciprocal discipline when informed of any public discipline imposed in any other jurisdiction;

(10) To forward a certified copy of the judgment of conviction to the disciplinary agency in each jurisdiction in which a lawyer is admitted when the lawyer is convicted of a serious crime (as hereinafter defined) in this state;

(11) To maintain permanent records of discipline and disability matters, subject to the expunction requirements of Rule 4(B)(12), and compile statistics to aid in the administration of the system, including but not limited to a single log of all complaints received,

19. Rec. 8.1, 8.2, 8.3, and 8.5.   **20.** Rec. 8.4.

investigative files, statistical summaries of docket processing and case dispositions, transcripts of all proceedings (or the reporter's notes if not transcribed), and other records as the board or court requires to be maintained. Statistical summaries shall contain, at a minimum:

(a) time records for all counsel and investigators, tracked by case or other task including time spent on non-disciplinary functions;

(b) the number of pending cases at each stage in the disciplinary process for each counsel and for the agency;

(c) the number of new cases assigned to each counsel during the year and the total for the agency;

(d) the number of cases carried over from the prior year for each counsel and the total for the agency;

(e) the number of cases closed by each counsel during the year and the total for the agency;

(f) the number of cases of special difficulty or complexity at each stage in the proceedings; and

(g) the ratio of staff turnover.[21]

(12) To expunge (i.e. destroy) after [three] years all records or other evidence of the existence of complaints terminated by dismissals or referrals to other component agencies pursuant to Rule 1(B)(4), except that upon disciplinary counsel's application, notice to respondent, and a showing of good cause, the board may permit disciplinary counsel to retain such records for one additional period of time not to exceed [three] years.

(i) Notice to Respondent. If the respondent was contacted by the agency concerning the complaint, or the agency otherwise knows that the respondent is aware of the existence of the complaint, the respondent shall be given prompt written notice of the expunction.

(ii) Effect of Expunction. After a file has been expunged, any agency response to an inquiry requiring a reference to the matter shall state that there is no record of such matter. The respondent may answer any inquiry requiring a reference to an expunged matter by stating that no complaint was made.

(13) To make referrals to the Alternatives to Discipline Program pursuant to Rule 11(G), to the central intake office or to any of the component agencies of the comprehensive system of lawyer regulation established by Rule 1; and

21. Rec. 14.1.

(14) To prepare an annual budget for the disciplinary counsel's office and submit it to the court for approval and to make reasonable and necessary expenditures pursuant to the approved budget to perform the duties of the office;[24]

C. *Advisory Opinions Prohibited.* Disciplinary counsel shall not render advisory opinions, either orally or in writing.[25]

D. *Ex Parte Communication With Disciplinary Counsel.*

(1) Members of a hearing committee, the board, or the court shall not communicate ex parte with disciplinary counsel regarding a pending or impending investigation or disciplinary matter except as explicitly provided for by law or for scheduling, administrative purposes or emergencies that do not deal with substantive matters or issues on the merits provided that:

(a) it is reasonable to believe that no party will gain a procedural or tactical advantage as a result of the ex parte communication; and

(b) provision is promptly made to notify all other parties of the substance of the ex parte communication and an opportunity to respond is allowed.

(2) A violation of this rule shall be a ground for lawyer or judicial discipline, as appropriate, and cause for removal from the hearing committee or the board.[26]

E. *Disqualification.* In addition to complying with the Rules of Professional Conduct regarding successive government and private employment (Model Rule of Professional Conduct 1.11), a former disciplinary counsel shall not personally represent a lawyer in any proceeding as provided in these Rules for a period of one year following completion of the disciplinary counsel's service.

Commentary

The court should appoint a permanent, full-time disciplinary counsel. The court should consider recommendations from many sources, including the board, state bar, civic groups, and other interested parties. The power to appoint should not be restricted by limiting the pool of potential candidates only to nominees from specific sources. Alternatively, instead of appointing disciplinary counsel directly, the court may wish to appoint a Commission on Lawyer Regulation, which would have the responsibility of appointing disciplinary counsel, as discussed in the Commentary to Rule 1.[29]

24. Rec. 6.1(a).

25. Rec. 6.1(e). The language "except upon the request of the court" is suggested to permit disciplinary counsel to provide opinions to, e.g., a court appointed committee drafting ethics or disciplinary procedural rules.

26. Rec. 6.2.

29. Rec. 6.1 and commentary.

Volunteers should be avoided if possible. They cannot devote the same time and attention to processing complaints as paid counsel, nor can they investigate complicated matters as thoroughly as one professionally trained to do so.

Disciplinary counsel may be allowed a reasonable amount of time for transition from private practice following appointment to phase out his or her private practice.

Since the court has the responsibility for the efficient operation of the agency, the court should appoint the board and disciplinary counsel. However, the court should not allow itself to become involved in the internal personnel management of the agency. The board and disciplinary counsel should have full authority to hire and fire their respective staffs.

Vesting all prosecutorial responsibility in disciplinary counsel is necessary if there is to be a separation of prosecutorial and adjudicative functions within a unitary agency.

Disciplinary counsel has the responsibility for investigating and prosecuting all matters. Disciplinary counsel must therefore have the authority to hire, compensate, and fire the staff necessary to carry out that responsibility in conformity with the applicable limits established by the board in the budget it has approved for the operation of the agency. All personnel assigned prosecutorial functions, whether lawyer or non-lawyer, full-time, part-time, or volunteer, should be appointed by and responsible to counsel. Full-time lawyer personnel hired by counsel should not be permitted to engage in the private practice of law.

Members of the public who come to the agency seeking its services are entitled to be advised of the disposition of their complaints. Fairness requires that no recommendation adverse to the respondent be made without providing an opportunity to be heard.

The clerk of the court in which the lawyer is convicted should send a certified copy of the judgment of conviction to counsel for the agency of the state in which the lawyer is admitted to practice. The certified copy of the judgment should be filed with the court to support the proposed order for immediate interim suspension.

Meaningful statistics can most effectively be recorded by using uniform terminology. The following terms are adopted to identify available sanctions in disciplinary matters: disbarment, suspension, reprimand, admonition, probation, and discipline by consent. The term adopted to indicate removal from practice on grounds of disability is transfer to disability inactive status.

* * *

RULE 5. Expenses

The salaries of disciplinary counsel and staff and their expenses, shall be paid by the court out of the funds collected under the provisions of Rule 8. Costs, and the expenses of the members of the board and of hearing committees shall be paid by the board [out of the funds collected under the provisions of Rule 8]. The board and disciplinary counsel shall annually obtain an independent audit by a certified public accountant of the funds entrusted to them and the disposition thereof and shall file a copy of the audit with this court.

Commentary

Disciplinary counsel and the board should be accountable for the expenditure of funds only to the court, except that unified bars may provide accounting and other financial services that do not impair the independence of disciplinary officials.

RULE 6. Jurisdiction

A. *Lawyers Admitted to Practice.* Any lawyer admitted to practice law in this state, including any formerly admitted lawyer with respect to acts committed prior to resignation, suspension, disbarment, or transfer to inactive status, or with respect to acts subsequent thereto which amount to the practice of law or constitute a violation of these Rules or of the Rules of Professional Conduct [Code of Professional Responsibility] or any Rules or Code subsequently adopted by the court in lieu thereof, and any lawyer specially admitted by a court of this state for a particular proceeding[, and any lawyer not admitted in this state who practices law or renders or offers to render any legal services in this state] is subject to the disciplinary jurisdiction of this court and the board.

B. *Former Judges.* A former judge who has resumed the status of a lawyer is subject to the jurisdiction of the board not only for conduct as a lawyer but also for misconduct that occurred while the lawyer was a judge and would have been grounds for lawyer discipline, provided that the misconduct was not the subject of a judicial disciplinary proceeding as to which there has been a final determination by the court. Misconduct by a judge that is not finally adjudicated before the judge leaves office falls within the jurisdiction of the lawyer disciplinary agency.

C. *Incumbent Judges.* Incumbent judges shall not be subject to the jurisdiction of the agency; however, if an incumbent judge is to be removed from office in the course of a judicial discipline or disability proceeding, the court shall first afford the board and the respondent an opportunity to submit a recommendation whether lawyer discipline should be imposed, and if so, the extent thereof.

D. *Powers Not Assumed.* These rules shall not be construed to deny to any court the powers necessary to maintain control over its proceedings.

Commentary

Admission to practice triggers the jurisdiction of the disciplinary authority, regardless of the location of the lawyer, the place where the act occurred, or whether the lawyer is qualified to practice; the court has the right and the obligation to inquire into any facts bearing upon the lawyer's fitness to practice.

A lawyer specially admitted in a state has a license for that limited appearance and is subject to the disciplinary authority of that jurisdiction. In the same way that the motorist has given his implied consent to be bound by the traffic laws of the states he travels, the lawyer admitted for a limited purpose subjects himself or herself to the rules of conduct in the jurisdiction.

It is inappropriate for the state in which the lawyer is specially admitted to rely exclusively upon the lawyer's home jurisdiction to enforce ethical standards. The witnesses and other evidence of misconduct are likely to be located in the adopted jurisdiction. Moreover, the jurisdiction in which the misconduct occurred will be far more interested in pursuing the matter. Finally, misconduct should in the first instance be judged by the ethical standards of the jurisdiction where it occurred.

If at the time a judge leaves office the entity responsible for bringing judicial disciplinary proceedings has an investigation in progress against him or her, the matter should be immediately transferred to the lawyer disciplinary agency. The only issue in that circumstance is the lawyer's fitness to continue to practice in light of the alleged misconduct. Since a judge may be subject to discipline as a judge for conduct that does not constitute misconduct as a lawyer, the allegations giving rise to the jurisdiction of the agency under paragraph B must cite conduct violating the Code of Judicial Conduct which also constitutes grounds for lawyer discipline.

The judicial discipline and disability retirement commission has special expertise to evaluate the conduct of sitting judges and to determine how that conduct reflects upon their continued ability to hold office. The status of a judge as a judge and discipline to be imposed during the judge's tenure should be determined by judicial discipline and disability retirement proceedings.

Consequently, even if the misconduct occurred prior to the judge's assumption of office, the commission should have jurisdiction since the judge's status as a judge is at issue. If a lawyer disciplinary agency has an investigation in progress against a judge at the time the judge takes office, it should immediately transfer the file to the commission. If the judge is to be removed from office and thus returned to the practice of law, the court should afford the lawyer disciplinary agency the opportunity to be heard on the issue of what lawyer discipline, if any, should be imposed. The agency has the special expertise to determine how conduct reflects upon a lawyer's continued qualification to practice law.

Affording the agency an opportunity to be heard on the subject of lawyer discipline protects the right of the profession to preserve the high standards of conduct that it maintains in the public interest.

RULE 7. Roster of Lawyers

Disciplinary counsel shall maintain or have ready access to current information relating to all lawyers subject to the jurisdiction of the board including:

   (a) full name and all names under which the lawyer has been admitted or practiced;

   (b) date of birth;

   (c) current law office address and telephone number;

   (d) current residence address;

   (e) date of admission in the state;

   (f) date of any transfer to or from inactive status;

   (g) all specialties in which certified;

   (h) other jurisdictions in which the lawyer is admitted and date of admission;

   (i) location and account numbers in which clients' funds are held by the lawyer;

   (j) nature, date, and place of any discipline imposed and any reinstatements in any other jurisdiction;

   (k) date of death; and

   (l) the universal lawyer identification number [together with the jurisdiction's prefix, if any, issued by the court].

Commentary

A permanent registration system should be established from which the agency can determine whether an individual is licensed to practice in the state, is living or deceased, and where the individual is located. The registration records may be maintained by the court, a court-designated agency, or in unified bar states by the state bar. Disciplinary counsel should have ready access to the records.

The individual lawyer has the responsibility of keeping his or her registration information current, and should be required to promptly inform the registration agency of any change. Generally, the address listed in the roster is the lawyer's legal address for purposes of service of process and any other notices. See Rule 13.

* * *

RULE 8. Periodic Assessment of Lawyers

A. *Requirement.* Every lawyer admitted to practice before this court shall pay to the clerk of this court [*state bar*] an annual fee for each fiscal year beginning [*date*] to be set by the court [*state bar*] from time to time. The fee shall be used to defray the costs of disciplinary administration and enforcement under these rules, other components of the system of lawyer regulation under other rules established by the court and for those other purposes the court shall from time to time designate. The annual fee until further order of the court shall be:

After Date of Admission to Practice Law	Annual fee
Up to five years:	$
Five years or more:	$

B. *Exemption of Judges.* Full-time judges shall be exempt from the payment of the fee during the time they serve in office.

C. *Suspension for Nonpayment.* Unless excused on grounds of financial hardship pursuant to procedures to be established by the board, any lawyer who fails to timely pay the fee required under paragraph A shall be summarily suspended, provided that a notice of delinquency, addressed to the lawyer's last known business address, has been forwarded to the lawyer by certified mail, return receipt requested, at least [thirty] days prior to such suspension.

D. *Reinstatement After Payment.* Any lawyer suspended under paragraph C shall be reinstated without further order if, within five years of the effective date of the suspension for nonpayment, the lawyer makes payment of all arrears and a penalty of 20% of the amount due from the date of the last payment to the date of the request for reinstatement. Any lawyer who fails to make these complete payments within five years of the effective date of the suspension for nonpayment may, in the discretion of the court, be required to petition for reinstatement under Rule 25.

E. *Registration Statement.* To facilitate the collection of the annual fee provided for in paragraph A and the regulation of lawyers, each lawyer required by this rule to pay an annual fee shall, on or before [*date*] of every year, commencing [*date*] file with the clerk of this court a registration statement, on a form prescribed by this court, setting forth the lawyer's residence and office addresses, other jurisdictions in which the lawyer is admitted to practice, the imposition of any public sanction or transfer to or from inactive status in any other jurisdiction, and such other information as this court may from time to time direct. Each lawyer shall file with the clerk of this court a supplemental statement of any change in the information previously submitted within [thirty] days of the change. All persons first becoming subject to these rules by admission to the practice of law before the courts of this state after [*date*] shall file the statement required by this rule at the time of admission, but no annual fee shall be payable until [*date*] next following such date of admission.

F. *Receipt Demonstrating Filing of Registration Statement.* Within [thirty] days of the receipt of a statement or supplement thereto filed by the lawyer in accordance with paragraph E, the clerk of this court shall acknowledge receipt on a form prescribed by the court in order to enable the lawyer on request to demonstrate compliance with the requirements of paragraphs A and E.

G. *Suspension for Failure to File Registration Statements.* Any lawyer who fails to file the statement or supplement in accordance with paragraph E shall be summarily suspended, provided a notice of delinquency has been forwarded to the lawyer by certified mail, return receipt requested, addressed to the lawyer's last known business address at least [thirty] days prior to the suspension. The lawyer shall remain suspended until compliance is demonstrated, whereupon the lawyer shall be reinstated without further order.

H. *Application for Transfer to Inactive Status.* A lawyer who has retired or is not engaged in practice shall advise the clerk of this court in writing that the lawyer desires to assume inactive status and discontinue the practice of law. Upon the filing of the notice, the lawyer shall no longer be eligible to practice law. A lawyer who is retired or on inactive status shall not be obligated to pay the annual fee imposed by this rule upon active practitioners. A lawyer on inactive status shall be removed from the roll of those classified as active until and unless the lawyer requests and is granted reinstatement to the active rolls.

I. *Reinstatement From Inactive Status.* Any lawyer on inactive status under paragraph H shall be reinstated without further order if the lawyer makes application within five years of the effective date of transfer to inactive status. Any lawyer who fails to make application for reinstatement within five years of the effective date of transfer to inactive status may, in the discretion of the court, be required to petition for reinstatement under Rule 25.

Any lawyer who is under an order of discipline in any other jurisdiction shall be required to petition for reinstatement under Rule 25.

Commentary

In some jurisdictions, statutory provisions vest ultimate authority and control over disciplinary agency budgets with the legislature. Within state constitutional constraints, the court should assert its inherent power to regulate the profession to provide for adequate funding of the disciplinary system. Lawyer discipline and other regulatory functions such as client protection funds, mandatory fee arbitration, voluntary arbitration, mediation, lawyer practice assistance, and lawyer substance abuse counseling should be funded by fees assessed on lawyers admitted to practice in the state. Funds collected by this assessment and disbursements made for lawyer discipline and other regulatory activities (such as mandatory fee arbitration, client protection funds, and lawyer practice assistance) should be controlled exclusively by the highest court in the jurisdiction. The court may choose to exercise these functions through a unified bar.

Inadequate funding is the major cause of inadequate enforcement. The availability of adequate funds for personnel and expenses will enable an agency to perform all essential duties and not just unavoidable tasks.

The profession recognizes that the creation and maintenance of an effective structure for discipline and disability proceedings is one of its primary responsibilities.

The level of funding for the agency will determine whether it can hire experienced, full-time lawyers as counsel, or whether it can rely upon volunteers, part-time participants and clerks. Adequate funding will enable the agency to unravel a complex or obscure fact situation with which it might not otherwise be able to cope. The level of funding will determine how promptly allegations can be resolved, thereby affecting the length of time the lawyer remains uncertain about his future, the extent to which clients are exposed to further harm, and the amount of public confidence in the system.

Disciplinary counsel should have sufficient staff and resources to: (1) fully investigate complaints by such means as sending investigators into the field to interview witnesses and examine records and evidence; and (2) regularly monitor sources of public information such as news reports and court decisions likely to contain information about lawyer misconduct.

* * *

RULE 9. Grounds for Discipline/Lesser Misconduct

A. It shall be a ground for discipline for a lawyer to:

(a) violate or attempt to violate the [State Rules of Professional Conduct], or any other rules of this jurisdiction regarding professional conduct of lawyers;

(b) engage in conduct violating applicable rules of professional conduct of another jurisdiction;

(c) willfully violate a valid order of the court or the board imposing discipline, willfully fail to appear before disciplinary counsel for admonition pursuant to Rule 10(A)(5), willfully fail to comply with a subpoena validly issued under Rule 14, or knowingly fail to respond to a lawful demand from a disciplinary authority, except that this rule does not require disclosure of information otherwise protected by applicable rules relating to confidentiality.

B. *Lesser Misconduct.* Lesser misconduct is conduct that does not warrant a sanction restricting the respondent's license to practice law. Conduct shall not be considered lesser misconduct if any of the following considerations apply:

(1) the misconduct involves the misappropriation of funds;

(2) the misconduct results in or is likely to result in substantial prejudice to a client or other person;

(3) the respondent has been publicly disciplined in the last three years;

(4) the misconduct is of the same nature as misconduct for which the respondent has been disciplined in the last five years;

(5) the misconduct involves dishonesty, deceit, fraud, or misrepresentation by the respondent;

(6) the misconduct constitutes a "serious crime" as defined in Rule 19(C); or

(7) the misconduct is part of a pattern of similar misconduct.

Commentary

When a lawyer is admitted to practice he or she becomes subject to rules of conduct in effect in that jurisdiction. A violation of those rules triggers the jurisdiction of the agency. This does not mean that every violation necessarily requires the imposition of a sanction, but merely that the agency can investigate the matter.

The agency's jurisdiction to investigate and to take whatever action is deemed to be appropriate is triggered by discipline imposed in another state. The imposition of discipline in one jurisdiction does not mean that every other jurisdiction in which the lawyer is admitted must necessarily impose discipline, but the burden is on the respondent to demonstrate that the imposition of the same discipline is inappropriate. See Rule 22.

All lawyers have an affirmative duty to cooperate, including keeping disciplinary counsel advised of current address for service of process, cooperating with disciplinary investigations, and appearing at disciplinary hearings.

This rule establishes the proper policy for the relationship of the disciplinary system to the bar. Respondents are entitled to due process in disciplinary proceedings and are protected by fifth amendment rights against self-incrimination. However, disciplinary proceedings are not criminal proceedings; respondents are not entitled to "stonewall."

* * *

RULE 10. Sanctions

A. *Types of Sanctions.* Misconduct shall be grounds for one or more of the following sanctions:

(1) Disbarment by the court.

(2) Suspension by the court for an appropriate fixed period of time not in excess of three years.

(3) Probation imposed by the court not in excess of two years, or imposed by the board or counsel with the consent of the respondent not in excess of two years; provided, however, that probation may be renewed for an additional [two year] period by consent or

after a hearing to determine if there is a continued need for supervision. If the respondent objects to the board or counsel's imposition of probation, the misconduct must either be made the subject of formal charges or a recommendation that probation be imposed must be filed with the court. The conditions of probation should be stated in writing. Probation shall be used only in cases where there is little likelihood that the respondent will harm the public during the period of rehabilitation and the conditions of probation can be adequately supervised. Probation shall be terminated upon the filing of an affidavit by respondent showing compliance with the conditions and an affidavit by the probation monitor stating that probation is no longer necessary and summarizing the basis for that statement.

(4) Reprimand by the court or the board. A reprimand shall be in writing and either imposed in person or served upon the respondent by certified mail. A reprimand issued by the court shall be published in the official reports for the guidance of other lawyers. A reprimand imposed by the board shall be published in the journal of the state bar and in a newspaper of general circulation in each judicial district in which the lawyer maintained an office for the practice of law.

(5) Admonition by disciplinary counsel imposed with the consent of the respondent and the approval of the chair of a hearing committee. An admonition cannot be imposed after formal charges have been issued. Admonitions shall be in writing and served upon the respondent. They constitute private discipline since they are imposed before the filing of formal charges. Only in cases of minor misconduct, when there is little or no injury to a client, the public, the legal system, or the profession, and when there is little likelihood of repetition by the lawyer, should an admonition be imposed. A summary of the conduct for which an admonition was imposed may be published in a bar publication for the education of the profession, but the lawyer shall not be identified. An admonition may be used in subsequent proceedings in which the respondent has been found guilty of misconduct as evidence of prior misconduct bearing upon the issue of the sanction to be imposed in the subsequent proceeding.

(6) Upon order of the court or the board, or upon stipulation, restitution to persons financially injured and reimbursement to the client security fund.

(7) Upon order of the court or the board, or upon stipulation, assessment of the costs of the proceedings, including the costs of investigations, service of process, witness fees, and a court reporter's services, in any case where discipline is imposed or there is a transfer to disability inactive status.

(8) Limitation by the court on the nature or extent of the respondent's future practice.

B. *Conditions.* Written conditions may be attached to an admonition or a reprimand. Failure to comply with such conditions shall be grounds for reconsideration of the matter and prosecution of formal charges against the respondent.

C. *Factors to Be Considered in Imposing Sanctions.* In imposing a sanction after a finding of lawyer misconduct, the court or board shall consider the following factors as enumerated in the ABA Standards for Imposing Lawyer Sanctions:

(1) whether the lawyer has violated a duty owed to a client, to the public, to the legal system, or to the profession;

(2) whether the lawyer acted intentionally, knowingly, or negligently;

(3) the amount of the actual or potential injury caused by the lawyer's misconduct; and

(4) the existence of any aggravating or mitigating factors.

D. *Public Nature of Sanctions.* Disposition of lawyer discipline shall be public in cases of disbarment, suspension, probation, and reprimand. In all cases of public discipline by the court, the court shall issue a written opinion setting forth its justification for imposing the sanction in that particular case.

Commentary

* * *

The *Standards for Imposing Lawyer Sanctions* were adopted by the ABA in 1986. These standards provide a framework to guide the courts in imposing sanctions, thereby giving the courts the flexibility to select the appropriate sanction in each particular case of lawyer misconduct.... The *Standards for Imposing Lawyer Sanctions* set forth a comprehensive system for determining sanctions, permitting flexibility and creativity in assigning sanctions in particular cases of lawyer misconduct. Use of the *Standards* will help achieve the degree of consistency in the imposition of lawyer discipline necessary for fairness to the public and the bar.

II. PROCEDURE FOR DISCIPLINARY PROCEEDINGS

RULE 11. Generally

A. *Evaluation.* The disciplinary counsel shall evaluate all information coming to his or her attention by complaint or from other sources alleging lawyer misconduct or incapacity. If the lawyer is not subject to the jurisdiction of the court, the matter shall be referred to the appropriate entity in any jurisdiction in which the lawyer is admitted. If the information, if true, would not constitute misconduct or incapacity, the matter may be referred to the central intake office or dismissed. If the lawyer is subject to the jurisdiction of the court and the information alleges facts which, if true, would constitute misconduct or incapacity, disciplinary counsel shall conduct an investigation.

B. *Investigation.*

(1) All investigations shall be conducted by disciplinary counsel. Upon the conclusion of an investigation, disciplinary counsel may dismiss or may recommend probation, admonition, the filing of formal charges, the petitioning for transfer to disability inactive status, participation in those programs listed in Rule 21(F), or a stay.

(2) Notice to Respondent. Disciplinary counsel shall not recommend a disposition other than dismissal or stay without first notifying the respondent in writing of the substance of the matter and affording him or her an opportunity to be heard. Notice to the respondent at his or her last known address is sufficient.

(3) Disciplinary counsel's recommended disposition shall not be subject to review upon the respondent's request for review. Disciplinary counsel's recommended disposition other than a dismissal or a referral to the Alternatives to Discipline Program shall be reviewed by the chair of a hearing committee selected in order from the roster established by the board. The complainant shall be notified of the disposition of a matter following investigation. The complainant may file a written request for review of counsel's dismissal within [thirty] days of receipt of notice of disposition pursuant to Rule 4(B)(6). Disciplinary counsel's dismissal shall be reviewed by the chair upon the complainant's request for review. The chair may approve, disapprove, or modify the recommendation or appealed dismissal. Disciplinary counsel may appeal a decision to disapprove or modify his or her recommendation to a reviewing chair of a second hearing committee also selected in order from the roster established by the board who shall approve either disciplinary counsel's recommendation or the action of the first reviewer, but the decision of the second reviewing chair shall not be appealable. Any hearing committee whose chair reviews a recommendation of disciplinary counsel is disqualified from participating in further consideration of the matter.

C. *Admonition or Probation—Imposition.*

(1) If a matter is recommended to be concluded by admonition or by probation, disciplinary counsel shall notify the respondent in writing of the proposed disposition and of the right to demand in writing within [fourteen] days that the matter be disposed of by a formal proceeding. Failure of the respondent to so demand within [fourteen] days after written notice of the proposed admonition or probation constitutes consent to the admonition or probation.

(2) If the respondent within [fourteen] days demands a formal hearing, formal charges may be instituted.

D. *Formal Charges.* If a matter is to be resolved by a formal proceeding, disciplinary counsel shall prepare formal charges in writing that give fair and adequate notice of the nature of the alleged misconduct.

(1) Disciplinary counsel shall file the charges with the board.

(2) Disciplinary counsel shall cause a copy of the formal charges to be served upon the respondent and proof of service to be filed with the board.

(3) The respondent shall file a written answer with the board and serve a copy on disciplinary counsel within [twenty] days after service of the formal charges, unless the time is extended by the chair of the hearing committee. In the event the respondent fails to answer within the prescribed time, or the time as extended, the factual allegations shall be deemed admitted as provided in Rule 33(A).

(4) If there are any material issues of fact raised by the pleadings or if the respondent requests the opportunity to be heard in mitigation, the [hearing committee] [board] shall serve a notice of hearing upon disciplinary counsel and the respondent, stating the date and place of hearing at least [twenty-five] days in advance thereof. The notice of hearing shall advise the respondent of the right to be represented by a lawyer, to cross-examine witnesses and to present evidence. The complainant, if any, shall have the right to make a statement to the [hearing committee] [board] concerning the respondent's alleged misconduct and the effect of the alleged misconduct on the complainant. The hearing shall be recorded. The [hearing committee] [board] shall promptly submit its report containing its findings and decision on dismissal or sanction to the [board] [court] and shall serve the report on disciplinary counsel and respondent.

(5) Information concerning prior discipline of the respondent shall not be divulged to the hearing committee until after the committee has made a finding of misconduct unless said information is probative of issues pending in the present matter.[47]

E. *Review by Board.* Review by the board shall be limited to a review of the report from the hearing committee and the record below. The board shall not review a matter unless (a) the respondent or disciplinary counsel files objections with the board within [20] days of the date of service of the report, or (b) a majority of the full board, at its

---

47. Standard 8.39 of the 1979 Standards for Lawyer Discipline and Disability Proceedings.

next meeting after submission of the report, votes to review the matter. If the board does not review the matter and the hearing committee has decided to dismiss the matter, the matter shall be dismissed. If the board does not review the matter and the sanction recommended by the hearing committee is not disbarment or suspension, the board shall impose the sanction upon the respondent. If the board does not review the matter and the sanction recommended by the hearing committee is disbarment or suspension, the board shall transmit the report of the hearing committee to the court with a statement that the parties have waived objections and the board has declined to review the matter. If the matter is to be reviewed by the board, the respondent and disciplinary counsel should be afforded an opportunity to file briefs and present oral argument during the review by the board. The board shall adopt rules establishing a timetable and procedure for the filing of briefs and presentation of argument.

(1) Decision by Board. Following its review, the board may approve, modify, or disapprove the recommendation of the hearing committee. The board shall prepare a written report containing its findings and decision on sanction or decision to dismiss the matter. A copy of the report shall promptly be submitted to the court and served on disciplinary counsel and the respondent. If the board determines that the matter shall be dismissed or that a sanction other than disbarment or suspension shall be imposed, and the court does not vote to review the matter, then the board shall dismiss the matter or impose the sanction upon respondent.

(2) During its review, the board shall not receive or consider any evidence that was not presented to the hearing committee, except upon notice to the respondent and disciplinary counsel and opportunity to respond. The hearing committee is the initial trier of fact; the board serves an appellate review function. If new evidence warranting a reopening of the proceeding is discovered, the case should be remanded to the hearing committee.

F. *Review by the Court.* The court may, within its discretion, review a matter if the respondent or disciplinary counsel files objections to the report of the board or if a majority of the court, within the time for filing objections, votes to review the matter. If the court does not review the matter and the sanction decided upon by the board or by the hearing committee with review declined by the board is suspension or disbarment, the court shall impose the sanction.

(1) The respondent and disciplinary counsel may file objections to the report of the board within [twenty] days from the date of service. Within [sixty] days after the court grants review, the respondent and disciplinary counsel may file briefs and present oral arguments pursuant to the rules governing civil appeals. Upon conclusion of the proceedings, the court shall promptly enter an appropriate order. The decision of the court shall be in writing and

state the reasons for the decision. Upon final disposition at any stage of the proceedings, the written findings shall be published in an appropriate journal or reporter and a copy shall be mailed to the respondent and the complainant and to the ABA National Discipline Data Bank.[53]

(2) During its review, the court shall not receive or consider any evidence that was not presented to the hearing committee, except upon notice to the respondent and disciplinary counsel and opportunity to respond.

(3) If new evidence warranting a reopening of the proceeding is discovered, the case shall be remanded to the hearing committee.

G. *Alternatives to Discipline Program*

(1) Referral to Program. In a matter involving lesser misconduct as defined in Rule 9(B), prior to the filing of formal charges, disciplinary counsel may refer respondent to the Alternatives to Discipline Program. The Alternatives to Discipline Program may include fee arbitration, arbitration, mediation, law office management assistance, lawyer assistance programs, psychological counseling, continuing legal education programs, ethics school or any other program authorized by the court.

(2) Notice to Complainant. Pursuant to Rule 4(B)(6), the complainant, if any, shall be notified of the decision to refer the respondent to the Alternatives to Discipline Program, and shall have a reasonable opportunity to submit a statement offering any new information regarding the respondent. This statement shall be made part of the record.

(3) Factors. The following factors shall be considered in determining whether to refer a respondent to the program:

(a) whether the presumptive sanction under the *ABA Standards for Imposing Lawyer Sanctions* for the violations listed in the complaint is likely to be no more severe than reprimand or admonition;

(b) whether participation in the program is likely to benefit the respondent and accomplish the goals set forth by the program;

(c) whether aggravating or mitigating factors exist; and

(d) whether diversion was already tried.

(4) Contract. Disciplinary counsel and the respondent shall negotiate a contract, the terms of which shall be tailored to the individual circumstances. In each case, the contract shall be signed by the respondent and the disciplinary counsel. The contract shall set forth the terms and conditions of the plan for the respondent and, if appropriate, shall identify the use of a practice monitor

---

53.   See also Rule 16(H).

and/or a recovery monitor and the responsibilities of the monitor(s). The contract shall provide for oversight of fulfillment of the contract terms. Oversight includes reporting of any alleged breach of contract to the disciplinary counsel. The contract shall also provide that the respondent will pay all costs incurred in connection with the contract. The contract shall include a specific acknowledgment that a material violation of a term of the contract renders voidable the respondent's participation in the program for the original charge(s) filed. The contract may be amended upon agreement of the respondent and disciplinary counsel. If a recovery monitor is assigned, the contract shall include respondent's waiver of confidentiality so that the recovery monitor may make necessary disclosures in order to fulfill the monitor's duties under the contract.

(5) Effect of Non-participation in the Program. The respondent has the right not to participate in the Alternatives to Discipline Program. If the respondent does not participate, the matter will proceed as though no referral to the program had been made.

(6) Status of Complaint. After an agreement is reached, the disciplinary complaint shall be held in abeyance [dismissed] pending successful completion of the terms of the contract.

(7) Termination.

(a) Fulfillment of the Contract: The contract is automatically terminated when the terms of the contract have been fulfilled. Successful completion of the contract constitutes a bar to any further disciplinary proceedings based upon the same allegations.

(b) Material Breach: A material breach of the contract shall be cause for termination of the respondent's participation in the program. After a material breach, disciplinary proceedings may be resumed or reinstituted.

Commentary

The evaluation process eliminates those matters over which the agency has no jurisdiction. It precedes investigation, which is reserved for those matters determined to involve a lawyer subject to the jurisdiction of the agency and allegations which, if true, would constitute misconduct.

If the matter is terminated at this stage because the matter does not involve allegations of misconduct, disciplinary counsel should notify the complainant and refer him or her to the central intake office. Disciplinary counsel may refer matters to the central intake office or directly to any of the component agencies included in the comprehensive lawyer regulation system established by Rule 1, such as the lawyer assistance program (which provides assistance for impairment problems) or the fee arbitration program.

Matters terminated at the evaluation stage because they concern a lawyer not admitted to practice in the jurisdiction should be forwarded by disciplinary counsel to the agency for the jurisdiction in which the lawyer is admitted. The complainant should be notified of the disposition if a matter is concluded at the screening stage.

A stay is appropriate only in extraordinary circumstances. Disciplinary counsel must determine whether the complainant or the respondent will suffer prejudice in the pending proceeding should the disciplinary action proceed immediately. In some cases, witnesses and evidence pertinent to both cases might not be obtainable at a later date; in other cases, the disciplinary action may be expedited by waiting for evidence to be adduced in another proceeding.

Fairness requires that no recommendation adverse to the respondent be made without providing him or her an opportunity to be heard. This does not mean that the respondent is entitled to notice immediately upon receipt of a complaint. In some instances, early notice would be harmful to the investigation. It does mean that the respondent has a right to be heard before the investigation is concluded and an adverse disposition formulated. If the matter is dismissed or stayed following investigation, respondent has no reason to appeal.

The review process preserves elements of bifurcation within the unitary system, because the recommendation of disciplinary counsel is subject to review and approval by a representative of the adjudicative body. The approval of counsel's recommendation to file formal charges by the reviewing member amounts to a finding of probable cause to proceed.

In order to prevent any possibility of forum shopping by disciplinary counsel, the hearing committee chairperson should be designated by the board. The hearing committee of which the reviewing chair is a member should be disqualified from any future consideration of the matter, in order to avoid being placed in the position of passing upon the correctness of his or her approval of the recommendation to prosecute formal charges.

The board supervises the operations of the agency. Any person dissatisfied with the action of the agency may complain to the board. The complaint should be submitted to a panel of the board, rather than the entire board, so that those members not serving on the panel will be available to participate in any future proceedings involving the matter.

If the first reviewing chairperson does not approve the recommendation, disciplinary counsel may submit the matter to a second reviewing chairperson who shall decide the issue by approving either the recommendation of disciplinary counsel or the modification thereon made by the first reviewer. The decision of the second reviewing chair shall be final within the agency.

The court, the board, or disciplinary counsel may impose probation. If probation is imposed by the board or by counsel, the consent of the respondent is required. The terms of the probation should specify periodic review of the order of probation, and provide a means to supervise the progress of the respondent.

Admonitions should be in writing and served upon the respondent. If the respondent does not consent to the admonition or probation, formal charges are instituted. The procedure is similar to the rejection of a settlement offer in a civil case or a plea bargain in a criminal case, which results in a trial.

The fact that refusal to consent to the admonition or probation subjects the respondent to formal charges and potentially more serious discipline does not violate due process any more than does the fact that a person charged with a crime is subject to conviction of a more serious offense when he or she refuses to plead to a lesser crime.

Prior discipline is relevant and material to the issue of the sanction to be imposed for the conduct which is the subject of the pending charges. Prior discipline is, except in unusual circumstances, not relevant or material to the issue of whether the conduct alleged has occurred. Consequently, introduction of evidence of prior discipline before a finding that the present charges have been sustained is prejudicial. Such records should not ordinarily be introduced until a finding of guilt has been made.

If evidence of prior discipline is necessary to prove the present charges (e.g. an allegation that the respondent continued to practice despite suspension) or to impeach (e.g. false testimony by respondent as to lack of prior discipline), it may be offered. However, it should not be used as a substitute for proving the allegations at issue.

The hearing may be recorded by any method authorized in the jurisdiction. The record will assist the hearing committee in the preparation and presentation of its report.

If the matter ultimately results in a recommendation for discipline, the record should be forwarded with the findings and recommendation. The recording should be available to the respondent upon request, and a transcript provided at cost.

The hearing committee is the initial trier of fact; the board serves an appellate review function. If new evidence warranting a reopening of the proceeding is discovered, the case should be remanded to the hearing committee.

Unless the decision of the hearing committee or the board is appealed or unless the board or court affirmatively decides to review a matter, cases should be disposed at the earliest possible stage. Of course, the court must retain ultimate responsibility for all disciplinary matters and, thus, must reserve the right to review any matter or even hold a *de novo* hearing if it so determines. This should occur only in extraordinary cases involving significant questions of law. In all other cases, the court should rely on its disciplinary counsel, the hearing committee, and the board to dispose of matters in accordance with established disciplinary law. This will both speed up the process and reduce the burden on the court.[54] If new evidence warranting a reopening of the proceeding is discovered, the case should be remanded to the hearing committee.

Written opinions of the court not only serve to educate members of the profession about ethical behavior, but also provide precedent for subsequent cases. Moreover, this requirement is manageable; the courts in the jurisdictions with the heaviest caseloads currently write opinions in every contested disciplinary case they decide. If a matter is concluded without review by the court, the report of the board or hearing committee should be published in the official reporter.

* * *

The overwhelming majority of complaints made against lawyers allege instances of lesser misconduct. Single instances of minor neglect or minor incompetence, while technically violations of the rules of professional conduct, are seldom treated as such. These complaints are almost always dismissed. Summary dismissal of these complaints is one of the chief sources of public dissatisfaction with the system.

These cases seldom justify the resources needed to conduct formal disciplinary proceedings. In most of these cases, the respondent's conduct does not justify imposing a disciplinary sanction. Therefore, these matters should be removed from the disciplinary system and handled administratively. It may be appropriate to compensate the client for the respondent's substandard performance by a fee adjustment or other arbitrated or mediated settlement. The respondent may need guidance to improve his or her skills or to overcome a problem with substance abuse.

A respondent has the right to refuse to participate in the Alternatives to Discipline Program. The only adverse consequence of a respondent's refusal to participate shall be that it is a factor to be considered by disciplinary counsel in determining whether to recommend the filing of formal charges. Disciplinary counsel may recommend formal charges even if the original complaint alleged lesser misconduct as defined in Rule 9(B). Disciplinary counsel, of course, retains the discretion to dismiss the complaint. If fee arbitration is mandatory in the jurisdiction, there is obviously no need for respondent's consent.

Participation in the program is not intended as an alternative to discipline in cases of serious misconduct or in cases that factually present little hope that participation will achieve program goals. In addition, the program will only be considered in cases where, assuming all the allegations against the respondent are true, the presumptive sanctions would be less than suspension or disbarment or other restrictions on the right to practice. See Rule 9(B). After the filing and service of formal charges, a referral to any of the component agencies

54. Rec. 11.

included in the comprehensive lawyer regulation system established by Rule 1 shall be made as written conditions pursuant to Rule 10(B).

The existence of one or more aggravating factors does not necessarily exclude participation in the program. For example, neglect cases often include a pattern of misconduct and multiple offenses, but do not involve dishonesty, bad faith, or a breach of fiduciary obligation. Thus, the existence of "a pattern of misconduct" and/or "multiple offenses" should not make a respondent ineligible for the program. A pattern of lesser misconduct may be a strong indication that office management is the real problem and that this program is the best way to address that underlying problem.

Factors that may indicate ineligibility for participation in the program include evidence of a dishonest or selfish motive, bad faith in, or the obstruction of, the disciplinary process, the submission of false evidence, or an indifference to making restitution. Both mitigating and aggravating factors should also be considered. The presence of one or more mitigating factors may qualify an otherwise ineligible respondent for the program.

The existence of prior disciplinary offenses would not necessarily make a respondent ineligible for referral to the Alternatives to Discipline Program. Consideration should be given to whether the respondent's prior offenses are of the same or similar nature, whether the respondent has previously been placed in the Alternatives to Discipline Program for similar conduct and whether it is reasonably foreseeable that the respondent's participation in the program will be successful.

Each participant in the program will become a party to a contract that is specifically designed to address the alleged violations. It will be the respondent's responsibility to carry out the contract provisions. The contract provisions will indicate who is responsible to oversee the fulfillment of the terms of the contract. The person overseeing the contract must report to the disciplinary counsel any non-compliance with the contract provisions.

In order to encourage voluntary participation in lawyer assistance programs, such programs provide confidentiality. Rule 8.3(c) of the ABA Model Rules of Professional Conduct states: "This Rule does not require disclosure of information ... gained by a lawyer or judge while serving as a member of an approved lawyers assistance program to the extent that such information would be confidential if it were communicated subject to the attorney-client privilege." However, participation in the Alternatives to Discipline Program differs from voluntary participation in a LAP program. The Alternatives to Discipline Rule recognizes this difference and requires the recovery monitor to make necessary disclosures in order to fulfill his or her duties under the contract.

RULE 12. Immunity

A. *From Civil Suits.* Communications to the board, hearing committees, or disciplinary counsel relating to lawyer misconduct or disability and testimony given in the proceedings shall be absolutely privileged, and no lawsuit predicated thereon may be instituted against any complainant or witness. Members of the board, members of hearing committees, disciplinary counsel, probation monitors, or any person acting on their behalf and staff shall be immune from suit for any conduct in the course of their official duties.

B. *From Criminal Prosecution.* Upon application by disciplinary counsel and notice to [appropriate prosecuting authority], the court may grant immunity from criminal prosecution to a witness in a discipline or disability proceeding.

Commentary

Agency personnel are an integral part of the judicial process and are entitled to the same immunity which is afforded to prosecuting lawyers. Immunity protects the independent judgment of the agency and avoids diverting the attention of its personnel as well as its resources toward resisting collateral attack and harassment.

The Rule recommends absolute privilege rather than qualified privilege; qualified privilege may not protect against harassment made possible by simply alleging malice in a lawsuit. Conduct on the part of agency personnel which is not authorized or exceeds assigned duties is not protected.

* * *

RULE 13. Service

A. *Service of Petition.* Service upon the respondent of the petition in any disciplinary or disability proceeding shall be made by personal service, by any person authorized by the chair of the board, or by registered or certified mail at an address shown in the current information roster filed by respondent pursuant to Rule 7 or other last known address.

B. *Service of Other Papers.* Service of any other papers or notices required by these rules may be made upon respondent or respondent's counsel and shall, unless otherwise provided by these rules, be made in accordance with Rule _____ of the [*state rules of civil procedure*].

RULE 14. Subpoena Power

A. *Oaths.* Any member of the board or of a hearing committee in matters before it, disciplinary counsel in matters under investigation by him or her, and any person authorized by law may administer oaths and affirmations.

B. *Investigatory Subpoenas.* Before formal charges have been filed, disciplinary counsel may, with the approval of the chairperson of a hearing committee, compel by subpoena the attendance of witnesses, and the production of pertinent books, papers, and documents, in accordance with [appropriate state rule of civil procedure].

C. *Subpoenas for Deposition or Hearing.* After formal charges are filed, disciplinary counsel or respondent may, in accordance with [appropriate state rule of civil procedure], compel by subpoena the attendance of witnesses and the production of pertinent books, papers, and documents at a deposition or hearing under these rules.

D. *Enforcement of Subpoenas.* The [appropriate court of general jurisdiction of the circuit, county, or city] in which the attendance or production is required may, upon proper application, enforce the attendance and testimony of any witnesses and the production of any documents subpoenaed.

E. *Quashing Subpoena.* Any attack on the validity of a subpoena so issued shall be heard and determined by the chair of the hearing committee before which the matter is pending or by the court wherein enforcement of the subpoena is being sought. Any resulting order is not appealable prior to entry of a final order in the proceeding.

F. *Witnesses and Fees.* Subpoena and witness fees and mileage shall be the same as those provided for proceedings in the [appropriate state court of general jurisdiction].

G. *Subpoena Pursuant to Law of Another Jurisdiction.* Whenever a subpoena is sought in this state pursuant to the law of another jurisdiction for use in lawyer discipline or disability proceedings, and where the issuance of the subpoena has been duly approved under the law of the other jurisdiction, the chair of the board, upon petition for good cause, may issue a subpoena as provided in this section to compel the attendance of witnesses and production of documents in the county where the witness resides or is employed or elsewhere as agreed by the witness. Service, enforcement, or challenges to this subpoena shall be as provided in these rules.

Commentary

If the complainant cannot furnish adequate evidence to substantiate his or her allegations and the respondent will not cooperate, counsel must seek independent evidence. If this evidence consists of testimony of a potential witness who does not want to get involved or the records of a third party, such as a bank that will not disclose the transcripts of its depositors' accounts voluntarily, disciplinary counsel without subpoena power will be unable to dispose of the complaint on the merits. Disciplinary counsel thus denied an indispensable investigatory tool can neither be effective nor command public confidence.

RULE 15. Discovery

A. *Scope.* Within [twenty] days following the filing of an answer, disciplinary counsel and respondent shall exchange the names and addresses of all persons having knowledge of relevant facts. Within [sixty] days following the filing of an answer, disciplinary counsel and the respondent may take depositions in accordance with [appropriate state rule of civil procedure], and shall comply with reasonable requests for (1) non-privileged information and evidence relevant to the charges or the respondent, and (2) other material upon good cause shown to the chair of the hearing committee [board].

B. *Resolution of Disputes.* Disputes concerning discovery shall be determined by the chair of the hearing committee [board] before which the matter is pending. All discovery orders by the chair are interlocutory and may not be appealed prior to the entry of the final order.

C. *Civil Rules Not Applicable.* Proceedings under these rules are not subject to the [state rules of civil procedure] regarding discovery except those relating to depositions and subpoenas.

Commentary

Liberal exchanges of non-privileged information should be encouraged, since they facilitate the trial of the charges. However, because a skillful advocate can convert unlimited discovery into a tool for delay, the time for discovery should be limited. An order regarding discovery should be interlocutory and should not be appealable prior to entry of a final order in the proceeding.

RULE 16.   Access to Disciplinary Information

A. *Availability of Information.* All records of the agency, except the work product of disciplinary counsel or the hearing committee or the board, shall be available to the public after a determination that probable cause exists to believe that misconduct occurred and after the filing and service of formal charges, unless the complainant or respondent obtains a protective order for specific testimony, documents or records.

B. *Confidentiality.* Prior to the filing and service of formal charges in a discipline matter, the proceeding is confidential within the agency, except that the pendency, subject matter, and status of an investigation may be disclosed by disciplinary counsel if:

(1) the respondent has waived confidentiality;

(2) the proceeding is based upon allegations that include either the conviction of a crime or reciprocal discipline;

(3) the proceeding is based upon allegations that have become generally known to the public; or

(4) there is a need to notify another person or organization, including the clients' security fund, in order to protect the public, the administration of justice, or the legal profession.

C. *Public Proceedings.* Upon a determination that probable cause exists to believe that misconduct occurred and the filing and service of formal charges in a discipline matter, or filing of a petition for reinstatement, the proceeding is public, except for:

(1) deliberations of the hearing committee, board, or court; or

(2) information with respect to which the hearing committee has issued a protective order.

D. *Proceedings Alleging Disability.* Proceedings for transfer to or from disability inactive status are confidential. All orders transferring a lawyer to or from disability inactive status are public.

E. *Protective Orders.* In order to protect the interests of a complainant, witness, third party, or respondent, the [hearing committee to which a matter is assigned] [board] may, upon application of any person and for good cause shown, issue a protective order prohibiting the disclosure of specific information otherwise privileged or confidential and direct that the proceedings be conducted so as to implement the order, including requiring that the hearing be conducted in such a way as to preserve the confidentiality of the information that is the subject of the application.

F. *Request for Nonpublic Information.* A request for nonpublic information other than that authorized for disclosure under paragraph B above shall be denied unless the request is from one of the following agencies:

(1) [*names of agencies authorized to investigate qualifications for admission to practice;*]

(2) lawyer disciplinary enforcement agencies;

(3) [*other agencies, if any, designated by the court.*]

G. *Notice to Lawyer.* Except as provided in paragraph H, if the board or counsel decides to provide nonpublic information requested, and if the lawyer has not signed a waiver permitting the requesting agency to obtain nonpublic information, the lawyer shall be notified in writing at his or her last known address of that information which has been requested and by whom, together with a copy of the information proposed to be released to the requesting agency. The notice shall advise the lawyer that the information shall be released at the end of [twenty-one] days following mailing of the notice unless the lawyer objects to the disclosure. If the lawyer timely objects to the disclosure, the information shall remain confidential unless the requesting agency obtains a court order requiring its release.

H. *Release Without Notice.* If an otherwise authorized requesting agency has not obtained a waiver from the lawyer to obtain nonpublic information, and requests that the information be released without giving notice to the lawyer, the requesting agency shall certify that:

(1) the request is made in furtherance of an ongoing investigation into misconduct by the lawyer;

(2) the information is essential to that investigation; and

(3) disclosure of the existence of the investigation to the lawyer would seriously prejudice that investigation.

I. *Notice to National Discipline Data Bank.* The board shall transmit notice of all public discipline imposed against a lawyer, transfers to or from disability inactive status, and reinstatements to the National Discipline Data Bank maintained by the American Bar Association.

J. *Duty of Officials and Employees of the Agency.* All officials and employees of the agency in a proceeding under these rules shall conduct themselves so as to maintain the confidentiality mandated by this rule.

Commentary

The confidentiality that attaches prior to a finding of probable cause and the filing of formal charges is primarily for the benefit of the respondent, and protects against publicity predicated upon unfounded accusations.

If the respondent waives confidentiality or if the nature of the accusation is already known to the public, the basis for confidentiality no longer exists. Where information has become widely known, interested individuals and particularly the media often seek comment from the disciplinary agency involved. The existence of privacy requirements places the disciplinary agency in the awkward position of being unable to acknowledge the existence of an investigation. This could lead to a mistaken notion that the agency is unaware of or uninterested in allegations of misconduct, without in any way protecting the reputation of the lawyer.

Once a finding of probable cause has been made, there is no longer a danger that the allegations against the respondent are frivolous. The need to assure the integrity of the disciplinary process in the eyes of the public requires that at this point further proceedings be open to the public. An announcement that a lawyer accused of serious misconduct has been exonerated after a hearing behind closed doors will be suspect. The same disposition will command respect if the public has had access to the evidence.

Disability proceedings remain confidential until the final order of the court, because medical evidence or other peculiarly personal information relating to the lawyer is often involved. An order of the court transferring the lawyer to disability inactive status is public. When a lawyer's license to practice has been limited in any way, public disclosure is necessary. Failure to reveal the fact of transfer to disability inactive status would mislead the public and others likely to come into contact with the lawyer into believing that he or she remains eligible to practice.

The order transferring the lawyer to disability inactive status should clearly state the conditions that must be met for the lawyer to be reinstated to active status. Orders of reinstatement to active status should be published in the journal of the state bar and in a newspaper of general circulation in each judicial district in which the lawyer maintained an office for the practice of law.

In most instances, requests to the agency for nonpublic information relating to a specific lawyer should be denied. The court in its discretion may direct that the agency cooperate with specific entities by providing them with nonpublic information. These will usually be entities charged with a public responsibility requiring that they investigate specific individuals, such as bar admissions committees, committees on judicial appointments, or law enforcement agencies.

Many of these agencies require the lawyer to sign a waiver authorizing the release of information. If the lawyer does not know what the file contains, he or she cannot knowingly authorize the disclosure of its contents. Therefore, if the lawyer requests it, a copy of any information which the agency proposes to disclose to the requesting entity should be furnished before a waiver is signed.

If the agency is asked to release information without a waiver from the lawyer, and is prepared to do so, it should first notify the lawyer of the request and furnish the lawyer with a copy of the information it proposes to release. This should be done sufficiently in advance of the release of the information to the requesting party to permit the lawyer to object to the release. The lawyer's timely objection places upon the requesting agency the burden of seeking a court order to release the information involved.

The requirement of notice to the lawyer prior to release does not apply to requests for information about a lawyer which are made in furtherance of an ongoing investigation into alleged misconduct on the part of the lawyer by an entity authorized to engage in such investigation. Before the agency releases information to an authorized entity without notice to the lawyer, the entity must provide the certification required by the rule.

Exchange of public information between agencies contributes to more effective enforcement. It is absurd for one agency to struggle with a substantive or procedural problem completely unaware that the same problem has been faced and resolved by an agency in another state. Nor should cases involving fundamental questions in disciplinary enforcement be litigated through the courts in the state in which they arise without agencies in other states which are likely to be vitally affected by the outcome being made aware of the existence of the proceeding until the Supreme Court of the United States renders a decision disposing of the issue.

The ABA Center for Professional Responsibility has full-time legal and administrative staff trained and educated in the discipline and disability field available to provide research information and consulting services. The Center maintains a file of the current rules of disciplinary enforcement of each jurisdiction, periodically updates an Index of case law, and operates the National Discipline Data Bank. Current information relating to the handling of particular problems or approaches to specific situations throughout the country is available.

RULE 17. Dissemination of Disciplinary Information

A. *Notice to Disciplinary Agencies.* Disciplinary counsel shall transmit notice of public discipline, transfers to or from disability inactive status, reinstatements, readmissions, and certified copies of judgments of conviction to the disciplinary enforcement agency of every other jurisdiction in which the respondent is admitted.

B. *Public Notice of Discipline Imposed.* Disciplinary counsel shall cause notices of suspension, disbarment, reinstatement, readmission, and transfers to or from disability inactive status to be published in the journal of the state bar and in a newspaper of general circulation in each judicial district in which the lawyer maintained an office for the practice of law.

C. *Notice to the Courts.* Disciplinary counsel shall promptly transmit a certified copy of the order of suspension, disbarment, reinstatement, and transfer to or from disability inactive status to all courts in this state. In addition, disciplinary counsel shall request the presiding judge of the court of the judicial district in which a respondent transferred to disability inactive status or otherwise unable to comply with the requirement of Rule 27 maintained an office for the practice of law to take such action under the provision of Rule 28 as may be indicated in order to protect the interests of the respondent and the respondent's clients.

Commentary

Broad dissemination of information concerning public discipline serves several important purposes. Notification to disciplinary agencies outside the jurisdiction where a sanction has been imposed facilitates appropriate action, such as reciprocal discipline, in jurisdictions where the lawyer is admitted or is seeking admission to practice. Transmittal of notice concerning criminal convictions provides disciplinary agencies with information that may form the basis of a petition for interim suspension. Publication in state bar journals and newspapers of general circulation helps protect the public and the legal community from being misled concerning the lawyer's eligibility to provide representation. In addition, public awareness of sanctions also enhances confidence in the disciplinary system as an effective means of responding to lawyer misconduct.

When a limitation on a lawyer's license has been removed through reinstatement, readmission or transfer to active status, publication and notification help the lawyer avoid a potential burden involved in correcting misunderstandings concerning his or her eligibility to practice. It is fair and reasonable to give notice of reinstatements, readmissions, and transfers to active status in the same manner as notice of public sanctions.

RULE 18. Additional Rules of Procedure

A. *Nature of Proceedings.* Disciplinary proceedings are neither civil nor criminal but are *sui generis.*

B. *Proceedings Governed by Rules of Civil Procedure and Evidence.* Except as otherwise provided in these rules, the [state rules of civil procedure] and the [state rules of evidence in civil nonjury matters] apply in discipline and disability cases.

C. *Standard of Proof.* Formal charges of misconduct, lesser misconduct, petitions for reinstatement and readmission, and petitions for transfer to and from disability inactive status shall be established by clear and convincing evidence.

D. *Burden of Proof.* The burden of proof in proceedings seeking discipline or transfer to disability inactive status is on disciplinary counsel. The burden of proof in proceedings seeking reinstatement, readmission, or transfer from disability inactive status is on the respondent.

E. *Prehearing Conference.* At the discretion of the [hearing committee] [board] or upon request of either party, a conference may be ordered for the purpose of obtaining admissions or otherwise narrowing the issues presented by the pleadings. The conference shall be held before the chair of the [hearing committee] [board] or another member of the [committee] [board] designated by the chair.

F. *Hearings Recorded.* The hearing should be recorded. Upon request, the board shall make the record of a hearing available.

G. *Related Pending Litigation.* Upon a showing of good cause to the board, the processing of a disciplinary matter may be stayed because of substantial similarity to the material allegations of pending criminal or civil litigation or disciplinary action.

H. *Hearings on Lesser Misconduct.* Hearings to adjudicate formal charges alleging lesser misconduct as defined in Rule 9(B) shall proceed in accordance with these rules except as follows:

(1) The hearing shall be held by a single adjudicator [member of a hearing committee] who shall be a lawyer and shall make written findings of fact and conclusions of law and shall:

(a) dismiss;

(b) recommend the imposition of no sanction other than reprimand, costs, restitution, probation not to exceed one year, or a combination thereof; or

(c) remand to a hearing committee if the misconduct is not lesser misconduct as defined in Rule 9(B).

(2) A prehearing conference need not be held. If no prehearing conference is held, the hearing shall commence within [30] days after the hearing committee member is designated.

(3) Respondent, complainant and disciplinary counsel shall have the right to seek review of the decision by a three member panel of

the board, which shall either adopt the decision of the single adjudicator or make written findings. The panel shall either dismiss the case or impose a sanction that does not constitute a restriction on the respondent's right to practice.

(4) The decision of the appellate adjudicator may be reviewed at the discretion of the court upon application by respondent, complainant or disciplinary counsel. The court shall grant review only in cases involving significant issues of law or upon a showing that the decision constituted an abuse of discretion. The court shall either adopt the decision or reject it. If the court rejects the decision, it shall make written findings and either dismiss the case or impose a sanction that does not constitute a restriction on the respondent's right to practice.

(5) Upon final disposition of the case, the written findings and conclusions of the final adjudicator shall be published in an appropriate journal or reporter and a copy shall be mailed to the respondent and to the complainant and to the ABA National Discipline Data Bank.

I. *Delay Caused by Complainant.* Neither unwillingness or neglect of the complainant to sign a complaint or prosecute a charge or settlement or compromise between the complainant and the lawyer or restitution by the lawyer, shall, in itself, justify abatement of the processing of any complaint.

J. *Effect of Time Limitations.* Except as is otherwise provided in these rules, time is directory and not jurisdictional. Failure to observe prescribed time intervals may result in sanctions against the violator but does not justify abatement of any discipline or disability investigation or proceeding.

K. *Complaints Against Disciplinary Agency Members.* If a complaint is filed against disciplinary counsel or disciplinary counsel's staff, a member of a hearing committee, or a member of the board, the matter shall proceed in accordance with these rules except that:

(1) If the respondent is disciplinary counsel or a member of the staff, the board shall appoint a special counsel to present the case;

(2) If the respondent is a member of a hearing committee, the chair of the board shall appoint a special hearing committee for the case; or

(3) If the respondent is a member of the board, the chief justice shall appoint a special board for the case.

Commentary

The holder of a license to practice law is subject to discipline for breaches of the standards of professional conduct; the license must not be arbitrarily taken away and the holder is entitled to procedural due process in any proceeding relating to such conduct. Such due process rights include fair notice of the charges, right to counsel, right to cross-examine witnesses, right to present arguments to the adjudicators, right of appeal (Rule 11); and right to subpoena and discovery (Rules 14 and 15).

The standard of proof for misconduct is higher than "preponderance of the weight of credible evidence" which is usually deemed sufficient in civil proceedings, yet not as stringent as "beyond a reasonable doubt" required in criminal cases.

A prehearing conference may be held by the chairman *sua sponte,* or upon request of counsel, the respondent (or respondent's counsel), or another hearing committee member. Prehearing conferences need not be held in lesser misconduct cases.

The hearing may be recorded by any method authorized in the jurisdiction. The record will assist the hearing committee in the preparation and presentation of its report. If the matter ultimately results in a recommendation for discipline, the record should be forwarded with the findings and recommendation. The recording should be available to the respondent upon request, and a transcript provided at cost.

Statutes of limitation are wholly inappropriate in lawyer disciplinary proceedings. Conduct of a lawyer, no matter when it has occurred, is always relevant to the question of fitness to practice. The time between the commission of the alleged misconduct and the filing of a complaint predicated thereon may be pertinent to whether and to what extent discipline should be imposed, but should not limit the agency's power to investigate.

This rule provides a rational basis for appointment of special counsel, special hearing committee, or special board by the next higher entity in the adjudicative process.

* * *

Lawyer discipline actions are in fact licensing proceedings. Due process accorded to respondent lawyers should be commensurate with the rights and privileges under review. Where the alleged misconduct would not warrant a sanction restricting the lawyer's right to practice, there is no justification for more elaborate procedures. The recommended expedited procedures preserve the rights to notice and hearing, to present evidence and confront witnesses, and to seek review.

At first, a respondent facing a possible reprimand or probation might think that full formal hearing and appeal procedures would provide more protection to his or her professional reputation. A more realistic assessment will show that the recommended expedited procedures are fair and equitable and offer sufficient protection, while full formal procedures are burdensome emotionally and financially compared to the rights at stake.

* * *

RULE 19. Lawyers Found Guilty of a Crime

A. *Transmittal of Proof of Determination of Guilt by Clerk of Trial Court.* The clerk of any court in this state in which a lawyer is found guilty of a crime shall within [ten] days after the finding of guilt transmit a certified copy of the proof of the finding of guilt to counsel for the lawyer disciplinary agency of every state in which the lawyer is admitted to practice.

B. *Determination of "Serious Crime."* Upon being advised that a lawyer subject to the disciplinary jurisdiction of this court has been found guilty of a crime, disciplinary counsel shall determine whether the crime constitutes a "serious crime" warranting immediate interim suspension. If the crime is a "serious crime," disciplinary counsel shall prepare an order for interim suspension and forward it to the court and the respondent with proof of finding of guilt. Disciplinary counsel shall in addition file formal charges against the respondent predicated upon the finding of guilt. On or before the date established for the entry of the order of interim suspension the lawyer may assert any jurisdictional deficiency that establishes that the suspension may not properly be ordered, such as that the crime did not constitute a "serious crime" or that the lawyer is not the individual found guilty. If the crime is not a "serious crime," counsel shall process the matter in the same manner as any other information coming to the attention of the agency.

C. *Definition of "Serious Crime."* A "serious crime" is any felony or any lesser crime that reflects adversely on the lawyer's honesty, trustworthiness or fitness as a lawyer in other respects, or any crime a necessary element of which, as determined by the statutory or common law definition of the crime, involves interference with the administration of justice, false swearing, misrepresentation, fraud, deceit, bribery, extortion, misappropriation, theft, or an attempt, conspiracy or solicitation of another to commit a "serious crime."

D. *Immediate Interim Suspension.* The court has exclusive power to place a lawyer on interim suspension.

    (1) Imposition. The court shall place a lawyer on interim suspension immediately upon proof that the lawyer has been found guilty of a serious crime regardless of the pendency of any appeal.

    (2) Termination. The court has exclusive power to terminate an interim suspension. In the interest of justice, the court may terminate an interim suspension at any time upon a showing of extraordinary circumstances, after affording disciplinary counsel notice and an opportunity to be heard.

E. *Conviction as Conclusive Evidence.* For purposes of a hearing on formal charges filed as a result of a finding of guilt, a certified copy of a judgment of conviction constitutes conclusive evidence that the lawyer committed the crime, and the sole issue in any such hearing shall be the nature and extent of the discipline to be imposed.

F. *Automatic Reinstatement From Interim Suspension Upon Reversal of Conviction.* If a lawyer suspended solely under the provisions of paragraph D demonstrates that the underlying finding of guilt or conviction has been reversed or vacated, the order for interim suspension shall be vacated and the lawyer placed on active status. The vacating of the interim suspension will not automatically terminate any formal proceeding then pending against the lawyer, the disposition of which shall be determined by the hearing committee and the board on the basis of the available evidence other than the finding of guilt or conviction.

G. *Notice to Clients and Others on Interim Suspension.* An interim suspension under this rule shall constitute a suspension of the lawyer for the purpose of Rule 27.

Commentary

Interim suspension is necessary both to protect members of the public and to maintain public confidence in the legal profession. The interim suspension not only removes any danger to clients and the public which the respondent may pose, but also serves to protect the profession and the administration of justice from the specter created where an individual found guilty of a "serious crime" continues to serve as an officer of the court in good standing.

Interim suspension is not final discipline; therefore counsel must proceed to file formal charges based upon the finding of guilt and subsequent conviction. Formal proceedings should not be conducted until all appeals from the conviction have been exhausted, unless the respondent requests that the hearing not be deferred.

Continued practice by a lawyer found guilty of a "serious crime" undermines the public confidence in the profession and the administration of justice. Because there may be delay between a determination of guilt and entry of a judgment of conviction, the disciplinary agency should seek interim suspension upon a finding of guilt. It is difficult to understand why a lawyer found guilty of stealing funds from a client can continue to handle client funds, why a lawyer found guilty of securities fraud can continue to prepare and certify registration statements, or why a lawyer found guilty of conspiracy to suborn perjury can continue to try cases and present witnesses. Immediate suspension of a lawyer so convicted, regardless of the pendency of any appeal, is essential to preserve public confidence.

* * *

RULE 20. Interim Suspension for Threat of Harm

A. *Transmittal of Evidence.* Upon receipt of sufficient evidence demonstrating that a lawyer subject to the disciplinary jurisdiction of this court has committed a violation of the [state Rules of Professional Conduct] or is under a disability as herein defined and poses a substantial threat of serious harm to the public, disciplinary counsel shall:

(i) transmit the evidence to the court together with a proposed order for interim suspension; and

(ii) contemporaneously make a reasonable attempt to provide the lawyer with notice, which may include notice by telephone, that a proposed order for immediate interim suspension has been transmitted to the court.

B. *Immediate Interim Suspension.* Upon examination of the evidence transmitted to the court by disciplinary counsel and of rebuttal evidence, if any, which the lawyer has transmitted to the court prior to the court's ruling, the court may enter an order immediately suspending the lawyer, pending final disposition of a disciplinary proceeding predicated upon the conduct causing the harm, or may order such other action as it deems appropriate. In the event the order is entered, the court may appoint a trustee pursuant to Rule 28 to protect clients' interests.

C. *Notice to Clients.* A lawyer suspended pursuant to paragraph B shall comply with the notice requirements in Rule 27.

D. *Motion for Dissolution of Interim Suspension.* On [two] days notice to disciplinary counsel, a lawyer suspended pursuant to paragraph B may appear and move for dissolution or modification of the order of suspension, and in that event the motion shall be heard and determined as expeditiously as the ends of justice require.

Commentary

Certain misconduct poses such an immediate threat to the public and the administration of justice that the lawyer should be suspended from the practice of law immediately pending a final determination of the ultimate discipline to be imposed. Interim suspension is also appropriate when the lawyer's continuing conduct is causing or is likely to cause serious injury to a client or the public, as, for example, where a lawyer abandons the practice of law or is engaged in an ongoing conversion of trust funds.

The procedures set forth in Rule 20 are similar to those applicable to civil temporary restraining orders, except that an immediate interim suspension order does not expire automatically, but requires a motion for dissolution or modification. Since immediate interim suspension may be imposed *ex parte* following reasonable efforts to notify the lawyer, a lawyer suspended without a hearing should be afforded an opportunity to seek dissolution or modification of the suspension order on an expedited basis.

RULE 21. Discipline by Consent

A. *Board Approval of Tendered Admission.* A lawyer against whom formal charges have been made may tender to disciplinary counsel a conditional admission to the petition or to a particular count thereof in exchange for a stated form of discipline. The tendered conditional admission shall be approved or rejected by the board [considering the recommendation of the hearing committee if the matter has already been assigned for hearing, and] subject to final approval or rejection by the court if the stated form of discipline includes disbarment, suspension or transfer to disability inactive status pursuant to Rule 11(F). If the stated form of discipline is rejected by the [adjudicative body] [board], the admission shall be withdrawn and cannot be used against the respondent in any subsequent proceedings.

B. *Review of Discipline by Consent.* The extent of discipline to be imposed is subject to review. If an agreement providing for admonition or probation is reached prior to the filing of formal charges, the agreement must be approved by the chair of a hearing committee [board].

C. *Discontinuance of Jurisdiction.* Approval of the discipline proposed by the board and, if required, by the court, shall divest the hearing committee of further jurisdiction and no report need be prepared in such cases. The final order of discipline shall be predicated upon the petition and the conditional admission tendered.

D. *Affidavit of Consent.* A lawyer who consents to a stated form of discipline shall present to the board an affidavit stating that he or she consents to the discipline and that:

(1) The consent is freely and voluntarily rendered; the lawyer is not being subjected to coercion or duress; the lawyer is fully aware of the implications of submitting the consent;

(2) The lawyer is aware that there is presently pending an investigation into, or proceeding involving, allegations that there exist grounds for discipline, the nature of which shall be specifically set forth;

(3) The lawyer acknowledges that the material facts so alleged are true; and

(4) The lawyer consents because the lawyer knows that if charges predicated upon the matters under investigation were filed, or if the pending proceeding were prosecuted, the lawyer could not successfully defend against them.

E. *Order of Discipline.* The board shall file the affidavit with the court. If the discipline by consent is a reprimand, the board shall enter the order. In all other instances in which proposed discipline has been approved the court shall enter the order disciplining the lawyer on consent. Whether the sanction is made public shall be governed by Rule 10(D).

Commentary

If an agreement provides for reprimand, suspension or disbarment, or if any agreement is reached after formal charges have been filed, the agreement must be approved by a panel of the board. Members of the panel are disqualified from any future consideration of the matter in the event the stipulated discipline is for any reason not imposed. If the stipulated discipline provides for suspension or disbarment, it must also be approved by the court.

Acceptance of stipulated discipline by a lawyer who has been guilty of misconduct and desires to avoid the trauma and expense of a proceeding is in the interest of the public and the agency. The public is immediately protected from further misconduct by the lawyer, who otherwise might continue to practice until a formal proceeding is concluded. The agency is relieved of the time-consuming and expensive necessity of prosecuting a formal proceeding.

The respondent should be required to admit the charges before discipline is stipulated, so that evidence of guilt will be available if the respondent later claims that he or she was not, in fact, guilty. Petitions for reinstatement are often filed years after discipline has been imposed, and if there is no admission it may be difficult for the agency to establish the misconduct because relevant evidence and witnesses may no longer be available.

Discipline by consent which results in the lawyer withdrawing from the practice of law should be recorded and treated as disbarment, not as resignation. An agreement made when the charges are before the board shall be reviewed by the court. In the event that proposed stipulated discipline is disapproved by the reviewing entity, or the matter is returned to formal proceedings for any reason, the respondent's admission of the charges cannot be used against the respondent.

RULE 22.   Reciprocal Discipline

A. *Disciplinary Counsel Duty to Obtain Order of Discipline or Disability Inactive Status From Other Jurisdiction.* Upon being disciplined or transferred to disability inactive status in another jurisdiction, a lawyer admitted to practice in [name of state] shall promptly inform disciplinary counsel of the discipline or transfer. Upon notification from any source that a lawyer within the jurisdiction of the agency has been disciplined or transferred to disability inactive status in another jurisdiction, disciplinary counsel shall obtain a certified copy of the order and file it with the board and with the court.

B. *Notice Served Upon Respondent.* Upon receipt of a certified copy of an order demonstrating that a lawyer admitted to practice in [name of state] has been disciplined or transferred to disability inactive status in another jurisdiction, the court shall forthwith issue a notice directed to the lawyer and to disciplinary counsel containing:

(1) A copy of the order from the other jurisdiction; and

(2) An order directing that the lawyer or disciplinary counsel inform the court, within [thirty] days from service of the notice, of any claim by the lawyer or disciplinary counsel predicated upon the grounds set forth in paragraph D, that the imposition of the identi-

cal discipline or disability inactive status in this state would be unwarranted and the reasons for that claim.

C. *Effect of Stay in Other Jurisdiction.* In the event the discipline or transfer imposed in the other jurisdiction has been stayed there, any reciprocal discipline or transfer imposed in this state shall be deferred until the stay expires.

D. *Discipline to Be Imposed.* Upon the expiration of [thirty] days from service of the notice pursuant to the provisions of paragraph B, this court shall impose the identical discipline or disability inactive status unless disciplinary counsel or the lawyer demonstrates, or this court finds that it clearly appears upon the face of the record from which the discipline is predicated, that:

(1) The procedure was so lacking in notice or opportunity to be heard as to constitute a deprivation of due process; or

(2) There was such infirmity of proof establishing the misconduct as to give rise to the clear conviction that the court could not, consistent with its duty, accept as final the conclusion on that subject; or

(3) The imposition of the same discipline by the court would result in grave injustice; or

(4) The misconduct established warrants substantially different discipline in this state.

(5) The reason for the original transfer to disability inactive status no longer exists.

If this court determines that any of those elements exists, this court shall enter such other order as it deems appropriate. The burden is on the party seeking different discipline in this jurisdiction to demonstrate that the imposition of the same discipline is not appropriate.

E. *Conclusiveness of Adjudication in Other Jurisdictions.* In all other aspects, a final adjudication in another jurisdiction that a lawyer has been guilty of misconduct or should be transferred to disability status shall establish conclusively the misconduct or the disability for purposes of a disciplinary or disability proceeding in this state.

Commentary

If a lawyer suspended or disbarred in one jurisdiction is also admitted in another jurisdiction and no action can be taken against the lawyer until a new disciplinary proceeding is instituted, tried, and concluded, the public in the second jurisdiction is left unprotected against a lawyer who has been judicially determined to be unfit. Any procedure which so exposes innocent clients to harm cannot be justified. The spectacle of a lawyer disbarred in one jurisdiction yet permitted to practice elsewhere exposes the profession to criticism and undermines public confidence in the administration of justice.

Disciplinary counsel in the forum jurisdiction should be notified by disciplinary counsel of the jurisdiction where the original discipline or disability inactive status was imposed. Upon receipt of such information, disciplinary counsel should promptly obtain and serve upon the lawyer an order to show cause why identical discipline or disability inactive status should not be imposed in the forum state. The certified copy of the order in the original jurisdiction should be incorporated into the order to show cause.

The imposition of discipline or disability inactive status in one jurisdiction does not mean that every other jurisdiction in which the lawyer is admitted must necessarily impose discipline or disability inactive status. The agency has jurisdiction to recommend reciprocal discipline or disability inactive status on the basis of public discipline or disability inactive status imposed by a state in which the respondent is licensed.

A judicial determination of misconduct or disability by the respondent in another jurisdiction is conclusive, and not subject to relitigation in the forum state. The court should impose identical discipline or disability inactive status unless it determines, after review limited to the record of the proceedings in the foreign jurisdiction, that one of the grounds specified in paragraph D exists.

RULE 23. Proceedings in Which Lawyer Is Declared to Be Incompetent or Alleged to Be Incapacitated

A. *Involuntary Commitment or Adjudication of Incompetency.* If a lawyer has been judicially declared incompetent or is involuntarily committed on the grounds of incompetency or disability, the court, upon proper proof of the fact, shall enter an order immediately transferring the lawyer to disability inactive status for an indefinite period until the further order of the court. A copy of the order shall be served, in the manner the court may direct, upon the lawyer, his or her guardian, or the director of the institution to which the lawyer has been committed.

B. *Inability to Properly Defend.* If a respondent alleges in the course of a disciplinary proceeding an inability to assist in the defense due to mental or physical incapacity, the court shall immediately transfer the lawyer to disability inactive status pending determination of the incapacity.

(1) If the court determines the claim of inability to defend is valid, the disciplinary proceeding shall be deferred and the respondent retained on disability inactive status until the court subsequently considers a petition for transfer of the respondent to active status. If the court considering the petition for transfer to active status determines the petition shall be granted, the court shall also determine the disposition of the interrupted disciplinary proceedings.

(2) If the court determines the claim of incapacity to defend to be invalid, the disciplinary proceeding shall resume and the respondent shall immediately be placed on interim suspension pending the final disposition of the matter.

C. *Proceedings to Determine Incapacity.* Information relating to a lawyer's physical or mental condition which adversely affects the lawyer's ability to practice law shall be investigated, and where warranted, shall be the subject of formal proceedings to determine whether the lawyer shall be transferred to disability inactive status. The hearings shall be conducted in the same manner as disciplinary proceedings, except that all of the proceedings shall be confidential. The court shall provide for such notice to the respondent of proceedings in the matter as it deems proper and advisable and may appoint a lawyer to represent the respondent if the respondent is without adequate representation. The court may take or direct whatever action it deems necessary or proper to determine whether the respondent is so incapacitated, including the examination of the respondent by qualified medical experts designated by the court. If, upon due consideration of the matter, the court concludes that the respondent is incapacitated from continuing to practice law, it shall enter an order transferring the respondent to disability inactive status for an indefinite period and until the further order of the court. Any pending disciplinary proceedings against the respondent shall be held in abeyance.

D. *Public Notice of Transfer to Disability Inactive Status.* The board shall cause a notice of transfer to disability inactive status to be published in the journal of the state bar and in a newspaper of general circulation in each judicial district in which the lawyer maintained an office for the practice of law.

E. *Reinstatement From Disability Inactive Status.*

(1) Generally. No respondent transferred to disability inactive status may resume active status except by order of this court.

(2) Petition. Any respondent transferred to disability inactive status shall be entitled to petition for transfer to active status once a year, or at whatever shorter intervals the court may direct in the order transferring the respondent to disability inactive status or any modifications thereof.

(3) Examination. Upon the filing of a petition for transfer to active status, the court may take or direct whatever action it deems necessary or proper to determine whether the disability has been removed, including a direction for an examination of the respondent by qualified medical experts designated by the court. In its discretion, the court may direct that the expense of the examination be paid by the respondent.

(4) Waiver of Doctor–Patient Privilege. With the filing of a petition for reinstatement to active status, the respondent shall be

required to disclose the name of each psychiatrist, psychologist, physician and hospital or other institution by whom or in which the respondent has been examined or treated since the transfer to disability inactive status. The respondent shall furnish to this court written consent to the release of information and records relating to the disability if requested by the court or court-appointed medical experts.

(5) Learning in Law; Bar Examination. The court may also direct that the respondent establish proof of competence and learning in law, which proof may include certification by the bar examiners of successful completion of an examination for admission to practice.

(6) Granting Petition for Transfer to Active Status. The court shall grant the petition for transfer to active status upon a showing by clear and convincing evidence that the disability has been removed.

(7) Judicial Declaration of Competence. If a respondent transferred to disability inactive status on the basis of a judicial determination of incompetence has been judicially declared to be competent, the court may dispense with further evidence that his disability has been removed and may immediately direct his reinstatement to active status upon terms as are deemed proper and advisable.

Commentary

Since the principal responsibility of the agency is to protect the public, it must concern itself with disabled lawyers who endanger the interests of clients, even if no misconduct has been committed. It is important that incapacity not be treated as misconduct, and to clearly distinguish willful conduct from conduct beyond the control of the lawyer.

* * *

RULE 24. Reinstatement Following a Suspension of Six Months or Less

A lawyer who has been suspended for six months or less pursuant to disciplinary proceedings shall be reinstated at the end of the period of suspension by filing with the court and serving upon disciplinary counsel an affidavit stating that he or she has fully complied with the requirements of the suspension order and has paid any required fees and costs.

Commentary

Reinstatement proceedings may take months to complete. Requiring a proceeding before a lawyer can be reinstated after a suspension of six months or less would unfairly prolong the period of suspension.

Consequently, reinstatement following a suspension for six months or less should be automatic upon the expiration of the prescribed period of time, a filing of an affidavit alleging compliance with the terms of the order of suspension and the payment of fees and costs.

RULE 25. Reinstatement After Suspension for More Than Six Months and Readmission

A. *Generally.* A lawyer suspended for more than six months or a disbarred lawyer shall be reinstated or readmitted only upon order of the court. No lawyer may petition for reinstatement until [six months before] the period of suspension has expired. No lawyer may petition for readmission until [five] years after the effective date of disbarment. A lawyer who has been placed on interim suspension and is then disbarred for the same misconduct that was the ground for the interim suspension may petition for readmission at the expiration of [five] years from the time of the effective date of the interim suspension.

B. *Petition.* A petition for reinstatement or readmission must be under oath or affirmation under penalty of perjury and shall specify with particularity the manner in which the lawyer meets each of the criteria specified in paragraph E or, if not, why there is good and sufficient reason for reinstatement or readmission. [Unless abated under Rule 26] the petition must be accompanied by an advance cost deposit in the amount set from time to time by the board to cover anticipated costs of the proceeding.

C. *Service of Petition.* The lawyer shall file a copy of the petition with disciplinary counsel and disciplinary counsel shall serve a copy of the petition upon each complainant in the disciplinary proceeding that led to the suspension or disbarment.

D. *Publication of Notice of Petition.* At the same time that a lawyer files a petition for reinstatement or readmission, the lawyer shall also publish a notice of the petition in the journal of the state bar and in a newspaper of general circulation in each judicial district in which the lawyer maintained an office for the practice of law when the lawyer was suspended or disbarred. The notice shall inform members of the bar and the public about the application for reinstatement or readmission, and shall request that any individuals file notice of their opposition or concurrence with the board within [sixty] days. In addition, the lawyer shall notify the complainant(s) in the disciplinary proceeding that led to the lawyer's suspension or disbarment that the lawyer is applying for reinstatement or readmission, and shall inform each complainant that he or she has [sixty] days to raise objections to or to support the lawyer's petition.

E. *Criteria for Reinstatement and Readmission.* A lawyer may be reinstated or readmitted only if the lawyer meets each of the following criteria, or, if not, presents good and sufficient reason why the lawyer should nevertheless be reinstated or readmitted:

(1) The lawyer has fully complied with the terms and conditions of all prior disciplinary orders except to the extent that they are abated under Rule 26.

(2) The lawyer has not engaged nor attempted to engage in the unauthorized practice of law during the period of suspension or disbarment.

(3) If the lawyer was suffering under a physical or mental disability or infirmity at the time of suspension or disbarment, including alcohol or other drug abuse, the disability or infirmity has been removed. Where alcohol or other drug abuse was a causative factor in the lawyer's misconduct, the lawyer shall not be reinstated or readmitted unless:

> (a) the lawyer has pursued appropriate rehabilitative treatment;

> (b) the lawyer has abstained from the use of alcohol or other drugs for at least [one year]; and

> (c) the lawyer is likely to continue to abstain from alcohol or other drugs.

(4) The lawyer recognizes the wrongfulness and seriousness of the misconduct for which the lawyer was suspended or disbarred.

(5) The lawyer has not engaged in any other professional misconduct since suspension or disbarment.

(6) Notwithstanding the conduct for which the lawyer was disciplined, the lawyer has the requisite honesty and integrity to practice law.

(7) The lawyer has kept informed about recent developments in the law and is competent to practice.

(8) In addition, a lawyer who has been disbarred must pass the bar examination and the character and fitness examination.

F. *Review of Petition.* Within [ninety] days after receiving a lawyer's petition for reinstatement or readmission, disciplinary counsel shall either: (1) advise the lawyer and the [board] court that disciplinary counsel will stipulate to the lawyer's reinstatement or readmission, or (2) advise the lawyer and the [board] court that disciplinary counsel opposes reinstatement or readmission and request the [board] court to set a hearing.

G. *Hearing; Report.* Upon receipt of disciplinary counsel's request for a hearing, the [board] court shall promptly refer the matter to a hearing committee. Within [ninety] days of the request, the hearing committee shall conduct a hearing at which the lawyer shall have the burden of demonstrating by clear and convincing evidence that he or she has met each of the criteria in paragraph E or, if not, that there is good and sufficient reason why the lawyer should nevertheless be reinstated or readmitted. The hearing committee shall file a report with the [board] court containing its findings and recommendations. [The board shall promptly review the report of the hearing committee and the record and shall file its own findings and recommendations with the court.]

H. *Decision as to Reinstatement or Readmission.* The court shall review the report filed by the [hearing committee] [board] or any stipulation agreed to by the lawyer and disciplinary counsel. If the court finds that the lawyer has complied with each of the criteria of paragraph E, or has presented good and sufficient reason for failure to comply, the court shall reinstate or readmit the lawyer. If the court reinstates or readmits the lawyer, the court shall issue a written opinion setting forth the grounds for its decision; if the court denies reinstatement or readmission, the court shall issue a written opinion setting forth the ground for its decision and shall identify the period after which the lawyer may reapply. Generally, no lawyer should be permitted to reapply for reinstatement or readmission within one year following an adverse judgment upon a petition for reinstatement or readmission.

I. *Conditions of Reinstatement or Readmission.* The court may impose conditions on a lawyer's reinstatement or readmission. The conditions shall be imposed in cases where the lawyer has met the burden of proof justifying reinstatement or readmission, but the court reasonably believes that further precautions should be taken to insure that the public will be protected upon the lawyer's return to practice.

The court may impose any conditions that are reasonably related to the grounds for the lawyer's original suspension or disbarment, or to evidence presented at the hearing regarding the lawyer's failure to meet the criteria for reinstatement or readmission. Passing the bar examination and the character and fitness examination shall be conditions to readmission following disbarment. The conditions may also include any of the following: limitation upon practice (to one area of law or through association with an experienced supervising lawyer); participation in continuing legal education courses; monitoring of the lawyer's practice (for compliance with trust account rules, accounting procedures, or office management procedures); abstention from the use of drugs or alcohol; active participation in Alcoholics Anonymous or other alcohol or drug rehabilitation program; monitoring of the lawyer's compliance with any other orders (such as abstinence from alcohol or drugs, or participation in alcohol or drug rehabilitation programs). If the monitoring lawyer determines that the reinstated or readmitted lawyer's compliance with any condition of reinstatement or readmission is unsatisfactory and that there exists a potential for harm to the public, the monitoring lawyer shall notify the court and, where necessary to protect the public, the lawyer may be suspended from practice under Rule 20(B).

J. *Reciprocal Reinstatement or Readmission.* Where the court has imposed a suspension or disbarment solely on the basis of imposition of discipline in another jurisdiction, and where the lawyer gives notice to the court that he or she has been reinstated or readmitted in the other jurisdiction, the court shall determine whether the lawyer should be reinstated or readmitted. Unless disciplinary counsel presents evidence demonstrating procedural irregularities in the other jurisdiction's proceeding or presents other compelling reasons, the court shall reinstate or readmit a lawyer who has been reinstated or readmitted in the jurisdiction where the misconduct occurred.

Commentary

Readmission occurs when a disbarred lawyer is returned to practice. Since the purpose of lawyer discipline is not to punish, readmission may be appropriate; the presumption, though, should be against readmission. In no event should a lawyer be considered for readmission until at least five years after the effective date of disbarment.

Reinstatement occurs when a suspended lawyer is returned to practice. Reinstatement is appropriate when a lawyer shows rehabilitation. Application for reinstatement should be permitted at the expiration of the ordered period of suspension. While reinstatement should not be ordered prior to the expiration of the ordered period of suspension, application for reinstatement may be allowed up to six months preceding the expiration so that the time required for a decision on the application does not unfairly prolong the suspension.

As a condition of readmission or reinstatement, a disbarred or suspended lawyer is usually required to establish rehabilitation, fitness to practice and competence, and may be required to pay the costs of the disciplinary proceedings, to make restitution, to disgorge all or part to the lawyer's or law firm's fee, to pass an examination in professional responsibility, and to comply with court orders.

There is a compelling reason not to grant reciprocal reinstatement under paragraph J if the forum jurisdiction imposed a longer suspension than the original jurisdiction or if there was a delay between the imposition of the original discipline and the imposition of the reciprocal discipline.

[RULE 26. Abatement or Modification of Conditions of Discipline, Reinstatement, or Readmission

Where the court has imposed conditions in an order of discipline or in an order of reinstatement or readmission, the lawyer may request of the court an order of abatement discharging the lawyer from the obligation to comply with the conditions, or an order modifying the conditions. The lawyer may so request either prior to or as part of lawyer's petition for reinstatement or readmission. The court may grant the request if the lawyer shows by clear and convincing evidence that the lawyer has made a timely, good faith effort to meet the condition(s) but it is impossible to fulfill the condition(s).]

Commentary

A jurisdiction adopting this Rule should also adopt the bracketed language in Rule 25(B).

RULE 27. Notice to Clients, Adverse Parties, and Other Counsel

A. *Recipients of Notice; Contents.* Within [ten] days after the date of the court order imposing discipline or transfer to disability inactive status, a respondent disbarred, transferred to disability inactive status, placed on interim suspension, or suspended for more than [six months] shall notify or cause to be notified by registered or certified mail, return receipt requested,

(1) all clients being represented in pending matters;

(2) any co-counsel in pending matters; and

(3) any opposing counsel in pending matters, or in the absence of opposing counsel, the adverse parties, of the order of the court and that the lawyer is therefore disqualified to act as lawyer after the effective date of the order.

The notice to be given to the lawyer(s) for an adverse party, or, in the absence of opposing counsel, the adverse parties, shall state the place of residence of the client of the respondent.

B. *Special Notice.* The court may direct the issuance of notice to such financial institutions or others as may be necessary to protect the interests of clients or other members of the public.

C. *Duty to Maintain Records.* The respondent shall keep and maintain records of the steps taken to accomplish the requirements of paragraphs A and B, and shall make those records available to the disciplinary counsel on request.

D. *Return of Client Property.* The respondent shall deliver to all clients being represented in pending matters any papers or other property to which they are entitled and shall notify them and any counsel representing them of a suitable time and place where the papers and other property may be obtained, calling attention to any urgency for obtaining the papers or other property.

E. *Effective Date of Order; Refund of Fees.* Orders imposing disbarment, suspension, or transfers to disability inactive status are effective on a date [15] days after the date of the order except where the court finds that immediate disbarment or suspension is necessary to protect the public. The respondent shall refund within [ten] days after entry of the order any part of any fees paid in advance that has not been earned.

F. *Withdrawal From Representation.* In the event the client does not obtain another lawyer before the effective date of the disbarment or suspension, it shall be the responsibility of the respondent to move in the court or agency in which the proceeding is pending for leave to withdraw. The respondent shall in that event file with the court, agency or tribunal before which the litigation is pending a copy of the notice to opposing counsel or adverse parties.

G. *New Representation Prohibited.* Prior to the effective date of the order, if not immediate, the respondent shall agree not to undertake any new legal matters between service of the order and the effective date of the discipline. Upon the effective date of the order, the respondent shall not maintain a presence or occupy an office where the practice of law is conducted. The respondent shall take such action as is necessary to cause the removal of any indicia of lawyer, counselor at law, legal assistant, law clerk or similar title.

H. *Affidavit Filed With Court.* Within [ten] days after the effective date of the disbarment or suspension order, or order of transfer to disability inactive status, the respondent shall file with this court an affidavit showing:

    (1) Compliance with the provisions of the order and with these rules;

    (2) All other state, federal and administrative jurisdictions to which the lawyer is admitted to practice;

    (3) Residence or other addresses where communications may thereafter be directed; and

    (4) Service of a copy of the affidavit upon disciplinary counsel.

Commentary

These notice provisions are necessary to ensure that the respondent's inability to practice does not prejudice the rights of existing clients or other parties, and that those who might otherwise have occasion to deal with the lawyer are made aware of the lawyer's suspension or disbarment. Compliance with the notice provision is an absolute precondition for reinstatement or readmission, and failure to comply may be grounds for further discipline.

Usually the effective date of discipline or transfer to disability inactive status should be the end of the period during which the final order may be appealed but at least fifteen days, unless the court finds immediate suspension or disbarment is necessary. The interval between the entry of the order and its effective date permits the respondent to wind up his or her practice in an orderly manner. The respondent should not accept new retainers during this period since it is unlikely he or she can adequately represent new clients before the effective date when practice must be discontinued.

RULE 28. **Appointment of Counsel to Protect Clients' Interests When Respondent Is Transferred to Disability Inactive Status, Suspended, Disbarred, Disappears, or Dies**

A. *Inventory of Lawyer Files.* If a respondent has been transferred to disability inactive status, or has disappeared or died, or has been suspended or disbarred and there is evidence that he or she has not complied with Rule 27, and no partner, executor or other responsible party capable of conducting the respondent's affairs is known to exist, the presiding judge in the judicial district in which the respondent maintained a practice, upon proper proof of the fact, shall appoint a lawyer or lawyers to inventory the files of the respondent, and to take such action as seems indicated to protect the interests of the respondent and his or her clients.

B. *Protection for Records Subject to Inventory.* Any lawyer so appointed shall not be permitted to disclose any information contained in any files inventoried without the consent of the client to whom the file relates, except as necessary to carry out the order of the court which appointed the lawyer to make the inventory.

Commentary

In any situation in which the lawyer is not available to protect clients, the agency has an obligation to protect them. When such information comes to the attention of the agency, it need not await the determination that misconduct has occurred before acting.

The cost of the inventory may be paid from the fees owing to the lawyer whose files are inventoried. The cost may also be paid by funds made available for that purpose by state and local bar associations. Often the lawyer appointed as trustee will waive all or part of his or her fee as a public service.

The trustee is appointed to inventory the files of the lawyer's clients, not to represent them. The trustee should review each file and recommend to the judge who appointed him or her a proposed disposition. The trustee may take only such action with respect to each client's file as is authorized by the judge who appointed him or her.

The lawyer-client privilege must be extended so that review of the file by the trustee is not deemed to be disclosure to a third party, which would waive the privilege.

RULE 29. Maintenance of Trust Funds in Approved Financial Institutions; Overdraft Notification

A. *Clearly Identified Trust Accounts in Approved Financial Institutions Required.*

(1) Lawyers who practice law in [name of state] shall deposit all funds held in trust in this jurisdiction [in accordance with Rule 1.15(a) of the Model Rules of Professional Conduct] in accounts clearly identified as "trust" or "escrow" accounts, referred to herein as "trust accounts," and shall take all steps necessary to inform the depository institution of the purpose and identity of the accounts. Funds held in trust include funds held in any fiduciary capacity in connection with a representation, whether as trustee, agent, guardian, executor or otherwise. Lawyer trust accounts shall be main-

tained only in financial institutions approved by the court [the board].

(2) Every lawyer engaged in the practice of law in [name of state] shall maintain and preserve for a period of at least five years, after final disposition of the underlying matter, the records of the accounts, including checkbooks, cancelled checks, check stubs, vouchers, ledgers, journals, closing statements, accountings or other statements of disbursements rendered to clients or other parties with regard to trust funds or similar equivalent records clearly and expressly reflecting the date, amount, source, and explanation for all receipts, withdrawals, deliveries and disbursements of the funds or other property of a client.

B. *Overdraft Notification Agreement Required.* A financial institution shall be approved as a depository for lawyer trust accounts if it files with the court an agreement, in a form provided by the court [board] to report to the disciplinary agency whenever any properly payable instrument is presented against a lawyer trust account containing insufficient funds, irrespective of whether or not the instrument is honored. The court [board] shall establish rules governing approval and termination of approved status for financial institutions, and shall annually publish a list of approved financial institutions. No trust account shall be maintained in any financial institution that does not agree to so report. Any such agreement shall apply to all branches of the financial institution and shall not be cancelled except upon [thirty] days notice in writing to the court [board].

C. *Overdraft Reports.* The overdraft notification agreement shall provide that all reports made by the financial institution shall be in the following format:

(1) In the case of a dishonored instrument, the report shall be identical to the overdraft notice customarily forwarded to the depositor, and should include a copy of the dishonored instrument, if such a copy is normally provided to depositors;

(2) In the case of instruments that are presented against insufficient funds but which instruments are honored, the report shall identify the financial institution, the lawyer or law firm, the account number, the date of presentation for payment, and the date paid, as well as the amount of overdraft created thereby.

D. *Timing of Reports.* Reports under paragraph C shall be made simultaneously with, and within the time provided by law for notice of dishonor, if any. If an instrument presented against insufficient funds is honored, then the report shall be made within [five] banking days of the date of presentation for payment against insufficient funds.

E. *Consent by Lawyers.* Every lawyer practicing or admitted to practice in this jurisdiction shall, as a condition thereof, be conclusively deemed to have consented to the reporting and production requirements mandated by this rule.

F. *Costs.* Nothing herein shall preclude a financial institution from charging a particular lawyer or law firm for the reasonable cost of producing the reports and records required by this rule.

G. *Definitions.* For purposes of this Rule:

(1) "Financial institution" includes a bank, savings and loan association, credit union, savings bank, and any other business or person that accepts for deposit funds held in trust by lawyers.

(2) "Properly payable" refers to an instrument which, if presented in the normal course of business, is in a form requiring payment under the laws of this jurisdiction.

(3) "Notice of dishonor" refers to the notice that a financial institution is required to give, under the laws of this jurisdiction, upon presentation of an instrument that the institution dishonors.

Commentary

Paragraph A sets forth the requirements for deposit of trust funds in clearly identified trust accounts in approved financial institutions. Funds held not in connection with a representation, such as a trust fund for a lawyer's own spouse or minor child, do not fall under the rule. The rule also does not concern a lawyer's own funds properly held in a non-fiduciary capacity, such as funds in a business or personal account.

Under Rule 1.15(a) of the Model Rules of Professional Conduct, trust property may be held outside the lawyer's home jurisdiction upon consent of the client. The overdraft notification rule governs funds held within the adopting state. A lawyer's obligation to deposit trust funds in an approved institution will arise upon adoption of the overdraft notification rule in a state where the lawyer deposits trust funds, whether that state is the state wherein the lawyer's office is situated or some other state.

The overdraft notification agreement requires that all overdrafts be reported, irrespective of whether the instrument is honored. In light of the purposes of Rule 29, and in view of ethical proscriptions concerning the preservation of client funds and commingling of client and lawyer funds, it would be improper for a lawyer to accept overdraft privileges or any other arrangement for a personal loan on a client trust account in exchange for the institution's promise to delay or not to report an overdraft.

Absence of discretion makes notification by a financial institution an administratively simple matter. An institution which receives an instrument for payment against insufficient funds need not evaluate whether circumstances require that notification be given; it merely provides notice. It then becomes the responsibility of the disciplinary agency to determine whether further action is necessary. In cases where an overdraft is a result of an accounting error (caused by either the lawyer or the institution), but notification has already been sent to the state agency, the institution should provide the lawyer with a written explanation (preferably, an affidavit from an officer of the institution) that the lawyer can then submit to the agency to verify the error.

The rule provides the proper format for overdraft reports. In so doing, the rule distinguishes between dishonored instruments and instruments that are presented against insufficient funds but honored. Where instruments are presented against insufficient funds but paid, the rule specifies the information that the institution should provide.

Ordinarily, within 24 hours of dishonor an institution gives notice of an overdraft to a depositor whose account is charged. See Uniform Commercial Code, Section 3–508. This is the same time period in which overdraft notification is given to the state disciplinary agency.

Where an instrument presented against insufficient funds is honored, the financial institution should send overdraft notification to the agency within five days of the date of presentation.

Upon receipt of an overdraft notification, Rule 29 contemplates that the state agency will contact the lawyer or firm by telephone and request an explanation for the overdraft. A letter requesting a documented explanation may also be sent. If the overdraft is an accounting error, the lawyer or firm submits a written explanation, including any documents to substantiate the claim. Where the lawyer or firm cannot supply an adequate or complete explanation for the overdraft, other action may be generated, including an audit or a demand for production of the lawyer's books and records.

The rule establishes that consent to the reporting and production requirements mandated by the rule is a condition of the privilege to practice law in a jurisdiction that has adopted the rule. This condition is intended to protect financial institutions from claims by lawyer-depositors based on disclosures made by financial institutions, provided that the disclosures are in accordance with the rule. Parties to an overdraft notification agreement are the court and a financial institution. The consent provision in the rule avoids the necessity for financial institutions to draft separate agreements with lawyers to establish consent to overdraft notification.

In addition to normal monthly maintenance fees on each account, a lawyer or firm can anticipate additional fees to be charged by the financial institutions for reporting overdrafts in accordance with this rule. However, because financial institutions already flag overdrafts and returned checks, it appears only slightly more burdensome for the institution to forward a copy to the local disciplinary agency. As a result, the additional cost to the lawyer should not be exorbitant.

Paragraph F should not be interpreted to allow a lawyer to permit trust account funds to be reduced through deductions made by a financial institution to cover costs of overdraft notification. Such costs should not be borne by clients.

Under the laws of most jurisdictions, the definition of "properly payable" will be contained in section 4–104 of the Uniform Commercial Code.

Under the laws of most jurisdictions, the definition of "notice of dishonor" will be determined by reference to section 3–508 of the Uniform Commercial Code, under which notice must be given by a bank before its midnight deadline and by any other person or institution before midnight on the third business day after dishonor or receipt of notice of dishonor.

RULE 30. Verification of Bank Accounts

A. *Generally.* Whenever disciplinary counsel has probable cause to believe that bank accounts of a lawyer that contain, should contain or have contained funds belonging to clients have not been properly maintained or that the funds have not been properly handled, disciplinary counsel shall request the approval of the chair of a hearing committee selected in order from the roster established by the board to initiate an investigation for the purpose of verifying the accuracy and integrity of all bank accounts maintained by the lawyer. If the reviewing member approves, counsel shall proceed to verify the accuracy of the bank accounts. If the reviewing member denies approval, counsel may submit the request for approval to one other chair of a hearing committee selected in order from the roster established by the board.

B. *Confidentiality.* Investigations, examinations, and verifications shall be conducted so as to preserve the private and confidential nature of the lawyer's records insofar as is consistent with these rules and the lawyer-client privilege.

Commentary

Evidence that one account of a lawyer has not been properly maintained or that funds of one client have not been properly handled should constitute cause for verifying the accuracy of all accounts containing the funds of any client maintained by the lawyer.

Examples of cause warranting audit include a check drawn on a client trust account returned for insufficient funds, failure to timely distribute funds to a client, or failure to file a certificate of compliance with the jurisdiction's audit rule.

RULE 31. Appeal by Complainant

A. *From Disposition by Central Intake Office.* A complainant who is not satisfied with the disposition of a matter by the central intake office may appeal, within [thirty] days of receipt of notice pursuant to Rule 1(B)(5), to a hearing committee chair, who may approve, modify or disapprove the dismissal, or direct that the matter be investigated by disciplinary counsel.

B. *From Disposition by Central Intake Office.* Except in matters involving lesser misconduct, which are governed by Rule 18(H)(3) and (4),[68] the determination of the board may be the subject of a petition for leave to appeal to the court, but leave shall not be granted unless the complainant shows that the board acted arbitrarily, capriciously, or unreasonably.

Commentary

It is very important that the disciplinary system be structured not only to actually protect the public, but also to inspire confidence in the public that the profession is acting to regulate itself. Thus it is important that complainants have the right to appeal a dismissal of their complaints.

It is important that complainants feel they have had their day in court on the basis for their complaint. Disciplinary hearings are neither civil nor criminal but *sui generis.* It is incorrect to assume that, as in a criminal proceeding, the complainant has no rights in regard to case disposition. It is also incorrect to assume that, as in a civil proceeding, a complainant has full participation in the litigation.

Without a limited right of appeal, complainants may feel that their grievances were not given sufficient consideration by the disciplinary system as a whole. Public sentiments of "lawyers protecting their own" can stem from this misunderstanding.

* * *

RULE 32.   Statute of Limitations

Proceedings under these rules shall be exempt from all statutes of limitations.

Commentary

Statutes of limitation are wholly inappropriate in lawyer disciplinary proceedings. Conduct of a lawyer, no matter when it has occurred, is always relevant to the question of fitness to practice. The time between the commission of the alleged misconduct and the filing of a complaint predicated thereon may be pertinent to whether and to what extent discipline should be imposed, but should not limit the agency's power to investigate. An unreasonable delay in the presentation of a charge of misconduct might make it impossible for an attorney to procure witnesses or the testimony available at an earlier time to meet such a charge.

Discipline and disability proceedings serve to protect the public from lawyers who are unfit to practice; they measure the lawyer's qualifications in light of certain conduct, rather than punish for specific trans-

68. Rec. 8.

gressions. Misconduct by a lawyer whenever it occurs reflects upon the lawyer's fitness.

EFFECTIVE DATE

These rules shall become effective on [*date*], and any discipline or disability investigation pending on that date shall be transferred to the board. Any matter then pending with respect to which a formal hearing has been commenced shall be concluded under the procedure existing prior to the effective date of these rules.

RULE 33. Failure to Answer/Failure to Appear

A. *Failure to Answer.* Failure to answer charges filed shall constitute an admission of the factual allegations.

B. *Failure to Appear.* If respondent should fail to appear when specifically so ordered by the committee or the board, the respondent shall have been deemed to have admitted the factual allegations which were to be the subject of such appearance and/or a concession to any motion or recommendations to be considered at such appearance. The committee or board shall not, absent good cause, continue or delay proceedings due to the respondent's failure to appear.

Commentary

This rule provides remedies for a lawyer's disregard of the duty to respond to a lawful demand for information from a disciplinary authority. Failure by respondents to answer or to appear in disciplinary matters is a significant problem. Rule 9(A)(3) applies if the court finds that the respondent has failed to answer or to appear.

Rule 18(B) provides that the rules of civil procedure apply unless otherwise provided; Rule 11(D)(3) provides that the respondent shall answer within [twenty] days after service of the formal charges unless the time is extended by the hearing committee chair.

RULE 34. Counsel for Indigent Respondent

Upon receipt of satisfactory proof of a respondent's indigency, the board may request a lawyer to serve as counsel for the respondent upon such terms and subject to such provisions as justice and equity may require. The respondent shall file with the board an affidavit demonstrating financial inability to retain counsel. The board's determination of indigency shall be based upon its review of the financial circumstances of the respondent. The board shall not consider a request for counsel if the respondent refuses to furnish proof of indigency.

Commentary

Upon satisfactory demonstration of a respondent's indigency, the board may request that a lawyer represent the respondent. While no simple formula can be devised for determining eligibility for representation by counsel based on indigency, the board should consider such factors as the respondent's income, fixed monthly expenditures, assets, fixed liabilities, borrowing capacity, and good faith efforts to secure representation.

The board may reserve the right to approve the rate of compensation for counsel who represents an indigent respondent. In any event, the fee for services rendered shall be supported by documentation of the time spent on the matter.

APPENDIX

A system in which inquiry officers, rather than hearing committees, are used may be established by adoption of the following two alternative provisions in place of Rules 2(G)(4), 2(G)(5), and 3:

AS AN ALTERNATIVE TO RULES 2(G)(4) AND (5), THE FOLLOWING SUBPARAGRAPH MAY BE ADOPTED:

(4) To conduct hearings into formal charges of misconduct, petitions for reinstatement, and petitions for transfer to and from disability inactive status, and prepare and forward to the court its own findings, if any, and recommendations together with the record of the hearing;

AS AN ALTERNATIVE TO RULE 3, THE FOLLOWING MAY BE ADOPTED: RULE 3. INQUIRY OFFICERS.

A. *Appointment.* The board shall appoint three or more inquiry officers [within each disciplinary district].

B. *Terms of Office.* All terms shall be three years and no inquiry officer shall serve for more than two consecutive three-year terms. An inquiry officer who has served two consecutive three-year terms may not be reappointed before the expiration of at least one year.

C. *Powers and Duties.* Inquiry officers shall review recommendations of counsel following investigation for disposition of disciplinary matters and petitions for transfer to and from disability inactive status.

AMERICAN BAR ASSOCIATION STANDARDS FOR IMPOSING LAWYER SANCTIONS

[In 1970, an ABA Report chaired by former Supreme Court Justice Tom Clark recognized that lawyers and judges needed standards for the enforcement of professional discipline. This report prompted the ABA to create a special commission to draft Standards for Lawyer Discipline and Disability Proceedings (1979). These standards, however, did not provide much guidance on the particular sanction that should be imposed upon a lawyer in a disciplinary proceeding. In 1980, the ABA commissioned another committee to study lawyer sanctions and to draft guidelines for imposing sanctions so that variations in punishment for the same offenses could be avoided. This committee studied all published disciplinary cases between 1980 and 1984 and developed Standards for Imposing Lawyer Sanctions. The ABA adopted these standards in 1986. They were amended in 1992. Ed.]

CONTENTS

C. Factors to Be Considered in Imposing Sanctions.
    4.0 Violations of Duties Owed to Clients.
        4.1 Failure to Preserve the Client's Property.
        4.2 Failure to Preserve the Client's Confidences.
        4.3 Failure to Avoid Conflicts of Interest.
        4.4 Lack of Diligence.
        4.5 Lack of Competence.
        4.6 Lack of Candor.
    5.0 Violations of Duties Owed to the Public.
        5.1 Failure to Maintain Personal Integrity.
        5.2 Failure to Maintain the Public Trust.
    6.0 Violations of Duties Owed to the Legal System.
        6.1 False Statements, Fraud, and Misrepresentation.
        6.2 Abuse of the Legal Process.
        6.3 Improper Communications With Individuals in the Legal System.
    7.0 Violations of Duties Owed to the Profession.
    8.0 Prior Discipline Orders.
    9.0 Aggravation and Mitigation.
        9.1 Generally.
        9.2 Aggravation.
        9.3 Mitigation.
        9.4 Factors Which Are Neither Aggravating Nor Mitigating.

Appendices
1. Cross-Reference Table: ABA Model Rules of Professional Conduct and Standards for Imposing Sanctions.
2. Cross-Reference Table: ABA Code of Professional Responsibility and Standards for Imposing Sanctions.
3. Frequency Statistics.

I. PREFACE

A. BACKGROUND

In 1979, the American Bar Association published the Standards for Lawyer Discipline and Disability Proceedings.[1] That book was a result of work by the Joint Committee on Professional Discipline of the American Bar Association. The Joint Committee was composed of members of the Judicial Administration Division and the Standing Committee on Professional Discipline of the American Bar Association. The task of the Joint Committee was to prepare standards for enforcement of discipline in the legal community.

The 1979 standards have been most helpful, and have been used by numerous jurisdictions as a frame of reference against which to compare their own disciplinary systems. Many jurisdictions have modified their procedures to comport with these suggested standards, and the Standing

---

1. Standards for Lawyer Discipline and Disability Proceedings (Chicago: Joint Committee of Professional Discipline of the Appellate Judges' Conference and the American Bar Association Standing Committee on Professional Discipline, 1979).

Committee on Professional Discipline of the American Bar Association has assisted state disciplinary systems in evaluating their programs in light of the approved standards.

It became evident that additional analysis was necessary in one important area—that of *appropriate sanctions* for lawyer misconduct. The American Bar Association Standards for Lawyer Discipline and Disability Proceedings (hereinafter "Standards for Lawyer Discipline") do not attempt to recommend the type of discipline to be imposed in any particular case. The Standards merely state that the discipline to be imposed "should depend upon the facts and circumstances of the case, should be fashioned in light of the purpose of lawyer discipline, and may take into account aggravating or mitigating circumstances" (Standard 7.1).

For lawyer discipline to be truly effective, sanctions must be based on clearly developed standards. Inappropriate sanctions can undermine the goals of lawyer discipline: sanctions which are too lenient fail to adequately deter misconduct and thus lower public confidence in the profession; sanctions which are too onerous may impair confidence in the system and deter lawyers from reporting ethical violations on the part of other lawyers. Inconsistent sanctions, either within a jurisdiction or among jurisdictions, cast doubt on the efficiency and the basic fairness of all disciplinary systems.

As an example of this problem of inconsistent sanctions, consider the range in levels of sanctions imposed for a conviction for failure to file federal income taxes. In one jurisdiction, in 1979, a lawyer who failed to file income tax returns for one year was suspended for one year,[2] while, in 1980, a lawyer who failed to file income tax returns for two years was merely censured.[3] Within a two-year period, the sanctions imposed on lawyers who converted their clients' funds included disbarment,[4] suspension,[5] and censure.[6] The inconsistency of sanctions imposed by different jurisdictions for the same misconduct is even greater.

An examination of these cases illustrates the need for a comprehensive system of sanctions. In many cases, different sanctions are imposed for the same acts of misconduct, and the courts rarely provide any explanation for the selection of sanctions. In other cases, the courts may give reasons for their decisions, but their statements are too general to be useful. In still other cases, the courts may list specific factors to support a certain result, but they do not state whether these factors *must* be considered in every discipline case, nor do they explain whether these factors are entitled to equal weight.

2. *In re* Gold, 77 Ill.2d 224, 396 N.E.2d 25 (1979).

3. *In re* Oliver, M.R. 2454, 79–CH–6 (1980).

4. *In re* Smith, 63 Ill.2d 250, 347 N.E.2d 133 (1976).

5. *In re* DiBella, 58 Ill.2d 5, 316 N.E.2d 771 (1974).

6. *In re* Sherman, 60 Ill.2d 590, 328 N.E.2d 553 (1975).

The Joint Committee on Professional Sanctions (hereinafter "Sanctions Committee") was formed to address these problems by formulating standards to be used in imposing sanctions for lawyer misconduct. The Sanctions Committee was composed of members from the Judicial Administration Division and the Standing Committee on Professional Discipline. The mandate given was ambitious: the Committee was to examine the current range of sanctions imposed and to formulate standards for the imposition of appropriate sanctions.

In addressing this task, the Sanctions Committee recognized that any proposed standards should serve as a *model* which sets forth a comprehensive system of sanctions, but which leaves room for flexibility and creativity in assigning sanctions in particular cases of lawyer misconduct. These standards are designed to promote thorough, rational consideration of all factors relevant to imposing a sanction in an individual case. The standards attempt to ensure that such factors are given appropriate weight in light of the stated goals of lawyer discipline, and that only relevant aggravating and mitigating circumstances are considered at the appropriate time. Finally, the standards should help achieve the degree of consistency in the imposition of lawyer discipline necessary for fairness to the public and the bar.

While these standards will improve the operation of lawyer discipline systems, there is an additional factor which, though not the focus of this report, cannot be overlooked. In discussing sanctions for lawyer misconduct, this report assumes that all instances of unethical conduct will be brought to the attention of the disciplinary system. Experience indicates that such is not the case. In 1970, the ABA Special Committee on Evaluation of Disciplinary Enforcement (the Clark Committee), was charged with the responsibility for evaluating the effectiveness of disciplinary enforcement systems. The Clark Committee concluded that one of the most significant problems in lawyer discipline was the reluctance of lawyers and judges to report misconduct.[7] That same problem exists today. It cannot be emphasized strongly enough that lawyers and judges must report unethical conduct to the appropriate disciplinary agency.[8] Failure to render such reports is a disservice to the public and the legal profession.

Judges in particular should be reminded of their obligation to report unethical conduct to the disciplinary agencies. Under the ABA Code of Judicial Conduct, a judge is obligated to "take or initiate appropriate disciplinary measures against a judge or lawyer for unprofessional con-

---

7. Problems and Recommendations in Disciplinary Enforcement (Chicago: American Bar Association, Special Committee on Evaluation of Disciplinary Enforcement, 1970), at 167.

8. Lawyers have a duty to report ethical misconduct of other lawyers under Rule 8.3 of the Model Rules of Professional Conduct (American Bar Association, 1983) and under DR1–103 of the Code of Professional Responsibility (American Bar Association, 1981). Judges have a similar duty under the Code of Judicial Conduct, Canon 3(B)(3) (American Bar Association, 1972).

duct of which the judge may become aware."[9] Frequently, judges take the position that there is no such need and that errant behavior of lawyers can be remedied solely by use of contempt proceedings and other alternative means. It must be emphasized that the goals of lawyer discipline are not properly and fully served if the judge who observes unethical conduct simply deals with it on an *ad hoc* basis. It may be proper and wise for a judge to use contempt powers in order to assure that the court maintains control of the proceeding and punishes a lawyer for abusive or obstreperous conduct in the court's presence. However, the lawyer discipline system is in addition to and serves purposes different from contempt powers and other mechanisms available to the judge. Only if all lawyer misconduct is in fact reported to the appropriate disciplinary agency can the legal profession have confidence that consistent sanctions are imposed for similar misconduct.

Consistency of sanctions depends on reporting of other types as well. The American Bar Association Center for Professional Responsibility has established a "National Discipline Data Bank" which collects statistics on the nature of ethical violations and sanctions imposed in lawyer discipline cases in all jurisdictions. The information available from the data bank is only as good as the reports which reach it. It is vital that the data bank promptly receive complete, accurate and detailed information with regard to all discipline cases.

Finally, the purposes of lawyer sanctions can best be served, and the consistency of those sanctions enhanced, if courts and disciplinary agencies throughout the country articulate the reasons for sanctions imposed. Courts of record that impose lawyer discipline do a valuable service to the legal profession and the public when they issue opinions in lawyer discipline cases that explain the imposition of a specific sanction. The effort of the Sanctions Committee was made easier by the well-reasoned judicial opinions that were available. At the same time, the Sanctions Committee was frustrated by the fact that many jurisdictions do not publish lawyer discipline decisions, and that even published decisions are often summary in nature, failing to articulate the justification for the sanctions imposed.

B. METHODOLOGY

The Standards for Lawyer Sanctions have been developed after an examination of all reported lawyer discipline cases from 1980 to June, 1984, where public discipline was imposed.[10] In addition, eight jurisdic-

---

9. *Id.*, Code of Judicial Conduct.

10. See Appendix 3 for a listing of the actual number of reported cases from each jurisdiction. The differences in the number of reported cases among the jurisdictions is a function not only of the differences in

lawyer populations, but in the operation of the state discipline systems. States differ dramatically in the sophistication of their disciplinary systems; most importantly for this study, states vary in the extent to which disciplinary orders are published. In tions, which represent a variety of disciplinary systems as well as diversity in geography and population size, were examined in depth. In these jurisdictions—Arizona, California, the District of Columbia, Florida, Illinois, New Jersey, North Dakota, and Utah—all published disciplinary cases from January 1974 through June 1984 were analyzed. In each case, data were collected concerning the type of offense, the sanction imposed, the policy considerations identified, and aggravating or mitigating circumstances noted by the court.[11]

These data were examined to identify the patterns that currently exist among courts imposing sanctions and the policy considerations that guide the courts. In general, the courts were consistent in identifying the following policy considerations: protecting the public, ensuring the administration of justice, and maintaining the integrity of the profession. In the words of the California Supreme Court: "The purpose of a disciplinary proceeding is not punitive but to inquire into the fitness of the lawyer to continue in that capacity for the protection of the public, the courts, and the legal profession." [12] However, the courts failed to articulate any theoretical framework for use in imposing sanctions.

In attempting to develop such a framework, the Sanctions Committee considered a number of options. The Committee considered the obvious possibility of identifying each and every type of misconduct in which a lawyer could engage, then suggesting either a recommended sanction or a range of recommended sanctions to deal with that particular misconduct. The Sanctions Committee unanimously rejected that option as being both theoretically simplistic and administratively cumbersome.[13]

those jurisdictions where disciplinary decisions are not published in the regional reporters, summaries in state bar publications or unreported cases (supplied by bar counsel) were examined. (To obtain copies of unreported decisions, contact the ABA Center for Professional Responsibility.) The states in which only reported cases were examined were: Alabama, Alaska, Arkansas, Colorado, Connecticut, Delaware, Georgia, Hawaii, Idaho, Indiana, Iowa, Kansas, Louisiana, Maryland, Minnesota, Mississippi, Missouri, Montana, Nebraska, Nevada, New Jersey, New Mexico, North Carolina, South Dakota, Ohio, Oklahoma, Oregon, Rhode Island, South Carolina, South Dakota, Utah, Vermont, Washington, West Virginia, and Wisconsin. In the following jurisdictions both reported and unreported cases were examined: Arizona, California, District of Columbia, Florida, Illinois, Kentucky, Massachusetts, New York, Pennsylvania, Tennessee, Virginia, and Wyoming. In the following jurisdictions, all data were collected from unreported decisions (supplied by bar counsel or taken from case summaries in bar publications): Maine, Michigan, New Hampshire, and Texas.

11. Because of the difficulty in getting complete factual statements, the report does not include cases which were the result of consent orders, or cases in which reciprocal discipline was imposed.

12. Ballard v. State Bar of California, 35 Cal.3d 274, 673 P.2d 226, 197 Cal.Rptr. 556 (1983).

13. An example of the problems which would be encountered in such an approach will suffice to demonstrate why that approach was rejected. It is improper for a lawyer to neglect a legal matter entrusted to him (Rule 1.3/DR 6–101(A)(3)). Sanctions which are imposed for violations of this ethical rule vary dramatically. Such conduct may be an intentional violation of

The Sanctions Committee next considered an approach that dealt with general categories of lawyer misconduct and applied recommended sanctions to those types of misconduct depending on whether or not—and to what extent—the misconduct resulted from intentional or malicious acts of the lawyer. There is some merit in that approach; certainly, the intentional or unintentional conduct of the lawyer is a relevant factor. Nonetheless, that approach was also abandoned after the Sanctions Committee carefully reviewed the purposes of lawyer sanctions. Solely focusing on the intent of the lawyer is not sufficient, and proposed standards must also consider the damage which the lawyer's misconduct causes to the client, the public, the legal system, and the profession. An approach which looked only at the extent of injury was also rejected as being too narrow.

The Committee adopted a model that looks first at the ethical duty and to whom it is owed, and then at the lawyer's mental state and the amount of injury caused by the lawyer's misconduct. (See Theoretical Framework, p. 5, for a detailed discussion of this approach.) Thus, one will look in vain for a section of this report which recommends a specific sanction for, say, improper contact with opposing parties who are represented by counsel [Rule 4.2/DR 7–104(A)(1)],[14] or for any other specific misconduct. What one will find, however, is an organizational framework that provides recommendations as to the type of sanction that should be imposed based on violations of duties owed to clients, the public, the legal system, and the profession.

To provide support for this approach, the Sanctions Committee has offered as much specific data and guidance as possible from reported cases.[15] Thus, with regard to each category of misconduct, the report provides the following:

— discussion of what types of sanctions have been imposed for similar misconduct in reported cases;

the rule (as where a lawyer takes a client's money never intending to perform the services requested), or it may result from negligence (as where an overworked or inexperienced lawyer does not meet a deadline relating to some aspect of the representation). The Sanctions Committee felt that a listing of sanctions based merely on the type of lawyer misconduct would not adequately differentiate between conduct which has an extremely deleterious effect on the client, the public, the legal system, and the profession, and conduct which has only a minimal effect. In short, the Sanctions Committee concluded that an approach that reviewed each type of misconduct would result in nothing more than a general statement that the individual circumstances of a case dictate the type of sanction which ought to be imposed.

14. Although the House of Delegates of the American Bar Association adopted the Model Rules of Professional Conduct on August 2, 1983, as the ethical standards for the legal profession, references to the Code of Professional Responsibility are included here because most states' ethical standards still follow the Code in both form and substance.

15. While it is not possible to discuss in detail each of the 2,991 cases which have been examined in preparing this report, statistical summaries are available from the American Bar Association Center for Professional Responsibility.

— discussion of policy reasons which are articulated in reported cases to support such sanctions; and,

— finally, a recommendation as to the level of sanction imposed for the given misconduct, absent aggravating or mitigating circumstances.

While it is recognized that any individual case may present aggravating or mitigating factors which would lead to the imposition of a sanction different from that recommended, these standards present a model which can be used initially to categorize misconduct and to identify the appropriate sanction. The decision as to the effect of any aggravating or mitigating factors should come only after this initial determination of the sanction.

The Sanctions Committee also recognized that the imposition of a sanction of suspension or disbarment does not conclude the matter. Typically, disciplined lawyers will request reinstatement or readmission. While this report does not include an in-depth study of reinstatement and readmission cases, a general recommendation concerning standards for reinstatement and readmission appears as Standard 2.10.

II. THEORETICAL FRAMEWORK

These standards are based on an analysis of the nature of the professional relationship. Historically, being a member of a profession has meant that an individual is some type of expert, possessing knowledge of high instrumental value such that the members of the community give the professional the power to make decisions for them. In the legal profession, the community has allowed the profession the right of self-regulation. As stated in the Preamble to the ABA Model Rules of Professional Conduct (hereinafter "Model Rules"), "[t]he legal profession's relative autonomy carries with it special responsibilities of self-government. The profession has a responsibility to assure that its regulations are conceived in the public interest and not in furtherance of parochial or self-interested concerns of the bar."[16]

This view of the professional relationship requires lawyers to observe the ethical requirements that are set out in the Model Rules (or applicable standard in the jurisdiction where the lawyer is licensed). While the Model Rules define the ethical guidelines for lawyers, they do not provide any method for assigning sanctions for ethical violations. The Committee developed a model which requires a court imposing sanctions to answer each of the following questions:

(1) What ethical duty did the lawyer violate? (A duty to a client, the public, the legal system, or the profession?)

(2) What was the lawyer's mental state? (Did the lawyer act intentionally, knowingly, or negligently?)

16. Preamble to Model rules, paragraph 11, *supra* note 8.

(3) What was the extent of the actual or potential injury caused by the lawyer's misconduct? (Was there a serious or potentially serious injury?) and

(4) Are there any aggravating or mitigating circumstances?

In determining the nature of the ethical duty violated, the standards assume that the most important ethical duties are those obligations which a lawyer owes to *clients*. These include:

(a) the duty of *loyalty* which (in the terms of the Model Rules and Code of Professional Responsibility) includes the duties to:
 (i) preserve the property of a client [Rule 1.15/DR9–102],
 (ii) maintain client confidences [Rule 1.6/DR4–101], and
 (iii) avoid conflicts of interest [Rules 1.7 through 1.13, 2.2, 3.7, 5.4(c) and 6.3/DR5–101 through DR5–105, DR9–101];
(b) the duty of *diligence* [Rules 1.2, 1.3, 1.4/DR6–101(A)(3)];
(c) the duty of *competence* [Rule 1.1/DR6–101(A)(1) & (2)]; and
(d) the duty of *candor* [Rule 8.4(c)/DR1–102(A)(4) & DR7–101(A)(3)].

In addition to duties owed to clients, the lawyer also owes duties to the *general public*. Members of the public are entitled to be able to trust lawyers to protect their property, liberty, and their lives. The community expects lawyers to exhibit the highest standards of honesty and integrity, and lawyers have a duty not to engage in conduct involving dishonesty, fraud, or interference with the administration of justice [Rules 8.2, 8.4(b) & (c)/DR1–102(A)(3)(4) & (5), DR8–101 through DR8–103, DR9–101(c)].

Lawyers also owe duties to the *legal system*. Lawyers are officers of the court, and must abide by the rules of substance and procedure which shape the administration of justice. Lawyers must always operate within the bounds of the law, and cannot create or use false evidence, or engage in any other illegal or improper conduct [Rules 3.1 through 3.6, 3.9, 4.1 through 4.4, 8.2, 8.4(d)(e) & (f)/DR7–102 through DR7–110].

Finally, lawyers owe duties to the *legal profession*. Unlike the obligations mentioned above, these duties are not inherent in the relationship between the professional and the community. These duties do not concern the lawyer's basic responsibilities in representing clients, serving as an officer of the court, or maintaining the public trust, but include other duties relating to the profession. These ethical rules concern:

(a) *restrictions on advertising and recommending employment* [Rules 7.1 through 7.5/DR2–101 through 2–104];

(b) *fees* [Rules 1.5, 5.4 and 5.6/DR2–106, DR2–107, and DR3–102];

(c) *assisting unauthorized practice* [Rule 5.5/DR3–101 through DR3–103];

(d) *accepting, declining, or terminating representation* [Rules 1.2, 1.14, 1.16/DR2–110]; and

(e) *maintaining the integrity of the profession* [Rules 8.1 & 8.3/DR1–101 and DR1–103].

The *mental states* used in this model are defined as follows. The most culpable mental state is that of intent, when the lawyer acts with the conscious objective or purpose to accomplish a particular result. The next most culpable mental state is that of knowledge, when the lawyer acts with conscious awareness of the nature or attendant circumstances of his or her conduct both without the conscious objective or purpose to accomplish a particular result. The least culpable mental state is negligence, when a lawyer fails to be aware of a substantial risk that circumstances exist or that a result will follow, which failure is a deviation from the standard of care that a reasonable lawyer would exercise in the situation.

The extent of the *injury* is defined by the type of duty violated and the extent of actual or potential harm. For example, in a conversion case, the injury is determined by examining the extent of the client's actual or potential loss. In a case where a lawyer tampers with a witness, the injury is measured by evaluating the level of interference or potential interference with the legal proceeding. In this model, the standards refer to various levels of injury: "serious injury," "injury," and "little or no injury." A reference to "injury" alone indicates any level of injury greater than "little or no" injury.

As an example of how this model works, consider two cases of conversion of a client's property. After concluding that the lawyers engaged in ethical misconduct, it is necessary to determine what duties were breached. In these cases, each lawyer breached the duty of loyalty owed to clients. To assign a sanction, however, it is necessary to go further, and to examine each lawyer's mental state and the extent of the injuries caused by the lawyers' actions.

In the first case, assume that the client gave the lawyer $100 as an advance against the costs of investigation. The lawyer took the money, deposited it in a personal checking account, and used it for personal expenses. In this case, where the lawyer acted intentionally and the client actually suffered an injury, the most severe sanction—disbarment—would be appropriate.

Contrast this with the case of a second lawyer, whose client delivered $100 to be held in a trust account. The lawyer, in a hurry to get to court, neglected to inform the secretary what to do with these funds and they were erroneously deposited into the lawyer's general office account. When the lawyer needed additional funds he drew against the general account. The lawyer discovered the mistake, and immediately replaced the money. In this case, where there was no actual injury and a potential for only minor injury, and where the lawyer was merely negligent, a less serious sanction should be imposed. The appropriate sanction would be either reprimand or admonition.

In each case, after making the initial determination as to the appropriate sanction, the court would then consider any relevant *aggravating or mitigating factors* (Standard 9). For example, the presence of aggravating factors, such as vulnerability of the victim or refusal to comply with an order to appear before the disciplinary agency, could increase the appropriate sanction. The presence of mitigating factors, such as absence of prior discipline or inexperience in the practice of law, could make a lesser sanction appropriate.

While there may be particular cases of lawyer misconduct that are not easily categorized, the standards are not designed to propose a specific sanction for each of the myriad of fact patterns in cases of lawyer misconduct. Rather, the standards provide a theoretical framework to guide the courts in imposing sanctions. The ultimate sanction imposed will depend on the presence of any aggravating or mitigating factors in that particular situation. The standards thus are not analogous to criminal determinate sentences, but are guidelines which give courts the flexibility to select the appropriate sanction in each particular case of lawyer misconduct.

The standards do not account for multiple charges of misconduct. The ultimate sanction imposed should at least be consistent with the sanction for the most serious instance of misconduct among a number of violations; it might well be and generally should be greater than the sanction for the most serious misconduct. Either a pattern of misconduct or multiple instances of misconduct should be considered as aggravating factors (see Standard 9.22).

IV. STANDARDS FOR IMPOSING SANCTIONS: BLACK LETTER RULES AND COMMENTARY

Definitions

"Injury" is harm to a client, the public, the legal system, or the profession which results from a lawyer's misconduct. The level of injury can range from "serious" injury to "little or no" injury; a reference to "injury" alone indicates any level of injury greater than "little or no" injury.

"Intent" is the conscious objective or purpose to accomplish a particular result.

"Knowledge" is the conscious awareness of the nature or attendant circumstances of the conduct but without the conscious objective or purpose to accomplish a particular result.

"Negligence" is the failure of a lawyer to heed a substantial risk that circumstances exist or that a result will follow, which failure is a deviation from the standard of care that a reasonable lawyer would exercise in the situation.

"Potential injury" is the harm to a client, the public, the legal system or the profession that is reasonably foreseeable at the time of the lawyer's misconduct, and which, but for some intervening factor or event, would probably have resulted from the lawyer's misconduct.

A. PURPOSE AND NATURE OF SANCTIONS

1.1 Purpose of Lawyer Discipline Proceedings

The purpose of lawyer discipline proceedings is to protect the public and the administration of justice from lawyers who have not discharged, will not discharge, or are unlikely properly to discharge their professional duties to clients, the public, the legal system, and the legal profession.

Commentary

A similar statement of purpose appears as Standard 1.1 of the Standards for Lawyer Discipline. While courts express their views on the purpose of lawyer sanctions somewhat differently, an examination of reported cases reveals surprising accord as to the basic purpose of discipline. As identified by the courts, the primary purpose is to protect the public.[17] Second, the courts cite the need to protect the integrity of the legal system, and to insure the administration of justice.[18] Another purpose is to deter further unethical conduct and, where appropriate, to rehabilitate the lawyer.[19] A final purpose of imposing sanctions is to educate other lawyers and the public, thereby deterring unethical behavior among all members of the profession.[20] As the courts have noted, while sanctions imposed on a lawyer obviously have a punitive aspect, nonetheless, it is not the purpose to impose such sanctions for punishment.[21]

To achieve these purposes, sanctions for misconduct must apply to all licensed lawyers. Lawyers who are not actively practicing law, but who are serving in such roles as corporate officers, public officials, or law professors, do not lose their association with the legal profession because of their primary occupation. The public quite properly expects that anyone who is admitted to the practice of law, regardless of daily occupational activities, will conform to the minimum ethical standards of the legal profession. If the lawyer fails to meet these standards, appropriate sanctions should be imposed.

17. *In re* Stout, 75 N.J. 321, 382 A.2d 630 (1978); Matter of Rubi, 133 Ariz. 491, 652 P.2d 1014 (1982).

18. *In re* Zderic, 92 Wash.2d 777, 600 P.2d 1297 (1979); *In re* Nadler, 91 Ill.2d 326, 438 N.E.2d 198 (1982).

19. Matter of McInerney, 389 Mass. 528, 451 N.E.2d 401 (1983).

20. Matter of Carroll, 124 Ariz. 80, 602 P.2d 461 (1979); Committee on Professional Ethics v. Gross, 326 N.W.2d 272 (Iowa 1982); The Florida Bar v. Lord, 433 So.2d 983 (Fla.1983).

21. Matter of Maragos, 285 N.W.2d 541 (N.D.1979); Matter of Grimes, 414 Mich. 483, 326 N.W.2d 380 (1982).

1.2 Public Nature of Lawyer Discipline Proceedings

Upon the filing and service of formal charges, lawyer discipline proceedings should be public, and disposition of lawyer discipline should be public in cases of disbarment, suspension, and reprimand. Only in cases of minor misconduct, when there is little or no injury to a client, the public, the legal system, or the profession, and when there is little likelihood of repetition by the lawyer, should private discipline be imposed.

Commentary

Standard 8.25 of the Standards for Lawyer Discipline states that "upon the filing and service of formal charges [against a lawyer] the proceeding should be public...."[22] Although the majority of jurisdictions still do not follow this procedure,[23] a combination of public proceedings, after probable cause is found, and public sanctions is the better approach. Individual lawyers may prefer to avoid the embarrassment and stigma associated with a public sanction, but the profession as a whole will benefit. The more the public knows about how effectively the disciplinary system works, the more confidence they will have in that system. If there is approval of the system, it is hoped that public confidence in the profession's ability to discipline itself will be assured. In the words of one court, "... the purpose of bar disciplinary proceedings is not to punish the respondent lawyer but to vindicate in the eyes of the public the overall reputation of the bar."[24] Public discipline accompanied by written opinions setting forth the court's rationale for imposing a particular sanction can enhance that reputation.

Public identification of a lawyer who has been sanctioned serves other purposes as well. Where only some of the misconduct is known and more than one lawyer appears to be involved, announcement of the names of those who are sanctioned permits others' names to be cleared. Where the lawyer sanctioned is particularly prominent, public identification demonstrates that the system does not play favorites. Where the lawyer sanctioned may have caused injury to others who did not know they could complain, identification enables other victims to make themselves known.

Public sanctions also serve other members of the legal profession. When all sanctions are public, lawyers themselves can observe whether the system is operating fairly, treating consistently lawyers who are disciplined for similar misconduct. Public sanctions also educate other

---

22. Lawyer Standards, *supra* note 1.

23. Only 19 jurisdictions currently follow the provision of Standard 8.25 (1983 Survey of Lawyer Disciplinary Procedures in the United States, American Bar Association Center for Professional Responsibility): Arkansas, Connecticut, Florida, Georgia, Idaho, Indiana, Kansas, Louisiana, Maryland, Michigan, Minnesota, Nebraska, New Hampshire, North Carolina, Oregon, Texas, Utah, Washington, and Wisconsin.

24. Levi and Denham v. Mississippi State Bar, 436 So.2d 781, 786 (Miss.1983).

lawyers, and help deter misconduct by others in the profession. The preventive aspect of discipline cannot be overlooked.

Even while recognizing these interests of the public and the profession, however, it is important to note that there are certain situations in which it may be appropriate to impose private discipline. In cases of minor misconduct, when there is little or no injury to a client, the public, the legal system, or the profession, and when there is little or no likelihood of repetition, the court or disciplinary counsel should consider imposing an admonition. A private sanction in such cases informs the lawyer that his or her actions are unethical, but does not unnecessarily stigmatize a lawyer from whom the public needs no protection. To deter other lawyers, the court can still issue a public report describing the facts in cases where admonitions are imposed, but omitting the names of the disciplined lawyers.

Finally, in discussing private discipline, it is important to examine cases of discipline "by consent" in cases of disbarment, suspension, and reprimand. While sanctions imposed after a consent agreement can be public, the process by which the sanction decision is reached is private. The respondent lawyer and disciplinary counsel stipulate as to the facts, and that private interpretation of the facts then becomes the basis for imposing a public sanction. While there are many practical reasons why this disciplinary "plea bargaining" occurs, it is inconsistent with the policies described above. At a minimum, where discipline by consent is imposed in cases of disbarment, suspension, or reprimand, the court should require that a statement of the facts be made public.

In cases of both public and private discipline, the court should state clearly and unambiguously what sanction or sanctions are to be imposed. The purposes of lawyer discipline are not served if the sanction is unclear or is conditioned on unnamed factors. Even when a private sanction is imposed, a disciplined lawyer is entitled to know exactly what is expected of him or her.

1.3 Purpose of These Standards

These standards are designed for use in imposing a sanction or sanctions following a determination by clear and convincing evidence that a member of the legal profession has violated a provision of the Model Rules of Professional Conduct (or applicable standard under the laws of the jurisdiction where the proceeding is brought). Descriptions in these standards of substantive disciplinary offenses are not intended to create grounds for determining culpability independent of the Model Rules. The Standards constitute a model, setting forth a comprehensive system for determining sanctions, permitting flexibility and creativity in assigning sanctions in particular cases of lawyer misconduct. They are designed to promote: (1) consideration of all factors relevant to imposing the appropriate level of sanction

in an individual case; (2) consideration of the appropriate weight of such factors in light of the stated goals of lawyer discipline; (3) consistency in the imposition of disciplinary sanctions for the same or similar offenses within and among jurisdictions.

Commentary

The Model Rules of Professional Conduct (or other standard under the laws of the particular jurisdiction) establish the ethical standards for lawyers, and lawyers who violate these standards are subject to discipline. When disciplinary proceedings are brought against lawyers alleged to have engaged in ethical misconduct, disciplinary counsel have the burden of proving misconduct by clear and convincing evidence (see Standards for Lawyer Discipline, Standard 8.40). Following such a finding, the court or disciplinary agency should impose a sanction.

The Standards for Imposing Lawyer Sanctions are guidelines which are to be used by courts or disciplinary agencies in imposing sanctions *following* a finding of lawyer misconduct. These standards are not grounds for discipline, but, rather, constitute a model for the courts to follow in deciding what sanction to impose for proven lawyer misconduct. While these standards set forth a comprehensive model to be used in imposing sanctions, they also recognize that sanctions imposed must reflect the circumstances of each individual lawyer, and therefore provide for consideration of aggravating and mitigating circumstances in each case.

The Standards for Imposing Lawyer Sanctions are designed to promote consistency in the imposition of sanctions by identifying the relevant factors that courts should consider (see Standard 3.0) and then applying these factors to situations where lawyers have engaged in various types of misconduct (see Standards 4.0 through 8.0). Because the Model Rules of Professional Conduct have been adopted by the American Bar Association as the ethical standards for the legal profession, the language of the Model Rules is used herein. However, because only a minority of jurisdictions have actually adopted the Model Rules, these Standards are phrased in terms of the fundamental duties owed to clients, the public, the legal system, and the profession. This general language should make these standards applicable in all jurisdictions regardless of whether the jurisdiction chooses to adopt the Model Rules, the former Code of Professional Responsibility, or some combination of these standards.

B. SANCTIONS

2.1 Scope

A disciplinary sanction is imposed on a lawyer upon a finding or acknowledgement that the lawyer has engaged in professional misconduct.

Commentary

Sanctions in disciplinary matters are neither criminal nor civil but *sui generis* and imposed under authority of the state's highest court.[25] Disciplinary sanctions are separate and apart from penalties which may be imposed solely for civil or criminal conduct, or contempt of court.[26] Disciplinary sanctions do not include restrictions upon a lawyer's practice which may be imposed solely as a result of a lawyer's disability. For example, a lawyer who has not engaged in professional misconduct, but whose ability to practice law is impaired, as by alcoholism or mental illness, should be helped to limit his practice or transferred to inactive status; disciplinary sanctions should not be imposed (see Standards for Lawyer Discipline, Standard 12). Disciplinary sanctions do not include penalties that may be imposed on lawyers who violate administrative rules or regulations applicable to members of the bar, such as by failing to pay dues or to attend mandatory continuing legal education programs.

2.2 Disbarment

Disbarment terminates the individual's status as a lawyer. Where disbarment is not permanent, procedures should be established for a lawyer who has been disbarred to apply for readmission, provided that:

(1) no application should be considered for five years from the effective date of disbarment; and

(2) the petitioner must show by clear and convincing evidence:

(a) successful completion of the bar examination,

(b) compliance with all applicable discipline or disability orders or rules; and

(c) rehabilitation and fitness to practice law.

Commentary

Disbarment is the most severe sanction, terminating the lawyer's ability to practice law. Disbarment enforces the purpose of discipline in that the public is protected from further practice by the lawyer; the reputation of the legal profession is protected by the action of the bench and bar in taking appropriate actions against unethical lawyers. Even though disbarment is reserved for the most serious cases, the majority of jurisdictions allow application for readmission after a period of time. For the protection of the public, however, the presumption should be against readmission, and, in order to insure that disbarment is in reality

25. Some states, for example, delegate this power to other agencies. See Standards for Lawyer Discipline, Standards 1.2, 2.1.

26. Attorney Grievance Commission v. Velasquez, 301 Md. 450, 483 A.2d 354 (1984); *In re* McDaniel, 470 N.E.2d 1327 (Ind.1984).

a more serious sanction than suspension, in no event should a lawyer even be considered for readmission until at least five years after the effective date of disbarment. After that time, a lawyer seeking to be readmitted to practice must show by clear and convincing evidence: successful completion of the bar examination, compliance with all applicable discipline or disability orders or rules, and rehabilitation and fitness to practice law (see Standards for Lawyer Discipline, Standards 6.1 and 6.2).

Disbarment includes disbarment by consent, resignation in lieu of disbarment, and reciprocal disbarment. Although a lawyer who has been disbarred on consent or who has resigned in lieu of disbarment may not be readmitted any earlier than any other lawyer who has been disbarred, the fact that the lawyer resigned or was disbarred on consent is a factor that can be considered if the lawyer applies for readmission.

2.3 Suspension

Suspension is the removal of a lawyer from the practice of law for a specified minimum period of time. Generally, suspension should be for a period of time equal to or greater than six months, but in no event should the time period prior to application for reinstatement be more than three years. Procedures should be established to allow a suspended lawyer to apply for reinstatement, but a lawyer who has been suspended should not be permitted to return to practice until he has completed a reinstatement process demonstrating rehabilitation, compliance with all applicable discipline or disability orders and rules, and fitness to practice law.

Commentary

Suspension includes suspension by consent, resignation in lieu of suspension and reciprocal suspension. Although jurisdictions impose suspensions for various time periods, the Standards for Lawyer Discipline recommend that suspension be for a definite period of time not to exceed three years. If the conduct is so egregious that a longer suspension seems warranted, the sanction of disbarment should be imposed.

In addition, the Standards draw a distinction between suspensions for six months or less, and suspensions for more than six months. Standard 6.4 states that a lawyer who has been suspended for six months or less should be reinstated automatically (i.e., without establishing rehabilitation). However, a lawyer who has been suspended for more than six months should *not* be reinstated without being required to show by clear and convincing evidence: rehabilitation, compliance with all applicable discipline or disability orders or rules, and fitness to practice law.

While the Standards for Lawyer Discipline currently provide for suspensions of less than six months, short-term suspensions with automatic reinstatement are not an effective means of protecting the public. If a lawyer's misconduct is serious enough to warrant a suspension from practice, the lawyer should not be reinstated until rehabilitation can be established. While it may be possible in some cases for a lawyer to show rehabilitation in less than six months, it is preferable to suspend a lawyer for at least six months in order to insure effective demonstration of rehabilitation. In order to insure that administrative procedures do not extend the period of actual suspension beyond that imposed, however, expedited procedures should be established to reinstate immediately lawyers who show rehabilitation, compliance with rules, and fitness to practice.

A six-month suspension is also necessary to protect clients. When shorter suspensions are imposed, lawyers can merely delay performing the requested services. If the lawyer eventually completes the work for the client and receives a fee, the suspension has only served to inconvenience the client. In reality, a short-term suspension functions as a fine on the lawyer, and fines are prohibited by the Lawyer Standards (see Standard 6.14).

The amount of time for which a lawyer should be suspended, then, should generally be for a minimum of six months. In no case should the time period prior to application for reinstatement be more than three years. The specific period of time for the suspension should be determined after examining any aggravating or mitigating factors in the case. At the end of this time period the lawyer may apply for reinstatement, and the lawyer must show: rehabilitation, compliance with all applicable discipline or disability orders and rules, and fitness to practice law (see Standard 6.4).

2.4 Interim Suspension

Interim suspension is the temporary suspension of a lawyer from the practice of law pending imposition of final discipline. Interim suspension includes:

    (a) suspension upon conviction of a "serious crime" or,

    (b) suspension when the lawyer's continuing conduct is or is likely to cause immediate and serious injury to a client or the public.

Commentary

Standard 6.5 of the Standards for Lawyer Discipline states that the court should place a lawyer on interim suspension immediately upon proof that the lawyer has been convicted of a "serious crime" or is causing great harm to the public. A "serious crime" is defined as any felony or any lesser crime a necessary element of which, as determined by the statutory or common law definition of such crime, involves interference with the administration of justice, false swearing, misrepresentation, fraud, extortion, misappropriation, theft; or an attempt or a conspiracy or solicitation of another to commit a "serious crime." [27] Interim suspension is necessary in such cases both to protect members of the public and to maintain public confidence in the legal profession. As explained in the commentary to Standard 6.5, it is difficult for members of the public to understand why a lawyer who has been convicted of stealing funds from a client can continue to handle client funds. Public confidence in the profession is strengthened when expedited procedures are available in such instances of lawyer misconduct.

Although due process does not require a hearing prior to imposing an interim suspension following a criminal conviction, an opportunity to show cause as to why it should not be imposed should be available. An interim suspension remains in effect until it is lifted by the court, or until the court imposes a final disciplinary sanction after compliance with relevant procedural rules.

Interim suspension is also appropriate when the lawyer's continuing conduct is causing or is likely to cause immediate and serious injury to a client or the public. The commentary to Standard 6.5 cites the example of a lawyer who has displayed a pattern of misconduct, such as ongoing conversion of trust funds, as warranting interim suspension. Interim suspension is also appropriate where a lawyer abandons the practice of law.

(As explained above in Section 2.1, cases of lawyer disability are not included in the scope of this report. See Standard 12.1 in the Standards for Lawyer Discipline for a discussion of transfer to disability inactive status.)

2.5 Reprimand

Reprimand, also known as censure or public censure, is a form of public discipline which declares the conduct of the lawyer improper, but does not limit the lawyer's right to practice.

Commentary

Publicity enhances the effect of the discipline and emphasizes the concern of the court with all lawyer misconduct, not only serious ethical violations. A reprimand is appropriate in cases where the lawyer's conduct, although violating ethical standards, is not serious enough to warrant suspension or disbarment. (See Definitions, Standards for Lawyer Discipline.) A reprimand serves the useful purpose of identifying lawyers who have violated ethical standards, and, if accompanied by a published opinion, educates members of the bar as to these standards.

A reprimand is not always sufficient to protect the public; it may also be appropriate to attach additional conditions to a reprimand. When a lawyer lacks competence in one area of practice, for example, the court could impose a reprimand and also require the lawyer to attend

27. See Definitions, Standards for Lawyer Discipline.

continuing education courses. In a case of neglect, the court could impose reprimand and probation, during which period of time the lawyer's diligence in handling client matters could be monitored.

2.6 Admonition

Admonition, also known as private reprimand, is a form of non-public discipline which declares the conduct of the lawyer improper, but does not limit the lawyer's right to practice.

Commentary

Admonition is the least serious of the formal disciplinary sanctions, and is the only private sanction. (See Definitions, Standards for Lawyer Discipline.) Because imposing an admonition will not inform members of the public about the lawyer's misconduct, admonition should be used only when the lawyer is negligent, when the ethical violation results in little or no injury to a client, the public, the legal system, or the profession, and when there is little or no likelihood of repetition. Relying on these criteria should help protect the public while, at the same time, avoid damage to a lawyer's reputation when future ethical violations seem unlikely. To enhance the preventive nature of lawyer discipline, the court or disciplinary agency should publish a fact description in admonition cases without disclosing the lawyer's name.

2.7 Probation

Probation is a sanction that allows a lawyer to practice law under specified conditions. Probation can be imposed alone or in conjunction with a reprimand, an admonition or immediately following a suspension. Probation can also be imposed as a condition of readmission or reinstatement.

Commentary

Probation is a sanction that should be imposed when a lawyer's right to practice law needs to be monitored or limited rather than suspended or revoked. The need for probation can arise under a variety of situations, and it can be imposed either alone or along with a sanction of reprimand or admonition. If probation is imposed with a reprimand, it would be a public sanction; if probation is imposed with an admonition, it would be a private sanction. If probation is the sole sanction imposed, it can be either public or private, but the sanction should be public in any case in which the lawyer has violated a duty owed to a client, the public, or the legal system. Probation can also be imposed as a condition of readmission following disbarment or as a condition of reinstatement following a period of suspension from practice.

By imposing probation, the court allows a lawyer to continue to practice, but also requires the lawyer to meet certain conditions that will protect the public and will assist the lawyer to meet ethical obligations. Conditions of probation can include:

(a) quarterly or semi-annual reports of caseload status, especially appropriate in neglect cases, see *Florida Bar v. Neale,* 432 So.2d 50 (Fla.1980);

(b) supervision by a local disciplinary committee member, see *In re Maragos,* 285 N.W.2d 541 (N.D.1979) and *In re Hessberger,* 96 Ill.2d 423, 451 N.E.2d 821 (1983);

(c) periodic audits of trust accounts, especially appropriate in cases where lawyers improperly handle client funds, see *Florida Bar v. Montgomery,* 418 So.2d 267 (Fla.1982);

(d) attendance at continuing education programs, especially appropriate in cases of incompetence, see *Florida Bar v. Glick,* 383 So.2d 642 (Fla.1980);

(e) participation in alcohol or drug abuse programs, especially appropriate where the lawyer's abuse of alcohol or drugs was a significant cause of his misconduct, see *Tenner v. State Bar,* 28 Cal.3d 202, 617 P.2d 486, 168 Cal.Rptr. 333 (1980) and *In re Heath,* 296 Or. 683, 678 P.2d 736 (1984);

(f) periodic physical or mental examinations, appropriate where the lawyer's physical or mental condition was a significant cause of his misconduct, see *In re McCallum,* 289 N.W.2d 146 (Minn. 1980) and *In re Mudge,* 33 Cal.3d 152, 654 P.2d 1307, 187 Cal.Rptr. 779 (1982);

(g) passing the bar examination or the appropriate professional responsibility examination, see *Florida Bar v. Peterson,* 418 So.2d 246 (Fla.1982) and *In re Morales,* 35 Cal.3d 1, 671 P.2d 857, 196 Cal.Rptr. 353 (1983);

(h) limitations on practice, see *Florida Bar v. Neely,* 417 So.2d 957 (Fla.1983); or

(i) such other conditions as are appropriate for the misconduct.

Probation may be terminated by the court after the respondent has filed an affidavit of compliance with all conditions of probation and the court is satisfied that the need for probation no longer exists. In the event that a lawyer is charged with violating the conditions of probation, a hearing is needed to determine whether a violation has occurred. The disciplinary authority has the burden of establishing any such violation by clear and convincing evidence. Upon a finding that a lawyer has violated probation conditions, the court may extend the probation, impose a more severe sanction, or otherwise handle the matter.

2.8 Other Sanctions and Remedies

Other sanctions and remedies which may be imposed include:

(a) restitution,

(b) assessment of costs,

(c) limitation upon practice,

(d) appointment of a receiver,

(e) requirement that the lawyer take the bar examination or professional responsibility examination,

(f) requirement that the lawyer attend continuing education courses, and

(g) other requirements that the state's highest court or disciplinary board deems consistent with the purposes of lawyer sanctions.

Commentary

These other sanctions and remedies are those that the court or the board may impose when it is deemed necessary to carry out the goals of the disciplinary system. The court should be creative and flexible in approaching those cases where there is some misconduct but where a severe sanction is not required. In less serious cases of incompetence, for example, a sanction requiring the lawyer to attend continuing legal education courses or to limit the lawyer's practice to handling certain types of cases may better protect the public than a period of suspension from practice. Fines are not an appropriate sanction (see Standard 6.14, Lawyer Standards).

2.9 Reciprocal Discipline

Reciprocal discipline is the imposition of a disciplinary sanction for conduct for which a lawyer has been disciplined in another jurisdiction.

Commentary

Public confidence in the profession is enhanced when lawyers who are admitted in more than one jurisdiction are prevented from avoiding the effect of discipline in one jurisdiction by practicing in another. Standard 10.2 of the Standards for Lawyer Discipline provides that a certified copy of the findings of fact in the disciplinary proceeding in the other jurisdiction should constitute conclusive evidence that the respondent committed the misconduct. Reciprocal discipline can be imposed without a hearing, but the court should provide the lawyer with an opportunity to raise a due process challenge or to show that a sanction different from the sanction imposed in the other jurisdiction is warranted. In order to facilitate the imposition of reciprocal discipline, bar counsel or other appropriate authority in each state should report all cases of public discipline to the ABA National Discipline Data Bank.[28]

28. The National Discipline Data Bank is operated by the American Bar Associa-

2.10 Readmission and Reinstatement

In jurisdictions where disbarment is not permanent, procedures should be established to allow a disbarred lawyer to apply for readmission. Procedures should be established to allow a suspended lawyer to apply for reinstatement.

Commentary

Readmission occurs when a disbarred lawyer is returned to practice. Since the purpose of lawyer discipline is not punishment, readmission may be appropriate; the presumption, however, should be against readmission. In no event should a lawyer even be considered for readmission until at least five years after the effective date of disbarment. After that time, a lawyer seeking to be readmitted to practice must show by clear and convincing evidence: rehabilitation, compliance with all applicable discipline or disability orders or rules, and fitness to practice law.

Reinstatement occurs when a suspended lawyer is returned to practice. Since the purpose of lawyer discipline is not punishment, reinstatement is appropriate when a lawyer can show rehabilitation. Application for reinstatement should not be permitted until expiration of the ordered period of suspension and generally not until at least six months after the effective date of suspension. A lawyer should not be reinstated unless he can show by clear and convincing evidence: rehabilitation, compliance with all applicable discipline or disability orders and rules and fitness to practice law (see Standard 6.4).

Conditional readmission and conditional reinstatement can occur when appropriate. Conditions that can be imposed include probation (see Standard 2.7) or other sanctions or remedies (see Standard 2.8).

C. FACTORS TO BE CONSIDERED IN IMPOSING SANCTIONS

3.0 Generally

In imposing a sanction after a finding of lawyer misconduct, a court should consider the following factors:

(a) the duty violated;

(b) the lawyer's mental state; and

(c) the actual or potential injury caused by the lawyer's misconduct; and

(d) the existence of aggravating or mitigating factors.

tion Center for Professional Responsibility. For further information on how to report or to receive current statistical data, contact the Center for Professional Responsibility at the American Bar Association, 750 N. Lake Shore Drive, Chicago, Illinois, 60611, or call (312) 988–5000.

Commentary

This system for determining an initial sanction upon a finding of lawyer misconduct requires courts to examine four factors: the nature of the duty violated, the lawyer's mental state, the actual or potential injury resulting from the lawyer's misconduct, and the existence of aggravating or mitigating factors. As explained above (see Theoretical Framework, p. 5), a lawyer's misconduct may be a violation of a duty owed to a client, the public, the legal system, or the profession. The lawyer's mental state may be one of intent, knowledge, or negligence. The injury resulting from the lawyer's misconduct need not be actually realized; in order to protect the public, the court should also examine the potential for injury caused by the lawyer's misconduct. In a case where a lawyer intentionally converts client funds, for example, disbarment can be imposed even where there is no actual injury to any client (see 4.11). In other situations, the standards make distinctions between various levels of actual or potential injury; disbarment may be reserved for cases of serious or potentially serious injury, while admonition may be imposed only in cases where there is little or no actual or potential injury. In any case, however, the court may then take account of any particular aggravating or mitigating factors (see Standard 9.0 for a list of these factors).

4.0 Violations of Duties Owed to Clients

Introduction

This duty arises out of the nature of the basic relationship between the lawyer and the client. The lawyer is not required to accept all clients,[29] but, having agreed to perform services for a client, the lawyer has duties that arise under ethical rules, agency law, and under the terms of the contractual relationship with the individual client. The lawyer must preserve the property of a client [Rule 1.15/DR 9–102], maintain client confidences [Rule 1.6/DR 4–101] and avoid conflicts which will impair the lawyer's independent judgment [Rules 1.7 through 1.13, 2.2, 3.7, 5.4(c), and 6.3/DR 5–101 through 5–105, DR 9–102]. In addition, the lawyer must be competent to perform the services requested by the client [Rule 1.1/DR 6–101(A)(1) and (2)] and be diligent in performing those services [Rules 1.2, 1.3, 1.4/DR 6–101(A)(3)]. The lawyer must also be candid with the client during the course of the professional relationship [Rule 8.4/DR 1–102(A)(4) and DR 7–101(A)(3)].

4.1 Failure to Preserve the Client's Property

Absent aggravating or mitigating circumstances, upon application of the factors set out in 3.0, the following sanctions are

---

29. Comment to Rule 6.2, paragraph 1, Model Rules, *supra* note 8; EC 2–26, Code of Professional Responsibility, *supra* note 8.

generally appropriate in cases involving the failure to preserve client property:

>   **4.11 Disbarment is generally appropriate when a lawyer knowingly converts client property and causes injury or potential injury to a client.**

Commentary

Some courts have held that disbarment is always the appropriate discipline when a lawyer knowingly converts client funds. For example, in the case of *In re Wilson*, 81 N.J. 451, 409 A.2d 1153 (1979), the Supreme Court of New Jersey discussed the rationale for imposing disbarment as a sanction on lawyers who misappropriate client funds:

> Like many rules governing the behavior of lawyers, this one has its roots in the confidence and trust which clients place in their attorneys. Having sought his advice and relying on his expertise, the client entrusts the lawyer with the transaction—including the handling of the client's funds. Whether it be a real estate closing, the establishment of a trust, the purchase of a business, the investment of funds, the receipt of proceeds of litigation, or any one of a multitude of other situations, it is common-place that the work of lawyers involves possession of their client's funds.... Whatever the need may be for the lawyer's handling of client's money, the client permits it because he trusts the lawyer.... [T]here are few more egregious acts of professional misconduct of which an attorney can be guilty than the misappropriation of a client's funds held in trust. [citing *In re Beckman*, 79 N.J. 402, 404–05, 400 A.2d 792, 793 (1979)].... Recognition of the nature and gravity of the offense suggests only one result—disbarment (81 N.J. at 454–55, 409 A.2d at 1154–55).

California has held that disbarment is appropriate even absent knowing conversion when a lawyer is grossly negligent in dealing with client property. As the California Supreme Court observed, "[e]ven if [the attorney's] conduct were not wilful and dishonest, gross carelessness and negligence constitute a violation of an attorney's oath faithfully to discharge his duties and involve moral turpitude." (*Chefsky v. State Bar*, 36 Cal.3d 116, at 123, 680 P.2d 82 (1984).)

Most courts, however, reserve disbarment for cases in which the lawyer uses the client's funds for the lawyer's own benefit. In *Carter v. Ross*, 461 A.2d 675 (R.I.1983), for example, the lawyer took money from an estate and used it to pay office and personal expenses. The Rhode Island Supreme Court cited the *Wilson* case and imposed disbarment: "We, like our New Jersey colleagues, are convinced that continuing public confidence in the judicial system and the bar as a whole requires that the strictest discipline be imposed in misappropriation cases" (461 A.2d at 676). Similarly, in *In re Freeman*, 647 P.2d 820 (Kan.App.1982), a lawyer was disbarred who caused checks from an insurance company to be issued to fictitious payees, and then converted that money for his own use. In these types of cases, where the lawyer's lack of integrity is clear, only the most compelling mitigating circumstances should justify a lesser sanction than disbarment.

In such cases, it may not even seem necessary to consider whether there is any injury to a client. Even though there will always be a potential injury to a client in such cases, the injury factor should still be considered. First, consideration of the extent of actual or potential injury can be important when it is especially serious: injury should be proved up at the disciplinary proceeding in order to make a record in the event that a lawyer applies for readmission. Second, even in jurisdictions where disbarment is permanent, consideration of injury reinforces the concept that a basic purpose of lawyer discipline is protection of the public. As the New York Supreme Court explained in a case where it imposed disbarment on a lawyer who misappropriated more than $31,000 from a client-descendent's estate by forging the administratrix's signature on checks: "This result is called for by the duty to protect the public and to vindicate the public's trust in lawyers as custodians of clients' funds" (*In re Marks,* 72 A.D.2d 399, 401, 424 N.Y.S.2d 229, 230 (1980)). (Note: Lawyers who convert the property of persons other than their clients are covered by Standard 5.11.)

> **4.12 Suspension is generally appropriate when a lawyer knows or should know that he is dealing improperly with client property and causes injury or potential injury to a client.**

Commentary

Suspension should be reserved for lawyers who engage in misconduct that does not amount to misappropriation or conversion. The most common cases involve lawyers who commingle client funds with their own, or fail to remit client funds promptly. While the court in *In re Wilson,* 81 N.J. 451, 409 A.2d 1153 (1979), defined misappropriation to include "any unauthorized use by the lawyer of clients' funds entrusted to him, ... whether or not he derives any personal gain or benefit therefrom" (81 N.J. at 455, n. 1, 409 A.2d at 1155, n. 1), most courts do not impose disbarment on lawyers who merely commingle funds. As the Washington Supreme Court recently concluded, "We do not now nor have we ever held that trust account violations per se result in disbarment" (*In re Salvesen,* 94 Wash.2d 73, 79, 614 P.2d 1264, 1266 (1980)).

For example, in *State v. Chartier,* 234 Kan. 834, 676 P.2d 740 (1984), the lawyer commingled a client's funds, and failed to notify a client of receipt of garnishment proceeds. The court imposed an indefinite suspension, stating that the lawyer "knew, or should have known though the exercise of reasonable diligence" that the garnishment funds collected exceeded the amounts actually due (234 Kan. at 836, 676 P.2d at 742). Similarly, in *Disciplinary Board of the Supreme Court v. Banks,* 641 S.W.2d 501 (Tenn.1982), the court imposed a one-year suspension where the lawyer took the client's money to invest but did not pay her interest on a regular basis or pay over the client's money upon her demand. The court noted that the lawyer did not intend to convert the client's funds to his own use: "At all times he acknowledged his responsibility for them and his indebtedness to her" (641 S.W.2d at 504). Because lawyers who commingle client's funds with their own subject the client's funds to the claims of creditors, commingling is a serious violation for which a period of suspension is appropriate even in cases when the client does not suffer a loss. As explained by the Illinois Supreme Court: "It is the risk of the loss of the funds while they are in the attorney's possession, and not only their actual loss, which the rule is designed to eliminate. . . ." *In re Bizar,* 97 Ill.2d 127, 454 N.E.2d 271 (1983).

4.13 Reprimand is generally appropriate when a lawyer is negligent in dealing with client property and causes injury or potential injury to a client.

Commentary

Reprimand should be reserved for lawyers who are merely negligent in dealing with client property, and who cause injury or potential injury to a client. Suspension or disbarment as applicable under Standards 4.11 and 4.12 and the commentary thereto is appropriate for lawyers who are grossly negligent. For example, lawyers who are grossly negligent in failing to establish proper accounting procedures should be suspended; reprimand is appropriate for lawyers who simply fail to follow their established procedures. Reprimand is also appropriate when a lawyer is negligent in training or supervising his or her office staff concerning proper procedures in handling client funds.

The courts have typically imposed reprimands in cases when lawyers fail to maintain adequate trust accounting procedures, or neglect to return the client's property promptly. In *The Florida Bar v. Golden,* 401 So.2d 1340 (Fla.1981), a public reprimand was imposed on a lawyer who failed to repay a loan made to him by a client for two years and who failed to keep adequate records of his trust accounting procedures. Similarly, in *Carter v. Gallucci,* 457 A.2d 269 (R.I.1983), because of inadequate records, a lawyer failed to pay real estate taxes out of funds disbursed to him. He did subsequently pay the taxes, and the court imposed a reprimand.

4.14 Admonition is generally appropriate when a lawyer is negligent in dealing with client property and causes little or no actual or potential injury to a client.

Commentary

Admonition should be reserved for cases where the lawyer's negligence poses little or no risk of injury to a client. An admonition would be appropriate, for example, when a lawyer's sloppy bookkeeping practices make it difficult to determine the state of a client trust account, but where all client funds are actually properly maintained. Imposing an admonition in such a case should serve as a warning to the lawyer to improve his or her accounting procedures, thus preventing any actual injury to any client.

4.2 Failure to Preserve the Client's Confidences

Absent aggravating or mitigating circumstances, upon application of the factors set out in 3.0, the following sanctions are generally appropriate in cases involving the failure to preserve client property:

> **4.21 Disbarment is generally appropriate when a lawyer, with the intent to benefit the lawyer or another, knowingly reveals information relating to representation of a client not otherwise lawfully permitted to be disclosed, and this disclosure causes injury or potential injury to a client.**

Commentary

Disbarment is warranted in situations when a lawyer intentionally abuses the client's trust by using the professional relationship to gain information which benefits the lawyer or another, and which causes injury or potential injury to a client. Because the violation of a client's confidence poses such a serious threat to the lawyer-client relationship, disbarment should be imposed whenever the lawyer acts with the intent to benefit the lawyer or another. Neither a ''serious'' injury nor a ''potentially serious'' injury to a client need be proved; any injury to a client will be sufficient to impose disbarment. An example of a case where disbarment is appropriate occurred in *In re Pool,* No. 83–37 BD, Sup.J.Ct., Suff.Cty., Mass. (1984), where a defendant's lawyer gave a federal prosecutor information about the location of a safety deposit box containing incriminating evidence in order to gain access to obtain funds to cover the costs of investigation. In the words of the court, ''[t]he disclosure of confidential information by a defense attorney to a prosecutor, without the client's consent, is a serious violation of the defense attorney's obligations'' (*Id.* at 4). (Note: This situation should be distinguished from the situation where a lawyer is acting under a good faith belief that there is no choice but to reveal a client's confidence, as in a case where a lawyer is called to testify as to the whereabouts of the client in a divorce proceeding and the lawyer's answer involves facts learned in the lawyer-client relationship. Here, the lawyer's good faith belief that the law requires disclosure of the information would be a mitigating factor, see Standard 9.32(b).)

> **4.22 Suspension is generally appropriate when a lawyer knowingly reveals information relating to the representation of a client not otherwise lawfully permitted**

to be disclosed, and this disclosure causes injury or potential injury to a client.

Commentary

Suspension is appropriate when the lawyer is not intentionally using the professional relationship to benefit himself or another, but nevertheless knowingly breaches a client's confidence such that the client suffers injury or potential injury. An appropriate case for a suspension would involve a lawyer who knowingly revealed confidential information to the opposing party in litigation, with the result that the client's position was weakened.

4.23 Reprimand is generally appropriate when a lawyer negligently reveals information relating to representation of a client not otherwise lawfully permitted to be disclosed and this disclosure causes injury or potential injury to a client.

Commentary

Reprimand should be imposed when a lawyer negligently breaches a client's confidence. Even when the client is not actually harmed, the potential for harm to the client and damage to the professional relationship is so significant that a public sanction should be imposed. In the words of one court: "This element of trust is the very essence of the attorney-client relationship" [*Matter of Roache*, 446 N.E.2d 1302, 1303 (Ind.1983)]. An appropriate case for a reprimand would involve a lawyer who negligently leaves a client's documents in a conference room following a meeting, or who discusses a client matter in a public place.

4.24 Admonition is generally appropriate when a lawyer negligently reveals information relating to representation of a client not otherwise lawfully permitted to be disclosed and this disclosure causes little or no actual or potential injury to a client.

Commentary

Maintaining a client's confidence is so fundamental to the professional relationship that generally it is inappropriate to impose a private sanction. At a minimum, a reprimand should be imposed (see Standard 4.23).

4.3 Failure to Avoid Conflicts of Interest

Absent aggravating or mitigating circumstances, upon application of the factors set out in Standard 3.0, the following sanctions are generally appropriate in cases involving conflicts of interest:

4.31 Disbarment is generally appropriate when a lawyer, without the informed consent of client(s):

   (a) **engages in representation of a client knowing that the lawyer's interests are adverse to the client's with the intent to benefit the lawyer or another, and causes serious or potentially serious injury to the client; or**

   (b) **simultaneously represents clients that the lawyer knows have adverse interests with the intent to benefit the lawyer or another, and causes serious or potentially serious injury to a client; or**

   (c) **represents a client in a matter substantially related to a matter in which the interests of a present or former client are materially adverse, and knowingly uses information relating to the representation of a client with the intent to benefit the lawyer or another, and causes serious or potentially serious injury to a client.**

Commentary

The courts generally disbar lawyers who intentionally exploit the lawyer-client relationship by acquiring an ownership, possessory, security or other pecuniary interest adverse to a client without the client's understanding or consent. For example, in *Matter of Easler,* 269 S.E.2d 765 (S.C.1980), a lawyer who engaged in a fraudulent scheme to obtain the client's property at a price well below market value was disbarred. The court noted that "in his attempt to acquire their property for his personal gain," the lawyer falsely notarized one of the clients' signature, and took advantage of the "domestic and financial difficulties the McFarlins [the clients] were undergoing" (269 S.E.2d at 766). In *In re Wolf,* 82 N.J. 326, 413 A.2d 317 (1980), a widow retained the lawyer who had represented her husband during his lifetime to handle her husband's estate. When she asked the lawyer to suggest an investment for a portion of her inheritance, he suggested that she invest in property which was owned by a company in which he was a stockholder and officer. Knowing that his client was naive and inexperienced in business matters, he directed her to invest her money in property worth only half of what he represented to her, and did not inform her as to the status of the mortgage, the title, or unpaid real estate taxes. Later on, he failed to notify her of a foreclosure action on the property or to defend the action on her behalf. In the words of the court, "It is clear that he exploited his client for his own financial benefit. It was unthinkable in the first place for respondent to have suggested such an investment, but, having done so, it was unconscionable for him to have continued to represent the widow. He should have insisted that she retain independent counsel or refused to consummate the transaction. Undoubtedly, independent counsel would never have allowed the widow to make this investment" (413 A.2d at 321). (Note: the lawyer, who was disbarred, also attempted to commit fraud on the court in order to secure a larger fee.) Similarly, in *In re Hills,* 296 Or. 526, 678 P.2d 262 (1984), the lawyer entered into a loan transaction with clients in which he intentionally misrepresented that funds were available to pay the note. He also entered into a partnership agreement with another client in which he misrepresented that the client would be a limited partner but, in fact, made the client a general partner. In neither of these cases did the lawyer advise the clients to seek independent legal counsel.

Disbarment is also appropriate in cases of multiple representation when a lawyer knowingly engages in conduct with the intent to benefit the lawyer or another. As one court has explained, "Although many ingredients go into the recipe for a successful lawyer-client relationship, one ingredient is indispensable: individual loyalty. The relationship cannot properly exist absent the lawyer's uncompromised commitment to the client's cause. DR 5–105 aims to insure undivided loyalty; in its absence, the lawyer cannot serve. The rule also seeks to maintain or increase public confidence in public institutions, for the appearance of impropriety that sometimes exists when a lawyer represents multiple clients ... erodes public confidence in the legal profession." *In re Jans,* 295 Or. 289, 666 P.2d 830, 832 (1983). In *In re Keast,* 497 P.2d 103 (Mont.1972), a lawyer represented a client charged with procuring girls for immoral purposes. Although the lawyer was named as one of the individuals for whom the girls were procured, he served as defense counsel in his client's criminal case. While this case was pending, the lawyer also filed an action for divorce against the client on behalf of the client's wife. The court imposed disbarment. In *Stanley v. Board of Professional Responsibility,* 640 S.W.2d 210 (Tenn.1982), a lawyer was disbarred who represented both the victim and the defendant in a criminal matter. After learning about the crime from the victim, the lawyer misled the defendant into employing him when the lawyer knew that the victim no longer wished to prosecute. In the words of the court, "Stanley [the lawyer] deceived an immature youth and his naive parents. He compounded the deception with his lack of understanding of the proper role of a lawyer—which does not include a self-appointed role as a paraclete, comforter, helper, or hand-holder, under the guise of legal services and at a lawyer's compensation rate" (640 S.W.2d at 213). (Note: the lawyer also was involved in another conflict of interest by entering into usurious loan transactions with two other clients.)

Finally, disbarment is appropriate when a lawyer knowingly uses information relating to representation of a former client with the intent to benefit the lawyer or another, and causes serious or potentially serious injury to a client. Although such cases are rare, disbarment is warranted when there is such an intentional abuse of the lawyer-client relationship.

4.32 Suspension is generally appropriate when a lawyer knows of a conflict of interest and does not fully

disclose to a client the possible effect of that conflict, and causes injury or potential injury to a client.

Commentary

Conflicts can take the form of a conflict between the lawyer and his or her client, between current clients, or between a former client and a present client. In the case of conflicts between a lawyer and a present client, suspension is appropriate when the lawyer knows that his or her interests may be or are likely to be adverse to that of the client, but does not fully disclose the conflict, and causes injury or potential injury to a client. For example, in *In re Boyer*, 295 Or. 624, 669 P.2d 326 (1983), the lawyer represented a client for a number of years, rendering both financial and legal advice. When another of his clients wanted to borrow money, the lawyer arranged for the first client to make a loan, and he prepared the note and a mortgage to secure the note, but the lawyer did not tell the first client either that such a loan might be usurious, and thus unenforceable, or that he had received a finder's fee from the second client for his efforts. The Oregon Supreme Court found that the lawyer violated DR 5–101(A) in his representation of the first client, and suspended him for seven months. [Note: the court also found a violation of DR 5–105(B).] Similarly, in *Joseph E. Chabat*, DP–161/80, DP 74/81 (Michigan Attorney Discipline Board, 1980), a lawyer in a divorce action was suspended for nine months when he lent himself money from the sale of a client's house and failed to advise the client to seek independent representation in regard to the loan.

Suspension is also appropriate when a lawyer knows of a conflict among several clients, but does not fully disclose the possible effect of the multiple representation, and causes injury or potential injury to one or more of the clients. For example, in *State v. Callahan*, 232 Kan. 136, 652 P.2d 708 (1982), the lawyer represented both the vendors and the purchaser in a land sale transaction. The lawyer failed to warn the vendors that they did not have a perfected security interest and failed to make full disclosure to the vendors of his close business and professional associations with the purchaser. The Supreme Court of Kansas imposed an indefinite suspension. Similarly, in *Matter of Krakauer*, 81 N.J. 32, 404 A.2d 1137 (1979), the New Jersey Supreme Court imposed a one-year suspension on a lawyer who represented both sides in a real estate transaction (and who also attempted to retain an unearned commission and called for a title search which was not ordered by the client).

Finally, suspension is appropriate when a lawyer knows or should know that the interests of a client are materially adverse to the interests of a former client in a substantially related matter, and causes injury or potential injury to the former or the subsequent client. For example, in *In re LaPinska*, 72 Ill.2d 461, 381 N.E.2d 700 (1978), the lawyer represented a contractor to secure title papers for a residence being sold. The lawyer, a city attorney, then represented the city in a suit brought by the purchasers of the residence against the contractor regarding a zoning violation of the property. When the purchasers complained about the leniency of the fine imposed on the contractor, the lawyer agreed to represent them in a civil suit against the contractor. Despite the fact that the lawyer had acted openly, and all the affected parties were aware of the dual representation, the Illinois Supreme Court suspended the lawyer for one year. Similarly, *In re Odendahl*, M.R. 2787 (Ill.1982), the Illinois Supreme Court suspended a lawyer for one year when, while a state's attorney, he represented individuals in nine divorce proceedings in which support payments were due. In one case, he represented the wife to obtain the divorce, and then the husband, in a petition to reduce the support payments. In another case, he prosecuted a defendant for disorderly conduct and then filed an answer for him in a divorce suit by his wife. The court noted that four of these cases occurred after motions to disqualify had been filed against the lawyer and that he knew or should have known of the impropriety of his conduct.

4.33 Reprimand is generally appropriate when a lawyer is negligent in determining whether the representation of a client may be materially affected by the lawyer's own interests, or whether the representation will adversely affect another client, and causes injury or potential injury to a client.

Commentary

The courts generally impose a reprimand when a lawyer engages in a single instance of misconduct involving a conflict of interest when the lawyer has merely been negligent and there is no overreaching or serious injury to a client. For example, in *State v. Swoyer*, 228 Kan. 799, 619 P.2d 1166 (1980), a public censure was imposed on a lawyer who was representing a client who owned his own business, and who also advised the client's former employee to sue the client for back wages. Although the lawyer stated that he was simply carrying out his client's wishes by attempting to secure payment for the employee, and that he merely advised her to file suit herself, the court found an ethical violation worthy of censure (reprimand) since her petition was actually typed in the lawyer's office and filed by the lawyer. In a multiple representation situation, the court in *Gendron v. State Bar of California*, 35 Cal.3d 409, 673 P.2d 260, 197 Cal.Rptr. 590 (1983), imposed a public reprimand on a public defender who neglected to obtain written waiver of conflict forms from three defendants who were jointly charged with robbery. In *Matter of Palmieri*, 76 N.J. 51, 385 A.2d 856 (1978), a public reprimand was imposed on a lawyer who represented the seller of a supermarket when, with the buyers unable to hire a lawyer and upon the insistence of the seller, he also represented the buyers. Although the lawyer made full disclosure of the relevant facts and pitfalls of multiple representation, he later filed suit against the buyers and eventually had to withdraw when he was required to be a witness concerning the nature of the agreement between the parties.

Courts also impose reprimands in cases of subsequent representation. For example, in *In re Drendel*, M.R. 1708 (Ill.1975), a lawyer represented a client in a divorce suit against his wife, but the parties reconciled before the hearing and the case was dismissed. About 18 months later, he represented the wife in a divorce action against the husband, but this suit was also dismissed. Similarly, in *In re Lewis*, M.R. 2766 (Ill.1982), the lawyer represented the executor of a will and later, while employed in another office, represented a client who was the devisee of the residence property who filed a petition alleging misconduct by the executor. The court ordered the lawyer censured [reprimanded], noting no evidence of secrecy, fraud, or financial benefit to the lawyer.

> **4.34 Admonition is generally appropriate when a lawyer engages in an isolated instance of negligence in determining whether the representation of a client may be materially affected by the lawyer's own interests, or whether the representation will adversely affect another client, and causes little or no actual or potential injury to a client.**

4.4 Lack of Diligence

Absent aggravating or mitigating circumstances, upon application of the factors set out in Standard 3.0, the following sanctions are generally appropriate in cases involving a failure to act with reasonable diligence and promptness in representing a client:

> **4.41 Disbarment is generally appropriate when:**
>
> **(a) a lawyer abandons the practice and causes serious or potentially serious injury to a client; or**
>
> **(b) a lawyer knowingly fails to perform services for a client and causes serious or potentially serious injury to a client; or**
>
> **(c) a lawyer engages in a pattern of neglect with respect to client matters and causes serious or potentially serious injury to a client.**

Commentary

Lack of diligence can take a variety of forms. Some lawyers simply abandon their practices, leaving clients completely unaware that they have no legal representation and often leaving clients without any legal remedy. Other lawyers knowingly fail to perform services for a client, or engage in a pattern of misconduct, demonstrating by their behavior that they either cannot or will not conform to the required ethical standards.

Disbarment is appropriate in each of these situations. For example, in *The Florida Bar v. Lehman*, 417 So.2d 648 (Fla.1982), a lawyer abandoned his practice and kept approximately 450 pending client matters. The clients suffered serious injuries; one client's statute of limitations ran, and many of the clients never recovered money paid to the lawyer as fees. See also: *In re Cullinam*, M.R. 2963 (Ill.1983) (with other charges). In a case demonstrating a pattern of neglect, *State v. Dixon*, 233 Kan. 465, 664 P.2d 286 (1983), a lawyer was disbarred after having been disciplined for 13 counts of neglect of probate cases, with each case involving a long period of neglect (16 years, 28 years, etc.). The court noted that, although there was no evidence of dishonesty on the part of the lawyer, disbarment was appropriate because "the extent of the neglect is extreme and had reached proportions never before considered by this court" (233 Kan. at 470, 644 P.2d at 289). See also: *The Florida Bar v. Mitchell*, 285 So.2d 96 (Fla.1980).

4.42 **Suspension is generally appropriate when:**

    (a) **a lawyer knowingly fails to perform services for a client and causes injury or potential injury to a client; or**

    (b) **a lawyer engages in a pattern of neglect and causes injury or potential injury to a client.**

Commentary

Suspension should be imposed when a lawyer knows that he is not performing the services requested by the client, but does nothing to remedy the situation, or when a lawyer engages in a pattern of neglect, with the result that the lawyer causes injury or potential injury to a client. Most cases involve lawyers who do not communicate with their clients. For example, in *In re Earl J. Taylor*, 666 Ill.2d 567, 363 N.E.2d 845 (1977), a lawyer was suspended for one year when he failed to appear at a criminal hearing, failed to file a divorce action, and failed to prosecute a civil case. In the third case, the lawyer told the client that "he'd take care of everything," yet did not contact her or return her telephone calls. This last client suffered a default judgment, which forced her to settle and pay a second lawyer; the first two clients suffered the loss of the fee. See also: *Hunt v. Disciplinary Board of the Alabama State Bar*, 381 So.2d 52 (Ala.1980); *People v. Dixon*, 616 P.2d 103 (Colo.1980).

4.43 **Reprimand is generally appropriate when a lawyer is negligent and does not act with reasonable diligence in representing a client, and causes injury or potential injury to a client.**

Commentary

Most courts impose a reprimand when the lawyer is negligent. For example, in *In re Logan*, 70 N.J. 222, 358 A.2d 787 (1976), a lawyer who neglected a client matter was reprimanded when, knowing that a motion for reduction of alimony was dependent on the court's examination of his client's tax return, he failed to file a copy of the tax return with the court. See also: *In re Donohue,* 77 A.D.2d 112, 432 N.Y.S.2d 498 (1980), where a lawyer neglected an estate matter, but where the estate was eventually closed to the satisfaction of all parties and with no financial loss, and *Louis Lan,* DP–194180 (Mich.Atty.Dis. Board 1980), where the lawyer attempted to transfer cases to other lawyers without adequately communicating with his clients.

> **4.44 Admonition is generally appropriate when a lawyer is negligent and does not act with reasonable diligence in representing a client, and causes little or no actual or potential injury to a client.**

4.5 Lack of Competence

Absent aggravating or mitigating circumstances, upon application of the factors set out in Standard 3.0, the following sanctions are generally appropriate in cases involving failure to provide competent representation to a client:

> **4.51 Disbarment is generally appropriate when a lawyer's course of conduct demonstrates that the lawyer does not understand the most fundamental legal doctrines or procedures, and the lawyer's conduct causes injury or potential injury to a client.**

Commentary

Disbarment should be imposed on lawyers who are found to have engaged in multiple instances of incompetent behavior. Since disbarment is such a serious sanction, it should rarely be imposed on a lawyer who has demonstrated only a single instance of incompetence; rather, disbarment should be imposed on lawyers whose course of conduct demonstrates that they cannot or will not master the knowledge and skills necessary for minimally competent practice. For example, in *The Florida Bar v. Blaha,* 366 So.2d 443 (Fla.1978), the court disbarred a lawyer who totally mishandled a guardianship and real estate transaction, and also filed a complaint for another client in the wrong court, such that relief was denied. In representing a third client, the lawyer mishandled a replevin action, filing replevin under old rules at a time when his client had not yet perfected a security interest necessary to support the action. As a result of this incompetence, the lawyer was eventually held in contempt and fined $3,000.

> **4.52 Suspension is generally appropriate when a lawyer engages in an area of practice in which the lawyer knows he or she is not competent, and causes injury or potential injury to a client.**

Commentary

In order to protect the public, a suspension should be imposed in cases when a lawyer engages in practice in areas in which a lawyer knows that he or she is not competent. In such cases, it may also be appropriate to attach certain conditions to the suspension, such as a requirement that the lawyer pass the bar examination or limit his or her practice to certain areas.

Such a situation arose in the case of *Office of Disciplinary Counsel v. Henry,* 664 S.W.2d 62 (Tenn.1983), where the lawyer mishandled four cases in a relatively short period of time. In one case, the lawyer attempted to represent a client charged with murder. The lawyer had never handled any felony case before, and yet did not associate any lawyer with him. He made little investigation of the crime, and filed motions based on statutes which had been superceded. Further, he severely damaged his client's case by filing an "amended answer" to the indictment, following the form which would be filed in a civil action, which set forth his client's version of the homicide. The court imposed a two-year suspension with reinstatement conditioned "upon a showing that he has obtained a level of competence adequate to justify the issuance of a license" (664 S.W.2d at 64).

4.53 Reprimand is generally appropriate when a lawyer:

> **(a) demonstrates failure to understand relevant legal doctrines or procedures and causes injury or potential injury to a client; or**
>
> **(b) is negligent in determining whether he or she is competent to handle a legal matter and causes injury or potential injury to a client.**

Commentary

Most courts impose reprimands on lawyers who are incompetent. For example, in *The Florida Bar v. Gray,* 380 So.2d 1292 (Fla.1980), the lawyer agreed to represent a client in a claim of violation of the truth in lending laws, but, although the evidence showed that he expected to become qualified in this area, he did not engage in sufficient study and investigation to become competent (only securing a number of laymen's publications). The court imposed a public reprimand. Similarly, in *State ex rel. Nebraska State Bar Association v. Holscher,* 193 Neb. 729, 230 N.W.2d 75 (1975), a county lawyer who filed a claim for services he rendered in foreclosing tax sale certificates without familiarizing himself with the statute prescribing the fee for such services received a reprimand.

While reprimand alone can be appropriate, a combination of reprimand and probation is often a more productive approach. Probation can be very effective in assisting lawyers to improve their legal skills. The court can use probation creatively, imposing whatever conditions are necessary to assist that particular lawyer. It may be appropriate, for example, to require an inexperienced lawyer to associate with co-counsel. In *Florida Bar v. Glick,* 383 So.2d 642 (Fla.1980), the court imposed a reprimand and one-year probation on a lawyer who mishandled a quiet title action. The court imposed the following conditions of probation: that the lawyer refrain from representing clients in real estate matters and that he complete 30 hours of approved continuing education courses in real property.

> **4.54 Admonition is generally appropriate when a lawyer engages in an isolated instance of negligence in determining whether he or she is competent to handle a legal matter, and causes little or no actual or potential injury to a client.**

4.6 Lack of Candor

Absent aggravating or mitigating circumstances, upon application of the factors set out in Standard 3.0, the following sanctions are generally appropriate in cases where the lawyer engages in fraud, deceit, or misrepresentation directed toward a client:

> **4.61 Disbarment is generally appropriate when a lawyer knowingly deceives a client with the intent to benefit the lawyer or another, and causes serious injury or potentially serious injury to a client.**

Commentary

Disbarment is appropriate when a lawyer intentionally abuses the fiduciary relationship, making misrepresentations to a client in order to benefit himself or another and causing serious injury or potentially serious injury to a client. (For a discussion of lack of candor before a court, see Standard 6.1). For example, in *Matter of Wolfson,* 313 N.W.2d 596 (Minn.1981), the court disbarred a lawyer who asked a client to help him arrange for a loan, and who misrepresented that the loan was for medical treatment for his daughter, when the loan was actually used in his wife's business. The client personally guaranteed payment of the loan and, when the lawyer failed to repay it, the client had to institute legal action against the lawyer to obtain an $832.61 judgment. In imposing disbarment, the court stated that the lawyer had not "hesitated to use his knowledge and skill as a lawyer for improper purposes" (313 N.W.2d at 602). (Note: The lawyer had also engaged in acts of neglect and abuse of the legal process.) Similarly, in (anonymous) 49 Cal.State Bar J. 73 (1974), a lawyer was disbarred after he borrowed money from two clients, falsely leading them to believe that he was solvent, with the result that the clients received an unsecured promissory note. In *Virginia State Bar ex rel. Eighth District Committee v. Fred W. Bender, Jr.,* No. 50228 (Va.App.Ct.1981), the court revoked the license of a lawyer who intentionally overstated the number of hours he worked on a client's estate to make it appear that he was entitled to $9,500.

4.62 Suspension is generally appropriate when a lawyer knowingly deceives a client, and causes injury or potential injury to the client.

Commentary

Suspension is appropriate when a lawyer knowingly deceives a client, although not necessarily for his own direct benefit, and the client is injured. The most common cases are those in which a lawyer misrepresents the nature or the extent of services performed. For example, in *Kentucky Bar Association v. Reed,* 623 S.W.2d 228 (Ky.1981), the court suspended a lawyer for one year when he misrepresented the status of three different cases and all three clients suffered injury (two clients suffered a summary judgment against them and another client was denied a settlement payment for an extensive period of time).

4.63 Reprimand is generally appropriate when a lawyer negligently fails to provide a client with accurate or complete information, and causes injury or potential injury to the client.

Commentary

Reprimand is justified when the lawyer is merely negligent and there is injury or potential injury to a client. In *Hawkins v. State Bar,* 23 Cal.3d 622, 591 P.2d 524, 153 Cal.Rptr. 234 (1979), a lawyer received a public reproval (reprimand) when he failed to fully explain to his clients the nature of a contingency interest which he possessed in insurance proceeds used to satisfy an adverse judgment against the clients in a personal injury action.

4.64 Admonition is generally appropriate when a lawyer engages in an isolated instance of negligence in failing to provide a client with accurate or complete information, and causes little or no actual or potential injury to the client.

5.0 Violations of Duties Owed to the Public

Introduction

The most fundamental duty which a lawyer owes the public is the duty to maintain the standards of personal integrity upon which the community relies. The public expects the lawyer to be honest and to abide by the law; public confidence in the integrity of officers of the court is undermined when lawyers engage in illegal conduct [Rules 8.4(b) and (c)/DR 1–102(A)(3)(4)) and (5)]. In addition, a lawyer who serves as a public official has the duty to avoid using his public position to obtain any special advantage for himself or a client, or to influence a tribunal to act in favor of himself or a client [Rules 3.5(a), 8.4(e) and (f)/DR 8–101 through DR 8–103, DR 9–101(c)]. Finally, prosecutors have a special obligation to protect the public interest by insuring that charges are brought only after a finding of probable cause, and that exculpatory evidence is turned over to the accused (Rule 3.8(a)/DR 7–103).

It is important to note that the ABA Standards for Lawyer Discipline provide that the court should place a lawyer on interim suspension immediately and without reference to the pendency of an appeal upon proof that the lawyer has been convicted of a "serious crime" or is causing great harm to the public (Standard 6.5). A "serious crime" is defined as any felony and any lesser crime a necessary element of which involves interference with the administration of justice, false swearing, misrepresentation, fraud, extortion, misappropriation, theft, or an attempt or a conspiracy to commit a "serious crime." The sanctions which are set out below are those which should be imposed as final discipline, at which time the interim suspension should be terminated (Standard 6.6).

5.1 Failure to Maintain Personal Integrity

Absent aggravating or mitigating circumstances, upon application of the factors set out in Standard 3.0, the following sanctions are generally appropriate in cases involving commission of a criminal act that reflects adversely on the lawyer's honesty, trustworthiness, or fitness as a lawyer in other respects, or in cases with conduct involving dishonesty, fraud, deceit, or misrepresentation:

5.11 Disbarment is generally appropriate when:

> **(a) a lawyer engages in serious criminal conduct, a necessary element of which includes intentional interference with the administration of justice, false swearing, misrepresentation, fraud, extortion, misappropriation, or theft; or the sale, distribution or importation of controlled substances; or the intentional killing of another; or an attempt or conspiracy or solicitation of another to commit any of these offenses; or**

> **(b) a lawyer engages in any other intentional conduct involving dishonesty, fraud, deceit, or misrepresentation that seriously adversely reflects on the lawyer's fitness to practice.**

Commentary

A lawyer who engages in any of the illegal acts listed above has violated one of the most basic professional obligations to the public, the pledge to maintain personal honesty and integrity. This duty to the public is breached regardless of whether a criminal charge has been brought against the lawyer. In fact, this type of misconduct is so closely related to practice and poses such an immediate threat to the public that the lawyer should be suspended from the practice of law immediately pending a final determination of the ultimate discipline to be imposed (see Standards for Lawyer Discipline, Standard 6.5).

In imposing final discipline in such cases, most courts impose disbarment on lawyers who are convicted of serious felonies. As the court noted in a case where a lawyer was convicted of two counts of federal income tax evasion and one count of subornation of perjury, "we cannot ask the public to voluntarily comply with the legal system if we, as lawyers, reject its fairness and application to ourselves." *In the Matter of Grimes*, 414 Mich. 483, 326 N.W.2d 380 (1982). See also: *In re Fry*, 251 Ga. 247, 305 S.E.2d 590 (Ga.1983), conviction of murder; *Sixth District Committee of the Virginia State Bar v. Albert C. Hodgson*, No. 80–18 (Va.Disciplinary Board, 1981), where a lawyer advised a client that he could make arrangements to have her husband killed in lieu of bringing a child custody suit.

> **5.12 Suspension is generally appropriate when a lawyer knowingly engages in criminal conduct which does not contain the elements listed in Standard 5.11 and that seriously adversely reflects on the lawyer's fitness to practice.**

Commentary

Lawyers who engage in criminal conduct other than that described above in Standard 5.11 should be suspended in cases where their conduct seriously adversely reflects on their fitness to practice. As in the case of disbarment, a suspension can be imposed even where no criminal charges have been filed against the lawyer. Not every lawyer who commits a criminal act should be suspended, however. As pointed out in the Model Rules of Professional Conduct:

> Although a lawyer is personally answerable to the entire criminal law, a lawyer should be professionally answerable only for offenses that indicate lack of those characteristics relevant to law practice. Offenses involving violence, dishonesty, or breach of trust, or serious interference with the administration of justice are in that category. A pattern of repeated offenses, even ones of minor significance when considered separately, can indicate indifference to legal obligation.[30]

The most common cases involved lawyers who commit felonies other than those listed above, such as the possession of narcotics or sexual assault. See: *In re Robideau*, 102 Wis.2d 16, 306 N.W.2d 1 (1981), suspension for three years for contributing to the delinquency of a minor and possession of a controlled substance; *In re Lanier*, 309 S.E.2d 754 (S.C.1983), indefinite suspension for possession of marijuana; *In re Safran*, 18 Cal.3d 134, 554 P.2d 329, 133 Cal.Rptr. 9 (1976), suspension for three years for conviction of two counts of child molesting.

---

30. Comment to Rule 8.4, Model Rules, *Id.*

5.13 Reprimand is generally appropriate when a lawyer knowingly engages in any other conduct that involves dishonesty, fraud, deceit, or misrepresentation and that adversely reflects on the lawyer's fitness to practice law.

Commentary

There are few situations not involving fraud or dishonesty which are sufficiently related to the practice of law to subject a lawyer to discipline. The Arizona Supreme Court applied this standard in *In re Johnson*, 106 Ariz. 73, 471 P.2d 269 (1970), a case where a lawyer was charged with assault, stating that "isolated, trivial incidents of this kind not involving a fixed pattern of misbehavior find ample redress in the criminal and civil laws. They have none of the elements of moral turpitude, arising more out of the infirmities of human nature. They are not the appropriate subject matter of a solemn reprimand by this court" (471 P.2d at 271). However, a pattern of repeated offenses, even ones of minor significance when considered separately, can indicate such indifference to legal obligation as to justify a reprimand.

There can be situations, however, in which the lawyer's conduct is not even criminal, but, because it is directly related to his or her professional role, discipline is required. For example, in *In re Lamberis*, 93 Ill.2d 222, 443 N.E.2d 549 (1982), the court imposed a censure [reprimand] on a lawyer who knowingly plagiarized two published works in a thesis submitted in satisfaction of the requirements for a master's degree. The court noted that although the lawyer's conduct might appear to be "fairly distant from the practice of law," discipline was "appropriate and required because both the extent of the appropriated material and the purpose for which it was used evidence the respondent's complete disregard for values that are most fundamental in the legal profession" (443 N.E.2d at 551). Specifically, the lawyer's plagiarism displayed "an extreme cynicism toward the property rights of others," and a "lack of honesty which cannot go undisciplined, especially because honesty is so fundamental to the functioning of the legal profession" (443 N.E.2d at 551–52).

5.14 Admonition is generally appropriate when a lawyer engages in any other conduct that reflects adversely on the lawyer's fitness to practice law.

5.2 Failure to Maintain the Public Trust

Absent aggravating or mitigating circumstances, upon application of the factors set out in Standard 3.0, the following sanctions are generally appropriate in cases involving public officials who engage in conduct that is prejudicial to the administration of justice or who state or imply an ability to influence improperly a government agency or official:

5.21 Disbarment is generally appropriate when a lawyer in an official or governmental position knowingly misuses the position with the intent to obtain a significant benefit or advantage for himself or another, or with the intent to cause serious or potentially serious injury to a party or to the integrity of the legal process.

Commentary

The public officials who are subject to disbarment generally engage in conduct involving fraud and deceit, and are generally subject to criminal sanctions as well. For example, in *In re Rosenthal*, 73 Ill.2d 46, 382 N.E.2d 257 (1978), two lawyers were disbarred who participated in an extortion scheme to benefit their client as part of a zoning request. One of the lawyers was an assistant Attorney General, a fact which the court emphasized as significant in imposing disbarment: "Despite his obligations as a law officer, he knowingly participated and furthered conduct which he knew to be illegal, and then, further, deliberately misled federal agents" (382 N.E.2d at 262). The court concluded, "corruption within government could not, in most instances, thrive but for those few attorneys, who, like respondents, are willing to tolerate such illegal activity if it will benefit their client. The practice of law is a privilege and demands a greater acceptance of responsibility and adherence to ethical standards than respondents have demonstrated" (382 N.E.2d at 261).

5.22 Suspension is generally appropriate when a lawyer in an official or governmental position knowingly fails to follow proper procedures or rules, and causes injury or potential injury to a party or to the integrity of the legal process.

Commentary

Suspension is an appropriate sanction when lawyers who are public officials knowingly act improperly, but not necessarily for their own benefit. For example, in *In re DeLucia*, 76 N.J. 329, 387 A.2d 362 (1978), a judge fixed a traffic ticket by entering a not guilty judgment when no hearing had been held. He later attempted to cover up his wrongdoing by preparing an affidavit with a backdated acknowledgment. Disciplinary proceedings were instituted after the lawyer had resigned from his part-time judgeship. The court imposed a one-year suspension, noting that he did not personally benefit. Similarly, in *In re Weishoff*, 75 N.J. 326, 382 A.2d 632 (1978), the court held that a municipal prosecutor's knowing participation in an improper disposition of a traffic ticket warranted a one-year suspension. In *In re Vasser*, 75 N.J. 357, 382 A.2d 1114 (1978), the court imposed a six-month suspension on a lawyer/part-time judge who improperly practiced law and also interceded in another court to obtain a postponement of a trial to give his client an advantage in an unrelated civil matter. The lawyer also used official court stationery with respect to a transaction relating solely to his private law practice. The court noted that "the instances of proved misconduct did not assume egregious proportions. His improper intercession in the neighboring municipal court apparently did not result in any tangible or lasting distortion of justice" (382 A.2d at 1117).

> **5.23 Reprimand is generally appropriate when a lawyer in an official or governmental position negligently fails to follow proper procedures or rules, and causes injury or potential injury to a party or to the integrity of the legal process.**

Commentary

In *In re Shafir,* 92 N.J. 138, 455 A.2d 1114 (1983), the court imposed a public reprimand on a county prosecutor who improperly placed his supervisor's signature on forms filed in plea bargaining cases. The lawyer stated that he believed he had explicit or implicit authority to sign what he thought were internal records and the disciplinary committee found that the lawyer "was not motivated by personal gain but only by a desire to move cases on his trial list" (455 A.2d at 1116). Similarly, in *State v. Socolofsky,* 233 Kan. 1020, 666 P.2d 725 (1983), the court imposed a public censure [reprimand] on a county attorney who anonymously mailed to discharged members of a jury a copy of a newspaper article describing that the acquitted defendant had subsequently pled guilty to a misdemeanor charge of delivery of L.S.D. in an unrelated case. Some of the jurors who received the mailing were called for service only a month later. The lawyer testified that he would not have mailed the article had he realized that the jurors were to be called for further service, and, that in his experience as a prosecutor, "he had never seen jurors called back for further duty so soon" (666 P.2d at 726).

> **5.24 Admonition is generally appropriate when a lawyer in an official or governmental position engages in an isolated instance of negligence in not following proper procedures or rules, and causes little or no actual or potential injury to a party or to the integrity of the legal process.**

6.0 Violations of Duties Owed to the Legal System

Introduction

Lawyers are officers of the court, and the public expects lawyers to abide by the legal rules of substance and procedure which affect the administration of justice. Lawyers must always operate within the bounds of the law, and cannot create or use false evidence, or make false statement of material fact [Rules 3.3, 3.4, and 4.1/DR 7–102(A)]. Ethical standards require that a lawyer refrain from filing frivolous suits (Rule 3.1/DR 7–102), delaying a trial (Rule 3.2/DR 7–102), improperly communicating with a party, juror, witness, or judge (Rules 3.5, 4.2,

4.3/DR 7–104, DR 7–108 through DR 7–110), threatening criminal prosecution (DR 7–105), or otherwise interfering with a legal process (Rules 3.4, 3.6, 4.1, 4.4/DR 7–106 and DR 7–107).

6.1 False Statements, Fraud, and Misrepresentation

Absent aggravating or mitigating circumstances, upon application of the factors set out in Standard 3.0, the following sanctions are generally appropriate in cases involving conduct that is prejudicial to the administration of justice or that involves dishonesty, fraud, deceit, or misrepresentation to a court:

> **6.11 Disbarment is generally appropriate when a lawyer, with the intent to deceive the court, makes a false statement, submits a false document, or improperly withholds material information, and causes serious or potentially serious injury to a party, or causes a significant or potentially significant adverse effect on the legal proceeding.**

Commentary

The lawyers who engage in these practices violate the most fundamental duty of an officer of the court. As the court noted in a case in which a criminal defense lawyer was disbarred for putting a client on the stand to testify falsely, "A lawyer's participation in the presentation of knowing false evidence is the clearest kind of ethical breach" [*Board of Overseers of the Bar v. James Dineen,* No. 83–46 (Maine 1983) at 4]. In *Office of Disciplinary Counsel v. Grigsby,* 493 Pa. 194, 425 A.2d 730 (1981), a lawyer was disbarred where he filed a false sworn pleading in connection with a pending garnishment proceeding. The pleading stated that the funds in the lawyer's checking account belonged to clients and could not be reached. The lawyer's action to save his money from garnishment was both intentional and damaging to his creditors. Similarly, in *Matter of Discipline of Agnew,* 311 N.W.2d 869 (Minn.1981), the court disbarred a lawyer who refused to return a client's documents after an initial consultation and, without the client's knowledge or consent, then instituted a suit on his behalf in which he made false allegations that the client had been harmed by the defendant. Because of the lawyer's actions, the client incurred legal bills of $8,000 and lost time appearing in court to obtain his own documents.

> **6.12 Suspension is generally appropriate when a lawyer knows that false statements or documents are being submitted to the court or that material information is improperly being withheld, and takes no remedial action, and causes injury or potential injury to a party to the legal proceeding, or causes an adverse or potentially adverse effect on the legal proceeding.**

1321

Commentary

Suspension is appropriate when a lawyer has not acted with intent to deceive the court, but when he knows that material information is being withheld and does not inform the court, with the result that there is injury or potential injury to a party, or an adverse or potentially adverse effect on the legal proceeding. For example, in *In re Nigohosian*, 88 N.J. 308, 442 A.2d 1007 (1982), the court suspended a lawyer for six months when he failed to disclose to the court or to opposing counsel the fact that he had previously conveyed property that was the subject of a settlement to someone else. The court noted that, while a lawyer does not have a continuing obligation to inform the court of the state of a client's assets, he "has a duty of disclosure of any significant fact" touching upon the status of an asset which is the subject matter of a stipulation before the court (442 A.2d at 1009).

6.13 Reprimand is generally appropriate when a lawyer is negligent either in determining whether statements or documents are false or in taking remedial action when material information is being withheld, and causes injury or potential injury to a party to the legal proceeding, or causes an adverse or potentially adverse effect on the legal proceeding.

Commentary

Reprimand is appropriate when a lawyer is merely negligent. For example, in *Gilbert E. Meltry*, D.P. 144/81 (Mich.Atty.Dis.Brd.1981), the lawyer was publicly reprimanded where he accidentally filed a motion for a bond which contained inaccurate statements. Similarly, in *In re Coughlin*, 91 N.J. 374, 450 A.2d 1326 (1982), the court held that a public reprimand should be imposed on a lawyer who did not follow proper procedures in acknowledging a deed (neglecting to secure the grantor's acknowledgement in his presence). The court noted that "his actions were not grounded on any intent of self-benefit, nor was any one harmed as a result of his actions" (450 A.2d at 1327). In *Davidson v. State Bar*, 17 Cal.3d 570, 551 P.2d 1211, 131 Cal.Rptr. 379 (1976), the court imposed a public reprimand on a lawyer who failed to disclose to the court the location of his client in a child custody case when his conduct occurred in confused circumstances caused by contradictory *ex parte* custody orders.

6.14 Admonition is generally appropriate when a lawyer engages in an isolated instance of neglect in determining whether submitted statements or documents are false or in failing to disclose material information upon learning of its falsity, and causes little or no actual or potential injury to a party, or causes little or no adverse or potentially adverse effect on the legal proceeding.

6.2 Abuse of the Legal Process

Absent aggravating or mitigating circumstances, upon application of the factors set out in Standard 3.0, the following sanctions are generally appropriate in cases involving failure to expedite litigation or bring a meritorious claim, or failure to obey any obligation under the rules of a tribunal except for an open refusal based on an assertion that no valid obligation exists:

> **6.21 Disbarment is generally appropriate when a lawyer knowingly violates a court order or rule with the intent to obtain a benefit for the lawyer or another, and causes serious injury or potentially serious injury to a party, or causes serious or potentially serious interference with a legal proceeding.**

Commentary

Lawyers should be disbarred for intentionally misusing the judicial process to benefit the lawyer or another when the lawyer's conduct causes injury or potentially serious injury to a party, or serious or potentially serious interference with a legal proceeding. For example, in *In the Matter of Daniel Friedland,* 416 N.E.2d 433 (Ind.1981), the lawyer filed charges against members of the Disciplinary Committee and witnesses in the lawyer disciplinary hearing. The lawyer attempted to use the lawsuit to intimidate and discredit those who administered and prosecuted grievances against him. In holding that the lawyer was not protected by the First Amendment, the court recognized the harm to judicial integrity. "It is the Constitutional duty of this Court, on behalf of sovereign interest, to preserve, manage, and safeguard the adjudicatory system of this State. The adjudicatory process cannot function when its officers misconstrue the purpose of litigation. The respondent attempted to influence the process through the use of threats and intimidation against the participants involved. This type of conduct must be enjoined to preserve the integrity of the system. The adjudicatory process, including disciplinary proceedings, must permit the orderly resolution of issues; Respondent's conduct impeded the order of this process" (416 N.E.2d at 438). See also: *In re Crumpacker,* 269 Ind. 630, 383 N.E.2d 36 (1978), where the court disbarred a lawyer who had engaged in nineteen acts of misconduct, including shouting at and verbally abusing witnesses and opposing counsel, taking an action merely to harass another, and generally using offensive tactics. In the words of the court, his misconduct showed that he was "a vicious, sinister person, tunnel-visioned by personal pique, willing to forego all professional responsibilities which conflict with acts of preconceived vengeance on personal enemies" (383 N.E.2d at 52).

> **6.22 Suspension is appropriate when a lawyer knows that he is violating a court order or rule, and there is injury**

or potential injury to a client or a party, or interference or potential interference with a legal proceeding.

Commentary

In many cases, lawyers are suspended when they knowingly violate court orders. Such knowing violations can occur when a lawyer fails to comply with a court order that applies directly to him or her, as in the case of lawyers who do not comply with a divorce decree ordering spousal maintenance or child support. Suspension is also appropriate where the lawyer interferes directly with the legal process. For example, in *In re Vincenti,* 92 N.J. 591, 458 A.2d 1268 (1983), the court imposed a suspension for one year and until further order of court where the lawyer made repeated discourteous, insulting and degrading verbal attacks on the judge and his rulings which substantially interfered with the orderly trial process. The court noted that it was not confronted with "an isolated example of loss of composure brought on by the emotion of the moment; rather, the numerous instances of impropriety pervaded the proceedings over a period of three months" (458 A.2d at 1274).

> **6.23 Reprimand is generally appropriate when a lawyer negligently fails to comply with a court order or rule, and causes injury or potential injury to a client or other party, or causes interference or potential interference with a legal proceeding.**

Commentary

Most courts impose a reprimand on lawyers who engage in misconduct at trial or who violate a court order or rule that causes injury or potential injury to a client or other party, or who cause interference or potential interference with a legal proceeding. For example, in *McDaniel v. State of Arkansas,* 640 S.W.2d 442 (Ark.1982), a lawyer who failed to file briefs in a timely manner after having been given extensions received a reprimand. In *Florida Bar v. Rosenberg,* 387 So.2d 935 (Fla.1980), the court imposed a reprimand on a lawyer who used harassing delay tactics at trial and who also refused to send copies of documents to opposing counsel. Courts also impose reprimands when lawyers neglect to respond to orders of the disciplinary agency. For example, in *In re Minor,* 658 P.2d 781 (Alaska 1983), the court imposed a public censure [reprimand] on a lawyer who, because of poor office procedures, neglected to respond to a letter from the Alaska Bar Association.

> **6.24 Admonition is generally appropriate when a lawyer engages in an isolated instance of negligence in complying with a court order or rule, and causes little or no actual or potential injury to a party, or causes little or no actual or potential interference with a legal proceeding.**

6.3 Improper Communications With Individuals in the Legal System

Absent aggravating or mitigating circumstances, upon application of the factors set out in Standard 3.0, the following sanctions are generally appropriate in cases involving attempts to influence a judge, juror, prospective juror or other official by means prohibited by law:

6.31 Disbarment is generally appropriate when a lawyer:

> **(a) intentionally tampers with a witness and causes serious or potentially serious injury to a party, or causes significant or potentially significant interference with the outcome of the legal proceeding; or**

> **(b) makes an ex parte communication with a judge or juror with intent to affect the outcome of the proceeding, and causes serious or potentially serious injury to a party, or causes significant or potentially significant interference with the outcome of the legal proceeding; or**

> **(c) improperly communicates with someone in the legal system other than a witness, judge, or juror with the intent to influence or affect the outcome of the proceeding, and causes significant or potentially significant interference with the outcome of the legal proceeding.**

Commentary

Disbarment is warranted in cases where the lawyer uses fraud or undue influence to injure a party or to affect the outcome of a legal proceeding. For example, in *In the Matter of Stroh*, 97 Wash.2d 289, 644 P.2d 1161 (1982), a lawyer was disbarred when he was convicted of tampering with a witness. The court justified imposing disbarment on the following basis: "First, the crime of tampering with a witness strikes at the very core of the judicial system and therefore necessarily involves moral turpitude.... An attorney presents his case almost entirely through the testimony of witnesses. Although an occasional witness may perjure him/herself, the presentation of the opponent's other witnesses and effective cross-examination frequently reveals the falsehood before a fraud has been perpetrated upon the court. A witness, tampered by an attorney, however, becomes much more destructive to the search for truth. That witness, privy to the testimony of other witnesses, can avoid the pitfalls of contradiction and refutation by judicious fabrication. Vigorous cross-examination may become ineffective as the coached witness would know both the questions and the proper answers. In sum, the legal system is virtually defenseless against the united forces of a corrupt attorney and a perjured witness" (644 P.2d at 1165).

Similarly, in *Matter of Holman,* 286 S.E.2d 148 (S.C.1982), a lawyer was disbarred who was convicted of contempt of court based on a communication with a member of a jury selected for trial.

6.32 Suspension is generally appropriate when a lawyer engages in communication with an individual in the legal system when the lawyer knows that such communication is improper, and causes injury or potential injury to a party or causes interference or potential interference with the outcome of the legal proceeding.

Commentary

In the case of *John Arnold Fitzgerald* (Tenn.1980) (unpublished decision), a lawyer was suspended for one year for threats to an opposing party. Similarly, in *The Florida Bar v. Lopez,* 406 So.2d 1100 (Fla. 1982), a lawyer was suspended for one year where he urged two parties he was suing on behalf of his client to change their testimony in exchange for general releases from prosecution. In imposing this sanction, the court rejected a referee's recommendation of a three-month suspension with automatic reinstatement, stating, "we feel that a three-month suspension is insufficient to impress upon respondent, the bar, and the public our dissatisfaction with and distress over his conduct. If Mr. Lopez had been convicted in a court of this state of tampering with a witness, he would have been subject to a one-year term of imprisonment. Using the witness-tampering statute as a guideline, we find a one-year suspension appropriate in this case" (406 So.2d at 1102). In *The Florida Bar v. Mason,* 334 So.2d 1 (Fla.1976), the court imposed a reprimand and suspension for one year and until proof of rehabilitation when a lawyer engaged in ex parte communications with justices of the Florida Supreme Court concerning the merits of a pending case and subsequently concealed his actions from opposing counsel.

6.33 Reprimand is generally appropriate when a lawyer is negligent in determining whether it is proper to engage in communication with an individual in the legal system, and causes injury or potential injury to a party or interference or potential interference with the outcome of the legal proceeding.

Commentary

Most courts impose reprimands on lawyers who engage in improper communications. For example, in *In re McCaffrey,* 549 P.2d 666 (Or. 1976), the court imposed a reprimand on a lawyer who unknowingly improperly communicated with a party represented by a lawyer. Even though the lawyer claimed that he thought the party, the husband in a dispute of visitation, was representing himself, the court stated that discipline could be imposed in cases of misconduct that the rule is designed to prevent, and it is "immaterial whether the communication is an intentional or a negligent violation of the rule" (549 P.2d at 668).

    6.34 Admonition is generally appropriate when a lawyer engages in an isolated instance of negligence in improperly communicating with an individual in the legal system, and causes little or no actual or potential injury to a party, or causes little or no actual or potential interference with the outcome of the legal proceeding.

7.0 Violations of Duties Owed to the Profession

Introduction

    The Model Rules include many ethical standards that are not fundamental to the professional relationship but which define certain standards of conduct. These standards concern restrictions on advertising (Rules 7.1, 7.2, 7.4, 7.5/DR 2–101, DR 2–102, DR 2–105), recommending employment (Rule 7.3/DR 2–103, DR 2–104), fees (Rules 1.5, 5.4 and 5.6/DR 2–106, DR 2–107 and DR 3–102), and assisting unauthorized practice (Rule 5.5/DR 3–101 and DR 3–103). Other such standards include the duty to comply with proper procedures for admission to the bar (Rule 8.1/DR 1–101), to report other lawyers who engage in unethical behavior (Rule 8.3/DR 1–103), and to properly withdraw from representation (Rule 1.16/DR 2–110).

    While these standards have been developed out of a desire to protect the public, such as by restricting practice to those persons who have met appropriate educational requirements, a violation of these standards generally is less likely to cause injury to a client, the public, or the administration of justice than the other standards discussed above. In fact, in the area of advertising, the United States Supreme Court has ruled that lawyer advertising is protected by the First Amendment and has struck down certain ethical prohibitions on advertising [see *Bates v. State Bar of Arizona*, 433 U.S. 350, 97 S.Ct. 2691, 53 L.Ed.2d 810 (1977); *In re R.M.J.*, 455 U.S. 191, 102 S.Ct. 929, 71 L.Ed.2d 64 (1982); *Zauderer v. Office of Disciplinary Counsel of the Supreme Court of Ohio*, 53 U.S.L.W. 4587, decided May 28, 1985].

    In general, then, a sanction of disbarment or suspension will rarely be required, and a sanction of reprimand, admonition or probation will be sufficient to insure that the public is protected and the bar is educated. While it will as a rule be inappropriate to impose a sanction of disbarment or suspension for six months or more, there are situations when a more severe sanction should be imposed. The standards set out below identify those exceptional situations.

    Absent aggravating or mitigating circumstances, upon application of the factors set out in Standard 3.0, the following sanctions are generally appropriate in cases involving false or misleading communication about the lawyer or the lawyer's services, improper communication of fields of practice, improper solicitation of professional employment from a prospective client, unreasonable or improper fees, unauthorized practice of law, improper withdrawal from representation, or failure to report professional misconduct.

7.1 Disbarment is generally appropriate when a lawyer knowingly engages in conduct that is a violation of a duty owed as a professional with the intent to obtain a benefit for the lawyer or another, and causes serious or potentially serious injury to a client, the public, or the legal system.

Commentary

Disbarment should be imposed in cases when the lawyer knowingly engages in conduct that violates a duty owed to the profession with the intent to benefit the lawyer or another, and which causes serious injury or potentially serious injury to a client, the public or the legal system. For example, disbarment is appropriate when a lawyer intentionally makes false material statements in his application for admission to the bar. For example, in *In re W. Jason Mitan,* 75 Ill.2d 118, 387 N.E.2d 278 (1979), *cert. denied,* 444 U.S. 916 (1979), the respondent made false statements and deliberately failed to disclose certain information on his application for admission to the bar. These false statements and omissions included his failure to disclose at least four of his previous addresses, the wrong birth date, his change of name, a previous marriage, a subsequent divorce, other law schools attended, application for admission to another state's bar, previous employers and occupations, prior civil suits and arrests, and conviction of a felony. The court felt that these falsehoods and omissions had a direct effect on the ability to practice law and be a competent member of the profession, and imposed disbarment.

7.2 Suspension is generally appropriate when a lawyer knowingly engages in conduct that is a violation of a duty owed as a professional, and causes injury or potential injury to a client, the public, or the legal system.

Commentary

Suspension is appropriate when the lawyer knowingly violates a duty owed to the profession and causes injury or potential injury to a client, the public, or the legal system, even when a lawyer does not intentionally abuse the professional relationship by engaging in deceptive conduct. Suspension is appropriate, for example, when the lawyer did not mislead a client but engages in a pattern of charging excessive or improper fees. A suspension is also appropriate when a lawyer solicits employment knowing that the individual is in a vulnerable state. For example, in *In re Teichner,* 75 Ill.2d 88, 387 N.E.2d 265 (1979), the court suspended a lawyer for two years who was invited by a minister to speak to victims of a railway disaster, but who then contacted victims whom he knew were still in a vulnerable state as a result of the tragedy.

7.3 Reprimand is generally appropriate when a lawyer negligently engages in conduct that is a violation of a duty owed as a professional, and causes injury or potential injury to a client, the public, or the legal system.

Commentary

Reprimand is the appropriate sanction in most cases of a violation of a duty owed to the profession. Usually there is little or no injury to a client, the public, or the legal system, and the purposes of lawyer discipline will be best served by imposing a public sanction that helps educate the respondent lawyer and deter future violations. A public sanction also informs both the public and other members of the profession that this behavior is improper. For example, in *Carter v. Falcarelli*, 402 A.2d 1175 (R.I. 1979), the court imposed public censure (reprimand) on a lawyer who failed to divulge the identity of another lawyer when matters had been forwarded and subsequently neglected.

Courts typically impose reprimands when lawyers engage in a single instance of charging an excessive or improper fee. See *In the Matter of Donald L. Fasig*, 444 N.E.2d 849 (Ind.1983), where the court imposed a public reprimand when the lawyer entered into an agreement for a contingent fee in a criminal case; *Russell J. Perry*, DP 63 (Mich.Atty. Dis.Board, 1983), where a lawyer charged an excessive fee by improperly adding investigation costs; and *The Florida Bar v. Sagrans*, 388 So.2d 1040 (Fla.1980), where the lawyer improperly split fees with a chiropractor.

Courts also impose reprimands on lawyers who are negligent in supervising their employees. For example, in the case of *Donald Franklin Kotter*, 52 Calif.State Bar J. 552–3 (Cal.1977), the court imposed a public reproval (reprimand) on a lawyer who neglected properly to instruct his employees regarding what acts constitute solicitation.

7.4 Admonition is generally appropriate when a lawyer engages in an isolated instance of negligence that is a violation of a duty owed as a professional, and causes little or no actual or potential injury to a client, the public, or the legal system.

8.0 Prior Discipline Orders

Introduction

Severe sanctions should be imposed on lawyers who violate the terms of prior disciplinary orders. While such lawyers may also demonstrate a pattern of misconduct that will serve as an aggravating factor (see Standard 9.22), these violations are so serious as to warrant special discussion.

Absent aggravating or mitigating circumstances, upon application of the factors set out in Standard 3.0, the following sanctions are generally appropriate in cases involving prior discipline.

8.1 Disbarment is generally appropriate when a lawyer:

(a) intentionally or knowingly violates the terms of a prior disciplinary order and such violation causes injury or potential injury to a client, the public, the legal system, or the profession; or

(b) has been suspended for the same or similar misconduct, and intentionally or knowingly engages in further acts of misconduct that cause injury or potential injury to a client, the public, the legal system, or the profession.

Commentary

Disbarment is warranted when a lawyer who has previously been disciplined intentionally or knowingly violates the terms of that order and, as a result, causes injury or potential injury to a client, the public, the legal system, or the profession. The most common case is one where a lawyer has been suspended but, nevertheless, practices law. The courts are generally in agreement in imposing disbarment in such cases. As the court explained in *Matter of McInerney*, 389 Mass. 528, 451 N.E.2d 401, 405 (1983), when the record establishes a lawyer's willingness to violate the terms of his suspension order, disbarment is appropriate "as a prophylactic measure to prevent further misconduct by the offending individual." See also: *In re Reiser*, M.R. 2269 (Ill.1980), where a lawyer was disbarred when he continued to practice law in violation of an order of suspension and caused serious injury to a client by neglecting her legal matter.

Disbarment is also appropriate when a lawyer intentionally or knowingly engages in the same or similar misconduct. For example, in *Benson v. State Bar*, 13 Cal.3d 581, 531 P.2d 1081, 119 Cal.Rptr. 297 (1975), the court disbarred a lawyer who induced a client to loan him money by making false representations and who then failed to repay the loan. The lawyer in that case had previously been suspended for one year (with a four-year probationary period) for misappropriation of client funds. See also: *Matter of Friedland*, 416 N.E.2d 433 (Ind.1981).

8.2 Suspension is generally appropriate when a lawyer has been reprimanded for the same or similar misconduct and engages in further acts of misconduct that cause injury or potential injury to a client, the public, the legal system, or the profession.

Commentary

Lawyers should be suspended when they engage in the same or similar misconduct for which they were previously disciplined when that misconduct causes injury or potential injury to a client, the public, the legal system, or the profession. As the court noted in *The Florida Bar v.*

Glick, 397 So.2d 1140, 1141 (Fla.1981), "[W]e must deal more severely with an attorney who exhibits cumulative misconduct."

8.3 Reprimand is generally appropriate when a lawyer:

(a) negligently violates the terms of a prior disciplinary order and such violation causes injury or potential injury to a client, the public, the legal system, or the profession; or

(b) has received an admonition for the same or similar misconduct and engages in further acts of misconduct that cause injury or potential injury to a client, the public, the legal system, or the profession.

Commentary

Reprimands are most commonly imposed on lawyers who have been disciplined and engage in the same or similar acts of misconduct. For example, in *Shalant v. State Bar of California,* 33 Cal.3d 485, 658 P.2d 737, 189 Cal.Rptr. 374 (1983), the court imposed a public reproval [reprimand] on a lawyer who failed to communicate with a client and who had received a private reproval for the same misconduct. See also: *Matter of Davis,* 280 S.E.2d 644 (S.C.1981), where the court explained that a reprimand for neglect was necessary because prior warnings for similar behavior were "ignored" (280 S.E.2d at 647).

8.4 An admonition is generally not an appropriate sanction when a lawyer violates the terms of a prior disciplinary order or when a lawyer has engaged in the same or similar misconduct in the past.

Commentary

An admonition is a sanction which should only be imposed in cases of minor misconduct, where the lawyer's acts cause little or no injury to a client, the public, the legal system, or the profession, and where the lawyer is unlikely to engage in further misconduct. Lawyers who do engage in additional similar acts of misconduct, or who violate the terms of a prior disciplinary order, have obviously not been deterred, and a more severe sanction should be imposed.

9.0 Aggravation and Mitigation

9.1 Generally

After misconduct has been established, aggravating and mitigating circumstances may be considered in deciding what sanction to impose.

Commentary

Each disciplinary case involves unique facts and circumstances. In striving for fair disciplinary sanctions, consideration must necessarily be given to the facts pertaining to the professional misconduct and to any aggravating or mitigating factors (see Standards for Lawyer Discipline, Standard 7.1). Aggravating and mitigating circumstances generally relate to the offense at issue, matters independent of the specific offense but relevant to fitness to practice, or matters arising incident to the disciplinary proceeding.

9.2 Aggravation

9.21 ***Definition.*** Aggravation or aggravating circumstances are any considerations, or factors that may justify an increase in the degree of discipline to be imposed.

9.22 ***Factors which may be considered in aggravation.*** Aggravating factors include:

(a) prior disciplinary offenses;

(b) dishonest or selfish motive;

(c) a pattern of misconduct;

(d) multiple offenses;

(e) bad faith obstruction of the disciplinary proceeding by intentionally failing to comply with rules or orders of the disciplinary agency;

(f) submission of false evidence, false statements, or other deceptive practices during the disciplinary process;

(g) refusal to acknowledge wrongful nature of conduct;

(h) vulnerability of victim;

(i) substantial experience in the practice of law;

(j) indifference to making restitution.

(k) illegal conduct, including that involving the case of controlled substances.

Commentary

Cases citing each of the factors listed above include: (a) prior disciplinary offenses: *Matter of Walton,* 251 N.W.2d 762 (N.D.1977); *People v. Vernon,* 660 P.2d 879 (Colo.1982); (b) dishonest or selfish motive: *In re: James H. Dineen,* SJC–535 (Maine 1980); (c) pattern of misconduct: *The Florida Bar v. Mavrides,* 442 So.2d 220 (Fla.1983); *State v. Dixon,* 233 Kan. 465, 664 P.2d 286 (1983); (d) multiple offenses: *State ex rel. Oklahoma Bar Association v. Warzya,* 624 P.2d 1068 (Okla.1981); *Ballard v. State Bar of California,* 35 Cal.3d 274, 673 P.2d 226, 197 Cal.Rptr. 556 (1983); (e) bad faith obstruction of disciplinary proceedings: *In re Brody,* 65 Ill.2d 152, 357 N.E.2d 498 (1976); *Committee on Prof. Ethics v. Brodsky,* 318 N.W.2d 180 (Iowa 1982); (f) lack of candor during the disciplinary process: *In re Stillo,* 68 Ill.2d 49, 368

N.E.2d 897 (1977); *Weir v. State Bar,* 23 Cal.3d 564, 591 P.2d 19, 152 Cal.Rptr. 921 (1979); (g) refusal to acknowledge wrongful nature of conduct: *Greenbaum v. State Bar,* 18 Cal.3d 893, 544 P.2d 921, 126 Cal.Rptr. 785 (1976); *H. Parker Stanley v. Bd. of Professional Responsibility,* 640 S.W.2d 210 (Tenn.1982); (h) vulnerability of victim: *People v. Lanza,* 613 P.2d 337 (Colo.1980); (i) substantial experience in the practice of law: *John F. Buckley,* 2 Mass.Atty.Dis.Rpt. 24 (1980); (j) indifference to making restitution: *The Florida Bar v. Zinzell,* 387 So.2d 346 (Fla.1980); *Bate v. State Bar of California,* 34 Cal.3d 920, 671 P.2d 360, 196 Cal.Rptr. 209 (1983).

9.3 **Mitigation**

9.31 *Definition.* Mitigation or mitigating circumstances are any considerations or factors that may justify a reduction in the degree of discipline to be imposed.

9.32 *Factors which may be considered in mitigation.* Mitigating factors include:

(a) absence of a prior disciplinary record;

(b) absence of a dishonest or selfish motive;

(c) personal or emotional problems;

(d) timely good faith effort to make restitution or to rectify consequences of misconduct;

(e) full and free disclosure to disciplinary board or cooperative attitude toward proceedings;

(f) inexperience in the practice of law;

(g) character or reputation;

(h) physical disability;

(i) mental disability or chemical dependency including alcoholism or drug abuse when:

(1) there is medical evidence that the respondent is affected by a chemical dependency or mental disability;

(2) the chemical dependency or mental disability caused the misconduct;

(3) the respondent's recovery from the chemical dependency or mental disability is demonstrated by a meaningful and sustained period of successful rehabilitation; and

(4) the recovery arrested the misconduct and recurrence of that misconduct is unlikely.

(j) delay in disciplinary proceedings;

(k) imposition of other penalties or sanctions;

(l) remorse;

(m)remoteness of prior offenses.

Commentary

While the courts generally agree that each of these factors can be considered in mitigation, the courts differ on whether restitution is a mitigating factor. Some courts hold that restitution should not be considered. See *Ambrose v. State Bar,* 31 Cal.3d 184, 643 P.2d 486, 481 Cal.Rptr. 903 (1982); *Oklahoma Bar Association v. Lowe,* 640 P.2d 1361 (Okla.1982); *In re Galloway,* 300 S.E.2d 479 (S.C.1983). Other courts do consider restitution. See *People v. Luxford,* 626 P.2d 675 (Colo.1981); *The Florida Bar v. Pincket,* 398 So.2d 802 (Fla.1980); *In re Suernick,* 100 Wis.2d 427, 321 N.W.2d 298 (1982). While restitution should not be a complete defense to a charge of misconduct, the better policy is to allow a good faith effort to make restitution to be considered as a factor in mitigation. Such a policy will encourage lawyers to make restitution, reducing the degree of injury to the client and helping insure that the lawyer has recognized the wrongfulness of his conduct. Restitution which is made upon the lawyer's own initiative should be considered as mitigating; lawyers who make restitution prior to the initiation of disciplinary proceedings present the best case for mitigation, while lawyers who make restitution later in the proceedings present a weaker case.

Cases citing personal and emotional problems as mitigating factors include a wide range of difficulties, most often involving marital or financial problems. The factor which has been treated most inconsistently by the courts is (h): physical/mental disability or impairment. The cases include the following types of behaviors or conditions: alcoholism, *The Florida Bar v. Ullensvang,* 400 So.2d 969 (Fla.1981); mental disorders, *In re Weyrich,* 339 N.W.2d 274 (Minn.1983); drug abuse, *In re Maragos,* 285 N.E.2d 541 (N.D.1979); and senility, *In re Hansen,* 318 N.W.2d 856 (Minn.1982). While most courts treat such disabilities or impairments as mitigating factors, it is important to note that the consideration of these factors does not completely excuse the lawyer's misconduct. In the words of the Illinois Supreme Court, "alcoholism is at most an extenuating circumstance, a mitigating fact, not an excuse." *In re Driscoll,* 85 Ill.2d 312, 423 N.E.2d 873, 874 (1981).

Cases citing each of the factors listed above include: (a) absence of a prior disciplinary record: *In re Battin,* 617 P.2d 1109, 168 Cal.Rptr. 477 (1980); *The Florida Bar v. Shannon,* 398 So.2d 453 (Fla.1981); (b) absence of selfish or dishonest motive: *People ex rel. Goldberg v. Gordon,* 607 P.2d 995 (Colo.1980); (c) personal/emotional problems: *In re Stout,* 75 N.J. 321, 382 A.2d 630 (1981); *Matter of Barron,* 246 Ga. 327, 271 S.E.2d 474 (1980); (d) timely good faith effort to make restitution or to rectify consequences of misconduct: *Matter of Byars,* 268 S.E.2d 155 (Ga.1980); *Matter of Rubi,* 133 Ariz. 491, 652 P.2d 1014 (1982); (e) full and free disclosure to disciplinary board/cooperative attitude toward proceedings: *Matter of Shaw,* 298 N.W.2d 133 (Minn.1980); *In the Matter of Rhame,* 416 N.E.2d 823 (Ind.1981); (f) inexperience in the practice of law: *In re: James M. Pool,* No. 83–37 BD (Sup.Jud.Ct.Suffolk Cty., Mass.1984); *Matter of Price,* 429 N.E.2d 961 (Ind.1982); (g) character/reputation: *Matter of Shaw,* 298 N.W.2d 133 (Minn.1980); *In re Bizar,* 97 Ill.2d 127, 454 N.E.2d 271 (1983); (h) physical/mental disability or impairment: *The Florida Bar v. Routh,* 414 So.2d 1023 (1982); *In re Hopper,* 85 Ill.2d 318, 423 N.E.2d 900 (1981); (i) delay in disciplinary proceedings: *Yokozeki v. State Bar,* 11 Cal.3d 436, 521 P.2d 858, 113 Cal.Rptr. 602 (1974); *The Florida Bar v. Thomson,* 429 So.2d 2 (Fla. 1983); (j) interim rehabilitation: *In re Barry,* 90 N.J. 286, 447 A.2d 923 (1982); *Tenner v. State Bar of California,* 617 P.2d 486, 168 Cal.Rptr. 333 (1980); (k) imposition of other penalties or sanctions: *In re Lamberis,* 93 Ill.2d 222, 443 N.E.2d 549 (1982); *In re: John E. Walsh,* SJC— 53.9 (Maine 1980); *Matter of Garrett,* 399 N.E.2d 369 (Ind.1980); (*l*) remorse: *In re Power,* 91 N.J. 408, 451 A.2d 666 (1982); *In re Nadler,* 91 Ill.2d 326, 438 N.E.2d 198 (1982); (m) remoteness of prior offenses: (no cases found).

9.4 Factors Which Are Neither Aggravating Nor Mitigating

The following factors should not be considered as either aggravating or mitigating:

(a) forced or compelled restitution;

(b) agreeing to the client's demand for certain improper behavior or result;

(c) withdrawal of complaint against the lawyer;

(d) resignation prior to completion of disciplinary proceedings;

(e) complainant's recommendation as to sanction;

(f) failure of injured client to complain.

Commentary

While courts have considered each of these factors, the purposes of lawyer discipline are best served by viewing them as irrelevant to the imposition of a sanction. Lawyers who make restitution voluntarily and on their own initiative demonstrate both a recognition of their ethical violation and their responsibility to the injured client or other party. Such conduct should be considered as mitigation (see Standard 8.32), even if the restitution is made in response to a complaint filed with the disciplinary agency. Lawyers who make restitution only after a disciplinary proceeding has been instituted against them, however, cannot be regarded as acting out of a sense of responsibility for their misconduct, but, instead, as attempting to circumvent the operation of the disciplinary system. Such conduct should not be considered in mitigation. See

Fitzpatrick v. State Bar of California, 20 Cal.3d 73, 141 Cal.Rptr. 169, 569 P.2d 763 (1977); *In re O'Bryant,* 425 A.2d 1313 (D.C.1981).

Similarly, mitigation should not include a lawyer's claim that "the client made me do it". Each lawyer is responsible for adhering to the ethical standards of the profession. Unethical conduct is much less likely to be deterred if lawyers can lessen or avoid the imposition of sanctions merely by blaming the client (see *In re Price,* 429 N.E.2d 961 (Ind.1982); *People v. Kennelly,* 648 P.2d 1065 (Colo.1982). In addition, neither the withdrawal of the complaint against the lawyer nor the lawyer's resignation prior to completion of disciplinary proceedings should mitigate the sanction imposed. In order for the public to be protected, sanctions must be imposed on lawyers who engage in unethical conduct. The mere fact that a complainant may have decided to withdraw a complaint should not result in a lesser sanction being imposed on a lawyer who has behaved unethically and from whom other members of the public need protection (see *In re McWhorter,* 405 Mich. 563, 275 N.W.2d 259 (1979), *on reh'g,* 407 Mich. 278, 284 N.W.2d 472 (1979)). Similarly, the lawyer's resignation is irrelevant; the purposes of deterrence and education can only be served if sanctions are imposed on all lawyers who violate ethical standards (see *In re Johnson,* 290 N.W.2d 604 (Minn.1980) and *In re Phillips,* 452 A.2d 345 (D.C.1982)).

The complainant's recommendation as to a sanction is a factor which should be neither aggravating nor mitigating. The consistency of sanctions cannot be assured if any individual's personal views concerning an appropriate sanction can either increase or decrease the severity of the sanction to be imposed by the court. Although the court should not consider the complainant's recommendation as to sanction, the complainant's feelings about the lawyer's misconduct need not be completely ignored. The complainant's views will be relevant and important in determining the amount of injury caused by the lawyer's misconduct, a factor which can be either aggravating [Standard 8.22(j)] or mitigating [Standard 8.32(i)].

Finally, the fact that an injured client has not complained should not serve as mitigation. The disciplinary system is designed to protect all members of the public. The fact that one injured person is willing to forgive and forget should not relieve or excuse the lawyer, who then has the capability of injuring others (see *In re Krakauer,* 81 N.J. 32, 404 A.2d 1137 (1979); *State ex rel. Oklahoma Bar Association v. Braswell,* 663 P.2d 1228 (Okla.1983)).

APPENDIX 1

Cross-Reference Table: ABA Model Rules of Professional Conduct and Standards for Imposing Sanctions

ABA Model Rules of Professional Conduct	*Standards for Imposing Sanctions*
Competence	
Rule 1.1	Standard 4.5
Scope of Representation	
Rule 1.2(a), (b), (c), (e)	Standard 4.4
Rule 1.2(d)	Standard 6.1
Diligence	
Rule 1.3	Standard 4.4
Communication	
Rule 1.4	Standard 4.4
Fees	
Rule 1.5	Standards 4.6 & 7.0
Confidentiality of Information	
Rule 1.6	Standard 4.2
Conflict of Interest	
Rule 1.7	Standard 4.3
Prohibited Transactions	
Rule 1.8	Standard 4.3
Former Client	
Rule 1.9	Standard 4.3
Imputed Disqualification	
Rule 1.10	Standard 4.3
Successive Government and Private Employment	
Rule 1.11	Standard 4.3
Former Judge or Arbitrator	
Rule 1.12	Standard 4.3
Organization as Client	
Rule 1.13	Standard 4.3
Disabled Client	
Rule 1.14	Standard 7.0
Safekeeping Property	
Rule 1.15	Standard 4.1
Declining or Terminating Representation	
Rule 1.16	Standard 7.0
Advisor	
Rule 2.1	Standard 7.0
Intermediary	
Rule 2.2	Standard 4.3
Evaluation for Use by Third Persons	
Rule 2.3	Standard 7.0
Meritorious Claims and Contentions	
Rule 3.1	Standard 6.2
Expediting Litigation	
Rule 3.2	Standard 6.2
Candor Toward the Tribunal	

ABA Model Rules of Professional Conduct	Standards for Imposing Sanctions
Rule 3.3	Standard 6.1
Fairness to Opposing Party and Counsel	
Rule 3.4	Standard 6.2
Impartiality and Decorum	
Rule 3.5	Standard 6.3
Trial Publicity	
Rule 3.6	Standard 6.2
Lawyer as Witness	
Rule 3.7	Standard 4.3
Special Responsibilities of a Prosecutor	
Rule 3.8	Standard 5.2
Advocate in Nonadjudicative Proceedings	
Rule 3.9	Standard 6.2
Truthfulness to Others	
Rule 4.1	Standard 6.1
Communication with Represented Persons	
Rule 4.2	Standard 6.3
Dealing with Unrepresented Persons	
Rule 4.3	Standard 6.3
Respect for Rights of Third Persons	
Rule 4.4	Standard 6.2
Responsibilities of a Partner or Supervisory Lawyer	
Rule 5.1	Standard 7.0
Responsibilities of a Subordinate Lawyer	
Rule 5.2	Standard 7.0
Responsibilities Regarding Nonlawyer Assistants	
Rule 5.3	Standard 7.0
Professional Independence of Lawyer	
Rule 5.4(a) & (b)	Standard 7.0
Rule 5.4(c)	Standard 4.3
Rule 5.4(d)	Standard 7.0
Unauthorized Practice of Law	
Rule 5.5	Standard 7.0
Restrictions on Right to Practice	
Rule 5.6	Standard 7.0
Pro Bono Publico Service	
Rule 6.1	No Applicable Standard
Accepting Appointments	
Rule 6.2	Standard 7.0
Membership in Legal Services Organization	
Rule 6.3	Standard 4.3
Law Reform Activities Affecting Client Interests	
Rule 6.4	Standard 5.2
Communication Concerning Lawyer's Services	
Rule 7.1	Standard 7.0
Advertising	
Rule 7.2	Standard 7.0
Direct Contact with Prospective Clients	
Rule 7.3	Standard 7.0
Communication of Fields of Practice	
Rule 7.4	Standard 7.0
Firm Names and Letterheads	
Rule 7.5	Standard 7.0
Bar Admission and Disciplinary Matters	
Rule 8.1	Standards 5.1 & 7.0
Judges and Legal Officials	

APPENDIX 1

ABA Model Rules of Professional Conduct	*Standards for Imposing Sanctions*
Rule 8.2	Standard 6.1
Reporting Professional Misconduct	
Rule 8.3	Standard 7.0
Misconduct	
Rule 8.4(a)	Standards 4.0, 5.0, 6.0, & 7.0
Rule 8.4(b)	Standard 5.1
Rule 8.4(c)	Standards 4.6 & 5.1
Rule 8.4(d)	Standard 6.0
Rule 8.4(e) & (f)	Standard 6.2
Jurisdiction	
Rule 8.5	None

APPENDIX 2

Cross-Reference Table: ABA Code of Professional Responsibility and Standards for Imposing Sanctions

ABA Code of Professional Responsibility	*Standards for Imposing Sanctions*
Canon 1: Integrity of Profession	
DR 1–101	Standard 7.0
DR 1–102	Standards 4.6, 5.1, 6.2
DR 1–103	Standard 7.0
Canon 2: Making Counsel Available	
DR 2–101	Standard 7.0
DR 2–102	Standard 7.0
DR 2–103	Standard 7.0
DR 2–104	Standard 7.0
DR 2–105	Standard 7.0
DR 2–106	Standard 7.0
DR 2–107	Standard 7.0
DR 2–108	Standard 7.0
DR 2–109	Standard 7.0
DR 2–110	Standard 7.0
Canon 3: Unauthorized Practice	
DR 3–101(A)	Standard 7.0
DR 3–101(B)	Standard 8.0
DR 3–102	Standard 7.0
DR 3–103	Standard 7.0
Canon 4: Confidences and Secrets	
DR 4–101	Standard 4.2
Canon 5: Independent Judgment	
DR 5–101	Standard 4.3
DR 5–102	Standard 4.3
DR 5–103	Standard 4.3
DR 5–104	Standard 4.3
DR 5–105	Standard 4.3
DR 5–106	Standard 4.3
DR 5–107	Standard 4.3
Canon 6: Competence	
DR 6–101(A)(1) & (2)	Standard 4.5
DR 6–101(A)(3)	Standard 4.4
DR 6–102	Standard 4.3
Canon 7: Zealous Representation	
DR 7–101(A)(1) & (2)	Standard 4.4
DR 7–101(A)(3)	Standard 4.6

APPENDIX 2

ABA Code of Professional Responsibility	*Standards for Imposing Sanctions*
DR 7–101(B)	Standard 7.0
DR 7–102	Standards 6.1 & 6.2
DR 7–103	Standard 5.2
DR 7–104	Standard 6.3
DR 7–105	Standard 6.2
DR 7–106	Standard 6.2
DR 7–107	Standard 6.2
DR 7–108	Standard 6.3
DR 7–109	Standard 6.3
DR 7–110	Standard 6.3
Canon 8: Improving the Legal System	
DR 8–101	Standard 5.2
DR 8–102	Standard 5.2
DR 8–103	Standard 5.2
Canon 9: Appearance of Impropriety	
DR 9–101(A) & (B)	Standard 4.3
DR 9–101(C)	Standard 5.2
DR 9–102	Standard 4.1

APPENDIX 3

Frequency Statistics

Jurisdiction	Total Number of Cases	Percentage of Total	Years
Alabama	13	.4%	1980–84
Alaska	8	.3%	1980–84
Arkansas	5	.2%	1980–84
Arizona	96	3.2%	1974–84
California	681	22.8%	1974–84
Colorado	56	1.9%	1980–84
Delaware	3	.1%	1980–84
D. of Columbia	126	4.2%	1974–84
Florida	347	11.6%	1974–84
Georgia	12	.4%	1980–84
Hawaii	4	.1%	1980–84
Idaho	10	.3%	1980–84
Illinois	198	6.6%	1974–84
Indiana	44	1.5%	1980–84
Iowa	39	1.3%	1980–84
Kansas	53	1.8%	1980–84
Kentucky	32	1.1%	1980–84
Louisiana	20	.7%	1980–84
Maine	17	.6%	1980–84
Maryland	3	.1%	1980–84
Massachusetts	92	3.1%	1980–84
Michigan	228	7.6%	1980–83
Minnesota	18	.6%	1980–84
Mississippi	4	.1%	1980–84
Missouri	1	0%	1980–84
Montana	3	.1%	1980–84
Nebraska	3	.1%	1980–84
Nevada	1	0%	1980–84
New Hampshire	0	0%	1980–84
New Jersey	69	2.3%	1974–84
New Mexico	4	.1%	1980–84
New York	243	8.1%	1979–82
North Carolina	1	0%	1980–84
North Dakota	16	.5%	1974–84
Ohio	16	.5%	1980–84
Oklahoma	15	.5%	1980–84
Oregon	47	1.6%	1980–84
Pennsylvania	4	.1%	1980–84
Rhode Island	6	.2%	1980–84
South Carolina	30	1.0%	1980–84
South Dakota	1	0%	1980–84
Tennessee	69	2.3%	1980–84
Texas	225	7.5%	1974–84
Utah	28	.9%	1980–84
Vermont	0	0%	1980–84
Virginia	56	1.9%	1980–84

APPENDIX 3

Jurisdiction	Total Number of Cases	Percentage of Total	Years
Washington	24	.8%	1980–84
West Virginia	2	.1%	1980–84
Wisconsin	12	.4%	1980–84
Wyoming	1	0%	1980–84
(Missing cases)	(5)	(.2%)	
	2991	100%	

ABA MODEL RULES FOR MEDIATION OF CLIENT–LAWYER DISPUTES (1998)

[In 1998, the ABA House of Delegates adopted without opposition a set of Model Rules for Mediation of Client–Lawyer Disputes.]

PREFACE

Mediation is a process by which those who have a dispute, misunderstanding or conflict come together and, with the assistance of a trained neutral mediator, resolve the issues and problems in a way that meets the needs and interests of both parties. The mediation process is an alternative to litigation or other more formal and expensive dispute resolution mechanisms.

The *Model Rules for Mediation of Client–Lawyer Disputes* implement Recommendation 3 of the 1992 Report of the Commission on Evaluation of Disciplinary Enforcement (the "McKay Commission,") in which the American Bar Association called for jurisdictions to expand their systems of lawyer regulation by establishing mechanisms to resolve disputes between lawyers and clients and to handle nondisciplinary complaints about lawyers. The McKay Commission included a mediation program among its court-established dispute resolution mechanisms. Comments do not add obligations to the Rules but provide guidance for conducting a mediation program in compliance with the Rules.

Rule 1. GENERAL PRINCIPLES AND JURISDICTION

A. Definitions.

(1) "Client" means a person or entity who directly or through an authorized representative consults or retains a lawyer in the lawyer's professional capacity.

(2) "Commission" means the Client–Lawyer Mediation Commission.

(3) "Lawyer" means any lawyer admitted to practice law in [name of jurisdiction], including any formerly admitted lawyer, any lawyer specially admitted by a court of this jurisdiction for a particular proceeding and any lawyer not admitted in this jurisdiction who practices law or renders or offers to render any legal services in this jurisdiction.

B. Establishment; Purpose.
It is the policy of the [highest court of the jurisdiction] to encourage the Informal resolution of disputes between lawyers who practice law in [name of Jurisdiction] and their clients. To that end, She [highest court of the jurisdiction] hereby

establishes through adoption of these rules, a program for mediation of client–lawyer disputes. The program Includes mediations referred by [the lawyer disciplinary agency] and voluntary mediation requests made by the client or by the lawyer, if both the client and the lawyer agree to mediate.

C. Jurisdiction.

(1) Any lawyer is subject to these rules for mediation.

(2) The Commission has jurisdiction over disputes which Involve lesser misconduct or no misconduct on the part of the lawyer and appear to be resolvable by mediation.

(3) The Commission has jurisdiction over disputes referred by [the lawyer disciplinary agency] and voluntary mediations in which a lawyer or client requests mediation and the other party agrees.

Comment

The mediation program described in these rules is part of this jurisdiction's comprehensive lawyer regulatory system. The comprehensive system includes: [a lawyer discipline and disability system, a client protection fund, mandatory arbitration of fee disputes, mediation, law office management assistance, and lawyer assistance programs].

Since mediation is a process that works by building consensus and agreement, the mediation process can preserve existing client-lawyer or other fiduciary relationships by allowing both sides to air their grievances and work together on a solution agreeable to all parties. When handled by a skilled mediator, the process can be simple and efficient, saving time and money for both parties. The lawyer's willingness to have a third party assist in resolving the dispute can demonstrate to the client that the lawyer's intention is to act in the client's best interest.

Mediation is not suitable when the dispute involves an allegation of lawyer misconduct which, if true, would warrant a sanction restricting the lawyer's license to practice law. Mediation is appropriate when the dispute involves no allegation of lawyer misconduct or an allegation of lesser misconduct as defined in [jurisdiction's rules of disciplinary enforcement]. It is appropriate because there is little or no injury to a client, the public, the legal system, or the profession, and there is little likelihood of repetition by the lawyer.

Examples of disputes that might be referred to mediation include allegations of a lawyer's failure or refusal to return a client's file based on a fee dispute with the client, release a lien on a client's recovery in a case in which the lawyer has been succeeded by another lawyer, withdraw from representation upon being discharged by the client, conclude a legal representation by preparing an essential dispositive document, such as the findings of fact and conclusions of law in a divorce or the final account in an estate, return an unearned fee or a portion of the fee, comply with his or her agreement with a medical provider on the client's behalf or communicate concerning the status of a matter.

Other examples of situations in which the parties might agree to voluntary mediation could include allegations of a client's failure to pay or fulfill the contract, pay for costs (including future costs) or communicate with the lawyer.

The primary purpose of the program is to resolve complaints referred from the jurisdiction's lawyer disciplinary agency. Therefore, such referrals should be given priority over voluntary mediations. Mediation can be used to complement fee arbitration proceedings. The Commission may accept jurisdiction in a dispute in which a fee arbitration proceeding is pending but has not yet begun. The intention is to solve the dispute in a less formal way, if possible, not to refer complainants back and forth between the two programs.

Rule 2. MEDIATION COMMISSION

A. Appointment of Commission. The [highest court of the jurisdiction] shall appoint a Mediation Commission to administer the Mediation Program. The [highest court of the jurisdiction] shall designate one member to serve as Chair of the Commission.

B. Composition. The Commission shall consist of [six] members, of whom at least one-third shall be nonlawyers. Members shall be appointed for terms of three years except where a vacancy has occurred in which event appointments shall be for the unexpired portion of the term being filled. Appointments shall be on a staggered basis so that the number of terms expiring shall be approximately the same each year. No members shall be appointed for more than two consecutive full terms, but members appointed for less than a full term (either originally or to fill a vacancy) may serve two full terms in addition to such part of a term.

C. Duties of the Commission. The Commission shall have the following powers and duties to:

(1) appoint and remove mediators and provide appropriate training;

(2) interpret these rules;

(3) establish written procedures not inconsistent with these rules;

(4) issue an annual report and periodic policy recommendations, as needed, to the [state's highest court] regarding the program;

(5) maintain all records of the Mediation Program;

(6) determine challenges for cause where a mediator has not voluntarily acceded to a challenge;

(7) educate the public and the bar about the Mediation Program;

(8) perform all acts necessary for the effective operation of the program; and

(9) establish fee schedules and oversee financial matters.

Comment

Overall authority to administer the Mediation Program is delegated by [the highest court of the jurisdiction] to the Commission. The court should ensure diversity in the membership of the Commission.

The Commission has authority to limit the types of matters accepted for mediation. Personal disputes and business matters where one of the parties is a lawyer but the allegations do not involve the practice of law are not appropriate for mediation under these rules. Mediation of disputes between lawyers is not precluded by these rules where the complaint otherwise meets the guidelines of matters that are appropriate for mediation.

The Commission has the authority to establish reasonable fees for the program and also to waive fees in cases of hardship. No fee should be charged a client if the charging of the fee would unduly restrict the client's access to the mediation process. Additionally, in mediations referred by [the lawyer disciplinary agency], the client should not be charged a fee for participating in the mediation.

With respect to the funding of the mediation program, it is envisioned that there will be minimal costs involved: lawyer and nonlawyer volunteers will be serving as mediators. The Commission may delegate the day-to-day administration of the Mediation Program to staff assigned to the lawyer disciplinary agency. However, a state or local bar association could administer this component of the lawyer regulation system.

Rule 3. MEDIATORS

A. List of Approved Mediators. The Commission shall maintain a list of approved mediators, both lawyers and nonlawyers, and shall adopt written standards for the appointment of the mediators. Mediators should represent all segments of the profession and the general population, including diversity on the basis of race, gender, and practice setting. Mediators shall be appointed for terms of [three] years and may be reappointed. The Commission may remove a mediator from the list of approved mediators for good cause, and may appoint a replacement member to serve the balance of the term of the removed member.

B. Conflicts of Interest. Within [20] days of the notification of appointment as a mediator, and prior to the initiation of the mediation, the mediator shall notify the Commission if he or she has previously acted as a mediator in the proceeding or in any other related proceeding or of any conflict of interest with a party to the mediation as defined in the [Code of Judicial Conduct] with respect to part-time judges. Upon notification of the conflict, the Commission shall appoint a replacement from the list of approved mediators.

C. Challenges for Cause. If either party has cause to object to participation by a mediator, a substitute shall be appointed by the

Commission. A challenge for cause shall be filed within [15] days after service of the notice of appointment. A mediator shall accede to a reasonable challenge and the Commission shall appoint a replacement. If a mediator does not voluntarily accede, the Commission shall decide whether to appoint a replacement. The decision of the Commission on challenges shall be final.

   D.   Duties. The mediator shall have powers and duties to:

   (1) grant extensions of time as deemed appropriate;

   (2) reschedule or terminate the mediation if a party fails to appear; and

   (3) perform all acts necessary to conduct an effective mediation conference.

Comment

Written standards for the appointment of mediators should ensure appropriate training and experience for mediators as well as diversity in the background and experience of the mediators. Mediators should also be dispersed throughout the jurisdiction to Increase access to the mediation process.

Mediators should be required to attend an appropriate training course, as determined by the Commission, which should include training in mediation theory, skills and the applicable provisions of the rules of professional conduct.

Mediators exercise a quasi-judicial role and should, therefore, be disqualified upon the same grounds and conditions applicable to part-time judges, The decisions of the mediators should be free from any appearance of outside influence.

Rule 4.   THE PROCESS

   A.   Commencement of Mediation.

   (1) Referral from Lawyer Disciplinary Agency. Within [15] calendar days after receipt by the Commission of a mediation referral from [the lawyer disciplinary agency], the Commission shall mail to both the lawyer and the complainant a copy of these rules and an agreement to mediate, together with a notice that shall Include the name, address and telephone number of the mediation program and the date on which the referral for mediation was received. If the signed agreement to mediate is not returned to the Commission by both parties within [30] calendar days of mailing, the Commission shall close the file, notify the parties that it is closing the file because one or both parties failed to return the agreement, and inform the [lawyer disciplinary agency] of the identity of the party or parties who did not consent to mediation.

   (2) Voluntary Mediation. Within [15] calendar days after receipt by the Commission of the approved written application for voluntary mediation of a dispute and a signed agreement to mediate, the Commission shall notify the other party of the request and shall forward to that party an agreement to mediate, together with a copy of these Rules and a copy of the written application. If the signed agreement is not returned to the program by the other party within [30] calendar days of mailing, the Commission shall close the file and notify the requestor that the other party did not consent to mediation.

B. Assignment of Mediators. The Commission shall notify the parties of the assignment of a mediator within [15] calendar days after receipt of the fully executed agreement to mediate. The notice shall include the name, address and telephone number of the mediator assigned. The mediator shall be assigned at random from the available pool of qualified individuals. Upon withdrawal or removal of a mediator, the Commission shall notify the parties within [10] calendar days of the name, address and telephone number of a new mediator.

C. Mediation Hearing Date. Within [15] calendar days after the date of mailing of the notice of the assignment of a mediator, the mediator shall arrange a mediation conference date which shall be scheduled to take place within [30] calendar days after the assignment notice mailing date, unless both parties to the mediation agree to a longer date. The mediator shall promptly notify the parties and the Commission of the place, date and time of the conference.

D. The Conference.

(1) Only the parties to the mediation, their lawyers, if any, and the mediator are required to be present during the mediation, but the mediator shall have authority to determine if others may be present at and participate in the mediation.

(2) The mediator shall have the authority to meet separately with the parties.

(3) If all parties and the mediator agree, the mediation may be conducted by telephone. In cases of hardship, the mediation may be conducted by telephone at the discretion of the mediator even if all parties do not agree.

(4) If upon completion of the mediation, the parties have an agreement, the mediator shall reduce the agreement of the parties to writing. The parties shall sign as many originals as there are parties to the mediation. A copy of the signed agreement shall be made for the Commission's records. The mediator shall report to the Commission on the Mediation Summary Report form, which will indicate if the dispute was resolved, was not resolved, or did not proceed because a party did not appear (with an indication of which party did not appear). Such agreement and/or report shall be submitted within [15] calendar days after the conclusion of the mediation.

(5) In the case of any mediation referred from the disciplinary agency, the following materials shall be transmitted to the [lawyer disciplinary agency] at the conclusion of the mediation:

> a. A duplicate original of the signed mediation agreement described in Rule 4.D.4 above; and

> b. the completed Mediation Summary Report form.

Comment

The overwhelming majority of complaints made against lawyers allege instances of lesser misconduct. Summary dismissal of these complaints is one of the chief sources of public dissatisfaction with the lawyer regulation system. These cases seldom justify the resources needed to conduct formal disciplinary proceedings and should be removed from the disciplinary system and handled administratively.

The mediation program established by these rules is designed to receive cases from a number of sources: the central intake office; the disciplinary agency; other agencies within the lawyer regulation system; the courts; or directly from the parties. Referrals from the disciplinary agency will usually be part of a diversion program or an agreement in lieu of discipline, in which a lawyer agrees to mediate a dispute with the understanding that the disciplinary matter will be dismissed upon successful completion of the mediation. Agreement of both the client and the lawyer is required for a matter to be referred to mediation from the disciplinary agency. Matters that come to the mediation program from the central intake office, other agencies, or directly from the parties are voluntary as described in these rules. The mediator is authorized to determine the rules by which the mediation will proceed. The mediator should conduct the conference informally. At the outset, the mediator should make clear to the parties that the mediator is serving as a mediator and not a judge. The mediators role is to facilitate communication and suggest ways of resolving the dispute; the mediator is not to impose a settlement on the parties. The mediator should make every effort to hear all the relevant facts, review all the relevant documents, become familiar with any controlling legal principles and seek to bring about an acceptable compromise between the parties. The mediator should make sure that any proposal offered for resolution of the matter is clearly understood by the parties and perceived to be fair.

Rule 5. CONFIDENTIALITY

A. Except as provided in Rule 4.D.5 above, and Rule 5.B below, all communications, negotiations or settlement discussions by and between participants and/or mediators in the mediation shall remain confidential. All parties attending a mediation shall sign a written agreement that the proceeding will be confidential.

B. Notwithstanding Rule 5.A above, lawyer mediators have a duty to, and nonlawyer mediators should, report conduct that would be reportable under the applicable rules of professional conduct or other applicable statutes or rules.

Comment

Confidentiality in a mediation hearing Is of paramount importance. Nevertheless, the need to report lawyer misconduct takes precedence. Lawyer mediators have a duty to, and nonlawyer mediators should, report conduct that would be reportable under the state's applicable rules or statutes. A lawyer having knowledge that another lawyer has committed a violation of the [rules of professional conduct] that raises a substantial question as to that lawyer's honesty, trustworthiness or fitness as a lawyer in other respects, must inform the appropriate professional authority. Nonlawyer mediators should refer to this standard in determining their responsibility to report lawyer misconduct. The fact that mediators have a duty to report lawyer misconduct should not have a chilling effect on those parties who are sincere in availing themselves of the benefits of mediation. All mediators may also be required by the laws in their jurisdiction to report to the appropriate agency evidence of other types of misconduct, i.e., child abuse or criminal conduct, that comes to light during a mediation.

Rule 6. IMMUNITY

Communications to the Commission, mediators, or disciplinary counsel relating to lawyer misconduct or disability and testimony given in the proceedings shall be absolutely privileged, and no lawsuit predicated thereon may be instituted against any client or witness. Members of the Commission, mediators, disciplinary counsel, or any person acting on their behalf, and staff shall be immune from suit for any conduct in the course of their official duties.

Comment

The personnel involved in the mediation process are an Integral part of the judicial process and are entitled to the same immunity, which is afforded prosecuting lawyers. Immunity protects the independent judgment of the mediation personnel and avoids diverting the attention of its personnel as well as its resources toward resisting collateral attack and harassment. A policy of conferring absolute immunity encourages those who have some doubt about a lawyer's conduct to submit the matter to the proper agency, where it may be examined and determined.

ABA MODEL RULES FOR FEE ARBITRATION

[In February 1995, the ABA House of Delegates approved the Model Rules for Fee Arbitration as a Model system for states to use in the resolution of fee disputes.]

Rule 1. GENERAL PRINCIPLES AND JURISDICTION

A. Definitions. The following definitions shall apply in all fee arbitration proceedings.

(1) "Client" means a person or entity who directly or through an authorized representative consults, retains or secures legal service or advice from a lawyer in the lawyer's professional capacity.

(2) "Commission" means the Fee Arbitration Commission.

(3) "Decision" means the determination made by the panel in a fee arbitration proceeding.

(4) "Lawyer" means a person admitted to the practice of law in [name of jurisdiction], or any other person who appears, participates or otherwise engages in the practice of law in this state, regardless of the status of his or her license. In these rules, the term "lawyer" includes a lawyer's assignee.

(5) "Panel" means the arbitrator(s) assigned to hear a fee dispute and to issue a decision.

(6) "Party" means the client, lawyer, the lawyer's assignee and any third person or entity who has been joined by the client or lawyer in the proceeding.

(7) "Petition" means a written request for fee arbitration in a form approved by the Commission.

(8) "Petitioner" means the party requesting fee arbitration.

(9) "Respondent" means the party with whom the petitioner has a fee dispute.

B. Establishment; Purpose. It is the policy of the [state's highest court] to encourage the informal resolution of fee disputes between lawyers who practice law in [name of jurisdiction] and their clients and, in the event such informal resolution cannot be achieved, to provide for the arbitration of such disputes. To that end, the [state's highest court] hereby establishes through adoption of these rules, a program and procedures for the arbitration of disputes concerning any and all fees and/or costs paid, charged, or claimed for professional services by lawyers.

C. Arbitration Mandatory for Lawyers. Fee arbitration pursuant to these rules is voluntary for clients and mandatory for lawyers if commenced by a client.

D. Effect of Arbitration.

(1) The Fee Arbitration is binding where all parties have agreed in writing that it will be binding.

(2) In the absence of a written agreement to be bound by the arbitration, the decision automatically becomes binding, unless, as permitted under Rule 7.B., any party seeks a trial de novo pursuant to the [jurisdiction's rules of civil procedure] within 30 days after service of the decision. This 30-day time period shall not be extended by an application for modification under these rules.

(3) After all parties have agreed in writing to be bound by an arbitration award, a party may not withdraw from that agreement unless all parties agree to the withdrawal in writing. At any time during the proceedings, the parties may agree in writing to be bound by the decision.

E. Jurisdiction. Any lawyer, as defined in Rule 1.A(4), is subject to these rules for fee arbitration.

F. Disputes not Subject to Arbitration. These rules do not apply to the following:

(1) Disputes where the lawyer is also admitted to practice in another jurisdiction, the lawyer maintains no office in [name of jurisdiction], and no portion of the legal services was rendered in [name of jurisdiction];

(2) Disputes where the client seeks affirmative relief for damages against the lawyer based upon alleged malpractice or professional misconduct;

(3) Disputes where entitlement to and the amount of the fees and/or costs charged or paid to a lawyer by the client or on the client's behalf have been determined by court order, rule, or decision;

(4) Disputes where a third person is responsible for payment of the fees and the client fails to join in the request for arbitration; and

(5) Disputes where the request for arbitration is filed more than [four] year(s) after the lawyer-client relationship has been terminated or more than [four] year(s) after the final billing has been received by the client, whichever is later, unless a civil action concerning the disputed amount is not barred by the statute of limitations.

G. Notice of Right to Arbitration; Stay of Proceedings; Waiver by Client.

(1) Prior to or at the time of service of a summons in a civil action against his or her client for the recovery of fees, costs, or both for professional services rendered, a lawyer shall serve upon the client [by certified mail return receipt requested] a written notice of the client's right to arbitrate. The notice, in a form approved by the Commission, shall include a provision advising the client that failure to file a Petition for Fee Arbitration within 30 days of service of notice of the right to arbitrate shall constitute a waiver of the right to arbitrate. Failure to give this notice shall be grounds for dismissal of the civil action.

(2) If a lawyer commences a fee collection action in any court, the court shall issue an order of stay upon the client giving notice to the court and the lawyer that a Petition for Arbitration was filed with the commission within [thirty] days of service of the notice of the right to arbitrate.

(3) After a client files a Petition, the lawyer shall refrain from any non-judicial collection activities related to the fees and/or costs in dispute pending the outcome of the arbitration.

(4) Unless all parties agree in writing to the arbitration, the right of the client to petition or maintain an arbitration is waived if:

(a) the client fails to file a Petition for Arbitration within [thirty] days of service of the notice of right to arbitrate pursuant to these rules; or

(b) the client commences or maintains a civil action or files any pleading seeking judicial resolution of the fee dispute, or seeking affirmative relief against the lawyer for damages based upon alleged malpractice.

Commentary

A fee arbitration system provides lawyers and clients with an out-of-court method of resolving fee disputes that is expeditious, confidential, inexpensive, and impartial. The court should ensure adequate funding for an effective program.

Although these rules only address fee arbitration, consideration should be given to the development of mediation as a component of the program as a prerequisite or alternative to fee arbitration.

A client who believes he or she may have been overcharged by a lawyer may have the lawyer's fee reviewed without incurring the expense of formal litigation. Participation in the Fee Arbitration Program is mandatory for lawyers if the request for arbitration is commenced by a client. The decision is binding only upon written agreement of the parties. In the absence of a written agreement to be bound by the arbitration decision, any party may seek a trial de novo within 30 days after service of the decision. The decision becomes binding if no party seeks a trial de novo within the 30-day period. The program is voluntary for the client since the lawyer regulatory system has no power to regulate the consumer of legal services. However, nothing in these rules precludes a lawyer and a client from entering into a contract to participate in binding arbitration under these rules as permitted by law.

A lawyer must notify a client of the availability of the Fee Arbitration Program prior to or at the time of service of a summons in a civil action against the client to recover fee and/or costs for professional services. The rule provides that notice be sent by certified mail return receipt requested. However, a jurisdiction may substitute such other means of service as will reasonably establish receipt. The client must file a Petition for Fee Arbitration within [thirty] days of service of such notice or the client waives the right to petition or maintain an arbitration proceeding under these rules. If all parties agree, the fee arbitration can proceed even if the client did not file the Petition for Fee Arbitration within the [thirty] day period. The client also waives the right to petition or maintain an arbitration if the client commences or maintains a civil action or files any pleading seeking judicial resolution of the fee dispute or seeking affirmative relief against the lawyer for damages based on alleged malpractice. This prevents the same facts from being the subject matter of the arbitration and a civil action. Nothing herein precludes a client from filing a complaint with the disciplinary authority. Nothing in these rules prevents the filing of a malpractice action after a decision is rendered in the fee arbitration proceeding. In accordance with Rule 7.B.(4), a decision under these rules is not admissible in a subsequent malpractice action.

The scope of these rules includes costs as well as fees. In many cases, fees and costs are inextricably linked. The fee arbitration process should be able to resolve both issues in one process.

The Fee Arbitration Program can be expanded to handle disputes between lawyers if all parties agree to be bound by the decision of the panel.

An alternative approach, which currently works effectively in those jurisdictions where it has been adopted, is to provide for arbitration which is both mandatory and binding in all cases. Under such a system, the arbitration decision is binding on the parties subject to appeal only in cases of demonstrable and fundamental unfairness in the procedures utilized in deciding the matter.

Rule 2. FEE ARBITRATION COMMISSION

A. Appointment of Commission. The [state's highest court] shall appoint a Fee Arbitration Commission to administer the Fee Arbitration Program. The [state's highest court] shall designate one member to serve as Chair of the Commission.

B. Composition. The Commission shall consist of [nine] members of whom one-third shall be nonlawyers. Members shall be appointed for terms of three years or until a successor has been appointed. Appointments shall be on a staggered basis so that the number of terms expiring shall be approximately the same each year. No members shall be appointed for more than two consecutive full terms, but members appointed for less than a full term (either originally or to fill a vacancy) may serve two full terms in addition to such part of a term.

C. Duties of the Commission. The Commission shall have the following powers and duties.

(1) to appoint, remove and provide appropriate training for lawyer and nonlawyer arbitrators and arbitration panels;

(2) to interpret these rules;

(3) to approve forms;

(4) to establish written procedures that afford a full and equal opportunity to all parties to present relevant evidence;

(5) to issue an annual report and periodic policy recommendations, as needed, to the [state's highest court] regarding the program;

(6) to maintain all records of the Fee Arbitration Program;

(7) to determine challenges for cause where an arbitrator has not voluntarily acceded to a challenge;

(8) to educate the public and the bar about the Fee Arbitration Program; and

(9) to perform all acts necessary for the effective operation of the program.

Commentary

Overall authority to administer the Fee Arbitration Program is delegated by the state's highest court to the Commission. Both lawyers and nonlawyer members serve on the Commission. Members are appointed by the court for three year terms. The court should ensure diversity in the membership of the Commission.

Members may be appointed for a period not to exceed two consecutive full terms and a portion of an additional term, if appointed originally to less than a full term. A rotation system is employed in the appointment of members so that, generally, the terms of one-third of the members expire annually. This procedure preserves continuity while inviting the fresh ideas which new personnel inevitably bring to a task.

The Commission has the duty to inform the bar and the public about the Fee Arbitration Program through such means as brochures, public service announcements, and any other means available. There should be a central place where the public can call with questions about lawyers and which can refer appropriate matters to the Fee Arbitration

Program. Members of the bar should be encouraged to inform any member of the public known to have a fee dispute with a lawyer about the right to seek fee arbitration or to pursue other available means to resolve the dispute, such as mediation.

Depending on funding, pro bono requirements, and other considerations, the Commission may authorize the reimbursement of reasonable costs and expenses to its members and to arbitrators. In larger jurisdictions, the Commission may employ staff to perform functions delegated by the Commission. The Commission can authorize local bar associations to sponsor and conduct fee arbitration programs. However, a client who believes he or she may not be able to obtain a fair resolution at the local level should be permitted to utilize the statewide program.

Rule 3. ARBITRATORS

A. List of Approved Arbitrators. The Commission shall maintain a list of approved arbitrators and shall adopt written standards for the appointment of the arbitrators. Such standards should ensure appropriate training and experience for arbitrators as well as diversity in the background and experience of the arbitrators. Arbitrators shall be appointed for terms of [three] years and may be reappointed. For good cause, the Commission may remove an arbitrator from the list of approved arbitrators, and may appoint a replacement member to serve the balance of the term of the removed member.

B. Panels. The Commission shall appoint panels from the list of approved arbitrators. For disputes involving [$7,500] or more, the panel shall consist of three arbitrators of whom one shall be a nonlawyer member. For disputes involving less than [$7,500], or in any case if the parties so stipulate, the panel shall consist of a sole arbitrator who shall be a lawyer. If the panel consists of three members, the Commission shall designate one member to act as Chair of the panel and to preside at the arbitration hearing.

C. Conflicts of Interest. Within [five] days of the notification of appointment to a panel, an arbitrator shall notify the Commission of any conflict of interest with a party to the arbitration as defined in the ABA Code of Judicial Conduct with respect to part-time judges. Upon notification of the conflict, the Commission shall appoint a replacement from the list of approved arbitrators.

D. Challenges for Cause. A party may challenge any arbitrator for cause. A challenge for cause naming the arbitrator and the reason for the challenge shall be filed within [fifteen] days after service of the notice of appointment. An arbitrator shall accede to a reasonable challenge and the Commission shall appoint a replacement. If an arbitrator does not voluntarily accede, the Commission shall decide whether to appoint a replacement. The decision of the Commission on challenges shall be final.

E. Duties. The panel shall have the following powers and duties:

(1) to take and hear evidence pertaining to the proceeding;

(2) to administer oaths and affirmations;

(3) to compel, by subpoena, the attendance of witnesses and the production of books, papers, and documents pertaining to the proceeding, and consider challenges to the validity of subpoenas;

(4) to issue decisions; and

(5) to perform all acts necessary to conduct an effective arbitration hearing.

Commentary

The Commission appoints both lawyers and nonlawyers to serve as arbitrators for [three] year renewable terms, and maintains a list of approved arbitrators. When a Petition is received, the Commission appoints from the list of approved arbitrators a panel of one or three arbitrators to hear the matter, depending on the amount in dispute. For larger jurisdictions, the Commission may hire staff or designate a presiding arbitrator to handle the appointment of panels or other administrative tasks as delegated by the Commission. The number of people on the list of approved arbitrators should not be so large as to prevent the participating arbitrators from obtaining sufficient experience in the program.

Appointments to the list of approved arbitrators should represent all segments of the profession and the general population, including diversity on the basis of race, gender and practice setting. Arbitrators should also be dispersed throughout the state to increase access to the fee arbitration process.

The Commission should adopt written standards for appointment of arbitrators which may include compliance with training requirements, ability to meet minimum time and case commitments, years in practice and experience. All panels of more than one arbitrator should include one nonlawyer member.

Members of panels exercise a quasi-judicial role and should, therefore, be disqualified upon the same grounds and conditions applicable to judges. The Commission may wish to provide that within [fifteen] days after service of the notice of appointment, any party may file one peremptory challenge. In the event of such a challenge, the Commission should relieve the challenged arbitrator and appoint a replacement.

Panels do not render advisory opinions but, rather, adjudicate fee controversies between lawyers and clients.

In jurisdictions with a high volume of arbitration cases, consideration should be given to having pre-set arbitration panels which meet at specified times to simplify the scheduling of hearings.

Rule 4. COMMENCEMENT OF PROCEEDINGS

A. Petition to Arbitrate. A fee arbitration proceeding shall commence with the filing of a Petition for Arbitration on a form approved by the Commission [and paying the appropriate filing fee as established by the (state's highest court)]. Any person who is not the client of the lawyer but who has paid or may be liable for the lawyer's fees may consent to be joined by the client as a party to the arbitration. The Petition for Arbitration must be signed by the client and any other party included by the client.

B. Commission Review. The Commission will review the Petition to determine if it is properly completed and if the Commission has jurisdiction. If the Petition is not properly completed, the Commission will return it to the petitioner and specify what clarification or additional information is required. If the Commission does not have jurisdiction, the petitioner shall be so advised.

C. Service of Petition; Response. Within [five] days of the receipt of a properly completed Petition, the Commission shall serve a copy of the Petition, along with a Fee Arbitration Response Form on the respondent. Within [twenty] days after service, the respondent shall file the completed Fee Arbitration Response Form with the Commission which shall forward a copy to all other parties. The Commission shall serve a copy of the Petition for Arbitration and a Fee Arbitration Response Form upon the law firm, if any, with which a lawyer-party is associated. If the respondent is a lawyer, the respondent shall set forth in the response the name of any other lawyer or law firm who the lawyer claims is responsible for all or part of the client's claim. Within [five] days of receipt of the response, the Commission shall serve on the lawyer(s) or law firm(s) named in the Response a copy of the Petition for Arbitration and a Fee Arbitration Response Form for completion. Within [twenty] days after service, the lawyer(s) or law firm(s) may file the completed Fee Arbitration Response Form with the Commission which shall forward a copy to all other parties.

D. Failure of a Lawyer Respondent to Respond. Failure of a lawyer respondent to file the Fee Arbitration Response Form shall not delay the scheduling of a hearing; however, in any such case the panel may, in its discretion, refuse to consider evidence offered by the lawyer which would reasonably be expected to have been disclosed in the response.

E. Client Consent Required. If a lawyer files a Petition for Arbitration, the arbitration shall proceed only if the client files a written consent within [thirty] days of service of the Petition.

F. Settlement of Disputes. If the dispute giving rise to the Petition for Arbitration has been settled, upon reasonable confirmation of that settlement, the matter shall be dismissed by the Commission or by the panel if one has been assigned.

G. Appointment of Panel. The Commission shall, within [ten] days after receipt of the Petition for Arbitration, appoint a panel and mail to the parties written notification of the name(s) of the panel member(s) assigned to hear the matter.

Commentary

The fee arbitration process begins with the filing of a Petition for Arbitration on a form approved by the Commission. The respondent has twenty days after service to return the Fee Arbitration Response Form. The process is commenced either unilaterally by a client or by the lawyer with the client's consent. If it is initiated by the client, participation is mandatory on the part of the lawyer.

The Fee Arbitration Program is designed to be simple and fast. Consequently, most cases should be concluded in an average of six months.

If a lawyer fails to timely file a Fee Arbitration Response Form, the hearing will nonetheless be held in the normal course and the panel may, in its discretion, refuse to consider evidence offered by the lawyer which would reasonably be expected to have been disclosed in the Response. This is not intended as a default procedure. It will still be necessary for the panel to determine the reasonableness of the fee.

The Commission must serve a copy of the Petition and the Fee Response Form on the law firm, if any, of which a lawyer is a member. The purpose of this rule is to assure that where a law firm is due a fee, or is obligated therefor, the law firm will have notice of the arbitration and an opportunity to participate.

Rule 5. HEARING

A. Notice of Hearing. The panel shall set the date, time and place for the hearing. The panel shall send notice of the hearing to the parties not less than [thirty] but no more than [sixty] days in advance of the hearing date, unless otherwise agreed by the parties.

B. Representation by Counsel. Any party may be represented by counsel.

C. Recording of Proceedings. A party to the proceedings may make arrangements to have the hearing reported at the party's own expense, provided notice is given to the other parties and the panel at least [five] days prior to the scheduled hearing. If a party orders a transcript, that party shall provide a copy of the transcript to the panel free of charge. Any other party is entitled at his or her own expense to acquire a copy of the transcript by making arrangements directly with the reporter. A panel, in its discretion, may make arrangements to have a hearing recorded and the parties may obtain a copy at their own expense.

D. Continuances. For good cause shown, a panel may continue a hearing upon the request of a party or upon the panel's own motion.

E. Oaths and Affirmations. The testimony of witnesses shall be by oath or affirmation.

F. Panel Quorums. All three arbitrators shall be required for a quorum where the panel consists of three members. A panel of three arbitrators shall act with the concurrence of at least two arbitrators.

G. Appearance; Failure of a Party to Appear. Appearance by a party at a scheduled hearing shall constitute waiver by said party of any deficiency with respect to the giving of notice of hearing. The panel may proceed in the absence of any party or representative who, after due notice, fails either to be present or to obtain a continuance. A decision shall not be made solely on the default of a party. The panel shall require parties who are present to submit such evidence as the panel may require to issue a decision.

H. Waiver of Personal Appearance. Any party may waive personal appearance and submit testimony and exhibits by written declaration under oath to the panel. Such declarations shall be filed with the panel at least [ten] days prior to the hearing. If all parties, in writing, waive appearances at a hearing, the matter may be decided on the basis of written submissions. If the panel concludes that oral presentations are necessary, the panel may schedule a hearing.

I. Telephonic Hearings. In its discretion, a panel may permit a party to appear or present witness testimony at the hearing by telephonic conference call. The costs of the telephone call shall be paid by the party.

J. Stipulations. Agreements between the parties as to issues not in dispute and the voluntary exchange of documents prior to the hearing are encouraged.

K. Evidence. The panel shall accept such evidence as is relevant and material to the dispute and request additional evidence as necessary to understand and resolve the dispute. The rules of evidence [of the jurisdiction] need not be strictly followed. The parties shall be entitled to be heard, to present evidence and to cross-examine parties and witnesses. The panel shall judge the relevance and materiality of the evidence.

L. Subpoenas. Upon request of a party and for good cause shown, or on its own initiative, the panel may issue subpoenas for witnesses or documents necessary to a resolution of the dispute. The requesting party shall be responsible for service of the subpoenas.

M. Reopening of Hearing. For good cause shown, the panel may reopen the hearing at any time before a decision is issued.

N. Death or Incompetency of a Party. In the event of death or incompetency of a party, the personal representative of the deceased party or the guardian or conservator of the incompetent may be substituted.

O. Burden of Proof. The burden of proof shall be on the lawyer to prove the reasonableness of the fee by a preponderance of the evidence.

Commentary

The goal of these rules is to provide a setting for hearings that is informal yet fair. To that end, the panel has discretion to grant postponements but need not permit the process to be subverted by unexcused absences. The panel will receive the evidence and testimony offered and judge its relevance and materiality. While the hearing may be conducted informally, witnesses should be required to testify under oath.

There is no provision for formal discovery; however, the panel has the power of subpoena, subject to rules of relevancy and materiality.

The burden of proof in fee arbitration is on the lawyer to prove the reasonableness of the fee by a preponderance of the evidence. This is consistent with the ABA Model Rules of Professional Conduct Rule 1.5 which provides that a lawyer's fee shall be reasonable.

The panel may consider evidence relating to claims of malpractice and professional misconduct, but only to the extent that those claims bear upon the fees, costs, or both to which the lawyer is entitled. The panel may not award affirmative relief in the form of damages for injuries underlying any such claim.

Rule 6. DECISION

A. Form of Decision. The panel's decision shall be in writing and shall include a clear statement of the amount in dispute, whether and to whom monies are due, and a brief explanation of the decision.

B. Issuance of Decision. The decision should be rendered within [thirty] days of the close of the hearing or from the end of any time period permitted by the panel for the filing of supplemental briefs or other materials. The arbitrator or panel chair shall forward the decision to the Commission which shall serve a copy of the decision on each party to the arbitration.

C. Modification of Decision.

(1) On application to the panel by a party to a fee dispute, the panel may modify or correct a decision if:

(a) there was an error in the computation of figures or a mistake in the description of a person, thing, or property referred to in the decision;

(b) the decision is imperfect in a matter of form not affecting the merits of the proceeding; or

(c) the decision needs clarification.

(2) Any party may file an application for modification with the panel within [twenty] days after service of the decision and shall serve a copy of the application on all other parties. An objection to the application must be filed with the panel within [ten] days after service of the application for modification.

(3) An application for modification shall not extend the thirty-day time period to seek trial de novo under these rules.

D. Retention of Files. The Commission shall maintain all fee arbitration files for a period of [three] years from the date a decision is issued.

Commentary

In order to bring a final and speedy conclusion to fee disputes, the decision of the panel is required to be in writing and should be rendered within thirty days. Discretion to extend the time period for unusually complicated or difficult matters should be provided.

Rule 7. EFFECT OF DECISION; ENFORCEMENT

A. Compliance with Decision.

(1) Where the parties have agreed to be bound by the arbitration or have settled the dispute, the parties shall have [thirty] days from service of the written decision or the date the stipulation of settlement is signed by the parties to comply with the decision or settlement.

(2) Where there is no agreement to be bound by the arbitration, any party is entitled to a trial de novo if sought within thirty days from service of the written decision, except that if a party willfully fails to appear at the arbitration hearing, that party shall not be entitled to a trial de novo. The determination of willfulness shall be made by the court. The party who failed to appear at the arbitration shall have the burden of proving that the failure to appear was not willful. In making its determination, the court may consider any findings made by the arbitrators on the subject of a party's failure to appear. If a trial de novo is not sought within 30 days, the decision becomes binding.

B. Trial De Novo.

(1) If there is an action pending, the trial de novo shall be initiated by filing a rejection of arbitration award and request for trial in that action within 30 days from service of the written decision.

(2) If no action is pending, the trial de novo shall be initiated by the commencement of an action in the court having jurisdiction over the amount in controversy within thirty days from the service of the written decision.

(3) The party seeking a trial de novo shall be the prevailing party if that party obtains a judgment more favorable than that provided by the arbitration award, and in all other cases the other party shall be the prevailing party. The prevailing party may, in the discretion of the court, be entitled to an allowance for reasonable attorney's fees and costs incurred in the trial de novo, which

allowance shall be fixed by the court. In fixing the attorney's fees, the court shall consider the decision and determinations of the arbitrators, in addition to any other relevant evidence.

(4) Except as provided in this rule, the decision and determinations of the arbitrators shall not be admissible in any action or proceeding and shall not operate as collateral estoppel or res judicata.

C. Petition to Confirm, Correct, or Vacate the Decision.

(1) If a civil action has been stayed pursuant to these rules, any petition to confirm, correct, or vacate the decision shall be filed with the court in which the action is pending, and shall be served in accordance with the [jurisdiction's statutes or rules of civil procedure.]

(2) If no action is pending in any court, the decision may be confirmed, corrected, or vacated by petition to the court having jurisdiction over the amount of the decision, in accordance with the [jurisdiction's statutes or rules of civil procedure.]

(3) A court confirming, correcting or vacating a decision under these rules may award to the prevailing party reasonable fees and costs including, if applicable, fees or costs on appeal, incurred in obtaining confirmation, correction or vacation of the award. The party obtaining judgment confirming, correcting, or vacating the decision shall be the prevailing party except that, without regard or consideration of who the prevailing party may be, if a party did not appear at the arbitration hearing in the matter provided by these rules, that party shall not be entitled to attorney's fees or costs upon confirmation, correction, or vacation of the award.

Commentary

Thirty days is considered a reasonable time period in which to expect the parties to comply with the decision. The thirty days begins to run when the decision in the fee arbitration process is served on the parties or when a settlement agreement is signed.

The Commission itself has no authority to enforce a decision. Either party may use the summary action mechanisms which are provided by the jurisdiction to obtain a judgment consistent with the panel's decision as expeditiously as possible.

Reasonable fees and costs may be awarded to the prevailing party in an action to confirm, correct or vacate a panel decision, unless the prevailing party failed to appear at the arbitration hearing in the manner provided in the rules. This exception should encourage full participation of the parties in the arbitration proceeding.

Every jurisdiction is encouraged to consider developing means of assisting clients in enforcing decisions. Some jurisdictions use a panel of pro bono lawyers to assist the clients in obtaining civil judgements.

Some jurisdictions refer lawyers who fail to comply with a decision or judgement to an appropriate agency for administrative, non-disciplinary action such as that used in the jurisdiction for failure to comply with mandatory continuing legal education requirements or failure to pay registration fees.

Rule 8. CONFIDENTIALITY

A. Confidentiality of Proceedings. Except as may be otherwise necessary for compliance with these rules or to take ancillary legal action with respect thereto, all records, documents, files, proceedings and hearings pertaining to the arbitration of any dispute under these rules shall be confidential and will be closed to the public, unless ordered open by a [court of general jurisdiction] upon good cause shown, except that a summary of the facts, without reference to the parties by name, may be publicized in all cases once the proceeding has been formally closed.

B. Confidentiality of Information. A lawyer may reveal information relating to the representation of the client to the extent necessary to establish his or her fee claim. In no event shall such disclosure be deemed a waiver of the confidential character of such matters for any other purpose.

Commentary

Rule 8.B is consistent with ABA Model Rule of Professional Conduct Rule 1.6, which permits limited disclosure of otherwise confidential information only "to the extent reasonably ... necessary to establish a claim or defense ... in a controversy between the lawyer and the client...."

Rule 9. IMMUNITY

A. Parties and Witnesses. Parties and witnesses shall have such immunity as is applicable in a civil action in the jurisdiction.

B. Commissioners; Arbitrators; Staff. Members of the Commission, panels and staff shall be immune from suit for any conduct in the course and scope of their official duties.

Rule 10. SERVICE

A. Method. Service on any party other than a lawyer or law firm shall be by personal delivery, by any person authorized by the Chair of the Commission, or by deposit in the United States mail, postage paid, addressed to the person on whom it is to be served at his or her office or home address as last given to the Commission.

B. Official Address of Lawyer. Service on an individual lawyer shall be at the latest address shown on the official membership records of the [highest court or state bar association.] Service on a law firm shall be at the address as shown in the Petition for Arbitration Form unless the law firm designates a lawyer to be responsible for the arbitration, in which case, service shall be at the designee's latest address shown on the official membership records of the [highest court or state bar association.] Service shall be in accordance with section 10.A. above.

C. Service on Represented Parties. If either party is represented by counsel, service shall be on the party as indicated in Rules 10.A. and 10.B., and on the counsel at the latest address shown on the official membership records of the [highest court or state bar association.]

D. Completion of Service. The service is complete at the time of deposit. The time for performing any act shall commence on the date service is complete and shall not be extended by reason of service by mail.